Lecture Notes in Computer Science

Edited by G. Goos and J. Hartmanis

354

J. W. de Bakker W.-P. de Roever G. Rozenberg (Eds.)

Linear Time, Branching Time and Partial Order in Logics and Models for Concurrency

School/Workshop, Noordwijkerhout, The Netherlands
May 30 – June 3, 1988

Springer-Verlag
Berlin Heidelberg New York London Paris Tokyo

Editors

J. W. de Bakker
Centre for Mathematics and Computer Science
Kruislaan 413, 1098 SJ Amsterdam, The Netherlands

W.-P. de Roever
Department of Computing Science
Eindhoven University of Technology
P.O. Box 513, 5600 MB Eindhoven, The Netherlands

G. Rozenberg
Institute of Applied Mathematics and Computer Science
University of Leiden
P.O. Box 9512, 2300 RA Leiden, The Netherlands

CR Subject Classification (1987): B.1, C.1–2, D.4, F.1, F.3–4

ISBN 3-540-51080-X Springer-Verlag Berlin Heidelberg New York
ISBN 0-387-51080-X Springer-Verlag New York Berlin Heidelberg

Printed in Germany

Printing and binding: Druckhaus Beltz, Hemsbach/Bergstr.
2145/3140-543210 – Printed on acid-free paper

PREFACE

Modelling the behaviour of concurrent and distributed systems has grown into one of the most challenging and vigorous research areas within theoretical computer science. The last decade has seen the emergence of three independent approaches to this problem, some of them capturing differences between systems that others ignore. The first one models a system by describing its execution runs, the second one by analysing the execution trees, and the third one models a system by describing the (in)dependencies and choices between the various events that may occur. Paradigmatic for these approaches are semantic domains with linear or branching elements, linear time and branching time temporal logic, and net theory. Although it seems that the more features a system captures the better, if one wants some measure of abstractness and parsimony, some of such features may be too detailed for a given level of description.

This volume reviews these intrinsically different approaches and evaluates their relative advantages. It is based on the "School/Workshop On Linear Time, Branching Time and Partial Order in Logics and Models for Concurrency" organized by the editors and held in the period May 30 - June 3, 1988 at Noordwijkerhout, The Netherlands. The School/Workshop was an activity of the project REX - Research and Education in Concurrent Systems sponsored by the Netherlands NFI (Nationale Faciliteit Informatica) Programme. The meeting was organized under auspices of the EATCS and was furthermore supported by the Centre for Mathematics and Computer Science, the University of Leiden, and the Eindhoven University of Technology.

The material presented in this volume has been prepared by the lecturers (and their coauthors) after the meeting took place - in this way the papers reflect also the vivid discussions that took place during the meeting. We are proud that we had such an excellent group of lecturers *and* such an eager and enthusiastic group of participants. We are very grateful to both groups for making the meeting both scientifically interesting and socially very pleasant, and to the Program Committee consisting of M. Hennessy, E.-R. Olderog, A. Pnueli, J. Sifakis, and P.S. Thiagarajan for their help in preparing the scientific program of the meeting.

We gratefully acknowledge the financial support from the Netherlands National Facility for Informatics (NFI).

The Centre for Mathematics and Computer Science was responsible for the technical organization of the meeting. The University of Leiden and the Eindhoven University of Technology have cooperated in the organization on a number of vital points. As directors of the School/Workshop we want to extend our special thanks to Ms. Loes Vasmel-Kaarsemaker, Ms. Marja Hegt, and Mr. Frans Snijders for organizational assistance beyond the call of duty.

We hope that in the *future* development of the theory of concurrent systems this volume may help in bringing at least *partial* order into the *branching* structure that this development undoubtedly will have.

January, 1989

The Editors,

J.W. de Bakker
W.P. de Roever
G. Rozenberg

THE REX PROJECT

The REX - Research and Education in Concurrent Systems-project investigates syntactic, semantic and proof-theoretic aspects of concurrency. In addition, its objectives are the education of young researchers and, in general, the dissemination of scientific results relating to these themes.

REX is a collaborative effort of the Leiden University (G. Rozenberg), the Centre for Mathematics and Computer Science in Amsterdam (J.W. de Bakker), and the Eindhoven University of Technology (W.P. de Roever), representing the areas syntax, semantics and proof theory, respectively. The project is supported by the Netherlands National Facility for Informatics (NFI); its expected duration is four years starting in 1988. In the years 1984-1988, the same groups worked together in the Netherlands National Concurrency Project (LPC), supported by the Netherlands Foundation for the Advancement of Pure Research (ZWO).

The research activities of the REX project will include, more specifically,

(i) Three subprojects devoted to the themes:
  - syntax of concurrent systems: a graph oriented framework for structures and processes
  - process theory and the semantics of parallel logic programming languages
  - high-level specification and refinement of real-time distributed systems.

(ii) Collaboration with visiting professors and post-doctoral researchers, in particular focused on the research themes mentioned above. In 1988/1989 these visitors include dr. E.-R. Olderog (Kiel), prof. P.S. Thiagarajan (Madras), dr. S. Ramesh (Indian Institute of Technology).

(iii) Workshops and Schools. The School/Workshop on Linear Time, Branching Time and Partial Order in Logics and Models for Concurrency was the first in a series of such events. For 1989, we plan a workshop on "Stepwise Refinement of Distributed Systems: Models, Formalisms, Correctness". In 1990, we shall organize a meeting on "Actor systems, object-oriented languages and massive parallelism" (tentative title).

The educational activities of REX include regular "concurrency days". A concurrency day may consist of tutorial introductions to selected topics, and of presentations of research results to a non-specialist audience. Often, experts from abroad are invited to contribute to these days. In addition, visiting professors are asked to present lecture series concerning recent developments in their fields of specialization. Clearly, the School/Workshops have as well an important educational function, providing their participants with an intensive introduction to new areas.

Finally, we mention another aspect of the REX project. We shall continue the regular contacts with other European projects in the area of concurrency built up during the LPC years. In particular, this applies to the French C^3 -Cooperation, Communication, Concurrency- program, to the British Computer Society - Formal Aspects of Computer Science group, and to groups within the Gesellschaft für Mathematik und Datenverarbeitung (GMD) in Bonn.

As mentioned already, REX continues the LPC cooperation. Some highlights of the LPC years are:

(i) the organization of the ESPRIT/LPC Advanced School on Current Trends in Concurrency (1985, proceedings appeared as Lecture Notes in Computer Science, Vol. 224, Springer, 1986);

(ii) Ph.D. research on the topics *vector synchronized systems, dataflow semantics*, and *real-time temporal logic*;

(iii) fruitful interaction with ESPRIT projects 415 (Parallel Architectures and Languages for AIP: a VLSI-directed approach) and 937 (Descartes, Debugging and Specification of ADA Real-Time Embedded Systems). LPC contributed to the local organization of ESPRIT 415 conference PARLE - Parallel Architectures and Languages Europe (1987, Proceedings appeared as Lecture Notes in Computer Science Vol. 258, 259, Springer);

(iv) the setting-up of the international exchanges referred to above.

We would like to conclude this brief presentation of the future (past) of the REX (LPC) project by inviting everyone who is interested in more information concerning REX (possibility of visits, plans for workshops, other forms of exchanges, etc.) to write to one of the project leaders.

J.W. de Bakker
W.P. de Roever
G. Rozenberg

CONTENTS

TIME, LOGIC AND COMPUTATION

Johan van Benthem
Faculty of Mathematics and Computer Science
University of Amsterdam
Roetersstraat 15, 1018 WB Amsterdam, Holland

ABSTRACT. This paper starts with a survey of temporal logic in its original guise, pointing at its connections with philosophy and linguistics. More specifically, a technical exposition is provided of the basic 'tense-logical' system, based on points or 'moments' of time, with the research program in model theory and proof theory which has grown around it. After that, a more recent stream of 'period' and 'event' based approaches to time is discussed, again with some of the new logical themes engendered by it. Finally, a review is given of some recent computational research in temporal logic. Here, a clear continuity of logical concerns emerges between philosophy, linguistics and computer science. But, the latter adds several new themes and perspectives which might well give it a significant impact on the earlier standard enterprise.

Keywords. Completeness, computational semantics, correspondence, event structure, first-order definability, period structure, point structure, temporal operator, tense logic.

CONTENTS

1. Introduction

The formal properties of Time have attracted the attention of philosophers and mathematicians ever since Antiquity (cf. the anthology Smart 1964). Moreover, abstract temporal structure finds its reflection in our linguistic habits of temporal reasoning, and hence logicians have entered this field too, creating a discipline of 'temporal logic' (Reichenbach 1947, Prior 1957, Prior 1967). But in fact, time is a phenomenon cutting across many academic boundaries: from physics (cf. Reichenbach 1957) to psychology (cf. Michon & Jackson 1985). [A reference spanning virtually this whole spectrum is Whitrow 1980.] Within this wider area, temporal logic finds itself in particularly close contact with philosophy, linguistics (cf. Dowty 1979) and increasingly also with computer science. For, these disciplines share an interest in creating exact systems of temporal representation, coming with calculi for reasoning about change or persistence over time.

The purpose of this paper is twofold. On the one hand, a discursive survey will be given of temporal logic as it has developed in this century - while on the other, there is a review of recent contacts with computer science; whose variety, after a mere decade of research, is already impressive. No complete coverage has been attempted, however, in either respect. For further details on temporal logic, there is an array of informative texts, such as Gabbay 1976, van Benthem 1983, Burgess 1984 and Goldblatt 1987a. Moreover, the present volume itself may be viewed as an anthology of computational research into temporal logic. Therefore, we shall feel free to choose our own path through the area, with an emphasis on general research lines, and an occasional new question or observation.

2. Points

2.1 Basic Framework

2.1.1 An instructive, and much-studied 'minimal' system of temporal logic was developed by Arthur Prior in the fifties and sixties. This so-called 'tense logic' has propositional operators P for *past* and F for *future*. The original motivation for concentrating on these was two-sided. Philosophically, these are the basic operators which assign changing temporal 'perspective' to events. I.e., they express the dynamic 'A-series' of McTaggart 1908, who contrasted this with the static 'B-series' of an immutable order of events. In Prior's system, B-series models provide the semantics for A-series languages, as we shall see. But also, linguistically, the operators P, F correspond to the most basic 'tenses' of natural language:

q	:	Mary cries	(present)
Pq	:	Mary cried	(past)
Fq	:	Mary will cry	(future).

Further iterations then reflect compound tenses:

PPq	:	Mary had cried	(past perfect)
FPq	:	Mary will have cried	(future perfect),

etcetera. The analogy is by no means without its problems: but it has had undeniable heuristic virtues.

Remark. The temporal system of expression in natural languages is much richer than these examples might suggest. In addition to tenses, there are many types of *temporal adverbs* ("now", "then", "yesterday", "for an hour",...), including an elaborate quantificational vocabulary ("always", "mostly", "often", "usually",...). Then, there are *temporal connectives* relating two events ("since", "until", "before", "after",...). And finally, there are so-called *aspects,* recording various kinds of temporal texture which an event can have: finished or unfinished, iterative or unique, and so on. Not all of these have yet received the systematic logical attention which they deserve. (But see Galton 1984 on the logic of aspect treated in a Priorean fashion, as well as Kamp & Rohrer 1988 on more general linguistic semantics of temporal expressions.) □

2.1.2 Semantic structures for the basic system are sets T of *points in time* equipped with a binary order of *precedence* : so-called *frames* $\mathbb{T}$ =

$(T, <)$.

These form the temporal pattern on which histories can take place, assigning to each $t \in T$ some interpretation of the original descriptive language on which the temporal operators have been superimposed. Our paradigm will be a temporal *propositional logic,* having a vocabulary of

proposition letters	:	p,q,r,...
Boolean connectives	:	$\neg, \wedge, \vee, \rightarrow, \leftrightarrow$
temporal operators	:	F, P

This allows us to define further temporal operators:

$G\phi$	=	$\neg F \neg \phi$	(always in the future)
$H\phi$	=	$\neg P \neg \phi$	(always in the past)

More generally, one can formulate and compare complex temporal statements.
Here is an illustration, involving relative scope of operators:

$p \rightarrow Gq$	:	if you sin, you will be punished ever after,
$G(p \rightarrow q)$	:	you will always be punished if you sin.

For the language, temporal *models* are structures $\mathbb{M}$ =

$(T, <, V)$,

where V is a *valuation* assigning to each atomic proposition p the set V(p) of times when it holds. A standard inductive truth definition then lifts this to complex formulas ϕ .

$\mathbb{M} \models \phi\ [t]$ (ϕ *is true in model* $\mathbb{M}$ *at point* t):

$\mathbb{M} \models p\ [t]$	iff	$t \in V(p)$
$\mathbb{M} \models \neg\phi\ [t]$	iff	*not* $\mathbb{M} \models \phi\ [t]$
$\mathbb{M} \models \phi \wedge \psi\ [t]$	iff	$\mathbb{M} \models \phi\ [t]$ *and* $\mathbb{M} \models \psi\ [t]$

and likewise for the other Boolean connectives;

$\mathbb{M} \models P\phi\ [t]$	iff	$\mathbb{M} \models \phi\ [t']$ *for some* $t'<t$
$\mathbb{M} \models F\phi\ [t]$	iff	$\mathbb{M} \models \phi\ [t']$ *for some* $t'>t$

But, one can also superimpose the temporal operators on an underlying *predicate logic*, allowing an interplay between temporal operators and quantifiers:

$F\exists x(Cx \wedge Mx)$:	there will be a child (then) landing on Mars
$\exists x(Cx \wedge FMx)$:	a child (now) will land (then) on Mars.

In this case, each point in time must carry a complete structure of individuals with relations and operations, in order to interpret the new vocabulary.

Remark. There are in fact some *options* here. For instance, should an atomic statement Px be false at point t if x does not exist at t, or should it be merely undefined? Likewise, should a formula GQx be true at t if Qx is true at all later points, or if it is merely true at all later points where x exists? (When we say that Napoleon was 'always' on the offensive, we obviously mean something like 'at all times of his existence'.) As we are not going to pursue temporal predicate logic here, these issues will not be explored. It should be noted, however, that the technical theory of this system can be rather complex, due to the interaction between quantification over points in time and quantification over individuals. (Cf. Garson 1984, Hughes & Creswell 1984.) □

2.1.3 The above frames only become more genuinely 'temporal structures' when further *constraints* are imposed. What are the basic properties of the temporal order? This is a question of what may be called 'mathematical metaphysics'.

Proposed principles here are of various logical kinds. First, there are simple *first-order* conditions which seem uncontroversial:

$\forall xyz: (x<y \wedge y<z) \rightarrow x<z$ (transitivity)

$\forall x: \neg x<x$ (irreflexivity)

Together, these imply asymmetry $\forall xy: x<y \rightarrow \neg y<x$. Note that all these conditions are *universal Horn* sentences. The first option encountered involves a non-Horn condition, viz.

$\forall xy: x<y \vee y<x \vee x=y$ (linearity)

A weaker form which has also been put forward is

$\forall xyzu: x<y \rightarrow (x<z \vee z<y)$ (almost-connectedness)

But both would exclude genuinely branching time with disjoint paths into the future.

Another option arises with *existence* principles, such as

$\forall x: \exists y\ x<y$ (succession)

An alternative would be to postulate an end to time. Likewise, there is a choice between

$\forall xy: x<y \rightarrow \exists z(x<z \wedge \neg\exists y(x<y \wedge y<z))$ (discreteness)

or

$\forall xy: x<y \rightarrow \exists z(x<z \wedge z<y)$ (density) .

And of course, these principles have leftward past variants too, with similar options.

On top of these first-order conditions, one can formulate *higher-order* postulates on the structure of time. A well-known mathematical example is *Dedekind Continuity*. But also, many philosophers and physicists would subscribe to a principle of *Homogeneity*: 'Time is structurally similar throughout' . Mathematically,

For any two points $t, t' \in T$, there exists an *order-automorphism* of $(T, <)$ mapping t to t'.

For instance, **R**, **Q**, **Z** are homogeneous, whereas **N** is not.

Note that, e.g., a homogeneous structure satisfies all formulas of the form

$\forall x\phi(x) \vee \forall x\neg\phi(x)$ *

In particular, taking $\phi(x) = \exists y(x<y \wedge \neg\exists z(x<z \wedge z<y))$, homogeneous structures must be either discrete or dense.

Remark. No stronger first-order condition than * can be derived from Homogeneity: see van Benthem 1984b. □

Another higher-order principle is *Isotropy*: 'There is no formally preferred direction of Time'. Mathematically,

Every frame $(T, <)$ is isomorphic to its converse $(T, >)$.

This principle enforces the same conditions for $<$ and $>$. [For a more global analogy, one might compare 'duality principles' in Graph Theory.] Actually, some of the earlier principles for $<$ automatically imply their $>$ form already (e.g., transitivity, irreflexivity and linearity). But this is not a general phenomenon, not even for Horn clause conditions. For instance, $\forall xyz(x<y \rightarrow x<z)$ does not imply $\forall xyz(x>y \rightarrow x>z)$.

Digression. Here is an illustration of the utility of classical model-theoretic methods in this area. The complete first-order theory of Isotropy is in fact given by the above conversion schema

$\phi(<) \leftrightarrow \phi(>)$, for all first-order sentences ϕ IS

For, suppose that some first-order sentence α is not a consequence of this schema. Then, by the Completeness and Loewenheim-Skolem theorems, there exists some countable frame $\mathbb{T}$ verifying the schema IS while falsifying α. Now, take any ω-saturated elementary extension $\mathbb{T}^+$ of $\mathbb{T}$ (cf. Chang & Keisler 1973): IS will remain true in $\mathbb{T}^+$, and α false. Let a_1 be any object in $\mathbb{T}^+$. The type of formulas $\{\psi(x) \mid \mathbb{T}^+ \models \psi[a_1]\}$, where $\psi=\psi(<)$, has an obvious transpose with $<$ replaced by $>$, which can be finitely satisfied in $\mathbb{T}^+$, thanks to the validity of IS. By saturation then, the whole transpose is realized by some object b_1 in $\mathbb{T}^+$. Continuing the resulting correspondence a_1,b_1 by the usual zigzag argument, we obtain two enumerations $a_1,a_2,...$ and $b_1,b_2,...$ of $\mathbb{T}^+$ such that $(\{a_1,a_2,...\}, <)$ is elementarily equivalent to $(\{b_1,b_2,...\}, <)$. Hence, the map $a_i \mapsto b_i$ $(i \in N)$ is an isomorphism between $\mathbb{T}^+$ and its converse. So, full second-order Isotropy holds for $\mathbb{T}^+$, and hence, α is not among its consequences either. ●

When viewed as a constraint on frames, however, the first-order schema IS will not be equivalent to Isotropy. For instance, the ordinal sum of $(\mathbf{Q}, <)$ and $(\mathbf{R}, <)$, in that order, validates IS, even though this frame is not isomorphic to its converse. But, the idea of the preceding proof is that, on suitably saturated models, first-order schemata approximate their second-order parents (cf. Barwise 1976). □

Evidently, the above considerations do not enforce one single formal picture of Time. Indeed, various mathematical structures still pass most tests. Examples are the classical reals, rationals or integers - but also a relativistic Minkowski Space $\mathbf{M}$ with 'causal precedence' between a point and its successors inside its future light cone. As a concrete, simplified example of the latter kind of structure, take $\mathbb{T} = (T, <)$ with

$T = \mathbf{R} \times \mathbf{R}$

$(x,y) < (u,v)$ if $x<u$ and $y<v$.

This is a branching temporal structure, which still allows 'confluence':

$\forall xy: \exists z(x<z \wedge y<z)$

$\forall xy: \exists z(z<x \wedge z<y)$

(See Goldblatt 1980, Shehtman 1983 for matching relativistic tense logics.)

There is no difficulty in this diversity. Our intuitions about Time, like those concerning other fundamental categories of thought, are rich enough to support different paradigms - and for the purpose of modelling certain phenomena, retaining an open mind toward such options is actually valuable. Moreover, the division into a small set of core conditions on temporal structures and further extras is also useful, in that a given application may need only a weak temporal calculus, rather than the full theory of some particular frame.

Example. Comparing Major Temporal Structures.

- **R, Q** have the same *first-order* theory, which differs from that of **M** or **Z**.
- **R, Q** have different *second-order* theories: the former, but not the latter, being Dedekind continuous.
- **R, Q, Z** all have the same *universal* first-order theory, which differs from that of **M**. (The latter is actually contained in the former, as **R** can be embedded as a substructure of **M**.)
- **R, Q, Z, M** all have the same universal *Horn* theory. (For, **M** is a *direct product* of **R**: and this frame operation preserves truth of Horn sentences.) □

Remark. If one takes this diversity of temporal structures quite seriously, then a reasonable next step would be to develop separate kinds of *topology* and *analysis* on them. (E.g., analysis on the rationals rather than the reals has a quite different flavour: cf. van Benthem 1983.) □

2.1.4 The preceding Section already introduced a typical logical theme, namely the interplay between properties of structures in general and what can be expressed about them in specific formal languages set up for the purpose of some genre of reasoning. In particular, one can study *correspondences* between structural properties of the temporal order and principles expressible in the earlier tense logical language. To see this, we must remove any dependence on the 'accidental facts' spread out over a temporal frame:

$(T, <) \models \phi\,[t]$ if $(T, <, V) \models \phi\,[t]$ *for all valuations* V on $(T, <)$

$(T, <) \models \phi$ if $(T, <) \models \phi\,[t]$ *for all points* $t \in T$.

Then, we get equivalences such as the following:

$(T, <) \models FFp \rightarrow Fp$ iff $<$ is *transitive*

$(T, <) \models Fp \rightarrow FFp$ iff $<$ is *dense*.

Often, however, these matches are not quite perfect, due to certain peculiarities of the tense-logical language. E.g., linearity is not definable as it stands, but

$(T, <) \models (Fp \wedge Fq) \rightarrow (F(p \wedge q) \vee F(p \wedge Fq) \vee F(q \wedge Fp))$ iff

$\forall x\colon \forall yz((x<y \wedge x<z) \rightarrow (y<z \vee z<y \vee y=z))$;

and analogously for a leftward variant. Likewise, discreteness can only be approximated:

$p \rightarrow FH(p \vee Fp)$ corresponds to $\forall x\colon \exists y(x<y \wedge \forall z{<}y(z=x \vee z<x))$.

In general, when viewed in this perspective, Prior's tense-logical formalism expresses *second-order* conditions on the temporal order (because of the above quantification over valuations). And indeed, some tense-logical principles do not correspond to first-order frame conditions on $<$ at all. An example is 'Loeb's Axiom':

$(T, <) \models H(Hp \rightarrow p) \rightarrow Hp$ iff $<$ is transitive and *well-founded.*

On the other hand, certain simple first-order principles are not tense-logically expressible. A well-known example is *irreflexivity* of $<$. Proofs of this and other assertions in this Section may be found in van Benthem 1983. What they presuppose is a deeper analysis of the semantic behaviour of this language. (Section 2.3.1 below has further information on this.)

With richer tense-logical formalisms, the correspondence situation changes. For instance, let us add an operator D ('difference'), whose interpretation is as follows:

$\mathbb{M} \models D\phi\,[t]$ if $\mathbb{M} \models \phi\,[t']$ *for some* $t' \neq t$.

(This proposal is due to several people independently, including Ron Koymans, Patrick Blackburn and Gargov, Passy & Tinchev 1987.) Then, irreflexivity becomes definable after all, by

$Fp \rightarrow Dp$;

and ordinary linearity is expresed by

$Dp \rightarrow Fp \vee Pp$.

Remark. In fact, all universal first-order conditions on $<$ are definable in the F, P, D formalism, as well as various other useful types of formula. □

Of course, one can also consider correspondence on *models* (T, <, V) rather than frames. We shall determine precisely which first-order formulas are tense-logically definable in Section 2.3, using their semantic invariance behaviour.

Remark. Correspondence also makes sense for other base logics than purely propositional ones. For instance, a quantifier / operator interchange principle such as

$\exists x G Q x \rightarrow G \exists x Q x$

expresses a condition of 'cumulation' on individual domains along successive points of time:

$\forall xy\!: x<y \rightarrow \forall u(u \in D_x \rightarrow u \in D_y)$. □

2.2 Axiomatics

2.2.1 In addition to the semantic aspect of temporal logic, there is also its proof-theoretic side. There, the focus is on syntactic calculi of deduction for temporal expressions. Many such calculi live in the literature, mainly stemming from two sources. On the one hand, philosophers have proposed certain forms of temporal argument, which can be systematized into logical systems. In this case, providing a proper semantics is only a second step. But more often, one starts from some preferred temporal picture, asking for a faithful and complete record of the argument patterns supported by it.

Here are some examples of tense-logical systems. The so-called *minimal tense logic* K_t has the following principles.

Axioms:

(1) all propositional tautologies

(2) $G(\phi \rightarrow \psi) \rightarrow (G\phi \rightarrow G\psi)$ (Temporal
$H(\phi \rightarrow \psi) \rightarrow (H\phi \rightarrow H\psi)$ Distribution)

(3) $\phi \rightarrow HF\phi$
$\phi \rightarrow GP\phi$

Definition:

(4) $F\phi \leftrightarrow \neg G \neg \phi$
$P\phi \leftrightarrow \neg H \neg \phi$

Rules of Inference:

(5) $\phi, \phi \rightarrow \psi \,/\, \psi$ (Modus Ponens)

(6) if ϕ is a theorem, then so are $G\phi$, $H\phi$ (Generalization)

On top of this, one can put any of a great number of possible axioms, reflecting special assumptions on the temporal order, such as the earlier-mentioned principles for transitivity, density or linearity. Here is an illustrative table (precise formulations of the relational conditions are left to the reader):

$FF\phi \rightarrow F\phi$	transitivity
$F\phi \rightarrow FF\phi$	density
$(F\phi \wedge F\psi) \rightarrow F(\phi \wedge F\psi) \vee F(\phi \wedge \psi) \vee F(\psi \wedge F\phi)$	right-linearity
$(P\phi \wedge P\psi) \rightarrow P(\phi \wedge P\psi) \vee P(\phi \wedge \psi) \vee P(\psi \wedge P\phi)$	left-linearity
F*true*	right succession
P*true*	left succession
$\phi \rightarrow FH(\phi \vee F\phi)$	right discreteness
$\phi \rightarrow PG(\phi \vee P\phi)$	left discreteness
$FG\phi \rightarrow GF\phi$	right confluence
$PH\phi \rightarrow HP\phi$	left confluence
$(F\phi \wedge FG\neg\phi) \rightarrow F(HF\phi \wedge G\neg\phi)$	Dedekind continuity

Different choices lead to different 'tense logics', which inhabit the *Lattice of Tense Logics*, lying in between the minimal system and, at the upper end, trivial systems in which (too) many temporal distinctions have collapsed, with principles such as

G*false* irreflexive isolated points

or

$G\phi \leftrightarrow \phi$ reflexive isolated points.

Thus, as in Section 2.1.3, the issue is not to locate one single preferred system, but rather to understand the varieties of temporal reasoning, by studying the properties of such logics and their inter-relationships.

Example. Relative Interpretation.

The lattice of tense logics cannot be taken at face value; since often, tense logics can be translated into each other. E.g., the transition

$$\tau(G\phi) \mapsto H\tau(\phi), \qquad \tau(H\phi) \mapsto G\tau(\phi)$$

will map an 'isotropic' logic like K_t into itself, whilst switching theorems. On the other hand, a translation like

$$\sigma(G\phi) \mapsto G\sigma(\phi) \wedge \sigma(\phi), \qquad \sigma(H\phi) \mapsto H\sigma(\phi) \wedge \sigma(\phi)$$

will embed K_t into the modal logic T, being K_t with the additional axiom

$G\phi \rightarrow \phi$, corresponding to *reflexivity*.

The latter illustrates the possible location of modalities inside temporal logics (cf. Smirnov 1982). Likewise, the definition of an operator 'somewhere'

$$\Diamond\phi := P\phi \vee \phi \vee F\phi$$

in the tense logic of linear orders will produce the modal logic S5. □

Remark. From certain points of view, K_t would not be a truly minimal system. For instance, it is also possible to treat it as a *bi-modal* system, having separate relations R_G, R_H for interpreting the two modalities G, H . Then, axiom (3) will correspond to an optional interaction condition on the two, namely

$$R_G^{\cup} \supseteq R_H, \qquad R_H \supseteq R_G^{\cup} .$$

Moreover, it is also possible to study weaker logics, lacking the Distribution axioms. Cf. Chellas 1980 on the 'neighbourhood semantics' appropriate for this purpose. (Even weaker basic calculi may also be obtained in the spirit of Lambek 1958, van Benthem 1986a and Girard 1987.) □

Actually, the definition of what constitutes a *tense logic* requires some care. The usual approach is 'extensional': one defines a tense logic by its theorems only, namely, as a set of formulas containing all axioms of K_t and being closed under the action of Modus Ponens, Generalization and *Substitution* for proposition letters. Sometimes, however, a more 'intensional' approach is preferable, defining tense logics by varying some prescribed format of deduction. Then, the choice of 'hard-wired' inference rules can be crucial.

Example. Promoting Derived Rules of Inference.
The following is a derived inference rule of K_t:

if $G\phi$ is a theorem, then so is ϕ itself.

But, if one were to require all tense logics to admit this rule, then certain candidates on the extensional account will be ruled out (such as the logic of 'two step time' axiomatized by GG*false*, F*true*$\vee P$*true*). □

2.2.2 Axiomatic tense logics can be related to classes of temporal frames via (soundness and) completeness results. First, the minimal tense logic K_t indeed captures precisely those truths which are valid at all points in all temporal models, without any constraints on the precedence relation:

Theorem. A tense-logical formula is provable in K_t if and only if it is universally valid.

The standard proof of this result yields even a little more.

Definition. Let Σ be a set of tense-logical formulas. Then ϕ is a *semantic consequence* of Σ if, for all models $\mathbb{M} = (T, <, V)$ and all points $t \in T$, $\mathbb{M} \models \Sigma\,[t]$ (i.e., $\mathbb{M} \models \sigma\,[t]$ for each $\sigma \in \Sigma$) only if $\mathbb{M} \models \phi\,[t]$. Notation: $\Sigma \models \phi$.

What we have in fact is the following *general completeness result:*

A formula ϕ is a semantic consequence of Σ if and only if
it is derivable from Σ using only principles from K_t.

Next, there are *special completeness theorems* of the form

'ϕ is a theorem of logic L if and only if ϕ is universally valid in all frames of class K'.

Such results may arise from two directions. Sometimes, a particular tense logic L is given axiomatically, and one asks for some frame class K modelling it. Or conversely, some frame or class of frames is given, and one looks for some (effective) complete axiomatization of its tense-logical validities.

Example. The full tense logic of the earlier transitive irreflexive frames is axiomatized by K_t4, being K_t plus the Transitivity axiom. □

Example. The full tense logic of the single frame $\mathbf{R}$ is axiomatized by K_t4 plus the earlier-mentioned axioms for density, succession and Dedekind continuity. Complete axiomatizations for e.g., $\mathbf{Q}$, $\mathbf{Z}$ or the earlier $\mathbf{M}$, may be found in the standard literature. □

As a matter of fact, the usual tense-logical calculi proposed in the literature have all found natural semantic modellings; while, vice versa, all natural temporal structures have turned out to possess elegantly axiomatized theories. These phenomena do not rest on any obvious a priori basis. For, if only for reasons of cardinality, there must be many temporal frames lacking effectively axiomatized tense logics. (There are only countably many of the latter, but uncountably many of the former.) Moreover, as we shall see more clearly in Section 2.3, the complete tense logic of a temporal frame actually comprises part of its *second-order* theory: a system which need not be axiomatizable at all, in view of the known incompleteness of second-order logic (cf. Doets & van Benthem 1983). And also in the other direction, at least as specimina of pathology, there exist many tense logics lacking adequate temporal modelling. The latter phenomenon is known as tense-logical *incompleteness*, first recorded in Thomason 1972.

Example. An Incomplete Tense Logic.

Consider the temporal structure $(\mathbf{Z}, <, \mathbb{W})$ which consists of the integers, provided with all *finite unions of convex subsets* of $\mathbf{Z}$. Call a tense-logical formula *valid* in this structure if it holds everywhere under all valuations taking their values in $\mathbb{W}$ only. The set of valid formulas forms a tense logic L, whose axioms include those for transitivity, left- and right-linearity as well as two restricted versions of Loeb's Axiom:

$$G(G\phi\to\phi)\to(FG\phi\to G\phi), \qquad H(H\phi\to\phi)\to(PH\phi\to H\phi).$$

All these are valid because of general properties of the underlying frame $(\mathbf{Z}, <)$. Not valid in general, but true here thanks to the restriction to valuations in $\mathbb{W}$, are two so-called 'McKinsey Axioms', forbidding infinite alternation in the truth value history of propositions:

$$GF\phi\to FG\phi, \qquad HP\phi\to PH\phi.$$

There can be no adequate frame class *K* whose logic this is; because of the following observation.

Claim. Any frame validating all axioms of L must consist of isolated reflexive points.

Proof. Consider any frame $\mathbb{T} = (T, <)$ validating L. By the basic axioms of this logic, $<$ is transitive and left- and right-linear. Moroever, on such a frame, the modified Loeb axioms enforce the property that no infinite upward sequence $t_1<t_2<\ldots$ is strictly bounded from above (and likewise for descending sequences). In particular, then, no reflexive point can occur strictly below or above another point. I.e., if a point is reflexive, it must be isolated. Finally, on full transitive frames, the McKinsey axioms correspond to the relational condition that every point has a reflexive final successor and predecessor. In combination with the preceding observation, this implies the claim. ◆

Now, on frames of this kind, the collapsing principle $p\to Gp$ will be universally valid. But, the latter is not a theorem of L, as it is not valid on $(\mathbf{Z}, <, \mathbb{W})$: for a counter-example, take $V(p) = \{0\}$. □

2.2.3 Individual tense-logical completeness theorems abound in the literature. This phenomenon has led to a search for *general methods* establishing completeness for wider ranges of cases at once. A related general question is, of course, to find some principled explanation of why the search for individual completeness theorems has been so succesful, by and large.

As to the second question, some general answers are available. For instance, because of the existence of a *translation* into standard logic (see section 2.3 below), the effective axiomatizability of general tense-logical consequence is derivable from that of ordinary first-order logic. Also, the fact that quite a few natural temporal frames possess effectively axiomatizable (and even decidable) tense logics follows from an observation made in Gabbay 1976: often, they are effectively embeddable into the *monadic second-order logic* of the structure of finite sequences of natural numbers with the relation of 'initial segment' and unary successor functions. By *Rabin's Theorem*, the latter logic is decidable: and hence, so is that of temporal frames such as $\mathbf{N}$, $\mathbf{Z}$ or $\mathbf{Q}$. An uncountable frame like $\mathbf{R}$ is beyond the scope of this method, however. (Incidentally, the axiomatizability of the tense logic of $\mathbf{Q}$ is also predictable on general logical grounds.)

Remark. Also relevant here is the analysis found in Doets 1987. Although the full second-order theory of structures such as **(N, <)** or **(R, <)** is highly complex, their monadic second-order fragment turns out to be axiomatizable in a natural way. For instance, for **(N, <)**, an adequate axiomatization consists of the complete first-order theory of left-bounded discrete linear orders plus Dedekind's Induction Axiom. (Thus, in a sense, Dedekind's well-known abstract proof of categoricity using the latter does have a constructive content after all.) But for **R**, one needs not just the obvious principles: being the complete first-order theory of unbounded dense linear orders plus Dedekind continuity, but also a monadic variant of the so-called Suslin Property (forbidding uncountable antichains of intervals). □

A penetrating general analysis of monadic second-order theories on linear frames may be found in Burgess & Gurevich 1985, who even prove *decidability* for such cases as: all elementary classes of linear frames, all continuous linear frames.

Remark. The above analysis is restricted to the case of propositional tense logics. For, the tensed *predicate* logic of even a structure like **Z** or **R** is not arithmetically definable, let alone effectively axiomatizable: a result due to Scott and Lindstroem independently (cf. Garson 1984). The reason is that, using the underlying predicate logic, one can encode enough of arithmetic into the tense logic to fall prey to Tarski's Theorem. □

In the reverse direction, from given tense logics to adequate frame classes, general results have been obtained by means of analysis of the *proof techniques* employed: usually, variants of Henkin set constructions or semantic Beth tableaus. (Cf. Segerberg 1970, Goldblatt 1987, Fitting 1983.) A central early result is *Bull's Theorem* (Bull 1966) concerning modal logics, or equivalently, pure future tense logics involving F,G only:

Theorem. All modal extensions of S4.3 have the finite model property.

What this means is the following. A logic L has the *finite model property* if every one of its non-theorems ϕ can be refuted on some finite model for L. From this, by 'modal collapsing', one can extract a finite *frame* for L which refutes ϕ. So, logics with the finite model property are also *complete* in the above sense. Moreover, provided that L be effectively axiomatizable (and all extensions of S4.3 are), such logics must also be decidable. In all this, S4.3 is the modal logic of the *reflexive linear orders*, whose characteristic axioms, on top of the minimal logic, express transitivity, right-linearity and reflexivity.

This result has been extended considerably in Fine 1974, 1985, where an intensive investigation is made of all modal logics containing the transitivity axiom plus at least one axiom 'Alt_n' restricting the number of incomparable <-successors for any point to at most n. (Thus, linearity is Alt_1.) Translating to tense logic, we may conclude at least that all pure future (or pure past) tense logics on strict linear time are complete. And this result may be extended to cases of branching with a fixed finite upper limit.

Remark. For a more negative result, see Thomason 1982, which shows that the general question whether a given modal formula axiomatizes a frame-complete logic is *undecidable*. □

Remark. There is also a curious *limitation* to current proof techniques - in that they do not explicate why not just the propositional tense logic of temporal frames, but often also their complete monadic second-order theory is effectively axiomatizable. □

Finally, we mention another possible type of general result, this time involving tense logics of temporal frames. Given that we know complete tense logics of certain frames, can we also describe the tense logic of other frames formed out of these by natural mathematical operations? For instance, our conjecture would be that the *ordinal sum* of two frames having effectively axiomatizable theories itself has such a theory, effectively obtainable from the two 'components'. And a similar issue may be raised for *direct products*: e.g., can the full tense logic of the earlier Minkowski frame $\mathbf{M} = \mathbf{R} \times \mathbf{R}$ be obtained effectively from that of $\mathbf{R}$ itself?

2.2.4 Much of the general (completeness) theory for intensional systems has been developed for *modal* logic, rather than for tense logic. One prevalent assumption is that generalization to the latter case is straightforward, since we are merely duplicating the modal operator into a bi-modal system. While this is true for many topics, there still remains a non-trivial problem of *transfer*:

Which techniques and results from modal logic generalize to tense logic?

First, here is a simple case of non-transfer.

Example. Disjunction Property.

The minimal modal logic has the following property:

If $G\phi \vee G\psi$ is provable, then so is either $G\phi$ or $G\psi$.

The proof of this uses a common model-theoretic technique called 'rooting'. Suppose that neither $G\phi$ nor $G\psi$ are theorems. Then there exist models $\mathbb{M}_1, \mathbb{M}_2$ refuting ϕ, ψ respectively, at some points t_1, t_2. Now, take the union of two disjoint copies of these models, held together by one new point, <-joined to only t_1, t_2. Thus, a new model is obtained in which $G\phi \vee G\psi$ fails at the new root: whence the latter formula is not a theorem either. ◆

This technique is no longer available in tense logic. The reason is as follows. Evaluation of pure future formulas in the separate models is not affected in their rooted join. But, for past formulas, changes may occur: e.g., rooting of two linear frames will produce leftward branching. And in fact, K_t does not have the disjunction property. For instance, $GP\phi \vee GP\neg\psi$ is among its theorems, whereas neither $GP\phi$ nor $GP\neg\psi$ is. □

Remark. The disjunction property and semantic rooting are also behind the notion of 'honesty' as developed in Halpern & Moses 1985. □

Next, here is a more serious example of non-transfer. *Bull's Theorem* no longer holds for tense logic. A counter-example is provided by the earlier case of an incomplete tense logic on discrete integer time (cf. Section 2.2.2). So, can anything be saved here? At least, we have a

Conjecture. Bull's Theorem holds for all tense logics on *dense* linear time.

2.3 Model Theory

2.3.1 The general theory of intensional logic has produced some useful model-theoretic tools. In particular, there are certain operations on frames and models which leave truth of modal or tense-logical formulas *invariant*. First, there is the following central notion and result.

- $\mathbb{M}_1 = (T_1, <_1, V_1)$ is a *generated submodel* of $\mathbb{M}_2 = (T_2, <_2, V_2)$ if

(1) $(T_1, <_1)$ is a subframe of $(T_2, <_2)$ which is closed under $<_2$- successors and $<_2$- predecessors (i.e., $\mathbb{T}_1$ is a 'generated subframe' of $\mathbb{T}_2$)

(2) for each proposition letter p , $V_1(p) = V_2(p) \cap T_1$.

- Then, for all tense-logical formulas ϕ , and all $t \in T_1$,

$\mathbb{M}_1 \models \phi[t]$ iff $\mathbb{M}_2 \models \phi[t]$.

It follows that tense-logical formulas valid in a frame are also valid in all its *generated subframes*, and also that formulas valid in a family of frames remain valid in their *disjoint union*.

Another invariance employs a notion of back-and-forth connection which is quite similar to the *bisimulations* of current process algebra (cf. Klop 1988):

- A binary relation C between T_1 and T_2 is a *zigzag relation* between two models $\mathbb{M}_1, \mathbb{M}_2$ if

(1) the domain of C equals T_1 and its range T_2

(2) for all $x \in T_1, y \in T_2$ with xCy, and each $z \in T_1$ such that $x <_1 z$ $(z <_1 x)$, there exists some $u \in T_2$ such that zCu and $y <_2 u$ $(u <_2 y)$; and vice versa

(3) for each proposition letter p, if xCy, then $x \in V_1(p)$ iff $y \in V_2(p)$.

- Then, for all tense-logical formulas ϕ, and all $x \in T_1, y \in T_2$ with xCy,

$\mathbb{M}_1 \models \phi[x]$ iff $\mathbb{M}_2 \models \phi[y]$.

As a consequence, tense-logical formulas valid in a frame are also valid in its *p-morphic images*; where a 'p-morphism' is a function preserving $<$, and obeying the above back-and-forth condition in the inverse direction.

Application. The following conditions on temporal precedence are not tense-logically definable:

$\exists x\ x<x$	(not preserved under generated subframes)
$\forall x \forall y\ (x<y \vee y<x \vee x=y)$	(not preserved under disjoint unions)
$\forall x\ \neg x<x$	(not preserved under p-morphic images) □

There are several further important operations on models, such as *filtration* ('modal collapsing') or *unraveling*: for which we refer to the literature (van Benthem 1983, Goldblatt 1987a).

Semantic invariances describe the characteristic behaviour of a certain (fragment of a) formal language. As such, they have a dual aspect. On the one hand, they are a sign of weakness: the language cannot detect genuine differences in temporal structure; on the other hand, they are useful, in that they allow transfer of truth from one temporal situation to another.

2.3.2 As has been observed already, tense logic can be related systematically to more standard systems of logic on binary orders. First, there is a *standard translation* from tense-logical formulas into formulas of a first-order language L_0 having one binary predicate letter $<$ as well as unary predicate letters P corresponding to proposition letters p. The latter have one free variable t_0, reflecting the 'current point of evaluation':

$(p)^* = Pt_0$

$(\neg\phi)^* = \neg(\phi)^*$

$(\phi\#\psi)^* = (\phi)^*\#(\psi)^*$, for all Boolean connectives #

$(F\phi)^* = \exists t(t_0<t \wedge [t/t_0](\phi)^*)$, where t is some

$(P\phi)^* = \exists t(t<t_0 \wedge [t/t_0](\phi)^*)$ fresh variable

Models (T, <, V) may be naturally regarded as semantic structures for the first-order language L_0 too - and then we have, properly viewed,

$\mathbb{M} \models \phi[t]$ iff $\mathbb{M} \models (\phi)^*[t]$.

Thus, many facts about standard first-order logic become available for tense logic too. For instance, tense-logical truth on models is insensitive to semantic operations which preserve first-order truth: such as the formation of elementary submodels or ultraproducts. In particular, one obtains *Loewenheim-Skolem* and *Compactness* theorems. Moreover, semantic consequence on models ("$\Sigma \models \phi$") reduces to first-order consequence: $(\Sigma)^* \models (\phi)^*$. The exact form of a properly tense-logical axiomatization requires additional scrutiny, of course. And so does the known *decidability* of the minimal tense logic: where a special purpose argument is needed - say, by filtration - to establish the finite model property.

The above translation takes tense-logical formulas into a *fragment* of the full corresponding first-order language L_0 . For instance, the only quantifiers required are *restricted*, being of the forms '$\exists y(x<y \wedge$' or '$\exists y(y<x \wedge$' . This fragment can be determined precisely, both syntactically and semantically (cf. van Benthem 1985).

Theorem. A first-order formula in L_0 with one free variable t_0 is equivalent to the translation of some tense-logical formula if and only if it is invariant for generated submodels and zigzag relations.

Thus, the basic tense logical formalism has an intimate connection with bisimulation: it is the largest description language for models which is invariant for such a structural connection.

With richer formalisms, this invariance disappears.

Example. Progressive Tense versus Bisimulation.

A tense operator not expressible in the basic P, F formalism is the progressive tense ("Mary is crying"):

$$\mathbb{M} \models \Pi\phi\,[t] \quad \text{iff} \quad \exists t_1<t\ \exists t_2>t\ \forall u\,(t_1<u<t_2 \Rightarrow \mathbb{M} \models \phi\,[u])\,.$$

This operator essentially involves *betweenness*, rather than mere succession or precedence. It is not even P, F definable on the rational frame $\mathbf{Q}$. For, consider the valuation $V(q) = \bigcup\{(i,i+1] \mid i \text{ is even}\}$. By induction, we have, for basic tense-logical formulas ϕ , and all points $t_1, t_2 \in V(q)$ that $(\mathbf{Q}, <, V) \models \phi\,[t_1]$ iff $(\mathbf{Q}, <, V) \models \phi\,[t_2]$. By contrast, Πq will be true in the topological interior of $V(q)$ only: not in its boundary points.

That the progressive Πq need not survive bisimulation, may be seen as follows. Consider the following bisimulation, where corresponding numbers indicate points to be identified ('fold the left-hand model'):

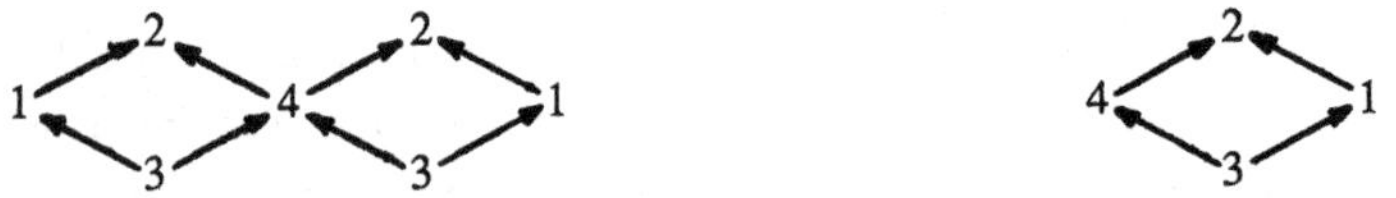

Set $V(q) = \{4\}$ in both cases. Then, Πq will be true on the left (consider, e.g., some upper 2 and its diagonally opposite 3); but, it fails on the right-hand side. □

Continuing the analysis behind the earlier characterization theorem, we can develop a hierarchy of ever finer notions of 'simulation', preserving ever stronger fragments of the first-order language L_0 .

Closer inspection reveals further syntactic peculiarities of the basic tense-logical fragment of L_0 . All translations can be taken into a fragment employing only *two variables*. The reason is that the 'fresh variables' for operators F, P may be chosen in an alternating manner.

Example. $G(FPq \wedge r)$ may be translated as

$$\forall t(t_0<t \rightarrow (\exists t_0(t<t_0 \wedge \exists t<t_0\ Qt) \wedge Rt)\,. \quad \square$$

This is quite significant, since fragments of predicate logic with a restriction to some fixed finite number of bound variables always allow a *functionally complete* variable-free *operator* formulation. (See Section 2.4.2

for more details.) Thus, tense logic is one of a larger family of operator formalisms approximating predicate logic.

Remark. In some respects, the basic tense logic is not yet well-chosen. For, its formulas do not exhaust the two-variable fragment of L_0 : as has been observed by various authors. For instance, none of its formulas expresses that $\exists y(t_0<y \wedge y<y)$ or $\exists y(t_0<y \wedge y<t_0 \wedge Py)$. Thus, there have been several attempts at increasing its coverage slightly, without losing pleasant axiomatizations and decidability. A systematic program to this effect is reported in Gargov, Passy & Tinchev 1987, who add various operations, such as 'window':

$$M \models W\phi\,[t] \quad \text{iff} \quad \forall t' (M \models \phi\,[t'] \Rightarrow t<t') .$$

What we need in general for two-variable L_0 are operators of the form

$$\exists x(\text{ 'some conjunction of atoms } \{x<y,\ y<x,\ x<x,\ y<y\} \text{ and their negations' } \wedge \phi(x)).$$

One elegant way of using an intensional logic framework here after all employs a small fragment of *Dynamic Logic* (cf. Harel 1984). Ordinary modal logic may be viewed as a poor dynamic logic of one binary relation (or atomic program) R , without any operations on the latter. Tense logic may be said to add the operation of *converse* here. But, we can also add the *Boolean* operations on programs: $-$, $\cap$ and $\cup$. The above first-order language is then captured by this dynamic logic, provided that one further propositional constant *loop* is added, true at only those points t where $t<t$. The resulting logic has been axiomatized in Gargov & Passy 1988. Its model theory still awaits further exploration (but cf. Goranko 1987). □

2.3.3 One strand in the above discussion is the more fundamental issue of *natural primitives* in setting up temporal logic. This may be approached in a more classical mathematical spirit as follows (cf. van Benthem 1986c).

Temporal propositional operators such as tenses may be viewed semantically as *operations* on sets of points in time: the latter being the correlates of propositions. Then, the question is which of these operations have a reasonable temporal motivation. For this purpose, fix some temporal frame $\mathbb{T} = (T, <)$. Because temporal operations are only concerned with temporal 'perspective', as encoded in the precedence order $<$, they should be insensitive to those transformations of the underlying points which preserve this precedence order. Thus (recall also the Homogeneity of Section 2.1.3),

f: $P(T) \rightarrow P(T)$ should be *invariant for automorphisms* of $(T, <)$, in the sense that,

for all subsets X of T and all <-automorphisms π , $\pi[f(X)] = f(\pi[X])$.

This commutation with automorphisms can also be formulated as follows:

$$t \in f(X) \quad \text{iff} \quad \pi(t) \in f(\pi[X]), \qquad \text{for all } t \in T .$$

Whether this is a restrictive requirement depends on the number of automorphisms in $\mathbb{T}$. E.g., $(\mathbf{N}, <)$ has only one (namely, the identity map), whereas $(\mathbf{R}, <)$ admits many translations and contractions. In the latter frame, then, automorphism invariance imposes a certain uniformity on temporal operations f , in that

(1) for any singleton $\{t\}$, $f(\{t\})$ is a union of certain of the three ranges
    $\{u \in T \mid u<t\}$, $\{t\}$ and $\{u \in T \mid t<u\}$,

(2) the choice under (1) is made uniformly .

Still, all temporal operations definable in standard logical languages, whether first-order or higher-order, pass this test.

Another kind of restriction which might be imposed concerns 'local computability' of temporal operations. For instance, here is a common condition of 'pointwise computability' or *Continuity*:

$f(\bigcup\{X_i \mid i \in I\}) = \bigcup\{f(X_i) \mid i \in I\}$, for all families of point sets $\{X_i \mid i \in I\}$ on $\mathbb{T}$.

In particular, this implies that $f(X) = \bigcup\{f(\{x\}) \mid x \in X\}$, for any set X .

Proposition. On **R** , the only automorphism-invariant and continuous temporal operations are F, P and identity, plus their disjunctions.

Thus, the Priorean basic framework captures the best-behaved operations on real time.

On other frames, however, this outcome may differ. For instance, on a discrete structure like **Z** , one would also have to allow "to-morrow", "yesterday" and their iterations.

This type of analysis can be extended, to create a structural hierarchy of temporal operations. For instance, instead of pointwise computability, one may require only computability by means of 'small episodes':

$f(X) = \bigcup\{f(Y) \mid Y \text{ is a } \textit{convex} \text{ subset of } X\}$.

Unlike Continuity, this would allow the earlier *progressive* tense, as well as various operations selecting *beginnings* or *endings* of convex intervals within propositions.

Moreover, a similar analysis can be given for *polyadic* temporal operations.

The attraction of this perspective is its language independence, giving us a separate stance from which to judge the design of temporal calculi.

2.3.4 Although the initial standard translation took tense-logical formulas to first-order ones, in L_0 , there is also a natural sense in which it makes them rather *second-order*. For, the earlier notion of truth in frames induces a correspondence with formulas in a *monadic* second-order logic over L_0 :

for formulas $\phi = \phi\,(p_1, \ldots, p_n)$,

$(T, <) \models \phi\,[t]$ iff $(T, <) \models \forall P_1 \ldots \forall P_n (\phi)^*\,[t]$.

More precisely, the latter formulas have a shape which is $\Pi^1{}_1$: all their second-order quantifiers occur in one universal block in front. Thus, on frames, tense logic behaves like a fragment of a higher-order logic; be it one whose logical properties are sometimes better than those of the full system. (Cf. van Benthem 1985 for some further technical background in higher-order logic.)

This is the proper setting, for instance, for pursuing the 'correspondences' of Section 2.1.4. See van Benthem 1984a for a survey of results, addressing such questions as

- Which model-theoretic behaviour is necessary and sufficient for first-order frame definability of tense-logical axioms?
- And conversely, for tense-logical frame definability of first-order conditions on precedence?
- Which algorithms (if any) produce standard ordering conditions equivalent to given tense-logical axioms?
- How can the account be extended to higher-order logic in general?

For instance, a tense-logical axiom defines a first-order condition on temporal frames if and only if it is preserved under the formation of *ultrapowers* of frames. And, e.g., a first-order sentence in $\{<, =\}$ is tense-logically definable on frames only if it is equivalent to one constructed from atoms $x<y$, $x=y$ and *false* using only one initial unrestricted universal quantifier, and after that only restricted ones $\forall u<v$, $\exists u<v$, $\forall v<u$, $\exists v<u$ as well as $\wedge, \vee$.

Remark. This type of question has a certain computational interest, in that one likes to see just where reductions are possible from second-order formalisms to first-order ones having better automated theorem provers. (For a parallel in the theory of *Circumscription*, cf. Lifschitz 1985, van Benthem 1988c.) □

Here, we shall consider a simpler question, however, related more directly to the expressive power of the basic tense logic on frames. For the purpose of illustration, let us restrict attention to unbounded strict linear orders which are also homogeneous in the sense of Section 2.1.3 . Thus, they are either dense or discrete. In this case, all equivalence classes of frames may be enumerated which have the same tense logic. Moreover, all these tense logics can be axiomatized effectively. The bare enumeration can be obtained by the method of 'filtration and inflation' found in van Benthem 1983 (theorem II.2.1.6), but also by means of a novel technique developed in De Jongh, Veltman & Verbrugge 1988. The latter also yields the axiomatizability of all logics concerned. The outcomes are as follows:

- On *dense* orders, the only types of frame which can be distinguished are those having exactly n exceptions to Dedekind Continuity (where $n = 0, 1, 2, .., \omega$).

Here, Dedekind Continuity itself is the special case with $n=0$.

Remark. This result shows that, even here, the basic tense logic is weaker in expressive power than the monadic $\Pi^1{}_1$ logic of $<$. For, Doets 1987 has a principle of the latter kind (being the $\Pi^1{}_1$ derivative of the Suslin Property mentioned in Section 2.2.3) which holds in **R** , but not in some of its Dedekind continuous non-Suslin homogeneous elementary equivalents. □

- On *discrete* orderings, the only types of frame which can be distinguished are those having exactly n consecutive copies of the integers **Z** (where $n = 1, 2, ..., \omega$).

Finally, despite its apparent simplicity, propositional tense logic on frames can also be intractable. Thus, Thomason 1974, 1975 establish that the notion of *frame-consequence* (as opposed to the earlier consequence relation on *models*) defined by:

$$\Sigma \models^* \phi \quad \text{if } \phi \text{ is true in every frame where } \Sigma \text{ holds},$$

is fully as complex as that of second-order logic in general.

2.3.5 *Appendix: Algebraic Semantics*

The basic tense logic can also be studied in an *algebraic* setting, as a formalism defining a Boolean algebra with two added operators p and f , which obey some minimal constraints, such as

$$p(x+y) = p(x)+p(y), \qquad f(x+y) = f(x)+f(y) .$$

Then, formulas become polynomials over algebras of the relevant similarity type: and different axiomatic systems correspond to different equational varieties. Here, general techniques from Universal Algebra may be applied. (Cf. Blok 1976, 1980; e.g., for many fundamental results about the extent of the incompleteness phenomenon among modal logics.)

For certain technical purposes, this algebraic approach seems more convenient than the (purely) model-theoretic one. Nevertheless, the two can be systematically related by introducing a somewhat more general notion of a temporal frame.

Definition. A *general frame* $(T, <, \mathbb{W})$ is a temporal frame $(T, <)$ together with a family $\mathbb{W}$ of subsets of T satisfying the following conditions:

(1) $\mathbb{W}$ is closed under the Boolean operations

(2) $\mathbb{W}$ is closed under the set-theoretic operations f, p defined by

$f(X) = \{t \in T \mid \exists x \in X\ t<x\}$ $p(X) = \{t \in T \mid \exists x \in X\ x<t\}$.

General frames implement the reasonable idea that the range of 'admissible propositions' on a temporal frame may obey certain restrictions: something which happened already with the structure $(\mathbf{Z}, <, \mathbb{W})$ used in Section 2.2.2, where only finite unions of convex sets were allowed.

Evaluation on general frames takes place as usual, but with only those valuations V whose values on proposition letters fall inside $\mathbb{W}$ .The stated closure conditions then guarantee that the set of valid formulas on a general frame will be a (substitution-closed) tense logic. All the earlier basic invariance relations between models are easily adapted to this new case, with corresponding outcomes for tense-logical formulas.

Remark. Another motivation for general frames stems from second-order logic. As in Henkin 1950, one can plausibly move from full 'standard models' for a higher-order formalism to a richer universe of 'general models', thereby restoring some form of general completeness. □

Now, there is a tight connection between general frames and temporal algebras. For, any general frame induces a temporal algebra of sets, whose universe is $\mathbb{W}$, and whose operations are the set-theoretic Booleans as well as the above-defined f and p . But also conversely, each temporal algebra may be *represented* as such a frame-induced set algebra, via the well-known Stone Ultrafilter Representation, adapted to this purpose (cf. Jonsson & Tarski 1951, Goldblatt 1976, van Benthem 1979). This two-way correspondence may be elaborated into a whole categorial correspondence, as the natural morphisms on either side are related too. The analogy is as follows:

generated subframes	homomorphic images
disjoint unions	direct products
p-morphic images	subalgebras .

The most elegant presentation of this categorial duality to date is Sambin & Vaccaro 1987.

Through this connection, many results have been obtained, such as the following (Goldblatt & Thomason 1975):

Theorem. An elementary class of frames K is tense-logically definable if and only if

(1) K is closed under the formation of p-morphic images, generated subframes and disjoint unions,

(2) both K and its complement are closed under the formation of ultrafilter extensions.

Remark. The algebraic viewpoint too, suggests certain generalizations of the basic tense-logical framework. For instance, it would also be quite natural to consider quasi-varieties, or classes of algebras defined by arbitrary *universal* statements of the algebraic language. Some corresponding changes (for the better) in the framework of modal logic are found in Kapron 1987. □

One reason why this framework has not been more prominent in our presentation is that it does not seem to adapt very easily to the richer formalisms to be considered below; where some form of *cylindric algebra* would be needed.

2.4 Further Developments

The account of temporal logic so far has concentrated on Prior's basic system, as a paradigm for developing a more general technical theory. From this base, one can set out in different directions.

2.4.1 *Locating Special Fragments*

We start with a direction which may not be the most obvious one, but which makes good computational sense, namely, looking for *fragments* of a formalism with better computational behaviour.

One important fragment provides a format for temporal axioms which guarantees two desirable properties for our logics, namely *frame completeness* and *first-orderness*. The relevant shapes are implications

$\phi \to \psi$, where ϕ is constructed using proposition letters and $\wedge, \vee, G, H, P, F$ such that no G or H governs a $\vee, F$ or P, and ψ is any *positive* formula constructed using proposition letters and $\wedge, \vee, G, H, F, P$.

The following result comes from Sahlqvist 1975:

Theorem. Each temporal logic extending K_t whose axioms consist of the above forms defines a first-order frame class, with respect to which it is complete.

In fact, the relevant frame condition on precedence may be obtained effectively from the axioms. Many of the earlier axioms are Sahlqvist forms (or can be transformed into them), witness

$FF\phi \to F\phi$, $F\phi \to FF\phi$, $FG\phi \to GF\phi$, $F\phi \wedge F\psi \to F(\phi \wedge F\psi) \vee F(\phi \wedge \psi) \vee F(\psi \wedge F\phi)$.

A typical non-example is the McKinsey Axiom $GF\phi \to FG\phi$, which is not first-order (cf. van Benthem 1984a).

A general Sahlqvist-type theorem for multi-modal logics occurs in Catach 1988.

These special forms can also be studied for their model-theoretic *transfer* behaviour (cf. Section 2.2.3). For instance, Sahlqvist forms without disjunctions in their antecedents define 'general Horn sentences' in the sense of Chang & Keisler 1973, which are all preserved under *direct products* of frames. (Can the preservation result of Section 2.3.4 be made to fit exactly those first-order conditions corresponding to tense-logical formulas preserved under direct products?) And also, the more general Sahlqvist format, consisting of 'generalized Horn clauses' having positive consequents, might be of interest by itself.

Remark. The search for fragments can also start inside the standard frame formalisms, of course. For instance, even though there is no known necessary *and sufficient* condition for a first-order sentence to be defined by a tense-logical axiom, one can in fact find such a result for all tense-logically definable *Horn clauses*, etcetera. □

Another type of syntactic fragmentation arises in the study of so-called 'normal forms' for intensional languages (cf. Fine 1975a; a topic rediscovered in Fagin & Vardi 1985). For instance, we can characterize the formulas up to nested operator depth n by means of their insensitivity to those parts of models which lie more than n $<$-successor / predecessor steps removed from their point of evaluation.

Even the process of generalization of a language itself always raises an inverse issue of fragmentation, viz. how to recognize the old language within the new. For instance, how can 'pure past' formulas be located within the full tense-logical language? (For a computational motivation of this type of question, see Pnueli's contribution to this volume, on the description of safety and liveness. See also Gabbay 1981b for a connection with functional completeness, via so-called 'separability'.) There is one trivial syntactic answer here: "look at the F, G - free formulas". But, the more interesting version would be a semantic one. Call a formula ϕ *pure past* if always

$M \models \phi[t]$ iff $(M\leftarrow, t) \models \phi[t]$,

where $(\mathbb{M}\leftarrow, t)$ is the submodel of $\mathbb{M}$ whose domain consists of just t together with all its ancestors in the precedence relation. What is the syntactic counterpart of this notion? In a full predicate logic, the answer is simple. For formulas $\phi=\phi(t_0)$, at least on *transitive* frames, pure past formulas are just those logically equivalent to one having all its quantifiers 'past-restricted' ('$\exists y(y\leq x$', '$\forall y(y\leq x$'). For, the latter formulas are obviously pure past in the semantic sense - and conversely, if ϕ is pure past, then it is logically equivalent to its own relativization to the predicate '$\lambda x.x\leq t_0$'.

For the tense-logical language, however, such a simple argument does not work. (Here is one instance where living inside a fragment has its drawbacks.) But, by more complex reasoning, similar to that proving the earlier invariance characterization of Section 2.3.2, one may show that a tense-logical formula is pure past if and only if it is logically equivalent to some formula without P, H operators.

More computationally, is being pure past a *decidable* notion? At least in general predicate logic, it is not, because of the following effective reduction of an undecidable problem to this one. Let α be an arbitrary predicate-logical sentence, not containing $<$. Let α^* be the syntactic restriction of α to the predicate '$\lambda x.x\leq t_0$'. Finally, set $\beta := \alpha \vee \exists y\ t_0<y$.

Claim. β is pure past if and only if α is universally valid.

Proof. 'If': With α universally valid, β is equivalent to the pure past formula *false*.

'Only if': Suppose that α is not universally valid. Say, $\mathbb{M}$ falsifies it. Then, expand $\mathbb{M}$ by choosing some t_0 and imposing a binary relation $<$ which makes all other points $<$-predecessors of t_0. Finally, add one new point which becomes an $<$-successor of t_0. In the new model $\mathbb{N}$, β holds, since $\exists y\ t_0<y$. But, in $(\mathbb{N}\leftarrow, t_0)$, both disjuncts of β are false: whence it is not pure past.

As for the question of decidability of pure pastness within the basic tense logic, we conjecture that the answer is positive.

2.4.2 *Ascending to Stronger Formalisms*

In many applications, the expressive limitations of the basic tense logic become a hindrance. Therefore, various enrichments have been studied. For instance, already in the study of tenses proper, we encountered the *progressive* tense, which is not P, F definable. This is even more striking with certain temporal connectives, such as "since" and "until", whose definitions may be rendered as

$$\mathbb{M} \models S\phi\psi\,[t] \quad \text{iff} \quad \exists u{<}t\,(\mathbb{M} \models \phi\,[u] \wedge \forall s(u{<}s{<}t \Rightarrow \mathbb{M} \models \psi\,[s])$$

$$\mathbb{M} \models U\phi\psi\,[t] \quad \text{iff} \quad \exists u{>}t\,(\mathbb{M} \models \phi\,[u] \wedge \forall s(t{<}s{<}u \Rightarrow \mathbb{M} \models \psi\,[s])$$

Such further operators may be viewed as successive steps towards drawing the full first-order language into the scope of temporal logic. Indeed, Kamp 1966 has the following functional completeness result.

Theorem. On continuous linear orders, S, U are sufficient for defining all first-order formulas in L_0.

This result has been generalized by Stavi, who found two additional operators S', U' such that the resulting set is functionally complete on arbitrary linear orders (cf. Gabbay 1981b).

Remark. Note that this result depends on the particular first-order language under consideration. For instance, if one also allows *binary* predicates over points as denotations of proposition letters (as in the temporal interval logics of Section 3), then no functional completeness exists, not even on $\mathbf{R}$ (cf. Venema 1988). □

Explicit completeness results for the S, U logic, both in general and on specific frames, may be found in Burgess 1982a, Goldblatt 1987a.

The general issue in the background here is that of the possible approximation of first-order logic by means of *variable-free* operator formalisms (cf. Section 2.3.2). As far as the present case is concerned, the situation was much clarified by Gabbay, Pnueli, Shelah & Stavi 1980 who showed that the following two statements are equivalent for temporal frames:

(1) the first-order predicate logic L_0 can be restricted without loss of expressive power to some fixed finite number of bound variables

(2) this logic has a finite functionally complete operator formalism.

Probably the most elegant presentation to date is to be found in Immerman & Kozen 1987, which characterizes these fixed bound variable fragments by means of the existence of winning strategies in an *Ehrenfeucht-Fraisse game* with pebbling. (Immerman 1982 has a connection with complexity measures for evaluation of first-order sentences.)

Concerning axiomatics, Gabbay 1981a, 1981b give a general (though abstract) method for producing completeness theorems for arbitrary temporal operators on *irreflexive* frames. (The trick here involves direct definition of the additional operators in terms of the old F, P, using proposition letters true at only one point as 'parameters'.) Also, the earlier-mentioned decidability results of Burgess & Gurevich 1985 are relevant here, as they were already about full first-order formalisms, rather than just the basic tense logic. As yet, however, there are few *explicit* completeness results for such natural special cases as the unary tense fragment of the full first-order language on **R** or **Z**.

Remark. Also in this full first-order setting, there is an issue of *incompleteness*, when looking in the opposite direction. Starting from a set of axioms, the following minimal system of $\Pi^1{}_1$ inference seems plausible and tractable: all deduction rules of *first-order* logic plus a *substitution rule* replacing universal second-order quantifiers by their first-order instances. But then, e.g., the earlier incomplete logic of Section 2.2.2 is still incomplete. For, on full frames, it implied $p \rightarrow Gp$ which does not follow from it on the general frame $(\mathbb{Z}, <, \mathbb{W})$. But, the latter range $\mathbb{W}$ is even closed under arbitrary sets which are parametrically first-order definable from it: and hence, it validates all consequences of our tense logic in the minimal $\Pi^1{}_1$ logic too. □

One prominent issue is how the earlier general tense-logical theory fares under successive extensions of the formalism. In fact, many results seem to generalize in one way or another. For instance, the earlier-mentioned Sahlqvist theorem will remain valid without any change in its proof for antecedents of the kind described in Section 2.4.1 with *arbitrary* positive first-order consequents. More technically, van Benthem 1986 has an extension of Goldblatt & Thomason type results (cf. Section 2.3.5) to definability of frame classes in monadic $\Pi^1{}_1$ logic (which corresponds to using full first-order languages on models).

Another direction of generalization in the literature has been toward 'multi-dimensional' tense logics, allowing evaluation of formulas at *sequences* of points. For instance, interpretation of sentences with temporal adverbs like "now", "then" will require a record of not just the current point of evaluation, but also certain auxiliary points. Thus, not just formulas $\phi(t_0)$, but also formulas with an arbitrary number of free temporal variables become relevant. See Segerberg 1973, Gabbay 1976, Burgess 1984a for some results in this area.

Remark. With arbitrary finite numbers of argument places, the issue of an adequate variable-free operator notation for first-order predicate logic starts shifting. For, in this area, there are several general candidates which do that job uniformly: witness Quine 1966 with a well-known proposal, and Bacon 1985 with a complete axiomatization of the latter. Van Benthem 1977 discusses the propriety of the latter kind of move for a genuine temporal logic. But also, one could use a formalism like Combinatory Logic (cf. Hindley & Seldin 1986) for the purpose.

There is a subtlety here, in that the earlier-mentioned (im)possibility results for temporal operator languages presuppose a narrower conception of what constitutes an 'admissible' operator; which would rule out the Quine apparatus, strictly speaking. It is perhaps too early to adjudicate the issue. □

Remark. There has been a lively debate on the utility, and indeed morality, of temporal operator formalisms versus predicate-logical ones employing explicit quantification over points in time (cf. Massey 1969, Needham 1975). There appears to be no uniform answer here. For certain purposes, restricted operator formalisms continue proving their value, in terms of perspicuity and simple computation. (A recent example of the virtues of 'operationalizing' may be found in so-called arithmetical 'provability logic': cf. Smorynski 1984.) On the other hand, the bounds of any particular operator formalism can sometimes become artificial - and then, displaying explicit variables can be definitely superior. □

As was already observed in Section 2.4.1, the very tendency toward increasing expressive power induces a general question as to what are *natural fragments* of first-order predicate logic. This issue can be approached in many different ways, depending on the intended application. For instance, in the semantics of natural language, a natural principle of division proceeds by various restrictions on the *binding patterns* for quantifiers: cf. van Benthem 1986a, 1988b. One possible route for temporal logic is to extend the analysis of invariant operations initiated in Section 2.3.3. For instance, we may generalize the result given there as follows:

> Any automorphism-invariant continuous n-ary operation on propositions in $\mathbf{R}$ may be defined using P, F, $\wedge$, $\vee$.

Not surprisingly, in view of Kamp 1966, a central role is played by Since and Until when it comes to enumerating all polyadic automorphism-invariant operations satisfying not continuity, but the earlier computability by convex subintervals. Thus, we can give a more principled underpinning of specific operators extending the basic framework.

2.4.3 *Further Directions*

The above survey of variants on the basic tense logic is by no means complete. Of the many other directions of research , we mention merely three.

- Linear versus branching time logics.

This topic is illustrated by various contributions in this volume. Basic publications in the logical tradition are Burgess 1980, Thomason 1984 and Gurevich & Shelah 1985. (See also de Jongh & Bowen 1986.)

The systems presented up till now allow branching models just as well as linear ones: witness the earlier Minkowski spaces. So, what is genuinely 'branching' temporal logic? One answer is that this is just a restriction to special branching frames; which then suggest a somewhat different set of basic temporal operators (often with a second-order flavour, as in 'eventual truth along all future branches'). Another, perhaps more principled answer is that branching indicates a two-sorted semantic perspective: of *points* in time and *paths* through them, requiring evaluation at point-on-path pairs. Philosophically, the question here is if this is really a temporal field, or whether we have crossed the border toward the land of *modality*.

Thus, on the previous pattern of this Section, the technical task would be to sort out possible choices of temporal structures, fundamental temporal operators and temporal axioms. For instance, should the set of paths always be 'full' in the set-theoretic sense, or could it be varied? (Such decisions affect the model theory considerably, inducing varying correspondences between axioms and structural conditions: cf. the appendix to Rodenburg 1986.) Then, what are appropriate basic temporal operators in such a setting? Probably the most plausible choice is the one found in much of the computational literature, namely to have an existential quantifier over paths diverging from the current one only at the time of evaluation, in addition to the ordinary future operator along the current path. Such systems have a nice axiomatic completeness theory (witness Emerson 1988, Stirling 1988), but they remain to be studied in the model-theoretic detail already obtained for the basic tense-logical framework.

- Introducing metric structure.

In basic research on Measurement (cf. Krantz et al. 1971), studying temporal order is just a prelude towards taking a second step, imposing *metric* structure for measuring duration. Little attention has been paid to this theme within temporal logic (see Burgess 1984a on what little there is). Nevertheless, there is no natural frontier here, since numerical representation may arise out of qualitative relational structure: witness the paradigm case of Geometry (Tarski 1969, Goldblatt 1987b) and Physics (Field 1980). For instance, what would be the proper temporal logic of the reals with precedence and *equidistance*? Probably, as in other cases of richer 'numerical' systems, the pure temporal logic component will be only a modest one, with much of the mathematical action occurring in the superstructure.

- Combinations of time and other phenomena.

It is often difficult to maintain a rigid separation between purely temporal phenomena and space, modality or causation. There is a good deal of philosophical and logical literature on such combinations, witness Chellas 1980, van Eck 1981, Thomason and Gupta 1981, van Benthem 1983, Thomason 1984 and van Benthem 1988a. Perhaps, in the final philosophical analysis, there is no such thing as a separate phenomenon of 'time' at all. Even so, to justify the enterprise of temporal logic, one may paraphrase an aphorism of the Dutch scholar Brandt Corstius as follows:

> "By 'science' we understand that immensely succesful human activity which proceeds by resolutely ignoring the fact that everything depends on everything else."

3. Intervals and Events

Over the past decade, a reappraisal has taken place of the choice of basic temporal entities. After all, the idea that these should be durationless *points* or moments in time, although prominent in modern science, reflects only one intuitive view of Time. But, even within mathematics, there has also been another broad intuition, viewing Time more 'continuously' as consisting of primitive pieces which always have duration: say, *periods*.

To be sure, the two views are not mutually exclusive. A 'point theorist' can understand periods as *intervals*, i.e., sets of points satisfying certain (convexity) constraints. And also conversely, a 'period theorist' can admit points as the result of a *limit* process extrapolating from ever smaller periods. In any case, by now, there has been a large number of attempts at (re)constructing a viable temporal period paradigm, of which we shall survey a few salient traits, in order to illustrate the workings of this new perspective in temporal logic.

3.1 Basic Period Ontology

The move from points to periods has had various motivations stemming from the original areas of application for temporal logic, being philosophy and linguistics. For instance, philosophers have become increasingly interested in so-called *part-whole* relations in addition to *element-set* relations, which leads to more 'continuous' approaches (cf. Smith 1982). But also in linguistic semantics, many temporal expressions in natural language seem to involve extended periods rather than points in time as their natural indices of evaluation. For instance, on dense structures like **Q** or **R**, the earlier account of the *progressive* tense (Sections 2.3.2, 2.4.2) would imply that, if I am suffering now, I have been suffering already (in some open interval far enough to the left in the ongoing interval of suffering). This inference seems unwarranted: and the problem highlights the fact that "be suffering" is more naturally predicated of extended intervals in the first place, without any direct reduction to points within these (if any). Further examples of mismatches may be found in Dowty 1979, Creswell 1985, van Benthem 1988a. Finally, there has been a number of proposals coming from Computer Science and Artificial Intelligence advocating this same move, for instance, by suggesting that in temporal data bases, periods rather than points are the most efficient carriers of temporal information (cf. Allen 1983).

Despite all these pointers to periods, no single ontological paradigm has emerged yet. As it turns out, there are a good many options as to the proper mathematical modelling. Clearly, there should be some form of *precedence* ; and also, at least one relation displaying the extended nature of periods, such as *inclusion* or *overlap* . But, many further candidates are around in the literature.

There are various possibilities here for a more principled selection. E.g., Ladkin & Maddux 1987 have a systematization in terms of *relational algebra.* And one could also extend the earlier *invariance* analysis of Sections 2.3.3, 2.4.2 on intervals of linear orders, in order to enumerate basic options. [A conceptual disadvantage of the latter procedure is that development of the period paradigm is made to depend essentially on pictures supplied by its point-based rival.]

Example. With two convex intervals on the reals **R**, there are only thirteen possible relative positions which are invariant under automorphisms: cf. Allen 1983, van Benthem 1983. For finite unions of convex intervals, however, the situation is less clear (cf. Ladkin 1987b), calling for further constraints. □

Incidentally, a period theorist is not committed to a sparse unitary ontology. For instance, another option might be to allow *co-existence* of different sorts of primitive temporal objects: periods, points and perhaps others as well.

Remark. A rather original perspective on the choice of primitive relations is found in Thomason 1987, who shows that a proper categorial duality between point structures and period structures may be set up only if we assume the following items:

'total precedence', 'beginning before', 'ending before' and 'abutment'. □

In addition to the choice of primitive relations, there is the issue of choosing appropriate *axioms*. Here, the same classification may be used as in Section 2.1.3. That is, there may be a core set of uncontroversial (Horn clause) first-order principles, surrounded by progressively more debatable further assumptions. Here is a reasonable system for precedence and overlap, due to Russell 1926:

(1) $\forall x: \neg x<x$

(2) $\forall x: xOx$

(3) $\forall xy: xOy \rightarrow yOx$

(4) $\forall xy: xOy \rightarrow \neg x<y$

(5) $\forall xyz: x<yOz<u \rightarrow x<u$

These principles imply transitivity for $<$.

For inclusion, one may require partial ordering:

(6) $\forall x: x \subseteq x$

(7) $\forall xyz: x \subseteq y \subseteq z \rightarrow x \subseteq z$

(8) $\forall xy: x \subseteq y \subseteq x \rightarrow x=y$

as well as *monotonicity*:

(9) $\forall xyzu: x \subseteq y<z \supseteq u \rightarrow x<u$

(10) $\forall xyzu: x \supseteq yOz \subseteq u \rightarrow xOu$.

Beyond these plausible properties of and connections between the primitive relations, there are also some less evident universal options, such as

$\forall xy: x<y \vee y<x \vee xOy$ (linearity)

$\forall xyzu: u \supseteq x<y<z \subseteq u \rightarrow y \subseteq u$ (convexity) .

On top of this, then, first-order principles with existential import may be formulated, expressing the existence of neighbours, subintervals, etcetera. Some full first-order theories of intervals may be found in van Benthem 1983, Allen & Hayes 1985, Ladkin 1987a, Ladkin & Maddux 1987. For instance, the complete first-order theory of $<, \subseteq$ on convex intervals of rational numbers is effectively axiomatizable (and indeed decidable), via a Cantor-style zigzag argument establishing countable categoricity.

Remark. Subtleties of formulation may matter here. For instance, some first-order interval theories will be decidable, whereas other related variants are not (cf. Schulz 1987). □

Then also, *higher-order* intuitions on period structures may be formulated. One example with a metaphysical pedigree is the idea of *Reflection*: 'The structure of the whole universe must be reflected in its smallest parts'. Technically, let $\mathbb{I} = (I, <, \subseteq, O)$ be some period structure, with $i \in I$. The substructure $\mathbb{I}_i$ has a universe $\{j \in I \mid j \subseteq i\}$ with the obvious restrictions of $<, \subseteq, O$. Then, one might require that:

For each $i \in I$, $\mathbb{I}$ is isomorphic to $\mathbb{I}_i$.

Note that this also makes all $\mathbb{I}_i$ isomorphic among themselves: Reflection involves a form of *Homogeneity*.

Remark. The pattern of the exposition here has followed that for point structures rather closely. Thus, whatever ontological rivalry may exist, the temporal point paradigm can serve as a model for its period alternative, at least in a methodological sense. □

3.2 Temporal Logic

First-order theories of intervals are one, direct way of describing period structures. But, it is also possible to proceed as before in the Priorean fashion, using period frames for the evaluation of suitable propositional languages. Again, there is a variety of possible 'temporal logics' here, differing in their choice of operators.

One relatively standard system of this kind is developed in van Benthem 1983. It has the earlier temporal operators P, F referring to total precedence, as well as one operator typically exploiting the additional inclusion structure, namely

$\mathbb{M} = (I, <, \subseteq, V) \models \Box\phi\,[i]$ iff $\forall j \subseteq i$: $\mathbb{M} \models \phi\,[j]$.

To preserve the symmetry here, we might add an upward dual of $\Box$.

This tense logic can be treated by the methods already developed in Section 2. For instance, various conditions on the period relations may correspond to principles expresssible in the temporal logic.

Example. The axioms $\Box\phi \rightarrow \Box\Box\phi$ and $\Box\Diamond\phi \rightarrow \Diamond\Box\phi$ together will now express that $\subseteq$ is an atomic transitive order. (Compare the McKinsey Axioms of Sections 2.2.2, 2.4.1.) $\Box$

Example. The axiom $F\phi \rightarrow \Box F\phi$ corresponds to leftward monotonicity, being $\forall xyz: x \subseteq y < z \rightarrow x < z$; and likewise, rightward monotonicity corresponds to $P\phi \rightarrow \Box P\phi$. $\Box$

Similarly, the basic model theory for this system can be developed using suitable notions of generated submodel and zigzag morphism.

Finally, as for completeness results, the following logic has been proposed as a 'minimal extended tense logic', and proved frame-complete in van Benthem 1983:

(1) a complete propositional base
(2) the modal logic S4 for $\Box$
(3) the minimal tense logic K_t for F, P
(4) the above two monotonicity axioms for $\Box$, F, P .

At the back of these results lies again a *translation* into a suitable first-order logic (on models), or a monadic second-order logic (on frames), as before.

Nevertheless, there is one important special case to be noted here. Quantification in the latter logics will be over individuals which are *periods* (and subsets of these, in the second-order case). But, when one is dealing with *intervals* which have been derived from some underlying point frame, quantification over periods itself may be viewed as being already second-order, vis-a-vis the underlying points. In many cases, however, the latter complexity can be reduced. Intervals are often given by their *boundary points*: and then, quantification over them reduces to mere quantification over ordered pairs of individual points, and hence to ordinary quantification over points.

Even thus, there remains a subtlety. Frame validity of an interval axiom will then involve quantification over all predicates of ordered pairs of points, that is, essentially, over all *binary relations* among points. Therefore, when measured in terms of the underlying points, frame validity of temporal axioms on interval structures becomes more complex than in Section 2 above, involving *dyadic* instead of *monadic* second-order logic. And, unlike the monadic theory of, say, the integers $\mathbf{Z}$, its dyadic second-order theory is non-effectively axiomatizable. (Cf. van Benthem 1983, Halpern & Shoham 1986.)

The observed smooth sailing along the path charted in Section 2 reflects the rather cautious selection of a minimal period tense logic. Many further choices of primitive predicates will lead to a more complex system, closer in spirit to the first-order generalizations of tense logic discussed in Section 2.4.2.

What is worth emphasizing are rather some *new* aspects of working with a period-based temporal logic, which have not emerged before.

One basic issue is this. Several authors have claimed that, on our intuitive understanding of even the standard *logical constants*, these no longer have their usual truth definitions in a period setting. For instance, Humberstone 1979 claims that *negation* now should have the following 'intuitionistic' reading (compare Troelstra & van Dalen 1988):

$\mathbb{M} \models \neg\phi\,[i]$ iff $\forall j \subseteq i$: *not* $\mathbb{M} \models \phi\,[j]$ ('nowhere during i') .

And Creswell 1977 has proposed that our natural temporal reading of conjunction involves a join of subperiods where the conjuncts hold:

$\mathbb{M} \models \phi\wedge\psi\,[i]$ iff $\exists j, k \in I$: $j \cup k = i$ *and* $\mathbb{M} \models \phi\,[j]$ *and* $\mathbb{M} \models \psi\,[k]$.

These views also come with general intuitions concerning the admissible truth value patterns of propositions across nested periods. Thus, Hamblin 1971 has stated that

"there are no indefinitely finely intermingled intervals of both truth and falsity for any statement".

Probably, a better strategy here is to leave the old logical constants undisturbed, while studying some of their compounds or variants. For instance, the above intuitionistic negation is already definable in our language as $\Box\neg\phi$. And, the Creswell conjunction might be added as a new connective, comparable to the computationally well-known chop operator CHOP $\phi\psi$, which says that a period can be divided up into two consecutive subperiods verifying ϕ, ψ in that order.

A more general new topic which arises naturally in this context is the semantic *preservation* behaviour of certain types of formula. For a long time, linguists have observed that temporal (verbal) expressions in natural language may be classified into various kinds, distinguishable by their behaviour under inclusion. For instance, some are downward preserved in passing from a period to its subperiods; others may be upward cumulative, in that they hold of any union of overlapping periods in which they hold. Moreover, there are linguistic constructions taking expressions from one such 'aspectual class' to another (cf. Dowty 1979). E.g., "Mary was writing" is preserved under subperiods, whereas its extended direct object form "Mary was writing a love letter" is not (cf. Krifka 1987). As a formal counterpart, we can study various types of preservation behaviour for syntactic classes of formulas in period tense logic.

Example. Temporal Propagation.

Here is a phenomenon which also makes sense within the framework of Section 2. Which formulas are such that, once true, they will remain true? Examples are all forms $G\phi$, $P\phi$(on transitive frames) as well as anything obtainable from them using $\wedge, \vee, \Box$. In fact, any future-propagated formula is equivalent to a form $G^*\phi$ (standing for: $G\phi\wedge\phi$). In particular, the class of formulas equivalent to some G^* shape is already closed under $\wedge, \vee, \Box$. □

Example. Temporal Descent.

Which formulas are such that their truth at any period trickles down to all its subperiods? Examples are all forms $P\phi$, $F\phi$, $\Box\phi$ as well as anything obtainable from them using $\wedge, \vee$. And conversely, any downward-preserved formula is equivalent to the form $\Box\phi$. Again, the class of such formulas is closed under P, F, $\Box$, $\wedge$ and $\vee$. □

Finally, here is an example of a richer interval logic, taken from Halpern & Shoham 1986. Structures are frames $(T, <)$ with intervals $[t_1,t_2]$ $(t_1 \leq t_2)$. Basic operators include the following:

BEGIN ϕ is true at $[t_1,t_2]$ iff there exists $t_3<t_2$ such that ϕ is true at $[t_1,t_3]$

START ϕ is true at $[t_1,t_2]$ iff there exists $t_3>t_2$ such that ϕ is true at $[t_1,t_3]$

BEFORE ϕ is true at $[t_1,t_2]$ iff there exists $t_3 \leq t_1$ such that ϕ is true at $[t_3,t_1]$, as well as their obvious duals (such as END opposite to BEGIN).

The expressive power of this formalism can be studied by the earlier techniques, viewing it as a two-dimensional multi-modal logic, whose primitive relations are required to show certain interactions, encodable in suitable axioms. See Venema 1988 for further details. Specifically,

(1) on linear orders, all point-based tense-logical statements are expressible, since the logic has the means of defining the functionally complete Stavi set S, U, S', U' of Section 2.4.2.

(2) as to interval expressions, the earlier CHOP operator is not definable

(3) the formalism is stronger than any point-based temporal logic, in that there exist two countable linear frames having the same monadic second-order theory which can be distinguished in this logic. (Recall the earlier remark about the *dyadic* second-order nature of the present formalism.)

Remark. Using an idea from van Benthem 1983, Venema reinterprets this interval logic as one of points in a direct product of the underlying frame with itself. Thus, the above operators become *topological* ones: and 'logic of time' becomes also 'logic of space'. □

As for completeness, Halpern & Shoham 1986 prove a number of negative results, establishing Π^1_1-hardness for the interval logics of e.g., **N**, **Z** or **R** . For general logical reasons, however, the rationals **Q** must remain an exception (as was observed already in Section 2.2.3) - and indeed, Venema provides a complete axiomatization of their interval logic, using the 'irreflexivity rule' of Gabbay 1981a. At the base of this lies a general interval logic, whose axioms include such typical cases as

BEGIN BEGIN $\phi \rightarrow$ BEGIN ϕ

END START $\phi \rightarrow$ START END ϕ

All these axioms express *first-order* conditions on the above topological structures, and hence on their underlying point frames. The reason is that all of them are *Sahlqvist* forms (cf. Section 2.4.1).

Remark. The last observation suggests that *fragments* of the full language may be better behaved (as is already pointed out by Halpern & Shoham themselves). In particular, are the Sahlqvist fragments of **N** , **Z** and **R** axiomatizable after all? □

Remark. The above logic is still traditional, in that intervals are convex sets on a *linear* order. P. Thiagarajan has suggested looking into similar logics of intervals on non-linear frames, such as the Minkowski spaces of section 2.2.1, 2.2.3 , whose convex intervals are geometric rectangles or , in higher dimensions, blocks. □

3.3 Relating Periods and Points

Not just philosophically, but also mathematically, the point-based paradigm of Time can peacefully coexist with the period-based one.

- Every point frame $(T, <)$ induces an interval structure $(I, <, \subseteq, O)$ where
  (1) I consists of all non-empty convex subsets of T
  (2) $i<i'$ if $\forall t \in i, t' \in i'$: $t<t'$
  (3) $i \subseteq i'$ if i is a subset of i'
  (4) iOi' if $i \cap i'$ is non-empty .

Such interval structures will validate almost all of the earlier basic postulates: and truly all, if one starts with an underlying transitive irreflexive frame $(T, <)$. See van Benthem 1983,1984b for details, including a proof that these principles axiomatize the complete first-order theory of convex interval structures on strict partial orders.

- Conversely, period structures may be *represented* as families of intervals on point frames via any one of a number of mathematical constructions, such as (maximal) filters (see van Benthem 1983) or Dedekind cuts (see Burgess 1984b, Thomason 1979). [Whitrow 1980 has an account of historically prior attempts, going back to Russell and Wiener.] A short exposition of the filter method and its mathematical properties is found in van Benthem 1984b. For instance, one interesting issue is the *correspondence* between the earlier basic constraints on the two kinds of temporal structure, when looking along the two representation maps. Likewise, one can try to relate Priorean tense logics interpreted at the two levels.
- This mathematical correspondence between point structures and period structures can be elaborated into a full-fledged *duality between categories* (cf. van Benthem 1983, Thomason 1987). The basic observation here is that natural kinds of morphism turn out to correspond on both sides. For instance, van Benthem 1984b correlates the following two notions (out of many possibilities):

(1) *positive extension* among period structures $\mathbb{I}_1, \mathbb{I}_2$:
I_1 is contained in I_2 , and likewise $<_1$ in $<_2 \restriction I_1$, $\subseteq_1$ in $\subseteq_2 \restriction I_1$.

(2) *anti-morphic surjective functions* between point structures $\mathbb{T}_1, \mathbb{T}_2$:
i.e., partial maps f from T_2 into T_1 such that $f(x)<_1 f(y) \rightarrow x<_2 y$,
which also satisfy a suitable continuity condition on distinguished intervals.

Intuitively, (1) describes a period structure $\mathbb{I}_1$ growing into a larger one $\mathbb{I}_2$ having new periods as well as (possibly) more precedence and inclusion facts about old periods. Thus, their induced point frames become richer, with the obvious notion of backward restriction among (suitable) filters satisfying (2). Further technical details may be found in the earlier references. What we have here, in fact, is an instance of the general mathematical duality between more point-based set-theoretic approaches and more interval-based topological ones , which also figures e.g. in the semantics of intuitionistic versus classical logic.

3.4 Extending to Events

In some ways, the move from temporal points to temporal periods seems only a half-way house towards more radical measures. Many recent authors in the philosophical and linguistic tradition have broken with the primacy, or at least independence, of a purely temporal ontology, by making *events* the major furniture of our universe. This is an old, and respectable idea. Already Leibniz tried to derive the structure of Time (and Space) out of the formal pattern of events in this world (cf. Winnie 1977). And also more recently, for quite different reasons, Davidson 1967 has been a very influential plea for making 'event' a basic category, both in the philosophy of language and in practical linguistics.

Remark. More recently, various formal theories of events have appeared, intended as a vehicle for the logical semantics of natural language (cf. Krifka 1987). One issue here is how to develop a good version of the *Lambda Calculus* based on both ordinary individuals and events. □

Events are not purely temporal entities, in that they also have (at least) spatial and causal aspects. Nevertheless, much of their formal theory, as far as temporality is concerned, has been similar to what we have already seen for period structures. For instance, the earlier basic axioms for the latter were originally put forward to capture the behaviour of events (cf. Russell 1926) - and a similar switch may be observed with many modern authors. What is different are rather the types of *question* suggested for logical investigation.

Example. Private and Public Time.

For Russell, one of the interesting phenomena to be clarified by logical analysis was the interplay between 'common sense' and 'scientific' notions of Time. Our private experiences come in the form of (finite) event structures, which may be pooled (via the earlier notion of positive extension) into some large public experience. In parallel, these event structures may be represented as point structures, running from private times to public time. The categorial perspective of Section 3.3 then allows us to make exact comparisons between various routes towards creating the public time of science (cf. Thomason 1979, van Benthem 1984b, 1988a). □

Example. Temporal Representation of Discourse.

In Kamp 1979, the process of interpreting natural language is analyzed as follows. Ongoing text produces 'discourse representations', whose temporal format is that of event structures. These should then be related to actual intervals in physical point-based time, in order to establish objective truth. In this perspective, the representation method of Section 3.3 turns out to explain some of the peculiarities of actual temporal expressions in natural language. □

Digression. Partial Models.

One of the other novelties in the paper just-mentioned (at least, as far as temporal logic is concerned) is the introduction of *partial* relations of precedence and inclusion, having positive parts to their extension, but also negative and undecided ones. The latter reflect temporary lack of information. We shall return to the underlying issue of *partial information* in Section 4 below. □

Partial information is just one of several computational issues which surface in the account so far. For instance, as we shall see, connections between various levels of temporal representation also arise naturally in computer science. And, on the topic of formal theories of events, much of the material in Winskel 1988 seems relevant in a wider philosophical / linguistic setting too.

In reality, the ontological picture behind natural language is more complex than has been suggested so far. We are living in a rich universe of not just individuals and events, but also such temporal entities as 'cases' (Lewis 1975), 'processes', 'states', etcetera. An interesting concrete reflection of this wealth is found in the aspectual calculus of Galton 1984, where states and events appear on a par as the basic temporal entities. The Priorean tenses F, P then become operators from states to states, whereas the progressive (PROG) as well as the perfect (PERF) change events into states. Conversely, there are operators turning states into events, such as INGR ('begin to') and PO ('spend a while'). A fair sample of Galton's principles reads as follows:

$$\text{PERF INGR } q \leftrightarrow P^*(P\neg q \wedge q) \qquad (\text{where } P^*q := Pq \vee q)$$

$$\text{PROG PO } q \leftrightarrow P\neg q \wedge q \wedge F\neg q$$

$$\text{PERF } q \rightarrow G \text{ PERF } q \,.$$

Thus, tense logic can be pursued in richer temporal ontologies too.

Although these theories have their motivation in linguistics and philosophy, they may be suggestive also as a source for computational accounts of storage of temporal information. Presumably, natural language has good reasons for preferring a rich many-sorted approach over some austere view of temporality.

4. Perspectives from Computer Science

The main topic of this survey has been temporal logic as it has developed from its original sources. But recently, there has been an outburst of application, and indeed independent development, of temporal logic within computer science: as is amply demonstrated by the present volume. Without any pretense at exhaustiveness or authority, the following is an attempt at stating some of the main phenomena which make this computational connection of interest to 'native' temporal logicians. Examples will be taken from both point-based and period or event-based paradigms.

4.1 Application with Innovation

Current applications of temporal logic in computer science look congenial to a temporal logician. This starts already with their general attitude. There seems to be a healthy engineering approach in computational work, stressing the construction of different temporal systems geared towards intended applications and *issues*, rather than the search for any single 'philosophers' stone'. This is quite in line with the tendency towards plurality and generality recorded earlier for classical temporal logic. Moreover, the kinds of technical question being studied are usually quite recognizable logical concerns, in particular, expressive power, axiomatizability and decidability. To an outsider, this might actually come as a surprise. A priori, one might expect computer scientists to arrive at quite different fundamental questions concerning known temporal logics. And perhaps, with time, this will yet come about.

Even so, not *all* logical concerns seem to have found computational application yet. For instance, there seems to be a relative neglect of other possible meta-properties of temporal calculi, such as *interpolation*, and likewise, of other types of model-theoretic question, such as *preservation*. It might be worth the effort to investigate their potential computational relevance too. After all, there are already quite surprising examples of new computational purposes for old logical notions, witness the use of the *finite model property* for deriving machines or protocols producing certain desired behaviour (cf. Clarke & Emerson 1981 and subsequent publications).

Computational research has not just been a customer of existing logic: it also has much of its own to offer which enriches traditional temporal logic in various ways.

For a start, it appears to have introduced one more 'standard concern' for research, in adddition to expressive power and axiomatization, namely that of precise *computational complexity* of proposed systems. Such concerns were largely absent from the classical literature, where 'decidability' was as far as practical concerns went. Moreover, issues of complexity have also started penetrating elsewhere in logic - witness the recent interest in deciding various other syntactic and semantic notions. Perhaps, we shall have a 'computational model theory' one day.

The concern with complexity may also be classified as an instance of another general trend in the computational literature, namely the study of the *fine-structure* of earlier logical systems. [In a sense, the fine-structure below logical Recursion Theory is what computer science is all about.] Often, there is as much to be gained by *restricting* as by *generalizing* from some standard temporal calculus. This is also true for expressive power and syntactic form; witness the emphasis on special syntactic shapes, such as those expressing 'liveness' and 'safety'. (See Pnueli 1988 and Katz 1988 for illustrations.)

Then, as is natural in any applied field, the computational perspective also highlights certain *concrete models* or model classes, whose temporal logic can then be developed in much more depth, using available special purpose tools. This may be observed, for instance, in the use of Automata Theory on discrete temporal frames of suitable order types in Thomas 1986, 1988. [The latter perspective may even be of general semantic significance after all: witness van Benthem 1987 on 'semantic automata' in a computational semantics.]

Another computational restriction is that to *finite models* (advocated in Gurevich 1985). Here, a number of results has been reached already within classical temporal logic. For instance, much of the earlier work on the finite model property falls under this heading. And there are also some results on expressive power of temporal logic on finite frames (cf. van Benthem 1986b). Contrary to prevailing prejudices among logicians, the finiteness restriction does not always make the original theory easier. For, useful classical methods based on Compactness fail, and have to be replaced by laborious combinatorial reasoning.

In addition to the process of specialization and concretization of classical temporal logic in a computational setting, it must be said that the area has also produced at least one important *generalization*. For, *Dynamic Logic* (see Harel 1984) may be viewed as a general form of temporal logic, where our earlier systems have become embedded in a theory of complex actions.

4.2 Semantic Parallels

The above examples were all taken from point-based temporal logic. Next, we review some topics from more recent period or event-based developments, which are sometimes surprisingly similar to those having occurrred in the classical framework. Since there are fewer ready-made tools here (compare Section 3), straightforward 'application' is not our main concern. What we want to demonstrate is rather how this parallel development by itself suggests a natural community of interests between logic, linguistics and computer science.

We have already seen a proposed temporal *interval logic* by Halpern & Shoham 1986, which turned out to be quite close to the standard tense-logical tradition (cf. Section 3.2).

Arguments put forward by computer scientists for making the move towards intervals or periods, rather than points, have been partly similar to classical ones ('greater ease and naturalness of expression': Halpern & Shoham 1986, Kowalski & Sergot 1985), partly new, stressing computational advantages of period-based inferential algorithms (Allen 1983). An interesting general philosophy supporting this ontological shift is found in the research program of *Naive Physics* in Artificial Intelligence (cf. Hayes 1979, Hobbs 1985). The guiding idea here is that efficient reasoning and computation requires knowledge representations which are similar to those used in the common sense world, rather than those found in abstract science. The technical elaboration of this program shows unmistakeable analogies with the research reported in Section 3 above. But of course, the scope of Naive Physics is much wider in principle than mere temporality.

Digression. As a matter of history of ideas, Naive Physics shows how 'lost causes' in science can still be of computational interest. What Hayes and his followers are doing seems close to an attempt at recapturing an Aristotelean, pre-Galilean physics. Thus, contrary to the tenets of modern orthodoxy, maintaining a plurality of scientific frameworks seems useful, even across so-called 'decisive turns' in history. □

There are also interesting analogies between more concrete proposals made in Artificial Intelligence, and Computer Science in general, concerning temporal representation and temporal inference, and the more linguistic/philosophical interests described earlier. For instance, the central issues in such papers as McDermott & Shoham 1985 or Kowalski & Sergot 1985 are quite close to those formulated in Section 3 concerning various forms of temporal persistence along precedence or inclusion orderings.

A final example, which brings together many earlier strands, arises from the much-cited recent work Lamport 1985 on the proper temporal modelling of *parallel computation*. Lamport presents a system of axioms for 'system executions', being sets of 'operation executions' ordered by two relations of total precedence and partial precedence. Moreover, he studies the connection between different 'views' of a system execution, arising from different groupings of individual actions into complex units. Without going into detail, we may note some interesting analogies with the themes developed in Section 3.

First, the choice of primitives is easily understood via Lamport's intuitive explanation in terms of subsets on a strict partial order $(T, <)$:

total precedence	$x<y$	$\forall e \in x\ \forall e' \in y:\ e<e'$
partial precedence	$x \leq y$	$\exists e \in x\ \exists e' \in y:\ e \leq e'$

Slightly more elegantly, we may rewrite the second notion as a disjunction of

overlap	xOy	$\exists e \in x\ \exists e' \in y:\ e=e'$
partial precedence*	$x<<y$	$\exists e \in x\ \exists e' \in y:\ e<e'$

Lamport's axioms express some obvious Horn clause conditions on these relations, which look similar to those encountered in the earlier literature (Kamp 1979, Allen 1983). That they are well-chosen may be seen from various mathematical results proven since (cf. Angers 1986, Ben-David 1987), which show that the models of the Lamport system, slightly extended, are precisely those admitting of a *representation* in terms of subsets on an underlying strict partial order. Such a result was also obtained independently using the methods of van Benthem 1983, with the outcome that the following Lamport-type calculus axiomatizes the complete first-order theory of point sets on strict partial orders:

(1) all Russell axioms on $<$, O listed in Section 3.1 (except for linearity)

(2) the further axioms

$x<y \rightarrow \neg y<<x$, $\quad x<<y<z<<u \rightarrow x<<u$, $\quad x<y<<z<u \rightarrow x<u$,

$xOy<z<<u \rightarrow x<<u$, $\quad x<<y<zOu \rightarrow x<<u$, $\quad xOy<zOu \rightarrow x<<u$

Remark. *Linearity* would be an optional item. Ben-David 1987 has some results on relating system executions to linear 'global time models' which is reminiscent of the embedding of discourse representations into real physical time discussed in Section 3.4. (This author also shows that, for certain types of modal statement, working with underlying partial orders or linear orders makes no difference. At the level of first-order relational conditions, this may also be shown to be true for *Horn clauses*.) □

Remark. In line with Section 3.1, *inclusion* may be added as a primitive relation. Then, the above representation result can be extended using some obvious axioms on $\subseteq$ and its interplay with $<<, <$, O .

□

Next, the idea of various related system executions, having different 'grain size', brings in the earlier categorial perspective of a wider world of event structures, with suitable morphisms connecting them. For instance, here are two candidates which may be discerned behind Lamport's presentation:

(1) f is an *embedding* from one system execution into another if it respects $<$ as well as $<<$.

(2) f is a *higher level view* if it is a surjection acting as follows:

$x<y \rightarrow f(x)<<f(y), \quad f(x)<f(y) \rightarrow x<y$.

Explanation. Higher level views may be interpreted as grouping several events into a single new one, and deriving the new relational structure from the old:

$u<v$ if $\forall x\in f^{-1}(u)\ \forall y\in f^{-1}(v)$: $x<y$

$u<<v$ if $\exists x\in f^{-1}(u)\ \exists y\in f^{-1}(v)$: $x<y$. □

Such morphisms can be studied model-theoretically as to their *transfer* behaviour. Which descriptions true in one approximation of a system remain valid in another? Notably, embeddings will preserve all existential positive statements concerning $<$ and $<<$. Higher level views will guarantee (amongst others) the following more complex transfer:

If $\phi = \phi(<)$ is true in the source, then ϕ^* is true in the image, where ϕ^* is obtained from ϕ by rewriting it to a form having negations only in front of atoms, and then replacing positive $x<y$ by $x<<y$ (negative atoms $\neg x<y$ remaining undisturbed).

Example. Succession $\forall x\ \exists y\ x<y$ induces $\forall x\ \exists y\ x<<y$; while discreteness $\forall x\ \exists y(\ x<y \wedge \neg\exists z(\ x<z \wedge\ z<y\ )\ )$ becomes $\forall x\ \exists y(\ x<<y\ \wedge \neg\exists z(\ x<z \wedge\ z<y\ )\ )$. □

In addition, of course, we may also study these morphisms in combination with their categorial counterparts at the level of the underlying point frames, by various representation methods.

Thus, the Lamport perspective too involves the richer temporal picture which was already required by philosophical and linguistic developments in current temporal logic. This final case of convergence concludes our survey of more tentative recent trends in temporal representation.

4.3 Reinterpreting Logic

One intriguing phenomenon to be observed these days is how computationally inspired ideas are making themselves felt even within the heartland of standard logic, leading to a reappraisal of basic semantic frameworks. It is too early yet to judge the intrinsic merits of this development: but it is certainly worth demonstrating in some detail here, for the case of the basic tense logic. We shall consider variations on all of its central aspects: whether its models, notions of inference or even modes of evaluation.

4.3.1 *Time Machines*

The imagery of *machines* is ubiquitous in computational logic, sometimes even occurring at several levels within one type of problem. This may be partly a matter of fashion. John Searle once pointed out in this connection how seventeenth century thinkers saw *clocks* everywhere, and their ancestors in Antiquity again whatever piece of technology was 'en vogue' then. Nevertheless, there is an interesting issue here concerning the nature of time. Traditional temporal logic has looked at time as a receptacle for histories, and accordingly, its models are regarded intuitively as sets of possible *traces* of the evolution of some system over time. What recent computational applications show, however, is that these models may also reflect the systems or *machines themselves* which produce these histories. [And of course, even on the classical view, one tries to see the grand System in or through the observed traces.]

The two perspectives mingle rather nicely in those semantics for branching time where some finite possible worlds frame, viewed as a machine, is considered together with the set of all its possible evolutions, so that statements about its 'states' and its 'paths' can be brought together. This also highlights a difference with traditional temporal logic of course: one is investigating 'machine time', rather than actual time. But on the other hand, this move toward conceptual, rather than actual temporal structure could also be observed already in those classical theories which were designed with an eye toward temporal representation (cf. Section 3).

In fact, classical logical techniques work just as well when dealing with machine-like temporal models. In particular, the semantic invariance relations of Section 2.3.1 make sense for machines too. For instance, given any finite state machine, its complete evolution tree is precisely its *unraveling* in the earlier sense, which is zigzag related to it: and hence the two verify the same tense-logical formulas at corresponding points. Conversely, given any temporal model, we may construct some minimal model verifying the same formulas at corresponding points by means of the earlier-mentioned technique of *filtration*. When the collapsed model is *finite*, we may view it as a machine producing the original 'behaviour'.

Remark. There are two subtleties here. One is that filtration may be *relativized* to work for special classes of formulas only. With a finite class of relevant formulas, the collapse is even guaranteed to be finite too. The other point is that the collapsing function is not necessarily a zigzag relation. For that to occur, one needs additional conditions on the original model, such as 'modal saturation' (cf. Fine 1975b). In particular, if the original model is only *finitely branching*, filtration will always produce p-morphic collapsing maps. □

Of course, the machine perspective suggests various new questions here, which would not be so evident in a more general modal or temporal perspective. One case in point are possible ways of *retrieving* machines from their output behaviour. (Compare the *Nerode representation* for finite automata.)

Also relevant is the earlier remark about bisimulation in process algebra and zigzag relations in temporal logic (cf. Sections 2.3.1, 2.3.2). Without going into details here about the encoding of transitions and states into propositions, we can make such simple observations as the following:

Two connected indeterministic finite automata bisimulate each other if and only if their initial states, when viewed as roots of possible worlds models, verify the same Priorean pure future formulas.

Example. Failure of Distribution.

The well-known example from Process Algebra concerning the difference between $a{\cdot}(b{+}c)$ and $(a{\cdot}b){+}(a{\cdot}c)$ is reflected in the temporal non-equivalence between $F(a \wedge (Fb \wedge Fc))$ and $F(a \wedge b) \wedge F(a \wedge c)$.

□

If one is merely interested in recognized sequences, then only a *fragment* of the temporal language will be relevant, using just syntactic forms $F(a_1 \wedge F(a_2 \wedge \ldots \wedge F(a_n \wedge \mathit{accept}) \ldots))$. Again, there is an analogy here between temporal logic and automata theory. Two deterministic finite automata bisimulate each other if and only if they recognize the same strings. But also, two corresponding 'deterministic' possible worlds models verify the same, possibly 'branching', pure future formulas if and only if they verify the same formulas of the above restricted 'linear' forms.

Thus, even though a precise elaboration is beyond the scope of this survey, predominantly machine-oriented formalisms for temporal behaviour and more traditional trace-oriented ones seem very closely connected - even though they may give rise to different points of emphasis in the agenda for research.

4.3.2 *Partial Information*

Another trend in current logic and semantics whose inspiration has clear computational roots is the interest in *information,* and potential lack of it. In particular, how can one draw inferences with *incomplete* information? *Partiality* is a broad concern by now (cf. Blamey 1986, Urquhart 1986), which again provides a fresh look at established logical systems. (Cf. Fenstad et al. 1987 on partial predicate logic and related theories.)

Within temporal logic, partiality may occur at several levels. Already in Section 3.4, we encountered temporal frames having 'positive', 'negative' as well as 'undecided' / 'unknown' parts to their relations of precedence and inclusion. This move can be made without losing the insights from the earlier 'total' framework.

Example. Partializing Temporal Constraints.
Let Σ be a set of first-order conditions on frames, defining a class K of admissible temporal structures. Let K_{part} be the class of those partial structures which can still be made into classical frames satisfying Σ by addition of individuals and appropriate closure of 'truth value gaps'. (Thus, K_{part} is a natural 'partial hull' for K .) Then, K_{part} is first-order definable too, in the obvious first-order companion language having two predicates $<^+, <^-$ and likewise for other temporal relations. (See Kamp 1979 for a proof.) Moreover, the new partial axioms may be extracted effectively from the original Σ . □

But not just the temporal *ontology* may be partialized. The same holds for the tense logic over it. For instance, even on standard frames, we may have partiality at the level of *interpretation*. Let us assume that propositional valuations V now have positive, negative and undecided parts to their extensions. Following a well-known pattern, one can then set up conditions of 'verification' and 'rejection':

$\mathbb{M} \models^+ p[t]$	iff	$t \in V^+(p)$
$\mathbb{M} \models^- p[t]$	iff	$t \in V^-(p)$
$\mathbb{M} \models^+ \neg\phi[t]$	iff	$\mathbb{M} \models^- \phi[t]$
$\mathbb{M} \models^- \neg\phi[t]$	iff	$\mathbb{M} \models^+ \phi[t]$
$\mathbb{M} \models^+ \phi\wedge\psi[t]$	iff	$\mathbb{M} \models^+ \phi[t]$ *and* $\mathbb{M} \models^+ \psi[t]$
$\mathbb{M} \models^- \phi\wedge\psi[t]$	iff	$\mathbb{M} \models^- \phi[t]$ *or* $\mathbb{M} \models^- \psi[t]$.

For the temporal operators, there seem to be *options*; of which we choose

$\mathbb{M} \models^+ F\phi[t]$	iff	*for some* $t'>t$: $\mathbb{M} \models^+ \phi[t]$
$\mathbb{M} \models^- F\phi\ [t]$	iff	*for each* $t'>t$: $\mathbb{M} \models^- \phi[t]$

An alternative would be to stipulate here: *for no* $t'>t$: $\mathbb{M} \models^+ \phi[t]$.

The option chosen here makes evaluation *persistent*, in that,

> If $\mathbb{M} \models^+ \phi[t]$, then $\mathbb{M}' \models^+ \phi\ [t]$, for every model $\mathbb{M}'$ differing from $\mathbb{M}$ only in that V'-values for proposition letters may have become 'more defined'; and likewise for $\mathbb{M} \models^- \phi\ [t]$.

The latter stipulation leads to possible non-persistence: growth of information may lead us to accept an already rejected statement after all. Eventually, having non-persistent operators available seems unavoidable when dealing with partial information - and the most natural candidate is the following two-valued negation:

$\mathbb{M} \models^+ \sim\phi\ [t]$	if	*not* $\mathbb{M} \models^+ \phi[t]$
$\mathbb{M} \models^- \sim\phi\ [t]$	otherwise.	

Then, the second reading of the future operator becomes definable as $\sim\sim F\phi$.

Again, this system can be translated into a classical 'total' variant, by a method of Gillmore (cf. Langholm 1988). In fact, it may be embedded back into the basic Priorean tense logic, so that its *decidability* and other meta-properties follow automatically.

Example. For the sake of illustration, here is the translation which embeds partial temporal logic into its total classical version. Each formula gets a 'positive' and a 'negative' counterpart, via the following mutual recursion:

$$(p)^+ = p^+ \qquad (p)^- = p^-$$
$$(\neg\phi)^+ = (\phi)^- \qquad (\neg\phi)^- = (\phi)^+$$
$$(\phi\wedge\psi)^+ = (\phi)^+\wedge(\psi)^+ \qquad (\phi\wedge\psi)^- = (\phi)^-\vee(\psi)^-$$
$$(F\phi)^+ = F(\phi)^+ \qquad (F\phi)^- = G(\phi)^- .$$

This allows us to reduce various proposed notions of partial consequence to their classical counterparts. □

Despite these reductions, the partial perspective also raises some interesting questions of its own, witness the characterization of persistence in an extended language proved in Langholm 1988. Further logical aspects of partiality are discussed in van Benthem 1988a.

4.3.3 *Circumscription*

One striking phenomenon in the field of automated reasoning is the emergence of computational systems having other modes of inference than just standard logical consequence. As such further inferences are often defeasible, the resulting logics will usually be non-monotonic. One such system, whose logical theory is relatively well-developed is the calculus of *circumscription* (cf. McCarthy 1980). Again, it is of interest to observe how even the basic temporal logic admits of circumscription, as an alternative to its standard notion of consequence.

Definition. Let ϕ be a tense-logical formula, and p some proposition letter. $(\mathbb{M}, t)$ is a *p-minimal* model for ϕ if (1) $\mathbb{M} \models \phi\,[t]$, and (2) for no $\mathbb{M}'$ differing from $\mathbb{M}$ only in that $V'(p)$ is properly contained in $V(p)$, $\mathbb{M}' \models \phi\,[t]$.

There is an immediate generalization to minimizing over several proposition letters simultaneously.

Remark. Actually, this notion is not foreign to standard tense logic. For instance, the proof of Sahlqvists's Theorem (Section 2.4.1) depends on the fact that its antecedent formulas admit of minimal models having first-order definitions for the extensions of the proposition letters involved (cf. van Benthem 1985). □

Now, circumscription gives us additional inferences, through the following notion of consequence, which looks only at special models for premises, where as few p-facts happen as possible:

$$\Sigma \models^{p}_{circ} \phi \quad \text{if} \quad \phi \text{ is true at all p-minimal models of } \Sigma .$$

Evidently, every standard consequence of Σ remains valid in this new sense; but in general, additional ones arise, such as $F(p \wedge q) \models^{p}_{circ} G(p \rightarrow q)$.

Many logical questions arise concerning circumscription in the basic tense logic. In particular, it is known that circumscription in *full* predicate logic is a highly complex, non-axiomatizable notion. On the other hand, for *monadic* predicate logic, circumscription is decidable. For the present formalism, intermediate between these two, we only have a

Conjecture. Circumscriptive inference in the minimal tense logic is decidable.

As for reduction to standard logics, the obvious translation matching the above definition takes circumscribed formulas (say) $\mu p \cdot \phi(p)$ to *monadic second-order* sentences (cf. van Benthem 1988c). Nevertheless, we may investigate just when tense-logical formulas have first-order circumscriptions, on the pattern of the earlier Correspondence Theory (cf. Lifschitz 1985, van Benthem 1988c).

Example. First-Order Circumscription.

By results of Lifschitz, all formulas of the following forms are first-order:

(1) $\mu p \cdot \phi(p)$ with only positive occurrences of p, (2) $\mu p \cdot \phi(p)$ with only negative occurrences of p.

E.g.,

$\mu p \cdot GFp$ is equivalent to $(\forall x>t_0\, \exists y>x\, Py) \wedge \forall u: \neg\forall x>t_0\, \exists y>x\, (Py \wedge \neg y=u)$,

$\mu p \cdot GF\neg p$ is equivalent to $(\forall x>t_0\, \exists y>x\, \neg Py) \wedge \neg\exists x Px$.

The following formula is not first-order, however: $\mu p \cdot (Fp \wedge G(p \rightarrow Fp) \wedge G(p \rightarrow Hp))$. For, it holds at 0 in the ordinal sum $(\mathbf{N}, <) + (\mathbf{Z}, <)$ when $V(p) = \mathbf{N}$. But, it fails in the many elementary equivalents of the latter structure having $V(p)$ true beyond the initial copy of $\mathbf{N}$. Therefore, no first-order definition can be adequate. □

4.3.4 *Dynamic Interpretation*

Logical formalisms are often contrasted with programming languages, as being *declarative* rather than *procedural* or 'imperative'. But recently, various authors have become interested in procedural aspects of logical interpretation, to the extent of giving procedural semantics for standard logical formalisms too. (Cf. Groenendijk & Stokhof 1987, taking up an earlier idea of Barwise; and van Benthem 1988c for further logical background.) When applied to the basic tense logic, the following mechanism of interpretation arises.

Intuitively, evaluation of tense-logical formulas in some model is a process taking us along various shifting points of evaluation. Thus, one might assign some set of succesful 'verification traces' to each formula. [This would be an alternative to the 'multi-dimensional' tense logics of Section 2.4.2.] But, as in Hoare-style operational semantics for programs, a convenient level of abstraction is provided by the mere *transition relation* associated with each formula, viewed as if it were an instruction for its own evaluation. Here is a formal implementation, restricted (for convenience only) to pure future tense logic.

Let $\mathbb{M}$ be a model $(T, <, V)$. We define a binary relation $[[\phi]]$ for each tense-logical formula ϕ through the following recursion:

$$[[q]] = \{ (t, t) \mid t \in V(p) \}$$

i.e., atomic propositions function as tests,

$$[[\phi \wedge \psi]] = [[\phi]] \circ [[\psi]]$$

i.e., conjunction denotes sequential composition,

$$[[F\phi]] = \{ (t, t') \mid \exists t'': t<t'' \textit{ and } (t'', t') \in [[\phi]] \}$$

i.e., future truth is established by making some succesful jump along $<$,

$$[[\neg\phi]] = \{ (t, t) \mid \forall t': (t, t') \notin [[\phi]] \}$$

i.e., negation is a test again, of 'strong failure'.

Remark. The third clause may also be rephrased as a composition of $[[\phi]]$ and $[[F]] = <$. □

On this account, interesting procedural differences emerge between formulas which used to be equivalent. For instance, $Fp \wedge Fq$ does not denote the same relation as $Fq \wedge Fp$. The reason behind this failure is in fact the *validity* of the following non-theorem of the standard system: formulas $Fp \wedge Fq$ denote the same relation as $F(p \wedge Fq)$. More generally, the effect of the new interpretation procedure is to widen scopes of F-operators toward the right. There are limits here, though, set by negation: $\neg Fp \wedge Fq$ is not equivalent to $\neg F(p \wedge Fq)$. Thus, *inference* in the new system will be startlingly unlike before.

In fact, there are several options for defining semantic consequence. One measures inclusion of interpretative transition relations:

$$\phi_1,\ldots,\phi_n \models^1 \psi \quad \text{if} \quad \text{in all models, } [[\phi_1 \wedge\ldots\wedge \phi_n]] \subseteq [[\psi]] .$$

Another notion would look at possible continuations for evaluating the conclusion after the premiscs have been processed:

$$\phi_1,\ldots,\phi_n \models^2 \psi \quad \text{if} \quad \text{in all models, } (t_1, t_2) \in [[\phi_1 \wedge\ldots\wedge \phi_n]] \text{ only if there exists some } t_3 \text{ such that } (t_2, t_3) \in [[\psi]] .$$

The reason why many properties of classical logic are lost here is that various 'side-effects' of interpretation become important to consequence. Nevertheless, one can still embed classical tense logic into the new one, for instance, by translating formulas so that every F-operator is packed in a double negation. (See the final example below, however, for a different principle.)

The purpose of this passage is merely to point out how even the well-known basic tense logic becomes challenging again under this oblique procedural perspective. For instance, one question now becomes whether the original set of *logical operators* is adequate to the new situation. The answer seems to be negative: on binary relations, many other operations become important (cf. van Benthem 1988c). For instance, it seems reasonable at least to have genuine *Booleans* too. This calls for the following alternatives for negation and conjunction:

$$[[\sim\phi]] \;=\; T\times T - [[\phi]] \qquad \text{('absence')}$$

$$[[\phi\cap\psi]] \;=\; [[\phi]] \cap [[\psi]] \qquad \text{('parallel success')}$$

Moreover, it seems reasonable to add a *modality* over extensions

$$[[\Box\phi]] \;=\; \{ (t, t) \mid \forall t' \in T: (t, t') \in [[\phi]] \} .$$

This makes the earlier negation $\neg$ definable, as well as other useful modalities of interpretation. Thus, the system with operators $\sim$, $\cap$, $\wedge$, $\Box$ and F seems a reasonable candidate for further investigation.

As for its complexity, we conjecture that the resulting system is still *decidable*. [But of course, in line with earlier remarks, one would like to know its *precise* complexity vis-a-vis K_t.]

What can be established a priori is the effective axiomatizability of these dynamic systems. The reason is that they admit of a*translation* into standard formalisms, be it a different one from that studied in Section 2.3.2. Tense logic now becomes a vehicle for defining binary *relations* rather than subsets over points in time:

$$\tau(p) \;=\; t_1=t_0 \wedge Pt_1$$

$$\tau(\sim\phi) \;=\; \neg\tau(\phi)$$

$$\tau(\phi\cap\psi) \;=\; \tau(\phi) \wedge \tau(\psi)$$

$$\tau(\phi\wedge\psi) \;=\; \exists x([x/t_1]\tau(\phi) \wedge [x/t_0]\tau(\psi))$$

$$\tau(F\phi) \;=\; \exists x(t_0<x \wedge [x/t_0]\tau(\phi))$$

$$\tau(\Box\phi) \;=\; t_1=t_0 \wedge \forall x([x/t_1]\, \tau(\phi))$$

Again, we can study the model theory of this system. For instance, which classes of relations can be tense-logically defined? Thus, the whole theory of Section 2 might be re-examined, under such a new embedding of tense logic as a fragment of first-order logic.

Remark. By exercising a little more care, the translation may even be taken into the *three-variable* fragment of L_0 with identity. The following instructions use only t_0, t_1, x to send every tense-logical ϕ to a first-order relation $\tau^*(\phi)$ with free variables t_0, t_1 :

$$\tau^*(p) \quad = \quad t_1=t_0 \wedge Pt_1$$
$$\tau^*(\sim\phi) \quad = \quad \neg\tau^*(\phi)$$
$$\tau^*(\phi\cap\psi) \quad = \quad \tau^*(\phi) \wedge \tau^*(\psi)$$
$$\tau^*(\phi\wedge\psi) \quad = \quad \exists x(\exists t_1(\tau^*(\phi) \wedge t_1=x) \wedge \exists t_0(\tau^*(\psi) \wedge t_0=x))$$
$$\tau^*(F\phi) \quad = \quad \exists x(t_0<x \wedge \exists t_0(\tau^*(\phi) \wedge t_0=x))$$
$$\tau^*(\Box\phi) \quad = \quad t_1=t_0 \wedge \forall t_1\tau^*(\phi)\ . \quad \Box$$

Remark. A more radical move would be to drop the clauses '$t_1=t_0$' in the above translation, and making evaluation of proposition letters a non-instantaneous action. (Thus, the formalism would become even more analogous to Dynamic Logic.) □

Digression. The above translation also suggests that dynamic point-based tense logic is closer to *interval* tense logic. Perhaps a better general perspective is this. We have a structure $\mathbb{T} = (T, <)$ modelling 'real time'. But, it also generates a notion of 'evaluation time', reflected in the structure $\mathbb{T}^*$ of all *finite sequences* of points from T ; which may be provided with various 'modalities' describing properties of the process of evaluation. Some of the Halpern & Shoham operators (see Section 3.2) would be appropriate here, but so would CHOP (in expressing that some sequence has recognized a conjunction $\phi\wedge\psi$ sequentially). □

Finally, we point out how, at least for the original system with operators $\wedge$, F, $\neg$, there is a classical road towards decidability by embedding the present dynamic system into classical tense logic.

Here is a sketch of a procedure for converting consequence problems in the dynamic system to those in classical tense logic. First, every formula ϕ can be transformed into an equivalent ϕ^*, working inside out, by widening scopes of F-operators as far as possible toward the right (until some negation boundary is hit). For formulas ϕ^* in this special form, it may be shown that their succesful transitions (x,y) are those having some finite sequence $x=t_1<t_2<...<t_n=y$, each of whose points corresponds to some outermost F operator (outside of the scope of any negation), while each t_i reflects some test (t_i, t_i) for a subformula p or $\neg\alpha$, which is satisfied if and only if the latter formulas are classically true at t_i . Using this perspective, various notions of dynamic consequence can be reduced. As a concrete illustration, one can check that

$$F\neg(Fp \wedge q) \wedge r \wedge Fp \models_2 Fr \wedge p \qquad \text{iff}$$
$$F(\neg F(p \wedge q) \wedge r \wedge F(p \wedge a)) \models FF(a \wedge F(r \wedge p)) \quad \text{classically.}$$

Explanation. The reason for this reduction lies in the following translation σ , where the *new* proposition letter a is used to mimick the second argument of the transition relation:

$$\sigma(p) \quad = \quad p \wedge a$$
$$\sigma(F\phi) \quad = \quad F\sigma(\phi)$$
$$\sigma(\phi\wedge\psi) \quad = \quad [\sigma(\psi)/a]\sigma(\phi)$$
$$\sigma(\neg\phi) \quad = \quad \neg[\mathit{true}/a]\sigma(\phi) \wedge a$$

By a straightforward induction, then, the following facts may be proven:

(1) $\mathbb{M} \models \sigma(\phi)\,[t]$ iff there exists some $t' \in V(a)$ such that $\mathbb{M}(t') \models \sigma(\phi)\,[t]$;
where $\mathbb{M}(t')$ is the model which differs from $\mathbb{M}$ only in that $V(a)$ is the singleton $\{t'\}$.
(2) $(t, t') \in [[\phi]]$ iff $\mathbb{M}(t') \models \sigma(\phi)\,[t]$.
As a corollary, e.g., the following reduction holds:

$$\phi \models^2 \psi \quad \text{iff} \quad \sigma(\phi) \models F^k(\, a \wedge [\mathit{true}/a]\sigma(\phi)\,)\ ;$$

where k is the number of outermost F-operators in ϕ (not governed by any negation). □

Here, our travels on the border-line between temporal logic and computer science come to an end. We have noticed short-term benefits of this contact, such as useful additions to the traditional logical fund of tools and applications. But, there may also be a long-term effect, as we have seen, in that logic itself might become transformed in a computational mode.

References

Allen, J., 1983, 'Maintaining Knowledge about Temporal Intervals', *Communications of the* ACM 26, 832-843.

Allen, J. & P. Hayes, 1985, 'A Commonsense Theory of Time', *Proceedings* IJCAI 1985, 528-531.

Anger, F., 1986, On Lamport's Interprocessor Communication Model, Department of Mathematics, University of Puerto Rico, Rio Piedras.

Apt, K., ed., 1985, *Logics and Models of Concurrent Systems*, Springer, Berlin.

Bacon, J., 1985, 'The Completeness of a Predicate-Functor Logic', *Journal of Symbolic Logic* 50, 903-926.

Bartsch, R., J. van Benthem & P. van Emde Boas, eds., 1989, *Meaning: Context and Expression*, Foris, Dordrecht.

Barwise, J., 1976, 'Some Applications of Henkin Quantifiers', *Israel Journal of Mathematics* 25, 47-63.

Bauerle, R., C. Schwarze & A. von Stechow, eds., 1979, *Semantics from Different Points of View*, Springer, Berlin.

Ben-David, S., 1987, The Global Time Assumption and Semantics for Concurrent Systems, Department of Computer Science, Technion, Haifa.

Benthem, J. van, 1977, 'Tense Logic and Standard Logic', *Logique et Analyse* 80, 47-83.

Benthem, J. van, 1979, 'Canonical Modal Logics and Ultrafilter Extensions', *Journal of Symbolic Logic* 44, 1-8.

Benthem, J. van, 1983, *The Logic of Time*, Reidel, Dordrecht.

Benthem, J. van, 1984a, 'Correspondence Theory', in D. Gabbay & F. Guenthner, eds., 1984, 167-247.

Benthem, J. van, 1984b, 'Tense Logic and Time', *Notre Dame Journal of Formal Logic* 25, 1-16.

Benthem, J. van, 1985, *Modal Logic and Classical Logic*, Bibliopolis, Napoli / The Humanities Press, Atlantic Heights.

Benthem, J. van, 1986a, *Essays in Logical Semantics*, Reidel, Dordrecht.

Benthem, J. van, 1986b, Notes on Modal Definability, report 86-11, Mathematical Institute, University of Amsterdam. (To appear in the *Notre Dame Journal of Formal Logic*.)

Benthem, J. van, 1986c, 'Tenses in Real Time', *Zeitschrift fuer mathematische Logik und Grundlagen der Mathematik* 32, 61-72.

Benthem, J. van, 1987, 'Towards a Computational Semantics', in P. Gardenfors, ed., 1987, 31-71.

Benthem, J. van, 1988a, *A Manual of Intensional Logic*, CSLI Lecture Notes 1, Center for the Study of Language and Information, Stanford University / The Chicago University Press, Chicago. (Second revised and expanded edition.)

Benthem, J. van, 1988b, 'Logical Syntax', to appear in *Theoretical Linguistics*.

Benthem, J. van, 1988c, 'Semantic Parallels in Natural Language and Computation', to appear in M. Garrido, ed., 1989.

Blamey, S., 1986, 'Partial Logic', in D. Gabbay & F. Guenthner, eds., 1986, 1-70.

Blok, W., 1976, *Varieties of Interior Algebras*, dissertation, Mathematical Institute, University of Amsterdam.

Blok, W., 1980, 'The Lattice of Modal Logics: An Algebraic Investigation', *Journal of Symbolic Logic* 45, 221-236.

Bull, R., 1966, 'That all Normal Extensions of S4.3 Have the Finite Model Property', *Zeitschrift fuer mathematische Logik und Grundlagen der Mathematik* 12, 341-344.

Burgess, J., 1980, 'Decidability for Branching Time', *Studia Logica* 39, 203-218.

Burgess, J., 1982a, 'Axioms for Tense logic I: "Since" and "Until"', *Notre Dame Journal of Formal Logic* 23, 367-374.

Burgess, J., 1982b, 'Axioms for Tense Logic II: Time Periods', *Notre Dame Journal of Formal Logic* 23, 375-383.

Burgess, J., 1984a, 'Basic Tense Logic', in D. Gabbay & F. Guenthner, eds., 1984, 89-133.

Burgess, J., 1984b, 'Beyond Tense Logic', *Journal of Philosophical Logic* 13, 235-248.

Burgess, J. & Y. Gurevich, 1985, 'The Decision Problem for Linear Time Temporal Logic', *Notre Dame Journal of Formal Logic* 26, 115-128.

Catach, L., 1988, Logiques Multimodales Normales,
Centre Scientifique, IBM-France, Paris.

Chang, C. & J. Keisler, 1973, *Model Theory*,
North-Holland, Amsterdam.

Chellas, B., 1980, *Modal Logic: An Introduction*,
Cambridge University Press, Cambridge.

Clarke, E. & E. Emerson, 1981, 'Synthesis of Synchronization Skeletons for Branching Time Temporal Logic', *Proceedings Workshop on Logic of Programs, Yorktown Heights NY*, Springer, Berlin, 52-71.

Creswell, M., 1977, 'Interval Semantics and Logical Words',
in Ch. Rohrer, ed., 1977, 7-29.

Creswell, M., 1985, *Adverbial Modification. Interval Semantics and its Rivals*,
Reidel, Dordrecht.

Crossley, J., ed., 1975, *Algebra and Logic*,
Springer, Berlin, (Lecture Notes in Mathematics 480).

Davidson, D., 1967, 'The Logical Form of Action Sentences',
in N. Rescher, ed., 1967, 81-95.

Doets, K., 1987, *Completeness and Definability: Applications of the Ehrenfeucht Game in Intensional and Second-Order Logic*, dissertation, Mathematical Institute, University of Amsterdam.

Doets, K. & J. van Benthem, 1983, 'Higher-Order Logic',
in D. Gabbay & F. Guenthner, eds., 1983, 275-329.

Dowty, D., 1979, *Word Meaning and Montague Grammar*,
Reidel, Dordrecht.

Earman, J., C. Glymour & J. Stachel, eds., 1977, *Foundations of Space-Time Theories*,
University of Minnesota Press, Minneapolis.

Eck, J. van, 1981, *A System of Temporally Relative Modal and Deontic Predicate Logic*,
dissertation, Department of Philosophy, University of Groningen.
(Also appeared in *Logique et Analyse*, 1983.)

Emerson, E., 1988, 'Branching Time Temporal Logics',
this volume.

Fagin, R. & M. Vardi, 1985, An Internal Semantics for Modal Logic,
report 85-25, Center for the Study of Language and Information, Stanford University.

Fenstad, J-E, P-K Halvorsen, T. Langholm, and J. van Benthem, 1987,
Situations, Language and Logic, Reidel, Dordrecht.

Field, H., 1980, *Science Without Numbers*,
Princeton University Press, Princeton.

Fine, K., 1974, 'Logics Extending K4. Part I',
Journal of Symbolic Logic 39, 31-42.

Fine, K., 1975a, 'Normal Forms in Modal Logic',
Notre Dame Journal of Formal Logic 16, 229-234.

Fine, K., 1975b, 'Some Connections between Elementary and Modal Logic', in S. Kanger, ed., 1975, 15-31.

Fine, K., 1985, 'Modal Logics Containing K4. Part II', *Journal of Symbolic Logic* 50, 619-651.

Fitting, M., 1983, *Proof Methods for Modal and Intuitionistic Logics*, Reidel, Dordrecht.

Gabbay, D., 1976, *Investigations in Modal and Tense Logics, with Applications to Problems in Philosophy and Linguistics*, Reidel, Dordrecht.

Gabbay, D., 1981a, 'An Irreflexivity Lemma', in U. Moennich, ed., 1981, 67-89.

Gabbay, D., 1981b, 'Expressive Functional Completeness in Tense Logic', in U. Moennich, ed., 1981, 91-117.

Gabbay, D. & F. Guenthner, eds., 1983, *Handbook of Philosophical Logic, vol. I: Elements of Classical Logic*, Reidel, Dordrecht.

Gabbay, D. & F. Guenthner, eds., 1984, *Handbook of Philosophical Logic, vol. II: Extensions of Classical Logic*, Reidel, Dordrecht.

Gabbay, D. & F. Guenthner, eds., 1986, *Handbook of Philosophical Logic, vol. III: Alternatives to Classical Logic*, Reidel, Dordrecht.

Gabbay, D., A. Pnueli, S. Shelah & Y. Stavi, 1980, 'On the Temporal Analysis of Fairness', *7th* ACM *Symposium on Principles of Programming Languages*, 163-173.

Galton, A., 1984, *The Logic of Aspect*, Clarendon Press, Oxford.

Gardenfors, P., ed., 1987, *Generalized Quantifiers. Logical and Linguistic Approaches*, Reidel, Dordrecht.

Garrido, M., ed., *Logic Colloquium. Granada 1987*, North-Holland, Amsterdam.

Gargov, G. & S. Passy, 1988, 'A Note on Boolean Modal Logic', Linguistic Modelling Laboratory / Sector of Mathematical Logic, University of Sofia.

Gargov, G., S. Passy & T. Tinchev, 1987, 'Modal Environment for Boolean Speculations', in D. Skordev, ed., 1987, 253-263.

Garson, J., 1984, 'Quantification in Modal Logic', in D. Gabbay & F. Guenthner, eds., 1984, 249-307.

Girard, J., 1987, 'Linear Logic', *Theoretical Computer Science* 50, 1-102.

Goldblatt, R., 1976, 'Metamathematics of Modal Logic', *Reports on Mathematical Logic* 6, 41-78; 7, 21-52.

Goldblatt, R., 1980, 'Diodorean Modality in Minkowski Space-Time', *Studia Logica* 39, 219-236.

Goldblatt, R., 1987a, Logics of Time and Computation, CSLI Lecture Notes 7, Center for the Study of Language and Information, Stanford University / The Chicago University Press, Chicago.

Goldblatt, R., 1987b, *Orthogonality and Space-Time Geometry*, Springer, New York.

Goldblatt, R. & S. Thomason, 1975, 'Axiomatic Classes in Propositional Modal Logic', in J. Crossley, ed., 1975, 163-173.

Goranko, V., 1987, 'Modal Definability in Enriched Languages', to appear in *Notre Dame Journal of Formal Logic*.

Groenendijk, J. & M. Stokhof, 1987, Dynamic Predicate Logic, Institute for Language, Logic and Information, University of Amsterdam. (To appear in the *Journal of Semantics*.)

Gurevich, Y., 1985, Logic and the Challenge of Computer Science, report TR-10-85, Computing Research Laboratory, The University of Michigan, Ann Arbor.

Gurevich, Y. & S. Shelah, 1985, 'The Decision Problem for Branching Time Logic', *Journal of Symbolic Logic* 50, 668-681.

Halpern, J. & Y. Moses, 1985, 'Towards a Theory of Knowledge and Ignorance', in K. Apt, ed., 1985, 459-476.

Halpern, J. & Y. Shoham, 1986, 'A Propositional Modal Logic of Time Intervals', *Proceedings Symposium on Logic in Computer Science*, IEEE, Boston.

Hamblin, C., 1971, 'Instants and Intervals', *Studium Generale* 24, 127-134.

Harel, D., 1984, 'Dynamic Logic', in D. Gabbay & F. Guenthner, eds., 1984, 497-604.

Harper, W., R. Stalnaker & G. Pearce, eds., 1981, *Ifs: Conditionals, Beliefs, Decision, Chance and Time*, Reidel, Dordrecht.

Hayes, P., 1979, 'The Naive Physics Manifesto', in D. Michie, ed., 1979.

Henkin, L., 1950, 'Completeness in the Theory of Types', *Journal of Symbolic Logic* 15, 81-91.

Hindley, J. & J. Seldin, 1986, *Introduction to Combinators and λ-Calculus*, Cambridge University Press, Cambridge.

Hintikka, J., ed., 1969, *The Philosophy of Mathematics*, Oxford University Press, Oxford.

Hobbs, J., ed., 1985, Commonsense Summer. Final Report, report 85-35, Center for the Study of Language and Information, Stanford University.

Hughes, G. & M. Creswell, 1984, *A Companion to Modal Logic*, Methuen, London.

Humberstone, L., 1979, 'Interval Semantics for Tense Logics', *Journal of Philosophical Logic* 8, 171-196.

Immerman, N., 1982, 'Upper and Lower Bounds for First-Order Expressibility', *Journal of Computer and Systems Sciences* 25, 76-98.

Immerman, N. & D. Kozen, 1987, 'Definability with Bounded Number of Bound Variables', *Proceedings* IEEE 1987, 236-244.

Jongh, D. de & K. Bowen, 1986, Some Complete Logics for Branched Time. Part I, report 86-05, Institute for Language, Logic and Information, University of Amsterdam.

Jongh, D. de, F. Veltman & R. Verbrugge, 1988, 'The Logics of Dense and Discrete Time', Institute for Language, Logic and Information, University of Amsterdam.

Jonsson, B. & A. Tarski, 1951, 'Boolean Algebras with Operators. Part I', *American Journal of Mathematics* 73, 891-939.

Kamp, H., 1966, *Tense Logic and the Theory of Linear Order*, dissertation, Department of Philosophy, University of California at Los Angeles.

Kamp, H., 1979, 'Instants, Events and Temporal Discourse', in R. Bauerle et al., eds., 1979, 376-417.

Kamp, H. & Ch. Rohrer, 1988, *Tense in Text*, Institut fuer Computerlinguistik, Universitaet Stuttgart.

Kanger, S., ed., 1975, *Proceedings of the Third Scandinavian Logic Symposium. Uppsala 1973*, North-Holland, Amsterdam.

Kapron, B., 1987, 'Modal Sequents and Definability', *Journal of Symbolic Logic* 52, 756-762.

Katz., S., 1988, 'Exploiting Interleaving Set Temporal Logic to Simplify Correctness Proofs', *this volume.*

Keenan, E., ed., 1975, *Formal Semantics of Natural Language*, Cambridge University Press, Cambridge.

Klop, J-W, 1988, 'Bisimulation Semantics', *this volume.*

Kowalski, R. & M. Sergot, 1985, A Logic-Based Calculus of Events, Department of Computing, Imperial College, London.

Krantz, D., R. Luce, P. Suppes & A. Tversky, 1971, *Foundations of Measurement*, Academic Press, New York.

Krifka, M., 1987, 'Nominal Reference and Temporal Constitution: Towards a Semantics of Quantity', to appear in R. Bartsch et al., eds., 1988.

Ladkin, P., 1987a, Models of Axioms for Time Intervals, The Kestrel Institute, Palo Alto.

Ladkin, P., 1987b, *The Logic of Time Representation*, dissertation, Department of Mathematics, University of California at Berkeley.

Ladkin, P. & R. Maddux, 1987, The Algebra of Convex Time Intervals, The Kestrel Institute, Palo Alto / Department of Mathematics, Iowa State University at Ames.

Lambek, J., 1959, 'The Mathematics of Sentence Structure', *American Mathematical Monthly* 65, 154-170.

Lamport, L., 1985, Interprocessor Communication. Final Report, SRI International, Menlo Park.

Langholm, T., 1988, *Partiality, Truth and Persistence*, CSLI Lecture Notes 15, Center for the Study of Language and Information, Stanford University / The Chicago University Press, Chicago.

Lewis, D., 1975, 'Adverbs of Quantification',
in E. Keenan, ed., 1975, 3-15.

Lifschitz, W., 1985, 'Computing Circumscription',
Proceedings IJCAI-85:1, 121-127.

Massey, G., 1969, 'Tense Logic! Why Bother?',
Nous 3, 17-32.

McCarthy, J., 1980, 'Circumscription. A Form of Non-Monotonic Reasoning',
Artificial Intelligence 13, 295-323.

McDermott, D. & Y. Shoham, 1985, 'Temporal Reasoning',
to appear in S. Shapiro, ed., *Encyclopedia of Artificial Intelligence*, Wiley-Interscience, New York.

McTaggart, J., 1908, 'The Unreality of Time',
Mind 18, 457-474.

Michie, D., ed., 1979, *Expert Systems*,
Edinburgh University Press, Edinburgh.

Michon, J. & J. Jackson, eds., 1985, *Time, Mind and Behavior*,
Springer, Berlin.

Moennich, U., ed., 1981, *Aspects of Philosophical Logic*,
Reidel, Dordrecht.

Needham, P., 1975, *Temporal Perspective*,
dissertation, Department of Philosophy, University of Uppsala.

Oberlander, J., ed., 1987, *Temporal Reference and Quantification: An IQ Perspective*,
Centre for Cognitive Science, University of Edinburgh.

Pnueli, A., 1981, 'The Temporal Semantics of Concurrent Programs',
Theoretical Computer Science 13, 45-60.

Pnueli, A., 1988, 'Linear Time Temporal Logic',
this volume.

Prior, A., 1957, *Time and Modality*,
Clarendon Press, Oxford.

Prior, A., 1967, *Past, Present and Future*,
Clarendon Press, Oxford.

Quine, W., 1966, 'Variables Explained Away',
in *Selected Logic Papers*, Random House, New York.

Reichenbach, H., 1947, *Elements of Symbolic Logic*,
The Free Press, New York.

Reichenbach, H., 1957, *The Philosophy of Space and Time*,
Dover, New York.

Rescher, N., ed., 1967, *The Logic of Decision and Action*,
University of Pittsburgh Press, Pittsburgh.

Rescher, N. & A. Urquhart, 1971, *Temporal Logic*,
Springer, Berlin.

Richards, B. & I. Bethke, 1987, 'The Temporal Logic IQ', in J. Oberlander, ed., 1987, 114-132.

Rodenburg, P., 1986, *Intuitionistic Correspondence Theory*, dissertation, Mathematical Institute, University of Amsterdam.

Roeper, P., 1980, 'Intervals and Tenses', *Journal of Philosophical Logic* 9, 451-469.

Rohrer, Ch., ed., 1977, *On the Logical Analysis of Tense and Aspect*, Gunter Narr Verlag, Tuebingen.

Russell, B., 1926, *Our Knowledge of the External World*, Allen & Unwin, London.

Sahlqvist, H., 1975, 'Completeness and Correspondence in the First and Second Order Semantics for Modal Logic', in S. Kanger, ed., 1975, 110-143.

Sambin, G. & V. Vaccaro, 1987, 'Topology and Duality in Modal Logic', to appear in *Annals of Pure and Applied Logic*.

Schulz, K., 1987, Event and Interval Structures: A Mathematical Comparison, Seminar fuer Natuerlich-Sprachliche Systeme, Universitaet Tuebingen.

Segerberg, K., 1970, 'Modal Logics with Linear Alternative Relations', *Theoria* 31, 301-322.

Segerberg, K., 1973, 'Two-Dimensional Modal Logic', *Journal of Philosophical Logic* 2, 77-96.

Shehtman, V., 1983, 'Modal Logics of Domains on the Real Plane', *Studia Logica* 42, 63-80.

Shoham, Y., 1986, *Reasoning about Change: Time and Causation from the Standpoint of Artificial Intelligence*, The MIT Press, Cambridge (Mass.).

Skordev, D., ed., 1987, *Mathematical Logic and its Applications*, Plenum Press, New York.

Smart, J., ed., 1964, *Problems of Space and Time*, McMillan, New York & London.

Smirnov, V., 1982, 'The Definition of Modal Operators by means of Tense Operators', *Acta Philosophica Fennica* 35, 50-69.

Smith, B., ed., 1982, *Parts and Moments. Studies in Logic and Formal Ontology*, Philosophia Verlag, Muenchen.

Smorynski, C., 1984, 'Modal Logic and Self-Reference', in D. Gabbay & F. Guenthner, eds., 1984, 441-495.

Stirling, C., 1988, Expressibility and Definability in Branching and Linear Time Temporal Logics, Department of Computer Science, University of Edinburgh.

Tarski, A., 1969, 'What is Elementary Geometry?', in J. Hintikka, ed., 1969, 164-175.

Thomas, W., 1986, Safety and Liveness Properties in Propositional Temporal Logic: Characterizations and Decidability, Lehrstuhl fuer Informatik II, Universitaet Aachen.

Thomas, W., 1988, 'Computation-Free Logic and Regular ω-Languages', *this volume.*

Thomason, R., 1984, 'Combinations of Tense and Modality', in D. Gabbay & F. Guenthner, eds., 1984, 135-165.

Thomason, R. & A. Gupta, 1981, 'A Theory of Conditionals in the Context of Branching Time', in W. Harper et al., eds., 1981, 299-322.

Thomason, S., 1972, 'Semantic Analysis of Tense Logics', *Journal of Symbolic Logic* 37, 150-158.

Thomason, S., 1974, 'Reduction of Tense Logic to Modal Logic', *Journal of Symbolic Logic* 39, 549-551.

Thomason, S., 1975, 'Reduction of Second-Order Logic to Modal Logic', *Zeitschrift fuer mathematische Logik und Grundlagen der Mathematik* 21, 107-114.

Thomason, S., 1979, Possible Worlds, Time and Tenure, Department of Mathematics, Simon Fraser University, Burnaby B. C.

Thomason, S., 1982, 'Undecidability of the Completeness Problem of Modal Logic', *Universal Algebra and Applications*, Banach Center Publications vol. 9, Warsaw.

Thomason, S., 1987, Free Construction of Time from Events, Department of Mathematics, Simon Fraser University, Burnaby B. C.

Troelstra, A. & D. van Dalen, 1988, *Constructivism in Mathematics*, North-Holland, Amsterdam.

Urquhart, A., 1986, 'Many-Valued Logic', in D. Gabbay & F. Guenthner, eds., 1986, 71-116.

Vardi, M., 1985, 'A Model-theoretic Analysis of Monotone Logic', *Proceedings* 9th IJCAI, 509-512.

Venema, Y., 1988, Expressiveness and Completeness of an Interval Tense Logic, report 88-02, Institute for Language, Logic and Information, University of Amsterdam. (Extended version to appear.)

Whitrow, G., 1980, *The Natural Philosophy of Time*, Clarendon Press, Oxford.

Winnie, J., 1977, 'The Causal Theory of Space-Time', in J. Earman et al., eds., 1977, 134-205.

Winskel, G., 1988, 'Event Structures', *this volume.*

PROCESS THEORY BASED ON BISIMULATION SEMANTICS

J.A. Bergstra
University of Amsterdam, Department of Computer Science
P.O. Box 19268, 1000 GG Amsterdam;
State University of Utrecht, Department of Philosophy,
P.O. Box 8810, 3508 TA Utrecht.

J.W. Klop
Centre for Mathematics and Computer Science,
P.O. Box 4079, 1009 AB Amsterdam;
Free University, Department of Mathematics and Computer Science,
De Boelelaan 1081, 1081 HV Amsterdam.

Note: Research partially supported by ESPRIT project 432, Meteor.
Chapter 1 of this paper is a modified version of 'Process algebra: specification and verification in bisimulation semantics', from CWI Monograph 4, Proc. of the CWI Symposium Mathematics and Computer Science II (eds. Hazewinkel, Lenstra, Meertens), North-Holland, Amsterdam 1986. Permission of the editors to include the present Chapter 1 here is gratefully acknowledged.

ABSTRACT
In this paper a process is viewed as a labeled graph modulo bisimulation equivalence. Three topics are covered: (i) specification of processes using finite systems of equations over the syntax of process algebra; (ii) inference systems which are complete for proving the equivalence of regular (finite state) processes; (iii) variations of the bisimulation model.

Introduction

We will discuss process theory on the basis of a given semantic concept. A process will be a rooted directed graph where arcs are labeled with actions. An example may clarify this matter (see Figure 1.1).

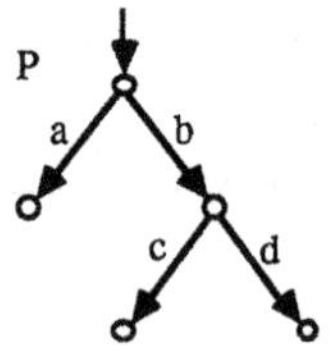

Figure 1.1

For instance the process P denotes a process that has two options for initial actions, a and b. After the a-step P will terminate, but after having done the b-step P has again two options, c and d.

Now obviously the concept of a process should be made independent of its incidental coding in a graph. So we must determine an appropriate equivalence relation on graphs. There are several possibilities for such equivalence relations. Relevant references are for instance: Brookes, Hoare & Roscoe [84], Hennessy [88], De Nicola & Hennessy [83], and Phillips [87]. However, bisimulation equivalence, as introduced in Park [81], stands out, in our view, as the most natural identification mechanism on process graphs discovered thus far.

Having thus established roughly the domain of processes as that of process graphs modulo bisimulation, the next step is to incorporate the major discovery of Milner [80], namely that processes have an algebraic structure. Our paper has to balance between two opposite poles: (a) the syntax of process algebra and its axioms and proof rules, (b) the extremely rich world of process graphs and bisimulations. The main relations between (a) and (b) are as follows:

(1) Using the syntax of process algebra we may write down equational axioms and axiom schemes that 'specify' bisimulation semantics. These axioms capture the intended process semantics in algebraic terms.

Chapter 1 contains a survey of a possible syntax of process algebra (ACP, Algebra of Communicating Processes, and extensions) and its axioms and rules: see Table 22. In this setting one finds the concept of a process algebra, i.e. a model of (the axioms of) process algebra: an appropriate class of process graphs, together with a definition of the algebraic operators on these process graphs such that bisimulation equivalence becomes a congruence relation. The main model is $\mathbb{G}/{\leftrightarrow}_{r\tau\delta}$, described in Chapter 1, Section 1.13.

(2) Equations over the syntax of process algebra having free variables ranging over processes can be solved in bisimulation semantics. In particular so-called systems of guarded recursion equations turn out to have unique solutions. These systems are used to specify processes.

Chapter 1 contains several examples of process specifications as well as a general theorem (1.14.2) that expresses the adequacy of finite guarded recursive equational specifications for the description of computable processes.

(3) Suppose that a particular class of process specifications in the sense of (2) is given. Then a major question is to decide whether or not two specifications specify the same process. This matter is undecidable in general, but in some cases positive results can be obtained.

Chapter 2 discusses the bisimulation equivalence problem for regular processes. For this case a complete inference system is presented.

(4) In the absence of the silent step τ, for each process algebra (based on graphs modulo bisimulation equivalence) one can define the corresponding algebra of processes modulo n with n a natural number. In this algebra processes are identified whenever the restrictions of their behaviour to the first n actions are bisimilar.

Complementary to this construction 'modulo n', there is the construction of projective limits of process algebras and processes. Equivalently, such a projective limit can be viewed as a topological completion in an appropriate topology. This leads to a topological view of process domains related to the work of De Bakker & Zucker [82a,b].

In Chapter 3 we study in detail the topological properties of process domains that result from general topological constructions on the basis of spaces with process graphs modulo bisimulation.

Contents

1. Specification and verification in bisimulation semantics

This chapter is a modified version of Bergstra & Klop [86c]. It serves as an introduction to both process algebra and bisimulation semantics. Sections 1-11 provide syntax and defining equations for our operator set of process algebra as well as several examples of process specifications including counters, bags, stacks and queues. Section 1.12 contains an extended example of a specification and verification in process algebra. To this end an alternating bit protocol is verified and specified in all detail. Sections 1.13, 1.14 introduce the bisimulation model and describe the expressive power of recursive specifications in the context of the bisimulation model.

1.1. Basic Process Algebra.

The kernel of all axiom systems for processes that we will consider, is Basic Process Algebra. The processes that we will consider are capable of performing atomic steps or actions a,b,c,..., with the idealization that these actions are events without positive duration in time; it takes only one moment to execute an action. The actions are combined into composite processes by the operations + and ·, with the interpretation that (a+b)·c is the process that first chooses between executing a or b and, second, performs the action c after which it is finished. (We will often suppress the dot and write (a+b)c.) These operations, 'alternative composition' and 'sequential composition' (or just sum and product), are the basic constructors of processes. Since time has a direction, multiplication is not commutative; but addition is, and in fact it is stipulated that the options (summands) possible at some stage of the process form a *set*. Formally, we will require that processes x,y,... satisfy the following axioms:

BPA	
	x+y = y+x
	(x+y)+z = x+(y+z)
	x+x = x
	(x+y)z = xz+yz
	(xy)z = x(yz)

Table 1

Thus far we used 'process algebra' in the generic sense of denoting the area of algebraic approaches to concurrency, but we will also adopt the following technical meaning for it: any model of these axioms will be a *process algebra*.. The simplest process algebra, then, is the term model of BPA (Basic Process Algebra), whose elements are BPA-expressions (built from the atoms a,b,c,... by means of the basic constructors) modulo the equality generated by the axioms. We will denote this structure with $\mathbb{A}_\omega$. This process algebra contains only finite processes; things get more lively if we admit recursion enabling us to define infinite processes. Even at this stage one can define, recursively, interesting processes; consider for instance the counter in Table 2.

COUNTER

X = (zero + up·Y)· X
Y = down + up·Y·Y

Table 2

Here 'zero' is the action that asserts that the counter has value 0, and 'up' and 'down' are the actions of incrementing, respectively decrementing, the counter by one unit. The process COUNTER is now represented by X; Y is an auxiliary process. COUNTER is a 'perpetual' process, that is, all its execution traces are infinite. Such a trace is e.g. zero·zero·up·down·zero·up·up·up· .... . A question of mathematical interest only is: can COUNTER be defined in a single equation, without auxiliary processes? The negative answer is an immediate consequence of the following fact:

1.1.1. THEOREM. *Let a system* $\{X_i = T(X_1,...,X_n) \mid i = 1,...,n\}$ *of guarded fixed point equations over* BPA *be given. Suppose the solutions* $\underline{X}_i$ *are all perpetual. Then they are regular.*

The solutions are in this case labeled transition graphs—modulo a certain equivalence relation which will be extensively discussed in the sequel. Two concepts in this statement need also an explanation: a fixed point equation (or recursion equation), like X = (zero + up·Y)·X is *guarded* if every occurrence of a recursion variable in the right hand side is preceded ('guarded') by an occurrence of an action. For instance, the occurrence of X in the right-hand side of X = (zero + up·Y)·X is guarded since, when this X is accessed, one has to pass either the guard zero or the guard up. A non-example: the equation X = X + a·X is not guarded. Furthermore, a process is *regular* if it has only finitely many 'states'; clearly, COUNTER is not regular since it has just as many states as there are natural numbers. Let us mention one other property of processes which have a finite recursive specification (by means of guarded recursion equations) in BPA: such processes are *uniformly finitely branching*. A process is finitely branching if in each of its states it can take steps (and thereby transform itself) to only finitely many subprocesses; for instance, the process defined by X = (a+b+c)X has in each state branching degree 3. 'Uniformly' means that there is uniform bound on the branching degrees throughout the process.

In fact, a more careful treatment is necessary to define concepts like 'branching degree' rigorously. For, clearly, the branching degree of a + a ought to be the same as that of the process 'a', since a + a = a. And the process X = aX will be the same as the process X = aaX; in turn these will be identified with the process X = aX + aaX. In the sequel we will extensively discuss the semantic criterion by means of which these processes are identified ('bisimilarity'). Milner [84] has found a simple axiom system (extending BPA) which is able to deal with recursion and which is complete for regular processes with respect to 'bisimilarity'. (See Section 2.3 in Chapter 2.)

Another non-trivial example is the following specification of the process behaviour of a Stack with data 0,1:

STACK

$X = 0{\downarrow}.YX + 1{\downarrow}.ZX$
$Y = 0{\uparrow} + 0{\downarrow}.YY + 1{\downarrow}.ZY$
$Z = 1{\uparrow} + 0{\downarrow}.YZ + 1{\downarrow}.ZZ$

Table 3

Here $0{\downarrow}$ and $0{\uparrow}$ are the actions 'push 0' and 'pop 0', respectively; likewise for 1. Now Stack is specified by the first recursion variable, X. Indeed, according to the first equation the process X is capable of performing either the action $0{\downarrow}$, after which the process is transformed into YX, or $1{\downarrow}$, after which the process is transformed into ZX. In the first case we have using the second equation $YX = (0{\uparrow} + 0{\downarrow}.YY + 1{\downarrow}.ZY)X = 0{\uparrow}\cdot X + 0{\downarrow}.YYX + 1{\downarrow}.ZYX$. This means that the process YX has three options; after performing the first one ($0{\uparrow}$) it behaves like the original X. Continuing in this manner we find a transition diagram or *process graph* as in Figure 1.2.

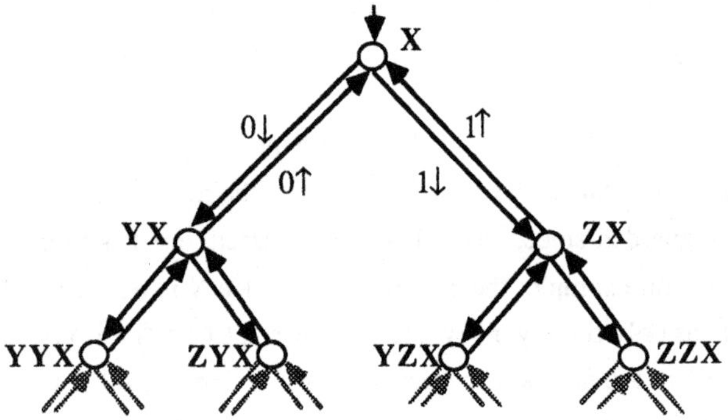

Stack

Figure 1.2

Before proceeding to the next section, let us assure the reader that the omission of the other distributive law, $z(x + y) = zx + zy$, is intentional. The reason will become clear after the introduction of 'deadlock'.

1.2. Deadlock. A vital element in the present set-up of process algebra is the process δ signifying 'deadlock'. The process ab performs its two steps and then stops, succesfully; but the process abδ deadlocks after the a- and b-action: it wants to do a proper action but it cannot. So δ is the acknowledgement of stagnation. With this in mind, the axioms to which δ is subject, should be clear:

DEADLOCK

$\delta + x = x$
$\delta \cdot x = \delta$

Table 4

(In fact, it can be argued that 'deadlock' is not the most appropriate name for the process constant δ. In the sequel we will encounter a process which can more rightfully claim this name: $\tau\delta$, where τ is the silent step. We will stick to the present terminology, however.)

The axiom system of BPA (Table 1) together with the present axioms for δ is called BPA_δ. We are now in a position to motivate the absence in BPA of the 'other' distributive law: $z(x+y) = zx+zy$. For, suppose it would be added. Then $ab = a(b + \delta) = ab + a\delta$. This means that a process with deadlock possibility is equal to one without, conflicting with our intention to model also deadlock behaviour of processes.

The essential role of the new process δ will only be fully appreciated after the introduction of communication, below.

1.3. The merge operator.

If x,y are processes, their 'parallel composition' $x \| y$ is the process that first chooses whether to do a step in x or in y, and proceeds as the parallel composition of the remainders of x,y. In other words, the steps of x,y are interleaved or *merged*. Using an auxiliary operator $⌊\!⌊$ (with the interpretation that $x ⌊\!⌊ y$ is like $x \| y$ but with the commitment of choosing the initial step from x) the operation $\|$ can be succinctly defined by the axioms:

MERGE

$x \| y$	$= x ⌊\!⌊ y + y ⌊\!⌊ x$
$ax ⌊\!⌊ y$	$= a(x \| y)$
$a ⌊\!⌊ y$	$= ay$
$(x + y) ⌊\!⌊ z$	$= x ⌊\!⌊ z + y ⌊\!⌊ z$

Table 5

The system of nine axioms consisting of BPA and the four axioms for merge will be called PA. Moreover, if the axioms for δ are added, the result will be PA_δ. The operators $\|$ and $⌊\!⌊$ will also be called *merge* and *left-merge* respectively.

The merge operator corresponds to what in the theory of formal languages is called *shuffle*. The shuffle of the words ab and cd is the set of words {abcd, acbd, cabd, acdb, cadb, cdab}. Merging the processes ab and cd yields the process

$$ab\|cd = ab⌊\!⌊cd + cd⌊\!⌊ab = a(b\|cd) + c(d\|ab) = a(b⌊\!⌊cd + cd⌊\!⌊b) + c(d⌊\!⌊ab + ab⌊\!⌊d) =$$
$$a(bcd + c(d\|b)) + c(dab + a(b\|d)) = a(bcd + c(db+bd)) + c(dab + a(bd+db)),$$

a process having as trace set the shuffle above.

An example of a process recursively defined in PA, is $X = a(b\|X)$. It turns out that this process can already be defined in BPA, by the system of recursion equations

$$\{X = aYX,\ Y = b + aYY\}.$$

To see that both ways of defining X yield the same process, one may 'unwind' according to the given equations:

$$X = a(b\|X) = a(b \mathbin{\lfloor\!\lfloor} X + X \mathbin{\lfloor\!\lfloor} b) = a(bX + a(b\|X) \mathbin{\lfloor\!\lfloor} b) = a(bX + a((b\|X)\|b))$$
$$= a(bX + a...),$$

while on the other hand

$$X = aYX = a(b + aYY)X = a(bX + aYYX) = a(bX + a...).$$

So at least up to level 2 the processes are equal. By further unwinding they can be proved equal up to each finite level. (Namely, by using the rule AIP, discussed in Section 1.8.)

Yet there are processes definable in PA but not in BPA. An example (from Bergstra & Klop [84b]) of such a process is given by the recursion equation

$$X = 0{\downarrow}\cdot(0{\uparrow} \| X) + 1{\downarrow}\cdot(1{\uparrow} \| X)$$

describing the process behaviour of a Bag (or multiset), in which arbitrarily many instances of the data 0,1 can be inserted (the actions $0{\downarrow}$, $1{\downarrow}$ respectively) or retrieved ($0{\uparrow}$, $1{\uparrow}$), with the restriction that no more 0's and 1's can taken from the Bag than were put in first. The difference with a Stack or a Queue is that all order between incoming and outgoing 0's and 1's is lost. The process graph corresponding to the process Bag is as in Figure 1.3.

We conclude this section on PA by mentioning the following fact (see Bergstra & Klop [84b]), which is useful for establishing non-definability results:

1.3.1. THEOREM. *Every process which is recursively defined in* PA *and has an infinite trace, has an eventually periodic trace.*

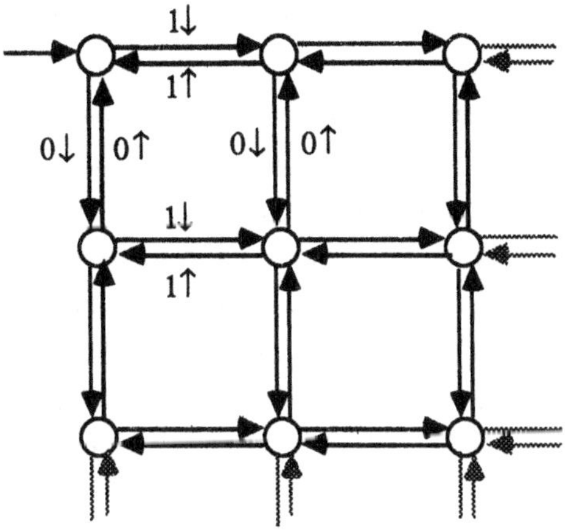

Figure 1.3

1.4. Fixed points. We have already alluded to the existence of infinite processes; this raises the question how one can actually construct process algebras (for BPA or PA) containing infinite processes in addition to finite ones. Such models can be obtained as:

(1) *projective limits* (Bergstra & Klop 84a, 86b]),

(2) *complete metrical spaces*, as in the work of De Bakker & Zucker [82a,b];

(3) *quotients of graph domains* (a graph domain is a set of process graphs or transition diagrams), as in Milner [80];

(4) the *'explicit' models* of Hoare [85];

(5) *ultraproducts of finite models* (Kranakis [86,87]).

In Section 1.13 we will discuss a model as in (3). As to (5), these models are only of theoretical interest: models thus obtained contain 'weird' processes such as $x = \sqrt{a^\omega}$, a process satisfying $x^2 = a^\omega = a \cdot a \cdot a \cdot \ldots$ while $x \neq x^2$.

Here, we look at (2). First, define the projection operators π_n $(n \geq 1)$, cutting off a process at level n:

PROJECTION

$\pi_1(ax)$	$= a$
$\pi_{n+1}(ax)$	$= a\pi_n(x)$
$\pi_n(a)$	$= a$
$\pi_n(x+y)$	$= \pi_n(x) + \pi_n(y)$

Table 6

E.g., for X defining BAG:

$$\pi_2(X) = in(0)(out(0) + in(0) + in(1)) + in(1)(out(1) + in(0) + in(1)).$$

By means of these projections a distance between processes x,y can be defined: $d(x,y) = 2^{-n}$ where n is the least natural number such that $\pi_n(x) \neq \pi_n(y)$, and $d(x,y) = 0$ if there is no such n. If the term model A_ω of BPA (or PA) as in Section 1.1 is equipped with this distance function, the result is an ultrametrical space (A_ω, d). By metrical completion we obtain a model of BPA (resp. PA) in which all systems of guarded recursion equations have a unique solution. In fact, the guardedness condition is exactly what is needed to associate a contracting operator on the complete metrical space with a guarded recursion equation. (E.g. to the recursion equation X = aX the contracting function f(x) = ax is associated; indeed $d(f(x),f(y)) \leq d(x,y)/2$.) Banach's contraction theorem then proves the existence of a unique fixed point. This model construction has been employed in various settings by De Bakker & Zucker [82a,b], who also posed the question whether *unguarded* fixed point equations, such as X = aX + X or Y = (aY ∥ Y) + b, always have a solution in the metric completion of (A_ω, d) as well. This turns out to be the case:

1.4.1. THEOREM. *Let* q *be an arbitrary process in the metric completion of* (A_ω, d) *and let* X = s(X) *be a recursion equation in the signature of* PA.
Then the sequence q, s(q), s(s(q)), s(s(s(q))), ... *converges to a solution* q* = s(q*).

For a proof see Bergstra & Klop [87]. In general, the fixed points q* = s(q*) are not unique. The proof of 1.4.1 in Bergstra & Klop [87] is combinatorial in nature; it is not at all clear whether this convergence result can be obtained by the 'usual' convergence proof methods, such as invoking Banach's fixed point theorem or (in a complete partial order setting) the Knaster-Tarski fixed point theorem. In Kranakis [87] the present theorem is extended to the case where s(X) may contain parameters.

1.4.2. REMARK. An alternative way to obtain this model (the metric completion of (A_ω, d)) is as follows. Let A_n denote A_ω modulo the equation $x = \pi_n(x)$; so A_n is the initial algebra of BPA $\cup$ $\{x = \pi_n(x)\}$, containing only processes of depth at most n. Now the family of models and projections $(A_n, \pi_n : A_{n+1} \rightarrow A_n \mid n \geq 0)$ has a projective limit A^∞. This structure is isomorphic to the metric completion of (A_ω, d). Therefore we will use A^∞ as an alternative notation for the metric completion of (A_ω, d).

1.5. Communication.

So far, the parallel composition or merge (∥) did not involve communication in the process x∥y: one could say that x and y are 'freely' merged or interleaved. However, some actions in one process may need an action in another process for an actual execution, like the act of shaking hands requires simultaneous acts of two persons. In fact, 'handshaking' is the paradigm for the type of communication which we will introduce now. If A = {a,b,c,...,δ} is the action alphabet, let us adopt a binary communication function $| : A \times A \rightarrow A$ satisfying the axioms in Table 7.

COMMUNICATION FUNCTION

$a \mid b$	$= b \mid a$
$(a \mid b) \mid c$	$= a \mid (b \mid c)$
$\delta \mid a$	$= \delta$

Table 7

Here a,b vary over A, including δ. We can now specify *merge with communication* ; we use the same notation $\|$ as for the 'free' merge in Section 1.3 since in fact 'free' merge is an instance of merge with communication by choosing the communication function trivial, i.e. $a \mid b = \delta$ for all $a,b \in A$. There are now two auxiliary operators, allowing a finite axiomatisation: left-merge ($\lfloor\!\lfloor$) as before and $\mid$ (*communication merge* or simply 'bar'), which is an extension of the communication function in Table 7 to all processes, not only the atoms. The axioms for $\|$ and its auxiliary operators are given in Table 8.

MERGE WITH COMMUNICATION

$x \| y$	$= x \lfloor\!\lfloor y + y \lfloor\!\lfloor x + x \mid y$
$ax \lfloor\!\lfloor y$	$= a(x \| y)$
$a \lfloor\!\lfloor y$	$= ay$
$(x + y) \lfloor\!\lfloor z$	$= x \lfloor\!\lfloor z + y \lfloor\!\lfloor z$
$ax \mid b$	$= (a \mid b)x$
$a \mid bx$	$= (a \mid b)x$
$ax \mid by$	$= (a \mid b)(x \| y)$
$(x+y) \mid z$	$= x \mid z + y \mid z$
$x \mid (y+z)$	$= x \mid y + x \mid z$

Table 8

We also need the so-called *encapsulation* operators ∂_H (for every $H \subseteq A$) for removing unsuccessful attempts at communication:

ENCAPSULATION

$\partial_H(a)$	$= a$ if $a \notin H$
$\partial_H(a)$	$= \delta$ if $a \in H$
$\partial_H(x+y)$	$= \partial_H(x) + \partial_H(y)$
$\partial_H(xy)$	$= \partial_H(x) \cdot \partial_H(y)$

Table 9

These axioms express that ∂_H 'kills' all atoms mentioned in H, by replacing them with δ. The axioms for BPA, DEADLOCK together with the present ones in Tables 7-9 constitute the axiom system ACP (Algebra of Communicating Processes). Typically, a system of communicating processes $x_1,...,x_n$ is now represented in ACP by the expression $\partial_H(x_1 \| ... \| x_n)$. Prefixing the encapsulation operator says that the system $x_1,...,x_n$ is to be perceived as a separate unit with respect to the communication actions mentioned in H; no communications between actions in H with an environment are expected or intended.

A useful theorem to break down such expressions is the *Expansion Theorem* (first formulated by Milner, for the case of CCS; see Milner [80]) which holds under the assumption of the *handshaking axiom* $x \mid y \mid z = \delta$. This axiom says that all communications are binary. (In fact we have to require associativity of '$\|$' first—see Table 10.)

1.5.1. EXPANSION THEOREM.

$$x_1 \| \ldots \| x_k = \Sigma_i\, x_i \lfloor\!\lfloor X_k^{\,i} + \Sigma_{i \neq j}\, (x_i \mid x_j) \lfloor\!\lfloor X_k^{\,i,j}$$

Here $X_k^{\,i}$ denotes the merge of $x_1,\ldots,x_k$ except x_i, and $X_k^{\,i,j}$ denotes the same merge except x_i, x_j ($k \geq 3$). For instance, for $k = 3$:

$$x \| y \| z = x \lfloor\!\lfloor (y \| z) + y \lfloor\!\lfloor (x \| x) + z \lfloor\!\lfloor (x \| y) + (y \mid z) \lfloor\!\lfloor x + (z \mid x) \lfloor\!\lfloor y + (x \mid y) \lfloor\!\lfloor z.$$

In order to prove the Expansion Theorem, one first proves by simultaneous induction on term complexity that for all closed ACP-terms (i.e. ACP-terms without free variables) the following *axioms of standard concurrency* hold:

AXIOMS OF STANDARD CONCURRENCY

$(x \lfloor\!\lfloor y) \lfloor\!\lfloor z$	$= x \lfloor\!\lfloor (y \| z)$
$(x \mid y) \lfloor\!\lfloor z$	$= x \mid (y \lfloor\!\lfloor z)$
$x \mid y$	$= y \mid x$
$x \| y$	$= y \| x$
$x \mid (y \mid z)$	$= (x \mid y) \mid z$
$x \| (y \| z)$	$= (x \| y) \| z$

Table 10

The defining power of ACP is strictly greater than that of PA. The following is an example (from Bergstra & Klop [84b]) of a process U, recursively defined in ACP, but not definable in PA: let the alphabet be $\{a,b,c,d,\delta\}$ and let the communication function be given by $c \mid c = a$, $d \mid d = b$, and all other communications equal to δ. Let $H = \{c,d\}$. Now we recursively define the process U as in Table 11:

$U = \partial_H\,(dcY \| Z)$
$X = cXc + d$
$Y = dXY$
$Z = dXcZ$

Table 11

Then, we claim, $U = ba(ba^2)^2(ba^3)^2(ba^4)^2....$ Indeed, using the axioms in ACP and putting

$$U_n = \partial_H (dc^nY \| Z)$$

for $n \geq 1$, a straightforward computation shows that

$$U_n = ba^nba^{n+1}U_{n+1}.$$

By Theorem 1.3.1, U is not definable in PA, since the one infinite trace of U is not eventually periodic.

We will often adopt a special format for the communication function, called *read-write communication*. Let a finite set D of *data* d and a set {1,...,p} of *ports* be given. Then the alphabet consists of *read* actions ri(d) and *write* actions wi(d), for i = 1,...,p and $d \in D$. The interpretation is: read datum d at port i, write datum d at port i respectively. Furthermore, the alphabet contains actions ci(d) for i = 1,...,p and $d \in D$, with interpretation: *communicate* d *at* i. These actions will be called *transactions* . The only non-trivial communications (i.e. not resulting in δ) are: $wi(d) | ri(d) = ci(d)$. Instead of wi(d) we will also use the notation si(d) (send d along i). Note that read-write communication satisfies the handshaking axiom: all communications are binary.

1.5.2. EXAMPLE. Using the present read-write communication format we can write the recursion equation for a Bag B_{12} (cf. Section 1.3) which reads data $d \in D$ at port 1 and writes them at port 2 as follows:

$$B_{12} = \Sigma_{d\in D}\, r1(d)(w2(d) \| B_{12}).$$

In order to illustrate the defining power of ACP, we will now give an infinite specification of the process behaviour of a queue with input port 1 and output port 2. Here D is a finite set of data (finite since otherwise the sums in the specification below would be infinite, and we do not consider infinite expressions), D* is the set of finite sequences σ of elements from D; the empty sequence is λ. The sequence $\sigma*\sigma'$ is the concatenation of sequences σ,σ'.

QUEUE

$Q = Q_\lambda$	$= \Sigma_{d\in D}\, r1(d).Q_d$	
$Q_{\sigma*d}$	$= s2(d).Q_\sigma + \Sigma_{e\in D}\, r1(e).Q_{e*\sigma*d}$	(for all $d\in D$ and $\sigma\in D^*$)

Table 12

Note that this infinite specification uses only the signature of BPA. We have the following remarkable fact:

1.5.2. THEOREM. *Using read-write communication, the process Queue cannot be specified in ACP by finitely many recursion equations.*

For the lengthy proof see Bergstra & Tiuryn [87]. It should be mentioned that the process Queue can be finitely specified in ACP if the read-write restriction is dropped and n-ary communications are allowed; in the next section it is shown how this can be done. In the sequel we will present some other finite specifications of Queue using features to be introduced later.

1.6. Renaming. A useful 'add-on' feature is formed by the renaming operators ρ_f, where $f: A \to A$ is a function keeping δ fixed. A renaming ρ_f replaces each action 'a' in a process by f(a). In fact, the encapsulation operators ∂_H are renaming operators; f maps $H \subseteq A$ to δ and fixes A - H pointwise. The following axioms, where 'id' is the identity function, are obvious:

RENAMING

$\rho_f(a)$	$= f(a)$
$\rho_f(x+y)$	$= \rho_f(x) + \rho_f(y)$
$\rho_f(xy)$	$= \rho_f(x) \cdot \rho_f(y)$
$\rho_{id}(x)$	$= x$
$(\rho_f \circ \rho_g)(x)$	$= \rho_{f \circ g}(x)$

Table 13

Again the defining power is enhanced by adding this feature. While Queue as in the previous section could not yet be finitely specified, it can now.

The actions are the r1(d), s2(d) as before; there are moreover 'auxiliary' actions r3(d), s3(d), c3(d) for each datum d. Communication is given by $r3(d) \mid s3(d) = c3(d)$ and there are no other non-trivial communications. If we let $\rho_{c3\to s2}$ be the renaming $c3(d) \to s2(d)$ and $\rho_{s2\to s3}$: $s2(d) \to s3(d)$, then for $H = \{s3(d), r3(d) \mid d \in D\}$ the following two guarded recursion equations give an elegant finite specification of Queue:

QUEUE, FINITE SPECIFICATION

$$Q = \Sigma_{d\in D}\, r1(d) \cdot (\rho_{c3\to s2} \circ \partial_H)(\rho_{s2\to s3}(Q) \parallel s2(d) \cdot Z)$$
$$Z = \Sigma_{d\in D}\, r3(d) \cdot Z$$

Table 14

(This specification was inspired by a similar specification in Hoare [84]. The present formulation is from Baeten & Bergstra [88].) The explanation that this is really Queue is as follows. We intend that Q processes data d in a queue-like manner, by performing 'input' actions r1(d) and 'output' actions s2(d). So $\rho_{s2\to s3}(Q)$ processes data in queue-like manner by performing input actions r1(d), output actions s3(d). First consider the parallel system $Q' = \partial_H(\rho_{s2\to s3}(Q) \parallel Z)$: since Z universally accepts s3(d) and transforms these into c3(d), this is just the queue with input r1(d), output c3(d). Now the process $Q^* = \partial_H(\rho_{s2\to s3}(Q) \parallel s2(d).Z)$ appearing in the recursion equation, is just like Q' but with the obligation to perform output action s2(d) *before all output actions* c3(d); this obligation is enforced since s2(d) must be passed before $\rho_{s2\to s3}(Q)$ and Z can communicate and thereby create the output actions c3(d). So $\rho_{c3\to s2}(Q^*) = Q_d$, the queue loaded with d, in the earlier notation used for the infinite specification of Queue (Table 10). But then $Q = \Sigma_{d\in D}\, r1(d).Q_d$ and this is exactly what we want.

In fact, the renamings used in this specification can be removed in favour of a more complicated communication format, as follows. Replace in the specification above $\rho_{s2\to s3}(Q)$ by $\partial_{s2}(Q \parallel V)$ where $V = \Sigma_d\, s2^*(d)\cdot V$ and $S2 = \{s2(d), s2^*(d) \mid d\in D\}$ with communications $s2(d)|s2^*(d) = s3(d)$ for all d. To remove the other renaming operator, put
$P = \partial_H(\partial_{S2}(Q \parallel V) \parallel s2(d)\cdot Z)$, and replace $\rho_{c3\to s2}(P)$ by $\partial_{C3}(P \parallel W)$ where $W = \Sigma_d\, c3^*(d)\cdot W$ and $c3(d)|c3^*(d) = s2(d)$ for all d. However, though the renamings are removed in this way, the communication is no longer of the read-write format, or even in the hand shaking format, since we have ternary nontrivial communications $s2(d) = c3(d)|c3^*(d) = r3(d)|s3(d)|c3^*(d)$. As we already stated in the last theorem, this is unavoidable.

1.7. Abstraction.

A fundamental issue in the design and specification of hierarchical (or modularized) systems of communicating processes is *abstraction*. Without having an abstraction mechanism enabling us to abstract from the inner workings of modules to be composed to larger systems, specification of all but very small systems would be virtually impossible. We will now extend the axiom system ACP, obtained thus far, with such an abstraction mechanism.

Consider two Bags B_{12}, B_{23} (cf. Example 1.5.1) with action alphabets $\{r1(d), s2(d) \mid d\in D\}$ and $\{r2(d), s3(d) \mid d\in D\}$, respectively. That is, B_{12} is a bag-like channel reading data d at port 1, sending them to port 2; B_{23} reads data at 2 and sends them to 3. (That the channels are bags means that, unlike the case of a queue, the order of incoming data is lost in the transmission.) Suppose the bags are connected at port 2; so we adopt communications $s2(d) \mid r2(d) = c2(d)$ where c2(d) is the transaction of d at 2.

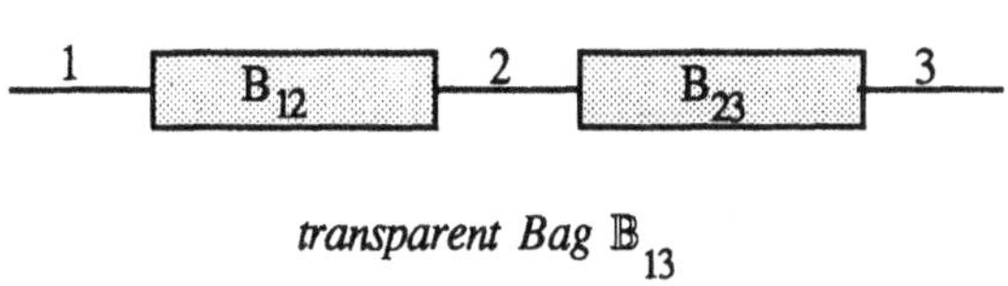

Figure 1.4

The composite system $\mathbb{B}_{13} = \partial_H(B_{12} \parallel B_{23})$ where $H = \{s2(d), r2(d) \mid d \in D\}$, should, intuitively, be again a Bag between ports 1,3. However, from some (rather involved) calculations we learn that

$$\mathbb{B}_{13} = \Sigma_{d\in D}\, r1(d)\cdot((c2(d)\cdot s3(d)) \parallel \mathbb{B}_{13}).$$

So $\mathbb{B}_{13}$ is a 'transparent' Bag: the passage of d through 2 is visible as the transaction event c2(d). (Note that this terminology conflicts with the usual one in the area of computer networks, where a network is called transparent if the internal structure is *not* visible.)

How can we *abstract* from such internal events, if we are only interested in the external behaviour at 1,3? The first step to obtain such an abstraction is to remove the distinctive identity of the actions to be abstracted, that is, to rename them all into one designated action which we call, after Milner, τ: the *silent* action. This renaming is realised by the *abstraction operator* τ_I, parameterized by a set of actions $I \subseteq A$ and subject to the following axioms:

ABSTRACTION

$\tau_I(\tau)$	$= \tau$
$\tau_I(a)$	$= a$ if $a \notin I$
$\tau_I(a)$	$= \tau$ if $a \in I$
$\tau_I(x+y)$	$= \tau_I(x) + \tau_I(y)$
$\tau_I(xy)$	$= \tau_I(x)\cdot\tau_I(y)$

Table 15

The second step is to attempt to devise axioms for the silent step τ by means of which τ can be removed from expressions, as e.g. in the equation $a\tau b = ab$. However, it is not possible to remove *all* τ's in an expression if one is interested in a faithful description of deadlock behaviour of processes (at least in bisimulation semantics, the framework adopted in this paper). For, consider the process (expression) $a + \tau\delta$; this process can deadlock, namely if it chooses to perform the silent action. Now, if one would propose naively the equations $\tau x = x\tau = x$, then $a + \tau\delta = a + \delta = a$, and the latter process has no deadlock possibility. It turns out that one of the proposed equations, $x\tau = x$, can be safely adopted, but the other one is wrong. Fortunately, R. Milner has devised some simple axioms which give a complete description of the properties of the silent step (complete with respect to a certain semantical notion of process equivalence called $r\tau\delta$-bisimulation, which does respect deadlock behaviour; this notion is discussed below), as follows.

SILENT STEP

$x\tau = x$
$\tau x = \tau x + x$
$a(\tau x + y) = a(\tau x + y) + ax$

Table 16

To return to our example of the 'transparent' Bag $\mathbb{B}_{13}$, after abstraction of the set of transactions I = {c2(d) | d∈D} the result is indeed an 'ordinary' Bag:

$$\tau_I(\mathbb{B}_{13}) =$$
$$\tau_I(\Sigma_{d\in D}\, r1(d)(c2(d).s3(d) \,\|\, \mathbb{B}_{13})) = \qquad (*)$$
$$\Sigma_{d\in D}\, r1(d)(\,\tau{\cdot}s3(d) \,\|\, \tau_I(\mathbb{B}_{13})) =$$
$$\Sigma_{d\in D}\, (r1(d){\cdot}\,\tau{\cdot}s3(d)) ⫽ \tau_I(\mathbb{B}_{13}) =$$
$$\Sigma_{d\in D}\, (r1(d).s3(d)) ⫽ \tau_I(\mathbb{B}_{13}) =$$
$$\Sigma_{d\in D}\, r1(d)(s3(d) \,\|\, \tau_I(\mathbb{B}_{13}))$$

from which it follows that $\tau_I(\mathbb{B}_{13}) = B_{13}$ (**), the Bag defined by

$$B_{13} = \Sigma_{d\in D}\, r1(d)(s3(d) \,\|\, B_{13}).$$

Here we were able to eliminate all silent actions, but this will not always be the case. For instance, 'chaining' two Stacks (see Figure 1.2) instead of Bags (Figure 1.3) yields a process with 'essential' τ-steps. Likewise for a Bag followed by a Stack. (Here 'essential' means: non-removable in bisimulation semantics.) In fact, the computation above is not as straightforward as was suggested: to justify the equations marked with (*) and (**) we need additional proof principles. As to (**), this equation is justified by the *Recursive Specification Principle* (RSP) stating that a *guarded system of recursion equations in which no abstraction operator τ_I appears, has a unique solution.*

1.8. Proof rules for recursive specifications. We have now presented a survey of ACP_τ; we refer to Bergstra & Klop [85] for an analysis of this proof system as well as a proof that (when the hand shaking axiom is adopted) the Expansion theorem carries over from ACP to ACP_τ unchanged. Note that ACP_τ (displayed in full in Section 1.11) is entirely equational. Without further proof rules it is not possible to deal (in an algebraical way) with infinite processes, obtained by recursive specifications, such as Bag; in the derivation above we tacitly used such proof rules and these will be made explicit below.

(i) RDP, the Recursive Definition Principle:
Every guarded and abstraction free recursive specification has a solution.
(ii) RSP, the Recursive Specification Principle:
Every guarded and abstraction free recursive specification has at most one solution.
(iii) AIP, the Approximation Induction Principle:
A process is determined by its finite projections.

In a more formal notation, AIP can be rendered as the infinitary rule

$$\frac{\forall n \quad \pi_n(x) = \pi_n(y)}{x = y}$$

As to (i), the restriction to guarded specifications is not very important (for an informal definition of 'guarded' see Section 1.1); in the process algebras that we have encountered and that satisfy RDP, also the same principle without the guardedness condition is true. More delicate is the situation in principle (ii): first, *τ-steps may not act as guards* : e.g. the recursion equation $X = \tau X + a$ has infinitely many solutions, namely $\tau(a + q)$ is a solution for arbitrary q; and second, the *recursion equations must not contain occurrences of abstraction operators* τ_I. That is, they are 'abstraction-free' (but there may be occurrences of τ in the equations). The latter restriction is in view of the fact that, surprisingly, the recursion equation $X = a\cdot\tau_{\{a\}}(X)$ possesses infinitely many solutions, even though it looks very guarded. (The solutions are: $a\cdot q$ where q satisfies $\tau_{\{a\}}(q) = q$.) That the presence of abstraction operators in recursive specifications causes trouble, was already noticed in Hoare [85].

As to (iii), we still have to define projections π_n in the presence of the τ-action. The extra clauses are:

PROJECTION, CONTINUED

$\pi_n(\tau)$	$= \tau$
$\pi_n(\tau x)$	$= \tau\cdot\pi_n(x)$

Table 17

So, τ-steps do not add to the depth; this is enforced by the τ-laws in Table 16 (since, e.g., $a\tau b = ab$ and $\tau a = \tau a + a$). Remarkably, there are infinitely many different terms t_n (that is, different in the term model of ACP_τ), built from τ and a single atom 'a', such that t_n has depth 1, i.e. $t = \pi_1(t)$. The t_n are inductively defined as follows:

$t_0 = a$, $t_1 = \tau a$, $t_2 = \tau$, $t_3 = \tau(a + \tau)$, $t_4 = a + \tau a$,
$t_{4k+i} = \tau\cdot t_{4k+i-1}$ for $i = 1,3$ and $k \geq 0$,
$t_{4k+i} = t_{4k+i-3} + t_{4k+i-5}$ for $i = 0,2$ and $k \geq 0$.

In fact, these are *all* terms (modulo provable equality in ACP_τ) with the properties as just stated. Furthermore, with respect to the "summand ordering" $\leq$ defined by $x \leq x + y$, the set of these term takes the form of the partial order in Figure 1.5, which has the same form (but for one point) as the Rieger-Nishimura lattice in intuitionistic propositional logic.

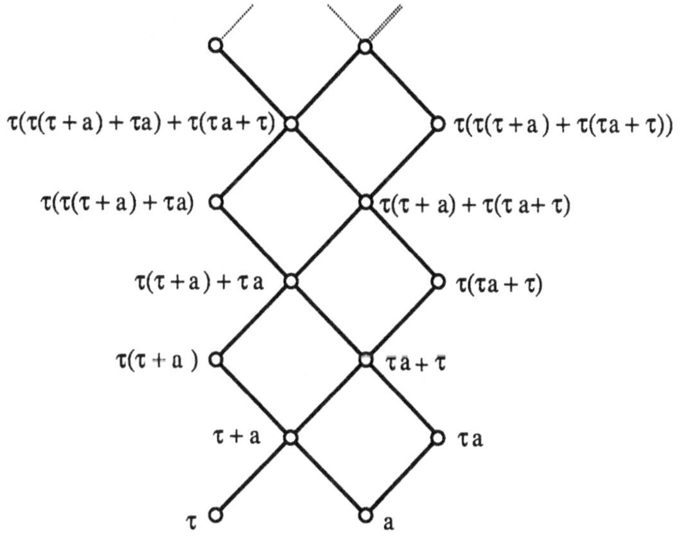

Figure 1.5

The unrestricted form of AIP as in (iii) will turn out to be too strong in some circumstances; it does not hold in one of the main models of ACP_τ, namely the graph model which is introduced in Section 1.13. Therefore we also introduce the following weaker form.

(iv) AIP^- (Weak Approximation Induction Principle):

Every process which has an abstraction-free guarded specification is determined by its finite projections .

Roughly, a process which can be specified without abstraction operators is one in which there are no infinite τ-traces (and which is definable). E.g. the process X_0 defined by the infinite specification $\{X_0 = bX_1, X_{n+1} = bX_{n+2} + a^n\}$, where a^n is a·a· ... ·a (n times), contains an infinite trace of b-actions; after abstraction with respect to b, the resulting process, $Y = \tau_{\{b\}}(X_0)$, has an infinite trace of τ-steps; and (at least in the main model of ACP_τ of Section 1.13) this Y is not definable without abstraction operators.

Even the Weak Approximation Induction Principle is rather strong. In fact a short argument shows the following:

1.8.1. THEOREM. $AIP^- \Rightarrow RSP$.

As a rule, we will be very careful in admitting abstraction operators in recursive specifications. Yet there are processes which can be elegantly specified by using abstraction inside recursion. The following curious specification of Queue is obtained in this manner. We want to specify Q_{12}, the queue from port 1 to 2, using an auxiliary port 3 and concatenating auxiliary queues Q_{13}, Q_{32}; then we abstract from the internal transaction at port 3. Write, in an ad hoc notation, $Q_{12} = Q_{13}{*}Q_{32}$. Now Q_{13} can be similarly split up: $Q_{13} = Q_{12}{*}Q_{32}$. This gives rise to six similar equations: $Q_{ab} = Q_{ac}{*}Q_{cb}$ where $\{a,b,c\} = \{1,2,3\}$. (See Figure 1.6.)

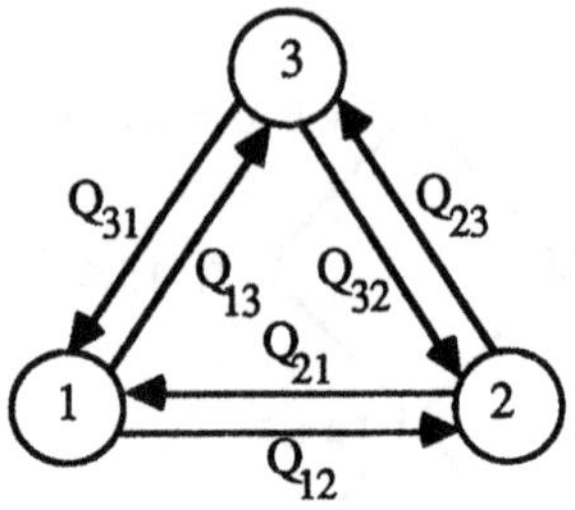

Figure 1.6

These six queues, which are merely renamings of each other, can now be specified in terms of each other as in the following table. One can prove that these recursion equations, though not abstraction-free, indeed have a unique solution.

QUEUE, FINITE SPECIFICATION WITH ABSTRACTION

$$\begin{aligned}
Q_{12} &= \Sigma_{d\in D}\, r1(d)\cdot\tau_3 \circ \partial_3(Q_{13} \parallel s2(d)\cdot Q_{32})\\
Q_{21} &= \Sigma_{d\in D}\, r2(d)\cdot\tau_3 \circ \partial_3(Q_{23} \parallel s1(d)\cdot Q_{31})\\
Q_{23} &= \Sigma_{d\in D}\, r2(d)\cdot\tau_1 \circ \partial_1(Q_{21} \parallel s3(d)\cdot Q_{13})\\
Q_{32} &= \Sigma_{d\in D}\, r3(d)\cdot\tau_1 \circ \partial_1(Q_{31} \parallel s2(d)\cdot Q_{12})\\
Q_{31} &= \Sigma_{d\in D}\, r3(d)\cdot\tau_2 \circ \partial_2(Q_{32} \parallel s1(d)\cdot Q_{21})\\
Q_{13} &= \Sigma_{d\in D}\, r1(d)\cdot\tau_2 \circ \partial_2(Q_{12} \parallel s3(d)\cdot Q_{23})
\end{aligned}$$

Table 18

Here the usual read-write notation is used: ri(d) means read d at i, si(d): send d at i, communications are $ri(d)|si(d) = ci(d)$; further $\tau_i = \tau_{\{ci(d)|d\in D\}}$ and $\partial_i = \partial_{\{ri(d),si(d)\,|\,d\in D\}}$. This example shows that even with the restriction to read-write communication, ACP_τ is stronger than ACP.

1.9. Alphabet calculus. In computations with infinite processes one often needs information about the *alphabet* $\alpha(x)$ of a process x. E.g. if x is the process uniquely defined by the recursion equation $X = aX$, we have $\alpha(x) = \{a\}$. An example of the use of this alphabet information is given by the implication $\alpha(x)\cap H = \emptyset \Rightarrow \partial_H(x) = x$. For finite closed process expressions this fact can be proved with induction to the structure, but for infinite processes we have to require such a property axiomatically. In fact, this example will be one of the 'conditional axioms' below (conditional, in contrast with the purely equational axioms we have introduced thus far). First we have to define the alphabet:

ALPHABET

$\alpha(\delta)$	$= \emptyset$
$\alpha(\tau)$	$= \emptyset$
$\alpha(a)$	$= \{a\}$
$\alpha(\tau x)$	$= \alpha(x)$
$\alpha(ax)$	$= \{a\} \cup \alpha(x)$
$\alpha(x+y)$	$= \alpha(x) \cup \alpha(y)$
$\alpha(x)$	$= \bigcup_{n\geq 1} \alpha(\pi_n(x))$
$\alpha(\partial_H(x)$	$= \alpha(x) - H$
$\alpha(\tau_I(x))$	$= \alpha(x) - I$

Table 19

To appreciate the non-triviality of the concept $\alpha(x)$, let us mention that a finite specification can be given of a process for which the alphabet is uncomputable (see Bergstra & Klop [84b] for an example).

Now the following conditional axioms will be adopted:

CONDITIONAL AXIOMS

$\alpha(x) \mid (\alpha(y) \cap H) \subseteq H$	$\Rightarrow$	$\partial_H(x \parallel y) = \partial_H(x \parallel \partial_H(y))$
$\alpha(x) \mid (\alpha(y) \cap I) = \emptyset$	$\Rightarrow$	$\tau_I(x \parallel y) = \tau_I(x \parallel \tau_I(y))$
$H = H_1 \cup H_2$	$\Rightarrow$	$\partial_H(x) = (\partial_{H1} \circ \partial_{H2})(x)$
$I = I_1 \cup I_2$	$\Rightarrow$	$\tau_I(x) = (\tau_{I1} \circ \tau_{I2})(x)$
$\alpha(x) \cap H = \emptyset$	$\Rightarrow$	$\partial_H(x) = x$
$\alpha(x) \cap I = \emptyset$	$\Rightarrow$	$\tau_I(x) = x$

Table 20

Using these axioms, one can derive for instance the following fact: if communication is of the read-write format and I is disjoint from the set of transactions (communication results) as well as disjoint from the set of communication actions, then the abstraction τ_I distributes over merges $x \parallel y$.

1.10. Koomen's Fair Abstraction Rule. Suppose the following statistical experiment is performed: somebody flips a coin, repeatedly, until head comes up. This process is described by the recursion equation X = flip·(tail·X + head). Suppose further that the experiment takes place in a closed room, and all information to be obtained about the process in the room is that we can hear the experimenter shout joyfully: 'Head!'. That is, we observe the process $\tau_I(X)$ where I = {flip, tail}. Now, if the coin is 'fair', it is to be expected that sooner or later the action 'head' will be perceived. Hence, intuitively, $\tau_I(X) = \tau\cdot$head. (This vivid example is from Vaandrager [86].)

Koomen's Fair Abstraction Rule (KFAR) is an algebraic rule enabling us to arrive at such a conclusion formally. (For an extensive analysis of this rule see Bateen, Bergstra & Klop [87].) The simplest form is

$$\frac{x = ix + y \quad (i \in I)}{\tau_I(x) = \tau\cdot\, \tau_I\,(y)} \qquad \text{KFAR}_1$$

So, KFAR_1 expresses the fact that the 'τ-loop' (originating from the i-loop) in $\tau_I(x)$ will not be taken infinitely often. In case this 'τ-loop' is of length 2, the same conclusion is expressed in the rule

$$\frac{x_1 = i_1x_2 + y_1,\ x_2 = i_2x_1 + y_2 \quad (i_1,i_2 \in I)}{\tau_I(x_1) = \tau\cdot\, \tau_I(y_1+y_2)} \qquad \text{KFAR}_2$$

and it is not hard to guess what the general formulation (KFAR_n, $n \geq 1$) will be. In fact, as observed in Vaandrager [86], KFAR_n can already be derived from KFAR_1 (at least in the framework of $\text{ACP}_\tau^{\#}$, to be discussed below).

KFAR is of great help in protocol verifications. An example is given in Section 1.12, where KFAR is used to abstract from a cycle of internal steps which is due to a defective communication channel; the underlying fairness assumption is that this channel is not defective forever, but will function properly after an undetermined period of time. (Just as in the coin flipping experiment the wrong option, tail, is not chosen infinitely often.)

An interesting peculiarity of the present framework is the following. Call the process τ^ω (= $\tau\cdot\tau\cdot\tau\cdot$....) *livelock*. Formally, this is the process $\tau_{\{i\}}(x)$ where x is uniquely defined by the recursion equation $X = i\cdot X$. Noting that $x = i\cdot x = i\cdot x + \delta$ and applying KFAR_1 we obtain $\tau^\omega = \tau_{\{i\}}(x) = \tau\delta$. In words: *livelock* = *deadlock*. There are other semantical frameworks for processes, also in the scope of process algebra but not in the scope of this paper, where this equality does not hold (see Bergstra, Klop & Olderog [86, 87]).

1.11. $\text{ACP}_\tau^{\#}$, a framework for process specification and verification.

We have now arrived at a framework which will be called $\text{ACP}_\tau^{\#}$, and which contains all the axioms and proof rules introduced so far. In Table 21 the list of all components of $\text{ACP}_\tau^{\#}$ is given; Table 22 contains the equational system ACP_τ. Note that for *specification* purposes one only needs ACP_τ or ACP_τ^{+}; for *verification* one will need $\text{ACP}_\tau^{\#}$ (an extensive example is given in Section 1.12). Also, it is important to notice that this framework resides entirely on the level of syntax and formal specifications and verification using that syntax—even though some proof rules are infinitary. No semantics for $\text{ACP}_\tau^{\#}$ has been provided yet; this will be done in Section 1.13. The idea is that 'users' can stay in the realm of this formal system and execute algebraical manipulations, without the need for an excursion into the semantics. That this can be done is demonstrated by the verification of a simple protocol in the next section; at that point the semantics of $ACP_\tau^\#$ (in the form of some model) has, on purpose, not yet been provided. This does not mean that the semantics is unimportant; it does mean that the user need only be concerned with formula manipulation. The underlying semantics is of great interest for the theory, if only to guarantee the consistency of the formal system; but applications should not be burdened with it, in our intention.

$ACP_\tau^\#$

Basic Process Algebra	A1-5
Deadlock	A6,7
Communication function	C1-3
Merge with communication	CM1-9
Encapsulation	D1-4
Silent step	T1-3
Silent step: auxiliary axioms	TM1,2;TC1-4
Abstraction	DT; TI1-5
Renaming	RN
Projection	PR1-4
Hand shaking	HA
Standard concurrency	SC
Expansion theorem	ET
Alphabet calculus	CA
Recursive Definition Principle	RDP
Recursive Specification Principle	RSP
Weak Approximation Induction Principle	AIP^-
Koomen's Fair Abstraction Rule	KFAR

Table 21

The system up to the first double bar is ACP; up to the second double bar we have ACP_τ, and up to the third double bar, ACP_τ^+.

So $ACP_\tau^\#$ is a medium for formal process specifications and verifications; let us note that we also admit infinite specifications. As the system is meant to have practical applications, we will only encounter *computable* specifications. A finite specification (of which an expression is a particular case) is trivially computable; an infinite specification $\{E_n \mid n \geq 0\}$, where E_n is the recursion equation $X_n = T(X_1,...,X_{f(n)})$, is computable if after some coding, in which E_n is coded as a natural number e_n, the sequence $\{e_n \mid n \geq 0\}$ is computable. Here an important question arises: *is every computable specification provably equal to a finite specification* ? At present we are unable to answer this question; but we can state that the answer is affirmative *relative to certain models* of $ACP_\tau^\#$. Before we elaborate this, a verification of a simple protocol is demonstrated.

ACP_τ

$x + y = y + x$	A1	$x\tau = x$	T1
$x + (y + z) = (x + y) + z$	A2	$\tau x + x = \tau x$	T2
$x + x = x$	A3	$a(\tau x + y) = a(\tau x + y) + ax$	T3
$(x + y)z = xz + yz$	A4		
$(xy)z = x(yz)$	A5		
$x + \delta = x$	A6		
$\delta x = \delta$	A7		
$a \mid b = b \mid a$	C1		
$(a \mid b) \mid c = a \mid (b \mid c)$	C2		
$\delta \mid a = \delta$	C3		
$x \| y = x \lfloor\!\lfloor y + y \lfloor\!\lfloor x + x \mid y$	CM1		
$a \lfloor\!\lfloor x = ax$	CM2	$\tau \lfloor\!\lfloor x = \tau x$	TM1
$ax \lfloor\!\lfloor y = a(x \| y)$	CM3	$\tau x \lfloor\!\lfloor y = \tau(x \| y)$	TM2
$(x + y) \lfloor\!\lfloor z = x \lfloor\!\lfloor z + y \lfloor\!\lfloor z$	CM4	$\tau \mid x = \delta$	TC1
$ax \mid b = (a \mid b)x$	CM5	$x \mid \tau = \delta$	TC2
$a \mid bx = (a \mid b)x$	CM6	$\tau x \mid y = x \mid y$	TC3
$ax \mid by = (a \mid b)(x \| y)$	CM7	$x \mid \tau y = x \mid y$	TC4
$(x + y) \mid z = x \mid z + y \mid z$	CM8		
$x \mid (y + z) = x \mid y + x \mid z$	CM9	$\partial_H(\tau) = \tau$	DT
		$\tau_I(\tau) = \tau$	TI1
$\partial_H(a) = a$ if $a \notin H$	D1	$\tau_I(a) = a$ if $a \notin I$	TI2
$\partial_H(a) = \delta$ if $a \in H$	D2	$\tau_I(a) = \tau$ if $a \in I$	TI3
$\partial_H(x + y) = \partial_H(x) + \partial_H(y)$	D3	$\tau_I(x + y) = \tau_I(x) + \tau_I(y)$	TI4
$\partial_H(xy) = \partial_H(x) \cdot \partial_H(y)$	D4	$\tau_I(xy) = \tau_I(x) \cdot \tau_I(y)$	TI5

Table 22

1.12. An algebraic verification of the Alternating Bit Protocol.

In this section we will demonstrate a verification of a simple communication protocol, the Alternating Bit Protocol, in the framework of $ACP_\tau^\#$. (In fact, not all of $ACP_\tau^\#$ is needed.) This verification is from Bergstra & Klop [86a]; the present streamlined treatment was kindly made available to us by F.W. Vaandrager (CWI Amsterdam).

Let D be a finite set of data. Elements of D are to be transmitted by the ABP from port 1 to port 2. The ABP can be visualized as follows:

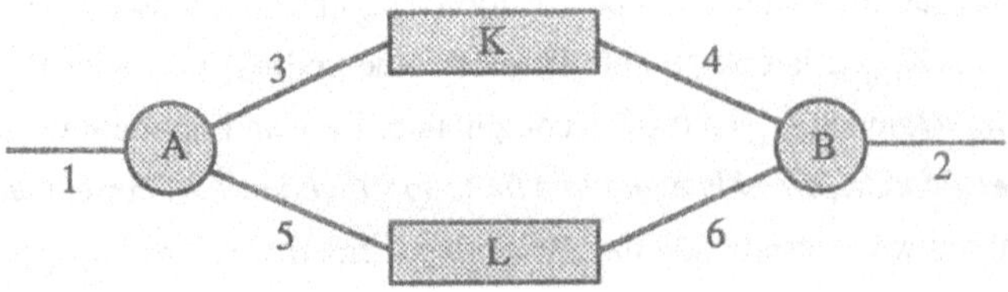

Figure 1.7

There are four components:

A: Reads a Message (RM) at 1. Thereafter it Sends a Frame (SF), consisting of the message and a control bit, into channel K until a correct Acknowledgement has been Received (RA) via channel L. The equations for A are as follows. We will always use the notations: datum $d \in D$, bit $b \in \{0,1\}$, frame $f \in D \times \{0,1\}$ (so a frame f is of the form db).

$$
\begin{aligned}
A &= RM^{0} \\
RM^{b} &= \Sigma_d\, r1(d) \cdot SF^{db} \\
SF^{db} &= s3(db) \cdot RA^{db} \\
RA^{db} &= (r5(1\text{-}b) + r5(e)) \cdot SF^{db} + r5(b) \cdot RM^{1\text{-}b}
\end{aligned}
$$

K: data transmission channel K communicates elements of $D \times \{0,1\}$, and may communicate these correctly or communicate an error value 'e'. K is supposed to be fair in the sense that it will not produce an infinite consecutive sequence of error outputs.

$$
\begin{aligned}
K &= \Sigma_f\, r3(f) \cdot K^{f} \\
K^{f} &= (\tau \cdot s4(e) + \tau \cdot s4(f)) \cdot K
\end{aligned}
$$

The τ's in the second equation express that the choice whether or not a frame f is to be communicated correctly, cannot be influenced by one of the other components.

B: Receives a Frame (RF) via channel K. If the control bit of the frame is OK, then the Message is Sent (SM) at 2. B Sends back Acknowledgement (SA) via L.

$$
\begin{aligned}
B &= RF^{0} \\
RF^{b} &= (\Sigma_d\, r4(d(1\text{-}b)) + r4(e)) \cdot SA^{1\text{-}b} + \Sigma_d\, r4(db) \cdot SM^{db} \\
SA^{b} &= s6(b) \cdot RF^{1\text{-}b} \\
SM^{db} &= s2(d) \cdot SA^{b}
\end{aligned}
$$

L: the task of acknowledgement transmission channel L is to communicate boolean values from B to A. The channel L may yield error outputs but is also supposed to be fair.

$$L = \Sigma_b\, r6(b)\cdot L^b$$
$$L^b = (\tau\cdot s5(e) + \tau\cdot s5(b))\cdot L$$

Define $\mathbb{D} = D \cup (D \times \{0,1\}) \cup \{0,1\} \cup \{e\}$. $\mathbb{D}$ is the set of 'generalized' data (i.e. plain data, frames, bits, error) that occur as parameter of atomic actions. We use the notation: $g \in \mathbb{D}$. For $t \in \{1,2,...,6\}$ there are send, read, and communication actions:

$$A = \{st(g), rt(g), ct(g) \mid g \in \mathbb{D}, t \in \{1,2,...,6\}\}.$$

We define communication by $st(g) \mid rt(g) = ct(g)$ for $g \in \mathbb{D}$, $t \in \{1,2,...,6\}$ and all other communications give δ. Define the following two subsets of A:

$$H = \{st(g), rt(g) \mid t \in \{3,4,5,6\}, g \in \mathbb{D}\}$$
$$I = \{ct(g) \mid t \in \{3,4,5,6\}, g \in \mathbb{D}\}.$$

Now the ABP is described by $ABP = \tau_I \circ \partial_H(A \parallel K \parallel B \parallel L)$. The fact that this is a correct protocol is asserted by

1.12.1. THEOREM. $ACP_\tau^{\#} \vdash ABP = \Sigma_d\, r1(d)\cdot s2(d)\cdot ABP$.

(Actually, we need only the part of $ACP_\tau^{\#}$ consisting of ACP_τ+SC+RDP+RSP+CA+KFAR—see Tables 21, 22.)

PROOF. Let $I' = \{ct(g) \mid t \in \{3,4,5\}, f \in \mathbb{D}\}$. We will use [x] as a notation for $\tau_{I'} \circ \partial_H(x)$. Consider the following system of recursion equations:

$$\begin{array}{lll}
(0) & X & = X_1^{\,0} \\
(1) & X_1^{\,b} & = \Sigma_d\, r1(d)\cdot X_2^{\,db} \\
(2) & X_2^{\,db} & = \tau\cdot X_3^{\,db} + \tau\cdot X_4^{\,db} \\
(3) & X_3^{\,db} & = c6(1\text{-}b)\cdot X_2^{\,db} \\
(4) & X_4^{\,db} & = s2(d)\cdot X_5^{\,db} \\
(5) & X_5^{\,db} & = c6(b)\cdot X_6^{\,db} \\
(6) & X_6^{\,db} & = \tau\cdot X_5^{\,db} + \tau\cdot X_1^{\,1-b}
\end{array}$$

We claim that $ACP_\tau^{\#} \vdash X = [A \parallel K \parallel B \parallel L]$. We prove this by showing that $[A \parallel K \parallel B \parallel L]$

satisfies the same recursion equations (0)-(6) as X does. In the computations below, the bold face part denotes the part of the expression currently being 'rewritten'.

(0) $[A \| K \| B \| L] = [RM^0 \| K \| RF^0 \| L]$

(1) $[\mathbf{RM^b} \| K \| RF^b \| L] =$
$\Sigma_d\, r1(d) \cdot [\,\mathbf{SF^{db}} \| \mathbf{K} \| RF^b \| L\,] =$
$\Sigma_d\, r1(d) \cdot \tau \cdot [RA^{db} \| K^{db} \| RF^b \| L\,] =$
$\Sigma_{d \in D}\, r1(d) \cdot [RA^{db} \| K^{db} \| RF^b \| L\,]$

(2) $[RA^{db} \| \mathbf{K^{db}} \| RF^b \| L\,] =$
$\tau \cdot [RA^{db} \| \mathbf{s4(e) \cdot K} \| \mathbf{RF^b} \| L] + \tau \cdot [RA^{db} \| \mathbf{s4(db) \cdot K} \| \mathbf{RF^b} \| L\,] =$
$\tau \cdot [RA^{db} \| K \| SA^{1\text{-}b} \| L\,] + \tau \cdot [RA^{db} \| K \| SM^{db} \| L\,]$

(3) $[RA^{db} \| K \| \mathbf{SA^{1\text{-}b}} \| \mathbf{L}\,] =$
$c6(1\text{-}b) \cdot [RA^{db} \| K \| RF^b \| \mathbf{L^{1\text{-}b}}\,] =$
$c6(1\text{-}b) \cdot (\, \tau \cdot [\mathbf{RA^{db}} \| K \| RF^b \| \mathbf{s5(e) \cdot L}\,] + \tau \cdot [\mathbf{RA^{db}} \| K \| RF^b \| \mathbf{s5(1\text{-}b) \cdot L}\,]) =$
$c6(1\text{-}b) \cdot \tau \cdot [\mathbf{SF^{db}} \| \mathbf{K} \| RF^b \| L\,] =$
$c6(1\text{-}b) \cdot \tau \cdot \tau \cdot [RA^{db} \| K^{db} \| RF^b \| L\,] =$
$c6(1\text{-}b) \cdot [RA^{db} \| K^{db} \| RF^b \| L\,].$

(4) $[RA^{db} \| K \| \mathbf{SM^{db}} \| L\,] =$
$s2(d) \cdot [RA^{db} \| K \| SA^b \| L\,].$

(5) $[RA^{db} \| K \| \mathbf{SA^b} \| \mathbf{L}\,] =$
$c6(b) \cdot [RA^{db} \| K \| RF^{1\text{-}b} \| L^b\,].$

(6) $[RA^{db} \| K \| RF^{1\text{-}b} \| \mathbf{L^b}\,] =$
$\tau \cdot [\mathbf{RA^{db}} \| K \| RF^{1\text{-}b} \| \mathbf{s5(e) \cdot L}\,] + \tau \cdot [\,\mathbf{RA^{db}} \| K \| RF^{1\text{-}b} \| \mathbf{s5(b) \cdot L}\,] =$
$\tau \cdot [\,SF^{db} \| K \| RF^{1\text{-}b} \| L\,] + \tau \cdot [\,RM^{1\text{-}b} \| K \| RF^{1\text{-}b} \| L\,].$

(7) $[\,\mathbf{SF^{db}} \| \mathbf{K} \| RF^{1\text{-}b} \| L\,] =$
$\tau \cdot [\,RA^{db} \| \mathbf{K^{db}} \| RF^{1\text{-}b} \| L\,] =$
$\tau \cdot (\, \tau \cdot [RA^{db} \| \mathbf{s4(e) \cdot K} \| \mathbf{RF^{1\text{-}b}} \| L\,] + \tau \cdot [\,RA^{db} \| \mathbf{s4(db) \cdot K} \| \mathbf{RF^{1\text{-}b}} \| L\,]) =$
$\tau \cdot [\,RA^{db} \| K \| SA^b \| L\,].$

Now substitute (7) in (6) and apply RSP + RDP. Using the conditional axioms (see Table 20, Section 1.9) we have ABP = $\tau_I(X) = \tau_I(X_1{}^0)$. Further, an application of $KFAR_2$ gives

$$\tau_I(X_2^{db}) = \tau\cdot \tau_I(X_4^{db}) \text{ and } \tau_I(X_5^{db}) = \tau\cdot \tau_I(X_1^{1-b}).$$

Hence,

$$\tau_I(X_1^{b}) = \Sigma_d\, r1(d)\cdot\tau_I(X_2^{db}) = \Sigma_d\, r1(d)\cdot \tau_I(X_4^{db}) =$$
$$\Sigma_d\, r1(d)\cdot s2(d)\cdot \tau_I(X_5^{db}) = \Sigma_d\, r1(d)\cdot s2(d)\cdot\tau_I(X_1^{1-b})$$

and thus

$$\tau_I(X_1^{0}) = \Sigma_d\, r1(d)\cdot s2(d)\cdot\Sigma_{d'}\, r1(d')\cdot s2(d')\cdot \tau_I(X_1^{0})$$
$$\tau_I(X_1^{1}) = \Sigma_d\, r1(d)\cdot s2(d)\cdot\Sigma_{d'}\, r1(d')\cdot s2(d')\cdot \tau_I(X_1^{1}).$$

Applying RDP + RSP gives $\tau_I(X_1^{0}) = \tau_I(X_1^{1})$ and therefore

$$\tau_I(X_1^{0}) = \Sigma_d\, r1(d)\cdot s2(d)\cdot \tau_I(X_1^{0}),$$

which finishes the proof of the theorem. □

More complicated communication protocols have been verified in $ACP_\tau^{\#}$ by Vaandrager [86]: a Positive Acknowledgement with Retransmission protocol and a One Bit Sliding Window protocol. There the notion of *redundancy in a context* is used as a tool which facilitates the verifications. A related method, using a modular approach, is employed in Koymans & Mulder [86], where a version of the Alternating Bit Protocol called the Concurrent Alternating Bit Protocol is verified in $ACP_\tau^{\#}$. (In fact, also in the verifications in Vaandrager [86] and Koymans & Mulder [86] one only needs the part of $ACP_\tau^{\#}$ mentioned after Theorem 1.12.1.) Another verification of the Concurrent Alternating Bit Protocol is given in Van Glabbeek & Vaandrager [88].

1.13. Bisimulation semantics for $ACP_\tau^{\#}$: the model of countably branching graphs.

We will now give a short description of what we consider to be the 'main' model of $ACP_\tau^{\#}$. The basic building material consists of the domain $\mathbb{G}$ of *countably branching, labeled, rooted , connected, directed multigraphs*. (In the notation of Chapter 3, $\mathbb{G}$ will be $\mathbb{G}_{\alpha,\aleph_1}$, where α is the alphabet cardinality.) Such a graph, also called a *process graph*, consists of a possibly infinite set of nodes s with one distinguished node s_0, the root. The edges, also called transitions or steps, between the nodes are labeled with an element from the action alphabet; also δ and τ may be edge labels. We use the notation $s \rightarrow_a t$ for an a-transition from node s to node t; likewise $s \rightarrow_\tau t$ is a τ-transition and $s\rightarrow_\delta t$ is a δ-step. That the graph is connected means that every node must be accessible by finitely many steps from the root node. Examples of process graphs where already given in Figures 1-3. Regarding δ-steps in process graphs, we will suppose that all process graphs are δ-normalised; the precise definition follows in Definition 1.13.3.

Corresponding to the operations +, ·, ||, ⌊⌊, | , ∂_H, τ_I, π_n, α in $ACP_\tau^\#$ we define operations in the domain **G** of process graphs. Precise definitions can be found in Baeten, Bergstra & Klop [87]; we will sketch some of them here. The sum g + h of two process graphs g, h is obtained by glueing together the roots of g and h; there is one caveat: if a root is cyclic (i.e. lying on a cycle of transitions leading back to the root), then the initial part of the graph has to be 'unwound' first so as to make the root acyclic. (In Chapter 2 we will be more precise about 'root-unwinding': see Definition 2.1.2 there.) The product g·h is obtained by appending copies of h to each terminal node of g; alternatively, one may first identify all terminal nodes of g and then append one copy of h to the unique terminal node if it exists. The merge g || h is obtained as a cartesian product of both graphs, with 'diagonal' edges for communications. (See Figure 1.8 for the merge of ab and cd, with communications b|c = g and a|d = f.) Definitions of the auxiliary operators ⌊⌊, | are somewhat more complicated and not discussed here. The encapsulation and abstraction operators are simply renamings, that replace the edge labels in H and I, respectively, by δ and τ, respectively. Definitions of the projection operators π_n and α should be clear from the axioms by which they are specified. As to the projection operators, it should be emphasized that τ-steps are transparent: they do not increase the depth.

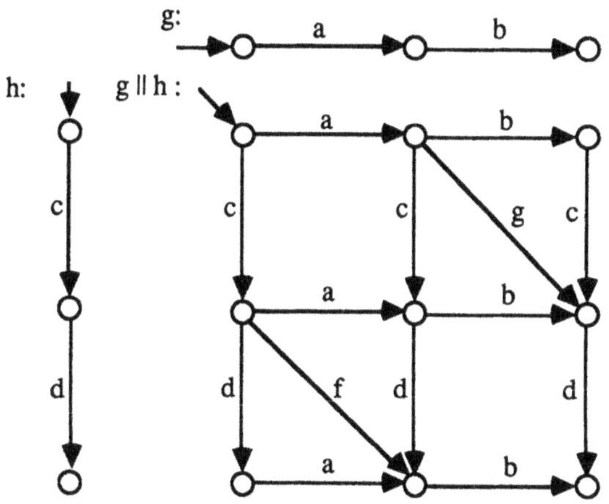

Figure 1.8

The domain **G** of process graphs equipped with the operations just introduced, is not yet a model of ACP_τ: for instance the axiom x + x = x does not hold. In order to obtain a model, we define an equivalence on the process graphs which is moreover a congruence with respect to the operations. This equivalence is called *bisimulation congruence* or *bisimilarity*. (The original notion is due to Park [81]; it was anticipated by Milner's observational equivalence, see Milner [80].)

1.13.1. DEFINITION. Let $g \in \mathbb{G}$.

(i) Steps $s \to_u t$ and $s \to_v t'$ (where $u, v \in A \to \{\tau, \delta\}$; s, t, t' are nodes of g) are *brothers*. A step $t \to_v t'$ is a *son* of the step $s \to_u t$.

(ii) g is said to be δ-*normalised* if δ-steps have no brothers and no sons.

(iii) End points of δ-steps are *virtual* nodes; all other nodes in g are *proper*.

(iv) A node is a *deadlock node* if all outgoing traces have only edges with labels τ, δ and end all in δ. (See Figure 1.9.)

(v) Nodes from which only infinite τ-traces start, are *livelock* nodes.

(vi) A *deadlock-livelock node* is a node from which all outgoing traces have as labels only τ, δ and such that there is no succesfully terminating trace.

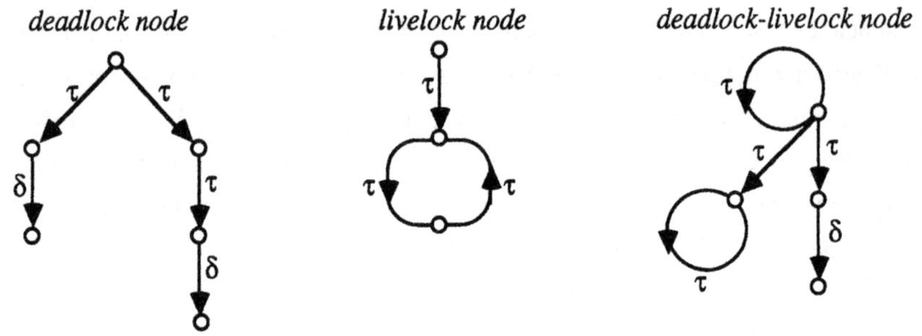

Figure 1.9

1.13.2. DEFINITION. A *path* π in g is a sequence

$$s_0 \to_{u0} s_1 \to_{u1} \cdots \to_{u(n-1)} s_n \qquad (n \geq 0)$$

of proper nodes and labelled edges. The node s_0 is *begin*(π), the node s_n is *end*(π). The path π determines a sequence of labels $u_0u_1...u_{n-1}$ ($u_i \in A \cup \{\tau\}$); *val*(π) is this sequence with all τ's skipped. Note that *val*(π) ∈ A*, the set of words over A, including the empty word λ.

1.13.3. DEFINITION. Let $g, h \in \mathbb{G}$ be δ-normalised. Let R be a relation between the proper nodes of g,h. We say that R relates path π in g to path π' in h (notation π R π') if

begin(π) R *begin*(π')
end(π) R *end*(π')
val(π) = *val*(π').

(s R t means: s,t are related by R.) If π R π', we also say that π is *transfered* by R to π', and vice versa.

(ii) Relation R has the *transfer property* if:

- whenever π is a path in g and *begin*(π) R t, t ∈ NODES(h), then π is transfered to some path

π' in h' with *begin*(π') = t;

- likewise with the role of g, h interchanged.

(Note that by definition the end points of π, π' are again related.)

1.13.4. DEFINITION. (i) Let g, h $\in \mathbb{G}$ be δ-normalised. Then g $\leftrightarrows_{r\tau\delta}^{R}$ h (g, h are $r\tau\delta$-bisimilar via R) if there is a relation between the proper nodes of g, h such that

(1) the roots of g, h are related,

(2) a root may only be related to a root,

(3) R has the transfer property,

(4) a deadlock-livelock node may only be related to a similar node.

(An equivalent definition is obtained by replacing (4) by:

(4') a node with possibly successful termination may only be related to a similar node. Here a node has 'possibly successful termination' if there is an outgoing trace ending succesfully.)

(ii) g $\leftrightarrows_{r\tau\delta}$ h if there is an R such that g $\leftrightarrows_{r\tau\delta}^{R}$ h.

1.13.5. EXAMPLES. (i) Figure 1.10 contains an example of a bisimulation in which only proper atoms (no τ, δ) are involved: the cyclic process graph g is bisimilar to the infinite process graph h obtained by unwinding.

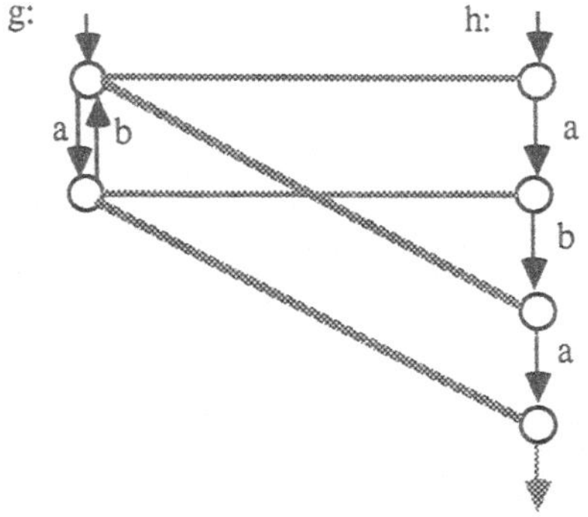

Figure 1.10

(ii) The two graphs in Figure 1.11 are bisimilar via the bisimulation relating nodes on the same level (i.e. joinable by a horizontal line).

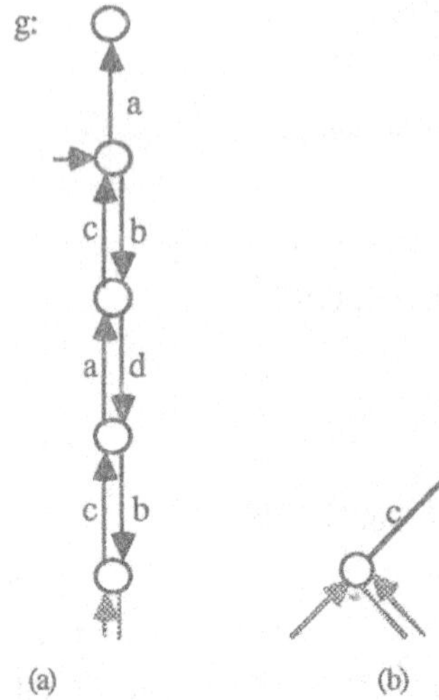

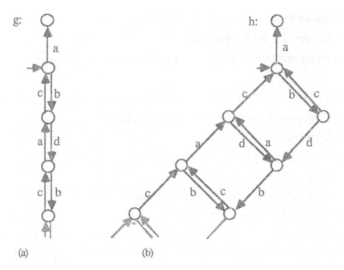

Figure 1. 11

(iii) Figure 1.12 demonstrates a bisimulation between process graphs involving τ-steps: nodes of the same 'color' are related.

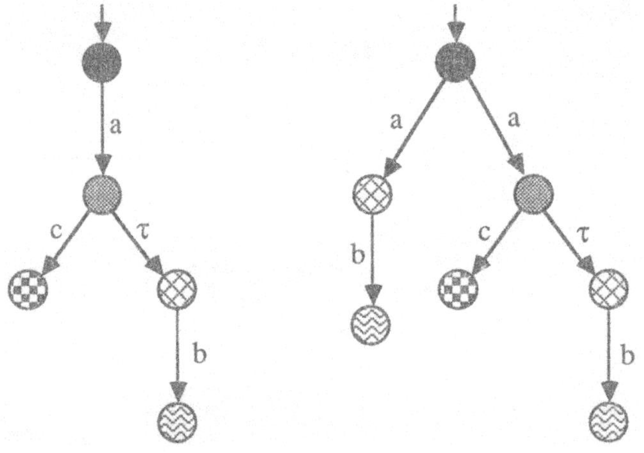

Example of r τδ-bisimulation: nodes of the same colour are related

Figure 1.12

We now are in the fortunate position that rτδ-bisimilarity is not only an equivalence relation on the domain **G** of process graphs, but even a congruence with respect to the operators on **G**. Thus we can take the quotient $\mathbf{G}/{\leftrightarrows_{\rho\tau\delta}}$, notation: $\mathbb{G}$. The following theorem is from Baeten, Bergstra & Klop [87].

1.13.6. THEOREM. $\mathbb{G}$ *is a model of* $ACP_\tau^{\#}$.

Remarkably, this *graph model* (as we will call it henceforth) does not satisfy AIP, the unrestricted Approximation Induction Principle. A counterexample is given (in a self-explaining notation) by the two process graphs $g = \Sigma_{n\geq1}\, a^n$ and $h = \Sigma_{n\geq1}\, a^n{+}a^\omega$ (see Figure 1.13(a)); while g and h have the same finite projections $\pi_n(g) = \pi_n(h) = a + a^2 + a^3 + ... + a^n$, they are not ($r\tau\delta$-)bisimilar due to the presence of the infinite trace of a-steps in h. It might be thought that it would be helpful to restrict the domain $\mathbb{G}$ of process graphs to finitely branching graphs, in order to obtain a model which does satisfy AIP, but there are two reasons why this is not the case: (1) the finitely branching graph domain would not be closed under the operations, in particular the communication merge (|); (2) a similar counterexample can be obtained by considering the finitely branching graphs $g' = \tau_{\{t\}}(g'')$ where g'' is the process graph defined by $\{X_n = a^n + tX_{n+1} \mid n \geq 1\}$ and $h' = g' + a^\omega$. (See Figure 1.14(b).)

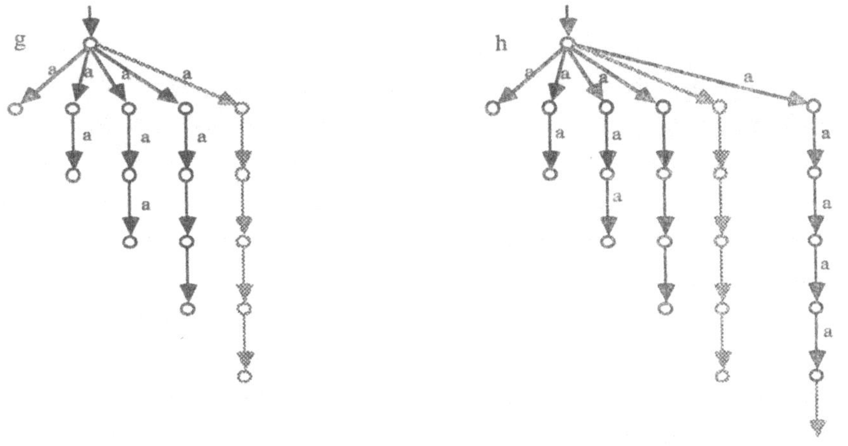

Figure 1.13

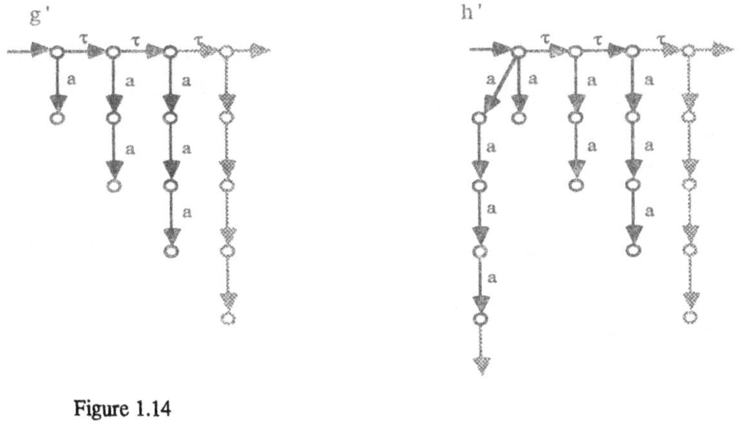

Figure 1.14

1.13.7. REMARK. It is not hard to see that the validity of AIP⁻ in the model $\mathbb{G}$ is a direct consequence of the following general lemma about bisimulations. Here, for a graph g, $\pi_n(g)$ is the n-th projection of g, i.e. what remains of g after cutting off everything below depth n. Furthermore, $\leftrightarrows$ is the restriction of $\leftrightarrows_{r\tau\delta}$ to the case where no τ or δ is present. (For an explicit definition, see 2.1.4.1 in Chapter 2.)

1.13.7.1. LEMMA. *Let* g, h *be process graphs containing only proper steps (not* τ *or* δ*). Let* g *be finitely branching (*h *may be infinitely branching). Then:*

$$\forall n\ \pi_n(g) \leftrightarrows \pi_n(h) \quad \Rightarrow \quad g \leftrightarrows h.$$

PROOF. We may suppose that g, h are process *trees*. Suppose g is finitely branching. Define relations $\equiv_n$ $(n \geq 1)$ and $\equiv$ between nodes s of g and t of h as follows: $s \equiv t$ iff $\forall n\ s \equiv_n t$ and $s \equiv_n t$ iff $\pi_n((g)_s \leftrightarrows \pi_n((h)t)$. Here $(g)_s$ is the subtree of g with root s. We will prove that $\equiv$ is a bisimulation.

For the roots s_0, t_0 of g, h respectively we have indeed $s_0 \equiv t_0$; this is just the assumption $\forall n$ $\pi_n(g) \leftrightarrows \pi_n(h)$. Next we show the easy half of the bisimulation requirements: let $s \equiv t$ and $t \to_a t'$. We have to show that there is an s' such that $s \to_a s'$ and $s' \equiv t'$. By definition of $\equiv_n$, and because we have $\forall n\ s \equiv_n t$, for every n there must be a step $s \to_a s_n'$ such that $s_n' \equiv_n t'$. Since s has only finitely many successors (g is finitely branching), there must be an s' among the s_n' such that $s \to_a s'$ and $s' \equiv_n t'$ for infinitely many n. Since the relations $\equiv_n$ are decreasing ($\equiv_0 \supseteq \equiv_1 \supseteq \equiv_2 \supseteq \ldots$) this means that $s' \equiv_n t'$ for *all* n, i.e. $s' \equiv_n t'$.

For the reverse bisimulation requirement, see Figure 1.15. Let $s \equiv t$ and $s \to_a s'$. To show that there is a t' such that $t \to_a t'$ and $s' \equiv t'$. We can find a-successors $t_1, t_2, \ldots, t_n, \ldots$ of t such that $s' \equiv_n t_n$. As was just proved, for every t_n there is an a-successor s_n of s with $s_n \equiv t_n$. Since s has only finitely many successors, the sequence $\{s_n\}_n$ is in fact finite. Hence there is an a-successor s* of s such that $s^* \equiv t_n$ for infinitely many n. So, $s' \equiv_n t_n \equiv s^*$ for infinitely many n. So $s' \equiv s^*$, and $s' \equiv t'$ where t' is one of the t_n with $t_n \equiv s^*$. □

The general case, where τ and δ may be present, follows by an entirely similar proof (see also Baeten, Bergstra & Klop [87]). Note however that $\pi_n(g)$ now is obtained by cutting away all steps that are reachable from the root only by passing n or more *proper* steps. (So $\pi_n(g)$ may contain infinite τ-paths.) Thus we have:

1.13.7.2. LEMMA. *Let* g, h *be process graphs. Let* g *have finite projections (i.e. every* $\pi_n(g)$ *is a finite graph.) Then:*

$$\forall n\ \pi_n(g) \leftrightarrows_{r\tau\delta} \pi_n(h) \quad \Rightarrow \quad g \leftrightarrows_{r\tau\delta} h.$$

Note that the assumption of finite projections is fulfilled for a graph which is defined by a system of guarded recursion equations; hence AIP^- holds in $\mathbb{G}$.

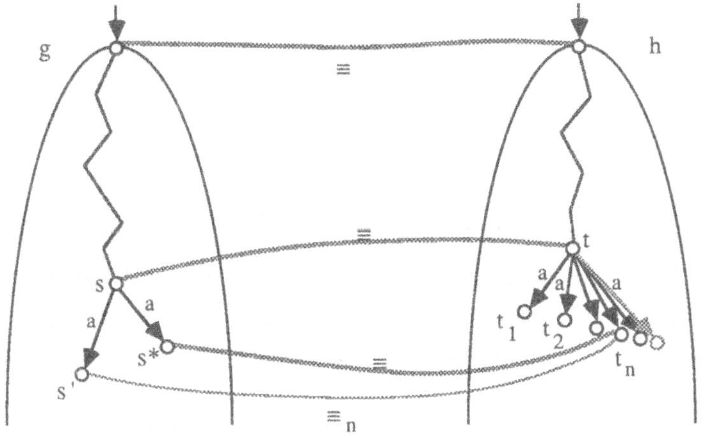

Figure 1.15

1.14. The expressive power of ACP_τ.

ACP_τ is a powerful specification mechanism; in a sense it is a universal specification mechanism: *every finitely branching, computable process can be finitely specified* in ACP_τ. We have to be more precise about the notion of 'computable process'. First, an intuitive explanation: suppose a finitely branching process graph g is actually given; the labels may include τ, and there may be even infinite τ-traces. That g is 'actually' given means that the process graph g must be 'computable': a finite recipe describes the graph, in the form of a coding of the nodes in natural numbers and recursive functions giving in-degree, out-degree, edge-labels. This notion of a computable process graph is rather obvious, and we will not give details of the definition here (these can be found in Baeten, Bergstra & Klop [87]).

Now even if g is an infinite process graph, it can be specified by an infinite computable specification, as follows. First rename all τ-edges in g to t-edges, for a 'fresh' atom t. Call the resulting process graph: g_t. Next assign to each node s of g_t a recursion variable X_s and write down the recursion equation for X_s according to the outgoing edges of node s. Let X_{s0} be the variable corresponding to the root s_0 of g_t. As g is computable, g_t is computable and the resulting 'direct' specification $E = \{X_s = T_s(\mathbf{X}) \mid s \in \text{NODES}(g_t)\}$ is evidently also computable (i.e.: the nodes can be numbered as s_n ($n \geq 0$), and after coding the sequence e_n of codes of equations E_n: $X_{sn} = T_{sn}(\mathbf{X})$ is a computable sequence). Now the specification which uniquely determines g, is simply: $\{Y = \tau_{\{t\}}(X_{s0})\} \cup E$. In fact all specifications below will have the form $\{X = \tau_I(X_0), X_n = T_n(\mathbf{X}) \mid n \geq 0\}$ where the guarded expressions $T_n(\mathbf{X})$ ($= T_n(X_{i1},...,X_{in})$) contain no abstraction operators τ_J. They may contain all other process operators. We will say that such specifications have *restricted abstraction.*

However, we want more than a computable specification with restricted abstraction: to describe process graph g we would like to find a *finite* specification with restricted abstraction for g. Indeed this is possible:

1.14.2. FINITE SPECIFICATION THEOREM. *Let the finitely branching and computable process graph* g *determine* $g^{\sim}$ *in the graph model* $\mathbb{G}$ *of* ACP_{τ}. *Then there is a finite specification with restricted abstraction* E *in* ACP_{τ} *such that* $[\![E]\!] = g^{\sim}$.

Here $[\![E]\!]$ is the semantics of E in the graph model. (The proof in Baeten, Bergstra & Klop [87] is by constructing a Turing machine in ACP_{τ}; the 'tape' is obtained by glueing together two stacks. A stack has a simple finite specification, already in BPA; see the example in Section 1.1.) A stronger fact would be the assertion that every computable specification with restricted abstraction in ACP_{τ} is provably equivalent (in $ACP_{\tau}^{\#}$) to a finite specification with restricted abstraction. At present we do not know whether this is true.

It should be noted that abstraction plays an essential role in this finite specification theorem. If $f: \mathbb{N} \to \{a,b\}$ is a sequence of a,b, let p_f be the process $f(0)\cdot f(1)\cdot f(2)\cdot ...$ (more precisely: the unique solution of the infinite specification $\{X_n = f(n)\cdot X_{n+1} \mid n \geq 0\}$). Now:

1.14.3. THEOREM. *There is a computable function* f *such that process* p_f *is not definable by a finite specification (in* ACP_{τ} *) without abstraction operator.*

A fortiori, p_f is not finitely definable in ACP. The proof in Baeten, Bergstra & Klop [87] is via a simple diagonalization argument.

1.14.4. REMARK. As we have seen, the graph model of $ACP_{\tau}^{\#}$ (Section 1.13) does not satisfy the unrestricted Approximation Induction Principle which states that every process is uniquely determined by its finite projections. It is natural to search for a model in which this principle does hold. However, Van Glabbeek [87] proves that such a model does not exist, if one wishes to adhere to the very natural assumption that composition of abstraction operators is commutative, and if one only allows models in which deadlock behaviour is respected (in which, therefore, the equation $\tau = \tau + \tau\delta$ does not hold). We will consider the following consequence of the axioms in Table 20: $\tau_{\{a\}} \circ \tau_{\{b\}} = \tau_{\{b\}} \circ \tau_{\{a\}}$ which we will denote by CA (commutativity of abstraction). Now Van Glabbeek [87] proves:

1.14.5. THEOREM. $ACP_{\tau} + KFAR_1 + RDP + RSP + CA + AIP \vdash \tau = \tau + \tau\delta$.

So, in every theory extending ACP_{τ}, the combination of features AIP, KFAR, CA, RDP+RSP is impossible. Among such theories are also theories where the equivalence on processes is much coarser, such as in Hoare's well-known failure model (see Hoare [85]).

2. Complete inference systems for regular processes

In the first chapter we have explained a proof system for specification of processes in bisimulation semantics (namely, in the graph model $\mathbb{G}$), which is 'complete' in the sense that every computable process in $\mathbb{G}$ can be finitely specified. In this chapter we will address the issue of completeness in the usual sense. In doing so, we restrict our attention to the submodel $\mathbb{R}$ of $\mathbb{G}$ consisting of processes having only finitely many 'states', i.e. to '*regular*' processes. Silent steps (τ-steps) are allowed in these processes. We will present a complete inference system for such processes; it is an improved version of the complete inference system in Bergstra & Klop [88].

To obtain the complete proof system we first explore various properties of bisimulations between process graphs with τ-steps ($r\tau$-bisimulation). This leads us to an analysis of $r\tau$-bisimulation which may be illuminating for its own sake. This part of the present chapter is taken from Bergstra & Klop [88]; Sections 2.1 and 2.2 are essentially 1.2-2.4 from Bergsta & Klop [88], with some modifications, and with some examples and proofs omitted.

In this chapter (and the next) we will not consider the process constant δ, deadlock. This is merely a matter of convenience, and in no way essential; all results can easily be adapted for the presence of δ. On the other hand, the presence of τ is very essential; without τ, complete proof systems for regular processes are relatively easy to find. Because δ is omitted from our considerations, we will refer to $r\tau\delta$-bisimulation (defined in Chapter 1, Definition 1.13.4) as $r\tau$-bisimulation.

2.1. Some properties of $r\tau$-bisimulation.

As in Chapter 1, $\mathbb{G}$ is the set of (at most) countably branching process graphs with edge labels from $A \cup \{\delta\} \cup \{\tau\}$. Here $A = \{a,b,c,...\}$ is the set of 'proper' atoms or actions. In the present chapter we will consider the set $\mathbb{R} \subseteq \mathbb{G}$ of finite process graphs in which no δ occurs; so the edge labels are from $A_\tau = A \cup \{\tau\}$. Notation: u,v,... vary over A_τ.

2.1.1. Root-unwinding

It will be convenient to have a canonical transformation of a process graph $g \in \mathbb{G}$ into an 'equivalent' root-acyclic one. (Here 'equivalent' is in a sense which will be explained below, in Proposition 2.1.4.3.)

2.1.2. DEFINITION. The map $\rho: \mathbb{G} \to \mathbb{G}$, *root-unwinding*, is defined as follows. Let $g \in \mathbb{G}$ have root r; then $\rho(g)$ is defined by the following clauses:

(i) NODES(ρ(g)) = NODES(g) $\cup$ {r'} where r' is a 'fresh' node;

(ii) the root of ρ(g) is r';

(iii) EDGES(ρ(g)) = EDGES(g) $\cup$ $\{r' \to_u s \mid r \to_u s \in$ EDGES(g)$\}$;

(iv) nodes and edges which are inaccessible from the new root r' are discarded.

2.1.3. EXAMPLE. Figure 2.1 gives two examples of root-unwinding.

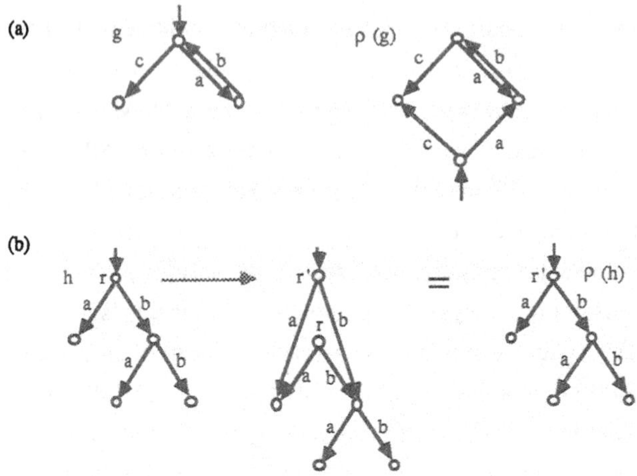

Figure 2.1

Observe that ρ is idempotent: $\rho^2(g) = \rho(g)$. Notation: $\mathbb{G}^\rho$ is the set of all root-unwound graphs in $\mathbb{G}$.

2.1.4. Bisimulations

In the previous chapter we have already defined rτδ-bisimulation; the concepts of 'ordinary' bisimulation $\underline{\leftrightarrow}$ (on $\mathbb{G} \times \mathbb{G}$), 'τ–bisimulation' $\underline{\leftrightarrow}_\tau$ (on $\mathbb{G} \times \mathbb{G}$) and 'rooted τ–bisimulation' $\underline{\leftrightarrow}_{r\tau}$ (on $\mathbb{G}^\rho \times \mathbb{G}^\rho$) are just restrictions of that of rτδ-bisimulation, but for the sake of clarity we give the successive definitions again, in a rephrased way which conforms more to the usual definition..

2.1.4.1. Bisimulation: $\underline{\leftrightarrow}$

Let g,h $\in \mathbb{G}$. The relation R $\subseteq$ NODES(g) $\times$ NODES(h) is a *bisimulation from* g *to* h, notation R: g $\underline{\leftrightarrow}$ h, if

(i) Domain(R) = NODES(g) and Range(R) = NODES(h)

(ii) (ROOT(g), ROOT(h)) $\in$ R

(iii) if (s,t) $\in$ R and $s \rightarrow_u s'$ $\in$ EDGES(g) then there is an edge $t \rightarrow_u t'$ $\in$ EDGES(h), such that (s',t') $\in$ R.

(iv) if (s,t) $\in$ R and $t \rightarrow_u t'$ $\in$ EDGES(h) then there is an edge $s \rightarrow_u s'$ $\in$ EDGES(g), such that (s',t') $\in$ R.

Further, we write g $\underline{\leftrightarrow}$ h if $\exists$R R: g$\underline{\leftrightarrow}$ h. In this case g,h are called *bisimilar*.

2.1.4.2. EXAMPLE. See Figure 2.2 for a bisimulation between a graph and its root-unwinding; the shaded lines denote the bisimulation.

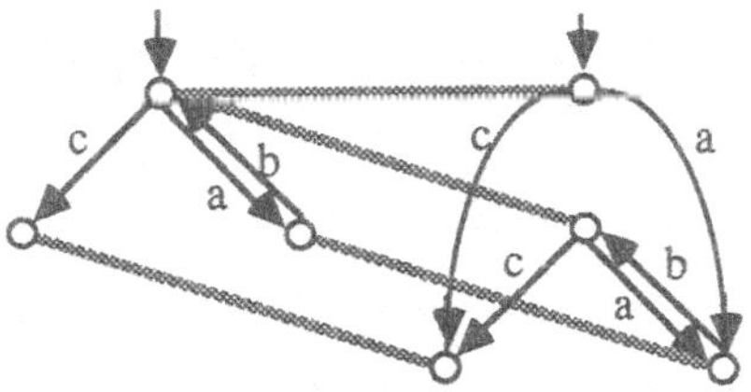

Figure 2.2

Bisimilar process graphs have the same sets of traces. The reverse, however, does not hold. We mention the following facts without proof:

2.1.4.3. PROPOSITION.

(i) *Let* $g \in \mathbb{G}$. *Then* $g \leftrightarrows \rho(g)$.

(ii) *The relation* $\leftrightarrows$ *(bisimilarity) is an equivalence relation on* $\mathbb{G}$.

(iii) *If* $g,h \in \mathbb{G}$, $R: g \leftrightarrows h$ *and for* $s \in$ NODES(g), $t \in$ NODES(h) *we have* $(s,t) \in R$, *then* $R': (g)_s \leftrightarrows (h)_t$, *where* R' *is the restriction of* R *to the nodes of* $(g)_s$ *and* $(h)_t$.

2.1.4.4. τ-Bisimulation: $\leftrightarrows_\tau$

An equivalent definition for ordinary bisimulation can be given as follows. Replace in the definition of 2.1.4.1. clauses (iii), (iv) by:

(iii)' if $(s,t) \in R$ and $\pi: s \twoheadrightarrow_w s'$ is a path in g (determining the 'word' $u_1u_2...u_k$ $(k \geq 0)$ of labels along the edges in π), then there is a path $\pi': t \twoheadrightarrow_{w'} t'$ in h such that $(s',t') \in R$ and such that $w \equiv w'$ (w,w' are identical).

(iv) likewise with the role of g, h interchanged.

The definition of $\leftrightarrows_\tau$ now parallels that for $\leftrightarrows$, with as only alteration that $w \equiv w'$ is replaced by $w \equiv_\tau w'$. Here $w \equiv_\tau w'$ ($w,w' \in A_\tau^*$ are equivalent modulo τ) if w,w' are identical after deletion of τ's. E.g. $\tau \equiv_\tau \tau\tau\tau \equiv_\tau \varepsilon$ (the empty word); $ab\tau\tau\tau c\tau \equiv_\tau \tau a\tau b\tau c$. Processes $g,h \in \mathbb{G}$ such that $g \leftrightarrows_\tau h$ are called *τ–bisimilar.*

2.1.4.5. Rooted τ-bisimulation: $\leftrightarrows_{r\tau}$

Suppose $g,h \in \mathbb{G}^\rho$ and $R: g \leftrightarrows_\tau h$ in such a way that

$(s,t) \in R \Rightarrow s = \text{ROOT}(g)$ and $t = \text{ROOT}(h)$, or: $s \neq \text{ROOT}(g)$ and $t \neq \text{ROOT}(h)$.

(So a non-root cannot be related in the bisimulation to a root.) Then R is called a *rooted τ–bisimulation* between g,h and we write $R: g \leftrightarrows_{r\tau} h$ or $g \leftrightarrows_{r\tau}^R h$. Such g,h are called *rτ–bisimilar* (via R). Note that $g \leftrightarrows h \Rightarrow g \leftrightarrows_\tau h$ and $g \leftrightarrows_{r\tau} h \Rightarrow g \leftrightarrows_\tau h$. As before, $\leftrightarrows_{r\tau}$ and $\leftrightarrows_\tau$ are equivalence relations on $\mathbb{G}^\rho$ and $\mathbb{G}$, respectively. Also $\leftrightarrows_\tau$, $\leftrightarrows_{r\tau}$ are invariant under ρ.

2.1.4.6. EXAMPLES.

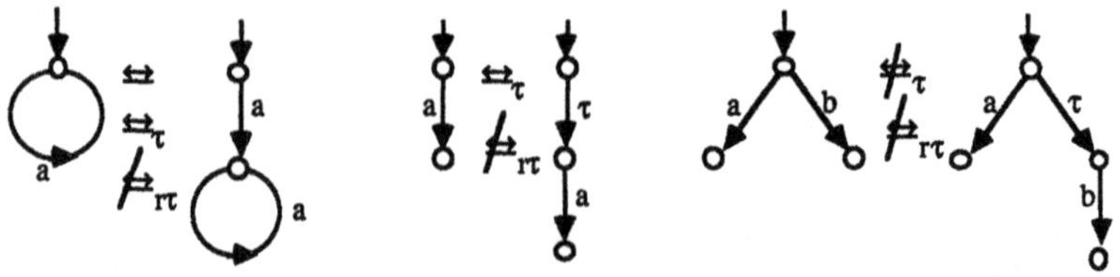

(a) (b) (c)

Figure 2.3

Some further obvious facts are:

2.1.4.7. PROPOSITION. (i) *Let* g,h $\in \mathbb{G}$ *be τ-bisimilar via* R. *Let* (s,t) $\in$ R. *Then* $(g)_s$ *and* $(h)_t$ *are τ-bisimilar (via the appropriate restriction of* R*). (The nodes* s,t *are called in this case τ-bisimilar.)*
(ii) *Let* g,h $\in \mathbb{G}^{\rho}$ *and* g $\underline{\leftrightarrow}_{r\tau}^{R}$ h. *Let* (s,t) $\in$ R. *Then* $(g)_s \underline{\leftrightarrow}_\tau (h)_t$ *(in general not* rτ*-bisimilar).* □

2.1.4.8. PROPOSITION. *Let* g,h $\in \mathbb{G}$ *and suppose R:* g $\underline{\leftrightarrow}$ h *as well as R':* g $\underline{\leftrightarrow}$ h. *Then* R∪R': g $\underline{\leftrightarrow}$ h. *Similar for* $\underline{\leftrightarrow}_\tau$ *and* $\underline{\leftrightarrow}_{r\tau}$. □

(Note that the *intersection* of bisimulations R, R' need not be a bisimulation.)

2.1.4.9. DEFINITION. (i) A *τ-cycle* in a process graph g is a cycle

$$\pi\colon s_0 \to_\tau s_1 \to_\tau \dots \to_\tau s_k \equiv s_0 \quad (k \geq 1).$$

(ii) A *τ–loop* is a τ-cycle of length 1:

$$\pi\colon s_0 \to_\tau s_0.$$

2.1.4.10. PROPOSITION. *Let* g $\in \mathbb{G}$ *contain a τ–cycle passing through the nodes* s,t. *Then* s,t *are τ-bisimilar (i.e.* $(g)_s \underline{\leftrightarrow}_\tau (g)_t$*).*

PROOF. (See Figure 2.4, next page.) Note that every point in g accessible form s is accessible from t and vice versa. Hence the node sets of $(g)_s$ and $(g)_t$ coincide. Now let Id be the identity relation on NODES($(g)_s$). Then it is easy to verify that Id ∪ {(s,t)} is a τ-bisimulation from $(g)_s$ to $(g)_t$. □

2.1.4.11. PROPOSITION. (i) *Let* g $\in \mathbb{G}$ *contain τ-bisimilar nodes* s,t. *Let* g* *be the result of adding a τ-edge from* s *to* t. *Then* g *and* g* *are τ-bisimilar.*
(ii) *Let* g $\in \mathbb{G}^{\rho}$ *contain non-root nodes* s,t *which are τ-bisimilar. Then* g $\underline{\leftrightarrow}_{r\tau}$ g*.

PROOF. (i) Let Id be the identity relation on NODES(g) (= NODES(g*)). Then Id ∪ {(s,t)} is a τ-bisimulation from g to g* as required. (ii) Similar. □

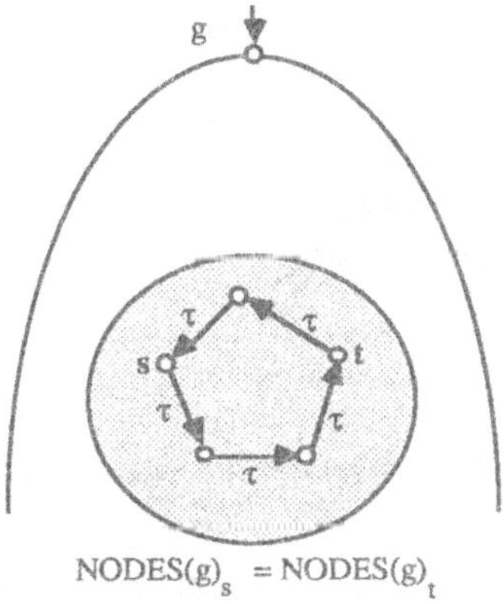

Figure 2.4

This proposition says that adding τ-steps between τ-bisimilar nodes in a graph g does not change the "τ-bisimilarity character" of g (and for the same reason, of any node q, or better, subgraph $(g)_q$ of g). Here the τ-bisimilarity character of g is the class of all g' ∈ 𝔾 which are τ-bisimilar with g. In particular, the τ-bisimilarity character is not disturbed by appending τ-loops to nodes of g. Vice versa, removing τ-loops also does not change the τ-bisimilarity character.

2.1.4.12. EXAMPLE.

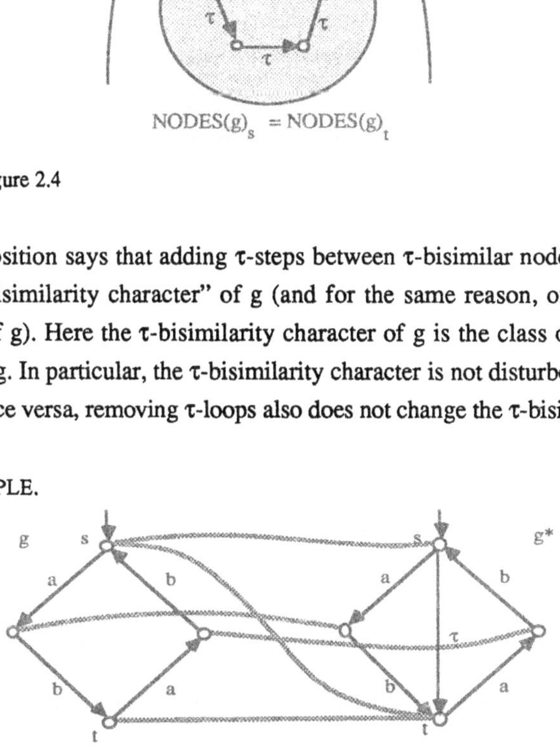

Figure 2.5

Just as all τ-loops can be removed from g without changing τ-bisimilarity (which follows from the previous proposition, by taking s = t), it is possible to remove all τ-cycles from g. We need a definition first:

2.1.4.13. DEFINITION. Let g ∈ 𝔾 contain nodes s,t. Then $g_{id(s,t)}$ is the process graph resulting from the identification of s and t, in the obvious sense.

2.1.4.14. EXAMPLE. Let g be as in Figure 2.5. Then $g_{id(s,t)}$ is:

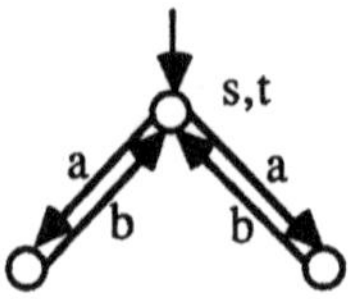

Figure 2.6

2.1.4.15. PROPOSITION. (i) *Let* $g \in \mathbb{G}$ *and suppose* s,t $\in$ NODES(g) *are* τ*-bisimilar. Then* g *and* $g_{id(s,t)}$ *are* τ*-bisimilar.*
(ii) *Let* $g \in \mathbb{G}^{\rho}$ *and suppose the non-root nodes* s,t $\in$ NODES(g) *are* τ*-bisimilar. Then* $g \,\underline{\leftrightarrow}_{r\tau}\, g_{id(s,t)}$.

PROOF. Obvious. □

2.1.4.16. COROLLARY. (i) *Every* $g \in \mathbb{G}$ *is* τ*-bisimilar with some* $g' \in \mathbb{G}$ *without* τ*-cycles.*
(ii) *Every* $g \in \mathbb{G}^{\rho}$ *is* $r\tau$*-bisimilar with some* $g' \in \mathbb{G}^{\rho}$ *without* τ*-cycles.*
(iii) *Every* $g \in \mathbb{R}$ *is* τ*-bisimilar to some* $g' \in \mathbb{R}$ *without infinite* τ*-paths.*

PROOF. Follows from considering Figure 2.7. □

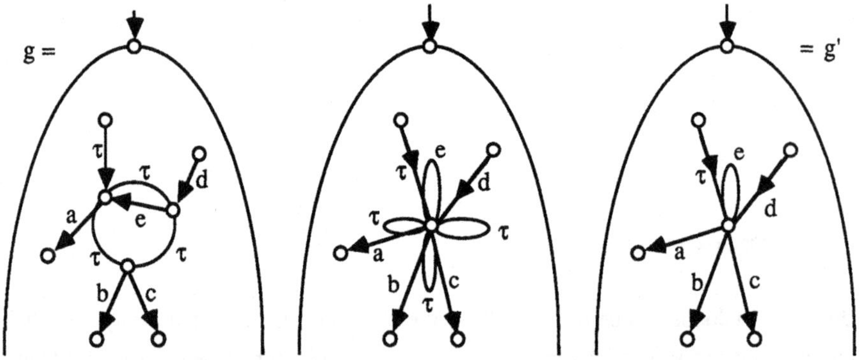

Figure 2.7

We conclude this section with an observation illuminating the difference between $\underline{\leftrightarrow}_{\tau}$ and $\underline{\leftrightarrow}_{r\tau}$. The easy proof is left to the reader (or, see Bergstra & Klop [88]).

2.1.4.17. REMARK. Let g,h $\in \mathbb{G}$ and let τg, τh be the result of prefixing a τ-step. Then:
$g \,\underline{\leftrightarrow}_{\tau}\, h \;\Leftrightarrow\; \tau g \,\underline{\leftrightarrow}_{r\tau}\, \tau h$.

2.2. An analysis of rτ-bisimulation.

The main result of this section is that an $r\tau$-bisimulation R between g,h $\in \mathbb{R}$ can be analysed into more simple parts:

$$\begin{array}{ccc} g & \underline{\leftrightarrow}_{r\tau} & h \\ \downarrow & & \downarrow \\ \Delta(g) & & \Delta(h) \\ \downarrow & & \downarrow \\ E(\Delta(g)) & \underline{\leftrightarrow} & E(\Delta(h)) \end{array}$$

(Corollary 2.2.4). I.e. $g \underline{\leftrightarrow}_{r\tau} h$ iff g,h after 'preprocessing' (by means of some simple operations Δ, E: $\mathbb{G} \to \mathbb{G}$), are bisimilar in the ordinary sense where τ does not play its special role. This analysis is the basis for the completeness theorem in the sequel where axioms are given describing rτ-bisimulation.

2.2.1. The operation Δ

First we need some terminology: if $g \in \mathbb{G}$, then an *arc* in g is a part of the form (a) in Figure 2.9 (here $u \in A_\tau$). In case $n = m = 0$, the arc is a *double edge* as in (b). Other special cases are in Figure 2.9(c), (d): these are called Δ-*arcs*. It is not required that the three nodes displayed in (a)–(d) are indeed pairwise different. The u-step between nodes s,t is called the *primary* edge of the arc.

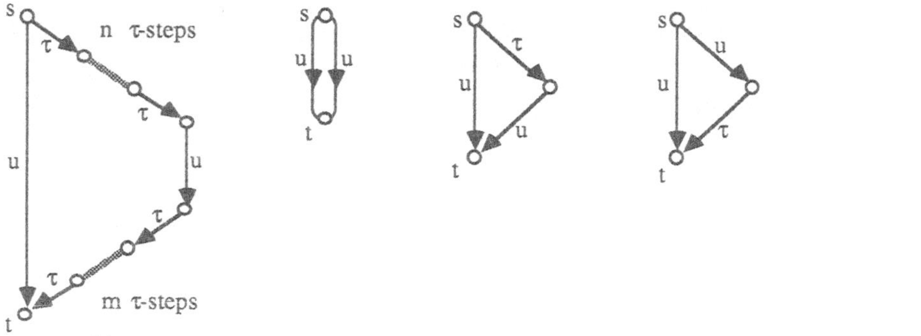

(a) (b) (c) (d)

Figure 2.9

Now the operation Δ: $\mathbb{G} \to \mathbb{G}$ is defined as follows: whenever $g \in \mathbb{G}$ contains a path $s_1 \to_\tau s_2 \to_u s_3$ (where s_1,s_2,s_3 need not be pairwise different), an edge $s_1 \to_u s_3$ is added if not yet present. Likewise for every path $s_1 \to_u s_2 \to_\tau s_3$. $\Delta(g)$ is the result of this completion of g with edges as indicated.

Further, we say that $g \in \mathbb{G}$ is Δ-*saturated* if $\Delta(g) = g$.

2.2.2. EXAMPLE.

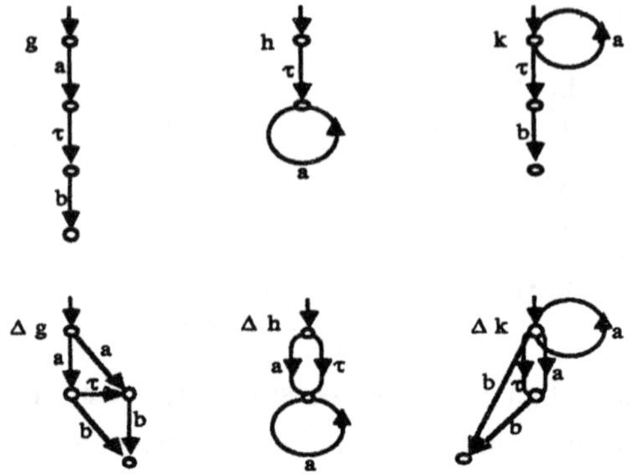

Figure 2.10

2.2.3. PROPOSITION. (i) $\Delta(g) \,\underline{\leftrightarrow}_{\tau}\, g$ *if* $g \in \mathbb{G}$; (ii) $\Delta(g) \,\underline{\leftrightarrow}_{r\tau}\, g$ *if* $g \in \mathbb{G}^{\rho}$.

PROOF. The identity relation R gives a (r)τ-bisimulation. □

2.2.4. The operation E

Call a node of $g \in \mathbb{G}^{\rho}$ *internal* if it is not the root, and an edge of g *internal* if it is between internal nodes. Further, call an internal τ-step $s \to_{\tau} t$ in $g \in \mathbb{G}^{\rho}$ an *ε-step* if s,t are τ-bisimilar. Finally, consider the set of internal nodes of $g \in \mathbb{G}^{\rho}$ and the equivalence relation on this set given by τ-bisimilarity. We will call the equivalence classes: *clusters*. So ε-steps always occur ‘inside’ a cluster (see Figure 2.11).

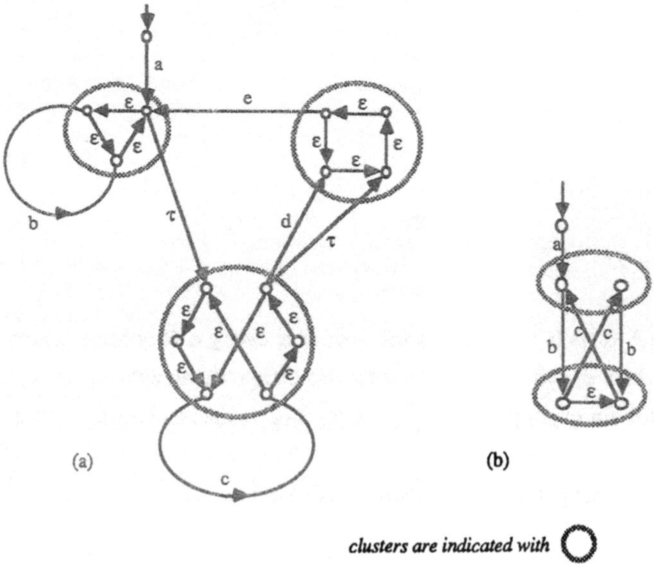

Figure 2.11

2.2.4.1. NOTATION. If s,s' are in the same cluster we write also s ~ s'.

The concept of clusters of nodes makes the structure of a process graph more perspicuous. In particular, Δ-saturated process graphs g have a local structure as indicated in Figure 2.12:

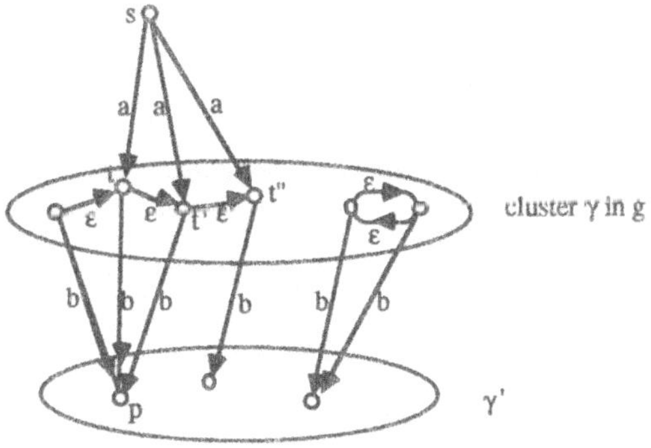

Figure 2.12

Namely, if γ is a cluster in g and $s \rightarrow_a t$ is an 'incoming' edge, then the endpoint t is carried in the direction of the ε-steps, thus providing arrows $s \rightarrow_a t'$, $s \rightarrow_a t''$. Vice versa, if $t' \rightarrow_b p$ is an outgoing edge, the starting point t' is carried backwards along ε-paths. This is a simple consequence of Δ-saturation and in fact it does not depend on the particular nature of ε-steps. Moreover, and this does depend on the definition of cluster in terms of $\leftrightarrows_\tau$, if γ has an outgoing edge $\rightarrow_b$ to some cluster γ', then from every point in γ there is an edge $\rightarrow_b$ to γ'. We will need this last fact so let us prove it:

2.2.4.2. PROPOSITION. *Let* g ∈ $\mathbb{G}^\rho$ *be Δ-saturated. Let* $s \rightarrow_u t$ *be an edge of* g *and let* s' ~ s. *Then* g *contains an edge* $s' \rightarrow_u t'$ *for some* t' ~ t.

PROOF. Consider an rτ-bisimulation R of g with itself relating s to s'. (R can be taken to be the union of the identity relation on g and a τ-bisimulation from $(g)_s$ to $(g)_{s'}$.) Now by definition of τ-bisimulation, given the edge $s \rightarrow_u t$ and s ~ s' there is a path π: s' ↠ t' with label $\tau^n u \tau^m$ in g for some n,m ≥ 0 and some t' with t' ~ t. By virtue of Δ-saturation, we now have an edge $s' \rightarrow_u t'$. □

Now we would like, in order to obtain the 'structure theorem' 2.2.4.7 concerning (r)τ-bisimulation as well as the completeness result in Section 2.3, to omit all ε-steps in a Δ-saturated graph g, resulting in a graph g' which is still rτ-bisimilar to g. Here the need for Δ-saturation comes in, for omitting ε-steps could make a non-Δ-saturated graph g disconnected, as in Example 2.2.2: there the τ-step in g (which clearly is an ε-step) cannot be removed, but it can in Δ(g).

2.2.4.3. DEFINITION. E is the operation from $\mathbb{G}^\rho$ to $\mathbb{G}^\rho$ which removes in $g \in \mathbb{G}^\rho$ all ε-steps (as well as parts of g which become disconnected in that process). If $g = E(g)$, g is called *prenormal.*

The straightforward proofs of the next two propositions are omitted (they can be found in Bergstra & Klop [88]).

2.2.4.4. PROPOSITION. E *preserves* Δ*-saturation.*

2.2.4.5. PROPOSITION. (i) *If* $g \in \mathbb{G}^\rho$ *is* Δ*-saturated, then* $g \leftrightarrow_{r\tau} E(g)$.
(ii) *For* $g \in \mathbb{G}^\rho$: $E(\Delta(g) \leftrightarrow_{r\tau} g$.

Now we arrive at a key lemma:

2.2.4.6. LEMMA. *Let* $g,h \in \mathbb{G}^\rho$ *be* Δ*-saturated and prenormal. Then:*

$$g \leftrightarrow_{r\tau} h \;\Rightarrow\; g \leftrightarrow h.$$

PROOF. (1) Let R be an $r\tau$-bisimulation between g,h. Then there is no τ-step in g which is "contracted" by R in h, as in Figure 2.13 (and likewise with g,h interchanged):

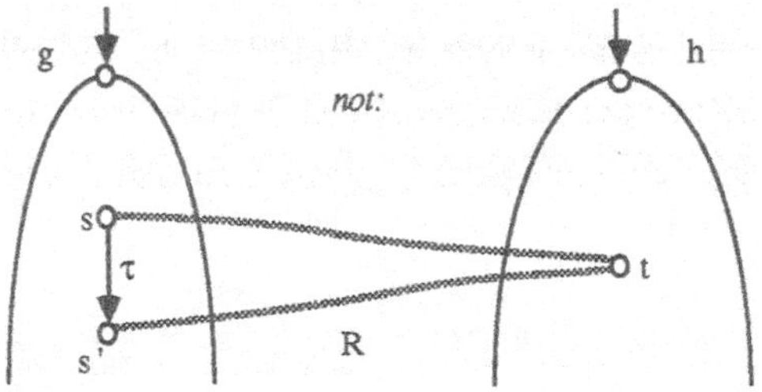

Figure 2.13

Namely, if s = r, the root of g, then this claim follows by definition of $\leftrightarrow_{r\tau}$. Otherwise, $s \to_\tau s'$ is an internal step ($s' \neq r$ since $g \in \mathbb{G}^\rho$) and now by Proposition 2.1.4.7(ii):

$$(g)_s \leftrightarrow_\tau (h)_t \leftrightarrow_\tau (g)_{s'}.$$

That is: $s \to_\tau s'$ is an ε-step. But then g is not prenormal.
(2) Let $s \to_u s'$ ($u \in A_\tau$) be a step in g (see Figure 2.14, next page). By definition of the $r\tau$-bisimulation R, there is given a t such that $(s,t) \in R$, a path $t \twoheadrightarrow t'$ with label $\tau^n u \tau^m$, for some t' such that $(s',t') \in R$. By Δ-saturation of h, there is now a step $t \to_u t'$. (1) and (2) together imply that the $r\tau$-bisimulation R is in fact an ordinary bisimulation. □

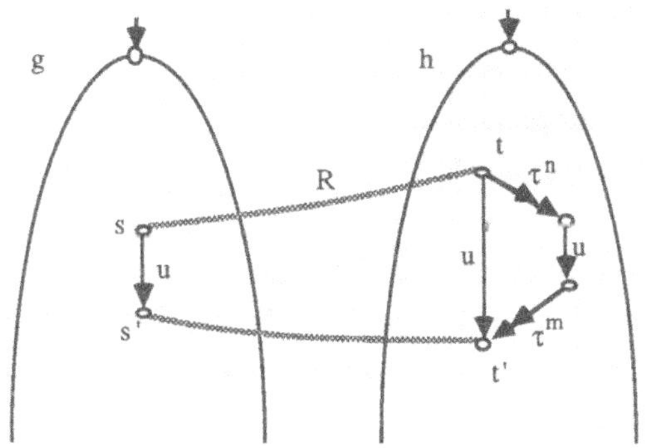

Figure 2.14

2.2.4.7. COROLLARY. *Let* g,h ∈ $\mathbb{G}^\rho$ *and let* g $\leftrightarrows_{r\tau}$ h. *Then* E(Δ(g)) $\leftrightarrows$ E(Δ(h)).

PROOF. By Proposition 2.2.3, Δg $\leftrightarrows_{r\tau}$ Δh. By Proposition 2.2.4.5, E(Δg) $\leftrightarrows_{r\tau}$ E(Δh). By Proposition 2.2.4.4, E(Δg) and E(Δh) are Δ-saturated. Hence by Lemma 2.2.4.6 these two graphs are bisimilar in the ordinary sense. □

2.3. Complete inference systems for rτ-bisimulation.

(This section will be slightly informal and gloss over some details; for these we refer to Bergstra & Klop [88].) A corollary of the preceding section (Corollaries 2.1.4.16 and 2.2.4.7) is that an rτ-bisimulation between two graphs g, h ∈ $\mathcal{R}^\rho$ can be analyzed in the following parts. (See Figure 2.15.)

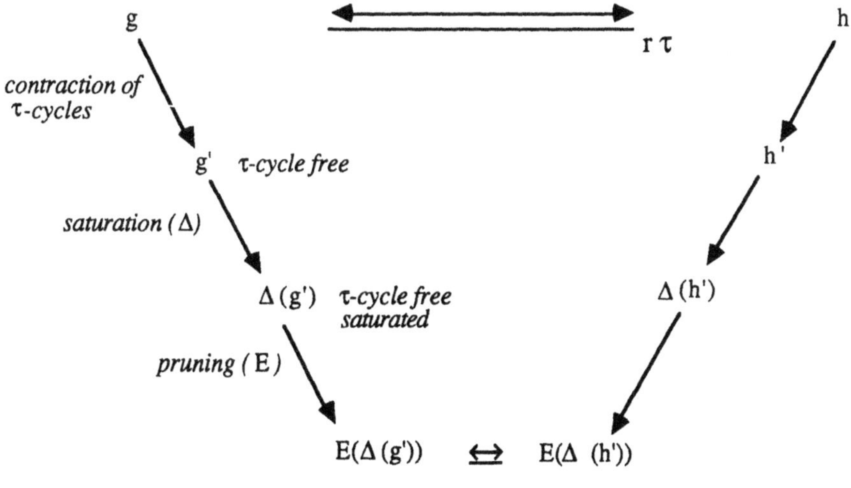

Figure 2.15

So, in order to have a complete proof system for $\leftrightarrows_{r\tau}$, it suffices to have:

I. A complete proof system for $\leftrightarrows$;
II. Proof rules which make '*contraction* of τ-cycles provable';
III. Likewise for *saturation* (the operation Δ);
IV. Likewise for *pruning* (the operation E).

First we have to explain the syntax used for regular processes, and the interpretation of expressions in that syntax into the semantic domain $\mathbb{R} = \mathfrak{R}/\leftrightarrows_{r\tau}$. Precise syntax definitions can be found in Bergstra & Klop [88]; here we will be more informal and give some suggestive examples instead.

Our syntactic expressions, denoting regular processes in $\mathbb{R}$, will be either of the form t where t is a closed BPA-term (see Table 1) or recursive expressions $\langle X_1 \mid E\rangle$ where $E = \{X_i = t_i(X_1,...,X_n) \mid i = 1,...,n\}$. Here $t_i(X)$ $(= t_i(X_1,...,X_n))$ is a BPA-term possibly involving formal recursion variables from $\{X_1,...,X_n\}$. Moreover, the $t_i(X)$ are 'simple' terms, defined as follows.*)

2.3.1. DEFINITION. (i) Every $u \in A_\tau$ is a simple term.
(ii) Let X be a recursion variable and let $u \in A_\tau$. Then uX is a simple term.
(iii) Let t, t' be simple terms. Then t + t' is a simple term.

So, aX + τY + c is a simple term, but abX + c, b(aX + c) and aXY + bYY are not.

The *semantics* of an expression $\langle X \mid E\rangle$ in $\mathbb{R}$ is obvious: to $\langle X \mid E\rangle$ there corresponds in an immediate way, suggested by the next example, a process graph in $\mathfrak{R}$, call it $g_{\langle X|E\rangle}$; now the semantics $[\langle X \mid E\rangle]_{\mathbb{R}}$ is $g_{\langle X|E\rangle} / \leftrightarrows_{r\tau}$.

2.3.2. EXAMPLE. The semantics of $\tau\cdot\langle X \mid X = \tau Y + aY, Y = \tau X + b\rangle$ is the graph g in Figure 2.19(a), modulo $\leftrightarrows_{r\tau}$. The semantics of $t\cdot\langle X \mid X = aX + b\rangle$ is h/ $\leftrightarrows_{r\tau}$, h as in Figure 2.16(b). Actually, g $\leftrightarrows_{r\tau}$ h; we will return to this example and show that the two expressions just mentioned are provably equal.

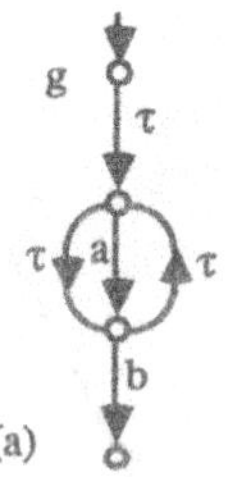

(a)

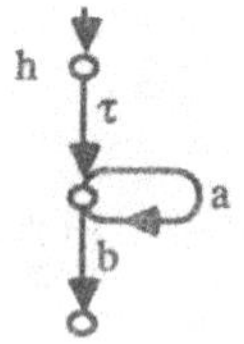

(b)

Figure 2.16

(*) (Actually, we have to be slightly more liberal w.r.t. the form of the t_i in $E = \{X_i = t_i(X_1,...,X_n) \mid i = 1,...,n\}$. In fact, we will allow substitutions for variables in the t_i, in order to have equalities like e.g. $\langle X \mid X = t(X,Y), Y = s(X,Y)\rangle = \langle X \mid X = t(X,Y), Y = s(t(X,Y),Y)\rangle$. For a more precise treatment see Bergstra & Klop [88].)

I. Having thus established our syntax and semantics, we turn to the question of finding a complete proof system for the easier case of bisimulation, $\leftrightarrows$. This question was solved in Milner [84b], using the syntax of μ-expressions. Milner's complete proof system 'M' for regular processes is given in Table 23.

M

$x + 0 = x$	A0
$x + y = y + x$	A1
$(x + y) + z = x + (y + z)$	A2
$x + x = x$	A3
$\mu X.T(X) = \mu Y.T(Y)$	μ0
$\mu X.T(X) = T(\mu X.T(X))$	μ1
$\dfrac{x = T(x)}{x = \mu X.T(X)}$ T(X) guarded	μ2
$\mu X(X + T) = \mu X(T)$	μ3

Table 23

2.3.3. EXAMPLE. Consider the μ-expressions μX. aX and μY. (aY + aμX.aX), denoting the graphs g, h (modulo $\leftrightarrows$) in Figure 2.17. Since g $\leftrightarrows$ h, we must be able to prove equality between the two μ-expressions. Indeed: abbreviate μX. aX by L, and the other μ-expression by R. Then, in M, one proves: L = aL = aL + aL and R = aR + aL. Hence L, R are solutions of the same guarded recursion equation X = aX + aL. Therefore L = R.

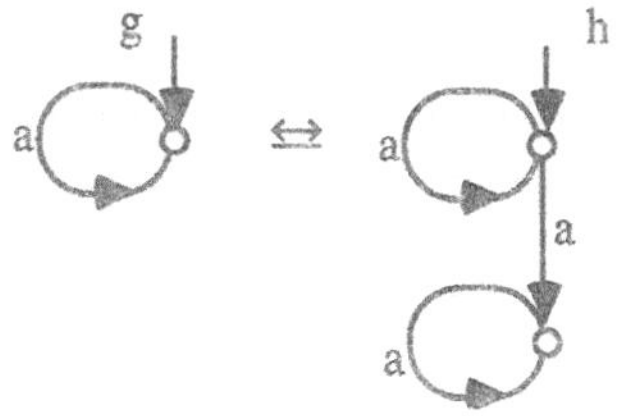

Figure 2.17

In the present framework we have the equivalent proof system BPA_{rec} (equivalent, modulo some inessential details, discussed in Bergstra & Klop [88]) as in Table 24 below. Here $E = \{X_i = T_i(X_1,...,X_n) \mid i = 1,...,n\}$. The rules R1,2 correspond to μ1,2 in Table 23. In particular, R1 implies the following axiom (which is equivalent to R1):

$$\langle X_1 \mid E\rangle = T_1(\langle X_1 \mid E\rangle, ..., \langle X_n \mid E\rangle)$$

and this axiom corresponds exactly to μ1.

The axiom μ3 in M has no counterpart in BPA_{rec}. The axioms A4, A5 come in here since multiplication is general (i.e. not merely 'prefix-multiplication').

Rule R3 states that 'conversions' in the right-hand sides of the equations in $\langle X \mid E\rangle$ are allowed.

BPA_{rec}

$x + y = y + x$	A1
$(x + y) + z = x + (y + z)$	A2
$x + x = x$	A3
$(x + y)z = xz + yz$	A4
$(xy)z = x(yz)$	A5
$\dfrac{x_i = \langle X_i \mid E\rangle,\ i=1,\ldots,n}{x_1 = T_1(x_1,\ldots,x_n)}$	R1
$\dfrac{x_i = T_i(x_1,\ldots,x_n),\ i = 1,\ldots,n}{x_1 = \langle X_1 \mid E\rangle}$ $T_i(X_1,\ldots,X_n)$ is guarded	R2
$\dfrac{E = E'}{\langle X_1 \mid E\rangle = \langle X_1 \mid E'\rangle}$	R3

Table 24

II. Next, we discuss the problem of making the contraction of τ-cycles provable. Of course, we start with adopting the τ-laws T1-3 as in Table 16 or 22. Now, for instance, we want to be able to prove

$$\langle X \mid X = \tau X + a\rangle = \langle X \mid X = \tau a\rangle \ (= \tau a)$$

in view of the $r\tau$-bisimilarity of the corresponding process graphs. Note that a proof rule like $x = \tau x + a \Rightarrow x = \tau a$ would not do the job; while it is true that τa is a solution of the equation $X = \tau X + a$ (since $\tau a = \tau(\tau a) + a$, using the τ-laws), it is unfortunately the case that also $\tau(a + q)$ for arbitrary q is a solution:

$$\tau(a + q) = \tau(a + q) + (a + q) = \tau(a + q) + (a + q) + a = \tau(a + q) + a = \tau(\tau(a + q)) + a.$$

The solution is the use of the abstraction operator τ_I (renaming every $i \in I$ into τ, see Table 15 or 22), and the proof rule KFAR (see Chapter 1, Section 1.10), enabling us to conclude from $x = ix + a$ that $\tau_{\{i\}}(x) = \tau a$. This is an instance of the proof rule $KFAR_1$:

$$\frac{x = ix + y}{\tau_{\{i\}}(x) = \tau\cdot\tau_{\{i\}}(y)}$$

which in turn can be derived from $KFAR_2$:

$$\frac{x = iy + z, \qquad y = jx + z'}{\tau_{\{i,j\}}(x) = \tau\cdot\tau_{\{i,j\}}(z + z')}$$

The desired equation can now be proved as follows. Put x = <X |X = iX + a>, so x = ix + a. By $KFAR_1$: $\tau_{\{i\}}(x) = \tau\cdot\tau_{\{i\}}(a) = \tau a$. Furthermore, $\tau_{\{i\}}(x) = \tau_{\{i\}}(\langle X \mid X = iX + a\rangle) = \langle X \mid X = \tau X + a\rangle$, which proves the result.

Using $KFAR_2$ we can "contract in a provable way" every τ-cycle in (the graph corresponding to) a system <X | E>. That $KFAR_2$ already suffices, and that one does not need $KFAR_n$ for n > 2, is demonstrated in Example 2.3.7 below.

III. Making the operation Δ (saturation) provable is no problem at all: here the τ-laws T1-3 suffice. We will not prove this here (see Bergstra & Klop [88]), but refer to the examples below.

IV. More consideration is required to see that also 'pruning' of internal ε-steps (by means of the operation E) is provable. Suppose g is a saturated, τ-cycle free graph $\in \mathcal{R}^\rho$. Then in order to execute operation E, we can successively remove the ε-steps. In each such removal the node set of g is not affected, since ε-steps are internal and g is saturated; furthermore, the "τ-bisimilarity character" of all nodes in g remains invariant. Hence also the cluster structure of the initial g remains invariant. At the end of the pruning operation, i.e. in E(g), each cluster still is a $\leftrightarrow_\tau$-equivalence class. Moreover, by similar arguments as used in the proof of Corollary 2.2.4.7 one proves:

2.3.4. PROPOSITION. *Let* $h_1, h_2 \in \mathcal{R}$ *be saturated, τ-cycle free, and suppose all ε-steps in* h_1, h_2 *(i.e. τ-steps between τ-bisimilar nodes) have been removed (including possible ones to or from the root). Then:*

$$h_1 \leftrightarrow_\tau h_2 \;\Rightarrow\; h_1 \leftrightarrow h_2.$$

Using this proposition we observe that in E(g) with g as above (saturated, τ-cycle free, $\in \mathcal{R}^\rho$) every cluster only contains nodes s, t which are bisimilar in the ordinary sense ($(g)_s \leftrightarrow (g)_t$). Here $(g)_s$, $(g)_t$ are h_1, h_2 from Proposition 2.3.4.

Now our way to make the transformation from g to E(g) provable, is to *start* with E(g) and then add ε-edges to arrive at g. Using the observation just made this is easy, and instead of a proof we just give an example.

2.3.5. EXAMPLE. Let E(g) and g be as in Figure 2.17.

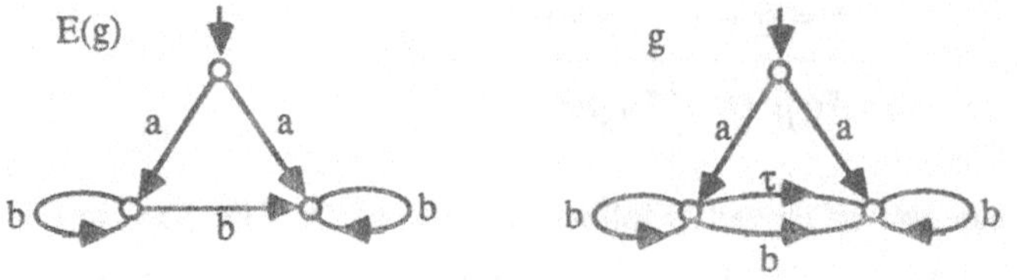

Figure 2.17

The corresponding expressions <X | E>, <X' | E'> (written as systems of equations where the first recursion variable is the 'designated' one) are:

E:	$X = aY + aZ$	E':	$X' = aY' + aZ'$
	$Y = bY + bZ$		$Y' = bY' + \tau Z' + bZ'$
	$Z = bZ$		$Z' = bZ'$

We now prove <X | E> = <X' | E'> as follows; here we use some of the proof rules from the proof system below in Table 25.

Abbreviating $\underline{X} = \langle\,|\,E\rangle$, $\underline{Y} = \langle Y\,|\,E\rangle$, $\underline{Z} = \langle Z\,|\,E\rangle$ and similarly for $\underline{X}'$, $\underline{Y}'$, $\underline{Z}'$, we have:

$$\underline{X} = a\underline{Y} + a\underline{Z}$$
$$\underline{Y} = b\underline{Y} + b\underline{Z}$$
$$\underline{Z} = b\underline{Z}.$$

Now consider the expression $\underline{Y}^* = \tau\underline{Y}$. Then $\vdash \underline{Y}^* = \underline{Y} + \tau\underline{Y} = \underline{Y} + \tau\underline{Z} = b\underline{Y} + b\underline{Z} + \tau\underline{Z} = b\tau\underline{Y} + b\underline{Z} + \tau\underline{Z} = b\underline{Y}^* + b\underline{Z} + \tau\underline{Z}$. Here we used that $\vdash \underline{Y} = \underline{Z}$, which follows from the fact that the graphs corresponding to Y, Z are bisimilar as stated in Proposition 2.3.4, and from the fact that the proof system is complete for ordinary bisimulation. Therefore:

$$\underline{X} = a\underline{Y} + a\underline{Z} = a\tau\underline{Y} + a\underline{Z} = a\underline{Y}^* + a\underline{Z}$$
$$\underline{Y}^* = b\underline{Y}^* + b\underline{Z} + \tau\underline{Z}$$
$$\underline{Z} = b\underline{Z}.$$

Hence $(\underline{X}, \underline{Y}^*, \underline{Z})$ satisfies E'. Hence $\vdash \underline{X} = \underline{X}'$. *)

The general case, where g and E(g) differ by more than one ε-step, is only notationally more complicated and left to the reader.

Table 25 presents the complete inference system $BPA_{\tau,rec}$.

---

*) We use here that E' is a *guarded* system of equations, which enables us to use rule R2 in Table 25. Actually, E' is only 'essentially' guarded; the τ occurring in E' is not a guard (a guard must be a *proper* atom), but substituting bZ' for Z' we arrive at a guarded system. It is not hard to prove that indeed, in general, the system E' corresponding to Δ(g') as in Figure 2.15 is essentially guarded (i.e. that Δ(g') is τ-cycle free).

$BPA_{\tau,rec}$

$x+y = y + x$	A1
$(x + y) + z = x + (y + z)$	A2
$x + x = x$	A3
$(x + y)z = xz + yz$	A4
$(xy)z = x(yz)$	A5
$x\tau = x$	T1
$\tau x + x = \tau x$	T2
$a(\tau x + y) = a(\tau x + y) + ax$	T3
$\tau_I(X) = X$	TI0
$\tau_I(\tau) = \tau$	TI1
$\tau_I(a) = \tau$ if $a \in I$	TI2
$\tau_I(a) = a$ if $a \notin I$	TI3
$\tau_I(x + y) = \tau_I(x) + \tau_I(y)$	TI4
$\tau_I(\tau y) = \tau \cdot \tau_I(y)$	TI5'
$\tau_I(ay) = \tau_I(a) \cdot \tau_I(y)$	TI5"
$\tau_I(\langle X_1 \mid E\rangle) = \langle X_1 \mid \tau_I(E)\rangle$	TI6
$\dfrac{x_i = \langle X_i \mid E\rangle,\ i = 1,\ldots,n}{x_1 = T_1(x_1,\ldots,x_n)}$	R1
$\dfrac{x_i = T_i(x_1,\ldots,x_n),\ i = 1,\ldots,n}{x_1 = \langle X_1 \mid E\rangle}$ $T_i(X_1,\ldots,X_n)$ is guarded	R2
$\dfrac{E = E'}{\langle X_1 \mid E\rangle = \langle X_1 \mid E'\rangle}$	R3
$\dfrac{x = iy + z, \quad y = jx + z'}{\tau_{\{i,j\}}(x) = \tau \cdot \tau_{\{i,j\}}(z + z')}$	$KFAR_2$

Table 25

A very elegant alternative complete proof system, employing the formalism of μ-expressions, is given in Milner [88]. It consists of the proof system in Table 23, extended with the τ-laws (T1-3) and the following two axioms, which play the role of $KFAR_2$:

$$\mu X(\tau X + E) = \mu X(\tau E)$$
$$\mu X(\tau(X + E) + F) = \mu X(\tau X + E + F).$$

Here E, F are arbitrary expressions.

We conclude this chapter with some examples showing the use of the proof system $BPA_{\tau,rec}$.

2.3.6. EXAMPLE. We resume the question in Example 2.3.2, to prove $\tau\cdot\langle X \mid X = \tau Y + aY,\ Y = \tau X + b\rangle = \tau\cdot\langle X \mid X = aX + b\rangle$. (See Figure 2.16.) Abbreviate:

$$\underline{X} = \langle X \mid E\rangle = \langle X \mid X = \tau Y + aY,\ Y = \tau X + b\rangle,\ \underline{Y} = \langle Y \mid E\rangle,$$
$$\underline{X}^i = \langle X \mid E^i\rangle = \langle X \mid X = iY + aY,\ Y = iX + b\rangle,\ \underline{Y}^i = \langle Y \mid E^i\rangle.$$

So we have $\underline{X}^i = i\underline{Y}^i + a\underline{Y}^i$ and $\underline{Y}^i = i\underline{X}^i + b$. Hence by $KFAR_2$:

$$\tau_{\{i\}}(\underline{X}^i) = \underline{X} = \tau\cdot\tau_{\{i\}}(a\underline{Y}^i + b)$$

which yields $\underline{X} = \tau\cdot(a\underline{Y} + b)$. Likewise $\underline{Y} = \tau(a\underline{Y} + b)$. Therefore $\underline{X} = \underline{Y}$, and so $\underline{X} = \tau(a\underline{X} + b)$. Thus

$$\underline{X} = \langle U \mid U = \tau(aU + b)\rangle = \langle U \mid U = \tau V,\ V = aU + b\rangle =$$
$$\langle U \mid U = \tau V,\ V = a\tau V + b\rangle = \langle U \mid U = \tau V,\ V = aV + b\rangle.$$

Now abbreviate: $\underline{U} = \langle U \mid U = \tau V,\ V = aV + b\rangle$, $\underline{V} = \langle V \mid U = \tau V,\ V = aV + b\rangle = \langle V \mid V = aV + b\rangle$. So we have proved $\tau\underline{X} = \tau\underline{U} = \tau\tau\underline{V} = \tau\langle V \mid V = aV + b\rangle$, which was our goal.

2.3.7. EXAMPLE. We want to prove that the expressions corresponding to the graphs in Figure 2.18 are equal.

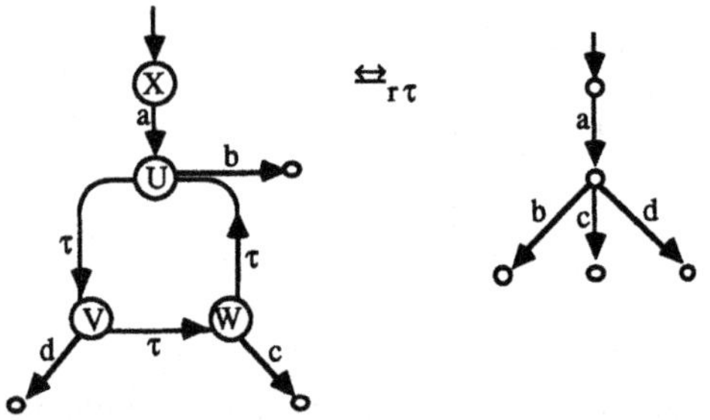

Figure 2.18

So, to prove:

$$\underline{X} = \langle X \mid E\rangle =$$
$$\langle X \mid X = aU,\ U = \tau V + b,\ V = \tau W + d,\ W = \tau U + c\rangle = a(b + c + d).$$

Now

$$\langle X \mid E\rangle = \langle X \mid X = aU,\ U = \tau V + b,\ V = \tau(\tau U + c) + d,\ W = \tau U + c\rangle =$$
$$\langle X \mid X = aU,\ U = \tau V + b,\ V = \tau(\tau U + c) + \tau U + d,\ W = \tau U + c\rangle =$$
$$\langle X \mid X = aU,\ U = \tau V + b,\ V = \tau W + \tau U + d,\ W = \tau U + c\rangle = \langle X \mid F\rangle.$$

The last system corresponds to the graph in Figure 2.19(a).

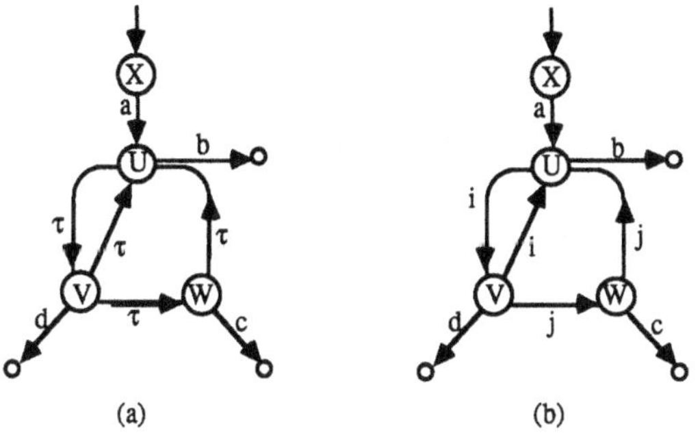

Figure 2.19

We now introduce:

$$X^{i,j} = \langle X \mid F^{i,j} \rangle = \langle X \mid X = aU,\ U = iV + b,\ V = jW + iU + d,\ W = jU + c \rangle.$$

So:

$$\underline{X}^{i,j} = a\underline{U}^{i,j},\ \underline{U}^{i,j} = i\underline{V}^{i,j} + b,\ \underline{V}^{i,j} = j\underline{W}^{i,j} + i\underline{U}^{i,j} + d,\ \underline{W}^{i,j} = j\underline{U}^{i,j} + c.$$

Now we apply $KFAR_2$ on the "i-cycle"; that is, from $\underline{U}^{i,j} = i\underline{V}^{i,j} + b$, $\underline{V}^{i,j} = j\underline{W}^{i,j} + i\underline{U}^{i,j} + d$ it follows that $\tau_{\{i\}}(\underline{U}^{i,j}) = \tau\cdot\tau_{\{i\}}(j\underline{W}^{i,j} + d + b)$ (*). Since

$$\tau_{\{i\}}(\underline{X}^{i,j}) = \underline{X}^{j} = \langle X \mid F^{j} \rangle =$$
$$\langle X \mid X = aU,\ U = \tau V + b,\ V = jW + \tau U + d,\ W = jU + c \rangle,$$

we now have: $\underline{X}^{j} = a\underline{U}^{j}$, $\underline{U}^{j} = \tau(j\underline{W}^{j} + d + b)$ (by (*)), $\underline{W}^{j} = j\underline{U}^{j} + c$. Here $\underline{U}^{j} = \langle U \mid F^{j} \rangle$ and $\underline{W}^{j} = \langle W \mid F^{j} \rangle$. Therefore

$$\underline{X}^{j} = \langle X \mid X = aU,\ U = \tau(jW + d + b),\ W = jU + c \rangle \text{ and}$$
$$\underline{X} = \tau_{\{j\}}(\underline{X}^{j}) = \langle X \mid X = aU,\ U = \tau(\tau W + d + b),\ W = \tau U + c \rangle =$$
$$\langle X \mid X = aU,\ U = \tau V,\ V = \tau W + d + b,\ W = \tau U + c \rangle =$$
$$\langle X \mid X = aV,\ V = \tau W + d + b,\ W = \tau V + c \rangle.$$

Here the last two recursion expressions correspond to the graphs in Figure 2.19(a,b) respectively.

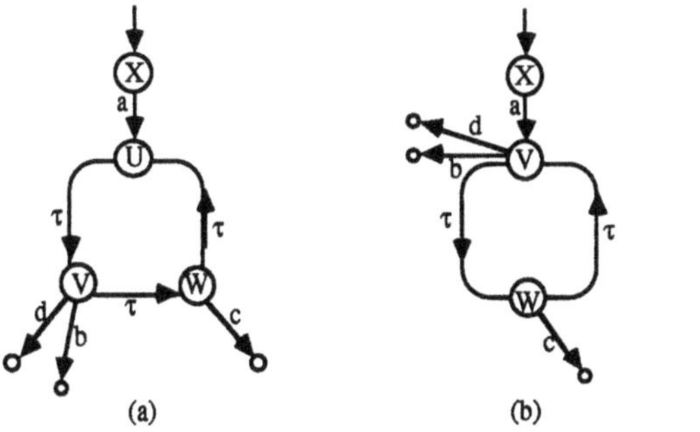

Figure 2.19

The remaining τ-cycle of two steps can now be contracted, as in the previous example, by one more application of $KFAR_2$. The result is: $\underline{X} = a(b + c + d)$.

3. A comparison of process models related to bisimulation semantics

In this chapter we compare the class of graph models as defined in Chapter 1 with a class of 'projective' models as well as with a class of metric models as in the work of De Bakker & Zucker [82a,b]. In doing so, we will restrict ourselves to the simple case of pure interleaving, without communication; that is, we will consider only models of the axiom system PA, in Tables 1 and 5 of Chapter 1. The alphabet involved will be $A = \{a,b,c,...\}$; it does not contain τ nor δ. Hence, the notion of bisimulation that is employed is $\leftrightarrow$, defined in 2.1.4.1. Two parameters will play an important role in this chapter: the cardinality α of alphabet A, and the branching degree β of process graphs.

3.1. DEFINITION. (i) Process graphs without cycles and without 'shared subgraphs' are process *trees*. (In Milner [80] these are called 'synchronisation trees'.) More precisely: a process graph is a process tree if every node has exactly one incoming arrow where the small root arrow also counts as an arrow. A process graph is finite if it contains finitely many edges and nodes.
(ii) If g is a process graph, and $s \in$ NODES(g) is a node of g, then the *branching degree* of s is the number of arrows leaving s. The branching degree of g is the maximum of the branching degrees of the nodes in g.
(iii) $\mathbb{G}_{\alpha,\beta}$ is the set of process graphs 'over' an alphabet of cardinality α and with branching degree $< \beta$. Here $\alpha \geq 1$ and $\beta \geq \aleph_0$. (The bound β on the branching degree must be infinite since otherwise the process graph domains below would not be closed under '+', as defined in 1.13.) On $\mathbb{G}_{\alpha,\beta}$ we define operations $+, \cdot, \|, \mathbin{\|\!\_}, (\,)_n$ $(n \geq 1)$; see Section 1.13 with the understanding that merge $\|$ is now simply the cartesian product graph, without 'diagonal' edges representing communications as in Chapter 1. Furthermore, in this chapter we employ the alternative notation $(\,)_n$ instead of $\pi_n(\,)$.This *projection* $(g)_n$ $(n \geq 1)$ is defined for trees g: it is the tree obtained by cutting away all nodes reachable from the root by a path of length $> n$. The corresponding edges are also left away. If g is not a tree, then $(g)_n$ is defined as $(g')_n$ where g' is the tree obtained by unwinding g.

As in Chapter 1, it turns out that bisimilarity $\leftrightarrow$ is a congruence on $\mathbb{G}_{\alpha,\beta}$ with respect to the operations just defined. Hence we can take the quotient

$$\mathbb{G}_{\alpha,\beta} = \mathbb{G}_{\alpha,\beta}/\leftrightarrow.$$

The quotient structures are models of PA, i.e. process algebras for PA. Using the usual distance function d, defined by

$$d(x,y) = \begin{cases} 2^{-m} & \text{if } \exists n\ (x)_n \neq (y)_n;\ m = \min\{n \mid (x)_n \neq (y)_n\} \\ 0 & \text{otherwise, i.e. } \forall n\ (x)_n = (y)_n \end{cases}$$

we have that $\mathbb{G}_{\alpha,\beta}$ is a pseudo-metric space but not yet a metric space. (For instance, in $\mathbb{G}_{1,\aleph_1}$ the elements determined by the process graphs $\Sigma_{n\geq 1}\ a^n$ and $\Sigma_{n\geq 1}\ a^n + a^\omega$ in Figure 1.13 are different but have distance 0.) It becomes a metric space after dividing out the congruence induced by the *Approximation Induction Principle* (AIP), discussed also in Chapter 1:

$$\frac{\forall n\ \ (x)_n = (y)_n}{x = y}$$

The result of 'dividing out' AIP is

$$\mathbb{G}^\circ_{\alpha,\beta} = \mathbb{G}_{\alpha,\beta}/\text{AIP}.$$

The $\mathbb{G}^\circ_{\alpha,\beta}$ have been defined as a 'double quotient' by first dividing out $\underline{\leftrightarrow}$ and next AIP. The same result can be obtained by defining a suitable equivalence relation at once; this is done in Golson & Rounds [83] where 'weak equivalence' is divided out. In Milner [80], p.42 this notion is called 'observation equivalence'. It is defined as follows:

3.2. DEFINITION. (i) If $s \in$ NODES(g), then $(g)_s$ is the subgraph of g with root s, and nodes: all nodes in g reachable from s, and edges as induced by g.
(Warning: the notation $(g)_s$ should not be confused with $(g)_n$ for the n-th projection of g.)
(ii) On a process graph domain $\mathbb{G}_{\alpha,\beta}$ we define transition relations $\Rightarrow_a$ for each atom a: if $s \rightarrow_a t$ is a step (edge) in $g \in \mathbb{G}_{\alpha,\beta}$, then $(g)_s \Rightarrow_a (g)_t$.
(Note the difference in notation: open arrows stand for transitions between process graphs, normal arrows denote steps between nodes in one process graph.)

3.3. DEFINITION. On $\mathbb{G}_{\alpha,\beta}$ we define equivalences $\equiv_n$ for each $n \geq 0$:
(i) $g \equiv_0 h$ for all g,h;
(ii) $g \equiv_{n+1} h$ if
  (1) whenever $g \Rightarrow_a g'$ there is a transition $h \Rightarrow_a h'$ with $g' \equiv_n h'$;
  (2) as (1) with the roles of g,h interchanged.

Furthermore, $g \equiv h$ if $g \equiv_n h$ for all $n \geq 0$.

An alternative, equivalent definition is:

3.4. DEFINITION. Let $g,h \in \mathbb{G}_{\alpha,\beta}$ be process graphs. Then $g \equiv_n h$ if $(g)_n \leftrightarrow (h)_n$ $(n \geq 1)$. Furthermore, $g \equiv h$ if $g \equiv_n h$ for all $n \geq 1$.

The proof that these definitions are indeed equivalent is left to the reader. We also omit the routine proof of the next proposition, where $\cong$ denotes *isometry*.

3.5. PROPOSITION. $\mathbb{G}^{\circ}_{\alpha,\beta} \cong \mathbb{G}_{\alpha,\beta}/\equiv$. □

3.5.1. REMARK. For *finitely branching* graphs (i.e. $\beta = \aleph_0$) and arbitrary alphabet, we have in fact

$$\mathbb{G}_{\alpha,\aleph_0}/\equiv \ = \ \mathbb{G}_{\alpha,\aleph_0}/\leftrightarrow.$$

That is, weak equivalence (or observational equivalence) coincides with bisimulation equivalence. In fact, the proof follows from Lemma 1.13.7.1. We give an alternative proof for the present simpler case here: Suppose g,h are finitely branching process graphs and suppose $g \equiv h$, or equivalently: $\forall n\ (g)_n \leftrightarrow (h)_n$. Now consider

$$B_n = \{R \mid R \text{ is a bisimulation from } (g)_n \text{ to } (h)_n\},$$
$$B = \bigcup_{n\geq 1} B_n.$$

This collection of 'partial' bisimulations between g,h is ordered by set-theoretic inclusion ($\subseteq$). In fact, $B' = B \cup \{(s_0,t_0)\}$ where s_0,t_0 are the roots of g,h respectively, is a tree w.r.t. $\subseteq$. Because g,h are finitely branching, this tree is also finitely branching: there are only finitely many extensions of a bisimulation between $(g)_n$, $(h)_n$ to a bisimulation between $(g)_{n+1}$, $(h)_{n+1}$. Moreover, because $\forall n\ (g)_n \leftrightarrow (h)_n$, the tree B' has infinitely many nodes. Therefore, by König's Lemma, B' has an infinite branch. This infinite branch is a chain of partial bisimulations R_i $(i\geq 1)$:

$$R_1 \subseteq R_2 \subseteq \ldots \subseteq R_n \subseteq \ldots$$

such that R_i is a bisimulation from $(g)_i$ to $(h)_i$. Now $R = \bigcup_{n\geq 1} R_i$ is a bisimulation from g to h.

The structures $\mathbb{G}^{\circ}_{\alpha,\beta}$ are also process algebras for PA. While all of the $\mathbb{G}^{\circ}_{\alpha,\beta}$ are metric spaces, they are not all *complete*. An example is given in Golson & Rounds [83]: $\mathbb{G}^{\circ}_{1,\aleph_0}$ is incomplete. (Consider the approximations of $\Sigma_{n\geq 1}\, a^n$.) Another example is as follows.

3.6. EXAMPLE. $\mathbb{G}^{\circ}_{\aleph_\omega,\aleph_\omega}$ is an incomplete metric space.

PROOF (sketch). The alphabet is $\{a_i \mid i < \aleph_\omega\}$. Define a sequence of process graphs g_n $(n \geq 1)$ by

$$g_n = \Sigma_{i1<\aleph 1}\ \Sigma_{i2<\aleph 2} \ldots \Sigma_{in<\aleph n}\ a_{i1}a_{i2}\ldots a_{in}.$$

Let brd(g) be the branching degree of process graph g, defined as follows: if s is a node of g, then brd(s) is the (cardinal) number of arrows leaving s; furthermore, brd(g) is the cardinal sum of the brd(s), s ∈ NODES(g). We claim:

(i) brd(g_n) = $\aleph_n$ for g_n as defined above,

(ii) brd($(g)_n$) ≤ brd(g) for all $g \in \mathbb{G}_{\alpha,\beta}$,

(iii) $h \leftrightarrows g_n \Rightarrow$ brd(h) ≥ brd(g_n) for g_n as defined above.

Claim (ii) is trivial; the inductive proofs of the other two claims are left to the reader. Using these claims, one shows immediately that there is no limit $g/\equiv$ for the sequence of elements $g_n/\equiv$ in $\mathbb{G}^\circ_{\aleph_\omega,\aleph_\omega}$ as this would require a process graph g with branching degree at least $\Sigma_{n<\omega} \aleph_n = \aleph_\omega$. □

We will now define *projective models* $A^\infty_{\alpha,\beta}$ of PA for arbitrary $\alpha \geq 1$ and $\beta \geq \aleph_0$. These will all be complete metric spaces. Furthermore, modulo isometry $A^\infty_{\alpha,\beta}$ is an extension of $\mathbb{G}^\circ_{\alpha,\beta}$, so the projective model can be considered as the metric completion of $\mathbb{G}^\circ_{\alpha,\beta}$. (In case $\mathbb{G}^\circ_{\alpha,\beta}$ is also complete, it is of course isometric to the projective model.) The projective models defined below differ from the ones in Kranakis [86,87]; there an element of a projective sequence is a sequence of *terms* (modulo derivable equality), below it is a sequence of finitely deep *process graphs* (modulo bisimilarity).

3.7. DEFINITION. (i) $\mathbb{G}^n_{\alpha,\beta} = \{g \in \mathbb{G}_{\alpha,\beta} \mid g = (g)_n\}$.

(ii) $\mathbb{G}^n_{\alpha,\beta} = \mathbb{G}^n_{\alpha,\beta}/\leftrightarrows$.

(iii) Let $g_i \in \mathbb{G}^n_{\alpha,\beta}$ ($i \geq 1$). Then the sequence $(g_1,g_2,...)$ is *projective* if for all i: $g_i = (g_{i+1})_i$.

(iv) $A^\infty_{\alpha,\beta}$ is the projective limit of the $\mathbb{G}^n_{\alpha,\beta}$ ($n \geq 1$); the elements of $A^\infty_{\alpha,\beta}$ are the projective sequences. The operators +, ·, ||, ⅬL are defined as follows: if $\gamma = (g_1,g_2,...)$ and $\gamma' = (g_1',g_2',...)$ then $\gamma \cdot \gamma' = ((g_1 \cdot g_1')_1, (g_2 \cdot g_2')_2,...)$ and likewise for the other operators.

3.8. THEOREM. $A^\infty_{\alpha,\beta}$ *is a complete metric space.*

PROOF (sketch). Consider a converging sequence $\gamma_i = (g_{i1}, g_{i2}, ...)$, $i \geq 1$. For growing i and fixed k, the sequence g_{ik} will eventually be constant, say after N(k) steps. We may suppose that N is a monotonic function. Now $\gamma = (g_{N(1),1}, g_{N(2),2}, ...)$ is the required limit. □

Van Glabbeek (personal communication) remarked that for finite α, there is no need to consider uncountably branching process graphs, see statement (i) in Corollary 3.12. His observation can be generalized to infinite α. First some notation.

3.9. NOTATION. Let α be a cardinal number (finite or infinite). Then $\alpha^* = \Sigma_{n<\omega} \alpha_n$, where $\alpha_0 =$

α, $\alpha_{n+1} = 2^{\alpha_n}$. For finite α, we have $\alpha^* = \aleph_0$. For $\alpha = \aleph_0$, the numbers α_n are known as the beth-numbers $\beth_n$ and $\alpha^* = \beth_\omega$. The cardinality of a set X is card(X). If κ is a cardinal, then κ^+ denotes the least cardinal larger than κ.

3.10. PROPOSITION. (i) *For infinite* α: $\text{card}(\mathbb{G}^n_{\alpha,\alpha^*}) = \alpha_n$.
(ii) $\text{card}(\bigcup_{n\geq 1} \mathbb{G}^n_{\alpha,\alpha^*}) = \alpha^*$.
(iii) *For any* α,κ: $\mathbb{G}^n_{\alpha,\alpha^*} \cong \mathbb{G}^n_{\alpha,\alpha^*+\kappa}$.

PROOF. (i) Induction on n. For n = 1 the statement is clear, since the process graphs $g_I = \sum_{a\in I} a$ for arbitrary non-empty $I \subseteq A$ are mutually non-bisimilar, and since every process graph in $\mathbb{G}^1_{\alpha,\alpha^*}$ is bisimilar with some g_I. Suppose the statement has been proved for n. Let $\mathcal{X}^n \subseteq \mathbb{G}^n_{\alpha,\alpha^*}$ be a set of representatives of the α_n bisimulation equivalence classes of $\mathbb{G}^{n+1}_{\alpha,\alpha^*}$, so $\text{card}(\mathcal{X}^n) = \alpha_n$. Now every element of $\mathbb{G}^{n+1}_{\alpha,\alpha^*}$ is bisimilar to one of the process graphs

$$g_{h,I,f} = h + \sum_{a\in I} \sum_{x\in f(I)} ax$$

where $h \in \mathcal{X}^n$, $I \subseteq A$ (possibly empty) and $f: I \rightarrow \wp(\mathcal{X}^n)$. Moreover, for different triples h,I,f the corresponding $g_{h,I,f}$ are not bisimilar. Hence $\text{card}(\mathbb{G}^n_{\alpha,\alpha^*}) = \alpha_n \cdot \alpha_1 \cdot \alpha_{n+1} = \alpha_{n+1}$. Here the factor α_n stems from the variation in h, α_1 from the variation in I while for each I the choice of f contributes a factor $(2^{\text{card}(\mathcal{X}_n)})^{\text{card}(I)} = 2^{\alpha_n} = \alpha_{n+1}$.

Part (ii) is by definition; (iii) is left to the reader. □

3.11. THEOREM. $A^\infty_{\alpha,\alpha^*} \cong A^\infty_{\alpha,\alpha^*+\kappa}$ *for any cardinal* κ.

PROOF. The isometry follows at once from Proposition 3.10(iii). □

3.12. COROLLARY.
(i) *For finite* α: $A^\infty_{\alpha,\aleph_0} \cong A^\infty_{\alpha,\aleph_0+\kappa}$ *for any cardinal* κ.
(ii) *For countably infinite alphabet:* $A^\infty_{\aleph_0,\beth_\omega} \cong A^\infty_{\aleph_0,\beth_\omega+\kappa}$ *for any cardinal* κ. □

We will now turn our attention to the models $\mathbb{G}^\circ_{\alpha,\beta}$ in order to compare them with the projective models.

3.13. PROPOSITION. *If* β *is sufficiently large,* $\mathbb{G}^\circ_{\alpha,\beta}$ *is complete.*

PROOF. We will try to prove that $\mathbb{G}^\circ_{\alpha,\beta}$ is isometric to $A^\infty_{\alpha,\beta}$ and deduce from that attempt a requirement on β.

We will drop the subscripts α,β. So let us try to establish an isometry φ from $\mathbb{G}^\circ$ to A^∞. Let $g \in \mathbb{G}^\circ$. Then $\varphi(g) = ((g)_1,(g)_2,\ldots)$. It is easy to prove that this is a projective sequence. The hard part is to prove that φ is a surjection. Consider an element $(g_1, g_2, \ldots) \in A^\infty$. Let g_i be a representing process graph of g_i ($i \geq 1$). We would like to find a graph g such that $(g)_i \;{\underline{\leftrightarrow}}\; g_i$ for all ≥ 1. (Cf. the construction in Theorem 3.5 of Golson & Rounds [83] by 'blowing up' trees; we wil use another construction.) For the rest of this proof, we will suppose that all process graphs are trees. Let g_i' be $(g_{i+1})_i$. So $g_i \;{\underline{\leftrightarrow}}\; g_i'$; say R_i is a bisimulation from g_i to g_i'. Let S_i: NODES(g_i') $\rightarrow$ NODES(g_{i+1}) be the obvious embedding function, obtained by the projection mapping. Now if s is a node of depth k in g_k (so s is 'appearing' for the first time in g_k), we define some sequences starting with s, which we will call *fibres*, as follows. Any sequence

$$s = s_k, s_k', s_{k+1}, s_{k+1}', s_{k+2}, s_{k+2}', \ldots$$

where $s_i \in$ NODES(g_i), $s_i' \in$ NODES(g_i'), $(s_i,s_i') \in R_i$ and $S_i(s_i') = s_{i+1}$ ($i \geq k$) is a fibre. We will say that this fibre starts in g_k. If σ,τ are fibres, starting in g_k and g_{k+1} respectively, we define transitions $\sigma \rightarrow_a \tau$ if there are a-steps between the elements of these sequences:

$$\begin{array}{llllll} \sigma: & s_k, s_k', & s_{k+1}, & s_{k+1}', & s_{k+2}, & s_{k+2}', \ldots \\ \downarrow a & & \downarrow a & \downarrow a & \downarrow a & \downarrow a \\ \tau: & & t_{k+1}, & t_{k+1}', & t_{k+2}, & t_{k+2}', \ldots \end{array}$$

Now we construct the process graph γ with as nodes the fibres and transitions as just defined. More precisely: the root of γ is the fibre through the roots of $g_1, g_1', g_2, \ldots$, and the other nodes of γ are those fibres reachable from the root of γ via transitions between fibres.

We claim that the projection $(\gamma)_n$ is bisimilar to g_n. A bisimulation ρ_n is given as follows: if s $\in$ NODES(g_n) and $\sigma \in$ NODES($(\gamma)_n$) then $(s,\sigma) \in \rho_n$ iff s is an element of σ. The verification of the claim is easy. An illustration is given in Figure 3.1 where γ is 'reconstructed' from the sequence of process graphs a, $a+a^2$, $a+a^2+a^3$, ... Interestingly, the result is not $\sum_{n\geq 1} a^n$ but $\sum_{n\geq 1} a^n + a^\omega$. (See the 'black fibers' in Figure 3.1.)

However, the problem is now to prove that the branching degree of γ is strictly bounded by β. We claim that this is so if $\beta > (\alpha^*)^{\aleph_0}$. Proof of the claim: let us take the g_i ($i \geq 1$) above as small as possible with respect to the cardinalities of their node sets. From the proof of Proposition 3.10(i) it is clear that we can take the g_i such that card(NODES(g_i)) $\leq \alpha_i$ (in fact we can even take card(NODES(g_i)) $\leq \alpha_{i-1}$). Hence we may suppose that the union of the node sets of the g_i, g_i' ($i\geq 1$) is bounded by α^*. Now every fibre (a node of the tree γ) is an ω-sequence of nodes of the g_i, g_i'. Hence there are at most $\kappa = (\alpha^*)^{\aleph_0}$ such fibres; so γ has at most κ nodes, so the branching degree of γ is bounded by κ. $\square$

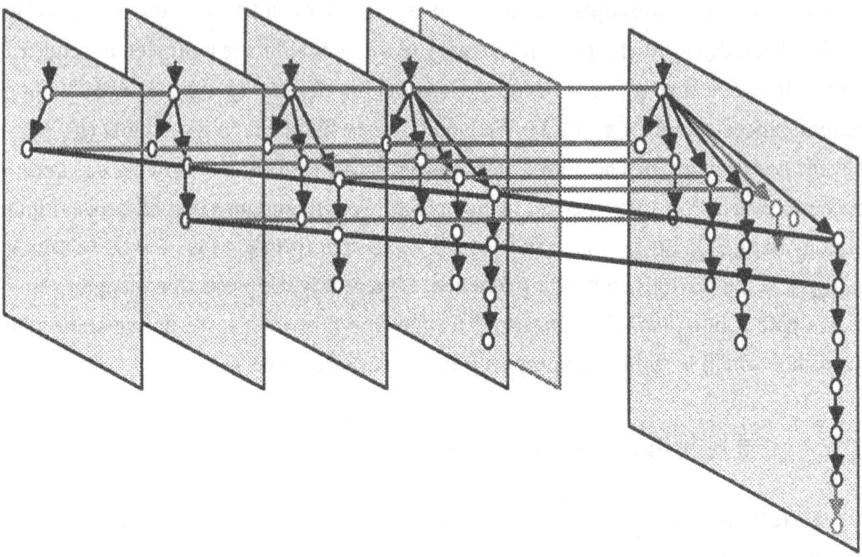

Figure 3.1

3.14. REMARK. (i) In the example above, in Figure 3.1, the process graph γ is closed (see Definition 3.23.1 for the definition of 'closed process graph'). In general, this needs not to be the case: e.g. if in the proof of Proposition 3.13, $g_i = (\Sigma_{n\geq 1}\ a^n)_i$ for $i \geq 1$ (so g_1 consists of infinitely many a-steps attached at the root) then $\gamma = \Sigma_{n\geq 1}\ a^n$ and this graph is not closed.
(ii) Another way of constructing a process graph g with projections $(g)_n$ bisimilar to g_n as in the proof above, is by taking g as the *canonical process graph* of the projective sequence $(g_1, g_2, ...) \in A^\infty$. See Definition 3.23.2. One can prove that this graph is closed indeed, for $\beta > (\alpha^*)^{\aleph_0}$.

3.15. DEFINITION. Let $X,X' \subseteq \mathbb{G}_{\alpha,\beta}$. (i) Then $(X)_n = \{(g)_n \mid g \in X\}$.
(ii) $X \equiv_n X'$ if $\forall g \in X\ \exists g' \in X'\ \ g \equiv_n g'$ and $\forall g' \in X'\ \exists g \in X\ \ g \equiv_n g'$.
(iii) $X \equiv X'$ if $X \equiv_n X'$ for all n.

3.16. DEFINITION. Let $g \in \mathbb{G}_{\alpha,\beta}$. The a-*derivation* of g is the set of all subgraphs of g reachable by an a-step from the root. Notation: g/a.

3.17. PROPOSITION. *Let* $g,h \in \mathbb{G}_{\alpha,\beta}$. *Then* g,h *determine the same element in* $\mathbb{G}^\circ_{\alpha,\beta}$ *iff for all* a, $g/a \equiv h/a$.

PROOF. Routine. □

3.18. PROPOSITION. *Let* $X \subseteq \mathbb{G}_{\alpha,\beta}$. *Then there is an* $X' \subseteq \mathbb{G}_{\alpha,\beta}$ *such that* $X \equiv X'$ *and* $\mathrm{card}(X') \leq \alpha^*$.

PROOF. Consider the collection $\bigcup_{n\geq 1}(X)_n$ of finitely deep process graphs. We will construct a graph (not a process graph) with node set $\bigcup_{n\geq 1}(X)_n$, and arrows $g \rightarrow h$ for $g \in (X)_n$, $h \in (X)_{n+1}$ whenever $g = (h)_n$. See Figure 3.2.

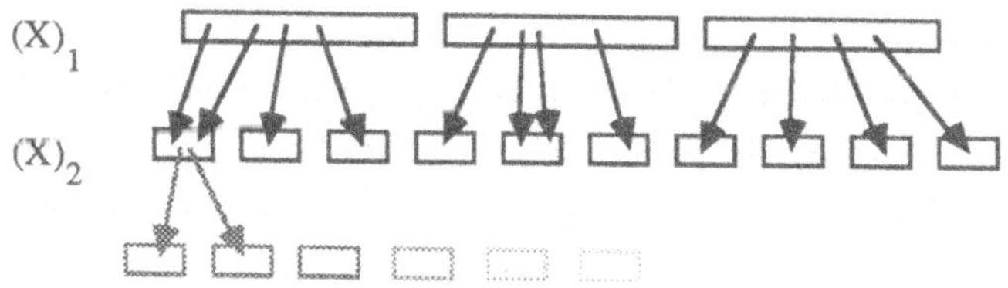

Figure 3.2

The boxes in Figure 3.2 are the $\Leftrightarrow$-equivalence classes. We note (Proposition 3.10(i)) that there are at most α_n boxes at level n, hence at most α^* boxes in total. Now every $g \in X$ corresponds with a path in this huge graph (not necessarily vice versa). We now construct X' as follows. If $g \in X$ is finitely deep (i.e. determines a terminating path in the graph of Figure 3.2), then $g \in X'$. Furthermore, in each box we select one node (i.e. a process graph $g \in (X)_n$ for some n) and choose an *arbitrary* path through this node. This path (which in fact is a projective sequence of process *graphs*) determines a process graph, call it $g^\sim$. Now we put $g^\sim \in X'$. Obviously, $\mathrm{card}(X') \leq \alpha^*$ and it is not hard to prove that $X \equiv X'$. □

3.19. PROPOSITION. *For all* α,κ: $\mathbb{G}^o_{\alpha,(\alpha^*)^+} \cong \mathbb{G}^o_{\alpha,(\alpha^*)^+ +\kappa}$

PROOF. Consider a process graph $g \in \mathbb{G}_{\alpha,(\alpha^*)^+ +\kappa}$. We must show that g can be pruned to a $g' \in \mathbb{G}_{\alpha,(\alpha^*)^+}$ such that g and g' determine the same element after dividing out $\Leftrightarrow$ and AIP (or dividing out $\equiv$ at once). This follows directly from the preceding two propositions. □

3.20. COROLLARY. *For all* α,κ,λ: $\mathbb{A}^\infty_{\alpha,\alpha^* + \kappa} \cong \mathbb{G}^o_{\alpha,(\alpha^*)^+ + \lambda}$

PROOF. This follows from Theorem 3.11 and Propositions 3.13 and 3.19. □

The cardinality of the models constructed above is for infinite alphabets quite large (this was already noticed in Golson & Rounds [83] for the process model of De Bakker & Zucker [82a,b];

see our remarks below). In fact:

3.21. PROPOSITION. (i) *For finite* α: card$(A^\infty{}_{\alpha,\aleph_0}) = 2^{\aleph_0}$

(ii) *For countably infinite alphabet*: card$(A^\infty{}_{\aleph_0,\beth_\omega}) = \beth_{\omega+1}$

(iii) *For general* α: card$(A^\infty{}_{\alpha,\alpha^*}) = 2^{(\alpha^*)} = (\alpha^*)^{\aleph_0}$.

PROOF. (We will assume the Axiom of Choice in our calculations with cardinals.) Statements (i) and (ii) follow from (iii). Proof of (iii): Let λ be card$(A^\infty{}_{\alpha,\alpha^*})$. Using Proposition 3.10 and noting that every element of $A^\infty{}_{\alpha,\alpha^*}$ is a map from ω into the union of the $\mathbb{G}^n{}_{\alpha,\alpha^*}$, we have $\lambda \le (\alpha^*)^{\aleph_0}$. In view of the isomorphism with the graph models (Corollary 3.20), we find $\lambda \ge 2^{(\alpha^*)}$. The argument is as follows: there are α^* finitely deep process graphs which are mutually not bisimilar. (This is in fact Proposition 3.10(ii).) Let $\mathfrak{F}$ be the set of these process graphs. For every subset $\mathfrak{X}$ of $\mathfrak{F}$ we define a process graph $g_{\mathfrak{X}}$ as $\Sigma_{g\in\mathfrak{X}}$ a.g for a fixed atom a. Now $g_{\mathfrak{X}} \leftrightarrows g_{\mathfrak{Y}}$ iff $\mathfrak{X} = \mathfrak{Y}$. Moreover, for different $\mathfrak{X},\mathfrak{Y}$ the corresponding graphs are not identified after dividing out AIP. So we now have:

$$2^{(\alpha^*)} \le \lambda \le (\alpha^*)^{\aleph_0}.$$

We also have: $2^{(\alpha^*)} = (\alpha^*)^{\alpha^*} \ge (\alpha^*)^{\aleph_0}$ (here AC is used, in the equality step). Hence the result follows. □

3.22. QUESTIONS. At present we do not know the answers to the following questions. For what α,β is $\mathbb{G}^\circ{}_{\alpha,\beta}$ a complete metric space? What is the cardinality of $\mathbb{G}^\circ{}_{\alpha,\beta}$ and $A^\infty{}_{\alpha,\beta}$? If $\mathbb{G}^\circ{}_{\alpha,\beta}$ is a complete metric space, is $\mathbb{G}^\circ{}_{\alpha,\beta'}$ for $\beta' > \beta$ also complete?

It is interesting to compare the projective model $A^\infty{}_{\alpha,\alpha^*}$ with the process model $\mathbb{P}_\alpha$ as constructed by De Bakker & Zucker [82a,b] as a solution of the domain equation

$$P \cong \{p_0\} \cup \wp_c(A \times P).$$

In $\mathbb{P}_\alpha$, processes can terminate with p_0 or with $\varnothing$ ('successfully' or 'unsuccesfully'). Leaving this double termination possibility aside (one can extend PA to PA_δ and have the same double termination possibility) or using a variant of the domain equation:

$$P \cong \wp_c(A \cup (A \times P)),$$

we can state that our projective model $A^{\infty}_{\alpha,\alpha^*}$ is *isometric* to the process domain $\mathbb{P}_\alpha$. For finite α, this follows from the proof in Golson & Rounds [83] that $\mathbb{P}_\alpha$ is isometric to the graph domain $\mathbb{G}^{\circ}_{\alpha,\aleph_1}$; hence it is also isometric to $A^{\infty}_{\alpha,\aleph_0}$, by Corollary 3.20. For infinite α the proof is similar. (The proof proceeds by noting that our spaces of finitely deep processes $\mathbb{G}^{n}_{\alpha,\alpha^*}$ are isometric to the P_n in De Bakker & Zucker [82a,b] or Golson & Rounds [83]; hence the completions of $\bigcup_{n\geq 1} \mathbb{G}^{n}_{\alpha,\alpha^*}$ and $\bigcup_{n\geq 1} P_n$, respectively, must also be isometric.) So the cardinality statements in Proposition 3.21 apply also to the models in De Bakker & Zucker [82a,b].

For a systematic (category-theoretic) treatment of De Bakker-Zucker domain equations like the two above, showing that they have unique solutions modulo isometry, we refer to America & Rutten [88].

3.23. Closed process graphs

We conclude with some remarks about a trade-off between closure properties of processes and the Approximation Induction Principle used in the construction of $\mathbb{G}^{\circ}_{\alpha,\alpha^*}$. These remarks are suggested by the fact that the model of De Bakker and Zucker is a solution of their domain equation; loosely speaking this means that the elements of that model can be perceived as 'hereditarily closed sets'. (Note, however, that these 'sets' are not well-founded. For a treatment of non-well-founded sets, including the connection with bisimulations, see Aczel [87].) One may ask whether the closure property can replace, when constructing a model from process graphs such as $\mathbb{G}^{\circ}_{\alpha,\alpha^*}$, taking the quotient with respect to AIP. We will make this question more precise using the definition of 'closed process tree' which was suggested to us by R. van Glabbeek (personal communication).

3.23.1. DEFINITION. (i) For process trees $g,h \in \mathfrak{G}_{\alpha,\beta}$ we define the distance $\delta(g,h)$ as follows:

$$\delta(g,h) = \begin{cases} 2^{-m} & \text{if } \exists n\ g \not\equiv_n h;\ m = \min\{n \mid g \not\equiv_n h\} \\ 0 & \text{otherwise, i.e. } g \equiv h. \end{cases}$$

(ii) Let $\mathcal{H} \subseteq \mathfrak{G}_{\alpha,\beta}$ be a set of process trees. Then $\mathcal{H}$ is *closed* if every Cauchy sequence $(g_i)_{i\geq 1}$ with respect to δ in $\mathcal{H}$ converges to a limit g in $\mathcal{H}$ (i.e. $\forall k\ \exists N\ \forall n{>}N\ \ g \equiv_k g_n$).

(iii) Let $g \in \mathfrak{G}_{\alpha,\beta}$ be a process tree. Then g is *closed* if all its nodes s are closed; and a node s in g is closed when $(g)_s/a$ is a closed set of trees for every $a \in A$. Here $(g)_s$ is the subtree of g at s. Futhermore, a process graph is closed if its tree unwinding is closed. The set of all closed process graphs is $\mathfrak{G}^{c}_{\alpha,\beta}$.

3.23.1.1. REMARK. Note that the closure property of process graphs is invariant under bisimulation equivalence: if g $\leftrightarrows$ h and g is closed, then h is closed.

3.23.2. DEFINITION. Let $\mathbb{M}$ be a a process algebra for PA.

(i) From the elements x,y,z,... of $\mathbb{M}$ we construct a transition diagram (i.e. a 'process graph' without root and not necessarily connected) as follows. Whenever x = ay + z there is a transition $x \rightarrow_a y$. In the case that x = ay we have the same transition. If x = a, then there is a transition $x \rightarrow_a \mathbf{o}$ where **o** is the *termination node*. More concisely, we have $x \rightarrow_a y$ iff x = ay + x and $x \rightarrow_a \mathbf{o}$ iff x = a + x. (To see this, use the axiom x + x = x.)

(ii) The *canonical process graph of* x *in* $\mathbb{M}$ is the process graph with root x, and as nodes all the elements of $\mathbb{M}$ reachable from x in zero or more transition steps as just defined, including possibly the termination node. Notation: $can_{\mathbb{M}}(x)$ or just can(x) when it is clear what $\mathbb{M}$ is meant. (See Figure 3.3 for the canonical process graph of $(\sum_{n\geq 1} a^n)/\equiv$ in $\mathbb{G}^{\circ}_{\alpha,\beta}$.)

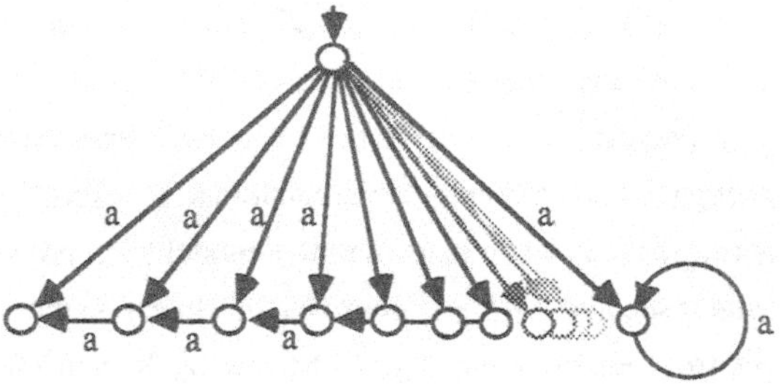

Figure 3.3

3.23.3. PROPOSITION. *Let g/≡ be an element of* $\mathbb{G}^{\circ}_{\alpha,\beta}$ *. Then:*

(i) can(g/≡) ≡ g.

(ii) can(g/≡) $\equiv_n$ can(h/≡) $\Leftrightarrow$ g $\equiv_n$ h.

(iii) can(g/≡) *is a closed proces graph.*

PROOF. (i) With induction on n we prove that g $\equiv_n$ can(g/≡) for $n \geq 0$ (see Definition 3.3). The basis of the induction, n = 0, is trivial. Suppose (induction hypothesis) that we have proved $\forall g$ g $\equiv_n$ can(g/≡). In order to prove g $\equiv_{n+1}$ can(g/≡), we have to show (1) and (2):

(1) *for every transition* $g \rightarrow_a g'$ *there is an initial step in* can(g/≡): $g/\equiv \rightarrow_a h/\equiv$ *such that*

$$g' \equiv_n (can(g/\equiv))_{(h/\equiv)} = can(h/\equiv).$$

(Remember that g/≡, h/≡ are nodes in can(g/≡).) Now $g/\equiv \rightarrow_a h/\equiv$ is (by definition of canonical process graph) the same as: $g/\equiv \ = a(h/\equiv) + r/\equiv$ for some graph r. Or, equivalently: $g \equiv ah + r$. So, given the transition $g \twoheadrightarrow_a g'$ we have to find h,r with $g \equiv ah + r$ and $g' \equiv_n \ can(h/\equiv)$. This is simple: take $h = g'$ and r as given by $g \twoheadrightarrow_a g'$ (i.e. $g = a{\cdot}g' + r$ for some r). Now apply the induction hypothesis.

(2) *For every initial step in* $can(g/\equiv)$: $g/\equiv \ \rightarrow_a h/\equiv$ *there is a transition* $g \twoheadrightarrow_a g'$ *such that* $g' \equiv_n \ can(h/\equiv)$.

So, let $g/\equiv \ \rightarrow_a h/\equiv$ be given. This means $g \equiv ah + r$ for some r. In particular, $g \equiv_{n+1} ah + r$, i.e.

$$(g)_{n+1} \leftrightarrows (ah + r)_{n+1} = a(h)_n + (r)_{n+1}. \qquad (*)$$

From the induction hypothesis we know that $h \equiv_n can(h/\equiv)$, i.e.

$$(h)_n \leftrightarrows (can(h/\equiv))_n. \qquad (**)$$

Combining (*),(**) we have

$$(g)_{n+1} \leftrightarrows a(can(h/\equiv))_n + (r)_n. \qquad (***)$$

Now we have to find a step $g \rightarrow_a g'$ such that $g' \equiv_n \ can(h/\equiv)$, i.e. $(g')_n \leftrightarrows (can(h/\equiv))_n$. This is easily obtained from (***): consider the a-occurrence displayed in the right-hand side of (***). By definition of $\leftrightarrows$, this a-step is matched in $(g)_{n+1}$ by an a-step $(g)_{n+1} \rightarrow_a (g')_n$ with $(g')_n \leftrightarrows (can(h/\equiv))_n$.

(ii) Write $g^* = can(g/\equiv)$. To prove ($\Leftarrow$), suppose $g \equiv_n h$. Then $g^* \equiv g \equiv_n h \equiv h^*$, using (i). So $g^* \equiv_n h^*$. The proof of ($\Rightarrow$) is similar.

(iii) Consider $can(g/\equiv)$. (See Figure 3.4.) Let s be a node of this graph (so $s \in \mathbb{G}^\circ_{\alpha,\beta}$). Consider the a-derivation of s, i.e. the set of subgraphs of $can(g/\equiv)$ determined by the a-successors of s. Clearly, this a-derivation is the set of canonical graphs of some elements t_i ($i \in I$) of $\mathbb{G}^\circ_{\alpha,\beta}$. Suppose this set $\{can(t_i) \mid i \in I\}$ contains a Cauchy sequence (with respect to δ as in Definition 3.23.1):

$$can(t_{i0}), can(t_{i1}), \dots , can(t_{in}), \dots .$$

We claim that the elements $t_{i0},t_{i1},\dots,t_{in},\dots$ form a Cauchy sequence in $\mathbb{G}^\circ_{\alpha,\beta}$. This follows at once from (ii) of this proposition. So there is a limit $t \in \mathbb{G}^{\circ}_{\alpha,\beta}$ of the last Cauchy sequence. Now can(t) is easily seen (using again (ii)) to be a limit (in the δ-sense) for the Cauchy sequence $\text{can}(t_{i0})$, $\text{can}(t_{i1})$, ...

We still have to prove that $s \to_a t$, or equivalently (see Definition 3.23.2(i)) $s = at + s$ in $\mathbb{G}^{\circ}_{\alpha,\beta}$. Let $\underline{s}$ denote a representing process graph from the ≡-equivalence class s, and likewise for t etc. Then we must prove that $\underline{s} \equiv a\underline{t} + \underline{s}$. To this end, take $\underline{t}_{ik}$ such that $\underline{t}_{ik} \equiv_n \underline{t}$. Since $\underline{s} \equiv a\underline{t}_{ik} + \underline{s}$ we have $\underline{s} \equiv_n a\underline{t} + \underline{s}$. Hence $\underline{s} \equiv a\underline{t} + \underline{s}$. □

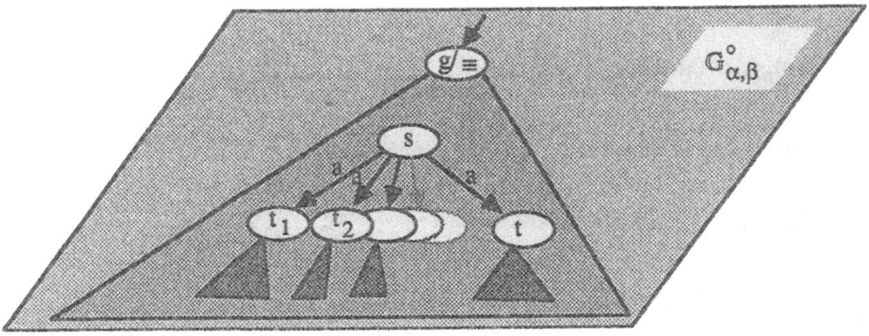

Figure 3.4

The preceding proposition enables us to define the *closure* of a process graph $g \in \mathfrak{G}_{\alpha,\beta}$, notation g^c, as can(g/≡) w.r.t. $\mathbb{G}^{\circ}_{\alpha,\beta}$, such that $g \equiv g^c$. Next, we define operations $+^c$, $\cdot^c$, $\|^c$, $\lfloor\!\lfloor^c$ on $\mathfrak{G}^c_{\alpha,\beta}$ as follows: $g \|^c h = (g \| h)^c$ and likewise for the other operators. Here $\|$ is the merge operation on $\mathfrak{G}_{\alpha,\beta}$.

5.4. REMARK. If $\mathfrak{G}^c_{\alpha,\beta}$ would have been closed under the operations $+, \cdot, \|, \lfloor\!\lfloor$ the preceding closure operation in $(g \| h)^c$ (etc.) would not have been necessary. However, for an *infinite* alphabet $\mathfrak{G}^c_{\alpha,\beta}$ is not necessarily closed under $\|$, as the following example shows. (We conjecture that for finite alphabets $\mathfrak{G}^c_{\alpha,\beta}$ is closed under the operations $\|$ etc.)

Let the alphabet be $\{a_i \mid i \geq 1\} \cup \{b,c\}$. We define process graphs H, G, g_n $(n \geq 1)$:

$$H = \|_{i\geq 1}\, a_i^{\omega}$$

$$g_n = a_n \| b^n$$

$$G = \Sigma_{n\geq 1}\, c \cdot g_n.$$

Now H is a closed process graph. This can be easily seen, noting that H is a *deterministic* process graph, i.e. a graph where two different edges leaving the same node must have different label, and noting that deterministic graphs are always closed. Also G is closed: the c-derivation G/c, consisting of the graphs g_n, does not contain a Cauchy sequence since the graphs g_n are already different in their first level, due to the 'spoiling effect' of the a_n in g_n. Now G || H is, we claim, not closed. For, consider the c-derivation

$$(G \parallel H)/c = \{H \parallel g_n \mid n \geq 1\}.$$

Since $H \parallel a_n \underline{\leftrightarrow} H$, we have

$$(G \parallel H)/c = \{H \parallel b^n \mid n \geq 1\},$$

modulo $\underline{\leftrightarrow}$ which does not affect the closure properties (as remarked in 5.1.1). The last set is a Cauchy sequence: in general, if $\{q_i \mid i \geq 1\}$ is a Cauchy sequence of process graphs, then $\{p \parallel q_i \mid i \geq 1\}$ is again a Cauchy sequence for arbitrary p. However, there is no limit for this sequence in the set (G || H)/c, and hence it is not closed. So G || H is not closed.

This counterexample may seem somewhat surprising in view of a related result in De Bakker, Bergstra, Klop & Meyer [84], where it is stated (Theorem 2.9) that the collection of closed *trace languages* (containing possibly infinite traces) is closed under the merge operation, for arbitrary alphabet. Here a trace language is obtained as the set of all maximal traces of a process (or process graph). Note however that closure of processes does not very well correspond to closure of the corresponding trace sets; cf. also Example 4.4 in De Bakker, Bergstra, Klop & Meyer [84] of a closed process graph with a trace set which is not closed.

Next, we define the quotient structure

$$\mathbb{G}^c_{\alpha,\beta} = \mathfrak{G}^c_{\alpha,\beta} / \underline{\leftrightarrow}.$$

Here $\mathfrak{G}^c_{\alpha,\beta}$ is supposed to be equipped with the operations as just defined. It is left to the reader to show that $\underline{\leftrightarrow}$ is indeed a congruence with respect to these operations. Now there is the following fact, showing that indeed taking the quotient with respect to the congruence induced by AIP can be exchanged for the restriction to closed process graphs:

3.23.5. THEOREM. $\mathbb{G}^c_{\alpha,\beta} \cong \mathbb{G}^\circ_{\alpha,\beta}$.

PROOF. Remember that $\mathbb{G}^c_{\alpha,\beta} = \mathbb{G}^c_{\alpha,\beta} / \leftrightarrows$ and $\mathbb{G}^\circ_{\alpha,\beta} = \mathbb{G}_{\alpha,\beta} / \equiv$. Define the map

$$\varphi: \mathbb{G}^c_{\alpha,\beta} / \leftrightarrows \ \to \mathbb{G}_{\alpha,\beta} / \equiv$$

by $\varphi(g/\leftrightarrows) = (g/\equiv)$. Here $g \in \mathbb{G}^c_{\alpha,\beta}$ and $g/\leftrightarrows$ is the equivalence class modulo $\leftrightarrows$; likewise $g/\equiv$ is the equivalence class of g modulo $\equiv$.

(1) To prove that φ is injective, let $g,h \in \mathbb{G}^c_{\alpha,\beta}$ and suppose $g \equiv h$. We must prove $g \leftrightarrows h$. Define $R \subseteq \text{NODES}(g) \times \text{NODES}(h)$ as follows: $(s,t) \in R$ iff $(g)_s \equiv (g)_t$. We claim that R is a bisimulation from g to h. Proof of the claim: The roots are related, by the assumption $g \equiv h$. Further, suppose $(s,t) \in R$ and suppose there is a step $s \to_a s'$ in g. (See Figure 3.5.)

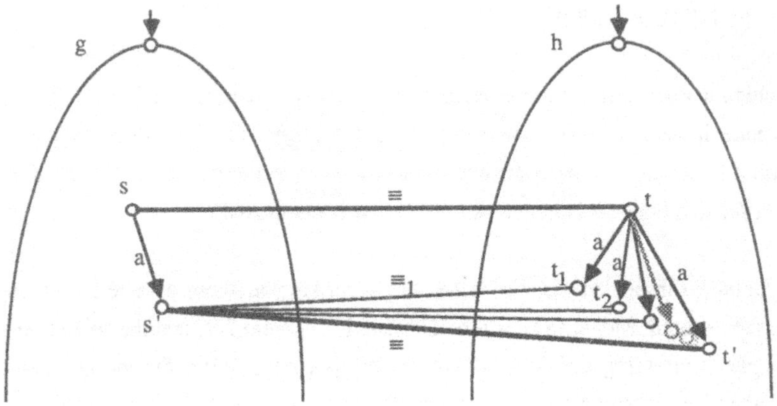

Figure 3.5

Since $(g)_s \equiv (h)_t$ we have for all $n \geq 1$: $(g)_s \equiv_n (h)_t$. This means that there are t_n such that $(g)_{s'} \equiv_n (h)_{tn}$ for all $n \geq 1$. The t_n (or rather the $(h)_{tn}$) form a Cauchy sequence with respect to δ, hence there is, since h is closed, a node t' such that $t \to_a t'$ and $(h)_{t'}$ is a limit for the Cauchy sequence t_n, $n \geq 1$. So $(h)_{t'} \equiv_n (h)_{tm}$ for some $m \geq n$. Therefore $(h)_{t'} \equiv_n (h)_{tm} \equiv_m (g)_{s'}$, and since $m \geq n$, $(h)_{t'} \equiv_n (g)_{s'}$. This holds for all $n \geq 1$, so $(h)_{t'} \equiv (g)_{s'}$, i.e. $(s',t') \in R$.

The same argument shows that if $(s,t) \in R$ and there is a step $t \to_a t'$ in h, then there is a step $s \to_a s'$ with $(s',t') \in R$.

This shows that R is a bisimulation from g to h, and ends the proof of (1).

(2) To prove that φ is surjective, we have to show that

$$\forall g \in \mathbb{G}^c_{\alpha,\beta} \ \exists g' \in \mathbb{G}^c_{\alpha,\beta} \ \ g \equiv g'.$$

This follows by taking $g' = \text{can}(g/\equiv)$ and applying Proposition 3.23.3(iii). □

In the case that β is large enough, so that $\mathbb{G}^c_{\alpha,\beta}$ is isometric to the process model $\mathbb{P}_\alpha$ of De Bakker and Zucker, this isometry leads to an 'explicit representation' of $\mathbb{P}_\alpha$, as follows. First a definition:

3.23.6. DEFINITION. (i) A process graph g is *minimal* if

$$\forall s,t \in \text{NODES}(g)\ \ (g)_s \leftrightarrows (g)_t \Rightarrow s = t.$$

(ii) A process graph is *normal* if

$$\forall s,t,t' \in \text{NODES}(g)\ \forall a \in A\ \ s \rightarrow_a t \ \&\ s \rightarrow_a t' \ \&\ (g)_s \leftrightarrows (g)_t \Rightarrow s = t.$$

Clearly, normality is implied by minimality. Also note that a process tree can never be minimal, unless it is linear (has only one branch); this is the reason for introducing the concept 'normal'.

It is not hard to prove that if g,h are minimal process graphs and $g \leftrightarrows h$, then g,h are in fact identical. Moreover, the canonical process graphs (of elements of $\mathbb{G}^\circ_{\alpha,\beta}$) are precisely the closed and minimal process graphs in $\mathfrak{G}_{\alpha,\beta}$. Thus every element in $\mathbb{P}_\alpha$ can be represented by a *closed, minimal process graph with branching degree at most* α^*, and the operations in $\mathbb{P}_\alpha$ can be represented by the corresponding operations in $\mathfrak{G}^c_{\alpha,\beta}$ followed by minimalisation (collapsing all bisimilar subgraphs). Another explicit representation can be given, using trees instead of graphs and observing that normal, bisimilar process trees are identical. Then the elements of $\mathbb{P}_\alpha$ correspond to *closed, normal process trees with branching degree at most* α^*. This representation is closer to the idea of elements of $\mathbb{P}_\alpha$ as 'hereditarily closed and possibly not well-founded sets'.

Summarizing our comparisons with $\mathbb{P}_\alpha$ we have established isometries (for all κ):

$$\mathbb{P}_\alpha \cong A^\infty_{\alpha,\alpha^*+\kappa} \cong \mathbb{G}^\circ_{\alpha,(\alpha^*)^++\kappa}.$$

Furthermore, writing $\mathfrak{G}^{cm}_{\alpha,\beta}$ for the set of closed minimal graphs in $\mathfrak{G}_{\alpha,\beta}$ and $\mathfrak{T}^{cn}_{\alpha,\beta}$ for the set of closed normal trees in $\mathfrak{G}_{\alpha,\beta}$, there are the isometries

$$\mathbb{P}_\alpha \cong \mathbb{G}^c_{\alpha,(\alpha^*)^++\kappa} \cong \mathfrak{G}^{cm}_{\alpha,(\alpha^*)^++\kappa} \cong \mathfrak{T}^{cn}_{\alpha,(\alpha^*)^++\kappa},$$

where the last two complete metric spaces can be seen as 'explicit representations' of $\mathbb{P}_\alpha$.

References

ACZEL, P. (87), *Lecture Notes on Non-Well-Founded sets*, CSLI, Lecture Notes Nr.9, 1987

AMERICA, P. & RUTTEN, J.J.M.M. (88), *Solving reflexive domain equations in a category of complete metric spaces*, in: Proc. of the Third Workshop on Mathematical Foundations of Programming Language Semantics (M. Main, A. Melton, M. Mislove, D. Schmidt, eds.), Springer LNCS 298, 1988, p.2540288. Also to appear in the Journal of Computer and System Sciences.

BAETEN, J.C.M. & BERGSTRA, J.A. (88), *Global renaming operators in concrete process algebra*, Information and Computation, Vol.78, Nr.3 (1988), 205-245.

BAETEN, J.C.M., BERGSTRA, J.A. & KLOP, J.W. (86), *Syntax and defining equations for an interrupt mechanism in process algebra*, Fund. Inf. IX (2), p.127-168, 1986.

BAETEN, J.C.M., BERGSTRA, J.A. & KLOP, J.W. (87) *On the consistency of Koomen's Fair Abstraction Rule*, TCS 51 (1987), 129-176.

BAETEN, J.C.M., BERGSTRA, J.A. & KLOP, J.W. (87a), *Decidability of bisimulation equivalence for processes generating context-free languages*, in: Proc. PARLE, Vol.II (Parallel Languages), (eds. J.W. de Bakker, A.J. Nijman, P.C. Treleaven), Eindhoven 1987, Springer LNCS 259, p.94-113, 1987.

BAETEN, J.C.M., BERGSTRA, J.A. & KLOP, J.W. (87b), *Conditional axioms and α/β calculus in process algebra*, in: Proc. IFIP Conf. on Formal Description of Programming Concepts—III, Ebberup 1986, (M. Wirsing, ed.) North-Holland, Amsterdam 1987, p.53-75.

BAETEN, J.C.M & VAN GLABBEEK, R.J. (87), *Another look at abstraction in process algebra*, in: Proc. 14th ICALP 87, Karlsruhe (Th. Ottman, ed.), Springer LNCS 267, p.84-94, 1987.

DE BAKKER, J.W., BERGSTRA, J.A., KLOP, J.W. & MEYER, J.-J.CH. (84), *Linear time and branching time semantics for recursion with merge*. Theoretical Computer Science 34 (1984), p.135-156.

DE BAKKER, J.W. & ZUCKER, J.I. (82a), *Denotational semantics of concurrency*, Proc. 14th ACM Symp. Theory of Comp., p. 153 - 158, 1982.

DE BAKKER, J.W. & ZUCKER, J.I. (82b), *Processes and the denotational semantics of concurrency*, Information and Control 54 (1/2), p. 70 - 120, 1982.

BERGSTRA, J.A. & KLOP, J.W. (84a), *Process algebra for synchronous communication*, Information & Control 60 (1/3), p. 109 - 137, 1984.

BERGSTRA, J.A. & KLOP, J.W. (84b), *The algebra of recurively defined processes and the algebra of regular processes*, in: Proc. 11th ICALP (ed. J. Paredaens), Antwerpen 1984, Springer LNCS 172, p.82-95, 1984.

BERGSTRA, J.A. & KLOP, J.W. (85), *Algebra of communicating processes with abstraction*, TCS 37 (1), p. 77 - 121, 1985.

BERGSTRA, J.A. & KLOP, J.W. (86a), *Verification of an alternating bit protocol by means of process algebra*, in: Math. Methods of Spec. and Synthesis of Software Systems '85 (eds. W. Bibel and K.P. Jantke), Math. Research 31, Akademie-Verlag Berlin, p.9-23. 1986.

BERGSTRA, J.A. & KLOP, J.W. (86b), *Algebra of communicating processes*, in: CWI Monographs I, Proceedings of the CWI Symposium Mathematics and Computer Science (eds. J.W. de Bakker, M. Hazewinkel & J.K. Lenstra) North-Holland, Amsterdam, 1986, p.89-138.

BERGSTRA, J.A. & KLOP, J.W. (86c), *Process algebra: specification and verification in bisimulation semantics*, in: CWI Monograph 4, Proceedings of the CWI Symposium Mathematics and Computer Science II (eds. M. Hazewinkel, J.K. Lenstra & L.G.L.T. Meertens), North-Holland, Amsterdam 1986, p.61-94.

BERGSTRA, J.A. & KLOP, J.W. (87), *A convergence theorem in process algebra*, CWI Report CS-R8733, Centre for Mathematics and Computer Science, Amsterdam, 1987.

BERGSTRA, J.A. & KLOP, J.W. (88), *A complete inference system for regular processes with silent moves*, in: Proc. of Logic Colloquium, Hull '86, (eds. F.R. Drake and J.K. Truss), North-Holland 1988.

BERGSTRA, J.A., KLOP, J.W. & OLDEROG, E.-R. (86), *Failure semantics with fair abstraction*, CWI Report CS-R8609, Amsterdam 1986.

BERGSTRA, J.A., KLOP, J.W. & OLDEROG, E.-R. (87), *Failures without chaos: a new process semantics for fair abstraction*, in: Proceedings IFIP Conference on Formal Description of Programming Concepts—III, Gl. Avernaes (Ebberup) 1986 (ed. M. Wirsing), North-Holland, Amsterdam, p.77-103, 1987.

BERGSTRA, J.A., KLOP, J.W. & OLDEROG, E.-R. (88), *Readies and failures in the algebra of communicating processes*, CWI Report CS-R8523, Amsterdam 1985. To appear in SIAM J. of Computing, 1988.

BERGSTRA, J.A. & TIURYN, J. (87), *Process algebra semantics for queues*, Fund. Inf. X, p.213-224, 1987.

BERGSTRA, J.A. & TUCKER, J.V. (84), *Top down design and the algebra of communicating processes*, Sci. of Comp. Progr. 5 (2), p. 171 - 199, 1984.

BROOKES, S.D. (83), *On the relationship of CCS and CSP* Proc. 10th ICALP (ed. J. Díaz), Barcelona 1983, Springer LNCS 154, 83-96.

BROOKES, S.D., HOARE, C.A.R. & ROSCOE, A.W. (84), A theory of Communicating Sequential Processes, JACM Vol.31, No.3 (1984) 560-599.

DE NICOLA, R. & HENNESSY, M. (83), *Testing equivalences for processes*, TCS 34, p.83-133.

VAN GLABBEEK, R.J. (87), *Bounded nondeterminism and the approximation principle in process algebra*. In: Proc. of the 4th Annual Symposium on Theoretical Aspects of Computer Science (eds. F.J. Brandenburg, G. Vidal-Naquet and M. Wirsing), Passau (W. Germany) 1987, Springer LNCS 247, 336-347.

VAN GLABBEEK, R.J. & VAANDRAGER, F.W. (88), *Modular specifications in process algebra—with curious queues*, Centre for Mathematics and Computer Science, Report CS-R8821, Amsterdam 1988; extended abstract to appear in: Proc. of the METEOR Workshop on Algebraic Methods: Theory, Tools and Applications, Springer LNCS.

GOLSON, W.G. & ROUNDS, W.C. (83), *Connections between two theories of concurrency: metric spaces and synchronization trees*. Information and Control 57 (1983), 102-124.

HENNESSY, M. (88), *Algebraic theory of processes*, The MIT Press, 1988.

HENNESSY, M. & MILNER, R. (85), *Algebraic laws for nondeterminism and concurrency*, JACM 32, 137-161.

HESSELINK, W. (88), *Deadlock and fairness in morphisms of transition systems*, Theor. Comp. Sci. 59 (1988) 235-257.

HOARE, C.A.R. (78), *Communicating sequential processes*, Comm. ACM 21, p. 666 - 677, 1978.

HOARE, C.A.R. (84), *Notes on communicating sequential processes*, International Summer School in Marktoberdorf: Control Flow and Data Flow, Munich 1984.

HOARE, C.A.R. (85), *Communicating sequential processes,* Prentice Hall 1985.

KOYMANS, C.P.J. & MULDER, J.C. (86), *A modular approach to protocol verification using process algebra,* Logic Group Preprint Series Nr.6, Dept. of Philosophy, State University of Utrecht, 1986; to appear in: Applications of Process Algebra, (J.C.M. Baeten, ed.), CWI Monograph, North-Holland, 1988.

KOYMANS, C.P.J. & VRANCKEN, J.L.M. (85), *Extending process algebra with the empty process* ε, Logic Group Preprint Series Nr.1, Dept. of Philosophy, State University of Utrecht, 1985.

KOSSEN, L. & WEIJLAND, W.P. (87), *Correctness proofs for systolic algorithms: palindromes and sorting,* Report FVI 87-04, Computer Science Department, University of Amsterdam, 1987.

KRANAKIS, E. (86), *Approximating the projective model,* in: Proc. Conf. on Math. Logic & its Applications, Druzhba (Bulgaria), 1986 (Pergamon Press).

KRANAKIS, E. (87), *Fixed point equations with parameters in the projective model,* Information and Computation, Vol.75, No.3, 1987.

MAUW, S. (87), *A constructive version of the Approximation Induction Principle,* Report FVI 87-09, Computer Science Department, University of Amsterdam, 1987.

MILNER, R. (80), *A calculus of communicating systems,* Springer LNCS 92, 1980.

MILNER, R. (84a), *Lectures on a Calculus for Communicating Systems,* Working Material for the Summer School Control Flow and Data Flow, Munich, July 1984.

MILNER, R. (84b), *A complete inference system for a class of regular behaviours,* Journal of Computer and System Sciences, Vol.28, Nr.3, 439-466, 1984.

MILNER, R. (85), *Lectures on a calculus for communicating systems,* in: Seminar on Concurrency, Springer LNCS 197 (1985), 197-220.

MILNER, R. (88), *A complete axiomatisation for observational congruence of finite-state behaviours,* Preprint, Univ. of Edinburgh 1985; to appear in Information and Computation 1988.

MOLLER, F. (88), *Non-finite axiomatisability in Process Algebras,* preprint, Univ. of Edinburgh, 1988

MULDER, J.C. (88), *On the Amoeba protocol,* CWI Report CS-R8827, Centre for Mathematics and Computer Science, Amsterdam 1988.

PARK, D.M.R. (81), *Concurrency and automata on infinite sequences.* Proc. 5th GI Conference, Springer LNCS 104, 1981.

PHILLIPS, I.C.C. (87), *Refusal testing,* TCS 50 (2), 1987.

VAANDRAGER, F.W. (86), *Verification of two communication protocols by means of process algebra,* CWI Report CS-R8608, Centre for Mathematics and Computer Science, Amsterdam 1986.

VRANCKEN, J.L.M. (86), *The Algebra of Communicating Processes with empty process,* Report FVI 86-01, Computer Science Department, University of Amsterdam, 1986.

WEIJLAND, W.P. (87), *A systolic algorithm for matrix-vector multiplication,* Report FVI 87-08, Computer Science Department, University of Amsterdam, 1987; also in: Proc. SION Conf. CSN 87, p.143-160, CWI, Amsterdam 1987.

Branching Time Temporal Logic†

E. Allen Emerson[1,2] *Jai* Srinivasan[1]

1. Department of Computer Sciences,
The University of Texas at Austin,
Austin, TX 78712, USA.

2. Mathematics and Computing Science Department,
Technical University of Eindhoven,
Eindhoven, The Netherlands.

Abstract. Many important parallel computer programs exhibit ongoing behaviour that is characterized naturally in terms of infinite execution traces, which can be organized into "branching" trees, and which reflect the high degree of nondeterminism inherent in parallel computation. In this paper, we give a systematic account of Branching Time Temporal Logics, which provide a formal system for describing and reasoning about the correct behaviour of such programs. Several systems of branching time temporal logic that have appeared in the literature are presented, and significant related issues such as their axiomatizations, and decision procedures for their satisfiability and model checking problems are discussed. The applicability of their axiomatizations to formulate deductive systems of these temporal logics to reason about the correctness of concurrent programs is then described as is that of their decision procedures to the tasks of mechanical synthesis and verification. A comparison of the relative expressive power of these systems of branching time temporal logic is also presented, and their ability to specify important correctness properties of programs, including those that involve fairness, is discussed. Moreover, their expressiveness is related to both, the expressiveness of corresponding linear time temporal logics, as well as that of other standard formalisms such as the monadic second-order theory of many successors and finite-state tree automata. Finally, a comparison is undertaken between branching time temporal logics and linear time ones, particularly with respect to their adequacy for such applications as specifying and reasoning about the correctness of concurrent programs.

Keywords: *Modal and Temporal Logic:* Branching time temporal logic, linear time temporal logic, dynamic logics, expressiveness, axiomatics, decidability, decision procedures, satisfiability, model checking; *Logics of Programs:* Reasoning about concurrent programs, program specification, program verification, specification of and reasoning about fairness; *Software Engineering:* Specification techniques, mechanical synthesis, automated verification techniques; *Computational Complexity; Automata Theory:* Finite-state automata on infinite objects, tree automata.

†This work was supported in part by NSF grant DCR–8511354, ONR URI contract N00014–86–K–0763, and Netherlands NWO grant nf–3/nfb 62–500.

Contents

1 Introduction

Many important parallel computer programs such as operating systems, network communication protocols, and air traffic control systems exhibit ongoing behaviour which is ideally nonterminating and thus infinite, reflecting their continuously operating nature. The behaviour of such programs is very naturally described in terms of a family of infinite execution traces, which may be viewed individually as being "linear" sequences, or which can be collectively organized into "branching" trees. There are, in general, infinitely many such traces describing the behaviour of a parallel program, engendered mainly by the high degree of nondeterminism inherent in such programs. This proliferation of traces implies that traditional program construction methodologies that are reasonably adequate for sequential programs (such as structured design and systematic testing) are wholly inadequate for dealing with the intricacies of parallel computation. It is therefore essential to develop an appropriate mathematical framework that makes it possible to deal with a parallel program as a mathematical object and to formally prove its correctness, viz., to prove that a program behaves as it is supposed to.

In a seminal paper ([Pn77]), Pnueli proposed the use of *temporal logic* as a basis for proving correctness of parallel programs. Until then, most of the research had revolved around extending the classical proof techniques introduced by Floyd ([Fl67]) for sequential programs and axiomatized by Hoare ([Ho69]). While the inductive assertion method for proving invariant properties (partial correctness) of programs generalized reasonably well, the method of using well-founded sets to prove termination (total correctness) was hampered by the intrinsic nondeterminism in parallel programs.

Temporal logic, a special type of modal logic, provides a formal system for qualitatively describing and reasoning about the occurrence of events in time, and, in fact, even for the occurrence of infinitely many events. In any system of temporal logic, various temporal operators or *modalities* are provided to specify how the truth of the properties of a temporal system vary over time. Typically, the modalities permit expression of such important properties of temporal systems as *invariances* (assertions that describe properties that are always true of a temporal system), *eventualities* (assertions that specify that a property must become true at some future instant of time), and *precedences* (assertions that state that one event must occur before another). Thus, temporal logic provides a suitable framework to model programs in general, be they sequential or parallel, terminating or nonterminating, and, in particular, it seems ideal for nonterminating parallel programs.

There is a consensus, nowadays, among many theoreticians and practitioners that temporal logic constitutes a promising approach to the problem of designing correct parallel programs. However, there is not yet a consensus regarding which specific system, or type, of temporal logic is best suited for this purpose. In this paper, we provide a systematic account of *branching time* temporal logics. Such systems of temporal logic view time as being a partially ordered collection of discrete instants and allow the specification of several alternative futures of any time instant; in contrast, the other principal systems of temporal logic, the *linear time* ones restrict themselves to dealing with a single future of a time instant with time still being considered discrete, but a linearly ordered collection of instants. (In that sense, a linear time temporal logic could be considered a sublogic of an appropriate branching time one; however, linear time temporal logics were formulated earlier, and have always enjoyed a special status because of their simpler structure.) We explain intuitively how this choice of the structure of time captures the nondeterministic behaviour of parallel programs. Then, with that as the primary motivation, we formally define several systems of branching time logic and demonstrate how various properties of programs can be expressed naturally in these systems. (Note that we shall restrict our discussion to *propositional* temporal logics, ones which augment ordinary propositional logic with temporal modalities. Such logics are surprisingly expressive in practice.)

After having outlined the syntax and the semantics of the main systems of branching time temporal logic that have appeared in the literature, we direct our attention to comparing them. One criterion to evaluate these systems of temporal logic is their *expressive power*, which, roughly, determines what correctness properties of programs are (and are not) expressible in the logic. Historically, in fact, it was this that played an important role in the formulation of the different systems of temporal logic (both linear and branching time), and, in a careful analysis of the relative merits of the application of branching time temporal logics to the reasoning of programs vis-à-vis linear time ones. Thus, we present a comparison of the relative expressiveness of the systems of branching time logic as well as the key points in the debate over branching and linear time logics.

Another issue over which there has been some divergence of opinion is just how temporal logic should be applied to reasoning about programs. Many applications of temporal logic to program reasoning have adopted the standard paradigm of manual program composition followed by manual program verification. The latter generally involves expressing facts known to be true of the program at hand and the correctness property to be proved within a system of temporal logic, and the correctness property is then formally derived as a theorem using a deductive proof system which is often based on an *axiomatization* of the temporal logic. One drawback of this approach is that the task of constructing the proof of correctness is generally quite tedious and often requires considerable ingenuity in its organization to be intellectually tractable. Moreover, if the program is incorrect, several iterations of this procedure may be necessary. An alternative approach is to automate program design and verification as much as possible. One ambitious such alternative is to mechanically synthesize a parallel program from the temporal specification of its intended behaviour. Another is to automate the verification of correctness properties of finite-state parallel programs. The methods used in the automated approach tap the natural correspondence between parallel programs and structures over which formulae of a temporal logic system are interpreted; in essence, the automated synthesis method uses a decision procedure that determines the *satisfiability* of the program specification cast as formula of a temporal logic system to derive a parallel program that satisfies the specification (cf. [EC82], [MW84]), and the automated verification method uses the *model checking* problem to determine the truth of the correctness property expressed as a temporal logic formula in a structure that may be viewed as the global flowgraph of the parallel program (cf. [CES83], [LP85]).

From a theoretical standpoint, however, the two approaches to reasoning about parallel programs, the manual and the automated, are related: the former may be viewed as motivating the development of a proof theory of a temporal logic, and the latter, a model theory. As is evident from the above, the related theoretical problems of significance are developing a sound and complete axiomatization of a temporal logic system (that could be the basis of a deductive proof system) to facilitate the manual approach, and formulating decision procedures for the satisfiability and model checking problems of the temporal logic for the automated one. Consequently, we outline the main results for branching time temporal logics in these areas, focussing on the techniques that have been used to arrive at the decision procedures and the axiomatizations. We also compare the complexity of the decision procedures, particularly for the satisfiability problem, for several systems of branching time temporal logic; as might be expected, in general, the complexity of deciding a branching time temporal logic increases with its expressive power. Thus, in choosing a system of temporal logic for an application domain, the systems designer must balance the efficiency with which he can reason about the modelled applications with the ease and generality that the temporal logic allows him to express relevant properties of the application domain.

The techniques used in the decision procedures for the satisfiability problem for many of the standard branching time temporal logics have evolved from attempting to solve similar problems for another distinctive class of modal logics called *dynamic logics*. A system of first-order dynamic logic was originally formulated by Pratt ([Pr76]) to reason primarily about programs using modal logic as a basis to provide a rigourous, relational semantics (cf. [deB80], [deR76]). Various propositional versions of such logics have since been proposed (cf. [FL77], [BHP81], [St81]). The structures over which dynamic logics are interpreted are essentially branching ones, and the logics themselves are closely related both in syntax and in semantics to branching time temporal logics. The essential difference between the derivatives of temporal logic as proposed by Pnueli and the dynamic logics is that the latter are *exogenous*, i.e., they provide a formalism that explicitly uses variables that range over programs, and composition operators over such variables to reason about several programs or program fragments. In contrast, the former are *endogenous* in that, when they are used to reason about programs, correctness assertions are presumed to deal with a single program though that program could be composed of several independent ones running in parallel. (One advantage of endogenous logics is that, though their development was motivated by an application area, viz., parallel programming, their formulation is quite independent of it, and, consequently, they can naturally be applied to a broad variety of areas. Indeed, that parallel programs can be modelled within the framework of such logics is incidental to their definition, and, thus, they deal with programs only implicitly.) Because of space restrictions, however, we shall focus on the endogenous temporal logics for the most part in this paper.

Throughout this paper, we have been intentionally informal in our presentation, our goal being largely to convey the motivation for, and the intuition behind, the results presented rather than to capture all their technical subtleties. No background in temporal logic is required of the reader; however, some knowledge of elementary classical mathematical logic, computational complexity, automata theory, and familiarity with the issues involved in reasoning about the correctness of parallel programs would be helpful.

2 Branching Time Logics: Syntax and Semantics

While several systems of branching time temporal logic of differing complexity and expressive power have been developed, most of them are subsumed by the temporal logic CTL* ([EH83], [CES83]). (The *CTL* in CTL* is an acronym for *Computation Tree Logic*. CTL is one of the precursors of CTL*, cf. [EC82], [EH82].) Hence, we shall formally define the syntax and the semantics of CTL*, and then informally indicate the appropriate restrictions to its syntax to define the other systems of branching time temporal logic. We also explore alternative definitions of CTL* to give a flavour of the variations possible in the choice of modalities when defining a temporal logic, and in the structures over which its formulae could be interpreted. We begin, however, with an informal overview of branching time temporal logic, motivated by its applications to reasoning about parallel programs.

2.1 An Informal Overview

As indicated in the introduction, temporal logic provides a formal system for describing the occurrence of events in time. It belongs to the class of modal logics which were originally developed by philosophers to deal with different "modes" of truth. For example, the assertion p may be false under the present circumstances, but the assertion *possibly* p would be true if there exist other circumstances in which p is true. In a system of temporal logic, the modalities are interpreted temporally to describe how the truth values of assertions vary with time. Typical temporal modalities include *sometime* p which is true at the present instant of time if there is a future moment at which p becomes true and *always* q which is true if q is true at all future moments.

A system of temporal logic specifies the *syntax* of legal formulae, and a *semantics* to interpret these formulae. All systems that we consider in this paper are *propositional* in that they augment ordinary propositional logic with temporal connectives to implicitly deal with time. Their semantics is defined over *structures*, which, for most systems of temporal logic, are, essentially, labelled, directed graphs. (These structures closely resemble, and have their roots in, Kripke structures originally proposed for modal logics; see, for example, [Kr63] or [HC72].) Intuitively, the *states* of a structure (vertices of the graphs) denote possible worlds or time instants, and are labelled with a set of atomic propositions that are true at that state. Note, therefore, that time is regarded as being *discrete*, rather than continuous. The edges denote the passage of time: an edge from state s to state t indicates that world t is a possible successor of world s. Thus, each path out of a state denotes a possible future of that state. The system of temporal logic is said to be *linear time* if structures over which formulae are interpreted are (one-way infinite) chains, and *branching time* if structures are arbitrary graphs (subject to the restriction that each state has at least one successor, i.e., every world has at least one future).

Regardless of the specifics of the syntax of a temporal logic system, the truth of a temporal formula is defined at each state of each structure. (We shall see that this is not completely accurate for some branching time logics, as they define the truth of some formulae at states, and others, along paths, but it serves to convey the intuition.) For purely propositional formulae, the truth of a formula at a state is determined by the atomic propositions true at the state. For other formulae, the temporal connectives in a formula relate the truth of the formula at a state to the truth of subformulae at other states; the precise nature of the relation is determined by the definition of the connective. In the systems of temporal logic that we consider, the truth of a formula is invariably determined by truth of subformulae at one or more *successor* states, i.e., by their truth along one or more possible futures.

Since the semantics of most systems of temporal logic is defined over directed graphs, this formalism is particularly well-suited for describing state-based systems whose temporal behaviour is an integral part of the system's functions. Consider, for example, continuously operating concurrent programs. Here, the model of concurrency is the usual one in which parallel execution of the sequential processes $P_1, P_2, \ldots, P_m$ is modelled by the nondeterministic interleaving of atomic steps of the individual processes. A concurrent program starting in a given state may follow any one of a (possibly infinite) number of computation paths (i.e., sequences of execution states) corresponding to the different nondeterministic choices the program might make. The initial state of a computation path represents the present, and subsequent states represent the future. The different computation paths thus represent alternate possible futures: at each moment, time may split into alternate courses and thus has a "branching" tree-like nature. The modalities of a temporal logic can be used to describe correctness properties of a concurrent program in terms of the program's future behaviour. The basic difference between linear and branching time temporal logics is that, while the former consider each execution sequence individually, which intuitively represents the future that the program will actually follow, the latter account for all the computation paths at once. Thus, when properties of a program are expressed in linear temporal logic, there is an implicit universal quantification over all possible futures that could turn out to be the actual future. In contrast, branching time modalities allow explicit quantification over the different possible futures beginning at the initial state. In either case, it is easily observed that there is a natural correspondence between computation paths and trees of parallel programs and linear and branching time structures, which are (respectively) one-way infinite chains and arbitrary directed graphs.

We now examine some of the commonly used temporal modalities, and show how program properties can be cast as temporal logic formulae. We note, first, that branching time logic formulae are classified as being either state formulae (ones true at states of a structure) or path formulae (ones true along an infinite path of the structure). Pure propositional formulae are state formulae. There are two *path modalities*, A and E, which can be prefixed to a path formula p to yield a state formula; intuitively, the state formula $A\,p$ is true at a state if p is true of all paths starting at that state, and $E\,p$ is true at a state if p is true of some path starting at that state. The modalities used to construct path formulae are the usual linear time ones: G (always), F (sometime), X (nexttime), and U (until). $G\,p$ is true of a path if p is true everywhere along the path, $F\,p$ is true of a path if p is true at some point in the path, $X\,p$ is true if p is true at the successor of the initial state of the path, and $p\;U\;q$ is true of a path if q eventually becomes true along the path and p is always true till then.

Some combinations of these modalities are particularly useful to specify program properties. For example, *safety* properties express the fact that a concurrent system is never in an undesirable state. The safety property p is expressible as the *invariance* assertion $AG\,p$, which intuitively says that p is true at all states of a computation tree viewed as a temporal logic structure (Fig. 1(a)). Thus if CS_1 and CS_2 are assertions true of a program state when processes 1 and 2 (respectively) are in their critical regions, the assertion $AG(\neg CS_1 \vee \neg CS_2)$ expresses the mutual exclusion of the two processes (at any time, either process 1 or process 2 is not in its critical region). Similarly *liveness* properties, which say that the system will progress to a desired state, can be expressed using the *inevitability* assertion $AF\,p$, which demarcates a frontier along the computation tree at which p is true (Fig. 1(b)). For example, the absence of starvation of process 1 can be expressed as $(TRY_1 \Rightarrow AF\,CS_1)$, i.e., if process 1 is in its trying region, and, thereby, is currently attempting to enter its critical region, it will eventually do so no matter what computation path is followed. A third useful combination is $EF\,p$, which expresses the *potentiality* of p (Fig. 1(c)). The U operator can be used to specify the relative order of events: e.g., the fact that process 1 must enter its trying region before gaining access to its critical region along all computation paths can be expressed as $A((\neg CS_1)\;U\;TRY_1)$.

There are two other combinations of the linear time operators that are interesting: $FG\,p$ (read more conveniently as "almost everywhere p", and often abbreviated to $\overset{\infty}{G}p$) is true of a path if p is true everywhere along the path except possibly for some finite initial segment of it, and $GF\,p$ ("infinitely often p", abbreviated to $\overset{\infty}{F}p$) is true of a path if p is true at infinitely many moments along the path. These two combinations are useful in expressing *fairness* constraints (cf. [GPSS80], [LPS81], [Pn83], [QS83], [FK84], [Fr86]) on scheduling a family of m processes. Consider, for example, a single computation path, and let $enabled_i$ be true at all moments along the path at which process i is ready for execution, and $executed_i$ be true each time it is actually scheduled for execution. Then the constraint that the computation path is *impartial* or *unconditionally fair* (i.e., each process is executed infinitely often along it) is expressed by $\bigwedge_{i=1}^{m} \overset{\infty}{F} executed_i$, and the fact that it is *just* or *weakly fair* (i.e., each process that clamours for execution persistently is eventually executed) by $\bigwedge_{i=1}^{m}(\overset{\infty}{G}\,enabled_i \Rightarrow \overset{\infty}{F}\,executed_i)$. Finally, *strong fairness* (every process that requests execution infinitely often is executed infinitely often) is expressed by $\bigwedge_{i=1}^{m}(\overset{\infty}{F}\,enabled_i \Rightarrow \overset{\infty}{F}\,executed_i)$.

2.2 A Formal Definition of CTL*

We now define CTL* formally in the "standard" way ([EH83]). CTL* formulae are constructed from a set of atomic propositions P, Q, etc. To define their syntax, we inductively define a class of *state formulae* (true or false of states) and a class of *path formulae* (true or false of paths):

S1. Any atomic proposition P is a state formula.

S2. If p, q are state formulae then so are $p \wedge q$ and $\neg p$.

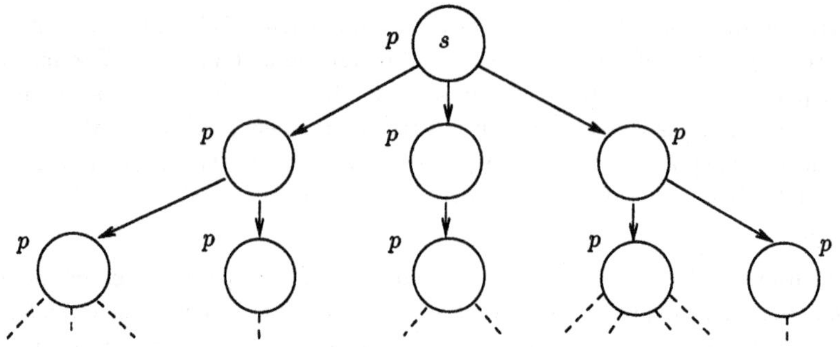

(a) The invariance assertion $AG\,p$ is true at s.

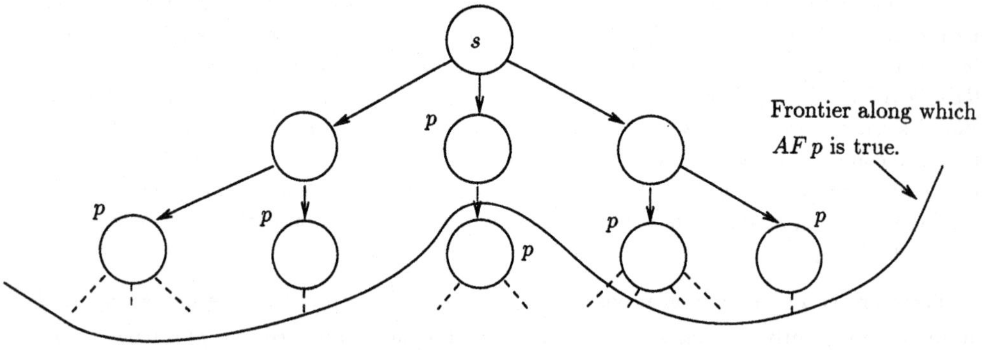

(b) The eventuality assertion $AF\,p$ is true at s.

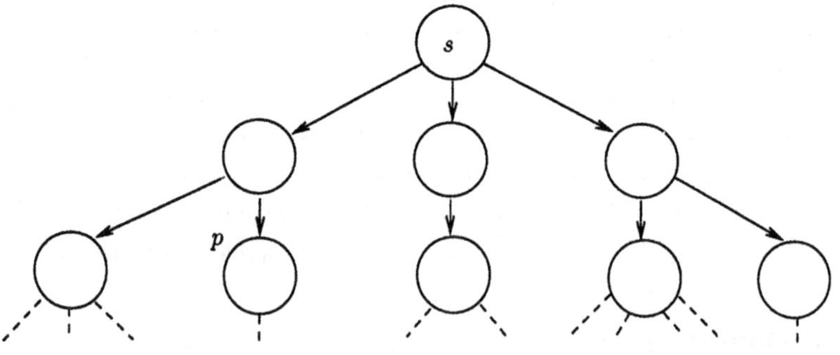

(c) The potentiality assertion $EF\,p$ is true at s.

Figure 1: Computation trees illustrating correctness properties of programs. (The assertion p is false at all states not marked with p.)

S3. If p is a path formula then $E\,p$ is a state formula.

P1. Any state formula p is also a path formula.

P2. If p, q are path formulae then so are $p \wedge q$ and $\neg p$.

P3. If p, q are path formulae then so are $X\,p$ and $(p\,U\,q)$.

The set of state formulae generated by the above rules forms the language CTL*. The other connectives are introduced as abbreviations in the usual way: $p \vee q$ abbreviates $\neg(\neg p \wedge \neg q)$, $p \Rightarrow q$ abbreviates $\neg p \vee q$, $p \equiv q$ abbreviates $(p \Rightarrow q) \wedge (q \Rightarrow p)$, $A\,p$ abbreviates $\neg E \neg p$, $F\,p$ abbreviates $true\,U\,p$, and $G\,p$ abbreviates $\neg F \neg p$. Also, the operators $\overset{\infty}{F}$ and $\overset{\infty}{G}$ are used as abbreviations for GF and FG respectively.

We define the semantics of a CTL* formula with respect to a structure $M = (S, R, L)$, where S is a non-empty set of *states*, R is a binary relation on S that is total (so each state has at least one successor), and L is a *labelling* which assigns to each state a set of atomic propositions, those intended to be true at that state. A *fullpath* $x = s_0, s_1, s_2, \ldots$ in M is an infinite sequence of states such that $(s_i, s_{i+1}) \in R$ for each i. We write $M, s \models p$ ($M, x \models p$) to mean that the state formula p (path formula p) is true in structure M at state s (of path x, respectively). When M is understood, we write simply $s \models p$ ($x \models p$). We define $\models$ inductively for an arbitrary state s and fullpath $x = s_0, s_1, s_2, \ldots$, using the convention that x^i denotes the suffix (full)path $s_i, s_{i+1}, s_{i+2}, \ldots$:

S1. $s \models P$ iff $P \in L(s)$ for any atomic proposition P.

S2. $s \models p \wedge q$ iff $s \models p$ and $s \models q$.
$s \models \neg p$ iff it is not the case that $s \models p$.

S3. $s \models E\,p$ iff for some fullpath y starting at s, $y \models p$.

P1. $x \models p$ iff $s_0 \models p$ for any state formula p.

P2. $x \models p \wedge q$ iff $x \models p$ and $x \models q$.
$x \models \neg p$ iff it is not the case that $x \models p$.

P3. $x \models X\,p$ iff $x^1 \models p$.
$x \models (p\,U\,q)$ iff $\exists\, i \geq 0$ such that $x^i \models q$ and $\forall\, j,\ 0 \leq j < i,\ x^j \models p$.

The modalities defined as abbreviations have the expected meaning as a consequence of the above definition. Specifically, $A\,p$ is true at a state s if p is true along all paths emanating from s, $F\,p$ (respectively, $G\,p$) is true of a path x if p is true of some (respectively, all) suffix fullpath(s) x^i, $i \geq 0$, and $\overset{\infty}{F}p$ (respectively, $\overset{\infty}{G}p$) is true of a fullpath x if p is true of infinitely many (respectively, all but a finite number of) suffix fullpaths x^i, $i \geq 0$. Note that in the latter two cases, if p is also a state formula, saying that p is true of a suffix fullpath x^i is equivalent to saying that it is true at state s_i.

As an aside, note that there are several other equivalent ways of defining the labelling of a structure. One obvious variant, for example, is to define it as a mapping from the set of atomic propositions to the powerset of the set of states.

We say that the state formula p is *valid*, and write $\models p$, if for every structure M and every state s in M, $M, s \models p$. We say that the state formula p is *satisfiable* if for some structure M and some state s in M, $M, s \models p$. In this case we also say that M is a *model* of p. We define validity and satisfiability similarly for path formulae. Note that a formula p is valid iff $\neg p$ is not satisfiable.

Example. All (substitution instances of) tautologies of ordinary propositional logic are valid. (A *substitution instance* of a tautology is any formula of a temporal logic that is inductively derived from a tautology by uniformly replacing all occurrences of an atomic proposition by any state formula. In the sequel, we shall use the term *tautology* to refer to all such substitution instances as well.) An example of a valid formula with temporal modalities is: $E(p\,U\,q) \Rightarrow EF\,q$. Some validities that we shall have occasion to use in this paper are:

1. $E(p \vee q) \equiv E\,p \vee E\,q$
2. $A(p \wedge q) \equiv A\,p \wedge A\,q$
3. $EG\,p \equiv p \wedge EXEG\,p$
4. $AG\,p \equiv p \wedge AXAG\,p$
5. $EF\,p \equiv p \vee EXEF\,p$
6. $AF\,p \equiv p \vee AXAF\,p$
7. $E(p\,U\,q) \equiv q \vee (p \wedge EXE(p\,U\,q))$
8. $A(p\,U\,q) \equiv q \vee (p \wedge AXA(p\,U\,q))$

The validities 3–8 above are examples of *fixpoint* characterizations of the branching time modalities that occur on the left of the equivalence. They can be informally verified by a close examination of the semantics of these modalities. For example, $EG\,p$ specifies the existence of a computation path along which p is always true; hence p must be true at the first state of the path, and $EG\,p$ true at the second, i.e., $EXEG\,p$ is also true at the first state of the path. Conversely, if both p and $EXEG\,p$ are true at a state, there is a fullpath starting at that state along which $EG\,p$ is true. Such fixpoint characterizations can be formally derived using the relation between branching time logics as presented here and *fixpoint* logics, for example, the propositional μ-calculus ([Ko82]).

A trivial example of a formula that is satisfiable, but not valid, is $P \wedge EX\,Q$, where P and Q are atomic propositions. A model for it is $M = (\{s\}, \{(s,s)\}, L)$, where $L(s) = \{P, Q\}$; the formula is true at the only state, s, of M. An example of an unsatisfiable formula is $\neg p \wedge AG\,p$. Note that its negation $(p \vee EF\neg p)$ is valid because $p \vee \neg p$ is a tautology (and, hence, valid) and $\neg p \Rightarrow EF\neg p$ is easily seen to be valid by inspecting the relevant definitions. □

We close this subsection with a definition of several related syntactic notions that we shall use in the sequel. First, a *pure path formula* is constructed by repeated applications of rules P2 and P3, using the rule

P0. Any atomic proposition P is a path formula.

as the basis. As usual, the modalities F, G, $\overset{\infty}{F}$, and $\overset{\infty}{G}$ may also appear in path formulae as they can be expressed in terms of X and U. Intuitively, pure path formulae have no path modalities (A or E); in fact, they are the formulae of the standard linear temporal logic ([Pn77], [GPSS80]). (Recall that as linear time formulae are typically interpreted over one-way infinite chains, there is only one fullpath stemming from each state, and so each fullpath can be naturally associated with a unique state. Hence a linear time temporal logic does not distinguish between state and path formulae.)

Similarly, a *pure propositional formula* is one with no temporal modalities; it is obtained by inductively applying the rules P0 and P2. Finally a pure path formula is said to be a *restricted path formula* if it meets both the following conditions: (a) The argument of each linear modality appearing in it is a pure propositional formula, and (b) Every instance of each atomic proposition in it appears within the scope of a temporal modality. Essentially, the first rule prevents nesting of the linear temporal modalities in the formula, and the second rule ensures that the formula is a boolean combination of subformulae, all of which are prefixed by some temporal connective. Thus, if P and Q are atomic propositions, $(F\,P)\,U\,Q$ and $P \wedge F\,Q$ are not restricted path formulae, while the formula $\neg((P \wedge\ Q)\ U\ (P \Rightarrow\ Q)) \wedge (X\,P \vee F(P \equiv Q))$ is an example of a restricted path formula.

2.3 Variations on the Definition of CTL*

In this subsection, we consider various modifications to the syntax or the semantics of the standard definition of CTL*. In general, all other branching time temporal logics that we define subsequently can be similarly modified. The variations that we consider here are primarily of two kinds: the first chooses a different set of temporal modalities, and the second, different kinds of structures to interpret formulae over.

2.3.1 Other Modalities

In the standard definition of CTL*, we have considered only *future* temporal operators that are also *reflexive*. A reflexive temporal operator is one that includes the present in the future. For example, assuming, for convenience of exposition, that p is a state formula, $F\,p$ holds along a fullpath x even if p is true at the first state of x. Clearly, an analogous operator F^+p, which requires p to hold strictly in the future, can be defined: it holds along the fullpath $x = s_0, s_1, s_2, \ldots$ iff p is true at a state s_i, $i \geq 1$. It is readily observed that both $F\,p$ and F^+p can be expressed in terms of each other: F^+p is true of a path iff $XF\,p$ is true of that path and $F\,p$ is true of a path iff $p \vee F^+p$ is true of it. Strict versions of other modalities (like G^+ and U^+) could also be adopted as the primitive operators instead of the reflexive versions.

A related notion is that of defining the *weak until* operator, U_w, instead of the strong until one, U, defined above. $p\ U_w\,q$ is true of a path either if $p\ U\ q$ is true of that path or if p holds throughout that path, i.e., $G\,p$ is true of it. Clearly, therefore, U_w can be expressed in terms of U; to express U in terms of U_w, note that $p\ U\ q$ is true of a path if both $p\ U_w\,q$ and $F\,q$ are true of it.

A *future* temporal operator is one which defines the truth of a formula in terms of the truth of subformulae at successor states. Analogues of X, F, G and U that define the truth of a formula along a fullpath in terms of the truth of subformulae at *predecessor* states on that path can as well be defined. Note that for such a definition to be feasible, one considers not just fullpaths starting at a state, but also ones that go through the state, or, alternatively, one defines the truth of a formula at each instant of time along a path. We do not give details of the definition of past temporal operators here mainly because this issue concerns primarily the linear time operators, and any reasonable definition can be carried over to branching time temporal logics.

Finally, we can add other path modalities to a branching time temporal logic. Two such that we shall find useful are A_ϕ and E_ϕ, where ϕ is a pure path formula. Typically, ϕ would specify a fairness constraint of the kinds discussed in Section 2.1. The path modalities E_ϕ and A_ϕ consider only those paths that satisfy ϕ, and, could be read as "for some (respectively, 'for all') path(s) that satisfy the constraint ϕ". Formally, $A_\phi\,p$ may be viewed as abbreviating the CTL* formula $A(\phi \Rightarrow p)$ and $E_\phi\,p$ as abbreviating $E(\phi \wedge p)$. Note that, as with A and E, A_ϕ and E_ϕ are duals of each other: $A_\phi p \equiv \neg E_\phi \neg p$. We shall explore these path modalities in more detail in the next subsection.

2.3.2 An Alternative Definition of the Semantics of CTL*

We now detail a more general semantics for the logic CTL*, which is, in fact, the one originally proposed in [EH83]. We shall also explain the reasons for choosing our more restrictive interpretation as the standard semantics.

The modified semantics is defined over a structure $M = (S, X, L)$, where S and L are as before (a set of states and a labelling from S to the set of atomic propositions respectively), and X is a set of paths (a *path* being any non-empty sequence of states). In essence, the set of paths in X replaces the set of fullpaths of the original interpretation. Thus, x is now an arbitrary path in X, and the phrase "for some fullpath y" in rule S3 is replaced by "for some path $y \in X$". Rules S1, S2, P1, and P2 remain unchanged. However, as the paths in X need not be infinite, rule P3 needs to be reformulated to:

P3′. $x \models X\,p$ iff $|x| \geq 1$ and $x^1 \models p$.
$x \models (p\ U\ q)$ iff $\exists i \geq 0$ such that $x^i \models q$ and $\forall j, 0 \leq j < i, x^j \models p$.

In the first clause, $|x|$ is the length of (one less than the number of states in) the path x. Note that the second clause is unchanged from the earlier interpretation.

Clearly, the modified semantics is more general than the original one: instead of interpreting a formula over the structure $M = (S, R, L)$, it can be interpreted over the modified structure $M' = (S, X, L)$, where X is the set of all fullpaths generated by the relation R on $S \times S$. Structures of this kind are called *R-generable* ones (note that R must be a *total* binary relation on the set of states), and the set of paths they generate have some pleasing properties that are naturally satisfied by many applications (e.g., the execution sequences of concurrent programs).

Specifically, it was shown in [Em83], that the set of paths generated by R-generable structures is:

1. *Suffix closed*, i.e., if $x = s_0, s_1, s_2 \ldots$ is in the set, so is x^1,
2. *Fusion closed*, i.e., if $x_1 s y_1$ and $x_2 s y_2$ are in the set (where x_1 and x_2 denote finite sequences of states, y_1 and y_2, infinite ones, s denotes a single state, and juxtaposition denotes the concatenation operator), then so is $x_1 s y_2$, and
3. *Limit closed*, i.e., if all the paths in the infinite sequence $\langle x_0 y_0,\ x_0 x_1 y_1,\ x_0 x_1 x_2 y_2, \ldots \rangle$ (where, as before, the x_i denote finite sequences of states, and the y_i denote infinite ones) are in the set, then the infinite path $x_0 x_1 x_2 \ldots$ is also in the set.

Conversely, any set of paths satisfying all these three properties is R-generable. It is readily observed that the set of *all* execution traces (and not just the ones that start at an initial state) of concurrent programs enjoys all these properties. In particular, fusion closure follows from the fact that the state (s) of a program completely determines all its possible future behaviours (y_1 and y_2) independent of the past history (x_1 or x_2), and limit closure formalizes the intuition that if a program can follow a computation path arbitrarily far, then it can follow it forever. This explains why R-generable structures are an apt choice for the definition of the standard semantics.

It is worthwhile pointing out that the set of fair, say, impartial, execution sequences of a concurrent program does *not* satisfy the the limit closure property. For though some process, say process 1, could be picked for execution consecutively arbitrarily many times along a fair computation path, the execution sequence in which only process 1 is executed is unfair. Thus, while R-generable structures are appropriate to reason about concurrent programs under pure nondeterministic scheduling, it might appear that programs operating under fair schedules should be modelled by some other kinds of structures. However, fairness can yet be naturally incorporated into R-generable structures using the path modalities A_ϕ and E_ϕ (where ϕ in this case is the appropriate fairness constraint), which restrict consideration to just the fair fullpaths in a structure. This approach was advocated in [Em83], and formalized in the temporal logic FCTL (Fair CTL) in [EL85]. We shall return to FCTL in the next subsection.

We conclude this subsection by remarking that the logic of time and chance, TC, a probabilistic temporal logic, introduced in [LS82] has a syntax that is essentially identical to the syntax of CTL* except that the modalities A (which is denoted by ∇ instead) and E (denoted by Δ) are interpreted differently: ∇p means that p is true for a set of paths of measure 1, i.e., it is almost certainly true, and Δp, that p holds for a set of paths of (some) positive measure. Thus, the semantics of two systems of temporal logic could be quite different even if their syntax is similar, and its choice is largely influenced by targeted applications of the temporal logic. (TC is intended to reason about probabilistic concurrent programs.)

2.3.3 Multi-Process Structures

One obvious way of extending the syntax of CTL* is by allowing the underlying language to have a set of *atomic arc assertions* in addition to (and disjoint from) the set of atomic propositions. Each atomic arc assertion is a primitive path formula in much the same way as each atomic proposition is a primitive state formula, and can be used to construct other formulae. Such an extended version of CTL* is interpreted with respect to an extended structure $M = (S, R, L, L_a)$, where S, R and L are defined as in Section 2.2, and L_a is a mapping from the set of atomic arc assertions to the powerset of the set R. The semantics of the arc assertions is given by the additional rule:

PO′. $x \models B$ iff $(s_0, s_1) \in L_a(B)$ for any atomic arc assertion B.

where, as before, $x = s_0, s_1, s_2 \ldots$ is an arbitrary fullpath in M.

An especially useful structure is obtained by considering a restricted class of extended structures: ones which have a finite set of atomic arc assertions and the union of whose images under the function L_a is exactly R. For convenience, let the arc assertions be denoted by $B_1, B_2, \ldots, B_m$. In such a case, the extended structure, $M = (S, R, L, L_a)$ could be equivalently described by the so called *multi-process structure* $M' = (S, \mathcal{R}, L)$, where $\mathcal{R}$ is a finite family $\{R_1, R_2, \ldots, R_m\}$ of binary relations such that $R_i = L_a(B_i)$. Note that $\bigcup_{i=1}^m R_i = \bigcup_{i=1}^m L_a(B_i) = R$, and, hence, the union of the family of relations is a total binary relation. Thus, the only difference between M and M' is that the set of arcs along which each arc assertion is true is specified separately (as the relations R_i) in M' rather than collectively (as the function L_a) in M.

Multi-process structures have been used to model concurrent programs with a fixed number of processes; as might be expected, R_i represents the transition relation of the ith process in this case, and S, the set of global program states. The atomic arc assertion B_i is true along all arcs which correspond to the state transitions (execution) of the ith process. In fact, we have used such arc assertions in Section 2.1 (we called them *executed*$_i$ then) to specify fairness constraints on scheduling a family of processes. (The predicates *enabled*$_i$ used there, on the other hand, are ordinary atomic propositions, true of states.) Multi-process structures have been used extensively to specify concurrent programs in a modular fashion, and, thereby, to automate the tasks of program synthesis and verification (see, for example, [EC82], [CG87], and [AE89]). It should also be noted that interpreting CTL* (and other branching time temporal logics) over multi-process structures provides a method of specifying assertions of individual programs separately, and, in that sense, these logics may be considered exogenous; however, they still differ from dynamic logics in that they do not provide operators to compose program units.

2.4 A Menagerie of Branching Time Logics

We now informally summarize the syntax of various branching time temporal logics that have appeared in the literature. As mentioned earlier, CTL* subsumes all of them, and, therefore, the semantics of the formulae of these systems is inherited from CTL*. Several of these logics are interesting in their own right for their curtailed expressiveness often suffices to specify temporal systems and permits more efficient decision procedures in the bargain as we shall see in a subsequent section.

Probably the branching time temporal logic most commonly used for reasoning about concurrent programs is CTL (Computation Tree Logic, cf. [EC82], [EH82]). Like CTL*, CTL comprises a set of state formulae. However, each occurrence of a path modality (A or E) in a CTL formula must be followed by precisely one instance of one of the linear time temporal modalities F, G, X or U. Thus, the set of CTL formulae is the maximal one generated by the rules S1 and S2 in Section 2.2 together with:

S3′. If p, q are formulae then so are $A(p\ U\ q)$, $E(p\ U\ q)$, $EX\ p$, and $AX\ p$.

(As before, the modalities AF and EF, and their duals, EG and AG, are viewed as abbreviations.) Examples of CTL formulae include $EGEX\ p$, which says that every state along a path has a successor state at which p is true, and $AG(TRY_1 \Rightarrow AF\ CS_1)$, which expresses the property that process 1 will always eventually enter its critical region every time it attempts to do so by transiting to its trying region (as in Section 2.1, CS_1 and TRY_1 are true at states when process 1 is in its critical and trying regions respectively).

Note that the definition above specifies CTL formulae without mention of path formulae. However, in order to extend CTL to include atomic arc assertions (as we did CTL* in Section 2.3.3), it is easiest to inductively define a class of path formulae together with the set of state formulae. This can be done in a manner similar to the definition of the syntax of CTL* formulae, and we shall assume such an extended definition for purposes of the examples that follow.

We now give some examples of CTL* formulae that are not CTL formulae. Among these are $f_0 = E((p\ U\ q) \vee G\,p)$, which expresses the weak until property along a fullpath, and $f_1 = E\overset{\infty}{G}\ executed_1$, which describes an unfair computation path along which, after a certain point in time, only process 1 is scheduled for execution. Similarly, the condition that all execution sequences of a family of m processes be impartial, given by $f_2 = A(\bigwedge_{i=1}^{m} \overset{\infty}{F} executed_i)$, is not a CTL formula. It is easily observed, however, that f_0 is formally equivalent to $E(p\ U\ q) \vee EG\,p$, which is a CTL formula.

CTL requires that each path quantifier be followed by a single linear time connective. Intuitively, CTL should be extendible to a logic that allows a restricted path formula to follow each occurrence of a path quantifier. This is what motivates the definition of CTL$^+$, a branching time temporal logic closely related to CTL. Loosely, CTL$^+$ differs from CTL in that it allows a path modality to be followed by a boolean combination of the linear time modalities F, G, X, and U in such a manner that nesting of these modalities is not permitted. The reader is referred to [EH82] for the rules that *generate* a CTL$^+$ formula; here, we offer the following technique for *recognizing* whether a formula is one belonging to CTL$^+$. To determine if f is a CTL$^+$ formula, for each subformula f_s that's the argument of some instance of a path quantifier occurring in f (i.e., for any subformula of f of the form $A\,f_s$ or $E\,f_s$), replace all subformulae of f_s whose main connective is a path quantifier by an arbitrary atomic proposition. The resulting formula must be a restricted path formula in which the only modalities that appear are one of F, G, X, and U. Thus f_0 is a CTL$^+$ formula, as are all CTL formulae. Note, that CTL$^+$ does not allow the linear time modalities following a path modality to be nested directly without an "intervening" path quantifier, nor does it permit $\overset{\infty}{F}$ and $\overset{\infty}{G}$ as linear time connectives; hence, f_1 and f_2 are not CTL$^+$ formulae.

One limitation of CTL and CTL$^+$ is that they do not allow the expression of fairness properties of programs. We could offer f_2 as an illustration of this claim; in reality, however, as the astute reader would have observed, there is a CTL formula equivalent to f_2, a point we shall dwell on in the next section. We shall also see there that there is no CTL formula equivalent to the constraint that requires that all schedules of a concurrent program satisfy *strong eventual fairness* (cf. [La80]) of, say, process 1 (i.e., if process 1 infinitely often demands to be executed, it should eventually be executed): $f_3 = A(\overset{\infty}{F}\,enabled_1 \Rightarrow F\,executed_1)$.

Two alternative extensions to CTL have been proposed to deal with fairness. First, the logic ECTL (Extended CTL) requires each path quantifier (A or E) occurring in its formulae to prefix a single instance of a linear time operator chosen from F, G, X, U, $\overset{\infty}{F}$, and $\overset{\infty}{G}$. Thus f_1 is an ECTL formulae, but none of f_0, f_2 or f_3 is. (f_0 illustrates the point that it is not immediately apparent that ECTL subsumes CTL$^+$ in expressiveness; it certainly does not do so syntactically.) It is easily seen, however, that $f_4 = \bigwedge_{i=1}^{m} A\overset{\infty}{F}\,executed_i$, is formally equivalent to f_2, and, clearly, f_4 is an ECTL formula.

Analogous to the extension of CTL to CTL$^+$, ECTL can be extended to ECTL$^+$. ECTL$^+$ is essentially the language studied in [EC80] and [Em81]. The method outlined above to recognize a CTL$^+$ formula could as well be applied to recognizing ECTL$^+$ formulae; in this case, the restricted path formulae may have the linear time modalities $\overset{\infty}{F}$ and $\overset{\infty}{G}$ in addition to F, G, X, and U. Hence, all of f_0, f_1, f_2, and f_3 are ECTL$^+$ formulae; note that ECTL$^+$ syntactically subsumes both ECTL and CTL$^+$. The formulae $f_5 = A((G\,request\_pending)\,U\,grant)$, which intuitively expresses the fact that, along all computation paths, a request (to a resource controller, say) always remains pending until it is granted, and $f_6 = EA\,p$ are examples of CTL* formulae that are not ECTL$^+$ formulae. In particular, f_5 illustrates that, of all the languages defined thus far, only CTL* allows a linear time modality to be directly nested in another without an "intervening" path modality, and f_6 exemplifies the fact that only CTL* permits two path quantifiers to be syntactically juxtaposed.

A second way of dealing with fairness properties of programs is embodied in the logic FCTL (Fair CTL) formulated in [EL85]. Instead of adding linear time temporal modalities to CTL as ECTL does, FCTL replaces CTL's path quantifiers with the path modalities A_ϕ and E_ϕ (discussed in Section 2.3.1) where ϕ is a *fairness constraint*, which (syntactically) is a restricted path formula in which the only linear temporal modalities that may appear are $\overset{\infty}{F}$ and $\overset{\infty}{G}$. Thus FCTL relativizes its path quantifiers to an underlying fairness constraint, and is designed to reason expressly about fair schedules of programs.

A related approach is presented in [CVW86]. Instead of defining new path quantifiers interpreted over the standard structures of branching time temporal logic, the structures over which CTL and CTL* are interpreted in [CVW86] are restricted to what are called the *fair structures*, which, in addition to the usual branching time structure, essentially specify a set of fair paths, but in a considerably more succinct fashion than explicitly listing all of them (as was done by the set X

in Section 2.3.2). The semantics is then the usual one except that only fair paths are considered in interpreting the path modalities. It is easily seen that the specified set of fair paths corresponds to the FCTL fairness constraint ϕ. Conversely, the CTL* rendition of FCTL formulae (Section 2.3.1) is essentially interpreted over fair structures.

The philosophy underlying this second approach to fairness (vis-à-vis using ECTL or CTL*) is that the temporal logic assertions (i.e., the syntactic part of the mathematical model) should be freely used to specify correctness properties of *only* the temporal systems they describe as opposed to properties of their implementation (of which fairness is one example). An appropriate way to account for the latter is to automatically incorporate them in the semantic portion of the mathematical framework that models the temporal systems. An unconstrained semantics could err by allowing the expression of properties unnecessary to specify the temporal systems.

We now mention some branching time systems subsumed by CTL. The logic UB (the Unified system of Branching time) was defined by Ben-Ari, Manna, and Pnueli [BMP81]. UB is just like CTL except that it does not have the modality U; thus, it has the basic modalities EF, EX, and EG (and their duals AG, AX, and AF) and consists of formulae in which each occurrence of a path quantifier (A or E) is followed by one instance of one of the linear time operators F, G, or X. UB thus allows the expression of such assertions as the *inevitability* of the property p, $AF\,p$, the *invariance* of p, $AG\,p$, and the *potentiality* of p, $EF\,p$. It does not, however, allow precedence properties like $A(p\;U\;q)$ to be expressed. The logic UB$^+$ extends UB in the same manner as CTL$^+$ extends CTL, and, as before, the above technique may be used to recognize UB$^+$ formulae; only, now, the restricted path formula may have only one of F, G or X as its linear time modalities. Thus, we can make assertions such as $E(Fp \wedge G\,q)$, i.e., there is a state on some computation path at which p holds, and q holds at all states on that path, in UB$^+$. Again, note that it is not immediately apparent that CTL subsumes UB$^+$ as some formulae of the latter are not (syntactically) CTL formulae. Finally, the logic UB$^-$ is a restriction of UB where we have only the modalities $EF\,p$ and $EX\,p$ (and their duals $AG\,p$ and $AX\,p$), i.e., each occurrence of E in a formula must be followed by one of F or X, and each instance of A, by one of G or X. It corresponds to the Nexttime system of [MP79]. UB$^-$ thus permits the potentiality and the invariance of p to be expressed.

The similarity in the definitions of CTL, ECTL, and UB motivates the following notation (cf. [EH83]): B(H_1, H_2, ..., H_k), where each H_i is a linear time modality, denotes the system of logic whose formulae are all state formulae in which each instance of a path modality (A or E) is followed by precisely one of the linear time modalities H_1, H_2, ..., H_k. Thus, B(X, U) denotes CTL. Note that F and G can be defined in terms of X and U without nesting linear time modalities, while $\overset{\infty}{F}$ and $\overset{\infty}{G}$ cannot; hence B(X, U) is the same as the logic B(F, G, X, U), but it is different from B(F, G, X, U, $\overset{\infty}{F}$, $\overset{\infty}{G}$). In fact, the latter is precisely ECTL and is more succinctly denoted by B(X, U, $\overset{\infty}{F}$). Similarly, B(F, X) denotes UB. Also, the system of logic B(H_1, H_2, ..., H_k)$^+$ is denoted by B(H_1, H_2, ..., H_k, $\wedge$, $\neg$), the $\wedge$ and $\neg$ serving as mnemonics for the fact that the restricted path formulae that may follow a path quantifier are obtained by boolean combinations of linear time path formulae with no nested modalities.

Finally, as alluded to in the introduction, every linear time temporal logic can also be thought of as a branching time one. Though most linear time temporal logics are formally defined only over one-way infinite chains, their semantics is easily extended to arbitrary directed graphs; this is done by defining the truth of a formula along each fullpath in much the same was as the truth of the path formulae generated by the rules P1–P3 is done in Section 2.2. Since a branching time logic generally has only state formulae, and linear time formulae are all path formulae, we associate with the linear time formula p, the branching time logic formula $A\,p$. The choice of A

(rather than E) as the prefix is because, in practical applications of linear time logics to reasoning about programs, this is the intuitive meaning assumed by linear time formulae: an assertion is true if it is holds along *all* execution sequences rather than some one. Thus, $A(Fp \vee FGX\,q)$ is a legitimate branching time formula corresponding to the linear time formula $Fp \vee FGX\,q$, but $EF\,p$ and $AGAF\,p$ are not (in the latter case because $GAF\,p$ is not a pure path formula). We use the notation B(L(H_1, H_2, ..., H_k)) to denote the branching time logic corresponding to the linear time one whose modalities are H_1, H_2, ..., H_k; note that, unlike B(H_1, H_2, ..., H_k) and B(H_1, H_2, ..., $H_k, \wedge, \neg$), B(L(H_1, H_2, ..., H_k)) does not restrict nesting of linear time modalities. Thus B(L(X, U)) is the branching time logic corresponding to the standard linear time temporal logic ([Pn77], [GPSS80]); this is the same as B(L(F, G, X, U, $\overset{\infty}{F}$, $\overset{\infty}{G}$)) because F, G, $\overset{\infty}{F}$, and $\overset{\infty}{G}$ can be defined in terms of X and U since the nesting of linear modalities is allowed.

3 Expressiveness of Branching Time Logics

The expressiveness of a temporal logic is one of two key criteria in evaluating it for potential applications. The question of expressive power specialized to concurrent programs, for example, is: What correctness properties of programs can and cannot be expressed in a given temporal logic with the modalities supplied by the logic? Note that it is often not immediately apparent whether a specific property is expressible in a particular temporal logic. As a trivial example, consider the weak until property: the formula f_0 of Section 2.4 is not a CTL formula, but there is an equivalent CTL formula that specifies the same property. For a less obvious example, the requirement that all schedules of a program with m processes be impartial is expressed by the ECTL formula $f = \bigwedge_{i=1}^{m} A\overset{\infty}{F}\,executed_i$ (the formula f_4 in Section 2.4). A little reflection shows that $A\overset{\infty}{F}\,p$ is equivalent to the CTL formula $AGAF\,p$ (and that its dual, $E\overset{\infty}{G}\,p$, to $EFEG\,p$); hence, the property that all schedules be impartial is expressed by the CTL formula $\bigwedge_{i=1}^{m} AGAF\,executed_i$. The property that at least *one* schedule be impartial, $E(\bigwedge_{i=1}^{m} \overset{\infty}{F}\,executed_i)$, however, cannot be expressed even in ECTL; in particular, note that the modalities $E\overset{\infty}{F}$, and its dual, $A\overset{\infty}{G}$, have no equivalents in CTL.

If two systems of temporal logic do have the same expressive power, the related question of *succinctness* of expression assumes importance. For, while both systems may be able to express the same properties, the formulae that specify them in the one may be considerably (say, exponentially) larger than assertions for those properties in the other; thus, one may prefer the system that is more economical in expression. Another facet of expressiveness, and one that is in general not subject to quantitative evaluation, is how *naturally* a set of properties relevant to describing a temporal system can be expressed in a temporal logic; again, a logic that allows only a contrived method of stating important temporal properties may be discarded in favour of one that permits more natural or elegant expression.

Motivated by the analogous problem in ordinary propositional logic, Kamp ([Ka68]) set out to determine a minimal set of independent linear temporal modalities in terms of which all other modalities were expressible. He showed that the strong, strict (irreflexive) *until*, and its past analogue, the strong, strict *since*, sufficed, and that the *nexttime* and *sometime* modalities were inadequate to express the (either the strict or the reflexive) *until*. Moreover, he demonstrated that linear temporal logic is equivalent in expressiveness to the (then) more widely studied formalism of first-order logic with arbitrary monadic (i.e., unary) predicates and the binary relation < (less than), known as the first-order logic of linear order. This problem was further explored in [GPSS80].

These pioneering works in this area have led to the investigation of similar problems for branching time temporal logics. In the following subsection, we shall summarize the results comparing the expressive power of the systems of branching time temporal logic introduced in Section 2.4. Then, we shall attempt to relate branching time temporal logic with other formalisms. Candidate formalisms with which such a relation could be formulated on account of the similarity in the objects they model include SnS, the monadic second-order theory of n successors, and languages accepted by finite-state automata on infinite trees. Finally, we shall explore the relation in expressiveness between branching and linear time temporal logics, and comment on the adequacy of each in being able to reason about the correctness of concurrent programs, which, historically, was an issue that caused CTL* to be formulated.

Before that, however, we should formulate precisely what is meant by saying that one system of logic (or one formalism) is as expressive as another. To provide a basis for comparison, it is clearly necessary that the class of mathematical objects being described by the formalisms (in the case of logics, the structures over which they are interpreted) be the same as it is the properties of these objects that are expressed in the formalisms being compared. Intuitively, to say that one formalism subsumes another in expressiveness is tantamount to saying that every property of these objects that can be captured by the less powerful formalism can also be expressed in the other. Hence, the following technical definition (cf. [GPSS80], [EH83]): Consider the systems of logics $\mathcal{T}_1$ and $\mathcal{T}_2$ whose formulae are interpreted over the same class, $\mathcal{C}$, of structures. We say that $\mathcal{T}_2$ *is at least as expressive as* $\mathcal{T}_1$, denoted by $\mathcal{T}_1 \leq^{\mathcal{C}} \mathcal{T}_2$, iff for each formula f of $\mathcal{T}_1$, there is a formula g in $\mathcal{T}_2$ such that, for all structures M in $\mathcal{C}$, f is true at precisely those states of M at which g is true. Also, $\mathcal{T}_1$ *is exactly as expressive as* $\mathcal{T}_2$, denoted by $\mathcal{T}_1 \equiv^{\mathcal{C}} \mathcal{T}_2$, iff each of $\mathcal{T}_1$ and $\mathcal{T}_2$ is at least as expressive as the other. Finally, $\mathcal{T}_1$ *is strictly less expressive than* $\mathcal{T}_2$, denoted by $\mathcal{T}_1 <^{\mathcal{C}} \mathcal{T}_2$, iff $\mathcal{T}_1 \leq^{\mathcal{C}} \mathcal{T}_2$ and it is not the case that $\mathcal{T}_2 \leq^{\mathcal{C}} \mathcal{T}_1$, i.e., there is a formula of $\mathcal{T}_2$ which is not equivalent (over the structures in $\mathcal{C}$) to any formula of $\mathcal{T}_1$. Note that these definitions that relate the expressiveness of $\mathcal{T}_1$ and $\mathcal{T}_2$ employ one notion of equivalence of formulae over structures. Other notions have also been used, yielding different definitions of expressiveness (cf. [La80]).

In the sequel, we omit explicit mention of the class $\mathcal{C}$ of structures as this will be apparent from context: in most cases, it will merely be the class of structures over which branching time temporal logics are interpreted, viz., the R-generable ones. Hence, we shall use the symbols $\leq$, $\equiv$, and $<$ instead of $\leq^{\mathcal{C}}$, $\equiv^{\mathcal{C}}$, and $<^{\mathcal{C}}$.

3.1 A Comparison of the Expressive Power of Several Branching Time Logics

We now relate the expressiveness of the various systems of temporal logic introduced in Section 2.4. (Note that all the systems of logic being compared are uniformly interpreted over the same class of structures, thus permitting such a comparison.) As has been hinted at in that subsection, the relation in the expressive power among these systems is:

$$\mathrm{UB}^- < \mathrm{UB} < \mathrm{UB}^+ < \mathrm{CTL} \equiv \mathrm{CTL}^+ < \mathrm{ECTL} < \mathrm{ECTL}^+ < \mathrm{CTL}^*$$

The relations $\mathrm{UB}^- \leq \mathrm{UB} \leq \mathrm{UB}^+$, $\mathrm{CTL} \leq \mathrm{CTL}^+$, and $\mathrm{ECTL} \leq \mathrm{ECTL}^+ \leq \mathrm{CTL}^*$ follow from the definition of the syntax of these temporal logics. The equivalence of CTL and CTL$^+$ together with the syntactic containment of UB$^+$ in CTL$^+$ establishes that $\mathrm{UB}^+ \leq \mathrm{CTL}$. Similarly, $\mathrm{CTL}^+ \leq \mathrm{ECTL}$.

The relation in expressiveness of the temporal logics UB$^-$ through CTL$^+$ is established in [EH82], and that of the systems CTL$^+$ through CTL*, in [EH83]. We list typical formulae that illustrate the strict containment in expressiveness of these systems (P and Q denote atomic propositions):

Formula	Expressible in	But not in
$AF\,P$	UB	UB^-
$E(F\,P \wedge G\,Q)$	UB^+	UB
$E(P\,U\,Q)$	CTL	UB^+
$E\overset{\infty}{F}\,P$	ECTL	CTL^+
$E(\overset{\infty}{F}\,P \wedge \overset{\infty}{F}\,Q)$	$ECTL^+$	ECTL
$A(F(P \wedge X\,P))$	CTL^*	$ECTL^+$

Later in this subsection, we shall outline the proofs of some of these results. Before that, a few remarks. First, we justify the claim made in Section 2.4 that the condition of strong eventual fairness of process 1 (expressed by the formula $f_3 = A(\overset{\infty}{F}\,enabled_1 \Rightarrow F\,executed_1)$ in that subsection) is not expressible in CTL. For if it were, then any formula of the form $A(\overset{\infty}{F}\,P \Rightarrow F\,q)$, where P is an atomic proposition and q is an arbitrary pure propositional formula would also be expressible. Setting q to *false*, this formula is equivalent to $A(\neg\overset{\infty}{F}\,P)$, which is equivalent to $\neg(E\overset{\infty}{F}\,P)$, which, as the table above indicates, is not expressible in CTL. Also, as an aside, note that formulae of the form $A(\overset{\infty}{F}\,P \Rightarrow F\,q)$ can be written as the FCTL formula $A_\phi F\,q$ (where ϕ is $\overset{\infty}{F}\,P$, and P could be *executed*$_1$, for example), indicating that, though the impartiality scheduling constraint over all paths is expressible in CTL, reasoning about correctness properties over fair schedules in general is not possible within the framework of CTL.

For a proof of the equivalence in expressiveness of CTL and CTL^+, the reader is referred to [EH82]. The essence of the proof is that it is possible to translate each CTL^+ formula into a CTL one (after having inductively transformed all subformulae whose main connective is a path modality) using a series of valid equivalences that allow the path modalities to distribute over the boolean connectives in the restricted path formula that follows. To do this, however, the U operator is required, and so the technique is inapplicable to transform formulae of UB^+ into UB. Note that the CTL formula obtained by the translation could, in the worst case, be exponential in the length of the original CTL^+ formula, and, so, the translation is not succinct. In general, however, it has been observed that most correctness properties of concurrent programs (that do not deal with fairness) can be expressed both succinctly and naturally in CTL itself. Thus, from the viewpoint of applications, CTL^+ is of limited interest.

We now turn to outlining the gist of the proofs of some of the inexpressiveness results stated above. Two techniques have been used. The first is to show that a particular temporal logic has some specific (meta-)property that a more powerful one lacks, and to use this property to separate the expressive powers of the two logics. The second technique constructs two sequences of models in such a manner that some formula of the more expressive logic can identify which sequence a model is from, but no formula in the less expressive logic can tell the models apart. The following two subsections illustrate these methods.

3.1.1 The Expressiveness of UB^- and UB

The first of the two methods has been used to show that the UB formula $AF\,P$ cannot be expressed in UB^-. Before a formal proof, however, we need to define several notions, which we shall also have occasion to use when discussing decision procedures for satisfiability of temporal logics; in fact, one of the reasons we have chosen to deal with this proof at length is to acquaint the reader with these concepts in the context of the syntactically simple temporal logic UB$^-$, and to demonstrate their versatility.

We begin by assuming that each UB$^-$ formula has only the temporal modalities AG and AX; their duals, EF and EX, can be converted to these modalities. Similarly, we assume that every formula has only the boolean connectives $\neg$ and $\wedge$, and we identify $\neg\neg f$ with f for any formula f. As is done for formulae of Propositional Dynamic Logic (PDL) in [FL79], we define the *Fischer-Ladner closure* $CL(f)$ of a UB$^-$ formula f as the smallest set of formulae containing f and satisfying the following four conditions:

1. $\neg p \in CL(f) \quad \Leftrightarrow \quad p \in CL(f)$,
2. $p \wedge q \in CL(f) \quad \Rightarrow \quad p,\, q \in CL(f)$,
3. $AX\,p \in CL(f) \quad \Rightarrow \quad p \in CL(f)$, and
4. $AG\,p \in CL(f) \quad \Rightarrow \quad p,\, AXAG\,p \in CL(f)$.

Note that all formulae in $CL(f)$ are UB$^-$ formulae. Intuitively, $CL(f)$ contains all subformulae of f. In addition, for each subformula $AG\,p$, $AXAG\,p$ is also in $CL(f)$. Note (from the fixpoint characterization of AG in Section 2.2) that $AG\,p$ is true at a state only if both p *and* $AXAG\,p$ are true at it; in this sense $AXAG\,p$ is a subformula of $AG\,p$. A formula that is either an atomic proposition or is of the form $AX\,p$ is said to be *elementary*. It is easily seen that the truth of any UB$^-$ formula at a state of a model is completely determined by the truth of its elementary subformulae at that state.

A second useful concept is that of a *quotient structure* of a model $M = (S,\, R,\, L)$ with respect to some set H of UB$^-$ formulae. First, we define the equivalence relation $\equiv_H$ on the set S of states of M as follows: for any s and t in S, $s \equiv_H t$ iff, for all formulae p in H, $M, s \models p$ iff $M, t \models p$, i.e., s and t agree on the truth of all formulae in H. It is readily observed that $\equiv_H$ is in fact an equivalence relation. The equivalence class (under $\equiv_H$) to which the state s belongs is denoted by $[s]$. Now, the quotient structure of M with respect to the set H of UB$^-$ formulae is defined as the structure $M/{\equiv_H} = (S',\, R',\, L')$, where S' is the set of equivalence classes under $\equiv_H$, i.e., $S' = \{[s] \mid s \in S\}$, $R' = \{([s],[t]) \mid (s,t) \in R\}$, and $L'([s])$ is $L(s)$ restricted to the set of atomic propositions appearing in some formula of H. Intuitively, M' may be thought of as being obtained from M by coalescing all states that agree on the truth of all formulae in H into a single "superstate" and re-directing any edge in M into or out of an ordinary state into its corresponding superstate.

Now, consider a UB$^-$ formula f and a state s of a structure M at which f is true. An important observation (that is true only of UB$^-$ and not even of UB) is that f continues to remain true at the state $[s]$ of the quotient structure $M/{\equiv_{CL(f)}}$ (which we shall denote by M') and conversely, i.e., $M, s \models f$ iff $M', [s] \models f$. This is easily proved by induction on the structure of f. The base case, when q is an atomic proposition, is trivially true by virtue of the definition of $L'([s])$. Similarly, if q is obtained by the boolean combination of simpler formulae. (When q is of the form $\neg p$, note that this follows from the fact that precisely one of p or $\neg p$ holds at any state of any structure.) Now, if q is of the form $AX\,p$ and is true at s in M, we need to show it is true at state $[s]$ of M', i.e., we need to show that p is true at all states $[t]$ that succeed $[s]$ in M'. But, if there is an edge from $[s]$ to $[t]$, there is a pair of states, say s' and t', in M such that t' succeeds s' and $[s'] = [s]$ and $[t'] = [t]$. Further, as s and s' agree on the truth of $AX\,p$, p is true at t', and, by the induction hypothesis, at $[t]$, as required. For the converse, note that whenever $(s,\, t) \in R$, $([s],\, [t]) \in R'$. The converse, when q is of the form $AG\,p$ follows similarly. For if q is true at $[s]$ in M', to show that it is true at s in M, one only needs to show that p is true at any state t in M

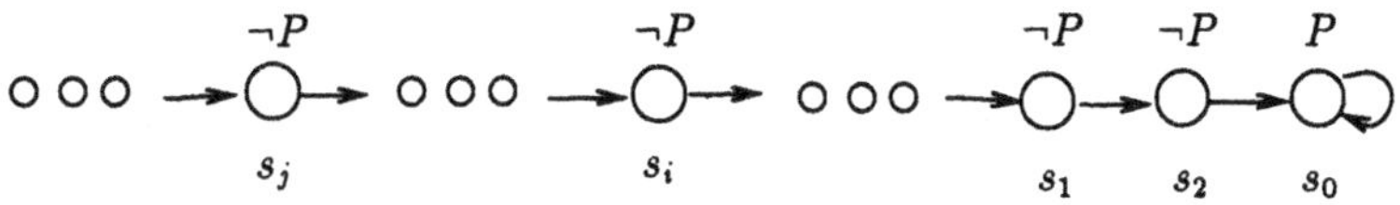

(a) A model for $AF\,P$

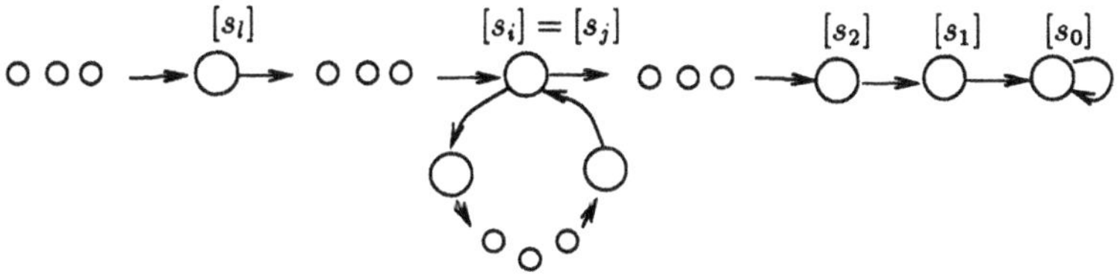

(b) Quotient structure of the model in (a).

Figure 2: Showing that $AF\,P$ is not true in a quotient structure.

reachable from s. But then, $[t]$ is reachable from $[s]$ in M', and p is true at $[t]$ as $AG\,p$ is true at $[s]$. Thus, from the induction hypothesis, p is true at t. The forward direction for the case when q is of the form $AG\,p$ is not as easy: specifically, there may be a path from $[s]$ to $[t]$ in M', but no path from s to t in M. Clearly, if there is a path from s to t in M, p is true at $[t]$ (as $AG\,p$ is true at s, and by the induction hypothesis). Otherwise, if there is a path from $[s]$ to $[t]$, there are states $u_1, u_2, \ldots, u_k$ and $v_1, v_2, \ldots, v_k$ in M such that $s = u_1$, $t = v_k$, and there is a path from each u_i to v_i in M, and, furthermore, u_{i+1} and v_i agree on the truth of all formulae in $CL(f)$, i.e., $[u_{i+1}] = [v_i]$. The truth of p at $[t]$ can now be argued by induction over the segments in this disjointed "path" in M.

The final argument to show that UB is more expressive than UB$^-$ is that the formula $f = AF\,P$ could be true at a state s of a structure M, but false at the state $[s]$ of the quotient structure $M' = M/{\equiv_{CL(f)}}$. Let, for example, M be the model shown in Fig. 2(a). Note that $AF\,P$ is true at each state of M, and $\neg P$ at each s_i, $i > 0$. As $CL(f)$ is finite, so is the set of equivalence classes of the relation $\equiv_{CL(f)}$; so some two states s_i and s_j, $0 < i < j$, must collapse to the state $[s_i]$ in the quotient structure. (Also, note that only s_0 collapses to $[s_0]$ as P is false at all other states of M.) A schematic diagram of the quotient structure M' is shown in Fig. 2(b). Note that there is a path in it (which could be a self-loop) from $[s_i]$ to itself; the states along the path correspond to $[s_k]$, where $i \le k \le j$. As P is false at all the states s_k, $F\,P$ is false along the fullpath starting at $[s_i]$ that repeatedly cycles along this path. Thus $AF\,P$ is false at $[s_i]$.

Clearly, therefore, $AF\,P$ cannot be equivalent to any UB$^-$ formula, p. If it were, p would be true both at s_i of M and $[s_i]$ of M' (as M' is the quotient structure of M), a contradiction.

The above technique, viz., showing that a quotient structure preserves the truth of a formula, was used by Fischer and Ladner ([FL79]) to arrive at a decision procedure for satisfiability of formulae of PDL. Their decision procedure can, therefore, be modified to determine satisfiability of UB$^-$ formulae, but cannot be directly used for UB or CTL as these logics have the modality AF. We shall elaborate on this in the next section.

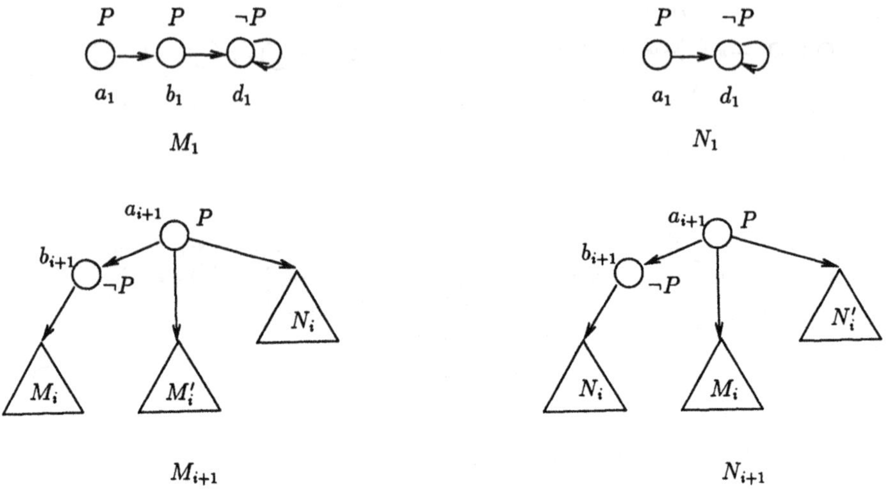

Figure 3: Models for $A(F(P \wedge X\,P))$ and $\neg A(F(P \wedge X\,P))$.

3.1.2 The Expressiveness of ECTL$^+$ and CTL*

We now illustrate the second technique that has been used to show that one temporal logic is more expressive than another. It constructs two series of models in such a manner that some formula in the more expressive logic can determine which series a specific model is from while all formulae of the less expressive logic are unable to do so. In fact, it is this second method that has been used to obtain all the results in the table above except for the $AF\,P$ one. However, except for the main outline of the proof, which we present here, the proof details for each of these results vary quite a bit as they are dependent on the syntax of the logics whose expressiveness is being considered. The interested reader is referred to [EH82] or [EH83] as appropriate.

We now show that the CTL* formula $f = A(F(P \wedge X\,P))$ is not expressible in ECTL$^+$. To do so, two sequences of models M_1, M_2, M_3, ... and N_1, N_2, N_3, ... are inductively defined as shown in Fig. 3. Note that the M_i' and the N_i' in the figures for the models of M_{i+1} and N_{i+1} are copies of the models M_i and N_i respectively. Also observe that, for each i, M_i, $a_i \models f$ and N_i, $a_i \models \neg f$. ($\neg f$ is formally equivalent to $E(G(\neg P \vee X \neg P))$.) In this sense, f can distinguish models from the two sequences. The proof in [EH83] shows that:

1. For each ECTL$^+$ formula p, there is a CTL formula q such that for all states s in M_i and t in N_i, M_i, $s \models p \equiv q$ and N_i, $t \models p \equiv q$, i.e., over this restricted class of models, CTL is at least as expressive as ECTL$^+$, and

2. For each CTL formula q, and all $i \geq |q|$, $M_i, a_i \models q$ iff $N_i, a_i \models q$. ($|q|$ denotes the length of the formula q.)

Now, suppose the ECTL$^+$ formula p is equivalent to f. Then, by (1) above, there is a CTL formula q that is equivalent to p, and, hence, to f, at all states of the models M_i and N_i, $i \geq 0$. Thus, by (2), $M_{|q|}, a_{|q|} \models q$ iff $N_{|q|}, a_{|q|} \models q$. Thus, either q is true at $a_{|q|}$ of both of $M_{|q|}$ and $N_{|q|}$ or false at both these states. However, f is true at the state $a_{|q|}$ of $M_{|q|}$ and false at the state $a_{|q|}$ of $N_{|q|}$, contradicting the fact that q is equivalent to f over these sequences of models.

The proofs of the other expressiveness results are built along similar lines, the ingenuity lying in constructing models that confound formulae of the less expressive logic, but are distinguishable by the formula listed in the table above of the more expressive logic.

3.2 Relating Branching Time Logic With Other Formalisms

As mentioned at the start of this section, the expressiveness of the standard linear time temporal logic has been shown to be equivalent to that of the first-order logic of linear order. Specifically, for each formula of either formalism, there is a formula in the other such that the two formulae are true at precisely the same states of all structures. Note that it is possible to interpret both formalisms over the same class of structures, viz., one-way infinite chains, and to set up a one-to-one correspondence between the atomic propositions of linear time temporal logic and the monadic predicates of first-order logic of linear order in such a way that a proposition is true at a state of the structure iff the corresponding predicate is true at that state. (The latter condition is necessary because a structure has a labelling in addition to the set of states and the binary relation.)

This result, established in [Ka68] and [GPSS80], was later extended by Wolper ([Wo81]) to include second-order quantification. Wolper introduced a temporal operator for each regular grammar. Other researchers (cf. [WVS83], [LPZ85]) have introduced automata connectives or quantification over the atomic propositions to achieve the same effect. Such an extended linear temporal logic has been shown to be equivalent in expressiveness to the second-order logic of linear order, which extends its first-order counterpart by allowing quantification over the monadic predicates. Other formalisms, notably automata- and formal language-theoretic, are known to be equivalent to both the first- and the second-order logics of linear order. For example, it is known that the class of *ω-regular languages* ([McN66]), which coincides with the class of languages of infinite strings accepted by nondeterministic finite-state Büchi automata and deterministic finite-state pairs automata over infinite strings ([Bü62], [McN66], [Sa88]), is exactly equivalent in expressiveness to the second-order logic of linear order.

It has been possible to relate the expressiveness of such varied formalisms to that of linear time temporal logic largely because of the simplicity of the structure of the models over which linear time logics are interpreted. Branching time temporal logics, on the other hand, are able to describe properties of considerably more general mathematical objects (arbitrary directed graphs), and there are not very many formalisms that are suited for this purpose. Hence, relatively little work has been done in relating the expressiveness of branching time temporal logic with other formalisms.

However, with certain restrictions, it is possible to compare the expressiveness of branching time logics with at least two other formalisms: finite state automata on infinite trees, and the monadic second-order theory of n successors, SnS. To do this, we modify the semantics of branching time temporal logics slightly by interpreting them only over infinite trees rather than over arbitrary graphs; it is evident, however, that each graph can be unwound into a tree.

One result that links the expressiveness of CTL* to the second-order theory of two successors is due to Hafer and Thomas ([HT87]): *CTL* is exactly as expressive as the monadic second-order theory of two successors over infinite binary trees, with set quantification restricted to infinite paths.* The authors note that, by allowing atomic arc assertions, the result can be extended to infinite n-ary trees.

Somewhat more is known about the relation between branching time temporal logics extended with existential quantification and tree automata. We first give a brief introduction to each of these. EQCTL* is a branching time temporal logic which allows second-order existential quantification over atomic propositions ([ES84]); so, in addition to the usual symbols in the logic of CTL*, EQCTL* has symbols (Y_1, Y_2, ...) that denote variable atomic propositions. An EQCTL* formula is of the form $\exists Y_1 \exists Y_2 \ldots \exists Y_k f$, where f is a CTL* formula in which the variable atomic propositions $Y_1, Y_2, \ldots, Y_k$ may or may not appear. EQCTL* formulae are also interpreted over CTL* structures: the EQCTL* formula $g = \exists Y_1 \exists Y_2 \ldots \exists Y_k f$ is true at a state s of a structure $M = (S, R, L)$ iff there exists a structure $M' = (S, R, L')$, where L' extends L by assigning a truth value to each of the Y_i at each of the states in S, such that the CTL* formula f is true at the state s of M'. The syntax and the semantics of EQUB and EQCTL are defined similarly, f being a UB and a CTL formula in these cases.

Tree automata ([Ra69], [HR72], [St81], [Em85]) are defined exactly like ordinary finite-state automata except that their input is a tree rather than a string. The tree automata that we consider here run on *infinite* trees, and, hence, their computations never terminate. Their acceptance of an input is given by an associated *acceptance condition* in much the same way as that of automata on infinite strings is specified. Specifically, a finite-state tree automaton that runs on infinite n-ary trees is a four-tuple $\mathcal{A} = (S, \Sigma, \delta, s_0)$, where S is a finite set of states, Σ is a finite input alphabet, s_0 is the initial state, and $\delta : S \times \Sigma \rightarrow \text{Powerset}(S^n)$ is the transition function to be described informally next (for a formal definition, the reader is referred to [ES84], for example), together with an acceptance condition, which too will be described shortly. $\mathcal{A}$ runs only on n-ary input trees, i.e., trees in which each node has exactly n children; note that the children of each node are ordered in some fixed fashion. Each node of an input tree T may be viewed as being labelled with some element of Σ. Each run of $\mathcal{A}$ down T ($\mathcal{A}$ has exactly one run down T only if it is deterministic) may be viewed as assigning a state to each node of T in a manner consistent with the transition function of $\mathcal{A}$ as follows. The state assigned to the root of T is s_0. Consider any node v that has been assigned the state s and is labelled with the input letter σ. $\mathcal{A}$ nondeterministically selects some element, say $(t_1, t_2, \ldots, t_n)$ in $\delta(s, \sigma)$ and assigns the state t_i to the ith child of v.

The acceptance conditions of tree automata can be used to classify them. We shall describe three of the standard acceptance conditions here. First the *Büchi acceptance condition* designates a subset, call it F, of states of S. The automaton $\mathcal{A}$ accepts an input tree T iff for some run down T, and every infinite path p in T starting at the root, one or more states of F is assigned infinitely many times by $\mathcal{A}$ to nodes along p. Similarly, the *pairs acceptance condition*, also known as the *McNaughton* or *Rabin* acceptance condition, designates a fixed number, say, k, of pairs of subsets of S, commonly denoted RED_i and $GREEN_i$. $\mathcal{A}$ accepts an input tree T iff for some run down T, and every infinite path p in T starting at the root, there is some pair, say, i, such that one or more states of $GREEN_i$ is assigned infinitely many times by $\mathcal{A}$ and every state of RED_i only finitely many times to nodes along p. Finally, the *complemented pairs* or *Streett* acceptance condition also designates a fixed number, k, of pairs of subsets of S, denoted RED_i and $GREEN_i$. This time, however, $\mathcal{A}$ accepts an input tree T iff for some run down T, every infinite path p in T starting at the root, and all pairs, i, $1 \leq i \leq k$, either every state of $GREEN_i$ is assigned only finitely many times by $\mathcal{A}$ to nodes along p or one or more states of RED_i is assigned infinitely many times as well to nodes along p (essentially, this is the complement of the pairs acceptance condition). The reader familiar with automata on infinite strings will recognize these acceptance conditions as obvious modifications of analogous ones for such automata.

Thus, both branching time temporal logics and tree automata deal with the same objects, viz., infinite trees. However, as branching time temporal logics cannot distinguish between the order of successors of a node, and tree automata accept only trees of fixed (and finite) branching, the class of structures over which the branching time logics are interpreted is limited to infinite binary trees, and only tree automata that run on binary trees and that have a symmetric transition

Figure 4: Models illustrating that $EF\,P$ is not equivalent to $A\,p$ for any path formula p.

function, i.e., for all $s \in S$ and all $\sigma \in \Sigma$, $(t_1, t_2) \in \delta(s, \sigma) \Leftrightarrow (t_2, t_1) \in \delta(s, \sigma)$, are considered here.

The following results are established in [ES84]: (i) EQCTL* *is exactly as expressive as symmetric pairs automata on infinite binary trees*, and (ii) EQUB *is exactly as expressive as symmetric Büchi automata on infinite binary trees*. The first result is proved by translating formulae of EQCTL* to those of $S2S$ (with the free set variables corresponding to the free atomic propositions in the EQCTL* formula); Rabin has shown ([Ra69]) that $S2S$ is at least as expressive as symmetric pairs automata on infinite binary trees. For the converse, it is shown that accepting runs of a symmetric pairs automaton can be encoded as an EQCTL* formula, with the existentially quantified atomic propositions, corresponding to the states of the automaton, being used to indicate the existence of an assignment of automaton states to the input tree, and with the formula itself ensuring that the assignment is consistent with the transition function of the automaton and accepts the input tree. The second result is proved in a similar fashion, but for the forward direction, the formulae of EQUB are translated to $S2S_{1.5}$, the second-order language of two successors, with one class of set variables ranging over only finite sets, and the second class over infinite sets; however, quantification is allowed only over the former class of variables. It may also be noted that, in fact, EQCTL and EQUB have exactly the same expressiveness, the power of the U operator being usurped by the ability to quantify over atomic propositions.

3.3 Branching versus Linear Time Temporal Logic

At the end of Section 2.4, we mentioned that every linear time temporal logic has a branching time analogue: in essence, each path formula p of the linear time logic is associated with the formula $A\,p$ of the branching time one. It was explained there that the choice of $A\,p$ rather than $E\,p$ arose from the way linear time temporal logic formulae have been interpreted in applications to reasoning about concurrent programs.

The following result proved in [EH83] should therefore be intuitively obvious: *The* B(F) *formula* $EF\,P$ *is not equivalent to any* B(L(F, X, U)) *formula*. (As usual, P is an atomic proposition.) In proof, suppose $EF\,P$ is equivalent to $A\,p$, where p is a pure path formula containing the temporal modalities F, X, and U. Consider the structures M and N shown in Fig. 4. Clearly, $M, s \models EF\,P$ and $N, s \models \neg EF\,P$. As $A\,p$ is equivalent to $EF\,P$, it is true at state s of M, and so p is true along each fullpath starting at s in M. As the only fullpath starting at s in N is also a fullpath starting at s in M, $A\,p$ is true at state s of N as well, a contradiction.

Note, however, this result does not imply that B(L(F, X, U)) is less expressive than B(F) for it does not say that all formulae of the former logic can be expressed as an equivalent formula of the latter. In fact, such is not the case, and the two logics are incomparable in expressive power, i.e., there are formulae of each not expressible in the other. However, it is shown in [EH83] that B(L(F, X, U)) $<$ CTL*, and, moreover, B(L(F, X, U)) is not comparable in expressiveness with even ECTL$^+$. Similarly, it is proved that B(L(F)) $<$ ECTL$^+$, and, as might be expected, from similar results established for linear time logics by Kamp, $B(L(F)) < B(L(F, U)) < B(L(F, X, U))$. Finally, like $B(L(F, X, U))$, $B(L(F, U))$ is not comparable in expressiveness with ECTL$^+$.

3.3.1 Suitability to Reasoning About Concurrent Programs

Finally, we discuss the suitability of branching and linear time temporal logics to reasoning about concurrent programs. Historically, it was this issue that motivated the formulation of CTL*, and, to some extent, led to a refinement in the definition that had been proposed by Lamport in [La80] to compare the expressive power of systems of temporal logic. We shall confine our discussion here to the arguments advanced therein to claim that linear time temporal logics are superior to branching time ones for reasoning about concurrent programs; to gain a fuller appreciation of the notions of expressiveness and validity of formulae discussed there, the reader is referred to the original, and to an analysis of those ideas in [EH83].

Two systems of temporal logic, one, a branching time one, and the other, a linear time one, were formulated in [La80]. The branching time system included the modalities $\Box$, with a semantics that we would recognize today as being the modality AG, and $\leadsto$, which is equivalent to the modality we now designate as AF. Also, $\Diamond p$ was defined as being equivalent to $\neg\Box\neg p$. Thus, $\Diamond$ is the modality EF, which indicates potentiality. The linear time temporal logic used the same symbols to denote linear time modalities: $\Box$ denoted G, $\leadsto$ denoted F, and $\Diamond$ was again defined to be an abbreviation of $\neg\Box\neg$. Thus, in linear time, $\Diamond$ is equivalent to $\leadsto$; however, in branching time, it is not. It was pointed out that in either the branching or the linear framework, $\Diamond p$ $(\neg\Box\neg p)$ is "not never p" and $\leadsto p$ is "sometime p". For linear time, the two are equivalent, but for branching time, they are not. (Hence, the title to [La80]: *"Sometime" is Sometimes "Not Never"*.)

A principle that is often employed in reasoning about concurrent programs, particularly to establish liveness properties, is that along *all* execution sequences of a program a predicate p eventually becomes true or remains false forever. Thus, Lamport claimed, it was necessary to have $\leadsto p \vee \Box\neg p$ as a valid formula, one that is true at all states of all models (i.e., at all states of all execution sequences of all programs). It was observed that this formula is valid under the linear time interpretation, but not under the branching time one. Hence the conclusion that linear time temporal logic is more suited to reasoning about concurrent programs. Of course, today, we can recognize the principle stated above as being incorrectly rendered in branching time logic. In effect, the *all* prefixing the execution sequences was allowed to distribute over the $\vee$ in the principle; a correct rendition would have been $A(F\,p \vee G\neg p)$, which, clearly, is valid. For linear time temporal logics, the translation is all right as execution sequences are considered individually.

Another argument forwarded in favour of linear time logics was that branching time logics were incapable of dealing with fairness. This followed from the definitions used in [La80] that compared the expressiveness of branching and linear time temporal logics, which, as was shown in [EH83], were based on a very coarse notion of equivalence of formulae of the two kinds of temporal logic. In any case, with those definitions of expressibility, it was shown that the linear time formula that required a process to be eventually fair ($\leadsto executed_1 \vee \leadsto\Box\neg enabled_1$ in Lamport's notation) was not expressible in branching time logic. Of course, that is only true of the branching time system Lamport proposed; as we now know, CTL* and several of its sublogics can express such fairness specifications.

As we have seen above, branching time temporal logics can express all the properties linear time ones can, and more. The most important difference between them is that branching time temporal logics can specify properties that are true only of some rather than all execution sequences e.g., a deadlock can occur under some circumstances), while linear time temporal logics can only specify properties that are universally true. Lamport had intuitively recognized this feature of branching time temporal logics and advocated their use for the study of nondeterministic algorithms (where the nondeterminism is inherent in the algorithm as opposed to the nondeterminism arising from the interleaving of the process steps as is done in modelling a concurrent program) as the computations of such algorithms are similar to those of nondeterministic automata and one needs to be able to express the condition that it suffices to have some one computation terminate successfully.

It is debatable whether one really needs to be able to specify existential properties when reasoning about concurrent programs. It is argued in [EH83] that making a distinction between the two sources of nondeterminism (the one arising from modelling concurrent programs, and the other inherent in the program itself) is not particularly appropriate as several programs display both kinds of nondeterminism. Furthermore, for such applications as automated program synthesis ([EC82]), one needs to be thorough in listing all the required specifications, and the ability to specify the existence of alternate computation paths is particularly important. Consider the example presented in [EH83] of a family of transaction server processes, P_1, P_2, ..., P_m, for updating a database system. Over and above the specifications that describe the fact that the process steps may be interleaved nondeterministically, one should be able to express all (i.e., the conjunction of) the following properties for each P_i: (*a*) P_i can await an input transaction forever in its noncritical region NCS_i: $EG\,NCS_i$, (*b*) P_i can receive a transaction and transit to its trying region TRY_i: $EF\,TRY_i$, and (*c*) along all execution sequences, P_i remains in its noncritical region forever or eventually enters its trying region: $A(G\,NCS_i \vee F\,TRY_i)$. No linear time formula is equivalent to the conjunction of the above three, and the "natural" specification, $A(G\,NCS_i \vee F\,TRY_i)$, permits programs in which all paths satisfy $F\,TRY_i$ and no path satisfies $G\,NCS_i$. Thus, without the ability to specify existential properties, methods external to the logic are necessary to ensure that the synthesized program exhibits an adequate degree of parallelism (see, for example, [MW84]). We shall discuss this point further in the next section.

On the other hand, in [La83], an argument to counter the above is reinforced, viz., that the ability to specify potentialities (or "possibilities" as they are called there) for reasoning about program *correctness* is inappropriate. In general, the need for restricting the expressiveness of the underlying temporal logic to the bare minimum necessary for the required application is articulated; as is pointed out, this is one of the hallmarks of a good mathematical tool. It is also argued that the *nexttime* operator is redundant for *specifications* as one generally needs to express only program properties that involve significant changes rather than properties that specify what should be true of the very next state in an execution sequence. We may mention as an aside that this paper provides a substantial example of how temporal logics in general can be used to specify and formally derive correct concurrent programs; in particular, it is illustrated how temporal logic allows hierarchical specifications of programs, and, thereby, permits modular development, aided by its *axiomatic* nature as opposed to the *constructive* approach of other methods.

4 Decision Procedures for Branching Time Logics

A standard problem in the theory of classical mathematical logic is to provide an axiomatization of a specific logic, i.e., to formulate a set of primitive validities (the axioms) and a set of inference rules using which all other validities can be derived. The corresponding problem has been investigated for temporal logics as well. From the computer science viewpoint, however, an equally important problem is to exhibit a *decision procedure* for the logic, i.e., an algorithm that determines whether a given formula of the logic is valid or not. Given that for all temporal logics we have encountered a formula is valid if, and only if, its negation is not satisfiable, and that the sets of formulae of all these logics are closed under logical negation, a closely related problem is to provide a decision procedure that determines the satisfiability of formulae of the temporal logic.

As we shall see, decision procedures of temporal logics for the satisfiability problem have applications to reasoning about temporal systems, e.g., they have been used to mechanically synthesize concurrent programs from temporal specifications. As a result, the (time) complexity of these algorithms has considerable practical significance. Thus, if the expressiveness of a branching time temporal logic is one criterion in evaluating it for potential applications, the complexity of its decision procedures must be another. We have seen that certain branching time temporal logics provide greater expressive power than others. An important question a designer of a temporal system is faced with is: How much expressive power does a specific application really require? A logic that is very expressive may provide great generality and ease of use for the specification of, and reasoning about, correctness properties of the system. However, there is likely to be a penalty associated with a high degree of expressiveness: as a general rule, the more expressive a temporal logic, the higher the complexity of the decision procedure for its satisfiability problem. Thus, the systems designer must trade off expressiveness for efficiency.

The following subsection reviews decision procedures and their complexity for the satisfiability problem for several branching time temporal logics. We also illustrate how this problem may be applied to the mechanical synthesis of concurrent programs. Then, we present axiomatizations of some branching time temporal logics, and discuss their applicability to the manual verification of concurrent programs.

Another problem for temporal logics that has proved to have several practical applications is the *model checking* problem, which is required to determine whether a given structure is a model of a given formula. Intuitively, this problem should be easier than the satisfiability problem, and, that, indeed, is the case for most temporal logics. In the last subsection, we discuss algorithms for model checking in the context of CTL, and list some of their applications. In particular, we shall illustrate how they can be applied to automating the task of verification of concurrent programs.

4.1 The Satisfiability Problem

Recall that the satisfiability problem for any particular temporal logic is: *Given a formula p of the temporal logic, does it have a model, i.e., a structure M and a state s of M such that $M, s \models p$?* For purposes of applications of this problem, if p is satisfiable, we would also like to construct (a finite representation of) some model of p.

For almost all branching time temporal logics, the satisfiability problem is decidable; in fact, a decision procedure can be obtained by translating formulae of the temporal logic into formulae of SnS, and using its decision procedure for satisfiability. However, even if the translation of formulae into SnS is succinct, the upper bound on the complexity of such a decision procedure would be nonelementary in the length of the formula since SnS cannot be decided in elementary time ([Me75]). (A function $f(n)$ is said to be *elementary* if it is of the order of $g_k(n)$ for some fixed k, where $g_k(n)$ is the function obtained by composing $\exp(n)$ with itself k times.) This approach thus has too severe a complexity penalty for applications. Moreover, we also wish to actually construct a finite model of satisfiable formulae. Hence, this solution is unacceptable.

Fortunately, there are several temporal logics, for which we can develop a suitable decision procedure of single or double exponential time complexity. (Note, as an aside, that all temporal ogics subsume ordinary propositional logic, and, thus their satisfiability problem is $\mathcal{NP}$-hard. Hence, it is extremely unlikely that decision procedures of considerably better complexity than exponential time can be formulated.) The first step is usually to establish that the logic has the *small model property:* if a formula is satisfiable, then it is satisfiable in a model whose size is bounded by some function, say, f, of the length of the formula. Having established this property, we have at once a nondeterministic algorithm to determine satisfiability of an input formula p that runs in time polynomial in $f(|p|)$: the algorithm merely guesses a structure of size no more than $f(|p|)$ and checks whether it is indeed a model of p. Thus, there is a deterministic algorithm that is exponential in $f(|p|)$.

There are two questions that naturally arise. First, how does one establish the small model property for a specific temporal logic? And, secondly, are there any techniques that can be used to optimize the naive deterministic algorithm outlined above if a temporal logic does have the small model property? In the following subsection, we answer these questions in the context of the temporal logic CTL; the techniques that are used, however, are sufficiently general, and have been applied to several other temporal logics including linear time ones.

In essence, the method builds a *tableau* (effectively, a graph, whose nodes are labelled with subformulae of the formula p whose satisfiability is being tested) that encodes potential models of p as described in the following. Intuitively, the nodes of the tableau are intended to correspond to states of potential models. Hence, to determine the set of subformulae labelling the nodes, the method exploits the fixpoint characteristics of temporal modalities listed in Section 2.2. Suppose we have determined that the subformula q of p should label a node u of the tableau, and the main connective of q is the temporal modality H. Using the fixpoint equivalent of H, q is decomposed into two assertions: one, q_1, that is required to be true of the state of the potential model to which the node u corresponds, and the other, q_2, that should be true at successor states of the state corresponding to u in the model. (Of course, depending on H, only one of these two assertions may need to be true; in any case, the truth of q_1 relates to the state corresponding to u, and the truth of q_2 to one or more successor states.) So q_1 is added to the label of u, and q_2 to the label of one or more successors of u in the tableau, as appropriate. Once constructed, the tableau is pruned with a small, fixed set of rules which ensure that the formulae labelling a node are in fact true at that node. If it is not possible for a formula labelling a node to be true there, then it can be shown that the conjunction of the formulae labelling that node cannot be true of any state of any model (i.e., the conjunction is invalid), and so that node is deleted. If p labels any node in the fully pruned tableau, the pruned tableau can be unwound into a model of p, otherwise, p is unsatisfiable. In general, the pruning procedure is polynomial in the size of the initial tableau, and the tableau can be constructed in time polynomial in its size; hence the factor governing the complexity is the size of the tableau in relation to the length of p. In any case, such an approach invariably yields a more efficient deterministic algorithm than the naive one described above.

A more recent approach to the satisfiability problem that has been used very effectively to develop a decision procedure for CTL*, for example, is an automata-theoretic one, the input to the automata being infinite objects rather than finite ones. This method of deciding the satisfiability problem is due to Streett ([St81]) and was originally proposed in the context of dynamic logics. It has since been advocated for both linear and branching time temporal logics; see, for example, [VW84], [Em85], [VS85]. We now describe the gist of the technique for branching time temporal logics; the only significant difference when it is applied to linear temporal logics is that the input to the automata are infinite strings rather than infinite trees for reasons that will be apparent from the following. In essence, the initial tableau constructed by the first method can be also viewed as the transition diagram of an automaton $\mathcal{A}$ (cf. [Em85]) that accepts as input infinite trees that correspond to models of the formula p whose satisfiability is being tested. (Tree automata have been discussed in Section 3.2.) Note that each node of the input tree is therefore a state of a structure and is thus labelled by a set of atomic propositions. Hence, the input alphabet is the powerset of the set of atomic propositions appearing in p. The nodes in the tableau roughly correspond to states of $\mathcal{A}$. The task of the automaton when it is at state s and after having last read the input letter σ of a node u of the input tree is to check that all formulae in the tableau node corresponding to the state s are in fact true at the u. Thus, the transitions out of the start state of $\mathcal{A}$ on input σ cause it to move nondeterministically to a state corresponding to one in the tableau labelled with both p and all atomic propositions appearing in σ. To check the truth of a formula, say, q, whose main connective is a temporal modality at the tree node u, the automaton implicitly uses the fixpoint characterization of the modality encoded in the tableau (and, hence, in its set of states) to check whether a simpler assertion (as before, call it q_1) is true at the current node, and/or another assertion (q_2) is true at (some or all) successor nodes of the input. The latter consideration (ensuring that q_2 is true of one or more input tree nodes to be scanned) dictates the transition function of the automaton: the automaton must transit to a state corresponding to a tableau node labelled with the formula q_2. Thus (in a sense made precise in [Em85]), the edges of the tableau correspond to the transitions of the automaton. In particular, as can be gleaned from the above, an edge from the tableau node V to W should be labelled with the input letter σ which contains precisely those atomic propositions in W.

It should therefore be intuitively clear that the automaton can be constructed by a method akin to the one that constructs the tableau. One aspect that needs to be resolved, however, is deciding which of the acceptance conditions described in Section 3.2 should be used and how the states of the automaton should be assigned to the subsets designated there as F for the Büchi acceptance condition, and as $GREEN_i$ and RED_i for the pairs and complemented pairs acceptance conditions. The acceptance condition is essentially used by $\mathcal{A}$ to indicate whether subformulae of the form $A(q\,U\,r)$ and $E(q\,U\,r)$ are true at a tree node if $\mathcal{A}$ assigns it a state corresponding to a tableau node containing such a formula. For example, if the complemented pairs condition is used, each subformula g of the form $A(q\,U\,r)$ or $E(q\,U\,r)$ of p has a corresponding designated pair of subsets RED_g and $GREEN_g$. For concreteness, let g be $A(q\,U\,r)$, and, for simplicity, let r be a pure propositional formula. $\mathcal{A}$ assigns a state of $GREEN_g$ to a tree node u precisely when (i.e., if and only if) it has to determine whether $A(q\,U\,r)$ is true at u and r is false at u. Once $\mathcal{A}$ assigns a state of $GREEN_g$ to a node u, its transition function (which, as we have seen, is determined in part by the fixpoint characterization of $A(q\,U\,r)$, viz., $A(q\,U\,r) \equiv r \vee (q \wedge AXA(q\,U\,r)))$, ensures that it continues to assign elements of $GREEN_g$ to nodes along any path in the input tree starting at u till it has verified that r is true at some input tree node, at which point it assigns an element of RED_g to that node. Thus, if r never becomes true along some path starting at u, i.e., $A(q\,U\,r)$ is false at u, $\mathcal{A}$ rejects because states in $GREEN_g$ are assigned infinitely often along that path, but the states of RED_g only finitely often. (Some thought will show that this technique can be generalized to work even if r is not a pure propositional formula by letting RED_g be the set of states of $\mathcal{A}$ which correspond to nodes of the tableau labelled with r.) The case when g is of the from $E(q\,U\,r)$ is handled in like fashion.

Thus, the satisfiability problem for the temporal logic now reduces to the non-emptiness problem for the class of Büchi, pairs, or complemented pairs tree automata: the formula is satisfiable iff the tree automaton accepts some input. We shall discuss this method in some more detail in a following subsection.

Finally, we show how the satisfiability problem can be applied to the mechanical synthesis of concurrent programs. Two different underlying models of computation have been used: a process-based one that uses test-and-set primitives to achieve synchronization in a shared memory environment ([EC82]), and a CSP-like framework which uses message passing for inter-process communication ([MW84]). Both methods, however, use similar theoretical techniques, and the latter uses an extended linear temporal logic ([Wo81]) to express temporal specifications of programs. Consequently, we shall illustrate the approach with a condensed example from [EC82].

4.1.1 Tableau-Based Methods

We now elaborate on the tableau-based approach to decide the satisfiability problem for the branching time logic CTL ([EH82]). The same technique has been applied to its sublogics (for example, UB, [BMP81]) and to related branching time logics like FCTL ([EL86]). It has also been classically used for dynamic logics like Propositional Dynamic Logic (PDL, cf. [FL79], [Pr80]) and Deterministic PDL ([BHP81]).

We first indicate how the small model property is established for CTL. An elegant way of doing this for UB^-, using the quotient construction method, was illustrated in Section 3.1.1. The method first "collapses" a (possibly infinite) model by identifying states according to an equivalence relation of small, finite index, and then shows that the resulting finite quotient structure is still a model of the formula in question. Unfortunately, as we have seen in Section 3.1.1, any method of trying to prove the small model property directly by using a quotient construction must fail when applied to UB or CTL on account of the modality $AF\,q$.

However, as is shown in [EH82], the quotient structure obtained from a CTL model (with respect to the Fischer-Ladner closure of a CTL formula which is defined in the same vein as that for a UB^- formula) may be viewed as a small *pseudo-model* which contains enough information to be unwound into a genuine (and still small) model. The essence of the argument is captured by Fig. 2. When a model is collapsed to a quotient structure, spurious cycles (in that they did not exist in the model) may be introduced along which eventualities like $AF\,q$ and $A(p\,U\,q)$ may remain unfulfilled forever. However, at every node at which such an eventuality is pending, there is a DAG (directed acyclic graph) rooted at that node at all of whose frontier nodes the eventuality is fulfilled, i.e., q is true at all the frontier nodes, and, moreover, in the case of the eventuality $A(p\,U\,q)$, p is true at all interior nodes of the DAG. (In actuality, the DAG also satisfies certain other constraints that we will detail in the technical presentation that follows.) In Fig. 2, for example, the DAG for the eventuality $AF\,P$ pending at $[s_i]$ is merely a chain from $[s_i]$ to $[s_0]$. Furthermore, a true model can be constructed from the quotient structure by splicing the DAGs for appropriate eventualities.

We now make this intuition somewhat more precise; our presentation of the algorithm, however, is deliberately informal, the intention only being to convey the substance of the technique. For a formal account, the reader is referred to [EH82]. The goal is to construct a pseudo-model for a CTL formula f. We begin, as in Section 3.1.1, by defining the *Fischer-Ladner closure* $CL(f)$ of f. We assume that f strictly abides by the syntax defined in Section 2.4 (only the rules S1 and S2 of Section 2.2 and the rule S3′ of Section 2.4 are used to construct it). Identifying $\neg\neg p$ with p for any CTL formula p, $CL(f)$ is the smallest set of formulae containing f and satisfying the following six conditions:

1. $\neg p \in CL(f) \quad \Leftrightarrow \quad p \in CL(f)$,
2. $p \wedge q \in CL(f) \quad \Rightarrow \quad p,\, q \in CL(f)$,
3. $AX\,p \in CL(f) \quad \Rightarrow \quad p \in CL(f)$,
4. $EX\,p \in CL(f) \quad \Rightarrow \quad p \in CL(f)$,
5. $A(p\,U\,q) \in CL(f) \quad \Rightarrow \quad p,\, q,\, AXA(p\,U\,q) \in CL(f)$, and
6. $E(p\,U\,q) \in CL(f) \quad \Rightarrow \quad p,\, q,\, EXE(p\,U\,q) \in CL(f)$.

Note that, in the case of formulae that are eventualities (i.e., formulae of the form $A(p\,U\,q)$ and $E(p\,U\,q)$), the fixpoint characterizations of their modalities (discussed in Section 2.2) determine their subformulae. As for UB^-, a formula is said to be *elementary* iff it is of the form $AX\,p$ or $EX\,p$.

We define a subset S of $CL(f)$ to be *maximally consistent* iff S satisfies all the following conditions:

1. For each $p \in CL(f)$, $\neg p \in S \Leftrightarrow p \notin S$,
2. $p \wedge q \in S \quad \Leftrightarrow \quad p, q \in S$,
3. $A(p\ U\ q) \in S \quad \Leftrightarrow \quad q \in S$ or $p, AXA(p\ U\ q) \in S$, and
4. $E(p\ U\ q) \in S \quad \Leftrightarrow \quad q \in S$ or $p, EXE(p\ U\ q) \in S$.

S is said to be *maximal* because for every subformula p of f (i.e., for each element in $CL(f)$), either p or $\neg p$ is in S. Note that the number of maximally consistent subsets of $CL(f)$ is no more than exponential in the length of f because the size of $CL(f)$ is linear in the length of f.

It is clear that the set of those formulae in $CL(f)$ that are true at any state of any structure is a maximally consistent subset of $CL(f)$, i.e., the quotient structure (or pseudo-model) with respect to $CL(f)$ of any model of f would have at most one state in it corresponding to each maximally consistent subset of $CL(f)$. Since we are attempting to construct a pseudo-model of f, a candidate structure is one that has one state corresponding to each maximally consistent subset of $CL(f)$. This state is labelled with the formulae in the subset it corresponds to, the intention being to have all these formulae true at it. We shall identify a state of our structure with the subset of $CL(f)$ that labels it. We shall call the structure itself the *initial tableau* and denote it by T_0.

We use the elementary formulae in a state to guide us in determining the edges of T_0. An edge is added from state V to state W iff (a) for every formula of the form $AX\,p$ in V, p is in W, and (b) for every formula of the form $\neg EX\,p$ in V, $\neg p$ is in W (note that $\neg EX\,p$ is equivalent to $AX\,\neg p$). Clearly, any quotient (with respect to $CL(f)$) of any structure cannot have any other edges.

The next step is to prune T_0 so that we in fact do have a pseudo-model: i.e., for each eventuality at each node, there is a DAG for that eventuality rooted at that node which certifies fulfillment of that eventuality at that node. We define this notion more carefully now. For an eventuality of the form $E(p\,U\,q)$ in the node V, there should be a (simple) path starting at V to some state W such that all states between V and W (including V, but excluding W) are labelled with p but not with q and W is labelled with q. For an eventuality of the form $A(p\,U\,q)$ in the node V, there should be a DAG rooted at V (which has no other root) such that all interior nodes of the DAG are labelled with p but not with q, all frontier nodes of the DAG are labelled with q, and, additionally, all interior nodes that contain $EX\,r$ (respectively, $\neg AX\,r$), for any formula r, must have a successor in the DAG labelled with r (respectively, $\neg r$). Moreover, for either kind of eventuality, any node of the tableau may appear at most once in the DAG.

Any node that contains an eventuality, but that that does not have a DAG that certifies fulfillment for that eventuality, can be deleted. (Once a node is deleted, other nodes that used it in a DAG to fulfill an eventuality, say, g, in their labels will need to determine for the new tableau whether it still contains a DAG that certifies fulfillment of g.) Similarly, a node that has no successor can be deleted, and one that is labelled with $EX\,r$ (respectively, $\neg AX\,r$), for any formula r, must have a successor in the tableau labelled with r (respectively, $\neg r$), otherwise, it too can be deleted. The pruning procedure stops when no more nodes can be deleted, and f is satisfiable iff it labels some one node in the pruned tableau.

To demonstrate the correctness of this algorithm, it can be shown by induction on the order of node deletions that the set of formulae labelling a deleted node cannot all be true together at any state of any structure (and, therefore, of any quotient structure of f), i.e., the conjunction of formulae in such a set is invalid. We have already argued this of any subset of formulae of $CL(f)$ that is not maximally consistent, and, hence, does not label some node of T_0. Also note that if all formulae in the maximally consistent subset S are true at a state u of a structure, then the maximally consistent set of formulae true at any successor state of u must be one that succeeds S in T_0. Thus, the above claim is easily verified if a node S is deleted because it has no successors (each state of a model must have a successor and none of the successors of S can label any state of any structure by the induction hypothesis), and when a node is deleted because it contains $EX\,r$, say, and none of its successors in the tableau contains r. A somewhat more involved argument establishes the truth of this hypothesis for the cases when S is deleted because it has an eventuality, but there is no DAG that certifies fulfillment of that eventuality rooted at it in the tableau.

For the other direction, we show how to construct a small model M of f if f does label some node of the pruned tableau. We construct M using the method described in [Em88]. M is best visualized as a two-dimensional matrix whose rows correspond to the eventualities in $CL(f)$ and whose columns, to nodes of the tableau. If the node S in the tableau is labelled with the eventuality $A(p\ U\ q)$, and S does not contain q, the matrix element in the row corresponding to $A(p\ U\ q)$ and in the column for S is a DAG rooted at S fulfilling the eventuality. Similarly, if the node S in the tableau is labelled with the eventuality $E(p\ U\ q)$, and S does not contain q, the matrix element in the row corresponding to $E(p\ U\ q)$ and in the column for S is constructed from a DAG, call it G, rooted at S fulfilling the eventuality; in essence, G is extended by adding fresh nodes so that each interior node of G has exactly the same successors as it does in the pruned tableau, and these new nodes are labelled with the same set of formulae as in the corresponding nodes of the tableau. In all other cases, this entry of the matrix is the subgraph of the pruned tableau induced by the node S and all its successors, except that if S is a successor of itself, the self-loop is deleted and an edge is directed instead to a fresh vertex labelled with exactly those formulae that appear in S. Note that all matrix entries are acyclic and each has only one root. Call each matrix entry a DAGG. Now, each frontier node V of each DAGG of the ith row is coalesced with the root of the DAGG in the column corresponding to V and in the $(i+1)$th row (with the last row wrapping around to the first). The resulting structure is M.

It is easy to see that each node in the pruned tableau labels some state of M, and also that if a state S has a formula $AX\,p$ (respectively, $EX\,p$) in its label, all (respectively, some one) of its successors is labelled with p. (This explains the additional clause in the definition of the DAGs that certify the eventuality $A(p\ U\ q)$ and the modification to the DAGs that certify fulfillment of eventualities of the form $E(p\ U\ q)$.) A little reflection shows that if an eventuality appears in the label of a state, it is in fact fulfilled along all fullpaths emanating from that state if it is of the form $A(p\ U\ q)$, and along some fullpath stemming from that state if it is of the form $E(p\ U\ q)$. To see this for eventualities of the form $A(p\ U\ q)$, observe that each fullpath goes through every row of the matrix (for each DAGG is acyclic and has a "depth" of at least two), and, hence, eventually through the frontier node of a DAGG for the appropriate eventuality. Thus if an eventuality, call it g, is incurred at S and remains unfulfilled along the path from a node S till the root node R of the DAGG for g, the DAGG must be a DAG fulfilling g, and thus the frontier node that the path goes through fulfills g. That the DAGG for g rooted at R must be a DAG for g follows from the fact that S is labelled with $g = A(p\ U\ q)$ and p, but not with q, and, so must be labelled with $AXA(p\ U\ q)$. Thus, all its successors are labelled with g as well (from the way edges are initially added to the T_0), and, inductively, so is R. The argument when the eventuality is of the form $E(p\,U\,q)$ is similar. Note how the fixpoint characterizations of the modalities AU and EU are used to "push" the pending eventualities down a fullpath till the path reaches a DAG that fulfills it. As for the model's size, note that each DAG contains at most one copy of each node in the tableau. Thus, the size of the model is polynomial in the size of the initial tableau and linear in the number of eventualities in f. As the size of the initial tableau is exponential in the length of f, the size of the model is bounded by some exponential function of this length.

We now examine the complexity of the algorithm. As noted, the size of the initial tableau is no more than exponential in the length of f. Only as many nodes can be deleted as there are nodes in the initial tableau, and to delete some one node in the tableau (at any intermediate stage), at most one needs to check that if $EX\,r$ (or $\neg AX\,r$) appears in a node, it has a successor with r ($\neg r$ respectively) in its label, and that all eventualities in all nodes are fulfilled. The former can be done in time linear in the size of the tableau. We shall show that we can determine all the nodes in an intermediate tableau that fulfill any eventuality in time proportional to the size of that tableau. Since there are at most as many eventualities as the length of the input formula f, the pruning procedure can be done in time linear in this length and polynomial in the size of the initial tableau, and, so, the overall complexity is exponential in the length of the input formula.

To see how to check whether a node S has a DAG fulfilling $A(p\,U\,q)$ in its label, all nodes in the tableau that are labelled with q are marked initially. On succeeding iterations, any unmarked node V labelled with $A(p\,U\,q)$ is marked provided that for every formula of the form $EX\,r$ (respectively, $\neg AX\,r$) that appears in its label, there is some successor node labelled with r (respectively, $\neg r$) that has been marked previously. At least one new node is marked on every iteration, and the algorithm terminates when no more nodes can be marked. (Hence, there are at most as many iterations as the size of the tableau.) S fulfills the eventuality $A(p\,U\,q)$ only if it is marked; if it is, a DAG can be constructed by using the marked nodes reachable from S. Note that a single run of this algorithm determines all nodes in the tableau labelled with $A(p\,U\,q)$ that fulfill it. A naive implementation of the algorithm may appear to run in time quadratic in the size of the tableau (as each iteration may appear to take time linear in the tableau's size), but it can be optimized to take only linear time overall by appending a marked node to a list, and, on each iteration, removing a node from the head of the list and considering its predecessors alone as candidates to be marked. Thus, the list has a frontier of marked nodes, and this frontier "radiates" out from the nodes marked with q till all nodes that satisfy the eventuality are marked.

Checking whether a node that has $E(p\,U\,q)$ in its label fulfills that eventuality is done similarly. All nodes labelled q are marked initially, and each iteration marks any unmarked node that is labelled with both p and $E(p\,U\,q)$ provided some one of its successors is marked.

Thus, we have a deterministic decision procedure for CTL whose complexity is at most exponential in the length of f. Unfortunately, though, the algorithm outlined above will always take time exponential in the length of f as all maximally consistent subsets of $CL(f)$ are always considered. An optimization that does not build the entire tableau initially, but constructs the initial tableau "bottom-up" (akin to the method used for Deterministic PDL in [BHP81], and having its origins in a similar method used for ordinary propositional logic in [Sm68]) is described in [EH82]. This method initially constructs an AND-OR graph from which the initial tableau is derived and the same set of rules described above is used to prune the initial tableau. Alternatively (as in [EC82]), the AND-OR graph itself can be viewed as a tableau, and the set of rules used to prune it are similar in spirit to the above, but modified slightly to account for the fact that the tableau has two kinds of nodes. The latter approach also makes clear the relation between the tableaux constructed from the fixpoint characterizations of modalities and the transition diagram of tree automata, which are also AND-OR graphs ([Em85]). For a coherent overview of all these methods described for the logic CTL itself (and for the relation of pseudo-models to *Hintikka structures*), the reader is referred to [Em88].

We conclude this section with a summary of the complexity results that have been established for the satisfiability problems of various branching time temporal logics that have been decided using a tableau-based approach. Historically, the technique used to establish the small model property for UB^- was done first for the dynamic logic PDL in [FL79], yielding a nondeterministic single exponential time algorithm for its satisfiability problem. A deterministic single exponential lower bound was also shown. Pratt ([Pr80]) used the tableau method similar to the one illustrated here to close the gap. It was shown in [BHP81] that the technique of [FL79] could not be used to establish the small model property for Deterministic PDL. They showed, as we have done for CTL, that the quotient structure is a small pseudo-model, and that the tableau technique of [Pr80] could be extended even in this case to get a pseudo-model and then unwind that to a true model; their single exponential deterministic algorithm is optimal for Deterministic PDL. This approach was also used for the temporal logic UB in [BMP81] to arrive at an optimal single exponential deterministic algorithm, and for CTL in [EH82]. (The deterministic single exponential lower bound for PDL carries over to UB^- because UB^- formulae can be succinctly translated to PDL.)

The same technique has been used for FCTL too ([EL86]). It is shown that when the fairness constraint ϕ is in the canonical form $\bigvee_{i=1}^{n} \bigwedge_{j=1}^{m}(\overset{\infty}{G}\, p_{ij} \vee \overset{\infty}{F}\, q_{ij})$, where the p_{ij} and the q_{ij} are pure path formulae, FCTL has the small model property (the model being bounded by an exponential function in the length of the input formula), and, hence, a nondeterministic exponential time algorithm, for its satisfiability problem. Also, if ϕ is of the form $\bigwedge_{i=1}^{m} \overset{\infty}{F} p_i$, FCTL has a single exponential deterministic procedure. (Note that the restricted constraint suffices to express impartiality and justice for example.) However, there are important technical differences between the procedure for FCTL and the one for CTL. For CTL the subgraph of the tableau certifying fulfillment of eventualities is acyclic. For FCTL, however, the subgraphs do contain (disciplined) cycles: for example, the subgraph certifying fulfillment of $A_\phi\, q$ will in general contain unfair cycles (corresponding to paths which violate the fairness specification ϕ), and that for $E_\phi\, q$ can even contain fair cycles.

More recently, in [ESS89], this approach has been used to formulate a temporal logic, SCTL (Simplified CTL), whose satisfiability problem is decidable in polynomial time. Among other constraints placed on the syntax of its formulae is that the atomic propositions out of which they are constructed be mutually exclusive. However, the logic is expressive enough to be able to express several important correctness properties of programs, and has been shown to have applications to the mechanical synthesis and verification of concurrent programs.

The tableau technique has been applied to linear time temporal logics as well: see, for example, [LPZ85], for a description of the procedure for a version of the logic that includes past as well as future temporal connectives. This procedure runs in deterministic exponential time and is very likely optimal as the satisfiability problem for linear time logic has been shown to be PSPACE-complete in [SC82].

4.1.2 The Automata-Theoretic Approach

Earlier in this section, we showed how the tableau for a formula f constructed in the tableau-based approach could be viewed as the transition diagram of a tree automaton which accepts infinite trees that correspond to models of f, and how the complemented pairs acceptance condition could be used to signal fulfillment of the eventualities in CTL along fullpaths of the model. (As an aside, note that the number of states in the automaton corresponds to the size of the tableau and is exponential in the length of f, while each designated pair in its acceptance condition corresponds to an eventuality of f, and, so, the number of such pairs is linear in the length of f. Hence, the number of designated pairs is logarithmic in the number of states of the automaton. This general relation is true of several other logics discussed below, and the intuition is the same. We mention it here because it plays an important role in formulating efficient algorithms in deciding the satisfiability of formulae of these logics.) Thus, if the satisfiability problem of a temporal logic is decidable by the tableau-based method, it is also reducible to the non-emptiness problem of tree automata.

It might appear, however, that there is no real benefit from using the automata-theoretic approach at all if the tableau-based one works well enough. But for some branching time temporal logics (like CTL*) which have a richer set of modalities than CTL, a tableau cannot be directly constructed (in part because there are no natural fixpoint characterizations of the modalities that splits assertions into two: one which needs to be true immediately, and the other, at one or more successor states). In such cases, the automata-theoretic approach often plays an integral role in obtaining a decision procedure; in particular, automata theory provides elegant methods to construct and combine their basic building blocks, viz., automata, and this has proved to be useful in tractably managing the combinatorially explosive number of different interactions of modalities that might otherwise need to be considered to formulate a decision procedure independently. Mainly to illustrate this point, for, unlike the tableau-based method, this is about as much the decision procedures that have been developed for various logics using this approach have in common, we outline the decision procedure for CTL* described in [ES84].

The first step is to reduce the kinds of modalities in CTL* formulae. This is done by succinctly translating each CTL* formula f into an equivalent one, f', which is in *normal form*, i.e., f' is constructed out of conjunctions and disjunctions of simpler formulae all of which have the form $A\,p$, $E\,p$ or $AGE\,p$ where p is a pure path formula. The algorithm used to convert f to normal form ensures that the length of f' is linear in the length of f. It is then shown that f' is satisfiable iff it has an infinite tree model, the branching at each node of which is restricted to at most the length of f'. This is crucial because, as seen in Section 3.2, tree automata accept input trees of finite branching only. Now, if a tree automaton for each conjunct and disjunct of f' can be constructed, they can be combined by taking their union or cross-product (for the cases of disjunctions and conjunctions respectively) to get a single tree automaton for f'. As is shown in [ES84], a complemented pairs tree automaton can be constructed for each type of conjunct or disjunct listed above that appears in f'; moreover, the size of the tree automaton for each conjunct or disjunct is no more than double exponential in the length of f' (and the number of designated pairs of *RED* and *GREEN* subsets is at most exponential in f'), and, as the number of such disjuncts and conjuncts in f' is no more than the length of f', the combined tree automaton (also a complemented pairs one) is also at most double exponential in the length of f' (and has at most an exponential number of designated pairs of subsets). An algorithm by Streett ([St81]) enables one to determine whether the language accepted by a complemented pairs tree automaton is non-empty in time single exponential in the size of (i.e., the number of states of) the automaton and double exponential in the number of designated pairs of subsets; thus, when the number of designated pairs of subsets of the automaton is logarithmic in the number of its states, the algorithm runs in time exponential in the size of the automaton. Hence, the overall decision procedure for the satisfiability of CTL* runs in time triple exponential in the length of the input formula. (Observe that two factors govern the complexity of decision procedures designed using the automata-theoretic approach. One is the complexity of the algorithm that determines non-emptiness of the language accepted by a given tree automaton, and the other is the size of the tree automaton obtained from the input formula.)

It turns out that constructing tree automata for formulae of the $E\,p$ and $AGE\,p$ with no more than a double exponential number of states (in the length of p) is relatively easy. But for formulae in f' of the form $A\,p$, the nondeterministic Büchi automaton (on infinite strings) constructed by the tableau method applied to the pure path (linear temporal logic) formula p is exponential in the length of p. This automaton needs to be determinized before it can be used to construct a tree automaton for $A\,p$, and the best known determinization procedure then (an ingenious one due to McNaughton, cf. [McN66]) involved a double exponential blow-up in the number of states. Thus, this method would yield only a triple exponential tree automaton for $A\,p$. One of the important results in [ES84] is that the special structure of the nondeterministic Büchi (strings) automaton for p could be used to determinize it in a way that caused only a single exponential blow-up in its size. (Recently, Safra [Sa88] has shown that a single exponential determinization is *always* possible; his construction uses McNaughton's techniques cleverly optimized in a way that had escaped several other prior efforts.)

We now summarize the research to date for several dynamic and branching time temporal logics that have been decided using this approach. The dynamic logic PDL-Δ and the propositional μ-calculus have also been shown to have elementary decision procedures for their satisfiability problems using tree automata. PDL-Δ (cf. [St81]) extends PDL, the Propositional Dynamic Logic, with the loop construct, and is similar to CTL*, but has ω-regular expressions instead of the path formulae of linear temporal logic. Streett showed in [St81] that its satisfiability problem is elementarily decidable by giving a deterministic triple exponential decision procedure. The propositional μ-calculus (cf. [Ko82]) is a language for expressing correctness properties of programs as extremal fixpoints of predicate transformers. (Several related algebraic methods for reasoning about program correctness have been developed; see, for example, [Pa70], [deR76], [Di76], [deB80], [EC80].) Kozen ([Ko82]) obtained a deterministic exponential time decision procedure using a tableau-based approach for a fragment of the propositional μ-calculus expressive enough to capture such modalities as $AF\,p$, $EF\,p$, and $AG\,p$, but not $A\overset{\infty}{G}\,p$. In [SE84], it was shown that the full μ-calculus is decidable in triple exponential time by reduction to the non-emptiness problem for tree automata. However, because of the discontinuous fixpoint characterizations of the μ-calculus modalities, even though its satisfiability problem is reduced to combinatorial properties of finite objects, transfinite ordinals are used in an essential way in the proof. In [Em85], a double exponential nondeterministic algorithm was presented for the satisfiability of CTL*; this was made possible by an improved nondeterministic method for testing non-emptiness of pairs automata, in fact, one that runs in polynomial time. Another nondeterministic algorithm that achieved the same bound for CTL* was independently given in [VS85]; moreover, nondeterministic single exponential upper bounds were established for both the μ-calculus and PDL-Δ, thus establishing double exponential deterministic upper bounds for both these logics. Also in [VS85], non-trivial lower bounds were established for the first time for the satisfiability problems of CTL* (deterministic double exponential) and the propositional μ-calculus (deterministic single exponential). A deterministic single exponential lower bound for PDL-Δ followed from that for PDL established in [FL79]. Automata-theoretic techniques have also been used in [CVW86] to derive optimal decision procedures for CTL (deterministic single exponential) and CTL* (deterministic double exponential) interpreted only over fair structures (see Section 2.4).

Recently, Emerson and Jutla ([EJ88]) have obtained vastly improved deterministic methods of testing non-emptiness of tree automata. They show that the non-emptiness problem for pairs automata is $\mathcal{NP}$-complete, but there is a deterministic algorithm that runs in time of the order of $(mn)^{3n}$, where m is the size of the automaton and n is the number of pairs designated in its acceptance condition (also see [PR89]). Similar bounds are also obtained for complemented pairs automata. Using the reduction described above ([ES84]), and this new deterministic algorithm, they exhibit an optimal (double exponential deterministic) algorithm for testing satisfiability of CTL*. Then, making use of Safra's more succinct construction to determinize Büchi automata on infinite strings together with their improved method of testing non-emptiness, they present optimal (deterministic single exponential) decision procedures for both the propositional μ-calculus and PDL-Δ.

As an aside, Abrahamson ([Ab80]) had shown that MPL (Modal Process Logic), which has a syntax very similar to that of CTL*, has a double exponential deterministic decision procedure for a semantics over structures that are not R-generable. (For R–generable structures, Abrahamson could give only a nonelementary decision procedure by embedding formulae of MPL in SnS.) The point to be noted is that such structures impose fewer constraints and thus there are "more" candidate structures for satisfiability of formulae. Hence, a decision procedure for the more natural semantics over R-generable structures should intuitively be harder to arrive at, and, historically, this has proved to be the case.

We conclude this sub-section by remarking on the symbiotic relationship between the two formalisms, viz., branching time temporal logic and automata theory. Without the use of automata theory, elementary decision procedures for many temporal logics may not have been possible. On the other hand, this theoretical application of automata to temporal logic has renewed interest in automata theory, and has been instrumental in formulating new concepts (such as various kinds of tree automata, cf. [St81], [VW84]), in providing better algorithms for classical problems (such as testing non-emptiness), and in sparking ingenious ways to combine automata (cf. [McN66], [Sa88]), a classical concern of automata theory.

4.1.3 Applications to Automated Program Synthesis

We now turn to more pragmatic matters, illustrating in this subsection a method to automatically synthesize concurrent programs from their temporal specifications. As mentioned earlier, we content ourselves by describing the technique presented in [EC82], and summarize related approaches at the end of this subsection.

The method assumes a process-based model operating in a shared memory environment with test-and-set primitives. Also, process interaction is assumed to be restricted to a well-defined, clean interface. Thus, each process may be viewed as having several sections of code (all of which are presumed to terminate) during the execution of which the process does not interact with the others; all interactions take place "between" these sections of code. As usual, it is assumed that the process' transitions from one section of code to another are instantaneous and simultaneously occurring transitions may be interleaved in any arbitrary order without affecting the correctness of the program.

For a set of such processes, the synthesis method automatically generates a *synchronization skeleton* from a high-level temporal logic specification expressed in CTL. The synchronization skeleton is essentially a state transition graph of the process, but the nodes represent the interaction-free regions of code alluded to above. Its edges, therefore, represent permitted sequences of terminating computations. Thus, the synchronization skeleton is an abstraction of the actual program where detail irrelevant to synchronization (i.e., the specifics of the interaction-free sections of code) is suppressed. For example, in the synchronization skeleton for a solution to the mutual exclusion problem each process' critical region may be viewed as a single node since the internal structure of the critical region is unimportant to the task of enforcing mutual exclusion. (Note that most solutions to synchronization problems in the literature are in fact given as synchronization skeletons.) Because synchronization skeletons are in general finite-state, propositional temporal logic suffices to specify their properties.

The synthesis method exploits the small model property of CTL. A decision procedure which, given a CTL formula, p, will decide whether p is satisfiable or not is its basis. For this application, unsatisfiability of p means that the specification is *inconsistent* (and should be reformulated). If p is satisfiable, then the specification it expresses is consistent. A model for p with a finite number of states is constructed by the decision procedure. In essence, the model represents the global flowgraph of the system of processes being synchronized: a state in it corresponds to a global state of the system, and an edge to a state transition of a single process (as simultaneous state transitions of two different processes are assumed to be interleavable in some arbitrary order). The synchronization skeleton of a program meeting the specification is then factored out of model. The small model property ensures that any program whose synchronization properties can be expressed in CTL can be realized by a system of concurrently running processes, each of which is a finite-state machine.

This method has been used to synthesize, for example, a starvation-free solution to the mutual exclusion problem for two processes, P_1 and P_2. Each process is always in one of three regions of code: N_i, the non-critical region of process i, T_i, the trying region of process i, and C_i, the critical region of process i. Each process always transits from its non-critical to its trying region, thence to its critical region, and then back to its non-critical region. Thus, a prototype synchronization skeleton for process i is shown in Fig. 5(a). The content of this figure is easily expressed formally in CTL, interpreted over a multi-process structure as discussed in Section 2.3.3. (Note that this includes the fact that each process be in precisely one of these three states at all times.) To formulate these assertions, each state of the synchronization skeleton is denoted by one atomic proposition, which, intuitively, is true precisely when the process is in that state. We shall use the symbols used to denote states to denote the atomic propositions as well. Other specifications for the problem can be expressed as follows:

1. The start state of each process is N_i, and, hence, that of the system is $N_1 \wedge N_2$.

2. Mutual exclusion should be enforced at all times (i.e., the two processes should not be in their critical regions at the same time): $AG(\neg C_1 \vee \neg C_2)$.

3. Neither process should starve (i.e., each time either process wishes to enter its critical region, it should eventually succeed): $AG(N_i \Rightarrow AF\, C_i)$.

Note that each assertion is a CTL one; their conjunction denotes the complete specification. The satisfiability procedure for CTL is used to construct a model for this formula. Each state in the model would have been labelled with one of each process' three states; if there is more than one state in the model in which the concurrent system's state is the same, they are distinguished by using different values of an *auxiliary variable* for that global state. Such variables are shared among all processes and used to enforce synchronization. For our example, the model constructed has two states labelled $T_1 \wedge T_2$, i.e., when both processes are in their trying regions, and the binary-valued auxiliary variable named *TURN* is used to distinguish them. Thus the synchronization variables are generated as required by the method.

From the global model, the synchronization skeletons can essentially be read off yielding the one shown in Fig. 5(b). (The value of j is 1 if i is 2, and 2 if i is 1.) Each arc in the figure is labelled with one or more conditional transitions $B? \rightarrow A$ (separated by the symbol $\vee$) used to

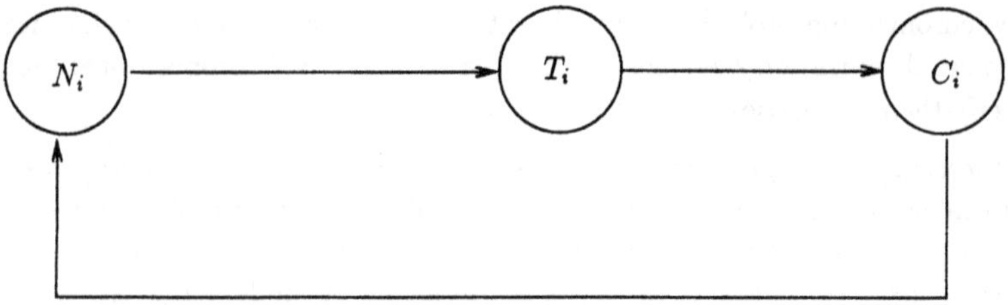

(a) Prototypical skeleton specified.

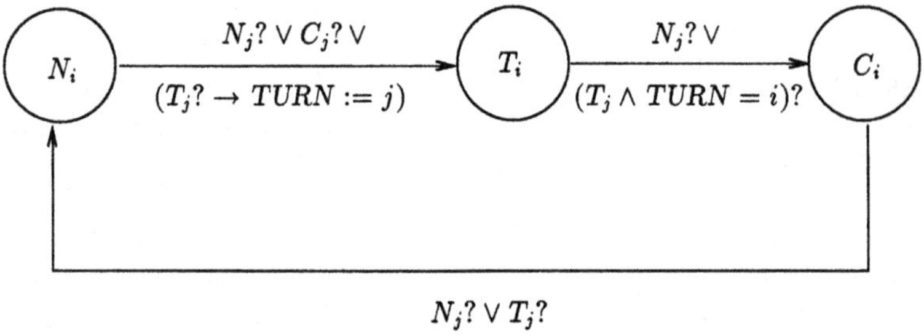

(b) Synthesized skeleton.

Figure 5: Synchronization skeletons for the mutual exclusion problem.

enforce synchronization constraints. For a process to make a transition, one of the conditional transitions labelling the corresponding arc should be true, and the action A associated with this conditional transition is taken to update the auxiliary variable. If a conditional transition does not change the value of any auxiliary variable, only $B?$ is written. Note that B is a predicate on the auxiliary variable and the process' states, which are assumed to be globally accessible in shared memory. Finally, note that the synthesized programs are correct under arbitrary schedules, and not just fair ones as no fairness constraints were imposed on the specifications.

Thus, this method obviates the need to compose a program as well as the need to construct a proof of its correctness. One only has to formulate a precise problem specification. An additional advantage of this method is that it is both *sound* in that any solution it yields does in fact meet the specification and *complete* in that, if the specification is satisfiable, a solution will be generated.

An implementation of this technique is discussed in [In84]. One problem with the method is that the procedure could potentially take exponential time because the satisfiability decision procedure for CTL is used. However, it has been shown ([ESS89]) that the assertions above, as well as those of several standard problems presented in the literature, can in fact be expressed in the more restrictive temporal logic SCTL (see Section 4.1.1, and note that the atomic propositions which denote process states are mutually exclusive and exhaustive), and, thus, the synthesis problem for any fixed number of (e.g., two) processes can be done in polynomial time. For a variable number of processes, the method is still exponential in the number of processes though. The state explosion problem for synthesis applications is addressed in [AE89].

Earlier methods of synthesis tended to be *heuristic* as opposed to *algorithmic*. Laventhal [Lav78]) used a specification language that is essentially predicate calculus augmented with a distinguished predicate to define the relative order of events in time. In [RK80], an applied linear time temporal logic is used. Instead of model-theoretic methods, both these techniques are *ad hoc*. They are illustrated on constructing resource synchronizers from specifications.

A similar technique of automatically synthesizing programs from specifications expressed in an extended linear temporal logic ([Wo81]) was established independently in [MW84]. The model of parallel computation in this case is based on message passing primitives in a distributed computing environment, and CSP programs are generated. Note, however, that their paradigm still involves "centralization" in that all interprocess communication occurs between a distinguished synchronizer process and one of its satellite processes. In some ways, a branching time logic is better for the synthesis problem because the existence of specific computation paths can be used to ensure that the synthesized program exhibits an adequate degree of parallelism (i.e., that the synthesized program can follow any one of a number of computation paths and is not a "degenerate" solution with only a single path). On the other hand, the extended temporal logic allows specifications of properties that are not expressible in CTL (counting modulo a fixed integer, for example). Also, CTL cannot express fairness constraints adequately. It is quite possible, however, that this approach can be used with FCTL to express the specifications rather than CTL. (As an aside, note that a finite model of the temporal specification f should be constructible if f is satisfiable. Thus, if the only known decision procedure for a temporal logic is based on the automata-theoretic approach, that logic cannot, in general, be used for this method of automated synthesis.)

4.2 Axiomatics and the Verification of Concurrent Programs

We now discuss the problem of formulating a sound and complete axiomatization for branching time temporal logics. An axiomatic system prescribes a series of primitive validities, the *axioms*, and a set of *inference rules*, which can be used to derive other assertions from the axioms. Such assertions are said to be *provable* within (and, sometimes *theorems* of) the axiomatic system, and their provability is denoted by $\vdash f$. The system is *sound* if all assertions derived from the axioms using the inference rules are valid, and it is *complete* if all validities of the temporal logic can be derived. Soundness of an axiomatic system, therefore, stipulates that if $\vdash f$, then $\models f$, and completeness, the converse. In our discussion, we shall say that f is *consistent* iff it is not the case that $\neg f$ is provable (i.e., not $\vdash \neg f$). Using the fact that f is valid iff $\neg f$ is not satisfiable, it is easily seen that an axiomatic system is sound if whenever f is satisfiable, it is consistent, and complete if the converse holds.

While sound axiomatizations of branching time temporal logics can be quite easily formulated, only one standard technique has been used to show that an axiomatization is complete. We shall outline this method in the context of CTL; the reader is referred to ([EH82]) for a complete proof. The same technique has been used for both dynamic logics (e.g., Deterministic PDL, cf. [BHP81]) and other systems of branching time logic (e.g., UB, cf. [BMP81]); however, it is applicable only to temporal logics whose satisfiability problem is solvable using the tableau-based approach. In fact, no sound and complete axiomatizations are known for most temporal logics (including CTL*) whose only known decision procedure for satisfiability uses the automata-theoretic method; that formalism does not provide any assistance in proving an axiomatic system complete.

The axioms in the system for CTL presented in [EH82] are as follows (p, q, and r are arbitrary CTL formulae):

A0. All tautologies of propositional logic
A1. $EX\,true \wedge AX\,true$
A2. $EF\,p \equiv E(true\; U\, p)$
A3. $AF\,p \equiv A(true\; U\, p)$
A4. $EX(p \vee q) \equiv EX\,p \vee EX\,q$
A5. $AX\,p \equiv \neg EX \neg p$
A6. $E(p\; U\, q) \equiv q \vee (p \wedge EXE(p\; U\, q))$
A7. $A(p\; U\, q) \equiv q \vee (p \wedge AXA(p\; U\, q))$

and the rules of inference are:

R0. $p,\, p \Rightarrow q \vdash q$ (modus ponens)
R1. $p \Rightarrow q \vdash EX\,p \Rightarrow EX\,q$
R2. $r \Rightarrow (\neg q \wedge EX\,r) \vdash r \Rightarrow \neg A(p\; U\, q)$
R3. $r \Rightarrow [\neg q \wedge AX(r \vee \neg E(p\; U\, q))] \vdash r \Rightarrow \neg E(p\; U\, q)$

An axiomatic system for UB is obtained by replacing p by *true* in A6 and A7 and in R2 and R3. (A related sound and complete axiomatization for CTL with fewer inference rules is presented in [Em88].)

Establishing the soundness of the system is easily done by inspection using the definition of validity of formulae. To show its completeness, every consistent formula f is shown to be satisfiable. This is done by showing that the pruned tableau of any consistent formula f contains a node labelled with f. As before, we identify a node S in the initial tableau with the maximally consistent subset of $CL(f)$ labelling it; the conjunction of the formulae in this subset is denoted by $\wedge S$.

The essence of the proof lies in proving the claim that if the node S is eliminated by the proof procedure, then $\wedge S$ is inconsistent, i.e., $\vdash \neg \wedge S$. Since $f \equiv \bigvee_{f \in S}(\wedge S)$ is clearly a tautology (recall each S is maximally consistent), it can be shown that $\vdash f \equiv \bigvee_{\{S \mid f \in S,\, \wedge S \text{ consistent}\}} \wedge S$, by using the claim to eliminate the inconsistent subsets to which f belongs from the tautology by repeated applications of the modus ponens inference rule, and, similarly, that $\vdash true \equiv \bigvee_{\{S \mid \wedge S \text{ consistent}\}} \wedge S$. These two can together be used to show that, if f is consistent, then so is some $\wedge S$, where $f \in S$, and so, by the contrapositive of the claim, S is not eliminated in the pruning procedure. Thus, f is satisfiable.

Before proving the claim, it is shown that if there is an edge in the initial tableau from V to W, then $\wedge V \wedge EX(\wedge W)$ is not consistent by proving its negation. Then (the contrapositive of) the claim is proved by showing that if $\wedge S$ is consistent, S cannot be eliminated by any of the pruning rules stated in Section 4.1.1, using induction on the order of the deleted nodes and considering each pruning rule separately. Details of the proof of the claim may be found in [EH82] (or, for a related axiomatization, in [Em88]).

An obvious application of sound and complete axiomatizations is that they can be used as the basis for a temporal deductive system for the manual verification of concurrent programs, or for manually refining temporal specifications from a high-level one to simpler ones that are easily implemented. This approach has been pursued in [MW78], [Ha80], [La80], [MP81a], [MP81b], [MP82], [OL82], [La83], [MP83], and [BKP84] among other places; note that many of these use the linear temporal logic formalism to prove a correctness property of a program, as one is generally required to prove that such properties are true of *all* execution sequences. We do not discuss the methods employed in detail here partly for this reason, and partly because this is probably the predominant application of temporal logics, and relevant literature is widely available.

In general, such methods place a heavy burden on the verifier's ingenuity to organize the proof well enough to make the task tractable, and often rely on his intimate knowledge of the working of the program to guide the proof through. In any case, the proof steps are seldom as small as those permitted by an axiomatic system like the one above; derived rules of inference that are first shown to be valid are commonly used (cf. [MP81b], [OL82]). An example of such a derived rule that is useful in demonstrating safety properties of programs is that if f is initially true and $AG(f \Rightarrow AX\, f)$ is true, then f is true everywhere, i.e., $AG\, f$ is true. To apply it, one must needs to show that f is true at the initial state of a program (this is like a basis step), and all execution steps of the program preserve the truth of f, essentially an induction step. Liveness properties, generally established only of fair execution sequences, are generally harder to show correct. Sometimes, simple derived principles (such as if $p \Rightarrow A_\phi\, F\, q$ and $AG(q \Rightarrow A_\phi\, F\, r)$ are both true, then so is $p \Rightarrow A_\phi\, F\, r$) suffice; at other times, one must use well-founded sets (much like in sequential program verification) to show that a liveness property holds.

Manna and Pnueli argue in [MP83] that the two phase procedure of first setting up an axiom system and then establishing derived principles for reasoning is unnecessary. They show that a deductive system for almost any concurrent programming language can be set up to have three parts, only one of which depends on the program being verified (its variables, reference to its states, etc.). One of the two other parts comprises general theorems of temporal logic enhanced with first-order logic quantifiers, and the other, the so-called *domain part*, has domain dependent axioms and theorems, that refer, for example, to general properties of common data structures used in all programs.

One alternative to the completely manual approach of verifying programs is to automate each proof step. This cuts down on the tedium of the method, while retaining its main advantage: allowing the verifier to use his understanding of the program to direct the proof to the goal. To do this, note that proving a formula f from the set $\mathcal{A}$ of axioms together with other known theorems is equivalent to showing that $\wedge\mathcal{A} \Rightarrow f$ is valid (assuming a sound and complete axiomatization). Thus this proof step can be automated using the decision procedure for satisfiability for the temporal logic. Of course, one expects that "most" proof steps would not force the decision procedure to its worst case time complexity (most often exponential deterministic time as we have seen), and that the verifier carefully selects a minimal subset of axioms and theorems needed to prove f. Such automated theorem provers are fairly standard in other areas of computer science.

Note that for this method to be useful, we test the satisfiability of the negation of $\wedge\mathcal{A} \Rightarrow f$, implicitly assuming that the set of formulae of the temporal logic is closed under negation. The logic SCTL (see Section 4.1.1) does not have this property. However, it is shown in [ESS89] that the problem of testing the validity of the inference of f from $\wedge\mathcal{A}$ can be done in small polynomial time, using SCTL's polynomial time decision procedure for satisfiability, and so proof steps are capable of being automated efficiently. The method is illustrated by proving liveness properties for example programs from [OL82].

One aspect related to providing axiomatizations is proving theorems (validities) of the axiomatization. Such validities are useful in tasks such as refining specifications for a program (cf. [La83]) or acting as mini derived rules of inference (largely to "simplify" assertions) in manual verification. Most such validities, however, concern the linear temporal operators (e.g., the connective F distributes over $\vee$, G, over $\wedge$, $G\, p \Rightarrow \overset{\infty}{G}\, p \Rightarrow \overset{\infty}{F}\, p \Rightarrow F\, p$, $F\overset{\infty}{F}\, p \equiv \overset{\infty}{F}\, p$, etc., etc.), and an extensive list may be found in, for example, [MP81a]. We have also had occasion to use some validities involving the branching time modalities in the course of the examples presented in this paper. A more complete list may be found, for example, in [BMP81].

4.3 The Model Checking Problem and its Applications

The model checking problem for a branching time logic may be stated as: *Given a formula f of the temporal logic, and a finite (or finitely represented) structure M, is M a model of f?* A natural variation of the problem may also specify a state of the structure and require that it be determined whether f is true at that state in M.

Unlike the problems of providing axiomatizations or determining satisfiability of formulae, the model checking problem has primarily been investigated only in endogenous temporal logic frameworks. The problem was first suggested in [CE81] for CTL. (A related model checking approach is described in [QS81].) Its simplicity and the efficiency of its solution for CTL ([CES83]) have led to its being applied to diverse areas. So we discuss the problem in the context of CTL, and then summarize results for other temporal logics.

Assume that we wish to determine whether formula f is true at some state of the finite structure $M = (S, R, L)$. The algorithm is designed so that when it finishes, each state s of M is labelled with the subformulae of f that are true at s. A simple way of understanding how the algorithm works is to consider the parse tree of the formula f, with operators (boolean ones and the temporal modalities AX, EX, AU, and AU, the first two of which are unary, and the third and the fourth, binary) at the interior nodes and atomic propositions at the leaves. The algorithm proceeds by working its way up the tree level by level: at each tree node n, which corresponds to the subformula p of f, say, it adds p to the labels of those states of the structure at which p is true. This is easily done if p is elementary (i.e., an atomic proposition or of the form $EX\,q$ or $AX\,q$) or if n has a boolean connective. For example if $p = q \wedge r$, each of q and r have been added to labels of all states at which they are true, and so the set of states of M is merely scanned to do the same for p. If p is of the form $A(q\,U\,r)$ or $E(q\,U\,r)$, a technique similar to the one used in the tableau-based method to determine if there is a DAG rooted at a state for these kinds of eventualities is used (see Section 4.1.1). For example, for $p = A(q\,U\,r)$, all nodes labelled with r are labelled with p, and then all nodes labelled with q but not with p such that all of their successors are labelled with $A(q\,U\,r)$ are labelled with p. This is done repeatedly till no more nodes can be labelled with p. (Note that this is simpler than determining if a state of the tableau has a DAG fulfilling p rooted at it because the internal nodes of the DAG were required to satisfy additional conditions.) The case when the modality is EU is handled similarly. Finally, M is a model of f iff some state of M is labelled with f when the algorithm terminates.

It is easy to see that the algorithm is linear in the length of f (each node of the parse tree is examined exactly once and there are no more nodes in the parse tree than the length of f). A more careful examination shows that it is also linear in the size of M (the number of states plus the number of elements of R) because labelling the states of M for each subformula takes time linear in the size of M. This is again apparent if the subformula is elementary or if its main connective is a boolean one. For the cases when the main connective is AU or EU, a linear time marking algorithm was outlined in Section 4.4.1. Thus, the overall complexity of the algorithm is of the order of $O(|M| \times |f|)$.

Surprisingly enough the model checking problem for the standard linear time temporal logic is PSPACE-complete ([SC82]), and, hence, unlikely to have as efficient a solution. (The model checking problem for linear temporal logics have to check the truth of an input *path* formula f as all linear time formulae are path formulae. By convention, however, the structure is not limited to being a chain, but is an arbitrary graph; the semantics of linear formulae over such structures is detailed at the end of Section 2.4. The problem for linear time temporal logics then requires one to determine if f is true of some one path of the given structure. Thus, in effect, the truth of the formula $A\,f$ is checked for in the branching time logic corresponding to the linear time one—see Section 2.4—as f is true along a fullpath of the structure iff $E\,f$ is true at some state of it, i.e., $\neg A \neg f$ is true at some state of the structure.) However, in [LP85] an algorithm that is *linear* in the size of the structure, but exponential in the length of the formula is presented. It is argued that as "interesting" temporal correctness properties tend to be small, but structures in general are not, the algorithm is efficient in practice. Moreover, linear temporal logic can express fairness properties, while CTL cannot. Thus, correctness properties that hold only under fair schedules cannot be checked with the CTL algorithm.

However, it is shown in [EL85] that an algorithm for model checking FCTL formulae can be developed that runs in time linear in the size of the structure and polynomial in the length of the formula provided that the fairness constraint ϕ is in the canonical form $\bigvee_{i=1}^{n} \bigwedge_{j=1}^{m} (\overset{\infty}{G}\, p_{ij} \vee \overset{\infty}{F}\, q_{ij})$, where the p_{ij} and the q_{ij} are pure path formulae. Most standard types of fairness, including all those discussed in Section 2.1, are succinctly expressible in this form; all other fairness constraints of the kind permitted in FCTL (see Section 2.4) can be translated to this form, but could blow-up exponentially in size. For FCTL, the model checking problem is solved by reduction (in linear time) to the *Fair State Problem:* Starting from which states does there exist some path along which ϕ holds? Both problems are shown to be $\mathcal{NP}$-complete when ϕ is an arbitrary fairness constraint.

Thus, the argument regarding fairness in favour of linear temporal logics is not a compelling one. It is still true, however, that there are correctness properties not involving fairness which are expressible in linear temporal logic, but not handled by the approach in [EL85], so that it might appear that linear time logic is still preferable for some applications of model checking. However, it is argued there that branching time logic is always better than linear time logic for model checking in the following way. Given a model checking algorithm for a system of linear time logic, there is a model checking algorithm of the same order of complexity (in both the structure and the formula sizes) for the corresponding full branching time logic which trivially subsumes the linear time logic in expressive power. (In particular, model checking for the *full* system of branching time logic CTL* is hence in PSPACE.)

This is shown by demonstrating that handling explicit path quantifiers and even nested path quantifiers costs (essentially) nothing: the real question for the model checking problem is what the *basic modalities* of a system of logic are. A basic modality of a branching time logic is the subset of its formulae of the form $A\,p$ or $E\,p$ where p is a pure path formula. As we have seen for CTL in Section 2.4, the syntax of the formulae of a branching time temporal logic can be defined by rules that essentially use just its basic modalities without reference to path formulae at all. Consider CTL*, for example. The basic modalities of CTL* are formulae of the form $A\,p$ or $E\,p$ where p is a pure path formula. Now, the the syntax of CTL* formulae can be equivalently be defined to be those generated by the rules S1 and S2 in Section 2.2 together with:

S3″. If p is a basic modality, $Q_1, Q_2, \ldots, Q_n$ are (instances of some) atomic propositions appearing in p, and $q_1, q_2, \ldots, q_n$ are arbitrary formulae derived by S1, S2, and previous applications of this rule, then the result of syntactically substituting the Q_i in p by the q_i is also a state formula.

The model checking algorithm works by recursive descent; when it encounters a subformula p of the form $A\,q$ or $E\,q$ where q is a pure path formula, it uses the linear temporal logic's algorithm for model checking. After that, it replaces p by a fresh atomic proposition, and proceeds to the previous level of recursion.

As for applications of model checking, one obvious one is to automate verification of finite-state concurrent programs (cf. [CE81], [CES83]). The global flowgraph of the program is viewed as a temporal structure and the property to be checked is expressed in an appropriate temporal logic. The method has been automated by Sifakis to be able to check network communication protocols; his implementation can handle models with of the order of 10^5 states and edges. Clearly, one problem with model checking for such an application is that the global state graph of the program is exponential in the number of processes. Recent work (cf. [CG87], [SG87]) has tried to overcome the state explosion problem. Model checking has also been used to verify hardware systems such as VLSI circuits ([Br86]).

5 Summary

In this paper, we have given a systematic account of branching time temporal logics and demonstrated how they provide a formal system for describing and reasoning about the correct behaviour of concurrent programs. We have seen that the system of branching time logic CTL* is expressive enough to be able capture many correctness properties including those that deal with the specification of fairness. On the other hand, its decision procedures have a high time complexity because of the expressiveness of its basic modalities. However, a key feature of branching time temporal logic is its ability to provide a rich variety of restricted mixes of path and linear time connectives, thereby permitting the definition of a wide range of systems of logic of varying expressiveness. Some of these, such as CTL and FCTL, have proved to be sufficiently expressive in practice to specify and reason about concurrent programs, and the simplicity of their modalities has allowed more efficient decision procedures to be developed for them. We have illustrated the applicability of their decision procedures for satisfiability and model checking (particularly those of CTL) to the tasks of automatically synthesizing and verifying finite-state concurrent programs respectively. We have also examined the relation between linear time and branching time temporal logics and discussed their suitability to reasoning about concurrent programs. Finally, we have outlined various techniques that have been used to arrive at decision procedures (for both satisfiability and model checking) for various systems of branching time temporal logic and shown how closely related formalisms such as automata theory have proved to be immensely useful for this purpose.

Bibliography

[Ab80] Abrahamson, K., Decidability and Expressiveness of Logics of Processes, Ph.D. Thesis, Univ. of Washington, 1980.

[AE89] Attie, P.C., E.A. Emerson, Synthesis of Concurrent Systems With Many Similar Sequential Processes, *to appear in Proc. 16th Annual ACM Symp. on Principles of Programming Languages*, Austin, 1989.

[Br86] Browne, M.C., An Improved Algorithm for the Automatic Verification of Finite State Systems Using Temporal Logic, *Proc. Symp. on Logic in Computer Science*, Cambridge, pp. 260–266, 1986.

[Bü62] Büchi, J.R., On A Decision Method in Restricted Second Order Arithmetic, *Logic, Methodology, and Philosophy of Science: Proc. 1960 International Congress*, Stanford Univ. Press, 1962.

[BHP81] Ben-Ari, M., J.Y. Halpern, A. Pnueli, Finite Models for Deterministic Propositional Dynamic Logic, *Proc. 8th Annual International Colloquium on Automata, Languages and Programming*, LNCS#115, Springer–Verlag, pp. 249–263, 1981; *a revised version entitled* Deterministic Propositional Dynamic Logic: Finite Models, Complexity, and Completeness, *appears in Journal of Computer and System Sciences*, vol 25, no. 3, pp. 402–417, 1982.

[BKP84] Barringer, H., R. Kuiper, A. Pnueli, Now you may Compose Temporal Logic Specifications, *Proc. of the 16th Annual ACM Symp. on Theory of Computing*, Washington D.C., pp. 51–63, 1984.

[BMP81] Ben-Ari, M., Z. Manna, A. Pnueli, The Temporal Logic of Branching Time, *Proc. 8th Annual ACM Symp. on Principles of Programming Languages,* Williamsburg, pp. 164–176, 1981; *also appeared in Acta Informatica*, **vol.** 20, no. 3, pp. 207–226, 1983.

[CE81] Clarke, E.M., E.A. Emerson, Design and Synthesis of Synchronization Skeletons Using Branching Time Temporal Logic, *Proc. of the Workshop on Logics of Programs*, Yorktown Heights, D. Kozen, editor, LNCS#131, Springer–Verlag, pp. 52–71, 1981.

[CES83] Clarke, E.M., E.A. Emerson, A.P. Sistla, Automatic Verification of Finite State Concurrent Systems Using Temporal Logic Specifications: A Practical Approach, *Proc. 10th Annual ACM Symp. on Principles of Programming Languages,* Austin, pp. 117–126, 1983; *also appeared in ACM Transactions on Programming Languages and Systems*, **vol.** 8, no. 2, pp. 244–263, 1986.

[CG87] Clarke, E.M., O. Grumberg, Avoiding the State Explosion Problem in Temporal Model Checking Algorithms, *Proc. of the 6th Annual ACM Symp. on Principles of Distributed Computing*, Vancouver, pp. 294–303, 1987.

[CVW86] Courcoubetis C., M.Y. Vardi, P. Wolper, Reasoning about Fair Concurrent Programs, *Proc. of the 18th Annual ACM Symp. on Theory of Computing*, Berkeley, pp. 283–294, 1986.

[deB80] de Bakker, J.W., *Mathematical Theory of Program Correctness*, Prentice–Hall, 1980.

[deR76] de Roever, W.P., *Recursive Program Schemes: Semantics and Proof Theory*, Mathematical Centre Tracts 70, Mathematisch Centrum, Amsterdam, 1976.

[Di76] Dijkstra, E.W., *A Discipline of Programming*, Prentice–Hall, 1976.

[Em81] Emerson, E.A., Branching Time Temporal Logic and the Design of Correct Concurrent Programs, Ph.D. Thesis, Harvard University, 1981.

[Em83] Emerson, E.A., Alternative Semantics for Temporal Logics, *Theoretical Computer Science*, **vol.** 26, no. 1–2, pp. 121–130, 1983.

[Em85] Emerson, E.A., Automata, Tableaux, and Temporal Logics, *Proc. Conf. on Logics of Programs*, Brooklyn, R. Parikh, editor, LNCS#193, Springer–Verlag, pp. 79–88, 1985.

[Em88] Emerson, E.A., Temporal and Modal Logic, *manuscript,* 1988; *to appear in* the *Handbook of Theoretical Computer Science*, J. van Leeuwen, editor, North–Holland.

[EC80] Emerson, E.A., E.M. Clarke, Characterizing Correctness Properties of Parallel Programs Using Fixpoints, *Proc. 7th Annual International Colloquium on Automata, Languages and Programming*, LNCS#85, Springer–Verlag, pp. 169–181, 1980.

[EC82] Emerson, E.A., E.M. Clarke, Using Branching Time Logic to Synthesize Synchronization Skeletons, *Science of Computer Programming*, **vol.** 2, pp. 241–266, 1982.

[EH82] Emerson, E.A., J.Y. Halpern, Decision Procedures and Expressiveness in the Temporal Logic of Branching Time, *Proc. of the 14th Annual ACM Symp. on Theory of Computing*, San Francisco, pp. 169–180, 1982; *also appeared in Journal of Computer and System Sciences*, **vol** 30, no. 1, pp. 1–24, 1985.

[EH83] Emerson, E.A., J.Y. Halpern, "Sometimes" and "Not Never" Revisited: On Branching versus Linear Time, *Proc. 10th Annual ACM Symp. on Principles of Programming Languages,* Austin, pp. 127–140, 1983; *also appeared in Journal ACM*, **vol** 33, no. 1, pp. 151–178, 1986.

[EJ88] Emerson, E.A., C.S. Jutla, The Complexity of Tree Automata and Logics of Programs, *29th Annual Symp. on Foundations of Computer Science*, White Plains, pp. 328–337, 1988.

[EL85] Emerson, E.A., C.L. Lei, Modalities for Model Checking: Branching Time Logic Strikes Back, *Proc. 12th Annual ACM Symp. on Principles of Programming Languages*, New Orleans, pp. 84–96, 1985; *also appeared in Science of Computer Programming*, **vol.** 8, pp. 275–306, 1987.

[EL86] Emerson, E.A., C.L. Lei, Temporal Reasoning under Generalized Fairness Constraints, *3rd Annual Symp. on Theoretical Aspects of Computer Science*, LNCS#210, Springer–Verlag, pp. 21–36, 1986.

[ES84] Emerson, E.A., A.P. Sistla, Deciding Full Branching Time Logic, *Information and Control*, **vol.** 61, no. 3, pp. 175–201, 1984; *also appeared in Proc. of the 16th Annual ACM Symp. on Theory of Computing*, Washington D.C., pp. 14–24, 1984.

[ESS89] Emerson, E.A., T.H. Sadler, J. Srinivasan, Efficient Temporal Reasoning (Extended Abstract), *to appear in Proc. 16th Annual ACM Symp. on Principles of Programming Languages*, Austin, 1989.

[Fl67] Floyd, R.W., Assigning Meaning to Programs, *Proceedings of Symposia in Applied Mathematics*, in *Mathematical Aspects of Computer Science*, J.T. Schwartz, editor, (American Mathematical Society), **vol.** 19, pp. 19–32, 1967.

[FL77] Fischer, M.J., R.E. Ladner, Propositional Modal Logic of Programs, *Proc. of the 9th Annual ACM Symp. on Theory of Computing*, Boulder, pp. 286–294, 1977.

[FL79] Fischer, M.J., R.E. Ladner, Propositional Dynamic Logic of Regular Programs, *Journal of Computer and System Sciences*, **vol.** 18, pp. 194–211, 1979.

[Fr86] Francez, N., *Fairness*, Springer–Verlag, 1986.

[FK84] Francez, N., D. Kozen, Generalized Fair Termination, *Proc. 11th Annual ACM Symp. on Principles of Programming Languages*, Salt Lake City, pp. 46–53, 1984.

[GPSS80] Gabbay, D., A. Pnueli, S. Shelah, J. Stavi, On the Temporal Analysis of Fairness, *Proc. 7th Annual ACM Symp. on Principles of Programming Languages*, Las Vegas, pp. 163–173, 1980.

[Ha80] Hailpern, B., Verifying Concurrent Processes Using Temporal Logic, Ph.D. Thesis, Stanford Univ. Computer Systems Lab Technical Report #195, 1980.

[HC72] Hughes, G.E., M.J. Creswell, *An Introduction to Modal Logic*, Methuen and Co. Ltd., 1972.

[Ho69] Hoare, C.A.R., An Axiomatic Basis for Computer Programming, *Communications ACM*, **vol.** 12, no. 10, pp. 576–583, 1969.

[HR72] Hossley, R., C. Rackoff, The Emptiness Problem For Automata On Infinite Trees, *Proc. 13th IEEE Symp. on Switching and Automata Theory* (*now called: Symp. on Foundations of Computer Science*), pp. 121–124, 1972.

[HT87] Hafer, T., W. Thomas, Computation Tree Logic CTL* and Path Quantifiers in the Monadic Theory of the Binary Tree, *Proc. 14th Annual International Colloquium on Automata, Languages and Programming*, LNCS#267, Springer–Verlag, pp. 269–279, 1987.

[In84] Inaba, Y., An Implementation of Synthesis of Concurrent Programs from Branching Time Temporal Logic Specifications, Master's Thesis, Univ. of Texas at Austin, 1984.

[Ka68] Kamp, H.W., Tense Logic and the Theory of Linear Order, Ph.D. Thesis, Univ. of California at Los Angeles, 1968.

[Ko82] Kozen, D., Results on the Propositional μ-Calculus, *Proc. 9th Annual International Colloquium on Automata, Languages and Programming*, LNCS#140, Springer–Verlag, pp. 348–359, 1982; *also appeared in Theoretical Computer Science*, **vol.** 27, no. 3, pp. 333–354, 1983.

[Kr63] Kripke, S.A., A Semantical Analysis of Modal Logic I: Normal Modal Propositional Calculi, *Zeitschr. f. Math. Logik Grundlagen d. Math.*, **vol.** 9, pp. 67–96, 1963.

[La80] Lamport, L., "Sometime" is Sometimes "Not Never"—On the Temporal Logic of Programs, *Proc. 7th Annual ACM Symp. on Principles of Programming Languages*, Las Vegas, pp. 174–185, 1980.

[La83] Lamport, L., What Good is Temporal Logic?, *Information Processing*, **vol.** 83, pp. 657–668, 1983.

[Lav78] Laventhal, M., Synthesis of Synchronization Code for Data Abstractions, Ph.D. Thesis, MIT, 1978.

[LS82] Lehmann, D., S. Shelah, Reasoning with Time and Chance, *Information and Control*, **vol.** 53, no. 3, pp. 165–198, 1982.

[LPS81] Lehmann, D., A. Pnueli, J. Stavi, Impartiality, Justice and Fairness: The Ethics of Concurrent Termination, *Proc. 8th Annual International Colloquium on Automata, Languages and Programming*, LNCS#115, Springer–Verlag, pp. 262–277, 1981.

[LP85] Lichtenstein, O., A. Pnueli, Checking That Finite State Concurrent Programs Satisfy Their Linear Specification, *Proc. 12th Annual ACM Symp. on Principles of Programming Languages*, New Orleans, pp. 97–107, 1985.

[LPZ85] Lichtenstein, O., A. Pnueli, L. Zuck, The Glory of The Past, *Proc. Conf. on Logics of Programs*, Brooklyn, R. Parikh, editor, LNCS#193, Springer–Verlag, pp. 196–218, 1985.

[McN66] McNaughton, R., Testing and Generating Infinite Sequences By a Finite Automaton, *Information and Control*, vol. 9, pp. 521–530, 1966.

[Me75] Meyer, A.R., Weak Monadic Second Order Theory of Successor Is Not Elementary-Recursive, *Logic Colloquium*, Symposium on Logic Held at Boston in 1972–73, Lecture Notes in Mathematics #453, R. Parikh, editor, Springer–Verlag, pp. 132–154, 1975.

[MP79] Manna, Z., A. Pnueli, The Modal Logic of Programs, *Proc. 6th Annual International Colloquium on Automata, Languages and Programming*, LNCS#71, Springer–Verlag, pp. 385–409, 1979.

[MP81a] Manna, Z., A. Pnueli, Verification of Concurrent Programs: The Temporal Framework, in *The Correctness Problem in Computer Science*, R.S. Boyer and J.S. Moore, editors, Academic Press, pp. 215–273, 1981.

[MP81b] Manna, Z., A. Pnueli, Verification of Concurrent Programs: Temporal Proof Principles, *Proc. of the Workshop on Logics of Programs*, Yorktown Heights, D. Kozen, editor, LNCS#131, Springer–Verlag, pp. 200-252, 1981.

[MP82] Manna, Z., A. Pnueli, Verification of Concurrent Programs: A Temporal Proof System, *Proc. 4th School on Advanced Programming*, Amsterdam, Holland, June 1982.

[MP83] Manna, Z., A. Pnueli, How to Cook a Proof System for Your Pet Language, *Proc. 10th Annual ACM Symp. on Principles of Programming Languages*, Austin, pp. 141–154, 1983.

[MW78] Manna, Z., R. Waldinger, Is "Sometime" Sometimes Bettar Than "Always"? Intermittent Assertions in Proving Program Correctness, *Communications ACM*, vol. 21, no. 2, pp. 159–172, 1978.

[MW84] Manna, Z., P. Wolper, Synthesis of Communicating Processes from Temporal Logic Specifications, *ACM Transactions on Programming Languages and Systems*, vol. 6, no. 1, pp. 68–93, 1984.

[OL82] Owicki, S., L. Lamport, Proving Liveness Properties of Concurrent Programs, *ACM Transactions on Programming Languages and Systems*, vol. 4, no. 3, pp. 455–495, 1982.

[Pa70] Park, D., Fixpoint Induction and Proofs of Program Properties, in *Machine Intelligence*, vol. 5, D. Mitchie, editor, Edinburgh University Press, 1970.

[Pn77] Pnueli, A., The Temporal Logic of Programs, *18th Annual Symp. on Foundations of Computer Science*, Providence, pp. 46–57, 1977.

[Pn83] Pnueli, A., On the Extremely Fair Treatment of Probabilistic Algorithms, *Proc. of the 15th Annual ACM Symp. on Theory of Computing*, Boston, pp. 278–290, 1983.

[PR89] Pnueli, A., R. Rosner, On the Synthesis of a Reactive Module, *to appear in Proc. 16th Annual ACM Symp. on Principles of Programming Languages*, Austin, 1989.

[Pr76] Pratt, V., Semantical Considerations on Floyd-Hoare Logic, *Proc. of the 10th Annual ACM Symp. on Theory of Computing*, San Diego, pp. 326–337, 1976.

[Pr80] Pratt, V., A Near-Optimal Method For Reasoning About Action, *Journal of Computer and System Sciences*, vol 20, no. 2, pp. 231–254, 1980.

[QS81] Queille, J.P., J. Sifakis, Specification and Verification of Concurrent Systems in CESAR, *Proc. of the 5th International Symposium on Programming*, LNCS#137, Springer–Verlag, pp. 337–350, 1981.

[QS83] Queille, J.P., J. Sifakis, Fairness and Related Properties in Transition Systems—A Temporal Logic To Deal With Fairness, *Acta Informatica*, vol. 19, no. 3, pp. 195–220, 1983.

[Ra69] Rabin, M., Decidability of Second-Order Theories and Automata on Infinite Trees, *Transactions of the American Mathematical Society*, vol. 141, pp. 1–35, 1969.

[RK80] Ramamritham, K., R. Keller, Specification and Synthesis of Synchronizers, *9th International Conf. on Parallel Processing*, 1980.

[RU71] Rescher, N., A. Urquhart, *Temporal Logic*, Springer–Verlag, 1971.

[Sa88] Safra, S., On the Complexity of ω-Automata, *29th Annual Symp. on Foundations of Computer Science*, White Plains, pp. 319–327, 1988.

[SC82] Sistla, A.P., E.M. Clarke, The Complexity of Propositional Linear Temporal Logics, *Proc. of the 14th Annual ACM Symp. on Theory of Computing*, San Francisco, pp. 159–168, 1982; *also appeared in Journal ACM*, vol. 32, no. 3, pp. 733–749, 1985.

[SG87] Sistla, A.P., S.M. German, Reasoning With Many Processes, *Proc. 2nd Annual Symp. on Logic in Computer Science*, Ithaca, pp. 138–152, 1987.

[Sm68] Smullyan, R.M., *First-Order Logic*, Springer–Verlag, 1968.

[St81] Streett, R.S., Propositional Dynamic Logic of Looping and Converse, Ph.D. Thesis, *MIT LCS* Technical Report TR-263, 1981; *alternatively, see:* Propositional Dynamic Logic of Looping and Converse is Elementarily Decidable, *Information and Control*, vol. 54, pp. 121–141, 1982.

[SE84] Streett, R.S., E.A. Emerson, The Propositional Mu-Calculus is Elementary, *Proc. 11th Annual International Colloquium on Automata, Languages and Programming*, LNCS#172, Springer–Verlag, pp. 465–472, 1984.

[VS85] Vardi, M., L. Stockmeyer, Improved Upper and Lower Bounds for Modal Logics of Programs, *Proc. of the 17th Annual ACM Symp. on Theory of Computing*, Providence, pp. 240–251, 1985.

[VW84] Vardi M., P. Wolper, Automata Theoretic Techniques for Modal Logics of Programs, *Proc. of the 16th Annual ACM Symp. on Theory of Computing*, Washington D.C., pp. 446–456, 1984; *also appeared in Journal of Computer and System Sciences*, vol 32, no. 2, pp. 183–221, 1984.

[VW86] Vardi, M., P. Wolper, An Automata-Theoretic Approach to Automatic Program Verification, *Proc. Symp. on Logic in Computer Science*, Cambridge, pp. 332–345, 1986.

[Wo81] Wolper, P., Temporal Logic Can Be More Expressive, *22nd Annual Symp. on Foundations of Computer Science*, Nashville, pp. 340–348, 1981; *also appeared in Information and Control*, vol. 56, pp. 72–99, 1983.

[Wo82] Wolper, P., Specification and Synthesis of Communicating Processes Using an Extended Temporal Logic, *Proc. 9th Annual ACM Symp. on Principles of Programming Languages*, Albuquerque, pp. 20–33, 1982; *also see* [MW84].

[WVS83] Vardi M., P. Wolper, A.P. Sistla, Reasoning about Infinite Computation Paths, *24th Annual Symp. on Foundations of Computer Science*, Tucson, pp. 185–194, 1983.

OBSERVING PROCESSES

M Hennessy

CSAI
University of Sussex,
Falmer, Brighton, BN1 9QH, U.K.

ABSTRACT. In this tutorial we discuss various behavioural theories of processes. The central theme is that processes should be semantically equivalent unless there is some observation or test which distinguishes them. By choosing different notions of observations a range of behavioural theories is obtained. They include bisimulation equivalence, testing equivalence and a number of equivalences which distinguish concurrency from nondeterminism.

KEY WORDS: Concurrent Processes, behavioural semantics, testing, process algebras.

CONTENTS

§0. Introduction

§0.1 In this tutorial we would like to give an overview of some recent developments in the semantics of concurrent systems. In particular, we will be discussing behavioural theories of process algebras. Process algebras are languages for describing processes which emphasise their structure. A particular process algebra consists of a set of combinators or constructors, and a particular description in this language consists of a set of recursive definitions over these combinators. Examples of process algebras may be found in [Mil80], [Ho85], [BK84], [AB84].

A denotational semantics for such a language could be given in a straightforward manner by choosing a semantic domain and a structure-preserving meaning function from expressions in the language into this domain. Unfortunately, it has been difficult to find adequate semantic domains for these languages and an alternative approach has been developed. The main use of a semantic domain is in determining whether two process descriptions have the same meaning, i.e. it induces an equivalence on expressions in the language. The alternative approach is to define these semantic equivalences directly without any recourse to a semantic domain. The central idea is that two processes are equivalent unless there is some way of observing a difference. There are many different ways in which one could formalise the idea of observing processes. One has to decide the nature of observations, how they are applied to processes and how the results are compared. Nevertheless, any theory based on such a formalisation is behavioural since it is based on a behavioural or operational view of processes. We will discuss a number of different formulations. In Part One we show that by choosing a particular notion of observation we obtain the well-known bisimulation equivalence, [Mil85]. This section is essentially a simple exposition of the results in [Ab87]. We will see that to apply the observations necessary to generate bisimulation equivalence one needs to have total control over the process being observed or tested. It is the kind of control which one has over a process running on a central machine if one owns the machine, has complete access to the operating system and an unlimited amount of memory. In Part Two we examine a much weaker notion of observation which is more in tune with the kind of observations one could make of independent processes which form part of a distributed system. Here one has no control over the process being observed. One can merely ask questions of it, by attempting to communicate with it. We will see a number of different formulations of these kinds of observations, all of which lead to the same behavioural equivalence, Testing equivalence [He88a].

Both of these theories explain concurrency in terms of nondeterminism; a concurrent process is equivalent to the purely nondeterministic process obtained by arbitrarily interleaving its basic actions. In Part Three, the final part, we examine to what extent the ideas of Chapters One and Two can be applied so as to obtain "noninterleaving" behavioural theories of processes, i.e. theories in which concurrency is not reduced to nondeterminism. This Chapter is much more speculative and is simply a brief sketch of continuing research, reported in [AH88], [Ca87], [CH87] and [He88b].

10.2 In this section we discuss briefly a general framework for testing. However we go about applying tests we will wish to compare their application to different processes. To this end we will take outcomes to particular applications of tests to be success or failure. These will be represented by the symbols $\top$, $\bot$ respectively. Since success is better than failure, these are naturally ordered as the two point lattice:

Θ =

Processes are in general nondeterministic and therefore may react to the same test in different ways. The results of all possible applications of a test to a process is therefore captured by a non-empty subset of Θ . It is non-empty because we view the tests as "partial-tests". When a test is applied success may be reported, represented by $\top$. The symbol $\bot$, on the other hand, simply means "lack of success"; this may be because a genuine failure is reported or because nothing is reported, e.g. there is a divergent computation.

The ordering on the basic set Θ may be lifted in three different ways to these nonempty subsets, using the three different varieties of powerdomain constructions. These may be graphically represented as follows:

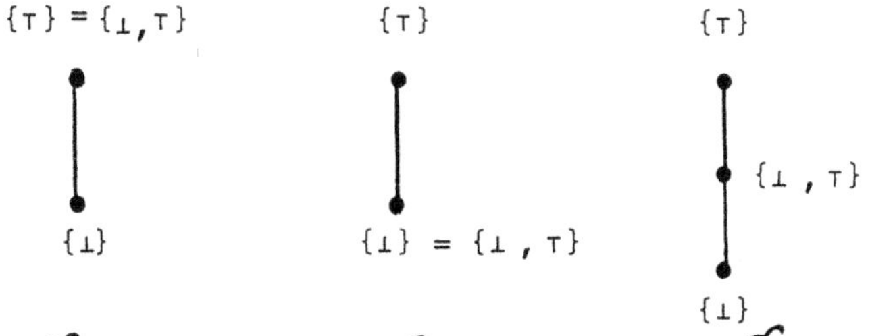

$\mathcal{P}_{MAY}(\Theta)$ $\mathcal{P}_{MUST}(\Theta)$ $\mathcal{P}(\Theta)$

They each represent different views of divergence or incomplete information. They may be used to formulate three different ways of comparing processes. Let $O(t,p)$ represent the set of possible outcomes from applying the test t to the process p. Then if T is the set of all appropriate tests we can define:

$$p \sqsubseteq_{*}^{T} q \quad \text{if} \quad \text{for every } t \text{ in } T \quad O(t,p) \leq_{*} O(t,q).$$

Here $*$ ranges over the possible constructions given above. So $p \sqsubseteq_{MAY}^{T} q$ means that if p may pass a test then q may also pass it, while $p \sqsubseteq_{MUST}^{T} q$ means that if p must pass a test, or guarantees it, then so does q; it is also easy to check that $\sqsubseteq^{T}$ is the conjunction of $\sqsubseteq_{MAY}^{T}$ and $\sqsubseteq_{MUST}^{T}$. We will also sometimes refer to the equivalences generated by these preorders by $\simeq_{MAY}$, $\simeq_{MUST}$ and $\simeq$ respectively.

Of course these behavioural relations depend on how we define T and $O(t,p)$ for particular processes and tests. Examples will be given in the remainder of the tutorial. Those in Parts One and Two, at least, will assume a basic operational semantics for processes in terms of a labelled transition system, lts. This consists of

- P a set of processes
- Act a set of actions
- $\longrightarrow \subseteq P \times Act \times P$.

Informally, $\langle p,a,p'\rangle \in \longrightarrow$ will be rendered as $p \xrightarrow{a} p'$ and may be read as: the process p may perform the action a and thereby be transformed into p'. The nature of the actions will depend on the language used for processes but the most common example is when the set of processes is some collection of communicating systems and the actions are the input or output of values at communication ports. We will not be very concerned with how one gives this style of operational semantics to particular languages although an example will be seen in Chapter Two. Other examples may be found in [Plo81], [Mil80], [He88a].

Part One : Bisimulations and General Testing

§1.1 A language for testing

The first language for testing which we consider is given in Figure 1.1. There are two primitive tests SUCC and FAIL; all processes always pass the first test whereas they always fail the second. So the sets of possible outcomes for these tests are defined by:

$$O(SUCC,p) = \{\top\}$$
$$O(Fail,p) = \{\bot\}$$

The next kind of test has the form at where t is a previously defined test. Informally this requires a process to perform the action a and then pass the test t. So if p cannot perform a, i.e. for no p' $p \xrightarrow{a} p'$, which we write as p ref a, then $O(at,p) = \{\bot\}$. If it can perform a then the outcome will depend on the process p evolves to by performing a:

$$\bot \in O(at,p) \text{ if for some } p',\ p \xrightarrow{a} p' \text{ and } \bot \in O(t,p')$$
$$\top \in O(at,p) \text{ if for some } p',\ p \xrightarrow{a} p' \text{ and } \top \in O(t,p').$$

The next type of test, $\tilde{a}t$, is very similar to at. The only difference is that p succeeds the test $\tilde{a}t$ if it cannot perform a, whereas it fails at.

Tests can also be combined using conjunction and disjunction. For example

$$\bot \in O(t_1 \wedge t_2,p) \quad \text{if} \quad \bot \in O(t_1,p) \quad \text{or} \quad \bot \in O(t_2,p)$$
$$\top \in O(t_1 \wedge t_2,p) \quad \text{if} \quad \top \in O(t_1,p) \quad \text{and} \quad \top \in O(t_2,p).$$

So it is possible to pass the combined test $t_1 \wedge t_2$ if it is possible to pass t_1 and it is possible to pass t_2. This definition is natural as it is generated by the pointwise extension of the usual conjunction operator on $\mathbb{O}$ where $\top$ represents true and $\bot$ false; if $f : \mathbb{O}^n \longrightarrow \mathbb{O}$ then the pointwise extension $f^*: \mathcal{P}(\mathbb{O})^n \longrightarrow \mathcal{P}(\mathbb{O})$ is defined by:

$$f^*(X_1,\ldots,X_n) = \{f(x_1,\ldots,x_n) \mid x_i \in X_i,\ 1 \le i \le n\}$$

This notation is used in Figure 1.1 to define formally the possible outcomes from conjunctive and disjunctive tests.

The tests defined so far are already quite powerful. Consider the processes in Figure 1.2. The reader should check that

$$O(a(bSUCC \wedge cSUCC),p_1) = \{\top\},\ O(a(bSUCC \wedge cSUCC),p_2) = \{\bot\}$$
$$O(a(bSUCC \wedge \tilde{c}FAIL),p_1) = \{\bot\},\ O(a(bSUCC \wedge \tilde{c}FAIL),p_2) = \{\bot,\top\}$$
$$O(abSUCC,p_3) = \{\top,\bot\},\quad O(abSUCC,p_4) = \{\top\}$$
$$O(a\tilde{b}FAIL,p_3) = \{\top,\bot\},\quad O(a\tilde{b}FAIL,p_4) = \{\bot\}.$$

Is it possible to find tests of this kind to distinguish between p_5 and p_6 or p_7 and p_8?

i) Test Language :

$$t ::= SUCC \mid FAIL \mid at \mid \tilde{a}t \mid t_1 \vee t_2 \mid t_1 \wedge t_2 \mid \forall t \mid \exists t$$

ii) Outcomes :

$$O(SUCC,p) = \{\top\}$$

$$O(FAIL,p) = \{\bot\}$$

$$O(at,p) = \begin{cases} \{\bot\} & \text{if } p \ \underline{ref} \ a \\ \dot{\cup}\{O(t,p') \mid p \xrightarrow{a} p'\} & \text{otherwise} \end{cases}$$

$$O(\tilde{a}t,p) = \begin{matrix} \{\top\} & \text{if } p \ \underline{ref} \ a \\ \cup\{O(t,p') \mid p \xrightarrow{a} p'\} & \text{otherwise} \end{matrix}$$

$$O(t_1 \wedge t_2,p) = O(t_1,p) \wedge^* O(t_2,p)$$

$$O(t_1 \vee t_2,p) = O(t_1,p) \vee^* O(t_2,p)$$

$$O(\forall t,p) = \forall O(t,p)$$

$$O(\exists t,p) = \exists O(t,p)$$

<u>Figure</u> 1.1 : A Test Language

It certainly is, if we allow the final two operators into the test language, $\forall$ and $\exists$. These may be defined as functions over $\mathcal{P}(O)$ as follows :

$$\forall X = \{\top\} \text{ if } \bot \notin X$$
$$= \{\bot\} \text{ otherwise}$$

$$\exists X = \{\top\} \text{ if } \top \in X$$
$$= \{\bot\} \text{ otherwise}$$

The possible outcomes from the application of tests $\forall t$, $\exists t$ may then be defined as in Figure 1.1. In other words, $O(\forall t,p)$ is $\{\top\}$ if and

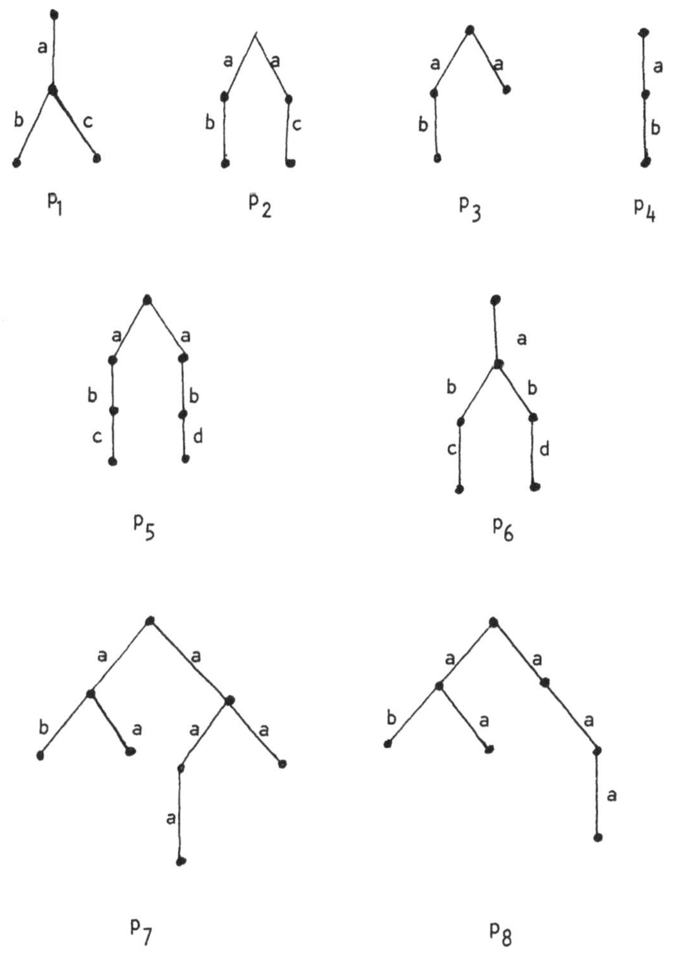

<u>Figure</u> 1.2. Simple Processes

only if every application of the test t is successful and is $\{\bot\}$ otherwise. $O(\exists t,p)$ is the converse: it is $\{\top\}$ if some application of t to p is successful and is $\{\bot\}$ otherwise. The reader might now like to check that :

$$O(\exists a \forall bcSUCC, p_5) = \{\top\} \quad , \quad O(\exists a\forall bcSUCC, p_6) = \{\bot\}$$

This set of tests is very powerful as they can be used to discover much of the structure of processes. We will discuss the exact nature of the resulting semantic preorders in the next section. However, because of the simplicity of the processes, we are considering the semantic preorders are actually equivalences, i.e. $p \sqsubseteq^T q$ implies $q \sqsubseteq^T p$.

This is because every test t has an inverse $\bar{t}$ with the property that for all p:

$$\bot \in O(t,p) \iff \top \in O(\bar{t},p)$$
$$\top \in O(t,p) \iff \bot \in O(\bar{t},p).$$

The definition of the inverse function is:

$$\overline{SUCC} = FAIL$$
$$\overline{FAIL} = SUCC$$
$$\overline{at} = \tilde{a}\bar{t}$$
$$\overline{\tilde{a}t} = a\bar{t}$$
$$\overline{t_1 \vee t_2} = \bar{t}_1 \wedge \bar{t}_2$$
$$\overline{t_1 \wedge t_2} = \bar{t}_1 \vee \bar{t}_2$$
$$\overline{\exists t} = \forall \bar{t}$$
$$\overline{\forall t} = \exists \bar{t}.$$

§1.2 Bisimulation Equivalence

Let us suppose that we have an operational semantics for a set of processes P in terms of an lts $\langle P, \rightarrow, Act \rangle$. A <u>bisimulation</u> is any symmetric relation $R \subseteq P \times P$ which satisfies:

if $\langle p,q\rangle \in R$ then $p \xrightarrow{a} p'$ implies $q \xrightarrow{a} q'$ for some q' such that $\langle p',q'\rangle \in R$.

Intuitively R provides a means by which q can simulate the actions of p, and vice versa because R is symmetric.
Let $p \sim_B q$ if $\langle p,q\rangle \in R$ for some bisimulation R. Then $\sim_B$ is an equivalence relation, called <u>strong bisimulation</u>. It possesses many interesting properties and has been used extensively as the semantic basis for a theory of communicating systems [Mil85], [Mil88]. For example, one can define properties of processes using a modal logic in such a way that $p \sim_B q$ if and only if they enjoy the same properties. If processes are defined using a process algebra such as CCS then $\sim_B$ is a congruence with respect to the combinators and may be characterised using a set of equations.

Bisimulation may also be connected with the notion of tests defined in the previous section. If the lts is sort-finite, i.e. every process can only ever perform actions from a finite set:

<u>Theorem</u>: $p \sim_B q$ if and only if $p \sqsubseteq^T q$.

The proof may be found in [Ab87]. In fact this paper considers the much more interesting case where the set of actions, Act, contains a distinguished action 1, representing silent or internal moves. Such moves arise naturally either by internal communication between subsystems or by internal computations which do not impinge on the environment, such as updating the memory. To take these internal actions into consideration various generalisations of strong bisimulation have been proposed. One essential idea is to generalise the relation $p \xrightarrow{a} q$ to $p \xRightarrow{a} q$. Intuitively $p \xrightarrow{a} q$ means that an observer may see the external action a when p evolves to q. But if invisible internal actions are allowed then p may perform some of these both before and after the externally visible action a. The relation $\xRightarrow{a}$ is defined by:

$$p \xRightarrow{a} q \quad \text{if} \quad \text{for some } p',q' \quad p \xrightarrow{1}{}^{*} \; p' \xrightarrow{a} q' \xrightarrow{1}{}^{*} \; q,$$

and is used in place of $\xrightarrow{a}$ in the definition of bisimulation.
One may also have divergent computations from a process, i.e. where the process p can perform an infinite sequence of internal actions. The definition of a bisimulation can be modified to take these potential divergences into consideration in such a way that the resulting relation is a pre-order, $\sqsubseteq_B$, rather than an equivalence; intuitively $p \sqsubseteq_B q$ if q is at least as defined as p and, apart from potential divergences they can simulate each other (wrt $\xRightarrow{a}$). One such definition, called <u>partial-bisimulation</u>, is given in [Wa87] where it is shown to have many of the properties of $\sim_B$.

This semantic pre-order can also be generated by essentially the same set of tests as given in §1.1. However, the definition of $O(t,p)$ is a little more complicated. One complication is the use of $\xRightarrow{a}$ rather than $\xrightarrow{a}$. Another is the fact now a process may both be able to perform an action and refuse it. For example, if p is the process

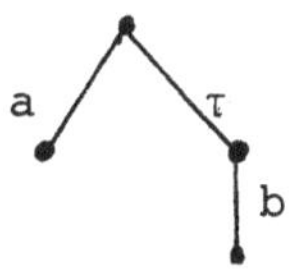

it can immediately perform a or it can evolve to a state where a is refused. So in this setting the appropriate definition is:

$$p \; \underline{ref} \; a \text{ if } \; p \xrightarrow{\tau^*} p' \quad \text{where} \quad p' \overset{1}{\nrightarrow}, \; p' \overset{a}{\nrightarrow} .$$

The precise definition of $O(t,p)$ may be found in [Ab87] but as an example one clause in the definition is

$$\begin{aligned} O(at,p) \;\; = \;\; & \cup\{O(t,p') \mid p \xRightarrow{a} p'\} \\ & \cup\{\bot \mid p \; \underline{ref} \; a \;\; \text{or} \;\; p \text{ diverges}\} \end{aligned}$$

With the appropriate definitions $\sqsubseteq^T$ is no longer an equivalence but we have once more that

$$p \sqsubseteq^T q \qquad \text{if and only if} \qquad p \sqsubseteq_B q,$$

i.e. partial bisimulation may be generated as a testing relation.

§1.3 Effective Testing

Although we have defined a set of tests we have only defined in a very abstract manner the outcome of applying a test to a process; the definition is denotational rather than operational. Is it possible to apply these tests in an effective manner so as to get the outcomes prescribed by the denotational definition? The tests actually look more like logical formulae rather than tests and, indeed, the theorem of §1.2 is proved by relating tests to a modal logic which characterises $\sim_B$. Nevertheless we will now see that they can be applied effectively.

The idea is to define a set of experiments and an effective binary relation $\longrightarrow$ between them. Intuitively $E \longrightarrow E'$ means that if we start the experiment E it may evolve into the experiment E'. One type of experiment is the initial application of a test t to a process p, which we write as $t \| p$. Another is the successful experiment denoted by $\top$; we also use $\bot$ to denote the unsuccessful experiment $\bot$. The result of applying t to p is defined by:

$$R(t,p) = \{\top \mid t\|p \longrightarrow^* \top\} \cup \{\bot \mid t\|p \longrightarrow^* E,\ E \text{ blocked}\} \cup \{\bot \mid t\|p \longrightarrow^{\omega}\}$$

where $t\|p \longrightarrow^{\omega}$ means that there is an infinite derivation from $t\|p$, and E is blocked if it is not $\top$ and $E \longrightarrow E'$ for no E'.

The definition of all possible experiments and $\longrightarrow$ is given in Figure 1.3. In this case, the only blocked experiment is $\bot$. Let us look at some clauses in the definition.

b) To apply successfully the test at to the process p, p must be able to perform the action a. If it cannot, i.e. p ref a then the experiment $at\|p$ will fail, i.e. $at\|p \longrightarrow \bot$. On the other hand, if $p \xrightarrow{a} p'$, then one possible way for the experiment $at\|p$ to proceed is to the new experiment $t\|p$.

The justification for the rules which apply to $\tilde{a}t\|p$ are similar.

d) To run the experiment $(t_1 \wedge t_2)\|p$ you run the two experiments

i) Experiments

$E ::= \top | \bot | t || p | E_1 \wedge E_2 | E_1 \vee E_2 | \forall E | \exists E$

ii) Running an experiment

a) $SUCC || p \longrightarrow \top$ $\qquad$ $FAIL || p \longrightarrow \bot$

b) $\dfrac{p \xrightarrow{a} p'}{at || p \longrightarrow t || p'}$ $\qquad$ $\dfrac{p \ \underline{\underline{ref}}\ a}{at || p \longrightarrow \bot}$

c) $\dfrac{p \xrightarrow{a} p'}{\tilde{a}t || p \longrightarrow t || p'}$ $\qquad$ $\dfrac{p \ \underline{\underline{ref}}\ a}{at || p \longrightarrow \top}$

d) i) $(t_1 \wedge t_2) || p \longrightarrow t_1 || p \wedge t_2 || p$

ii) $\dfrac{E_1 \longrightarrow E_1' \ . \ E_2 \longrightarrow E_2'}{E_1 \wedge E_2 \longrightarrow E_1' \wedge E_2'}$

iii) $\top \wedge E \longrightarrow E \quad , \quad E \wedge \top \longrightarrow E$

iv) $\bot \wedge E \longrightarrow \bot \quad , \quad E \wedge \bot \longrightarrow \bot$

e) i) $(t_1 \vee t_2) || p \longrightarrow t_1 || p \vee t_2 || p$

ii) $\dfrac{E_1 \longrightarrow E_1' \ , \ E_2 \longrightarrow E_2'}{E_1 \wedge E_2 \longrightarrow E_1' \wedge E_2'}$

iii) $\top \vee E \longrightarrow \top \quad , \quad E \vee \top \longrightarrow \top$

iv) $\bot \vee E \longrightarrow E \quad , \quad E \vee \bot \longrightarrow E$

f) i) $(\forall t) || p \longrightarrow \forall (t || p)$

ii) $\forall \top \longrightarrow \top \quad , \quad \forall \bot \longrightarrow \bot$

iii) $\dfrac{\delta_1(E) = \{E_1, \ldots, E_n\}}{\forall E \longrightarrow \wedge^{n}_{i=1} \forall E_i}$

g) i) $\exists t|p \longrightarrow \exists(t|p)$

ii) $\exists\bot \longrightarrow \bot$, $\exists\top \longrightarrow \top$

iii) $$\frac{\delta_1(E) = \{E_1,\ldots,E_n\}}{\exists E \longrightarrow \vee_{i=1}^{n} \exists E_i}$$

Note: $\delta_1(E) = \{E', E \longrightarrow E'\}$

Figure 1.3 Experiments

$t_1\|p$ and $t_2\|p$ separately and compare the results. If both succeed the overall experiment also succeeds and otherwise it fails; this can happen by either experiment returning a definite failure or by either or both continuing indefinitely.
To run $(t_1 \vee t_2)\|p$ you also run the two experiments $t_1\|p$ and $t_2\|p$ separately but the results are compared disjunctively.

f) To run the experiment $(\forall t)\|p$ essentially one "conjunctively dovetails" through all possible computations from $t|p$. The first possible move is to $\forall(t\|p)$. From there one can only go to $\wedge_{i=1}^{n}\forall E_i$ where $E_1,\ldots,E_n$ are all possible experiments which result in one-step from $t|p$. Each E_i is in turn expanded out and so on. All these computations must eventually halt successfully or otherwise the experiment will result in failure.

The reasoning for $(\exists t)\|p$ is similar, with $\wedge$ replaced by $\vee$.

This effective notion of applying a test gives the required outcomes. If we assume that the lts of processes is image-finite, i.e. for every process p and action a $\{p', p \xrightarrow{a} p'\}$ is finite, then

Theorem: $R(t,p) = O(t,p)$

Proof: See [Ab87]. □

Although this definition of $\longrightarrow$ is an effective definition, many of the rules which comprise the definition imply that to carry out a test one needs to have considerable control over the process being tested. For example, to apply $t_1 \wedge t_2$ to p one needs to duplicate the process p and run independently the experiments $t_1 \| p$ and $t_2 \| p$. This implies the ability to copy (an arbitrary number of times) the state of a process at any time during its execution. The application of $\forall t$ or $\exists t$ implies even further control over the process; to apply it one essentially has to dovetail all one-step evolutions of the experiment.

As mentioned in the introduction, this form of testing is appropriate if the process resides on a central processor and the tester has complete control over the operating system. We will refer to it as tightly-controlled testing. In the next section we examine a looser form of testing which is more appropriate when the tester has no control over the process being examined.

PART TWO: Testing Equivalence

§2.1 Testing Distributed Systems

Suppose we wish to apply a test to a distributed system or more generally a part of a distributed system. We view a distributed system as an independent process or collection of independent processes which computes or evolves independently of its environment. Periodically it may communicate with its environment by sending it a message or, conversely, the environment may wish to communicate with it and attempt to send it a message. Because the process is independent it may, if it wishes, choose to accept the message and subsequently may or may not respond.

A tester can be considered as another process in the environment. But now the only way of experimenting on a process is to send it a message and hope for a reply. In this testing scenario most of the constructs in the testing language are inappropriate. Conjunction and disjunction are out as they presuppose the ability to copy at any stage the state of the process being tested. $\forall$ and $\exists$ also presuppose at least this and probably more. Even $\tilde{a}t$, called refusal testing in [Ab87], enables one to conclude success by the absence of a response from the process. This rules out virtually every construct in the language. However, in a distributed world we can take as a test simply another process, and the application of this test to a process proceeds by both processes attempting to communicate with each other. But there should be some way of knowing when a test succeeds, the role played by the distinguished test SUCC in the previous chapter. So let us say that a test is simply a process which contains a distinguished action w, which reports success.

To sum up this discussion we have as the set of experiments:

$$E ::= t \| p \mid \top$$

and the evolution of experiments, $\longrightarrow$, is defined by

i) $$\frac{t \xrightarrow{a} t',\ p \xrightarrow{a} p'}{t \| p \longrightarrow t' \| p'}$$

ii) $$\frac{t \xrightarrow{w}}{t \| p \longrightarrow \top}$$

If processes can perform internal silent moves we would also include the rules

iii) $$\frac{t \xrightarrow{1} t'}{t \| p \xrightarrow{1} t' \| p} \qquad \frac{p \xrightarrow{1} p'}{t \| p \xrightarrow{1} t \| p.}$$

This form of testing is very weak or loose as it presupposes no control over the process being tested. With these revised definitions we obtain new result sets $R(t,p)$ and thereby new testing preorders:

$$p \sqsubseteq^{T}_{*} q \quad \text{if for every test } t \quad R(t,p) \leq_{*} R(t,q).$$

These testing preorders have been studied for a number of languages in [DH83], [He83], [He88a] and enjoy many of the properties of the bisimulation based relations: they can be equationally characterised and even have a reasonably natural denotational semantics which is fully-abstract. They are also much weaker than the bisimulation based relations: in general they distinguish far fewer processes. We will not go into the details of this theory as it is explained in depth in [He88a]. This book uses a language which is a cross between CSP, [Ho85], and CCS, [Mil80]. Its syntax and operational semantics are given in Figure 2.1. The syntax consists of the set of recursive words over a collection of combinators. The construct recx.- binds free variables and we assume the usual conventions about free and bound variables. Processes are taken to be the closed words in the language. The set of actions consists of a basic set Λ together with the set of their complements

i) The language

$$t ::= x \mid NIL \mid \Omega \mid at_1 \mid t_1 + t_2 \mid t_1 \oplus t_2 \mid t_1 | t_2 \mid t_1 \backslash c \mid recx.t$$

ii) The operational semantics

i) $ap \xrightarrow{a} p$

ii) $p_1 \oplus p_2 \rightarrowtail p_1 \;,\; p_1 \oplus p_2 \rightarrowtail p_2$

iii) $p_1 \xrightarrow{a} p_1'$ implies $p_1 + p_2 \xrightarrow{a} p_1', \; p_2 + p_1 \xrightarrow{a} p_1'$

$p_1 \rightarrowtail p_1'$ implies $p_1 + p_2 \rightarrowtail p_1' + p_2, \; p_2 + p_1 \rightarrowtail p_2 + p_1'$

iv) $p_1 \xrightarrow{a} p_1'$ implies $p_1 | p_2 \xrightarrow{a} p_1' | p_2, \; p_2 | p_1 \xrightarrow{a} p_2 | p_1'$

$p_1 \rightarrowtail p_1'$ implies $p_1 | p_2 \rightarrowtail p_1' | p_2, \; p_2 | p_1 \rightarrowtail p_2 | p_1'$

v) $p_1 \xrightarrow{a} p_1' \;,\; p_2 \xrightarrow{\bar{a}} p_2'$ implies $p_1 | p_2 \rightarrowtail p_1' | p_2'$

vi) $p_1 \xrightarrow{a} p_1' \;,\; a \neq c, \bar{c}$ implies $p_1 \backslash c \xrightarrow{a} p_1' \backslash c$

$p_1 \rightarrowtail p_1'$ implies $p_1 \backslash c \rightarrowtail p_1' \backslash c$

vii) $\Omega \rightarrowtail \Omega$

viii) $recx.t \rightarrowtail t[recx.t/x]$

<u>Figure 2.1</u> A process description language

$\bar{\Lambda} = \{ \bar{a} \mid a \in \Lambda \}$. The operational semantics is given in terms of the arrows $\xrightarrow{a}$, relations over processes, which are defined inductively. Internal moves are modelled using the arrow $\rightarrowtail$ to emphasise that they are different from the usual internal moves in CCS [Mil80].

We will use this language in the next section but here we will simply discuss briefly the use of this language to define tests. The simple test abw, which asks for an a action followed by a b action, will distinguish between p_1 and p_2 and between p_3 and p_4 in Figure 1.2 This is because $R(abw, p_1) = R(abw, p_4) = \{\top\}$ whereas $R(abw, p_2) = R(abw, p_3) = \{\top, \bot\}$. The test acw distinguishes between p_1 and p_4 while $a(bw + cw)$ distinguishes between p_2 and p_3. On the other hand, p_5 and p_6 cannot be distinguished by any tests, nor can p_7 and p_8.

One can show that, although infinite tests are allowed, finite tests suffice: if two processes are distinguishable they are distinguishable using a finite test. Also, if a process guarantees a finite test, then there is a finite approximation to the process which also guarantees it. This means that the behaviour of a process is determined by that of its finite approximations which in turn implies that the resulting denotational model is ω-algebraic. Although any expression in the language may be used as a test, it turns out that the preorders are determined by a small class of (finite) tests of a very particular kind. They consist of three types. The first characterises the possibles actions a process can make after having performed an initial sequence of actions. The second determines when processes have potential divergences while the last is used to discover the sequences of actions a process cannot perform.

§2.2 System Testing

In the previous section we saw a very simple kind of loosely controlled test, namely another process which is allowed to interrogate the process under investigation. In this section we examine even simpler kinds of tests.

One kind of test is to ask a process to guarantee a particular action a; in other words, to take as tests only processes which have the particularly simple form aw for some action a. Then $R(aw,p) = \{\top\}$ if and only if p does not diverge and every stable process which p may reach can perform a, i.e. if $p \rightarrowtail\!\!\!\!\longrightarrow^* p' \not\rightarrowtail$ implies $p' \xrightarrow{a}$. Let us denote the resulting preorder by $\underset{\sim}{\sqsubset}_A$:

$$p \underset{\sim}{\sqsubset}_A q \quad \text{if for every } aw, \ R(aw,p) \leq_{MUST} R(aw,p)$$

This is a very weak form of testing. For example, it will not distinguish p_1 from p_2 nor p_3 from p_4 in Figure 1.2. To increase its power we introduce a new method for testing processes. The intuitive idea is to use systems to test sub-systems. If two processes are supposed to be equivalent, then they should behave in the same way as part of larger systems. So to test a process we could place it within a larger system and apply a simple basic test to this larger system. We will call this method <u>systems-testing</u>. Used in this manner a system is simply a process with a 'hole', [ ], in it. These are often called contexts and written as C[ ]. The result of filling in the hole with a process p is written as C[p].

As an example of systems-testing take the case when the basic test to be applied to the overall system is to guarantee an action. The experiment scenario is:

$$t ::= aw, \; a \in Act$$

$$E ::= C[\;] \| t \mid \top$$

An experiment proceeds by placing the process p into the system and allowing the experiment to run in the normal way. We use $\sqsubseteq^C_A$ to denote the resulting preorder :

$$p \sqsubseteq^C_A q \quad \text{if for every context } C[\;], \quad C[p] \sqsubseteq_A C[q].$$

Referring again to Figure 1.2 we can now distinguish p_1 from p_2 and p_3 from p_4. In both cases the required system is $[\;]|\bar{a}NIL$:

$$R(p_1|\bar{a}NIL,bw) = R(p_4|\bar{a}NIL,bw) = \{\top\} \text{ whereas}$$

$$R(p_2|\bar{a}NIL,bw) = R(p_3|\bar{a}NIL,bw) = \{\top,\bot\}.$$

Another basic form of test is to ask for all the maximal sequences of actions which a process can perform. This is analogous to placing a process in a cosy environment, where all of its communication requests will be granted, and recording the resulting interactions. Formally the set of tests is now

$$t ::= sw, \quad s \in Act^*$$

and the possible experiments are as before:

$$E ::= t \| p \mid \top$$

The evolution of experiments is a little different as we are looking for maximal sequences. The required rules are:

$$\frac{t \xrightarrow{a} t',\; p \xrightarrow{a} p'}{t \| p \rightarrow t' \| p'} \qquad \frac{p \rightarrowtail p'}{t \| p \rightarrow t \| p'}$$

$$\frac{t \xrightarrow{w},\; p \text{ terminated}}{t \| p \rightarrow \top}$$

Here terminated is a predicate which tests whether a process can perform any action.

In order to relate this notion of testing with the previous ones we will order processes simply by comparing the set of maximal a sequences they can produce:

$$p \sqsubseteq_{MT} q \quad \text{if for every test } t \quad R(t,q) \leq_{MAY} R(t,p).$$

Once more this form of testing is very weak. It will not distinguish p_1 from p_2 since they have exactly the same set of maximal sequences {ab,ac}. It will not even distinguish recx.ax from recx.bx since neither has any maximal(finite) sequence.However,if we introduce systems-testing they can be distinguished. In the first case we use the context $[\,]\backslash b$. Then $R(aw, p_1\backslash b) = \{\bot\}$ while $R(aw, p_2\backslash b) = \{\top,\bot\}$. The required context and test in the second case is $([\ ]\,|\,\bar{a}c)\backslash a,b$ and cw respectively. We use $\sqsubseteq^{c}_{MT}$ to denote the resulting preorder generated from $\sqsubseteq_{MT}$ using systems-testing.

As a final example of a combination of systems-testing and a basic test we consider testing for the possibility of termination. A process p is terminated, as we have already stated, if it can do no action, including no internal action. So here the basic test is very simple: a process passes if it can evolve to a terminated process. There is no apparatus necessary to carry out a test:

$$E ::= p \mid \top$$

The evolution of a test, $\longrightarrow$, is defined as follows:

$$\frac{p \text{ terminated}}{p \longrightarrow \top}$$

$$\frac{p \succ\!\!\longrightarrow p' \;,\quad p' \longrightarrow \top}{p \longrightarrow \top}$$

Let us write $p \sqsubseteq_{md} q$ if $R(q) \leq_{MAY} R(p)$.

This form of test is practically useless. It will not even distinguish aNIL from bNIL or indeed aNIL from a process which can only diverge such as Ω. Nevertheless if we include systems-testing we get a reasonable ability to distinguish process. In fact, under mild restrictions all the testing preorders discussed in this section coincide.

A process is <u>strongly convergent</u> if every process to which it can evolve is convergent. It means that at no time during the execution of the process will it ever diverge.

<u>Theorem</u>: If p and q are strongly convergent then

$$p \sqsubseteq_{MUST} \qquad p \sqsubseteq^{c}_{A} q$$

$$p \sqsubseteq^{c}_{MT} q$$

$$p \sqsubseteq^{c}_{MD} q. \qquad \square$$

The proof of this theorem for CCS may be found in [Ma88]; it is easily adaptable to our language. The theorem may also be extended to processes which are not strongly convergent by mild generalisations of the basic tests involved.

This theorem shows that the loosely controlled testing preorder $\sqsubseteq_{MUST}$ defined in the previous sub-section, is relatively stable. It can be obtained in a number of different ways from the notion of systems-testing.

PART THREE: Nonsequential Testing

§3.1 Limitations

In the previous two sections we have described two well-known behavioural equivalences and we have seen that they may be viewed as testing equivalences, if we adopt a suitable notion of testing. It is also well known that both of these equivalences do not distinguish concurrency from interleaving. More specifically, every concurrent process is equivalent to a purely sequential, but possibly nondeterministic process. The typical example is the concurrent process aNIL|bNIL. This is considered to be equivalent to the purely sequential process abNIL + baNIL. More generally, any concurrent process can be reduced to an equivalent sequential process, obtained by interleaving its possible events.

We would like to develop behavioural equivalences for process algebras in which concurrency plays a fundamental role; in particular it should not be reducible to nondeterminism. It is relatively easy to define such equivalences - a multitude may be found in [GV87]. The main problem is to assess the adequacy of suggested equivalences. For example, syntactic identity is an equivalence which certainly distinguishes concurrency from nondeterminism but it could not seriously be suggested as a reasonable behavioural equivalence. But what is a reasonable behavioural equivalence? The answer is to a certain extent aesthetic. The thesis of this tutorial is that it should at least be generated from a reasonable notion of test. So we need a set of tests which distinguish concurrency from nondeterminism. But this is not sufficient. One of the major attractions of the equivalences of the previous sections is that they can abstract away from internal details. This is not so apparent from our exposition but it is necessary if we wish to consider equivalent specifications and their implementations. They are also tractable, at least mathematically. In view of the fact that they are applied to process algebras, we could take this to mean that they can be characterised equationally, although this is open to debate.

The problem of finding an adequate non-sequential behavioural equivalence is being addressed by many researchers, some of whose efforts may be seen elsewhere in this volume. In this last section we will give a brief survey of the attempts made by the author and co-workers to extend the ideas of the two previous sections so as to obtain such equivalences. These do not yet satisfy the three criteria, given rather informally above. In particular it is difficult to define nonsequential behavioural equivalences which abstract from internal details in an adequate way. This is the object of our current research.

The underlying feature of the equivalences of the two previous sections is the operational semantics of processes as labelled transition systems. Already at this level all reference to concurrency has been eliminated. So any attempt at defining nonsequential behavioural equivalences starting with labelled transition systems seems doomed to failure. However all is not lost. The relation $p \xrightarrow{a} q$ may be interpreted as saying that as a result of performing a simple experiment on p, an a-experiment, p it evolves to q. For example, we could imagine defining $p \xrightarrow{e} q$ where e is a labelled partial-order, encoding the independence or causality of events which p can perform so as to evolve into q. We will not take this approach as it is far from obvious that causal relations can be observed. Indeed, in the next two sections we examine different generalisations. The first assumes that p is a distributed process and the observer has some knowledge of its distributed nature. The second assumes that in $p \xrightarrow{a} q$ the a-action is no longer atomic.

§3.2 Distributed Bisimulation

Let us assume that p is a distributed system, i.e. it is distributed amongst a number of locations. If an observer sees p perform an a action he will see it at some particular location. This a action will have a global effect on p as usual, which is recorded by $p \xrightarrow{a} p'$. In addition it has a local effect and we assume that the user has access to this local effect. So the combined effect of the action may be recorded by

$$p \xrightarrow{a} \langle p_L, p_G \rangle \ .$$

Here p_L is the local residual of p and p_G is the global residual. An example of this generalised action is given in Figure 3.1 for a very simple toy language, TL. The only interesting rule is c) which says that if, in $p|q$, p performs an a action then q will be part of the global residual but not the local residual.

We can now modify the definition of a bisimulation so as to apply to these new arrows:

$R \subseteq P \times P$ is a d-bisimulation if it is symmetric and whenever $\langle p,q \rangle \in R$ if $p \xrightarrow{a} \langle p_L, p_G \rangle$ then $q \xrightarrow{a} \langle q_L, q_G \rangle$ for some q_L, q_G such that $\langle p_L, q_L \rangle \in R$, $\langle p_G, q_G \rangle \in R$.

i) The language, TL

$p ::= NIL \mid ap \mid p + q \mid p|q$

ii) The observations

a) $ap \xrightarrow{a} \langle p,p \rangle$

b) $p \xrightarrow{a} \langle p_L, p_G \rangle$ implies $p + q \xrightarrow{a} \langle p_L, p_G \rangle$
$q + p \xrightarrow{a} \langle p_L, p_G \rangle$

c) $p \xrightarrow{a} \langle p_L, p_G \rangle$ implies $p|q \xrightarrow{a} \langle p_L, p_G|q \rangle$
$q|p \xrightarrow{a} \langle p_L, q|p_G \rangle$

Figure 3.1

Now mimicing (strong) bisimulation equivalence we can define (strong) distributed bisimulation equivalence as follows:

$$p \; d{\sim} q \quad \text{if} \quad \langle p,q\rangle \in R \quad \text{for some d-bisimulation } R.$$

This relation is indeed an equivalence and is preserved by the operators in the language of Figure 3.1. It also distinguishes concurrency from nondeterminism. For example

$$aNIL|bNIL \;\; d{\sim} \;\; abNIL + baNIL.$$

This is because

$$aNIL|bNIL \xrightarrow{a} \langle NIL,\ NIL|bNIL\rangle$$

whereas the only possible a-move from abNIL + baNIL is

$$abNIL + baNIL \xrightarrow{a} \langle bNIL,\ bNIL\rangle$$

and obviously the local components are not equivalent. The reader might also check that

$$aNIL|(bNIL + cNIL) \;\; d{\sim} \;\; aNIL|bNIL + aNIL|cNIL$$

$$aNIL|bNIL + abNIL \;\; d{\sim} \;\; aNIL|bNIL.$$

Is d~ a testing equivalence? Yes: the required modification to the tightly-controlled testing of Part one. The tests at and $\tilde{a}t$ are replaced by a<t,t'> and $\tilde{a}$<t,t'> respectively. Intuitively t is to test the local component and t' the global one. The definition of $\longrightarrow$, the evolution of experiments, is changed by replacing b) with

b') $$\frac{p \xrightarrow{a} \langle p',p''\rangle}{a\langle t',t'\rangle \| p \longrightarrow t'\|p' \wedge t''\|p''} \qquad \frac{p \; \underline{ref} \; a}{a\langle t',t''\rangle \| p \longrightarrow \bot}$$

and c) with an analogous c'). Then, if we assume image-finiteness of the derivation relations, we have that d~ coincides with the testing equivalence generated from these tests.

This new nonsequential behavioural equivalence can also be equationally characterised, at least if we are willing to augment the language with a new operator, the asymmetric parallel operator $|\!\!/$. The operational semantics for this new operator consists of one of the inductive rules for $\lfloor$:

d) $p \xrightarrow{a} \langle p_L, p_G \rangle$ implies $p \lfloor q \xrightarrow{a} \langle p_L, p_G | q \rangle$.

The complete axiomatisation for $d{\sim}$ over this extended language is given in Figure 3.2. The reader may wish to experiment with these equations by deriving the following identities:

$$(x|y)|z = x|(y|z)$$
$$(x + z)| y + x|(y + z') = (x + z)|y + x|(y + z') + x|y$$
$$p = p + (x_1 + x_2)|(y_1 + y_2)$$

where

p is $x_1|(y_1 + y_2) + x_2|(y_1 + y_2) + (x_1 + x_2)|y_1 + (x_1 + x_2)|y_2$

The language we have considered is very simple but these results have been extended to more complicated languages which allow communication and silent actions. They have not yet been applied to languages with abstraction features such as hiding in CSP and restriction in CCS. One difficulty is to define an adequate notion of local residual for processes which have hidden communication links with other processes.

Distributed Bisimulations are discussed in detail in [Ca87], [CH87].

$$x + (y + z) = (x + y) + z$$
$$x + y = y + x$$
$$x + x = x$$
$$x + NIL = x$$

$$x|y = x \lfloor y + y \lfloor x$$
$$(x + y) \lfloor z = x \lfloor z + y \lfloor z$$
$$(x \lfloor y) \lfloor z = x \lfloor (y|z)$$
$$NIL \lfloor x = NIL$$
$$x \lfloor NIL = x$$

Figure 3.2 Equations for $d{\sim}$

§3.3 Nonatomic actions

When describing the operational semantics of processes in terms of labelled transition systems it is assumed that the actions are instantaneous or atomic. Let us relax this assumption and suppose that actions take time. We do not wish to be very specific in assigning durations to specific actions. Instead we take the minimal consequence of the supposition: namely, that actions have distinct beginnings and endings. We may view these as actions in their own right, s(a) representing the beginning of the action a and f(a) its finish. We may now describe the operational semantics of processes in terms of these sub-actions. As an example we give the operational semantics of the example language in Figure 3.3. We use $a_s p$ to denote a process which is performing the action a and when it is completed will continue to act like the process p.

a) $ap \xrightarrow{s(a)} a_s p$

b) $a_s p \xrightarrow{f(a)} p$

c) $p \xrightarrow{e} p'$ implies $p + q \xrightarrow{e} p'$
$\qquad q + p \xrightarrow{e} p'$

d) $p \xrightarrow{e} p'$ implies $p|q \xrightarrow{e} p'|q$
$\qquad q|p \xrightarrow{e} q|p'$
$\qquad p/\!\!/q \xrightarrow{e} p'|q$

Figure 3.3 Nonatomic actions

Once more the notion of bisimulation may be modified to apply to these sub-actions. Let us call the resulting equivalence $\sim_t$, timed-observational equivalence. It distinguishes concurrency from non-determinism. For example, aNIL|bNIL $\not\sim_t$ abNIL + baNIL. The former can begin an a action and evolve to the state a_sNIL|bNIL whereas the latter cannot begin an a action and evolve to any comparable state. The only possible state might be a_sbNIL which is not equivalent to a_sNIL|bNIL since it cannot immediately start a b action.

For our toy language $\sim_t$ coincides with $d\sim$ so that the equations in Figure 3.2 are also a complete axiomatisation for $\sim_t$. There is also a complete axiomatisation obtainable from that for strong bisimulation by extending the language and replacing ap with $a_s a_f p$. However, this is not interesting. In general there would be an enormous increase in the size of proofs based on equations. The attraction of the characterisation in Figure 3.2 is that reasoning based on these equations will be in terms of the original language itself, rather than the semantic notions of the beginnings and endings of actions. However, these equivalences differ if one adds silent moves. In this case $\sim_t$ is contained in $d\sim$ but not the converse: $d\sim$ satisfies the equation

$$a(x + 1y) = a(x + 1y) + ay$$

which is violated by $\sim_t$.

This timed equivalence may also be viewed in a trivial way as being induced by testing. One merely phrases the tightly-controlled tests in terms of the sub-actions s(a) and f(a) rather than the instantaneous action a. However, as with distributed-bisimulation, there is as yet no adequate treatment of abstraction mechanisms.

Details concerning $\sim_t$ may be found in [He88].

§3.4 Other Directions

The two previous equivalences are variations on the theme of bisimulation equivalence. Let us now look briefly at some variations on the theme of loosely-controlled testing and systems-testing. There is virtually no published work in this area so what follows is mostly speculation.

The normal operators in process algebras usually preserve observational equivalence and the testing equivalence of Part two. So in order to use systems-testing to define a nonsequential behavioural equivalence we need to introduce new operators for defining systems which do not preserve these standard equivalences. One such operator is action-refinment. Let us introduce the notation $p[a \longrightarrow q]$ to mean the process p with the action a refined to the process q. Even without seeing the formal definitions the reader should still be convinced that although

$$aNIL|bNIL \sim_B abNIL + baNIL,$$

$$(aNIL|bNIL)[a \longrightarrow bcNIL] \not\sim_B (abNIL + baNIL) [a \longrightarrow bcNIL].$$

So a natural question to ask is what equivalences do we obtain if we use systems-testing where the systems may use action-refinement? It is rather surprising that action-refinement has not been studied in the context of process algebras so very little is known about it. Of course, the equivalence obtained will depend on the kind of basic test used.

It is known that if we take tightly-controlled testing as the basic testing method then the resulting equivalence coincides with $\sim_t$ (and therefore d~), at least for a mild generalisation of TL. That is $p \sim_t q$ if and only if $p \sim_B^c q$ for p and q in a language similar to TL augmented by action refinement. The proof, which is quite involved, may be found in [AH87]. If $\sim_B$ is replaced with maximal sequence equivalence, $\approx_{MS}$, of with $\approx_A$, then other behavioural equivalences are obtained, $\approx_{MS}^c$ and $\approx_A^c$, respectively. Another possibility is to use as the basic text maximal sequences of the sub-sections s(a) and s(b) instead of a. All of these certainly distinguish aNIL|bNIL from abNIL + baNIL but, apart from that, not much is known about them even for the toy language TL, although some progress has been made in [NEL88]. Their equivalences ignore entirely the branching structure of processes. Modulo this factorisation, they characterise $\approx_{MS}^c$ in terms of the semi-words of actions that a process can "perform", for a process language similar to TL but without auto-parallelism [GV87] and, of course, their systems-testing includes systems with action-refinement.

ACKNOWLEDGEMENTS

Financial assistance from the SERC, under grant number GR/D/97368 is gratefully acknowledged. I should also like to thank F Williams for typing the difficult manuscript, and L Aceto for a careful reading of a first draft.

REFERENCES

[Ab87] Abramsky, S., Observational Equivalence as a Testing Equivalence, TCS, 53, pp.225-241, 1987

[AB84] Austry, D. and Boudol G., Algèbre de processus et synchronisation, TCS, 30, pp.91-131, 1984

[AH88] Aceto, L. and Hennessy M., Towards Action-Refinement in Process Algebras, University of Sussex Technical Report, 1988

[BK84] Bergstra, J. and Klop, J., Process Algebra for Synchronous Communication, Information and Control, 60,

[Ca87] Castellani, I., Distributed Bisimulations, Ph.D.Thesis, University of Edinburgh, 1987

[CH87] Hennessy, M. and Castellani, I., Distributed Bisimulations, University of Sussex Technical Report, 1987

[DH83] DeNicola, R. and Hennnesy, M., Testing Equivalences for Process, TCS, 34, pp.83-133, 1983

[GV87] van Glabbeek, R. and Vaandrager, F., Petri Net Models for Algebraic Theories of Concurrency, University of Aarhus, 1988

[He83] Hennessy, M., Synchronous and Asynchronous Experiments on Processes, Information and Control, 59, pp.36-83, 1983

[He88a] Hennessy, M., An Algebraic Theory of Processes, MIT Press, 1988

[He88b] Hennessy, M., Axiomatising Finite Concurrent Processes, SIAM Journal of Computing, October 1988

[Ho85] Hoare, C., Communicating Sequential Processes, Prentice-Hall, 1985

[Main88] Main, M., Trace, Failure and Testing Equivalences for Communicating Processes, IJPP, vol.16, No.5, pp 383-401

[Mil80] Milner, R., A Calculus of Communicating Systems, LNCS,94,1980

[Mil83] Milner, R., Synchrony and Asynchrony, TCS,25, pp.267-310,1983

[Mil88] Milner, R., Operational and Algebraic Semantics of Concurrent Processes, Technical Report ECS-LFCS-88-46, University of Edinburgh

[NEL88] Nielson, M. Engberg, U. and Larsen, K.S., Partial Order Semantics for Concurrency, University of Aarhus, 1988

[Ph85] Philipps, I., Refusal Testing, TCS,50, 1985

[Plo81] Plotkin, G., A Structural Approach to Operational Semantics, Lecture Notes, University of Aarhus, 1981

[Wa87] Walker, D., Bisimulation and Divergence, Proceedings of LICS 88 conference, pp.186-192. Also Technical Report ECS-LFCS-87-29, University of Edinburgh

The Anchored Version of the Temporal Framework *

Zohar Manna
Department of Computer Science
Stanford University, Stanford, CA 94305
&
Department of Applied Mathematics
Weizmann Institute of Science, Rehovot

Amir Pnueli
Department of Applied Mathematics
Weizmann Institute of Science, Rehovot

ABSTRACT. In this survey paper we present some of the recent developments in the temporal formal system for the specification, verification and development of reactive programs. While the general methodology remains very much the one presented in some earlier works on the subject, such as [MP83c,MP83a,Pnu86], there have been several technical improvements and gained insights in understanding the computational model, the logic itself, the proof system and its presentation, and connections with alternative formalisms, such as finite automata. In this paper we explicate some of these improvements and extensions.

The main difference between this and preceding versions is that here we consider a notion of validity for temporal formulae, which is *anchored* at the initial state of the computation. The paper discusses some of the consequences of this decision.

Key words: Temporal Logic, Reactive Systems, Concurrent Programs, Specification, Verification, Proof System, Classification of Properties, Safety, Liveness, Recurrence, Responsiveness, Progress, Fairness, Fair Transition System.

Contents

*This research was supported in part by the National Science Foundation under grants DCR-8413230 and CCR-8812595, by the Defense Advanced Research Projects Agency under contract N00039-84-C-0211, and by the United States Air Force Office of Scientific Research under contracts AFOSR 87-0149 and 88-0281.

1 Introduction

Over the last several years we have witnessed the evolution of a formal methodology for the specification, verification, and development of reactive programs (and more general reactive systems), based on temporal logic. This methodology consists of several elements which we list below.

- *A computational model*, which provides a general uniform representation for the various programming languages and diverse suggested mechanisms for synchronization and communication between the concurrent processes comprising a reactive system. The generic computational model used in the temporal methodology presented in this paper is that of *Fair Transition System*. The computation model assigns a semantics to each reactive system. This semantics associates with each program a *behavior*, which is a single or a set of computation structures which represent its possible executions. In the case considered here, the semantics of a program is the set of its computation, where each computation is a sequence of states that can be generated in a single execution of the program.

- *A specification language*, which is essentially temporal logic augmented by some program specific predicates and functions, referring to the additional programming constructs needed to fully describe a state in the computation of a reactive program. In order to relate a specification presented by a formula in the logic to the program it is supposed to specify, it is necessary that the computational structures defined to be the semantics of a program can serve as *models* (in the logical sense) for the formula, which means that we can evaluate the formula on each of these structures and find whether it holds (is true) on the structure. Then, we say that the program *satisfies* (or *implements*) the specification given by a formula φ if φ holds over each of the computation structures. For example, in the linear semantics we consider here, the specification language is *linear* temporal logic, whose models are arbitrary sequences of states. Since the semantics of a program is a set of computations, which are also sequences of states, the specification φ is valid over the program P if it holds over all the computations of P.

- *Classification of Properties.* While not absolutely necessary, it is often very convenient and instructive to classify the properties that can be expressed in the specification language into several classes which share some common characteristics. After all, we should never forget that, even if our fondest dreams become true, and every constructed program is rigorously verified, the only guarantee this gives us is that the program precisely and unambiguously implements the specification, namely the program is correct relative to the specification. However, how do we know that the *specification* is correct, relative to the informal requirements or intuition about the intended behavior of the system? Formal tools can only help us in comparing two formal presentations of a system, but cannot help us in reconciling a formal description with an informal one. Usually we should be concerned with two aspects of the specification, which are its *consistency* and *completeness.* Consistency of a specification is something that can yield to formal tools, since we are comparing some parts of the specification with some other parts. Completeness, on the other hand, must be judged against the informal requirements. By recognizing some standard classes of properties, which usually occur in systems of a certain kind, we are alerted to the possibility of incompleteness by noticing that a specification of such system does not contain any properties of one of these classes. For example, it is now a folk axiom that no specification of a system can be complete without containing some *safety* properties and some *liveness* properties.

  Indeed, one of the most important classifications of properties of reactive systems, is their partition into safety and liveness properties. In this paper, we present a more detailed classification of properties which distinguishes many more subclasses than those two, but which serves the same purpose of structuring the specification and its proof methods into several frequently occurring patterns.

- *A proof system* which enables us to formally prove that a given program satisfies a given specification. Such a proof system can be partitioned into three parts (see [MP83c,MP83a]):

  ⋆ *A General Part.* This part provides axioms and rules to establish the validity of formulae which are generally valid, i.e., over any model, not necessarily associated with a given program. For example, for linear temporal logic this part is used to establish the validity of formulae that hold over any sequence of states. Thus, this part provides us with the tools to conduct program and domain independent reasoning over temporal models.

  ⋆ *A Domain Part.* This part provides axioms and rules to reason about the data domain which both the program and the specification refer to. Thus, for a program over the integers, we usually employ a specification which refers to the predicates and operations specific to the integers, such as $>, +$, etc. Similar theories should be provided for other data domains such as strings, lists, etc. While the general part enables us to establish validity of uninterpreted temporal formulae, the combination of the general part and the domain part extends this ability to deal also with interpreted temporal formulae. Still, the validity considered is over arbitrary interpreted sequences of states. An important function of the domain part is that it provides us with multiple induction principles, corresponding to the various well founded domains we may study.

  ⋆ *A Program Part.* This is the part that restricts the set of considered models to those that correspond to the behavior of the specific program we wish to analyze. By having deduction rules which are specific to a particular program, we can establish temporal properties which are not valid over all possible models, but just over the models associated with the behavior of the program. Together with the more general tools presented in the previous parts, the combined system gives us sufficient power to prove most of the properties that can be specified in temporal logic. This statement is made precise by several completeness results for the proof system.

- *Decision Procedures* and tools for *Automatic Verification.* While the main tool for verifying that a program satisfies its specification is still the deductive proof system discussed above, it depends very much on the skill and ingenuity of the person performing the verification. In some cases, the verification problem is decidable, and then it is possible to perform some verification tasks fully automatically, without any need for human intervention. The most prevalent of these cases is the case of *finite state systems*, in which all the data domains over which the program variables vary are finite. In this case the specification can always be represented by a propositional temporal formula, and the verification problem becomes decidable. Differently from sequential programs, there are many finite state reactive programs whose verification problem is far from trivial. Notably, many synchronization problems can, with some degree of abstraction, be faithfully represented as finite state programs. There has been quite an intense activity over the last several years, concentrating on the construction and efficient implementation of algorithms for automatic verification of finite state programs. See for example [CES86,LP84,QS83], etc.

- *Development* Paradigms. While the ability to verify an existing program relative to its specification is a very important element of a methodology for the systematic development of a program from its specification, it cannot serve as the sole basis for such a methodology. A proper methodology cannot wait until a full implementation is constructed and then attempt to verify it. The more constructive approach is to design a set of development strategies, which gradually transform the specification into a correct implementation. Several such development schemes have been successfully suggested for sequential programs by works such as [Dij76,Gri81], etc., and recently for reactive programs by [CM88]. To carry such a program for the temporal methodology requires a better understanding of the two major transformations that can be considered for reactive systems, which are *decomposition* and *refinement*. By refinement we mean the replacement of relatively moderate size actions, that at a certain level of abstraction can be considered atomic, by a more detailed implementation that necessarily makes them non atomic on the next level. Such a replacement is usually orthogonal to the process structure of the system and may affect uniformly many of the processes at the same time, but does not alter the process structure itself. Some general approaches to this important problem are discussed in [AL88,Bac80] as well as many other places. Decomposition, on the other hand, usually involves breaking some process into composition of smaller processes. To properly handle decomposition, we need a *compositional* proof system, in which the temporal properties of a composite process can be deduced from the properties of its components. We refer the reader to [dRZ87] for discussion of some of the requisites from such a system, and to a sequence of works [BKP84,NGO85,WGS87,Zwi88], which attempt to construct such a compositional proof system.

As can be seen from the short account of the main elements, of which the temporal methodology consists, some of them are in a more advanced stage of development, and are better understood than the others. However, there seems to be an accumulated evidence indicating that this methodology, or a one similar to it, can provide a feasible formal approach to the systematic development of reactive systems. This does not necessarily implies that we expect all parts of a big real time system to be rigorously developed and formally verified. According to a more modest and realistic view, the methodology or various parts of it can be used to develop small but critical parts of the system, most often subject to a certain degree of abstraction and simplification.

While there may be a consensus about this general principle, at least among the afictionados of the formal approach to programming, opinions vary greatly as to the precise details and parameters of the different constituents of the methodology. We will consider below the main parameters involved, and then indicate the choice selected by us and maintained for the rest of the paper.

1.1 Some Parameters of the Methodology

Type of Semantics

One of the important parameters of the methodology is the type of semantics which is assigned to programs. Some of the possible choices are, respectively:

- *Linear Semantics.* Under this choice, the semantics of a program P is the set of all the computations of P, where each computation is a (possibly infinite) sequence of states generated by performing the basic actions of the program (transitions) one at a time. Concurrent activity of two parallel processes in the program is represented by the *interleaving* of their atomic actions. To compensate for this much simpler, but perhaps less natural, representation of concurrency by interleaving, we add the notion of *fairness* to the computational model. One of the main functions of the fairness requirements is to exclude the interleaving between two processes in which, beyond a certain point all the actions taken are taken from only one of the processes, while the other has some enabled actions which never get executed. One of the simplifications taken in the linear approach is that we do not retain the information of where did the program take a choice between several possibilities. This can be illustrated by saying that the linear approach considers the program $a(b+c)$ to be (semantically) equivalent to the program $ab+ac$, even though the first program decides between taking b or c only after performing a, while the second program decides a priori whether it is going to perform ab or ac. Another obvious simplification inherent in the linear approach is its inability to distinguish between the non-determinism caused by a non-deterministic choice existing in the program for one of the processes, and the one introduced by the interleaving representation of concurrency, which in the case of two independent actions a and b being enabled in two processes, can choose to perform a before b, or vice versa. This can be illustrated by claiming that the linear approach also considers the programs $ab+ba$ and $a\|b$ to be semantically equivalent, even though, in the first program there is a non-deterministic choice in the program for the single process, while in the second program each of the processes is deterministic, and it is only our attempt to describe their possible behavior by linear sequences which causes the possibility of two such sequences, namely $a;b$ and $b;a$.

- *Branching Semantics.* Under this choice, the semantics of a program P is a single (possibly infinite) tree of states, where each node representing a state s in the computation, has as direct descendants all the states that can be derived from s by the execution of one of the atomic transitions which can be performed from s. This semantics certainly distinguishes between the program $a(b+c)$ and the program $ab+ac$, which differ in the point at which the choice between the two possibilities is made. On the other hand, this approach still represents concurrency by interleaving, and considers the programs $a\|b$ and $ab+ba$ equivalent.

- *Partial Order Semantics.* Under this view, the semantics of a program is a (possibly infinite) structure of states (or events), on which we recognize two basic relations. One is a partial order which represents the *precedence* ordering between events, and constrains certain events to occur only *following* some other events. Typically, this will be the case of two actions a and b, where b follows a in a sequential program of one of the processes (such as acb). The other relation is that of *conflict.* Two events are considered to be conflicting if they can never participate in the same execution. A typical case of conflict is associated with choice. Thus, in the program $ab+cd$, the actions a and c are in conflict. If we execute the action a, we lose the possibility of executing the action c. The conflict relation is extended by the precedence relation. Thus, if a is in conflict with c, and a and c, respectively precede b and d, it follows that each of $\{a,b\}$ is in conflict with each of $\{c,d\}$. If two events are neither related by the precedence relation, nor are in conflict, we say that they are *independent*, which can be interpreted as being concurrent, i.e., can be executed in parallel. An execution is any maximal substructure which does not contain two conflicting actions. Note that in describing a computation we refuse to commit ourselves to the ordering between actions which are independent. This is the reason that the partial order semantics is the only one from those we consider, which identify concurrency as a unique phenomena which is not translatable to any interleaved representation. To illustrate these concepts, we consider the trivial programs we have mentioned above. For the program $a\|b$, we have two actions, a and b, which are identified as independent. For the program $ab+ba$, we have to consider *four* actions a',b',a^*,b^*, where $a' \prec b'$ and $b^* \prec a^*$, and each of $\{a',b'\}$ is in conflict with each of $\{b^*,a^*\}$. Clearly, these two programs correspond to completely different structures. Similarly $a(b+c)$ differs from $ab+ac$ because, for example, the structure corresponding to $ab+ac$ contains two actions a,a^*, which are in conflict. Thus, it is obvious that the partial order semantics is sensitive both to the location of choice and to concurrency as different from interleaving. We refer the reader to some of the standard references to Petri Nets, such as [Rei85] for a fuller description of this approach.

This variety of semantics naturally leads to a variety of corresponding temporal logics. Consequently, we observe the following proposed logics to deal with each of the semantic views:

- Linear Temporal Logic. This is the logic considered in this paper, and the one studied previously in [GPSS80,MP83c,MP83a]. Tailored for a semantics consisting of a set of linear executions, formulae in this language define predicates over sequences.
- Branching Temporal Logic. Different variants of branching temporal logics have been considered, starting with the simpler logic presented in [BMP83], and culminating in the most expressive CTL^* of [EH86]. All these logics are interpreted on a branching structure that can be viewed as a tree. For a semantics of a program represented by a single computation tree, a formula in the language defines a predicate over such trees.
- Temporal Logic over Partial Orders. Here the situation is much more fluid. Only very recently have there been suggestions for formulating such a logic. Some of them are presented in this volume.

We can summarize the four different combinations of the two distinguishing criteria in the table below:

	Does not Distinguish Concurrency	Distinguishes Concurrency
Does Not Distinguishes Branching Points	Linear Semantics Linear Temporal Logic	Sets of Partial Order Executions Interleaving Sets Logic [KP87]
Distinguishes Branching Points	Computation Trees Branching Time Logics	Full Event Structures Logics?

The Expressive Power of the Specification Language

Even if we settle on the linear type of semantics, there are still many choices of the exact syntactic features and the expressive power of the chosen specification language. Some of the issues and alternatives that can be considered are listed below.

- One can choose (as a starting point) the future fragment of the temporal logic, including the *Until* and *Next* operator, as suggested in [GPSS80], and further developed in [MP83c] to include quantification over *static* (called there *global*) variables.
- Various arguments have been advanced against the use of the *Next* operator, claiming that it can express distinctions (such as whether an identical state repeats twice or three times in succession), which a properly abstract semantics should not make. This has been claimed in [Lam83b] which provides strong evidence that all the properties one wishes to express for asynchronous systems do not require this operator.

- Another important observation was made in [Wol83] pointing that there are simple properties, usually referring to counting events, which are not expressible in the regular version of temporal logic. This makes temporal logic less expressive than the formalism of ω–automata which is another attractive formalism for expressing properties of sequences. Wolper suggested in [Wol83] to remedy this problem by the introduction of special *grammar operators*. Meanwhile, there have been additional suggestions for extending temporal logic to attain the full expressive power of ω–automata. Some of these suggestions include the use of quantifiers over *dynamic* variables (also referred to as *local*), and the use of fixpoint operators. Both of these extensions leave the propositional version of the logic decidable, even though undisciplined use of quantifiers may significantly boost up the complexity of the decision procedure. Quantification over dynamic variables turned out to be a very useful device for abstraction, and has been shown to be necessary for attaining compositional completeness.

- An interesting alternative to temporal logic is specification by ω–automata. The utility of automata for automatic verification of finite state programs has been long realized (see [VW86]). However, a relatively recent development, suggested first in [AS89], generalized the use of automata to specify also infinite state programs (see also [MP87]). We will expand on this alternative later in the paper.

- Somewhat related to the automata approach, is the suggestion to use *fair transitions systems* not only, as we do, as a computational model, but also as a specification language. This suggestion has a strong appeal of uniformity, in that the specification and implementation languages coincide, and we can immediately conceive of a multi-level process of refinement from a most abstract transition system to a concrete one, at the end, which defines the implementation. This approach to specification and associated development has been suggested by many researchers, including [Lam83a,Jon87,BK83]. In some sense we can view [CM88] as one of the most complete accounts of specification and refinement by fair transition systems.

1.2 The Anchored Version of Temporal Logic

The original version of the temporal language presented in [GPSS80], and which serves as the basis for the temporal methodology described in [MP83c,MP83a,Pnu86], is based on two major design decisions:

- Only the future fragment is considered. In that the approach deviates from Kamp's version of temporal logic ([Kam68]), which serves as the major inspiration for [GPSS80]. Kamp considers a language with both future and past operators. The decision to adopt only the future fragment was based on the fact, established in [GPSS80], that this fragment by itself is expressively complete, meaning that it can express any property expressible by temporal logic (and the first order theory of linear order, which serves as the standard yardstick for temporal expressibility). It also appeared to provide natural expressions for the main classes of program properties one may wish to formalize. For example:

  - The formula $\Box p$ expresses the invariance of the assertion p over all executions of the program.
  - The formula $p \rightarrow \Diamond q$ expresses an eventuality property that guarantees the single occurrence of the event q, such as termination of the program that is expected to occur only once.

- The formula $\Box(p \rightarrow \Diamond q)$ expresses a repeated eventuality property (also called *response* properties), which guarantees that *every* occurrence of p must be followed by an occurrence of q.
- The formula $\Box(p \rightarrow (\neg r)\,\mathsf{U}\,q)$, using the *Unless* operator U (a weak version of the *Until* operator $\mathcal{U}$), expresses a (continuous) precedence property, ensuring that from any occurrence of p, the first following occurrence of r (if any) must be preceded by an occurrence of q (see [MP83b] for applications of such formulae).
- The formula $\Box\Diamond p \rightarrow \Box\Diamond q$ expresses a strong fairness property, ensuring that if there are infinitely many p's then there are also infinitely many q's. This property can represent a strong fairness requirement, which states that if a certain transition is infinitely often enabled, then it is also infinitely often taken. It can also represent a situation of response to persistence, in which the response q is guaranteed only if the request p is repeated sufficiently many times (infinitely many in the limit).

- A second basic feature of the [GPSS80] temporal logic is that satisfiability and validity are evaluated at *all* positions in the computation. Thus, a valid formula is expected to hold at all positions of a computation, and a formula is considered to be satisfiable if it holds at *some* position in some computation. This view treats all states in the computation uniformly and does not assign any special significance to the initial state. The best representation of this view is by the *Generalization* rule of the proof system of [GPSS80], given by:

$$p \vdash \Box p$$

  This rule claims that if the formula p is valid (anywhere) then it is valid at all states of the computation, and in fact *always* p is also valid. We refer to this feature of the logic as the *floating* interpretation of formulae.

The first indications that something can be gained by relaxing one or both of these design decision came when it was realized that some properties, in particular *precedence* properties, have a more natural expression, when using the past operators. For example, consider the property of *the absence of unsolicited response*, which states that the response q can only happen if it was preceded by the request p. Assuming, for simplicity, that both p and q can occur at most once, this is expressed in the [GPSS80] logic as

$$init \rightarrow (\neg q)\,\mathsf{U}\,p$$

Note that because of the floating interpretation of the logic, we cannot use the simpler $(\neg q)\,\mathsf{U}\,p$ expression. This is because, even in a good computation, i.e., one in which q is preceded by a p, there are some positions, namely all those which come after p and before q, at which it is not true that the first following occurrence of q must be preceded by an occurrence of p. Thus, to state this property we must anchor the observation point, at which the formula is evaluated, to the beginning of the computation. This is done by the special state predicate *init*, which characterizes the initial point in the computation. However, if we are allowed to use past operators in our logic, we may express the same property by the more intuitive formula ([KdR83,KVdR83])

$$\Box(q \rightarrow \diamondminus p),$$

which uses the *Once in the past* operator $\diamondminus$, to claim that every q is preceded by a p. This form, which states that there is no effect without a cause, also has the aesthetically pleasing symmetry with the formula $\Box(p \rightarrow \Diamond q)$, stating that there is no cause without effect.

Indeed, when carrying out a more thorough investigation of what is involved with adding the past fragment to temporal logic ([LPZ85]), it has been found that, while it does not (mathematically) increase the expressive power of the language, it does make the following important contributions to the utility of the language:

- Many properties, such as the one illustrated above, have much more natural expression when using the past.
- The past operators enable a syntactic characterization of an important classification of the properties expressible by temporal logic into several classes. This classification is very helpful for structuring the specification of a complex system, and for deriving a correlated system of proof principles specifically tailored for each of the classes. These are most useful for guiding the user to use for each property the proof strategy most appropriate for its class.
- The past forms (in particular the normal form on which the mentioned classification is based) are very useful for the establishment of the close connections between temporal logic and transition based formalisms such as $\omega-$automata.
- The relative cost of this expansion of the logic, has been found to be quite modest. The decision procedure for the propositional segment has the same complexity as that of the pure future fragment. A deductive system, proven complete (for the propositional segment), and a model checking procedure have been derived by a straightforward extension of the same constructs for the future logic.

We intend to illustrate some of these advantages in the following sections.

For awhile, we have experimented with the full logic (consisting of both past and future), still retaining the floating interpretation of formulae. However, it soon became apparent that this second basic assumption should also be removed when expanding the logic. We list below some points of dissatisfaction with the floating interpretation, not all of which are directly connected to the introduction of the past.

- The generalization rule $p \vdash \Box p$ is a continuous source of irritation. Technically, it invalidates the important *deduction* rule, which is an important tool in the predicate calculus, claiming that

  $$p \vdash q \text{ iff } \vdash p \rightarrow q.$$

  To see this it is sufficient to observe that $p \vdash \Box p$ according to the generalization rule itself, yet $p \rightarrow \Box p$ is not a generally valid formula.
- The proof system should be applicable not only to the universal set of all possible sequences, but also to more restricted sets of models, for example to those which correspond to computations of a given program. Thus, in addition to the notions of unrestricted validity and provability, which we may denote by $\models p$ and $\vdash p$, respectively, we are also interested in the same notions relativized to a restricted set of models C, and denoted by $C \models p$ and $C \vdash p$, respectively. It is easy to see that while the generalization rule is sound over the universal set of models, it is not valid over an arbitrary set of models C. To retain the generalization rule in such a relativization, it is necessary to require that C be *suffix closed*, i.e., contain with each sequence σ, all the suffixes of σ. This is the reason why, when working with the

floating framework, we always define the set of computations, over which the temporal formulae are evaluated, to consist of all the *initialized* computations of the program, together with all their suffixes. One may easily argue that this not a very natural definition.

For example, let us reconsider the property of no effect without cause, which requires that, every computation containing a q at some position, should contain a p at some preceding position. While we would expect this property to hold over all initialized computations of a good program which is expected to satisfy this property, we certainly cannot expect it to hold also over suffixes of such computations. This is because some suffix may contain the q event, but start only after the p event which existed in the full initialized computation. Thus, the true expression of this property in the floating framework must be

$$init \rightarrow \Box(q \rightarrow \Diamond p),$$

again relying on the special *init* predicate to restrict our attention to initialized computations only.

- While extra effort, expressed by the need for the *init* precondition, is required to represent anchored properties, such as the precedence property mentioned above or the eventual occurrence of an event that happens only once, it is too easy to represent really floating properties, i.e., those that do hold at all positions of all computations. For example, we are used to express the fact that p happens infinitely many times by the formula $\Box\Diamond p$. However, according to the floating interpretation it is sufficient to claim (and prove) that $\Diamond p$ is valid over the program, since by the floating interpretation (and the generalization rule) there is always an implicit $\Box$ operator standing in front of every valid formula. This is at times both inconvenient and misleading.

Based on these arguments, we have attempted in some of our later works (e.g., [MP87]) to operate in the anchored framework of temporal logic, using the full logic with both the past and future operators. As long as we do not present the full proof system for the logic, the differences between the floating and the anchored versions are not very apparent. They are mainly felt in the following points:

- Suffix closure is no longer required for the set of computations. We only consider initialized computations.
- A formula φ is defined to be *valid* over a set of sequences C, if it holds at position 0 of *every* sequence of C.

  The formula φ is defined to be *satisfiable* over C, if it holds at position 0 of *some* sequence of C.
- The default mode for expressing properties is the anchored mode, which does not require the special predicate *init*. For example, consider a sequential program with terminal location l_t. We will use l_t also as a state predicate, stating that the control is currently at l_t. To express unconditional termination of such a program, we write simply $\Diamond l_t$. To express termination conditional on some data precondition p holding at the beginning of the computation, we write $p \rightarrow \Diamond l_t$. To express the precedence property, claiming that every q is preceded by a p, we write $\Box(q \rightarrow \diamondminus p)$. On the other hand, to express floating properties, such as $\Box\Diamond p$, we must always include the preceding $\Box$ operator.

In these limited experiments, we found the anchored version much more systematic and unambiguous. Encouraged by this, we present in this paper most of the relevant proof system for supporting the anchored version.

2 Programs and Computations

2.1 An Abstract Computational Model

The basic computational model we use to represent programs is that of a *fair transition system* ([MP83a,Pnu86]). According to this model, a program P consists of the following components.

- $V = u_1, ..., u_n$ – A finite set of *state variables*. Some of these variables represent *data* variables, which are explicitly manipulated by the program text. Other variables are *control* variables, which represent, for example, the location of control in each of the processes in a concurrent program. We assume each variable to be associated with a domain, over which it varies.

- Σ – A set of *states*. Each state $s \in \Sigma$ is an interpretation of V, assigning to each variable $y \in V$ a value over its domain, which we denote by $s[y]$.

- $\mathcal{T}$ – A finite set of *transitions*. Each transition $\tau \in \mathcal{T}$ is associated with an assertion $\rho_\tau(V, V')$, referring to both an unprimed and a primed version of the state variables. The purpose of a transition assertion is to express a relation between a state s and its successor s', and we use the unprimed version to refer to values in s, and the primed version to refer to values in s'. For example, the assertion

  $$x' = x + 1$$

  states that the value of x in s' is greater by 1 than its value in s.

- Θ – The *initial condition*. This is an assertion characterizing all the *initial* states, i.e., states at which the computation of the program can start. A state satisfying Θ is called an initial state.

- $\mathcal{W} = \{W_1, ..., W_r\}$ – A family of *weak fairness* requirements (called *justice* requirements in [MP83a,Pnu86]). Each requirement $W_i = (E_i, T_i) \in \mathcal{W}$ consists of two sets of transitions, $E_i, T_i \subseteq \mathcal{T}$, on which the requirement of joint weak fairness is imposed. Intuitively, this forbids a computation in which, beyond a certain point, transitions in E_i are continuously enabled, but no transition of T_i is taken.

- $\mathcal{F} = \{F_1, ..., F_t\}$ – A family of *strong fairness* requirements (called *fairness* requirements in [MP83a,Pnu86]). Each requirement $F_i = (E_i, T_i) \in \mathcal{F}$ consists of two sets of transitions, $E_i, T_i \subseteq \mathcal{T}$, on which the requirement of joint strong fairness is imposed. Intuitively, this forbids a computation in which, beyond a certain point, transitions in E_i are enabled infinitely many times, but no transition of T_i is taken.

We define the state s' to be a *τ-successor* of the state s if

$$\langle s, s' \rangle \models \rho_\tau(V, V'),$$

where $\langle s, s' \rangle$ is the joint interpretation which interprets $x \in V$ as $s[x]$, and interprets x' as $s'[x]$. Following this definition, we can view the transition τ as a function $\tau : \Sigma \mapsto 2^\Sigma$, defined by:

$$\tau(s) = \{s' \mid s' \text{ is a } \tau\text{-successor of } s\}$$

We say that the transition τ is *enabled* on the state s, if $\tau(s) \neq \phi$. Otherwise, we say that τ is *disabled* on s. We say that a state s is *terminal* if all the transitions $\tau \in \mathcal{T}$ are disabled on it. The enableness of a transition τ can be expressed by the formula

$$En(\tau) : (\exists V')\rho_\tau(V, V'),$$

which is true in s iff s has some successor.

For a set of transitions $T \subseteq \mathcal{T}$, we say that T is enabled on s if *some* transition $\tau \in T$ is enabled on s, and that T is disabled on s if *all* transitions $\tau \in T$ are disabled on s.

Given a program P for which the above components have been specified, we define a *computation* of P to be a finite or infinite sequence of states

$$\sigma : s_0, s_1, s_2, \ldots,$$

satisfying the following requirements:

- **Initiality** The state s_0 is inital, i.e., $s_0 \models \Theta$.
- **Consecution** For each $j = 0, 1, \ldots$, $s_{j+1} \in \tau(s_j)$, for some $\tau \in \mathcal{T}$. In this case, we say that the transition τ is *taken* at position j in σ. For a set of transitions $T \subseteq \mathcal{T}$, we say that T is taken at position j, if some $\tau \in T$ is taken at j.
- **Termination** Either σ is infinite, or it ends in a state s_k which is terminal.
- **Weak Fairness** For each $(E_i, T_i) \in \mathcal{W}$ it is required that, if E_i is continuously enabled beyond some point in σ, then T_i must be taken at infinitely many positions in σ.
- **Strong Fairness** For each $(E_i, T_i) \in \mathcal{F}$ it is required that, if E_i is enabled on infinitely many states of σ, then T_i must be taken at infinitely many positions in σ.

Note that, by the definition of a transition τ being taken at a position, it is possible for more than one transition to be considered as taken at one position. Note also that any finite computation automatically satisfies all the weak and strong fairness requirements. For a finite computation σ, we denote by $|\sigma|$ the length of the computation, i.e., the number of states it contains. For an infinite computation, we write $|\sigma| = \omega$.

For a program P, we denote by $\mathcal{C}(P)$ the set of all computations of P.

2.2 Concrete Model I: Shared Variables

In general, we prefer in this exposition not to repeat material that has appeared previously, and prefer to refer the reader to [Pnu86] which provides a wide coverage of the temporal framework. However, we do present topics that have been refined (and hopefully improved) over the version appearing in [Pnu86]. One of them is the computational model, both abstract and concrete, in which we have refined the notions of fairness requirements. This is why we present several concrete models that illustrate, in particular, the meaning of the fairness requirements.

In the shared variables model, a program has the form:

$$P : \{\varphi\}[P_1 \| \ldots \| P_m]$$

Each program is associated with a set of shared variables $Y = y_1, \ldots, y_n$.

the formula φ, called the *data precondition* of P, is an assertion restricting the initial values of the variables in Y.

Each P_i, called a process, is a sequential program that may access and modify each of the shared variables in Y. We will often represent each P_i as a *transition diagram*. A transition diagram for the process P_i is a directed graph with nodes $\mathcal{L}^i = \{l_0^i, \ldots, l_t^i\}$, called *locations*. the location l_0^i is considered to be the entry location, and optionally l_t^i is a stopping location. Each edge in the graph is labeled by a guarded instruction of the form:

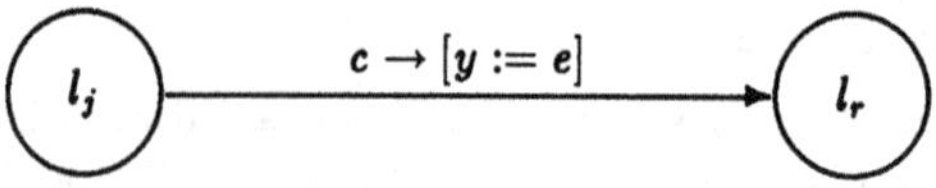

where c is a boolean expression (condition), $y \in Y$ is a variable, and e is an expression. We also allow multiple assignment $\overline{y} := \overline{e}$, in which a list of expressions $\overline{e} = e_1, ..., e_k$ is evaluated and simultaneously assigned to a corresponding list of variables $\overline{y} = y_1, ..., y_k$. The intended meaning of such an instruction is that when c holds, execution may proceed from l_j to l_r while assigning the current value of e to y.

Alternately, we may choose to represent processes by a text program, assuming the correspondence between the two representations to be obvious.

To assign to a program such as this the semantics of a fair transition system, we identify as follows:

- $V = Y \cup \{\pi_1, ... \pi_m\}$. As state variables we take all the data variables Y, to which we add a set of control variables $\pi_1, ..., \pi_m$. Each variable π_i for $i = 1, ..., m$ ranges over $\mathcal{L}^i$ and indicates the current location of control for the process P_i.

- As states we take all interpretations of V over the appropriate domain.

- As transitions we take all the edges in the diagrams for the processes. Consider a typical transition τ associated with an edge which connects location l_j to location l_r in process P_i, and labeled by the instruction $c \rightarrow [y := e]$. For such a transition we define $^\bullet\tau$, called the *source* of τ to be l_j, and $\tau^\bullet$, called the *target* of τ, to be l_r. For such a transition, we define the transition assertion ρ_τ by:

$$\rho_\tau \ : \ (\pi_i = l_j) \wedge c \wedge (\pi_i' = l_r) \wedge (y' = e) \wedge \bigwedge_{u \in V - \{\pi_i, y\}} (u' = u)$$

 Thus, this assertion states that, in order for the assertion to be enabled, it is necessary that P_i be at l_j, and that c holds, and when taken, the new value of π_i is l_r, the new value of y is the current value of e, and all other variables retain their values.

 Two transitions, τ and τ', are defined to be *in conflict*, if they share the same source, i.e., $^\bullet\tau = ^\bullet\tau'$. For a transition τ, we define the *competition set* of τ, denoted by $Comp(\tau)$ to be the set consisting of τ itself and all the transitions that are in conflict with τ.

- The initial condition is defined by:

$$\Theta \ : \ \varphi \wedge (\pi_1 = l_0^1) \wedge ... \wedge (\pi_m = l_0^m)$$

 Thus, it is required that initially, the data precondition φ holds, and all processes reside in their entry locations.

- The weak fairness family includes the requirement $(\{\tau\}, Comp(\tau))$ for each $\tau \in \mathcal{T}$. Thus, we require that if a certain transition is continuously enabled beyond a certain point, then, either this transition, or one competing with it must be taken infinitely many times.

- The strong fairness family is empty at this point, implying that no strong fairness requirements are made yet.

We would like to explain why the weak fairness requirements assume the particular form presented above, rather than the simpler form $(\{\tau\},\{\tau\})$, requiring that if τ is continuously enabled then τ itself should be taken infinitely many times. The reason is that the main purpose of the weak fairness is to compensate for the interleaving representation of concurrency, and ensure that every *process* will eventually progress (provided it is enabled, of course). Therefore, we wanted our fairness requirements to ensure this progress, but nothing more. In particular, we did not want the requirements to automatically imply *fairness in selection*, meaning that if a non-deterministic choice in one of the processes is repeated infinitely many times, then the process must choose fairly between the transitions involved in the choice. This is not because we are against fairness in selection, but rather that we prefer to separate the two issues, and have separate requirements that will represent process progress and nothing more, and another set that will represent fairness in selection. This leaves he designer of the programming language (in particular its semantics) the option to adopt one type of fairness without the other, or to adopt both.

To illustrate why the simpler $(\{\tau\},\{\tau\})$ implies fairness in selection, while our requirement $(\{\tau\}, Comp(\tau))$ does not, consider the following simple program.

$$\{\ y = 1\ \}$$

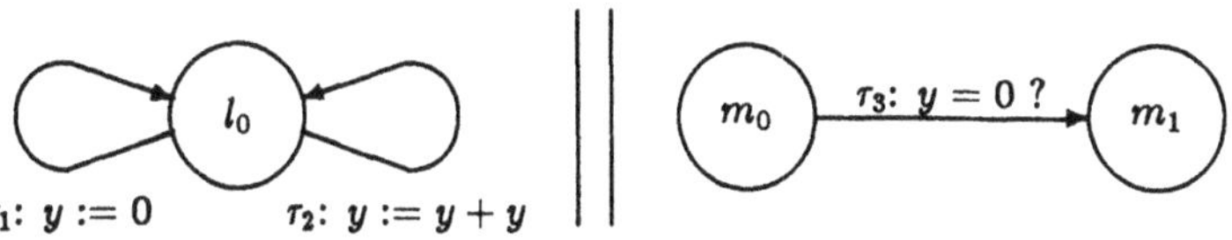

$- P_1 -$ $\qquad$ $- P_2 -$

This program consists of two processes, P_1 and P_2. Process P_2 continuously waits for the variable y, which initially is positive, to become 0. The process P_1 has two transitions τ_1 and τ_2 in tight loops around the location l_0. The transition τ_1 sets the value of y to 0. The transition τ_2 doubles the value of y. Note that once y becomes 0, the transition τ_2 preserves this value, so eventually P_2 will sense that $y = 0$ and proceed to location m_1.

The question is: is it guaranteed that in all computations of this program, eventually τ_1 will be taken, causing P_2 to eventually reach m_1? In other words, is the following sequence of states (each state presented by listing the current values of π_1, π_2, y, respectively):

$$\sigma : \langle l_0, m_0, 1\rangle, \langle l_0, m_0, 2\rangle, \langle l_0, m_0, 4\rangle, ...,$$

obtained by continuously taking only the transition τ_2, acceptable as a computation of the above program?

The answer depends on the fairness requirements we adopt, in particular the ones concerned with τ_1. The weak fairness requirement associated with τ_1, as defined in our semantics for the shared variable model, is given by $(\{\tau_1\},\{\tau_1,\tau_2\})$. Under this requirement, the sequence above is weakly fair with respect to τ_1, since even though it is continuously enabled and never taken, one of its competitors, τ_2, is taken infinitely many times. Obviously this sequence is also weakly fair with respect to τ_2, which is taken infinitely many times, and also to τ_3, which is never enabled. Thus, according to our official semantics this sequence is admissible as a computation.

If, on the other hand, we take instead the naive requirement $(\{\tau_1\}, \{\tau_1\})$, then the sequence above is not weakly fair with respect to this requirement. This means that the naive requirement forces the process P_1 to be fair in its selection, and eventually take τ_1.

2.3 Semaphores

For additional synchronization and coordination between processes we introduce two special instructions, *request*(y) and *release*(y), called *semaphore* instructions. Operationally, they perform the same transition (and therefore have the same transition assertion ρ_τ) as the guarded commands:

$$\begin{aligned} \textit{request}(y) &: (y > 0) \rightarrow [y := y + 1] \\ \textit{release}(y) &: y := y + 1 \end{aligned}$$

To illustrate their use, consider the following program:

$$\{\ y = 1\ \}$$

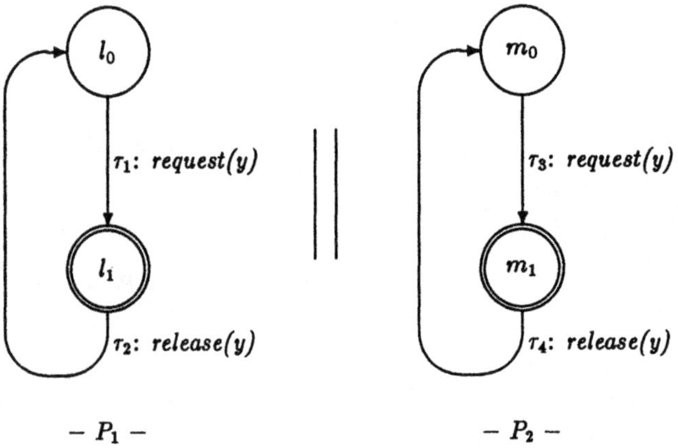

This program uses semaphores in order to coordinate mutual exclusion between the locations l_1 and m_1, i.e., to ensure that at no state in the computation can P_1 be at l_1, while at the same time, P_2 is at m_1. This is ensured by this program, because the first process to enter one of those *critical* locations sets y to 0, which disbales the *request*(y) of the other process, until the first process exits its critical location and resets y to 1.

However, another property we would expect from a good implementation of a mutual exclusion program is *accessibility*. This property requires that any process that wishes to enter its critical location will eventually do so. In the simpler program above, the processes continuously wish to enter their critical location (as represented by the fact that the non-critical location has only one exit), and therefore accessibility means that each process should visit its critical location infinitely many times. Unfortunately, this property is not guaranteed under our current fairness assumptions. Consider for example the sequence of states:

$$\sigma : \langle l_0, m_0, 1\rangle, \langle l_1, m_0, 0\rangle, \langle l_0, m_0, 1\rangle, \langle l_1, m_0, 0\rangle, \langle l_0, m_0, 1\rangle, ...,$$

obtained by taking only transitions of P_1. This sequence satisfies all our fairness requirements. It is certainly weakly fair to τ_1, τ_2, which are taken infinitely many times. It is also trivially fair to τ_4, which is never enabled. What about τ_3? While it is enabled infinitely many times, at all occurrences of the state $\langle l_0, m_0, 1\rangle$, it is also disabled infinitely many times, at all occurrences of the state $\langle l_1, m_0, 0\rangle$. Thus, τ_3 is not continuously enabled at any point, and hence the sequence above is also fair to τ_3. It follows that this sequence is a computation, and hence the property of accessibility does not hold for this program.

To remedy this situation we extend our fairness requirements as follows:

- For each transition τ associated with a *request* instruction, we add the strong fairness requirement $(\{\tau\}, Comp(\tau))$ to the strong fairness family $\mathcal{F}$.

Note that there is no need to make a similar requirement for the *release* instruction, since when the control is in the location which is the source for this transition, the transition is always enabled. The requirement of strong fairness imposed above makes the sequence σ, considered previously, inadmissible as a computation, since it is not strongly fair with respect to the transition τ_3, which is enabled infinitely many times but never taken. It is not difficult to see that, with the strong fairness requirements imposed for both τ_1 and τ_3, every computation must visit both l_1 and m_1 infinitely many times.

2.4 Concrete Model II : Synchronous Message Passing

As our next concrete model, we take a programming language in which communication between processes is performed by synchronous (hand-shaking) message passing, similar to CSP or CCS. For describing programs we may still use the diagram language, but enrich its repertoire of instructions that may label edges in the diagrams, by two new instructions:

- **Send**

$$c \rightarrow [\alpha \Leftarrow e]$$

  This instruction sends on channel α the current value of the expression e. The enableness of this instruction is, in general, conditional on a boolean expression c

- **Receive**

$$c \rightarrow [\alpha \Rightarrow y]$$

  This instruction reads from channel α a value into the variable y. Its execution is conditional on the boolean condition c.

According to the synchronous communication protocol, a *receive* instruction in one process can be executed only jointly with a *send* instruction of a parallel process, which addresses the same channel. The joint execution causes both processes to advance across their respective edges, while the value of e evaluated in the sending process is assigned to the variable y in the receiving process. Consequently, we define the set of transitions $\mathcal{T}$ for a synchronously communicating program as follows:

- **Assignment**

  With each edge labeled by an assignment instruction, we associate a transition whose transition assertion is defined identically to the shared variable case.

- **Communication**

  Consider a *pair* of edges a_k, a_r belonging to two parallel processes, P_i, P_j, respectively, which are labeled by a send and receive instructions, addressing the same channel, i.e.,

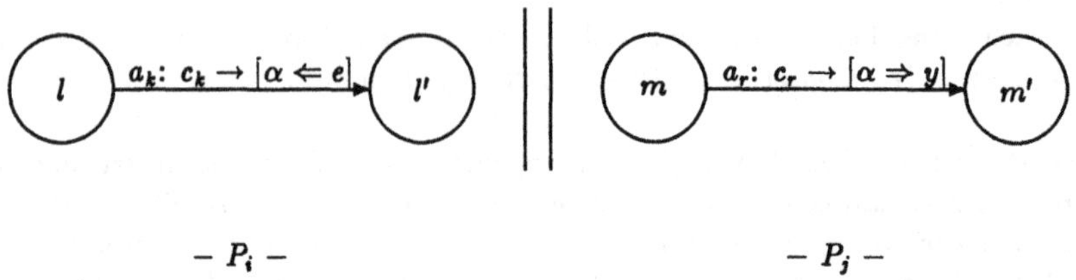

We refer to such a pair as a *matching* pair of communication instructions. For each such pair we define a transition τ_{kr}, whose transition relation is given by:

$$\rho_{\tau_{kr}} : (\pi_i = l) \wedge (\pi_j = m) \wedge c_k \wedge c_r \wedge (\pi_i' = l') \wedge (\pi_j' = m') \wedge (y' = e) \wedge \bigwedge_{u \in V - \{\pi_i, \pi_j, y\}} (u' = u)$$

Joint transitions, such as the ones considered above, have more than one source. For example, the transition τ_{kr} has as sources the locations l in P_i, and m in P_j. Consequently it has several *competition sets*, one associated with each source, or each process to which the transition belongs. As before we denote by $Comp(\tau)$ the *family* of competitions sets of the transition τ. For the case that the transition τ is an assignment, the family $Comp(\tau)$ contains only a single competition set.

We formulate now the fairness requirements associated with synchronously communicating programs.

- Weak Fairness. For each transition τ and each competition set $C \in Comp(\tau)$, we include in $\mathcal{W}$ the requirement $(\{\tau\}, C)$.
- Strong Fairness. For each *communication* transition τ and each competition set $C \in Comp(\tau)$, we include in $\mathcal{F}$ the requirement $(\{\tau\}, C)$.

Thus, we associate strong fairness requirements only with the communication transitions, interpreting them as coordination transitions similar to semaphores. Let us examine the implications of these definitions.

Consider first the following situation:

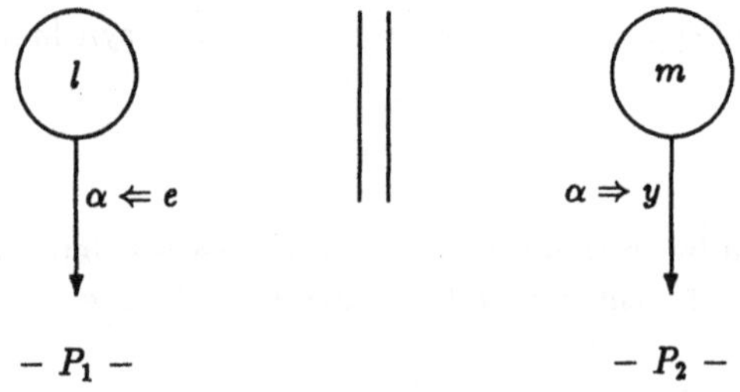

In this case we have two processes with two matching communication instructions. However, none have competitors (we assume that the only edges departing from l and m, are those depicted in the diagram). Consequently, the competition family of τ_{12} consists of a single set $\{\tau_{12}\}$. It follows that if a computation ever arrives to a state in which control is both at l and m, then weak fairness alone is sufficient to guarantee that τ_{12} will eventually be taken. This is because, otherwise, it will be continuously enabled and never taken.

Next consider the following situation.

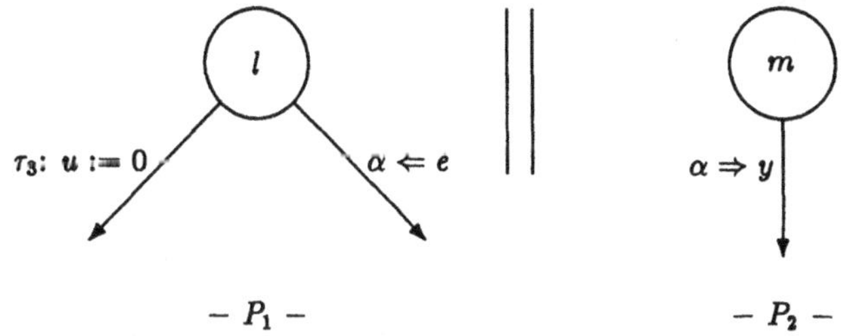

Here there are two alternatives departing from l, the communication and also another transition, which being a local assignment, is always enabled. Consider the situation in which P_2 arrives at m and waits there for a communication, while P_1 visits l infinitely often, always exiting via τ_3. Is such a behavior allowed by our fairness requirements?

Let us examine the competition family of τ_{12}. It is given by

$$Comp(\tau_{12}) = \{\{\tau_{12}, \tau_3\}, \{\tau_{12}\}\}$$

As we observe, it consists of two sets: $\{\tau_{12}, \tau_3\}$ – the competition set in P_1, and $\{\tau_{12}\}$ – the competition set in P_2. The behavior described above is strongly fair with respect to the requirement $(\{\tau_{12}\}, \{\tau_{12}, \tau_3\}$, since the transition τ_3 is taken infinitely many times. However, this behavior is not strongly fair with respect to the second fairness requirement associated with τ_{12}, namely $(\{\tau_{12}\}, \{\tau_{12}\})$. This is because τ_{12} is not taken even once. Thus, our fairness requirements guarantee that, in a situation such as above, where P_2 steadily waits at m, while P_1 visits l infinitely many times, the communication will eventually take place.

Next consider a third situation.

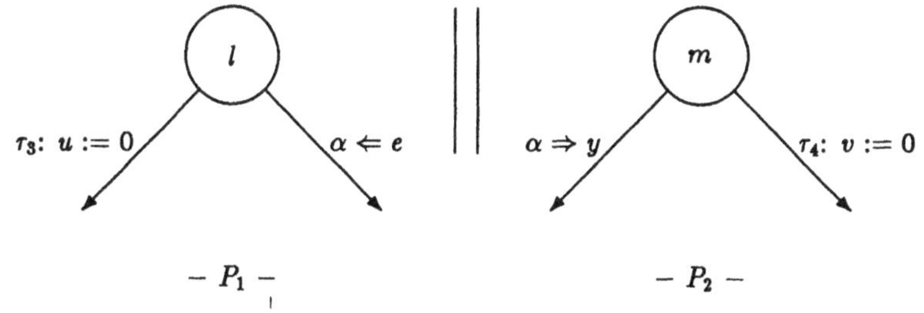

Here, both processes have local alternatives to the joint transition. Assume a behavior containing infinitely many states in which both P_1 is at l while P_2 is at m, but yet not taking the joint transition even once. This of course means that both processes consistently choose the local alternative. Does such a behavior satisfy our fairness requirements? Yes, because the two competition sets are $\{\tau_3, \tau_{12}\}$ and $\{\tau_{12}, \tau_4\}$, respectively, and each of them contains a transition that is taken infinitely many times.

One may wonder whether the distinction we make between the two last cases is not somewhat arbitrary. We claim it is not. There is a certain degree of robustness we would like our definitions and concepts to have. For example, they should be robust against interchanging the order of two adjacent transitions which are independent of one another, i.e., belong to different processes and do not access the same variable or channel. Any behavior of the last example in which the processes jointly visited the locations l, m infinitely many times, can be modified by such interchanges into an equivalent behavior in which P_1 is never at l at the same time that P_2 is at m. This is because the entry transitions to this location in one of the processes must be independent of the exit local exit transition in the other. Consequently, we can make sure that one of the processes leaves the critical position before the other enters his. Clearly in such a modified behavior the question of the joint transition never arise, because it is never enabled. We claim that this should be the case with the original behavior. In such a situation we consider it quite coincidental that they visited their respective critical locations (i.e., l and m) together.

The situation is quite different for the example where one of the processes is frozen in a waiting position, while the other visits its critical location infinitely often. Any interchanged behavior would retain the same characterization. We can make the entries and exits from the locations of the active process come a little earlier or later, but we cannot alter the fact that the other process is steadly waiting.

We can summarize this discussion by saying that the form of strong fairness we have adopted for synchronously communicating processes has the following characterization:

> If a communication transition between two processes is enabled infinitely often, then it is guaranteed to be taken only if one of the processes waits steadily, while the other may wander in and out of the communication location.

We conclude this discussion by showing how this approach can be used to implement mutual exclusion between two processes, using synchronous communication.

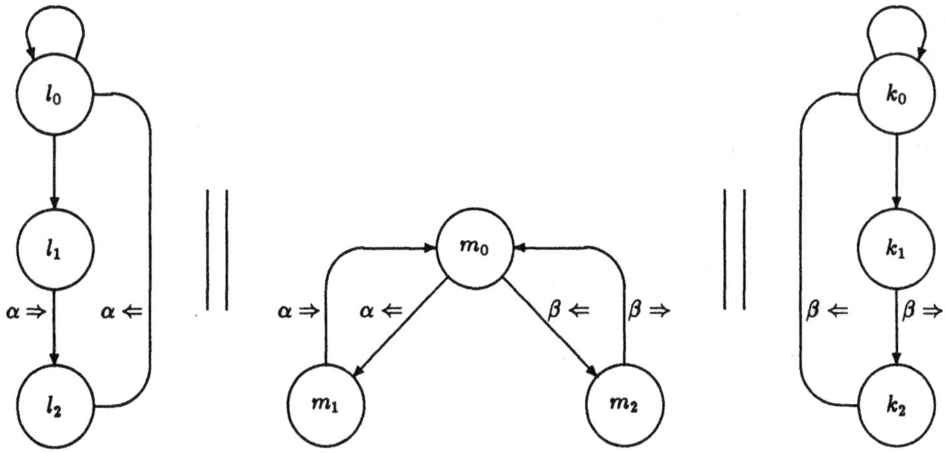

– P_1 – — *Arbiter* — – P_2 –

This program uses an arbiter process to mediate between the rivals P_1 and P_2. The arbiter synchronizes with P_1 by communicating along channel α, and with P_2 along channel β. The reason that process P_1, for example, if it waits at l_1 long enough is guaranteed to eventually perform its communication is that P_1 in this case is the steady waiter, while the arbiter may wander in and out of m_0 several times. If P_1 had an internal transition allowing it to change its mind and go from l_1 back to l_0, then this guarantee would not have held any longer.

3 Temporal Logic

We assume an underlying assertional language, which contains at least the predicate calculus, and interpreted symbols for expressing the standard operations and relations over the integers. We refer to a formula in the assertion language as a *state formula*, or simply as an *assertion*.

A *temporal formula* is constructed out of state formulae to which we apply the boolean operators, $\neg$ and $\vee$ (the other boolean operators can be defined from these), and the following basic temporal operators.

$\bigcirc$ – Next $\ominus$ – Previous
$\mathcal{U}$ – Until $\mathcal{S}$ – Since

A *model* for a temporal formula p is a finite or infinite sequence of states

$$\sigma : s_0, s_1, ...,$$

where each state s_j provides an interpretation for the variables mentioned in p. If σ is finite, i.e., $\sigma : s_0, s_1, ..., s_k$, we define the *length* of σ to be the number of states in σ, i.e., $|\sigma| = k+1$. If σ is infinite, we write $|\sigma| = \omega$.

Given a model σ, as above, we present an inductive definition for the notion of a temporal formula p holding at a position $j, 0 \leq j < |\sigma|$, in σ, denoted by $(\sigma, j) \models p$.

- For a state formula p

$$(\sigma, j) \models p \iff s_j \models p.$$

For the case that p is a state formula it can be evaluated locally, using the interpretation given by s_j to the free variables appearing in p.

- $(\sigma, j) \models \neg p \iff (\sigma, j) \not\models p$
- $(\sigma, j) \models p \vee q \iff (\sigma, j) \models p$ or $(\sigma, j) \models q$
- $(\sigma, j) \models \bigcirc p \iff j+1 < |\sigma|$ and $(\sigma, j+1) \models p$
- $(\sigma, j) \models p \mathcal{U} q \iff$ for some $k, j \leq k < |\sigma|, (\sigma, k) \models q$, and for every $i, j \leq i < k, (\sigma, i) \models p$
- $(\sigma, j) \models \ominus p \iff j > 0$ and $(\sigma, j-1) \models p$
- $(\sigma, j) \models p \mathcal{S} q \iff$ for some $k, 0 \leq k \leq j, (\sigma, k) \models q$, and for every $i, j \geq i > k, (\sigma, i) \models p$

Additional temporal operators can be defined as follows:

$\circledcirc p = \neg \bigcirc \neg p$	– Weak Next	$\circleddash p = \neg \ominus \neg p$	– Weak Previous
$\diamondsuit p = \mathrm{T} \mathcal{U} p$	– Eventually	$\diamondminus p = \mathrm{T} \mathcal{S} p$	– Sometimes in the past
$\square p = \neg \diamondsuit \neg p$	– Henceforth	$\boxminus p = \neg \diamondminus \neg p$	– Always in the past
$p \mathsf{U} q = \square p \vee p \mathcal{U} q$	– Unless, Weak Until	$p \mathsf{S} q = \boxminus p \vee p \mathcal{S} q$	–Weak Since

Two additional useful derived operators are the *entailment* operator, defined by:

$$p \Rightarrow q \iff \square (p \rightarrow q),$$

and the *strong equivalence* operator, defined by

$$p \Leftrightarrow q \iff \Box(p \equiv q).$$

A formula that contains no future operators is called a *past* formula. A formula that contains no past operators is called a *future* formula. Note that a state formula, to which we also refer as an *assertion*, is both a past and a future formula. For a state formula p and a state s such that p holds on s, we say that s is a p-state.

If $(\sigma, 0) \models p$, we say that p holds on σ, and denote it by $\sigma \models p$. A formula p is called *satisfiable* if it holds on some model. A formula is called *valid* if it holds on all models.

Two formulae p and q are defined to be *equivalent*, denoted by $p \approx q$, if the formula $p \equiv q$ is valid, i.e., $\sigma \models p$ iff $\sigma \models q$.

The notion of validity defined above is the notion of *temporal validity*, i.e., a temporal formula holding at position 0 of all possible sequences of states. A simpler notion we need now and then is that of *assertional validity*, which is that of an assertion p holding over every possible state. When we have to discuss the two together, we denote the temporal validity of a formula p by $\models_T p$, and the assertional validity of an assertion q by $\models_A q$. Obviously, an assertion q is assertionally valid iff it is temporally valid, because any state can be used as the first state in a sequence. That is:

$$\models_A q \iff \models_T q.$$

For the use of temporal formulae for specifying the properties of programs, we need to restrict the two notions of validity to a smaller sets of models, i.e., the models corresponding to computations of a given program. First we will give a general definition for an arbitrary set of models. Let $\mathcal{C}$ be a set of models, i.e., a set of finite or infinite sequences of states. We define a temporal formula to be (temporally) $\mathcal{C}$-valid, denoted by $\mathcal{C} \models_T p$ (or simply $\mathcal{C} \models p$, when there is no danger of confusion), if p holds at the first position of every sequence of $\mathcal{C}$. Similarly, we define an assertion q to be (assertionally) $\mathcal{C}$-valid, denoted by $\mathcal{C} \models_A q$, if q holds at all the states appearing at any position in the sequences of $\mathcal{C}$. Note that under a restriction to some subset $\mathcal{C}$, it is no longer the case that an assertion q is assertionally valid iff it is temporally valid, i.e.,

$$\neg(\mathcal{C} \models_A q \iff \mathcal{C} \models_T q)$$

This is because, in a restricted set of models, the states appearing at the first position in sequences may be a strict subset of the states appearing anywhere in the sequences of $\mathcal{C}$.

Given a program P, we can restrict our attention to the set of models which correspond to computations of P, i.e., $\mathcal{C}(P)$. This leads to the corresponding notions of validity over P. Thus, for a temporal formula p, we say that p is (temporally) P-valid, denoted by $P \models_T p$, if p holds at the first position of all the computations of P. For an assertion q, we say that q is (assertionally) P-valid, denoted by $P \models_A q$, if q holds over all *accessible* states of p, i.e., states appearing at some position in a computation of P. Similarly, we obtain the notions of P-satisfiability and P-equivalence.

4 The Classification of Properties

Having defined the notions of programs and their computations, which are sequences of states, and how temporal formulae are interpreted over sequences, it is obvious how a temporal formula may serve as a specification for a program. A program P is said to satisfy (or implement) the specification φ, if φ is P-valid. In general, a specification is structured as a conjunction of *requirements*, each of them describing some property that the program is supposed to have. One of the main advantages of this conjunctive structure of the specification is its *incrementality*. This means that if, at a later stage we wish to add, delete, or modify, one of the requirements, this can be done by dealing with this requirement alone, without directly interfering with any of the others. Similarly, in order to verify that a proposed implementation satisfies the specification, it is sufficient to verify each of the properties separately. In that, it is superior to some of the alternative specification methods, such as those based on process algebra formalisms, and provide an abstract modeling of the specified system. There the model integrates all the requirements together, and any modification of one of them, may require a major overhaul of the complete model.

However, there is another aspect, in which the abstract modeling approach is superior to the logic based approach, and this is the question of completeness of the specification. In the conjunctive form of the specification, there is always the question whether we have included all the properties that are relevant to the program we wish to specify. As we indicated in the introduction, one of the ways to try to ensure completeness of the specification is to classify the properties into several classes of frequently occurring properties. Then, when we contemplate a specification, we can at least compare it against a check list of types of properties, and for each class ask whether we have included a property of this type in the specification, or perhaps recognize that this class is irrelevant to the considered program.

This is the reason why there is a great interest in structuring the universe of expressible properties into several classes, each of which typically represents a certain type of phenomena, and is associated with a a unique style of verification needed for its establishment.

The first such classification of properties into the classes of *safety* and *liveness* properties has been suggested by Lamport in [Lam77]. The definition of the two classes has been given informally, by the descriptions:

- A *safety* property states that some bad thing *never* happens.
- A *liveness* property states that some good thing *eventually* happens.

Examples of safety properties are those which are expressible by an invariance formula of the form $\Box p$, and state that some state property p continuously holds on all states in the computation of the program. For example, p may state that mutual exclusion is maintained in the current state, i.e., that if one of the processes is critical then the other is not. Then, $\Box p$ claims that mutual exclusion always holds.

Examples of liveness properties are those which are expressible by an eventuality formula of the form $\Diamond q$, and state that some state property will eventually hold on each computation of the program. For example, if q designates termination, then $\Diamond q$ claims that the program always terminates.

As has been established over the years, this partition also distinguishes between two distinct proof approaches which are needed to establish the validity of properties in the two classes. To prove safety properties one uses essentially *computational induction* (using the terminology of [Man74]), based on an invariance principle. According to this principle, one shows that p holds in the initial state, and then, that p is preserved by any transition of the program. Consequently, based on an induction argument on the position in the computation, it follows that p holds at all positions. Note that the inductive argument appears only in the justification of the proof principle, but not in its application. That is, the user of the principle only establishes the two facts mentioned above, i.e., that p holds initially, and that it is preserved over any transition. Thus the induction is *implicit*.

Liveness properties, on the other hand, are proven using ***structural induction*** (using the terminology of [Man74]), i.e., explicit induction on some element of the state. This induction is often represented as an application of a well-founded argument. The reason we need explicit induction for liveness properties, such as $p \to \Diamond q$, is that when the program starts at a p-state, there are in general, several important intermediate stages that the computation has to evolve through on the way from p to q. The well-founded argument is used to measure how close we are to the goal q. We refer the reader to [OL82,MP84] for a discussion of the uniques proof principles associated with each class.

A more formal definition of the semantic nature of safety properties has been given in [Lam83b], and a semantic formalization of liveness properties has been given in [AS85]. These two formal definitions lead to the following pleasing consequences:

- The classes of safety and liveness properties are disjoint (except for the trivial formulae T, F).
- Every property can be represented as the intersection of a safety property and a liveness property.
- The classes contain the obvious properties that are informally associated with them, i.e., $\Box p$ in the safety class, and $\Diamond q, p \to \Diamond q, \Box \Diamond q$, etc. in the liveness class, for state formulae p, q.
- All the properties classified as safety properties can be proven using an invariance principle, while the properties classified as liveness properties can be proven using a well-founded principle.

Alpern and Schneider (see [AS89,AS87]) studied this classification in terms of predicate automata, a topic we will cover in a later subsection. They provided syntactic characterization of the two classes by imposing structural constraints on the automata describing such properties.

Unfortunately, the situation is less satisfactory when we try to give a syntactic characterization of these two classes in terms of the temporal logic formulae expressing them. Sistla gave in [Sis85] a syntactic characterization of the safety class, as the set of formulae constructed from state formulae to which we apply the positive boolean operations $(\wedge, \vee)$, and the temporal operator U (***Unless***). Note that $\Box$ is a special case of U, since $\Box p = p \mathsf{U} \text{F}$. He also gave some characterizations of some subclasses of the liveness class, which however do not cover the full class. Another problem with these characterizations, which are all done within the future fragment, is that they do not lead directly to a useful proof principle.

An intersting development occurred when, incorporating the past fragment into the logic, it was realized ([LPZ85]) that the full class of safety properties expressible in temporal logic, can be expressed by a formula of the form $\Box p$ for some ***past*** formula p. This seems a most natural generalization of the classical example of safety formulae which have the form $\Box p$ for a ***state*** formula p. Based on this observation, we have developed a small hierarchy of classes of properties, of which safety is the lowest class. Unfortunately, while agreeing with the safety-liveness classification on the safety class, we do not have any class in the hierarchy which corresponds to the liveness class, which makes our classification somewhat orthogonal to the safety-liveness partition.

In the current section we present our classification of the temporal properties, to which we refer as the Borel hierarchy, since it coincides with the two lower levels of the Borel topological hierarchy. We examine this classification from three points of view. The first is semantic or topological, in which we characterize the classes as sets of sequences. Next, we consider properties which are expressible in temporal logic, and for those give for each class a syntactic characterization of the formulae which express properties falling in this class. Finally we consider the expression of properties by predicate automata, and give syntactic characterization of the automata describing properties falling in each class. We show that these three view coincide, i.e., any property expressible by temporal logic, which is semantically classified as belonging to class κ, is expressible by a κ-type formula. A similar result holds for properties expressible by automata. In the last section dealing with the program part of the proof system, we will indicate what are the proof principles associated with each of the classes.

4.1 Semantic View

We introduce the following notation. Let Σ denote the set of states. We denote by Σ^+ the set of all finite but non empty sequences of states, and by Σ^ω the set of all infinite state sequences. Let $\Sigma^\infty = \Sigma^+ \cup \Sigma^\omega$ denote the set of both finite and infinite sequences. For a finite sequence $\sigma \in \Sigma^+$ and a sequence $\sigma' \in \Sigma^\infty$, we denote by $\sigma \prec \sigma'$ the fact that σ is a finite prefix of σ' but different from σ' (a proper finite prefix). We denote by $\sigma \preceq \sigma'$ the more general relation $(\sigma \prec \sigma') \vee (\sigma = \sigma' \in \Sigma^+)$. We denote by $\sigma \cdot \sigma'$ the sequence, obtained by concatenating σ' to the end of σ. Note that the concatenation is defined only if σ is finite.

We (semantically) define a property to be a set $\Pi \subseteq \Sigma^\infty$. Intuitively, since we have no language to express the requirements the property should fulfill, the only way we can describe a property is by the set of all sequences that have this property. A property is called *finitary* if it contains only finite sequences (may still be an infinite set of such sequences), and it is called an *infinitary* property if it only contains infinite sequences. For a property $\Pi \subseteq \Sigma^\infty$, we denote by $Pref(\Pi)$ the set of all *finite* prefixes of Π:

$$Pref(\Pi) = \{\sigma \in \Sigma^+ \mid \sigma \preceq \sigma' \text{ for some } \sigma' \in \Pi\}.$$

We denote by $\sigma[0..k]$ the finite prefix $s_0, s_1, ..., s_k$ of the sequence $\sigma : s_0, s_1, ..., s_k, s_{k+1}, ...$

The intuition behind the classification is based on a loose generalization of the basic informal characterization given by Lamport for the two classes. We distinguish four different modalities that can describe the frequency of occurrences of "good things" in a sequence. Informally:

- A *safety* property states that a good thing happens at *all* states of the sequence.
- A *termination* property states that a good thing happens at *some* states of the sequence.
- A *recurrence* property states that a good thing happens at *infinitely many* states of the sequence.
- A *persistence* property states that a good thing happens at *all but finitely many* states of the sequence.

It can be claimed that the above definition makes sense only if we can check at any state of the sequence, whether the good thing holds there or not. Consequently, we identify the good thing as a general property of finite prefixes of a sequence, i.e., as a finitary property. Thus, we can view the classification as based on the different ways we can derive an infinitary property from a finitary one.

To formalize these notions, we introduce four operators A, E, R, and P, which map finitary properties on properties contained in Σ^∞. They are defined as follows:

- $\sigma \in A(\Pi) \iff \forall \sigma'(\sigma' \preceq \sigma) : \sigma' \in \Pi.$

  Obviously, $\sigma \in A(\Pi)$ iff *every* finite prefix of σ is in Π.

- $\sigma \in E(\Pi) \iff \exists\sigma'(\sigma' \preceq \sigma) : \sigma' \in \Pi$

  Obviously, $\sigma \in E(\Pi)$ iff *some* finite prefix of σ is in Π.

- $\sigma \in R(\Pi) \iff \forall\sigma'(\sigma' \preceq \sigma) : \exists\sigma''(\sigma' \preceq \sigma'' \preceq \sigma) : \sigma'' \in \Pi.$

  Obviously, $\sigma \in R(\Pi)$ iff

  either σ is finite and belongs to Π,
  or σ is infinite and *infinitely many* finite prefixes of σ are in Π.

- $\sigma \in P(\Pi) \iff \exists\sigma'(\sigma' \preceq \sigma) : \forall\sigma''(\sigma' \preceq \sigma'' \preceq \sigma) : \sigma'' \in \Pi.$

  Obviously, $\sigma \in P(\Pi)$ iff

  either σ is finite and belongs to Π,
  or σ is infinite and *all but finitely many* finite prefixes of σ are in Π.

For X, one of the four operators A, E, R, P, we define the finitary and infinitary versions of X by:

$$X_f(\Pi) = X(\Pi) \cap \Sigma^+ \quad \text{and} \quad X_\omega(\Pi) = X(\Pi) \cap \Sigma^\omega$$

We call $A_\omega(\Pi), E_\omega(\Pi), R_\omega(\Pi)$, and $P_\omega(\Pi)$, the *safety, termination, recurrence,* and *persistence* properties induced by Π, respectively. We classify an infinitary property $\Pi \subseteq \Sigma^\omega$ as follows:

- Π is a *safety* property if $\Pi = A_\omega(\Pi')$ for some finitary Π'.
- Π is a *termination* property if $\Pi = E_\omega(\Pi')$ for some finitary Π'.
- Π is a *recurrence* property if $\Pi = R_\omega(\Pi')$ for some finitary Π'.
- Π is a *persistence* property if $\Pi = P_\omega(\Pi')$ for some finitary Π'.

We refer to these four classes of properties, denoted by $\mathcal{S}, \mathcal{T}, \mathcal{R}, \mathcal{P}$, respectively, as the *basic* classes. In addition we have four more classes that can be constructed by boolean combinations of the basic classes.

We define a property Π to be an *intermittence* property, belonging to the class $\mathcal{I}$,if

$$\Pi = A_\omega(\Pi') \cup E_\omega(\Pi''),$$

for some finitary Π' and Π''.

We define a property Π to be a *multiple intermittence* property, belonging to the class $\mathcal{MI}$, if it can be obtained by a finite boolean combination, i.e., union, intersection, and complementation (relative to Σ^ω) of safety and termination properties.

We define a property Π to be a *progress* property, belonging to the class $\mathcal{G}$, if

$$\Pi = R_\omega(\Pi') \cup P_\omega(\Pi''),$$

for some finitary Π' and Π''.

We define a property Π to be a *multiple progress* property, belonging to the class $\mathcal{MG}$, if it can be obtained by a finite boolean combination of recurrence and persistence properties.

The motivation for these names will be given in the next subsection.

We observe the following facts about the defined classes.

Fact 4.1 Duality: *The classes $\mathcal{S}$ and $\mathcal{T}$ are dual under complementation, i.e.,* $\Pi \subseteq \Sigma^\omega$ *is a* **safety** *property iff* $\Sigma^\omega - \Pi$ *is a* **termination** *property. Similarly, the classes $\mathcal{R}$ and $\mathcal{P}$ are dual. The classes $\mathcal{MI}$ and $\mathcal{MG}$ are closed under complementation.*

To show that $\mathcal{S}$ and $\mathcal{T}$ are complementary, we observe that for a finitary $\Pi \subseteq \Sigma^+$:

$$\begin{aligned} \Sigma^\omega - A_\omega(\Pi) &= E_\omega(\Sigma^+ - \Pi), \quad \text{and} \\ \Sigma^\omega - E_\omega(\Pi) &= A_\omega(\Sigma^+ - \Pi) \end{aligned}$$

This is because

$$\begin{aligned} \sigma \in (\Sigma^\omega - A_\omega(\Pi)) &\leftrightarrow \sigma \notin A_\omega(\Pi) \\ &\leftrightarrow \neg(\forall \sigma'(\sigma' \preceq \sigma) : \sigma' \in \Pi) \\ &\leftrightarrow \exists \sigma'(\sigma' \preceq \sigma) : \sigma' \notin \Pi \\ &\leftrightarrow \exists \sigma'(\sigma' \preceq \sigma) : \sigma' \in (\Sigma^+ - \Pi). \\ &\leftrightarrow \sigma \in E_\omega(\Sigma^+ - \Pi) \end{aligned}$$

Similarly:

$$\begin{aligned} \Sigma^\omega - R_\omega(\Pi) &= P_\omega(\Sigma^+ - \Pi), \quad \text{and} \\ \Sigma^\omega - P_\omega(\Pi) &= R_\omega(\Sigma^+ - \Pi) \end{aligned}$$

The class $\mathcal{MI}$, being defined as a boolean combination of safety and termination properties, is certainly closed under an additional boolean operation such as complementation. The same holds for the class $\mathcal{MG}$.

Fact 4.2 Closure: *The classes $\mathcal{S}, \mathcal{T}, \mathcal{MI}, \mathcal{R}, \mathcal{P}, \mathcal{MG}$ are closed under union and intersection. The classes $\mathcal{I}, \mathcal{G}$ are closed under union.*

To show these closure properties, we need some operations on *finitary* properties. We use freely the boolean operations of union and intersection, and complementation with respect to Σ^+. we also use concatenation of properties:

$$\Pi_1 \cdot \Pi_2 = \{\sigma_1 \cdot \sigma_2 \mid \sigma_1 \in \Pi_1 \,,\ \sigma_2 \in \Pi_2\}.$$

the special property Σ is the set of all singleton sequences, i.e., sequences of length 1.

Note that using concatenation between properties, we can express the operator $E(\Pi)$ and its restricted versions, for a finitary Π, as:

$$E(\Pi) = \Pi \cdot \Sigma^\infty, \quad E_f(\Pi) = \Pi \cdot \Sigma^+, \quad E_\omega(\Pi) = \Pi \cdot \Sigma^\omega$$

An additional finitary operator is the *since* operator, modeled after the corresponding temporal operator. It is defined by:

$$(\Pi_1)\mathbf{S}(\Pi_2) = \{\sigma \in \Sigma^+ \mid \exists \sigma'(\sigma' \preceq \sigma) : [(\sigma' \in \Pi_2) \wedge (\forall \sigma''(\sigma' \prec \sigma'' \preceq \sigma) : \sigma'' \in \Pi_1)]\}.$$

According to this definition $\sigma \in (\Pi_1)\mathbf{S}(\Pi_2)$ iff σ has a finite prefix σ' in Π_2 and all other prefixes of σ, longer than σ', are in Π_1.

The closure properties under the positive boolean operations are shown as follows:

- For *safety* they are justified by:

$$\begin{aligned} A_\omega(\Pi_1) \cap A_\omega(\Pi_2) &= A_\omega(\Pi_1 \cap \Pi_2), \\ A_\omega(\Pi_1) \cup A_\omega(\Pi_2) &= A_\omega(A_f(\Pi_1) \cup A_f(\Pi_2)). \end{aligned}$$

To support the last equality, we show inclusion in both directions.

Assume that $\sigma \in A_\omega(\Pi_1)$. This means that every finite prefix $\sigma' \preceq \sigma$ is in Π_1. Take any finite prefix $\sigma'' \preceq \sigma$. Obviously, any finite prefix of σ'' is also a finite prefix of σ and hence is in Π_1. It follows that $\sigma'' \in A(\Pi_1)$. Since σ'' is finite, actually $\sigma'' \in A(\Pi_1) \cap \Sigma^+ = A_f(\Pi_1)$. Clearly $\sigma'' \in A_f(\Pi_1) \cup A_f(\Pi_2)$. Hence, any finite prefix of σ is in $A_f(\Pi_1) \cup A_f(\Pi_2)$. We conclude that $\sigma \in A_\omega(A_f(\Pi_1) \cup A_f(\Pi_2))$, and therefore:

$$A_\omega(\Pi_1) \subseteq A_\omega(A_f(\Pi_1) \cup A_f(\Pi_2)).$$

By symmetry, also $A_\omega(\Pi_2)$ is contained in the same right hand side, and we conclude

$$A_\omega(\Pi_1) \cup A_\omega(\Pi_2) \subseteq A_\omega(A_f(\Pi_1) \cup A_f(\Pi_2)).$$

To show inclusion in the other direction, assume that $\sigma \notin A_\omega(\Pi_1) \cup A_\omega(\Pi_2)$. Then σ must have a finite prefix $\sigma_1 \notin \Pi_1$ and another finite prefix $\sigma_2 \notin \Pi_2$. Without loss of generality assume $\sigma_1 \preceq \sigma_2$. It follows that $\sigma_2 \notin A_f(\Pi_2)$, and since σ_2 has a prefix $\sigma_1 \notin \Pi_1$, also $\sigma_2 \notin A_f(\Pi_1)$. Hence, $\sigma_2 \notin A_f(\Pi_1) \cup A_f(\Pi_2)$, and therefore $\sigma \notin A_\omega(A_f(\Pi_1) \cup A_f(\Pi_2))$.

- For the *termination* class, we use the previously established duality with *safety* to claim:

$$\begin{aligned} E_\omega(\Pi_1) \cup E_\omega(\Pi_2) &= E_\omega(\Pi_1 \cup \Pi_2), \\ E_\omega(\Pi_1) \cap E_\omega(\Pi_2) &= E_\omega(E_f(\Pi_1) \cap E_f(\Pi_2)). \end{aligned}$$

- For *recurrence*, we claim:

$$R_\omega(\Pi_1) \cup R_\omega(\Pi_2) = R_\omega(\Pi_1 \cup \Pi_2).$$

Obviosuly, σ contains either infinitely many Π_1-prefixes or infinitely many Π_2-prefixes iff it contains infinitely many $(\Pi_1 \cup \Pi_2)$-prefixes.

Closure under intersection is given by the equality:

$$R_\omega(\Pi_1) \cap R_\omega(\Pi_2) = R_\omega(\Pi_1 \cap [(\overline{\Pi_1})\mathcal{S}(\Pi_2)] \cdot \Sigma),$$

where we denote, for a finitary property Π, $\overline{\Pi} = \Sigma^+ - \Pi$.

We observe that $\sigma \in (\Pi_1 \cap [(\overline{\Pi_1})\mathcal{S}(\Pi_2)] \cdot \Sigma)$ iff $\sigma \in \Pi_1$, σ has a prefix $\sigma' \prec \sigma$ such that $\sigma' \in \Pi_2$, and all other prefixes, longer than σ' and shorter than σ, are not in Π_1. This characterizes a finite sequence σ in Π_1, such that its longest proper prefix which belongs to $\Pi_1 \cup \Pi_2$ belongs in fact to Π_2.

Obviously, σ has infinitely many Π_1-prefixes as well as infinitely many Π_2-prefixes iff it has infinitely many Π_1-prefixes whose longest proper $(\Pi_1 \cup \Pi_2)$-prefix is a Π_2-prefix.

- For *persistence*, we use duality with the *recurrence* class. This yields:

$$\begin{aligned} P_\omega(\Pi_1) \cap P_\omega(\Pi_2) &= P_\omega(\Pi_1 \cap \Pi_2), \\ P_\omega(\Pi_1) \cup R_\omega(\Pi_2) &= P_\omega(\Pi_1 \cup \overline{[(\Pi_1)\mathcal{S}(\overline{\Pi_2})] \cdot \Sigma}). \end{aligned}$$

- The class of *intermittence* properties is closed under unions. To see this, we observe that

$$[A_\omega(\Pi_1) \cup E_\omega(\Pi_2)] \cup [A_\omega(\Pi'_1) \cup E_\omega(\Pi'_2)] \;=\; A_\omega(\Pi''_1) \cup E_\omega(\Pi''_2),$$

  where
  $A_\omega(\Pi''_1) = A_\omega(\Pi_1) \cup A_\omega(\Pi'_1)$, guaranteed by the closure properties of $\mathcal{S}$, and
  $E_\omega(\Pi''_2) = E_\omega(\Pi_2) \cup E_\omega(\Pi'_2)$, guaranteed by the closure properties of $\mathcal{T}$

- The class of *progress* properties is handled similarly, using the closure under union of the classes $\mathcal{R}, \mathcal{P}$.

- The closure of $\mathcal{MI}, \mathcal{MG}$ is obvious.

Fact 4.3 Inclusion: *The classes of properties are related by the inclusion relations depicted in the diagram of Figure 1. The edges in the diagram represent strict inclusions.*

Note that the families of intermittence and progress properties are only subsets of the topological families $G_\delta \cap F_\sigma$ and $G_{\delta\sigma} \cap F_{\sigma\delta}$, respectively. The families of multiple intermittence and multiple progress, on the other hand, coincide precsicely with these topological families.

To show the inclusions $\mathcal{S} \cup \mathcal{T} \subseteq \mathcal{R}$ and $\mathcal{S} \cup \mathcal{T} \subseteq \mathcal{P}$, we observe that:

$$A_\omega(\Pi) = R_\omega(A_f(\Pi)) = P_\omega(A_f(\Pi)),$$

$$E_\omega(\Pi) = R_\omega(E_f(\Pi)) = P_\omega(E_f(\Pi)).$$

For example, an infinite $\sigma \in R_\omega(E_f(\Pi))$ iff σ has infinitely many prefixes $\sigma' \in E_f(\Pi)$, i.e., prefixes σ' containing a prefix $\sigma'' \preceq \sigma'$ such that $\sigma'' \in \Pi$. This is true iff σ has some prefix $\sigma'' \prec \sigma$ such that $\sigma'' \in \Pi$, Hence $R_\omega(E_f(\Pi)) = E_\omega(\Pi)$.

The other inclusions are equally easy to show. The strictness of the inclusions, not related to the classes $\mathcal{MI}$ and $\mathcal{MG}$ are also straightforward.

Corollary 4.1 Normal Form: *Any* multiple intermittence *property is expressible as the intersection of several* intermittence *properties. Similarly, any* multiple progress *property is expressible as the intersection of several* progress *properties.*

Thus, any *multiple intermittence* property Π is expressible as:

$$\Pi = \bigcap_{i=1}^{k} (A_\omega(\Pi'_i) \cup E_\omega(\Pi''_i)),$$

for some finitary Π'_i and $\Pi''_i, i = 1, ..., k$.

Similarly, any *multiple progress* property Π is expressible as:

$$\Pi = \bigcap_{i=1}^{k} (R_\omega(\Pi'_i) \cup P_\omega(\Pi''_i)),$$

for some finitary Π'_i and $\Pi''_i, i = 1, ..., k$.

Let $\Pi \subseteq \Sigma^\omega$ be a multiple intermittence property. By definition it can be expressed as a boolean combination of safety and termination properties. We perform the following transformations on the boolean expressions:

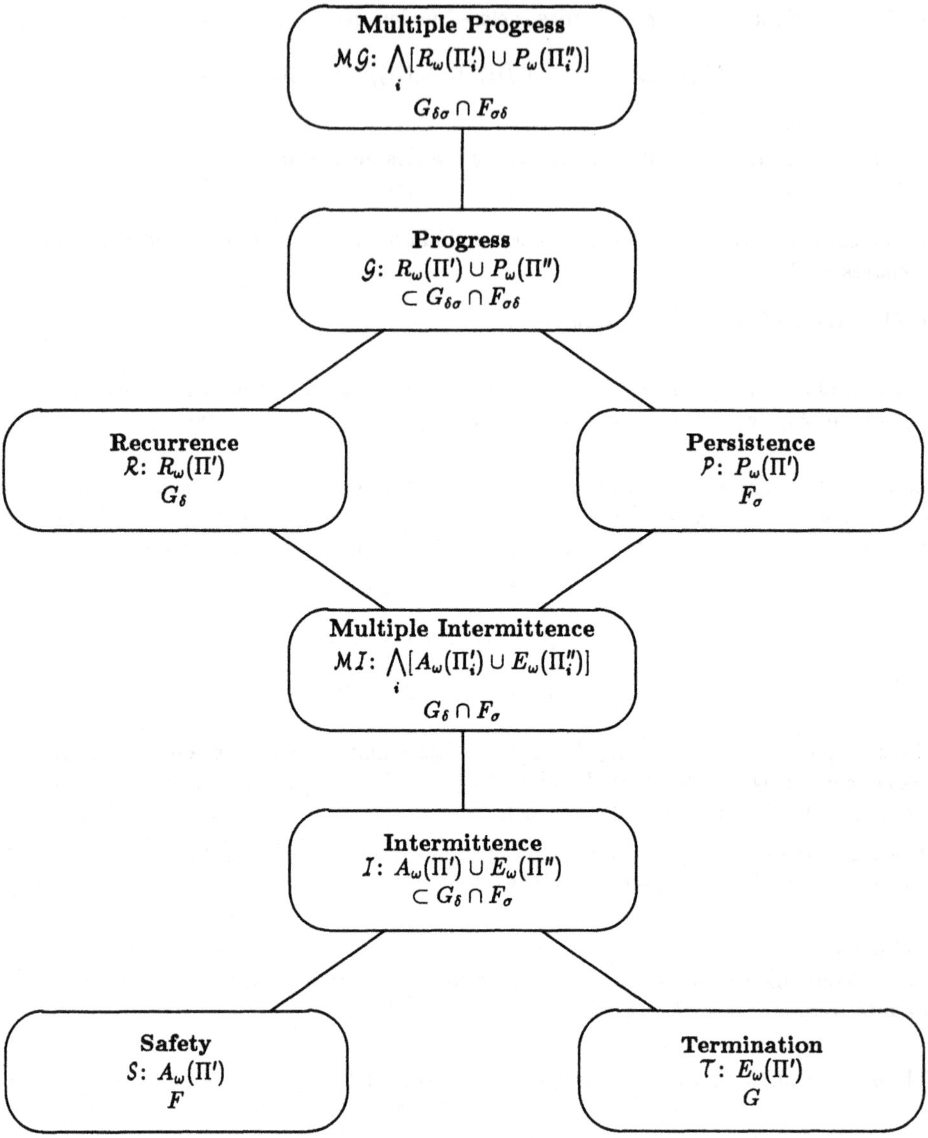

Figure 1: Inclusion Relations between the Classes

First we push all the complementations inside, using De Morgan laws. By the duality properties described in fact 4.1, all the complementations can be reduced to operations on finitary properties.

We are left with a positive boolean combination of safety and termination properties. We expand the resulting expression by distributivity to obtain a conjunctive normal form, i.e., an intersection of unions of safety and termination properties. By associativity of the union, we can group each union of safety properties and use the closure of the safety class under union to replace the union of safety properties by a single safety property. Similarly, we union together several termination properties into a single termination property. Thus we are left with an intersection of several clauses, each of which is a union of a single safety property and a single termination property. This leads directly to the normal form for the *multiple intermittence* class.

An identical argument leads to the normal form for the *multiple progress* properties.

We may in fact split the class of *multiple intermittence* properties into an infinite hierarchy, $\mathcal{I} = \mathcal{I}_1 \subset \mathcal{I}_2 \subset \ldots$, where $\mathcal{I}_k$ for $k \geq 1$ is defined as the class of all properties that can be expressed as the intersection of (at most) k *intermittence* properties. It can be shown that this hierarchy is strict, i.e., for every k, there are properties which belong to $\mathcal{I}_{k+1}$ but not to $\mathcal{I}_k$. Obviously, $\mathcal{MI} = \bigcup_{k \geq 1} \mathcal{I}_k$, and the strictness of the hierarchy implies the strict inclusion of $\mathcal{I} = \mathcal{I}_1$ in $\mathcal{MI}$.

The hierarchy we study here is a *conjunctive* hierarchy, meaning that the outermost operator is an intersection or a conjunction. Previous discussions in the literature consider a *disjunctive* hierarchy of the *multiple progress* properties (at least those which are definable by an ω-automaton). This hierarchy has been studied in [Lan69],[Wag79], and [Kam85], and is related to the Rabin's index of an ω-automaton. The k'th layer in this hierarchy is given as:

$$\Pi = \bigcup_{i=1}^{k} (R_\omega(\Pi'_i) \cap P_\omega(\Pi''_i))$$

Obviously, these two versions are dual, and properties of one can be mapped to properties of the other by complementation.

Comparison with the Safety–Liveness Partition

In this section we would like to compare our definition with the characterizations of safety and liveness as given in [AS85].

A safety property is characterized in [AS85] as a property $\Pi \subseteq \Sigma^\omega$ such that

$$\sigma \in \Pi \iff \forall \sigma'(\sigma' \preceq \sigma) : \exists \sigma''(\sigma'' \in \Sigma^\omega) : \sigma' \cdot \sigma'' \in \Pi \tag{1}$$

To see that this characterization precisely matches ours, we observe that the expression

$$\exists \sigma''(\sigma'' \in \Sigma^\omega) : \sigma' \cdot \sigma'' \in \Pi$$

Can be written as $\sigma' \in Pref(\Pi)$ for an infinitary Π. Hence, the characterization is equivalent to:

$$\sigma \in \Pi \iff \forall \sigma'(\sigma' \preceq \sigma) : \sigma' \in Pref(\Pi) \iff \sigma \in A_\omega(Pref(\Pi)).$$

This is the same as

$$\Pi = A_\omega(Pref(\Pi)).$$

It follows that any property satisfying (1) can be expressed as $A_\omega(\Pi')$, where Π' happens to be $Pref(\Pi)$. It is not difficult to see that, if $\Pi = A_\omega(\Pi')$ for an arbitrary Π', then in fact Π can also be expressed as $A_\omega(Pref(\Pi))$.

Liveness is characterized in [AS85] as an infinitary property $\Pi \subseteq \Sigma^\omega$, such that

$$\forall \sigma (\sigma \in \Sigma^+) : \exists \sigma'(\sigma' \in \Sigma^\omega) : \sigma \cdot \sigma' \in \Pi.$$

That is, every arbitrary finite sequence can be extended to an infinite sequence which belongs to Π.

As we already commented, the liveness class is orthogonal to our classification. For one, the liveness class is disjoint to the safety class. In our case we have an inclusive hierarchy, in which all the classes, excepting the termination class contain the safety class as a subclass. Because of the orthogonality of the two concepts, it is possible to inquire about properties which are *κ-live*, which means that they are both a liveness property and a property of class $\kappa \in \{\mathcal{T}, \mathcal{I}_k, \mathcal{R}, \mathcal{P}, \mathcal{G}_k\}$ in our hierarchy. In fact, for every property Π, of class κ, as defined above (i.e., in any class but the safety class), we can define the *liveness closure* of Π, denoted by $\mathcal{L}(\Pi)$, which is the smallest liveness property containing Π. In fact, the liveness closure of Π is given by

$$\mathcal{L}(\Pi) = \Pi \cup E_\omega(\Sigma^+ - Pref(\Pi)).$$

and can be shown to be also of class κ. Clearly, $\sigma \in \mathcal{L}(\Pi)$ iff either $\sigma \in \Pi$ or σ contains a prefix $\sigma' \prec \sigma$ that *cannot* be extended to a sequence in Π. Take any finite sequence σ_0. Either it can be extended to a sequence in Π, or it belongs to $\Sigma^+ - Pref(\Pi)$, in which case any infinite extension of it will belong to $E_\omega(\Sigma^+ - Pref(\Pi))$. This shows that $\mathcal{L}(\Pi)$ is a liveness property. Due to the closure properties of the classes $\mathcal{T}, \mathcal{I}, \mathcal{R}, \mathcal{P}, \mathcal{G}$, the property $\mathcal{L}(\Pi)$ belongs also to the class κ to which Π belongs.

One of the results of [AS85] is that each property is the intersection of a safety property and a liveness property. We can extend this result by claiming that every property of class $\kappa \in \{\mathcal{T}, \mathcal{I}_k, \mathcal{R}, \mathcal{P}, \mathcal{G}_k\}$ is the intersection of a liveness property of class κ and a safety property. This is due to the equality

$$\Pi = \mathcal{L}(\Pi) \cap A_\omega(Pref(\Pi)).$$

Topological Characterization

It is possible to locate the classes of properties in our hierarchy in the lower two (and a half) levels of the Borel topological hierarchy. The set Σ^ω can be made into a metric space by defining the distance between two sequences σ and $\sigma' \in \Sigma^\omega$ to be

$$\delta(\sigma, \sigma') = 2^{-j},$$

where j is the minimal index such that $\sigma[j] \neq \sigma'[j]$.

With this topology we can establish the following correspondence between our classification and the first several levels of the Borel hierarchy:

$(\mathcal{S} = F)$	Π is a *safety* property	iff	it is a *closed* set
$(\mathcal{T} = G)$	Π is a *termination* property	iff	it is an *open* set
$(\mathcal{MI} = G_\delta \cap F_\sigma)$	Π is a *multiple intermittence* property	iff	it is a $G_\delta \cap F_\sigma$ set
$(\mathcal{R} = G_\delta)$	Π is a *recurrence* property	iff	it is a G_δ set
$(\mathcal{P} = F_\sigma)$	Π is a *persistence* property	iff	it is an F_σ set
$(\mathcal{MG} = G_{\delta\sigma} \cap F_{\sigma\delta})$	Π is a *multiple progress* property	iff	it is a $G_{\delta\sigma} \cap F_{\sigma\delta}$ set

In the above, we have denoted by F the family of all closed sets, by G the family of all open sets, by G_δ all sets obtainable as a countable intersection of open sets, and by F_σ all sets obtainable by a countable union of closed sets.

For example, let us show that the class of termination properties coincides with the class of open sets.

- Let $\Pi = E_\omega(\Pi')$ be a termination set. Let $\sigma \in \Pi$ be any sequence in Π. By definition, σ has a finite prefix $\sigma' \prec \sigma$ which belongs to Π'. Assume its length to be k. Then we claim that all infinite sequences whose distance from σ does not exceed $2^{-(k+1)}$ are also in Π. Let σ'' be such an infinite sequence. Obviously, σ and σ'' must agree on at least the first k states. Consequently, σ'' also has σ' as a finite prefix. Consequently, $\sigma'' \in \Pi$.

- Let Π be an open set. Take any infinite sequence $\sigma \in \Pi$. Since Π is open, there must be some distance $2^{-(k+1)}$ such that all infinite sequences closer to σ than that distance are in Π. Let σ' be the prefix of length k of σ. We define Π' to be the set of all such prefixes. It is not difficult to see that $E_\omega(\Pi') = \Pi$.

4.2 Expressiveness in Temporal Logic

Next, we restrict our attention to infinitary properties that can be expressed in temporal logic.

A temporal formula p specifies a property $\Pi(p)$ given by:

$$\Pi(p) = \{\sigma \in \Sigma^\infty \mid \sigma \models p\}.$$

Note that two formulae p and q are equivalent, denoted by $p \approx q$, iff $\Pi(p) = \Pi(q)$.

Since we are interested (for simplicity) in infinitary properties only, we define the *infinitary* property specified by the formula p to be $\Pi_\omega(p) = \Pi(p) \cap \Sigma^\omega$. Alternately, we can define $\Pi_\omega(p) = \Pi(p \wedge \Box \bigcirc \mathrm{T})$, where $\Box \bigcirc \mathrm{T}$ specifies Σ^ω. Corresponding to the restriction to infinite sequences, we define two formulae p and q to be ω-equivalent, denoted by $p \approx_\omega q$, if $\Box \bigcirc \mathrm{T} \rightarrow (p \equiv q)$ is valid, i.e., p is equivalent to q on any infinite sequence. Obviously $p \approx_\omega q$ iff $\Pi_\omega(p) = \Pi_\omega(q)$.

Below, we present for each class of properties a syntactic characterization of the formulae that specify properties in that class, examples of some formulae of alternative forms that also specify properties in that class, and some comments about the boolean closure of the class.

- *Safety*

A formula of the form $\Box p$ for some past formula p is called a *safety* formula. Obviously, every safety formula specifies a safety property.

Conversely, every safety property which is specifiable in temporal logic, is specifiable by a safety formula. This means that every infinitary property Π, that is expressible on one hand as $A_\omega(\Pi')$ for some finitary Π', and is specifiable, on the other hand, by *some* temporal formula, is specifiable in fact by a safety formula.

To see this, we observe that for every temporal formula φ, there exists an effectively derivable past formula *prefix*(φ) such that for each $\sigma \in \Sigma^\omega$, and $k \geq 0$

$$(\sigma, k) \models \mathit{prefix}(\varphi) \quad \leftrightarrow \quad \exists \sigma' \in \Sigma^\omega : \sigma[0..k] \cdot \sigma' \models \varphi.$$

This means that *prefix*(φ) characterizes all the finite computations that can be extended to an infinite computation satisfying φ. Then, if φ specifies a safety property it can be shown that $\varphi \approx_\omega \Box(\mathit{prefix}(\varphi))$.

Examples of properties specified by safety formulae are partial correctness, mutual exclusion, absence of deadlock, etc. The closure of safety formulae under conjunction and disjunction is based on the following equivalences:

$$(\Box p \wedge \Box q) \approx \Box(p \wedge q)$$
$$(\Box p \vee \Box q) \approx \Box(\boxminus p \vee \boxminus q).$$

Note the analogy with the corresponding proof of closure for the semantic view.

- *Termination*

A formula of the form $\Diamond p$ for some past formula p is called a *termination* formula. Obviously every termination formula specifies a termination property.

Conversely, every termination property which is specifiable in temporal logic can be specified by a termination formula. To see this we observe that if φ specifies a termination property, then $\varphi \approx_\omega \Diamond(\neg \mathit{prefix}(\neg\varphi))$.

Examples of properties specifiable by termination formulae are, of course, termination, total correctness, and guarantee of a goal that has to be reached *once*. Closure of termination formulae under conjunction and disjunction is ensured by the equivalences:

$$(\Diamond p \vee \Diamond q) \approx \Diamond(p \vee q)$$
$$(\Diamond p \wedge \Diamond q) \approx \Diamond(\diamondminus p \wedge \diamondminus q).$$

Note that $p\mathcal{U}q$, for past formulae p and q, expresses a termination property, since it is equivalent to:

$$p\mathcal{U}q \approx \Diamond(q \wedge \circleddash \boxminus p).$$

- *Intermittence*

A Formula of the form $(\Box p \vee \Diamond q)$ for some past formulae p and q is called an *intermittence* formula. An equivalent form for such formulae is give by the implication:

$$\Diamond p \rightarrow \Diamond q,$$

which states that if p will eventually happen, then so will q. This type of statement is the basis for the intermittent assertions proof method ([MW78]).

Clearly, a multiple intermittence formula is a formula of the form:

$$\bigwedge_{i=1}^{k}(\Box p_i \vee \Diamond q_i),$$

which allows several intermittence conjuncts.

- *Recurrence*

A formula of the form $\Box\Diamond p$ for some past formula p is called a *recurrence* formula. A recurrence formula obviously specifies a recurrence property.

Conversely, every recurrence property, which is specifiable in temporal logic can be specified by a recurrence formula. This fact will be shown later.

An alternative useful form for recurrence properties is the entailment $p \Rightarrow \Diamond q$ or equivalently $\Box(p \rightarrow \Diamond q)$, to which we refer as a *response* formula. To see that this formula specifies a recurrence property we observe:

$$(p \Rightarrow \Diamond q) \quad \approx \quad \Box\Diamond((\neg p)\mathcal{S}q)$$

The formula on the right states the existence of infinitely many states such that the last observed p was followed (or coincided with) q. Because of that, we often refer to the class of recurrence properties also as the *response* class.

Recurrence formulae can specify all the properties specifiable by safety formulae. This is due to the equivalence:

$$\Box p \approx \Box\Diamond(\boxminus p)$$

They can also specify all the properties specifiable by termination formulae:

$$\Diamond p \approx \Box\Diamond(\Diamond\!\!\!\!-\, p)$$

Examples of properties specifiable by recurrence formulae are accessibility, lack of individual starvation, responsiveness to requests, etc. Recurrence formulae can also express weak-fairness requirements. For simplicity, let us consider a transition τ with no competitors, i.e., $Comp(\tau) = \{\tau\}$. A weak-fairness requirement for such a transition τ is that, if τ is continuously enabled beyond some point, it will eventually be taken. This can be expressed by:

$$(\Box En(\tau) \Rightarrow \Diamond taken(\tau)) \;\approx\; \Box\Diamond(\neg En(\tau) \vee taken(\tau))$$

Closure of recurrence formulae under conjunction and disjunction is ensured by the equivalences:

$$\begin{array}{lcl} (\Box\Diamond p \vee \Box\Diamond q) & \approx & \Box\Diamond(p \vee q) \\ (\Box\Diamond p \wedge \Box\Diamond q) & \approx_\omega & \Box\Diamond[p \wedge \ominus[(\neg p)\, \mathcal{S}\, q]] \end{array}$$

- *Persistence*

A formula of the form $\Diamond\Box p$ for some past formula p is called a *persistence* formula. Persistence formulae obviously specify persistence properties.

Conversely, every persistence property, which is specifiable in temporal logic, can be specified by a persistence formula. This follows by duality from the corresponding result for recurrence formulae.

Similarly to recurrence, persistence formulae can specify all the properties specifiable by safety or termination formulae. This is supported by:

$$\begin{array}{l} \Box p \approx \Diamond\Box\,(\boxminus p) \\ \Diamond p \approx \Diamond\Box\,(\Diamond\!\!\!\!-\, p). \end{array}$$

Closure of persistence formulae under conjunction and disjunction can be obtained by duality from the closure properties of recurrence formulae.

- *Progress*

A formula of the form $\Box\Diamond p \vee \Diamond\Box q$ for some past formulae p and q is called a *progress* formula. Obviously, a progress formula specifies a progress property.

Conversely, every progress property, which is specifiable in temporal logic, can be specified by a progress formula. This will be shown later.

It is easy to see that progress formulae generalize both recurrence and persistence formulae. An alternative form to progress formulae is: $\Box\Diamond p \Rightarrow \Box\Diamond q$. In this form they are useful for specifying *strong* fairness requirements, such as $\Box\Diamond En(\tau) \Rightarrow \Box\Diamond taken(\tau)$, which states that a transition, which is enabled infinitely many times, must be taken infinitely many times. Progress formulae can also describe systems whose response is guaranteed only if there are infinitely many requests for this response. An example of such a system is an eventually reliable channel.

Progress formulae are closed under disjunction but not under conjunction. A conjunction of progress formulae leads to the most general normal form of temporal formulae:

$$\bigwedge_{i=1}^{n} (\Box\Diamond p_i \vee \Diamond\Box q_i)$$

which are identified as *multiple progress* formulae.

We can summarize the relation of the property hierarchy to the formula hierarchy by the following proposition.

Proposition 4.1 *A property* Π, *that is specifiable by a temporal formula, is a* κ*-property iff it is specifiable by a* κ*-formula, where* $\kappa \in$ {*safety, termination, intermittence, recurrence, persistence, progress*}.

The fact that a κ-formula specifies a κ-property is straightforward. The other direction has been proved for the *safety* and *termination* cases. For the other cases we have to rely on a similar proof for automata that we discuss next.

In Figure 2 we present the hierarchy between the temporal characterizations of the properties.

4.3 Predicate-Automata

An alternative formalism for specifying temporal properties is that of finite-state predicate automaton (see [AS89], [MP87]). In the version we consider here, a predicate-automaton $\mathcal{M}$ consists of the following components:

- Q – A finite set of automaton-states.
- $q_0 \in Q$ – An initial automaton-state.
- $T = \{t(q_i, q_j) \mid q_i, q_j \in Q\}$ – A set of *transition conditions*. For each $q_i, q_j \in Q, t(q_i, q_j)$ is a state formula specifying the computation states under which the automaton may proceed from q_i to q_j. We assume that each $t(q_i, q_j)$ is either syntactically identical to the constant F, or holds over some computation state s.
- $R \subseteq Q$ – A set of *recurrent* automaton-states.
- $P \subseteq Q$ – A set of *persistent* automaton-states.

Let

$$\sigma: s_0, s_1, \ldots \in \Sigma^\omega$$

be an infinite computation. Computations are fed as input to the automaton which either accepts or rejects them. An infinite sequence of automaton-states

$$r: q_0, q_1, \ldots \in Q^\omega,$$

is called a *run* of $\mathcal{M}$ over σ if:

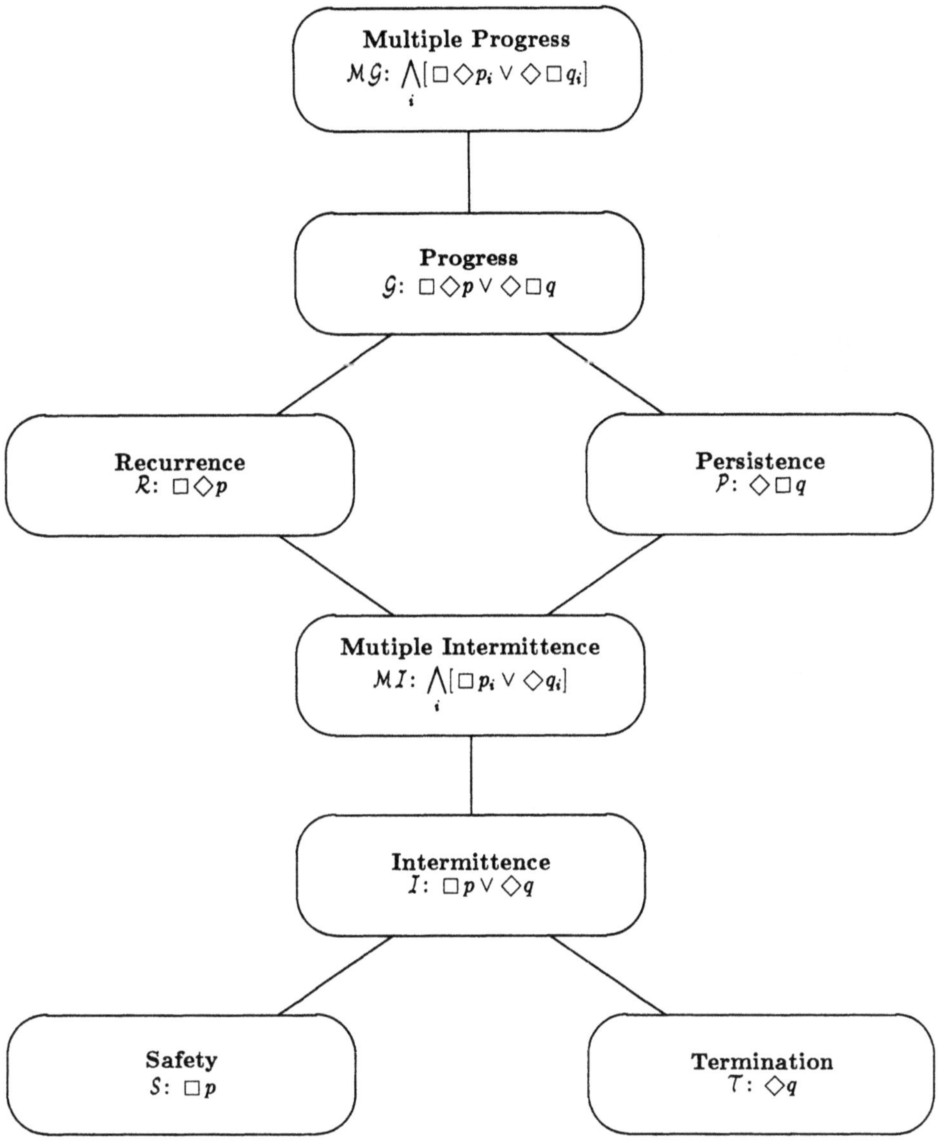

Figure 2: Inclusion Relations between the Temporal Classes

1. The first state of the run q_0 is the initial state of $\mathcal{M}$.
2. For every $i > 0$, $s_{i-1} \models t(q_{i-1}, q_i)$.

Note that the automaton always starts at q_0, and s_0 causes it to move from q_0 to q_1.

We define the infinity set of r, $Inf(r)$, to be the set of automaton-states that occur infinitely many times in r.

A run r is defined to be *accepting* if either $Inf(r) \cap R \neq \phi$ or $Inf(r) \subseteq P$. The automaton $\mathcal{M}$ *accepts* the computation σ if there exists a run of $\mathcal{M}$ over σ which is accepting. This definition of acceptance has been introduced by Streett ([Str82]).

An alternative definition, given in [MP87] is that *all* runs of A over σ are accepting.

The automaton $\mathcal{A}$ is called *complete* if for each $q \in Q$,

$$\bigvee_{q' \in Q} t(q, q') = \mathrm{T}.$$

It is called *deterministic*, if for every q and $q' \neq q''$, $t(q, q') \rightarrow \neg t(q, q'')$, that is, we cannot have both $t(q, q')$ and $t(q, q'')$ true.

In this paper we restrict our attention to complete deterministic automata. Deterministic automata have exactly one run r corresponding to each input computation σ, and hence the definition of acceptance in [MP87] coincides with the one used here.

Let $G = R \cup P$ and $B = Q - G$. We refer to G and B as the "good" and "bad" sets of states, respectively. We define the following classes of automata by introducing restrictions on their transition conditions and accepting states.

- A *safety* automaton is such that there is no transition from $q \in B$, to $q' \in G$, i.e., for every $q \in B, q' \in G$, $t(q, q') \equiv \mathrm{F}$. That is, the automaton cannot move from a bad state ($q \in B$) to a good state ($q' \in G$).
- A *termination* automaton is such that there is no transition from $q \in G$ to $q' \in B$.
- A *intermittence* automaton is such that:
  - There is no transition from $q \notin P$ to $q' \in P$.
  - There is no transition from $q \in R$ to $q' \notin R$.

  The above definition implies that once a run exits P, it can never reenter P again, and once it enters R, it can never get out. This can be generalized to multiple intermittence as follows:
- A *multiple intermittence* automaton (of degree k) is an automaton, in which each state $q \in Q$ has a rank $\rho(q)$, $0 \leq \rho(q) \leq k$, such that:
  - There is a transition from q to q', i.e., $t(q, q') \neq \mathrm{F}$, only if $\rho(q) \leq \rho(q')$.
  - There is a transition from $q \in B$ to $q' \in G$ only if $\rho(q) < \rho(q')$.
  - There is no transition from a state $q \in G$ of rank k to a state $q' \in B$.

  This definition leads to the fact that a run can enter from B to G (equivalently, exit from G into B), at most k times. It is easy to see that the case of $k = 1$ corresponds to the definition of an intermittence automaton, with P being the set of G-states with rank 0, and R being the set of G-states with rank 1.

- A *recurrence* automaton is such that $P = \phi$.
- A *persistence* automaton is such that $R = \phi$.
- A *progress* automaton is an unrestricted automaton of the above type.

We define the property specified by an automaton $\mathcal{M}$, $\Pi_{\mathcal{M}}$, as the set of all infinite computations that are accepted by $\mathcal{M}$.

In order to attain expressive power comparable to (and even exceeding, see [Wol83]) that of temporal logic we have to consider a more general type of automaton.

We define a *Streett Predicate Automaton* to be a structure

$$\mathcal{M} = \langle Q, q_0, T, L \rangle$$

where Q, q_0, and T are as defined above, and L is a finite list of pairs of acceptance sets.

$$L = (R_1, P_1), \ldots (R_k, P_k)$$

A run r of a Streett automaton is accepting if for *each* $i = 1, \ldots, k$, either $\mathit{Inf}(r) \cap R_i \neq \phi$ or $\mathit{Inf}(r) \subset P_i$. The notions of computations accepted by such automaton and the properties specified by it are similar to the simpler case. This type of automaton has been studied by Streett in [Str82], and is the dual of Rabin's automaton ([Rab72]).

Obviously, all the preceding types of automata are special cases of a Streett automaton with $k = 1$. We associate a general Streett automaton with the class of multiple progress properties.

An infinitary property $\Pi \subseteq \Sigma^\omega$ is defined to be *specifiable by automata*, if there exists a Streett automaton $\mathcal{M}$, which accepts an infinite sequence σ iff $\sigma \in \Pi$. The following proposition relates the syntactic characterization of the different types of automata to the semantic characterization of the properties they specify.

Proposition 4.2 *A property Π, that is specifiable by automata, is a κ-property iff it is specifiable by a κ-automaton, where $\kappa \in$ {safety, termination, intermittence, recurrence, persistence, progress}.*

For most of these types, this proposition has been proved in [Lan69], with some minor differences in the definitions of a safety and termination automata. The case of progress, and in fact the complete hierarchy above, has been solved in [Wag79].

For completeness, we include below our version of a proof of the proposition, which for most of the cases is straightforward.

Proof

It is simple to show that a κ-automaton specifies an κ-property. Let $\mathcal{M}$ be a κ-automaton. Since $\mathcal{M}$ is deterministic and complete, there is, for each finite computation $\sigma \in \Sigma^+$, a unique state q, denoted by $\delta(q_0, \sigma)$, such that the run of $\mathcal{M}$ on σ terminates (σ is finite) at q.

Define $\Pi(q) = \{\sigma \in \Sigma^+ \mid \delta(q_0, \sigma) = q\}$ for each $q \in Q$.

Obviously, an infinite σ is accepted by $\mathcal{M}$ iff its corresponding run r, either visits infinitely many times states in R, or is constrained from a certain point to visit only P-states. This means that either σ contains infinitely many prefixes in $\Pi(q)$ for $q \in R$, or that all but finitely many prefixes of σ are in $\Pi(q)$ for some $q \in P$. It follows that

$$\Pi_{\mathcal{M}} = R_\omega(\bigcup_{q \in R} \Pi(q)) \cup P_\omega(\bigcup_{q \in P} \Pi(q)).$$

Consequently, every property specifiable by a single automaton is a progress property. However, as we will show for the special cases of κ-automata, this expression can be further simplified.

- For a safety automaton, it is clear that no finite prefix of an acceptable computation can be in $\Pi_B = \bigcup_{q \in B} \Pi(q)$. This is because, once a run visits a bad state $q \in B$, it can never return to a good state. Hence for safety automata we also have

$$\Pi_{\mathcal{M}} = A_\omega(\bigcup_{q \in G} \Pi(q)),$$

which establishes $\Pi_{\mathcal{M}}$ as a safety property.

- For a termination automaton, once a run visits a good state it can never visit a bad state. It follows that

$$\Pi_{\mathcal{M}} = E_\omega(\bigcup_{q \in G} \Pi(q)),$$

which shows that $\Pi_{\mathcal{M}}$ is a termination property.

- For a recurrence automaton, we are given that $P = \phi$, and therefore $\Pi_{\mathcal{M}} = R_\omega(\bigcup_{q \in R} \Pi(q))$.

- For a persistence automaton, we are given that $R = \phi$, and therefore $\Pi_{\mathcal{M}} = P_\omega(\bigcup_{q \in P} \Pi(q))$.

Consider now the other direction of the proposition. It states that a κ-property specifiable by automata can be specified by a κ-automaton. Assume that a κ-property Π is specifiable by automata. Thus, there exists a Streett automaton

$$\mathcal{M} = \langle Q, q_0, T, L\rangle, \qquad L = \{(R_i, P_i), \quad i = 1, \ldots, k\}$$

specifying Π.

Let $\delta: Q \times \Sigma^+ \rightarrow Q$ be the function, based on T, that, for each state $q \in Q$ and each finite computation $\sigma \in \Sigma^+$, yields the state $\delta(q, \sigma) \in Q$ reached by the automaton starting at q and reading the computation σ.

- Consider first the case that Π is a *safety* property, and hence, satisfies $\Pi = A_\omega(\mathit{Pref}(\Pi))$.

  We construct an automaton:

$$\mathcal{M}' = \langle Q, q_0, T', G, G\rangle,$$

where Q and q_0 are as before. G and B are defined by

$$\begin{aligned} &G = \{q_0\} \cup \{q \in Q \mid \delta(q_0, \sigma) = q \text{ for some } \sigma \in \mathit{Pref}(\Pi)\}, \\ &B = Q - G. \end{aligned}$$

The transition conditions $T' = \{t'(q, q') \mid q, q' \in Q\}$ are given by:

$$t'(q, q') = \begin{cases} \mathbf{T} & q \in B,\ q' = q \\ \mathbf{F} & q \in B,\ q' \neq q \\ t(q, q') & q \notin B \end{cases}$$

We claim that, for a finite computation $\sigma \in \Sigma^+$,

$$\sigma \in \mathit{Pref}(\Pi) \longleftrightarrow \delta(q_0, \sigma) \in G.$$

By the construction of G, if $\sigma \in \mathit{Pref}(\Pi)$, then $\delta(q_0, \sigma) \in G$.

Assume that $\sigma \notin Pref(\Pi)$. This means that σ cannot be a prefix of a computation in Π. Let $\delta(q_0, \sigma) = q$. We would like to show that $q \notin G$.

Assume to the contrary that $q \in G$. This can only be caused by another finite computation $\sigma' \in Pref(\Pi)$ such that also $\delta(q_0, \sigma') = q$. If $\sigma' \in Pref(\Pi)$, there must exist an extension $\sigma'' \in \Sigma^\omega$, such that $\sigma' \cdot \sigma'' \in \Pi$. Consider the mixed computation $\sigma \cdot \sigma'' \in \Sigma^\omega$. Let r be the run of $\langle Q, q_0, T\rangle$ over $\sigma \cdot \sigma''$, and r' the run of $\langle Q, q_0, T\rangle$ over $\sigma' \cdot \sigma''$. Since $\delta(q_0, \sigma) = \delta(q_0, \sigma') = q$, these runs coincide after a finite segment. It follows that $Inf(r) = Inf(r')$, and hence $\sigma \cdot \sigma''$ should be accepted. This contradicts our assumption that $\sigma \notin Pref(\Pi)$. Hence our claim is established.

It is now easy to show that $\sigma \in \Sigma^\omega$ is accepted by $\mathcal{M}'$ iff $\sigma \in \Pi$.

Denote by δ' the transition function based on T'. Assume that σ is accepted by $\mathcal{M}'$, and let r be its corresponding run. To be accepting, r must go infinitely many times through G states. By the way we defined T', this means that $\mathcal{M}'$ only visits G-states. Since T and T' are identical as long as we only visit G-states, this means that for every $\sigma' \prec \sigma$, $\delta(q_0, \sigma') = \delta'(q_0, \sigma') \in G$. It follows that every $\sigma' \prec \sigma$ is in $Pref(\Pi)$, and since Π is a safety property, that $\sigma \in \Pi$.

In the other direction, assume that σ is rejected by $\mathcal{M}'$. This implies the existence of a *minimal* $\sigma' \prec \sigma$ such that $\delta'(q_0, \sigma') \notin G$. Since σ' is minimal, the run caused by σ' visits only G-states except the last. It follows that $\delta'(q_0, \sigma') = \delta(q_0, \sigma')$, and hence $\sigma' \notin Pref(\Pi)$. Thus, σ' cannot be the prefix of a computation in Π, and therefore $\sigma \notin \Pi$.

- Consider the case that Π is a *termination* property.

In that case, we have that $\Pi = E_\omega(\Pi')$ for some finitary property Π'. We define the sets G and B, as follows:

$$G = \{q \mid \delta(q_0, \sigma) = q \ \text{ for some } \sigma \in \Pi'\},$$
$$B = Q - G.$$

Construct the automaton:

$$\mathcal{M}' = \langle Q, q_0, T', G, G\rangle$$

where T' is given by:

$$t'(q, q') = \begin{cases} \text{T} & q \in G,\ q' = q \\ \text{F} & q \in G, q' \neq q \\ t(q, q') & q \notin G \end{cases}$$

We show that $\sigma \in \Sigma^\omega$ is accepted by $\mathcal{M}'$ iff $\sigma \in \Pi$.

Assume that σ is accepted by $\mathcal{M}'$. Then there exists some prefix $\sigma_1 \prec \sigma$ which causes $\mathcal{M}'$ to visit a state in G for the first time while reading σ. Let $q = \delta'(q_0, \sigma_1)$. Since q is the first visit to a $G-$state, it follows that the behavior of $\mathcal{M}'$ on σ_1 is identical to that of $\mathcal{M}$ on σ_1, and therefore also $\delta(q_0, \sigma_1) = q$. By the definition of G, there exists a finite sequence $\sigma_2 \in \Pi'$ such that $\delta(q_0, \sigma_2) = q$. Let $\sigma' \in \Sigma^\omega$ be the suffix of σ following σ_1, i.e., $\sigma = \sigma_1 \cdot \sigma'$. Denote by r_1 the run of $\mathcal{M}$ over $\sigma = \sigma_1 \cdot \sigma'$, and by r_2 the run of $\mathcal{M}$ over $\sigma_2 \cdot \sigma'$. Obviously, r_1 and r_2 can differ only by a finite prefix. $\mathcal{M}$ accepts $\sigma_2 \cdot \sigma'$ because $\sigma_2 \in \Pi'$. Since $Inf_{\mathcal{M}}(r_1) = Inf_{\mathcal{M}}(r_2)$, $\mathcal{M}$ must also accept $\sigma_1 \cdot \sigma' = \sigma$. Thus, $\sigma \in \Pi$.

Assume that $\sigma \in \Pi$. There must exist a prefix $\sigma' \prec \sigma$ such that $\sigma' \in \Pi'$. let σ' be the minimal such prefix of σ. Let $q = \delta(q_0, \sigma')$. Obviously $q \in G$, and q is the first $G-$ state that $\mathcal{M}$ visits on reading σ. It follows that also $q = \delta'(q_0, \sigma')$. By the way $\mathcal{M}'$ is constructed, once it visits a $G-$state, it stays in G forever. Consequently, $\mathcal{M}'$ accepts σ.

■ Next, consider the case that Π is a *recurrence* property. This means that $\Pi = R_\omega(\Pi')$ for some finitary Π'.

We perform a series of modifications on the individual pairs of sets R_i, P_i, $i = 1, \ldots, k$, until all the members $P_i' = \phi$. These modifications will preserve the property defined by the automaton.

Without loss of generality, we define the modifications on the first pair R_1, P_1. After obtaining a $P_1' = \phi$, we move on to the other pairs.

Assume that all the states in the automaton are reachable. A *cycle* C in the automaton is a set of states such that there exists a cyclic path in the automaton that passes only through the states in C, and at least once through each of them. We only consider *accessible cycles*. These are cycles such that the path leading from q_0 to some q in C, and the cyclic path traversing C are accessible, i.e., never pass through transitions such that $t(q_i, q_j) = \text{F}$. A *good cycle* is a cycle such that a run r with $Inf(r) = C$ is accepting. A *persistent* cycle is a good cycle C such that $C \cap R_1 = \phi$, and hence $C \subseteq P_1$. Define A_1 to be the set of automaton states participating in persistent cycles.

Let $\mathcal{M}$ be the automaton accepting Π with accepting pairs (R_i, P_i), $i = 1, \ldots, k$, and consider the automaton $\mathcal{M}'$ coinciding with $\mathcal{M}$ in all but the accepting pairs. The list of accepting pairs for $\mathcal{M}'$ is (R_1', P_1'), (R_i, P_i), $i = 2, \ldots, k$, where we define:

$$\begin{aligned} R_1' &= R_1 \cup A_1 \\ P_1' &= \phi. \end{aligned}$$

We wish to show that $\mathcal{M}$ and $\mathcal{M}'$ accept precisely the same computations.

Consider first a computation σ accepted by $\mathcal{M}$. Let J be the infinity set $Inf_{\mathcal{M}}(r(\sigma))$. Clearly J satisfies the requirements presented by (R_i, P_i), $i > 1$, in both automata. The acceptance for $i = 1$ implies that either $J \cap R_1 \neq \phi$ or $J \subseteq P_1$. In the first case obviously $J \cap R_1' \neq \phi$. In the second case, if $J \cap R_1 = \phi$, then J is a persistent cycle. It follows that $J \subseteq A_1$, and hence $J \cap R_1' \neq \phi$.

Consider next, an infinite computation σ accepted by $\mathcal{M}'$. We will prove that σ is also accepted by $\mathcal{M}$. Assume, to the contrary, that σ is rejected by $\mathcal{M}$. Let J be as before. Since $\mathcal{M}'$ accepts σ, $J \cap R_1' \neq \phi$. The rejection by $\mathcal{M}$ imply that $J \cap R_1 = \phi$. Hence there must be some $q \in A_1$ in J. Let π be a cyclic path from q to itself precisely traversing J. In order for σ to be rejected by $\mathcal{M}$, J must also contain a state $q' \notin R_1 \cup P_1$. Since $q \in A_1$ there must exist another cycle J', such that $q \in J'$, and J' is a persistent cycle. Let π' be the cyclic path from q to itself precisely traversing J'. Let σ' a finite computation that causes the automaton to move from q back to q along π'.

The state q and computation σ' have the following property:

For every finite computation σ^*, such that $\delta(q_0, \sigma^*) = q$, there exists a positive integer n (possibly dependent on σ^*) such that $\sigma^* \cdot (\sigma')^n$ contains a prefix $\sigma \prec \sigma^* \cdot (\sigma')^n$, $|\sigma| \succ |\sigma^*|$, which belongs to Π'.

To see this, we observe that the computation $\sigma^* \cdot (\sigma')^\omega$ has J' as infinity set, and is therefore in Π. Consequently, $\sigma^* \cdot (\sigma')^\omega$ must have infinitely many prefixes in Π', most of which are longer than σ^*. The shortest of these is a prefix of $\sigma^* \cdot (\sigma')^n$ for an appropriate $n > 0$.

Let now σ_0 be a computation such that $\delta(q_0, \sigma) = q$, and $\hat{\sigma}$ a computation leading the automaton from q to q along the path π, which precisely traverses J. Consider the following infinite computation:

$$\sigma'' = \sigma_0 \hat{\sigma} (\sigma')^{n_1} \hat{\sigma} (\sigma')^{n_2} \cdots$$

where the n_j's are chosen so that σ'' has infinitely many prefixes in Π'. That is, for each

$$\sigma''_{j-1} = \sigma_0 \hat{\sigma} (\sigma')^{n_1} \dots (\sigma')^{n_{j-1}} \hat{\sigma}$$

we choose an $n_j > 0$ such that $\sigma''_{j-1} \cdot (\sigma')^{n_j}$ has a prefix in Π', longer than σ''_{j-1}.

It follows, on one hand, that since σ'' has infinitely many prefixes in Π', $\sigma'' \in \Pi$.

On the other hand, the infinity set corresponding to σ'' is $J \cup J'$ which has an empty intersection with R_1 and at least one state $q' \notin P_1$. This contradicts the assumption that $\mathcal{M}$ specifies Π.

Consequently, there cannot exist a computation σ which is accepted by $\mathcal{M}'$ and rejected by $\mathcal{M}$.

It follows that $\mathcal{M}'$ is equivalent to $\mathcal{M}$. We can repeat the process for each $i = 2, \dots, k$ until we obtain an automaton with all $P'_i = \phi$, $i = 1, \dots, k$.

It only remains to show that such an automaton is equivalent to an automaton with a single R and a single $P = \phi$. This is essentially a closure property that states that the intersection of recurrence automata is equivalent to a single recurrence automaton. The construction is similar in spirit to the formula for the intersection of recurrence formulas. The automaton detects visits to R_2-states such that the most recent previous visit to an $R_1 \cup R_2$-state was in fact a visit to an R_1-state (for $k = 2$).

- The case of a persistence property Π that is specifiable by an automaton is handled by duality. We consider $\overline{\Pi} = \Sigma^\omega - \Pi$ which can be shown to be a recurrence property also specifiable by an automaton.

By the construction for recurrence properties, there exists a recurrence automaton

$$\mathcal{M} = \langle Q, q_0, T, R, \phi \rangle$$

specifying $\overline{\Pi}$. The following persistence automaton obviously specifies Π

$$\mathcal{M}' = \langle Q, q_0, T, \phi, Q - R \rangle.$$

- The case of progress properties specifiable by automata is handled as follows.

Let Π be a progress property specifiable by the automaton

$$\mathcal{M} = \langle Q, q_0, T, \{(R_i, P_i), \quad i = 1, \dots, k\} \rangle.$$

Clearly the role of the list of pairs (R_i, P_i), $i = 1, \dots, k$, is to define the subsets $J \subseteq Q$ such that every computation σ with $Inf(r(\sigma)) = J$ is accepted. Let F denote the family of these sets. Obviously, $J \in F \longleftrightarrow (R_i \cap J \neq \phi \text{ or } J \subseteq P_i)$ for each $i = 1, \dots, k$.

A characterization property that can be derived from Wagner [Wag79] (see also [Kam85]) is the following:

If $\mathcal{M}$ specifies a progress property, then for each accessible accepting set $J \in F$,

$$\begin{array}{rl} \text{Either} & A \in F \text{ for every accessible cycle } A \supseteq J, \\ \text{Or} & B \in F \text{ for every accessible cycle } B \subseteq J. \end{array}$$

An equivalent statement of this fact is that we cannot have a chain of three accessible cycles

$$B \subseteq J \subseteq A,$$

such that $J \in F$, but $B \notin F$ and $A \notin F$.

According to this characterization we can partition the family of accessible accepting sets into:

$$F = \{A_1, \dots, A_m, B_1, \dots, B_n\},$$

where, for each A_i and an arbitrary accessible cycle X, $A_i \subseteq X \longrightarrow X \in F$ and for each B_j, and an arbitrary accessible cycle X, $X \subseteq B_j \longrightarrow X \in F$.

This leads to the construction of the following automaton:

$$\mathcal{M}' = \langle Q', q_0', T', R', P' \rangle$$

$Q' = Q \times Q^m \times 2 \times n \times 2.$

Each state $q' \in Q'$ has the following structure:

$$q' = \langle q, q_1, \dots, q_m, f_R, j, f_P \rangle,$$

where $q \in Q$, $q_i \in A_i$, $i = 1, \dots, m$, $f_R, f_P \in \{0, 1\}$ and $1 \leq j \leq n$.

We assume that the states of $\mathcal{M}$ are ordered in some linear order. For each A_i, $i = 1, \dots, m$, we define $min(A_i)$ to be the state of A_i appearing first in the linear order. For $q \in A_i$ we define $next(q, A_i)$ to be the first state $\hat{q} \in A_i$ appearing after q in the linear order. If $q \in A_i$ is the last A_i-state in the linear order then $next(q, A_i) = min(A_i)$.

The role of the different components in q' is as follows:

- The state q simulates the behavior of the original automaton. Each $q_i \in A_i$ anticipates the next A_i-state we expect to meet. If the run visits all the A_i's infinitely many times, each anticipated q_i will be matched infinitely many times.
- The recurrence flag f_R is set to 1 each time one of the anticipated A_i-states is matched.

  The index j checks whether the run of $\mathcal{M}$ stays completely within one of the sets $B_1, ..., B_n$ from a certain point on. It moves cyclically over $1, ..., n$, and at any point checks whether the next automaton state is in B_j. If the next automaton state is in B_j, then j retains its value and the next value of f_P will be 1. Otherwise, j is incremented (modulo n), and the next value of f_P is 0.

$$q_0' = \langle q_0, min(A_1), \dots, min(A_m), 0, 1, 0 \rangle$$

- T' is defined as follows:

$$\begin{aligned} & t'(\langle q, q_1, \dots, q_m, f_R, j, f_p \rangle, \ \langle \tilde{q}, \tilde{q}_1, \dots, \tilde{q}_m, \tilde{f}_R, \tilde{j}, \tilde{f}_P \rangle) = \\ & \quad t(q, \tilde{q}) \ \wedge \\ & \quad \bigwedge_{i=1}^{m} \{[(\tilde{q} = q_i) \wedge (\tilde{q}_i = next(q_i, A_i))] \vee [(\tilde{q} \neq q_i) \wedge (\tilde{q}_i = q_i)]\} \ \wedge \\ & \quad ((\tilde{f}_R = 1) \equiv \bigvee_{i=1}^{m} (\tilde{q} = q_i)) \ \wedge \\ & \quad ([(\tilde{q} \in B_j) \wedge (\tilde{j} = j)] \vee [(\tilde{q} \notin B_j) \wedge (\tilde{j} = \lfloor j \ mod m \rfloor + 1)]) \ \wedge \\ & \quad ((\tilde{f}_P = 1) \equiv (\tilde{q} \in B_j)). \end{aligned}$$

  - The first clause in this definition states that the first component q follows the same path that would be followed by the original automaton.

- The second clause states that either the newly visited automaton-state $\tilde{q}$ matches the anticipated state of A_i, and then we modify q_i to the next A_i-state in sequence, or there is no match and then q_i remains the same.
- The third clause states that f_R is set to one iff $\tilde{q}$ matches one of the anticipated states. If different from 1 it must be 0.
- The fourth clause states that if $\tilde{q}$ belongs to B_j then j is preserved. Otherwise it is incremented by one in a cyclic manner.
- The last clause states that f_P is set to 1 whenever $\tilde{q}$ is in B_j.

- The acceptance sets are defined by

$$\begin{aligned} R' &= \{\langle q, q_1, \ldots, q_m, 1, j, f_P\rangle \mid \text{ for some } q, q_1, \ldots, q_m, j, f_P\} \\ P' &= \{\langle q, q_1, \ldots, q_m, f_R, j, 1\rangle \mid \text{ for some } q, q_1, \ldots, q_m, f_R, j\}. \end{aligned}$$

Let σ be a computation and r' the corresponding run of $\mathcal{M}'$ over σ. If r' visits R' infinitely many times, this implies that r, the run of $\mathcal{M}$ over σ, visits infinitely many times *all* the states of some A_i. This shows that $Inf(r) \supseteq A_i$ and hence σ is accepted by $\mathcal{M}$ as well as by $\mathcal{M}'$.

If r' stays contained in P' from a certain point on, it means that the value of j is never changed beyond that point and hence r is contained in B_j from that point on. Again, this means that σ is accepted by $\mathcal{M}$ as well as by $\mathcal{M}'$.

As similar argument shows that all computations accepted by $\mathcal{M}$ are also accepted by $\mathcal{M}'$. ┘

4.4 Deciding the Type of a Property

In this section we consider the following problem:

Problem 4.1 *Given a Streett automaton $\mathcal{M}$, decide whether the property specified by this automaton is a κ-property, where $\kappa \in$ {safety, termination, intermittence, recurrence, persistence, progress}*

The following proposition gives an answer to this general question:

Proposition 4.3 *It is decidable whether a given Streett automaton specifies a κ-property, for $\kappa \in$ {safety, termination, recurrence, persistence, progress}.*

Again, for the first types, the answer has been given by Landweber in [Lan69]. For the case of progress, as well as the complete hierarchy below, it is provided by Wagner in [Wag79].

In the context of specification, this question was tackled in [AS87], where a decision procedure is given for safety and liveness which is not covered by the previous results.

Since the decision procedures for the cases we consider here are relatively simple, we repeat them below, using our terminology.

First, some definitions.

A set of automaton states $A \subset Q$ is defined to be *closed* if for every $q, q' \in Q$

$$q \in A \;\wedge\; t(q, q') \neq \text{F} \;\longrightarrow\; q' \in A$$

The closure $\hat{A}$ of a set of states is the smallest closed set containing A.

For a given Streett automaton $\mathcal{M}$, we define $G = \bigcap_{i=1}^{k} (R_i \cup P_i)$.

- Checking for a *safety* property.
  Let $B = Q - G$. The automaton $\mathcal{M}$ specifies a safety property iff $\hat{B} \cap G = \phi$.

- Checking for a *termination* property.
  $\mathcal{M}$ specifies a termination property iff $\hat{G} \cap B = \phi$.

To check for the other levels of the hierarchy, we define the family of accepting sets F.

$$F = \{J \mid J \text{ is an accessible cycle, } J \cap R_i \neq \phi \text{ or } J \subseteq P_i \text{ for each } i = 1, \ldots, k\}.$$

The following are direct consequences of the characterizations in [Wag79]:

- Checking for a *recurrence* property.
  $\mathcal{M}$ specifies a recurrence property iff for every $J \in F$ and every accessible cycle $A \supseteq J$, $A \in F$.

- Checking for a *persistence* property.
  $\mathcal{M}$ specifies a persistence property iff for every $J \in F$ and every accessible cycle $B \subseteq J$, $B \in F$.

- Checking for a *progress* property.
  $\mathcal{M}$ specifies a progress property iff there do not exist three accessible cycles

  $$B \subseteq J \subseteq A$$

  such that $J \in F$, but $B, A \notin F$.

As a matter of fact, the methods of [Wag79] identify the exact location of an automaton specifiable property in the progress hierarchy, i.e., the minimal k such that the property can be specified by a Streett automaton with $|L| = k$.

According to the characterization, this minimal k is the maximal n admitting a chain of accessible cycles of the form

$$B_1 \subset J_1 \subset B_2 \subset J_2 \subset \cdots \subset J_n,$$

where $B_i \notin F$ and $J_i \in F$ for $i = 1, \ldots, n$.

4.5 Connections Between Temporal Logic and Automata

Temporal logic and predicate automata have been considered as alternatives for specifying properties of programs. A comparison of their expressive power is considered next.

Proposition 4.4 *A property specifiable by a κ-formula is specifiable by an κ-automaton, for κ ranging over the different types.*

This is based on the following construction, studied in [LPZ85] and [Zuc86].

For each finite set of past formulae $p_1, \ldots, p_k$ it is possible to construct a deterministic automaton $\mathcal{M}$ with a set of states Q and designated subsets $F_1, \ldots, F_k \subseteq Q$. The automaton $\mathcal{M}$ has the property that for each $i = 1, \ldots, k$, each infinite computation $\sigma \in \Sigma^\omega$, and each position $j \geq 0$,

$$\delta(q_0, \sigma[0 \ldots j]) \in F_i \quad \textit{iff} \quad (\sigma, j) \models p_i .$$

Thus, the automaton $\mathcal{M}$ identifies, while reading σ up to position j, which p_i's hold at that position.

Using this basic construction, it is straightforward to build a κ-automaton corresponding to a κ-formula.

For example, for the progress formula $\Box\Diamond p_1 \vee \Diamond\Box p_2$, let the automaton mentioned above be $\langle Q, q_0, T\rangle$ with the designated sets F_1 and F_2. Then the corresponding progress automaton is

$$\langle Q, q_0, T, F_1, F_2\rangle.$$

In the other direction, not every property specifiable by an automaton can be specified in temporal logic. Only a restricted class of automata, called *counter-free* automata (see [MP71]) can be translated into temporal logic. A (Street) automaton is defined by be counter-free if there exists no finite computation σ and a state q, such that $q = \delta(q, \sigma^n)$ for some $n > 1$ but $\delta(q, \sigma) \neq q$. The existence of such q and σ would have enabled the automaton to count occurrences of σ modulo n.

It has been shown in [Zuc86] that:

> An automaton specifies a property specifiable by temporal logic iff it is counter-free.

This result can be refined to provide a translation from counter-free κ-automata to κ-formulae.

Proposition 4.5 *A property specifiable by a counter-free κ-automaton is specifiable by a κ-formula.*

The translation is essentially the one studied in [Zuc86], but showing that the structure required in a κ-automaton corresponds to the structure required in a κ-formula.

It is based on the construction of a past formula φ_q for each $q \in Q - \{q_0\}$ of a given counter-free automaton table $\langle Q, q_0, T\rangle$. The formula φ_q characterizes all the finite computations leading from q_0 to q, i.e., for each infinite computation $\sigma \in \Sigma^\omega$ and position $j \geq 0$,

$$\delta(q_0, \sigma[0..j]) = q \quad \longleftrightarrow \quad (\sigma, j) \models \varphi_q.$$

For example, the formula corresponding to the (counter-free) progress automaton $\langle Q, q_0, T, R, P\rangle$ is

$$\Box\Diamond\Big(\bigvee_{q\in R} \varphi_q\Big) \quad \vee \quad \Diamond\Box\Big(\bigvee_{q\in P} \varphi_q\Big).$$

The above two ways translation, subject to counter-freedom, provides a standard reduction of results about automata into the corresponding results about temporal logic. We can use this reduction to prove the other direction of proposition 4.1.

We illustrate this method on the following part of the proposition.

> A progress property Π that is specifiable by temporal logic, is specifiable by a progress formula.

Proof

Let φ be the formula specifying Π. Using the translation described in proposition 4.4, we construct a counter-free automaton $\mathcal{M}_\varphi$, specifying the progress property Π. Using the construction described in proposition 4.2 for the case of a progress property, we construct a progress automaton $\tilde{\mathcal{M}}$ that specifies the same property. The construction of $\tilde{\mathcal{M}}$ only *refines* the structure of $\mathcal{M}_\varphi$, splitting each state of $\mathcal{M}_\varphi$ into many distinct states, respecting the transitions. It follows that since $\mathcal{M}_\varphi$ is counter-free so is $\tilde{\mathcal{M}}$. We can now use the translation from counter-free automata to temporal formulae, described in proposition 4.5, to construct a progress formula $\varphi_{\tilde{\mathcal{M}}}$ specifying Π.

This method was used in [Zuc87] to establish the strict hierarchy for temporal formulae, based on [Kam85].

5 Proof System – General Part

In this section we present a deductive proof system for the general part of temporal logic.

5.1 Validity and Provability

We consider two types of validity. A state formula φ is defined to be *assertionally valid*, denoted by $\models_A \varphi$, if

$s \models \varphi$ for every state $s \in \Sigma$.

A temporal formula φ is defined to be *temporally valid*, denoted by $\models_T \varphi$, if

$(\sigma, 0) \models \varphi$ for every finite or infinite sequence of states $\sigma \in \Sigma^* \cup \Sigma^\omega$.

Note that if the formula φ contains some temporal operator, then only one type of validity, the temporal validity can be applied to it. In that case we can simply refer to it as valid, and denote this fact by writing $\models \varphi$. On the other hand, in the case that φ is an *assertion* (synonymous term for a state formula), both types of validity apply. Since we are mainly interested in temporal validity, we will drop the subscript $_T$ from the validity notation, and interpret the simpler $\models$ as $\models_T$.

Corresponding to these two types of validity, we may consider two possible deductive proof systems. The first proof system supports proving assertional validity of state formulae, while the second system supports proving (general) temporal validity of temporal formulae. This leads to two notions of *provability*. We say that a state formula α is *assertionally provable*, denoted by $\vdash_A \alpha$, if its assertional validity can be proven using the assertional proof system. Similarly, we say that a formula φ is *temporally provable*, denoted by $\vdash_T \varphi$, if its (general) temporal validity can be proven by the temporal proof system we describe in this section. To alleviate the notation, we use $\vdash$ to denote $\vdash_T$ whenever it causes no ambiguity. In most of the presentation of our proof system, we write simply φ as a premise, conclusion, or line in a proof, as representing the provability statement $\vdash_T \varphi$.

The notions of validity and provability can be extended to *consequential* validity and provability. Let Φ denote a set of formulae, $\Phi = \{\varphi_1, ..., \varphi_n\}$, to which we refer as *assumptions*. We say that a formula p is a *valid consequence* of the assumptions Φ, denote by $\Phi \models \varphi$ if every sequence that satisfies all the assumptions in Φ, also satisfies p.

We present below the temporal proof system. First we will introduce the future fragment of the operators and their associated proof system, and then extend it by the addition of the past operators.

5.2 Future Fragment – Operators and Axioms

We use the boolean operators $\rightarrow, \neg, \vee, \wedge$ and $\equiv$.

As basic temporal (future) operators we take the *Weak Next* operator $\bigcirc$, and the *Unless* operator U. The semantic definition of these two operators is given by:

- $(\sigma, j) \models \bigcirc q \iff j+1 = |\sigma|$ or $(\sigma, j+1) \models q$
  Note that the last state in a sequence satisfies $\bigcirc q$ for any q, including $q = \text{F}$.
- $(\sigma, j) \models p \mathsf{U} q \iff \forall k\,(j \leq k < |\sigma|) : [(\sigma, k) \models p \;\vee\; \exists i\,(j \leq i \leq k) : (\sigma, i) \models q]$
  Thus, $p \mathsf{U} q$ holds at position j iff p holds continuously at all positions greater or equal to j, either to the end of the sequence σ, or at least to the first occurrence of q.

We can define all the other future operators in terms of these basic two.

Strong Next $\quad \bigcirc q = \neg \bigcirc \neg q$
Obviously, $\bigcirc q$ holds at a position in a sequence if there exists a next position, and q holds there.

Henceforth $\quad \Box p = (p \mathsf{U} \text{F})$
Obviously, $\Box p$ holds at a position j if p holds at all positions $i \geq j$.

Eventually $\quad \Diamond q = \neg \Box \neg q$
Obviously, $\Diamond q$ holds a at a position j if q holds at some position $i \geq j$.

Until $\quad p \mathcal{U} q = (p \mathsf{U} q) \wedge \Diamond q$
Obviously, $p \mathcal{U} q$ holds if p holds continuously until the next occurrence of q, which is guaranteed to happen.

Entailment $\quad p \Rightarrow q = \Box(p \rightarrow q)$
Clearly, p entails q over a sequence if p implies q at all positions in the sequence.

Strong equivalence $\quad p \Leftrightarrow q = \Box(p \equiv q)$
Clearly, p is strongly equivalent to q over a sequence if p is equivalent to q at all positions in the sequence.

Axioms

F1. $\bigcirc p \Rightarrow \bigcirc p$

F2. $\bigcirc(p \rightarrow q) \Rightarrow (\bigcirc p \rightarrow \bigcirc q)$

F3. $\Box(p \rightarrow q) \Rightarrow (\Box p \rightarrow \Box q)$

F4. $\Box p \rightarrow \Box \bigcirc p$

F5. $(p \Rightarrow \bigcirc p) \rightarrow (p \Rightarrow \Box p)$

F6. $(p \mathsf{U} q) \Leftrightarrow [q \vee (p \wedge \bigcirc(p \mathsf{U} q))]$

F7. $\Box p \Rightarrow p \mathsf{U} q$

Inference Rules

For the first inference rule, we need the notion of the *temporal instantiation* of a state formula. Let α be a state formula containing the proposition symbol Q, and φ some temporal formula. We denote by $\alpha[\varphi/Q]$ the temporal formula obtained from α by replacing all occurrences of Q by φ. We call $\alpha[\varphi/Q]$ a temporal instantiation of the state formula α by the replacement $Q \leftarrow \varphi$. For example, the formula

$$[r \wedge (r \rightarrow (p\mathcal{U}q))] \rightarrow (p\mathcal{U}q))$$

is a temporal instantiation of the state formula

$$\alpha \;:\; [r \wedge (r \rightarrow Q)] \rightarrow Q,$$

obtained by the replacement $Q \leftarrow (p\mathcal{U}q)$. It is easy to extend this notion to a multiple replacement, where a list of proposition symbols is replaced by a matching list of temporal formulae. We consider only *safe* replacements, which do not cause free variables appearing in the temporal formula φ to be captured by quantifications appearing in α.

INS TEMPORAL INSTANTIATION

For φ, a temporal instantiation of the state formula α,

$$\frac{\models_A \alpha}{\vdash_T \Box\varphi}$$

MP MODUS PONENS

$$\frac{p \rightarrow q\;,\; p}{q}$$

PAR PARTICULARIZATION

$$\frac{\Box p}{p}$$

The **INS** rule enables us to derive the temporal validity of the formula $[r \wedge (r \rightarrow (p\mathcal{U}q))] \rightarrow (p\mathcal{U}q))$ from the assertional validity of the state formula $[r \wedge (r \rightarrow Q)] \rightarrow Q$. Note that the premise for the rule requires validity of α rather than provability, which makes the temporal proof system independent of the assertional proof system that may be used to derive α. In principle, we can use alternative means, such as specific decision procedures, for establishing the assertional validity of α.

On the other hand, the price of this generality is that it makes the deductive system non-recursive. This is because the set of assertionally valid statements (allowing quantification and general interpretations into concrete structures) is in general non-recursive. To avoid this situation, we will usually restrict the assertions α to purely propositional formulae. With this restriction, the system becomes recursive. We will maintain this assumption unless we explicitly say otherwise.

Note that, in some sense, the **PAR** rule can be viewed as the inverse of the **INS** rule. While the **INS** rule deduces the validity of φ at all states in a sequence from the validity of α at an arbitrary single step, the **PAR** deduces the validity of p at a single step, the first in the sequence, from its validity at all states in the sequence.

5.3 Theorems and Derived Rules

In the following, we use the axioms and rules given above to derive some additional theorems and derived rules. A theorem is a statement of the form $\vdash_T p$, claiming that the formula p is provable in the presented deductive system, and hence is valid.

The proof of a theorem is presented as a sequence of lines. A line in a proof can be an instantiation of an axiom, i.e., particularizing symbols such as p and q, appearing in the axiom and denoting arbitrary formulae, to more concrete forms, which may in turn contain other symbols standing for arbitrary formulae. For example, having the axiom **F1**: $\diamondsuit p \Rightarrow \bigcirc p$, we may instantiate p to $\Box q$ and include $\diamondsuit \Box q \Rightarrow \bigcirc \Box q$ as a line in a proof, quoting **F1** as justification. Alternately, a line in a proof may be justified by an application of a *rule*. For example, the **MP** rule allows us to infer q from $p \rightarrow q$ and p. Using instantiation again, this enables us to write $\bigcirc r$ at a line k of the proof, provided we have already derived $\Box r \rightarrow \bigcirc r$ at line $i < k$, and $\Box r$ at line $j < k$. In this case, we will include **MP** i, j as the justification for line k. Once a theorem is established, we are allowed to use it as an axiom in subsequent rules. This is because we can view a theorem as an abbreviation for its proof, which means that in any proof using the theorem as a justification for a line, we could have expanded the derivation of the line by substituting the proof of the theorem at this point.

A derived rule is a statement of the form:

$$\frac{\begin{array}{c} p_1 \\ p_2 \\ \cdot \\ \cdot \\ p_n \end{array}}{q}$$

This statement claims that if the formulae $p_1, ..., p_n$, called *premises*, are provable in the deductive system, then so is the *conclusion* q.

The proof of a derived rule is similar to the proof of a theorem in that it includes lines resulting from instantiation of axioms (or previously established theorems), or application of rules. In addition, it may also include lines which list one of the premises p_i, with the justification *Premise*. Again, once a rule is proven, we may use it in subsequent proofs to justify additional steps. This is justified again by the claim that any such application at some step in a proof could have been proven without the use of the derived rule, by substituting the proof of the rule (properly instantiated) at that step. In many cases rules are easier to use than their formulation as axioms. Consequently, many of our derivations below will transform axioms into rules.

Rule PR PROPOSITIONAL REASONING

$$\frac{\begin{array}{c} (p_1 \wedge p_2 \wedge ... \wedge p_n) \rightarrow q \\ p_1, p_2, ..., p_n \end{array}}{q}$$

Proof:

1. $(p_1 \wedge p_2 \wedge ... \wedge p_n) \rightarrow q$ Premise.
2. $p_1, p_2, ..., p_n$ Premise.
3. $[(p_1 \wedge p_2 \wedge ... \wedge p_n) \rightarrow q] \rightarrow [p_1 \rightarrow (p_2 \rightarrow (...(p_n \rightarrow q)...)]$ INS

4. $p_1 \rightarrow (p_2 \rightarrow (...(p_n \rightarrow q)...)$ **MP** 3, 1, def. of $\Rightarrow$.
5. $p_2 \rightarrow (p_3 \rightarrow (...(p_n \rightarrow q)...)$ **MP** 4, 2(1).
6. ...

...

q

∎

Often, we use the **PR** rule without explicitly designating the first premise. This is done whenever the first premise is an obvious propositional tautology.

Rule GMP GENERALIZED MODUS PONENS

$$\frac{p \Rightarrow q\ ,\ \Box p}{\Box q}$$

Proof:

1. $\Box(p \rightarrow q) \Rightarrow (\Box p \rightarrow \Box q)$ **F3**
2. $\Box(p \rightarrow q) \rightarrow (\Box p \rightarrow \Box q)$ **PAR**
3. $p \Rightarrow q$ Premise
4. $\Box(p \rightarrow q)$ Definition of $\Rightarrow$
5. $\Box p \rightarrow \Box q$ **MP** 2, 4
6. $\Box p$ Premise
7. $\Box q$ **MP** 5, 6

∎

Rule GPR GENERALIZED PROPOSITIONAL REASONING

$$\frac{\begin{array}{c}(p_1 \wedge p_2 \wedge ... \wedge p_n) \Rightarrow q \\ \Box p_1, \Box p_2, ..., \Box p_n\end{array}}{\Box q}$$

Proof:

1. $(p_1 \wedge p_2 \wedge ... \wedge p_n) \Rightarrow q$ Premise.
2. $\Box p_1, \Box p_2, ..., \Box p_n$ Premise.
3. $[(p_1 \wedge p_2 \wedge ... \wedge p_n) \rightarrow q] \Rightarrow [p_1 \rightarrow (p_2 \rightarrow (...(p_n \rightarrow q)...)]$ **INS**
4. $p_1 \Rightarrow (p_2 \rightarrow (...(p_n \rightarrow q)...)$ **GMP** 3, 1, def. of $\Rightarrow$.
5. $p_2 \Rightarrow (p_3 \rightarrow (...(p_n \rightarrow q)...)$ **GMP** 4, 2(1).
6. ...

...

$\Box q$

∎

Often, we use the **GPR** rule without explicitly designating the first premise. This is done whenever the first premise is a substitution instance of an obvious propositional tautology.

Rule R1

$$\frac{p \Leftrightarrow q}{p \Rightarrow q}$$

Proof:

1. $\sqcup[p \equiv q]$ — Premise
2. $[p \equiv q] \Rightarrow (p \rightarrow q)$ — **INS.**
3. $p \Rightarrow q$ — **GMP** 2, 1 ; def. of $\Rightarrow$.

∎

Rule R2

$$\frac{p \Rightarrow q \ , \ q \Rightarrow p}{p \Leftrightarrow q}$$

Proof:

1. $[(p \rightarrow q) \wedge (q \rightarrow p)] \Rightarrow (p \equiv q)$ — **INS.**
2. $\square(p \rightarrow q)$ — Premise.
3. $\square(q \rightarrow p)$ — Premise.
4. $p \Leftrightarrow q$ — **GPR**, 1, 2, 3

∎

5.4 Theorems and Rules for $\circledcirc$

Rule $\circledcirc$G $\circledcirc$ GENERALIZATION

$$\frac{\square p}{\square \circledcirc p}$$

Proof:

1. $\square p$ — Premise
2. $\square p \rightarrow \square \circledcirc p$ — **F4**
3. $\square \circledcirc p$ — **MP** 2, 1

∎

Rule $\circledcirc$M $\circledcirc$ IS MONOTONIC

(a) $$\frac{p \Rightarrow q}{\circledcirc p \Rightarrow \circledcirc q}$$ (b) $$\frac{q \Leftrightarrow p}{\circledcirc p \Leftrightarrow \circledcirc q}$$

Proof:

(a)

1.	$p \Rightarrow q$	Premise.
2.	$\Box \bigcirc (p \to q)$	$\bigcirc$**G.**
3.	$\bigcirc (p \to q) \Rightarrow (\bigcirc p \to \bigcirc q)$	**F2.**
4.	$\bigcirc p \Rightarrow \bigcirc q$	**GMP** 3, 2.

(b)

1.	$p \Leftrightarrow q$	Premise.
2.	$p \Rightarrow q$	**R1.**
3.	$\bigcirc p \Rightarrow \bigcirc q$	$\bigcirc$**M**(a).
4.	$\bigcirc q \Rightarrow \bigcirc p$	Similarly.
5.	$\bigcirc p \Leftrightarrow \bigcirc q$	**R2,** 3, 4.

∎

Theorem T1 $\bigcirc$ IS CONJUNCTIVE

$$\bigcirc (p \wedge q) \Leftrightarrow (\bigcirc p \wedge \bigcirc q)$$

Proof:

1.	$p \Rightarrow (q \to (p \wedge q))$	**INS**
2.	$\bigcirc p \Rightarrow \bigcirc (q \to (p \wedge q))$	$\bigcirc$**M**
3.	$\bigcirc (q \to (p \wedge q)) \Rightarrow (\bigcirc q \to \bigcirc (p \wedge q))$	**F2**
4.	$\bigcirc p \Rightarrow (\bigcirc q \to \bigcirc (p \wedge q))$	**GPR** 2,3
5.	$(\bigcirc p \wedge \bigcirc q) \Rightarrow \bigcirc (p \wedge q)$	**GPR**
6.	$(p \wedge q) \Rightarrow p$	**INS**
7.	$\bigcirc (p \wedge q) \Rightarrow \bigcirc p$	$\bigcirc$**M**
8.	$\bigcirc (p \wedge q) \Rightarrow \bigcirc q$	Similarly
9.	$\bigcirc (p \wedge q) \Rightarrow (\bigcirc p \wedge \bigcirc q)$	**GPR** 7,8
10.	$\bigcirc (p \wedge q) \Leftrightarrow (\bigcirc p \wedge \bigcirc q)$	**R2** 5,9

∎

Theorem T2 $\bigcirc$ IS DISJUNCTIVE

$$\bigcirc (p \vee q) \Leftrightarrow (\bigcirc p \vee \bigcirc q)$$

Proof:

1.	$\bigcirc ((\neg p) \to q) \Rightarrow (\bigcirc (\neg p) \to \bigcirc q)$	**F2**
2.	$\bigcirc (p \vee q) \Rightarrow (\neg \bigcirc (\neg p) \vee \bigcirc q)$	$\bigcirc$**M, GPR**
3.	$\bigcirc (p \vee q) \Rightarrow (\Diamond p \vee \bigcirc q)$	Definition of $\Diamond$, **GPR**
4.	$\bigcirc (p \vee q) \Rightarrow (\bigcirc p \vee \bigcirc q)$	**F1, GPR**
5.	$p \Rightarrow (p \vee q)$	**INS**
6.	$\bigcirc p \Rightarrow \bigcirc (p \vee q)$	$\bigcirc$**M**
7.	$\bigcirc q \Rightarrow \bigcirc (p \vee q)$	Similarly
8.	$(\bigcirc p \vee \bigcirc q) \Rightarrow \bigcirc (p \vee q)$	**GPR** 6,7
9.	$\bigcirc (p \vee q) \Leftrightarrow (\bigcirc p \vee \bigcirc q)$	**R2** 4, 8

∎

Theorem $\bigcirc$D$\Diamond$ $\bigcirc$ IS DUAL TO $\Diamond$

$$\neg \bigcirc p \Leftrightarrow \Diamond (\neg p)$$

Proof:

1. $p \Leftrightarrow \neg(\neg p)$	**INS**
2. $\Box p \Leftrightarrow \Box(\neg(\neg p))$	**$\Box$M**
3. $\neg\Box p \Leftrightarrow \neg\Box(\neg(\neg p))$	**GPR**
4. $\neg\Box p \Leftrightarrow \Diamond(\neg p))$	Definition of $\Diamond$

∎

Theorem T3

$$\Box(p \rightarrow q) \Leftrightarrow (\Box p \rightarrow \Box q)$$

Proof:

1. $\Box(p \rightarrow q) \Rightarrow (\Box p \rightarrow \Box q)$	**F2**
2. $(\Box p \rightarrow \Box q) \Rightarrow (\neg\Box p \vee \Box q)$	**GPR**
3. $(\Box p \rightarrow \Box q) \Rightarrow (\Diamond(\neg p) \vee \Box q)$	**ND, GPR**
4. $(\Box p \rightarrow \Box q) \Rightarrow (\Box(\neg p) \vee \Box q)$	**F1**
5. $(\Box p \rightarrow \Box q) \Rightarrow \Box((\neg p) \vee q))$	**T2**
6. $(\Box p \rightarrow \Box q) \Rightarrow \Box(p \rightarrow q)$	**$\Box$M, GPR**
7. $\Box(p \rightarrow q) \Leftrightarrow (\Box p \rightarrow \Box q)$	**R2**, 1, 6

∎

5.5 Theorems and Rules about $\Diamond$

Rule $\Diamond$M $\Diamond$ IS MONOTONIC

$$\text{(a)} \quad \frac{p \Rightarrow q}{\Diamond p \Rightarrow \Diamond q} \qquad \text{(b)} \quad \frac{q \Leftrightarrow p}{\Diamond p \Leftrightarrow \Diamond q}$$

Proof:

(a)

1. $p \Rightarrow q$	Premise.
2. $(\neg q) \Rightarrow (\neg p)$	**GPR**
3. $\Box(\neg q) \Rightarrow \Box(\neg p)$	**$\Box$M**
4. $\neg\Box(\neg p) \Rightarrow \neg\Box(\neg q)$	**GPR**
5. $\Diamond p \Rightarrow \Diamond q$	Definition of $\Diamond$

(b) From (a) and **R2**.

∎

Theorem T4 $\Diamond$ IS CONJUNCTIVE

$$\Diamond(p \wedge q) \Leftrightarrow (\Diamond p \wedge \Diamond q)$$

By **T2** and duality. That is, apply **T2** to $\neg p$ and $\neg q$, and then introduce appropriate negations. ∎

Theorem T5 $\Diamond$ IS DISJUNCTIVE

$$\Diamond(p \vee q) \Leftrightarrow (\Diamond p \vee \Diamond q)$$

By **T1** and duality. ▪

Theorem T6

$$\bigcirc(p \rightarrow q) \Leftrightarrow (\bigcirc p \rightarrow \bigcirc q)$$

By **T3** and duality. ▪

5.6 Theorems about $\Box$

Rule $\Box$M $\Box$ IS MONOTONIC

$$\text{(a)} \quad \frac{p \Rightarrow q}{\Box p \Rightarrow \Box q} \qquad \text{(b)} \quad \frac{q \Leftrightarrow p}{\Box p \Leftrightarrow \Box q}$$

Proof:

(a)

1. $p \Rightarrow q$ — Premise.
2. $\Box\Box(p \rightarrow q)$ — Definition of $\Rightarrow$
3. $\Box(p \rightarrow q) \Rightarrow (\Box p \rightarrow \Box q)$ — **F3**.
4. $\Box p \Rightarrow \Box q$ — GMP 3,2.

(b) From (a) and **R2**.

▪

Rule CI COMPUTATIONAL INDUCTION

$$\frac{p \Rightarrow \bigcirc p}{p \Rightarrow \Box p}$$

Proof:

1. $p \Rightarrow \bigcirc p$ — Premise.
2. $(p \Rightarrow \bigcirc p) \rightarrow (p \Rightarrow \Box p)$ — **F5**
3. $p \Rightarrow \Box p$ — MP 2,1

▪

Theorem T7

$$\Box p \Leftrightarrow [p \wedge \bigcirc(\Box p)]$$

Proof:

1. $p\mathcal{U}_F \Leftrightarrow F \vee [p \wedge \bigcirc(p\mathcal{U}_F)]$ — **F6**
2. $p\mathcal{U}_F \Leftrightarrow [p \wedge \bigcirc(p\mathcal{U}_F)]$ — **GPR**
3. $\Box p \Leftrightarrow [p \wedge \bigcirc(\Box p)]$ — Definition of $\Box$

▪

Rule $\Box$I $\Box$ INTRODUCTION

$$\frac{q \Rightarrow [p \wedge \bigcirc q]}{q \Rightarrow \Box p}$$

Proof:

1. $q \Rightarrow [p \wedge \bigcirc q]$	Premise.
2. $q \Rightarrow \bigcirc q$	**GPR**
3. $q \Rightarrow \Box q$	**CI**
4. $q \Rightarrow p$	**GPR 1**
5. $\Box q \Rightarrow \Box p$	$\Box$**M**
6. $q \Rightarrow \Box p$	**GPR 3, 5**

∎

Theorem **T7** and the $\Box$**I** rule identify $\Box p$ as the *maximal* solution of the following equation for X

$$[X \Rightarrow (p \wedge \bigcirc X)] \tag{2}$$

Theorem **T7** shows that $\Box p$ satisfies the entailment (2) when substituted for X. The $\Box$**I** rule shows that any other solution q of the entailment must be smaller than $\Box p$, where the ordering between formulae is defined by

$p \prec q$ iff $p \Rightarrow q$.

Theorem T8 $\Box$ IS REFLEXIVE

$$\Box p \Rightarrow p$$

Proof: **T7** + **GPR** ∎

Theorem T9

$$\Box p \Rightarrow \bigcirc \Box p$$

Proof: **T7** + **GPR** ∎

Theorem T10

$$\Box p \Rightarrow \bigcirc p$$

Proof:

1. $\Box p \Rightarrow p$	**T8**
2. $\bigcirc \Box p \Rightarrow \bigcirc p$	$\bigcirc$**M**
3. $\Box p \Rightarrow \bigcirc \Box p$	**T9**
4. $\Box p \Rightarrow \bigcirc p$	**GPR** 3,2

∎

Theorem T11 $\Box$ IS IDEMPOTENT

$$\Box p \Leftrightarrow \Box \Box p$$

Proof:

1. $\Box \Box p \Rightarrow \Box p$	**T8**
2. $\Box p \Rightarrow \bigcirc \Box p$	**T9**
3. $\Box p \Rightarrow [\Box p \wedge \bigcirc \Box p]$	**GPR**
4. $\Box p \Rightarrow \Box \Box p$	$\Box$**I**
5. $\Box p \Leftrightarrow \Box \Box p$	**R2** 1,4

The following theorem generalizes **F4** from implication to entailment.

Theorem T12

$$\Box p \Rightarrow \Box \bigcirc p$$

Proof:

1. $\Box p \Rightarrow \bigcirc p$ **T10**
2. $\Box \Box p \Rightarrow \Box \bigcirc p$ **□M**
3. $\Box p \Rightarrow \Box \Box p$ **T11,GPR**
4. $\Box p \Rightarrow \Box \bigcirc p$ **GPR 3,2**

Rule □G □ GENERALIZATION

$$\frac{\Box p}{\Box \Box p}$$

Proof:

1. $\Box p$ Premise.
2. $\Box p \Rightarrow \Box \Box p$ **T11,R1**
3. $\Box p \rightarrow \Box \Box p$ **PAR**
4. $\Box \Box p$ **MP 3,1**

Theorem T13 □ IS CONJUNCTIVE

$$\Box(p \wedge q) \Leftrightarrow (\Box p \wedge \Box q)$$

Proof:

1. $p \wedge q \Rightarrow p$ **INS**
2. $\Box(p \wedge q) \Rightarrow \Box p$ **□M**
3. $\Box(p \wedge q) \Rightarrow \Box q$ Similarly
4. $\Box(p \wedge q) \Rightarrow (\Box p \wedge \Box q)$ **GPR 2,3**
5. $p \Rightarrow (q \rightarrow (p \wedge q))$ **INS**
6. $\Box p \Rightarrow \Box(q \rightarrow (p \wedge q))$ **□M**
7. $\Box p \Rightarrow (\Box q \rightarrow \Box(p \wedge q))$ **T8, GPR**
8. $(\Box p \wedge \Box q) \Rightarrow \Box(p \wedge q)$ **GPR**
9. $\Box(p \wedge q) \Leftrightarrow (\Box p \wedge \Box q)$ **R2 4,8**

5.7 Theorems about $\Diamond$

Theorem T14 $\Diamond$ IS REFLEXIVE

$$p \Rightarrow \Diamond p$$

Proof:

1. $\Box(\neg p) \Rightarrow (\neg p)$ **T8**
2. $p \Rightarrow \neg\Box(\neg p)$ **GPR**
3. $p \Rightarrow \Diamond p$ Definition of $\Diamond$

∎

Theorem T15 $\Diamond$ IS IDEMPOTENT

$$\Diamond p \Leftrightarrow \Diamond\Diamond p$$

Proof:

1. $\Box(\neg p) \Leftrightarrow \Box\Box(\neg p)$ **T11**
2. $\neg\Box(\neg p) \Leftrightarrow \neg\Box\Box(\neg p)$ **GPR**
3. $\neg\Box(\neg p) \Leftrightarrow \neg\Box(\neg\neg\Box(\neg p))$ **□M, GPR**
4. $\Diamond p \Leftrightarrow \Diamond\Diamond p$ Definition of $\Diamond$

∎

Rule ◇M $\Diamond$ IS MONOTONIC

$$\text{(a)} \quad \frac{p \Rightarrow q}{\Diamond p \Rightarrow \Diamond q} \qquad \text{(b)} \quad \frac{q \Leftrightarrow p}{\Diamond p \Leftrightarrow \Diamond q}$$

Proof:

(a)

1. $p \Rightarrow q$ Premise.
2. $\neg q \Rightarrow \neg p$ **GPR**
3. $\Box(\neg q) \Rightarrow \Box(\neg p)$ **□M**
4. $\neg\Box(\neg p) \Rightarrow \neg\Box(\neg q)$ **GPR**
5. $\Diamond p \Rightarrow \Diamond q$ Definition of $\Diamond$

(b) From (a) and **R2**.

∎

Theorem T16 $\Diamond$ IS DISJUNCTIVE

$$\Diamond(p \vee q) \Leftrightarrow (\Diamond p \vee \Diamond q)$$

Proof:

1. $\Box((\neg p) \wedge (\neg q)) \Leftrightarrow (\Box(\neg p) \wedge \Box(\neg q))$ **T13**
2. $\Box(\neg(p \vee q)) \Leftrightarrow (\Box(\neg p) \wedge \Box(\neg q))$ **□M, GPR**
3. $\neg\Box(\neg(p \vee q)) \Leftrightarrow (\neg\Box(\neg p) \vee \neg\Box(\neg q))$ **GPR**
4. $\Diamond(p \vee q) \Leftrightarrow (\Diamond p \vee \Diamond q)$ Definition of $\Diamond$

Rule $\Diamond$T $\Diamond$ IS TRANSITIVE

$$\frac{p \Rightarrow \Diamond q \ , \ q \Rightarrow \Diamond r}{p \Rightarrow \Diamond r}$$

Proof:

1. $p \Rightarrow \Diamond q$ — Premise.
2. $q \Rightarrow \Diamond r$ — Premise.
3. $\Diamond q \Rightarrow \Diamond \Diamond r$ — $\Diamond$**M**
4. $\Diamond q \Rightarrow \Diamond r$ — **T15, GPR**
5. $p \Rightarrow \Diamond r$ — **GPR 1,4**

Rule $\Diamond$C $\Diamond$ IS CONFLUENT

$$\frac{p \Rightarrow \Diamond (q \vee r) \ , \ q \Rightarrow \Diamond s \ , \ r \Rightarrow \Diamond s}{p \Rightarrow \Diamond s}$$

Proof:

1. $q \Rightarrow \Diamond s$ — Premise.
2. $r \Rightarrow \Diamond s$ — Premise.
3. $(q \vee r) \Rightarrow \Diamond s$ — **GPR 1,2**
4. $\Diamond (q \vee r) \Rightarrow \Diamond \Diamond s$ — $\Diamond$**M**
5. $\Diamond (q \vee r) \Rightarrow \Diamond s$ — **T15**
6. $p \Rightarrow \Diamond (q \vee r)$ — Premise.
7. $p \Rightarrow \Diamond s$ — **GPR 6,5**

Theorem T17

$$\Diamond p \Leftrightarrow p \vee \pmb{\bigcirc} (\Diamond p)$$

Proof:

1. $\Box \neg p \Leftrightarrow (\neg p) \wedge \pmb{\bigcirc} (\Box \neg p)$ — **T7**
2. $\neg \Box \neg p \Leftrightarrow p \vee \neg \pmb{\bigcirc} \neg (\neg \Box \neg p)$ **GPR**
3. $\Diamond p \Leftrightarrow p \vee \pmb{\bigcirc} (\Diamond p)$ — Definitions of $\Diamond$, $\pmb{\bigcirc}$

Rule $\Diamond$I $\Diamond$ INTRODUCTION

$$\frac{p \vee \pmb{\bigcirc} q \Rightarrow q}{\Diamond p \Rightarrow q}$$

Proof: By duality from $\Box$**I**.

Theorem **T17** and the $\Diamond$**I** rule identify $\Diamond p$ as the *minimal* solution of the following equation for X

$$[p \vee \pmb{\bigcirc} X \Rightarrow X] \tag{3}$$

Theorem **T17** shows that $\Diamond p$ satisfies the entailment (3) when substituted for X. The $\Diamond$**I** rule shows that any other solution q of the entailment must be greater or equal to $\Diamond p$.

6 General Proof System - The Past

Let us now add the set of *past* operators to the language. Similarly to the future set, they can all be defined in terms of the two basic past operators, the *Weak Previous* operator $\widetilde{\ominus}$, and the *Weak Since* operator S. The semantic definition of these two operators is given by:

- $(\sigma, j) \models \widetilde{\ominus} q \iff j = 0$ or $(\sigma, j-1) \models q$

  Note that the first state in a sequence satisfies $\widetilde{\ominus} q$ for any q, including $q = \text{F}$.

- $(\sigma, j) \models p \mathsf{S} q \iff \forall k\,(j \geq k \geq 0) : [(\sigma, k) \models p \ \vee \ \exists i\,(j \geq i \geq k) : (\sigma, i) \models q]$

  Thus, $p\mathsf{S}q$ holds at position j iff p holds continuously at all positions lesser than or equal to j, either to the beginning of the sequence σ, or at least to the first preceding occurrence of q.

We can define all the other past operators in terms of these basic two.

Strong Previous $\ominus q \ = \ \neg \widetilde{\ominus} \neg q$

Obviously, $\ominus q$ holds at a position in a sequence if there exists a previous position, and q holds there.

Has Always $\boxminus p \ = \ (p \mathsf{S} \text{F})$

Obviously, $\boxminus p$ holds at a position j if p holds at all positions $i \leq j$.

Once $\diamondminus q \ = \ \neg \boxminus \neg q$

Obviously, $\diamondminus q$ holds a at a position j if q holds at some position $i \leq j$.

Strong Since $p\,\mathcal{S}\,q \ = \ (p \mathsf{S} q) \wedge \diamondminus q$

Obviously, $p\,\mathcal{S}\,q$ holds if p held continuously since the previous occurrence of q, which is guaranteed to have happened.

The following additional axioms complete the proof system, enabling it to also deal with the past operators.

Axioms

P1. $\ominus p \Rightarrow \widetilde{\ominus} p$
P2. $\widetilde{\ominus}(p \rightarrow q) \Rightarrow (\widetilde{\ominus} p \rightarrow \widetilde{\ominus} q)$
P3. $\boxminus(p \rightarrow q) \Rightarrow (\boxminus p \rightarrow \boxminus q)$
P4. $\Box p \rightarrow \Box \widetilde{\ominus} p$
P5. $(p \Rightarrow \widetilde{\ominus} p) \rightarrow (p \Rightarrow \boxminus p)$
P6. $(p \mathsf{S} q) \Leftrightarrow [q \vee (p \wedge \widetilde{\ominus}(p \mathsf{S} q))]$
P7. $\widetilde{\ominus} \text{F}$

As we can easily see, axioms **P1**–**P6** are almost symmetric to axioms **F1**–**F6** of the future fragment. They deviate from full symmetry in that the principal operator is still the $\Rightarrow$ operator, which is a future operator. However, this is only natural in the anchored mode, where a formula of the form $\boxminus p$ is equivalent (because it is evaluated at position 0, which has no past) to p. Due to this, there is no sense in writing a formula whose highest temporal operator is a past operator. For the same reason, the two factors of the implication in **P4** start with the future operator $\square$.

The last axiom **P7** is unique to the past, and claims that the first position of each sequence (and this is where we test validity) has no preceding position. This is done by stating that all preceding positions satisfy F. Axiom **P7** is one of the few exceptions (and in some sense the only necessary one) to the advice we have just given, not to have a past operator at a top level position in the formula. On the other hand, note that we do not have the past analogue of **F7**, which should have been $\boxminus p \Rightarrow p \mathcal{S} q$. This is because, using **P7** it can be proven as a theorem, as we do below in **T44**.

In addition to these two sets, each dealing mainly with the operators within its respective fragment, we have two *mixed* axioms, mixing the future with the past.

F8. $p \Rightarrow \bigcirc \ominus p$
P8. $p \Rightarrow \boxminus \bigcirc p$

The future axiom **F8** states that if we take one step forward from a p-state, we can always take one step backwards, and return to a (actually the same) p-state. Axiom **P8** describes a similar situation when the first step is taken backwards.

No additional rules are needed to deal with the past.

6.1 Theorems and Derived Rules for the Past

Most of the theorems and derived rules for the past fragment can be obtained by symmetry from the corresponding theorems and rules for the future fragment. We include a proof for the first two rules to illustrate the symmetry elements.

Rule $\boxminus$G $\boxminus$ GENERALIZATION

$$\frac{\square p}{\square \boxminus p}$$

Proof:

1. $\square p$ — Premise
2. $\square p \rightarrow \square \boxminus p$ — **P4**
3. $\square \boxminus p$ — **MP 2, 1**

∎

Rule $\boxminus$M $\boxminus$ IS MONOTONIC

$$\text{(a)} \quad \frac{p \Rightarrow q}{\boxminus p \Rightarrow \boxminus q} \qquad \text{(b)} \quad \frac{q \Leftrightarrow p}{\boxminus p \Leftrightarrow \boxminus q}$$

Proof:

(a)
1. $p \Rightarrow q$ — Premise.
2. $\square \boxminus (p \rightarrow q)$ — $\boxminus$G.
3. $\boxminus (p \rightarrow q) \Rightarrow (\boxminus p \rightarrow \boxminus q)$ — **P2.**
4. $\boxminus p \Rightarrow \boxminus q$ — **GMP 3,2.**

∎

For the rest of the theorems and rules that can be established by symmetry, we list them below without proof.

Theorem T18 $\ominus$ IS CONJUNCTIVE

$$\ominus(p \land q) \Leftrightarrow (\ominus p \land \ominus q)$$

Theorem T19 $\ominus$ IS DISJUNCTIVE

$$\ominus(p \lor q) \Leftrightarrow (\ominus p \lor \ominus q)$$

Theorem $\ominus$D$\circleddash$ $\ominus$ IS DUAL TO $\circleddash$

$$\neg \ominus p \Leftrightarrow \circleddash(\neg p)$$

Theorem T20

$$\ominus(p \rightarrow q) \Leftrightarrow (\ominus p \rightarrow \ominus q)$$

Rule $\circleddash$M $\circleddash$ IS MONOTONIC

$$\text{(a)} \quad \frac{p \Rightarrow q}{\circleddash p \Rightarrow \circleddash q} \qquad \text{(b)} \quad \frac{q \Leftrightarrow p}{\circleddash p \Leftrightarrow \circleddash q}$$

Theorem T21 $\circleddash$ IS CONJUNCTIVE

$$\circleddash(p \land q) \Leftrightarrow (\circleddash p \land \circleddash q)$$

Theorem T22 $\circleddash$ IS DISJUNCTIVE

$$\circleddash(p \lor q) \Leftrightarrow (\circleddash p \lor \circleddash q)$$

Theorem T23

$$\circleddash(p \rightarrow q) \Leftrightarrow (\circleddash p \rightarrow \circleddash q)$$

6.2 Theorems about $\boxminus$

Rule $\boxminus$G $\boxminus$ GENERALIZATION

$$\frac{\Box p}{\Box \boxminus p}$$

Proof:

1.	$\Box p$	Premise
2.	$\Box \ominus p$	$\ominus$G
3.	$\ominus p \Rightarrow (p \rightarrow \ominus p)$	INS
4.	$\Box \ominus p \Rightarrow \Box(p \rightarrow \ominus p)$	$\Box$M
5.	$\Box \ominus p \rightarrow (p \Rightarrow \ominus p)$	PAR, Definition of $\Rightarrow$
6.	$\Box \ominus p \rightarrow (p \Rightarrow \boxminus p)$	P5, PR
7.	$p \Rightarrow \boxminus p$	MP 6,2
8.	$\Box \boxminus p$	GMP 7,1

∎

Rule $\boxminus$M $\boxminus$ IS MONOTONIC

(a) $\dfrac{p \Rightarrow q}{\boxminus p \Rightarrow \boxminus q}$ (b) $\dfrac{q \Leftrightarrow p}{\boxminus p \Leftrightarrow \boxminus q}$

Proof:

(a)

1.	$p \Rightarrow q$	Premise.
2.	$\square(p \rightarrow q)$	Definition of $\Rightarrow$
3.	$\square \boxminus(p \rightarrow q)$	$\boxminus$G
4.	$\boxminus(p \rightarrow q) \Rightarrow (\boxminus p \rightarrow \boxminus q)$	**P3**
5.	$\square(\boxminus p \rightarrow \boxminus q)$	**GMP** 4,3
6.	$\boxminus p \Rightarrow \boxminus q$	Definition of $\Rightarrow$

(b) From (a) and **R2**.

∎

Rule RI REVERSE INDUCTION

$$\frac{p \Rightarrow \ominus p}{p \Rightarrow \boxminus p}$$

Theorem T24

$$\boxminus p \Leftrightarrow p \wedge \ominus \boxminus p$$

Rule $\boxminus$I $\boxminus$ INTRODUCTION

$$\frac{p \Rightarrow q \wedge \ominus p}{p \Rightarrow \boxminus q}$$

Theorem **T24** and the $\boxminus$**I** rule identify $\boxminus p$ as the *maximal* solution of the following equation for X

$$[X \Rightarrow (p \wedge \ominus X)] \tag{4}$$

Theorem T25 $\boxminus$ IS REFLEXIVE

$$\boxminus p \Rightarrow p$$

Theorem T26

$$\boxminus p \Rightarrow \ominus \boxminus p$$

Theorem T27

$$\boxminus p \Rightarrow \ominus p$$

Theorem T28 $\boxminus$ IS IDEMPOTENT

$$\boxminus p \Leftrightarrow \boxminus \boxminus p$$

Theorem T29

$$\boxminus p \Rightarrow \boxminus \ominus p$$

Rule $\boxminus$PG $\boxminus$ PAST GENERALIZATION

$$\frac{\boxminus p}{\boxminus \boxminus p}$$

Theorem T30 $\boxminus$ IS CONJUNCTIVE

$$\boxminus(p \wedge q) \Leftrightarrow (\boxminus p \wedge \boxminus q)$$

6.3 Theorems about $\diamondminus$

Theorem T31 $\diamondminus$ IS REFLEXIVE

$$p \Rightarrow \diamondminus p$$

Theorem T32 $\diamondminus$ IS IDEMPOTENT

$$\diamondminus p \Leftrightarrow \diamondminus\diamondminus p$$

Rule $\diamondminus$M $\diamondminus$ IS MONOTONIC

$$\text{(a)} \quad \frac{p \Rightarrow q}{\diamondminus p \Rightarrow \diamondminus q} \qquad \text{(b)} \quad \frac{q \Leftrightarrow p}{\diamondminus p \Leftrightarrow \diamondminus q}$$

Theorem T33 $\diamondminus$ IS DISJUNCTIVE

$$\diamondminus(p \vee q) \Leftrightarrow (\diamondminus p \vee \diamondminus q)$$

Rule $\diamondminus$T $\diamondminus$ IS TRANSITIVE

$$\frac{p \Rightarrow \diamondminus q \ , \ q \Rightarrow \diamondminus r}{p \Rightarrow \diamondminus r}$$

Rule $\diamondminus$C $\diamondminus$ IS CONFLUENT

$$\frac{p \Rightarrow \diamondminus(q \vee r) \ , \ q \Rightarrow \diamondminus s \ , \ r \Rightarrow \diamondminus s}{p \Rightarrow \diamondminus s}$$

Theorem T34

$$\diamondminus p \Leftrightarrow p \vee \ominus(\diamondminus p)$$

Rule $\diamondminus$I $\diamondminus$ INTRODUCTION

$$\frac{p \vee \ominus q \Rightarrow q}{\diamondminus p \Rightarrow q}$$

Theorem **T34** and the $\diamondminus$**I** rule identify $\diamondminus p$ as the *minimal* solution of the following equation for X

$$[p \vee \ominus X \Rightarrow X] \tag{5}$$

6.4 Theorems about U

In this section we consider theorems governing the behavior of the *unless* operator U. First, we establish the monotonicity of U with respect to both arguments.

Rule UI U INTRODUCTION

$$\frac{r \Rightarrow [q \vee (p \wedge \boxcircle r)]}{r \Rightarrow (p \mathsf{U} q)}$$

Proof: Define $\varphi : r \wedge \neg(p\,\mathcal{U}\,q)$

1.	$\varphi \Rightarrow [q \vee (p \wedge \bigcirc r)]$	Premise
2.	$p\mathcal{U}q \Leftrightarrow q \vee [p \wedge \bigcirc (p\mathcal{U}q)]$	**F6**
3.	$\neg(p\mathcal{U}q) \Rightarrow \neg q \wedge [\neg p \vee \bigcirc \neg(p\mathcal{U}q)]$	**GPR**, definition of $\bigcirc$
4.	$\varphi \Rightarrow \neg q \wedge [\neg p \vee \bigcirc \neg(p\mathcal{U}q)]$	Definition of φ, **F1, GPR**
5.	$\varphi \Rightarrow p \wedge \bigcirc r \wedge \bigcirc \neg(p\mathcal{U}q)$	**GPR** 1,4
6.	$\varphi \Rightarrow p \wedge \bigcirc [r \wedge \neg(p\mathcal{U}q)$	**T1**
7.	$[r \wedge \neg(p\mathcal{U}q)] \Rightarrow p \wedge \bigcirc [r \wedge \neg(p\mathcal{U}q)]$	definition of φ
8.	$r \wedge \neg(p\mathcal{U}q) \Rightarrow \Box p$	$\Box$**I**
9.	$r \wedge \neg(p\mathcal{U}q) \Rightarrow p\mathcal{U}q$	**F7**
10.	$r \wedge \neg(p\mathcal{U}q) \Rightarrow \mathrm{F}$	**GPR**
11.	$r \Rightarrow p\mathcal{U}q$	**GPR**

Axiom **F6** and the **UI** rule identify $p\mathcal{U}q$ as the *maximal* solution of the following equation for X

$$X \Rightarrow [q \vee (p \wedge \bigcirc X)] \tag{6}$$

Axiom **F6** shows that $p\mathcal{U}q$ satisfies the entailment (6) when substituted for X. The **UI** rule shows that any other solution r of the entailment must be smaller than $p\mathcal{U}q$.

Rule UM U IS MONOTONIC

(a) $$\frac{p \Rightarrow p' \qquad q \Rightarrow q'}{p\mathcal{U}q \Rightarrow p'\mathcal{U}'q}$$ (b) $$\frac{p \Leftrightarrow p' \qquad q \Leftrightarrow q'}{p\mathcal{U}q \Leftrightarrow p'\mathcal{U}q'}$$

Proof:

(a)

1. $p \Rightarrow p'$ — Premise.
2. $q \Rightarrow q'$ — Premise.
3. $p\mathcal{U}q \Rightarrow [q \vee (p \wedge \bigcirc (p\mathcal{U}q))]$ — **F6**
4. $p\mathcal{U}q \Rightarrow [q' \vee (p' \wedge \bigcirc (p\mathcal{U}q))]$ — **GPR** 3, 2, 1
5. $p\mathcal{U}q \Rightarrow p'\mathcal{U}'q$ — **UI**

(b) From (a) and **R2**.

Theorem T35

$$\Box((\neg p)\,\mathcal{U}\,p)$$

Proof:

1. $\Box \mathrm{T}$ — **INS**
2. $\Box \bigcirc \mathrm{T}$ — $\bigcirc$**G**
3. $p \Leftrightarrow (p \wedge \bigcirc \mathrm{T})$ — **GPR**
4. $\mathrm{T} \Rightarrow [\neg p \vee (p \wedge \bigcirc \mathrm{T})]$ — **GPR**
5. $\Box((\neg p)\,\mathcal{U}\,p$ — **UI**

The following theorem shows that U is conjunctive in its first argument.

Theorem T36

$$(p \wedge q)\,\mathsf{U} r \Leftrightarrow (p\,\mathsf{U} r) \wedge (q\,\mathsf{U} r)$$

Proof:

1. $(p \wedge q) \Rightarrow p$ **INS**
2. $(p \wedge q)\,\mathsf{U} r \Rightarrow p\,\mathsf{U} r$ **UM**
3. $(p \wedge q)\,\mathsf{U} r \Rightarrow q\,\mathsf{U} r$ Similarly
4. $(p \wedge q)\,\mathsf{U} r \Rightarrow (p\,\mathsf{U} r) \wedge (q\,\mathsf{U} r)$ **GPR** 2,3
5. $p\,\mathsf{U} r \Rightarrow [r \vee (p \wedge \bigcirc(p\,\mathsf{U} r))]$ **F6**
6. $q\,\mathsf{U} r \Rightarrow [r \vee (q \wedge \bigcirc(q\,\mathsf{U} r))]$ **F6**
7. $(p\,\mathsf{U} r) \wedge (q\,\mathsf{U} r) \Rightarrow \{r \vee [(p \wedge q) \wedge \bigcirc(p\,\mathsf{U} r \wedge q\,\mathsf{U} r)]\}$ **GPR** 5,6
8. $(p\,\mathsf{U} r) \wedge (q\,\mathsf{U} r) \Rightarrow (p \wedge q)\,\mathsf{U} r$ **UI**
9. $(p \wedge q)\,\mathsf{U} r \Leftrightarrow (p\,\mathsf{U} r) \wedge (q\,\mathsf{U} r)$ **GPR** 4, 8

The following theorem shows that U is disjunctive in its second argument.

Theorem T37

$$p\,\mathsf{U}(q \vee r) \Leftrightarrow (p\,\mathsf{U} q) \vee (p\,\mathsf{U} r)$$

Proof:

1. $q \Rightarrow (q \vee r)$ **INS**
2. $p\,\mathsf{U} q \Rightarrow p\,\mathsf{U}(q \vee r)$ **UM**
3. $p\,\mathsf{U} r \Rightarrow p\,\mathsf{U}(q \vee r)$ Similarly
4. $(p\,\mathsf{U} q \vee p\,\mathsf{U} r) \Rightarrow p\,\mathsf{U}(q \vee r)$ **GPR** 2,3
5. $p\,\mathsf{U}(q \vee r) \Rightarrow \{(q \vee r) \vee [p \wedge \bigcirc(p\,\mathsf{U}(q \vee r))]\}$ **F6**
6. $p\,\mathsf{U} q \Leftrightarrow \{q \vee [p \wedge \bigcirc(p\,\mathsf{U} q)]\}$ **F6**
7. $\neg(p\,\mathsf{U} q) \Leftrightarrow \{\neg q \wedge [\neg p \vee \neg\bigcirc(p\,\mathsf{U} q)]\}$ **GPR**
8. $\neg(p\,\mathsf{U} q) \Rightarrow \{\neg q \wedge [\neg p \vee \bigcirc\neg(p\,\mathsf{U} q)]\}$ **GPR, $\bigcirc$D$\bigcirc$**
9. $\neg(p\,\mathsf{U} q) \Rightarrow \{\neg q \wedge [\neg p \vee \bigcirc\neg(p\,\mathsf{U} q)]\}$ **GPR, F1**
10. $[p\,\mathsf{U}(q \vee r) \wedge \neg(p\,\mathsf{U} q)] \Rightarrow \{r \vee [p \wedge \bigcirc(p\,\mathsf{U}(q \vee r)) \wedge \bigcirc\neg(p\,\mathsf{U} q)]\}$ **GPR** 5, 9
11. $[p\,\mathsf{U}(q \vee r) \wedge \neg(p\,\mathsf{U} q)] \Rightarrow \{r \vee [p \wedge \bigcirc(p\,\mathsf{U}(q \vee r)) \wedge \bigcirc\neg(p\,\mathsf{U} q))]\}$ **T1, GPR**
12. $[p\,\mathsf{U}(q \vee r) \wedge \neg(p\,\mathsf{U} q)] \Rightarrow p\,\mathsf{U} r$ **UI**
13. $p\,\mathsf{U}(q \vee r) \Rightarrow (p\,\mathsf{U} q \vee p\,\mathsf{U} r)$ **GPR**
14. $p\,\mathsf{U}(q \vee r) \Leftrightarrow (p\,\mathsf{U} q) \vee (p\,\mathsf{U} r)$ **GPR** 4, 13

The following two theorems display some idempotence properties of the U operator, meaning that if we apply it twice, we get back the original formula. Obviously, since the U operator has two arguments we can perform a double application in either of them.

Theorem T38

$$(p\,\mathsf{U} q)\,\mathsf{U} q \Leftrightarrow p\,\mathsf{U} q$$

Proof:

1. $(p\,\mathsf{U} q)\,\mathsf{U} q \Rightarrow [q \vee (p\,\mathsf{U} q \wedge \bigcirc((p\,\mathsf{U} q)\,\mathsf{U} q))]$ **F6**
2. $(p\,\mathsf{U} q)\,\mathsf{U} q \Rightarrow [q \vee p\,\mathsf{U} q]$ **GPR**
3. $q \Rightarrow p\,\mathsf{U} q$ **F6, GPR**

4. $(p\,\mathcal{U}\,q)\,\mathcal{U}\,q \Rightarrow p\,\mathcal{U}\,q$ **GPR 2, 3**
5. $p\,\mathcal{U}\,q \Rightarrow (q \vee \bigcirc(p \wedge \bigcirc(p\,\mathcal{U}\,q)))$ **F6**
6. $p\,\mathcal{U}\,q \Rightarrow (q \vee \bigcirc(p\,\mathcal{U}\,q \wedge \bigcirc(p\,\mathcal{U}\,q)))$ **GPR**
7. $p\,\mathcal{U}\,q \Rightarrow (p\,\mathcal{U}\,q)\,\mathcal{U}\,q$ **GPR**
8. $(p\,\mathcal{U}\,q)\,\mathcal{U}\,q \Leftrightarrow p\,\mathcal{U}\,q$ **GPR 4, 7**

Theorem T39

$$p\,\mathcal{U}\,(p\,\mathcal{U}\,q) \Leftrightarrow p\,\mathcal{U}\,q$$

Proof:

1. $q \Rightarrow p\,\mathcal{U}\,q$ **F6, GPR**
2. $p\,\mathcal{U}\,q \Rightarrow p\,\mathcal{U}\,(p\,\mathcal{U}\,q)$ **UM**
3. $p\,\mathcal{U}\,(p\,\mathcal{U}\,q) \Rightarrow [p\,\mathcal{U}\,q \vee [p \vee \bigcirc(p\,\mathcal{U}\,(p\,\mathcal{U}\,q))]]$ **F6**
4. $p\,\mathcal{U}\,(p\,\mathcal{U}\,q) \Rightarrow \{q \vee [p \wedge \bigcirc(p\,\mathcal{U}\,q)] \vee [p \wedge \bigcirc(p\,\mathcal{U}\,(p\,\mathcal{U}\,q))]\}$ **F6, GPR**
5. $p\,\mathcal{U}\,(p\,\mathcal{U}\,q) \Rightarrow \{q \vee [p \wedge \bigcirc(p\,\mathcal{U}\,q \vee p\,\mathcal{U}\,(p\,\mathcal{U}\,q))]\}$ **T1, GPR**
6. $[p\,\mathcal{U}\,q \vee p\,\mathcal{U}\,(p\,\mathcal{U}\,q)] \Rightarrow p\,\mathcal{U}\,(p\,\mathcal{U}\,q)$ **GPR 2**
7. $p\,\mathcal{U}\,(p\,\mathcal{U}\,q) \Rightarrow \{q \vee [p \wedge \bigcirc(p\,\mathcal{U}\,(p\,\mathcal{U}\,q))]\}$ **$\bigcirc$M, GPR 6, 5**
8. $p\,\mathcal{U}\,(p\,\mathcal{U}\,q) \Rightarrow p\,\mathcal{U}\,q$ **UI**
9. $p\,\mathcal{U}\,(p\,\mathcal{U}\,q) \Leftrightarrow p\,\mathcal{U}\,q$ **GPR 2, 8**

The following rule establishes transitivity of $\mathcal{U}$.

Rule UT $\mathcal{U}$ IS TRANSITIVE

$$\frac{p \Rightarrow q\,\mathcal{U}\,r\ ,\ r \Rightarrow q\,\mathcal{U}\,t}{p \Rightarrow q\,\mathcal{U}\,t}$$

Proof:

1. $p \Rightarrow q\,\mathcal{U}\,r$ Premise.
2. $r \Rightarrow q\,\mathcal{U}\,t$ Premise.
3. $p \Rightarrow q\,\mathcal{U}\,(q\,\mathcal{U}\,t)$ **UM 1, 2**
4. $p \Rightarrow q\,\mathcal{U}\,t$ **T39**

We list below several additional theorems concerning the $\mathcal{U}$ operator without proofs. They appear together with their proofs in a form that uses implication instead of entailment in [MP83c]. The changes from the implication proofs to entailment proofs is very uniform, and has been amply demonstrated above.

Theorem T40

$$[p\,\mathcal{U}\,q \wedge (\neg q)\,\mathcal{U}\,r] \Rightarrow p\,\mathcal{U}\,r$$

The following two theorems are referred to as *collapsing* theorems, since they collapse a nested unless formula into an unnested one, at the cost of losing some sequencing information.

Theorem T41

$$(p\,\mathcal{U}\,q)\,\mathcal{U}\,r \Rightarrow (p \vee q)\,\mathcal{U}\,r$$

Theorem T42

$$p\,\mathsf{U}(q\,\mathsf{U}r) \Rightarrow (p \vee q)\,\mathsf{U}r$$

The following theorem establishes in some sense the linearity of time. It states that for every two events, p and q, either p weakly precedes q, or q weakly precedes p. Weak precedence of p before q, for example, means that *if* q happens, then p must occur before it or simultaneously with it. If q does not happen, then there is no obligation concerning p. This weak precedence is expressed by the formula $(\neg q)\,\mathsf{U}p$, meaning that q will not happen unless p happened before or together with it.

Theorem T43

$$\Box[(\neg p)\,\mathsf{U}q \vee (\neg q)\,\mathsf{U}p]$$

6.5 Theorems about S

In this section we consider theorems governing the behavior of the *Weak Since* operator S. First, we derive some auxiliary theroems leading to the past analogue of axiom **F7**.

The first theorem states that form any position it is possible to go back to the start point of the sequence.

Theorem T43 The Start Point is reachable

$$\Box \diamondminus \ominus \mathrm{F}$$

Proof:

1.	$\diamondminus \ominus \mathrm{F} \Rightarrow \bigcirc \widetilde{\ominus} \diamondminus \ominus \mathrm{F}$	**P8**
2.	$\widetilde{\ominus} \diamondminus \ominus \mathrm{F} \Rightarrow \diamondminus \ominus \mathrm{F}$	**T34, GPR**
3.	$\bigcirc \widetilde{\ominus} \diamondminus \ominus \mathrm{F} \Rightarrow \bigcirc \diamondminus \ominus \mathrm{F}$	**$\bigcirc$M**
4.	$\diamondminus \ominus \mathrm{F} \Rightarrow \bigcirc \diamondminus \ominus \mathrm{F}$	**GPR** 1,3
5.	$\diamondminus \ominus \mathrm{F} \Rightarrow \Box \diamondminus \ominus \mathrm{F}$	**CI**
6.	$\diamondminus \ominus \mathrm{F} \rightarrow \Box \diamondminus \ominus \mathrm{F}$	**PAR**
7.	$\ominus \mathrm{F} \Rightarrow \diamondminus \ominus \mathrm{F}$	**T34, GPR**
8.	$\ominus \mathrm{F} \rightarrow \diamondminus \ominus \mathrm{F}$	**PAR**
9.	$\ominus \mathrm{F}$	**P7**
10.	$\diamondminus \ominus \mathrm{F}$	**MP** 8,9
11.	$\Box \diamondminus \ominus \mathrm{F}$	**MP** 6,10

∎

The next theorem provides the past analogue of **F7**.

Theorem T44

$$\boxminus p \Rightarrow p\,\mathsf{S}q$$

Proof: Define $\varphi : \boxminus p \wedge \neg(p\,\mathsf{S}q)$

1.	$\varphi \Rightarrow p \wedge \ominus \boxminus p$	**T24,GPR**
2.	$\varphi \Rightarrow \neg[q \vee (p \wedge \ominus(p\,\mathsf{S}q))]$	**P6**
3.	$\varphi \Rightarrow [\neg q \wedge (\neg p \vee \widetilde{\ominus}\neg(p\,\mathsf{S}q))]$	**GPR** definition of $\widetilde{\ominus}$

4.	$\varphi \Rightarrow [p \wedge \widetilde{\ominus} \boxminus p \wedge \ominus \neg(p\mathsf{S}q)]$	**GPR 1,3**
5.	$\varphi \Rightarrow [\widetilde{\ominus} \boxminus p \wedge \ominus \neg(p\mathsf{S}q)]$	**GPR**
6.	$\varphi \Rightarrow [\widetilde{\ominus} \boxminus p \wedge \widetilde{\ominus} \neg(p\mathsf{S}q)]$	**P1**
7.	$\varphi \Rightarrow \widetilde{\ominus} \varphi$	**T18** definition of φ
8.	$\varphi \Rightarrow \boxminus \varphi$	**RI**
9.	$\varphi \Rightarrow \ominus \neg(p\mathsf{S}q)$	**GPR 4**
10.	$\neg(p\mathsf{S}q) \Rightarrow \mathrm{T}$	**INS**
11.	$\ominus \neg(p\mathsf{S}q) \Rightarrow \ominus \mathrm{T}$	**$\ominus$M**
12.	$\varphi \Rightarrow \ominus \mathrm{T}$	**GPR 9,11**
13.	$\boxminus \varphi \Rightarrow \boxminus \ominus \mathrm{T}$	**$\boxminus$M**
14.	$\varphi \Rightarrow \boxminus \ominus \mathrm{T}$	**GPR 8,13**
15.	$\diamondminus \widetilde{\ominus} \mathrm{F} \Rightarrow (\varphi \rightarrow \diamondminus \widetilde{\ominus} \mathrm{F})$	**INS**
16.	$\Box \diamondminus \widetilde{\ominus} \mathrm{F}$	**T43**
17.	$\Box(\varphi \rightarrow \diamondminus \widetilde{\ominus} \mathrm{F})$	**GMP 15,16**
18.	$\varphi \Rightarrow \diamondminus \widetilde{\ominus} \mathrm{F}$	Definition of $\Rightarrow$
19.	$\varphi \Rightarrow (\boxminus \ominus \mathrm{T} \wedge \diamondminus \widetilde{\ominus} \mathrm{F})$	**GPR 14,18**
20.	$\varphi \Rightarrow \mathrm{F}$	**GPR** definitions of $\ominus$, $\diamondminus$ and monotonicity
21.	$\Box(\varphi \rightarrow \mathrm{F})$	Definition of $\Rightarrow$
22.	$\Box(\boxminus p \wedge \neg(p\mathsf{S}q) \rightarrow \mathrm{F})$	definition of φ
23.	$\Box(\boxminus p \rightarrow (p\mathsf{S}q)$	**GPR,$\Box$M**
24.	$\boxminus p \Rightarrow p\mathsf{S}q$	Definition of $\Rightarrow$

∎

Now that we have brought the past part to a symmetric situation to the future part, we may prove the other S theorems similarly to the proofs of the corresponding U theorems.

Rule SI S INTRODUCTION

$$\frac{r \Rightarrow [q \vee (p \wedge \widetilde{\ominus} r)]}{r \Rightarrow (p\mathsf{S}q)}$$

Rule SM S IS MONOTONIC

$$\text{(a)} \quad \frac{\begin{array}{c} p \Rightarrow p' \\ q \Rightarrow q' \end{array}}{p\mathsf{S}q \Rightarrow p'\mathsf{S}'q} \qquad \text{(b)} \quad \frac{\begin{array}{c} p \Leftrightarrow p' \\ q \Leftrightarrow q' \end{array}}{p\mathsf{S}q \Leftrightarrow p'\mathsf{S}q'}$$

Theorem T45

$$\Box((\neg p)\mathsf{S}p)$$

Theorem T46

$$(p \wedge q)\mathsf{S}r \Leftrightarrow (p\mathsf{S}r) \wedge (q\mathsf{S}r)$$

Theorem T47

$$p\mathsf{S}(q \vee r) \Leftrightarrow (p\mathsf{S}q) \vee (p\mathsf{S}r)$$

Theorem T48

$$(p\mathsf{S}q)\mathsf{S}q \Leftrightarrow p\mathsf{S}q$$

Theorem T49

$$p\mathsf{S}(p\mathsf{S}q) \Leftrightarrow p\mathsf{S}q$$

Rule ST S IS TRANSITIVE

$$\frac{p \Rightarrow q\,\mathcal{S}\,r\ ,\ r \Rightarrow q\,\mathcal{S}\,t}{p \Rightarrow q\,\mathcal{S}\,t}$$

Theorem T50

$$[p\,\mathcal{S}\,q \wedge (\neg q)\,\mathcal{S}\,r] \Rightarrow p\,\mathcal{S}\,r$$

Theorem T51

$$(p\,\mathcal{S}\,q)\,\mathcal{S}\,r \Rightarrow (p \vee q)\,\mathcal{S}\,r$$

Theorem T52

$$p\,\mathcal{S}(q\,\mathcal{S}\,r) \Rightarrow (p \vee q)\,\mathcal{S}\,r$$

Theorem T53

$$\Box[(\neg p)\,\mathcal{S}\,q \vee (\neg q)\,\mathcal{S}\,p]$$

6.6 Completeness and Connections with [LPZ]

In [LPZ85], we presented a proof system for the full temporal logic, including the past operators. Naturally, the version presented there is the *floating* version, for which validity of a formula p is defined by requiring that p holds at *all* positions of all sequences. In order to compare the two approaches, we denote the floating validity by $\models^{fl}$. Denoting the anchored validity used in this paper by $\models$, we observe the following relations holding between the two notions of validity:

$$\begin{array}{lcl} \models p & \longleftrightarrow & \models^{fl} (\widetilde{\ominus}\,\mathrm{F} \rightarrow p) \\ \models^{fl} p & \longleftrightarrow & \models \Box p \end{array}$$

Thus, the two notions can be reduced to one another, and it is only a question of convenience, but not of expressibility, which one we prefer to use.

For completeness, we repeat below the proof system of [LPZ85]. We denote provability according to this proof system by $\vdash^{fl}$.

Axioms

	Past Axioms		Future Axioms
FP1.	$\neg\ominus p \equiv \widetilde{\ominus}\neg p$	FF1.	$\neg\bigcirc p \equiv \widetilde{\bigcirc}\neg p$
FP2.	$\ominus p \rightarrow \widetilde{\ominus} p$	FF2.	$\bigcirc p \rightarrow \widetilde{\bigcirc} p$
FP3.	$p \rightarrow \widetilde{\ominus}\bigcirc p$	FF3.	$p \rightarrow \widetilde{\bigcirc}\ominus p$
FP4.	$\widetilde{\ominus}(p \rightarrow q) \rightarrow (\widetilde{\ominus} p \rightarrow \widetilde{\ominus} q)$	FF4.	$\widetilde{\bigcirc}(p \rightarrow q) \rightarrow (\widetilde{\bigcirc} p \rightarrow \widetilde{\bigcirc} q)$
FP5.	$\neg\diamondminus p \equiv \boxminus\neg p$	FF5.	$\neg\Diamond p \equiv \Box\neg p$
FP6.	$\boxminus(p \rightarrow q) \rightarrow (\boxminus p \rightarrow \boxminus q)$	FF6.	$\Box(p \rightarrow q) \rightarrow (\Box p \rightarrow \Box q)$
FP7.	$\boxminus p \rightarrow \widetilde{\ominus} p$	FF7.	$\Box p \rightarrow \widetilde{\bigcirc} p$
FP8.	$\boxminus(p \rightarrow \widetilde{\ominus} p) \rightarrow (p \rightarrow \boxminus p)$	FF8.	$\Box(p \rightarrow \widetilde{\bigcirc} p) \rightarrow (p \rightarrow \Box p)$
FP9.	$p\,\mathcal{S}\,q \equiv q \vee [p \wedge \ominus(p\,\mathcal{S}\,q)]$	FF9.	$p\,\mathcal{U}\,q \equiv q \vee [p \wedge \bigcirc(p \ominus q)]$
FP10.	$\diamondminus\widetilde{\ominus}\,\mathrm{F}$	FF10.	$p\,\mathcal{U}\,q \rightarrow \Diamond q$

Inference Rules

R1. For each p, a temporal instantiation of a propositional tautology, $\vdash^{fl} p$.

R2. If $\vdash^{fl} p \rightarrow q$ and $\vdash^{fl} p$ then $\vdash^{fl} q$ (Modus Ponence).

R3. If $\vdash^{fl} p$ then both $\vdash^{fl} \boxminus p$ and $\vdash^{fl} \Box p$.

Following the presentation of the floating proof system, [LPZ85] proves its completeness. This shows that if $\models^{fl} p$ then $\vdash^{fl} p$. We can follow the same ideas, with very little changes, to prove the completeness of the anchored proof system we have presented here.

Instead, we will reduce the completeness problem of the anchored system to that of the floating system. This will also demonstrate the relations between the two.

Proposition 6.1 *For every temporal formula p, if* $\vdash^{fl} p$ *then* $\vdash \Box p$.

the proposition claims that whenever p is provable in the floating proof system, then $\Box p$ is provable in the anchored system.

To prove this proposition, it is sufficient to show for each axiom p of the floating system, that $\Box p$ is provable in the anchored system, and for each rule $p_1, ..., p_n \vdash^{fl} q$ of the floating system, that the rule $\Box p_1, ..., \Box p_n \vdash \Box q$ is provable in the anchored system. For most of the axioms, we have already proven $\Box p$ as one of our theorems above. It is not difficult to prove it for the reamining ones. The situation is similar for the rules. For example, for R2 we have to prove $\Box(p \to q), \Box p \vdash \Box q$, which is precisely our **GMP** rule.

Using this proposition and the observations above, we can prove immediately the completeness of the anchored proof system presented in this paper.

Proposition 6.2 Completeness: *The anchored proof system presented here is complete for the propositional fragment of temporal logic.*

Proof:

Assume that $\models p$. By the observation above, it follows that $\models^{fl} \circleddash \mathrm{F} \to p$. By the completeness of the floating proof system it follows that $\vdash^{fl} \circleddash \mathrm{F} \to p$. By the proposition above $\vdash \Box \circleddash \mathrm{F} \to p$. Using the **PAR** rule, we can infer $\vdash \circleddash(\mathrm{F} \to p)$. By **P7** and **MP** we can infer $\vdash p$. ┛

7 The Program Part

In this section we present the program part of the proof system.

In principle, we should provide a separate proof rule for each of the property classes in our hierarchy. In practice, we concentrate on three particular classes, which have special significance as expressing most of the interesting program properties, and forming a natural generalization of the two classes of invariance and eventuality properties considered in the previous proof systems. These are the classes of:

- *Safety* Properties. These are all the properties which can be expressed by a temporal formula of the form

$$\Box q$$

for some *past* formula q.

- *Response (Recurrence)* Properties. These are all the properties which can be expressed by a temporal formula of the form

$$\Box(p \to \Diamond q), \text{ or alternately, } \Box\Diamond q$$

for some *past* formulae p, and q. Note that we use the names *response* and *recurrence* synonymously.

- *Progress* Properties. These are all the properties which can be expressed by a temporal formula of the form

$$\Box\Diamond p \rightarrow \Box\Diamond q$$

for some *past* formulae p, and q.

We provide complete rules for each of these classes. This provides full coverage for the complete temporal logic, since by [LPZ85] (see also [Tho81]), any temporal formula φ is equivalent to a conjunction of progress properties. Therefore, to prove the $\mathcal{P}$-validity of φ, it is sufficient to prove the $\mathcal{P}$-validity of each of the conjuncts, for which we can use the rule for progress properties.

7.1 Rules for Safety

In this section we consider proof rules for establishing the $\mathcal{P}$-validity of a safety formula. As we recall, a safety formula has the form $\Box p$ for some past formula p. Let us review first the appropriate rule given in [MP83a] for the simpler case that p is a state-formula.

For a transition τ, and state-formulae p, and q, we define the *verification condition* of τ, relative to p and q, to be the implication:

$$\rho_\tau \wedge p \rightarrow q',$$

where ρ_τ is the transition assertion corresponding to τ, and q', the *primed version* of the assertion q, is obtained from q by replacing each variable occurring in q by its primed version. We denote this verification condition by $\{p\}\tau\{q\}$. Since ρ_τ holds for two states s and s' iff s' is a τ-successor of s, and q' states that q holds on s', it is not difficult to see that

> If the verification condition $\{p\}\tau\{q\}$ is valid, then every τ-successor of a p-state is a q-state.

For a set of transitions $T \subseteq \mathcal{T}$, we denote by $\{p\}T\{q\}$ the verification condition requiring that $\{p\}\tau\{q\}$ holds for each $\tau \in T$. Let us denote by $\mathcal{T}_P$ the set of transitions for the program P. Then the following rule is sound and complete for establishing the P-validity of the invariance formula $\Box q$ for a state formula q.

Rule INV INVARIANCE OF STATE FORMULAE

$$\begin{array}{ll} \text{I1.} & \Theta \rightarrow \varphi \\ \text{I2.} & \varphi \rightarrow q \\ \text{I3.} & \{\varphi\}\mathcal{T}_P\{\varphi\} \\ \hline & \Box q \end{array}$$

This rule uses an auxiliary assertion φ which, by premise I1 holds initially, and by premise I3 is propagated form each state to its successor. This shows that φ holds continuously over all computations of P. Since, by I2 φ implies q, it follows that q is also an invariant of the program.

Generalizing to Past Formulae

Next, we have to extend the **INV** rule to deal with formulae q, which are past formula. First, we extend the notion of the primed version of a formula, to apply also to a past formula. Recall that the intended meaning of a primed formula is express the value of a formula in the next state, in terms of the values of the variables in the next state and in terms of values in the current state. This is inductively defined as follows:

- For a state formula $p(\bar{u})$, we define as before
$$(p(\bar{u}))' = p(\bar{u}')$$
- For a *Previous* formula
$$(\circleddash p)' = p$$
This corresponds to our intuition that $\circleddash p$ holds in the next state iff p holds now.
- For a *Since* formula
$$(p\,\mathcal{S}\,q)' = q' \vee ((p\,\mathcal{S}\,q) \wedge p')$$
This corresponds to the intuition that $p\,\mathcal{S}\,q$ holds in the next state if, either q holds there, or $p\,\mathcal{S}\,q$ holds now and p holds next.

With this definition, we extend the notion of the verification condition $\{p\}\tau\{q\}$ to apply also to past formulae p and q, and mean
$$\rho_\tau \wedge p \Rightarrow q'$$
Note that since we work with temporal formulae, we replaced the previous implication by an entailment, because we expect the implication to hold at *all* positions of the computation, not only at the first one.

With this extension, the general single rule for establishing safety properties is given by

Rule SAFE PROVING SAFETY

$$\begin{array}{ll} \text{I1.} & \Theta \wedge \textbf{first} \rightarrow \varphi \\ \text{I2.} & \varphi \Rightarrow q \\ \text{I3.} & \{\varphi\}\mathcal{T}_P\{\varphi\} \\ \hline & \Box q \end{array}$$

In this rule, we replaced the implication in I2 by an entailment. In I1 we also added the conjunct **first** which is an abbreviation for the formula $\circleddash$F, characterizing the first position in the computation as the only position that has no predecessor. This conjunct is sometimes necessary to ensure that φ holds in the first position.

The premises I1 – I3 of the rule are temporal, i.e., each contains at least one temporal operator. How are these to be proven? We remind the reader of the **INS** rule, presented in the general part of the proof system, and recommend it as a general tool for deriving temporal validities from assertional ones. Let p be a state formula containing Q as a propositional symbol, and let φ be a temporal formula. We denote by $p[\varphi/Q]$ be the temporal formula obtained from p by replacing all occurrences of Q by φ. We repeat below the rule.

Rule INS TEMPORAL INSTANTIATION

$$\frac{\models_A p}{\Box p[\varphi/Q]}$$

Note, in particular, that if p has the form $t \rightarrow r$ then the temporal conclusion is an entailment of the form $t[\varphi/Q] \Rightarrow r[\varphi/Q]$.

Example 7.1 *Consider the trivial program with a single state variable x, the data precondition $x = 0$, and a single transition τ whose assertion is given by $\rho_\tau : x' = x + 1$. We wish to prove for this program the trivial safety property*

$$\Box((x = 10) \rightarrow \diamondminus(x = 5)).$$

This property claims that any state in which $x = 10$ must have been preceded by a state in which $x = 5$. Note that this trivial property would not be true for a program that advances in steps of 2, rather then steps of 1. To prove this property, we identify q as $(x = 10) \rightarrow \diamondminus(x = 5)$ and intend to use the **SAFE** rule. As the auxiliary formula φ, we take $(x \geq 5) \rightarrow \diamondminus(x = 5)$. The rule requires showing the following three premises:

I1. $(x = 0) \wedge \textbf{first} \Rightarrow ((x \geq 5) \rightarrow \diamondminus(x = 5))$

I2. $((x \geq 5) \rightarrow \diamondminus(x = 5)) \Rightarrow ((x = 10) \rightarrow \diamondminus(x = 5))$

I3. $(x' = x + 1) \wedge ((x \geq 5) \rightarrow \diamondminus(x = 5)) \Rightarrow ((x' \geq 5) \rightarrow (\diamondminus(x = 5) \vee (x' = 5)))$

In I3 we have already expanded $(\diamondminus(x = 5))$ into $(\diamondminus(x = 5) \vee (x' = 5))$. All of these apparently temporal formulae can be established by the **INS** rule, using the following three valid state formulae, and their associated instantiations.

S1. $(x = 0) \wedge p \rightarrow ((x \geq 5) \rightarrow r)$

with the replacement of $(\textbf{first}, \diamondminus(x = 5))$ for the proposition symbols (p, r), respectively.

S2. $((x \geq 5) \rightarrow p) \rightarrow ((x = 10) \rightarrow p)$

with the replacement of $\diamondminus(x = 5)$ for the proposition symbol p.

S3. $(x' = x + 1) \wedge ((x \geq 5) \rightarrow p) \rightarrow ((x' \geq 5) \rightarrow (p \vee (x' = 5)))$

with the replacement of $\diamondminus(x = 5)$ for the proposition symbol p.

The following theorem establishes that these two rules are adequate for proving all the safety properties.

Theorem 7.1 *The* **SAFE** *and the* **INS** *rules are complete for proving the $\mathcal{P}$-validity of any safety property, based on pure assertional reasoning.*

The proof of the theorem is based on the construction of a big past invariant which relates the values of variables in an accessible state (i.e., appearing in some computation of P) to the boolean values of the temporal sub-formulae of the past formula q, whose invariance we wish to establish. Details will be given in the full version of the paper.

Causality Formulae

Even though, in theory, the completeness theorem above fully settles the question of proving the validity of safety formulae, there is a practical interest in identifying special forms of safety formulae, for which a specific proof methodology exists. One of these subclasses contains the properties expressible by the *causality* formula

$$p \Rightarrow \diamondminus q$$

for state formulae p and q, which states that every p-state is necessarily preceded by a q-state.

To present a proof rule for causality properties, we define first the *inverse verification condition*, denoted by $\{p\}\tau^{-1}\{q\}$ and standing for the entailment

$$\rho_\tau \wedge p' \Rightarrow q$$

The validity of this condition ensures that any τ-predecessor of a p-state must be a q-state. The condition is extended to sets of transitions $T \subseteq \mathcal{T}$ in the usual way. Then, the following rule is adequate for proving causality properties.

Rule CAUS PROVING CAUSALITY PROPERTIES

$$\begin{array}{ll} \text{C1.} & p \rightarrow (\varphi \vee q) \\ \text{C2.} & \Theta \rightarrow \neg\varphi \\ \text{C3.} & \{\varphi\}\mathcal{T}_P^{-1}\{\varphi \vee q\} \\ \hline & p \Rightarrow \diamondminus q \end{array}$$

By premise C1, any state satisfying p, either already satisfies q, or satisfies the auxiliary state formula φ. By premise C3, the predecessor of any φ-state must satisfy $\varphi \vee q$. Thus, if we do not find a q preceding p, φ propagates all the way to the initial position. However, this contradicts premise C2, according to which the initial position cannot satisfy φ.

There are several advantages in using this rule, even for proving invariance properties $\Box p$. To prove such an invariance as a causality property, we reformulate it as $\neg p \Rightarrow \diamondminus \text{F}$, i.e., any instance of a $\neg p$ must be preceded by a contradiction.

Incremental Proofs

In the previous paragraphs, we have considered how to establish the invariance of some past formulae. Having established some basic invariants of this form, we may want to use them in order to derive more complex properties. For this purpose, we use the generalized Modus Ponens rule **GMP**, introduced in the general part of the proof system, which allows us, once we have established the invariance $\Box p$, to use p as an extra assumption.

Rule GMP GENERALIZED MODUS PONENS

$$\begin{array}{ll} \text{A1.} & p \Rightarrow q \\ \text{A2.} & \Box p \\ \hline & \Box q \end{array}$$

The premise A1 states that, having p as a constant assumption, we can prove q at all positions. Premise A2 guarantees that p is indeed an invariant of the program. Then from these two we infer that q holds at all states of the computations of the program P.

7.2 Rules for Response (Recurrence)

Response properties are those which can be expressed by a formula of the form

$$p \Rightarrow \Diamond q, \text{ or equivalently, } \Box(p \rightarrow \Diamond q)$$

for some past formulae p and q. Now that we have learned, in the previous section, how to generalize rules having assertional premises into rules with temporal premises involving past formulae, it is straightforward to properly adapt the set of rules from [MP83a]. The rules for establishing response properties can be partitioned into *single step* rules and *extended* rules. We consider each group in turn.

Single Step Response Rules

These are the rules that establish properties which depend on the execution of a single helpful transition (or one of several candidates) to accomplish the guaranteed response q. We have three rules in this group, which differ by the type of *fairness* on which they rely.

The first rule is unconditional of any fairness assumption, and only relies on the fact that as long as there are enabled transitions, some transition will eventually be taken.

Rule B-RESP BASIC RESPONSE RULE

$$\begin{array}{ll} \text{B1.} & p \Rightarrow (q \vee \varphi) \\ \text{B2.} & \{\varphi\}\mathcal{T}_P\{q\} \\ \text{B3.} & \varphi \Rightarrow En(\mathcal{T}_P) \\ \hline & p \Rightarrow \Diamond q \end{array}$$

The rule considers three past formulae p, q, and the auxiliary φ. Premise B1 requires that any p state, either already satisfies q, or satisfies φ. Premise B2 requires that taking any transition from a φ-state, must lead to a q-state. Premise B3 requires that at least one transition must be enabled on each φ-state. Clearly such a transition must be taken next, resulting in a q-state.

The next single step rule relies on weak fairness to ensure that eventually a helpful transition, leading to q will be taken. It assumes a weak fairness requirement $(E, T) \in \mathcal{W}$. We denote by $\overline{T}$ the complementary set of transitions, i.e., the transitions in $\mathcal{T}_P - T$.

Rule W-RESP RESPONSE UNDER WEAK FAIRNESS

$$\begin{array}{ll} \text{W1.} & p \Rightarrow (q \vee \varphi) \\ \text{W2.} & \{\varphi\}T\{q\} \\ \text{W3.} & \{\varphi\}\overline{T}\{q \vee \varphi\} \\ \text{W4.} & \varphi \Rightarrow En(E) \\ \hline & p \Rightarrow \Diamond q \end{array}$$

Premise W1 ensures, as before, that p entails q or φ. Premise W2 states that any transition in T leads from φ to q. Premise W3 states that any transition not in T, either leads from φ to q, or preserves φ. Premise W4 ensures that E is enabled as long as φ holds. It is not difficult to see that if p happens, but is not followed by a q, then φ must hold continuously beyond this point, and no transition of T is taken. However, due to W4, this means that E is continuously enabled yet no transition of T is ever taken, which violates the requirement of weak fairness for (E, T).

The last rule relies on a strong fairness requirement $(E,T) \in \mathcal{F}$.

Rule S-RESP RESPONSE UNDER STRONG FAIRNESS

$$\begin{array}{ll} \text{S1.} & p \Rightarrow (q \vee \varphi) \\ \text{S2.} & \{\varphi\} T \{q\} \\ \text{S3.} & \{\varphi\} \overline{T} \{q \vee \varphi\} \\ \text{S4.} & \varphi \Rightarrow \Diamond(q \vee En(E)) \\ \hline & p \Rightarrow \Diamond q \end{array}$$

The difference between this rule and its **W**-version is in the fourth premise. While W4 requires that φ entails $En(E)$ now, S4 requires the eventual enabling of E. Here an occurrence of p not followed by a q, leads, as before, to φ holding continuously, and no transition of T being taken. However, the weaker premise S4 guarantees that E is enabled infinitely many times, which suffices to violate the strong fairness requirement with respect to (E,T).

Rules for Extended Response

These rules combine single step response properties to form general response properties, which need more than a single helpful transition for their achievement.

First, we list two basic rules, which can be derived in the general part, and which express the monotonicity and transitivity of the response connective.

Rule RM THE RESPONSE CONNECTIVE IS MONOTONIC

$$\begin{array}{l} p \Rightarrow q \\ q \Rightarrow \Diamond r \\ r \Rightarrow t \\ \hline p \Rightarrow \Diamond t \end{array}$$

The next rule represents transitivity

Rule RT THE RESPONSE CONNECTIVE IS TRANSITIVE

$$\begin{array}{l} p \Rightarrow \Diamond q \\ q \Rightarrow \Diamond r \\ \hline p \Rightarrow \Diamond r \end{array}$$

The most important rule for establishing extended response properties is based on well founded induction. We assume a *well founded* relation $(\mathcal{A}, \prec)$, and a partial *ranking function* δ, mapping states into the domain $\mathcal{A}$. We denote the fact that δ is defined by $\delta \in \mathcal{A}$. The following rule uses well founded induction to establish an extended response property.

Rule WELL WELL FOUNDED RULE FOR RESPONSE

$$\begin{array}{ll} \text{L1.} & p \Rightarrow (q \vee \varphi) \\ \text{L2.} & \varphi \Rightarrow (\delta \in \mathcal{A}) \\ \text{L3.} & [\varphi \wedge (\delta = \alpha)] \Rightarrow \Diamond[q \vee (\varphi \wedge (\delta \prec \alpha))] \\ \hline & p \Rightarrow \Diamond q \end{array}$$

Premise L1 ensures that any state satisfying p must satisfy q or φ. Premise L2 ensures that δ is defined as long as φ holds. Premise L3 guarantees that if φ holds with a certain rank α, then eventually we will reach a state, in which either q holds, or φ is maintained but with a rank lower than α. Since a well founded ranking cannot go on decreasing forever, we must eventually reach a q-state.

The adequacy of this set of rules for establishing response properties is summarized in the following theorem.

Theorem 7.2 *The rules given above are complete for proving the $\mathcal{P}$-validity of any response property, based on pure assertional reasoning.*

7.3 Rules for Progress

In this section we deal with *progress* properties, which are the properties that can be expressed by a formula of the form

$$\Box\Diamond p \vee \Diamond\Box q,$$

for some past formulae p and q. There are several alternative forms in which every progress property can be recast. They are given by

$$\Box\Diamond r \rightarrow \Box\Diamond q, \text{ and } \Box\Diamond r \Rightarrow \Diamond q.$$

We prefer to work with an extended form of the last formula

$$p \wedge \Box\Diamond r \Rightarrow \Diamond q$$

This formula states that any occurrence of p, which is followed by infinitely many occurrences of r, must eventually be followed by a q.

Progress under Weak Fairness

If we work only under the assumption of weak fairness, that is, the family of strong fairness requirements happens to be empty, then we can base the proof of progress properties on some response properties and a well founded argument. This is given by the **W-PROG** rule.

Rule W-PROG PROGRESS UNDER WEAK FAIRNESS

$$\begin{array}{ll} \text{W1.} & p \Rightarrow (q \vee (\varphi \wedge (\delta \in \mathcal{A}))) \\ \text{W2.} & [\varphi \wedge (\delta = \alpha)] \Rightarrow [(\varphi \wedge (\delta \preceq \alpha)) \,\mathcal{U} q] \\ \text{W3.} & [r \wedge \varphi \wedge (\delta = \alpha)] \Rightarrow \Diamond[q \vee (\delta \prec \alpha)] \\ \hline & p \wedge \Box\Diamond r \Rightarrow \Diamond q \end{array}$$

This rule uses the $\mathcal{U}$ operator (*Unless*).

Premise W1 of the rule ensures that any position that satisfies p, either already satisfies q, or satisfies φ and has a defined rank. In the later case it initiates a gradual process evolving towards the eventual realization of q. Premise W2 ensures that, starting at a position satisfying φ and having a defined rank α, φ is continuously maintained and the rank never increases above α until q occurs, if ever. Premise W3 indicates that an additional occurrence of r, strengthens the non-increase, guaranteed by W2, into a decrease. Thus, if there are infinitely many occurrences of r then, either δ decreases infinitely often, which is impossible due to well foundedness, or q is eventually realized.

The adequacy of this rule is stated by the following proposition

Proposition 7.1 *For a program with no strong fairness requirements, the* **W-PROG** *rule is complete for proving the $\mathcal{P}$-validity of any progress property.*

Obviously, a progress property $p \wedge \Box\Diamond r \Rightarrow \Diamond q$ can be valid over a program due to the fact that the simpler response property $p \Rightarrow \Diamond q$ is valid. The proposition above essentially identifies the main mechanism, by which the occurrence of infinitely many r's can help a progress property to be realized. This mechanism is associated with a ranking function, which measures the distance away from the realization of q, such that each additional occurrence of r causes an eventual decrease in the rank.

Progress under Strong Fairness

When we have strong fairness requirements, a well founded decrease is not the only mechanism by which infinitely many occurrences of r can cause the program to progress from p to q. Another candidate mechanism is that we have a strong fairness requirement $(E, T) \in \mathcal{F}$, such that each transition in T leads from p to q, and each occurrence of r causes E to eventually become enabled (at least once). Consequently, the **W-PROG** is no longer adequate.

To cover the case of strong fairness, we present first a single step rule for progress under strong fairness. The rule concerns a strong fairness requirement $(E, T) \in \mathcal{F}$, and past formulae p, r, q, and φ.

Rule S-PROG PROGRESS UNDER STRONG FAIRNESS

$$\begin{array}{ll} \text{S1.} & p \Rightarrow (q \vee \varphi) \\ \text{S2.} & \{\varphi\} T \{q\} \\ \text{S3.} & \{\varphi\} \overline{T} \{q \vee \varphi\} \\ \text{S4.} & [\varphi \wedge \Box\Diamond(\varphi \wedge r)] \Rightarrow \Diamond(q \vee En(E)) \\ \hline & [p \wedge \Box\Diamond r] \Rightarrow \Diamond q \end{array}$$

This rule establishes one step progress, under the assumption of strong fairness for (E, T). This and other progress properties can now be combined, using several properties of the progress connective, such as monotonicity and transitivity. These are summarized below.

Rule PM THE PROGRESS CONNECTIVE IS MONOTONIC

$$\begin{array}{l} p' \Rightarrow p \\ r' \Rightarrow r \\ q \Rightarrow q' \\ [p \wedge \Box\Diamond r] \Rightarrow \Diamond q \\ \hline [p' \wedge \Box\Diamond r'] \Rightarrow \Diamond q' \end{array}$$

The next rule represents transitivity

Rule PT THE PROGRESS CONNECTIVE IS TRANSITIVE

$$\begin{array}{l} [p \wedge \Box\Diamond r] \Rightarrow \Diamond q \\ [q \wedge \Box\Diamond r] \Rightarrow \Diamond t \\ \hline [p \wedge \Box\Diamond r] \Rightarrow \Diamond t \end{array}$$

Finally, we have a well founded rule for combining together progress properties into an unbounded chain.

Rule WELL-PROG WELL FOUNDED RULE FOR PROGRESS

$$\frac{\begin{array}{ll} \text{L1.} & p \Rightarrow (q \vee \varphi) \\ \text{L2.} & \varphi \Rightarrow (\delta \in \mathcal{A}) \\ \text{L3.} & [\varphi \wedge (\delta = \alpha) \wedge \Box\Diamond r] \Rightarrow \Diamond[q \vee (\varphi \wedge (\delta \prec \alpha))] \end{array}}{[p \wedge \Box\Diamond r] \Rightarrow \Diamond q}$$

We summarize this more general case by the following proposition.

Proposition 7.2 *The rules given above are complete for proving the $\mathcal{P}$-validity of any progress property, based on pure assertional reasoning.*

Acknowledgement

We gratefully acknowledge the help rendered by Orna Lichtenstein and Ascher Wilk in the preparation of this manuscript. Special thanks are due to Roni Rosner for his dedicated technical help and most helpful suggestions.

References

[AL88] M. Abadi and L. Lamport, The existence of refinement mappings, *Proc. 3rd IEEE Symp. Logic in Comp. Sci.*, 1988, pp. 165–175.

[AS85] B. Alpern and F.B. Schneider, Defining liveness, *Info. Proc. Lett.* **21**, 1985.

[AS87] B. Alpern and F.B. Schneider, Recognizing safety and liveness, *Distributed Computing* **2**, 1987, pp. 117–126.

[AS89] B. Alpern and F.B. Schneider, Verifying temporal properties without temporal logic, *ACM Trans. Prog. Lang. Syst.* **11**, 1989.

[Bac80] R.J.R. Back, *Correctness preserving program refinements: Proof theory and applications*, Mathematical Center Tracts, 131, Center for Mathematics and Computer Science (CWI), Amsterdam, 1980.

[BK83] R.J.R Back and R. Kurki-Suonio, Decentralization of process nets with a centalized control, *Proc. 2nd ACM Symp. Princ. of Dist. Comp.*, 1983, pp. 131–142.

[BKP84] H. Barringer, R. Kuiper, and A Pnueli, Now you may compose temporal logic specifications, *Proc. 16th ACM Symp. Theory of Comp.*, 1984, pp. 51–63.

[BMP83] M. Ben-Ari, Z. Manna, and A Pnueli, The temporal logic of branching time, *Acta Informatica* **20**, 1983, pp. 207–226.

[CES86] E.M. Clarke, E.A. Emerson, and A.P. Sistla, Automatic verification of finite state concurrent systems using temporal logic specifications, *ACM Trans. Prog. Lang. Syst.* **8**, 1986, pp. 244–263.

[CM88] K.M. Chandy and J Misra, *Parallel Program Design*, Addison-Wesley, 1988.

[Dij76] E.W. Dijkstra, *A Discipline of Programming*, Prentice-Hall, New Jersey, 1976.

[dRZ87] W.P. de Roever and J. Zwiers, *Different Styles of Compositional and Modular Proof-systems for a CCS/CSP-like Language*, Technical Report, Philips Research, 1987.

[EH86] E.A. Emerson and J.Y. Halpern, 'Sometimes' and 'not never' revisited: On branching time versus linear time, *J. ACM* **33**, 1986, pp. 151–178.

[GPSS80] D. Gabbay, A. Pnueli, S. Shelah, and J. Stavi, On the temporal analysis of fairness, *Proc. 6th ACM Symp. Princ. of Prog. Lang.*, 1980, pp. 163–173.

[Gri81] D. Gries, *The Science of Programming*, Springer, New-York, 1981.

[Jon87] B. Jonsson, *Compositional Verification of Distributed Systems*, Ph.D. thesis, Uppsala University, Sweden, 1987.

[Kam68] J.A.W. Kamp, *Tense Logic and the Theory of Order*, Ph.D. thesis, UCLA, 1968.

[Kam85] M. Kaminski, A classification of $\omega-$regular languages, *Theor. Comp. Sci.* **36**, 1985, pp. 217–229.

[KdR83] R. Koymans and W.P. de Roever, Examples of a real-time temporal logic specifications, *The Analysis of Concurrent Systems*, Springer, 1983, pp. 231–252.

[KP87] S. Katz and D. Peled, *Interleaving Set Temporal Logic*, Technical Report 456, Dept. of Computer Science, Technion, Haifa, Israel, 1987.

[KVdR83] R. Koymans, J. Vytopyl, and W.P. de Roever, Real-time programming and asynchronous message passing, *Proc. 2nd ACM Symp. Princ. of Dist. Comp.*, 1983.

[Lam77] L. Lamport, Proving the correctness of multiprocess programs, *Trans. on Software Engineering* **1**, 1977.

[Lam83a] L. Lamport, Specifying concurrent program modules, *ACM Trans. Prog. Lang. Syst.* **5**, 1983, pp. 190–222.

[Lam83b] L. Lamport, What good is temporal logic, *Proc. IFIP Congress* (R.E.A. Mason, ed.), North-Holland, 1983, pp. 657–668.

[Lan69] L.H. Landweber, Decision problems for $\omega-$automata, *Mathematical Systems Theory* **4**, 1969, pp. 376–384.

[LP84] O. Lichtenstien and A. Pnueli, Checking that finite state concurrent programs satisfy their linear specification, *Proc. 10th ACM Symp. Princ. of Prog. Lang.*, 1984, pp. 97–107.

[LPZ85] O. Lichtenstien, A. Pnueli, and L. Zuck, The glory of the past, *Proc. Conf. Logics of Programs*, Lec. Notes in Comp. Sci. 193, Springer, 1985, pp. 196–218.

[Man74] Z. Manna, *Mathematical Theory of Computation*, McGraw-Hill, 1974.

[MP71] R. McNaughton and S. Papert, *Counter Free Automata*, MIT Press, 1971.

[MP83a] Z. Manna and A. Pnueli, How to cook a temporal proof system for your pet language, *Proc. 9th ACM Symp. Princ. of Prog. Lang.*, 1983, pp. 141–154.

[MP83b] Z. Manna and A. Pnueli, Proving precedence properties: the temporal way, *Proc. 10th Int. Colloq. Aut. Lang. Prog.*, Lec. Notes in Comp. Sci. 154, Springer, 1983, pp. 491–512.

[MP83c] Z. Manna and A. Pnueli, Verification of concurrent programs: A temporal proof system, *Foundations of Computer Science IV, Distributed Systems: Part 2* (J.W. De-Bakker and J. Van Leuwen, eds.), Mathematical Centre Tracts 159, Center for Mathematics and Computer Science (CWI), Amsterdam, 1983, pp. 163–255.

[MP84] Z. Manna and A. Pnueli, Adequate proof principles for invariance and liveness properties of concurrent programs, *Sci. Comp. Prog.* **32**, 1984, pp. 257–289.

[MP87] Z. Manna and A. Pnueli, Specification and verification of concurrent programs by $\forall$-automata, *Proc. 14th ACM Symp. Princ. of Prog. Lang.*, 1987, pp. 1–12.

[MW78] Z. Manna and R. Waldinger, Is 'sometime' sometimes better than 'always'?: intermittent assertions in proving program correctness, *Comm. ACM* **21**, 1978, pp. 159–172.

[NGO85] V. Nguyen, D. Gries, and S. Owicki, A model and temporal proof system for network of processes, *Proc. 12th ACM Symp. Princ. of Prog. Lang.*, 1985, pp. 121–131.

[OL82] S. Owicki and L. Lamport, Proving liveness properties of concurrent programs, *ACM Trans. Prog. Lang. Syst.* **4**, 1982, pp. 455–495.

[Pnu86] A. Pnueli, Applications of temporal logic to the specification and verification of reactive systems: A survey of current trends, *Current Trends in Concurrency*, Lec. Notes in Comp. Sci. 224, Springer, 1986, pp. 510–584.

[QS83] J.P. Queille and J. Sifakis, Fairness and related properties in transition systems — A temporal logic to deal with fairness, *Acta Informatica* **19**, 1983, pp. 195–220.

[Rab72] M.O. Rabin, *Automata on Infinite Objects and Churc's Problem*, Volume 13 of *Regional Conference Series in Mathematics*, Amer. Math. Soc., 1972.

[Rei85] W. Reisig, *Petri Nets: An Introduction*, Volume 4 of *EATCS Monographs on Theoretical Computer Science*, Springer, 1985.

[Sis85] A.P. Sistla, On caracterization of safety and liveness properties in temporal logic, *Proc. 4th ACM Symp. Princ. of Dist. Comp.*, 1985, pp. 39–48.

[Str82] R.S. Street, Propositional dynamic logic with converse, *Information and Control* **54**, 1982, pp. 121–141.

[Tho81] W. Thomas, A combinatorial approach to the theory of ω-automata, *Inf. and Cont.* **48**, 1981, pp. 261–283.

[VW86] M.Y. Vardi and P. Wolper, Automata theoretic techniques for modal logics of programs, *J. Comp. Sys. Sci.* **32**, 1986, pp. 183–221.

[Wag79] K. Wagner, On $\omega-$regular sets, *Information and Control* **43**, 1979, pp. 123–177.

[WGS87] J. Widom, D. Gries, and F.B. Schneider, Completeness and incompleteness of trace-based network proof system, *Proc. 14th ACM Symp. Princ. of Prog. Lang.*, 1987, pp. 27–38.

[Wol83] P. Wolper, Temporal logic can be more expressive, *Inf. and Cont.* **56**, 1983, pp. 72–99.

[Zuc86] L. Zuck, *Past Temporal Logic*, Ph.D. thesis, Weizmann Institute, 1986.

[Zuc87] L. Zuck, Manuscript, 1987.

[Zwi88] J. Zwiers, ***Compositionality, Concurrency and Partial Correctness: Proof theories for networks of processes and their connection***, Ph.D. thesis, University of Eindhoven, The Netherlands, 1988. To appear in the LNCS-series, Springer.

BASIC NOTIONS OF TRACE THEORY

Antoni Mazurkiewicz
Institute of Computer Science
Polish Academy of Sciences
P.O.Box 22, PL-00-901 Warsaw

ABSTRACT. The concept of traces has been introduced for describing non-sequential behaviour of concurrent systems via its sequential observations. Traces represent concurrent processes in the same way as strings represent sequential ones. The theory of traces can be used as a tool for reasoning about nets and it is hoped that applying this theory one can get a calculus of the concurrent processes analogous to that available for sequential systems. The following topics will be discussed: algebraic properties of traces, trace models of some concurrency phenomena, fixed-point calculus for finding the behaviour of nets, moduiarity, and some applications of the presented theory.

Key words: concurrency, traces, processes, partial ordering, Petri nets.

CONTENTS:

0. INTRODUCTION

In concurrent system activities the ordering of event occurrences is partial: there is no means to decide which one from independent events occurs earlier than the other. The only way to establish objective ordering of event occurrences in such systems is to find their mutual causal dependencies and to agree that a cause must be always earlier than its effect. Therefore, the dependency (or independency) of event occurrences should be a basis for a concurrent behaviour description. On the other hand, a single observer of a concurrent system notices a sequence of events occurring in the system; thus, it would be useful to combine sequential observations (expressed as strings of events) with a dependency relation (expressed as a relation in the set of event occurrences) in order to grasp some concurrency phenomena and to investigate the nonsequential behaviour of systems via their sequential observations.

The algebra of strings and of sets of strings (languages) has been proved to be of great importance for the theory of sequential systems. Many various models of computations have been investigated by means of sets of strings they can generate (or accept). Such notions as finite automata, sequential machines, regular languages, regular expressions, are strongly connected with strings of symbols representing actions occurring in real systems, since the behaviour of such systems can be described by sets of interpreted strings. The algebra of strings has established a basis for all subsequent theoretical investigations.

In case of concurrent systems, strings of symbols, perfectly suited for modelling sequential processes, are not so generally and directly available. Since some events occurring in concurrent systems are independent of each other, there is no causal relationship putting them in one linearly ordered sequence; instead, their occurrences form a partially ordered set. Therefore an attempt should be made to adjust string oriented methods and techniques to the reality of concurrency.

The theory of traces was motivated by the above arguments. It started in 1977 as a tool for analysing the behaviour of Petri nets. Since then a considerable progress has been made in the theory itself as well as in its applications in related branches of concurrency theory, especially in the theory of Petri nets. On the other hand, trace theory is closely related to the algebraic theory of free partially commutative monoids which is recently intensively developed.

Nowadays, there are several research directions in developing the theory. One is connected with graph representation of traces and the theory of graph grammars; the aim is to overcome some limitations caused by strings and to deal with explicit partial ordering of event occurrences. The second, algebraic, is connected with theory of trace languages, as a basis for concurrent systems specification and description techniques. Issues connected with trace models for temporal logic lead to another research direction.

The paper aims to present briefly some facts and methods offered by trace theory. The proofs of theorems are not included; they are either obvious, or can be found elsewhere. The paper does not pretend to give the whole review of the theory; it would be impossible within the limited size of the paper. The choice of topics reflects the personal interest of the author. The enclosed bibliography gives references to source papers connected with trace theory and those references to papers on Petri nets which are directly related to the topics discussed here.

The standard mathematical denotations are used through the paper. By the ordering relation in a set X we understand any reflexive, transitive and antisymmetric relation in X, i.e. a relation R such that for each x, y, z in X we have xRx (reflexivity), xRyRz => xRz (transitivity), xRyRx => x = y (antisymmetry). If, moreover, xRy or yRx for any x, y in X, R is said to be a linear or total ordering. By a <u>strict</u> ordering in X we understand a transitive and irreflexive relation in X i.e. a relation Q such that xQyQz => xQz, xQy => not(yQx), for all x, y, z in X. If, moreover, for any x, y in X, xQy or yQx or x = y, Q is a strict linear ordering in X. The set of nonnegative integers is denoted by ω. The braces around singletons are omitted if it causes no ambiguity.

1. SEQUENTIAL LANGUAGES

We start this section with some notions concerning strings and string languages. Since traces are generalizations of strings, the theory of traces needs a basis created by that of strings. Section 1 is just thought as a collection of facts and notions useful later on for developing the trace theory.

1.1. **Strings.** Let A be a finite set of symbols (an <u>alphabet</u>). The ordered triple $S = (A^*, \circ, \varepsilon)$, where A^* is the set of all finite sequences (<u>strings</u>) of symbols in A, ε is the empty string, and $\circ$ is the concatenation operation on strings, is the well known monoid of strings over A (usually the sign $\circ$ for concatenation is omitted in expressions). Interpreting symbols in alphabet A as elementary (atomic) actions, strings over A can be viewed as composed actions; the effect of such a composed action is the join effect of the constituent atomic actions executed in the sequence indicated by the string.

For each string $w \in A^*$ define

$$Rng(w) = \{a \in A \mid \exists w_1, w_2 \in A^*: w = w_1 a w_2\};$$

Rng(w) is called the range of w. Clearly, for each string w over an alphabet A we have $Rng(w) \subseteq A$ but not necessarily $Rng(w) = A$.

Let w be a string over an alphabet A. Elements of the set

$$Pref(w) = \{u \mid \exists v \in A^*: uv = w\}$$

are called prefixes of w. Obviously, $w \in Pref(w)$ and $\varepsilon \in Pref(w)$ for each string w.

Let A be an alphabet, $w \in A^*$. For any alphabet B denote by w/B the (string) projection of w onto B, i.e. a string over $A \cap B$ defined as follows:

$$\varepsilon/B = \varepsilon,$$
$$(wa)/B = (w/B)a, \text{ if } w \in A^*, a \in B,$$
$$(wa)/B = (w/B), \text{ if } w \in A^*, a \notin B.$$

Intuitively, projection from A onto B "erases" from a string over A all symbols not belonging to B.

Let u, v be strings; any string

$$u_1v_1u_2v_2 \ldots u_nv_n, \quad n \geq 0,$$

such that $u_1u_2 \ldots u_n = u$, $v_1v_2 \ldots v_n = v$, is called a shuffle of u with v. The set of all shuffles of u with v is denoted by Shuffle(u,v).

1.2. **String languages**. Let A be an alphabet; any subset of A^* is called a (string) language over A. If L_1, L_2 are languages over A, then their concatenation L_1L_2 is defined as

$$L_1L_2 = \{uv \mid u \in L_1, v \in L_2\}.$$

If w is a string, L is a language, then (according to our convention of omitting braces aroud singletons)

$$wL = \{wu \mid u \in L\}, \quad Lw = \{uw \mid u \in L\}.$$

The power of a language L is defined recursively:

$$L^0 = \{\varepsilon\},$$
$$L^{n+1} = L^n L,$$

for each $n \in \omega$. The iteration L^* of L is the union:

$$\bigcup_{n\in\omega} L^n.$$

Extend the projection function from strings to languages defining for each language L over an alphabet A and any alphabet B the projection of L onto B as a language L/B over $A \cap B$ defined as

$$L/B = \{u/B \mid u \in L\}.$$

Extend also the notion of shuffling from strings to languages defining for arbitrary languages L_1, L_2:

$$\mathrm{Shuffle}(L_1,L_2) = \bigcup \{\mathrm{Shuffle}(u,v) \mid u \in L_1,\ v \in L_2\}.$$

For any language L over A set

$$\mathrm{Pref}(L) = \bigcup_{w\in L} \mathrm{Pref}(w).$$

Elements of Pref(L) are called prefixes of L. Obviously, $L \subseteq \mathrm{Pref}(L)$. A language L is prefix closed, if $L = \mathrm{Pref}(L)$. Clearly, for any language L the language Pref(L) is prefix closed. An ordered set $(X,\leq)$ is a tree, if:

(i) for each $x \in X$ the set $\{y \in X \mid y \leq x\}$ is linearly ordered;

(ii) for each $x, y \in X$ there is $z \in X$ with $z \leq x$, $z \leq y$.

PROPOSITION 1.2.1. For each prefix closed string language L the ordered set $(L,\sqsubseteq)$ is a tree. □

A language L is <u>directed</u>, if for each u, v in L there is w in L such that $u \sqsubseteq w$, $v \sqsubseteq w$.

PROPOSITION 1.2.2. Any directed string language is linearly ordered by the prefix relation. □

EXAMPLE 1.2.1. The prefix ordering of languages $Pref((ab)^*)$ and $Pref((ac)^*ad)$ is presented in Fig.1.2.1; both languages are prefix closed; the first is directed; it represents the infinite sequence (a,b,a,b,a,b,...). Both languages will be discussed later on. □

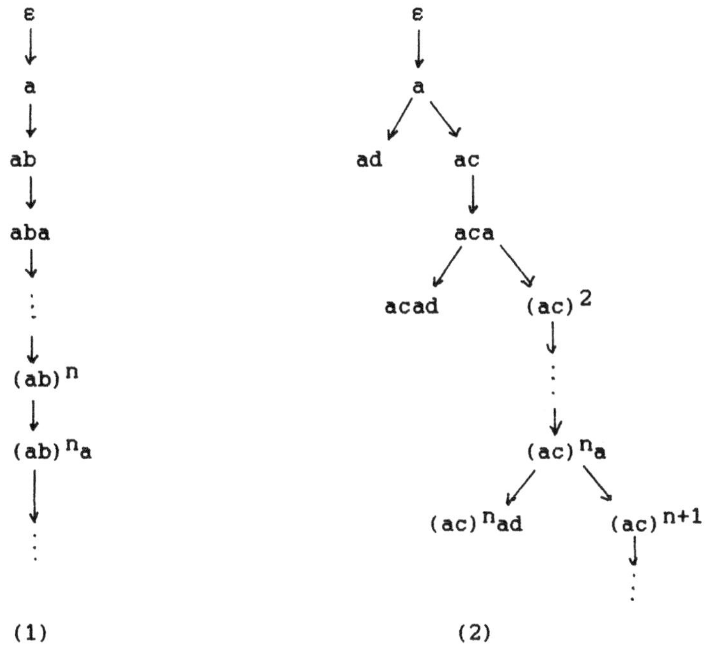

Fig.1.2.1: Prefix structure of $Pref((ab)^*)$ (1) and $Pref((ac)^*(ad))$ (2)

1.3. **String systems**. Call a <u>string system</u>, or <u>system</u> for short, any ordered pair (A,L) where A is an alphabet, $L \subseteq A^*$, and $L = \emptyset$ implies $A = \emptyset$. If $X = (A,L)$ is a string system, A is the <u>alphabet</u> of X denoted by $\alpha(X)$ and L is the <u>language</u> of X denoted by $\lambda(X)$. The difference between string languages and string systems is that different systems can have identical languages, as e.g. systems $(\{a\},a^*)$, $(\{a,b\},a^*)$. While a language gives information which sybols are present in strings of the language, a string system gives also information which symbols are absent in those strings; in other words, within systems represented by string systems it is possible to speak not only about executions of some actions but also about their omissions.

Let X be a string system. The prefix ordering of $\lambda(X)$ will be called the prefix ordering of X and the diagram of this ordering will be called the diagram of X.

Denote by $\emptyset$ and call empty the system $(\emptyset,\emptyset)$. For each system X and each string w over $\alpha(X)$ define

$$wX = (\alpha(X), w\lambda(X)),$$
$$Xw = (\alpha(X), \lambda(X)w);$$

and extend this definition for string languages over $\alpha(X)$:

$$LX = (\alpha(X), L\lambda(X)),$$
$$XL = (\alpha(X), \lambda(X)L)$$

for each string language L over $\alpha(X)$ and each string system X.

We say that a system X is contained in another system Y and write $X \subseteq Y$, if $\alpha(X) \subseteq \alpha(Y)$ and $\lambda(X) \subseteq \lambda(Y)$. Denote the class of all string systems by Ω. Define <u>merging</u> as a binary operation & on string systems:

$$\&: \Omega \times \Omega \longrightarrow \Omega$$

such that for all string systems X, Y

$$\alpha(X\&Y) = \alpha(X) \cup \alpha(Y),$$
$$\lambda(X\&Y) = \{w \in (\alpha(X\&Y))^* \mid w/\alpha(X) \in \lambda(X),\ w/\alpha(Y) \in \lambda(Y)\}$$

(we use here the infix notation and assume & to bind weaker than the concatenation and stronger than other set-theoretical operations).

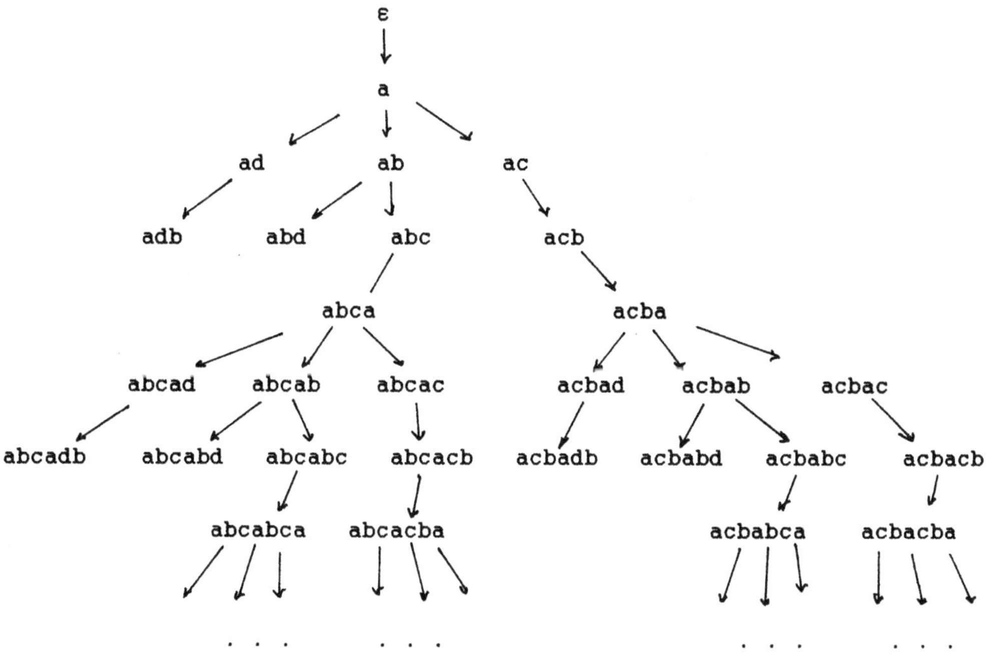

Fig. 1.3.1: Prefix structure of $Pref((ab)^*)\&Pref((ac)^*ad)$.

Let X, Y, Z be string systems. The following equalities hold:

$$X\&X = X,$$
$$X\&Y = Y\&X,$$
$$X\&(Y\&Z) = (X\&Y)\&Z$$
$$(\varepsilon,A)\&(\varepsilon,B) = (\varepsilon,A \cup B),$$
$$X\&\emptyset = \emptyset,$$
$$(X \cup Y)\&Z = X\&Z \cup Y\&Z.$$

Observe that for any string systems X, Y

$$\alpha(X) = \alpha(Y) \Rightarrow \lambda(X\&Y) = \lambda(X) \cap \lambda(Y),$$
$$\alpha(X) \cap \alpha(Y) = \emptyset \Rightarrow \lambda(X\&Y) = Shuffle(\lambda(X),\lambda(Y)).$$

Note also that if $\lambda(X)$, $\lambda(Y)$ are singletons, then in general it is not so in case of $\lambda(X\&Y)$. $\lambda(X\&Y)$ is not empty if and only if

$$\lambda(Y)/\alpha(X) = \lambda(X)/\alpha(Y).$$

EXAMPLE 1.3.1. Let X, Y be string systems,

$$X = (\{a,b\},(ab)^*(a \cup \varepsilon)),$$
$$Y = (\{a,c,d\},(ac)^*(ad \cup a \cup \varepsilon));$$

observe that $\lambda(X) = \mathrm{Pref}((ab)^*)$, $\lambda(Y) = \mathrm{Pref}((ac)^*ad)$ (cf. Example 1.1). The merging of X and Y is the system

$$X\&Y = (\{a,b,c,d\},$$
$$(abc \cup acb)^*(abd \cup adb \cup ab \cup ac \cup ad \cup a \cup \varepsilon)).$$

The diagram of X&Y is presented in Fig.1.3.1 (cf. diagrams from Example 1.2.1). □

2. DEPENDENCY AND TRACES

2.1. **Concurrent alphabets.** By a concurrent alphabet we shall mean any ordered pair $\Sigma = (A,D)$ where A is a finite set (the alphabet of Σ) and D is a symmetric and reflexive binary relation in A (the dependency in Σ). In particular, $(\emptyset,\emptyset)$ (the empty alphabet), (A,id_A) and (A,A^2) (alphabets with minimum and full dependency) are concurrent alphabets for each alphabet A. For any concurrent alphabets $\Sigma_1 = (A_1,D_1)$, $\Sigma_2 = (A_2,D_2)$, define

$$\Sigma_1 \cup \Sigma_2 = (A_1 \cup A_2,\ D_1 \cup D_2),$$
$$\Sigma_1 \cap \Sigma_2 = (A_1 \cap A_2,\ D_1 \cap D_2),$$
$$\Sigma_1 \subseteq \Sigma_2 \iff A_1 \subseteq A_2 \text{ and } D_1 \subseteq D_2.$$

It is clear that $\Sigma_1 \cup \Sigma_2$ and $\Sigma_1 \cap \Sigma_2$ are concurrent alphabets, and

$$\Sigma_1 \cap \Sigma_2 \subseteq \Sigma_i \subseteq \Sigma_1 \cup \Sigma_2, \qquad i = 1,2.$$

For any alphabet A by D(A) we shall denote the concurrent alphabet (A,A^2) and call it the full dependency alphabet (over A). If A =

$\{a_1, a_2, \ldots, a_n\}$, we shall write

$$D(a_1, a_2, \ldots, a_n)$$

rather than D(A). It is clear that each concurrent alphabet is the union of a finite number of full dependency alphabets. Define $I_\Sigma = A^2 \setminus D$; I_Σ will be called the <u>independency</u> in Σ; obviously, I_Σ is a symmetric and irreflexive relation in A. Two symbols a, b in A will be called mutually <u>dependent</u> in Σ, if $(a,b) \in D$; otherwise they are said to be <u>independent</u> in Σ. Any triple (A,I,D) where A is an alphabet, $I \subseteq A^2$ is symmetric and irreflexive, and $D = A^2 \setminus I$ is called a <u>reliance alphabet</u>; this construct is sometimes used as a primitive concept of trace theory and then the concurrent alphabet (A,D) is a derived notion.

EXAMPLE 2.1.1. Concurrent alphabet $(\{a,b,c\}, \{a,b\}^2 \cup \{a,c\}^2)$ is the union of D(a,b) and D(a,c); symbols b, c are (the only) independent symbols in this alphabet. □

2.2. **Traces**. Let $\Sigma = (A,D)$ be a concurrent alphabet. Define $\equiv_\Sigma$ as the least congruence in the monoid $(A^*, \circ, \varepsilon)$ such that

$$(a,b) \in I_\Sigma \;\Rightarrow\; ab \equiv_\Sigma ba.$$

for all a,b in A. In other words, $w' \equiv_\Sigma w''$ if and only if there is a finite sequence of strings

$$(w_0, w_1, \ldots, w_n), \quad n \geq 0,$$

such that

$$w_0 = w', \quad w_n = w'',$$

and for each i, $1 \leq i \leq n$, there are strings u, v, and symbols a, b, $(a,b) \in I_\Sigma$, with

$$w_{i-1} = uabv, \; w_i = ubav.$$

The relation $\equiv_\Sigma$ will be referred to as the <u>trace equivalence</u> over Σ. Equivalence classes of $\equiv_\Sigma$ are called <u>traces</u> over Σ; a trace generated by a string w will be denoted by $[w]_\Sigma$. By $[A^*]_\Sigma$ we shall denote the set $\{[w]_\Sigma \mid w \in A^*\}$, and by $[A]_\Sigma$ the set $\{[w] \mid e \in A\}$. We shall omit subscript Σ, if Σ is understood.

It is clear that $w_1 \equiv w_2$ implies $Rng(w_1) = Rng(w_2)$; thus, for all strings w, we can define Rng([w]) as Rng(w).

By definition, a single trace arises by identifying all strings which differ only in the ordering of adjacent independent symbols. If symbols in A are thought as atomic system actions, traces represent composed actions in which some elementary actions occur independently (i. e. without any causal relationship) of each other. The notion of traces allows to eliminate from strings the ordering between some process actions occurring independently of each other.

EXAMPLE 2.2.1. Let $\Sigma = D(a,b) \cup D(a,c)$. Then b, c are independent in Σ; the equivalence class generated by string "abbca" is:

$$[abbca]_\Sigma = \{abbca,\ abcba,\ acbba\}. \ \square$$

The quotient monoid $T = (A^*,\circ,\varepsilon)/\equiv_\Sigma \ = \ ([A^*]_\Sigma,\circ,[\varepsilon]_\Sigma)$ is called the <u>trace monoid</u> over Σ. Clearly, T is generated by [A]; it is a monoid in which the concatenation operation $\circ$ may be commutative for some different symbols (in contrast to the monoid of strings, where $a \neq b$ implies $ab \neq ba$). The monoid T is also called a <u>free partially commutative monoid</u> over A. It is clear that in case of full dependency ($D = A^2$) T is isomorphic to the ordinary algebra $(A^*,\circ,\varepsilon)$ of strings over A. We are going to develop the algebra of traces along the same lines as it was presented above in case of the algebra of strings. Let us recall that the mapping

$$[\,]_\Sigma : A^* \longrightarrow [A^*]_\Sigma : w \longmapsto [w]_\Sigma$$

is a homomorphism of $(A^*,\circ,\varepsilon)$ onto $([A^*]_\Sigma,\circ,[\varepsilon]_\Sigma)$ (called the <u>natural</u> homomorphism onto a quotient algebra).

Let fix a concurrent alphabet Σ and let w, w_1, w_2, ... denote strings over Σ, and e, e_1, e_2, ... denote symbols in Σ. Since the alphabet is fixed, indices Σ will be omitted. We shall give now some facts about the trace equivalence.

PROPOSITION 2.2.1. If $w \equiv u$, then w is a permutation of u.

Proof. In the definition of $\equiv$ relation, ab is a permutation of ba; if u', w' are permutation of u'', w'', respectively, then $u'w'$ is a permutation of $u''w''$; finally, composition of permutations is a permutation. □

For each string $w = e_1e_2...e_n$, by w^R denote the mirror image of w, i.e. the string $e_n...e_2e_1$. Operation $w \longmapsto w^R$ will be called the <u>mirror reflexion</u>. Define $[w]^R$ by $[w^R]$; this definition is correct because of the following proposition.

PROPOSITION 2.2.2 (Mirror rule). For any strins w, u: $w \equiv u \iff w^R \equiv u^R$.

Proof. Obvious, since the definition of $\equiv$ is invariant under the mirror reflexion. □

Write $w_1 = (w\backslash e)$ and say that w_1 arise from w by deleting from w the last occurrence of e in two cases: either if $w_1 = w$ and e does not occur in w, or there are strings u, v such that $w = uev$, $w_1 = uv$, and e does not occur in v.

PROPOSITION 2.2.3 (Cancellation rule). If $w_1 \equiv w_2$, then $(w_1\backslash e) \equiv (w_2\backslash e)$.

Proof. By symmetry, reflexivity and transitivity of $\equiv$ it suffices to prove the implication:

$$uabv \equiv ubav \Rightarrow (uabv\backslash e) \equiv (ubav\backslash e)$$

for any strings u,v, any independent symbols a,b, and any symbol e. Indeed, if e occur in v or if e does not occur in abv, the implication is obvious. If e does not occur in v and it occurs in abv, then either $e = a$ or $e = b$. If $e = a$, then $(uabv\backslash e) = ubv = (ubav\backslash e)$; if $e = b$, then $(uabv\backslash e) = uav = (ubav\backslash e)$. Thus, in all cases $(uabv\backslash e) \equiv (ubav\backslash e)$. □

We can easily generalize the cancellation rule to the case of an arbitrary (not neccessarily the last) occurrence of a symbol.

PROPOSITION 2.2.4. For any strings w_1, w_2, u, v: $w_1 \equiv w_2$ if and only if $uw_1v \equiv uw_2v$.

Proof. Clearly, $w_1 \equiv w_2$ implies $uw_1v \equiv uw_2v$. Assume now $uw_1v \equiv uw_2v$. By cancellation rule $uw_1 \equiv uw_2$; by the mirror rule $w_1{}^Ru^R \equiv w_2{}^Ru^R$; and again by cancellation rule $w_1{}^R \equiv w_2{}^R$, and by mirror rule $w_1 \equiv w_2$. □

PROPOSITION 2.2.5 (Reduction rule). For any strings $u_1, v_1, w_1, u_2, v_2, w_2$:

$$u_1 \equiv u_2,\ v_1 \equiv v_2,\ u_1w_1v_1 \equiv u_2w_2v_2 \ \Rightarrow\ w_1 \equiv w_2.$$

Proof. Assume the premise of the above implication. Because of $u_1 \equiv u_2$ and of $v_1 \equiv v_2$, $u_1w_1v_1 \equiv u_2w_1v_2$; thus, $u_2w_1v_2 \equiv u_2w_2v_2$. Therefore, by Proposition 2.6, $w_1 \equiv w_2$. □

PROPOSITION 2.2.6. Let w_1, w_2 be strings, e_1, e_2 be symbols, $e_1 \neq e_2$. If $w_1e_1 \equiv w_2e_2$, then e_1, e_2 are independent and there is a string w such that $w_1 \equiv we_2$, $w_2 \equiv we_1$.

Proof. Assume $w_1e_1 \equiv w_2e_2$, $e_1 \neq e_2$. Applying twice the cancellation rule we get $w_1\backslash e_2 \equiv w_2\backslash e_1$; denote $w_1\backslash e_2$ by w. By the same rule we get $w_1 \equiv (w_2\backslash e_1)e_2 \equiv we_2$, and $w_2 \equiv (w_1\backslash e_2)e_1 \equiv we_1$. Thus, since $w_1e_1 \equiv w_2e_2$, $we_2e_1 \equiv we_1e_2$. By the cancellation rule $e_2e_1 \equiv e_1e_2$, what proves independency of e_1, e_2. □

PROPOSITION 2.2.7. The following equalities hold for any symbol e, strings u,w, and traces τ, τ_1, τ_2, τ_3, σ', σ'':

$$[u][w] = [uw],$$
$$[w] = [\varepsilon] \iff w = \varepsilon,$$
$$\tau[\varepsilon] = [\varepsilon]\tau = \tau,$$
$$\tau_1(\tau_2\tau_3) = (\tau_1\tau_2)\tau_3,$$
$$\tau_1 = \tau_2 \iff \tau_1{}^R = \tau_2{}^R,$$
$$\sigma'\tau_1\sigma'' = \sigma'\tau_2\sigma'' \iff \tau_1 = \tau_2,$$
$$\tau_1[e_1] = \tau_2[e_2] \iff \text{either } e_1 = e_2, \text{ or } (e_1,e_2) \in I \text{ and there is } \tau \text{ s.t. } \tau_1 = \tau[e_2],\ \tau_2 = \tau[e_1].$$

Proof is a direct consequence of the definition of traces and of properties of the trace eqivalence shown above. □

2.3. **Dependency graphs**. Dependency graphs are thought as graphical representations of traces which make explicit the ordering of symbol occurrences within traces. It turns out that for a given concurrent alphabet algebra of traces is isomorphic with the algebra of dependency graphs defined below. Therefore, it is only a matter of taste which objects are chosen for representing concurrent processes: equivalence classes of strings or labelled graphs.

Let $\Sigma = (A,D)$ be a concurrent alphabet. Dependency graphs over Σ (or d-graphs for short) are finite, oriented, acyclic graphs with nodes labelled with symbols from A in such a way that two nodes of a d-graph are connected with an arc if and only if they are different and labelled with dependent symbols. Formally, a triple

$$\gamma = (V,R,\varphi)$$

is a _dependency graph_, (_d-graph_) over Σ, if

V is a finite set (of nodes of γ),
$R \subseteq V \times V$ (the set of arcs of γ),
$\varphi: V \longrightarrow A$ (the labelling of γ),

such that

$$R^{+} \cap id_V = \emptyset, \text{ (acyclicity)}$$
$$R \cup R^{-1} \cup id_V = \varphi D \varphi^{-1}, \text{ (dependence connectivity)}$$

where for any mappings $\varphi: X \longrightarrow A$, $\psi: Y \longrightarrow A$, $\varphi D \psi^{-1}$ denotes a relation in $X \times Y$ such that

$$(x,y) \in \varphi D \psi^{-1} \iff (\varphi(x),\varphi(y)) \in D.$$

Two d-graphs γ', γ'' are isomorphic, $\gamma' \cong \gamma''$, if there exists a bijection between their nodes preserving labelling and arc connections. As usual, two isomorphic graphs are identified; all subsequent properties of d-graphs are given up to isomorphism. The empty d-graph

$(\emptyset,\emptyset,\emptyset)$ will be denoted by λ and the set of all isomorphism classes of d-graphs over Σ by Γ_Σ.

EXAMPLE 2.3.1. Let $\Sigma = D(a,b) \cup D(a,c)$. Then the node labelled graph (V, R, φ), with

$V = \{1,2,3,4,5\}$,

$R = \{(1,2), (1,3), (1,4), (1,5), (2,4), (2,5), (3,5), (4,5)\}$,

$\varphi(1) = a$, $\varphi(2) = b$, $\varphi(3) = c$, $\varphi(4) = b$, $\varphi(5) = a$,

is a d-graph. It is (isomorphic to) the graph in Fig. 2.3.1. □

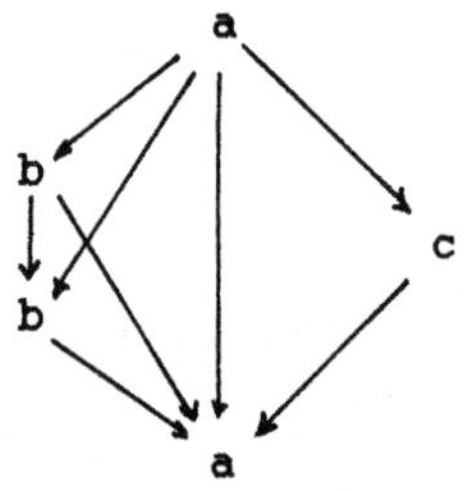

Fig. 2.3.1: A dependency graph over $D(a,b) \cup D(a,c)$.

Since d-graph is acyclic, the transitive and reflexive closure of its arc relation is an ordering. Thus, each d-graph uniquely determines an ordering of symbol occurrences. This ordering will be discussed later on.

By definition, d-graphs are finite, oriented, acyclic, node labelled graphs. Moreover, it is clear that in an arbitrary d-graph any nodes labelled with the same symbol must be joined with an arc; and that, if two nodes of a d-graph are joined with an arc, then any other two nodes of this graph labelled with the same symbols must be also joined with an arc. Are the above requirements sufficient for a graph to be a d-graph? The answer is "no"; a full characterization of d-graphs gives the Ehrenfeucht - Rozenberg theorem quoted here in slightly modified version. Before formulating it we need some auxiliary notions.

We shall consider only finite, acyclic, oriented, node labelled graphs, called here simply graphs. Let $\gamma = (V.R,\varphi)$ be a graph. We say that γ is a d-graph candidate, if there exists a concurrent alphabet Σ such that γ is a d-graph over Σ. Let R', R" be two equivalence relations; we say that R' is a refinement of R", if $R' \subseteq R''$.

Define for any graph $\gamma = (V.R,\varphi)$ two binary relations in V, Q_γ and L_γ, as follows:

$$(v_1,v_2) \in Q_\gamma \iff (v_1,v_2) \in R \cup R^{-1}, \text{ and}$$
$$\forall v \in V-\{v_1,v_2\}: (v_1,v) \in R \iff (v_2,v) \in R;$$
$$(v_1,v_2) \in L_\gamma \iff \varphi(v_1) = \varphi(v_2).$$

THEOREM 2.3.1 (Characterization of d-graphs, Ehrenfeucht, Rozenberg 1987). For each graph γ relations Q_γ, L_γ are equivalence relations; γ is a d-graph candidate if and only if L_γ is a refinement of Q_γ.

Proof can be found in [ER]. □

Define in Γ_Σ the composition operation $\circ$ (this sign will be frequently omitted in expressions) as follows: for each graphs γ_1, γ_2 in Γ_Σ the composition $(\gamma_1 \circ \gamma_2)$ of γ_1 with γ_2 is a graph arising from the disjoint union of γ_1 and γ_2 by adding to it new arcs leading from each node of γ_1 to each node of γ_2 provided they are labelled with dependent symbols. Formally, $(V,R,\varphi) \cong \gamma' \circ \gamma''$ iff there are instances (V',R',φ'), (V'',R'',φ'') of γ', γ'', respectively, such that

$$V = V' \cup V'',\ V' \cap V'' = \emptyset,$$
$$R = R' \cup R'' \cup \varphi' D (\varphi'')^{-1},$$
$$\varphi = \varphi' \cup \varphi''.$$

Interpreting d-graphs as descriptions of some processes, composition of d-graphs can be viewed as "sequential" as well as "parallel": composing two independent d-graphs (i.e. d-graphs such that any node of one of them is independent of any node of the other) we get the result intuitively understood as "parallel" composition of processes, while composing two d-graphs such that any node of one of them is dependent of any label of the other the result can be viewed as the "sequential" or "serial" composition of processes. In general, the d-graph composition is a mixture of "parallel" and "sequential" compositions, when some (but not all) nodes of one d-graph are dependent on some (but not all) nodes of the other. The nature of composition of d-graphs depends on the nature of dependency relation given in the concurrent alphabet.

THEOREM 2.3.2. The algebra $G = (\Gamma_\Sigma, \circ, \lambda)$ is a monoid.

Proof. It suffices to show that $\circ$ is associative and that $\lambda \circ \gamma \cong \gamma \circ \lambda \cong \gamma$ for each d-graph δ. Let (V_i, R_i, φ_i) be instances of d-graphs γ_i such that $V_i \cap V_j = \emptyset$ for $i \neq j$, $i = 1,2,3$. By simple calculation we prove that $(\gamma_1 \circ \gamma_2) \circ \gamma_3$ is (isomorphic to) the d-graph (V, R, φ) with

$$V = V_1 \cup V_2 \cup V_3,$$
$$R = R_1 \cup R_2 \cup R_3 \cup \varphi_1 D \varphi_2^{-1} \cup \varphi_1 D \varphi_3^{-1} \cup \varphi_2 D \varphi_3^{-1},$$
$$\varphi = \varphi_1 \cup \varphi_2 \cup \varphi_3,$$

and the same result we obtain for $\gamma_1 \circ (\gamma_2 \circ \gamma_3)$. The isomorphism $\lambda \circ \gamma \cong \gamma \circ \lambda \cong \gamma$ is obvious. □

Let $\Sigma = (A,D)$ be a concurrent alphabet; define a mapping

$$\langle\rangle_\Sigma : A^* \longrightarrow \Gamma_\Sigma : w \longmapsto \langle w \rangle_\Sigma$$

by setting for each w', w'' in A^*, e in A:

$$\langle \varepsilon \rangle_\Sigma \cong \lambda;$$
$$\langle e \rangle_\Sigma \cong (\{e\}, \emptyset, \{(e,e)\});$$
$$\langle w'w'' \rangle_\Sigma \cong \langle w' \rangle_\Sigma \circ \langle w'' \rangle_\Sigma.$$

Denote $\{\langle e \rangle_\Sigma \mid e \in A\}$ by $\langle A \rangle_\Sigma$ and $\{\langle w \rangle_\Sigma \mid w \in A^*\}$ by $\langle A^* \rangle_\Sigma$. The subscript Σ will be omitted if Σ is understood from a context. From the above definition it follows that for any string w and symbol e $\langle we \rangle$ is a graph arising from $\langle w \rangle$ by adding to $\langle w \rangle$ a new node labelled with e and new arcs, leading to this new node from all nodes of $\langle w \rangle$ labelled with symbols dependent on e. If e.g. $\Sigma = D(a,b) \cup D(a,c)$, then $\langle abbca \rangle_\Sigma$ is the d-graph presented in Fig. 2.3.1.

PROPOSITION 2.3.1. For any d-graph δ over $\Sigma = (A,D)$ there is a string $w \in A^*$ such that $\delta \cong \langle w \rangle_\Sigma$.

Proof. It is true if δ is the empty d-graph. By induction, for any nonempty d-graph δ remove any of its maximal nodes (they always exist, since d-graphs are acyclic). It is clear that the resulting graph δ' is a d-graph. Now, by induction hypothesis there is a string w' s.t. $\langle w'\rangle_\Sigma \cong \delta'$; then the string $w = w'e$, where e is the label of the removed node, is the required string, since δ is evidently isomorphic with $\langle w'e\rangle_\Sigma = \langle w\rangle_\Sigma$. □

Therefore, $\langle\rangle_\Sigma$ is a surjection, hence $\Gamma_\Sigma = \langle A^*\rangle_\Sigma$ and $(\Gamma_\Sigma, \circ, \lambda) = (\langle A^*\rangle_\Sigma, \circ, \langle\varepsilon\rangle_\Sigma)$.

EXAMPLE 2.3.2. Let $\Sigma = D(a,b) \cup D(a,c)$. In Fig. 2.3.2 the composition of dependence graphs $\langle abb\rangle$, $\langle ca\rangle$ is depicted; the dotted arrows represent arcs added in the composition. □

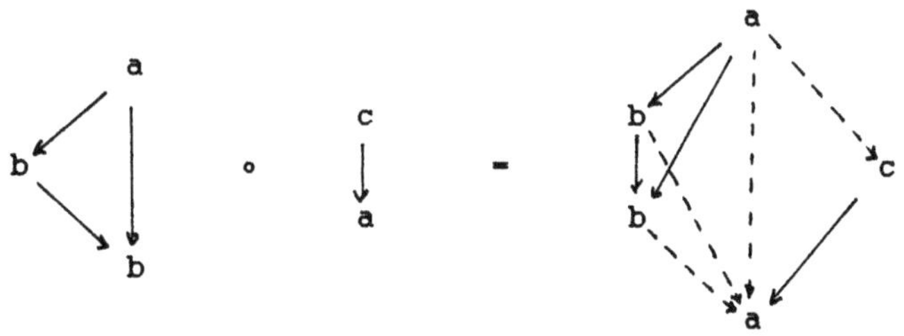

Fig. 2.3.2: Composition of dependency graphs

Call a linearization of a d-graph γ any string $e_1e_2...e_n$ such that there are Q and e with

(i) $(\{1,2,...,n\},Q,e) \cong \gamma$,

(ii) $e(i) = e_i$, $(i = 1,2,...,n)$,

(iii) $(i,j) \in Q \Rightarrow i < j$, $(i,j = 1,2,...,n)$.

THEOREM 2.3.3. For each d-graph γ and string w:

$$\langle w\rangle \cong \gamma \iff w \text{ is a linearization of } \gamma.$$

Proof. ($\Rightarrow$). Assume $\langle w\rangle \cong \gamma$. It is clear that w meets all requirements for strings to be linearizations of γ.

(<=). By induction on w. Assume w is linearization of γ. If w = ε, γ must be empty and clearly $\langle\varepsilon\rangle \cong \lambda$. Assume u to be a string, e to be a symbol, and w = ue. Then, by condition (iii) of the linearization definition, γ has a maximal node labelled with e; let γ' arises from γ by removing this maximal node. It is clear that u is a linearization of γ'; by induction hypothesis $\langle u\rangle \cong \gamma'$; by composition definition $\langle ue\rangle \cong \gamma$. □

PROPOSITION 2.3.2. For any strings w', w": $\langle w'\rangle\circ\langle w''\rangle \cong \langle w'w''\rangle$; i.e. $\langle\,\rangle$ is a homomorphism from the monoid of strings over A onto the monoid of d-graphs over (A,D).

Proof is straightforward. □

THEOREM 2.3.4. Monoid $(\langle A^*\rangle_\Sigma, \circ, \langle\varepsilon\rangle_\Sigma)$ is generated by the set $\langle A\rangle_\Sigma$. □

Proof follows from the equality $\langle e_1e_2\ldots e_n\rangle = \langle e_1\rangle\langle e_2\rangle\ldots\langle e_n\rangle$, for each string $e_1e_2\ldots e_n$. □

The relationship between traces and d-graphs over Σ is expressed by the following theorem.

THEOREM 2.3.5. For each strings w', w" in A^*

$$[w']_\Sigma = [w'']_\Sigma \text{ iff } \langle w'\rangle_\Sigma \cong \langle w''\rangle_\Sigma.$$

Proof by induction w.r. to the length of w'. If w' = ε the assertion of the theorem is obviously true, since the only trace equal to the empty trace is empty and the only d-graph isomorphic to the empty d-graph is also empty. Let now w' = u'e' for a string w and symbol e'. Assume $w' \equiv w''$. Thus, $u'e' \equiv w''$; w" cannot be empty, hence w" = u"e" for a string u and symbol e". We have then $u'e' \equiv u''e''$ and by Proposition 2.2.6 either e' = e" and $u' \equiv u''$ or there is a string u such that $u' \equiv ue''$, $u'' \equiv ue'$ and e', e" are independent. In the first case $\langle u'\rangle \cong \langle u''\rangle$ by induction hypothesis and since e' = e" $\langle u'e'\rangle \cong \langle u''e''\rangle$. In the second case e', e" are independent, hence $\langle ue'e''\rangle \cong \langle ue''e'\rangle$ by the composition definition of d-graphs. Since by induction hypothesis $\langle u'\rangle \cong \langle ue''\rangle$ and $\langle u''\rangle \cong \langle ue'\rangle$, we have $\langle u'e'\rangle \cong \langle u''e''\rangle$. Thus, in both cases $\langle u'e'\rangle \cong \langle u''e''\rangle$, i.e. $\langle w'\rangle \cong \langle w''\rangle$.

Assume now $\langle w'\rangle \cong \langle w''\rangle \cong \gamma$. Since γ is not empty, strings w', w'' are also not empty and there are strings u', u'', and symbols e', e'' such that $w' = u'e'$, $w'' = u''e''$. Thus, $\langle u'e'\rangle \cong \langle u''e''\rangle$. If $e' = e''$, $\langle u'\rangle \cong \langle u''\rangle$ and, by induction hypothesis, $u' \equiv u''$. It implies $u'e' \equiv u''e''$. If $e' \neq e''$, d-graph γ contains two maximal nodes labelled with e' and e''. Remove both these nodes from γ; let u be a string such that $\langle u\rangle$ is isomorphic to the resulting d-graph. Thus, $\langle ue'e''\rangle \cong \gamma \cong \langle ue''e'\rangle$. We have clearly $\langle ue'\rangle \cong \langle u''\rangle$ and $\langle ue''\rangle \cong \langle u'\rangle$. By induction hypothesis $ue' \equiv u''$ and $ue'' \equiv u$, hence $ue'e'' \equiv u''e''$ and $ue''e' \equiv ue'e''$. Since by definition of trace congruence $ue'e'' \equiv ue''e'$, we have $u''e'' \equiv u'e'$, i.e. $w' \equiv w''$; it completes the proof. □

The main theorem of this section is a direct consequence of Theorem 2.3.5:

THEOREM 2.3.6. For each concurrent alphabet $\Sigma = (A,D)$, the monoid $(\langle A^*\rangle_\Sigma, \circ, \langle \varepsilon\rangle_\Sigma)$ is isomorphic to the trace monoid $([A^*]_\Sigma, \circ, [\varepsilon]_\Sigma)$; the isomorphism is induced by the bijection

$$[A]_\Sigma \longrightarrow \langle A\rangle_\Sigma : \ [e]_\Sigma \longmapsto \langle e\rangle_\Sigma .$$

□

The above theorem states that traces and d-graphs over the same concurrent alphabet can be viewed as two faces of the same coin; the same concepts can be here expressed in two different ways: speaking about traces the algebraic character of the concept is stressed out, while speaking about d-graphs its causality (or ordering) features are emphasized. We can consider some graph - theoretical features of traces as well as some algebraic properties of dependence graphs; e.g. the notion of connectivity of traces will be used in the sequel, and the string representation of d-graphs has been just used. In fact, this dual character of traces, algebraic and graph-theoretic, was a principal motivation for introducing them as representations of concurrent processes.

Using this isomorphism, one can prove facts about traces using d-graph methods and the other way around; as an example of this technique we prove a trace generalization of the well-known Levi Lemma for strings (and a generalization of the last assertion of Proposition 2.2.7 given above).

Let v', v" be two nodes of a d-graph (V,R,φ); we say that v' is earlier than v", if $(v',v") \in R$, and not earlier otherwise, and that v', v" are independent, if neither v' is earlier than v" nor v" is earlier than v'. Let γ be a d-graph (V,R,φ) and U be a subset of V. Then any graph isomorphic to $(U, R \cap (U \times U), \varphi|U)$ is a d-graph again, called the subgraph of γ induced by U. As in case of traces, let $Rng(\gamma)$ denote the set of all labels of nodes of D, for any d-graph γ.

PROPOSITION 2.3.3. For any d-graphs γ_1, γ_2, γ_3, γ_4 over a common concurrent alphabet:

$$\gamma_1\gamma_2 \cong \gamma_3\gamma_4 \iff \exists\ \delta_1,\delta_2,\delta_3,\delta_4: \gamma_1 \cong \delta_1\delta_2,\ \gamma_2 \cong \delta_3\delta_4,\ \gamma_3 \cong \delta_1\delta_3,\ \gamma_4 \cong \delta_2\delta_4,\ Rng(\delta_2) \times Rng(\delta_3) \subseteq I_\Sigma.$$

Proof. Let $\gamma_i = (V_i, R_i, \varphi_i)$ $(i = 1,2,3,4)$ and let $\gamma \cong (V, R, \varphi) \cong \gamma_1\gamma_2 \cong \gamma_3\gamma_4$. Let ψ_1 be isomorphism from $\gamma_1\gamma_2$ to γ and ψ_2 be isomorphism from $\gamma_3\gamma_4$ to γ. Set

$$U_1 = \psi_1(V_1) \cap \psi_2(V_3),$$
$$U_2 = \psi_1(V_1) \cap \psi_2(V_4),$$
$$U_3 = \psi_1(V_2) \cap \psi_2(V_3),$$
$$U_4 = \psi_1(V_2) \cap \psi_2(V_4).$$

We have then $U_1 \cup U_2 = \psi_1(V_1)$ and $U_3 \cup U_4 = \psi_2(v_2)$ and by definition of d-graphs composition $U_1 \cap U_2 = \emptyset$, $U_3 \cap U_4 = \emptyset$. Let δ_i be the subgraph of γ induced by U_i, for each i=1,2,3,4. By properties of isomorphisms it is not difficult to see that $\gamma_1 \cong \delta_1\delta_2$, $\gamma_2 \cong \delta_3\delta_4$, $\gamma_3 \cong \delta_1\delta_3$, $\gamma_4 \cong \delta_2\delta_4$. Moreover, since any node of V_2 is not earlier than any node of V_1 and isomorphisms preserve the node ordering, any node of U_2 (contained in V_2) is not earlier than any node of U_3 (contained in V_1); similarly, since any node of V_4 is not earlier than any node of V_3, any node of U_3 (contained in V_4) is not earlier than any node of U_2 (contained in V_3). Thus, any node of U_2 is independent of any node of U_3 (Fig. 2.3.3). It completes the proof. □

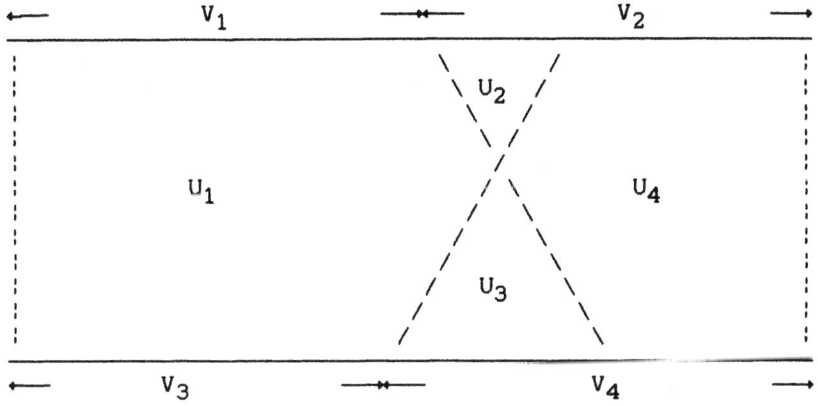

Fig. 2.3.3: Illustration of Levi Lemma for d-graphs.

By Theorem 2.3.6 the above proposition can be reformulated as follows:

COROLLARY (Levi Lemma for traces). For any traces $\tau_1, \tau_2, \tau_3, \tau_4$ over Σ:

$$\tau_1\tau_2 = \tau_3\tau_4 \iff \exists\, \sigma_1, \sigma_2, \sigma_3, \sigma_4: \quad \tau_1 = \sigma_1\sigma_2,\ \tau_2 = \sigma_3\sigma_4,\ \tau_3 = \sigma_1\sigma_3,\ \tau_4 = \sigma_2\sigma_4,\ Rng(\sigma_2) \times Rng(\sigma_3) \subseteq I_\Sigma. \ \Box$$

The interested reader can compare this result with the classical Levi Lemma (for strings).

Similarly as infinite strings can be defined as directed and prefix closed string languages (consisting of all finite prefixes of such an infinite string), infinite traces can be defined as directed and prefix closed trace languages; an infinite trace can be identified with a trace language consisting of all finite trace prefixes of such a trace. The notion of dependency graph can be easily generalized to this case. To do it, we need some auxiliary definitions. Let Σ be a concurrent alphabet; we shall consider oriented and acyclic graphs with nodes labelled with symbols from Σ. A subgraph G_0 of such a graph G is the <u>initial part</u> of G, if, together with a node v, G_0 contains all arcs in G leading to v. The class of all initial parts of a graph G will be denoted by $Init(G)$.

THEOREM 2.3.7. For each directed and prefix closed trace language T over Σ there exists unique (up to isomorphism) oriented and acyclic graph G with nodes labelled with symbols in Σ such that for each γ

$$\exists \tau \in T: \ \delta(\tau) \cong \gamma \ \Leftrightarrow \ \exists g \in Init(G): \ g \cong \gamma$$

for each γ ($\cong$ denotes the isomorphism of oriented labelled graphs). □

Proof (sketch). It is easy to show that the quadruple S,

$$S = (\Gamma, T, \langle\rangle, \varphi),$$

where T is the given set of traces, Γ is the set of all d-graphs corresponding to traces from T, $\langle\rangle: T \longrightarrow \Gamma$, and φ is the family of isomorphisms (embeddings):

$$\{\varphi_{t_1 t_2} \mid t_1, t_2 \in T, t_1 \sqsubseteq t_2\}$$

such that $\varphi_{t_1 t_2}$ is the isomorphism of t_1 with a prefix of t_2, is a direct system. Then the graph G from the claim of the theorem is the direct limit of S. □

For each directed trace language T over Σ denote by $\delta(T)$ and call the d-graph of T the graph the existence of which is ensured by Theorem 4. Clearly, $\delta(T)$ need not be finite. Dependency graphs of directed trace languages are intended to describe explicitly the ordering of symbols (elementary actions) in processes represented by such languages.

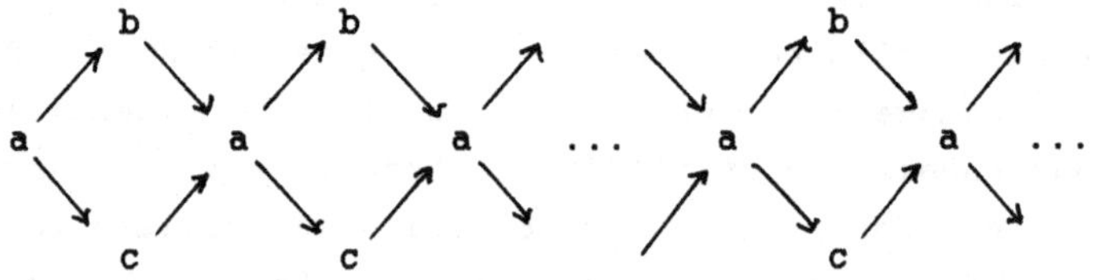

Fig. 6: An infinite dependency graph

EXAMPLE 2.3.3. Let $\Sigma = D(a,b) \cup D(a,c)$. The trace language $T = [(abc)^*]$ over Σ is directed; $\delta(T)$ is the (infinite) graph given in Fig. 6 (as usual, arcs following by transitivity from others are omitted). □

2.4. **Histories.** The concepts presented in this section originate in papers of M.W. Shields [Sh1,Sh2,Sh3]. The main idea is to represent concurrent processes by a collection of individual histories of objects involved; such an individual history is a string of events concerning only one object, and the global history is a collection of individual ones. This approach, appealing directly to the intuitive meaning of parallel processing, is particularly well suited to COSY system [LSB] and CSP-like systems [H] where individual components run independently of each other with one exception: an event concerning a number of (in CSP at most two) components can occur coincidently in all these components ("shake hands" or "rendez vous" synchronization principle, or "simultaneity = coincidence" principle, as stated in Net Theory [Pet1]). The presentation and the terminology used here are adjusted to the present purposes and differ from those of the authors.

Let $S = (A_1, A_2, \ldots, A_n)$ be a n-tuple of finite alphabets (concurrent <u>components</u> of S) fixed from now on.

Denote by $\mathbf{M}$ the product algebra

$$(A_1^*, \circ, \varepsilon) \times (A_2^*, \circ, \varepsilon) \times \ldots \times (A_n^*, \circ, \varepsilon)$$

of free monoids; $\mathbf{M}$ is clearly a monoid, as a product of monoids. The composition in $\mathbf{M}$ is componentwise:

$$(uv)_i = u_i v_i, \qquad (i=1,2,\ldots,n),$$

for all u, v in $A_1^* \times A_2^* \times \ldots \times A_n^*$. Let $A = \bigcup_i A_i$. For each $e \in A$ define $\underline{e}$ as the n-tuple:

$$\underline{e} = (e_1, e_2, \ldots, e_n)$$

with $e_i = e$ if $e \in A_i$, and $e_i = \varepsilon$ otherwise. Elements of $E_0 = \{\underline{e} \mid e \in A\}$ will be referred to as <u>elementary</u> actions of S. Thus, elementary action $\underline{e}$ is common for all components having e in their repertoire. Define $\mathbf{H}$ as the submonoid of $\mathbf{M}$ generated by E_0; elements of $\mathbf{H}$ call <u>global histories</u> (or simply, <u>histories</u>), and components of global histories – <u>individual histories</u> in S.

EXAMPLE 2.4.1. Let $A_1 = \{a,b\}$, $A_2 = \{a,c\}$, $S = (A_1, A_2)$. Then elementary actions of S are: (a,a), (b,ε), (c,ε). The pair:

$$h = (abba, aca)$$

is a global history in S, since $h = (a,a)(b,\varepsilon)(b,\varepsilon)(\varepsilon,c)(a,a)$; the pair (abba, cca) is not a history. □

The algebra **H** of histories can be interpreted as follows. There is n sequential components of a concurrent system. Each of them is capable to execute (sequentially) some elementary actions being at its disposal; such elementary actions form the repertoire of the component, denoted by A_i for i-th component. All of them can act independently of each other, but an action common to a number of components can be executed by all such components coincidently. Then the join action executed by all of them is n-tuple of individual histories of components; individual histories must be consistent, i.e. the condition for coincident execution of common actions must be observed. The following theorem offers a criterion for such a consistency.

Let $S = (A_1, A_2, \ldots, A_n)$, $A = \bigcup_i A_i$; define the <u>component projection</u> function π_S as the mapping

$$\pi_S\colon A^* \longrightarrow A_1^* \times A_2^* \times \ldots \times A_n^*\colon w \longmapsto (w/A_1, w/A_2, \ldots, w/A_n).$$

The subscript S will be omitted if S is known.

THEOREM 2.4.1. Let $h = (w_1, w_2, \ldots w_n)$; h is a global history in S if and only if there is a string w over A such that $\pi(w) = h$.

Proof. The n-tuple h is a global history if, and only if, there are symbols $e_1, e_2, \ldots, e_m$ in A such that

$$h = \underline{e}_1\underline{e}_2\ldots\underline{e}_m;$$

since $\underline{e}_i = \pi(e_i)$ and π respects composition,

$$h = \pi(e_1)\pi(e_2)\ldots\pi(e_m) = \pi(e_1 e_2 \ldots e_m).$$

It means that h is a history if and only if there is a string w with $\pi(w) = h$. □

Now, we are going to explain the relationship between histories and traces. Let S be as above, and let $\Sigma = D(A_1) \cup D(A_2) \cup \ldots \cup D(A_n)$.

THEOREM 2.4.2. For any strings w', w" over A:

$$w' \equiv_\Sigma w'' \iff \pi_S(w') = \pi_S(w'').$$

Proof. (=>). Since the trace equivalence ≡ is the least congruence in A^* s.t. $(a,b) \in I$ implies $ab \equiv ba$, it suffices to show that the equivalence w'Ew" defined by $\pi(w') = \pi(w'')$ for all w', w" in A^* is also such a congruence. By properties of projection functions we can easily check that

$$\pi(w') = \pi(w'') \text{ and } \pi(u') = \pi(u'') \Rightarrow \pi(w'u') = \pi(w''u''),$$
$$\pi(\varepsilon) = \pi(w) \Rightarrow w = \varepsilon,$$

hence E is a congruence in A^*. Assume that $(a,b) \in I$; by definition of components $(A_1, A_2, \ldots, A_n)$ we see that there is no component A_i containing both a and b; it means that, for all i, $(ab)/A_i = (ba)/A_i = a/A_i$ if b is not in A_i, or $(ab)/A_i = (ba)/A_i = b/A_i$ if a is not in A_i. Thus, $\pi(ab) = \pi(ba)$. Therefore, $\equiv \subseteq E$, i.e. $w' \equiv w''$ implies $\pi(w') = \pi(w'')$.

(<=). We prove by induction on the length of w that $\pi(w) = \pi(u)$ implies $w \equiv u$. If $w = \varepsilon$ then $u = \varepsilon$ and $w \equiv u$. Assume $\pi(we) = \pi(u)$ with w in A^*, e in A, i.e. e is in A_i for some i; by definition of π e must occur in u. Thus, $u = u'eu''$ for some u', u" in A^*. Observe that e is independent of any symbol occurring in u"; otherwise e could not occur in we as the last symbol. It proves $eu'' \equiv u''e$, and $u'eu'' \equiv u'u''e$. It remains to show that $u'u'' \equiv w$, which is equivalent to $u'u_2e \equiv we$. By definition of projection $\pi(we) = \pi(u'eu'') = \pi(u'u''e)$ and consequently $\pi(we) = \pi(u'u'')$; by induction hypothesis $w \equiv u'u''$ and by Proposition 2.2.4 $we \equiv u'u''e$. It completes the proof. □

Denote by $\pi(A)$ the set $\{\pi(e) \mid e \in A\}$; thus, elements of $\pi(A)$ are n-tuples $(e/A_1, e/A_2, \ldots, e/A_n)$ for each e in A; clearly, if $(s_1, s_2, \ldots, s_n)$ is such a n-tuple, s_i is either e (if e is in A_i) or ε (if e is not in A_i). Therefore, $\pi(e)$ = $\underline{e}$. Denote also by $\pi(A^*)$ the set $\{\pi(w) \mid w \in A^*\}$ and define the composition operation $\circ$ in the set $\pi(A^*)$ by the equality:

$$\pi(u) \circ \pi(v) = \pi(uv).$$

Clearly, $\circ$ is an associative operation in $\pi(A^*)$ and $\pi(\varepsilon)$ is the neutral element of $\circ$. Thus we have the following theorem:

THEOREM 2.4.3. $\mathbf{H} = (\pi(A^*),\circ,\pi(\varepsilon))$; the component projection π is a homomorphism from $(a^*,\circ,\varepsilon)$ onto $\mathbf{H}$. □

THEOREM 2.4.4. Let $S = (A_1,A_2,\ldots,A_n)$, $n>0$, be n-tuple of finite alphabets, $A = \bigcup_i A_i$, $\Sigma = D(A_1) \cup D(A_2) \cup \ldots \cup D(A_n)$. The monoid $(\pi_S(A^*),\circ,\pi_S(\varepsilon))$ is isomorphic to the trace monoid $([A^*]_\Sigma,\circ,[\varepsilon]_\Sigma)$; the isomorphism is induced by the bijection

$$[A]_\Sigma \longrightarrow \pi_S(A): [e]_\Sigma \longmapsto \pi_S(e). \ \Box$$

Proof follows directly from Theorem 2.4.2 and well known properties of projections. □

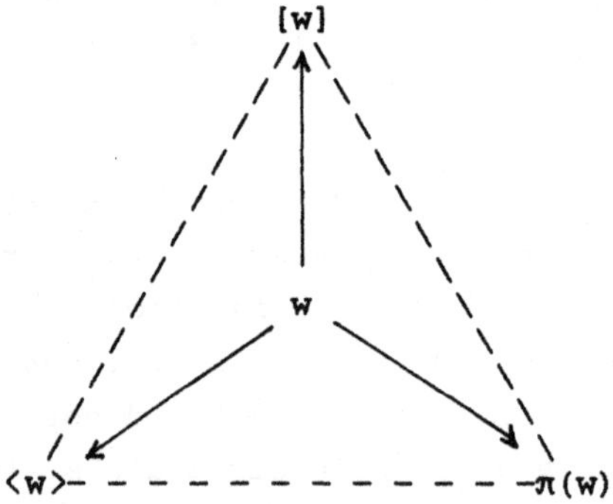

Fig. 2.4.1: The relationship between traces, graphs and histories.

Observe that the system S is not uniquely determined by the concurrent alphabet Σ = (A,D). The only condition relating Σ to S is the equality

$\Sigma = \bigcup_i D(A_i)$ saying that components of S are cliques of the dependency relation of Σ. There is a freedom in choosing these cliques: e.g. one can define S as consisting of two element components only; clearly, any finite relation is the union of two element cliques. Or one can take as components the maximal cliques of D; then the number of components is the smallest possible. Or, accepting systems with some identical components, one can make the number of components arbitrary large. In spite of this differences in "dimensions", all of them are isomorphic with each other as monoids.

The results of this section concerning a comparison of trace monoids with related algebras can be summarized by the diagram in Fig.2.4.1. The outer sides of the triangle represent correspondences between objects (placed at the vertices) of algebras; each correspondence establishes an isomorphism between the corresponding algebras. The inner arrows indicate correspondences establishing epimorphisms from the string monoid onto suitable algebras.

3. TRACES AND PARTIAL ORDER

There are two kinds of ordering defined by strings: the ordering of symbols within a string, called in the sequel the <u>occurrence ordering</u>, and the ordering of strings themselves by the prefix relation, the <u>prefix ordering</u>. Looking at strings as at models of sequential processes, the first determines the order of event occurrences within a process. The second is the order of process states, since each prefix of a string can be interpreted as a partial execution of the process interpreting by this string, and such a partial execution determines uniquely an intermediate state of the process. Both orderings, although different, are closely related: given one of them, the second can be reconstructed.

Traces are intended to be generalizations of strings, hence the ordering given by traces should be a generalization of that given by strings. Actually, it is a case; as we could expect, the orderings resulting from traces are partial. In this chapter we shall discuss in details the ordering resulting from trace approach.

We start from string ordering, since it gives us some tools and notions used next for defining the trace ordering. We shall consider both kinds of ordering: first the prefix ordering and next the occurrence ordering. In the whole chapter Σ will denote a fixed (except examples) concurrent alphabet, $\Sigma = (A,D)$; all subsequent notions will be related to Σ; all strings are assumed to be strings over A. The set of all traces over Σ will be denoted by θ.

3.1. **Prefix ordering.** Let $\sqsubseteq$ be a relation in A^* such that

$$v \sqsubseteq w \iff v \in Pref(w).$$

PROPOSITION 3.1.1. A^* is (partially) ordered by $\sqsubseteq$; for any string w, the set Pref(w) is linearly ordered by $\sqsubseteq$.

Proof is straightforward. □

Relation $\sqsubseteq$ is called the <u>prefix ordering</u> of strings.

Similarly as in case of strings, a trace σ is a <u>prefix</u> of a trace τ, if there is γ such that $\tau = \sigma\gamma$. The set of all prefixes of a trace τ will be denoted by $Pref(\tau)$. Extend now $\sqsubseteq$ to the set θ of all traces over Σ defining

$$\tau_1 \sqsubseteq \tau_2 \iff \tau_1 \in Pref(\tau_2).$$

If $\tau_1 \sqsubseteq \tau_2$, we say that τ_1 is <u>dominated</u> by τ_2 or that τ_2 <u>dominates</u> τ_1.

PROPOSITION 3.1.2. θ is (partially) ordered by $\sqsubseteq$.

Proof. Since $\tau = \tau\varepsilon$, $\sqsubseteq$ is reflexive; because of associativity of the trace composition, $\sqsubseteq$ is transitive; and since $\tau = \tau\sigma$ implies $\sigma = \varepsilon$, $\sqsubseteq$ is antisymmetric. □

For each trace τ the set $Pref(\tau)$ ordered by the prefix relation will be called the <u>prefix</u> <u>structure</u> of τ. The following example shows that in general the prefix structure of a trace is not linear.

EXAMPLE 3.1.1. Let $\Sigma = D(a,b) \cup D(a,c)$. In Fig. 3.1.1 the dependency graph of trace [abbca] and the prefix structure of [abbca] are presented. In both diagrams the arrows following from others by transitivity or reflexivity are omitted. □

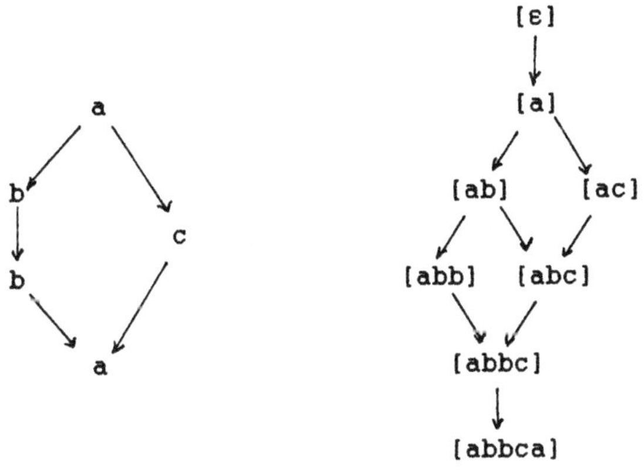

(a) (b)

Fig. 3.1.1: Dependency graph (a) and prefix structure (b) of [abbca] with bc ≡ cb

Thus, in contrast to linearly ordered prefixes of a string, the set Pref(τ) is ordered by ⊑ only partially. Interpreting a trace τ as a single run of a system, the ordering of symbol occurrences in τ (given by the dependence graph of τ) can be viewed as the ordering of event occurrences and the prefix structure of τ as the ordered set of all intermediate (global) system states reached during the run interpreted by τ. Since the ordering of event occurrences is partial, the ordering of states (the prefix structure) is also partial. In this interpretation [ε] represents the initial state, incomparable prefixes represent states arising in effect of events occurring concurrently; if τ_2 dominates τ_1, τ_1 represents a partial execution of a run leading to τ_2.

3.2 **Occurrence ordering in strings.** At the beginning of this section we give a couple of recursive definition of auxiliary notions. All of them define some functions on A^*; let in these definitions w denotes always a string over A, e, e', e" - symbols in A.

The <u>occurrence</u> <u>number</u> of e in w is an integer denoted by $\#(w,e)$ and defined recursively as follows:

$$\#(\varepsilon,e) = 0,$$
$$\#(we',e) = \#(w,e) + 1, \quad \text{if } e' = e,$$
$$\#(we',e) = \#(w,e), \quad \text{otherwise.}$$

The <u>occurrence</u> <u>set</u> of w is a set denoted by Occ(w) and defined recursively as follows:

$$Occ(\varepsilon) = \emptyset,$$
$$Occ(we) = Occ(w) \cup \{(e,\#(we,e))\}.$$

PROPOSITION 3.2.1. For each w, e, and $n \geq 0$: $(e,n) \in Occ(w) \iff n \leq \#(w,e)$.

Proof. Obvious. □

PROPOSITION 3.2.2. $Occ(w) = \{(e,n) \mid e \in A,\ 0 < n \leq \#(w,e)\}$.

Proof. Follows from Proposition 3.2.1. □

The above equality might be the alternative definition of Occ(w). It implies that a string and its permutation has a common occurrence set, as having the same occurrence number of symbols.

EXAMPLE 3.2.1. The occurrence set of the string "abbca" is the set $\{(a,1),(a,2),(b,1),(b,2),(c,1)\}$. □

The <u>occurrence</u> <u>ordering</u> in a string w is the set of pairs denoted by Ord(w) and defined recursively as follows:

$$Ord(\varepsilon) = \emptyset,$$
$$Ord(we) = Ord(w) \cup (Occ(we) \times \{(e,\#(we,e))\}).$$

Thus, $Ord(w) \subseteq Occ(w) \times Occ(w)$.

EXAMPLE 3.2.2. A diagram of (the transitive and reflexive reduction of) Ord(abbca) is shown in Fig. 3.2.1. □

$$(a,1) \longrightarrow (b,1) \longrightarrow (b,2) \longrightarrow (c,1) \longrightarrow (a,2)$$

Fig. 3.2.1: Ord(abbca)

PROPOSITION 3.2.3. Ord is a linear ordering of Occ(w).

Proof. It is true for $w = \varepsilon$. Assume that Ord(w) linearly orders Occ(w). Let $n = \#(w,e)$; then Ord(we) is the extension of Ord(w) by all pairs from $Occ(we) \times \{(e,n+1)\}$. Since

$$\begin{aligned} Occ(we) &= Occ(w) \cup \{(e,n+1)\} \\ Ord(we) &= Occ(we) \times \{(e,n+1)\} \\ &= Occ(w) \times \{(e,n+1)\} \cup \{((e,n+1),(e,n+1))\}, \end{aligned}$$

Ord(we) is a linear ordering of Occ(we). □

PROPOSITION 3.2.4. $Ord(w) \subseteq Ord(we)$.

Proof follows directly from the definition. □

Let $B \subseteq A$ and w be a string over A; recall that w/B denotes the projection of w onto alphabet B. We have the following propositions.

PROPOSITION 3.2.5. $\#(w/B,e) = \#(w,e)$ if $e \in B$, and $\#(w/B,e) = 0$ otherwise.

Proof is obvious. □

PROPOSITION 3.2.6. $Occ(w/B) \subseteq Occ(w)$.

Proof. If $w = \&$, the inclusion is trivial. Assume $Occ(w/B) \subseteq Occ(w)$ and consider Occ(we/B). If $e \in B$, then

$$\begin{aligned} Occ(we/B) &= Occ(w/B) \cup \{(e,\#(w/B,e)+1)\} \\ &= Occ(w/B) \cup \{(e,\#(w,e)+1)\} \\ &\subseteq Occ(w) \cup \{(e,\#(w,e)+1)\} \\ &= Occ(we). \end{aligned}$$

If $e \notin B$, then

$$\begin{aligned} Occ(we/B) &= Occ(w/B) \\ &\subseteq Occ(w) \\ &\subseteq Occ(w) \cup \{(e,\#(w,e)+1)\} \\ &= Occ(we). \end{aligned}$$

Thus, in both cases $Occ(we/B) \subseteq Occ(we)$. It completes the proof. □

3.3. **Occurrence ordering in traces.** In this section we generalize the notion of occurrence ordering from strings to traces.

PROPOSITION 3.3.1. For any strings u, v: $u \equiv v$ implies $Occ(u) = Occ(v)$.

Proof. If $u \equiv v$, then u is a permutation of v. The proof then follows from Proposition 3.2.2. □

The above proposition allows us to define the occurrence set for a trace τ as the occurrence set of an arbitrary representant of τ. We define now the occurrence ordering of a trace τ as the intersection of occurrence orderings of all representants of τ. Formally, the occurrence ordering of τ is the relation

$$Ord(\tau) = \bigcap \{Ord(u) \mid [u] = \tau\}.$$

$Ord(\tau)$ is indeed an ordering relation in $Occ(\tau)$ as the intersection of ordering relations of $Occ(\tau)$. From this definition it follows that the occurrence orderings of instances of a trace τ are all possible linearizations (extensions to the total ordering) of the occurrence ordering of τ and that the occurrence ordering of a trace τ is the greatest ordering common for all representants of τ. In the rest of this section we give some properties of this ordering and its alternative definitions.

We can interprete the ordering $Ord(\tau)$ as follows. Suppose there is a number of observers looking at the same concurrent process represented by τ. Observation made by each of them is sequential; each of them sees only one representant of τ. If two observers discover an opposite ordering of the same events in the observed process, it means that these events are not actually ordered in the process and that the difference noticed by observers results only because their specific points of view. Thus, such an ordering should not be taken into account, and consequently, two events can be considered as really ordered in the process if and only if they are ordered in the same way in <u>all</u> possible observations of the process (all observers agree on the same ordering).

3.4. **D-graph ordering**. Consider now d-graphs over Σ. Let γ = (V,R,φ) be a d-graph fixed for the rest of this section. Define

$$\xi : V \longrightarrow A \times \omega : v \longmapsto (\varphi(v), \#(v)),$$

where

$$\#(v) = \text{card } \{u \mid \varphi(u)=\varphi(v),\ (u,v) \in R\} + 1.$$

Since out of two nodes labelled with the same symbols one must precede the other, ξ is a one-to-one mapping assigning to each node of γ an occurrence of its label, i.e. an occurrence of a symbol from A. Since each d-graph determines a partial ordering of its nodes, and ξ is a one-to-one function, γ determines (via ξ) a partial ordering of symbol occurrences. The formal construction is the following. First, set $Occ(\gamma) = \xi(V)$.

PROPOSITION 3.4.1. For any string w: $Occ(\langle w\rangle) = Occ(w)$.

Proof. Clearly, $Occ(\langle\varepsilon\rangle) = \emptyset = Occ(\varepsilon)$. Assume $Occ(\langle w\rangle) = Occ(w)$, $e \in A$, and $\#(w,e) = n$. Then $Occ(\langle we\rangle) = Occ(\langle w\rangle) \cup \{(e,n+1)\} = Occ(w) \cup \{(e,n+1)\} = Occ(we)$. □

Next, define <u>occurrence</u> <u>relation</u> for $\gamma = (V,R,\varphi)$ as the binary relation $\xi(\gamma)$ in $Occ(\gamma)$:

$$\xi(\gamma) = \{(\xi(u),\xi(v)) \mid (u,v) \in R\}.$$

EXAMPLE 3.4.1. The diagram of the occurrence relation for the d-graph $\langle abbca\rangle$ over $D(a,b) \in D(a,c)$ is given in Fig. 3.4.1. □

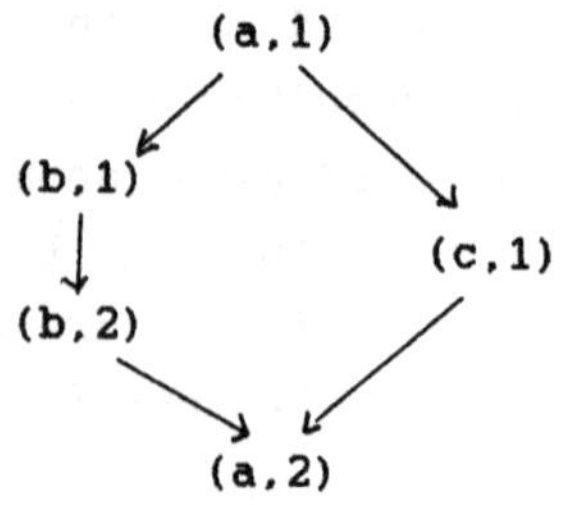

Fig. 3.4.1: The occurrence relation for <abbca> over D(a,b) ∪ D(a,c).

The transitive and reflexive closure of $\xi(\gamma)$ will be called the occurrence ordering of γ and denoted by Ord(γ). Since $\xi(\gamma)$ is acyclic, Ord(γ) is an ordering in Occ(γ).

PROPOSITION 3.4.2. For each string u, Ord(u) is an extension of Ord(<u>) to a linear ordering.

Proof. Let u be a string. It suffices to show that $\xi(\langle u\rangle) \subseteq \mathrm{Ord}(u)$, since then $\mathrm{Ord}(\langle u\rangle) = (\xi(\gamma))^* \subseteq (\mathrm{Ord}(u))^* = \mathrm{Ord}(u)$. Let $((e',n'),(e'',n'')) \in \xi(\langle u\rangle)$. Since Ord(u) is linear, either $((e',n'),(e'',n'')) \in \mathrm{Ord}(u)$, or $((e'',n''),(e',n')) \in \mathrm{Ord}(u)$, or $(e',n') = (e'',n'')$. But, because of the definition of <u>, only the first case is possible; it means that $\mathrm{Ord}(\xi(\langle u\rangle) \subseteq \mathrm{Ord}(u)$. □

THEOREM 3.4.1. For each string w: Ord([w]) = Ord(<w>).

Proof. Let w be a string and set $\Omega(w) = \{u \mid \langle u\rangle \cong \langle w\rangle\}$. By Theorem 2.3.3 $\Omega(w)$ is the set of all linearizations of <w>. Then $\{\mathrm{Ord}(u) \mid u \in \Omega(w)\}$ is the family of all extensions of Ord(<w>) to linear orderings; hence, because any ordering is the intersection of all its extensions to the total ordering,

$$\mathrm{Ord}(\langle w\rangle) = \bigcap \{\mathrm{Ord}(u) \mid u \in \Omega(w)\}.$$

By Theorem 2.3.5 $\Omega(w) = \{u \mid [u] = [w]\}$; thus, by definition of trace ordering, Ord([w]) = Ord(<w>). □

Each occurrence (e,n) of symbol e in a d-graph γ define the least prefix $\gamma(e,n)$ of γ containing n occurrences of e.

For each d-graph $\gamma = (V,R,\varphi)$ and each node v in V define $U = \{u \in V \mid u R^* v\}$ and $\downarrow_\gamma v$ as the d-graph $(U, R \cap (U\times U), \varphi|U)$.

PROPOSITION 3.4.3. For each d-graph γ, if $(e,n) = \xi(v)$, then

$$\gamma(e,n) \cong \downarrow_\gamma v.$$

In words: $\gamma(e,n)$ is the subgraph of γ induced by all nodes of γ preceding the node corresponding to the occurrence (e,n)).

Proof. Any prefix of γ containing n occurrences of e must contain the node v with $\xi(v) = (e,n)$; because $\gamma(e,n)$ is a prefix of γ, it must contain $\downarrow_\gamma v$; thus, $\downarrow_\gamma v$ is the least prefix with the required property. □

PROPOSITION 3.4.4. $((e',n'),(e'',n'')) \in Ord(\gamma) \iff \gamma(e',n') \subseteq \gamma(e'',n'')$.

Proof. Let v', v" be two nodes of γ such that $\xi(v') = (e',n')$, $\xi(v'') = (e'',n'')$. If $(v',v'') \in R$, then $\downarrow_\gamma v' \subseteq \downarrow_\gamma v''$ and by Proposition 3.4.3 $\gamma(e',n') \subseteq \gamma(e'',n'')$. If $\gamma(e',n') \subseteq \gamma(e'',n'')$, then $\downarrow_\gamma v' \subseteq \downarrow_\gamma v''$; it means that $(v',v'') \in R^*$, hence $((e',n'),(e'',n'')) \in Ord(\gamma)$. □

3.5. **History ordering**. Now, Let $S = (A_1,A_2,\ldots,A_n)$, n>0, be n-tuple of finite alphabets (concurrent components of S), fixed for the rest of this section, such that $\Sigma = D(A_1) \cup D(A_2) \cup \ldots \cup D(A_n)$. Let π be the component projection function w.r. to S. Let $h = (h_1,h_2,\ldots,h_n)$ be a global history in S; define <u>history ordering</u> in h as

$$Ord(h) = (\bigcup \{Ord(h_i) \mid 1 \leq i \leq n\})^*.$$

THEOREM 3.5.1. $Ord(\pi(w)) = Ord(\langle w\rangle)$.

Proof. Let $\pi(w) = (w_1,w_2,\ldots,w_n)$. and $1\leq i\leq n$. Consider w_i. By Proposition 3.2.6, since $w_i = w/A_i$, $Occ(w_i) \subseteq Occ(w) = Occ(\langle w\rangle)$. Since any two symbols in A_i are dependent, $Ord(w_i) \subseteq \xi(\langle w\rangle)$. Hence

$$\bigcup_i \mathrm{Ord}(w_i) \subseteq \xi(\langle w\rangle),$$

and

$$\mathrm{Ord}(\pi(w)) = (\bigcup_i \mathrm{Ord}(w_i))^* \subseteq (\xi(\langle w\rangle))^* = \mathrm{Ord}(\langle w\rangle).$$

To prove the inverse inclusion observe that if $((e',n'),(e'',n'')) \in \xi(\langle w\rangle)$, then (e',e'') must be dependent; hence it must be i, $1\leq i\leq n$, such that $e',e'' \in A_i$. It means that there is i such that $((e',n'),(e'',n'')) \in \mathrm{Ord}(w_i)$. Thus, $\xi(\langle w\rangle) \subseteq \mathrm{Ord}(\langle w_i\rangle)$, hence

$$\xi(\langle w\rangle) \subseteq \bigcup_i \mathrm{Ord}(w_i),$$

and consequently

$$\mathrm{Ord}(\langle w\rangle) = (\xi(\langle w\rangle))^* \subseteq (\bigcup_i \mathrm{Ord}(w_i))^* = \mathrm{Ord}(\pi(w)). \square$$

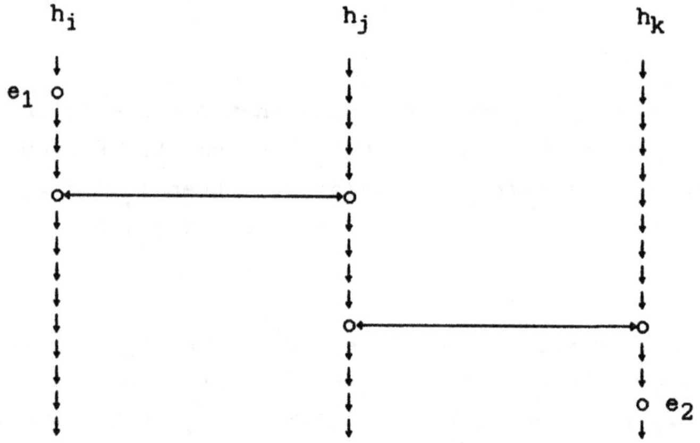

Fig. 3.5.1. History ordering: e_2 follows e_1.

The principle of history ordering Ord(h) is illustrated in Fig. 3.5.1. Let us interprete ordering Ord(h) in similar way as we have done it in case of traces. Each individual history of a component can be viewed as the result of a local observation of a process limited to events belonging to the repertoire of the component. From such a viewpoint, an observer can notice only events local to the component he is localized at; remaining actions are invisible for him. Thus, being localized at i-th component, he notices the ordering Ord(h_i) only. To discover the global ordering of events in the whole history, all such individual histories have to be put together; then events observed coincidently from different components form a sort of links between individual observations and make possible to discover an ordering between events local to separate and remote components. The rule is: an event occurrence (e",n") follows another event occurrence (e',n'), if there is a sequence of event occurrences beginning with (e',n') and ending with (e",n") in which every element follows its predecessor according to the individual history containing both of them (Fig.3.5.1). Such a principle is used by historians to establish a chronology of events concerning remote and separate historical objects.

Let us comment and compare all three ways of defining ordering within graphs, traces, and histories. They have been defined in the following way:

Ord(<w>):	as the transitive and reflexive closure of arc relation of <w>;
Ord([w]):	as intersection of linear orderings of all representants of [w];
Ord(π(w))	as the transitive closure of the union of linear orderings of all π(w) components.

All of them describe processes as partially ordered sets of event occurrences. They have been defined in different way: in natural way for graphs, as the intersection of individually observed sequential orderings in case of traces, and as the union of individually observed sequential orderings in case of histories. In case of traces, observations were complete, containing every action, but sometimes discovering different orderings of some events; in case of histories, observations were incomplete, limited only to local events, but discovering always the proper ordering of noticed events. In the case of traces the way of obtaining the global ordering is by comparing all individual observations and rejecting a subjective and irrelevant information (by intersection of individual orderings); in case of histories, all individual observations are collected together to gain complementary and relevant information (by unifying individual observations). While the second method has been compared to the method of historians, the first one can be compared to that of physicists. In all three cases the results are the same; it gives an additional argument for the above mentioned definitions and indicates their soundness.

4. TRACE SYSTEMS.

In this section sets of traces are the main object of consideration. If a single trace can represent a run of a concurrent system (the effect of a single execution of the system), a set of traces is thought as representing all possible runs (the behaviour) of a system. Different elements of such a set correspond to different choices (decisions) made in the course of the system run. Sets of traces will be called traditionally trace languages. Because of specific features of an important operation on concurrent systems (synchronization operation), we shall consider not languages themselves, but languages together with underlying alphabets. The constructs (concurrent alphabet, trace language) will be called trace systems.

4.1. **Trace languages.** Let $\Sigma = (A,D)$ be a concurrent alphabet. Each subset of the set $[A^*]_\Sigma$ (denoted in the sequel by θ) is called a <u>trace language</u> over Σ. Concatenation of trace languages is defined in usual way; for each trace languages T, S, their concatenation is the language

$$TS = \{\tau_1\tau_2 \mid \tau_1 \in T,\ \tau_2 \in S\}.$$

For each nonnegative integer n the power T^n of a trace language T over Σ is defined recursively:

$$T^0 = [\varepsilon]_\Sigma,$$
$$T^{n+1} = T^nT, \quad n \in \omega.$$

The iteration of T is the union

$$T^* = \bigcup_{n\in\omega} T^n.$$

PROPOSITION 4.1.1. The following formulas are valid for arbitrary (string) languages over A: L, L_1, L_2, and an arbitrary family $\{L_i\}_{i\in J}$ of such languages:

$[\emptyset] = \emptyset,$
$[L_1][L_2] = [L_1L_2],$
$L_1 \subseteq L_2 \Rightarrow [L_1] \subseteq [L_2],$
$[L_1] \cup [L_2] = [L_1 \cup L_2],$
$\bigcup_{i\in J} [L_i] = [\bigcup_{i\in J} L_i],$
$[L]^* = [L^*].$

Proof follows directly from the definition of traces and of trace languages. □

For each trace language T define, similarly to the sequential case,

$$\mathrm{Pref}(T) = \bigcup_{\tau\in T} \mathrm{Pref}(\tau).$$

A trace language T is <u>prefix closed</u>, if T = Pref(T); in other words, T is prefix closed, if

$$\tau \in T,\ \sigma \sqsubseteq \tau \Rightarrow \sigma \in T.$$

A trace language T is <u>directed</u>, if

$$\tau_1 \in T,\ \tau_2 \in T \Rightarrow \exists\tau\in T\colon \tau_1 \sqsubseteq \tau,\ \tau_2 \sqsubseteq \tau$$

4.2. **Regular trace languages.** Call two traces τ_1, τ_2 over Σ <u>independent</u>, if

$$\mathrm{Rng}(\tau_1) \times \mathrm{Rng}(\tau_2) \subseteq I_\Sigma,$$

and <u>dependent</u> otherwise. A trace τ over Σ is <u>connected</u>, if any nonempty traces τ_1, τ_2 with $\tau = \tau_1\tau_2$ are dependent. In other words, τ is connected if $\delta(\tau)$ is a connected graph.

Assign to each trace τ over Σ a set $\Delta_\Sigma(\tau) = \{\tau_1,\tau_2,\ldots,\tau_n\}$ of traces over Σ such that

$\tau = \tau_1\tau_2\ldots\tau_n,$
τ_i is nonempty and connected for each i, $1 \le i \le n$,
τ_i, τ_j are independent for each i, j, $1 \le i < j \le n$.

Elements of $\Delta_\Sigma(\tau)$ will be called <u>independent components</u> of τ, and the set $\Delta_\Sigma(\tau)$ the <u>decomposition</u> of τ. If Σ is known, we shall write $\Delta(\tau)$ rather than $\Delta_\Sigma(\tau)$.

EXAMPLE 4.2.1. Let $\Sigma = D(a) \cup D(b)$; then

$$\Delta([abbab]) = \{[aa], [bbb]\}. \square$$

It is clear that in case of full dependency $\Delta(\tau) = \{\tau\}$ for each trace τ.

Let T be a trace language over Σ; the <u>decomposition</u> of T is defined as the set

$$\Delta_\Sigma(T) = \bigcup_{\tau \in T} \Delta_\Sigma(\tau).$$

As usual, we write $\Delta(T)$ instead of $\Delta_\Sigma(T)$, if Σ is understood. From the above definition it follows that $\Delta(T)$ contains connected traces only. Furthermore, operation Δ has the following properties:

$T^* \subseteq \Delta(T)^*$;

$T = \Delta(T)$, if the dependency in Σ is full;

$\Delta(\Delta(T)) = \Delta(T)$.

We say that a trace language T is <u>connected</u>, if $T = \Delta(T)$. Obviously, if T, S are connected trace languages, then $T \cup S$ is also connected.

EXAMPLE 4.2.2. Let $\Sigma = D(a) \cup D(b)$. Then the language [ab] is not connected, since $[a] \in \Delta([ab]) = \{[a], [b]\}$ and $[a] \notin [ab]$; the language $[a \cup b]$ is connected. $\square$

The <u>trace iteration</u> $T^\#$ of a trace language T is defined as

$$T^\# = (\Delta(T))^*.$$

Roughly speaking, in $T^\#$ connected components of a trace in T are iterated independently of each other (being treated as separate elements of T), in contrast to the ordinary iteration T^*, where all components of a trace in T are iterated simultaneously. If dependency is full, then clearly $T^* = T^\#$.

EXAMPLE 4.2.3. Let $\Sigma = D(a) \cup D(b)$. Then $[ab]^* \neq [ab]^\#$, since $[ab]^* = \{[a^n b^n] \mid n \in \omega\}$, while $[ab]^\# = \{[a^n b^m] \mid n \in \omega, m \in \omega\} = [a^* b^*]$. □

Let T be a trace language over a concurrent alphabet Σ. For each trace τ over Σ denote by $Cont(\tau,T)$ and call the <u>continuation</u> of τ in T the set $\{\sigma \mid \tau\sigma \in T\}$.

Similarly to the case of string languages, call a trace language T <u>regular</u>, if the family of sets

$$\{Cont(\tau,T) \mid \tau \in \theta(\Sigma)\}$$

is finite. The following theorem characterizes regular trace languages in a similar way to the characterization of regular string languages; in fact, this theorem is a generalization of the Kleene characterization of regular string languages.

THEOREM 4.2.1 (Ochmański 1985). The class of all regular trace languages over Σ is the least class of languages containing all finite trace languages over Σ and closed w.r. to the union, concatenation, and the trace iteration operations.

Proof is too complex and involved to be quoted here. The reader is referred to [O1]. □

Observe that in case of full dependency, i.e. when traces are isomorphic with strings, this theorem is reduced to the Kleene theorem, since in this case trace and string iterations are identical (up to isomorphism).

An auxiliary result needed to prove the above theorem is interesting by itself. A binary relation $<$ in A^* is called a <u>lexicographical order</u> in A^*, if there is a strict linear ordering $<_0$ of elements of A such that $a_1 a_2 \ldots a_n < b_1 b_2 \ldots b_m$ holds iff either

$$a_1 = b_1,\ a_2 = b_2,\ \ldots,\ a_{j-1} = b_{j-1},\ a_j <_0 b_j$$

for an integer $j \leq n$, $j \leq m$, or $n \leq m$ and

$$a_1 = b_1,\ a_2 = b_2,\ \ldots,\ a_n = b_n.$$

Let now $\Sigma = (A,D)$ be a concurrent alphabet. For a given lexicographical ordering $<$ in A^* and any trace τ over Σ denote by $\mu(\tau)$ the minimal representant of τ (according to $<$). For any set T of traces the set $\mu T = \{\mu\tau \mid \tau \in T\}$ is the set of strings called the set of minimal representants of T w.r. to $<$. Now we can formulate the theorem.

THEOREM 4.2.2. For arbitary lexicographic ordering, a set T of traces is regular if and only if the set of minimal representants of T is regular.

Proof. See [O1]. □

This theorem can serve as a simple and useful criterion for checking regularity of trace languages.

EXAMPLE 4.2.4. Let $\Sigma = D(a,b) \cup D(a,c)$ and $a <_0 b <_0 c$; then the string "abbca" is the minimal representant of the trace [abcba]. The trace language $[(acb)^*]$ is regular, since the (string) language $(abc)^*$ of its minimal representants is regular. The trace language $[(bc)^*]$ is not regular, since the language $\{b^n c^n \mid n = 0,1,2,\ldots\}$ of its minimal representants is not regular. If we change the lexicographic ordering to e.g. $c <_0 a <_0 b$, the results remain the same: the regular string language $(acb)^*$ is the language of minimal representants of $[(acb)^*]$, and non-regular language $\{c^n b^n \mid n = 0,1,2,\ldots\}$ is the language of minimal representants of $[(bc)^*]$. □

4.3. **Fixed-point equations.** Let $\Sigma_1 = (A,D_1)$, $\Sigma_2 = (B,D_2)$ be concurrent alphabets and let φ be a function:

$$\varphi:\ 2^{A^*} \longrightarrow 2^{B^*}.$$

We say that φ is <u>monotonic</u>, if for each $X, Y \subseteq A^*$

$$X \subseteq Y \Rightarrow \varphi(X) \subseteq \varphi(Y),$$

and that φ is <u>congruent</u> (w.r. to Σ_1, Σ_2), if for each $X, Y \subseteq A^*$

$$[X]_{\Sigma_1} = [Y]_{\Sigma_1} \Rightarrow [\varphi(X)]_{\Sigma_2} = [\varphi(Y)]_{\Sigma_2}.$$

If φ is congruent, then there exists a function ψ,

$$\psi: 2^{\theta(\Sigma_1)} \longrightarrow 2^{\theta(\Sigma_2)}$$

such that for each $X \subseteq A^*$

$$\psi([X]_{\Sigma_1}) = [\varphi(X)]_{\Sigma_2}.$$

Clearly, arbitrary superpositions of monotonic and congruent functions are monotonic and congruent. For any set X and any function

$$\varphi: 2^X \longrightarrow 2^X,$$

a subset X_0 of X is the least fixed point of φ, if

$$\varphi(X_0) = X_0,$$

and for each $Y \subseteq X$

$$\varphi(Y) = Y \Rightarrow X_0 \subseteq Y.$$

The following theorem expresses the relationship between solving equations (finding fixed points) in the domain of string languages and that of trace languages.

THEOREM 4.3.1. Let $\Sigma = (A,D)$ be a concurrent alphabet. If

$$\varphi: 2^{A^*} \longrightarrow 2^{A^*}$$

is monotonic and congruent, X_0 is the least fixed point of φ, then $[X_0]_\Sigma$ is the least fixed point of function $[\varphi]_\Sigma$ defined for all $X \subseteq A^*$ by the equality

$$[\varphi]_\Sigma([X]_\Sigma) = [\varphi(X)]_\Sigma.$$

Proof. Let $\Sigma = (A,D)$ be a concurrent alphabet, φ be a monotonic and congruent function from subsets to subsets of A^*, and let X_0 be the least fixed point of φ. First, observe that for any language Y satifying $\varphi(Y) \subseteq Y$ we have $X_0 \subseteq Y$. Indeed, let Y_0 be the least language such that $\varphi(Y_0) \subseteq Y_0$; hence $Y_0 \subseteq Y$. Since φ is monotonic

$\varphi(\varphi(Y_0)) \subseteq \varphi(Y_0)$, hence $\varphi(Y_0)$ meets also the inclusion and consequently $Y_0 \subseteq \varphi(Y_0)$. It implies $Y_0 = \varphi(Y_0)$ and by the definition of X_0 we get $X_0 \subseteq Y_0 \subseteq Y$. Now,

$$[X_0] = [\varphi(X_0)] = [\varphi]([X_0])$$

by congruency of φ. It means that $[X_0]$ is a fixed point of $[\varphi]$. It remains to show that $[X_0]$ is the least such a point. Let T be a trace language such that $[\varphi](T) = T$ and let $X = \bigcup T$. Thus $[X] = T$ and $\bigcup T = \bigcup [X] = X$. Since $Z \subseteq \bigcup [Z]$ for any language Z and since T is the least fixed point of φ,

$$\varphi(X) \subseteq \bigcup[\varphi(X)] = \bigcup([\varphi]([X])) = \bigcup([\varphi](T)) = \bigcup T = X;$$

hence $\varphi(X) \subseteq X$. Thus, as we have already proved, $X_0 \subseteq X$, hence $[X_0] \subseteq [X] = T$. It proves $[X_0]$ to be the least fixed point of $[\varphi]$. □

This theorem can be easily generalized for tuples of monotonic and congruent functions. Functions built up from variables and constants by means of union, concatenation and iteration operations can serve as examples of monotonic and congruent functions. Another example of congruent functions are trace projections.

4.4. **Trace systems**. By a <u>trace system</u> we shall understand any ordered pair (Σ,T), where Σ is a concurrent alphabet and $T \subseteq \theta(\Sigma)$. The class of all trace systems will be denoted by Π. Similarly to string systems, let for each trace system $X = (\Sigma,T)$

$$\alpha(X) = \Sigma, \ \lambda(X) = T.$$

We shall write $\emptyset$ for the empty trace system $((\emptyset,\emptyset),\emptyset)$ and $X \subseteq Y$, if $\alpha(X) \subseteq \alpha(Y)$ and $\lambda(X) \subseteq \lambda(Y)$. Clearly, Π is partially ordered by $\subseteq$. By $X \cup Y$, $X \cap Y$ we shall mean systems $(\alpha(X)\cup\alpha(Y),\lambda(X)\cup\lambda(Y))$, $(\alpha(X)\cap\alpha(Y),\lambda(X)\cap\lambda(Y))$, respectively. A trace system X is said to be: <u>sequential</u>, if $\alpha(X) = D(A)$ for some alphabet A, i.e. if the dependency in $\alpha(X)$ is full; <u>regular</u> (<u>directed</u>, <u>prefix closed</u>), if $\lambda(X)$ is a regular (directed, prefix closed, resp.) trace language over $\alpha(X)$. To simplify the notation, if X,Y are trace systems, τ is a trace, we shall write $\theta(X)$, $\theta(X \cup Y)$, τ/X, etc, rather than $\theta(\alpha(X))$, $\theta(\alpha(X) \cup \alpha(Y))$, $\tau/\alpha(X)$, etc. If τ is a trace in $\theta(X)$, define

$$\tau X = (\alpha(X), \tau\lambda(X)), \quad X\tau = (\alpha(X), \lambda(X)\tau);$$

and extend this definition for trace languages:

$$TX = (\alpha(X), T\lambda(X)), \quad XT = (\alpha(X), \lambda(X)T),$$

for each trace language T over $\alpha(X)$.
The motivation for introducing trace systems is the same as that for string systems: within trace systems we can speak not only about occurrences of sybols in traces, but also about their absence.

4.5. **Trace projection** . Let Σ_1, Σ_2 be concurrent alphabets, $\Sigma = \Sigma_1 \cap \Sigma_2$, A be the alphabet of Σ, τ be a trace over Σ_1, $\tau = [w]$. Denote by τ/Σ_2 the (trace) projection of τ onto Σ_2, i.e. a trace over Σ, defined by the following equality

$$[w]_{\Sigma_1}/\Sigma_2 = [w/A]_{\Sigma}.$$

It can be easily checked that the above definition is correct, i.e. that if $[w]_{\Sigma_1} = [u]_{\Sigma_1}$, then $[w]_{\Sigma_1}/\Sigma_2 = [u]_{\Sigma_1}/\Sigma_2$.

Let Σ_1, Σ_2 be concurrent alphabets, $\Sigma = \Sigma_1 \cup \Sigma_2$. The following equalities hold:

$$\tau/(\emptyset,\emptyset) = [\varepsilon]_{(\emptyset,\emptyset)},$$
$$(\tau\sigma)/\Sigma = (\tau/\Sigma)(\sigma/\Sigma),$$
$$(\tau/\Sigma_1)/\Sigma_2 = \tau/(\Sigma_1 \cap \Sigma_2).$$

for all traces τ, σ over Σ.

4.6. **Trace synchronization.** The synchronization operation on traces is a trace analogue of the merging operation for string systems. By synchronization we mean a binary operation in Π, i.e. a function

$$\|: \Pi \times \Pi \longrightarrow \Pi$$

such that for each trace systems X, Y, using the infix notation,

$$\alpha(X\|Y) = \alpha(X) \cup \alpha(Y),$$

$$\lambda(X\|Y) = \{\tau \in \theta(X \cup Y) \mid (\tau/X) \in X,\ (\tau/Y) \in Y\}.$$

Synchronization operation $\|$ is assumed to bind weaker than the concatenation and stronger than other set-theoretical operations.

PROPOSITION 4.6.1. Let X, Y be trace systems. If $\alpha(X) = \alpha(Y)$, then $X\|Y = X \cap Y$.

Proof. Assume $\alpha(X) = \alpha(Y)$, $\tau \in \theta(X \cup Y)$; then $\tau/X = \tau/Y = \tau$, hence $\tau \in X\|Y$ iff $\tau \in X$ and $\tau \in Y$. □

PROPOSITION 4.6.2. Let X, Y, Z be trace systems, Σ_1, Σ_2 be concurrent alphabets, τ be a trace over $\alpha(X) \cup \alpha(Y)$. The following equalities hold:

(a) $X\|X = X$,

(b) $X\|Y = Y\|X$,

(c) $X\|(Y\|Z) = (X\|Y)\|Z$

(d) $(\Sigma_1,[\varepsilon])\|(\Sigma_2,[\varepsilon]) = (\Sigma_1 \cup \Sigma_2,\ [\varepsilon])$,

(e) $X\|\emptyset = \emptyset$,

(f) $(X \cup Y)\|Z = X\|Z \cup X\|Z$,

(g) $(X\|Y)\tau = X(\tau/X)\|Y(\tau/Y)$,

(h) $\tau(X\|Y) = (\tau/X)X\|(\tau/Y)Y$.

Proof. (a) follows from the previous proposition. (b) is obvious. Let σ be a trace; $\sigma \in X\|(Y\|Z)$ iff $\sigma/X \in X$ and $\sigma/(Y\|Z) \in (Y\|Z)$, i.e. iff $\sigma/X \in X$, $\sigma/Y \in Y$, and $\sigma/Z \in Z$. The same condition we get for $\sigma \in (X\|Y)\|Z$, which proves (c). (d) is obvious. (e) holds since there is no trace with a projection belonging to the empty set. Let σ be a trace; $\sigma \in (X \cup Y)\|Z$ iff $\sigma/(X \cup Y) \in (X \cup Y)$ and $\sigma/Z \in Z$ i.e. iff ($\sigma/X \in X$ or $\sigma/Y \in Y$) and $\sigma/Z \in Z$; this condition holds iff ($\sigma/X \in X$ and $\sigma/Z \in Z$) or ($\sigma/Y \in Y$ and $\sigma/Z \in Z$), which means $\sigma \in (X\|Z) \cup (Y\|Z)$. It proves (f). To prove (g), observe that $\sigma \in (X\|Y)\tau$ iff there is a trace ρ in $(X\|Y)$ s.t. $\sigma = \rho\tau$, i.e. iff there is ρ with ρ/X in X, ρ/Y in Y, and $\sigma = \rho\tau$. Since τ is in $\alpha(X) \cup \alpha(Y)$, this last condition is equivalent to the condition: there is ρ with $(\rho\tau)/X \in X(\tau/X)$ and $(\rho\tau)/Y \in Y(\tau/Y)$. It proves (g). Proof of (h) is similar. □

The essential difference between the (string) merging & and the (trace) synchronization $\|$ is that the last operation applied to singletons returns either a singleton or the empty set, which (in general) is not true for the merging operation; it means that $\|$ restricted to singletons is a partial function, while & similarly restricted is not.

The following propositions express some preservation properties of the synchronization operation.

PROPOSITION 4.6.3. If X, Y are regular trace systems, then so is $X \| Y$.

Proof. First we prove the following equality:

$$\mathrm{Cont}(\tau, X\|Y) = \mathrm{Cont}(\tau/X, X) \;\|\; \mathrm{Cont}(\tau/Y, Y).$$

By definition of continuations $\sigma \in \mathrm{Cont}(\tau, X\|Y)$ iff $\tau\sigma \in X\|Y$; by definition of synchronization operation $\tau\sigma \in X\|Y$ iff $(\tau\sigma)/X \in X$ and $(\tau\sigma)/Y \in Y$; by definition of projections $(\tau\sigma)/X \in X$ and $(\tau\sigma)/Y \in Y$ iff $(\tau/X)(\sigma/X) \in X$ and $(\tau/Y)(\sigma/Y) \in Y$. It means that $(\sigma/X) \in \mathrm{Cont}(\tau/X, X)$ and $(\sigma/Y) \in \mathrm{Cont}(\tau/Y, Y)$, i.e. that

$$\sigma \in \mathrm{Cont}(\tau/X, X) \;\|\; \mathrm{Cont}(\tau/Y, Y).$$

Now, let τ be an arbitrary trace. Since X, Y are regular, there are finite families $\{X_1, X_2, \ldots, X_n\}$, $\{Y_1, Y_2, \ldots, Y_m\}$ of all continuations in X and Y, respectively. Since the above families are families of all continuations, there are i, j such that

$$\mathrm{Cont}(\tau/X, X) = X_i, \quad \mathrm{Cont}(\tau/Y, Y) = Y_j.$$

Thus,

$$\mathrm{Cont}(\tau, X\|Y) = \mathrm{Cont}(\tau/X, X) \;\|\; \mathrm{Cont}(\tau/Y, Y) = X_i \;\|\; Y_j.$$

It proves that the finite family $\{Z_{11}, Z_{12}, \ldots, Z_{ij}, \ldots, Z_{nm}\}$ with $Z_{ij} = X_i \| Y_j$ is the family of all continuations in $X\|Y$. Therefore, $X\|Y$ is regular. □

PROPOSITION 4.6.4. If X, Y are prefix closed trace systems, then so is $X\|Y$.

Proof. Let X, Y be prefix closed trace systems, $\tau \in (X\|Y)$ and $\tau = \tau_1\tau_2$.

We have to prove that $\tau_1 \in (X\|Y)$. Since $\tau_1\tau_2 \in (X\|Y)$,

$$(\tau_1\tau_2)/X \in X \text{ and } (\tau_1\tau_2)/Y \in Y,$$

hence by distributivity of projections

$$(\tau_1/X)(\tau_2/X) \in X \text{ and } (\tau_1/Y)(\tau_2/Y) \in Y.$$

Since X and Y are prefix closed, $(\tau_1/X) \in X$ and $(\tau_1/Y) \in Y$; thus, by definition of synchronization, $\tau_1 \in (X\|Y)$. It completes the proof. □

The next theorem enables us to find the synchronization of trace languages by solving fixed point equations.

THEOREM 4.6.1. The synchronization operation $\|$ is the least binary operation in Π (w.r. to the inclusion ordering of Π) meeting the following properties:

(i) $(A,[\varepsilon])\|(B,[\varepsilon]) = (A \cup B,[\varepsilon])$

(ii) $(X \cup Y)\|Z = X\|Z \cup Y\|Z$,

(iii) $\tau(X\|Y) = (\tau/X)X\|(\tau/Y)Y$,

(iv) $X\|Y = Y\|X$,

for any concurrent alphabets A, B, any trace systems X, Y, Z, and any trace τ in $\theta(X \cup Y)$. □

Proof. By Proposition 4.6.2 the synchronization operation $\|$ satisfies conditions (i) - (iv). To prove that $\|$ is the least such operation, let $\varphi: \Pi \times \Pi \longrightarrow \Pi$ be another operation satisfying (i) - (iv), X, Y be two trace systems, τ be a trace in $\theta(X \cup Y)$, and prove by induction

$$\tau \in X\|Y \Rightarrow \tau \in X\varphi Y. \tag{*}$$

Observe first that by (ii) φ is additive, hence monotonic, w.r. to the first argument, and by (iv) monotonic w.r. to the both arguments. Assume $\tau \in X\|Y$, hence $\tau/X \in X$, $\tau/Y \in Y$. If $\tau = [\varepsilon]$, then $(\alpha(X),[\varepsilon]) \subseteq X$, $(\alpha(Y),[\varepsilon]) \subseteq Y$. By monotonicity of φ

$$(\alpha(X),[\varepsilon])\varphi(\alpha(Y),[\varepsilon]) \subseteq X\varphi Y,$$

and by (i)

$$(\alpha(X)\cup\alpha(Y),[\varepsilon]) \subseteq X\varphi Y$$

which means that $\tau \in X\varphi Y$. Assume now (*) to hold and let $[e]\tau \in X\|Y$ for some symbol e in $\alpha(X)\cup\alpha(Y)$. Since obviously $\tau \in (\alpha(X),\tau/X)\|(\alpha(Y),\tau/Y)$, by induction hypothesis

$$\tau \in (\alpha(X),\tau/X)\varphi(\alpha(Y),\tau/Y);$$

and by (iii)

$$[e]\tau \in ((\alpha(X),[e]\tau)/X)\varphi(\alpha(Y),([e]\tau)/Y).$$

Since $[e]\tau \in X\|Y$, $([e]\tau)/X \in X$ and $([e]\tau)/Y \in Y$; by monotonicity again

$$(\alpha(X),([e]\tau)/X)\varphi((\alpha(Y),[e]\tau)/Y) \subseteq X\varphi Y.$$

That is, $[e]\tau \in X\varphi Y$. Therefore, by induction, (*) holds for any trace τ. □

EXAMPLE 4.6.1. Let $A = D(a,b)$, $B = D(a,c,d)$ and let $X = (A,[(ab)^*(a \cup \varepsilon)])$, $Y = (B,[(ac)^*(ad \cup a \cup \varepsilon)])$ be trace systems. Find $X\|Y$.

First, put $X_0 = (A,[\varepsilon])$, $Y_0 = (B,[\varepsilon])$, and $Z_0 = (A \cup B,[\varepsilon])$. Next, write equations for X and Y:

$$X = [ab]X \cup ([a] \cup [\varepsilon])X_0,$$
$$Y = [ac]Y \cup ([ad] \cup [a] \cup [\varepsilon])Y_0.$$

Hence, by Theorem 4.6.1, $X\|Y$ is the least solution of the following equation:

$$X\|Y = ([ab]X \cup [a]X_0 \cup X_0)\|([ac]Y \cup [ad]Y_0 \cup [a]Y_0 \cup Y_0).$$

By (ii) we have

$$X\|Y = ([ab]X\|[ac]Y) \cup ([a]X_0\|[ac]Y) \cup (X_0\|[ac]Y) \cup$$

$$([ab]X \| [a]Y_0) \cup ([a]X_0 \| [a]Y_0) \cup (X_0 \| [a]Y_0) \cup$$
$$([ab]X \| [ad]Y_0) \cup ([a]X_0 \| [ad]Y_0) \cup (X_0 \| [ad]Y_0) \cup$$
$$([ab]X \| Y_0) \cup ([a]X_0 \| Y_0) \cup (X_0 \| Y_0);$$

by (i) and (iii) we get

$$[ab]X \| [ac]Y = [abc](X \| Y);$$
$$[a]X_0 \| [ac]Y = [ac](X_0 \| Y);$$
$$X_0 \| [ac]Y = \emptyset;$$
$$[ab]X \| [a]Y_0 = [ab](X \| Y_0);$$
$$[a]X_0 \| [a]Y_0 = [a](X_0 \| Y_0);$$
$$X_0 \| [a]Y_0 = \emptyset;$$
$$[ab]X \| [ad]Y_0 = [abd](X \| Y_0);$$
$$[a]X_0 \| [ad]Y_0 = [ad](X_0 \| Y_0);$$
$$X_0 \| [ad]Y_0 = \emptyset;$$
$$[a]X_0 \| Y_0 = \emptyset.$$

Thus, we have

$$X \| Y = [abc](X \| Y) \cup [ac](X_0 \| Y) \cup [ab](X \| Y_0) \cup [a](X_0 \| Y_0) \cup$$
$$[abd](X \| Y_0) \cup [ad](X_0 \| Y_0) \cup [\varepsilon](X_0 \| Y_0).$$

Now we need to calculate $X_0 \| Y_0$, $X_0 \| Y$, and $X \| Y_0$:

$$X_0 \| Y_0 = Z_0, \text{ (by (i))},$$
$$X_0 \| Y = X_0 \| ([ac]Y \cup [a]Y_0 \cup [ad]Y_0 \cup Y_0) = X_0 \| Y_0 = Z_0,$$
$$X \| Y_0 = ([ab]X \cup [a]X_0 \cup X_0) \| Y_0 = X_0 \| Y_0 = Z_0.$$

Denote $X \| Y$ by Z; then Z satisfies the following equation:

$$Z = [abc]Z \cup ([ab] \cup [ac] \cup [abd] \cup [ad] \cup [a] \cup [\varepsilon])Z_0.$$

By Theorem 4.3.1 the least solution of this equation is

$$[(abc)^*(abd \cup ab \cup ad \cup ac \cup a \cup \varepsilon]Z_0$$
$$= \mathrm{Pref}[(abc)^*abd]Z_0$$
$$= (A \cup B, \mathrm{Pref}[(abc)^*abd])$$
$$= (A \cup B, \mathrm{Pref}([abc]^*[abd])).$$

Since [abc] is a connected trace language over $A \cup B$ we have as well

$$X \| Y = (A \cup B, Pref([abc]^{*}[abd])).$$

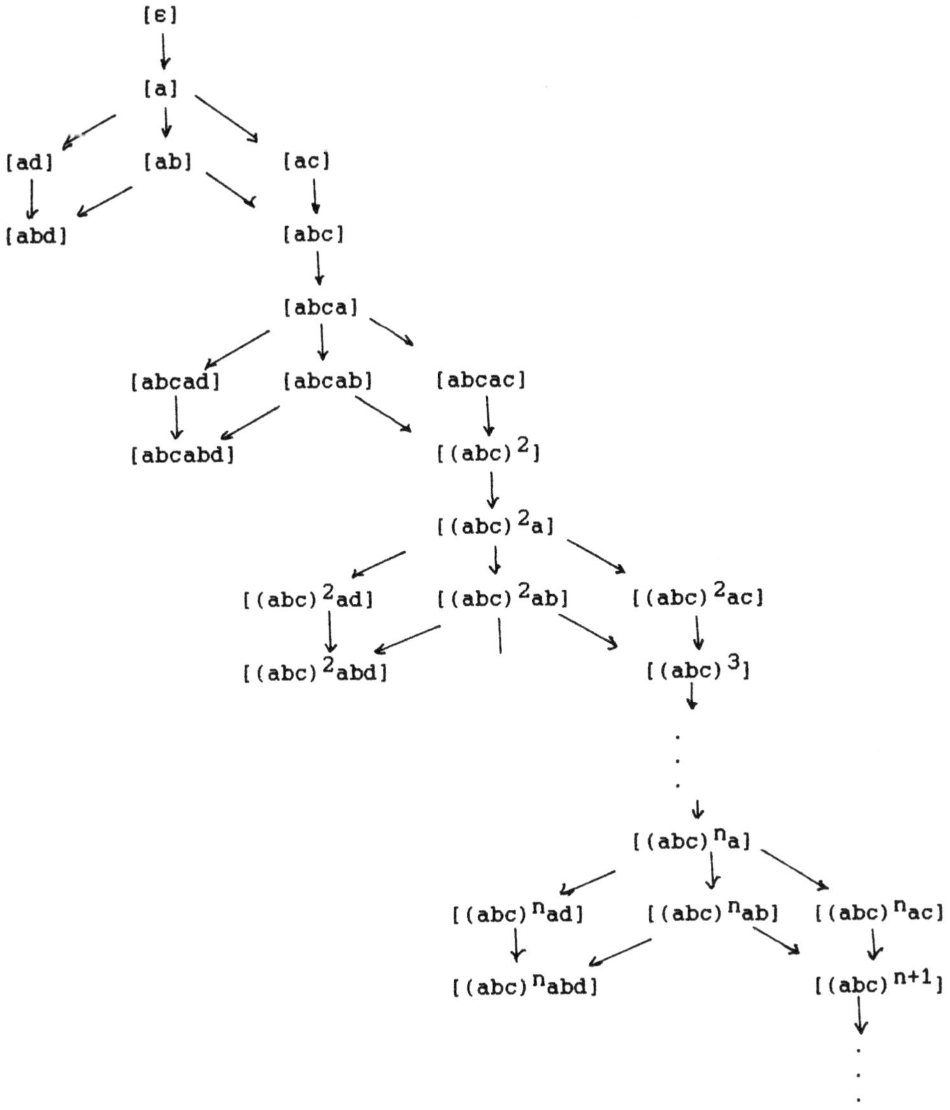

Fig. 4.6.1: Prefix structure of $Pref[(abc)^{*}abd]$ with $bc \equiv cb$, $bd \equiv db$.

The right-hand side of the above equality gives an explicit form of the synchronization of X and Y. Observe that while X and Y are sequential systems, $X\|Y$ is non-sequential trace system. Since $\alpha(X\|Y) = A \cup B = D(a,b) \cup D(a,c,d)$, (b,c) and (b,d) are independent. The diagram in Fig. 4.6.1 represents the prefix ordering of $X\|Y$. □

5. NETS AND TRACES

5.1. Condition - event systems. By a condition - event net system (CE system, for short), we understand any ordered quadruple

$$N = (B,E,F,C_{in}),$$

where B and E are finite, disjoint, nonempty sets (of conditions (or places) and events (or transitions) of N, respectively), $F \subseteq B\times E \cup E\times B$ (the flow relation of N), with $dom(F) \cup cod(F) = B \cup E$, and $C_{in} \subseteq B$ (the initial case of N). As all other types of nets, CE systems are represented graphically using boxes to represent events, circles to represent conditions, and arrows leading from circles to boxes or from boxes to circles to represent the flow relation; in such a representation circles corresponding to conditions in the initial case are marked with dots.

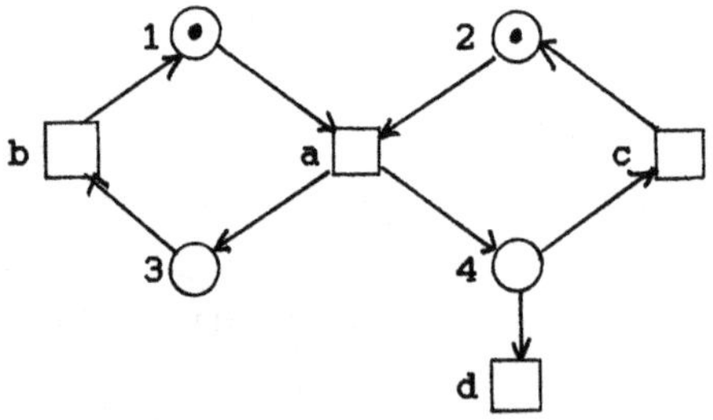

Fig. 5.1.1: A condition - event net system

EXAMPLE 5.1.1. The following quadruple is an CE system:

$N = (\{1,2,3,4\}, \{a,b,c,d\},$

$\{(1,a),(a,3),(3,b),(b,1),(2,a),(a,4),(4,c),(4,d),(c,2)\}$,
$\{1,2\})$.

In Fig. 5.1.1 this system is represented graphically. □

Let $N = (B,E,F,C_{in})$ be an CE system. For each $x \in B \cup E$, the sets:

$$Pre(x) = \{y \mid (y,x) \in F\},$$
$$Post(x) = \{y \mid (x,y) \in F\},$$
$$Prox(x) = Pre(x) \cup Post(x),$$

are called respectively the <u>preset</u>, the <u>postset</u>, and the <u>proximity</u> of x. Sets of conditions will be called <u>configurations</u>. Two CE systems are said to be <u>B-disjoint</u> (<u>E-disjoint</u>), if their sets of conditions (events, resp.) are disjoint.

5.2. **Firing sequences**. Let $N = (B,E,F,C_{in})$ be an CE system. The <u>transition function</u> δ_N of N is a partial function:

$$\delta_N: 2^B \times E \longrightarrow 2^B$$

such that

$$\delta_N(C_1,e) = C_2 \iff Pre(e) \subseteq C_1,\ Post(e) \subseteq C_2,$$
$$C_1 \backslash Pre(e) = C_2 \backslash Post(e).$$

It can be easily seen that this definition is correct, i.e. that for each configuration C and transition e there exists at most one C' such that $\delta_N(C,e) = C'$. Function δ_N describes a change of conditions holding caused by a single event occurrence, if it is defined; otherwise we say that the event has no concession to occur. The <u>reachability function</u> R_N of N is a partial function:

$$R_N: E^* \longrightarrow 2^B,$$

such that

$$R_N(\varepsilon) = C_{in},$$
$$R_N(we) = \delta_N(R_N(w),e),$$

for all $e \in E$, $w \in E^*$. Set

$$S_N = \mathrm{Dom}(R_N),\ C_N = \mathrm{Cod}(R_N),$$

and call elements of S_N (i.e. some sequences of events) firing sequences of N, and those of C_N (i.e. some configurations) cases of N. If w is a firing sequence and $R_N(w) = C$, then w is said to lead to the case C of N.

The string system (E,S_N) will be referred to as the sequential behaviour of N and denoted by SB_N. Clearly, SB_N is prefix closed and ordered into a tree by the prefix ordering. Maximal directed subsets of S_N are then full paths through this tree and can be viewed as sequential observations of the behaviour of N, i.e. observations made by observers capable to see only a single event occurrence at a time. The ordering of symbols in strings of SB_N reflects not only the (objective) causal ordering of event occurrences but also a (subjective) observational ordering resulting from a specific view over concurrent actions. Therefore, the structure of SB_N alone does not allow to decide whether the difference in ordering is caused by a conflict resolution (a decision made in the system), or by different observations of concurrency. In order to extract from SB_N the causal ordering of event occurrences we must supply SB_N with an additional information; as such information we take here the dependency of events.

5.3. **Firing traces**. Let $N = (B,E,F,C_{in})$ be an CE system fixed for this section. Define dependency in N as a relation $D_N \subseteq E\times E$ such that:

$$(e_1,e_2) \in D_N \iff \mathrm{Prox}(e_1) \cap \mathrm{Prox}(e_2) \neq \emptyset.$$

Clearly, D_N is a reflexive and symmetric. The complement of D_N in E will be called the independency in N. By definition, two events are independent in N, if and only if they have no adjacent conditions in common; if such events occur next to each other in a firing sequence, the order of their occurrences is irrelevant, since (according to our understanding of CE system activity) they occur concurrently in this execution. In order to get rid of this ordering we intend to replace the sequential description of CE systems behaviour by nonsequential one, expressing the behaviour of CE systems by traces rather than sequences. To this end, set $\Sigma_N = (E,D_N)$ and call Σ_N the concurrent alphabet <u>associated</u> with N; let $\equiv_N$ denote the trace equivalence over Σ_N and $[w]_N$ the equivalence class of $\equiv_N$ represented by w. As usual, the subscript N will be omitted if it causes no ambiguity.

The <u>trace behaviour</u> of N is defined as the trace system $TB_N = (\Sigma_N, [S_N])$; elements of TB_N will be called <u>firing traces</u> of N.

It is clear that each firing sequence of N is contained in some equivalent class belonging to TB_N. Conversely, from the theorem below it follows that each representant of a firing trace of N is a firing sequence of N and all equivalent firing sequences lead to the same case of N.

THEOREM 5.3.1. The reachability function R_N is congruent w.r. to Σ_N, i.e. for each two strings w_1, w_2 in E^*

$$w_1 \equiv_N w_2 \Rightarrow R_N(w_1) = R_N(w_2)$$

(here, the equality in the conclusion means that either both sides are defined and equal, or both of them are undefined). □

Proof. Let $w_1 \equiv w_2$; we have to prove $R_N(w_1) = R_N(w_2)$. Because of the definition of trace equivalence it suffices to consider the case with $w_1 = we_1e_2u$ and $w_2 = we_2e_1u$, for independent events e_1, e_2 and arbitrary w, u in E^*. Because of the reachability function definition, we have to prove only

$$\delta_N(\delta_N(C,e_1),e_2) = \delta_N(\delta_N(C,e_2),e_1)$$

for an arbitrary configuration C. By simple inspection we conclude that, because of independency of e_1 and e_2, i.e. because of disjointness of proximities of e_1 and e_2, both sides of the above condition are equal to a configuration C' with

$$C\backslash(Pre(e_1) \cup Pre(e_2)) = C'\backslash(Post(e_1) \cup Post(e_2)),$$
$$Pre(e_1) \cup Pre(e_2) \subseteq C,\ Post(e_1) \cup Post(e_2) \subseteq C',$$

or both of them are undefined. It completes the proof. □

This is another motivation for introducing traces for describing concurrent systems behaviour. Representing traces by their dependency graphs, firing traces can be viewed as partially ordered sets of symbol occurrences; the ordering within firing traces is determined by mutual dependencies of events and then it reflects the causal relationship between event occurrences rather than the non - objective ordering following from the string representation of the CE system activity.

PROPOSITION 5.3.1. TB_N is a prefix closed trace system. □

Proof follows directly from the recursive definition of reachability function. □

Let Σ be a concurrent alphabet. Two traces over Σ are said to be <u>consistent</u>, if both of them are prefixes of a common trace over Σ. A trace system (Σ, X) is <u>proper</u>, if each two consistent traces in X are prefixes of a common trace in X. Levi Lemma for traces and the transition function definition implies the following proposition.

PROPOSITION 5.3.2. TB_N is a proper trace system. □

Proof. Let t_1, t_2 be two traces in TB_N dominated by a trace t in Σ_N. Hence, for some t_3, t_4 we have $t_1t_3 = t = t_2t_4$. By generalized Levi Lemma there are traces s_1, s_2, s_3, s_4 such that $t_1 = s_1s_2$, $t_2 = s_1s_3$ and s_2, s_3 are independent. The reachability function is defined for t_1 and t_2, i.e. R_N is defined for s_1s_2 and for s_1s_3; because of independency of s_2 and s_3, R_N is also defined for the trace $s = s_1s_2s_3 = s_1s_3s_2$; thus, $s_1s_2s_3$ is in TB_N. Clearly, t_1 and t_2 are prefixes of s. □

Each firing trace uniquely determines a case of the CE system reached from its initial case. Moreover, each firing trace determines uniquely the way of reaching this case (the history of the CE system activity resulting with this case). Therefore, firing traces can be identified with (global) states of an CE system. In this approach a state defines, roughly speaking, what has already happened in the system. This identification would be impossible while dealing with firing sequences, since some different strings might represent the same history of the considered system; the one to one correspondence between firing sequences and states would not be achieved before identifying some of sequences into equivalence classes.

Maximal directed subsystems of TB_N will be called (trace) processes in N. If P is a process in N, then by its directedness and prefix closedness there exists a (generalized) dependency graph of P; thus, processes in N can be viewed as (possibly infinite) dependency graphs over Σ_N. The set of all processes in N describes all possible executions of the system represented by N.

5.4. **Composition and decomposition of systems.** In this section a modular way of finding the behaviour of CE systems is presented. It will be shown how to construct the behaviour of an CE system from behaviours of some parts of this CE system. The method is to decompose a given CE system into modules, to find their behaviours, to put them together, and to get in this way the behaviour of the original CE system.

We say that an CE system $N = (B,E,F,C_{in})$ is composed of CE systems $N_1 = (B_1,E_1,F_1,(C_{in})_1)$, $N_2 = (B_2,E_2,F_2,(C_{in})_2)$, and write

$$N = N_1 + N_2,$$

if N_1, N_2 are B-disjoint (i.e. $B_1 \cap B_2 = \emptyset$), $E = E_1 \cup E_2$, $B = B_1 \cup B_2$, $F = F_1 \cup F_2$, and $C_{in} = (C_{in})_1 \cup (C_{in})_2$. Obviously, $(C_{in})_1 \cap (C_{in})_2 = \emptyset$. If $N = N_1 + N_2$, N_1 and N_2 are called components of N.

PROPOSITION 5.4.1. For each pairwise B-disjoint CE systems N_1, N_2, N_3:

$$N_1 + N_2 = N_2 + N_1,$$
$$(N_1 + N_2) + N_3 = N_1 + (N_2 + N_3). \; \Box$$

Thus, + is a symmetric and associative operation on B-disjoint CE systems; it makes possible to omit parentheses and disregard the order of terms in composition.

PROPOSITION 5.4.2. For each B-disjoint CE systems N_1, N_2:

$$\Sigma_{N_1+N_2} = \Sigma_{N_1} \cup \Sigma_{N_2}. \; \Box$$

The main theorem of this section is the following:

THEOREM 5.4.1. If $N_1, N_2, \ldots, N_k$, $k \geq 1$, are pairwise B-disjoint CE systems, then

$$TB_{N_1+N_2+\ldots+N_k} = TB_{N_1} \| TB_{N_2} \| \ldots \| TB_{N_k}. \ \square$$

Proof. Let $N_1, N_2, \ldots, N_k$ be pairwise place-disjoint CE systems, $N = (B,E,F,C_0) = N_1+N_2+\ldots+N_k$; for each i, $1 \leq i \leq k$, let $N_i = (B_i,E_i,F_i,C_{0i})$ and let Σ_i be the concurrent alphabet of N_i; R_i, pre_i, $post_i$, $prox_i$ denote reachability, preset, postset, and proximity functions for N_i; R, pre, post, prox be those functions for N. Let, for each $C \subseteq B$, $C_i = C \cap B_i$. Finally let $\Sigma = \Sigma_1 \cup \Sigma_2 \cup \ldots \cup \Sigma_k$. Let $Q_i(C)$ denotes the set $\{w \mid R_i(w) = C\}$ and $Q(C)$ the set $\{w \mid R(w) = C\}$.

We have to prove that for each string w and for each C in B:

$$w \in Q(C) \iff \forall\, i: w/E_i \in Q_i(C_i).$$

The proof will be carried on by induction w.r. to the length of w.

(a) $w = \varepsilon$. Then

$$\begin{aligned}
&\varepsilon \in Q(C)\\
\iff\ & C = C_0\\
\iff\ & \forall\, i: C_i = C_{0i}\\
\iff\ & \forall\, i: \varepsilon \in Q_i(C_i).
\end{aligned}$$

(b) $w = ue$, $e \in E$, $w \in E^*$.

$$\begin{aligned}
&w \in Q(C) \iff ue \in Q(C)\\
\iff\ & \exists\, C': u \in Q(C'),\ \delta(c',e) = C\\
\iff\ & \exists\, C': \forall\, i: u/E_i \in Q_i(C'_i),\ \delta(C',e) = C, \quad \text{(by ind. hyp.)}\\
\iff\ & \exists\, C': \forall\, i: u/E_i \in Q_i(C'_i),\ pre(e) \subseteq C',\ post(e) \subseteq C,\\
& \quad C'\backslash pre(e) = C\backslash post(e)\\
\iff\ & \exists\, C': \forall\, i: u/E_i \in Q_i(C'_i),\\
& \quad (e \notin E_i,\ C'_i = C_i, \text{ or}\\
& \quad e \in E_i,\ pre_i(e) \subseteq C'_i,\ post_i(e) \subseteq C_i, C'_i\backslash pre_i(e) = C_i\backslash post_i(e))\\
\iff\ & \forall\, i: ue/E_i \in Q_i(C_i)\\
\iff\ & \forall\, i: w/E_i \in Q_i(C_i).
\end{aligned}$$

By induction, the theorem is proved. □

This theorem allows us to find the behaviour of an CE system knowing behaviours of its components. One can expect the behaviour of components to be easier to compute than that of the whole CE system. In fact, there exists a standard set of very simple CE systems, with behaviours already known, such that an arbitrary CE system can be composed from systems in this set; these CE systems, containing only one condition, will be called atomic CE systems or simply atoms.

Let $N = (B,E,F,C_{in})$ be an CE system; for each $b \in B$ the CE system

$$N_b = (\{b\}, Prox(b), F_b, (C_{in})_b),$$

where

$$F_b = \{(e,b) \mid e \in Pre(b)\} \cup \{(b,e) \mid e \in Post(b)\},$$
$$(C_{in})_b = C_{in} \cap \{b\},$$

is called an atom of N (determined by b). Clearly, the following proposition holds:

PROPOSITION 5.4.3. Each CE system is the composition of all its atoms.
□

In Fig. 5.4.1 atoms of the CE system from Example 5.1.1 are presented.

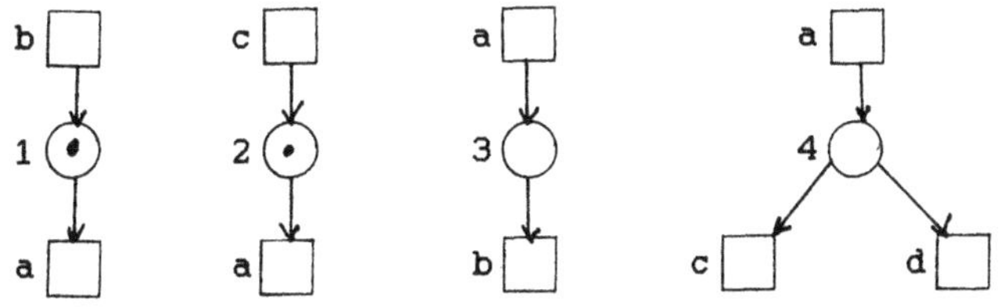

Fig. 5.4.1: Atomic CE systems

PROPOSITION 5.4.4. Let N = (b,Prox(b),F,C) be an atomic CE system, U = Pre(b)\Post(b), V = Post(b)\Pre(b), W = Pre(b)∩Post(b), A = Prox(b) (Fig. 5.4.2). Then

$TB_N = (D(A), [(W^*VU)^*W^*(V \cup \varepsilon)])$, if $b \in C$, and
$TB_N = (D(A), [(UW^*V)^*(UW^* \cup \varepsilon)])$, if $b \notin C$.

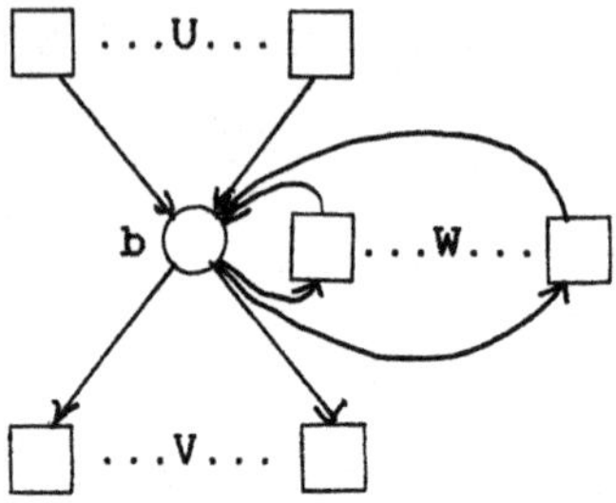

Fig. 5.4.2

Proof. Observe first that any atomic CE system is sequential, since the dependency relation of its alphabet is full. It implies that its firing traces are isomorphic with its firing sequences, hence we shall consider sequences rather than traces. If $b \in C$, then such a sequence may look as follows: first zero or more occurrences of some events from W, then an occurrence of an event from V; at this moment condition b ceases to hold; next an occurrence of an event from U, turning back condition b to hold, and all over again, zero or more times. Such a behaviour is described by the expression $(W^*VU)^*$. If we add to such a behaviour all its possible prefixes, we obtain the expression $(W^*VU)^*W^*(V \cup \varepsilon)$. It is clear that there is no sequences outside this set possible in this case. If $b \notin C$, then each non-empty sequence must start with an occurrence of an event from U, to start holding condition b, and next the situation is similar to that discussed above. All such sequences, together with their prefixes, are described by the expression $(UW^*V)^*(UW^* \cup \varepsilon)$. It ends the proof. □

Observe that in case of absence of events in W the expressions for the behaviour of atomic CE systems reduce to:

$$TB_N = (D(A),[(VU)^*(V \cup \varepsilon)]), \quad \text{if } b \in C, \text{ and}$$
$$TB_N = (D(A),[(UV)^*(U \cup \varepsilon)]), \quad \text{if } b \notin C,$$

since then $W^* = \emptyset^* = \varepsilon$ by the definition of iteration *. If, moreover, U (or V) is empty, then the expressions look as follows:

$$TB_N = (D(A),[V \cup \varepsilon]), \text{if } b \in C, \text{ and } TB_N = (D(A),[\varepsilon]), \text{if } b \notin C$$

or, respectively,

$$TB_N = (D(A),[\varepsilon]), \text{if } b \in C, \text{ and } TB_N = (D(A),[U \cup \varepsilon]), \text{ if } b \notin C.$$

Proposition 5.4.4 together with Theorem 5.4.1 is to the effect that the activity of an arbitrary CE system can be found by performing the synchronization operation applied to trace behaviours of atoms of the system; these behaviours are given by the above expressions. Thus, for an arbitrary CE system it is possible to write down an explicit expression built up from (unique) event names and operations: ε (nullary), $*$ (unary), and $\cup$, $\circ$, $\|$ (binary).

EXAMPLE 5.4.1. Consider CE system N from Example 5.1.1. Trace behaviours of its atoms (presented in Fig. 5.4.1) are:

$$TB_{N_1} = (D(a,b),[(ab)^*(a \cup \varepsilon)]),$$
$$TB_{N_2} = (D(a,c),[(ac)^*(a \cup \varepsilon)]),$$
$$TB_{N_3} = (D(a,b),[(ab)^*(a \cup \varepsilon)]),$$
$$TB_{N_4} = (D(a,c,d),[(a(c \cup d))^*(a \cup \varepsilon)]).$$

By idempotency of $\|$ we get

$$TB_{N_1+N_3} = TB_{N_1} \| TB_{N_3} = (D(a,b),[(ab)^*(a \cup \varepsilon)]).$$

Now, set

$$X = TB_{N_2},\ Y = TB_{N_4},\ X_0 = (D(a,c),[\varepsilon]),\ Y_0 = (D(a,b,c),[\varepsilon]);$$

by Theorem 4.3.1 we have the following equations for X and Y:

$$X = [ac]X \cup [a \cup \&]X_0, \quad Y = [ac \cup ad]Y \cup [a \cup \varepsilon]Y_0;$$

and by Theorem 4.6.1(ii) we get the following equation for $X \| Y$:

$$\begin{aligned} X\|Y &= [ac]X\|[ac]Y \cup [ac]X\|[ad]Y \cup [ac]X\|[a \cup \varepsilon]Y_0 \cup \\ &\qquad [a \cup \varepsilon]X_0\|[ac \cup ad]Y \cup [a \cup \varepsilon]X\|[a \cup \varepsilon]Y_0 \\ &= [ac]X\|[ac]Y \cup [a]X_0\|[ad]Y \cup [a]X_0\|[a]Y_0 \cup [\varepsilon]X_0\|[\varepsilon]Y_0 \end{aligned}$$

(all remaining terms vanish); by Theorem 4.6.1(iii) we obtain

$$X\|Y = [ac](X\|Y) \cup [ad](X_0\|Y) \cup [a](X_0\|Y_0) \cup [\varepsilon](X_0\|Y_0);$$

set $Z = X\|Y$, $Z_0 = X_0\|Y_0$; since $X_0\|Y = (D(a,c,d),[\varepsilon]) = Z_0$ we have the following equation:

$$Z = [ac]Z \cup [ad \cup a \cup \varepsilon]Z_0$$

for $X\|Y$. By Theorem 4.3.1 the least solution of this equation is $[(ac)^*(ad \cup a \cup \varepsilon)]Z_0$; thus,

$$TB_{N_2+N_4} = (D(a,c,d),[(ac)^*(ad \cup a \cup \varepsilon)]).$$

To get TB_N we need to calculate

$$TB_{N_1+N_3}\|TB_{N_2+N_4};$$

which has already been done in Example 4.6.1; thus, finally

$$\begin{aligned} TB_N &= (\Sigma, [(abc)^*(abd \cup ab \cup ad \cup a \cup \varepsilon)]) \\ &= (\Sigma, Pref([(abc)^*(abd)])), \end{aligned}$$

where $\Sigma = D(a,b) \cup D(a,c,d)$. Independent events in Σ are then (b,c) and (b,d). The structure of states of TB_N is given in Fig. 4.6.1. □

THEOREM 5.4.2. The trace behaviour of any CE system is a trace regular language.

Proof. Since the dependency of alphabets of atoms is full, the minimal representant of a trace $[w]$ is simply w, for any lexicographic ordering. Thus, by Proposition 5.4.4 the set of minimal representants of the behaviour of atoms is regular. Therefore, by Theorem 4.2.2, the behaviour of atomic CE systems is regular. Hence, Proposition 4.6.3 together with Proposition 5.4.3 proves the theorem. □

Naturally, to find the behaviour of an CE system we do not need to decompose it into atoms; it suffices to decompose it into some modules of already known behaviours, e.g. into sequential subnets the behaviour of which can be found by methods elaborated within the theory of sequential systems.

6. TRACES AND PROCESSES

6.1. **State space.** In the last chapter the behaviour of CE systems was expressed in terms of some prefix closed and proper trace systems. In the present chapter concurrent processes viewed as trace languages will be discussed in an abstract framework, i.e. without referring to concrete mechanisms (as e.g. CE systems) generating them. Here, the basic notions will be that of an (atomic) action, represent by a symbol (letter) and that of the dependency / independency of such symbolic actions; let then $\Sigma = (A,D)$ be a concurrent alphabet, fixed for the rest of this chapter, and θ be the set of all traces over Σ. Elements of Σ will represent atomic actions and pairs in D – their mutual dependency. Because of our intended interpretation, traces over Σ will be called <u>states</u>, and the set θ of all states over Σ – the <u>state space</u>; θ is partially ordered by the domination relation $\sqsubseteq$:

$$\sigma_1 \sqsubseteq \sigma_2 \iff \sigma_1 \in \mathrm{Pref}(\sigma_2).$$

For any subset Q of θ define

$$\uparrow Q = \{\tau \in \theta \mid \exists \sigma \in Q: \sigma \sqsubseteq \tau\},$$
$$\downarrow Q = \{\tau \in \theta \mid \exists \sigma \in Q: \tau \sqsubseteq \sigma\}.$$

We say that a subset Q of θ <u>dominates</u> another subset R of θ (or that R is <u>dominated</u> by Q), if $R \subseteq \downarrow Q$. Two states are <u>consistent</u>, if there is a state in the state space dominating both of them and <u>inconsistent</u> otherwise. A set P of states is said to be <u>proper</u>, if any two of its consistent states are dominated by a state in P, and <u>directed</u>, if arbitrary two states in P are dominated by a state in P. Clearly, any directed set of states is proper, but not the other way around. A maximal chain in P will be called a line in P. A set of states is conflict-free, if any two of its states are consistent; and it is sequential, if any two its consistent states are comparable. Thus, each sequential set of states is proper.

6.2. **Trace structures.** By a trace structure over Σ we shall mean any prefix closed and proper trace language over Σ; traces in a trace structure T will be called states of T.

From Propositions 5.3.1 and 5.3.2 it follows that if (Σ,T) is the trace behaviour of any CE system, T is a trace structure over Σ; the convers is not true in general. By the diagram of a trace structure T we shall understand the graph of the poset $(T,\sqsubseteq)$; in such a graph arcs resulting from others by transitivity or reflexivity will be omitted. Examples of such graphs were given in Fig. 3.1.1(b) and Fig. 4.6.1.

Trace structures are intended to represent the behaviour of concurrent systems. Let T be a trace structure and let σ', σ'' be states in T. As it has been mentioned above, if a state σ' is dominated by another state σ'', it means that there is a run of the represented concurrent system, containing both of them, in which σ'' comes up not earlier than σ'. Thus, two states are comparable, if and only if they appear in the same execution of the concurrent system and the history of one of them is an initial part of the history of the other. If σ' is incomparable with σ'', two cases are possible: either both of them are dominated by a common state (then they are consistent), or such a common state does not exist (then they are inconsistent). In the first case σ' and σ'' are two states of the same run of the concurrent system, but resulting in effect of concurrent actions of the system; they identify different pieces of the same history, exhibited later by the common dominating state. In the second case σ' and σ'' are states identifying pieces of two different histories, resulting in effect of a choice (a conflict resolution) made earlier during the system action.

A trace structure T is sequential (conflict free), if T is a sequential (conflict free) trace language.

PROPOSITION 6.2.1. A trace structure is sequential iff its diagram is a rooted tree; a trace structure is conflict free, iff it is directed.

Proof is obvious. □

Maximal (w. r. to the inclusion ordering) directed subsets of a trace structure T will be called <u>processes</u> in T. Clearly, all processes are prefix closed. Because of directedness, any process contains only states appearing in a single run of the represented system, since all of them can be viewed as prefixes of the same history. Because of maximality, processes describe full executions of the concurrent system being interpreted.

EXAMPLE 6.2.1. It has been shown that the trace behaviour of the CE system from Example 5.1.1 is (Σ,T) where

$$\Sigma = D(a,b) \cup D(a,c,d), \quad T = Pref[(abc)^{*}abd];$$

T is a trace structure; the diagram of T has been presented in Fig. 4.6.1. Processes in T are trace languages

$$P_0, P_1, \ldots, P_n, \ldots, P_\omega,$$

where $P_n = Pref[(abc)^n abd]$ for each $n \in \omega$, and $P_\omega = Pref[(abc)^{*}]$. Observe that for each n process P_n is finite, and P_ω is infinite.

Diagrams of P_n and of P_ω are given in Fig. 6.2.1.

PROPOSITION 6.2.2. The set of processes of any trace structure is not empty.

Proof. The set of directed subsets of any trace structure is not empty; each such subset can be extended to a process, hence the Proposition is proved. □

Let T be a trace structure; a state is <u>terminal</u> in T, if it is a maximal state of T; clearly, if a trace structure T contains a terminal state σ, then $Pref(\sigma)$ is a finite process in T; conversely, any finite process in T is equal to $Pref(\sigma)$ for some terminal state σ.

PROPOSITION 6.2.3. The only process in a conflict free trace structure is the trace structure itself.

Proof. Conflict free trace structure is directed. □

PROPOSITION 6.2.4. A subset of a sequential trace structure T is a process in T if and only if it is a line in T.

Proof. Any directed subset of a tree is a line. □

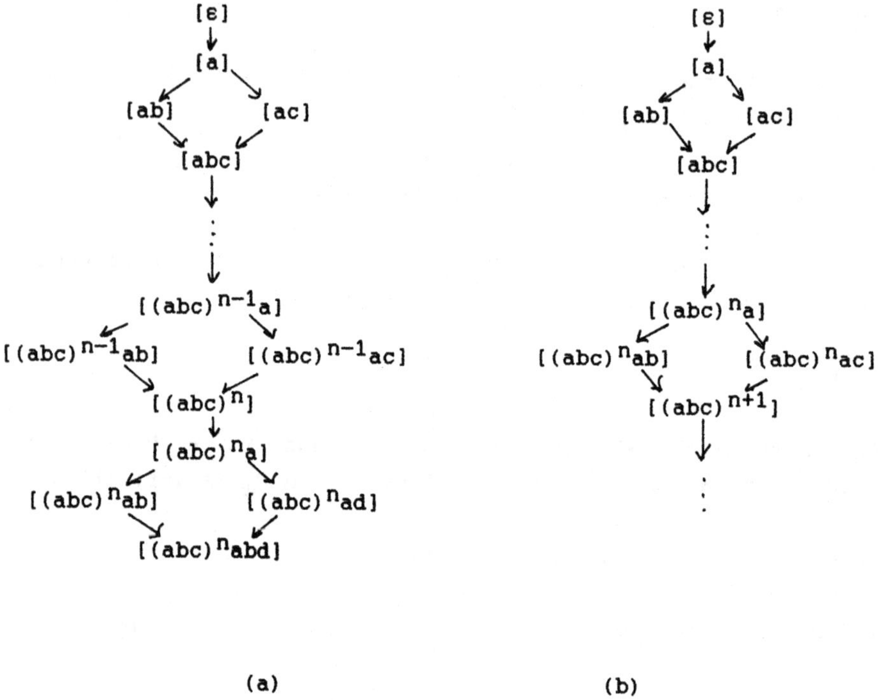

Fig. 6.2.1: Processes P_n (a) and P_ω (b)

6.3. **Observations**. To prove inevitable properties of concurrent systems (discussed in the next section) we need the notion of an observation. Intuitively speaking, an observation is a finite or infinite sequence of states as seen by a sequential observer of a system. Because of possible concurrency, different observers can notice different order of action execution and, consequently, their observations consist of different system states. Objective properties of the system behaviour are independent on particular observations, hence such properties should be discovered by all system observations provided they are faithful, i.e. they do not overlook any action performed by the system. These intuitions give rise to the following formal definition.

By an <u>observation</u> of a trace structure T we mean any line V in T such that $\downarrow V$ is a process in T.

Recall here that any process is a maximal directed subsystem of T, i.e. it contains every possible state of a single run of the represented system; each line is a maximal sequential observation of the system run; to guarantee the "faithfulness" of such an observation we require the maximality of $\downarrow V$. The set $\downarrow V$ of states is obviously directed for any line V in T, but not necessarily it is a maximal directed subsystem of T. Because of this maximality property, one can say that an observation is a line that dominates everything possible to be dominate by a line.

THEOREM 6.3.1. For each system T and each process P in T there exists an observation of T dominating P.

Proof. Let P be a process in T. If P is empty, then P is (the only) observation of P. Assume P to be not empty. As a set of traces over a finite alphabet P is countable; let then

$$(\sigma_0, \sigma_1, \ldots, \sigma_n, \ldots)$$

be an enumeration of P (i.e. $P = \{\sigma_n \mid n \in \omega\}$). Define a sequence $V = (\tau_0, \tau_1, \ldots, \tau_n, \ldots)$ inductively as follows:

$\tau_0 = \sigma_0$;

τ_{n+1} is a trace in P dominating τ_n and σ_{n+1}.

Such a trace exists since P is directed. Clearly, V is linearly ordered since $\tau_n \sqsubseteq \tau_{n+1}$ for each n; moreover, V dominates P. Indeed, let $\sigma' \in P$; then $\sigma' = \sigma_j$ for some j, hence $\sigma' \sqsubseteq \tau_j$. Thus, each trace in P is dominated by a trace in V. Extending V to a line we get an observation of P. □

EXAMPLE 6.3.1. Let $\Sigma = D(a) \cup D(b)$, $T = (a \cup b)^*$. T is clearly a system. The diagram of T is given in Fig. 6.3.1.

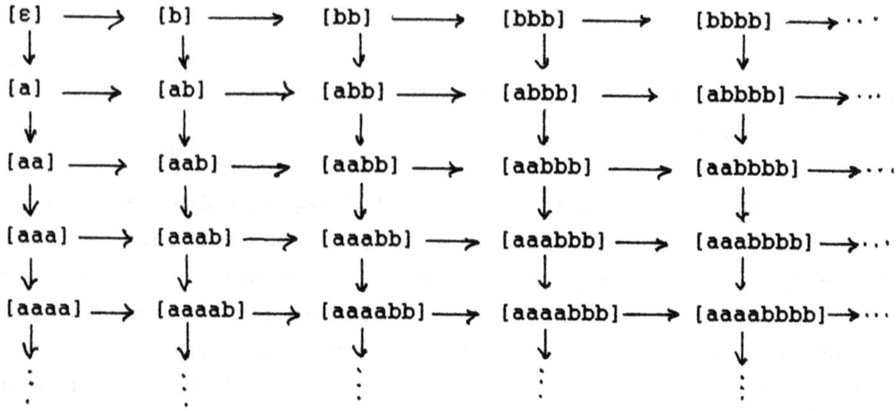

Fig. 6.3.1.

Observe first that the system is conflict free (all its states are consistent); thus, any observation must dominate the whole system. The line

$$V = ([\varepsilon],[a],[ab],[aba],[abab],\ldots[(ab)^n],[(ab)^n a],\ldots)$$

is an observation of T, since any state in T is dominated by a state in V, e.g. [abbbaabaaa] = [aaaaaabbbb] $\subseteq$ [aaaaaabbbbbb] = [abababababab] $\in$ V. However, not all lines in T are observations; e.g. the line

$$U = ([\varepsilon],[a],[aa],\ldots[a^n],\ldots),$$

is not an observation, since it leaves undominated all states $[a^i b^j]$ with $j>0$.

Observe that in T there is infinitely many lines that are observations of T as well as infinitely many lines that are not such observations. Observe also that each finite chain in T can be extended to an observation of T as well as to a line being not an observation of T. It means that the property of a line "to be an observation" is not finitary: it is not sufficient to know a finite part of a line to decide whether the line is an observation or not. □

Call a trace structure T _strongly synchronized_, if for each state σ of T there exists a finite number of states of T incomparable and consistent with σ.

PROPOSITION 6.3.1. Every line in a strongly synchronized trace structure is an observation.

Proof. Assume T be a strongly synchronized and let P be a process in T, V be a line of P, and $\sigma \in P$. We have to prove that $\sigma \in \downarrow V$. If $\sigma \in V$, the proof is finished. Assume $\sigma \notin V$. Since V is a maximal line in P, there are some traces in V incomparable with σ. Since S is strongly synchronized, there is a finite number of such traces. Let σ_0 be the greatest of them; it cannot be the greatest element of V, since then V would be strictly contained in the chain $V \cup \{\sigma'\}$, where σ' is a trace dominating both σ_0 and σ; hence, there is a trace σ'' in V dominating σ_0 and different from σ_0; by definition of σ_0, σ'' dominates σ. Thus, $\sigma \in \downarrow V$. □

EXAMPLE 6.3.2. The system presented in Fig. 4.6.1 is strongly synchronized; consequently, every line in it is an observation. The system presented in Fig. 6.3.1 is not strongly synchronized: for each $n \in \omega$ trace $[a^{n+1}]$ is consistent and incomparable with the trace $[b]$. □

6.4. **Invariancy and inevitability**. Let T be a trace structure over Σ; by a _property_ we shall mean any subset of states in $\theta(\Sigma)$. We say that a property Q is _invariant_ in T, if and only if

$$T \cap \uparrow Q \subseteq Q.$$

It means that once the system reaches a state with an invariant property, all subsequent states will have this property.

THEOREM 6.4.1. A property Q is invariant in a trace structure T over (A,D), if for each $\sigma \in Q$ and each $a \in A$

$$\sigma \in Q,\ \sigma[a] \in T \Rightarrow \sigma[a] \in Q.$$

Proof. Simple induction. □

Thus, checking the invariancy of a property in concurrent systems is relatively simple and similar to that in sequential ones: Q is invariant, if for each state in Q any possible next state is also in Q.

PROPOSITION 6.4.1. $\emptyset$ is an invariant property; T is an invariant property; if Q_1 and Q_2 are invariant properties, then

$$Q_1 \cup Q_2,\ Q_1 \cap Q_2$$

are also invariant properties.

Proof. Directly from the definition. □

In order to define inevitability in trace structures we have to refer to observations. Intuitively, a property is inevitable in a system, if sooner or later the system reaches a state with this property. Inevitability of a property must be objective, i.e. it must not depend on particular observations of the system; hence, if a property is inevitable, any observer of the system must sooner or later notice a state with this property. The formal definition is as follows.

A property Q is inevitable in T, if each observation of T intersects Q (i.e. if $V \cap Q \neq \emptyset$ for any observation V of T).

A property that is not inevitable is called avoidable.

EXAMPLE 6.4.1. Consider system T from Example 6.3.1. The (one state) property Q_{nm}:

$$Q_{nm} = \{[a^n b^m]\},$$

is avoidable in T for any $n,m \in \omega$, since the following line is an observation of T not intersecting Q_{nm}:

$$([\varepsilon],[a],\ldots[a^{n+1}],[a^{n+1}b],\ldots[a^{n+1}b^m],[a^{n+1}b^m a],$$
$$\ldots[a^{n+1}b^m(ab)^n],\ldots).$$

The property R_{nm}:

$$R_{nm} = \{[a^i b^j] \mid i \geq n,\ j \geq m\}$$

is inevitable in T for each n,m $\in \omega$, since any observation of T must contain a state dominating $[a^k b^k]$ with $k = \max(n,m)$; such a state clearly belongs to R. □

In general, it is more difficult to prove inevitability than invariancy, mainly because of the nonlocal character of the observation definition. The following proposition gives simple facts about inevitability that can be useful in checking inevitability of some properties.

PROPOSITION 6.4.2. T is inevitable in T; $[\varepsilon]$ is inevitable in T; if $Q_1 \subseteq Q_2$ and Q_1 is inevitable in T, then Q_2 is inevitable in T; if each process in T contains a state in Q, then $\uparrow Q$ is inevitable in T.

Proof. Only the last claim of the proposition needs a proof. Let P be a process in T and V be an observation of P. If P contains a state τ in Q and V is an observation of P, then there is σ in V dominating τ. Since σ dominates τ, τ is in Q, $\sigma \in \uparrow Q$; thus $V \cap \uparrow Q \neq \emptyset$. Thus, $\uparrow Q$ is inevitable in T. □

The last claim in Proposition 6.4.2 can be paraphrased as follows: the future is inevitable.

Proving invariancy and/or inevitability of some properties (and some combination of them) is of primary interest in analysis and design of concurrent systems. The above formulated notions are thought as some "trace" primitives which can be helpful in creating a partial order model for developing a temporal logic with concurrency.

6. BIBLIOGRAPHICAL NOTES

The motivation for developing the presented theory was to create means for analysing the behaviour of Petri nets as introduced in [Pet1-Pet2], [R1], [RT1]. It was intended to find tools similar to those used succesfully in automata theory or other sequential systems. The notion of traces and of dependency graphs has been introduced in [M1] and presented at Aarhus Workshop on Concurrency in 1977. Since then the theory started to develop in several directions: investigation of algebraic properties [AW1], [BBMS1], [BG1], [BMS1-BMS7], [Kn1-Kn2], [KG], [M4], [Sz1], [T1], [O1], [S1], [Ry1]; connections with graph theory [AR1]; applications to the analysis of concurrent systems [FR], [J1-J4], [Z1-Z2], [Zu1]; comparison with other formalisms [KG1], [M4]. One important topic investigated by Zielonka in [Z2] has not been discussed in the present paper, namely the relation between regular trace languages and concurrent systems called asynchronous automata. Unfortunately, introducing these notions within a limited frame of this paper is impossible. This subject will be presented elsewhere.

Independently of the concurrency theory, since 1978 the algebra of free partially commutative monoids started to develop [[CdL1], [CF1], [CL1-CL2], [CM1], [CP1], [D1-D2], [F1], [Me1-Me2], [P1]. Since the application of traces is limited to finite (0,1)-marked nets, some more sophisticated tools has been proposed in [G1], [St1-St2]. Traces introduced in [Re1] correspond to traces presented here but without independency of events; anyway, the concept of string systems used here is due to Rem.

Condition event systems considered here are very closed to elementary net systems introduced in [Ro1], [Th1], . In [Ro1] an application of traces for the behaviour description is given. The synchronization operation for trace systems has been defined in [M5] with an extensive use of projections due to [GKR1], [KG1]. Modular and fixed point technique for calculating the trace behaviour of nets is given in [M5]. Trace structures are similar to the event structures introduced in [NPW1], but based on dependency / independency relation rather than the conflict relation. The notion of inevitability in the trace structure framework is a particular case of a more general concept discussed in a forthcoming paper.

Acknowledgements. The author gratefully acknowledges the help of Prof. G. Rozenberg in preparation of this paper. Thanks are also due to my colleagues E. Ochmański and W. Penczek who were the first readers of the paper. The author is indebted to IJ. J. Aalbersberg for his effort in collecting the bibliography on traces.

7. REFERENCES

[AR1]: **AALBERSBERG, IJ. J., ROZENBERG, G.**: "Traces, dependency graphs and DNLC grammars", Discrete Applied Mathematics 11 (1985) 299 - 306

[AR2]: **AALBERSBERG, IJ. J., ROZENBERG, G.**: "Trace languages defined by context-free languages", manuscript, (1985)

[AW1]: **AALBERSBERG, IJ. J., WELZL, E.**: "Trace languages defined by regular string languages", to appear (1985)

[BBMS1]: **BERTONI, A., BRAMBILLA, M., MAURI, G., SABADINI, N.**: "An application of the theory of free partially commutative monoids: asymptotic densities of trace languages", Lecture Notes in Computer Science 118 (1981) 205 - 215

[BG1]: **BERTONI, A. and GOLDWURM, M.**: "Average analysis of an algorithm for a membership problem of trace languages", manuscript, (1986)

[BMS1]: **BERTONI, A., MAURI, G., SABADINI, N.**: "A hierarchy of regular trace languages and some combinatorial applications", Proc. 2nd World Conf. on Math. at the Serv. of Men, Las Palmas (1982) 146 - 153

[BMS2]: **BERTONI, A., MAURI, G., SABADINI, N.**: "Equivalence and membership problems for regular trace languages", Lecture Notes in Computer Science 140 (1982) 61 - 71

[BMS3]: **BERTONI, A., MAURI, G., SABADINI, N.**: "Context - free trace languages", Proc. 7th CAAP, Lille (1982) 32 - 42

[BMS4]: **BERTONI, A., MAURI, G., SABADINI, N.**: "Equivalence and membership problems for regular and context - free trace languages", manuscript (1982)

[BMS5]: **BERTONI, A., MAURI, G., SABADINI, N.**: "Concurrency and commutativity", manuscript (1982)

[BMS6]: **BERTONI, A., MAURI, G., SABADINI, N.**: "Unambiguous regular trace languages", Proc. Colloq. on Algebra, Combinat. and Comp. Science, Gyor (1983)

[BMS7]: **BERTONI, A., MAURI, G., SABADINI, N.**: "Representation of prefixes of a trace and membership problem for context - free trace languages", manuscript (1985)

[BFP1]: **BEST, E., FERNANDEZ, C. and PLUNNECKE, H.**: "Concurrent systems and processes", manuscript (1985)

[CdL1]: **CARPI, A. and LUCA, A. de**: "Square - free words on partially commutative free monoids", Information Processing Letters 22 (1986) 125 - 132

[CF1]: **CARTIER, P. and FOATA, D.**: "Problemes combinatoires de commutation et rearrangements", Lecture Notes in Mathematics 85 (1969)

[CL1]: **CLERBOUT, M. and LATTEUX, M.**: "Partial commutations and faithful rational transductions", Theoretical Computer Science 34 (1984) 241 - 254

[CL2]: **CLERBOUT, M. and LATTEUX, M.**: "Semi - commutations", Techn. Rep. IT-63-84, Equipe Lilloise d'Inform. Theor., Univers. de Lille 1, Villeneuve d'Ascq. (1984)

[CM1]: **CORI, R. and METIVIER, Y.**: "Recognizable subsets of some partially abelian monoids", Theoretical Computer Science 35 (1984) 179 - 189

[CP1]: **CORI, R. and PERRIN, D.**: "Automates and commutations partielles", RAIRO Informatique Theorique 19 (1985) 21 - 32

[D1]: **DUBOC, C.**: "Some properties of commutation in free partially commutative monoids", Information Processing Letters 20 (1985) 1 - 4

[D2]: **DUBOC, C.**: "Equations in free partially commutative monoids", Lecture Notes in Computer Science 210 (1986) 192 -202

[ER]: **EHRENFEUCHT, A., ROZENBERG, G.**: "On the Structure of Dependence Graphs", Rapport 87-02, Dept. of Computer Science, University of Leiden (1987)

[FR1]: **FLE, M. P. and ROUCAIROL, G.**: "On serializability of iterated transactions", Proc. ACM SIGACT-SIGOPS Symp. on Princ. of Distrib. Comp., Ottawa (1982) 194 - 200

[FR2]: **FLE, M. P. and ROUCAIROL, G.**: "Fair serializability of iterated transactions using FIFO - nets", Lecture Notes in Computer Science 188 (1985) 154 - 168

[FR3]: **FLE, M. P. and ROUCAIROL, G.**: "Maximal serializability of iterated transactions", Theoretical Computer Science 38 (1985) 1 - 16

[F1]: **FOATA, D.**: "Rearrangements of words", in M. Lothaire: Combinatorics on words, Addison-Wesley, Reading, (1983) Chapter 10

[G1]: **GRABOWSKI, J.**: "On partial languages", Fundamenta Informaticae 4 (1981) 427 - 498

[GKR]: **GYORY, G., KNUTH, E., RONYAI, L.**: "Grammatical projections 1. Elementary constructions", Working Paper II/3, MTA SZTAKI, Budapest (1979)

[J1]: **JANICKI, R.**: "Synthesis of concurrent schemes", Lecture Notes in Computer Science 64 (1978) 298 - 307

[J2]: **JANICKI, R.**: "On the design of concurrent systems", Proc. 2nd Intern. Conf. on Distrib. Comp. Systems, Paris (1981) 455 - 466

[J3]: **JANICKI, R.**: "Mazurkiewicz traces semantics for communicating sequential processes", Proc. 5th European Workshop on Appl. and Theory of Petri Nets, Aarhus (1984) 50 - 70

[J4]: **JANICKI, R.**: "Trace semantics for communicating sequential processes", Techn. Rep. R-85-12, Inst. for Elektr. Syst., Aalborg Univ., Aalborg (1985)

[K1]: **KELLER, R. M.**: "A solvable program-schema equivalence problem", Proc. 5th Ann. Princeton Conf. on Inf. Sciences and Systems, Princeton (1971) 301 - 306

[Kn1]: **KNUTH, E.**: "Petri nets and regular trace languages", manuscript (1978)

[Kn2]: **KNUTH, E.**: "Petri nets and trace languages". Proc. 1st Europ. Conf. on Parallel and Distr. Processing, Toulouse (1979) 51 - 56

[KG1]: **KNUTH, E. and GYORY, G.**: "Paths and traces", Computational Linguistics and Computer Languages 13 (1979) 31 - 42

[LSB]: **LAUER, P.E., SHIELDS, M.W., BEST, E.**: "Formal Theory of the Basic COSY Notation", Technical Report 143, Computing Laboratory, University of Newcastle upon Tyne (1979)

[L1]: **LEVI F. W.**: "On semigroups", Bull. of the Calcutta Math. Soc. 36 (1944) 141 - 146

[M1]: **MAZURKIEWICZ, A.**: "Concurrent program schemes and their interpretations", DAIMI Rep. PB-78, Aarhus Univ., Aarhus (1977)

[M2]: **MAZURKIEWICZ, A.**: "Equational semantics of concurrent systems", Proc. 8th Spring School on Comp. Sci., Colleville sur mer (1980)

[M3]: **MAZURKIEWICZ, A.**: "A calculus of execution traces for concurrent systems", manuscript (1983)

[M4]: **MAZURKIEWICZ, A.**: "Traces, histories, graphs: instances of a process monoid", Lecture Notes in Computer Science 176 (1984) 115 - 133

[M5]: **MAZURKIEWICZ, A.**: "Semantics of concurrent systems: a modular fixed-point trace approach", Lecture Notes in Computer Science 188 (1985) 353 - 375

[M6]: **MAZURKIEWICZ, A.**: "Trace Theory", Advances in Petri Nets 1986, Part II, Proceedings of an Advanced Course Lecture Notes in Computer Science 255 (1987) 279 - 324

[Me1]: **METIVIER, Y.**: "Une condition suffisante de reconaissabilite dans un monoide partiellement commutatif", Techn. Rep. 8417, U.E.R. de Math. et d'Inform., Univ. de Bordeaux, Bordeaux (1984)

[Me2]: **METIVIER, Y.**: "Sous-ensemble reconnaisable d'un monoide partiellment commutatif libre", manuscript (1985)

[NPW1]: **NIELSEN, M., PLOTKIN, G., WINSKEL, G.**: "Petri nets, event structures and domains, Part 1", Theoretical Computer Science 13 (1981) 85-108

[O1]: **OCHMANSKI, E.**: "Regular trace languages", Ph. D. Thesis (1985) (summary in Bull. of EATCS 27, 1985)

[P1]: **PERRIN, D.**: "Words over a partially commutative alphabet", NATO ASI Series F12 (1985) 329 - 340

[Pet1]: **PETRI, C.A.**: "Concepts of Net Theory", Proceedings of the Symposium and Summer School on MFCS'73, High Tatras (1973)

[Pet2]: **PETRI, C.A.**: "Non-Sequential Processes", GMD-ISF Report 77.05, Gesellschaft fuer Mathematik und Datenverarbeitung mbH Bonn (1977)

[R1]: **REISIG, W.**: "Petri nets - an introduction", EATCS Monographs on Theoretical Computer Science, Springer Verlag (1985)

[Re1]: **REM, M.**: "Concurrent Computations and VLSI Circuits", Control Flow and Data Flow: Concepts of Distributed Programming (M. Broy, editor), Springer (1985) 399 - 437

[Ro1]: **ROZENBERG, G.**: "Behaviour of elementary net systems", Advances in Petri Nets 1986, Part I, Proceedings of an Advanced Course Lecture Notes in Computer Science 254 (1987) 60 - 94

[RT1]: **ROZENBERG, G., THIAGARAJAN, P.S.**: "Petri Nets: Basic Notions, Structure and Behaviour", Lecture Notes in Computer Science 224, (1986) 585 - 668

[Ry1]: **RYTTER, W.**: "Some properties of trace languages", Fundamenta Informaticae 7 (1984) 117 - 127

[S1]: **SAKAROVITCH, J.**: "On regular trace languages", to appear (1986)

[Sh1]: **SHIELDS, M.W.**: "Adequate Path Expressions", Lecture Notes in Computer Science 70, (1979) 249 - 265

[Sh2]: **SHIELDS, M.W.**: "Non-Sequential Behaviour", Part 1, Int. Report CSR-120-82, Dept. of Computer Science, University of Edinburgh (1982)

[Sh3]: **SHIELDS, M.W.**: "Concurrent Machines", The Computer Journal 28, Nr. 5 (1988) 449 - 466

[St1]: **STARKE, P. H.**: "Processes in Petri Nets", Elektron. Inf. und Kyb. 17 (1981)

[St2]: **STARKE, P. H.**: "Traces and semiwords", Lecture Notes in Computer Science 208 (1985) 332 - 349

[Sz1]: **SZIJARTO, M.**: "A classification and closure properties of languages for describing concurrent system behaviours", Fundamenta Informaticae 4 (1981) 531 - 549

[T1]: **TARLECKI, A.**: "Notes on the implementability of formal languages by concurrent systems", ICS PAS Report 481, Inst. of Comp. Science, Polish Academy of Sciences, Warszawa (1982)

[Th1]: **THIAGARAJAN, P.S.**: "Elementary net systems", Advances in Petri Nets 1986, Part I, Proceedings of an Advanced Course Lecture Notes in Computer Science 254 (1987) 26 - 59

[Z1]: **ZIELONKA, W.**: "Proving assertions about parallel programs by means of traces", ICS PAS Report 424, Inst. of Comp. Science, Polish Academy of Sciences, Warszawa (1980)

[Z2]: **ZIELONKA, W.**: "The notes on finite state asynchronous automata and trace languages", manuscript (1982)

[Z3]: **ZIELONKA, W.**: "Notes on Finite Asynchronous Automata", Informatique Theorique et Applications 21, Nr. 2, (1987) 99-135

[Zu1]: **ZUIDWEG, H.**: "Trace approach to synchronic distances" (manuscript), University of Leiden, Leiden (1986)

An introduction to event structures

by
Glynn Winskel

Computer Science Department,
Aarhus University,
Denmark.

ABSTRACT: Event structures are models of processes as events constrained by relations of consistency and enabling. These notes are intended to introduce the mathematical theory of event structures, show how they are related to Petri nets and Scott domains, and how they can be used to provide semantics to programming languages for parallel processes as well as languages with higher types.

Key words: Event structures, Petri nets, traces, concurrency, nondeterminism, parallel computation, semantics, communicating processes, higher types, lambda calculus.

CONTENTS

0. Introduction.

Event structures are models of processes as events constrained by relations of consistency and enabling. Their study in denotational semantics first arose as a biproduct in the pioneering work of G.Kahn and G.Plotkin on some foundational questions in denotational semantics (see [KP]). The concrete data structures of Kahn and Plotkin were later realised to be closely related to confusion-free Petri nets (see [NPW]) and this led to the more general definitions discussed here. Since then they have been developed as a model in their own right and for certain applications (*e.g.* see section 7 on higher-type event structures) they are easier and less clumsy to use than Petri nets, to which they are closely related however. These notes are intended to introduce the mathematical theory of event structures, show how they are related to Petri nets and Scott domains, and how they can be used to provide semantics to programming languages for parallel processes as well as languages with higher types.

The notes [W1] provide another description of event structures, in many ways fuller than the presentation here. They overlap a great deal with the notes here, and fairly often the reader is referred to [W1] for proofs or further details. These notes do however try to compensate for the terse presentation in [W1] and should be easier to read.

1. Modelling concurrency.

The models of computation we shall consider in these notes are based on the primitive notion of an *event*. We all have an intuitive idea, from everyday experience and science, of what an event is. Attempting a rough definition we might say an event is an action which one can choose to regard as indivisible—it either has happened or has not according to our description of some process. This is not to say that an event is indivisible, and without detailed structure, in any absolute sense; it might well have internal structure, and consist of a complicated process, which it is sensible to analyse at another level of abstraction. But then, of course, at that more detailed level of abstraction what was originally an event is no longer a single event, but several or many. From their far perspective, historians may talk of the event of a battle or the birth of a famous person—not just single events to the people involved at the time! An event can have detailed structure in another sense—its occurrence may be very significant a change a great deal—though this is determined more by how the event influences other events. How we catch this will be discussed shortly. Another property we expect of an event is that it is localised in space and time, that as far as our description is concerned it occurs in a small area and over a small period of time. Speaking informally, this really follows from our understanding of an event as being without detailed structure—if we were to understand an event as occupying some extended region of space and time then its dimensions would presumably be important. Again, of course, there is nothing absolute about this; what we think of as small depends on what we are modelling and how we go about it.

In viewing the events of a distributed computation, it may well be that we can ascribe precise places and times to all the events of interest. True, if the computation is very distributed, so that relativistic effects become important, these may not be agreed on by all observers. But even without relativistic effects, and even if it is feasible, there is generally no point in analysing the computation at such a level of detail—the precise places and times are most often incidental details. What is important in designing and analysing distributed computations are the significant events and how the occurrence of an event causally depends on the previous occurrence of others. For example, the event of a process transmitting a message would presumably depend on it first performing some events, so it was in the right state to transmit, including the receipt of the message which in turn would depend on its previous transmission by another process. This outlook has been proposed by Lamport among others (see *e.g.* [Lam]).

The scale at which it is sensible to view a computation as distributed can vary immensely. For example, similar ideas have been used in the analysis of self-timed circuits in VLSI (See *e.g.* [Rem]).

Such ideas suggest that we view distributed computations as event occurr . :es together with a relation expressing causal dependency, and this we may reasonably take to be a partial order. As a definition we take:

1.1 Definition. An *elementary event structure* $(E, \leq)$ is a partially ordered set. The set E is to be thought of as a set of event occurrences and the partial order relation as expressing *causal dependency*; for two events e, e' we have $e \leq e'$ when the occurrence of the event e' depends on the previous occurrence of the event e.

Guided by our interpretation we can formulate a notion of computation state of an elementary event structure $(E, \leq)$. Taking a computation state of a process to be represented by the set x of events which have occurred in the computation, we expect that

$$e' \in x \;\;\&\;\; e \leq e' \Rightarrow e \in x;$$

if an event has occurred then all events on which it causally depends have occurred too. Say a subset $x \subseteq E$ which satisfies this property is *left-closed*, and collect all such subsets together in the family described as $\mathcal{L}(E)$.

A particular left-closed set is determined by an event e of an event structure $(E, \leq)$. Define

$$\lceil e \rceil = \{e' \in E \mid e' \leq e\},$$

which is clearly left-closed.

Viewing computation states as such subsets, progress in a computation is measured by the occurrence of more events. Let $x, y \in \mathcal{L}(E)$ for an event structure E. If $x \subseteq y$ then x can be regarded as a subbehaviour of y. The relation of inclusion between left-closed subsets is an information order of the sort familiar from denotational semantics, but special in that more information corresponds to more events having occurred. The least element of information in an order $(\mathcal{L}(E), \subseteq)$ is the empty set, when no events have occurred, and there is a maximum element, the set containing all events. In fact the partial orders of left-closed subsets are complete lattices. Recall:

1.2 Definition. A complete lattice is a partial order which has least upper bounds (joins or suprema) $\bigsqcup X$ and greatest lower bounds (meets or infima) $\prod X$ of arbitrary subsets X. We write $x \sqcup y$ and $x \sqcap y$ for the least upper bound and greatest lower bound respectively of two elements x, y.

As we shall see the lattices associated with left-closed sets are lattices of a rather special sort.

This view of a process as a domain of computation states is a little nonstandard and unusual—one is used to processes being denotated by elements of a domain, not by a domain itself. Domains are more usually used as denotations of types. However, thinking of a domain of computation states $\mathcal{L}(E)$ as the "type" of computation states of a process makes the idea less strange, and more familiar.

One can ask: precisely what class of domains are represented in this way? In fact the class is exactly that of algebraic lattices which are infinitely distributive in that they satisfy the following laws:

$$(\bigsqcup X) \sqcap y = \bigsqcup\{x \sqcap y \mid x \in X\} \tag{1}$$
$$(\prod X) \sqcup y = \prod\{x \sqcup y \mid x \in X\} \tag{2}$$

It is straightforward to verify one part of this statement. First, recall the definition of algebraic lattice.

1.3 Definition.

A *directed subset* of a partial order L is a subset $S \subseteq L$ with the property that for any finite set $X \subseteq S$ there is an element $s \in S$ such that $\forall x \in X.\ x \sqsubseteq s$.
(In particular, a chain is directed.)

A *finite element* of a complete lattice is an element f with the property that for all directed sets S, if $f \sqsubseteq \bigsqcup S$ then there is some $s \in S$ for which $f \sqsubseteq s$.

A complete lattice is *algebraic* if for any element d the set $\{x \sqsubseteq d \mid x \text{ is finite}\}$ is directed and has least upper bound d.

1.4 Theorem. *Let $(E, \leq)$ be a partial order. Then $(\mathcal{L}(E), \subseteq)$ is an algebraic lattice which satisfies the distributive laws (1) and (2) above.*

Proof. Verifying that left-closed subsets of a partial order, ordered by inclusion, form an algebraic lattice with meets and joins given as intersections and unions is routine, as is the verification of the distributivity laws. ∎

The converse is harder. A first, simpler representation of the lattices represented by elementary event structures starts by observing that an event e in an event structure corresponds with the left-closed set

$$\lceil e \rceil = \{e' \mid e' \leq e\}.$$

Such configurations are characterised in the domain order as being complete primes. Moreover as every left-closed subset is the union of such configurations they form a subbasis in the domain of configurations of an event structure.

1.5 Definition. Let $(L, \sqsubseteq)$ be a complete lattice.

A *complete prime* of L is an element $p \in L$ such that

$$p \sqsubseteq \bigsqcup X \Rightarrow \exists x \in X.\, p \sqsubseteq x$$

for any set X.

L is *prime algebraic* iff

$$x = \bigsqcup \{p \sqsubseteq x \mid p \text{ is a complete prime}\},$$

for all $x \in L$.

1.6 Example. Consider the lattice:

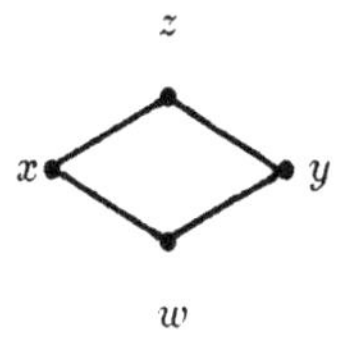

As in any finite lattice, all the elements are finite, and the lattice is algebraic. The least element w, like all least elements, is the least upper bound $\bigsqcup \emptyset$ without there being an element in $\emptyset$ which dominates it. It can not therefore be a complete prime. The element z is dominated, in fact equal to, the least upper bound $x \bigsqcup y$ without being dominated by either x or y. It can not be a complete prime either. On the other hand both x and y are complete primes—any least uper bound of a set dominating them must contain an element which does so.

1.7 Proposition. *Let E be an elementary event structure. In the partial order $(\mathcal{L}(E), \subseteq)$ the complete primes are precisely those left-closed subsets of the form $\lceil e \rceil$ for $e \in E$.*

Conversely, any complete lattice which is prime algebraic domain is associated with an elementary event structure in which the events are its complete primes.

1.8 Definition. Let L be a complete lattice which is prime algebraic. Define $\mathcal{P}r(L) = (P, \leq)$, where P consists of the complete primes of L and

$$p \leq p' \Leftrightarrow p \sqsubseteq p'$$

for $p, p' \in P$

1.9 Theorem. *Let L be a complete lattice which is prime algebraic. Then $\mathcal{P}r(L)$ is an elementary event structure, with $\phi : L \cong (\mathcal{L}\mathcal{P}r(L), \subseteq)$ giving an isomorphism of partial orders where $\phi(d) = \{p \sqsubseteq d \mid p \text{ is a complete prime}\}$ with inverse $\theta : \mathcal{L}\mathcal{P}r(L) \to L$ given by $\theta(x) = \bigsqcup x$.*

Proof. Let P be the complete primes of L. Obviously the maps θ and ϕ are monotonic *i.e.* order preserving. We show they are mutual inverses and so give the required isomorphism.

Firstly we show $\theta\ \phi = 1$. Thus we require $x = \bigsqcup\{p \in P \mid p \sqsubseteq x\}$ for all $x \in L$. But this is just the condition of prime algebraicity.

Now we show $\phi\ \theta = 1$. Let $X \in \mathcal{L}(P, \leq)$. We require $X = \phi\ \theta(X)$ *i.e.* $X = \{p \in P \mid p \sqsubseteq \bigsqcup X\}$. Clearly $X \subseteq \{p \in P \mid p \sqsubseteq \bigsqcup X\}$. Conversely if $p \sqsubseteq \bigsqcup X$, where p is a complete prime, then certainly $p \sqsubseteq q$ for some $q \in X$. However X is left-closed so $p \in X$, showing the converse inclusion

Thus we have established the required isomorphism. ∎

To show prime algebraicity for infinitely distributive, algebraic lattices we use another idea. Events in $(E, \leq)$ also manifest themselves in the lattice $(\mathcal{L}(E), \subseteq)$ as prime intervals. We say x is *covered* by x' in a partial order, written $x \prec x'$ iff

$$x \sqsubseteq x' \ \ \& \ \ x \neq x' \ \ \& \ \ (\forall z.\ x \sqsubseteq z \sqsubseteq x' \Rightarrow x = z \ \text{ or } \ z = x').$$

The relation $\prec$ is called the *covering* relation. A *prime interval* is a pair $[x, x']$ such that $x \prec x'$. In $(\mathcal{L}(E), \subseteq)$ a prime interval is associated with the occurrence of an event at some element $x \in \mathcal{L}(E)$; in $(\mathcal{L}(E), \subseteq)$, the relation $x \prec x'$ holds iff there is an event e such that $e \notin x$ and $x' = x \cup \{e\}$ with $x, x' \in \mathcal{L}(E)$. Note that an event is not in general associated with a unique prime interval but many.

In a complete lattice which is prime algebraic, $x \prec x'$ means there is a unique complete prime p such that $x' = x \sqcup p$, and in fact p can be recovered as

$$p = \prod\{z \mid x' \sqsubseteq x \sqcup z\}.$$

This observation and the following lemma, which ensures there are enough prime intervals, give the heart of the proof.

1.10 Lemma. *Let $L = (L, \sqsubseteq)$ be an algebraic lattice. Then*

$$\forall x, y \in L.\ x \sqsubseteq y \ \ \& \ \ x \neq y \Rightarrow \exists z, z' \in L.\ x \sqsubseteq z \prec z' \sqsubseteq y.$$

Proof. Suppose x, y are distinct elements of L such that $x \sqsubseteq y$. Because L is algebraic there is a finite element b such that $b \not\sqsubseteq x \ \ \& \ \ b \sqsubseteq y$. By Zorn's lemma there is a maximal chain C of elements above x and strictly below $x \sqcup b$. As b is finite, from the construction of C we must have $x \sqsubseteq \bigsqcup C \prec x \sqcup b \sqsubseteq y$. ∎

1.11 Theorem. *Let L be a complete lattice. Then L is prime algebraic iff it is algebraic and infinitely distributive (i.e. satisfies the distributive laws (1) and (2)).*

Proof.

"only if":

Let L be a prime algebraic complete lattice. Let P be the ordering of L restricted to its complete primes. By the previous theorem we know $L \cong \mathcal{L}(P)$ so it is sufficient to prove properties for $\mathcal{L}(P)$. We have already seen the distributivity laws follow from the corresponding laws for sets.

The finite elements of $(\mathcal{L}(P), \subseteq)$ are easily shown to be precisely the left-closures of finite subsets of P. Suppose $x \in \mathcal{L}(P)$ is finite. Obviously $x = \bigcup\{[X] \mid X \subseteq_{fin} x\}$. But the set $\{[X] \mid X \subseteq_{fin} x\}$ is clearly directed so, because x is finite, $x = [X]$ for some finite set $X \subseteq P$. Conversely, it is clear that an element of the form $[X]$, for a finite $X \subseteq P$, is necessarily finite; if $[X] \subseteq \bigcup S$ for a directed subset S of $\mathcal{L}(P)$ then X, and so $[X]$, is included in the union of a finite subset of S, and so in an element of S. Clearly now every element of $\mathcal{L}(\mathrm{P})$ is the least upper bound of the finite elements below it, making $\mathcal{L}(\mathrm{P})$ algebraic.

Thus L is an algebraic lattice satisfying the distributive laws (1) and (2).

"*if*":

Let $\mathrm{L} = (L, \sqsubseteq)$ be an algebraic lattice satisfying the distributive laws (1) and (2).

Let $x \prec x'$ in L. Define $pr[x,x'] = \prod\{y \in L \mid x' \leq x \sqcup y\}$. We show $p = pr[x,x']$ is a complete prime of L. Note first that $x \sqcup p = \prod\{x \sqcup y \mid x' \sqsubseteq x \sqcup y\} = x'$ by distributive law (2). Now suppose $p \sqsubseteq \bigsqcup Z$ for some $Z \subseteq L$. Then $p = (\bigsqcup Z) \sqcap p = \bigsqcup\{z \sqcap p \mid z \in Z\}$ by the distributive law (1). Write $Z' = \{z \sqcap p \mid z \in Z\}$, so $p = \bigsqcup Z'$. Then $x' = x \sqcup p = x \sqcup (\bigsqcup Z') = \bigsqcup\{x \sqcup z' \mid z' \in Z'\}$. Clearly $x \sqsubseteq x \sqcup z' \sqsubseteq x'$ for all $z \in Z'$. As $x \prec x'$ we must have $x' = x \sqcup z'$ for some $z' \in Z'$; otherwise $x = x \sqcup z'$ for all $z' \in Z'$ giving the contradiction $x = \bigsqcup\{x \sqcup z' \mid z' \in Z'\} = x'$. But then $p \sqsubseteq z'$ from the definition of p. However $z' = z \sqcap p$ for some $z \in Z$. Therefore $p \sqsubseteq z$ for some $z \in Z$. Thus p is a complete prime of L.

That L is prime algebraic follows provided for $z \in L$, we have $z = \bigsqcup\{pr[x,x'] \mid x \prec x' \sqsubseteq z\}$. Let $z \in L$. Write $w = \bigsqcup\{pr[x,x'] \mid x \prec x' \sqsubseteq z\}$. Clearly $w \sqsubseteq z$. Suppose $w \neq z$. Then, by the lemma, $w \sqsubseteq x \prec x' \sqsubseteq z$ for some $x, x' \in L$. Write $p = pr[x,x']$. Then $p \sqsubseteq w$ making $x \sqcup p = x$, a contradiction as $x \sqcup p = x'$. Thus each element of L is the least upper bound of the complete primes below it, as required.

Thus we have established the required equivalence between prime algebraic complete lattices and algebraic lattices satisfying (1) and (2). ∎

So far we have fed very little intuition into our definition of event structure. True, our interpretation of the partial order as one of causal dependency motivated our choice of formulation of computation state. But our physical understanding of what events are invokes more than is caught there. For example, should it be possible for an event to occur when it causally depends on an infinite set of events, as in the following examples? In the diagrams we represent a single link in the causal dependency relation, say $e_0 < e_1$, by drawing $e_0\bullet \rightarrow \bullet e_1$ or $e_1\bullet \leftarrow \bullet e_0$.

$$e_0\bullet \rightarrow e_1\bullet \rightarrow e_2\bullet \rightarrow \cdots e_n\bullet \rightarrow \cdots \bullet\, e$$

$$\cdots \rightarrow e_n\bullet \rightarrow \cdots \rightarrow e_2\bullet \rightarrow e_1\bullet \rightarrow e\bullet$$

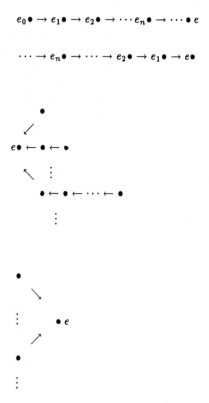

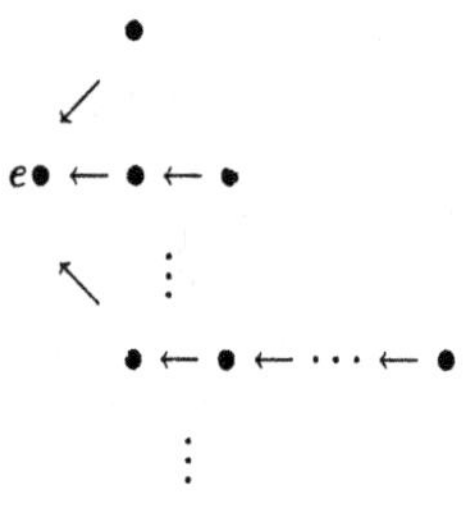

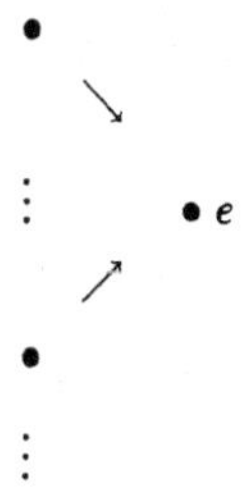

In the first example, an event e can only occur after a chain of events, first e_0, then e_1, then e_2 *etc.* , have occurred. Such an event structure is of the kind that arises in describing the processes in the paradoxes of Zeno. Zeno, to point out the illusory nature of reality, argued that a door could never close because the event of it doing so would depend on the events of it first half closing, then three-quarters closing, then seven-eighths closing *etc.* . Nowadays, familiar as we are with the calculus and the physics of continuous processes, it is hard to appreciate the difficulties Zeno saw. But still, we would not expect such an event structure to arise when describing processes where the events are discrete, meaning roughly that the events do not blur into one another. Attempting a tentative definition of what we mean by "discrete", we shall say a set of events in space and time is discrete when we can uniformly choose some real number r so that any two events can be separated by spheres of space and time of radius r.*

The remaining examples are a little more subtle. The second example represents a process where in order for an event e to occur e_1 must have occurred before, before that e_2 *etc.* . The third example represents a process where the occurrence of an event e depends on the previous occurrence of chains of events of unbounded length. The fourth shows an event e whose occurrence depends

* Another definition which works equally well for our purposes is to say a set of events in space and time is discrete when it is a closed subset such that any two events can be separated by an open neighbourhood. I do not know how to choose between the two definitions.

on the previous occurrence of an infinite number of events all independent of each other. When the events are understood to be discrete the reasonableness of these three descriptions is determined by whether or not there is an initial state, at which no events have occurred. If there is such an initial state the second, third and fourth examples cannot be discrete.

To see this, we use the fact there is an upper bound on the speed at which causal influence can travel. Any point in space and time determines a future-cone of points in space and time which it can effect and a past-cone of points which can have affected it. Assume a process begins with some "initial event" i, marking a state where no process events have occurred, and includes the occurrence of an event e. Then the intersection of the future-cone of i and the past-cone of e is a bounded closed region which therefore has the property that any infinite subset of points has an accumulation point. Because this region must contain all the process events on which e depends we cannot have discreteness for any of the examples above.

In fact the argument entails that to obtain discreteness under the assumption that there is an initial state, at which no events have occurred, we should insist on the following strong discreteness axiom on event structures.

1.12 Definition. Say an elementary event structure satisfies the *axiom of finite causes* when

$$\forall e \in E.\ \{e' \in E \mid e' \leq e\} \text{ is finite.}$$

We have just seen an attempt to argue for an axiom on event structures based on simple physical principles. As a computational argument for the axiom we shall show how it is implied by Scott's thesis, once we make certain assumptions about how to get datatypes and functions between them from an elementary event structure. Dana Scott proposed the thesis that computable functions between datatypes are continuous, it being understood that datatypes are associated with domains of information and that computable functions between datatypes are associated with functions between their domains of information. A function $f : D \to E$ from one complete lattice D to another E is *continuous* iff it preserves least upper bounds of directed sets *i.e.* for all directed sets S

$$\bigsqcup fS = f(\bigsqcup S).$$

Note a continuous function is *monotonic*, *i.e.*

$$\forall x, y \in D.\ x \sqsubseteq y \Rightarrow f(x) \sqsubseteq f(y),$$

In particular, a continuous function should preserve least upper bounds of ω-chains, *i.e.* for all chains $x_0 \sqsubseteq x_1 \sqsubseteq \cdots \sqsubseteq x_n \sqsubseteq \cdots$ in D we have

$$\bigsqcup_{n\in\omega} f(x_n) = f(\bigsqcup_{n\in\omega} x_n).$$

Intuitively the ultimate output value should be no more than the limit of the values determined at finite stages in delivering the input, so we can approximate the ultimate output value arbitrarily closely by the output values at finite stages. Scott's thesis has an intuitive justification (see *e.g.* [St]), and plays a key part in the mathematical basis of denotational semantics.

We show $\mathrm{E} = (E, \leq)$ will obey Scott's thesis iff it satisfies the axiom of finite causes. Of course we need to make clear what we mean by "obey Scott's thesis". This hinges on associating datatypes and continuous functions with E.

We can choose to imagine some of the events of E as being events of input E_0 from some datatype, some as internal events, and others as events of output E_1 to some datatype. The datatypes may have their own causal dependencies, which contribute to the dependency of the full process, so the input datatype can carry an partial order $\mathrm{E}_0 = (E_0, \leq_0)$ and the output datatype a partial order $\mathrm{E}_1 = (E_1, \leq_1)$. The orderings of the datatypes should be sub-partial orders of that of the process, *i.e.*

$$\mathrm{E}_0 \subseteq \mathrm{E} \ \ \& \ \ \mathrm{E}_1 \subseteq \mathrm{E},$$

meaning $\leq_0 \subseteq \leq$ and $\leq_1 \subseteq \leq$. There are natural domains of information associated with the two datatypes, *viz.* their domains of left-closed sets of events. The process induces a function between the domains. Define

$$f_{E_0,E_1} : \mathcal{L}(\mathrm{E}_0) \to \mathcal{L}(\mathrm{E}_1) \text{ to map } x \mapsto \{e \in E_1 \mid \lceil e \rceil \cap E_0 \subseteq x\}.$$

The idea is that an event of E occurs once the necessary input events have occurred. It is clear that:

1.13 Proposition. *The function f_{E_0,E_1} is monotonic.*

However for partial orders in general the function may not be continuous. Consider, for example, the partial order

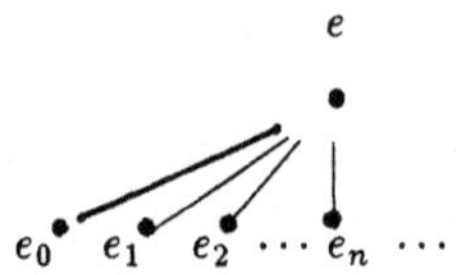

with $E_0 = \{e_n \mid n \in \omega\}$ and $E_1 = \{e\}$ ordered by the identity relation. Then taking S to be the directed set consisting of all finite subsets of E_0 we see (as in the proof of the theorem below) that the least upper bound of S is not preserved by f_{E_0,E_1}. If E is to represent a computable process, according to Scott's thesis, f_{E_0,E_1} should be continuous. Furthermore it should be for any choice of events for the input and output datatypes.

1.14 Definition. We say E *obeys Scott's thesis* iff

$$\forall \mathrm{E}_0, \mathrm{E}_1. \, (\mathrm{E}_0 \subseteq \mathrm{E} \;\;\&\;\; \mathrm{E}_1 \subseteq \mathrm{E} \Rightarrow f_{E_0,E_1} \text{ is continuous}).$$

Now by a simple argument we can show those elementary event structures E which obey Scott's thesis are precisely those which satisfy the axiom of finite causes.

1.15 Theorem. *The elementary event structure E obeys Scott's thesis iff it satisfies the axiom of finite causes.*

Proof.

"only if" Suppose E obeys Scott's thesis. Suppose for some e in E we had $\lceil e \rceil$ infinite. Take

$$E_0 = \{e' \in E \mid e' < e\} \text{ and } E_1 = \{e\},$$

with both ordered by the identity relation. Define S to consist of all finite subsets of E_0. Then S is a directed subset of $\mathcal{L}(\mathrm{E}_0)$. Moreover no element of S is E_0 as E_0 is infinite. However now $f_{E_0,E_1}(\bigcup S) = \{e\}$ while $\bigcup f_{E_0,E_1} S = \emptyset$. Thus f_{E_0,E_1} is not continuous which contradicts the assumption that E obeys Scott's thesis. Thus $\lceil e \rceil$ is finite for all $e \in E$.

"if" Suppose $\lceil e \rceil$ is finite for all e in E. Assume $E_0 \subseteq E$ and $E_1 \subseteq E$. Let S be a directed subset of $\mathcal{L}(\mathrm{E}_0)$. Abbreviate f_{E_0,E_1} to f. As f is always monotonic we have $\bigcup fS \subseteq f(\bigcup S)$. Suppose $e \in f(\bigcup S)$. Then $\lceil e \rceil \cap E_0 \subseteq \bigcup S$. As $\lceil e \rceil$ is finite so is $\lceil e \rceil \cap E_0$. Thus because S is directed $\lceil e \rceil \cap E_0 \subseteq s$ for some $s \in S$. Then $e \in f(s)$. This shows $f(\bigcup S) \subseteq \bigcup fS$ so $f(\bigcup S) = \bigcup fS$. Therefore f is continuous. Hence $(E, \leq)$ obeys Scott's thesis, as required. ∎

It should be stressed that the argument does rest on assumptions about how to obtain datatypes and functions between them from an elementary event structure; in the presence of, for example, a topology on events, when they are not discrete, these are likely to be obtained differently.

It is a slippery business arguing for axioms on event structures, resting as it does on assumptions about common understanding and intuitions. Henceforth we shall just assume the axiom of finite causes, or an equivalent, for our models of processes.

The axiom of finite causes on event structures has its lattice-theoretic analogue.

1.16 Definition. Say an algebraic lattice is *finitary* iff every finite element dominates only a finite number of elements, *i.e.* $\{d \mid d \sqsubseteq x\}$ is finite for every finite element x.

Not surprisingly, the algebraic lattices represented by elementary event structures satisfying the axiom of finite causes are finitary. Because of this the infinite distributivity laws are implied by distributivity, just in a finite form.

1.17 Definition. Say a lattice is *distributive* iff it satisfies

$$x \sqcap (y \sqcup z) = (x \sqcap y) \sqcup (x \sqcap z) \qquad (3).$$

Theorem. *Let L be an an algebraic lattice which is finitary. Then L is prime algebraic iff L satisfies the finite distributive law (3).*

1.18 Corollary.
(i) Let E be an elementary event structure satisfying the axiom of finite causes. Then $(\mathcal{L}(E), \subseteq)$ *is an algebraic lattice which is finitary and satisfies the finite distributive law (3).*
(ii) Let L be an algebraic lattice which is finitary and satisfies the finite distributive law (3). Then there is an elementary event structure E satisfying the axiom of finite causes such that $L \cong (\mathcal{L}(E), \subseteq)$.

A word on our formulation of computation state as a left-closed subset: Here the most generous formulation has been given, in that it allows the most general set of left-closed subsets. It includes all infinite left-closed subsets of events which according to our interpretation could only be realised after an infinite period of time. A more refined analysis of what is to be meant by "computation state" might rule out some of them. Questions of "fairness" might rule out all infinite left-closed subsets but the maximal one.

2. Adding nondeterminism.

So far we have postulated that concurrency or parallelism is to be modelled through a partial order expressing causal dependency. Clearly, one thing is missing from such descriptions, and this is the ability to model a process which, perhaps influenced by the environment, can behave in different and incompatible ways, the phenomenon of nondeterminism. To model nondeterminism we adjoin further structure in the form of a conflict relation to express how the occurrence of certain events rules out the occurrence of others. In these notes we shall assume that events exclude each other in a binary fashion (see [W1] for a more general treatment). As an example of such a binary conflict, the event of an "a" being typed in the first position of a line conflicts with the event of a "b" being typed in that same position.

2.1 Definition. Define a *prime event structure* to be a structure $\mathrm{E} = (E, \#, \leq)$ consisting of a set E, of *events* which are partially ordered by $\leq$, the *causal dependency relation*, and a binary, symmetric, irreflexive relation $\# \subseteq E \times E$, the *conflict relation*, which satisfy

$$\{e' \mid e' \leq e\} \text{ is finite,}$$
$$e\#e' \leq e'' \Rightarrow e\#e''.$$

for all $e, e', e'' \in E$.

2.2 Definition. Let $(E, \#, \leq)$ be a prime event structure. Define its *configurations*, $\mathcal{L}(\mathrm{E})$, to consist of those subsets $x \subseteq E$ which are

conflict-free: $\forall e, e' \in x.\ \neg(e\#e')$ and
left-closed: $\forall e, e'.\ e' \leq e \in x \Rightarrow e' \in x$.

In particular, define $\lceil e \rceil = \{e' \in E \mid e' \leq e\}$.

We study the kind of domains which are represented by prime event structures. As we have chosen to work with a binary conflict relation we rightly expect that compatibility in the domain of configurations will be determined in a binary fashion.

2.3 Definition. Let $(D, \sqsubseteq)$ be a partial order.

Say a set $X \subseteq D$ is *finitely compatible* iff if every finite $Y \subseteq X$ has an upper bound. (A directed set is finitely compatible.)

Say D is *consistently complete* iff every finitely compatible subset $X \subseteq D$ has a least upper bound $\bigsqcup X$.

A partial order is a *Scott domain* (or simply a domain) iff it is consistently complete and the restriction of the order to $\{x \in D \mid x \sqsubseteq d\}$ is an algebraic lattice for all $d \in D$; its *finite elements* are precisely those elements which are finite in some such lattice.

Say D is *coherent* iff all subsets $X \subseteq D$ such that

$$\forall d_0, d_1 \in X.\ d_0 \uparrow d_1$$

have least upper bounds $\bigsqcup X$.

(Note a consistent complete partial order has a least element, *viz.* $\bot = \bigsqcup \emptyset$, though it may not have a greatest. It follows the same is true also for coherent partial orders.)

Remark. Note any consistent complete partial order has greatest lower bounds of any nonempty subsets: For X nonempty, $\prod X = \bigsqcup\{d \mid \forall x \in X.\ d \sqsubseteq x\}$.

There is another characterisation of finite elements of a domain:

2.4 Proposition. *Let $(D, \sqsubseteq)$ be a domain, as defined above. An element $x \in D$ is finite iff for every directed subset S of D $x \sqsubseteq \bigsqcup S$ implies there is some $s \in S$ for which $x \sqsubseteq s$.*

Proof. The proof of the proposition uses the fact that meets in an algebraic lattice L are continuous *i.e.*

$$\bigsqcup S \sqcap d = \bigsqcup\{s \sqcap d \mid s \in S\}$$

for all elements d and directed subsets S. It is clear that $\bigsqcup\{s \sqcap d \mid s \in S\} \sqsubseteq \bigsqcup S \sqcap d$. To see the converse, let x be a finite element of L with $x \sqsubseteq \bigsqcup S \sqcap d$. Then as $x \sqsubseteq \bigsqcup S$, a directed set, there is an $s \in S$ so $x \sqsubseteq s$. Hence $x \sqsubseteq s \sqcap d$, giving $x \sqsubseteq \bigsqcup\{s \sqcap d \mid s \in S\}$. In an algebraic lattice this is enough to establish the converse ordering, and hence the equality.

Suppose x is an element of D with the property that for every directed subset S if $x \sqsubseteq \bigsqcup S$ then $x \sqsubseteq s$ for some $s \in S$. Take any d such that $x \sqsubseteq d$. The element x is finite in the lattice $\{y \in D \mid y \sqsubseteq d\}$, and so is finite in D. Conversely, suppose x is finite in D. Then x is finite in a lattice $L = \{y \in D \mid y \sqsubseteq d\}$ for some $d \in D$. Suppose S is a directed subset of D such that $x \sqsubseteq \bigsqcup S$. Then by the fact above

$$x \sqsubseteq \bigsqcup S \sqcap d = \bigsqcup\{s \sqcap d \mid s \in S\},$$

the least upper bound of a directed set in the lattice L. Thus $x \sqsubseteq s \sqcap d$, so $x \sqsubseteq s$, as required. ∎

For those familiar with another definition of domain, we remark that the proposition above is the key to showing our definition of domain is equivalent to the usual definition.

As in the section on elementary event structures, the simplest representation of the domains represented by prime event structures starts by observing that an event e in an event structure corresponds with the configuration $\lceil e \rceil$. Such elements are characterised as being complete primes, extending the definition used before.

2.5 Definition.

A domain D is a *prime algebraic* iff each sublattice $\{x \in D \mid x \sqsubseteq d\}$ is prime algebraic; the complete primes of D are those elements which are complete primes in any sublattice $\{x \in D \mid x \sqsubseteq d\}$.

A domain D is a *distributive (respectively infinitely)* iff each sublattice $\{x \in D \mid x \sqsubseteq d\}$ is distributive (respectively infinitely).

A domain D is a *finitary* iff each sublattice $\{x \in D \mid x \sqsubseteq d\}$ is finitary.

From earlier results it follows that several concepts coincide. For example it is a direct consequence of the definition and the result 1.11 that a domain is prime algebraic iff it is infinitely distributive. Similarly, if a domain is finitary then it is prime algebraic iff it is distributive. Elsewhere, in [NPW,W,W1], other definitions have been given of the concepts above so we spend a moment checking the new definitions agree with the old. A standard way to say a domain is distributive is expressed in the next proposition as an equivalent to the definition above.

2.6 Proposition. *A domain is distributive iff it satisfies:*

$$x \uparrow y \Rightarrow (x \sqcup y) \sqcap z = (x \sqcap z) \sqcup (y \sqcap z) \qquad (*)$$

Proof. Suppose the condition $(*)$ holds in some domain D. Then certainly any sublattice $\{x \in D \mid x \sqsubseteq d\}$ is distributive for any $d \in D$. Conversely, suppose D is distributive in the sense of the definition above. Let $x, y, z \in D$ with $x \uparrow y$. Then $x, y \sqsubseteq d$ for some $d \in D$. Take $z' = z \sqcap d$. Then, as the sublattice $\{x \in D \mid x \sqsubseteq d\}$ is distributive with elements x, y, z'

$$(x \sqcup y) \sqcap z = (x \sqcup y) \sqcap z' = (x \sqcap z') \sqcup (y \sqcap z') = (x \sqcap z) \sqcup (y \sqcap z).$$

∎

Similar, more standard, reformulations are possible for the definitions of the stronger notions of distributivity of a domain.

2.7 Proposition. *Let D be a prime algebraic domain. Its complete primes are precisely those elements p with the property that for any compatible subset $X \subseteq D$ if $p \sqsubseteq \bigsqcup X$ then $p \sqsubseteq x$ for some $x \in X$.*

We remark that the fact above is the key to showing the present definition and the alternative definition of prime algebraicity in [W,NPW,W1] are equivalent.

Earlier results make it straightforward to characterise the order of configurations of prime event structures.

2.8 Theorem. *Let E be a prime event structure. The partial order $(\mathcal{L}(E), \subseteq)$ is a coherent, finitary prime algebraic domain; the complete primes are the set $\{\lceil e \rceil \mid e \in E\}$.*

Conversely, any coherent, finitary prime algebraic domain is associated with a prime event structure in which the events are its complete primes.

2.9 Definition. Let D be a coherent, finitary prime algebraic domain. Define $\mathcal{P}r(\mathrm{D}) = (P, \#, \leq)$, where P consists of the complete primes of D,

$$p \leq p' \Leftrightarrow p \sqsubseteq p',$$

and

$$p \# p' \Leftrightarrow p \not\uparrow p',$$

for $p, p' \in P$

2.10 Theorem. *Let D be a coherent, finitary prime algebraic domain. Then $\mathcal{P}r(D)$ is a prime event structure, with $\phi : D \cong (\mathcal{L}\mathcal{P}r(D), \subseteq)$ giving an isomorphism of partial orders where $\phi(d) = \{p \sqsubseteq d \mid p$ is a complete prime$\}$ with inverse $\theta : \mathcal{L}\mathcal{P}r(D) \to D$ given by $\theta(x) = \bigsqcup x$.*

Thus prime event structures and coherent, finitary prime algebraic domains are equivalent; one can be used to represent the other.

As we have seen in section 1, events also manifest themselves in a domain of configurations as prime intervals. Recall a *prime interval* is a pair $[d, d']$ such that $d \prec d'$. In a domain of configurations a prime interval is associated with the occurrence of an event at some configuration; in a domain of configurations $(\mathcal{L}(E), \subseteq)$, the relation $x \prec x'$ holds iff there is an event e such that $e \notin x$ and $x' = x \cup \{e\}$ with $x, x' \in \mathcal{L}(E)$. Define

$$[c, c'] \leq [d, d'] \Leftrightarrow d' = c' \sqcup d \ \ \& \ \ c = c' \sqcap d.$$

Form the equivalence relation $\sim$ as the symmetric, transitive closure of $\leq$, and write $[d, d']_\sim$ for the equivalence class of $[d, d']$ with respect to $\sim$. In a domain of configurations, $[c, c'] \sim [d, d']$ implies

$c' \backslash c = d' \backslash d = \{e\}$ for the same event e. So $\sim$-classes are associated with unique events. For domains represented as families of configurations of complete primes this association is a 1-1 correspondence.

2.11 Proposition. *Let D be a coherent, finitary prime algebraic domain. Let $\phi : D \cong \mathcal{L}Pr(D)$ be the isomorphism $d \mapsto \{p \sqsubseteq d \mid p$ is a complete prime$\}$. Define the following map from $\sim$-classes to complete primes:*

$$[d, d']_\sim \mapsto p$$

where p is the unique member of $\phi(d') \setminus \phi(d)$. This map is a 1-1 correspondence with inverse

$$p \mapsto [d, d']_\sim$$

where $d = \bigsqcup\{c \mid c \sqsubseteq p \;\&\; c \neq p\}$ and $d' = p$.

Sometimes one makes use of the fact that if d is a finite element of a coherent, finitary prime algebraic domain D then there is a *covering chain*

$$\bot = d_0 \prec d_1 \prec \cdots \prec d_n = d$$

in D up to d. This is obvious because we can represent any such domain as the left closed consistent subsets of some prime event structure.

Another characterisation of finitary, coherent prime algebraic domains can be obtained from the results in the last section.

2.12 Theorem. *A finitary, coherent domain is prime algebraic iff it is distributive.*

Remark. Prime event structures represent finitary, coherent prime algebraic domains. These are precisely the coherent dI-domains of Gérard Berry (see [Be]).

3. Stable event structures.

Not all the constructions we want to use are easily defined on prime event structures. For example, parallel compositions and function space constructions are not easily defined directly on them and to do so involves fairly complicated inductive definitions. The problem arises because in a prime event structure each event has the property that it causally depends on a *unique* set of events—it is enabled in a unique way. There are situations where this property does not arise naturally. Consider the event of typing a second character on a line, say "b" to be precise. It depends on having typed a first character, and any character "a", "b", "c" *etc.* will do. The occurrence of typing "b" in the second space cannot be said to causally depend on any particular one occurring in the first place. The only way to describe such a situation by a prime event structure is to work with an idea of event different than that which first suggests itself. In this case, instead of a single event, standing for putting "b" in the second place, we could use events called ab, bb, cb *etc.* meaning "b" after "a", "b" after "b", "b" after "c" *etc.* . And as we mentioned, analogous problems arise in defining some constructions like parallel composition on prime event structures and give some technical difficulties to do with encoding the history of their dependency into the naming of events.

Such difficulties can be avoided by working with more general event structures, which allow an event to be enabled in several different ways. For simplicity we shall not be quite as general as we might be and keep to a binary conflict relation.

3.1 Definition. An *event structure* is a triple $(E, \#, \vdash)$ where:

(i) E is a set of *events*.

(ii) $\#$ is a binary symmetric, irreflexive relation on E, the conflict relation. We shall write Con for the set of finite conflict-free subsets of E, *i.e.* those finite subsets $X \subseteq E$ for which

$$\forall e, e' \in X.\ \neg(e \# e').$$

(iii) $\vdash \subseteq \mathrm{Con} \times E$ is the *enabling* relation which satisfies

$$X \vdash e \ \&\ X \subseteq Y \in \mathrm{Con} \Rightarrow Y \vdash e.$$

Our intuitive understanding of the conflict relation is the same as before. The enabling relation is expressed in the notion of configuration we adopt for event structures. A configuration is a set of events which have occurred by some stage in a process. According to our understanding of the conflict relation a configuration should be conflict-free. According to our understanding of the enabling relation every event in a configuration should have been enabled by events which have occurred previously. However the chain of enablings should not be infinite but eventually end with events which are enabled by the null set, and so need no events to occur previously.

3.2 Definition. Let $\mathrm{E} = (E, \#, \vdash)$ be an event structure. Define a *configuration* of E to be a subset of events $x \subseteq E$ which is

(i) *conflict-free:* $\forall e, e' \in x.\ \neg(e \# e')$,

(ii) *secured:* $\forall e \in x \exists e_0, \cdots, e_n \in x.\ e_n = e \ \&\ \forall i \leq n.\ \{e_0, \cdots, e_{i-1}\} \vdash e_i$.

The set of all configurations of an event structure is written as $\mathcal{F}(\mathrm{E})$.

It is helpful to unwrap condition (ii) a little. It says an event e is secured in a set x iff there is a sequence of events $e_0, \cdots, e_n = e$ in x such that

$$\emptyset \vdash e_0,\ \{e_0\} \vdash e_1, \cdots, \{e_0, \cdots, e_{i-1}\} \vdash e_i, \cdots, \{e_0, \cdots, e_{n-1}\} \vdash e_n.$$

We call such a sequence $e_0, e_1, \ldots, e_n = e$ a *securing* for e in x. The following proposition expresses when an event can be added to a configuration to obtain another configuration. We use $X \subseteq_{fin} Y$ to mean X is a finite subset of Y.

3.3 Proposition. *Let $E = (E, \#, \vdash)$ be an event structure. Suppose $x \in \mathcal{F}(E)$ and $e \in E$. Then $x \cup \{e\} \in \mathcal{F}(E)$ iff*

(i) $\forall X \subseteq_{fin} x.\ X \cup \{e\} \in Con$ and

(ii) $\exists X \subseteq_{fin} x.\ X \vdash e$.

Each event structure determines a family of subsets of events, the configurations of the event structure. Such families have a simple characterisation.

3.4 Definition. Let F be a family of subsets. Say a subset X of F is *pairwise compatible* iff for all $x, x' \in X$ there is some $z \in \mathrm{F}$ with $x, x' \subseteq z$.

3.5 Theorem. *Let E be an event structure. Its configurations $F = \mathcal{F}(E)$ form a set of subsets of E which satisfy*

(i) coherence: If X is a pairwise compatible subset of F then $\bigcup X \in F$,

(ii) finiteness:

$$\forall x \in F \forall e \in x \exists z \in F.\ (z \text{ is finite} \ \&\ e \in z \ \&\ z \subseteq x),$$

(iii) coincidence-freeness:

$$\forall x \in F \forall e, e' \in x.\ e \neq e' \ \Rightarrow\ (\exists y \in F.\ y \subseteq x \ \&\ (e \in y \Leftrightarrow e' \notin y)).$$

3.6 Lemma. *Let F be a family of subsets satisfying (i), (ii) and (iii) above. For all $x, y \in F$*

$$x \subset y \Rightarrow \exists e \in y \setminus x.\ x \cup \{e\} \in F.$$

We can use this fact to show any family satisfying (i), (ii) and (iii) above can be got as the family of configurations of an event structure.

3.7 Theorem. *Let F be a family of configurations of a set E. Define a structure $\mathcal{E}(F) = (E, \#, \vdash)$ on E by taking*

$e\#e'$ iff $\forall x \in F.\ e \in x \Leftrightarrow e' \notin x$,
$X \vdash e$ iff X is conflict-free and $\exists x \in F.\ e \in x \ \&\ x \subseteq X \cup \{e\}$.
If F is a family of configurations then $\mathcal{E}(F)$ *is an event structure such that* $\mathcal{F}\mathcal{E}(F) = F$.

Notice we do not have $\mathcal{E}\mathcal{F}(\mathrm{E})$ and E equal in general for event structures E, and two different event structures can determine the same family of configurations. However, for two families of configurations F_0 and F_1, if $\mathcal{E}(\mathrm{F}_0) = \mathcal{E}(\mathrm{F}_1)$ then $\mathrm{F}_0 = \mathrm{F}_1$.

A characterisation of the domains which can be obtained as configurations of an event structure $(E, \#, \vdash)$ will be given, though without proofs, which can be found in [W] and [C]. Our concern will be largely with the more restricted class of stable event structures, the domains of which have a much simpler characterisation along the lines of that for elementary event structures.

Certainly, the partial order $(\mathrm{F}(E), \subseteq)$, of an event structure E, will be finitary domain. In addition it satisfies further axioms on domains which involve the covering relation, prime intervals and the equivalence $\sim$ on them. They are:

Axiom C: $x \prec y \ \&\ x \prec z \ \&\ y \uparrow z \ \&\ y \neq z \Rightarrow y \prec y \sqcup z \ \&\ z \prec y \sqcup z$

Axiom R: $[x, y] \sim [x, y'] \Rightarrow y = y'$

Axiom V: $[x, x'] \sim [y, y'] \ \&\ [x, x''] \sim [y, y''] \ \&\ x' \uparrow x'' \Rightarrow y' \uparrow y''$

3.8 Theorem.
(i) Let E be an event structure. The partial order $(F(E), \subseteq)$ *is a finitary domain which satisfies axioms C, R and V. Furthermore it is coherent.*
(ii) Let D be a finitary domain which satisfies axioms C, R and V. Then there is an event structure E such that $D \cong (F(E), \subseteq)$. *Furthermore D is coherent.*

Proof. See the thesis [W] or the book [C] for the proof. The verification of (i) is routine. That of (ii) requires the construction of an event structure from the domain—its events are $\sim$-classes of prime intervals. ∎

Consider an event structure consisting of three events a, b, c with empty conflict relation but where the enabling relation is the least such that $\emptyset \vdash a$, $\emptyset \vdash b$, $\{a\} \vdash c$ and also $\{b\} \vdash c$. In this case the set $\{a, b, c\}$ is a configuration. Because the event c is enabled by either of a or c its occurrence can not be said to causally depend on either one or the other or both. We might say that c has been caused by a and b in parallel. We can not ascribe a partial order of causal dependency to the events as they stand. This is not to say that such an event structure is not a legitimate description of any process. It might well be, but not one to which our intuitions about a partial order of causal dependency apply directly. In a great many examples of processes there are no "parallel causes" and a form of causal dependency, local to configurations, can be seen on the events. For them the event structures are *stable* in the following sense:

3.9 Definition. Let $\mathrm{E} = (E, \#, \vdash)$ be an event structure. Say E is *stable* if it satisfies the following axiom

$$X \vdash e \ \&\ Y \vdash e \ \&\ X \cup Y \cup \{e\} \in \mathrm{Con} \Rightarrow X \cap Y \vdash e.$$

The stability axiom ensures that an event in a configuration is enabled in an essentially unique way. Assume e belongs to a configuration x of a stable event structure. Suppose $X \vdash e$ and $X \subseteq x$. Then $X \cup \{e\} \in \mathrm{Con}$—the enabling $X \vdash e$ is consistent. Take

$$X_0 = \bigcap\{Y \mid Y \subseteq X \ \&\ Y \vdash e\}.$$

Because X is finite this is an intersection of a finite number of sets and we see by the stability axiom that $X_0 \vdash e$. Moreover X_0 is the unique minimal subset of X which enables e. More formally, for any event structure, stable or otherwise, we can define the *minimal enabling* relation $\vdash_{min}$ by

$$X \vdash_{min} e \Leftrightarrow X \vdash e \ \&\ (\forall Y \subseteq X.\ Y \vdash e \Rightarrow Y = X).$$

Then for any event structure

$$Y \vdash e \Rightarrow \exists X \subseteq Y.\ X \vdash_{min} e.$$

But for stable event structures we have uniqueness too, at least for consistent enablings:

$$Y \vdash e \ \ \&\ \ Y \cup \{e\} \in \text{Con} \Rightarrow \exists! X \subseteq Y.\ X \vdash_{min} e.$$

It follows that for stable event structures

$$X \vdash_{min} e \ \ \&\ \ Y \vdash_{min} e \ \ \&\ \ X \cup Y \cup e \in \text{Con} \Rightarrow X = Y.$$

Consequently the families of configurations of stable event structures satisfy the following intersection property.

3.10 Theorem. *Let E be a stable event structure. Then its family of configurations $\mathcal{F}(E)$ satisfies*

$$\forall X \subseteq \mathcal{F}(E).\ X \neq \emptyset \ \ \&\ \ X\uparrow \Rightarrow \bigcap X \in \mathcal{F}(E).$$

3.11 Definition. Say a family of sets F is *stable* when it satisfies the following axiom (in addition to those in theorem 3.5)

(stability) $\qquad \forall X \subseteq \text{F}.\ X \neq \emptyset \ \ \&\ \ X\uparrow \Rightarrow \bigcap X \in \text{F}.$

Thus the configurations of a stable event structure form a stable family. For a stable family there is a partial order of causal dependency on each configuration of events.

3.12 Definition. Let F be a stable family of configurations. Let x be a configuration. For $e, e' \in x$ define

$$e' \leq_x e \Leftrightarrow \forall y \in \text{F}.\ e' \in y \ \ \&\ \ y \subseteq x \Rightarrow e \in y.$$

When $e \in x$ define

$$\lceil e \rceil_x = \bigcap \{y \in \text{F} \mid e \in y \ \ \&\ \ y \subseteq x\}.$$

We say a set y is $\leq_x$-left closed when it satisfies

$$e' \leq_x e \ \ \&\ \ e \in y \Rightarrow e' \in y.$$

As usual, we write $e' <_x e$ for $e \leq_x e'$ $\ \&\ $ $e \neq e'$.

3.13 Proposition. *Let x be a configuration of a stable family F. Then $\leq_x$ is a partial order and $\lceil e \rceil_x$ is a configuration such that*

$$\lceil e \rceil_x = \{e' \in x \mid e' \leq_x e\}.$$

Moreover the configurations $y \subseteq x$ are exactly the left–closed subsets of $\leq_x$.

Let x be a configuration of a stable family. Intuitively an event e in x can only occur once all its predecessors $\{e' \in x \mid e' <_x e\}$ have occurred.

A special form of stable event structure is obtained from a prime event structure $(E.\#, \leq)$ in the following way: Define

$$X \vdash e \Leftrightarrow \lceil e \rceil \subseteq X \cup \{e\}.$$

Then $(E, \#, \vdash)$ is a stable event structure such that $\mathcal{F}(E, \#, \vdash) = \mathcal{L}(E.\#, \leq)$. For such stable families all the orders $\leq_x$, for a configuration x, are restrictioons of a common causal dependency relation $\leq$. This is not the case for stable families in general.

3.14 Example. Let E be the event structure with events $\{0,1,2\}$ with conflict relation the least one such that $0\#1$, and enabling relation the least one such that

$$\emptyset \vdash 0,\ \emptyset \vdash 1,\ \{0\} \vdash 2,\ \{1\} \vdash 2.$$

Then E is a stable event structure and the configurations $\mathcal{F}(\mathrm{E})$ have the form

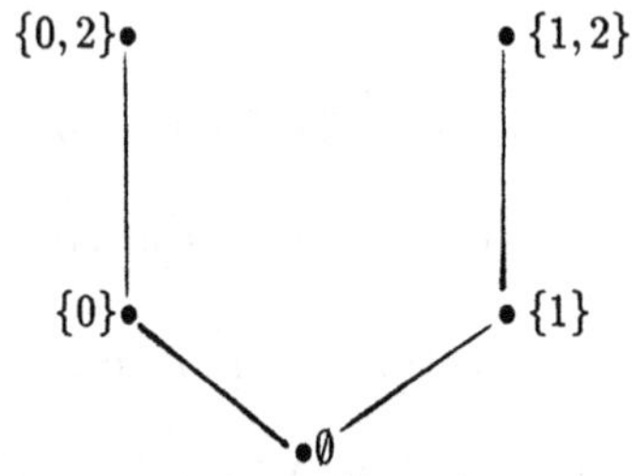

Let $x = \{0,2\}$ and $y = \{1,2\}$ be particular configurations. Then $0 \leq_x 2$ and $1 \leq_y 2$ but $0 \not\leq_y 2$ and $1 \not\leq_x 2$. The orderings $\leq_x$ and $\leq_y$ are not restrictions of a "global" partial order on events.

3.14 Theorem.

Let E be a stable event structure. Then its family of configurations $\mathcal{F}(E)$ is stable.

Let F be a stable family of configurations. Then $\mathcal{E}(F)$ is a stable event structure.

Families of configurations of stable event structures are prime algebraic. The axiom of stability on event structures has as its counterpart the axiom of distributivity on domains.

3.15 Theorem. *Let F be a family of sets which satisfies (i), (ii), (iii) in theorem 3.5 and is stable (3.11). The partial order $(F, \subseteq)$ is a finitary, coherent, prime algebraic domain; the complete primes are the set $\{\lceil e \rceil_x \mid e \in x \ \&\ x \in \mathcal{F}(E)\}$.*

Referring to theorem 2.12:

3.16 Corollary. *Let E be a stable event structure. The domain of configurations $(\mathcal{F}(E), \subseteq)$ is a coherent, distributive domain.*

Thus stability of event structures appears as distributivity of the domains of configurations. The fact that events must be secured in configurations, expressing the intuition that an event's occurrence can only depend on a finite number of previous occurrences, reappears as the fact that domains of configurations are finitary.

Conversely, given a finitary, coherent, prime algebraic domain D we can generate an isomorphic stable family *viz.* the family $\mathcal{LPr}(D)$ got by taking the configurations of the prime event structure corresponding to D. Hence we can produce prime, and stable, event structures with domains of configurations isomorphic to D.

4. A complete partial order of event structures.

There is an ordering on event structures which is useful for giving meaning to recursively defined event structures. The order is based on an idea of substructure.

4.1 Definition. Let $\mathrm{E}_0 = (E_0, \#_0, \vdash_0)$ and $\mathrm{E}_1 = (E_1, \#_1, \vdash_1)$ be event structures. Define

$$\begin{aligned} \mathrm{E}_0 \trianglelefteq \mathrm{E}_1 \Leftrightarrow & E_0 \subseteq E_1, \\ & \forall e, e'.\ e \#_0 e' \Leftrightarrow e, e' \in E_0 \ \&\ e \#_1 e' \quad \text{and} \\ & \forall X, e.\ X \vdash_0 e \Leftrightarrow X \subseteq E_0 \ \&\ e \in E_0 \ \&\ X \vdash_1 e. \end{aligned}$$

In this case say E_0 is a *substructure* of E_1.

The notion of substructure is closely tied to that of restriction, an important operation in its own right.

4.2 Definition. Let $\mathrm{E} = (E, \#, \vdash)$ be an event structure. Let $A \subseteq E$. Define the *restriction* of E to A to be

$$\mathrm{E}\lceil A = (A, \#_A, \vdash_A)$$

where

$$X \in \mathrm{Con}_A \Leftrightarrow X \subseteq A \;\;\&\;\; X \in \mathrm{Con},$$
$$X \vdash_A e \Leftrightarrow X \subseteq A \;\;\&\;\; e \in A \;\;\&\;\; X \vdash e.$$

4.3 Proposition. *Let $\mathrm{E} = (E, \#, \vdash)$ be an event structure. Let $A \subseteq E$. Then $\mathrm{E}\lceil A$ is an event structure.*

Let $\mathrm{E}_0 = (E_0, \#_0, \vdash_0)$ and $\mathrm{E}_1 = (E_1, \#_1, \vdash_1)$ be event structures. Then

$$\mathrm{E}_0 \trianglelefteq \mathrm{E}_1 \Leftrightarrow \mathrm{E}_0 = \mathrm{E}_1\lceil E_0.$$

If $\mathrm{E}_0 \trianglelefteq \mathrm{E}_1$ and $E_0 = E_1$ then $\mathrm{E}_0 = \mathrm{E}_1$.

Proof. Obvious from the definitions. ∎

This definition of substructure almost gives a complete partial order (cpo) of event structures. There is a least event structure, the unique one with the empty set of events. Each ω-chain of event structures, increasing with respect to $\trianglelefteq$ has a least upper bound, with events, consistency and enabling relations the union of those in the chain. But of course event structures form a class and not a set and for this reason alone they do not quite form a cpo. We call structures like cpos but on a class rather than a set *large cpos*. This is all we need. (Very similar approaches for solving domain equations, or equations for structures like domains, occur elsewhere.)

4.4 Theorem. *The relation $\trianglelefteq$ is a partial order on event structures. It has a least event structure $\mathbf{0} =_{def} (\emptyset, \{\emptyset\}, \emptyset)$. An ω-chain of event structures $\mathrm{E}_0 \trianglelefteq \mathrm{E}_1 \cdots \trianglelefteq \mathrm{E}_n \trianglelefteq \cdots$ where $\mathrm{E}_n = (E_n, \#_n, \vdash_n)$ has a least upper bound*

$$\bigcup_{n\in\omega} \mathrm{E}_n = (\bigcup_{n\in\omega} E_n, \bigcup_{n\in\omega} Con_n, \bigcup_{n\in\omega} \vdash_n).$$

Proof. Routine. ∎

The substructure relation on event structures is closely related to the rigid embeddings of Kahn and Plotkin [KP].

4.5 Definition. Let D_0 and D_1 be domains. Let $f : \mathrm{D}_0 \to \mathrm{D}_1$ be a continuous function. Say f is an *embedding* iff there is a continuous function $g : \mathrm{D}_1 \to \mathrm{D}_0$, called a *projection*, such that

$$gf(d) = d \text{ for all } d \in D_0 \text{ and}$$
$$fg(c) \sqsubseteq c \text{ for all } c \in D_1.$$

Say f is a *rigid embedding* iff it is an embedding with projection g such that

$$c \sqsubseteq f(d) \Rightarrow fg(c) = c$$

for all $d \in D_0, c \in D_1$.

4.6 Proposition. *Let E_0 and E_1 be event structures such that $\mathrm{E}_0 \trianglelefteq \mathrm{E}_1$. The inclusion map $i : \mathcal{F}(\mathrm{E}_0) \to \mathcal{F}(\mathrm{E}_1)$ is a rigid embedding with projection $j : \mathcal{F}(\mathrm{E}_1) \to \mathcal{F}(\mathrm{E}_0)$ given by $j(y) = \bigcup\{x \in \mathcal{F}(\mathrm{E}_0) \mid x \subseteq y\}$ for $y \in \mathcal{F}(\mathrm{E}_1)$.*

The next lemma is a great help in proving operations continuous on the large cpo of event structures. Generally it is very easy to show that a unary operation is monotonic with respect to $\trianglelefteq$ and continuous on the sets of events, a notion we now make precise.

4.7 Definition. Say a unary operation **F** on event structures is *continuous on events* iff for any ω-chain, $E_0 \trianglelefteq E_1 \cdots \trianglelefteq E_n \trianglelefteq \cdots$, each event of $F(\bigcup_i E_i)$ is a event of $\bigcup_i F(E_i)$.

4.8 Lemma. *Let F be a unary operation on event structures. Then F is continuous iff F is monotonic with respect to $\trianglelefteq$ and continuous on events.*

4.9 Definition. Let **D** be a large cpo ordered by $\trianglelefteq$, with least upper bounds $\bigcup X$ when they exist. Let F be a continuous operation on **D**. Define *fix* F to be the least upper bound

$$\bigcup_{n\in\omega} F^n(\underline{\emptyset}).$$

4.10 Proposition. *For the situation in the above definition, the element fix F of* **D** *is the least fixed point of F.*

As a simple example of a recursively defined event structure we consider the fixed point of an operation called *prefixing* (sometimes called lifting, or guarding) whose effect on an event structure is to adjoin an extra initial event. Then once it has occurred the behaviour resumes as that of the original event structure.

4.11 Definition. Let a be an event. For an event structure $E = (E, \#, \vdash)$ define aE to be the event structure $(E', \#', \vdash')$ where

$$\begin{aligned}
&E' = \{(0,a)\} \cup \{(1,e) \mid e \in E\},\\
&e_0' \#' e_1' \Leftrightarrow \exists e_0, e_1.\ e_0' = (1,e_0)\ \&\ e_1' = (1,e_1)\ \&\ e_0 \# e_1,\\
&X \vdash' e' \Leftrightarrow e' = (0,a) \text{ or } [e' = (1,e_1)\ \&\ (0,a) \in X\ \&\ \{e \mid (1,e) \in X\} \vdash e_1].
\end{aligned}$$

4.12 Proposition. *For any event a the operation a( ) is $\trianglelefteq$-continuous on event structures. The least fixed point fix a( ) has events in 1-1 correspondence with strings in the regular language 1^*0a; any finite subset of events is consistent and the enabling relation satisfies*

$$\begin{aligned}
&\emptyset \vdash 0a,\\
&X \vdash 1^n 0a \Leftrightarrow \{0a, \cdots, 1^{n-1}0a\} \subseteq X,
\end{aligned}$$

for $n \geq 1$.

Only fixed points of unary operators on event structures have been considered so far. The generalisation to n-ary operators is straightforward following the scheme familiar from domain theory. Such operators are continuous iff they are continuous in each argument separately. They compose to give other continuous operators and we can take their least fixed points to deal with simultaneous recursive definitions. Note that other orderings can sometimes work just as well to handle recursive definitions; for example, simple coordinatewise inclusion gives a large cpo with respect to which most operations are continuous, though it will not work for function space constructions like those mentioned in section 7.

5. Semantics of communicating processes.

One use of event structures is to give a denotational semantics of a language of parallel processes which reflects the parallelism in processes as causal independence between events. The nature of the events, how they interact with the environment, is specified in the language by associating each event with a label from the synchronisation algebra L. The language we shall use is one where processes communicate by events of synchronisation with no value passing. Its syntax has the form:

$$p ::= nil \mid \alpha p \mid p_0 + p_1 \mid p_0 \times p_1 \mid p\lceil\Lambda \mid p[\Xi] \mid x \mid rec x.p$$

where x is in some set of variables X over processes, α is a label, Λ is a subset of labels, in $p[\Xi]$ the symbol Ξ denotes a relabelling function between tow sets of labels.

Informally, the product $p_0 \times p_1$ is a form of parallel composition which introduces arbitrary events of synchronisation between processes. Unwanted synchronisations can be restricted away with the help of the restriction operation $p\lceil\Lambda$ and then existing events renamed with the relabelling operation $p[\Xi]$. So in this way we can define specialised parallel compositions of the kind that appear in CCS and CSP, for example.

To explain formally the behaviour of the constructs in the language we describe them as constructions on labelled event structures, so a closed process term in this language is to denote a stable event structure but where the events are labelled.

5.1 Definition. A *labelled event structure* consists of $(E, \#, \vdash, L, l)$ where $(E, \#, \vdash)$ is an event structure, L is a set of labels, not including the element $*$, and l is a function $l : E \to L$ from its events to its labels.

Remark. The special role of the element $*$ will become clear soon.

It shortens some definitions if we use the reflexive conflict relation:

5.2 Notation. In an event structure we shall write $\mathrel{W}$ for the reflexive conflict relation by which we mean that $e \mathrel{W} e'$ in an event structure iff either $e\#e'$ or $e = e'$. With this notation instead of describing the conflict-free sets of an event structure as those sets X such that

$$\forall e, e' \in X.\ \neg(e\#e')$$

we can say they are those sets X for which

$$\forall e, e' \in X.\ e \mathrel{W} e' \Rightarrow e = e'.$$

The term *nil* represents the *nil* process which has stopped and refuses to perform any event; it will denoted by the empty labelled event structure $(\emptyset, \emptyset, \emptyset, \emptyset, \emptyset)$—no events, no labels.

A *prefixed* process αp first performs an event of kind α to become the process p. Its denotation is given using the prefixing construction of the last section.

5.3 Definition. Let (E, L, l) be a labelled event structure. Let α be a label. Define $\alpha(\mathrm{E}, L, l)$ to be the labelled event structure $(\alpha E, L', l')$ with labels

$$L' = \{\alpha\} \cup L$$

and

$$l'(e') = \begin{cases} \alpha & \text{if } e = (0, \alpha) \\ l(e) & \text{if } e = (1, e) \end{cases}$$

for all $e' \in E'$.

The configurations of $\alpha\mathrm{E}$, a prefixed labelled event structure, have the simple and expected characterisation. (By $\mathcal{F}(\mathrm{E})$ of a labelled event structure E we shall understand the set of configurations of the underlying event structure.)

5.4 Proposition. *Let E be a labelled event structure. Let α be a label.*

$$x \in \mathcal{F}(\alpha E) \Leftrightarrow x = \emptyset \ \text{ or } \ [(0,0) \in x \ \&\ \{e \mid (1,e) \in x\} \in \mathcal{F}(E)].$$

A *sum* $p_0 + p_1$ behaves like p_0 or p_1; which branch of a sum is followed will often be determined by the context and what kinds of events the process is restricted to.

5.5 Definition. Let $\mathrm{E}_0 = (E_0, \#_0, \vdash_0, L_0, l_0)$ and $\mathrm{E}_1 = (E_1, \#_1, \vdash_1, L_1, l_1)$ be labelled event structures. Their *sum*, $\mathrm{E}_0 + \mathrm{E}_1$, is defined to be the structure $(E, \#, \vdash, l)$ with

events $E = \{(0,e) \mid e \in E_0\} \cup \{(0,e) \mid e \in E_1\}$, the disjoint union of sets E_0 and E_1, with injections $\iota_k : E_k \to E$, given by $\iota_k(e) = (k,e)$, for $k = 0,1$,
conflict relation

$$\begin{aligned} e\#e' \Leftrightarrow & \exists e_0, e_0'.\ e = \iota_0(e_0) \ \&\ e' = \iota_0(e_0') \ \&\ e_0 \#_0 e_0' \\ \text{or } & \exists e_1, e_1'.\ e = \iota_1(e_1) \ \&\ e' = \iota_1(e_1') \ \&\ e_1 \#_1 e_1' \\ \text{or } & \exists e_0, e_1.\ (e = \iota_0(e_0) \ \&\ e' = \iota_1(e_1)) \text{ or } (e' = \iota_0(e_0) \ \&\ e = \iota_1(e_1)) \end{aligned}$$

and enabling relation

$$\begin{aligned} X \vdash e \Leftrightarrow & X \in \mathrm{Con} \ \&\ e \in E \ \& \\ & [(\exists X_0 \in \mathrm{Con}_0, e_0 \in E_0.\ X = \iota_0 X_0 \ \&\ e = \iota_0(e_0) \ \&\ X_0 \vdash_0 e_0) \text{ or} \\ & (\exists X_1 \in \mathrm{Con}_1, e_1 \in E_1.\ X = \iota_1 X_1 \ \&\ e = \iota_1(e_1) \ \&\ X_1 \vdash_1 e_1)]. \end{aligned}$$

Its set of labels is the disjoint union $L_0 \uplus L_1$, with injections $\kappa_i : L_i \to L_0 \uplus L_1$ for $i = 0,1$. Its labelling function acts so

$$l(e) = \begin{cases} \kappa_0(l_0(e_0) & \text{if } e = \iota_0(e_0)) \\ \kappa_1(l_1(e_1) & \text{if } e = \iota_1(e_1)). \end{cases}$$

The choice to take disjoint sets of labels is somewhat arbitrary, though later it does lead to a direct categorical characterisation, and afterall we can obtain another form of sum where copies of events keep their original labels by using relabelling.

The configurations of a sum are obtained from copies of the configurations of the components identified at their empty configurations.

5.6 Proposition. *Let E_0 and E_1 be labelled event structures.*

$$x \in \mathcal{F}(E_0 + E_1) \Leftrightarrow (\exists x_0 \in \mathcal{F}(E_0).\ x = \iota_0 x_0) \text{ or } (\exists x_1 \in \mathcal{F}(E_1).\ x = \iota_1 x_1).$$

For purposes like modelling value-passing it can be useful to generalise the definition of sum to indexed families of event structures. The definition is straightforward (it can be found in [W1]).

A *product* process $p_0 \times p_1$ behaves like p_0 and p_1 set in parallel. Their events of synchronisation are those pairs of events (e_0, e_1), one from each process; if e_0 is labelled α_0 and e_1 is labelled α_1 the synchronisation event is then labelled (α_0, α_1). Events need not synchronise however; an event in one component may not synchronise with any event in the other. We shall use events of the form $(e_0, *)$ to stand for the occurrence of an event e_0 from one component unsynchronised with any event of the other. Such an event will be labelled by $(\alpha_0, *)$ where α_0 is the original label of e_0 and $*$ is a sort of undefined.

In fact we shall often want to take the first or second coordinates of such pairs and, of course, this could give the value $*$ which we think of as undefined, so that, in effect, we are working with partial functions with $*$ understood to be undefined. We can keep expressions tidier by adopting some conventions about how to treat this undefined value when it appears in expressions and assertions.

5.7 Notation. We shall be working with partial functions θ on events. We indicate that θ is a partial function from E_0 to E_1 by writing $\theta : E_0 \to_* E_1$. Then it may not be the case that $\theta(e)$ is defined and we use $*$ to represent undefined, so $\theta(e) = *$ means the same as $\theta(e)$ is undefined. It is a nuissance when using predicates like $\theta(e) \in X$ to always have to say "provided $\theta(e)$ is defined". Instead we adopt the convention that the basic predicates of equality, membership, conflict, and reflexive conflict are strict in the sense that if they mention $\theta(e)$ this implies $\theta(e)$ is defined. Under this convention, for example,

$$\begin{aligned} &\theta(e) \in X \Rightarrow \theta(e) \text{ is defined, and} \\ &\theta(e) = \theta(e') \Rightarrow \theta(e) \text{ is defined } \ \&\ \theta(e') \text{ is defined.} \end{aligned}$$

We adopt a similar strict interpretation for function application. So if f is a function applied to some value, denoted by a, then $f(a)$ is undefined (gives $*$) if a is undefined.

As usual we represent the image of a set under a partial function by

$$\theta X = \{\theta(e) \mid e \in X \ \ \& \ \ \theta(e) \text{ is defined}\}.$$

5.8 Definition. Let $\mathrm{E}_0 = (E_0, \#_0, \vdash_0, L_0, l_0)$ and $\mathrm{E}_1 = (E_1, \#_1, \vdash_1, L_1, l_1)$ be labelled event structures. Define their *product* $\mathrm{E}_0 \times \mathrm{E}_1$ to be the structure $\mathrm{E} = (E, \#, \vdash, L, l)$ consisting of events E of the form

$$E_0 \times_* E_1 = \{(e_0, *) \mid e_0 \in E_0\} \cup \{(*, e_1) \mid e_1 \in E_1\} \cup \{(e_0, e_1) \mid e_0 \in E_0 \ \ \& \ \ e_1 \in E_1\},$$

with projections $\pi_i : E \rightarrow_* E_i$, given by $\pi_i(e_0, e_1) = e_i$, for $i = 0, 1$, reflexive conflict relation $\mathrel{W}$ given by

$$e \mathrel{W} e' \Leftrightarrow \pi_0(e) \mathrel{W_0} \pi_0(e') \ \text{ or } \ \pi_1(e) \mathrel{W_1} \pi_1(e')$$

for all e, e'—we use Con for the conflict-free finite sets, enabling relation $\vdash$ given by

$$X \vdash e \Leftrightarrow X \in \mathrm{Con} \ \ \& \ \ e \in E \ \ \& \\ (\pi_0(e) \text{ is defined} \Rightarrow \pi_0 X \vdash_0 \pi_0(e)) \ \ \& \ \ (\pi_1(e) \text{ is defined} \Rightarrow \pi_1 X \vdash_1 \pi_1(e)).$$

Its set of labels is

$$L_0 \times_* L_1 = \{(\alpha_0, *) \mid \alpha_0 \in L_0\} \cup \{(*, \alpha_1) \mid \alpha_1 \in L_1\} \cup \{(\alpha_0, \alpha_1) \mid \alpha_0 \in L_0 \ \ \& \ \ \alpha_1 \in L_1\},$$

with projections $\lambda_i : E \rightarrow_* E_i$, given by $\lambda_i(\alpha_0, \alpha_1) = \alpha_i$, for $i = 0, 1$. Its labelling function is defined to act on an event e so

$$l(e) = (l_0 \pi_0(e), l_1 \pi_1(e)).$$

We characterise the configurations of the product of two event structures in terms of their configurations.

5.9 Proposition. *Let $\mathrm{E}_0 \times \mathrm{E}_1$ be the product of labelled event structures with projections π_0, π_1. Let $x \subseteq E_0 \times_* E_1$, the events of the product. Then $x \in \mathcal{F}(\mathrm{E}_0 \times \mathrm{E}_1)$ iff*

a) $\pi_0 x \in \mathcal{F}(\mathrm{E}_0) \ \ \& \ \ \pi_1 x \in \mathcal{F}(\mathrm{E}_1)$,

b) $\forall e, e' \in x.\ \pi_0(e) = \pi_0(e') \ \text{ or } \ \pi_1(e) = \pi_1(e') \Rightarrow e = e'$,

d) $\forall e \in x \exists y \subseteq x.\ \pi_0 y \in \mathcal{F}(\mathrm{E}_0) \ \ \& \ \ \pi_1 y \in \mathcal{F}(\mathrm{E}_1) \ \ \& \ \ e \in y \ \ \& \ \ |y| < \infty$ and

c) $\forall e, e' \in x.\ e \neq e' \Rightarrow \exists y \subseteq x.\ \pi_0 y \in \mathcal{F}(\mathrm{E}_0) \ \ \& \ \ \pi_1 y \in \mathcal{F}(\mathrm{E}_1) \ \ \& \ \ (e \in y \Leftrightarrow e' \notin y)$.

The proposition above expresses the intuition that an allowable behaviour of the product of two processes is precisely that which "projects" to allowable behaviours in the component processes—the complicated-looking conditions (c) and (d) are there just to ensure that the family of sets is finitary and coincidence-free.

The *restriction* $t \lceil \Lambda$ behaves like the process p but with its events restricted to those with labels which lie in the set Λ.

5.10 Definition. Let $\mathrm{E} = (E, \#, \vdash, L, l)$ be a labelled event structure. Let Λ be a subset of labels. Define the restriction $\mathrm{E} \lceil \Lambda$ to be $(E', \#', \vdash', L \cap \Lambda, l')$ where $(E', \#', \vdash')$ is the restriction of $(E, \#, \vdash)$ to the events $\{e \in E \mid l(e) \in \Lambda\}$ and the labelling function l' is the restriction of the original labelling function to the domain $L \cap \Lambda$.

5.11 Proposition. *Let* $\mathrm{E} = (E, \#, \vdash, L, l)$ *be a labelled event structure. Let* $\Lambda \subseteq L$.

$$x \in \mathcal{F}(\mathrm{E}\lceil\Lambda) \Leftrightarrow x \in \mathcal{F}(\mathrm{E}) \;\;\&\;\; \forall e \in x.\; l(e) \in \Lambda.$$

A relabelled process $p[\Xi]$ behaves like p but with the events relabelled according to Ξ.

5.12 Definition. Let $\mathrm{E} = (E, \#, \vdash, L, l)$ be a labelled event structure. Let Λ, L' be sets of labels and $\Xi : \Lambda \to L'$. Define the relabelling $\mathrm{E}[\Xi]$ to be $(E, \#, \vdash, L', l')$ where

$$l'(e) = \begin{cases} \Xi l(e) & \text{if } l(e) \in \Lambda, \\ l(e) & \text{otherwise.} \end{cases}$$

In order to give a meaning to the recursively defined processes of the form *recx.p* we use the fact that the operations are continuous with respect to a large c.p.o. of labelled event structures. The large c.p.o. of event structures $\trianglelefteq$ extends naturally to labelled event structures in such a way that operations like parallel composition are continuous.

Define the ordering $\trianglelefteq_L$ on labelled event structures by:

$$(\mathrm{E}_0, L_0, l_0) \trianglelefteq_L (\mathrm{E}_1, L_1, l_1) \Leftrightarrow \mathrm{E}_0 \trianglelefteq \mathrm{E}_1 \;\;\&\;\; L_0 \subseteq L_1 \;\;\&\;\; l_0 = l_1 \lceil E_0.$$

The null labelled event structure $(\underline{\emptyset}, \emptyset, \emptyset)$ is the least L-labelled event structure with respect to $\trianglelefteq_L$. Of course, $\trianglelefteq_L$ has least upper bounds of ω-chains; the lub of a chain $(\mathrm{E}_0, L_0, l_0), \ldots, (\mathrm{E}_n, L_n, l_n), \ldots$ takes the form $(\bigcup_n \mathrm{E}_n, \bigcup_n L_n, \bigcup_n l_n)$. All the operations prefixing, sum, restriction, relabelling and parallel composition are continuous with respect to $\trianglelefteq_L$. The proofs follow by applying lemma 4.8. It is straightforward to check that each operation is monotonic and continuous on events for each argument separately, and so is $\trianglelefteq$–continuous. Thus we can give a denotational semantics to $\mathbf{Proc}_L$by representing recursively defined processes as the least fixed points of continuous operation.

5.13 Definition. *Denotational semantics:* Define an *environment* for process variables to be a function ρ from process variables X to labelled event structures. For a term t and an environment ρ, define the denotation of t with respect to ρ written $[\![t]\!]\rho$ by the following structural induction—syntactic operators appear on the left and their semantic counterparts on the right.

$$\begin{array}{llll} [\![nil]\!]\rho & = (\underline{\emptyset}, \emptyset) & [\![t\lceil\Lambda]\!]\rho & = [\![t]\!]\rho\lceil\Lambda \\ [\![x]\!]\rho & = \rho(x) & [\![t[\Xi]]\!]\rho & = [\![t]\!]\rho[\Xi] \\ [\![\alpha t]\!]\rho & = \alpha([\![t]\!]\rho) & [\![t_1 \times t_2]\!]\rho & = [\![t_1]\!]\rho \times [\![t_2]\!]\rho \\ [\![t_1 + t_2]\!]\rho & = [\![t_1]\!]\rho + [\![t_2]\!]\rho & [\![recx.t]\!]\rho & = \mathit{fix}\ \Gamma \end{array}$$

where Γ is an operation on labelled event structures given by $\Gamma(\mathrm{E}) = [\![t]\!]\rho[\mathrm{E}/x]$ and *fix* is the least–fixed–point operator.

Remark. A straightforward structural induction shows that Γ above is indeed continuous with respect to $\trianglelefteq_L$ so the denotation of a recursively defined process is really the least fixed point of the associated functional Γ.

It can be shown that each operation preserves the stability axiom on event structures and so restricts to an operation on stable event structures. Consequently, according to the denotational semantics each closed process term denotes a labelled stable event structure. By taking events to be complete primes in the families of configurations—using the operation $\mathcal{P}r$—we obtain labelled prime event structures as denotations.

5.14 Example. With respect to any environment ρ, the terms $\alpha\beta nil$ and γnil denote event structures with domains of configurations of the form below:

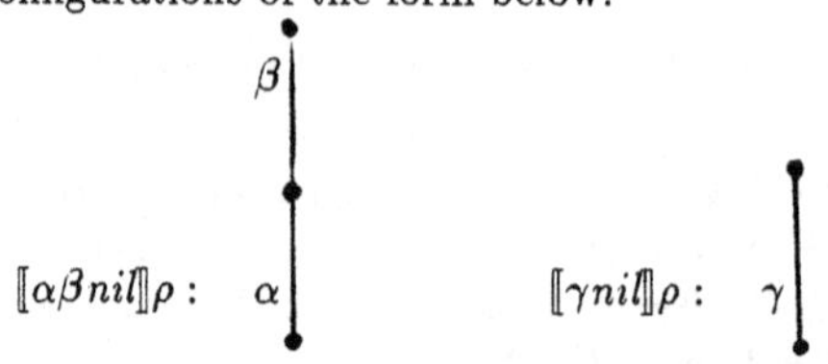

where we label prime intervals by the labels of the corresponding events. The domains of configurations of $[\![\alpha\beta nil \times \gamma nil]\!]\rho$ look like:

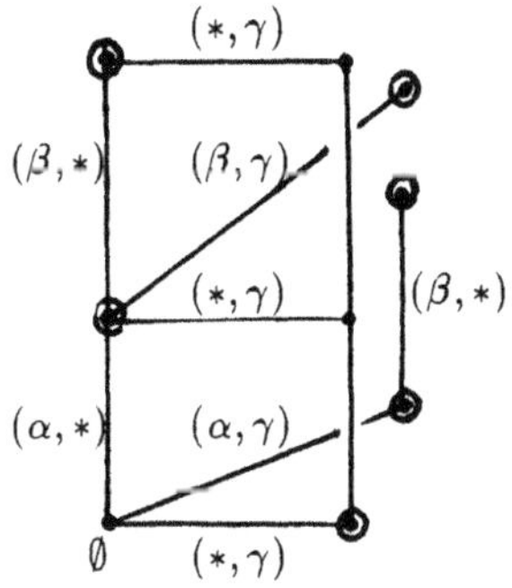

where we have encircled the complete primes. A labelled prime event structure is obtained by taking the complete primes as new events and the causal dependency and conflict relations as restrictions of the ordering and incompatibility relations. (We leave this to the reader.)

Labelled stable event structures are fairly complicated things, and constructions on them are complicated too. Originally, for the most part, languages like the one we are using were given an "interleaving semantics" in the sense that parallelism was simulated by nondeterministically interleaving the events of two processes set in parallel, except where they were synchronised together. How are we to check that our semantics agrees with such semantics even though it expresses more about the computations?

Part of the answer lies in taking a more abstract view of the constructions used by employing elementary category theory. Category theory not only provides abstract characterisations of constructions like product, restriction and relabelling, which determine the constructions to within isomorphism, but also provides techniques for proving the consistency of one semantics with respect to another.

Examples of morphisms have been introduced implicitly in the definition of sum and product, and, for example, the definition of product used projection functions on the events and labels. Through them, proposition 5.9 formalises the intuition that an allowable behaviour of the product of two processes is precisely that which "projects" to allowable behaviours in the component processes.

The following gives the general definition of morphism between labelled event structures.

5.15 Definition. Let $\mathrm{E}_0 = (E_0, \#_0, \vdash_0, L_0, l_0)$ and $\mathrm{E}_1 = (E_1, \#_1, \vdash_1, L_1, l_1)$ be labelled event structures. A *(partially synchronous) morphism* from E_0 to E_1 is a pair (η, λ) of partial functions $\eta : E_0 \to_* E_1$ on events and $\lambda : L_0 \to_* L_1$ on labels which satisfies

(i) $\eta(e) \mathrm{W}_1 \eta(e') \Rightarrow e \mathrm{W}_0 e'$,

(ii) $X \vdash_0 e$ & $\eta(e)$ is defined $\Rightarrow \eta X \vdash_1 \eta(e)$ and

(iii) $l_1 \eta = \lambda l_0$.

(Note by our strictness convention in handling undefined the truth of $\eta(e) \mathrm{W}_1 \eta(e')$ asserts also that $\eta(e)$ and $\eta(e')$ are defined.)

Remark. The partially synchronous morphisms here are are a little different from those presented in [W1]. Firstly, because conflict is based on a binary relation in these notes, the conditions are expressed differently—though with the same effect on configurations. Secondly, here event structures carry labels and we have made the morphisms respect them. While this addition does permit a categorical characterisation of restriction and relabelling, it does not complicate many of the proofs.

A morphism $(\eta, \lambda) : \mathrm{E}_0 \to \mathrm{E}_1$ between labelled event structures E_0 and E_1 expresses how behaviour in E_0 determines behaviour in E_1. The partial function η expresses how the occurrence of events in E_0 imply the simultaneous occurrence of events in E_1; the fact that $\eta(e_0) = e_1$ means that the event e_1 is a component of the event e_0 and, in this sense, that the occurrence of e_0 implies the simultaneous occurrence of e_1. The final condition (iii) simply ensures the agreement of the functions on events and the function on labels. To understand condition (i) it is helpful to break it into an equivalent conjunction of the following two conditions:

(ia) $\eta(e) = \eta(e') \Rightarrow e \mathbb{W}_0 e'$,

(ib) $\eta(e) \#_1 \eta(e') \Rightarrow e \#_0 e'$

for all events e, e' in E_0. The condition (ia) says if two distinct events e, e' have the same image then they are in conflict. This formalises the idea that if two distinct events in E_0 have the same image e_1 in E_1 then they cannot belong to the same configuration. Otherwise, by the property of coicidence-freeness of configurations, there would be a configuration containing both events but with a subconfiguration which separated them. Considering the effect of the occurrence of the two events, under the morphism, this would lead to the contradiction of e_1 occurring twice. Condition (1b) says that if two events have images in conflict then they must themselves be in conflict. It says conflict-free sets in E_0 determine conflict-free behaviour in E_1. Condition (ii) in the definition says that a morphism preserves enabling. Together conditions (i) and (ii) ensure that a configuration in E_0 determines a configuration in E_1, in other words that morphisms preserve configurations.

5.16 Proposition. *Let $(\eta, \lambda) : E_0 \to E_1$ be a morphism of stable event structures. Then*

$$x \in \mathcal{F}(E_0) \Rightarrow (\eta x \in \mathcal{F}(E_1) \ \ \& \ \ \forall e, e' \in x.\ \eta(e) = \eta(e') \Rightarrow e = e').$$

5.17 Proposition. *Labelled event structures with partially synchronous morphisms form a category with composition the coordinatewise composition of partial functions and identity morphisms pairs of identity functions on events and labels.*

The product and sum are familiar categorical constructions:

5.18 Proposition. *The product of labelled event structures is the categorical product in the category of labelled event structures with partially synchronous morphisms. The sum is the categorical coproduct.*

These facts determine the product and sum to within isomorphism.

Restriction and relabelling are constructions which depend on labelling sets and functions between them. Seeing them as categorical constructions involves dealing explicitly with functions on labelling sets and borrowing a couple of fundamental ideas from indexed category theory.

We can project a morphism (η, λ) between labelled event structures to a partial function $p(\eta, \lambda) = \lambda$ on labelling sets, determining a functor p from the category of labelled event structures to the category of labelling sets with functions. Suppose E is an event structure with labelling set L. We will lose no generality if we assume the restricting set Λ is a subset of L. Then there is an inclusion morphism $j : \Lambda \to L$ in the category of labelling sets with partial functions. The restriction $E \lceil \Lambda$ has labelling set Λ and there is a morphism $(i, j) : E \lceil \Lambda \to E$ where i is the inclusion map on events. This morphism is characterised abstractly as the *cartesian lifting* of j with respect to E. A morphism $f : E' \to E$ between event structures is said to be a *cartesian lifting* of the morphism $p(f)$ between labelling sets with respect to E if for any morphism $g : E'' \to E$ on event structures and morphism $\lambda : p(E'') \to p(E')$ between labelling sets for which $p(f)\lambda = p(g)$ there is a unique morphism $h : E'' \to E'$ such that $p(h) = \lambda$ and $fh = g$.

Relabelling can be characterised in a similar way but using a dual notion. Suppose E is a labelled event structure with labelling set L. To simplify the explanation, as we lose no generality, we assume $\Xi : L \to L'$ is a total function. The labelled event structure $E[\Xi]$ has labelling set L' and there is a morphism $(1, \Xi) : E \to E[\Xi]$, where 1 is the identity function on the set of events. This morphism is a *cocartesian lifting* of Ξ with respect to E. A morphism $f : E \to E'$ between event structures is said to be a *cocartesian lifting* of the morphism $p(f)$ between labelling sets with respect to E if for any morphism $g : E \to E''$ on event structures and morphism $\lambda : p(E') \to p(E'')$ between labelling sets for which $\lambda p(f) = p(g)$ there is a unique morphism $h : E' \to E''$ such that $p(h) = \lambda$ and $hf = g$.

It is not hard to see that the notions of cartesian and cocartesian liftings are general notions which make sense whenever we have a functor p from one category to another. It can be checked that the domain of a cartesian lifting and the codomain of a cocartesian lifting are determined to within isomorphism, and moreover, by isomorphisms which project to the identity.

To summarise:

5.19 Proposition. *Operations of restriction are obtained as cartesian liftings of an inclusion between labelling sets. Operations of relabelling are obtained as cocartesian liftings of total functions between labelling sets.*

I do not know a categorical characterisation of prefixing. Nor do I know a categorical way of expressing hiding (the operation of making certain specified events hidden or internal, so that they can occur within a process but cannot synchronise further with any events in the environment).

The abstract and general constructions of the operations used to describe our language of processes are useful when we come to consider different models. The same abstract constructions apply in many different models. We can draw on some general results about functors preserving constructions in order to show how semantics in terms of one model is preserved when it is translated to semantics in terms of another.

For example, a well-known interleaving model is that of synchronisation trees in which nodes represent states and arcs carrying labels are thought of as labelled events. By regarding such trees as (families of configurations of) special kinds of labelled prime event structures we inherit a notion of partially synchronous morphism on them. In the category of synchronisation trees the coproduct is an operation which "glues" trees together at their roots, while the product is of the kind one would hope for from Milner's expansion theorem. Again cartesian and cocartesian liftings give restriction and relabelling operations. The identification of synchronisation trees with certain kinds of labelled event structures is essentially an inclusion functor from the category of synchronisation trees to the category of labelled event structures. There is another functor, going the other way from labelled event structures to synchronisation trees, which given a labelled event structure serialises its event occurrences to produce a synchronisation tree whose behaviour is an interleaved version of that of the original event structure. These two functors bear a useful relationship with each other: the serialisation functor is right adjoint to the inclusion functor, a fact which characterises it to within isomorphism. The adjunction is, in fact, of a special form: if we serialise a synchronisation tree we obtain a synchronisation tree isomorphic to the original. This makes the adjunction a coreflection.

Armed with this knowledge we can make use of some general results. Right adjoints preserve all limits, and products in particular. This immediately yields that the serialisation of the product of labelled event structures is the product (as a tree) of their serialisations. There are other useful facts like that left adjoints preserve coproducts, and results on the preservation of cartesian and cocartesian liftings. Such facts are clearly useful in showing how semantics is preserved by operations, like serialisation, across different models. They can save us calculations in another way. To give the idea, rather than work out the product in trees we can see they exist from the existence of a coreflection, given that we know we have products of event structures. If T_0 and T_1 are synchronisation trees, we can regard them as event structures, form their product $T_0 \times_E T_1$ as event structures, serialise this to get $S(T_0 \times_E T_1)$ and know this is the product of $S(T_0)$ and $S(T_1)$ because the right adjoint S preserves products. As S is part of a coreflection $S(T_0) \cong T_0$ and $S(T_1) \cong T_1$. So $S(T_0 \times_E T_1)$ is the product of T_0 and T_1 in the category of synchronisation trees.

For a a detailed account of categories of models for parallel computation see [W1] (although the treatment of labels there is different, the presence of labels does not complicate the proofs much) and [W2] (where labels are taken into account but largely for the model of Petri nets).

6. Nets, traces and event structures.

In this section we sketch the relationship between event structures and two other models of parallel computation, Petri nets and trace languages. All three follow a similar philosophy in the way they represent concurrency.

In defining Petri nets and constructions on them we shall use multisets and their notation—see the appendix for a quick summary. Note, especially, that we call a multiset a *set* when its multiplicities are all less than or equal to 1.

6. Definition. A *Petri net* is a structure $(B, M_0, E, pre, post)$ where,

B is a set of *conditions*,
M_0 is a multiset of conditions, called the *initial marking*,
E is a set of *events*,
pre and *post* are multirelations $E \to_m B$, called the *pre* and *post* condition maps respectively,

which satisfy the restriction:

$$\forall b \in B.\ M_{0b} \neq 0 \text{ or } (\exists e \in E.\ pre(e)_b \neq 0 \text{ or } post(e)_b \neq 0).$$

6.2 Notation. When the context makes it clear we shall use $^\bullet(\ )$ and $(\ )^\bullet$ for the pre and post condition maps.

The restriction in the definition of Petri nets is there for the technical reason that in the full treatment with morphisms on nets it ensures that we can always manage with multisets in which the multiplicities are finite.

6.3 Definition. The behaviour of nets:

Let $N = (B, M_0, E, pre, post)$ be a Petri net.
A *marking* M is a multiset of conditions, *i.e.* $M \in m(B)$.
Let M, M' be markings. Let A be a finite multiset of events. Define

$$M \xrightarrow{A} M' \Leftrightarrow {}^\bullet A \leq M \ \ \&\ \ M' = M - {}^\bullet A + A^\bullet.$$

This gives the *transition relation* between markings. The transition $M \xrightarrow{A} M'$ means that the finite multiset of events A can occur concurrently from the marking M to yield the marking M'.

A *reachable marking* of N is a marking M for which

$$M_0 \xrightarrow{A_0} M_1 \xrightarrow{A_1} \cdots \xrightarrow{A_{n-1}} M_n = M$$

for some markings and finite multisets of events.

6.4 Notation. We write $M \xrightarrow{A} M' : N$ to mean M is a reachable marking of N and $M \xrightarrow{A} M'$ is a transition of N. We write $M \xrightarrow{A}: N$ to mean $M \xrightarrow{A} M' : N$, for some M'.

6.5 Definition. Say a Petri net N is *safe* iff $^\bullet e$ and $e^\bullet$ are sets, for all events e, and whenever $M \xrightarrow{A}: N$ then M and A are sets.

As Mazurkiewicz has shown, the behaviour of safe nets can be analysed through the notion of trace, and we refer the reader to his lecture notes in this volume for a fuller account. (Please be prepared for our definitions to appear superficially different from his.)

6.6 Definition. A *trace language* consists of (A, I, T) where A is a set of *events*, I is a binary, symmetric, irreflexive relation on A called the *independence* relation and T is a nonempty subset of sequences A^* which is

prefix closed: $sa \in T \Rightarrow s \in T$ for all $s \in A^*, a \in A$,
I-closed: $sabt \in T \ \&\ aIb \Rightarrow sbat \in T$ for all $s, t \in A^*, a, b \in A$.

Say a trace language is *coherent* iff

$$sa \in T \ \ \&\ \ sb \in T \ \ \&\ \ aIb \Rightarrow sab \in T$$

for all $s \in A^*, a, b \in A$.

Probably more familiar is the definition of a trace language as a set of equivalence classes along the following lines.

6.7 Definition. Let (A, I, T) be a trace language. Define the relation $=_I$ on T to be the smallest equivalence relation such that

$$t_0 =_I t_1' \text{ if } \exists s, s' \in T, a, b \in A.\ aIb \ \&\ t_0 = sabs' \ \&\ t_1 = sbas'.$$

For $s \in T$ write $\{s\}_I$ for the $=_I$-equivalence class of s. For $=_I$-equivalence classes x, y, define $x \leq y$ iff there are s, s' such that $x = \{s\}_I$ and $y = \{t\}_I$ and s is a prefix of t.

Write T_I for the set of $=_I$ equivalence classes ordered by $\leq_I$; call its members traces.

Of course, all traces are equivalence classes of finite sequences. They represent finite computations. Not having limit points, traces do not form domains. However, we can add limit points by taking a *completion by ideals*.

6.8 Definition. Let $(P, \leq)$ be a partial order. An *ideal* of P is a left-closed, directed subset. In particular the *principal ideals* are those subsets of the form $\{q \in P \mid q \leq p\}$, for some $p \in P$. Define the *completion by ideals*, P^∞, to be the partial order of ideals ordered by inclusion.

6.9 Proposition. *Let P be a partial order. The ideal completion P^∞ is a domain iff P has least upper bounds of all finite compatible subsets. In the case where P^∞ is a domain its finite elements are precisely the principal ideals.*

Remark. The proposition holds in further generality, for what are known as algebraic complete partial orders. These can be characterised as those partial orders which arise, to within isomorphism, as ideal completions of partial orders with a least element.

6.10 Lemma. *Let (A, I, T) be a trace language. The order T_I^∞ is a finitary, prime algebraic domain.*

Proof. A proof can be found in Bednarczyk's thesis [B] thoughthere they are given just for full trace languages with all sequences. Bednarczyk's proofs (p.54–58) apply in the wider context of all trace languages, to show that T_I has least upper bounds of finite compatible sets and is distributive *i.e.*

$$x \uparrow y \Rightarrow (x \sqcup y) \sqcap z = (x \sqcap z) \sqcup (y \sqcap z).$$

T_I can thus be identified with the finite elements of a distributive domain T_I^∞. Built out of finite sequences ordered by extension, the domain has to be finitary and hence prime algebraic. ∎

6.11 Lemma. *If a trace language (A, I, T) is coherent then the domain T_I^∞ is coherent.*

Proof. Again, Bednarczyk's proof (p.58) applies more generally. Another proof follows from the representation theorem 3.8. It is easily checked that all the axioms C, R, V hold of the finitary domain T_I^∞ (Notice that if two prime intervals are $\sim$-equivalent then their event symbols from the trace language are the same). The domain T_I^∞ is thus coherent by 3.8(ii). ∎

6.12 Definition. Let N be a safe net. Define $Trace(N) = (A, I, T)$ where A is the set of events of N, $e_0 I e_1$ holds between events e_0, e_1 iff $({}^\bullet e_0 \cup e_0{}^\bullet) \cap ({}^\bullet e_1 \cup e_1{}^\bullet) = \emptyset$, and T consists of the set of firing sequences $\langle e_1, \ldots, e_{n-1}\rangle$ from the initial marking (*i.e.* $M_0 \xrightarrow{e_1} \cdots \xrightarrow{e_{n-1}}$ where M_0 is the initial marking).

6.13 Proposition. *Let N be a safe net. Then $Trace(N)$ is a coherent trace language.*

Proof. Well-known, and fairly easy to see (See [Maz]). ∎

6.14 Corollary. *Let N be a safe net. Let $Trace(N) = (A, I, T)$. Then T_I^∞ is a coherent, finitary prime algebraic domain.*

Thus via traces we have defined an operator from safe nets to coherent, finitary prime algebraic domains. As prime event structures are equivalent to such domains we can as well obtain an operator $\mathcal{E}$ taking a safe net to a prime event structure whose events correspond to occurrences of events in the net.

There is an operator in the opposite direction from prime event structures to safe nets. Given an event structure we can form a Petri net with the same behaviour by adding enough conditions to the events to express the causal dependency and conflict of the original event structure: if $e < e'$

in the event structure then we put in a condition as a precondition of e' and a postcondition of e; if $e\#e'$ we make e and e' share a common precondition. More precisely we can build conditions out of events in accord with the causal dependency and conflict relations in the following way:

6.15 Definition. Let $\mathrm{E} = (E, \#, \leq)$ be an event structure. Define $\mathcal{N}(\mathrm{E})$ to be (B, E, F, M) where

$$M = \{(\emptyset, A) \mid A \subseteq E \ \& \ (\forall a, a' \in A.\ a(\# \cup 1)a')\}$$
$$B = M \cup \{(e, A) \mid e \in E \ \& \ A \subseteq E \ \& \ (\forall a, a' \in A.\ a(\smile)a') \ \& \ (\forall a \in A.\ e < a)\}$$
$$F = \{(e, (e, A)) \mid (e, A) \in B\} \cup \{((c, A), e) \mid (c, A) \in B \ \& \ e \in A\}.$$

This shows how we can translate between the different models of safe Petri nets and prime event structures, or equivalent prime algebraic domains. Notice $\mathcal{EN}(\mathrm{E}) \cong \mathrm{E}$. In fact the scheme extends to the situation when we label events and endow nets with morphisms on the same lines as those for event structures. The operations $\mathcal{E}$ and $\mathcal{N}$ between the two models extend to functors which form a coreflection. The presence of morphisms makes $\mathcal{E}$ less arbitrary than it might otherwise seem—there are many ways of building a net with the same behaviour as a prime event structure (see *e.g.* ch.6 of [W2] for another).

The story extends to many more categories of models. The morphisms on the different models also express synchronisation. The appropriate constructions to give denotations to our language of processes have the same abstract characterisation in all the different categories. The fact that they are preserved in moving from one model to another follows from general properties of the adjoints (see [W1] and [B] for details, though just for unlabelled structures).

7. Higher-type event structures.

So far we have focussed on one particular interpretation of events, as actions of synchronisation between processes. Of course other interpretations are possible. We now look at another specific interpretation in which event structures are used to represent higher types. We have seen how stable event structures represent domains. In fact such domains can be made into a cartesian closed category. Not only does this yield a model for various typed λ-calculi but, using the techniques of section 4, we can produce models of so called untyped λ-calculi. We shall not present any proofs in this section—they can be found in [W1].

As morphisms between stable event structures we take *stable* functions between their domains of configurations.

7.1 Definition. Let E_0 and E_1 be stable event structures. A stable function from E_0 to E_1 is a continuous function $f : (\mathcal{F}(\mathrm{E}_0), \subseteq) \to (\mathcal{F}(\mathrm{E}_1), \subseteq)$ on their configurations which is continuous and satisfies

$$\forall X \subseteq \mathcal{F}(\mathrm{E}_0).\ X \neq \emptyset \ \& \ X\uparrow \Rightarrow f(\bigcap X) = \bigcap fX.$$

7.2 Proposition. *Stable event structures with stable functions composed as functions and the usual identities form a category.*

The key idea to the treatment of higher types is the general construction of an event structure to represent the function space of stable functions between two event structures. We must somehow represent the space of stable, continuous functions $f : \mathrm{E}_0 \to \mathrm{E}_1$ between two stable event structures E_0 and E_1 as an event structure itself. This is done by taking the events of a "function space" event structure to be basic parts of functions (x, e) standing for the event of outputting e at input x, a finite configuration of E_0. The function f will correspond to a configuration of events (x, e) in which x is a minimal input configuration at which e is output.

7.3 Definition. Let $\mathrm{E}_0 = (E_0, \#_0, \vdash_0)$ and $\mathrm{E}_1 = (E_1, \#_1, \vdash_1)$ be stable event structures. Their *stable function space*, $[\mathrm{E}_0 \to \mathrm{E}_1]$ is defined to be the event structure $(E, \#, \vdash)$ with events E

consisting of pairs (x, e) where x is a finite configuration in $\mathcal{F}(\mathrm{E}_0)$ and $e \in E_1$, a reflexive conflict relation $\mathbb{W}$ given by

$$(x, e)\mathbb{W}(x', e') \text{ iff } x \uparrow x' \ \& \ e\mathbb{W}_1 e'$$

and an enabling relation given by

$$\{(x_0, e_0), \cdots, (x_{n-1}, e_{n-1})\} \vdash (x, e) \text{ iff } \{e_i \mid x_i \subseteq x\} \vdash_1 e.$$

7.4 Proposition. *The stable function space of two stable event structures is a stable event structure. The stable function space construction is $\trianglelefteq$-continuous.*

The configurations of a stable function space $[\mathrm{E}_0 \to \mathrm{E}_1]$ correspond to stable, continuous functions $\mathcal{F}(\mathrm{E}_0) \to \mathcal{F}(\mathrm{E}_1)$.

7.5 Definition. Let E_0 and E_1 be stable event structures.

For $F \in \mathcal{F}([\mathrm{E}_0 \to \mathrm{E}_1])$ define

$$(\phi(F))(x) = \{e \in E_1 \mid \exists x' \subseteq x.\ (x', e) \in F\}$$

for $x \in \mathcal{F}(\mathrm{E}_0)$.

For $f : \mathcal{F}(\mathrm{E}_0) \to \mathcal{F}(\mathrm{E}_1)$ a stable, continuous function define $\mu(f)$ a subset of events of $[\mathrm{E}_0 \to \mathrm{E}_1]$ by

$$(x, e) \in \mu(f) \Leftrightarrow e \in f(x) \ \& \ (\forall x' \subseteq x.\ e \in f(x') \Rightarrow x' = x).$$

7.6 Theorem. *Let E_0 and E_1 be stable event structures.*
(i) For $F \in \mathcal{F}([\mathrm{E}_0 \to \mathrm{E}_1])$, the function $\phi(F) : \mathcal{F}(\mathrm{E}_0) \to \mathcal{F}(\mathrm{E}_1)$ is continuous and stable.
(i) For $f : \mathcal{F}(\mathrm{E}_0) \to \mathcal{F}(\mathrm{E}_1)$ a stable, continuous function, the subset $\mu(f) \in \mathcal{F}([\mathrm{E}_0 \to \mathrm{E}_1])$.
(iii) Further, ϕ and μ are mutual inverses giving a 1-1 correspondence between configurations $\mathcal{F}([\mathrm{E}_0 \to \mathrm{E}_1])$ and stable, continuous functions $\mathcal{F}(\mathrm{E}_0) \to \mathcal{F}(\mathrm{E}_1)$.

The product in the category is obtained very simply. The event structures are allowed to operate disjointly, completely in parallel, neither one having an effect on the other. It is easily defined for all event structures not just the stable ones.

7.7 Definition. Let $\mathrm{E}_0 = (E_0, \#_0, \vdash_0)$ and $\mathrm{E}_1 = (E_1, \#_1, \vdash_1)$ be stable event structures. Their *disjoint product*, $\mathrm{E}_0 \oplus \mathrm{E}_1$, is the structure $(E, \#, \vdash)$ where the events are

$$E = \{0\} \times E_0 \cup \{1\} \times E_1,$$

a disjoint union, the consistency predicate is given by

$$X \in \mathrm{Con} \Leftrightarrow \{e \mid (0, e) \in X\} \in \mathrm{Con}_0 \ \& \ \{e \mid (1, e) \in X\} \in \mathrm{Con}_1,$$

and the enabling by

$$\begin{aligned} X \vdash e \Leftrightarrow & X \in \mathrm{Con} \ \& \ e \in E \ \& \\ & [(\exists e_0 \in E_0.\ e = (0, e_0) \ \& \ \{e' \mid (0, e') \in X\} \vdash_0 e_0) \text{ or} \\ & (\exists e_1 \in E_1.\ e = (1, e_1) \ \& \ \{e' \mid (1, e') \in X\} \vdash_1 e_1)]. \end{aligned}$$

Define the *projections* $p_k : \mathcal{F}(\mathrm{E}_0 \oplus \mathrm{E}_1) \to \mathcal{F}(\mathrm{E}_k)$ by taking $p_k(x) = \{e \mid (k, e) \in x\}$, for $k = 0, 1$.

7.8 Proposition. *Let E_0 and E_1 be event structures with events E_0, E_1 respectively. Then*

$$x \in \mathcal{F}(E_0 \oplus E_1) \Leftrightarrow x \subseteq E_0 \uplus E_1 \ \& \ p_0(x) \in \mathcal{F}(E_0) \ \& \ p_1(x) \in \mathcal{F}(E_1).$$

There is a 1-1 correspondence between $\mathcal{F}(E_0 \oplus E_1)$ and $\mathcal{F}(E_0) \times \mathcal{F}(E_1)$ given by

$$x \mapsto (p_0(x), p_1(x)).$$

The disjoint product is $\trianglelefteq$-continuous.

Thus we can identify x, a configuration of a disjoint product, with the pair $(p_0(x), p_1(x))$.

7.9 Theorem. *The disjoint product $E_0 \oplus E_1$ of stable event structures E_0 and E_1, with projections π_0, π_1, is a product in the category $\mathbf{E}_{stab}$.*

At this point we can directly prove the cartesian closure of $\mathbf{E}_{stab}$, based on the observation that, for stable event structures E, E_0, E_1 the two event structures

$$[E \oplus E_0 \to E_1]$$

and

$$[E \to [E_0 \to E_1]]$$

are the same up to a natural renaming of events.

7.10 Lemma. *Let E, E_0, E_1 be stable event structures. There is a 1-1 correspondence θ between the events of $[E \oplus E_0 \to E_1]$ and $[E \to [E_0 \to E_1]]$ given by*

$$\theta : ((w, x), e) \longleftrightarrow (w, (x, e)),$$

for w, x finite configurations of E, E_0 and event e of E_1, such that θ gives an isomorphism of event structures in the strong sense that

$$a \#_p a' \Leftrightarrow \theta(a) \#_f \theta(a')$$

and

$$X \vdash_p a \Leftrightarrow \theta X \vdash_f \theta(a),$$

where $\#_p, \vdash_p$ are the conflict and entailment relations of $[E_0 \oplus E_1 \to E_2]$ and $\#_f, \vdash_f$ are the relations of $[E_0 \to [E_1 \to E_2]]$.

Certainly the category of stable event structures with stable functions has products including the null event structure as terminal object. The above results yield a natural 1-1 correspondence between morphisms $E_0 \oplus E_1 \to E_2$ and $E_0 \to [E_1 \to E_2]$ and so show the category is cartesian closed [Mac. p.95-96]. We show the exponentiation more explicitly.

7.11 Theorem. *The category $\mathbf{E}_{stab}$ is cartesian closed. It has products as shown and an exponentiation of two stable event structures E_0 and E_1 has the form $[E_0 \to E_1]$, ap where $ap : [E_0 \to E_1] \oplus E_0 \to E_1$ is given by*

$$ap(f, x) = (\phi f)(x)$$

for $f \in \mathcal{F}([E_0 \to E_1])$ and $x \in \mathcal{F}(E_0)$.
(We have identified (f, x) with the corresponding configuration of the disjoint product.)

In the traditional function space used in denotational semantics the functions in the function space $[D \to E]$, where D and E are domains are ordered pointwise, *i.e.* two continuous functions f, g are ordered by

$$f \sqsubseteq g \Leftrightarrow \forall d \in D.\ f(d) \sqsubseteq g(d).$$

This ordering is called the *extensional* order. The inclusion order on the configurations of $[E_0 \to E_1]$ induces another order on stable, continuous functions $(\mathcal{F}(E_0), \subseteq) \to (\mathcal{F}(E_1), \subseteq)$ which we have seen can be expessed as

$$f \leq g \Leftrightarrow \mu f \subseteq \mu g.$$

This order is called the *stable* order (a name due to Berry). We give an example.

7.12 Example. The two point domain O consisting of $\bot \sqsubseteq T$ can be represented as the the configurations of the obvious event structure with a single event $\bullet$, so $\bot = \emptyset$ and $T = \{\bullet\}$. All the monotonic functions $O \to O$ are stable and continuous. Ordered extensionally they are

$$(\lambda x.\bot) \sqsubseteq (\lambda x.\ x = T \to T|\bot) \sqsubseteq (\lambda x.T)$$

while according to the stable ordering we only have

$$(\lambda x.\bot) \leq (\lambda x.\ x = T \to T|\bot) \quad \text{and} \quad (\lambda x.\bot) \leq (\lambda x.T),$$

because $(\lambda x.\ x = T \to T|\bot) \not\leq (\lambda x.T)$. For two functions to be in the stable order it is not only necessary that they are ordered extensionally but also that if they both output a value for common input then they do so for the same minimal value.

As an example we indicate how the category can be used to give a model for a λ-calculus with atoms.

7.13 Example. We can use the sum construction on event structures (it extends to a functor) and a constant event structure **A** of atomic events to define an operation

$$\mathrm{E} \mapsto \mathbf{A} + [\mathrm{E} \to \mathrm{E}].$$

This operation is $\trianglelefteq$-continuous, being the composition of continuous things, and so has a least fixed point which can serve as a model for the λ-calculus with atoms following standard lines.

Recent work of Girard has pointed the way to another appplication for the category of event structures with stable functions, or the equivalent category of dI-domains. In [G], Girard works with a full subcategory of ours with objects called *coherent spaces* and shows how they give a model to his System F, the polymorphic λ-calculus. From the point of view of denotational semantics, coherent spaces are too restrictive because they are not closed under the useful operations of lifting (prefixing) or separated sum. However Girard's ideas can be extended to our category (see [CGW]) which supports such constructions as well as polymorphism. (It should also be mentioned that Girard's ideas also extend, though less directly, to the more traditional category of Scott domains with continuous functions—see [CGW1].)

Another possible use of stable event structures is as a model of Girard's "linear logic" [G1] though this is not yet widely understood (and certainly not yet by me). By restricting the category of stable event structures to stable functions which are also additive (*i.e.* preserve all least uper bounds when they exist) we obtain the subcategory with so-called *linear maps*. This category forms a model for Girard's intuitionistic linear logic (see [YL]) with coherent spaces and linear maps, a model for classical linear logic, as a reflective subcategory. Although these categories are not cartesian closed, they are monoidal closed, a property which means there is a function space but with respect to a bifunctor which is not necessarily a categorical product. Monoidal closed categories have arisen in another context, in the work of Meseguer and Montanari on categories of Petri nets, in generalising the partially synchronous morphisms on nets (see [MM]). The mathematical structure they uncover, as with the monoidal closed categories of event structures, holds great promise, I think, though, at present I don't know how to use it; whereas the partially synchronous morphisms yield familiar and intuitively understandable constructions, underlying working languages like Occam, the linear morphisms give constructions not so familiar in Computer Science. The tie-in with linear logic may be fruitful. While on the topic, I'll mention a that there is a right adjoint to the inclusion functor from stable event structures with partially synchronous morphisms (ignoring labels) and that of stable event structures with finitary linear maps (linear maps preserving finite elements); the right adjoint makes new events out of subsets of the original event structure. Whether this provides any reduction of a linear logic to another more basic one, along the lines of Girard's reduction of intuitionistic to linear logic, I don't know.

8. Further work.

There are two holes in these notes. One is that left by omitting any discussion of logic and proof systems on event structures, and the other is the absence of any treatment of operational semantics and its relation to the event structure models of processes. Some work has been done in both these areas but it is patchy, at least as I perceive it.

A representation of certain kinds of domains was first carried out by G.Kahn and G.Plotkin in their attempt to define a general notion of sequential function (see [KP]). Their work on sequentiality was made higher order by G.Berry and P-L.Curien (see [BC], [C]) though at the expense of moving to algorithms rather than functions. Berry's thesis [Be] is rich in results including the beginnings of an operational characterisation of the stable order between stable functions. As for event structure models of parallel processes and attempts to justify them in operational or observational terms we mention [BoCa], [Ca], [EN], [MDN].

A compositional proof system for Petri nets with categorical combinators of the sort seen here and a recursively defined Hennessy-Milner logic is presented in [W2]. Its generalisation to event structures has proved elusive so far—the thesis [Z] will indicate some of the difficulties. For examples of logics on prime event structures see [TL] and [P].

Appendix: Multisets and multirelations.

Let X and Y be sets. A *multirelation* from X to Y is a function $\alpha : Y \times X \rightarrow \omega$, with *entries* $\alpha_{y,x}$ which are nonnegative numbers; we indicate such a multirelation by writing $\alpha : X \rightarrow_m Y$. Multirelations are composed as matrices: Let $\alpha : X \rightarrow_m Y$ and $\beta : Y \rightarrow_m Z$. Define their *composition* $\beta\alpha : X \rightarrow_m Z$ to be given by

$$(\beta\alpha)_{z,x} = \Sigma_{y \in Y} \beta_{z,y} \cdot \alpha_{y,x},$$

which exists provided no infinite sums of nonzero integers arise in this way.

A multiset over a set X is a multirelation $\alpha : \mathbf{1} \rightarrow_m X$ from a distinguished one-element set $\mathbf{1}$. We write $\alpha \in m(X)$ to mean α is a multiset over X, and write the entry of the multiset α at $x \in X$ as α_x.

Regarded as matrices we can form entrywise sums and scalar products of multirelations, and provided the results never go negative we can subtract one multirelation from another. We write $\alpha + \beta$ and $\alpha - \beta$ for the sum and difference of $\alpha, \beta : X \rightarrow_m Y$. Similarly, we can write $\alpha \leq \beta$, for $\alpha, \beta : X \rightarrow_m Y$, when $\alpha_{x,y} \leq \beta_{x,y}$ for all $x \in X, y \in Y$.

We identify subsets of a set X with those multisets over it whose entries never exceed 1. In particular, the *null* multiset $\mathbf{0}$ of X for which every entry is 0 corresponds to the empty set. For $x \in X$, we shall write simply x for the singleton multiset which has entry 1 at x and 0 elsewhere. We shall identify *relations* between a set X and a set Y with those multirelations $\theta : X \rightarrow_m Y$ for which all entries are at most 1. In particular, a partial function $f : X \rightarrow_* Y$, between sets X and Y, is identified with a multirelation $f : X \rightarrow_m Y$ in which $f_{y,x} \leq 1$, for all $x \in X, y \in Y$, and for any $x \in X$ there is at most one $y \in Y$ so $f_{y,x} = 1$; the fact that an application $f(x)$ of a partial function f to an element x is undefined corresponds to the application fx of the multirelation f to the singleton multiset x being $\mathbf{0}$.

Acknowledgements: Thanks to Mogens Nielsen for helpful comments.

References

[Be] Berry, G., Modèles complètement adéquats et stables des lambda-calculs typés. Thèse de Doctorat d'Etat, Université de Paris VII (1979).

[B] Bednarczyk, M.A., Categories of asynchronous systems. PhD in Comp Sc, University of Sussex, report no.1/88 (1988).

[BC] Berry, G., and Curien, P-L., Sequential algorithms on concrete data structures. TCS vol 20 (1982).

[BoCa]Boudol,G., and Castellani,I., On the semantics of concurrency: partial orders and transition systems. Springer Lec Notes in Comp Sc vol 249 (1987).

[C]Curien, P-L., Categorical combinators, sequential algorithms and functional programming. Research notes in theoretical comp. sc., Pitman, London (1986).

[Ca] Castellani, I., Permutations of transitions. This volume.

[EN] Engberg,U., Nielsen,M., and Larsen,K.S., Fully abstract models of a language with refinement. This volume.

[CGW] Coquand, T., Gunter, C., and Winskel, G., Polymorphism and domain equations. In the proc of Third Workshop on the Mathematical Foundations of Programming Language Semantics, New Orleans, LA 1987.

[CGW1] Coquand, T., Gunter, C., and Winskel, G., Domain theoretic models of polymorphism. To appear in Information and Computation, 1987.

[G] Girard, J-Y., The system F of variable types, fifteen years later. TCS vol.45 (1986).

[G1] Girard, J-Y., Linear logic. TCS 1987.

[KP] Kahn, G., and Plotkin, G., Domaines Concrètes. Rapport IRIA Laboria No. 336 (1978).

[YL] Lafont, Y., Linear logic and lazy computation. Springer Lec Notes in Comp Sc vol 249 (1987).

[Lam] Lamport, L., Time clocks and the ordering of events in a distributed system. CACM 21, (1978).

[Mac] Maclane, S., Categories for the Working Mathematician. Graduate Texts in Mathematics, Springer (1971).

[Maz] Mazurkiewicz, A., Traces. This volume.

[Mil]Milner, R., A Calculus of Communicating Systems. Springer Lecture Notes in Comp. Sc. vol. 92 (1980).

[MM] Meseguer, J., and Montanari, U., Petri nets are monoids: a new algebraic foundation for net theory. Proc of LICS, Computer Society Press (1988).

[MDN] Degano, P., De Nicola,R. and Montanari, U., On the consistency of "truly concurrent" operational and denotational semantics. Proc of LICS, Computer Society Press (1988).

[NPW] Nielsen, M., Plotkin, G., Winskel, G., Petri nets, Event structures and Domains, part 1 . Theoretical Computer Science, vol. 13 (1981).

[P] Penczek,W., The temporal logic of event structures. Report 616, Inst of Comp Sc, Polish Academy of Science, Warsaw, 1987.

[Rem] Rem, M., Partially ordered computations, with an application to VLSI design. In "Foundations of Computer Science IV, part 2", Mathemtical Centre, Amsterdam (1983).

[TL] Lodaya,K., and Thiagarajan, P.S., A modal logic for a subclass of event structures. Proc of ICALP 1987 published in Springer Lecture Notes in C.S. (1987).

[W] Winskel, G., Events in Computation. Ph.D. thesis, available as a technical report, Comp. Sc. Dept., University of Edinburgh (1980).

[W1]Winskel, G., Event structures. Invited lectures for the Advanced Course on Petri nets, September 1986. Appears as a report of the Computer Laboratory, University of Cambridge, 1986, and in the proceedings of the school, published in Springer Lecture Notes in C.S., vol.255 (1987).

[W2] Winskel, G., A category of labelled nets and compositional proof system. Proc of LICS, Computer Society Press (1988).

[Z] Zhang, G.Q., Logic and semantics in computation. PhD in progress, Computer Laboratory, Cambridge University.

A Logic for the Description of Behaviours and Properties of Concurrent Systems

(Extended Abstract)

A. Bouajjani, S. Graf, J. Sifakis

Laboratoire de Génie Informatique-IMAG
BP 53 X, 38041 Grenoble Cedex, France

ABSTRACT We present two logics *LSP* (Logic of Sequential Processes) and *LP* (Logic of Processes) which are propositional μ-calculi with both logical operators and standard operators of process algebras such as prefixing, non-deterministic choice, parallel composition and restriction. The process algebra operators are extended on unions of bisimulation classes.
LSP is an extension of an algebra of sequential processes with strong bisimulation. A deductive system is proposed for this logic and a comparison with the propositional μ-calculus of Kozen is carried out.
LP is an extension of an algebra of communicating processes with strong bisimulation. A deductive system is proposed for this logic and its use is illustrated by an example.

Keywords : Program logic, μ-calculus, compositional proof methods, process algebra, adequacy, expressivity.

CONTENTS

1. Introduction

The idea of combining approaches for the specification of concurrent systems has motivated the research for the definition of languages enjoying advantages unique to each approach. The most promising combination is that of a logic based approach and a transition based approach [Pn86] [Si86]. In the logic based approach, specifications of a system are expressed as a set of properties described by formulas of a logic. Typical examples of logics used for this purpose are the various program logics. In the transition based approach, a system is described in a language directly interpretable by some abstract machine (transition system).

One of the advantages of the logic based approach is that logic specifications are conjunctive in character [Pn86]. That is, a logic formula represents a class of behaviours and the specification of a system is given as the conjunction of formulas describing the intersection of the classes of the behaviours represented by the conjuncts. As a consequence, logic specifications are easily modifiable and the specification process is flexible. Another obvious advantage of this approach is abstractness i.e., independence with respect to implementation choices.

Compared to logic based formalisms, transition based formalisms have some very attractive features, too. They use very primitive concepts : the concepts of state and transition. Descriptions are concrete and easier to understand by people not familiar with logics. Furthermore, the possibility of graphic representation is a substantial advantage.

Logics and transition systems are also different in the types of the properties they describe easily. Logics lend themselves better to the description of global properties such as termination, mutual exlusion and fairness. On the contrary, transition based formalisms are better adapted to the characterisation of situations where there exist "tight" relations between events, such as sequencing and precedence properties. Clearly, the direct expression of global properties in such formalisms, seems to be difficult if not impossible, due to their nature.

All these considerations make it very desirable to develop specification languages that combine logic based and transition based approaches. The problem of combining program logics and process algebras can be summarized as follows [HM82] [Pn85] [GS86a] [GS86b] [GS86c].

Consider a process algebra with language of terms $\mathcal{T}$ for the description of processes and a given congruence relation $\approx$ for their comparison. If the language of formulas F of a logic is used as a specification language for processes of $\mathcal{T}$, then a satisfaction relation $\models$ subset of $\mathcal{T}\times F$, must be given. This relation induces on $\mathcal{T}$ an equivalence $\equiv$ defined by, $t_1 \equiv t_2$ iff $\forall f \in F$ ($t_1 \models f$ iff $t_2 \models f$). Clearly, a minimal requirement for $(F, \models)$ to be an appropriate specification language for $(\mathcal{T},\approx)$ is that $\approx\, =\, \equiv$. This requirement, known as *adequacy*, has first been considered in [HM82] where a simple modal language adequate for CCS with observational congruence, is given. A stronger compatibilty requirement between $(\mathcal{T},\approx)$ and $(F, \models)$, is *expressivity* [Pn85]. $(F, \models)$ is said to be expressive for $(\mathcal{T},\approx)$, if it is adequate for it and there exists a function φ: $\mathcal{T}\rightarrow F$ such that, $t\approx t'$ iff $t' \models \varphi(t)$ i.e., $\varphi(t)$ represents the congruence class of t. Using logics expressive for a given process algebra allows to use a single language - the language of the formulas of the logic - to decribe both processes and their properties.

In [GS86c] a logic is given which is expressive for a process algebra with strong bisimulation. Its language of formulas is obtained by consistently extending the operators of the process algebra on unions of bisimulation classes. Thus, terms of the process algebra are given the status of formulas. This paper extends the results of [GS86c] and is organized as follows.

In section 2, we present a logic which can be considered as a μ-calculus with both logical operators and operators on processes such as, prefixing by a set of actions, and non deterministic choice. We call this logic *Logic of Sequential Processes* (*LSP*) as a subset of its formulas corresponds to the language of terms often used to describe (sequential) processes in process algebras. Adequacy and expressivity of the proposed logic, is shown for bisimulation semantics. In section 3, a comparison is given with μ-calculus of Kozen [Ko83]. It is shown that if the vocabulary of actions is finite then a fragment of *LSP* is as expressive as $L\mu$. However, *LSP* allows a more direct description of behaviours due to the use of process constructors. In section 4, is presented an extension of *LSP*, called *Logic of Processes* (*LP*), by using parallel composition and restriction operators and providing actions a structure encoding communication capabilities. *LP* characterizes systems of communicating processes modulo strong bisimulation. A deductive system is proposed for this logic and its use is illustrated by an example.

2. The Logic of Sequential Processes *LSP*

2.1. Syntax

Let $\mathcal{P}$ be a set of atomic propositions, $\mathcal{A}$ a set of actions and $\mathcal{X}$ a set of variables. The language of formulas of *LSP* is given by the following grammar :

$f ::= \mathrm{T} \mid P\in \mathcal{P} \mid X\in \mathcal{X} \mid Bf\ ,\ B\in 2^{\mathcal{A}} \mid Nil \mid \neg f \mid f\vee f \mid f+f \mid \mu X.f(X)$ where, $f(X)$ is syntactically monotonic in X, i.e., any occurrence of X is under an even number of negations in $f(X)$.

The formulas $\bot, f\wedge g, f\supset g, f\equiv g$, and $\nu x.f(X)$ are abbreviations for $\neg\mathrm{T}$, $\neg(\neg f\vee\neg g)$, $\neg f\vee g$, $(f\supset g)\wedge(g\supset f)$, and $\neg\mu X.\neg f(\neg X)$ respectively. The symbol θ is used to represent an occurrence of μ or ν and $-B$ is the complement of B in $\mathcal{A}$. To simplify notation, whenever B is a singleton, $B=\{a\}$, we write af instead of $\{a\}f$.

A formula is said to be *well-guarded* if any occurrence of a variable X is under the scope of a prefixing operator B. For a formula, we use the notions of free and bound variables as in predicate calculus by considering μ and ν as quantifiers. Let $\underline{X}=(X_1,\ldots,X_n)\in \mathcal{X}^n$. The notation $f(\underline{X})$ means that the free variables of f belong to $\underline{X}$. In the sequel, a closed formula is called *sentence*. We represent by $S(LSP)$ the set of sentences of *LSP*.

2.2. Semantics

A *transition system* is a tuple $M=(Q,R,\mathcal{I})$ where Q is a set of states, $R\subseteq Q\times\mathcal{A}\times Q$ is a transition relation and $\mathcal{I} : Q\rightarrow 2^{\mathcal{P}}$ a function associating with a state a finite set of propositions which are true at that state. Hereafter, we consider only transition systems such that $\forall q\in Q.\ \forall a\in \mathcal{A}.$ $\{(q,a,q')\in R : q'\in Q\}$ is finite i.e., that are finite branching for transitions with the same label.

Represent by $Trans(R,q)=\{(q,a,q')\in R :\ a\in \mathcal{A},\ q'\in Q\}$, the set of transitions from a state $q\in Q$.

We consider a binary equivalence relation ~ on Q which is a *strong bisimulation* [Mi80] preserving the interpretation function $\mathcal{I}$ and defined as the largest relation such that $\forall q_1,q_2\in Q.$ $q_1\sim q_2$ if and only if

- $\mathcal{I}(q_1)=\mathcal{I}(q_2)$,
- $\forall a\in \mathcal{A}.\ \forall q_1'\in Q.\ (q_1,a,q_1')\in R \Rightarrow \exists q_2'\in Q.\ (q_2,a,q_2')\in R$ and $q_1'\sim q_2'$,
- $\forall a\in \mathcal{A}.\ \forall q_2'\in Q.\ (q_2,a,q_2')\in R \Rightarrow \exists q_1'\in Q.\ (q_1,a,q_1')\in R$ and $q_1'\sim q_2'$.

Given a transition system $M_0=(Q_0,R_0,\mathcal{I}_0)$ and $q_1,q_2\in Q_0$, q_1+q_2 is considered as a state of a transition system $M=(Q,R,\mathcal{I})$ such that :

(a) $Q=Q_0\cup\{q_1+q_2\}$,

(b) R is the least relation such that :

- $R_0\subseteq R$,
- $(q_1,a,q')\in R_0$ or $(q_2,a,q')\in R_0 \Rightarrow (q_1+q_2,a,q')\in R$,

(c) $\mathcal{I}$ is the extension of $\mathcal{I}_0$ such that :

- $\mathcal{I}(q)=\mathcal{I}_0(q)$ for $q\in Q_0$,
- $\mathcal{I}(q_1+q_2)=\mathcal{I}(q_1)\cup\mathcal{I}(q_2)$

Notice that the operation of + on states and the bisimulation ~ can be defined between states of two different transition systems ; it is sufficient to consider them on the union of the transition systems.

Models of *LSP* are transition systems $M=(Q,R,\mathcal{I})$ such that :

(r1) $\forall q\in Q, \exists Q_1, Q_2, q_1\in Q_1, q_2\in Q_2, q\sim q_1+q_2 \Rightarrow \exists q_1',q_2'\in Q.\ q_1\sim q_1'$ and $q_2\sim q_2'$,

i.e., for any state obtained from q by considering a non empty subset of outgoing transitions, there exists a state of Q equivalent to it.

(r2) $\forall q_1,q_2\in Q.\ \exists q\in Q.\ q\sim q_1+q_2$,

i.e., the set of the states of Q is closed for the + operation.

For such a transition system $M=(Q,R,\mathcal{I})$, the semantics of *LSP* is given by a *satisfaction relation* $\models\subseteq Q\times S(LSP)$. A formula $f(\underline{X})$ is interpreted as a function of $(2^Q)^n\rightarrow 2^Q$. For a valuation $\underline{V}=(V_1,\ldots,V_n)\in(2^Q)^n$ and a state $q\in Q$, the relation $\models$ is inductively defined by :

$q\models \mathrm{T}$

$q\models P$	$\Leftrightarrow$	$q\in \mathcal{I}(P)$
$q\models X_i(\underline{V})$	$\Leftrightarrow$	$q\in V_i$
$q\models\neg f(\underline{V})$	$\Leftrightarrow$	$q\not\models f(\underline{V})$
$q\models f\vee g(\underline{V})$	$\Leftrightarrow$	$q\models f(\underline{V})$ or $q\models g(\underline{V})$
$q\models Nil$	$\Leftrightarrow$	$Trans(R,q)=\varnothing$
$q\models Bf(\underline{V})$	$\Leftrightarrow$	$Trans(R,q)\neq\varnothing$ and $(q,a,q')\in Trans(R,q) \Rightarrow (a\in B$ and $q'\models f(\underline{V}))$
$q\models f+g(\underline{V})$	$\Leftrightarrow$	$\exists q_1,q_2\in Q.\ q\sim q_1+q_2$ and $q_1\models f(\underline{V})$ and $q_2\models g(\underline{V})$
$q\models \mu Y.f(Y,\underline{X})(\underline{V})$	$\Leftrightarrow$	$q\in\bigcap\{Q'\subseteq Q : \{q' : q'\models f(Q',\underline{V})\}\subseteq Q'\}$

A sentence f is *valid* ($\models f$) if and only if for any model $M=(Q,R,\mathcal{I})$, $\forall q\in Q.\ q\models f$.

2.3. Adequacy and expressivity for strong bisimulation

Proposition 1 (Adequacy)

Let $M=(Q,R,\mathcal{I})$ be a model. $\forall q_1,q_2\in Q.\ q_1\sim q_2 \Rightarrow \forall f\in S(LSP).\ (q_1\models f \Leftrightarrow q_2\models f)$.

Proof : The proof is carried out by induction on the structure of formulas and the number of μ-formulas they contain. We give hereafter proofs for a few cases. Let $q_1,q_2 \in Q$ such that $q_1 \sim q_2$.

- $q_1 \models Bf(\underline{V})$.

By definitions of $\models$ and $\sim$ and from $q_1 \sim q_2$, we deduce $Trans(R,q_2) \neq \emptyset$ and $\forall (q_2,a,q) \in Trans(R,q_2).\ \exists (q_1,a,q') \in Trans(R,q_1).\ q \sim q'$ and $a \in B$ and $q' \models f(\underline{V})$.

Thus, by induction hypothesis, $Trans(R,q_2) \neq \emptyset$ and $(q_2,a,q) \in Trans(R,q_2) \Rightarrow a \in B$ and $q \models f(\underline{V})$ which is equivalent to $q_2 \models Bf$.

- $q_1 \models f+g(\underline{V})$.

By definition of $\models$, $\exists q_{11},q_{12} \in Q.\ q_1 \sim q_{11}+q_{12}$ and $q_{11} \models f(\underline{V})$ and $q_{12} \models g(\underline{V})$. From $q_1 \sim q_2$, we obtain $q_2 \models f+g(\underline{V})$.

- $q_1 \models \mu Y.f(Y,\underline{X})(\underline{V})$.

In [GS86c] is proved that formulas of *LSP* are both ∨-continuous and ∧-continuous due to the finite branching restriction on models. Thus, $q_1 \models \mu Y.f(Y,\underline{X})(\underline{V})$ if and only if $\exists k.\ q_1 \models f^k(\bot,\underline{V})$. The formula $f^k(\bot,\underline{V})$ contains one μ-formula less than $\mu Y.f(Y,\underline{X})(\underline{V})$. Thus, by induction hypothesis, $q_2 \models f^k(\bot,\underline{V})$ and then $q_2 \models \mu Y.f(Y,\underline{X})(\underline{V})$. □

Proposition 2 (Expressivity)

Consider that $\mathcal{P}$ is finite and let $M=(Q,R,\mathcal{I})$ be a model. For $q \in Q$, if $\{q' : qR^*q'\}$ is finite, then $\exists \varphi(q) \in S(LSP).\ \forall q'.\ q \sim q' \Leftrightarrow q' \models \varphi(q)$.

Proof: We associate with a state $q \in Q$ a variable X_q and consider the following system of fixpoint equations :

$$\{X_q = (\wedge_{P_i \in \mathcal{I}(q)} P_i) \wedge (\wedge_{P_i \notin \mathcal{I}(q)} \neg P_i) \wedge \Sigma_{(q,a_i,q_i) \in R}\, a_i X_{q_i}\}_{q \in Q}$$

Let $\{f_q\}_{q \in Q}$ be the greatest fixpoint of this system. Clearly, formulas f_q can be characterized by formulas of $S(LSP)$ by using the ν-operator. It can be proved that $\varphi(q)=f_q$ by using a similar result in [GS86c] for *LSP* without atomic propositions. □

Example Consider a model with a transition relation represented by the graph in figure 1.

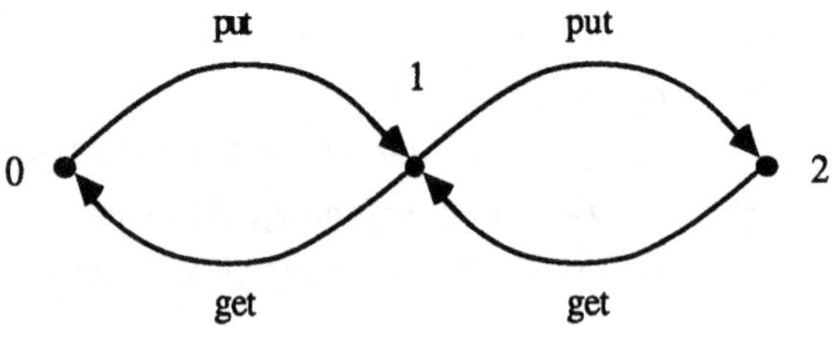

figure 1

Let P_0, P_1, P_2 be the propositions characterizing the states 0, 1, 2 respectively. The system of fixpoint equations associated with this model is,

$$X_0 = P_0 \wedge put X_1$$
$$X_1 = P_1 \wedge (put X_2 + get X_0)$$
$$X_2 = P_2 \wedge get X_1$$

The formulas $\varphi(0)$, $\varphi(1)$, $\varphi(2)$ are respectively

$$\varphi(0) = P_0 \wedge put\ \varphi(1)$$

$$\varphi(1) = \nu X_1.P_1 \wedge [put\ (P_2 \wedge get X_1) + get(P_0 \wedge put X_1)]$$

$$\varphi(2) = P_2 \wedge get\ \varphi(1).$$

2.4. Deductive system

We give hereafter a deductive system for *LSP*. The soundness of this system can be proved as in [GS86c] where all the axioms, except A9, have been proved sound for a slightly different semantics.

PC axioms and rules for propositional calculus

A1 $f+(g+h) \equiv (f+g)+h$

A2 $f+g \equiv g+f$

A3 $f+f \equiv f$

A4 $f+Nil \equiv f$

A5 $f+(g \vee h) \equiv (f+g) \vee (f+h)$

A6 $(B_1 \cup B_2)f \equiv B_1 f \vee B_2 f \vee B_1 f + B_2 f$

A7 $B(f \vee g) \equiv Bf \vee Bg \vee Bf + Bg$

A8 $B_1 f \wedge B_2 g \equiv (B_1 \cap B_2)(f \wedge g)$

A9 $(P \wedge f)+g \equiv P \wedge (f+g)$

A10 $(\Sigma_I f_i) \wedge (\Sigma_J g_j) \equiv \Sigma_I \bigvee_J (f_i \wedge g_j) + \Sigma_J \bigvee_I (f_i \wedge g_j)$ where $f_i, f_j ::= Bf | \mathrm{T}$

A11 $\neg(\mathrm{T}+Bf) \equiv -B\mathrm{T} \vee B\neg f \vee (-B\mathrm{T}+B\neg f) \vee Nil$

A12 $\neg(\Sigma_I B_i f_i) \equiv \neg(\mathrm{T}+\Sigma_I B_i f_i) \vee (\mathrm{T}+\bigwedge_I(-B_i\mathrm{T} \vee B_i \neg f_i))$

A13 $\emptyset f \equiv \perp$

A14 $B\perp \equiv \perp$

A15 $f+\perp \equiv \perp$

A16 $Nil \vee \mathcal{A}\mathrm{T} \equiv \mathrm{T}$

A17 $f \supset g \vdash Bf \supset Bg$

A18 $(f_1 \supset g_1) \wedge (f_2 \supset g_2) \vdash f_1+f_2 \supset g_1+g_2$

LFA $f(\mu X.f(X)) \supset \mu X.f(X)$

FIR $f(g) \supset g \vdash \mu X.f(X) \supset g$

Notice that the language of terms t defined by the grammar :

$$t ::= Nil \mid X \in \mathcal{X} \mid at \mid t+t \mid \nu X.t(X)$$

is contained in the language of formulas of *LSP*. The set of the closed well-guarded terms of this language whith axioms A1 to A4 and the duals of LFA and FIR (replace implication by equivalence) characterizes exactly regular transition systems modulo strong bisimulation [Mi84].

Axioms A6 to A12 are distributivity properties between logical operators and process constructors. A13 to A15 are strictness axioms. Axiom A16 simply expresses the fact that either a process is blocked or it can perform at least one initial move. Rules A17 and A18 express monotonicity of prefixing and + operators. Finally, LFA and FIR are standard axiom and rule for least fixpoints.

From the deductive system above, the following theorems can be proved :

T1 $\mathcal{A}\mathrm{T}+\mathrm{T} \equiv \mathcal{A}\mathrm{T}$

T2 $\neg Nil \equiv \mathcal{A}\mathrm{T}$

T3 $\mathrm{T}+Bf \equiv \bigvee_{C\subseteq B}(\mathrm{T}+Cf)$

T4 $\mathrm{T}+B(\bigvee_I f_i) \equiv \mathrm{T}+(\bigvee_I Bf_i)$

T5 $P+f \equiv P\wedge(\mathrm{T}+f)$

T6 $Nil\wedge\Sigma_I B_i f_i \equiv \bot$

T7 $(\mathrm{T}+\Sigma_I f_i)\wedge(\mathrm{T}+\Sigma_J g_j) \equiv \mathrm{T}+\Sigma_I f_i+\Sigma_J g_j$

T8 $\neg(\Sigma_I B_i f_i+\mathrm{T}) \equiv \big(\bigvee_I -B_i\mathrm{T}\big)\vee\big(\bigvee_I B_i(\neg f_i)\big)\vee\big(\bigvee_I(-B_i\mathrm{T}+B_i(\neg f_i))\big)\vee Nil$

T9 $\neg(\Sigma_I B_i f_i) \equiv \neg(\Sigma_I B_i f_i+\mathrm{T})\vee$

$$\big(\bigvee_{J\subset I}((-\cup_J B_j)\cap(\cap_K B_k))(\mathrm{T}+\wedge_K\neg f_k)\big)\vee(\mathrm{T}+(-\cup_I B_i)\mathrm{T})$$

where $K=I-J$

FT $f(\theta X.f(X)) \equiv \theta X.f(X)$

FID $g\supset f(g)\vdash g\supset \nu X.f(X)$

3. Relationship with the μ-calculus $L\mu$

In this section, we establish relations between the process logic *LSP* and the propositional μ-calculus $L\mu$ of Kozen [Ko83]. We reduce decidability of a sublanguage of *LSP* when finiteness of $\mathcal{A}$ is assumed, to decidability of $L\mu$. The main purpose of this comparison is to show that although the two formalisms have the same descriptive power, *LSP* leads to more concise descriptions of behaviours due to the use of the non deterministic choice operator + and the prefixing operators *B*.

For $\mathcal{P}$, $\mathcal{A}$, $\mathcal{X}$ as in section 2, the language of formulas of $L\mu$ is defined by :

$f ::= \mathrm{T} \mid P\in\mathcal{P} \mid X\in\mathcal{X} \mid \langle a\rangle f\ ,\ a\in\mathcal{A} \mid \neg f \mid f\vee f \mid \mu X.f(X)$ where $f(X)$ is syntactically monotonic in X.

In addition to the usual abbreviations, we take $[a]f=\neg\langle a\rangle\neg f$.

Let $S(L\mu)$ be the set of sentences of $L\mu$. The semantics of $L\mu$ for a model $M=(Q,R,\mathcal{I})$ is given by a satisfaction relation $\models\subseteq Q\times S(L\mu)$ defined as the satisfaction relation of *LSP* for operators common to both languages. The meaning of $\langle a\rangle f$ is :

$q\models\langle a\rangle f(\underline{V}) \Leftrightarrow \exists q'\in Q.\ (q,a,q')\in R$ and $q'\models f(\underline{V})$

A sound deductive system for $L\mu$ is given in [Ko83]. For a sentence f of $L\mu$ we write $\vdash_{L\mu} f$ if f is provable in this system.

In the rest of this section, we consider a logic *LSP* with $\mathcal{A}$ finite. Consider the subset LSP_r of the formulas of *LSP* such that, in their syntactic tree, between a variable and a + operator there exists a prefixing operator B. We show that $LSP_r/\equiv_{LSP}$ is isomorphic to $L\mu/\equiv_{L\mu}$, where $\equiv_{LSP}$ and $\equiv_{L\mu}$ are the equivalence relations induced by the respective semantics. To this aim, we define a canonical form for formulas of LSP_r.

Definition Let CF be the set of formulas of LSP inductively defined by :

- $\mathrm{T} \in CF$ and $\bot \in CF$
- $Nil \in CF$
- $P \in \mathcal{P} \Rightarrow P \in CF$ and $\neg P \in CF$
- $X \in \mathcal{X} \Rightarrow X \in CF$
- $\forall i.\ a_i \in \mathcal{A}$ and $f_i \in CF \Rightarrow \Sigma_I a_i f_i \in CF$ and $\mathrm{T}+\Sigma_I a_i f_i \in CF$
- $f \in CF$ and $g \in CF \Rightarrow f \vee g \in CF$
- $f \in CF$ and $g \in CF \Rightarrow f \wedge g \in CF$
- $f(X) \in CF \Rightarrow \theta X.f(X) \in CF$

Proposition 3 $\forall f \in LSP_r.\ \exists f_n \in CF.\ \vdash_{LSP} f \equiv f_n$

Proof : Any formula of LSP_r can be transformed into a fomula of CF by using the deductive system of LSP. The syntactic restrictions on formulas ensure that, by using distributivity properties, we can obtain a formula in which all the negations are on atomic propositions and any term of a sum is either a prefixed formula or T. □

We define hereafter two homomorphisms relating LSP and $L\mu$.

Definition Let $\phi : CF \rightarrow L\mu$ be the function such that :

- $\phi(\mathrm{T}) = \mathrm{T}$
- $\phi(\bot) = \bot$
- $\phi(P) = P$
- $\phi(\neg P) = \neg P$
- $\phi(X) = X$
- $\phi(Nil) = \bigwedge_{a \in \mathcal{A}}[a]\bot$
- $\phi(f \vee g) = \phi(f) \vee \phi(g)$
- $\phi(f \wedge g) = \phi(f) \wedge \phi(g)$
- $\phi(\Sigma_I a_i f_i) = \left(\bigwedge_I \langle a_i \rangle \phi(f_i)\right) \wedge \left(\bigwedge_{a \in \mathcal{A}(I)}[a]\left(\bigvee_{ai=a} \phi(f_i)\right)\right) \wedge \left(\bigwedge_{b \notin \mathcal{A}(I)}[b]\bot\right)$
  where $\mathcal{A}(I) = \{a_i : i \in I\}$
- $\phi(\mathrm{T}+\Sigma_I a_i f_i) = \bigwedge_I \langle a_i \rangle \phi(f_i)$
- $\phi(\theta X.f(X)) = \theta X.\phi(f(X))$

Definition Let $\psi : L\mu \rightarrow LSP$ be the function such that :

- $\psi(\mathrm{T}) = \mathrm{T}$
- $\psi(\bot) = \bot$
- $\psi(P) = P$
- $\psi(X) = X$
- $\psi(\langle a \rangle f) = a\psi(f)+\mathrm{T}$
- $\psi(\neg f) = \neg\psi(f)$

- $\psi(f \vee g) \quad = \quad \psi(f) \vee \psi(g)$
- $\psi(\mu X.f(X)) \quad = \quad \mu X.\psi(f(X))$

Proposition 4 $\forall f \in CF.\ \vdash_{LSP} \psi(\phi(f)) \equiv f$.

Proof: The proof is done by induction on the syntax of formulas of CF. It is obvious for the cases $\mathrm{T}, \bot, P, \neg P, X, f \vee g, f \wedge g, \theta X.f(X)$. We give proofs for the remaining cases.

$$
\begin{aligned}
(1)\ \psi(\phi(Nil)) &\equiv \psi(\wedge_{a \in \mathcal{A}}[a]\bot) = \psi(\wedge_{a \in \mathcal{A}} \neg \langle a \rangle \mathrm{T}) \text{ by definition,}\\
&\equiv \neg \vee_{a \in \mathcal{A}} \psi(\langle a \rangle \mathrm{T}) \text{ by PC and by definition,}\\
&\equiv \neg \vee_{a \in \mathcal{A}} (a\mathrm{T}+\mathrm{T}) \text{ by definition,}\\
&\equiv \neg(\mathcal{A}\mathrm{T}+\mathrm{T}) \text{ by T3,}\\
&\equiv \neg \mathcal{A}\mathrm{T} \text{ by T1,}\\
&\equiv Nil \text{ by T2.}
\end{aligned}
$$

$$
\begin{aligned}
(2)\ \psi(\phi(\mathrm{T}+\Sigma_I a_i f_i)) &\equiv \psi(\wedge_I \langle a_i \rangle \phi(f_i)) \text{ by definition,}\\
&\equiv \wedge_I \psi(\langle a_i \rangle \phi(f_i)) \text{ by definition,}\\
&\equiv \wedge_I \big(\mathrm{T}+a_i \psi(\phi(f_i))\big) \text{ by definition,}\\
&\equiv \wedge_I (\mathrm{T}+a_i f_i) \text{ by induction hypothesis,}\\
&\equiv \mathrm{T}+\Sigma_I a_i f_i \text{ by T7.}
\end{aligned}
$$

$$
\begin{aligned}
(3)\ \psi(\phi(\Sigma_I a_i f_i)) &\equiv \psi\big(\wedge_I \langle a_i \rangle \phi(f_i) \wedge (\wedge_{a \in \mathcal{A}(I)} [a] \vee_{ai=a} \phi(f_i)) \wedge \neg \vee_{b \notin \mathcal{A}(I)} \langle b \rangle \mathrm{T}\big) \text{ by definition,}\\
&\equiv \big(\wedge_I \psi(\langle a_i \rangle \phi(f_i))\big) \wedge\\
&\quad \big(\wedge_{a \in \mathcal{A}(I)} \neg \psi(\langle a \rangle \wedge_{ai=a} \neg \phi(f_i))\big) \wedge\\
&\quad \big(\neg \vee_{b \notin \mathcal{A}(I)} \psi(\langle b \rangle \mathrm{T})\big) \text{ by definition,}\\
&\equiv \big(\mathrm{T}+\Sigma_I a_i \psi(\phi(f_i))\big) \wedge\\
&\quad \big(\wedge_{a \in \mathcal{A}(I)} \neg(\mathrm{T}+a \wedge_{ai=a} \neg \psi(\phi(f_i)))\big) \wedge\\
&\quad \big(\neg \vee_{b \notin \mathcal{A}(I)} (\mathrm{T}+b\mathrm{T})\big) \text{ by definition,}\\
&\equiv (\mathrm{T}+\Sigma_I a_i f_i) \wedge\\
&\quad (\wedge_{a \in \mathcal{A}(I)} \neg(\mathrm{T}+a \wedge_{ai=a} \neg f_i)) \wedge\\
&\quad (\neg \vee_{b \notin \mathcal{A}(I)} (\mathrm{T}+b\mathrm{T})) \text{ by induction hypothesis,}\\
&\equiv \neg\big(\neg(\mathrm{T}+\Sigma_I a_i f_i) \vee (\vee_{a \in \mathcal{A}(I)} (\mathrm{T}+a \wedge_{ai=a} \neg f_i)) \vee (\mathrm{T}+(-\mathcal{A}(I))\mathrm{T})\big) \text{ by PC and T3,}\\
&\equiv \neg(\neg(\Sigma_I a_i f_i)) \text{ by T9}\\
&\equiv \Sigma_I a_i f_i \text{ by PC } \square
\end{aligned}
$$

Proposition 5

1. $\forall f \in CF.\ \forall q \in Q.\ q \models_{LSP} f \Rightarrow q \models_{L\mu} \phi(f)$
2. $\forall f \in L\mu.\ \forall q \in Q.\ q \models_{L\mu} f \Rightarrow q \models_{LSP} \psi(f)$

Proof: By induction on the structure of f. $\square$

Proposition 5 says that LSP_r is as expressive as $L\mu$ and conversely. That is, $LSP_r/\equiv_{LSP}$ is isomorphic to $L\mu/\equiv_{L\mu}$. It is known [EL86] that $L\mu$ is strictly more expressive than logics of programs such as CTL [CES83], CTL^* [EH83]. For example, as it was shown in [GS86c], the formulas $EF(f)$ and $AF(f)$ of CTL are represented in LSP by $\mu X.(f \vee T{+}\mathcal{A}X)$ and $\mu X.(f \vee \mathcal{A}X)$ respectively.

However, from proposition 5 can also be deduced that

(a) $\forall f \in CF.\ \models_{LSP} f \Rightarrow \models_{L\mu} \phi(f)$,

(b) $\forall f \in L\mu.\ \models_{L\mu} f \Rightarrow \models_{LSP} \psi(f)$.

From (a), (b) and propositions 4, one can obtain $\forall f \in CF.\ \models_{LSP} f \Leftrightarrow \models_{L\mu} \phi(f)$, and prove by using proposition 3 decidability for LSP_r from decidability of $L\mu$ [KP83], [SE84].

4. The Logic of Processes *LP*

In this section we define an extension of *LSP* called *Logic of Processes* which allows a characterization of systems of communicating processes. For this, we consider that actions are provided with a structure encoding communication capabilities and introduce parallel composition and restriction operators as in [Mi80] on both models and formulas.

4.1. Syntax

Let S be the language of sentences of *LSP* on a set $\mathcal{P}$ of atomic propositions and a set $\mathcal{A}$ of actions such that $\mathcal{A}=\mathcal{G}\times\{?,!,.\}$ where $\mathcal{G}$ is a set of *gates*. The formulas of *LP* are given by the grammar :

$$f ::= s \in S \mid Bf,\ B \in 2^{\mathcal{A}} \mid \neg f \mid f \vee f \mid f{+}f \mid f \| f \mid f\backslash G,\ G \in 2^{\mathcal{G}}.$$

This syntax forbids the use of $\|$ or $\backslash$ operators in the scope of a fixpoint operator and ensures that the processes described are regular.

4.2. Semantics

Let $M_0=(Q_0,R_0,\mathcal{I}_0)$ be a transition system.

(1) For $q_1,q_2 \in Q_0$, $q_1 \| q_2$ is considered as a state of a transition system $M=(Q,R,\mathcal{I})$ such that :

(a) $Q=Q_0 \cup \{q_1 \| q_2\}$,

(b) R is the least relation such that :

- $R_0 \subseteq R$,
- $(q_1,a,q_1') \in R \quad \Rightarrow \quad (q_1\|q_2,a,q_1'\|q_2) \in R$,
- $(q_2,a,q_2') \in R \quad \Rightarrow \quad (q_1\|q_2,a,q_1\|q_2') \in R$,
- $(q_1,g!,q_1') \in R$ and $(q_2,g?,q_2') \in R$

  $\Rightarrow \quad (q_1\|q_2,g.,q_1'\|q_2') \in R$ and $(q_2\|q_1,g.,q_2'\|q_1') \in R$,

(c) $\mathcal{I}$ is the extension of $\mathcal{I}_0$ such that :

- $\mathcal{I}(q)=\mathcal{I}_0(q)$ for $q \in Q_0$,
- $\mathcal{I}(q_1\|q_2)=\mathcal{I}(q_1) \cup \mathcal{I}(q_2)$.

(2) For $q \in Q$ and $G \in 2^{\mathcal{G}}$, $q\backslash G$ is considered as a state of a transition system $M=(Q,R,\mathcal{I})$ such that :

(a) $Q=Q_0\cup\{q\backslash G\}$,

(b) R is the least relation such that :

- $R_0 \subseteq R$,
- $(q,g.,q')\in R_0 \quad \Rightarrow \quad (q\backslash G,g.,q'\backslash G)\in R$,
- $(q,gx,q')\in R_0$ and $x\in\{?,!\}$ and $g\notin G$

  $\Rightarrow \quad (q\backslash G,gx,q'\backslash G)\in R$,

(c) $\mathcal{J}$ is the extension of $\mathcal{J}_0$ such that :

- $\mathcal{J}(q)=\mathcal{J}_0(q)$ for $q\in Q_0$,
- $\mathcal{J}(q\backslash G)=\mathcal{J}(q)$.

Models of LP are transition systems $M=(Q,R,\mathcal{J})$ such that :

($r1$) and ($r2$) in 2.2,

($r3$) $\forall q\in Q, \exists Q_1, Q_2, q_1\in Q_1, q_2\in Q_2, q\sim q_1\|q_2 \Rightarrow \exists q_1',q_2'\in Q.\ q_1\sim q_1'$ and $q_2\sim q_2'$,

i.e., if a state $q\in Q$ is the parallel composition of two states q_1 and q_2 then there exist for them equivalent states in Q.

($r4$) $\forall q_1,q_2\in Q.\ \exists q\in Q.\ q\sim q_1\|q_2$,

i.e., the set of the states of Q is closed for the $\|$ operation.

($r5$) $\forall q\in Q, \exists Q_1, q_1\in Q_1, q\sim q_1\backslash G \Rightarrow \exists q'\in Q.\ q_1\sim q'$,

($r6$) $\forall q\in Q.\ \forall G\in 2^{\mathcal{G}}.\ \exists q'\in Q.\ q'\sim q\backslash G$.

For a valuation $\underline{V}=(V_1,\ldots,V_n)\in(2^Q)^n$ and a state $q\in Q$, we extend the satisfaction relation $\models$ of LSP to formulas of LP by :

$q\models f\|g(\underline{V}) \;\Leftrightarrow\; \exists q_1,q_2\in Q.\ q\sim q_1\|q_2$ and $q_1\models f(\underline{V})$ and $q_2\models g(\underline{V})$

$q\models f\backslash G(\underline{V}) \;\Leftrightarrow\; \exists q'\in Q.\ q\sim q'$ and $q'\models f(\underline{V})$.

4.3. Deductive system

We propose hereafter a sound deductive system for LP. It is the extension of the one for LSP given in 2.4. by the following axioms and rules :

A19 $(f_1\|f_2)\|f_3 \equiv f_1\|(f_2\|f_3)$

A20 $f_1\|f_2 \equiv f_2\|f_1$

A21 $f\|Nil \equiv f$

A22 If $f=\Sigma_I a_i f_i$ and $f'=\Sigma_J b_j f_j'$ then

$f\|f' \supset \Sigma_I a_i(f_i\|f')+\Sigma_J b_j(f\|f_j')+(\Sigma g.(f_i\|f_j')$ for $a_i=gx$ and $b_j=g\underline{x})$

where, for $x\in\{?,!\}$, $\underline{x}=?$ if $x=!$ and vice versa.

A23 $(f_1\vee f_2)\|f_3 \equiv (f_1\|f_3)\vee(f_2\|f_3)$

A24 $(P\wedge f_1)\|f_2 \equiv P\wedge(f_1\|f_2)$

A25 $\mathrm{T}\|\mathcal{A}\mathrm{T} \equiv \mathcal{A}\mathrm{T}$

A26 $\bot\|f \equiv \bot$

A27 $Nil\backslash G \equiv Nil$

A28 $(f_1+f_2)\backslash G \equiv f_1\backslash G+f_2\backslash G$

A29 $(f_1\vee f_2)\backslash G \equiv f_1\backslash G\vee f_2\backslash G$

A30 $(Bf)\backslash G \equiv Nil$ if $B \subseteq (G! \cup G?)$ and

$(Bf)\backslash G \equiv (B\text{-}(G! \cup G?))(f\backslash G)$ otherwise

A31 $(P \wedge f)\backslash G \equiv P \wedge (f\backslash G)$

A32 $\bot\backslash G \equiv \bot$

A33 $f \supset Nil \vee (\mathcal{A}\text{-}(G! \cup G?))f) \vdash T\backslash G$

A34 $f_1 \supset f_2 \vdash (f_1 \| f_3) \supset (f_2 \| f_3)$

A35 $f_1 \supset f_2 \vdash (f_1\backslash G) \supset (f_2\backslash G)$

Notice that the language of terms t defined by the grammar :

$t ::= Nil \mid X \in \mathcal{X} \mid at \mid t+t \mid I \mid t \| t \mid t\backslash G \mid \nu X.st(X)$ where st is a sequential term,

is contained in the language of formulas of *LP*. It can be shown that for f and f' terms of this language, implication in A22 can be replaced by equivalence. In this case, A22 becomes a version of the expansion theorem of pocess algebras.

The set of the closed well-guarded terms with axioms A1 to A4, A19 to A22, A27, A28, A30 and the duals of LFA and FIR (replace implication by equivalence) characterizes systems of communicating processes modulo strong bisimulation. Axioms A19 to A22 (resp. A27, A28, A30) are standard axioms for parallel composition (resp. restriction).

Example The aim of this example is to illustrate the use of the deductive system of *LP*. Consider two processes $p_1 = \nu X_1.(a.c!X_1)$ and $p_2 = \nu X_2.(b.c?X_2)$ and the formulas $f_1 = F(a.\mathrm{T})$, $f_2 = F(b.\mathrm{T})$ and $f_3 = F(a.\mathrm{T}+b.\mathrm{T})$ where $F(f) = \nu Z.(\mathcal{A}Z \wedge \mu Y.(\mathcal{A}Y \vee f))$. Informally speaking, $F(f)$ expresses the property "always eventually f". We give proofs for $p_1 \supset f_1$ and $(p_1 \| p_2)\backslash\{c\} \supset f_3$.

(I) *Proof of* $p_1 \supset f_1$:

We first prove $p_1 \supset f_1'$ where $f_1' = \nu Z.(\mathcal{A}\mathcal{A}Z \wedge \mu Y.(\mathcal{A}Y \vee a.\mathrm{T}))$. By rule FID it is sufficient to prove $p_1 \supset \mathcal{A}\mathcal{A}p_1 \wedge \mu Y.(\mathcal{A}Y \vee a.\mathrm{T})$, equivalent to $p_1 \supset \mathcal{A}\mathcal{A}p_1$ and $p_1 \supset \mu Y.(\mathcal{A}Y \vee a.\mathrm{T})$. These goals are proved by applications of FT and monotonicity of prefixing.

To complete the proof we show that $f_1' \supset f_1$. By application of FID it is sufficient to prove $f_1' \supset \mathcal{A}f_1' \wedge \mu Y.(\mathcal{A}Y \vee a.\mathrm{T})$, equivalent to $f_1' \supset \mathcal{A}f_1'$ and $f_1' \supset \mu Y.(\mathcal{A}Y \vee a.\mathrm{T})$. The later goal is equivalent by FT to $\mathcal{A}\mathcal{A}f_1' \wedge \mu Y.(\mathcal{A}Y \vee a.\mathrm{T}) \supset \mu Y.(\mathcal{A}Y \vee a.\mathrm{T})$ which is true by PC.

Let us prove $f_1' \supset \mathcal{A}f_1'$. By FT, PC and A8, we have $f_1' \equiv \mathcal{A}(\mathcal{A}f_1' \wedge \mu Y.(\mathcal{A}Y \vee a.\mathrm{T})) \vee a.\mathcal{A}f_1'$. Thus, it is sufficient to prove $\mathcal{A}f_1' \supset f_1'$ (PC and A17). By FID, it is sufficient to prove $\mathcal{A}f_1' \supset \mathcal{A}\mathcal{A}\mathcal{A}f_1' \wedge \mu Y.(\mathcal{A}Y \vee a.\mathrm{T})$, equivalent to $\mathcal{A}f_1' \supset \mathcal{A}(\mathcal{A}\mathcal{A}f_1' \wedge \mu Y.(\mathcal{A}Y \vee a.\mathrm{T})) \vee a.\mathcal{A}\mathcal{A}f_1'$ (FT, PC and A8). Finally, by PC and A17, it is sufficient to prove $f_1' \supset \mathcal{A}\mathcal{A}f_1' \wedge \mu Y.(\mathcal{A}Y \vee a.\mathrm{T})$ which is true by FT.

(II) *Proof of* $(p_1 \| p_2)\backslash\{c\} \supset f_3$:

Let $p_3 = (p_1 \| p_2)\backslash\{c\}$. To prove $p_3 \supset f_3$ we can first show that $p_3 \supset p_3'$ where $p_3' = \nu Y.(a.b.c.Y + b.a.c.Y)$. This proof can be carried out as proofs of equivalence in process algebras by application of FT, FID and the expansion theorem A22. Finally, we prove $p_3' \supset f_3$ as in (I), by showing $p_3' \supset f_3'$ and $f_3' \supset f_3$ where $f_3' = \nu Z.(\mathcal{A}\mathcal{A}\mathcal{A}Z \wedge \mu Y.(\mathcal{A}Y \vee a.\mathrm{T}+b.\mathrm{T}))$.

To prove $p_3'\supset f_3'$ it is sufficient to show $p_3'\supset \mathcal{A}\mathcal{A}\mathcal{A}p_3'\wedge\mu Y.(\mathcal{A}Y\vee a.\mathrm{T}+b.\mathrm{T}))$ (FID), equivalent to $p_3'\supset \mathcal{A}(\mathcal{A}\mathcal{A}p_3'\wedge\mu Y.(\mathcal{A}Y\vee a.\mathrm{T}+b.\mathrm{T}))\vee a.\mathcal{A}\mathcal{A}p_3'+b.\mathcal{A}\mathcal{A}p_3'$ (FT, A8, PC). It is sufficient to prove $p_3'\supset a.\mathcal{A}\mathcal{A}p_3'+b.\mathcal{A}\mathcal{A}p_3'$. As $p_3'\equiv a.b.c.p_3'+b.a.c.p_3'$ (FT), the proof is obtained by application of monotonicity rules.

To prove $f_3'\supset f_3$ it is sufficient to show $f_3'\supset \mathcal{A}f_3'\wedge\mu Y.(\mathcal{A}Y\vee a.\mathrm{T}+b.\mathrm{T})$ (FID), equivalent to $f_3'\supset \mathcal{A}(f_3'\wedge\mu Y.(\mathcal{A}Y\vee a.\mathrm{T}+b.\mathrm{T}))\vee a.f_3'+b.f_3'$ (FT, A8, PC).

As $f_3'\equiv \mathcal{A}(\mathcal{A}\mathcal{A}f_3'\wedge\mu Y.(\mathcal{A}Y\vee a.\mathrm{T}+b.\mathrm{T}))\vee a.\mathcal{A}\mathcal{A}f_3'+b.\mathcal{A}\mathcal{A}f_3'$ it is sufficient to prove $\mathcal{A}\mathcal{A}f_3'\supset f_3'$. By FID, it is sufficient to prove $\mathcal{A}\mathcal{A}f_3'\supset \mathcal{A}^5f_3'\wedge\mu Y.(\mathcal{A}Y\vee a.\mathrm{T}+b.\mathrm{T})$, equivalent to

$$\mathcal{A}\mathcal{A}f_3'\supset \mathcal{A}(\mathcal{A}^4f_3'\wedge\mu Y.(\mathcal{A}Y\vee a.\mathrm{T}+b.\mathrm{T}))\vee a.\mathcal{A}^4f_3'+b.\mathcal{A}^4f_3' \text{ (FT, A8, PC).}$$

It is sufficient to prove $\mathcal{A}f_3'\supset \mathcal{A}^4f_3'\wedge\mu Y.(\mathcal{A}Y\vee a.\mathrm{T}+b.\mathrm{T})$, equivalent to

$$\mathcal{A}f_3'\supset \mathcal{A}(\mathcal{A}^3f_3'\wedge\mu Y.(\mathcal{A}Y\vee a.\mathrm{T}+b.\mathrm{T}))\vee a.\mathcal{A}^3f_3'+b.\mathcal{A}^3f_3' \text{ (FT, A8, PC).}$$

It is sufficient to prove $f_3'\supset \mathcal{A}^3f_3'\wedge\mu Y.(\mathcal{A}Y\vee a.\mathrm{T}+b.\mathrm{T})$ which is true by FT.

References

[CES83] Clarke E.M., Emerson E.A., Sistla A.P. *Automatic Verification of Finite State Concurrent Systems Using Temporal Logic*, 10th Annual ACM Symp. on Principles of Programming Languages, 1983.

[EH83] Emerson E.A., Halpern J.Y. *"Sometimes" and "Not Never" Revisited : on Branching versus Linear Time*, 10th Annual ACM Symp. on Principles of Programming Languages, 1983.

[EL86] Emerson E.A., Lei C-L. *Efficient Model Checking in Fragments of the Propositional Mu-Calculus*, LICS 1986.

[GS86a] Graf S., Sifakis J. *A Modal Characterisation of Observational Congruence of Finite Terms of CCS*, Information and Control Vol.68, 1-3, 1986.

[GS86b] Graf S., Sifakis J. *A Logic for the Specification and Proof of Controllable Terms of CCS*, Acta Informatica 23, 1986.

[GS86c] Graf S., Sifakis J. *A Logic for the Description of Non-deterministic Programs and their Properties*, Information and Control Vol.68, 1-3, 1986.

[HM82] Hennessy M., Milner R. *Observing Non-determinism and Concurrency*, Proceedings of 7th ICALP, LNCS 92, 1982.

[Ko83] Kozen D. *Results on the Propositional μ-calculus*, TCS 27, 1983.

[KP83] Kozen D., Parikh R. J. *A decision Procedure for the Propositional Mu-calculus*, Second Workshop on Logics of Programs, 1983.

[Mi80] Milner R. *A Calculus of Communicating Systems*, LNCS 92, 1980.

[Mi84] Milner R. *A Complete Inference System for a Class of Regular Behaviours*, JCSS 28, 439-466, 1984.

[Pn85] Pnueli A. *Linear and Branching Time Structures in the Semantics and Logics of Reactive Systems*, Proceedings of ICALP, LNCS 194, 1986.

[Pn86] Pnueli A. *Specification and Development of Reactive Systems*, Proceedings IFIP 1986.

[Si86] Sifakis J. *A Response to Amir Pnueli's "Specification and Development of Reactive Systems"*, Proceedings IFIP 1986.

[SE84] Streett R.S., Emerson E.A. *The propositional Mu-calculus is Elementary*, Proc. 12th ICALP, LNCS 172, 465-472, 1984.

Permutation of Transitions:
An Event Structure Semantics for CCS and SCCS

Gérard Boudol & Ilaria Castellani
INRIA Sophia-Antipolis
06560-VALBONNE FRANCE

Abstract. We apply Berry & Lévy's notion of equivalence by permutations to CCS and EIJE/SCCS, thus obtaining a pomset transition semantics for these calculi. We show that this ovides an operational counterpart for an event structure semantics for CCS and SCCS similar the one given by Winskel.

Keywords: process algebras, pomset-labelled transition systems, event structures.

Contents

Introduction.

computational system evolves by elementary computations from one state to the other, in nota- n $s \longrightarrow s'$. Examples of state changes are transitions of a machine, β-reductions of λ-terms and writings in a term rewriting system. When states are abstract programs one may extract from eir syntactical structure some indication of *what* has been performed and *where* it has happened. other words, one may decorate transitions with a label w, thus obtaining $s \xrightarrow{w} s'$, where w is occurrence of action. Now assume that $s \xrightarrow{u} s_0$ and $s \xrightarrow{v} s_1$: in many cases we may have the tuition that these two moves are *compatible*, or independent. This means that we are able to fine what remains of one move after the other, in notation v/u and u/v, in such a way that v/u n happen in state s_0, that is $s_0 \xrightarrow{v/u} s'$, and similarly $s_1 \xrightarrow{u/v} s''$. If u and v are really compatible, should be able to perform them in any order, without affecting the result, that is: $s' = s''$. is is known as the *diamond property*, or the parallel moves property. Moreover, two sequences transitions should be regarded as equivalent, if they are equal up to commutation of compatible moves, typically:

$$s \xrightarrow{u} s_0 \xrightarrow{v/u} s' \simeq s \xrightarrow{v} s_1 \xrightarrow{u/v} s'$$

This is the essence of Berry and Lévy's *equivalence by permutations* for sequences of (elementary) computations.

This equivalence was first elaborated by Lévy in his thesis (*cf.* [15]) upon Church notion of residual for the λ-calculus, and then used for recursive program schemes in [1]. It was further extended to deterministic term rewriting systems by Huet and Lévy in [14], and to non-deterministic ones by Boudol in [3]. In any case, this equivalence allows one to associate with each "state" a complete partial order of computations. These computations are equivalence classes of sequences of elementary moves, ordered by the prefix ordering, up to commutations. A similar notion is used for Petri nets by Nielsen, Plotkin and Winskel, who define in [20] an equivalence that "*abstracts away from the ordering of concurrent firings of transitions*" (this is also used by van Glabbeek and Vaandrager in [13], and by Best and Devillers in [2]; a similar idea is that of *trace* of Mazurkiewicz [16]). Moreover they show that for nets the ordered space of computations has a nice characterization: it is the space of configurations of an *event structure*. As a matter of fact, the three basic connectives of event structures – causality, concurrency and conflict – are already present in computations. Roughly speaking, two occurrences of actions (events) u and v are *consistent* (non-conflicting), with respect to a state s if they can appear in the same computation of s:

$$s \cdots \xrightarrow{u} \cdots \xrightarrow{v} \cdots$$

In this case they are concurrent if they may be permuted:

$$s \cdots \xrightarrow{u} \cdots \xrightarrow{v} \cdots \simeq s \cdots \xrightarrow{v} \cdots \xrightarrow{u} \cdots$$

Otherwise they are causally related: one of them must precede the other.

In this note we propose an equivalence by permutations for Milner's calculi CCS and SCCS [17,18], and show that the ordered space of computations of a term is the poset of configurations of an event structure. The events are simply occurrences of actions, and, roughly speaking, they are compatible if they lie on different sides of a parallel system, though some complications arise from communication. We show that each equivalence class of computations (up to permutations) may be represented as a one step transition, where the action is a labelled poset of events. With the exception of communication, this corresponds exactly to our semantics for "true concurrency" in [6,7]. Our operational semantics for CCS is similar to the one given by Degano, De Nicola and Montanari in [11], who obtain a poset transition from a sequence of "atomic transitions" that they call atomic concurrent histories. The poset transition semantics provides us with an operational counterpart to the interpretation of CCS terms as event structures. However it remains to be checked that our constructions coincide, at least in interpreting CCS, with those given by Winskel in [22] (see also [23]).

2. Pure CCS: terms and transitions.

As in [17], we assume a fixed set Δ of *names*. We use $\alpha, \beta, \ldots$ to stand for names. We assume a set $\overline{\Delta}$ of *co-names* (complementary names), disjoint from Δ and in bijection with it: the co-name of α is $\bar{\alpha}$, and its name is $\mathsf{nm}(\alpha) = \alpha = \mathsf{nm}(\bar{\alpha})$. Then $\Lambda = \Delta \cup \overline{\Delta}$ is the set of *labels*. We shall use

λ to range over Λ, and extend the bijection so that $\bar{\bar{\lambda}} = \lambda$. As usual the set A of CCS *actions* is $A = \Lambda \cup \{\tau\}$, where τ is a new symbol, not in Λ; by convention the name of τ is τ. We use a, b, $c, \ldots$ to range over A. We presuppose a collection X (disjoint from A) of *identifiers*, and use x, y, $z, \ldots$ to range over identifiers.

The *action* construct of CCS will be denoted by $a\colon p$, while the parallel composition is $(p \parallel q)$. We shall not use the relabelling operator, although it would not introduce any difficulty. The syntax of (pure) CCS terms is given by the following grammar:

$$p \ ::= \ \mathsf{nil} \mid x \mid a\colon p \mid (p \parallel p') \mid (p + p') \mid (p \backslash \alpha) \mid \mu x.p$$

We shall use p, q, $r, \ldots$ to range over terms; finite terms – built without fixpoint $\mu x.p$ – should be viewed as *finite trees*, with parallel composition and sum as binary node constructors, action and restriction as unary ones (with a parameter in A and Δ respectively), and nil as constant. However this representation will remain implicit throughout this paper. For instance the term

$$r = ((\alpha\colon \mathsf{nil} \parallel (\bar{\alpha}\colon \mathsf{nil} + \beta\colon \mathsf{nil}))\backslash \alpha)$$

will be identified with the tree:

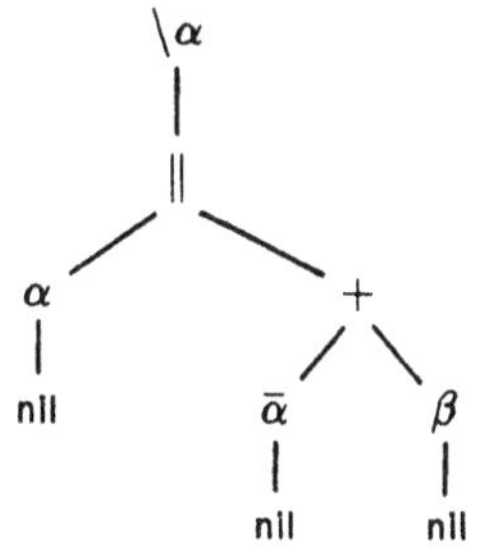

As is standard, the fixpoint construction binds the defined identifier, and substituting q for x in p may require renaming the bound variables of p in order to avoid captures; the result of such a substitution is denoted $p[q/x]$. Terms involving fixpoint define *infinite trees*, obtained by unfolding $\mu x.p$ into $p[\mu x.p/x]$ ad infinitum. As it is usual, we assume that there is a constant Ω, which is not a CCS term, in order to interpret diverging terms such as $\mu x.x$ for instance.

The semantics of CCS terms is given by means of *inference rules*, allowing one to prove *transitions* of the form $p \xrightarrow{a} p'$ for terms. We assume these rules to be known (see [17]). Modern proof theory shows that there are some advantages to reap from a *syntax* for proofs – if we think of inference rules as proof constructions. The case of CCS is very simple, since the validity of a "proposition" $p \xrightarrow{a} p'$ only depends on the structure of the term p. More precisely, a proof of such a transition is just an indication of how we get the action a from the term p. In the simplest case, this indication is a path which leads to an (outermost) subterm $a\colon q$. But the action can also be a communication τ, in which case this indication is a path to a pair of complementary subterms $\lambda\colon q$ and $\bar{\lambda}\colon q'$. Then we have to devise a syntax for these paths, which are some kind of initial subterms. Let F be a set of function symbols, which are symbols with arity, from which we build terms. Then with each $f \in F$ of arity n we can associate a collection of new symbols f_m, one for each $m \subseteq \{1, \ldots, n\}$, so that the arity of f_m is the cardinality of m. For instance the "split" term $f_{\{i_1,\ldots,i_k\}}(t_{i_1}, \ldots, t_{i_k})$ represents an initial subterm of $f(t_1, \ldots, t_n)$ obtained by deleting some arguments of f.

In the case of CCS, we only need some of these constructs, namely $a\colon_{\emptyset}$, $\|_{\{1\}}$, $\|_{\{2\}}$ and $\|_{\{1,2\}}$, $+_{\{1\}}$ and $+_{\{2\}}$, $\backslash\alpha_{\{1\}}$. We shall use specific names for these, respectively γ_a, π_0, π_1, δ, σ_0, σ_1 and ρ_α. The syntax for proofs of CCS transitions is thus given by the grammar:

$$\theta \ ::= \ \gamma_a \mid \pi_0(\theta) \mid \pi_1(\theta) \mid \delta(\theta,\theta') \mid \sigma_0(\theta) \mid \sigma_1(\theta) \mid \rho_\alpha(\theta)$$

One should note that although we call them proof terms, the θ's will not in general represent *valid* proofs; for instance $\rho_\alpha(\gamma_\alpha)$ does not correspond to any CCS transition, and the reader should be able to find other kinds of examples. The valid proofs are those built by means of the formation rules below. Usually one denotes by $\theta\colon\Phi$ the fact that θ is a proof of the proposition Φ; since we shall use sequences of transitions, we prefer the notation $p \xrightarrow{a\,,\,\theta} p'$ for: *θ is a proof of the fact that p performs the action a and becomes p' in doing so.* We call these enriched transitions *proved transitions*. The rules of inference (and formation of proofs) are the following:

action	$\vdash\ a\colon p \xrightarrow{a\,,\,\gamma_a} p$
parallel composition 1	$p \xrightarrow{a\,,\,\theta} p'\ \vdash\ (p \parallel q) \xrightarrow{a\,,\,\pi_0(\theta)} (p' \parallel q)$
parallel composition 2	$q \xrightarrow{b\,,\,\theta'} q'\ \vdash\ (p \parallel q) \xrightarrow{b\,,\,\pi_1(\theta')} (p \parallel q')$
communication	$p \xrightarrow{\lambda\,,\,\theta} p'\ ,\ q \xrightarrow{\bar\lambda\,,\,\theta'} q'\ \vdash\ (p \parallel q) \xrightarrow{\tau\,,\,\delta(\theta,\theta')} (p' \parallel q')$
sum 1	$p \xrightarrow{a\,,\,\theta} p'\ \vdash\ (p+q) \xrightarrow{a\,,\,\sigma_0(\theta)} p'$
sum 2	$q \xrightarrow{b\,,\,\theta'} q'\ \vdash\ (p+q) \xrightarrow{b\,,\,\sigma_1(\theta')} q'$
restriction	$p \xrightarrow{a\,,\,\theta} p'\ ,\ \mathsf{nm}(a) \neq \alpha\ \vdash\ (p\backslash\alpha) \xrightarrow{a\,,\,\rho_\alpha(\theta)} (p'\backslash\alpha)$
fixpoint	$p[\mu x.p/x] \xrightarrow{a\,,\,\theta} p'\ \vdash\ \mu x.p \xrightarrow{a\,,\,\theta} p'$

It should be clear that if we drop the proof terms these rules are exactly those of CCS. Note also that the proofs actually hold for the (infinite) trees that we get by unfolding the $\mu x.p$'s, since the (meta) rule for fixpoint does not introduce any special proof constructor. Let us see an example: we have for the previous term $r = ((\alpha\colon \mathsf{nil} \parallel (\bar\alpha\colon \mathsf{nil} + \beta\colon \mathsf{nil}))\backslash\alpha)$

$$r \xrightarrow{\beta\,,\,\rho_\alpha(\pi_1(\sigma_1(\gamma_\beta)))} ((\alpha\colon \mathsf{nil} \parallel \mathsf{nil})\backslash\alpha)$$

and

$$r \xrightarrow{\tau\,,\,\rho_\alpha(\delta(\gamma_\alpha,\sigma_0(\gamma_{\bar\alpha})))} ((\mathsf{nil} \parallel \mathsf{nil})\backslash\alpha)$$

Decorating the transitions with their proofs provides us with a "maximal" concrete information. This can be weakened in various ways to obtain more abstract semantics. For instance we can extract from a proof θ of a transition $p \xrightarrow{a} p'$ the *local residual* associated with this proof, as defined by Castellani and Hennessy [8,9] (we omit the formal definition). Then one may consider decorated transitions of the form $p \xrightarrow{a\,,\,p''} p'$ where p'' is the local residual, and devise an enriched notion of bisimulation.

As a matter of fact, we could have used transitions $p \xrightarrow{\theta} p'$, since the action itself is determined by the proof: it is the *label* $\ell(\theta)$ of the proof, defined as:

(i) $\ell(\gamma_a) = a$;

(ii) $\ell(f(\theta)) = \ell(\theta)$ for all unary proof constructor f;

(iii) $\ell(\delta(\theta, \theta')) = \tau$.

3. Permutation of transitions.

In order to define the equivalence by permutations on sequences of transitions, we first need a notion of *concurrent* proved transitions. Roughly speaking, two transitions are concurrent if they occur on different sides of a parallel composition, whereas they are in conflict if they occur on different sides of a sum. However some complications arise from communication, which may introduce new conflicts. Typically, two communications will be in conflict if they share one component. Conversely, they will be concurrent if they are pairwise concurrent – i.e. they have concurrent (corresponding) components.

The relation of concurrency on proved transitions is induced from a relation of concurrency between proof terms, denoted $\theta \smile \theta'$. The relation $\smile$ on proof terms is the least symmetric relation *compatible with the proof constructors* which satisfies the following clauses:

(A1) $\pi_0(\theta) \smile \pi_1(\theta')$

(A2) $\theta \smile \theta' \;\Rightarrow\; \begin{cases} \pi_0(\theta) \smile \delta(\theta', \theta'') \\ \pi_1(\theta) \smile \delta(\theta'', \theta') \end{cases}$

For instance, considering the term $((\alpha : \mathsf{nil} \parallel \beta : \mathsf{nil}) \parallel \bar{\alpha} : \mathsf{nil})$, we have $\pi_0(\pi_1(\gamma_\beta)) \smile \delta(\pi_0(\gamma_\alpha), \gamma_{\bar{\alpha}})$. As regards communication, compatibility of $\smile$ with the constructor δ amounts to requiring:

$$\theta_0 \smile \theta_0' \text{ and } \theta_1 \smile \theta_1' \;\Rightarrow\; \delta(\theta_0, \theta_1) \smile \delta(\theta_0', \theta_1')$$

Note that $\theta \smile \theta' \Rightarrow \theta \neq \theta'$.

DEFINITION (CONCURRENT TRANSITIONS). *Let* $t_0 = p \xrightarrow{a,\, \theta_0} p_0$ *and* $t_1 = p \xrightarrow{b,\, \theta_1} p_1$ *be two proved transitions for the same* CCS *term* p. *The transitions are concurrent, in notation* $t_0 \smile t_1$, *if and only if* $\theta_0 \smile \theta_1$.

Note that the concurrency relation between transitions is symmetric and irreflexive. The two transitions of the example above are not concurrent since they made two different choices at the subterm $(\bar{\alpha} : \mathsf{nil} + \beta : \mathsf{nil})$. Let us see another example of conflict, arising from communication: if q is the term $(\bar{\alpha} : \mathsf{nil} \parallel (\alpha : \mathsf{nil} \parallel \alpha : \mathsf{nil}))$ then the two transitions

$$q \xrightarrow{\tau,\, \delta(\gamma_{\bar{\alpha}}, \pi_0(\gamma_\alpha))} (\mathsf{nil} \parallel (\mathsf{nil} \parallel \alpha : \mathsf{nil})) \quad , \quad q \xrightarrow{\tau,\, \delta(\gamma_{\bar{\alpha}}, \pi_1(\gamma_\alpha))} (\mathsf{nil} \parallel (\alpha : \mathsf{nil} \parallel \mathsf{nil}))$$

are not concurrent, since they share the same "sub-transition" $\pi_0(\gamma_{\bar{\alpha}})$. The conflict relation will be formalized later.

We define now the *residual* θ/θ' of a proof term by a concurrent one, namely what is left of the proof θ after θ'. This residual may differ from the proof term itself because of nondeterministic choices. For any concurrent proofs θ, θ', the residual θ/θ' is defined by:

$i \neq j \;\Rightarrow\; \pi_i(\theta)\,/\pi_j(\theta') = \pi_i(\theta)$

$$\theta \smile \theta' \;\Rightarrow\; \begin{cases} \pi_0(\theta)\,/\delta(\theta',\theta'') = \pi_0(\theta/\theta') \text{ and} \\ \delta(\theta',\theta'')/\pi_0(\theta) = \delta(\theta'/\theta,\theta'') \\ \pi_1(\theta)\,/\delta(\theta'',\theta') = \pi_1(\theta/\theta') \text{ and} \\ \delta(\theta'',\theta')/\pi_1(\theta) = \delta(\theta'',\theta'/\theta) \end{cases}$$

$$\theta \smile \theta' \;\Rightarrow\; \begin{cases} \pi_i(\theta)/\pi_i(\theta') = \pi_i(\theta/\theta') \\ \sigma_i(\theta)/\sigma_i(\theta') = \theta/\theta' \\ \rho_\alpha(\theta)/\rho_\alpha(\theta') = \rho_\alpha(\theta/\theta') \end{cases}$$

$\theta_0 \smile \theta_0'$ and $\theta_1 \smile \theta_1' \;\Rightarrow\; \delta(\theta_0,\theta_1)/\delta(\theta_0',\theta_1') = \delta(\theta_0/\theta_0',\theta_1/\theta_1')$

Let us look at an example, which shows in which way residuals are affected by choices. The term $p = ((a\colon \mathsf{nil} \parallel b\colon \mathsf{nil}) + c\colon \mathsf{nil})$ may do the proved transitions:

$$p \xrightarrow{\sigma_0(\pi_0(a))} (\mathsf{nil} \parallel b\colon \mathsf{nil}), \qquad p \xrightarrow{\sigma_0(\pi_1(b))} (a\colon \mathsf{nil} \parallel \mathsf{nil})$$

So the proof of the b-transition is $\sigma_0(\pi_1(b))$. On the other hand, once the a-transition has happened, the proof of the b-transition becomes $\pi_1(b) = \sigma_0(\pi_1(b))/\sigma_0(\pi_0(a))$, and we have:

$$(\mathsf{nil} \parallel b\colon \mathsf{nil}) \xrightarrow{(\pi_1(b))} (\mathsf{nil} \parallel \mathsf{nil})$$

The following result, also known as the parallel moves lemma, states a "conditional Church-Rosser property", namely that two transitions are confluent whenever they are concurrent. It is much simpler in CCS than in λ-calculus or term rewriting systems, since a proof of a transition cannot be duplicated or deleted by another concurrent one; it is always left unchanged, up to the resolution of choices.

LEMMA (THE DIAMOND LEMMA). *Let $t_0 = p \xrightarrow{a,\,\theta_0} p_0$ and $t_1 = p \xrightarrow{b,\,\theta_1} p_1$ be two proved transitions. If they are concurrent then there exists a unique term $\bar{p}$ such that $p_0 \xrightarrow{b,\,\theta_1/\theta_0} \bar{p}$ and $p_1 \xrightarrow{a,\,\theta_0/\theta_1} \bar{p}$.*

This property is in fact much stronger than confluence: it says that a (proved) transition survives any concurrent one. Therefore we can adopt the standard terminology ([1,3,14,15]): the transition $t_1' = p_0 \xrightarrow{b,\,\theta_1/\theta_0} \bar{p}$ (with the notations of the diamond lemma) is the *residual* of t_1 by t_0, denoted t_1/t_0 and similarly $t_0/t_1 = p_1 \xrightarrow{a,\,\theta_0/\theta_1} \bar{p}$ is the residual of t_0 by t_1. This is the basis of the equivalence by permutations.

Each CCS term p determines a set $\mathcal{T}^\infty(p)$ of finite or infinite sequences of proved transitions of the form

$$p \xrightarrow{a_1,\,\theta_1} p_1 \;\cdots\; p_{n-1} \xrightarrow{a_n,\,\theta_n} p_n \;\cdots$$

Equivalently we could have presented these as sequences of steps:

$$t_1 \cdots t_n \cdots \quad \text{where} \quad t_n = p_{n-1} \xrightarrow{a_n,\,\theta_n} p_n \quad (\text{and } p_0 = p)$$

The set of finite such sequences is denoted $\mathcal{T}(p)$, and we shall denote ss' the concatenation of $s \in \mathcal{T}(p)$ and $s' \in \mathcal{T}^\infty(q)$, which is only defined if s ends at q. We are now ready to define the permutation equivalence and the permutation preorder on $\mathcal{T}(p)$: intuitively two (finite) sequences of proved transitions are equivalent if they are the same up to permutations of concurrent steps; the preorder is just the prefix order up to permutations. We shall denote by $\ll$ the usual prefix order:

$$\forall s \in \mathcal{T}^{\infty}(p)\ \forall s' \in \mathcal{T}^{\infty}(p)\ s \ll s' \ \Leftrightarrow_{\text{def}}\ s = s' \text{ or } \exists s''\ ss'' = s'$$

DEFINITION (THE PERMUTATION EQUIVALENCE AND PREORDER). *Let p be a CCS term. The equivalence by permutations on $\mathcal{T}(p)$ is the least equivalence $\simeq$ such that*

$$s_0 t_0 (t_1/t_0) s_1 \ \simeq\ s_0 t_1 (t_0/t_1) s_1$$

(provided that $t_0 \smile t_1$ and that concatenation is defined). The preorder $\lesssim$ is given by

$$s_0 \lesssim s_1 \Leftrightarrow_{\text{def}} \exists s\ s_0 \ll s\ \&\ s \simeq s_1$$

The typical example of equivalent sequences of transitions is (omitting the obvious proofs):

$$(a:p \parallel b:q) \xrightarrow{a} (p \parallel b:q) \xrightarrow{b} (p \parallel q) \simeq (a:p \parallel b:q) \xrightarrow{b} (a:p \parallel q) \xrightarrow{a} (p \parallel q)$$

Here one can commute the two steps. There is another kind of sequences of transitions where this is not possible, for a step is *caused*, or created, by a previous one. The typical example is obviously

$$a:b:\mathsf{nil} \xrightarrow{a} b:\mathsf{nil} \xrightarrow{b} \mathsf{nil}$$

The main idea of this note is that, if we only retain the actions and their possible permutations, we can represent the equivalence class of a sequence

$$s = p \xrightarrow{a_1\,,\,\theta_1} \cdots \xrightarrow{a_n\,,\,\theta_n} p'$$

as a *one step transition* $p \xrightarrow{P} p'$ where P is a *pomset* (partially ordered multiset [21]) of actions of A, – that is an isomorphism class of posets labelled in A. Such pomset transitions were introduced in [6] for a subset of CCS. Let us formalize this idea: we shall write $s \sim_{\varsigma} s'$ if s' results from s by the transposition of the steps i and $i+1$, and ς is the corresponding transposition of $\{1, \ldots, n\}$, where n is the length of s (obviously $\simeq$ preserves the length of sequences). So $\varsigma(i) = i+1$ and $\varsigma(i+1) = i$. It should be clear that $s' \simeq s$ if and only if there is a sequence $\varsigma_1, \ldots, \varsigma_k$ of such transpositions from s to s'. Let us denote this fact by $s \sim_{\varsigma_1, \ldots, \varsigma_k} s'$. Then the equivalence class of $s = p \xrightarrow{a_1\,,\,\theta_1} \cdots \xrightarrow{a_n\,,\,\theta_n} p'$ determines a transition $p \xrightarrow{P} p'$, where $P = (E, l, \leq)$ is the labelled poset defined by

$$\begin{cases} E = \{e_1, \ldots, e_n\} \\ l(e_i) = a_i \\ e_i \leq e_j \ \Leftrightarrow\ \forall s'.\ s' \sim_{\varsigma_1, \ldots, \varsigma_k} s \ \Rightarrow\ \eta(i) \leq \eta(j) \quad \text{where } \eta = \varsigma_k \circ \cdots \circ \varsigma_1 \end{cases}$$

Note that P is defined up to isomorphism, since the events e_i are taken arbitrarily. A similar definition is given in [13] for Petri nets. For instance the equivalence class of

$$(a:p \parallel b:c:q) \xrightarrow{a} (p \parallel b:c:q) \xrightarrow{b} (p \parallel c:q) \xrightarrow{c} (p \parallel q)$$

may be represented as a transition whose label is a pomset consisting of events e_1, e_2 and e_3 labelled a, b and c respectively, where e_2 precedes e_3 and e_1 is incomparable with e_2 and e_3, that is:

$$(a : p \parallel b : c : q) \xrightarrow{\left\{\begin{array}{cc} a & b \\ & | \\ & c \end{array}\right\}} (p \parallel q)$$

As we shall see, we can interpret a term as an event structure, so that the pomsets of actions of the term are the configurations of this event structure.

The preorder $\lesssim$ is naturally extended to (possibly infinite) sequences of proved transitions $s \in \mathcal{T}^\infty(p)$:

$$s_0 \lesssim s_1 \Leftrightarrow_{\mathrm{def}} \forall s \in \mathcal{T}(p)\ s \ll s_0 \ \Rightarrow\ \exists s' \in \mathcal{T}(p)\ s' \ll s_1 \ \&\ s \lesssim s'$$

It is easy to show that for finite sequences of transitions s and s' of the same term

$$s \simeq s' \Leftrightarrow s \lesssim s' \ \&\ s' \lesssim s$$

Therefore we shall keep the notation $\simeq$ for the equivalence on $\mathcal{T}^\infty(p)$ induced by the preorder $\lesssim$. We have

$$s_0 \simeq s'_0 \ \&\ s_1 \simeq s'_1 \ \Rightarrow\ s_0 \lesssim s_1 \ \Leftrightarrow\ s'_0 \lesssim s'_1$$

Then the quotient $\mathcal{C}^\infty(p) = \mathcal{T}^\infty(p)/\simeq$, which is the set of *computations* of p, is a partially ordered set – the ordering on equivalence classes will be denoted $\sqsubseteq$.

In [3], the maximal computations (w. r. t. $\sqsubseteq$) were called *terminating*, since, roughly speaking, it does not remain anything to do after a maximal computation. More precisely, if an action is possible at some point of a maximal computation, then after a finite amount of time, this possibility disappears – either because the action has been done or because it is no longer enabled. Then for CCS the maximal computations set up a notion of *fairness*: these are the computations satisfying a *finite delay property*. For instance

$$(a^\omega \parallel b^\omega) = (\mu x.a : x \parallel \mu x.b : x) \xrightarrow{a} (\mu x.a : x \parallel \mu x.b : x) \ \cdots \ \xrightarrow{a} \ \cdots$$

is not maximal since the proved transition

$$(a^\omega \parallel b^\omega) \xrightarrow{b,\ \pi_1(\gamma_b)} (a^\omega \parallel b^\omega)$$

has a residual along the whole computation. On the other hand

$$(a+b)^\omega = \mu x.(a : x + b : x) \xrightarrow{a} \mu x.(a : x + b : x) \ \cdots \ \xrightarrow{a} \ \cdots$$

is a maximal computation. Not too surprisingly, our proof terms are similar to the labels used by Costa and Stirling in [10] to define various notions of fairness. However a maximal computation is not what is usually called (weakly or strongly) fair computation. This is so because our notion of proved transition is rather discriminating. For instance in $r = \mu x.(\alpha : x + \beta : \mathsf{nil})$, the action β has infinitely many distinct proofs (this is apparent in the infinite tree of this term): informally, at each point of choice in r, a "new" β is available. Then

$$(r \parallel \bar{\beta} : \mathsf{nil})\backslash\beta \xrightarrow{\alpha} (r \parallel \bar{\beta} : \mathsf{nil})\backslash\beta \ \cdots \ \xrightarrow{\alpha} \ \cdots$$

is a maximal computation: at each step the potential communication is different, and at each step it is discarded. There is no proved transition which is "infinitely often" or "almost always" enabled along this computation. Similarly if $q = \mu x.a\colon (\alpha\colon x + \beta\colon \mathsf{nil})$ then

$$(q \parallel \bar{\beta}\colon \mathsf{nil})\backslash\beta \xrightarrow{a} \xrightarrow{\alpha} (q \parallel \bar{\beta}\colon \mathsf{nil})\backslash\beta \cdots \xrightarrow{a} \xrightarrow{\alpha} \cdots$$

is a maximal computation.

4. Event Structures.

It is known that the posets of computations $\mathcal{C}^\infty(p)$ are complete partial orders (*cf.* [1,3]). But we can say much more: the main result of this note is that $\mathcal{C}^\infty(p)$ is the poset of configurations of an event structure. The following definition is a slight variation of Winskel's one [23] – the domain of configurations will be coherent, for inconsistency is given by a binary relation:

DEFINITION (LABELLED EVENT STRUCTURES). *An A-labelled event structure is a structure* $(E, \prec, \#, \ell)$ *where*

(i) E *is the (denumerable) set of events,*

(ii) $\prec \subseteq E \times E$ *is an irreflexive relation (i.e.* $e \prec e' \Rightarrow e \neq e'$*), the flow relation;*

(iii) $\# \subseteq E \times E$ *is a symmetric relation, the conflict relation;*

(iv) $\ell\colon E \to A$ *is the labelling function.*

Here too we denote $\sharp$ the reflexive closure of #. Note that we do *not* assume that the conflict relation is irreflexive. We shall use *self-conflicting* (or inconsistent) events, which are the events $e \in E$ such that $e \# e$, in the interpretation of the restriction operator.

We shall always draw event structures up to isomorphism, that is omitting the name of events; moreover in the figures we shall represent $e \prec e'$ by $e \rightarrowtail e'$. For instance

∇'

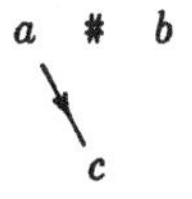

is a structure with three events e, e' and e'' respectively labelled a, b and c such that $e \prec e''$ and $e \# e'$.

In [6] we have introduced a notion of computation of an event structure, which is a labelled poset of events. This is just what Winskel calls a configuration, supplied with the causality ordering on events which holds in that configuration. To define the computations of an event structure $S = (E, \prec, \#, \ell)$ we need to introduce an *enabling* relation $F \vdash e$, for $e \in E$ and $F \subseteq E$. Let us denote by C_S the set of conflict-free subsets of E, that is:

$$F \in C_S \ \Leftrightarrow_{\text{def}} \ F \subseteq E \ \&\ \forall e, e' \in F\ \neg(e \# e')$$

We interpret $e' \prec e$ as meaning "e' is a condition for e". Then $F \vdash e$ means that F is a maximal set of non-conflicting conditions for e, that is:

$F \vdash e \quad \Leftrightarrow_{\text{def}} \quad e' \in F \Rightarrow e' \prec e$ and
$F \cup \{e\}$ is conflict-free: $F \cup \{e\} \in C_S$ and
F is closed under non-conflicting conditions for e:
$e' \prec e \ \&\ e' \notin F \Rightarrow \exists e'' \in F\ e' \# e''$

One can see that the structure $(E, C_S, \vdash)$ is what Winskel calls a *stable* event structure – where $\vdash$ is the minimal enabling relation (*cf.* [23]) – if we relax the hypothesis that the consistent sets are finite.

DEFINITION (CONFIGURATIONS). *Given an A-labelled event structure $S = (E, \prec, \#, \ell)$ a configuration of S is a set of events $F \subseteq E$ such that*

(i) F satisfies the finite causes property: for all $e \in F$ there exists $\{e_1, \dots, e_n\} \subseteq F$ such that $e_n = e$ & $\forall i\, \exists G \subseteq \{e_1, \dots, e_{i-1}\}\quad G \vdash e_i$

(ii) F is conflict-free (or consistent): $F \in C_S$

We denote by $\mathcal{F}^\infty(S)$ the set of configurations of the event structure S. This set, ordered by inclusion, has a nice property: the poset $(\mathcal{F}^\infty(S), \subseteq)$ is a finitary prime algebraic coherent poset, that is a coherent dI-domain, *cf.* [20,23] – in fact our event structures are just another concrete presentation of such domains. For F a configuration of S, we denote $\leq_F =_{\mathrm{def}} (\prec \cap (F \times F))^*$, the reflexive and transitive closure of the restriction of $\prec$ to F. Then we have:

LEMMA. *For any configuration $F \in \mathcal{F}^\infty(S)$ of S the relation $\leq_F$ is an ordering such that*

$$e \leq_F e' \Leftrightarrow \forall G \in \mathcal{F}^\infty(S)\ G \subseteq F \;\&\; e' \in G \Rightarrow e \in G$$

Moreover $G \subseteq F$ is a configuration of S if and only if it is a left-closed subset of F:

$$\forall G \subseteq F.\ G \in \mathcal{F}^\infty(S) \Leftrightarrow e \in G \;\&\; e' \leq_F e \Rightarrow e' \in G$$

The proof is given in [23]. The ordering $\leq_F$ is the (local) *causality* relation in F. The restriction $\ell\lceil F$ of the labelling ℓ to F is denoted ℓ_F.

DEFINITION (COMPUTATIONS). *Given an A-labelled event structure $S = (E, \prec, \#, \ell)$ a computation of S is a labelled poset $(F, \leq_F, \ell_F)$ where F is a configuration of S.*

We shall denote by $\mathcal{G}^\infty(S)$ the set of computations of S. The previous result allows us to regard this set as ordered by inclusion, without ambiguity since for any configuration F there is only one ordering $\leq$ and only one labelling ℓ such that $(F, \leq, \ell)$ is a computation of S. As we have shown in [6], we can define a transition relation on event structures, where at each step the performed action is a computation – that is a labelled poset. For any computation $P = (F, \leq_F, \ell_F)$ of $S = (E, \prec, \#, \ell)$, let us define the *remainder* $S[P]$ of S after P by:

$$S[P] =_{\mathrm{def}} (E', \prec', \#', \ell') \quad \text{where} \quad \begin{cases} E' = E - F \\ \prec' = \prec \cap (E' \times E') \\ e \;\#'\; e' \Leftrightarrow e \;\#\; e' \text{ or } e = e' \;\&\; \exists e'' \in F\ e \;\#\; e'' \\ \ell' = \ell\lceil E' \end{cases}$$

Then the transitions are

$$S \xrightarrow{P} S[P] \quad \text{for} \quad P \in \mathcal{G}^\infty(S)$$

There are two ways of interpreting a CCS term as an event structure: either we directly define from the syntactical materials a structure $\mathcal{S}(p)$ for each closed term p, or we define a construction on event structures for each CCS operator and interpret CCS by a morphism of algebra $\mathcal{I}^\infty$. We shall take both ways; the constructions we use are adapted from those of Winskel [22,23].

4.1 Let us first define $\mathcal{S}(p) = (\mathcal{E}(p), \prec, \#, \ell)$. The events are occurrences of possible future actions for a term, so we define the set $\mathcal{O}$ of *occurrences*. We just have to extend the syntax of proofs, allowing them to pass through a guard $a\colon p$, using the symbol $a\colon_{\{1\}}$, which will be denoted γ'_a. The syntax of occurrences is thus

$$o \ ::= \ \gamma_a \mid \gamma'_a(o) \mid \pi_0(o) \mid \pi_1(o) \mid \delta(o, o') \mid \sigma_0(o) \mid \sigma_1(o) \mid \rho_\alpha(o)$$

For instance the occurrence of the action b in $a: b: \mathsf{nil}$ is $\gamma'_a(\gamma_b)$. We extend the labelling to occurrences, in an obvious way: $\ell(\gamma'_a(o)) = \ell(o)$. Let us now define the notions of conflict and flow on occurrences. The *conflict* relation $o \# o'$ is the least symmetric relation which satisfies the following, where we denote by $\sharp$ the reflexive closure of $\#$:

(B1) $i \neq j \Rightarrow \sigma_i(o) \# \sigma_j(o')$

(B2) $o \sharp o' \Rightarrow \begin{cases} \pi_0(o) \# \delta(o', o'') \\ \pi_1(o) \# \delta(o'', o') \end{cases}$

(B3) $o \# o' \Rightarrow \begin{cases} \pi_i(o) \# \pi_i(o') \\ \sigma_i(o) \# \sigma_i(o') \\ \rho_\alpha(o) \# \rho_\alpha(o') \\ \gamma'_a(o) \# \gamma'_a(o') \end{cases}$

(B4) $\mathsf{nm}(\ell(o)) = \alpha \Rightarrow \rho_\alpha(o) \# \rho_\alpha(o)$

(B5) $o_0 \sharp o'_0$ or $o_1 \sharp o'_1$ and $(o_0, o_1) \neq (o'_0, o'_1) \Rightarrow \delta(o_0, o_1) \# \delta(o'_0, o'_1)$

$o_0 \# o_0$ or $o_1 \# o_1 \Rightarrow \delta(o_0, o_1) \# \delta(o_0, o_1)$

In the structure $S(p)$, the flow represents possible immediate precedence. Quite obviously the relation $o \prec o'$ is brought out by the action construct $a: p$ – loosely speaking $\gamma_a \prec \gamma'_a(\theta)$. More precisely $\prec$ is the least relation on $\mathcal{O}$ compatible with the occurrence constructors that satisfies the following clauses:

(C1) $\gamma_a \prec \gamma'_a(\theta)$ where θ is any proof term

(C2) $o \prec o' \Rightarrow \begin{cases} \delta(o, o'') \prec \pi_0(o') \\ \delta(o'', o) \prec \pi_1(o') \end{cases}$ and $\begin{cases} \pi_0(o) \prec \delta(o', o'') \\ \pi_1(o) \prec \delta(o'', o') \end{cases}$

(C3) $o \prec o' \Rightarrow \begin{cases} \delta(o, o_1) \prec \delta(o', o'_1) \\ \delta(o_0, o) \prec \delta(o'_0, o') \end{cases}$

The relation $\prec$ is irreflexive; note on the other hand that it is not transitive: for instance if $o_0 \prec o'_0$ and $o_1 \prec o'_1$ then $\pi_0(o_0) \prec \delta(o'_0, o_1)$ and $\delta(o'_0, o_1) \prec \pi_1(o'_1)$ but we do not have $\pi_0(o_0) \prec \pi_1(o'_1)$. Let us see some examples: in the term $r = (\alpha: \alpha: \mathsf{nil} \parallel \bar{\alpha}: \mathsf{nil})$ we have

$$\delta(\gamma_\alpha, \gamma_{\bar{\alpha}}) \prec \delta(\gamma'_\alpha(\gamma_\alpha), \gamma_{\bar{\alpha}})$$
$$\delta(\gamma_\alpha, \gamma_{\bar{\alpha}}) \# \delta(\gamma'_\alpha(\gamma_\alpha), \gamma_{\bar{\alpha}})$$

This shows that $\#$ and $\prec$ are not necessarily disjoint. The following example shows that the transitive closure of $\prec$ is not disjoint from $\smile$ (extended to occurrences in the obvious way): in the term $q = (a: \alpha: \mathsf{nil} \parallel \bar{\alpha}: b: \mathsf{nil})$ we have

$$\pi_0(\gamma_a) \prec \delta(\gamma'_a(\gamma_\alpha), \gamma_{\bar{\alpha}}) \prec \pi_1(\gamma'_{\bar{\alpha}}(\gamma_b))$$
$$\pi_0(\gamma_a) \smile \pi_1(\gamma'_{\bar{\alpha}}(\gamma_b))$$

Note also that $\prec$ is not asymmetric; for instance in the term $(\alpha: \beta: \mathsf{nil} \parallel \bar{\beta}: \bar{\alpha}: \mathsf{nil})$ we have

$$\delta(\gamma_\alpha, \gamma'_{\bar{\beta}}(\gamma_{\bar{\alpha}})) \prec \delta(\gamma'_\alpha(\gamma_\beta), \gamma_{\bar{\beta}}) \prec \delta(\gamma_\alpha, \gamma'_{\bar{\beta}}(\gamma_{\bar{\alpha}}))$$

To define the structure $S(p)$ it just remains to define the set $\mathcal{E}(p)$ of events, which is a subset of the set $\mathcal{O}$ of occurrences – it should be understood that in $S(p) = (\mathcal{E}(p), \prec, \#, \ell)$ the flow and conflict relations are the restrictions to $\mathcal{E}(p)$ of the relations we just defined on occurrences. The set $\mathcal{E}(p)$ of events of p is defined inductively as follows:

(E1) $\gamma_a \in \mathcal{E}(a\colon p)$;
if $o \in \mathcal{E}(p)$ then $\gamma'_a(o) \in \mathcal{E}(a\colon p)$;

(E2) if $o \in \mathcal{E}(p_i)$ then $\pi_i(o) \in \mathcal{E}(p_0 \parallel p_1)$;
if $o \in \mathcal{E}(p_0)$ and $o' \in \mathcal{E}(p_1)$ and $\ell(o) = \overline{\ell(o')}$, then $\delta(o, o') \in \mathcal{E}(p_0 \parallel p_1)$;

(E3) if $o \in \mathcal{E}(p_i)$ then $\sigma_i(o) \in \mathcal{E}(p_0 + p_1)$;

(E4) if $o \in \mathcal{E}(p)$ then $\rho_\alpha(o) \in \mathcal{E}(p \backslash \alpha)$;

(E5) if $o \in \mathcal{E}(p[\mu x.p/x])$ then $o \in \mathcal{E}(\mu x.p)$.

For instance if $r = (a\colon \alpha\colon \mathsf{nil} \parallel \bar{\alpha}\colon b\colon \mathsf{nil})\backslash\alpha$ then $S(r)$ may be drawn

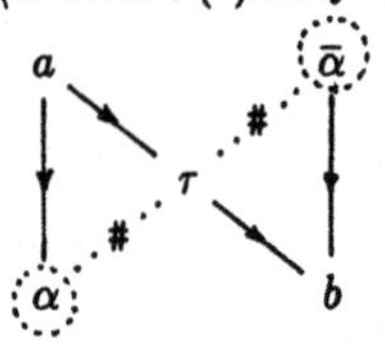

where the dotted circles around α and $\bar{\alpha}$ indicate that the corresponding events are self-conflicting. In this structure the enabling consists of (identifying the events with their labels) $\{a\} \vdash \tau$ and $\{\tau\} \vdash b$. Clearly α and $\bar{\alpha}$ cannot occur in a configuration since they are inconsistent.

4.2 On the other hand, the constructions on event structures corresponding to CCS operators are as follows:

(i) nil is the empty event structure;

(ii) if $S = (E, \prec, \#, \ell)$ then $a\colon S = (\{\varepsilon\} \cup E, \prec', \#, \ell')$ where

- $\varepsilon \notin E$
- $e \prec' e' \Leftrightarrow e \prec e'$ or $(e = \varepsilon \;\&\; \emptyset \vdash e')$
- $\ell'(\varepsilon) = a$ and $\ell'(e) = \ell(e)$ for $e \in E$;

(iii) if $S_i = (E_i, \prec_i, \#_i, \ell_i)$ for $i = 0, 1$ then $S_0 \parallel S_1 = (E, \prec, \#, \ell)$ where

- $E = (E_0 \times \{*\}) \cup (\{*\} \times E_1) \cup \{(e_0, e_1) \mid e_i \in E_i \;\&\; \ell(e_0) = \overline{\ell(e_1)}\}$

where $* \notin E_0 \cup E_1$

- $e \prec e' \Leftrightarrow e = (x, y) \;\&\; e' = (x', y')$ and $x \prec_0 x'$ or $y \prec_1 y'$

where, by convention, $* \not\prec_i z$ and $z \not\prec_i *$ for any z.

- $e \# e' \Leftrightarrow \begin{cases} e = (x, y) \;\&\; e' = (x', y') \;\&\; e \neq e' \text{ and } x \,\sharp_0\, x' \text{ or } y \,\sharp_1\, y', \text{ or} \\ e = (x, y) = e' \;\&\; x \#_0 x \text{ or } y \#_1 y \end{cases}$

where, by convention, $\neg(* \,\sharp_i\, z)$ for any z.

- $\ell(e, *) = \ell_0(e)$, $\ell(*, e) = \ell_1(e)$ and $\ell(e_0, e_1) = \tau$

(iv) if $S_i = (E_i, \prec_i, \#_i, \ell_i)$ for $i = 0, 1$ then $S_0 + S_1 = (E, \prec, \#, \ell)$ where

- $E = \{(i, e_i) \mid e_i \in E_i\}$
- $e \prec e' \Leftrightarrow e = (i, e_i) \;\&\; e' = (i, e'_i) \;\&\; e_i \prec_i e'_i$
- $e \# e' \Leftrightarrow \begin{cases} e = (i, e_i) \;\&\; e' = (i, e'_i) \;\&\; e_i \#_i e'_i \quad \text{or} \\ e = (i, e_i) \;\&\; e' = (j, e'_j) \;\&\; i \neq j \end{cases}$
- $\ell(i, e) = \ell_i(e)$.

(v) if $S = (E, \prec, \#, \ell)$ then $S\backslash\alpha = (E, \prec, \#', \ell)$ where

- $e \#' e' \Leftrightarrow e \# e'$ or $e = e' \;\&\; \mathsf{nm}(\ell(e)) = \alpha$

The interpretation $\mathcal{I}^\infty(p)$ is given by the unique continuous morphism $\mathcal{I}^\infty$ from the free algebra of infinite trees to the algebra of labelled event structures ($\mathcal{I}^\infty(\mu x.p)$ is defined by a standard fixpoint construction, *cf.* [22,6]). Let us see some examples. The structure $\mathcal{I}^\infty((\alpha : \beta : \mathsf{nil} \parallel \bar{\alpha} : \mathsf{nil}))$ may be drawn:

This example shows that $\mathcal{I}^\infty(p)$ may contain a substructure ∇' (*cf.* [6]). The interpretations of $(\alpha : a : \alpha : \mathsf{nil} \parallel \bar{\alpha} : \mathsf{nil})$ and $(a : \alpha : \mathsf{nil} \parallel \bar{\alpha} : b : \mathsf{nil})$ may be drawn respectively

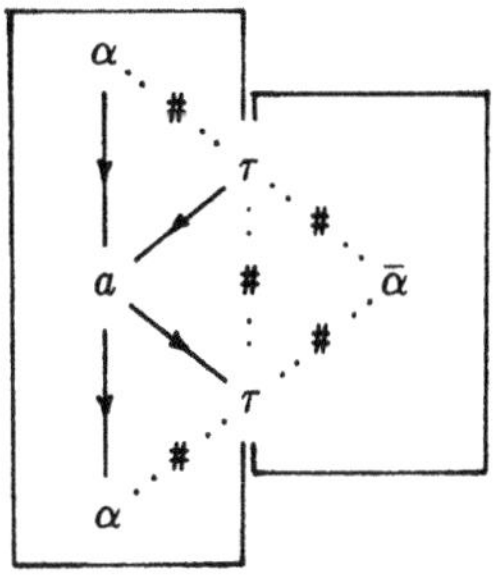

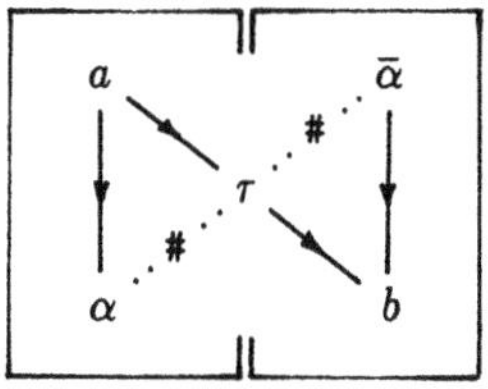

The second structure contains a substructure N and a substructure ∇, *cf.* [6]. An example, suggested by M. Nielsen, shows that $\prec^*$ is not an ordering: if we interpret $(\alpha : a : \beta : \mathsf{nil} \| \bar{\beta} : b : \bar{\alpha} : \mathsf{nil})$ we get

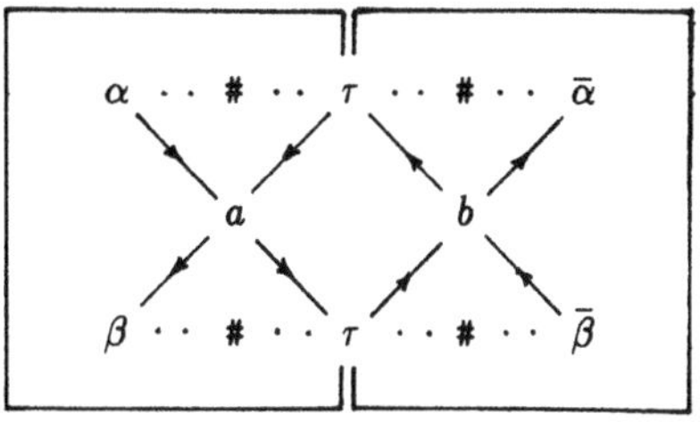

Note that if $r = (\alpha : a : \beta : \mathsf{nil} \parallel \bar{\beta} : b : \bar{\alpha} : \mathsf{nil})\backslash\alpha\backslash\beta$ then in the structure $\mathcal{I}^\infty(r)$ the enabling is such that $F \vdash e \;\Rightarrow\; F \neq \emptyset$, so that it has no configuration. The same is true for the interpretation of $(\alpha : \beta : \mathsf{nil} \parallel \bar{\beta} : \bar{\alpha} : \mathsf{nil})\backslash\alpha\backslash\beta$, where the enabling relation is empty. One can also see that in the interpretation of $((\alpha : \beta : \mathsf{nil} \parallel \bar{\alpha} : \mathsf{nil}) \parallel \alpha : \bar{\beta} : \mathsf{nil})\backslash\alpha,\beta$, there is no enabling for the β communication.

THEOREM 1. *For all closed CCS terms p the poset $(\mathcal{C}^\infty(p), \sqsubseteq)$ of computations of p is isomorphic to the poset $(\mathcal{G}^\infty(\mathcal{S}(p)), \subseteq)$ of computations of the labelled event structure $\mathcal{S}(p)$. Moreover the structure $\mathcal{S}(p)$ is isomorphic to $\mathcal{I}^\infty(p)$.*

We could prove moreover that there is an exact correspondence (as in [6]) between equivalence classes of finite computations and the pomset transitions on event structures, that is between the pomset transitions $p \xrightarrow{P} p'$ associated with the sequences of proved transitions

$$p \xrightarrow{a_1\,,\,\theta_1} p_1 \;\cdots\; p_{n-1} \xrightarrow{a_n\,,\,\theta_n} p'$$

up to permutations, and the transitions

$$\mathcal{S}(p) \xrightarrow{P} \mathcal{S}(p)[P]$$

Therefore we can say that we have given an operational meaning to the event structure semantics for CCS. This provides also for a "truly concurrent" operational semantics for CCS, which generalizes the one we have given in [6] for a restricted language. This "poset semantics" is similar to the one given, via concurrent histories, by Degano, De Nicola and Montanari in [11].

Its seems fair to say that, due to communication, the mathematical theory for CCS is not especially aesthetic. Communication may be achieved by other means, as proposed in [5,7] – but there, no mathematical theory is given. If we abandon communication, we get a more satisfactory theory: the syntax for concurrent – but non communicating – systems is

$$p \ ::= \ \mathsf{nil} \mid x \mid a : p \mid (p \parallel p') \mid (p + p') \mid \mu x.p$$

where $a \in A$, and the set A of actions does not need to have any particular structure. The operational semantics is the same, but obviously without the communication rule. Then the "permutations of transitions semantics" is exactly the semantics we have given in [6] for this calculus (if sequential composition $p\,;q$ of [6] is restricted to $p \in A$), and the corresponding constructions on event structures are much more pleasant than the ones presented here. However, as is noted in [5] and [7], the resulting calculus is too asynchronous. The next section presents a first attempt to remedy this deficiency.

5. Synchrony and Asynchrony.

In [18], Milner proposed the synchronous calculus SCCS, based on a structured set of actions – namely a commutative semigroup $(A\,,\cdot)$. The main new construction was the synchronous product $(p \times q)$. However, Milner noted in [19] that "*It was not made sufficiently clear that* SCCS *provides an asynchronous process model which stands in its own right*". To some extent, the calculus MEIJE of [4] – which is a variant of SCCS – does not suffer this defect. It was shown in [4] that, among several equivalent formulations, this calculus can be built upon two basic kinds of parallelism: interleaving $(p \mid q)$ and synchronous product $(p \times q)$. In this formulation of MEIJE, the sum is not primitive, but may be derived using communication. From now on we shall deal with this calculus, parameterized on a *free commutative semigroup* $(A^\circ\,,\cdot)$ of actions, generated by the set A of atomic actions. We let aside communication, as well as the restriction operator, which could be handled as in the previous sections, with respect to a commutative group of actions. Since we ignore communication, we need to regard sum as a primitive operator here. We shall give a so-called "non-interleaving" semantics for $(p \mid q)$, thus it is better to rename the two parallel operators *asynchronous* and *synchronous parallelism* respectively. Moreover we shall denote the synchronous parallelism by $(p \otimes q)$, in order to avoid confusion with the cartesian product, and we denote asynchronous parallelism by $(p \parallel q)$, as done so far in this paper. Therefore the syntax of our calculus for synchrony and asynchrony – let us call it **C** – is

$$p \ ::= \ \mathsf{nil} \mid x \mid a : p \mid (p \parallel p') \mid (p + p') \mid (p \otimes p') \mid \mu x.p$$

where a belongs to the set A of atomic actions. The syntax for proofs of transitions is now

$$\theta \ ::= \ \gamma_a \mid \pi_0(\theta) \mid \pi_1(\theta) \mid \sigma_0(\theta) \mid \sigma_1(\theta) \mid \kappa(\theta,\theta')$$

and the inference rules are

action	$\vdash\ a : p \xrightarrow{a\,,\,\gamma_a} p$
asynchronous parallelism 1	$p \xrightarrow{a\,,\,\theta} p'\ \vdash\ (p \parallel q) \xrightarrow{a\,,\,\pi_0(\theta)} (p' \parallel q)$
asynchronous parallelism 2	$q \xrightarrow{b\,,\,\theta'} q'\ \vdash\ (p \parallel q) \xrightarrow{b\,,\,\pi_1(\theta')} (p \parallel q')$
sum 1	$p \xrightarrow{a\,,\,\theta} p'\ \vdash\ (p + q) \xrightarrow{a\,,\,\sigma_0(\theta)} p'$
sum 2	$q \xrightarrow{b\,,\,\theta'} q'\ \vdash\ (p + q) \xrightarrow{b\,,\,\sigma_1(\theta')} q'$
synchronous parallelism	$p \xrightarrow{a\,,\,\theta} p'\ ,\ q \xrightarrow{b\,,\,\theta'} q'\ \vdash\ (p \otimes q) \xrightarrow{a \cdot b\,,\,\kappa(\theta,\theta')} (p' \otimes q')$
fixpoint	$p[\mu x.p/x] \xrightarrow{a\,,\,\theta} p'\ \vdash\ \mu x.p \xrightarrow{a\,,\,\theta} p'$

We shall not repeat the definition of the equivalence by permutations and the associated preorder: it suffices to redefine the notion of concurrency – the diamond lemma will be the same as before. In **C**, the source of concurrency is asynchronous parallelism, therefore $\smile$ is the least relation compatible with the proof constructors such that

$$\forall \theta\, \forall \theta'\ i \neq j\ \Rightarrow\ \pi_i(\theta) \smile \pi_j(\theta')$$

We still denote by $\simeq$ the permutation equivalence on sequences of (proved) transitions, and by $(\mathcal{C}^\infty(p), \sqsubseteq)$ the ordered space of computations of p. We could define an event structure $S(p)$ for each term p of **C**, as in the previous section, but it is more instructive to give the constructions on event structures which allow us to define $\mathcal{I}^\infty(p)$ for each closed term p of **C**.

As noted by Girard ([12]) there are (at least) two natural ways to combine two sets of events E_0 and E_1: either we *juxtapose* these sets, by a disjoint union $E_0 \uplus E_1$, or we form their *cartesian product* $E_0 \times E_1$. In Girard's terminology, the first kind of construction defines *additive* operators whereas the second one defines *multiplicative* operators (as a matter of fact, Girard proposes his constructions for what he calls *coherent spaces*, which are event structures without causality). For what regards the additive operators on event structures, there are three natural constructions, according to which relation, among causality, concurrency and conflict, is set between the events of E_0 and E_1. These are the constructions we used in [6], where our calculus only stands on the additive (asynchronous) side. On the other hand, one of the additive operators, asynchronous parallelism, is missing in SCCS. The construction $a : S$ is a special case of sequential composition, namely *lifting*; it is the same as for CCS, and so is $S_0 + S_1$. For what regards the construction $S_0 \parallel S_1 = (E, \prec, \#, \ell)$, it is given as follows, assuming $S_i = (E_i, \prec_i, \#_i, \ell_i)$ for $i \in \{0,1\}$:

- $E = E_0 \uplus E_1 = \{0\} \times E_0 \cup \{1\} \times E_1$
- $(i,e) \prec (j,e')\ \Leftrightarrow\ i = j\ \&\ e \prec_i e'$
- $(i,e)\ \#\ (j,e')\ \Leftrightarrow\ i = j\ \&\ e\ \#_i\ e'$
- $\ell(i,e) = \ell_i(e)$

The asynchronous parallel composition and sum are analogous to Girard's additive conjunction and additive disjunction respectively. On the other side, for what regards concurrency in the multiplicatives, Girard proposes three constructions: conjunction, disjunction and implication (*times*, *par* and *entail*, or linear implication, in Girard's terminology). We cannot see however what could be a diamond lemma if we allowed multiplicative disjunction or implication as process constructors. Moreover, our interpretation of the synchronous product, though a multiplicative one, is slightly different from Girard's multiplicative conjunction, since here the same event cannot be used twice in a computation. We define thus $S_0 \otimes S_1 = (E_0 \times E_1, \prec, \#, \ell)$ where

- $(e_0, e_1) \prec (e_0', e_1') \Leftrightarrow e_0 \prec_0 e_0'$ or $e_1 \prec_1 e_1'$

- $(e_0, e_1) \# (e_0', e_1') \Leftrightarrow \begin{cases} (e_0, e_1) \neq (e_0', e_1') \ \& \ e_0 \#_0 e_0' \text{ or } e_1 \#_1 e_1', \text{ or} \\ (e_0, e_1) = (e_0', e_1') \text{ and } e_0 \#_0 e_0 \text{ or } e_1 \#_1 e_1 \end{cases}$

- $\ell(e_0, e_1) = \ell_0(e_0) \cdot \ell_1(e_1)$

The morphism I^∞ from $\mathbf{C}$ to event structures is now fully determined. For instance the interpretation of $(a : b : \text{nil}) \otimes c : \text{nil}$ is a structure with two events e and e' labelled $a \cdot c$ and $b \cdot c$ such that $e \prec e'$ and $e \# e'$, therefore e' cannot occur in a computation of this structure. Similarly the interpretation of $(a : \text{nil} \parallel b : \text{nil}) \otimes c : \text{nil}$ consists of two events such that $e \# e'$, therefore the only two non-empty computations are $a \cdot c$ and $b \cdot c$. In both these examples, conflict arises from the *sharing* of a "sub-action". As another example, we can draw the interpretation of the term $(a : \text{nil} \parallel b : \text{nil}) \otimes (c : d : \text{nil})$ as

$$
\begin{array}{ccccc}
a \cdot c & \cdots & \# & \cdots & a \cdot d \\
\vdots & & & & \vdots \\
\# & & \prec & & \# \\
\vdots & & & & \vdots \\
b \cdot c & \cdots & \# & \cdots & b \cdot d
\end{array}
$$

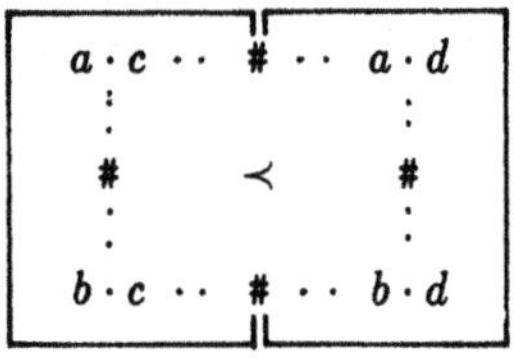

The result we had for CCS, relating the event structure semantics to permutations of transitions, holds also for $\mathbf{C}$:

THEOREM 2. *For any closed term p of $\mathbf{C}$ the poset $(C^\infty(p), \sqsubseteq)$ of computations of p is isomorphic to the poset $(\mathcal{F}^\infty(I^\infty(p)), \subseteq)$ of computations of the labelled event structure $I^\infty(p)$.*

We have announced that this result remedies the lack of synchrony one finds in CCS without communication. Let us state this point more formally: in [6] we gave a *direct* operational meaning to the event structure semantics for the asynchronous part of the language $\mathbf{C}$ (without $\otimes$). This was achieved by giving rules to prove transitions $p \xrightarrow{u} p'$ where u is a pomset, but it was not clear how to describe such transitions for $p = (q \otimes r)$. The equivalence by permutations brings an answer to this question. Indeed, the problem is the same as for CCS communication: it lies in the fact that parallel composition (either CCS composition with communication, or SCCS synchronous product) does not preserve the computations, since it may introduce conflicts.

REFERENCES

[1] G. BERRY, J.-J. LÉVY, *Minimal and Optimal Computations of Recursive Programs*, J. of ACM 26 (1979) 148-175.

[2] E. BEST, R. DEVILLERS, *Interleaving and Partial Orders in Concurrency: A Formal Comparison*, in Formal Description of Programming Concepts III, North-Holland (1987) 299-321.

[3] G. BOUDOL, *Computational Semantics of Term Rewriting Systems*, in Algebraic Methods in Semantics (M. Nivat, J.C. Reynolds, Eds), Cambridge University Press (1985) 169-236.

[4] G. BOUDOL, *Notes on Algebraic Calculi of Processes*, in Logics and Models of Concurrent Systems (K. Apt, Ed.) NATO ASI Series F13 (1985) 261-303.

[5] G. BOUDOL, *Communication is an Abstraction*, Actes du Second Colloque C³ (1987) 45-63, and INRIA Res. Rep. 636.

[6] G. BOUDOL, I. CASTELLANI, *On the Semantics of Concurrency: Partial Orders and Transition Systems*, TAPSOFT 87, Lecture Notes in Comput. Sci. 249 (1987) 123-137.

[7] G. BOUDOL, I. CASTELLANI, *Concurrency and Atomicity*, Theoretical Comput. Sci. 59 (1988) 1-60.

[8] I. CASTELLANI, M. HENNESSY, *Distributed Bisimulations*, Comput. Sci. Rep. 5-87, University of Sussex (1987).

[9] I. CASTELLANI, *Bisimulations for Concurrency*, Ph. D. Thesis, University of Edinburgh (1988).

[10] G. COSTA, C. STIRLING, *Weak and Strong Fairness in* CCS, Information and Computation 73 (1987) 207-244.

[11] P. DEGANO, R. DE NICOLA, U. MONTANARI, *Partial Ordering Derivations for CCS*, FCT 85, Lecture Notes in Comput. Sci. 199 (1985) 520-533.

[12] J.-Y. GIRARD, *Linear Logic*, Theoretical Comput. Sci. 50 (1987) 1-102.

[13] R. van GLABBEEK, F. VAANDRAGER, *Petri Net Models for Algebraic Theories of Concurrency*, Proceedings PARLE Conference, Eindhoven, Lecture Notes in Comput. Sci. 259 (1987) 224-242.

[14] G. HUET, J.-J. LÉVY, *Call-by-need Computations in Non-ambiguous Linear Term Rewriting Systems*, IRIA-LABORIA Report 359 (1979).

[15] J.-J. LÉVY, *Optimal Reductions in the Lambda Calculus*, in To H. B. CURRY: Essays on Combinatory Logic, Lambda Calculus and Formalism (J.P. Seldin, J.R. Hindley, Eds), Academic Press (1980) 159-191.

[16] A. MAZURKIEWICZ, *Concurrent Program Schemes and their Interpretations*, Aarhus Workshop on Verification of Parallel Programs, Daimi PB-78, Aarhus University (1977).

[17] R. MILNER, *A Calculus of Communicating Systems*, Lecture Notes in Comput. Sci. 92 (1980) reprinted in Report ECS-LFCS-86-7, Edinburgh University.

[18] R. MILNER, *Calculi for Synchrony and Asynchrony*, Theoret. Comput. Sci. 25 (1983) 267-310.

[19] R. MILNER, *Process Constructors and Interpretations*, IFIP 86 (1986) 507-514.

[20] M. NIELSEN, G. PLOTKIN, G. WINSKEL, *Petri Nets, Event Stuctures and Domains*, Theoret. Comput. Sci. 13 (1981) 85-108.

[21] V.R. PRATT, *Modelling Concurrency with Partial Orders*, Intern. J. of Parallel Programming 15 (1986) 33-71.

[22] G. WINSKEL, *Event Structure Semantics for CCS and Related Languages*, Daimi PB-159, Aarhus University (1983) s.a. 9th ICALP, Lecture Notes in Comput. Sci. 140 (1982) 561-576.

[23] G. WINSKEL, *Event Structures*, Advances in Petri Nets 86, Lecture Notes in Comput. Sci. 255 (1987) 325-392.

Expressibility Results for Linear-Time and Branching-Time Logics

E. M. Clarke, I. A. Draghicescu

Computer Science Department
Carnegie Mellon University
Pittsburgh, PA 15213

Abstract We investigate the expressive power of linear-time and branching-time temporal logics as fragments of the logic CTL*. We give a simple characterization of those CTL* formulas that can be expressed in linear-time logic. We also give a simple method for showing that certain CTL* formulas cannot be expressed in the branching-time logic CTL. Both results are illustrated with examples.

key words: temporal logic, linear-time logic, branching-time logic, computation tree logics, fairness

Contents

This research was partially supported by NSF grant CCR-87-226-33.

1. Introduction

Temporal Logics are widely used for reasoning about concurrent programs and reactive systems. We will model such programs by labelled state-transition graphs, called *Kripke structures* [8]. If some state is designated as the *initial* state, then the Kripke structure can be unwound into an infinite tree with that state as the root. Since paths in the tree represent possible computations of the program, we will refer to the infinite tree obtained in this manner as the *computation tree* of the program. Temporal logics may differ according to how they handle branching in the underlying computation tree. In *linear-time logic*, operators are provided for describing events along a single computation path. In a *branching-time logic* the temporal operators quantify over the paths that are possible from a given state. Each type of logic has its advantages and disadvantages. Testing satisfiability for linear-time formulas appears easier than for branching-time formulas [1], while automatic verification techniques based on *model checking* [5] have lower complexity in the case of branching-time logics.

Lamport [9] was the first to investigate the expressive power of the two types of temporal logic from the perpsective of computer science. His 1980 POPL paper discussed two logics: a simple linear-time logic and a simple branching-time logic. He showed that each logic could express certain properties that could not be expressed in the other. For example, branching-time logic cannot express certain natural fairness properties that can easily expressed in the linear-time logic. Linear-time logic, on the other hand, cannot express the possibility of event occuring at sometime in the future along some computation path, even though this can be expressed in the branching time logic. There were some difficulties with the method that Lamport used for obtaining these results, however. In particular, his approach was somewhat like comparing "apples and oranges", since the truth of a branching-time formula was determined with respect to a state while the truth of a linear-time formula was determined with respect to an individual computation path. This resulted in a notion of *expressive equivalence* that classified some satisfiable formulas as being equivalent to *false*.

Emerson and Halpern [7] provided a uniform framework for investigating this question. They formulated the problem in terms of the expressive power of various fragments of a single logic called CTL* (Computation Tree Logic), which was first discussed in [4] and [6]. This logic combines both linear-time and branching-time operators; its syntax is given in terms of *path formulas* that are interpreted over computation paths and *state formulas* that are true or false in a state. The path formulas use the standard temporal operators **G** (*always*), **F** (*sometimes*), **X** (*nexttime*), and **U** (*until*) and are like the formulas of traditional linear-time logic except that both atomic propositions and state formulas are allowed as primitive components of formulas. A state formula may be obtained from a path formula by prefixing it with a *path quantifier* that can either be an "**A**" (*for every path*) or a "**E**" (*there exists a path*). Linear-time logic (LTL) is identified with the set of all CTL* state formulas that have the form **A***f* where *f* is a path formula that does not contain any state sub-formulas. The branching-time part (called CTL) consists of all CTL* state formulas in which every linear-time operator is immediately preceded by a path quantifier.

Since both LTL and CTL consist entirely of state formulas, Emerson and Halpern were able to avoid the uniform framework problem in Lamport's paper. They showed that there exists a formula of LTL that cannot be expressed in CTL and vice versa. In general, the proofs of their inexpressibility results are quite long and complicated. For example, the proof that the linear-time formula for strong fairness is not expressible in CTL uses a complicated inductive argument that requires 3 1/2 journal pages to present. Furthermore, the technique that they use in this proof does not easily generalize to other examples. One reason for this difficulty is that formulas, which superficially appear similar, can have very different properties. For example, although **A**(**FG***p*) cannot be expressed as a CTL formula, **A**(**GF***p*) can be expressed as a CTL formula and in fact is equivalent to **AG**(**AF***p*). Likewise, the CTL formula **AG**(**AF**p) is expressible in LTL since it is equivalent to **A**(**FG**p), but the formula **AF**(**AG**p), obtained by reversing the operators **AF** and **AG**, is not expressible in LTL.

Our paper gives a simple characterization of those CTL* formulas that can be expressed in LTL. We show that a CTL* formula f can be expressed in LTL if and only if it is equivalent to the formula **A**f' where f' is obtained from f by deleting the path quantifiers. We also give a necessary condition that a CTL* formula must satisfy in order to be expressible in CTL. The condition is formulated in terms of models that are labelled state transition graphs with *fairness constraints* . Intuitively, a CTL formula is unable to distinguish between two such models when the second is obtained from the first by adding a fairness constraint that extends some constraint of the first model. By using these two results we are able to give simple arguments to show that a number of example formulas cannot be expressed in LTL (in CTL). An additional advantage of our approach is that it provides insight into why CTL and LTL have different expressive powers.

The paper is organized as follows: In Section 2 we describe the logics LTL, CTL and CTL*. Section 3 contains the characterization of those CTL* formulas that can be expressed in LTL. Section 4 gives the necessary condition that a CTL* formula must satisfy in order to be expressible in CTL. It also contains several examples that show how this result can be used to give simple proofs that certain properties like strong fairness cannot be expressed in CTL. The paper concludes in Section 5 with a discussion of some remaining open problems.

2. Computation Tree Logics (CTL, LTL, and CTL*)

There are two types of formulas in CTL*: *state formulas* (which are true in a specific state) and *path formulas* (which are true along a specific path). Let AP be the set of atomic proposition names. A state formula is either:

- A, if $A \in AP$.
- If f and g are state formulas, then $\neg f$ and $f \vee g$ are state formulas.
- If f is a path formula, then **E**f is a state formula.

A path formula is either:

- A state formula.
- If f and g are path formulas, then $\neg f$, $f \vee g$, **X**f, and f**U**g are path formulas.

CTL* is the set of state formulas generated by the above rules.

CTL ([2], [4]) is a restricted subset of CTL* that permits only branching-time operators–each path quantifier must be immediately followed by exactly one of the operators **G**, **F**, **X**, or **U**. More precisely, CTL is the subset of CTL* that is obtained if the path formulas are restricted as follows:

- If f and g are state formulas, then **X**f and f**U**g are path formulas.
- If f is a path formula, then so is $\neg f$.

Linear temporal logic (LTL), on the other hand, will consist of formulas that have the form **A**f where f is a path formula in which the only state subformulas that are permitted are atomic propositions. More formally, a path formula is either

- An atomic proposition.
- If f and g are path formulas, then $\neg f$, $f \vee g$, **X**f, and f**U**g are path formulas.

We define the semantics of CTL* with respect to a structure $M = (\mathcal{S}, \mathcal{R}, \mathcal{L})$, where

- $\mathcal{S}$ is a set of states.
- $\mathcal{R} \subseteq \mathcal{S} \times \mathcal{S}$ is the transition relation, which must be total. We write $s_1 \rightarrow s_2$ to indicate that $(s_1, s_2) \in \mathcal{R}$.
- $\mathcal{L} : \mathcal{S} \rightarrow \mathcal{P}(AP)$ is a function that labels each state with a set of atomic propositions true in that state.

Unless otherwise stated, all of our results apply only to *finite* Kripke structures.

We define a *path in M* to be a sequence of states, $\pi = s_0 s_1 \ldots$ such that for every $i \geq 0$, $s_i \rightarrow s_{i+1}$. π^i will denote the *suffix* of π starting at s_i.

We use the standard notation to indicate that a state formula f holds in a structure: $M, s \models f$ means that f holds at state s in structure M. Similarly, if f is a path formula, $M, \pi \models f$ means that f holds along path π in structure M. The relation $\models$ is defined inductively as follows (assuming that f_1 and f_2 are state formulas and g_1 and g_2 are path formulas):

1.	$s \models A$	*iff*	$A \in L(s)$.
2.	$s \models \neg f_1$	*iff*	$s \not\models f_1$.
3.	$s \models f_1 \vee f_2$	*iff*	$s \models f_1$ or $s \models f_2$.
4.	$s \models \mathbf{E}(g_1)$	*iff*	there exists a path π starting with s such that $\pi \models g_1$.
5.	$\pi \models f_1$	*iff*	s is the first state of π and $s \models f_1$.
6.	$\pi \models \neg g_1$	*iff*	$\pi \not\models g_1$.
7.	$\pi \models g_1 \vee g_2$	*iff*	$\pi \models g_1$ or $\pi \models g_2$.
8.	$\pi \models \mathbf{X} g_1$	*iff*	$\pi^1 \models g_1$.
9.	$\pi \models g_1 \mathbf{U} g_2$	*iff*	there exists a $k \geq 0$ such that $\pi^k \models g_2$ and for all $0 \leq j < k$, $\pi^j \models g_1$.

We will also use the following abbreviations in writing CTL* (CTL and LTL) formulas:

•$f \wedge g$	$\equiv$	$\neg(\neg f \vee \neg g)$	•$\mathbf{A}(f)$	$\equiv$	$\neg\mathbf{E}(\neg f)$
•$\mathbf{F}f$	$\equiv$	$true\mathbf{U}f$	•$\mathbf{G}f$	$\equiv$	$\neg\mathbf{F}\neg f$.

The necessary condition for expressability in CTL is given for Kripke structures with fairness consraints. The fairness constraints are specified in essentially the same way as the acceptance sets for Muller automata [10]. A *Kripke structure with fairness constraints* is a 4-tuple $M = (\mathcal{S}, \mathcal{R}, \mathcal{L}, \mathcal{F})$ where

- $\mathcal{S}, \mathcal{R}, \mathcal{L}$ are as in the definition of the standard Kripke structures.

- $\mathcal{F} \subseteq 2^S$ is a set of fairness constraints.

Let $M = (\mathcal{S}, \mathcal{R}, \mathcal{L}, \mathcal{F})$ be a Kripke structure with fairness constraints and $\pi = s_0 s_1 \ldots$ a path in M. Let $inf(\pi)$ denote the set of states occurring infinitely often on π. π is fair iff $inf(\pi) \in \mathcal{F}$.

The semantics of CTL* with respect to a Kripke structure with fairness constraints $M = (\mathcal{S}, \mathcal{R}, \mathcal{L}, \mathcal{F})$ is defined using only the fair paths of the structure. Thus, the relation $\models$ is defined inductively for all states s and fair paths π of M using the same clauses as in the case of ordinary CTL* except the clause 4 is replaced by

4'. $s \models \mathbf{E}(g_1)$ *iff* there exists a fair path π starting with s such that $\pi \models g_1$.

3. Linear Time

For every $n \geq 0$, let $\sim_n$ be the equivalence relation over infinite paths given by

$$\sigma' \sim_n \sigma'' \quad \textit{iff} \quad \text{for any linear formula } f \text{ with } \mathit{length}(f) \leq n,\ \sigma' \models f \iff \sigma'' \models f$$

Lemma 1 *Suppose AP, the set of atomic propositions is finite. Let M be a Kripke structure and σ a path in M. Let $n \geq 0$.*

Then there exists a prefix xy of σ such that xy^ω is an infinite path in M and $\sigma \sim_n xy^\omega$.

Proof: It will be given in the completed version.

If ϕ is a CTL* formula, we will denote by ϕ^d the linear formula obtained from ϕ by deleting all its path quantifiers. For instance, if $\phi = \mathbf{AG}(p\mathbf{U}(\mathbf{EX}q))$ then $\phi^d = \mathbf{G}(p\mathbf{U}(\mathbf{X}q))$.

For a Kripke structure M and a path $\sigma = s_0 s_1 \ldots s_{i-1}(s_i \ldots s_{j-1})$ in M we will denote by $M(\sigma)$ the single-path Kripke structure defined by σ. $M(\sigma) = (\mathcal{S}(\sigma), \mathcal{R}(\sigma), \mathcal{L}(\sigma))$, where :
$\mathcal{S}(\sigma) = \{\bar{s}_0, \ldots, \bar{s}_{j-1}\}$
$\mathcal{R}(\sigma) = \{(\bar{s}_0, \bar{s}_1), \ldots, (\bar{s}_{j-2}, \bar{s}_{j-1}), (\bar{s}_{j-1}, \bar{s}_i)\}$
$\mathcal{L}(\sigma) : \mathcal{S}(\sigma) \rightarrow 2^{AP}$, $\mathcal{L}(\sigma)(\bar{s}_k) = \mathcal{L}(s_k)$

Let us notice that for any path of the form xy^ω of a Kripke structure M and for any CTL* formula ϕ, we have

$$M(xy^\omega), \bar{s}_0 \models \phi \quad \textit{iff} \quad M(xy^\omega), xy^\omega \models \phi^d$$

Theorem 1 *Let ϕ be a CTL* state formula.*

Then ϕ is expressible in LTL iff ϕ is equivalent to $\mathbf{A}\phi^d$.

Proof: Suppose that ϕ is equivalent to $\mathbf{A}f$, where f is a linear formula. We have to show that ϕ is equivalent to $\mathbf{A}\phi^d$.

Let M be a Kripke structure and s_0 a state in M. We have :

$M, s_0 \models \phi$	iff	for all paths σ in M,	$M, \sigma \models f$
	iff	for all paths of the form xy^ω in M,	$M, xy^\omega \models f$
		(by Lemma 1)	
	iff	for all paths of the form xy^ω in M,	$M(xy^\omega), xy^\omega \models f$
	iff	for all paths of the form xy^ω in M,	$M(xy^\omega), \overline{s_0} \models \phi$
	iff	for all paths of the form xy^ω in M,	$M(xy^\omega), xy^\omega \models \phi^d$
		(as noticed above)	
	iff	for all paths of the form xy^ω in M,	$M, xy^\omega \models \phi^d$
	iff	for all paths σ in M,	$M, \sigma \models \phi^d$
		(by Lemma 1)	
	iff	$M, s_0 \models \mathbf{A}\phi^d$	

Theorem 2 *Let ϕ be a CTL* formula.*

Then ϕ is expressible in LTL iff there exists a set $\mathcal{P}$ of paths such that

$M, s_0 \models \phi$ *iff for any path σ starting in s_0, there exists a path $\sigma' \in \mathcal{P}$ such that $\sigma \sim_{length(\phi)} \sigma'$*

Proof: Suppose ϕ is expressible in LTL. Then, by Theorem 1, ϕ is equivalent to $\mathbf{A}\phi^d$. Let $\mathcal{P} = \{\sigma \mid \sigma \models \phi^d\}$.

For any Kripke structure M and any state s_0 in M, we have

$M, s_0 \models \phi$	iff	for any path σ in M starting in s_0,	$M, \sigma \models \phi^d$
	iff	for any path σ in M staring in s_0,	$\sigma \in \mathcal{P}$
	iff	for any path σ in M staring in s_0, there exists a path $\sigma' \in \mathcal{P}$ such that $\sigma \sim_{length(\phi)} \sigma'$	
		(as $\sigma \sim_{length(\phi)} \sigma'$ and $\sigma' \in \mathcal{P}$ imply, by the definition of $\mathcal{P}$, that $\sigma \in \mathcal{P}$)	

In order to prove the converse, suppose $\mathcal{P}$ is a set of paths with the following property :

$M, s_0 \models \phi$ iff for any path σ starting in s_0, there exists a path $\sigma' \in \mathcal{P}$ such that $\sigma \sim_{length(\phi)} \sigma'$.

By Theorem 1, it is enough to show that $M, s_0 \models \phi \iff M, s_0 \models \mathbf{A}\phi^d$.

Suppose that $M, s_0 \models \phi$. Then, by the above property of $\mathcal{P}$, for any path $\sigma = xy^\omega$ in M starting in s_0, there exists a path $\sigma' \in \mathcal{P}$ such that $\sigma \sim_{length(\phi)} \sigma'$. Thus, for any $\sigma = xy^\omega$, the unique path of $M(\sigma)$ is $\sim_{length(\phi)}$-equivalent with some path in $\mathcal{P}$. Using again the property of $\mathcal{P}$, we obtain that $M(\sigma), \overline{s}_0 \models \phi$. This implies that for any $\sigma = xy^\omega$, $M, \sigma \models \phi^d$. Therefore, by Lemma 1, for any path σ in M starting in s_0, $M, \sigma \models \phi^d$, which implies $M, s_0 \models \mathbf{A}\phi^d$.

Suppose $M, s_0 \models \mathbf{A}\phi^d$. In particular, for any path xy^ω in M starting in s_0, $M(xy^\omega), xy^\omega \models \phi^d$, which implies $M(xy^\omega), \overline{s}_0 \models \phi$ and therefore there exists $\sigma' \in \mathcal{P}$ such that $xy^\omega \sim_{length(\phi)} \sigma'$. Thus, by Lemma 1, for any path σ in M starting in s_0, there exists a path $\sigma' \in \mathcal{P}$ such that $\sigma \sim_{length(\phi)} \sigma'$. Therefore $M, s_0 \models \phi$.

Using the above characterizations, it is easy to check, for instance, whether $\mathbf{AFAG}p$ is expressible in LTL.

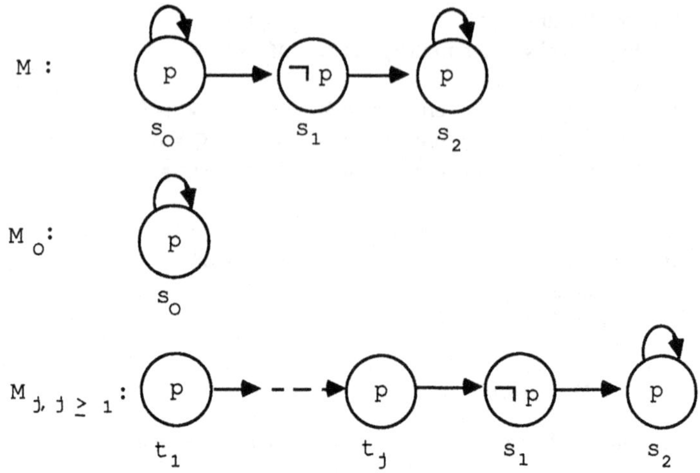

Figure 1: Kripke Structures for **AFAG**p

Consider the Kripke structures shown in Figure 1,
$M = (\{s_0, s_1, s_2\}, \{(s_0, s_0), (s_0, s_1), (s_1, s_2), (s_2, s_2)\}, L)$, where $\mathcal{L}(s_0) = \mathcal{L}(s_2) = \{p\}$ and $\mathcal{L}(s_1) = \{\neg p\}$,
$M_0 = (\{s_0\}, \{(s_0, s_0)\}, \mathcal{L}\mid_{M_0}\})$,
$M_j = (\{t_1, \ldots, t_j, s_1, s_2\}, \{(t_1, t_2), \ldots, (t_{j-1}, t_j), (t_j, s_1), (s_1, s_2), (s_2, s_2)\}, \mathcal{L}_j)$, for any $j \geq 1$,
where $calL_j(t_k) = \mathcal{L}(s_2) = \{p\}$ and $\mathcal{L}_j(s_1) = \{\neg p\}$.

It is easy to see that $M, s_0 \not\models$ **AFAG**p but $M, s_0 \models$ **A**((**AFAG**p)^d). This implies, by Theorem 1, that **AFAG**p is not expressible in LTL.

We also have $M_0, s_0 \models$ **AFAG**p and for any $j \geq 1$, $M_j, t_1 \models$ **AFAG**p but $M, s_0 \not\models$ **AFAG**p. As any path of M is $\sim_{length(\mathbf{AFAG}p)}$-equivalent to a path in some M_j, $j \geq 0$, we obtain again, by Theorem 2 this time, that **AFAG**p is not expressible in LTL.

4. Branching Time

A strongly connected component C of a directed graph $G = (\mathcal{V}, \mathcal{R})$ is *non-trivial* if either $\mid C \mid > 1$ or $C = \{c\}$ and c has a self loop—i.e. $(c, c) \in R$. If $M = (\mathcal{S}, \mathcal{R}, \mathcal{L}, \mathcal{F})$ is a Kripke structure with fairness constraints, then we can assume without loss of generality that each set $F \in \mathcal{F}$ determines a non-trivial strongly connected subgraph of the graph of M. If $\mathcal{F}$ and $\mathcal{F}'$ are two sets of fairness constraints, then we will say that $\mathcal{F}'$ *extends* $\mathcal{F}$ if $\mathcal{F}' = \mathcal{F} \cup \{F'\}$ where F' is a superset of some set $F \in \mathcal{F}$.

Theorem 3 *Let $M = (\mathcal{S}, \mathcal{R}, \mathcal{L}, \mathcal{F})$ be a Kripke structure with fairness constraints, and let $M' = (\mathcal{S}, \mathcal{R}, \mathcal{L}, \mathcal{F}')$ where the set of constraints $\mathcal{F}'$ extends $\mathcal{F}$. Then for all CTL formulas f and all states $s \in S$,*

$$M, s \models f \quad \text{iff} \quad M', s \models f$$

Proof: We prove the theorem by induction on the structure of f. We have the following cases:

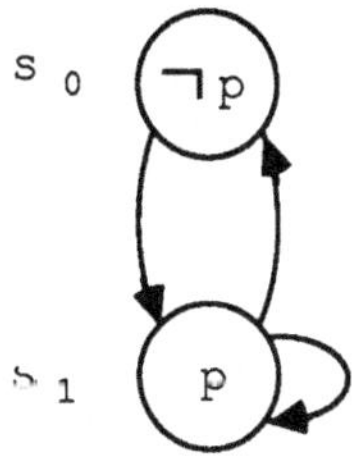

Figure 2: Kripke Structure for **A**(**FG**p)

- f is an atomic proposition: This case is trivial.
- $f = f_1 \vee f_2$ or $f = \neg f_1$: This case follows directly from the inductive hypothesis.
- $f = \mathbf{EX}f_1$ or $f = \mathbf{E}[f_1 \mathbf{U} f_2]$: We consider $f = \mathbf{E}[f_1 \mathbf{U} f_2]$; the other case is similar. We first show that the set of finite prefixes of the M-fair paths coincides with the set of finite prefixes of M'-fair paths. To see that this is true let P be the set of prefixes of M-fair paths that start at s and let P' be the corresponding set for M'. We must show that $P = P'$. It is easy to see that $P \subseteq P'$. Since $\mathcal{F} \subseteq \mathcal{F}'$, it must be the case that every M-fair path starting at s is also M'-fair path. To show that $P' \subseteq P$, let $p' \in P'$. Assume that p' is a prefix of some M'-fair path π'. If $inf(\pi') \in \mathcal{F}$, then π' is also an M-fair path and $p \in P$. If $inf(\pi') = F'$, then π must pass infinitely often through F since $F \subseteq F'$. Let p be a prefix of π' that includes all of p' and ends in a state of F. Since F determines a nontrivial strongly connected component of the graph of M, we can extend p to an M-fair path π such that $inf(\pi) = F$. Consequently, $p \in P$.

  Assume that $M, s \models \mathbf{E}[f_1 \mathbf{U} f_2]$. There must be a M-fair path π that starts at s such that for some $k \geq 0$ $M, \pi^k \models f_2$ and for all $0 \leq j < k$, $M, \pi^k \models f_1$. By the above observation there is an M'-fair path π' that has the same prefix of length k as π. By the inductive hypothesis $M', (\pi')^k \models f_2$ and for all $0 \leq j < k$, $M', (\pi')^k \models f_1$. It follows that $M', \pi' \models f_1 \mathbf{U} f_2$ and that $M', s \models \mathbf{E}[f_1 \mathbf{U} f_2]$. Exactly the same argument can be used to show that if $M', s \models \mathbf{E}[f_1 \mathbf{U} f_2]$, then $M, s \models \mathbf{E}[f_1 \mathbf{U} f_2]$.
- $f = \mathbf{EG}f_1$: If $M, s \models \mathbf{EG}f_1$ then, as any M-fair path is also a M'-fair path, it follows by the inductive hypothesis that $M, s \models \mathbf{EG}f_1$. For the other direction suppose that $M', s \models \mathbf{EG}f_1$ and let π be the M'-fair path that satisfies $\mathbf{G}f_1$. If $inf(\pi) \in \mathcal{F}$ then we are done. Otherwise $inf(\pi) = F'$ and F' is strongly connected. As $F \subseteq F'$ is also strongly connected, there exists a path π_1 starting in s such that $inf(\pi_1) = F$ and any state on π_1 is also on π. It follows π_1 is M-fair and, by inductive hypothesis, $M, \pi_1 \models \mathbf{G}f_1$, which implies $M, s \models \mathbf{EG}f_1$.

We illustrate how the Theorem 3 can be used to prove that **A**(**FG**p) is not expressible in CTL. Let M be the Kripke structure shown in Figure 2 with the fairness constraint $\mathcal{F} = \{\{s_1\}\}$. The set $\{s_1\}$ determines a non-trivial strongly connected component of the graph of M. **A**(**FG**p) is true in state s_0 of M, since all fair paths must eventually loop forever in state s_1. The set $\{s_0, s_1\}$ is certainly a superset of the set $\{s_1\}$. If we let $\mathcal{F}' = F \cup \{\{s_0, s_1\}\}$ and M' be the corresponding Kripke structure with $\mathcal{F}'$ replacing $\mathcal{F}$, then M and M' will satisfy the same CTL formulas. However, **A**(**FG**p) is not true in state s_0 of M' since the path $\pi = s_0 s_1 s_0 s_1 \ldots$ is fair, but does not satisfy the path formula **FG**p. It follows that no CTL formula is equivalent to **A**(**FG**p).

The same two Kripke structures M and M' can be used to show that the formula $\mathbf{AF}(p \wedge \mathbf{X}p)$ is not expressible in CTL. If π is a fair path in M, then p must hold almost always on π. Consequently,

$\pi \models \mathbf{F}(p \wedge \mathbf{X}p)$. It follows that $\mathbf{AF}(p \wedge \mathbf{X}p)$ is true in state s_0 of M. However, $\pi' = s_0 s_1 s_0 s_1 \ldots$ is a fair path in M' that does not satisfy $\mathbf{F}(p \wedge \mathbf{X}p)$, so $\mathbf{AF}(p \wedge \mathbf{X}p)$ is false in state s_0 of M'.

5. Conclusion

In the linear-time case we have obtained two necessary and sufficient conditions for a CTL* formula to be expressible in LTL. In the branching-time case we have only given a necessary condition for a CTL* formula to be expressible in CTL. It would be useful to have a complete characterization in this case as well. One possibility would be to prove the converse for Theorem 3, which we state as a conjecture below:

Conjecture 1 *If f is not expressible in CTL, then it is possible to find two Kripke structures $M = (\mathcal{S}, \mathcal{R}, \mathcal{L}, \mathcal{F})$ and $M' = (\mathcal{S}, \mathcal{R}, \mathcal{L}, \mathcal{F}')$ with $\mathcal{F}'$ an extension of $\mathcal{F}$ such that for some state $s \in \mathcal{S}$*

$$\textit{either} \quad M, s \models f \textit{ and } M', s \not\models f \quad \textit{or} \quad M, s \not\models f \textit{ and } M', s \models f.$$

So far, we have been unable to prove or disprove this conjecture. If it is true, we believe that the proof is likely to be difficult.

Another problem with the result in Section 4 is that it is possible to have a CTL* formula that is equivalent to *false* over ordinary Kripke models and, therefore, is expressible in CTL, but is not expressible in CTL when the models are fair Kripke structures. In order to construct such an example we use a result from [3], which shows that it is possible to completely characterize an ordinary Kripke structure in the logic CTL. Let M and M' be two Kripke structures. Let s_0 be a state of M and s_0' be a state of M'. Then M, s_0 is *CTL*-equivalent* to M', s_0' iff for all CTL* formulas f, $M, s_0 \models f$ *iff* $M', s_0' \models f$.

Given a Kripke structure M and a state s_0 of M, there is a CTL formula $C(M, s_0)$ such that $M', s_0' \models C(M, s_0)$ iff M, s_0 is CTL*-equivalent to M', s_0'. For the model shown in Figure 2, $C(M, s_0)$ is given by

$$p \wedge \mathbf{AG}(p \rightarrow (\mathbf{EX}(\neg p) \wedge \mathbf{AX}(\neg p)) \wedge \mathbf{AG}(\neg p \rightarrow (\mathbf{EX}(\neg p) \wedge \mathbf{EX}(p)).$$

Now, consider the formula $C(M, s_0) \wedge \mathbf{A}(\mathbf{FG}p)$. This formula is equivalent to *false* if the models are ordinary Kripke structures. Since $\mathbf{A}(\mathbf{FG}p)$ is false in M, s_0, it follows that if $M', s_0' \models C(M, s_0)$ then $M', s_0' \models \neg\mathbf{A}(\mathbf{FG}p)$. If we modify M to include the fairness constraint $\mathcal{F} = \{\{s_1\}\}$, then $C(M, s_0) \wedge \mathbf{A}(\mathbf{FG}p)$ is true in s_0. Thus, the formula is not equivalent to *false* over fair Kripke structures. Essentially the same argument as in the first example of Section 4 shows that it is not expressible in CTL in this case. It would be useful to have a version of Theorem 3 that applied to ordinary Kripke structures and avoided such pathological examples.

References

[1] E.M. Clarke A.P. Sistla. Complexity of propositional temporal logics. *Journal of the Association for Computing Machinery*, 32(3):733–749, July 1986.

[2] M. Ben-Ari, Z. Manna, and A. Pneuli. The temporal logic of branching time. In *8th Annual ACM Symp. on Principles of Programming Languages*, pages 164–177, 1981.

[3] M. C. Browne, E. M. Clarke, and O. Grumberg. Characterizing Kripke structures in temporal logic. In *1987 Colloquium on Trees in Algebra and Programming*, Pisa, Italy, March 1987.

[4] E.M. Clarke and E.A. Emerson. Synthesis of synchronization skeletons for branching time temporal logic. In *Proc. of the Workshop on Logic of Programs*, Springer-Verlag, Yorktown Heights, NY, 1981.

[5] E.M. Clarke, E.A. Emerson, and A.P. Sistla. Automatic verification of finite-state concurrent systems using temporal logic specifications. *ACM Transactions on Programming Languages and Systems*, 8(2):244–263, 1986.

[6] E.A. Emerson and J.Y. Halpern. Decision procedures and expressiveness in the temporal logic of branching time. *J. Comput. System Sci.*, 30(1):1–24, 1985.

[7] E.A. Emerson and J.Y. Halpern. 'Sometimes' and 'not never' revisited: on branching versus linear time. In *Proc. 10th ACM Symp. on Principles of Programming Languages*, 1983.

[8] G.E. Hughes and M.J. Creswell. *An Introduction to Modal Logic*. Methuen and Co., 1977.

[9] L. Lamport. 'Sometimes' is sometimes 'not never'. In *Seventh Annual ACM Symposium on Principles of Programming Languages*, pages 174–185, Association for Computing Machinery, Las Vegas, January 1980.

[10] D. E. Muller. Infinite sequences and finite machines. In *Proc. 4th Annual IEEE Symposium of Switching Theory and Logical Design*, pages 3–16, 1963.

Partial Orderings Descriptions and Observations of Nondeterministic Concurrent Processes

Pierpaolo Degano
Dipartimento di Informatica, Università di Pisa,
Corso Italia, 40 I-56100 Pisa ITALY, e_mail: degano@dipisa.uucp

Rocco De Nicola
Istituto di Elaborazione dell'Informazione, C.N.R.
Via S. Maria, 46 I-56100 Pisa ITALY, e_mail: denicola@icnucevm.bitnet

Ugo Montanari
Dipartimento di Informatica, Università di Pisa
Corso Italia, 40 I-56100 Pisa ITALY, e_mail: ugo@dipisa.uucp

ABSTRACT. A methodology is introduced for defining truly concurrent semantics of processes as equivalence classes of Labelled Event Structures (LES). The construction of a les providing the operational semantics of systems consists of three main steps. First, systems are decomposed into sets of sequential processes and a set of rewriting rules is introduced which describe both the actions sequential processes may perform and their causal relation. Then, the rewriting rules are used to build an occurrence net. Finally, the required event structure is easily derived from the occurrence net. As a test case, a partial ordering operational semantics is introduced first for a subset of Milner's CCS and then for the whole calculus. The proposed semantics are consistent with the original interleaving semantics of the calculus and are able to capture all and only the parallelism present in its multiset semantics. In order to obtain more abstract semantic definitions, new notions of observational equivalence on Labelled Event Structures are introduced that preserve both concurrency and nondeterminism.

Key words: Semantics of Programming Languages, Communicating Processes, Observational Equivalence, Concurrency, Nondeterminism, CCS, LES.

CONTENTS

1. Introduction

The operational semantics of a concurrent language has often been described as a labelled transition system [Kel76]. The states of the transition system are terms of the language which also denote processes. These may perform certain actions to become other processes and this fact is represented by labelled transitions between states, e.g., the transition p—α→q describes the evolution of a process p to a process q via an action α.

A drawback of this approach is that it describes transitions between global states only, and does not offer a full account of the causal dependencies between the actions (possibly due to independent/parallel subsystems) which are performed when passing from one state to another. As a result, standard transition systems permit descriptions of systems through a so-called *interleaving operational semantics*, where the operator for the parallel composition is not primitive: given any finite term containing this operator, another term always exists without it which exhibits the same behaviour. More precisely, concurrency between actions is expressed by saying that they may occur in any order; thus concurrency is reduced to interleaving plus nondeterminism. A slight variation of transition systems permits multisets of actions (or steps as they are called in the Petri Net setting [Rei85]) as possible transition labels; languages like Meije [AB84] and SCCS [Mil83] are equipped with an operational semantics based on this generalization. Multiset labels give a direct representation of the amount of "parallelism" available in the system and help in distinguishing the behaviour of systems in some obvious cases. For example, this approach can distinguish the CCS agents αNIL|βNIL and αβNIL + βαNIL. However, within this framework, causal dependencies are still not recoverable. For instance, the behaviour of αNIL|βNIL + αβNIL and that of αNIL|βNIL cannot be differentiated. Hence, labelled transition systems are capable of describing the temporal dependencies of systems, but are not capable of properly representing their causal dependencies.

Our goal is to equip concurrent languages and systems with operational definitions which also describe their causal behaviour. In this paper, we show how the centralized assumption on transition systems can be relaxed by resorting to rewriting systems which describe the independent evolution of parts of the global states. Indeed, rewriting rules can be fruitfully used as the basis for defining different types of operational semantics. In this paper we will show that they are a natural starting point for defining operational semantics in terms of a subclass of Winskel's Labelled Event Structures.

Event Structures [CFM83, MS81, NPW81 and Win80, 87] are a suggestive domain for describing true concurrency. We will use their oldest and simplest version [NPW81] which we call Conflict Event Structures, to distinguish it from more recent variants, also called Event Structures. Within this model, concurrent processes are represented via sets of event occurrences equipped with two relations which describe how events are causally related and when the occurrences of certain events exclude others. Actually, in the model we use here, events are labelled by actions; thus we will call it Conflict Labelled Event Structures, CLES for short. They turn out to be a rich and versatile model. On one hand, CLES generalize Synchronization Trees [Mil80], a model suitable for interleaving semantics. On the other hand, they are reminiscent of many partial ordering models designed for explicitly representing concurrency and causality, like those of [GR83, Wink80, Pra86, DM87]. The advantage of CLES is that the nondeterministic aspects of concurrent systems are explicitly described and both global and local choices can be naturally expressed.

In order to use CLES as a semantic domain, a further step is needed for defining a notion of abstraction from unwanted details; indeed, a semantics in terms of CLES is still very intensional. Like in the case of interleaving semantics based on synchronization trees [Mil80], the abstraction is obtained by introducing an observational equivalence on the semantic domain. Some notions of equivalence for CLES which preserve concurrency have been proposed in the literature. In [ADF87], a notion of testing equivalence for CLES is defined by mimicking the definition of those testing equivalences already introduced for labelled transition systems [DeN87]. In [BC87] a notion of observational equivalence based on bisimulation [Par81] is introduced for more general event structures. Both these equivalences preserve concurrency, but they are not completely satisfactory in that the branching structure of CLES is not always respected (see Figure 2.3 of next section for an example).

In this paper, we introduce a new class of equivalences which use bisimulation to check whether two cles's will have the same future behaviour. There is an essential difference between our CLES equivalence and those presented in the literature: unwanted identifications are avoided by keeping track of the history which has lead to a stage from where a particular step of a given computation is observed. The definition of the new class of equivalence directly derives from the equivalences based on bisimulation of Nondeterministic Measurement Systems (NMS) [DDM87a] and was originally presented in [Mon85]. These are a particular class of trees the nodes of which are labelled by what is observed of systems computations. Like the equivalences defined on NMS, the class of equivalences relation on CLES we introduce is parametric with respect to a notion of observation of computations. Interestingly enough, by choosing a notion of sequential observation we are able to obtain an interleaved semantics for CLES which essentially flattens them to synchronization trees. Moreover, by defining more sophisticated observations, different types of partial ordering semantics are captured, the more discriminating of which fully respects causality, nondeterminism and their interplay.

As an example of our approach to partial ordering semantics of concurrent systems, we provide CCS [Mil80] with an Event Structures semantics. More precisely, we will show how to associate to every CCS term an equivalence class of cles's which only differ for those details considered uninteresting at a given level of abstraction. At first, we will not present the truly concurrent semantics for whole CCS, but we will deal with a significant subset of the calculus which has been already studied in [Nie87] and called *Simple CCS*. This calculus contains no terms in which two parallel processes appear in a choice or recursion context. For example, we shall not provide a truly concurrent semantics for the agent (αNIL | βNIL) + γNIL or rec x. (αNIL | βNIL). Afterward, we will discuss the necessary modifications to our rules in order to deal with the whole calculus. Restricting our attention to *Simple CCS*, enables us to concentrate on the essence of our approach. The simplicity of the construction should permit separating our concerns, and thus an easier understanding of our general approach to partial ordering semantics.

Like in the traditional interleaving semantics, we follow the Structured Operational Semantics (SOS) approach [Plo81] for describing the new operational semantics for both Simple CCS and the full calculus, and describe the evolution of systems in a syntax-driven way. Since we aim at describing also causal relations, a *rewriting system* is introduced, rather than a transition system. It relates sets of sequential (sub)processes of CCS agents, rather than their whole global states. Sequential processes are obtained by decomposing CCS agents, and the actual relation describes both the actions the sequential processes may perform and their effects.

In order to build cles's from the rewriting rules we follow [DDM88b]. We took advantage of the fact that this operational semantics may be used to associate Condition/Event Systems [DDM88] or one-safe Petri Nets [Old87] to CCS, and of the fact that Occurrence Nets [NPW81] can be seen as behaviours of systems. Indeed, occurrence nets can be easily obtained by unfolding nets, and the unfolding uniquely determines an event structure; it is sufficient to strip the conditions away. It is worth noting that the construction of the occurrence net is not essential; it could be skipped at the price of a much more complicated construction which builds the cles directly from the rewritings.

After the presentation of the rewriting rules for Simple CCS and the construction of the cles's from them, we discuss the adequacy of the new semantics. It is checked against the two requirements which we proposed in [DDM88] to make less arbitrary the choice of a truly concurrent semantics for a language previously equipped with an interleaving and/or a multiset semantics. Our requirements are that:

i) the interleaving semantics is retrievable from the true concurrent semantics;
ii) the true concurrent semantics captures all and only the parallelism present in the (multiset semantics of the) language.

We will show that the CLES semantics of Simple CCS satisfies criterion i) by considering the identifications of simple agents induced by the strong bisimulation within the two semantics. We will show that two agents are identified in the original interleaving transition system if and only if they are identified by the CLES semantics when interleaving observations are used. For proving that also criterion ii) is satisfied, we compare our semantics with a new transition system for CCS which precisely defines the multisets of independent actions that agents may perform, in the spirit of SCCS [Mil83] and Meije [AB84]. We will prove that a set of concurrent actions can take place if and only if there is a corresponding derivation in the multiset transition system. Of course, the statement itself of ii) assumes we agree that the multiset transition system expresses all the parallelism of a CCS agent; however the rules for SCCS and Meije have stirred little controversy, and in fact it is difficult to conceive, as multiset semantics of CCS, anything different from what we propose.

The paper will proceed by showing that it is not possible to straightforwardly extend the semantics presented for the simple calculus to the full one. Indeed, while property i) would still hold, property ii) would not be satisfied: there are terms whose "simple" semantics does not always exhibit a truly concurrent behaviour. The literature reports possible ways of defining semantics of full CCS which give a faithful account of concurrency [DDM88, 88a, Old87]. In the last part of the paper, we will briefly discuss these approaches and then present a new semantics which relies on a notion of atomic actions.

The basic idea is that both choice operators and recursive definitions operationally consist of two different steps. In the former case, one of the two alternatives has first to be chosen and the actual actions can then be performed. In the latter case, the recursive definition has to be unwind and only then actions can occur. Thus, we introduce a new kind of silent moves which processes can perform for choosing between two alternatives or unwinding recursive definitions. These silent moves are eventually hidden within those actions which could not take place without them, thus leading to sequences of actions which we will consider as atomic. It is important to notice that talking of actions which are essential for the execution of other is only meaningful if the semantic model permits recovering the causal relations among events. Hence, the idea of atomic actions can be easily exploited within a partial ordering based semantics but this would not be possible within an interleaving or a multiset approach without resorting to explicit mechanisms [GMM88].

It is worth noting that all the equivalences and the comparisons of the paper have been carried on by resorting to quite a demanding bisimulation. Silent τ-actions are considered to be always visible; this assumption led to strong observational equivalences. However, more abstract equivalences that forget τ's can be easily obtained by modifying our observation functions. Actually, weak observational equivalences are obtained by ignoring the events labelled by τ when defining the observation functions, yet keeping them in the observed cles.

The paper is organized as follows. In Section 2, the relevant definitions of Conflict Labelled Event Structure and the new class of observational equivalences are introduced and the relationships between the equivalences are discussed. In Section 3, the CLES semantics for Simple CCS is presented. Its adequacy and possible extensions are discussed in Section 4. Finally, Section 5 contains the new semantics for CCS based on atomic actions together with a discussion of its adequacy. The relevant notions of CCS and of Occurrence Nets are relegated in the Appendix. There, we present both the interleaving and the multiset transition systems for the calculus and the definition of the interleaving strong observational equivalence. Most of the proofs are sketched, they either have appeared or will appear in other papers.

2. Event Structures, Observations and Equivalences

The basic model we will use for describing processes are *Event Structures* as proposed in [NPW81]. Often one is interested only in the types of events; because of this a function is introduced to label events with action names, thus obtaining *Labelled Event Structures* (LES). The actions are used to identify the external aspect of the rôle a process plays when an event happens. Since different event occurrences can "look the same", the labelling function may associate the same label to different events.

Throughout the paper we only consider *Conflict Labelled Event Structures* (CLES), a subset of the original model which is sufficient to describe concurrent systems [Win82, Win85]. This subclass includes only those les's which have at most a countable set of events and relies on the relations of partial ordering and conflict, rather than on the general notions of *enabling condition* and *configuration*. A process is then represented by a set of labelled events equipped with the relations of partial ordering and conflict which describe how events are causally related and when the occurrence of certain events excludes others.

In this section, we shall first recall the basic notions of CLES, then we will introduce various ways of observing their computations and a machinery which, by exploiting these observations, permits identifying of those event structures which "look the same" to chosen observers. We will define three observational equivalences for Event Structures which rely on the notion of bisimulation [Par81] in much the same fashion as observational equivalence for Synchronization Trees [Mil80].

2.1. Definition (*The basic model*)

Let Λ be a countable set of actions, a *conflict labelled event structure* is a quadruple
$L = (\mathbf{E}, \leq, \#, l)$, where:

i) $(\mathbf{E}, \leq)$ is a partial ordering of events, such that for all $e \in \mathbf{E}$, $[e] = \{e' \in \mathbf{E} \mid e' \leq e\}$ is finite;

ii) #, the conflict relation, is a symmetrical, irreflexive binary relation on $\mathbf{E}$.
is hereditary, i.e., $e \# e'$ and $e' \leq e''$ implies $e \# e''$.

iii) $l: \mathfrak{E} \to \Lambda$ is a labelling function from events to actions. ♦

The set of all cles's will be denoted by CLES; isomorphic cles's will be identified.

2.2. Definition

Two cles's are identified if and only if there exists a label- and order- and conflict-preserving bijection between them. ♦

2.3. Notation

Let $L = (\mathfrak{E}, \leq, \#, l)$, $e', e'' \in \mathfrak{E}$ with $e' \neq e''$, and $\mathfrak{E}' \subseteq \mathfrak{E}$

i) we let $co = \mathfrak{E} \times \mathfrak{E} - \leq - \geq - \#$, where - denotes set difference;

ii) we write $co(\mathfrak{E}')$ if and only if e' co e'' for all $e \in \mathfrak{E}'$;

iii) two events are in either relation:

- $e' \leq e''$, i.e., e' *causes* e'';
- $e'' \leq e'$, i.e., e'' *causes* e';
- $e' \# e''$, i.e., e' and e'' are *mutually exclusive*;
- e' co e'', i.e., e' and e'' are *concurrent*. ♦

2.4. Definition

Let $L = (\mathfrak{E}, \leq, \#, l)$; a subset $\mathfrak{E}'$ of $\mathfrak{E}$ is

i) *left closed* if $e \in \mathfrak{E}'$ and $e' \leq e$ implies $e' \in \mathfrak{E}'$;

i) *conflict free* if for every $e, e' \in \mathfrak{E}'$ not($e \# e'$);

iii) is a *computation* if it is left closed and conflict free. ♦

In order to use CLES as a semantic domain, a further step is needed for defining a way of abstracting from unwanted details. Indeed, a semantics in terms of CLES is still very intensional; as was the case for the interleaving semantics based on synchronization trees, we need to define an equivalence relation on the model. When defining equivalences on synchronization trees, care was taken not to identify those processes with a different branching structure. When considering event structures, we need also to be careful about respecting the causal dependencies between actions and the interplay of causality and branching.

The definition of the new equivalences for CLES is directly derived by that of [DDM87a] and was originally presented in [Mon85]. In that paper a general framework for defining behavioural equivalences is introduced, based on Nondeterministic Measurement Systems (NMS), a particular class of trees the nodes of which are labelled by what is observed of systems computations. Roughly speaking, in our case the labels of the nodes correspond to observation of CLES computations. As in [DDM87a], the equivalence relation for CLES we introduce is parametric with respect to a notion of observation of CLES computations (called also configuration in [Win87]) and relies on the bisimulation approach.

Generally, two processes E_1 and E_2 are considered as equivalent if and only if there exists a relation $\mathfrak{R}$, called *bisimulation*, which contains the pair $\langle E_1, E_2 \rangle$ and only pairs of processes which are able to perform computations which permit the same observations (whatever these are: strings, sequences of multisets, labelled partial orderings) evolving to equal (up to $\mathfrak{R}$) processes. In order to be able to fully capture the interplay between nondeterminism and concurrency we cannot just follow this approach. Our approach differs in one important aspect from the usual definition based on bisimulation. Whenever processes perform a step we need to use also information about the actions they have performed before (their past) and compare their computations up to the next states.

Because of this, we introduce the class of *Extended CLES*, which are pairs consisting of a cles and a sequence of events keeping track of all the events whose actions have been observed up to a given stage of the observations, i.e. the past of the les. The latter will be represented as an ordering of events (*mixed ordering*) which keeps into account both the causal dependencies between events and their generation ordering (see also [DDM88a]). We also introduce an observation function which, provided with the past of an extended cles, yields an element of the chosen semantic domain of the observation function.

2.5. Definition (*Computations and generation orderings*)

Let $L = (\mathbf{E}, \leq, \#, l)$ be a cles, and s, s_1, s_2, s_3 be sequences of events of L without repetitions,

i) s *represents a computation* $\mathbf{E}'$ of L if and only if $\mathbf{E}'$ consists of all the events in s, and $s = s_1e_1s_2e_2s_3$ implies $e_1 \leq e_2$ or e_1 co e_2;

ii) if s represents a computation $\mathbf{E}'$, the total ordering it imposes on $\mathbf{E}'$ will be called *generation ordering*;

iii) given a sequence s_1 which represents a computation, it *extends* s if and only if $s_1 = ss_2$. ♦

2.6. Definition (*Orderings of events*)

Let Λ be a countable set of *event labels*.

i) A *partial ordering (po) of events* is a triple $h = \langle S, l, \leq \rangle$, where
   - S is a set of *events*;
   - $l : S \to \Lambda$ is a *labelling function*;
   - $\leq$ is a partial ordering relation on S, called *causal relation*;

ii) A *total ordering (to) of events* is a po of events $t = \langle S, l, \underline{\ll} \rangle$ such that $\underline{\ll}$ is total;

iii) A *mixed ordering (mo) of events* is a quadruple $d = \langle S, l, \leq, \underline{\ll} \rangle$, where $\langle S, l, \leq \rangle$ is a po and $\langle S, l, \underline{\ll} \rangle$ is a to of events such that $\leq \subseteq \underline{\ll}$. ♦

Similarly to cles's, also isomorphic orderings of events will be identified.

2.7. Definition

Two orderings of events are identified if and only if there exists a label- and order-preserving bijection between them. ♦

Note that the definition above permits writing a to of events $\langle S, l, \underline{\ll} \rangle$ as a sequence of event labels $s = l(e_1)\ldots l(e_n)$, where $e_i \underline{\ll} e_j$, $i \leq j$.

2.8. Definition (*Extended CLES and observation functions*)

Let $L = (\mathbf{E}, \leq, \#, l)$ be a cles,

i) An *extended cles* is a pair $\langle L, s \rangle$, where L is a cles, and s is a sequence of events representing one of its computations;

ii) $past\langle L, s \rangle = \langle S, l', \leq', \underline{\ll} \rangle$ where S consists of all the events in s; l' and $\leq'$ are the obvious restriction of l and $\leq$; finally $\underline{\ll}$ is the total ordering of s.

iii) Given a domain of observations D, an observation function is a function

obs: Extended CLES $\rightarrow$ D. ♦

We are now ready to introduce our class of equivalences; it is based on bisimulation and is parametric with respect to the observation function **obs**.

2.9. Definition (*Observational Equivalences for CLES*)
Given two cles's L and L' and an observation function **obs**, we have that L *is obs-bisimilar to* L', written as $L \cong_{obs} L'$, if and only if $\langle L, \varepsilon \rangle \approx_{obs} \langle L', \varepsilon \rangle$, where $\approx_{obs}$ is the maximal fixed point of the following function.

Let Ψ be the function over binary relations S between extended cles's defined as follows:
$\langle\langle L, s\rangle, \langle L', s'\rangle\rangle \in \Psi(S)$ if and only if

- **obs**(*past*$\langle L, s\rangle$) = **obs**(*past*$\langle L', s'\rangle$);
- for every sequence s_1 of events of L which extends s, there exists a sequence s'_1 of L' which extends s' such that $\langle\langle L, s_1\rangle, \langle L', s'_1\rangle\rangle \in S$;
- for every sequence s'_1 of events of L' which extends s', there exists a sequence s_1 of L which extends s such that $\langle\langle L, s_1\rangle, \langle L', s'_1\rangle\rangle \in S$. ♦

Actually, the observation function **obs** can be as abstract as needed. It might simply keep track of the labels of the events of a configuration and of their generation ordering, thus reducing CLES to an interleaving model. But it might also record the causal relations between events or, even more, both their causal relation and their generation ordering. Correspondingly, we define below three observation functions. The first of them (int) enables us to compare our semantics with interleaving one. The second observation function (po) leads to identifications which respect the interplay between nondeterminism and causality. The third one (mo) is sufficiently robust to preserve equivalence on CLES also when actions are refined into more elementary ones.

2.10. Definition (*Observation of the past*)
Let $L = (\mathfrak{E}, \leq, \#, l)$ be a cles; s be a sequence of events representing a computation of L and *past*$\langle L, s\rangle$ = $\langle S, l, \leq, \underline{\ll}\rangle$. We define three observation functions as follows:

i) *from CLES to sequences of actions or Labelled Total Orderings:*

int($\langle S, l, \leq, \underline{\ll}\rangle$) = $\langle S, l, \underline{\ll}\rangle$,

ii) *from CLES to Labelled Partial Orderings:*

po($\langle S, l, \leq, \underline{\ll}\rangle$) = $\langle S, l, \leq\rangle$;

iii) *from CLES to Labelled Mixed Orderings:*

mo($\langle S, l, \leq, \underline{\ll}\rangle$) = $\langle S, l, \leq, \underline{\ll}\rangle$. ♦

The following proposition clarifies the increasingly discriminating power of the three observation functions above, and can be easily proved to hold by noting that the sequences which represent computations of a cles L induce all and only the total orderings which result from the linearizations of the partial ordering ≤ of L.

2.11. Proposition

Given two CLES L, L', we have that

i) $L \cong_{mo} L'$ implies $L \cong_{po} L'$ implies $L \cong_{int} L'$;

ii) $L \cong_{int} L'$ does not imply $L \cong_{po} L'$ does not imply $L \cong_{mo} L'$. ♦

The examples of Figure 2.1 provide the necessary counterexamples to part (ii) of the above proposition. We have that the interleaving based equivalence identifies two concurrent events with their nondeterministic interleavings and that po and mo observations provide us with more discriminating power than the interleaving one. Graphically, the events of a cles will be represented by labelled dots, the conflict relation by arcs labelled by #, and the causal relation by its Hasse diagram growing downwards. Moreover, thanks to the hereditarity assumption, we will draw only the initial conflicts and not the inherited ones. As we will see in Section 5, the three cles's of Figure 2.1 correspond to the following CCS agents

$E_1 = \alpha NIL|\beta NIL$, $E_2 = \alpha NIL|\beta NIL + \alpha\beta NIL$, and $E_3 = \alpha\beta NIL + \beta\alpha NIL$.

In passing, it is worth noting that the same figure shows that po and mo observation functions are the basis for defining a semantics which is more detailed than a multiset based one. Indeed, a semantics based on multisets would identify the cles's corresponding to agents E_1 and E_2.

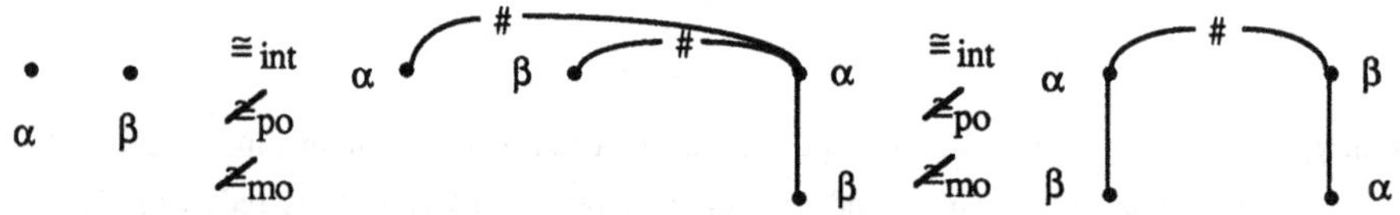

Figure 2.1
Three cles's.

Figure 2.2 gives evidence that the mo observation function is indeed more powerful than the po one. This example was shown to us by Alex Rabinovich whom we would like to thank for prompting us to reconsider the notion of mixed ordering of [DDM88a] as a possible observation. It has now been shown [GG89] that the equivalence based on mo observations is resistant to action refinement, i.e. to the replacement of all events labelled by the same actions by a conflict-free cles. Instead, po equivalence does not even preserve splitting of actions. For example, if we split all events labelled by α in the two cles's of Figure 2.2. i.e. if we replace each of them with a pair of causally related events labelled α_1 and α_2, we obtain two cles's which are not po equivalent anymore.

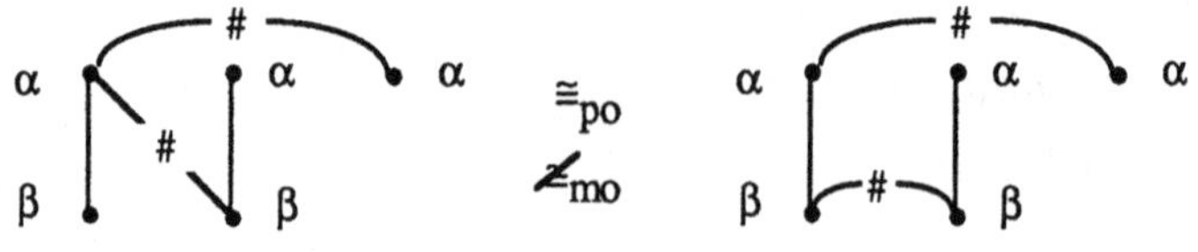

Figure 2.2.
Two cles's which are po, but not mo equivalent

Some considerations are in order for relating our approach to CLES equivalences with that of [BC87] and [DDM88a] and for motivating the introduction of Extended CLES. Had we defined the equivalence on CLES without the (past) history of the actual step, we would have identified some structures which on reasonable grounds should be considered as different. For example the two cles's of Figure 2.3 would be considered as equivalent. In Section 5, we will show how to generate them starting from the CCS terms

$\alpha.(\beta.NIL+\gamma.NIL) + \alpha.NIL|\beta.NIL + \alpha.\beta.NIL$ and

$\alpha.(\beta.NIL+\gamma.NIL) + \alpha.NIL|\beta.NIL.$

We claim that these agents should be differentiated whenever causal dependencies are felt as important. Indeed, the first agent may *cause* via an α either (β.NIL+γ.NIL) or just β.NIL, while the second has no choice.

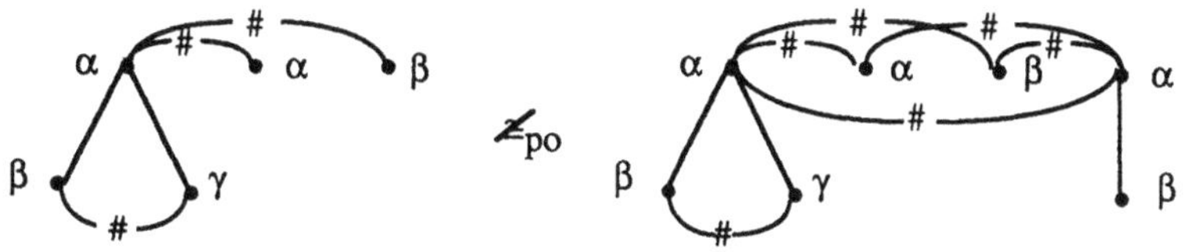

Figure 2.3.
Two cles's which are not po equivalent.

3. Truly Concurrent Semantics for Simple CCS

In this section, we will show how to associate an event structure to CCS agents. Indeed, at first, we will not consider the whole language; for didactic reason we will restrict our attention to a significant subset of CCS which does not permit terms in which the operator for parallel composition appears in a + or rec context. Thus, we consider the class of *simple agents* as defined in [Nie87]. In the following sections our approach will be extended to the whole calculus.

First, a rewriting system will be defined, from which the possible concurrency among the actions performed by agents are recoverable. Then, the rewriting rules will be used as the starting point for defining the occurrence net, a "sequential interpretation" of which can be proved isomorphic to the standard operational semantics of CCS. Finally, the wanted cles will be obtained from the occurrence net by simply forgetting its conditions.

3.1. Definition (*Simple Agents*)
The set S of simple agents, expressed in terms of sequential agents F, is generated by the following BNF-like grammar

$S ::= F \mid S\backslash\alpha \mid S[\phi] \mid S|S \mid x$

$F ::= NIL \mid \mu S \mid F+F \mid rec\ x.\ F.$ ♦

The set S is clearly a subset of the set of CCS agents presented in the Appendix. Although in this section we deal with simple agents only, our definitions will cover the whole language, whenever possible. This is because it is easier to give structural definitions for the whole language due to its more compact syntactical definition, and because definitions can be directly reused in the following sections. Thus, we will use the same notation of the Appendix, e.g. E will denote also a simple agent.

We now present a new set of inference rules for Simple CCS which define a set of rewriting rules relating parts of simple agents, rather than whole global states. Agents are decomposed into sets of sequential processes, called grapes, and the rewriting rules not only tell the actions an agent E may perform, but also which sequential processes of E actually moves. The rewriting rules have the form $I_1 -\mu\rightarrow I_2$, and their intuitive meaning is that the set of grapes I_1 may become the set I_2 by performing the action μ. The new axioms and inference rules are in direct correspondence with the interleaving based ones presented in the Appendix. The next definitions introduce grapes and the decomposition function. Since these definitions will be needed also in Section 5 they are given for the whole language.

3.2. Definition (*defining CCS sequential processes*)

A **grape** is a term defined by the following BNF-like grammar

$$G ::= NIL \mid \mu E \mid E + E \mid rec\ x.\ E \mid id|G \mid G|id \mid G\backslash\alpha \mid G[\phi]$$

where E, $\backslash\alpha$ and $[\phi]$ have the standard CCS meaning.

We will use I, I_1, I_2,... to denote sets of grapes, and g, g_1, g_2,... to denote single grapes. ♦

Intuitively speaking, a grape represents a subagent of an agent, together with its access path. The latter is used to take into account the environment in which sequential processes operate. We have an operator on grapes for each CCS operator and keep the same name for all operators apart for parallel composition. This is replaced by two unary operators, |id and id|, which are used as tags for recording that there are other processes which can perform actions concurrently with those of the given sequential process. An agent can be decomposed by the following function dec into a set of grapes.

3.3. Definition (*decomposing CCS agents into sequential processes*)

Function dec decomposes a CCS agent into a set of grapes and is defined by structural induction as follows:

$dec(NIL) = \{NIL\}$ $\qquad$ $dec(\mu E) = \{\mu E\}$

$dec(E\backslash\alpha) = dec(E)\backslash\alpha$ $\qquad$ $dec(E[\phi]) = dec(E)[\phi]$

$dec(E_1+E_2) = \{E_1+E_2\}$ $\qquad$ $dec(rec\ x.\ E) = \{rec\ x.\ E\}$.

$dec(E_1|E_2) = dec(E_1)|id \cup id|dec(E_2)$ ♦

We understand constructors $\backslash\alpha$, $[\phi]$ and |id as extended to operate on sets elementwise, e.g., $I\backslash\alpha = \{g\backslash\alpha \mid g \in I\}$. Note that the decomposition stops when an action, a sum or a recursion is encountered, since these are considered as atomic sequential processes.

3.4. Example

$dec(((\alpha NIL+\gamma NIL)|\beta\bar{\gamma}NIL)\backslash\gamma) = \{((\alpha NIL+\gamma NIL)|id)\backslash\gamma,\ (id|\beta\bar{\gamma}NIL)\backslash\gamma\}$ ♦

3.5. Definition

A set I of grapes is *complete* if there exists a CCS agent E such that dec(E) = I. ♦

3.6. Property (*complete sets of grapes are isomorphic to CCS agents*)

Function dec is injective and thus defines a bijection between CCS agents and complete sets of grapes. ♦

The inverse of function dec is standard unification, provided that distinct variables are substituted for each occurrence of id, and that $\{\mu E\}$, $\{E_1+E_2\}$ and $\{\text{rec } x.\ E\}$ are considered as atomic. In other words, the most general unifier of a complete set of grapes I is the CCS agent of which I is the decomposition. Note also that complete sets of grapes can be used to represent the *global states* of the system.

Below we define our new partial ordering rewriting relation which is given in the SOS style. The operator - denotes set difference, and is defined only if its second argument is a subset of the first one.

3.7. Definition (*partial ordering rewriting relation*)

The *partial ordering rewriting relation* $I_1 \text{—}\mu\!\rightarrow I_2$ is defined as the least relation satisfying the following axiom and inference rules

act) $\{\mu E\} \text{—}\mu\!\rightarrow \text{dec}(E)$

res) $I_1 \text{—}\mu\!\rightarrow I_2$ *and* $\mu \notin \{\alpha, \alpha^-\}$ *imply* $I_1\backslash\alpha \text{—}\mu\!\rightarrow I_2\backslash\alpha$,

rel) $I_1 \text{—}\mu\!\rightarrow I_2$ *implies* $I_1[\phi] \text{—}\phi(\mu)\!\rightarrow I_2[\phi]$

sum) $\{E_1\} \text{—}\mu\!\rightarrow I_2$ *implies* $\{E_1+E\} \text{—}\mu\!\rightarrow I_2$ *and* $\{E+E_1\} \text{—}\mu\!\rightarrow I_2$

com) $I_1 \text{—}\mu\!\rightarrow I_2$ *implies* $I_1|\text{id} \text{—}\mu\!\rightarrow I_2|\text{id}$ *and* $\text{id}|I_1 \text{—}\mu\!\rightarrow \text{id}|I_2$

$I_1 \text{—}\lambda\!\rightarrow I_2$ *and* $I'_1 \text{—}\lambda^-\!\rightarrow I'_2$ *imply* $I_1|\text{id} \cup \text{id}|I'_1 \text{—}\tau\!\rightarrow I_2|\text{id} \cup \text{id}|I'_2$

rec) $\{E_1[\text{rec } x.\ E_1/x]\} \text{—}\mu\!\rightarrow I_2$ *implies* $\{\text{rec } x.\ E_1\} \text{—}\mu\!\rightarrow I_2$. ♦

We can now comment on our axiom and rules. In axiom **act)**, a single grape is rewritten as a set of grapes, since the occurrence of the action makes explicit the (possible) parallelism of E. The rules **res)** and **rel)** and the first two rules for **com)** simply say that if a set of grapes I_1 can be rewritten as I_2 via μ, then the access paths of the grapes in I_1 and I_2 can be combined with either path constructors $.\backslash\alpha$, $.[\phi]$, .|id or id|., and still obtain a rewriting rule, labelled, say, by μ'. Clearly, when dealing with restriction μ' is μ, but the inference is possible only if $\mu \notin \{\alpha, \alpha^-\}$; in **rel)** μ' is $\phi(\mu)$ and in the first two rules of **com)** μ' is simply μ. The third rule for **com)** is just the synchronization rule. The rules for **sum)** and **rec)** are similar to those of the original interleaving transition system; this is because we are dealing with simple agents only, and both summands of + and the body of rec are always sequential agents. We will see in the next section that these inference rules cannot be easily extended when the whole calculus is considered.

3.8. Example (*Example 3.4 continued*)

The rewriting rules of the simple agent of Example 3.4. are

$r_1 = \{((\alpha\text{NIL}+\gamma\text{NIL})|\text{id})\backslash\gamma\} \text{—}\alpha\!\rightarrow \{(\text{NIL}|\text{id})\backslash\gamma\}$

$r_2 = \{(\text{id}|\beta\gamma^-\text{NIL})\backslash\gamma\} \text{—}\beta\!\rightarrow \{(\text{id}|\gamma^-\text{NIL})\backslash\gamma\}$

$r_3 = \{((\alpha\text{NIL}+\gamma\text{NIL})|\text{id})\backslash\gamma,\ (\text{id}|\gamma^-\text{NIL})\backslash\gamma\} \text{—}\tau\!\rightarrow \{(\text{NIL}|\text{id})\backslash\gamma,\ (\text{id}|\text{NIL})\backslash\gamma\}$. ♦

3.9. Proposition (*asynchrony of the partial ordering rewriting relation*)
If I_1—μ→I_2 is a rewriting rule, then for any set of grapes I_3 with $I_3 \cap I_1 = \emptyset$ and $I_1 \cup I_3$ complete, we have that $I_2 \cup I_3$ is complete and $I_3 \cap I_2 = \emptyset$.

Proof. Immediate by induction on the structure of the proof of the rewriting. ♦

The proposition above amounts to saying that the initial set of grapes of a rewriting rule can always be seen as a part of a global state. Moreover, rewritings are independent of those grapes which are concurrent with the rewritten ones; hence the same rules can be used in many different global contexts.

3.10. Proposition (*correspondence between interleaving transitions and partial ordering rewritings*)
E_1—μ→E_2 is an interleaving transitions if and only if there exist a rewriting rule I_1—μ→I_2 and a set of grapes I_3 such that dec(E_1) = $I_1 \cup I_3$ and dec(E_2) = $I_2 \cup I_3$.

Proof. Given a rewriting rule or a derivation, use the structure of its deduction to obtain the other one. ♦

Our operational semantics in terms of CLES for an agent E is obtained from the rules above. First an occurrence net is generated, and then its conditions are dropped to get a cles. Actually, the intermediate step consisting in defining Occurrence Nets could be skipped, at the price of a much more complicated construction. A more intensional semantics can be found in [DDM87b] where, starting from the same set of rewriting rules, a Condition/Event system is built which generalizes CCS transition system. Actually, sequential processes are conditions; decompositions of CCS agents are cases; and elements of the relation are events.

The construction of the occurrence net associated to a simple agent E consists roughly in unfolding the condition/event system starting from the set of grapes dec(E) [DDM88b].

- Its **conditions** are pairs: the first element is an event of the occurrence net or the mark "init" and the second element is a grape.
- Its **events** are also pairs: the first element is a set of conditions and the second element is a rewriting rule.

Roughly speaking, a grape occurring as second element of a condition b is a post-condition of the rewriting rule which is the second component of the event taken as first element of b. When there is no such event, we are in the initial case. Symmetrically, the (set of) conditions which are the first component of an event, say e, stay for the pre-conditions of the rewriting rule acting as second component of e.

It is worth noting that, in this case, we will not identify isomorphic occurrence nets. Indeed, the actual structure of events and conditions is important for determining both the causal and the conflict relations. However, as we have already stressed, the occurrence net we will obtain from the transition relation is only an intermediate step toward the construction of a cles defined of course up to isomorphism.

3.11. Definition (*From agents to occurrences nets*)

The set of conditions $\mathfrak{B}$ and the set of events $\mathfrak{E}$, the flow relation $\mathfrak{F}$, and the initial marking $\mathfrak{M}_0$ of the occurrence net associated to term E are defined as follows.

- $g \in$ dec(E) **implies** ‹init, g› $\in \mathfrak{B}$;
- $\underline{B} \subseteq \mathfrak{B}$, co($\underline{B}$), $\{g \mid$ ‹e, g› $\in \underline{B}\}$ = I' **implies**

  ‹$\underline{B}$, I—μ→ I'› $\in \mathfrak{E}$ **and** ‹‹$\underline{B}$, I—μ→ I'›, g› $\in \mathfrak{B}$ for all $g \in$ I';
- e $\mathfrak{F}$ ‹e, g›; b $\mathfrak{F}$ ‹{b} $\cup \underline{B}$, t›;

  ‹{b} $\cup \underline{B}$, t› # ‹{b} $\cup \underline{B}'$, t'› and # is made hereditary;
- $\mathfrak{M}_0$ = {‹init, g› | g $\in$ dec(E)}. ♦

3.12. Example (*Examples 3.4 and 3.8 continued*)

Given the agent of Example 3.4 and the rewriting rules of Example 3.8, our construction generates the following occurrence net with six conditions and three events:

b_1 = ‹init, ((αNIL+γNIL)|id)\γ›

b_2 = ‹init, (id|βγ̄NIL)\γ›

e_1 = ‹{b_1}, r_1›; with b_1 F e_1

b_3 = ‹e_1, (NIL|id)\γ›; with e_1 F b_3

e_2 = ‹{b_2}, r_2›; with b_2 F e_2

b_4 = ‹e_2, (id|γ̄)\γ›; with e_2 F b_4

e_3 = ‹{b_1, b_4}, r_3›; with b_1 F e_3, b_4 F e_3

b_5 = ‹e_3, (NIL|id)\γ›; with e_3 F b_5

b_6 = ‹e_3, (id|NIL)\γ›; with e_3 F b_6.

Note that e_1 # e_3, for they share b_1.

Figure 3.1 depicts the occurrence net relative to the example above. ♦

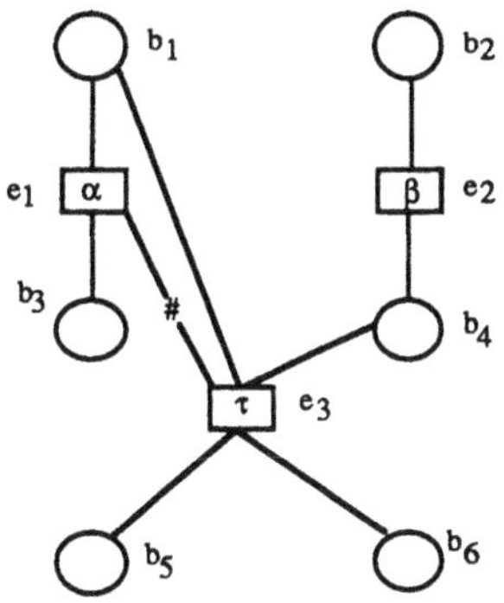

Figure 3.1.

The occurrence net corresponding to the agent ((αNIL+γNIL)|βγ̄NIL)\γ.
The transitions of the net are decorated with the actions of the rewriting rules they contain.

3.13. Definition (*From occurrences nets to event structures*)

Given the occurrence net ($\mathfrak{B}$, $\mathfrak{E}$, $\mathfrak{F}$, $\mathfrak{M}_0$) for a simple agent E, the cles associated to it, called $\mathcal{OP}$(E), is L= ($\mathfrak{E}$, ≤, #, l), where

- relation ≤ is the reflexive, transitive closure of $\mathfrak{F}$ when restricted to $\mathfrak{E}$;
- # is as in Definition 3.11, again restricted to $\mathfrak{E}$; and
- l(‹$\underline{B}$, I—μ→I'›) = μ. ♦

3.14. Example (*Examples 3.4, 3.8 and 3.12 continued*)

The occurrence net of Example 3.12, once restricted to the events, becomes the cles described formally below, and depicted in Figure 3.2. Note again that $e_1 \# e_3$ for they share b_1.

$e_1 = \langle\{b_1\}, r_1\rangle$ with label α $\qquad$ $e_2 = \langle\{b_2\}, r_2\rangle$ with label β; e_1 co e_2

$e_3 = \langle\{b_1, b_4\}, r_3\rangle$ with label τ; $e_1 \# e_3$, $e_2 \le e_3$. ♦

Figure 3.2.

The cles corresponding to the agent $((\alpha NIL+\gamma NIL)|\beta\bar{\gamma}NIL)\backslash\gamma$.

4. Adequacy and problems

In this section we prove that the distributed semantics we have proposed satisfies the criteria i) and ii) discussed in the introduction. Actually, we will establish item i) by proving that the identifications between simple agents induced by strong observational equivalence (all τ's are visible) on the original interleaving transition system for CCS [Mil80] coincide with those induced by the CLES semantics with interleaving observations. For proving criterion ii), we compare our semantics with the multiset transition system for CCS presented in the Appendix. Given a simple agent and its associated cles, we prove that the cles contains a set of concurrent events if and only there is a corresponding transition in the multiset transition system.

The next proposition establishes a clear correspondence between an interleaving transition from an agent E_1 to an agent E_2 of the original transition systems, and a sequence of rewritings in our rewriting system from E_1 to E_2. It will be essential for proving that the occurrence net of a simple CCS agent contains two sets of conditions corresponding to E_1 and E_2 which are connected by a set of events labelled consistently with the sequence of rewritings s, and partially ordered by a relation compatible with the total ordering induced by s.

We introduce below a notion of computation from an agent E_1 to an agent E_2, in the framework of partial ordering rewritings.

4.1. Definition (*computation*)

Given an agent E_1, the sequence

$$\xi = \{G_0\ I_1 \text{—}\mu_1\text{→} I'_1\ G_1 \ldots G_{n-1}\ I_n \text{—}\mu_n\text{→} I'_n\ G_n\}$$

is a *computation* from E_1 to E_2 if

i) • G_i is a complete set of grapes, $0 \le i \le n$,
- $G_0 = dec(E_1)$, $G_n = dec(E_2)$, and
- $I_i \text{—}\mu_i\text{→} I'_i$ is in the partial ordering rewriting relation, $0 < i \le n$;

ii) • $I_i \subseteq G_{i-1}$, and

• $G_i = (G_{i-1} - I_i) \cup I'_i$, $0<i\leq n$. ♦

4.2. Proposition (*interleaving and po computations are in direct correspondence*)
$E_1 \text{—}\mu_1\rightarrow E_2 \text{—}\mu_2\rightarrow \dots E_n \text{—}\mu_n\rightarrow E_{n+1}$ if and only if there is a computation
$dec(E_1)\ I_1 \text{—}\mu_1\rightarrow I'_1\ G_1 \dots G_{n-1}\ I_n \text{—}\mu_n\rightarrow I'_n\ dec(E_{n+1})$. ♦

4.3. Theorem (*interleaving observations give interleaving semantics*)
Given two simple CCS agents E and E', then $E \approx E'$ if and only if $\mathbf{Op}(E) \cong_{int} \mathbf{Op}(E')$. ♦

Proof. Hint.
We have to show that if there exists a bisimulation (as defined in the appendix) which contains the pair $\langle E_1, E_2\rangle$ then there exists also a bisimulation based on interleaving observations of extended Cles (Definition 2.8) which contains $\langle\langle \mathbf{Op}(E), \varepsilon\rangle, \langle \mathbf{Op}(E'), \varepsilon\rangle\rangle$ and viceversa. In order to prove this, we rely on the fact that the past of a cles plays no role when only interleaving observations are allowed. Then, because of Proposition 4.2, to prove the claim it is sufficient to show that:
a) If there exists a sequence of rewritings
$$\xi = \{dec(E_1) = G_1\ I_1 \text{—}\mu_1\rightarrow I'_1\ G_2 \dots G_n\ I_n \text{—}\mu_n\rightarrow I'_n\ G_{n+1} = dec(E_2)\}$$
then $\mu_1 \dots \mu_n$ represents a computation c of $\mathbf{Op}(E_1)$ and $\mathbf{Op}(E_1)$ reduces to $\mathbf{Op}(E_2)$ once the events of c and those in conflict with them are removed.
b) If in $\mathbf{Op}(E_1)$ the sequence $\mu_1 \dots \mu_n$ represents a computation c which leads to $\mathbf{Op}(E_2)$, there always exists a sequence of rewritings such that the generation ordering of the events coincides with $\mu_1 \dots \mu_n$.
These two facts are proved by exploiting first the relationships between our rewriting system and the derived occurrence net and then the correspondence between the partial ordering of the occurrence nets and that of the cles.
For additional detail about the proof techniques used we refer the interested reader to [DDM87a and 88a]. ♦

4.4. Corollary (*interleaving semantics is retrievable from partial ordering semantics*)
Given two simple CCS agents E and E', then $\mathbf{Op}(E) \cong_{po} \mathbf{Op}(E')$ implies $E \approx E'$

Proof. Follows from Theorem 4.3 and Proposition 2.11.i). ♦

The next theorem establishes criterion ii) of the Introduction about the adequacy of the operational semantics defined so far in that all the potential parallelism of simple agents is exploited. We will prove that a cles associated to a given agent E contains a set of concurrent actions if and only if there is a corresponding derivation in the multiset transition system for CCS defined in the Appendix. Of course, the statement of ii) assumes we agree that the multiset transition system expresses all the parallelism of a CCS agent; indeed it is difficult to conceive, as multiset semantics of CCS, anything different from what we propose.

4.5. Theorem (*no concurrency is lost*)

Let E be a simple agent, $E—\{\mu_1\mu_2...\mu_n\}—>> E'$ if and only if there exists a set of grapes I_0 such that

- $dec(E) = I_1 \cup I_2 \cup ... \cup I_n \cup I_o, I_i \cap I_j = \emptyset, 0 \le i \ne j \le n$;
- $I_i - \mu_i \rightarrow I'_i$; for $i \ge 1$
- $dec(E') = I'_1 \cup I'_2 \cup ... \cup I'_n \cup I_0, I'_i \cap I'_j = \emptyset, 0 \le i \ne j \le n$.

Proof. Hint. By induction on the cardinality of the multiset. The base is $E—\{\mu\}—>> E'$ if and only if $I_1—\mu_1\rightarrow I'_2$, with $dec(E) = I_1 \cup I_0$, the proof of which relies on the close relationship between $E—\{\mu\}—>> E'$ and $E—\mu\rightarrow E'$ and on Proposition 3.10. The proof of the inductive step goes on by case analysis exploiting Proposition 3.9. Note that the inductive step is needed when dealing with non-sequential agents only, since cases μE, E_1+E_2, and rec x. E are completely covered by the base one. ♦

In the previous section we have defined the notion of grapes and the decomposition function for the full language. There is a straightforward extension to the rewriting rules of Definition 3.7 that covers the full language [DDM87b]. Everything is left unchanged except for the following inference rules which are used in place of those for sum and recursion.

sum) $dec(E_1) - I_3 —\mu\rightarrow I_2$ *implies* $\{E_1+E\} —\mu\rightarrow I_2 \cup I_3$ *and* $\{E+E_1\} —\mu\rightarrow I_2 \cup I_3$

rec) $dec(E_1[rec\ x.\ E_1/x]) - I_3 —\mu\rightarrow I_2$ *implies* $\{rec\ x.\ E_1\} —\mu\rightarrow I_2 \cup I_3$.

After these modifications, we have that property i) holds also for the full language; but potential concurrency among actions is lost whenever a pair of parallel processes is put either in a sum or in a recursion context. Thus, Theorem 4.5 does not hold when considering the full calculus.

As an example, consider agent $E = \alpha NIL \mid \beta NIL$ which, when decomposed, originates the set of grapes $\{\alpha NIL \mid id, id \mid \beta NIL\}$. Our construction builds up a cles in which actions α and β (or rather *events* corresponding to *rewriting rules* whose actions are α and β) are concurrent. When we plug the agent E into a sum context, for example to obtain the agent $(\alpha NIL \mid \beta NIL) + \gamma NIL$, the decomposition function originates the singleton $\{\alpha NIL \mid \beta NIL + \gamma NIL\}$. In the corresponding cles (see Fig. 4.1.a) the events labelled by α and β are always causally dependent (in the occurrence net both of them share the same precondition $\{\langle init, (\alpha NIL \mid \beta NIL) + \gamma NIL\rangle\}$). The expected cles is instead the one shown in Figure 4.1.b). Indeed, the original agent as the following as a possible multiset transition:

$(\alpha NIL \mid \beta NIL) + \gamma NIL —\{\alpha, \beta\}—>> NIL \mid NIL.$

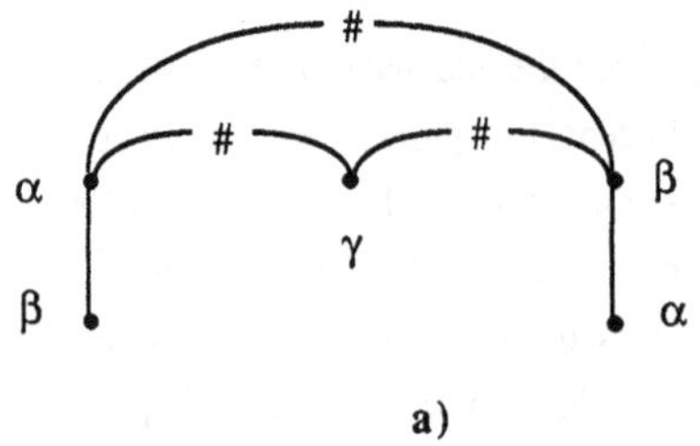

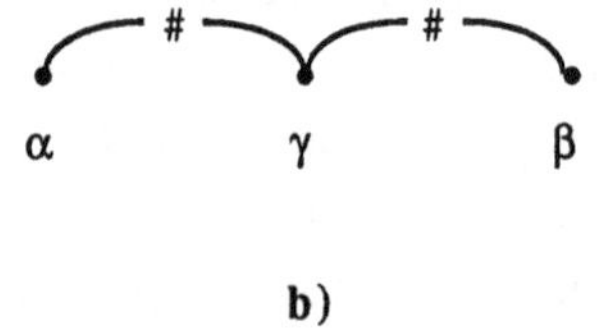

Figure 4.1
Two conflict labelled event structures.

The same problems arise when E is put in a rec context like rec x. αNIL | βNIL. Recall that the sets of grapes obtained by decomposing those agents the most external operator of which is a + or a rec, are always singletons. Thus, all non simple agents are never further decomposed even if one of the summands or the body of the recursion contains the parallel composition operator at the top level; they will be decomposed only after an action has been performed. This is why initial concurrent actions are interleaved.

In previous papers we have proposed different ways to overcome these problems either by resorting to more complex decompositions of agents [DDM88], or to more complex rewriting rules [DDM88a]. In [DDM88] we introduce a new decomposition relation which goes on decomposing terms also after the two critical operators have been encountered. More precisely, we extend the syntax of grapes by allowing grapes of the form G + G, and define an alternative decomposition relation **decrel** which is an extension of and plays the same role as function dec. The main difference concerns those agents of the form $E_1 + E_2$ in that both E_1 and E_2 are further decomposed. Moreover, we operate on recursive terms on a "by need" basis by performing a single unwinding whenever rec appears not prefixed by an action. Note that rec is no more considered as an operator, but simply as a shorthand for the infinite term obtained by unwinding recursion. Also, the rewriting system is accordingly modified: no inference rule is needed for dealing with recursion, and the following rules replaces rules **sum**) of Definition 3.7

sum') $I_1 \cup I_3 \text{—}\mu\text{→} I_2$ *and* I is complete *implies* $I_1 \cup (I_3 + I) \text{—}\mu\text{→} I_2$
and $I_1 \cup (I + I_3) \text{—}\mu\text{→} I_2$.

An immediate consequence of this approach is that there exist sequences of rewritings leading to global states which do not immediately correspond to CCS agents because discarded choices may still be recorded in some grapes. The problem is originated by the fact that those grapes which do not contribute to an action are not involved in control, and thus they are not updated at all. Still, they are part of the global state. For example, we have that (αNIL | βNIL) + γNIL originates via decrel {αNIL | id + γNIL, id | βNIL + γNIL}, and that this set of grapes can perform an α-rewriting to become {NIL | id, id | βNIL + γNIL}. Such a set of grapes is not in direct correspondence with any CCS term, although, as one would expect, its behaviour will be the same of {NIL | id, id | βNIL}. Thus, the bijection given by function dec between global states reachable via rewritings and complete sets of grapes (i.e., CCS agents) is lost; a many-to-one correspondence holds, instead.

Another solution to the problems above is proposed in [DDM88a], which keeps the same decomposition function presented in Section 3, but introduces a more complicated arrow. The new rewriting rules have the form $I_1 \text{–}[\mu,\Re]\text{→} I_2$ where I_1 and I_2 are sets of grapes, and $\Re$ is a binary relation on grapes which records other grapes which may be caused by those in I_1, but not by μ. The intended dynamic meaning of the rules is that, by performing an event labelled by μ, the set of grapes I_1 occurring in the current state can be replaced by the grapes in I_2 and by those related to I_1 via $\Re$, thus obtaining the new state. The rewriting rule (shown in Fig. 4.2) of the agent (α.NIL|β.NIL)+γ.NIL, when it evolves to NIL|β.NIL after resolving the nondeterministic choice in favour of α is the following:

{(α.NIL|β.NIL)+γ.NIL} –[α, {(α.NIL|β.NIL)+γ.NIL $\leq$ id|β.NIL}]→ {NIL|id}

This notation describes the fact that grape (α.NIL|β.NIL)+γ.NIL causes both the grape id|β.NIL and the event labelled by α which in turn causes the grape NIL|id. Note that the possibility that id|β.NIL has to perform β independently of the occurrence of α is expressed by the absence of any causal relation between α and id|β.NIL.

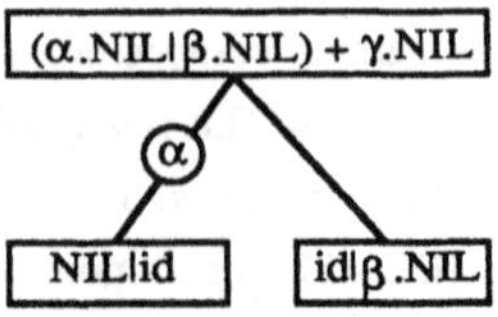

Figure 4.2.

The rewriting rule {(α.NIL|β.NIL)+γ.NIL} −[α, {(α.NIL|β.NIL)+γ.NIL ≤ id|β.NIL}]→ {NIL|id}. (Grapes are represented by labelled boxes, events by labelled circles and the causal relation is expressed through its Hasse diagram growing downwards.)

A rewriting rule of the above form may look a bit unnatural. We are used to conceiving labelled rules as relations between a set of processes and an action, and between that action and *all* the new processes. Instead, in the example above, the grape id|β.NIL is directly related to the grape (α.NIL|β.NIL)+γ.NIL. This happens because the evolution of nondeterministic processes of this kind requires first choosing one of the alternatives, and then performing an action of the chosen grapes. A possible way of describing the above rule in detail is illustrated in Fig. 4.3.a). First, a choice-event causes two concurrent grapes α.NIL|id and id|β.NIL; the former then performs an α. It is however important to note that, in order to be faithful to the original semantics, the decision and the action must be considered as a single indivisible action. Since the original CCS has no mechanisms for defining atomic actions from sequences, we are left with two alternatives: either to hide the decision, and obtain rewriting rules such as those of Fig. 4.2, or to incorporate the decision into the action itself, and obtain a rule which enforces a causal dependence of β on α (Fig. 4.3.b). In the previous section, we have followed the latter approach, and this has lead us to the above mentioned problems.

The next section will provide the calculus with a third solution based on a notion of atomic sequence of actions.

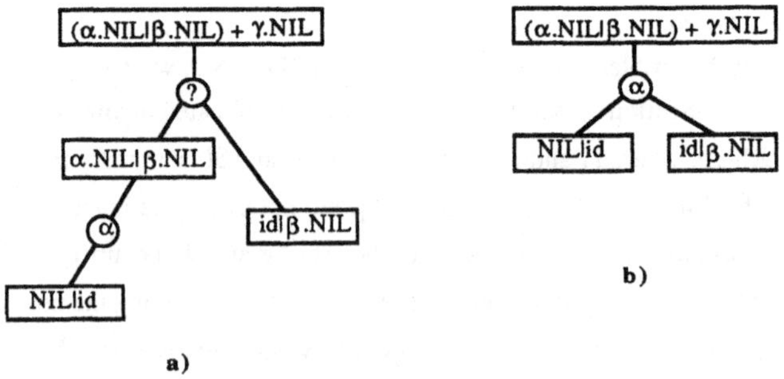

Figure 4.3.

Alternative descriptions of the α-rule of agent (α.NIL|β.NIL)+γ.NIL.

5. A Truly Concurrent Semantics for CCS Based on Atomic Actions

In this section we will introduce the partial ordering semantics for full CCS. The approach we will follow is essentially the same as the one of Section 3, where a cles was associated to a CCS term by relying on four basic steps, consisting in the definition of:

i) a decomposition function which determines the sequential components of agents;

ii) a set of rewriting rules which describe the elementary steps of the sequential components;

iii) the occurrence net which will be used to obtain le cles by dropping the conditions;

iv) the associated cles to models the dynamics of a given term.

Indeed, also for full CCS, we will use steps i) and iii) of Section 3. More precisely, we will again use function dec for decomposing CCS agents and exactly the same approach to build an occurrence net from the new set of rewriting rules. The actual rules of the full calculus (step ii) will be similar to those of Definition 3.7 in that they relate two sets of grapes through a label; but the set of possible labels will be enriched with three distinct elements π_l, π_r and π_{rec}. Label π_l (π_r) will be used to mirror that the left (right) alternative of a nondeterministic processes has been chosen to proceed with the rewritings; label π_{rec} will be used for performing unwindings of recursive terms. Step iv), i.e. the construction of cles's from occurrence nets, this time will not only forget the conditions, but also all those events which have been originated by rewritings labelled by π_l, π_r or π_{rec}. In spite of the fact that completely new actions are introduced, we will show that both the retrievability of the original interleaving semantics and the ability of fully describing the parallelism of the multiset semantics are kept.

Below, we introduce the enriched set of actions which will be used to label arrows.

5.1. Definition *(enriched set of actions)*

The set of basic actions $\Lambda = \{\alpha, \beta, \gamma, ...\} \cup \{\alpha^-, \beta^-, \gamma^-, ...\} \cup \{\tau\}$ as defined in the Appendix is extended with three distinct actions π_l, π_r, π_{rec}.

We will use

- ρ to range over the new set of actions;
- π, possibly indexed, to range over π_x, x = l, r, rec. ♦

We now are ready to introduce the new set of rewriting rules. This set is simpler than the one of Definition 3.7, and even simpler than the interleaving transition system presented in the Appendix. The main differences between the new rewriting system and the others is that it has three more axioms in place of the three inference rules of **sum**) and **rec**). The new axioms permit, via a π-move, choosing between the agents in a sum and unfolding recursive agents. Then, a basic action μ of an agent E_1+E_2 can be understood as consisting of concatenating (at least) two rewriting rules. Starting from the singleton $\{E_1+E_2\}$ the first rewriting rule, inferred by axiom **Sum**), discards alternative E_2 and decomposes E_1 into a set of grapes I; the second rule rewrites a subset of I, via action μ. Note that, if E_1 is again a sum or a rec, the process is iterated, as long as necessary. The intuition behind rule **Rec**) is similar to that behind **Sum**). Obviously, the first rewriting rule will unfold the recursive agent by replacing all the occurrences of the bound variable with the body of the recursive definition.

5.2. Definition (*Π-rewriting relation*)

The *Π-rewriting relation* $I_1 \text{—}\rho\text{→} I_2$ is defined as the least relation satisfying the following axioms and inference rules.

Act) $\{\mu E\} \text{—}\mu\text{→} dec(E)$

Sum) $\{E_1+E_2\} \text{—}\pi_l\text{→} dec(E_1)$ *and* $\{E_1+E_2\} \text{—}\pi_r\text{→} dec(E_2)$

Rec) $\{rec\ x.\ E_1\} \text{—}\pi_{rec}\text{→} dec(E_1[rec\ x.\ E_1/x])$

Res) $I_1 \text{—}\rho\text{→} I_2$ *and* $\rho \notin \{\alpha,\alpha^-\}$ *imply* $I_1\backslash\alpha \text{—}\rho\text{→} I_2\backslash\alpha$

Rel) $I_1 \text{—}\rho\text{→} I_2$ *implies* $I_1[\phi] \text{—}\phi(\rho)\text{→} I_2[\phi]$

Com) $I_1 \text{—}\rho\text{→} I_2$ *implies* $I_1|id \text{—}\rho\text{→} I_2|id$ *and* $id|I_1 \text{—}\rho\text{→} id|I_2$

$I_1 \text{—}\lambda\text{→} I_2$ *and* $I'_1 \text{—}\lambda^-\text{→} I'_2$ *imply* $I_1|id \cup id|I'_1 \text{—}\tau\text{→} I_2|id \cup id|I'_2$. ♦

We can now establish a few properties similar to those proved for Simple CCS. These will be useful for establishing adequacy and completeness of our new semantics.

5.3. Property

If $I_1\text{—}\rho\text{→}I_2$ is a Π-rewriting rule, then for any set of grapes I_3 with $I_3 \cap I_1 = \emptyset$ and $I_1 \cup I_3$ complete, we have that $I_2 \cup I_3$ is complete and $I_3 \cap I_2 = \emptyset$.

Proof. The proof is immediate by a case analysis on why $I_1 \text{—}\rho\text{→} I_2$. ♦

Of course, the notion of computation given by Definition 5.4 can easily be modified to fit with the present rewriting system. We can now introduce the notion of transaction, i.e. of a sequence of elementary actions which is considered as a single action; it cannot be interrupted and leaves no traces of the intermediate states. This notion permits incorporating (hiding) a sequence of π-actions into the μ-action they have caused. It is worth noting that the causal relations between π- and μ-actions are naturally expressed by the latter condition of Definition 5.4. Our new computations will be defined as sequences of μ-transactions.

5.4. Definition (*μ-transaction*)

A computation

$$\{G_0\ I_1\text{—}\pi_1\text{→}I'_1\ G_1 \ldots G_{n-1}\ I_n\text{—}\pi_n\text{→}I'_n\ G_n\ I_{n+1}\text{—}\mu\text{→}I'_{n+1}\ G_{n+1}\}$$

is a *μ-transaction* (written $G_0 \sim\pi_1\ldots\pi_n\mu\sim> G_{n+1}$) if for every i there exists j, $i < j \leq n+1$ such that $I'_i \cap I_j \neq \emptyset$. ♦

5.5. Example

Let us consider the following agent

$$E = ((\alpha NIL+\beta NIL) \mid (\beta^- NIL+ \gamma NIL))\backslash\beta + \delta NIL.$$

It originates the following computation

$$\{E\} \quad \{E\}\text{—}\pi_l\text{→}\{((\alpha NIL+\beta NIL) \mid id)\backslash\beta,\ (id \mid (\beta^- NIL+\gamma NIL))\backslash\beta\}$$

$$\{((\alpha NIL+\beta NIL) \mid id)\backslash\beta,\ (id \mid (\beta^- NIL+\gamma NIL))\backslash\beta\} \quad \{((\alpha NIL+\beta NIL) \mid id)\backslash\beta\}\text{—}\pi_r\text{→}\{(\beta NIL \mid id)\backslash\beta\}$$

$$\{(\beta NIL \mid id)\backslash\beta,\ (id \mid (\beta^- NIL+\gamma NIL))\backslash\beta\} \quad \{(id \mid (\beta^- NIL+\gamma NIL))\backslash\beta\}\text{—}\pi_l\text{→}\{()id \mid (\beta^- NIL)\backslash\beta\}$$

$$\{(\beta NIL \mid id)\backslash\beta,\ (id \mid \beta^- NIL)\backslash\beta\} \quad \{(\beta NIL \mid id)\backslash\beta,\ (id \mid \beta^- NIL)\backslash\beta\}\text{—}\tau\text{→}\{(NIL \mid id)\backslash\beta,\ (id \mid NIL)\backslash\beta\}$$

$$\{(NIL \mid id)\backslash\beta,\ (id \mid NIL)\backslash\beta\}$$

which yields the following τ-transaction

$$\{E\} \sim\pi_l\ \pi_r\ \pi_l\ \tau \sim> \{(NIL \mid id)\backslash\beta,\ (id \mid NIL)\backslash\beta\},$$

Instead, the following is not an α-transaction

$$\{E\} \sim\pi_l\ \pi_l\ \pi_l\ \alpha \sim> \{(NIL \mid id)\backslash\beta,\ (id \mid \beta^- NIL)\backslash\beta\},$$

since the computations which may generate it contain at least one π_l that does not cause the α. See also Example 5.11 below. ♦

5.6. Definition (*atomic computation*)
A computation is *atomic* if it is a concatenation of *μ-transactions*. ♦

The correspondence between the interleaving transition system and the Π-rewriting system is given by the following theorem, which establishes a bijection between the μ-transactions and the original interleaving transitions. This theorem will play the same rôle of Proposition 3.10 when proving the adequacy of the new semantics.

5.7. Theorem (*correspondence between interleaving transitions and μ-transactions*)
We have a derivation $E_1\text{—}\mu\text{→}E_2$ if and only if there exists a μ-transaction $dec(E_1)\sim\pi_1...\pi_n\mu\sim> dec(E_2)$.

Proof. (Hint of) One direction is proved by induction on the number of π; the other by induction on the length of the proof. ♦

5.8. Corollary (*correspondence between interleaving and atomic Π-computations*)

$$E_1\text{—}\mu_1\text{→}E_2\text{—}\mu_2\text{→} \dots E_n\text{—}\mu_n\text{→}E_{n+1}$$

if and only if there is an atomic computation

$$dec(E_1)\ I_1\text{—}\rho_1\text{→}I'_1\ G_1...G_{m-1}\ I_m\text{—}\rho_m\text{→}I'_m\ dec(E_{n+1})$$

such that $\rho_1\rho_2...\rho_m = \pi^{i_1}\mu_1\pi^{i_2}\mu_2 \dots \pi^{i_n}\mu_n$, with $m = n + \Sigma_{1\le j\le n}\ i_j$.

Proof. The proof is by induction on the number of computation steps, and relies on Theorem 5.7. ♦

Given a CCS agent, we build its associated occurrence net exactly as in Section 3, Definition 3.11. The corresponding cles is obtained almost like in Definition 3.13, the only difference is that also those events labelled by π are stripped away. This last abstraction step is sound because of Theorem 5.7.

5.9. Definition (*From occurrences nets to event structures*)

Given the occurrence net $(\mathcal{B}, \mathcal{E}, \mathcal{F}, \mathcal{M}_0)$ for agent E, the CLES associated to it, called $\mathcal{A}op$(E), is $L = (\mathcal{E}', \leq, \#, l)$, where

- $\mathcal{E}' = \mathcal{E} - \{\langle \underline{B}, I \text{—}\pi\text{→} I'\rangle \mid \pi \in \{\pi_l, \pi_r, \pi_{rec}\}\}$;
- relation $\leq$ is the reflexive, transitive closure of $\mathcal{F}$ when restricted to $\mathcal{E}'$;
- # is as in Definition 3.11, again restricted to $\mathcal{E}'$; and
- $l(\langle \underline{B}, I \text{—}\mu\text{→} I'\rangle) = \mu$. ♦

5.10. Theorem (*interleaving observations give interleaving semantics*)

$E \approx E'$ if and only if $\mathcal{A}op(E) \cong_{int} \mathcal{A}op(E')$.

Proof. Hint.

Basically, the proof follows the same pattern as that for Theorem 4.3. However, some additional complications do arise because in the final cles's we drop also the events labelled by π. It is then necessary to establish a relation between atomic computations and certain computation nets; i.e. those which have no maximal event with label π. They are called atomic computation nets. Hence we have to establish that:

a) if there exists an atomic computation

$$\xi = \{dec(E_1) = G_1\ I_1 \text{—}\rho_1\text{→} I'_1\ G_2 \ldots G_n\ I_n \text{—}\rho_n\text{→} I'_n\ G_{n+1} = dec(E_2)\}$$

then there exists *an atomic computation net from* $dec(E_1)$ *to* $dec(E_2)$ such that its partial ordering is compatible with the sequence $\rho_1 \ldots \rho_n$;

b) given an atomic computation net from $dec(E_1)$ and $dec(E_2)$ with partial ordering $\leq$ we have that for any sequence s of μ-labels compatible with $\leq$, there exists an atomic computation from E_1 to E_2 whose sequence of μ-labels is s;

and then we have to establish that:

c) given an atomic computation net from $dec(E_1)$ to $dec(E_2)$ with partial ordering $\leq$ and a sequence of μ-labels s compatible with $\leq$, s represents a computations of $\mathcal{A}op(E_1)$ which leads to $\mathcal{A}op(E_2)$;

d) if s represents a computations of $\mathcal{A}op(E_1)$ which leads to $\mathcal{A}op(E_2)$ then there exists an atomic computation net from $dec(E_1)$ to $dec(E_2)$ with partial ordering $\leq$ compatible with s. ♦

5.11. Example

Let us have the following agent

$$E = ((\alpha NIL+\beta NIL) \mid (\beta^- NIL+ \gamma NIL))\backslash\beta + \delta NIL,$$

the following set of grapes

$g_1 = ((\alpha NIL+\beta NIL) \mid (\beta^- NIL+ \gamma NIL))\backslash\beta + \delta NIL$; $\quad g_2 = ((\alpha NIL+\beta NIL) \mid id)\backslash\beta$

$g_3 = (id \mid (\beta^- NIL+ \gamma NIL))\backslash\beta$ $\quad g_4 = \delta NIL$

$g_5 = NIL$ $\quad g_6 = (\alpha NIL \mid id)\backslash\beta$

$g_7 = (\beta NIL \mid id)\backslash\beta$ $\quad g_8 = (id \mid \beta^- NIL)\backslash\beta$

$g_9 = (id \mid \gamma NIL)\backslash\beta$ $\quad g_{10} = (NIL \mid id)\backslash\beta$

$g_{11} = (id \mid NIL)\backslash\beta$

and the following rewriting rules

$r_1 = \{g_1\} \xrightarrow{\pi_l} \{g_2, g_3\}$ $\quad$ $r_2 = \{g_1\} \xrightarrow{\pi_r} \{g_4\}$

$r_3 = \{g_4\} \xrightarrow{\delta} \{g_5\}$ $\quad$ $r_4 = \{g_2\} \xrightarrow{\pi_l} \{g_6\}$

$r_5 = \{g_2\} \xrightarrow{\pi_r} \{g_7\}$ $\quad$ $r_6 = \{g_3\} \xrightarrow{\pi_l} \{g_8\}$

$r_7 = \{g_3\} \xrightarrow{\pi_r} \{g_9\}$ $\quad$ $r_8 = \{g_6\} \xrightarrow{\alpha} \{g_{10}\}$

$r_9 = \{g_9\} \xrightarrow{\gamma} \{g_{11}\}$ $\quad$ $r_{10} = \{g_7, g_8\} \xrightarrow{\tau} \{g_{10}, g_{11}\}$

Figures 5.1 and 5.2 show the occurrence net and the cles associated to E (note that dec(E) = $\{g_1\}$). ♦

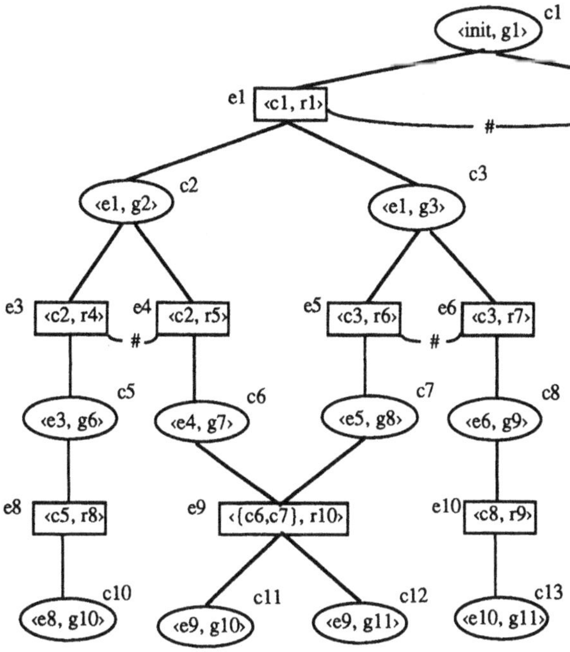

Figure 5.1.

The occurrence net associated to the agent $((\alpha NIL+\beta NIL) \mid (\beta^{-}NIL+\gamma NIL))\backslash\beta + \delta NIL$.

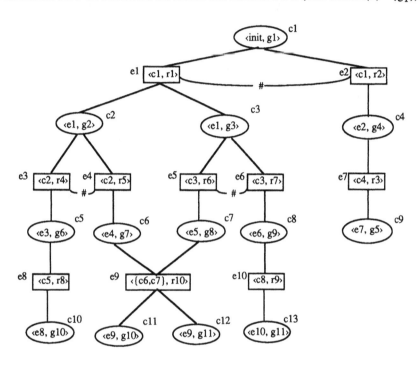

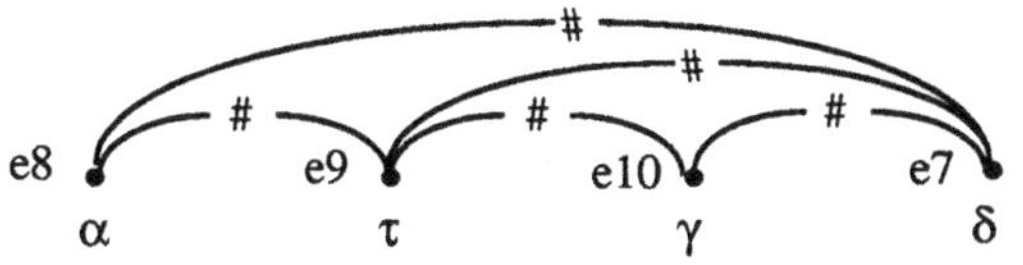

Figure 5.2.

The cles derived from the occurrence net depicted in Figure 5.1.

It is worth noting that the notion of atomicity cannot be introduced in such a simple way within the interleaving framework. If a set of rules similar to those of Definition 5.2 is used for defining the interleaving semantics of CCS, then a different semantics for the calculus is obtained which does introduce non existent deadlocks. Actually, if rules

sum) $E_1+E_2 \xrightarrow{\pi_l} E_1$ **and** $E_1+E_2 \xrightarrow{\pi_r} E_2$ and

rec) rec x. $E_1 \xrightarrow{\pi_{rec}} E_1[\text{rec x. } E_1/x]$

are substituted for rules **sum)** and **rec)** of the Appendix and we consider again agent

$E = ((\alpha NIL+\beta NIL) \mid (\beta^- NIL+ \gamma NIL))\backslash\beta + \delta NIL.$

we would have the following as a possible sequence of transitions

$$E \xrightarrow{\pi_l} ((\alpha NIL+\beta NIL) \mid (\beta^- NIL+ \gamma NIL))\backslash\beta \xrightarrow{\pi_l} (\alpha NIL \mid (\beta^- NIL+ \gamma NIL))\backslash\beta$$

$$\xrightarrow{\pi_l} (\alpha NIL \mid \beta^- NIL)\backslash\beta \xrightarrow{\alpha} (NIL \mid \beta^- NIL)\backslash\beta.$$

Thus, in the new interleaving system we would have an α-transaction E~α~> (NIL | β^-NIL)\β which leads to a deadlocked state, while in the original transition system after an α-transition there is always the possibility of performing a γ-transition. (Note that this possibility is reflected in the occurrence net of Figure 5.1; see also Example 5.5.) The problem with the "interleaving transactions" is that the causal dependencies between π- and μ-transitions cannot be recovered at all. A proposal for enriching CCS with transactions in within the interleaving framework can be found in [GMM88].

We finally prove that the Π-rewriting system does indeed capture all the concurrency of a CCS agent; as in Section 4, we will resort to the CCS multiset transition system of the Appendix.

5.12. Theorem (*no concurrency is lost*)

Let E be a CCS agent, E—$\{\mu_1\mu_2\ldots\mu_n\}$—>> E' if and only if there exists a set of grapes I_0 such that

- $dec(E) = I_1 \cup I_2 \cup \ldots \cup I_n \cup I_0$, $I_i \cap I_j = \emptyset$, $0 \le i \ne j \le n$;
- I_i~μ_i~> I'_i for $i \ge 1$;
- $dec(E') = I'_1 \cup I'_2 \cup \ldots \cup I'_n \cup I_0$, $I'_i \cap I'_j = \emptyset$, $0 \le i \ne j \le n$.

Proof. Similar to the proof of Theorem 4.5. ♦

All the equivalences and the comparisons of the paper have been carried on by resorting to quite a demanding bisimulation. Silent τ-actions are considered to be always visible; this assumption led to strong observational equivalences. However, more abstract equivalences that forget τ's can be easily obtained by modifying our observation functions. Actually, weak observational equivalences can be obtained by ignoring the events labelled by τ when defining the observation function, yet keeping them in the observed cles.

Appendix: CCS and Occurrence Nets

Here, we briefly introduce the relevant definitions of Milner's Calculus of Communicating Systems [Mil80], and of Occurrence Nets [Win87, NPW81].

A Calculus of Communicating Systems - CCS

The concrete syntax of "pure" CCS, i.e., without value passing, is as follows

$E ::= NIL \mid \mu E \mid E\backslash\alpha \mid E[\phi] \mid E+E \mid E|E \mid x \mid rec\ x.\ E$

where x is a variable; $\Delta = \{\alpha,\beta,\gamma,...\}$; $\Delta^- = \{\alpha^- \mid \alpha\in\Delta\}$; $\tau\notin\Delta$; $\Delta \cup \Delta^- \cup \{\tau\}$ is the set of *basic actions*, ranged over by μ; $\Lambda = \Delta \cup \Delta^-$ is ranged over by λ; ϕ is a permutation of $\Lambda \cup \tau$ which preserves τ and the operation $^-$ of complementation. CCS *agents* are terms generated by the above BNF the variables of which are bound within a recursive definition (*closed*).

NIL represents an agent which cannot perform any action. μ**E** denotes an agent which can only perform action μ and then behave like E. The actions of **E[ϕ]** are renamings via ϕ of those of E. Agent **E\\α** behaves like E but cannot perform actions α and α^-. Agent $\mathbf{E_1+E_2}$ can act either as E_1 or as E_2. Agent $\mathbf{E_1|E_2}$ can perform in parallel the actions of E_1 and E_2; moreover they can synchronize, through a τ, whenever they are able to perform complementary actions. Agent **rec x. E** denotes a recursive agent.

The *interleaving operational semantics* is given in terms of labelled interleaving transitions over CCS agents, defined by the following inference rules.

act) $\mu E -\mu\rightarrow E$

res) $E_1 -\mu\rightarrow E_2$ *and* $\mu \notin \{\alpha, \alpha^-\}$ *imply* $E_1\backslash\alpha -\mu\rightarrow E_2\backslash\alpha$

rel) $E_1 -\mu\rightarrow E_2$ *implies* $E_1[\phi] -\phi(\mu)\rightarrow E_2[\phi]$

sum) $E_1 -\mu\rightarrow E_2$ *implies* $E_1+E -\mu\rightarrow E_2$ *and* $E+E_1 -\mu\rightarrow E_2$

com) $E_1 -\mu\rightarrow E_2$ *implies* $E_1|E -\mu\rightarrow E_2|E$ *and* $E|E_1 -\mu\rightarrow E|E_2$

$E_1 -\lambda\rightarrow E_2$ *and* $E'_1 -\lambda^-\rightarrow E'_2$ *imply* $E_1|E'_1 -\tau\rightarrow E_2|E'_2$

rec) $E_1[rec\ x.E_1 /x] -\mu\rightarrow E_2$ *implies* $rec\ x.E_1 -\mu\rightarrow E_2$.

The *strong observational equivalence* is defined as follows.

1. Let Ψ be the function over binary relations **S** between CCS agents defined as follows: $\langle E_0, E_1\rangle \in \Psi(S)$ if and only if , for every $s \in (\Lambda \cup \{\tau\})^*$,
   i) whenever $E_0-s\rightarrow E'_0$ there exists E'_1 such that $E_1-s\rightarrow E'_1$ and $\langle E'_0, E'_1\rangle \in \mathbf{S}$
   ii) whenever $E_1-s\rightarrow E'_1$ there exists E'_0 such that $E_0-s\rightarrow E'_0$ and $\langle E'_0, E'_1\rangle \in \mathbf{S}$.
2. A relation $\Re$ is a *bisimulation* if $\Re \subseteq \Psi(\Re)$
3. The strong observational equivalence $\approx$ is the maximal fixed point of Ψ.

Another transition system is introduced which extends the original system in that all the interleaved transitions are kept, but also transitions labelled by multisets of concurrent actions are introduced in the spirit of SCCS [Mil83] and Meije [AB84], and of steps in Petri Nets [Rei85]. As for the interleaving semantics, the simultaneous execution of complementary actions results in a τ-action. The synchronization algebra can be extended to multisets as follows.

Let M, M' and M" be multisets of actions (notation $\{\mu_1, \ldots, \mu_n\}$) and $\cup_m$ denote multiset union; the *multiset synchronization relation* is the least relation which satisfies:

i) Synch(M', M", M' $\cup_m$ M") and

ii) Synch(M', M", M) **implies** Synch(M' $\cup_m$ $\{\lambda\}$, M" $\cup_m$ $\{\lambda^-\}$, M $\cup_m$ $\{\tau\}$).

The *multiset derivation relation* E_1—M→E_2, where M is a multiset of CCS actions and ϕ is extended to operate on multisets, is defined as the least relation satisfying the following axiom and inference rules:

ACT) μE —$\{\mu\}$—>> E

RES) E_1 —M—>> E_2 *and* $\alpha,\alpha^- \notin$ M *imply* $E_1\backslash\alpha$ — M—>> $E_2\backslash\alpha$

REL) E_1 —M—>> E_2 *implies* $E_1[\phi]$ —ϕ(M)—>> $E_2[\phi]$

SUM) E_1 —M—>> E_2 *implies* E_1+E — M—>> E_2 *and* E+E_1 — M—>> E_2

COM) E_1 —M—>> E_2 *implies* E_1|E — M—>> E_2|E *and* E|E_1 — M—>> E|E_2

E_1 —M'—>>E_2 *and* E'_1 —M"—>>E'_2 *and* Synch(M', M", M)

imply E_1|E'_1 — M—>> E_2|E'_2.

REC) E_1[rec x.E_1 /x] —M—>> E_2 *implies* rec x.E_1 —M—>>E_2.

Occurrence Nets

An Occurrence Net is a 4-tuple $(\mathcal{B}, \mathcal{E}, \mathcal{F}, \mathcal{M}_0)$ where

- $\mathcal{B}$ is a non-empty set of conditions;
- $\mathcal{E}$ is a set of events disjoint from B;
- $\mathcal{F} \subseteq (\mathcal{B}\times\mathcal{E}) \cup (\mathcal{E}\times\mathcal{B})$ is the flow relation;
- $\mathcal{M}_0 \subseteq \mathcal{B}$ is a non-empty set, called the initial marking;

and, letting $^\bullet x = \{y \in \mathcal{B} \cup \mathcal{E} \mid y\ F\ x\}$,

i) a condition $b \in \mathcal{M}_0$ if and only if $^\bullet b = \emptyset$;

ii) $\forall b \in \mathcal{B}.\ |^\bullet b| \leq 1$;

iii) $\mathcal{F}^+$ is irreflexive and $\forall e \in \mathcal{E}. \{e' \mid e'\ \mathcal{F}^*\ e\}$ is finite;

iv) $\forall x \in B \cup E$ either $x \in M_0$ or $\exists\, y \in B \cup E$ such that xFy or yFx;

v) # is irreflexive, where x' # x" if and only if
$\exists$ e', e" $\in$ E such that e' $\#_m$ e" *and* e' F^* x' *and* e" F^* x",
where e' $\#_m$ e" iff e', e" $\in$ E *and* $^\bullet e' \cap {}^\bullet e'' \neq \emptyset$.

Given x,y $\in$ B $\cup$ E and X $\subseteq$ B $\cup$ E

- x co y if and only if neither x F^* y, nor y F^* x, nor x # y.
- co(X) if and only if x co y for all x, y $\in$ B $\cup$ E.
- An occurrence net is *conflict free* if the relation # is empty.

References

[ADF87] Aceto,L., De Nicola,R. and Fantechi,A. Testing Equivalences for Event Structures, in *Mathematical Models for the Semantics of Parallelism* (M. Venturini Zilli, Ed.), LNCS, **280**, Springer -Verlag, Heidelberg, 1987, pp. 1-20.

[AB84] Austry,D. and Boudol,G. Algèbre de Processus et Synchronization, *Theoret. Comput. Sci.*, **30**, 1 (1984), 91-131.

[BC87] Boudol,G. and Castellani,I. On the Semantics of Concurrency: Partial Orders and Transition Systems, in Proc. *TAPSOFT-CAAP '87*, Lecture Notes in Computer Science, **249**, Springer-Verlag, Heidelberg, 1987, pp. 123-137.

[CFM83] Castellani,I. Franceschi,P. and Montanari,U. Labeled Event Structures: A Model for Observable Concurrency, in *Formal Description of Programming Concepts II* (D. Bijørner, Ed.), North Holland, Amsterdam, 1983, pp. 383-400.

[DDM87a] Degano,P., De Nicola,R. and Montanari,U. Observational Equivalences for Concurrency Models, in *Formal Description of Programming Concepts* III (M. Wirsing, Ed.), North Holland, Amsterdam, 1987, pp. 105-132.

[DDM87b] Degano, P., De Nicola, R. and Montanari, U. CCS is an (Augmented) Contact-Free C/E System, in *Mathematical Models for the Semantics of Parallelism* (M. Venturini Zilli, Ed.), LNCS, **280**, Springer-Verlag, Heidelberg, 1987, pp. 144-165.

[DDM88] Degano,P., De Nicola,R. and Montanari,U. A Distributed Operational Semantics for CCS based on Condition/Event Systems. *Acta Informatica,* **26**, (1988), 59-91.

[DDM88a] Degano,P., De Nicola,R. and Montanari,U. A Partial Ordering Semantics for CCS, Nota Interna 88-3, Dip. Informatica, University of Pisa, 1988. Submitted for Publication.

[DDM88b] Degano,P., De Nicola,R. and Montanari,U. On the Consistency of Operational and Denotational Semantics for True Concurrency, Proc. LICS '88, (IEEE Computer Society Press, Washington, 1988), pp. 133-141.

[DeN87] De Nicola,R. Extensional Equivalences for Transition Systems, *Acta Informatica*, **24**, (1987), 211-237.

[DM87] Degano,P. and Montanari,U. Concurrent Histories: A Basis for Observing Distributed Systems, *Journal of Computer and System Sciences*, **34** (1987), 442-461.

[GG89] van Glabeek,R. and Goltz,U. Equivalence Notions for Concurrent Systems and Refinement of Actions, *Draft* (1989).

[GMM88] Gorrieri,R., Marchetti,S. and Montanari,U. A^2CCS: Atomic Action for CCS, Proc. CAAP '88, LNCS, **299**, (Springer-Verlag, Heidelberg, 1987), pp. 258-270.

[GR83] Goltz,U. and Reisig,W. The Non-sequential Behaviour of Petri Nets, *Info. and Co.* **57**, (1983), 125-147.

[Kel76] Keller, R. Formal Verification of Parallel Programs. *Communication of ACM*, **7**, (1976) 561-572.

[Mil80] Milner,R. *A Calculus of Communicating Systems*. LNCS, **92**, (Springer-Verlag, Heidelberg, 1980).

[Mil83] Milner,R. Calculi for Synchrony and Asynchrony, *Theoret. Comput. Sci.*, **25**, (1983) 267-310.

[Mon85] Montanari,U. Observational Equivalence Revisited, minutes of the IFIP W.G. 2.2 meeting, Passau 1985.

[MS81] Montanari,U. and Simonelli,C. On Distinguishing Between Concurrency and Nondeterminism, Proc. Ècole de Printemps on Concurrency and Petri Nets, Colleville sur Mer, 1980, available as Tech. Rep. PFI-Cnet No 7, 1981.

[NPW81] Nielsen,M., Plotkin,G., Winskel,G. Petri Nets, Event Structures and Domains, Part 1, *Theoret. Comput. Sci.*, **13**, (1981) 85-108.

[Nie87] Nielsen,M. CCS - and its relationship to Net Theory, In *Advances in Petri Nets 1987*, (G. Rozenberg, Ed.) LNCS, **266**, (Springer-Verlag, Heidelberg, 1987), pp. 393-415.

[Old87] Olderog,E.-R. Operational Petri Net Semantics for CCSP. In *Advances in Petri Nets 1987*, (G. Rozenberg, Ed.) LNCS, **266**, (Springer-Verlag, Heidelberg, 1987), pp. 196-223.

[Par81] Park,D. Concurrency and Automata on Infinite Sequences, Proc. GI, LNCS, **104**, (Springer-Verlag, Heidelberg, 1981), pp. 167-183.

[Plo81] Plotkin, G. A Structural Approach to Operational Semantics. Technical Report DAIMI FN-19, Aarhus University, Department of Computer Science, Aarhus, 1981.

[Pra86] Pratt,V. Modelling Concurrency with Partial Orders, *International Journal of Parallel Programming*, **15**, (1986) 33-71.

[Rei85] Reisig, W.: *Petri Nets: An Introduction*, EATCS Monographs on Theoretical Computer Science, Springer-Verlag, 1985.

[Wink80] Winkowski,J. Behaviours of Concurrent Systems, *Theoret. Comput. Sci.*, **12** (1980), 39-60.

[Win80] Winskel,G. Events in Computation, Ph. D. Thesis, Univ. of Edinburgh, CST-10-80, (1980).

[Win82] Winskel,G. Event Structures for CCS and Related Languages, Proc. 9th ICALP, (M. Nielsen, and E. M. Schmidt, Eds), LNCS, **140**, Springer-Verlag, Heidelberg, 1982, pp. 561-576.

[Win85] Winskel, G.: Categories of Models of Concurrency, in: *Seminar on Concurrency* (S.D. Brookes, A. W. Roscoe, G. Winskel, eds.), LNCS 197, Springer-Verlag, Heidelberg, 1985, pp. 246-267,

[Win87] Winskel, G. Event Structures, in *Advances in Petri Nets 1987*, (G. Rozenberg, ed.) LNCS, **266**, Springer-Verlag, Heidelberg, 1987, pp. 196-223.

MODELING CONCURRENCY BY PARTIAL ORDERS AND NONLINEAR TRANSITION SYSTEMS

Haim Gaifman
Institute of Mathematics and Computer Science
Hebrew University Jerusalem Israel

ABSTRACT In the first part we give a general analysis of concurrency. We model computations as structures over multisets of actions with two strict partial orders: *causal* precedence (in a wide sense of "causal") and *temporal* precedence. The first is included in the second. Concurrent events are those incomparable under causal precedence, simultaneous events are those incomparable under temporal precedence. Thus, simultaneity implies concurrency but not vice versa. In this setting we can define precisely how computing devices are specified by partial orders and how pomsets express concurrency. The causal parts of the possible computations of a computing device constitute the *core* of the corresponding process. They turn out to be the least constrained members in the set of pomsets which specifies the device. The core of the process is insensitive to the way we model time and events, the temporal components are not. In the second part of the work we propose a generalization of linear transition systems. The nonlinear systems act like automata that spew out pomsets instead of strings. Various intuitions can be carried over from the linear to the nonlinear case without sacrificing true concurrency. Nonlinear automata can be used to generate the cores of processes associated with a great variety of computing devices. In particular, we show how they provide useful descriptions of shared resource situations (Dining Philosophers with and without Locking). The avoidance of deadlock by an implementation can be defined and proved. Similarly, we can define formally what it means for an implementation to involve loss of parallelism. Such a loss shows in the form of extra order constraints that have to be added to core members of the original process. Nonlinear transition systems appear to be natural candidates for modeling concurrency and hidden branching within a manageable framework.

Key words: concurrent, computation, partial order, pomset, process, action, event, causal precedence, simultaneous, transition system, automaton, state, shared resource, dining philosophers, deadlock.

CONTENTS

1 Partially Ordered Multisets And Concurrent Behaviors

When modeling computations, or for that matter any activity, it is customary to distinguish between *actions* and *events*. An action may occur more than once. An occurrence of an action is an event. A computation produces a *multiset* of actions. Formally, a multiset is a structure of the form

$$(V, \mu)$$

where V is a set (of events) and μ is a labeling which assigns each $e \in V$ the object (action) of which e is an occurrence. We say that e is an occurrence of $\mu(e)$ and that $\mu(e)$ is the type of e.

A **pomset** (partially ordered multiset) consists of a multiset (V, μ) and a strict (i.e., irreflexive) partial order, $<$, of V. The partial order is meant to imply temporal precedence: if $e_1 < e_2$ then e_1 precedes e_2; but not all temporal precedences have to be represented in $<$. We think of the inequalities as order constraints and of $<$ as a set of such constraints. A pomset can be written in the form

$$(V, <, \mu)$$

If desirable, we can display the range of μ in the notation, writing: $(V, \Sigma, <, \mu)$ where $\Sigma = \{\mu(e) : e \in V\}$. We also say that a pomset is *over* Σ if Σ includes the range of μ. This is analogous to a string being over an alphabet. Indeed, strings are pomsets in which $<$ is total.

(Pomsets appear to have originated with Grabowski [Gr] in the study of Petri nets. Independently, they were exemplified by Brock and Ackerman's scenarios, [BA]. The name "pomset" is due to Pratt [Pr] who has been advocating pomsets for the last six years and who supplied many of the basic concepts concerning them. Certain algebraic aspects of pomsets have been investigated by Gischer [Gi]. Further developments have been carried out by the author, in a joint work with Pratt [GP].

Note that our definition differs a little from that of [Pr], which originated in [Gi] and appears also in [GP]. Pomsets are defined there as structures $(V, \Sigma, <, \mu)$ where Σ is any superset of the range of μ. Such a definition is handy for some purposes but has unpleasant side effects which are avoided by our present simpler version.[1] On the whole the difference is not essential.)

[1] By the version of [Pr] strings are not exactly pomsets and formal languages are not exactly special cases of processes. It is as if we defined a string to be a pair (Σ, s) where s is an ordinary string and Σ is a set containing all the symbols appearing in s and, possibly, more. This version leads to a semantics which is not fully abstract. Processes may differ by virtue of having different action alphabets, even though the difference concerns only actions which never occur in the behaviors of these processes.

An *isomorphism* of the pomsets $(V, <, \mu)$ and $(V', <', \mu')$ is a bijection, say $'$, of V onto V' which is a structure isomorphism: (i) $e_1 < e_2 \iff e_1' <' e_2'$ and (ii) $\mu(e) = \mu'(e')$. For our purposes isomorphic pomsets can be considered equal. We do however distinguish isomorphic pomsets when they occur as different substructures of the same pomset.

We use p, q, p_1, q_1,... for pomsets.

A (pomset-) *process* is a class of pomsets closed under isomorphisms.

We use P, Q, P_1, Q_1,... for processes.

Processes are used to model computing devices, i.e., to represent sets of possible computations. The intuition behind pomsets is that *pomsets should be to concurrent computations what strings are to sequential ones.* They make for a true representation of concurrency which is impossible in the interleaving semantics (i.e., the one based on strings). To see this point consider the following very simple example:

Example 1.1 M_1 is a computing device which does sequentially in nondeterministic order the actions a and b, each action ones.

M_2 is a device consisting of two concurrently working components. One does a (once) the other does b (once).

The possible linear behaviors of M_1 and M_2 are the same: ab ba

Thus we cannot distinguish in the interleaving semantics between concurrent performance and sequential performance in nondeterministic order.

With pomsets this distinction is brought out by means of $a||b$ — the pomset obtained by "placing side by side" an occurrence of a and an occurrence of b with no order constraints. This pomset is included in the process representing M_2 but excluded from the one representing M_1. The reason for the exclusion is the following rule of pomset modeling:

Lack of order constraints implies concurrent performance.

Sequentially performed events must be therefore totally ordered by the pomset ordering. The ordering may however relate also concurrent events: we can have $e < e'$ for concurrently performed e and e'.

We still need a precise and general account of how sets of pomsets represent computing devices. So far such an account has been missing from the literature (which is perhaps the reason for some complaints about unclarity in the meaning of pomsets.) We shall presently propose such an account. In order to do that we analyze the very concept of "concurrent performance" and propose a general definition of "computation". First another, more interesting, example.

Example 1.2 (Simple Channel) This device accepts data values ("messages") at one end and outputs them in the same order at the other end. At each end the activity is sequential. The activities at the two ends are concurrent. The delay between input and corresponding output may vary nondeterministically.

If Δ = set of data values the actions are:

$in\delta$ (accept δ at the input end), $out\delta$ (emit δ at the output end), $\delta \in \Delta$.

A typical pomset of this process is drawn below.

Here as elsewhere we use $\rightarrow$ to show orderings provided in the pomset. The order $<$ is the transitive closure of all arrow-connected pairs.

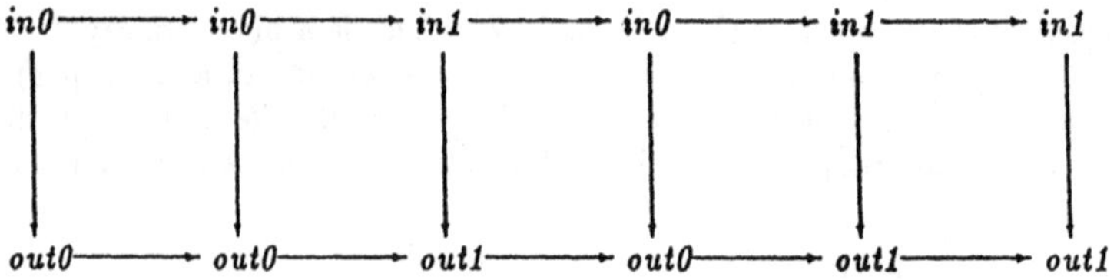

Figure 1

Note that the vertical arrows reflect a causal relation between input and output. The horizontal arrows reflect merely the sequentiality of each channel end. (But both can be fruitfully incorporated in a wider "causality" concept.)

There is no inequality in either direction between the first *out*0 and the second *in*0 and this marks them as being performed concurrently. We might augment the given partial order by adding an arrow between them. Such augments provide more temporal order information but less information about concurrent performance.

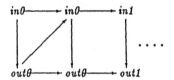

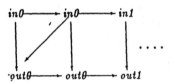

Note that the same actions can be sometimes concurrent and sometimes not: The first *out*0 is performed concurrently with the second *in*0, but not with the first *in*0 (because it must always come after it). For this reason the Simple Channel cannot be modeled by traces. In the trace model (cf. [AR], [Ma]) the concurrency of the first *out*0 with the second *in*0 would imply its concurrency with the first *in*0.

Computations

Example 1.1 shows that a computation is insufficiently characterized by the temporal order of its events. We can have e preceding e' in a sequential computation or in a concurrent one and we want to distinguish between the two.

A computations will be therefore a structure over a multiset of actions with a component for expressing temporal order and another component for expressing concurrency.

The temporal order is to be given by temporal precedence (or precedence, for short). We take it to be a strict partial order (i.e., irreflexive and transitive). We use $<^t$ for precedence.

If $e \neq e'$ and neither $e <^t e'$ nor $e' <^t e$ then we say that e and e' are *simultaneous*.

Note that simultaneity for us is nothing more than incomparability under $<^t$. Evidently it is symmetric. We find it convenient to construe it as irreflexive, i.e., an event is not considered simultaneous with itself. This is a technical convenience and not essential.

Simultaneity is empty iff $<^t$ is a total order.

The properties of $<^t$ depend on how we model time and events. For example, if we take time as a linear order and we model events as occupying time points, then two events are simultaneous iff they occupy the same time point. In that case simultaneity is an equivalence relation and the partial order given by Fig. 1 cannot be a temporal precedence. To become one it has to be augmented by additional arrows. But the partial order of Fig. 1 is a possible temporal precedence if events occupy intervals. We shall say more on the subject later.

As for concurrency, it is more convenient to handle it through its negation: ***sequentiality***. Two distinct events are performed sequentially iff they are not performed concurrently. (Also an event is not performed sequentially with itself.)

Write $Seq(e, e')$ for: e and e' are performed sequentially.

Then Seq is a symmetric irreflexive relation. The following two conditions are now imposed:

(S1) If $Seq(e, e')$ then either $e <^t e'$ or $e' <^t e$.

(S2) If $e <^t e'$ and $e' <^t e''$ and if $Seq(e, e')$ and $Seq(e', e'')$, then $Seq(e, e'')$.

(S1) says that two sequential events cannot be simultaneous, in other words: simultaneous events are performed concurrently.

To see the point of (S2), consider Fig. 1. The first *in0* and the second *in0* are performed sequentially, also the second *in0* and the second *out0* are performed sequentially. The precedences being what they are, (S2) implies that the first *in0* and the second *out0* are performed sequentially. Thus (S2) makes performance in separate components sequential when the events can be connected by a mixed chain of "local" (horizontal) and causal (vertical) arrows.

In general, sequential performance signifies that there is some dependence between the performed events, over and above mere temporal order. This is the case when the events use a common resource which cannot be shared at the same time. A narrow location (like the channel end of the Simple Channel) is a particular case of such a resource. A dependence is also established by causal relations. The vertical arrows in Fig. 1 are such an example.

It is very convenient to use an extended notion of "causality" which covers the common notion of cause and effect as well as the dependencies which are due to shared resources. In Petri nets ([Pe], [Re], [RT]) such a notion arises naturally, because in that model the performance of the first *in0* produces conditions which enable the performance of the second *in0*. Here we do not assume any operational model like Petri nets. But we shall use "causal dependency" in an extended sense which covers also the horizontal arrows of Fig. 1.

We therefore define *causal precedence*, to be denote by $<^c$, by:

$$e <^c e' \iff_{Df} Seq(e, e') \text{ and } e <^t e'$$

We shall use 'precedence' unqualified for temporal precedence.

From (S2) we get easily: $e <^c e' <^c e'' \Rightarrow e <^c e''$. Hence $<^c$ is a partial order included in $<^t$. (S1) is easily seen to imply:

$$Seq(e, e') \iff e <^c e' \text{ or } e' <^c e.$$

So we can recover Seq from $<^c$. Consequently, *two distinct events are concurrent iff they are incomparable under* $<^c$.

We find it convenient to construe concurrency as irreflexive (again, a technical convenience, not an essential point).

The upshot of this is that *concurrency is to causal precedence what simultaneity is to temporal precedence.*

We formalize all this in:

Definition 1.1 (computation) A *computation* is a structure $(V, <^c, <^t, \mu)$, where (V, μ) is a multiset and $<^c$ and $<^t$ are (strict) partial orders of V, such that $<^c$ is included in $<^t$. Moreover $<^t$ should be a possible temporal ordering of V, under the presupposed modeling of time and events.

The members of V are called the *computation events* and $<^t$ and $<^c$ are called, respectively, *(temporal) precedence* and *causal precedence*.

Two events are *performed sequentially* if they are related (i.e., comparable) by $<^c$. Two events are *simultaneous* if distinct and incomparable under $<^t$; they are *performed concurrently*, or for short *concurrent*, if distinct and incomparable under $<^c$.

Computations and Pomsets

Now we can see how pomsets provide partial descriptions of computations:

Definition 1.2 (covers a computation) A pomset $p = (V, <, \mu)$ *covers* a computation if the computation has the same multiset and for all e, e' in V we have:

$$e <^c e' \Rightarrow e < e' \Rightarrow e <^t e'$$

The second implication says that all order constraints of the pomset are satisfied in the computation by temporal precedence . The first implication says that all causal precedences are represented in the pomset. It means that any two distinct events which are incomparable under $<$ are also incomparable under $<^c$. This is our old rule that $<$-incomparable events must be concurrent.

For example, $a||b$ covers all computations with two events in which a is performed concurrently with b. (We identify actions with events if each action occurs once.) And $a \rightarrow b$ covers all computations with two events in which a precedes b.

We shall use $||$ for the $<$-incomparability relation over distinct members of V. That is to say:

$$e \;||\; e' \textit{ iff } e \neq e' \textit{ and neither } e < e' \textit{ nor } e' < e.$$

We shall however use $||$ also for the "placing-side-by-side" operation on pomsets, [Pr]. In particular, $a||b$ is the two-event pomset with no order constraints. The context will make clear the intended meaning of $||$.

In general, it takes two pomsets to characterize completely a computation:

Definition 1.3 (causal and temporal pomsets) The *causal part* (or *causal pomset*) of a computation $(V, <^c, <^t, \mu)$ is the pomset $(V, <^c, \mu)$. The *temporal part* (or *temporal pomset*) of the computation is the pomset is $(V, <^t, \mu)$.

In the causal pomset we have a complete representation of concurrency by $||$. In addition, we have partial information on temporal order. The temporal pomset gives us the full temporal picture but only partial information on concurrency. The pomset in Fig. 1 is the causal pomset of some computation of the Simple Channel.

As mentioned above, whether some partial order can be the full temporal precedence relation depends on the modeling of time and events. Usually there are severe restrictions. We do not want to commit ourselves to a particular model, but the restrictions, whatever they are, should be indicated. So we define:

Definition 1.4 (full pomsets) A pomset $(V, <, \mu)$ is *full* if $<$ can be interpreted as a temporal precedence relation over V.

What the full pomsets are depends on the choice of the time/events model, which we leave open.

On the other hand there appear to be no limitations on causal pomsets (at least not in the finite case). The reason is that, given a (finite) pomset, we can make up a computing device capable of producing a computation for which causal precedence is exactly the given $<$. Use concurrently working components to produce $<$-incomparable events and wire the device so as to introduce the "right" dependencies that make $<$-related events sequential. (This can be made into a precise claim, using some modeling of computing devices, e.g., Petri nets.)

Definition 1.5 ([Pr] augment) A pomset q is an *augment* of p, denoted: $p \preceq q$, if q has the same multiset of actions and its partial order includes that of p.

The augment is *proper*, denoted $p \prec q$, if it is different from p.

A process P is *augment closed* if it contains with every pomset all its augments. The *augment closure* of P is the process consisting of all augments of members of P. (It is the smallest augment closed process which includes P.)

We can now set up the one-to-one correspondence between certain pairs of pomsets and computations.

Definition 1.6 ((p,q)-computation) Let $p = (V, <_p, \mu)$ be any pomset and let $q = (V, <_q, \mu)$ be a full pomset which augments p. Then the *(p,q)-computation* is $(V, <_p, <_q, \mu)$. In other words, it is the unique computation with causal pomset p and temporal pomset q.

Processes and Sets of Computations

To specify a computing device is to give information about its possible computations. We shall therefore consider natural ways in which processes (sets of pomsets) determine sets of computations.

Call $p \in P$ a **least constrained** pomset of P if it is not a proper augment of any other pomset in P.

Every finite pomset in P augments some least constrained pomset (because any decreasing augment chain of finite pomsets is finite, there being only finitely many partial orders over a finite V). From now on we require that this should hold in general, that is to say, all processes are required to satisfy: *Every $p \in P$ augments some least constrained pomset of P.*
The following is trivial:

Proposition 1.1 *Among all pomsets which cover a given computation the causal pomset is the least constrained.*

This provides the clue for determining the set of computations represented by a process:

- The least constrained pomsets in the process are the causal pomsets of the represented computations.
- Additional information about temporal order is obtained via those augments of the causal pomsets which are in the process.

The strongest notion is that of *complete representation.* Here all computations are given by spelling out both the causal and the temporal parts:

A process P *represents (completely)* the set of all (p,q) computations such that p is a least constrained member of P and $q \in P$ is a full pomset augmenting p.

In the next section we shall argue that, in the context of specification problems, this is too strong. Knowing the causal parts is in many cases sufficient. But let us see first how complete representation works.

Example 1.3 (Loose and tight concurrency) Let P_1, P_2 and P_3 be the following processes:

P_1: $a \to b$, $b \to a$
P_2: $a \to b$, $b \to a$, $a \,||\, b$
P_3: $a \,||\, b$

The least constrained pomsets in P_1 are $a \rightarrow b$ and $b \rightarrow a$. Each of P_2 and P_3 have one least constrained pomset: $a||b$.

P_1 represents the sequential device M_1 of Example 1.1.

Each of P_2 and P_3 represents a device which performs concurrently a and b. In the case of P_2 the concurrency is *loose*. Each of: *a precedes b*, *b precedes a* is possible. This is shown by the presence of $a \rightarrow b$ and $b \rightarrow a$ in the process. If our time/events model allows simultaneities, then they can be also performed simultaneously (because $a||b$ is a full pomset and the $(a||b,\ a||b)$-computation performs a and b simultaneously).

In the case of P_3 the concurrency is *tight*, no precedence is possible; if it were, there should have been a pomset in P_3 testifying to it. This implies that the actions are always performed simultaneously. (Imagine a device in which one action triggers the concurrent performance of the other "at the same time", i.e., in the same time slot. Or imagine events occupying time-intervals where the triggering is such that the time intervals overlap. Simultaneity can be also enforced by clocks that have been synchronized by a hidden event.)

An intermediate degree of tightness is exemplified by $\{a||b,\ a \rightarrow b\}$.

In augment closed processes each pomset can be augmented arbitrarily. This implies that concurrently performed events are performable in either order and any global choice of the order is possible, provided that it is compatible with the given order constraints. *Augment closed processes model completely loose concurrency.*

In the following example we use $\rightarrow$ for pomset concatenation e.g., $(a||b) \rightarrow c$ has three events and two order constraints: $a < b$ and $a < c$. (Actions that occur once are identified with their corresponding events.)

Example 1.4 Consider the following processes, where $Q_2 \subset Q_1$:

Q_1 :	$(a \rightarrow c)\|\|b$,	$(a\|\|b) \rightarrow c$,	$a \rightarrow (b\|\|c)$,	$b \rightarrow a \rightarrow c$,	$a \rightarrow b \rightarrow c$,	$a \rightarrow c \rightarrow b$
Q_2 :		$(a\|\|b) \rightarrow c$,	$a \rightarrow (b\|\|c)$,	$b \rightarrow a \rightarrow c$,	$a \rightarrow b \rightarrow c$,	$a \rightarrow c \rightarrow b$

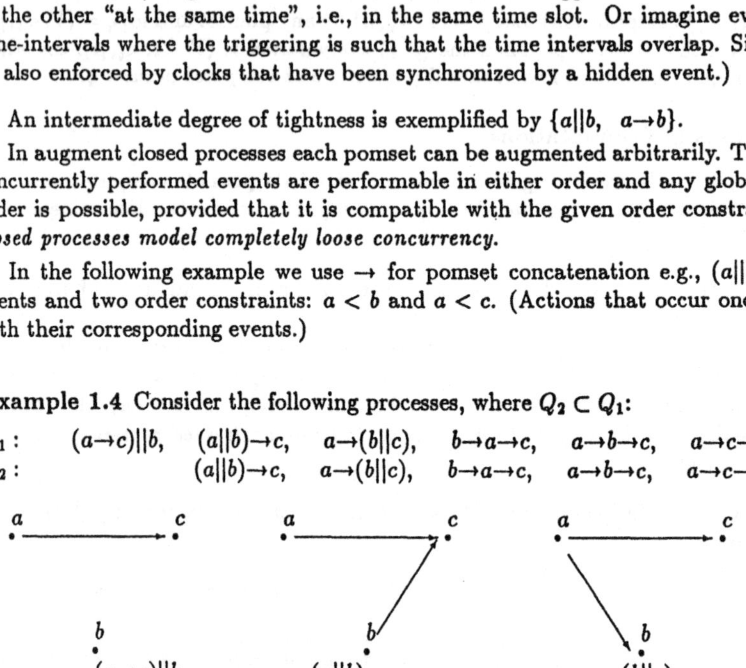

$(a \rightarrow c)||b$ $\qquad$ $(a||b) \rightarrow c$ $\qquad$ $a \rightarrow (b||c)$

Q_1 has one least constrained pomset: $(a \rightarrow c)||b$. It represents a device made of two concurrently working components. One performs sequentially a then c, the other performs b.

Q_2 has two least constrained pomsets $(a||b) \rightarrow c$ and $a \rightarrow (b||c)$. Here the device chooses nondeterministically between (i) a concurrent performance of a and b, all this followed by c and (ii) a performance of a followed by a concurrent performance of b and c.

Q_1 and Q_2 are augment closed, so the concurrency is loose in both cases.

Note the non-distributivity of concatenation over $||$.

Modeling Time and Events

We shall now outline some of the possibilities for modeling time and events:

(I) No Simultaneity. Simultaneity is impossible. Temporal precedence is always a total ordering.

(II) Linear time, point-like events. Every event has an associated time point (or temporal slot). Precedence of events is the precedence of their time points. Events are simultaneous iff they have the same time point.

(III) Linear time, interval-like events. Every event has an associated closed time-interval. Precedence of events is the precedence of their intervals (the right end of one interval precedes the left end of the other). Events are simultaneous iff their intervals overlap. Such a model has been used in [La].

(IV) Models based on relative time. There are many clocks. An event e precedes e' iff it precedes it according to all clocks. Events are simultaneous iff either they are simultaneous in all clocks or two clocks disagree on their ordering. (Models of this type have been suggested by Pratt).

In the case of (I) a pomset is full iff it is linear, i.e., if $<$ is a linear order. In (II) a pomset is full iff it is *prelinear*, meaning that $||$ is an equivalence relation which is a congruence for $<$ and $<$ induces a total order on the equivalence classes. In (III) a pomset is full iff $<$ is what is known as an interval-order (cf [Fi]).

We refer to models other than (I) as *models with simultaneity.*

(I) is the strongest model in the sense that all linear pomsets are full in all other natural models. Similarly (II) is strongest in the class of all natural models with simultaneity.

When a particular time/events model is assumed it is natural to restrict accordingly the processes to be considered. For example, any pomset in the process should have a full augment in it. Else, it does not cover any of the process' computations. The pomset framework is however not committed to a particular modeling. Results obtained without presuppositions on time and events will apply equally in all models.

Example 1.5 Let $Q = \{(a{\rightarrow}c)||b,\quad (a||b){\rightarrow}c,\quad a{\rightarrow}(c||b),\quad b{\rightarrow}a{\rightarrow}c\}$.

All computations of Q consist of a sequential performance of: *a then c* and, concurrently with it, a performance of b. For linear time and point-like events there are three computations: *b simultaneous with a, b simultaneous with c, b precedes a.* For interval-like events there is a fourth computation: *b simultaneous with a and with c,* which is impossible for point-like events (because a precedes c).

Note that in the No Simultaneity model Q represents only one computation, that in which the temporal order is: $b{\rightarrow}a{\rightarrow}c$. This does not seem natural in view of the fact that b is performed concurrently with a. Cases of this kind are excluded by each of the following requirements. The first is natural for the No Simultaneity model, the second — for models with simultaneity.

Order Reversibility If p is least constrained in P and $e \; ||_p \; e'$ (i.e., e and e' are $<$-incomparable in p) then there are full pomsets in P augmenting p, such that $e < e'$ in one and $e' < e$ in the other.

Possible Simultaneity If p is least constrained in P and $e \; ||_p \; e'$ then there is a full augment of p in P for which $e \; || \; e'$.

Intuitively, the first condition says that concurrently performed events can be performed in either order and the second condition says that they can be performed simultaneously. These intuitions can be formalized, as shown in the following subsection.

Modal Interpretations of Concurrency

The satisfaction of either of Order Reversibity or Possible Simultaneity enables us to define concurrency in terms of possible temporal orderings. The first reduction assumes that Order Reversibility holds, the second and, I think, the more useful one assumes Possible Simultaneity.

(C1) *e and e′ are performed (in a given computation) concurrently iff it is possible for the computing device to perform them in either order.*

(C2) *e and e' are performed (in a given computation) concurrently iff it is possible for the computing device to perform them simultaneously.*

(C1) and (C2) are actually theorems, provided that "possible" is made precise by using the following Kripke model:

Let the possible worlds be all the computations of the device. Define *computation*$_1$ to be accessible from *computation*$_2$ iff they have the same causal pomset. (Recall: "it is possible that X" is true in *world*$_1$ iff X is true in some world accessible from *world*$_1$).[2]

If the process is augment closed, Order Reversibility holds for all (natural) time/event models and Possible Simultaneity holds for all (natural) models with simultaneity. Moreover, for models with simultaneity we have:

(SIM) *Two events are simultaneous iff it is possible for the device to perform them in either order*

All this follows from the following proposition and from the fact that all linear pomsets are full in all (natural) time/events models and all prelinear pomsets are full in all (natural) models with simultaneity.

Proposition 1.2 *If $<$ is a partial order and two distinct members e, e' are $<$-incomparable then (i) there are linear augments of $<$ which order e and e' in either way and (ii) there exists a prelinear augment of $<$ for which e and e' are in the same equivalence class.*

(i) is a basic theorem on partial orders, (ii) is not more difficult to prove.

(SIM) appears to vindicate Hoar, [Ho], who proposed to define simultaneous performance as performability in either order. Note however that, for sequentially performed events, order reversal is *not* possible in this Kripke model, even when the order is chosen nondeterministically. (Being sequential in a (p,q)-computation means that the events are comparable in p. Their order in p is inherited by all (p,q')-computations, hence by all computations accessible from the given (p,q)-computation.) Therefore nondeterministic sequential choice cannot be used, as Hoar suggested, to express simultaneity. The possibility of reversal is due here to concurrency not to sequential nondeterminism.

Limits of the Representation

Not every set of computations can be represented completely by a set of pomsets. This should be obvious from the fact that a computation is essentially a pair of pomsets. A simple counting argument shows that, on a given multiset of more than one event, there are more sets of computations than sets of pomsets. For example, the set of computations of the following device cannot be represented:

Capricious Device This device chooses nondeterministically between a concurrent performance of a and b and a sequential performance of *a then b* .

We must use $a||b$ to cover the first alternative and $a \to b$ for the second. But then $a \to b$ will be interpreted as the temporal part of the $(a||b,\ a \to b)$-computation (a concurrent performance of a and b in which a precedes b).

We could have used other codings, but the counting argument shows that no method is exhaustive. The representation proposed here appears to hit the best compromise between

[2] Here, for example, is the argument for the "only if" direction of (C2). Let e and e' be events in the (p,q)-computation. It is possible for e and e' to be simultaneous iff there is a (p',q')-computation, accessible from (p,q), in which they are simultaneous, i.e., $e||_{q'}e'$. Since $p' \preceq q'$ we have $e||_{p'}e'$. The accessibility means that $p = p'$. Thus $e||_p e'$, implying that they are concurrent. The "if" direction follows from the Possible Simultaneity condition.

expressibility and simplicity. Cases of the Capricious Device type are not likely to play an important role in natural specification problems. The simplicity gained by replacing computations (pairs of partial orderings) by pomsets (single partial orderings) is worth the price of the limitations.

2 Specifications

To represent completely a device the process should represent completely the set of its possible computations. (It is also natural to require that every pomset in the process should cover some computation of the device.)

In the case of augment closed processes it suffices to describe only the causal parts of the computations, the rest is gotten by taking the augment closure. In other cases, as well, we might be content with specifying the causal pomsets, leaving the finer details of temporal ordering open. We thus concentrate on the least constrained pomsets:

Definition 2.1 (core) The *core* of a process P, denoted $Cor(P)$, is the set of all least constrained pomsets of P.

P is a *core* if $P = Cor(Q)$ for some Q.

Two processes P, Q, are *core equivalent* if $Cor(P) = Cor(Q)$

Proposition 2.1 *(i)* $Q \subseteq Cor(P) \Rightarrow Q = Cor(Q)$

(ii) P is a core iff it consists of members incomparable under $\prec$ (the augment ordering).

(iii) $Cor(P)$ is the minimal set (with respect to inclusion) which is core equivalent to P.

The first two claims derives directly from the fact that the core consists of all minimal elements under the partial order $\prec$. The third claim follows from the first.

Proposition 2.2 *P and Q are core equivalent iff they have the same augment closure.*

Proof Assume, for the "if" direction, that P and Q have the same augment closure. If $p \in Cor(P)$ then $p \in P$ and, a fortiori, p is in the augment closure of P, hence also of Q. Therefore $q \preceq p$ for some $q \in Q$. Now, for some $q' \in Cor(Q)$, $q' \preceq q$. By the same reasoning, going back to P, $p' \preceq q'$ for some $p' \in P$. Since p is least augmented in P none of the augments in the chain $p' \preceq q' \preceq q \preceq p$ is proper. Hence $p = q'$. The "only if" direction follows from the trivial fact that P and $Cor(P)$ have the same augment closure. □.

Call p a *causal pomset of the device M* if p is a causal pomset of some computation of M.

Definition 2.2 (specification) A process P is a *specification* of the computing device M if

(1) $Cor(P)$ consists of all the causal pomsets of M.

(2) Every $p \in P$ covers some possible computation of M.

A *core-specification* of M is a specification of M which is a core.

A specification gives us through its core the full information on causal precedence and concurrency. It might also give us additional partial information on possible temporal orderings.

Example 2.1 Let $P = \{p_1, p_2\}$ where $p_1 = (a \rightarrow b)||(c \rightarrow d)$ and p_2 is an augment of p_1 obtained by adding the constraint $a < c$.

Evidently, $Cor(P) = \{p_1\}$.

P specifies a device which performs *a then b* concurrently with *c then d*; this much is given by the core. Since p_2 covers some computation, it is possible for the device to compute so as to satisfy all order constraints of p_2. In our case this means that a can precede c. All the rest is left open, we are not told whether c can precede a, or whether b can precede c, etc.

The core specification tells us that *a then b* is concurrently performed with *c then d* and nothing more.

The specification of the Simple Channel by pomsets of the type of Fig. 1 (we shall presently see how to characterize them) is its core specification.

The following derives directly from the definitions and from the fact that a core is just a set of pomsets incomparable under $\prec$.

Proposition 2.3 *A device M has a specification iff its causal pomsets are incomparable under $\prec$. If it has a specification then it has a unique core-specification consisting of all its causal pomsets.*

The Capricious Device of the previous section has no specification, because one causal pomset properly augments another.

Core specifications can be regarded as optimal for the following reasons:

(1) When the processes to be considered are augment closed it suffices to describe them up to core equivalence, with the understanding that in any case all augments are included. Each core equivalence class is characterized by its core which is its minimal (under set inclusion) member. In this case core specifications amount to full representations.

(2) The core provides exactly all the information about causal precedence and concurrency, which is extremely valuable even when the finer details of temporal order are left unspecified. Moreover, providing additional temporal order information may clutter unnecessarily the description. Imagine, for example the result of putting many additional arrows in Fig. 1.

(3) The information provided by the core is insensitive to the modeling of time and events. We can therefore ignore issues arising from choices of particular time/events models.

Quite aside from the question of true concurrency, pomsets can be very useful for specifying sets of interleavings. Consider for example the Simple Channel and the associated set of all its interleaved computations. A clear and simple description is to say that this is the set of all linearizations of pomsets of the type of Fig. 1. And pomsets of the type of Fig. 1 have, we shall see, a very simple formal definition.

Definition 2.3 (normal) A core P is *normal* if every two distinct members of P have disjoint sets of linearizations.

A process is *normal* if its core is.

The process Q_2 of Example 1.4 is not normal, because $a \to b \to c$ is a linearization of two different least constrained pomsets.

In normal processes every member of the process is an augment of a uniquely determined member of the core (otherwise, two distinct members of the core will have a common augment, hence also a common linearization).

We can decode in such a process the core member from any linearization of it. This means that the causal part of any computation can be decoded from each of its interleavings . (This of course does not mean that the interleavings characterize the process. The decoding depends on the process which, as our trivial starting example illustrates, is *not* determined by the interleavings.) Therefore the temporal part of a computation determines it uniquely.

As an illustration consider all pomsets of the type of Fig. 1 (a precise definition of this family will be given in the next section). Each of the pomsets can be reconstructed from any of its linearizations: Namely, the substring consisting of all input actions must be the "upper row" and this determines the pomset completely.

It appears that many natural specification problems (those motivated by concrete cases) give rise to normal processes.

3 Nonlinear Transition Systems

Dependent Actions and Local Concatenations

$(V, <, \mu)$ is a *subpomset* of $(V', <', \mu')$ if $V \subseteq V'$ and $<$ and μ are the restrictions of $<'$ and μ' to V.

The *concatenation*, $p_1; p_2$, of two pomsets p_1 and p_2 is the pomset obtained by placing p_2 after p_1. Formally:

Let $p_i = (V_i, <_i, \mu_i)$ where V_1 and V_2 are disjoint. (If they are not, use disjoint isomorphic copies.) Then $p_1; p_2$ is the pomset containing p_1 and p_2 as subpomsets, whose set of events is $V_1 \cup V_2$ and whose partial order is obtained from $<_1 \ \cup \ <_2$ by adding all order constraints: $e_1 \ < \ e_2$ where $e_1 \in V_1, e_2 \in V_2$.

Now assume that p_1 and p_2 are over the action alphabet Σ. Let D be a binary relation over Σ. Then the **D-local concatenation** of p_1 and p_2 is defined like concatenation except that we add to $<_1 \ \cup \ <_2$ only the constraints $e_1 < e_2, \quad e_1 \in V_1 \ e_2 \in V_2,$ such that $(\mu_1(e_1), \mu_2(e_2)) \ \in \ D$ (and we close under transitivity).

Think of D as expressing dependencies between actions. When we form a D-local concatenation, additional action-occurrences which are dependent on "previous" ones follow them sequentially. But when there is no dependence concurrency is allowed.

Symmetric dependency relations have been introduced in the context of trace theory, by Mazurkiewicz, [Ma] (cf. also [AR]). A restricted type of local concatenation, where D is the equivalence relation holding between co-located events, has been defined in [Pr]. In this paper we assume throughout that D is reflexive and symmetric. Note though that our definition of D- local concatenation makes sense for an arbitrary D.

We denote the D-local concatenation of p and q by $p \ |;|_D q$. We omit 'D' when the intended dependency relation is clear. (Think of $|;|$ as composed of concatenation with concurrence, which is what local concatenation is).

Here is an example how local concatenations can make for simple descriptions of processes. Consider the Simple Channel.

Let $In = \{in\delta : \delta \in \Delta\}, \quad Out = \{out\delta : \delta \in \Delta\}$

Put: $D = In \times In \ \cup \ Out \times Out$.

D consists here of all pairs of co-located actions, where the locations are the input end and the output end of the channel.

Let $Q = \{in\delta; out\delta \ : \ \delta \in \Delta\}$.

Then the core of the Simple Channel, i.e., the set of pomsets exemplified by Fig. 1, consists of all pomsets of the form :

$$p_1 \ |;| \ p_2 \ |;| \ \dots \ |;| \ p_n \quad \text{where } p_i \in Q.$$

(Note how each additional local concatenation produces an additional column. The horizontal arrows are due to $|;|$, the vertical arrows are due to the ordinary concatenation which is used inside the pomsets of Q.)

The core can be written also as $Q^{|*|}$ where $^{|*|}$ expresses repeated local concatenation (in the way * expresses repeated concatenation). We can see already how regular expressions can be generalized so as to define partial orderings.

Transition Systems

Transition systems (defined first by Myhill [My]) are a most common tool for defining formal languages. At the heart of a transition system is a transition relation, $\mathrm{T} \subseteq St \times \Sigma^* \times St$ where St is a set of states and Σ^* is the set of all finite strings over the alphabet Σ.

Tuples $(S, s, S') \in \mathrm{T}$ are called *transitions*. A *transition sequence is a sequence* $S_0, s_1, S_1, \dots, s_n$, such that every (S_{i-1}, s_i, S_i) is a transition.

Let us say that the transition sequence *carries* S_0 *to* S_n and *produces*, or *generates*, the concatenation of the s_i's : $s_1 \dots s_n$.

With each pair of states (S, S') we can associate the set of all strings producible by transition sequences which carry S to S'.

The transition system has also designated sets of initial and final states. It defines the language consisting of all strings producible by transition sequences which carry an initial state to a final one.

Regular sets are sets of strings definable in this way by finite transition systems.

We generalize this to nonlinear transition systems which produce pomsets instead of strings:

- Use transitions of the form $(S, \ p, \ S')$, where p ranges over pomsets.
- Having obtained a string of pomsets, interpret juxtaposition as local concatenation, i.e, the generated pomset is the local concatenation of the p_i's: $p_1 \ |;| \ p_2 \dots \ |;| \ p_n$.

The intuition is that the system passes from one state to another by producing a pomset and that we "connect" all these pomsets by specifying only order constraints that are due to dependencies, as given by the presupposed dependency relation D.

Nonlinear transition systems are related, though not directly, to Stark's interesting concept of concurrent transition systems, [St]. Stark construes his systems as categories (with states as objects and transitions as morphisms) with an additional two place operation through which concurrency is handled. Though the present framework is differently based and aims at different issues, our nonlinear transition systems can provide models for interpreting Stark's abstract algebra.

Note that a transition system can generate infinite pomsets as well. This, again, is analogous to the linear case. When considering infinite transition sequences one usually requires that there be infinitely many occurrences of final states. In order to avoid issues not directly related to our main concerns, we shall restrict ourselves henceforth to finite pomsets. (The forthcoming theorems are nontheless true also for the infinite case).

In listing transitions we write (S, p, S') as:

$S \mid;\mid p \Longrightarrow S'$

Read: " From S, by producing p, go to S'."

The empty pomset is denoted by Λ.

A transition of the form $\Lambda \Longrightarrow S$ ("go to S by doing nothing") means that S is an initial state.

We use $\leftrightarrow_D$ to express dependencies between actions: $a \leftrightarrow_D b$ means that a and b are related by D. Reflexive dependencies $a \leftrightarrow_D a$ are always assumed whether listed or not. We write $a \leftrightarrow_D \Sigma$ for the collection of all $a \leftrightarrow_D b$, $b \in \Sigma$ and $\Sigma \leftrightarrow_D \Sigma'$ for the collection of all $a \leftrightarrow_D a'$, $a \in \Sigma, b \in \Sigma'$.

For the specification of the Simple Channel we need only one state. Here is how the specification looks:

Actions: $in\delta$, $out\delta$, $\delta \in \Delta$

Dependencies: Put $In = \{in\delta : \delta \in \Delta\}$, $Out = \{out\delta : \delta \in \Delta\}$, then:

$$In \leftrightarrow_D In, \qquad Out \leftrightarrow_D Out.$$

States: S

Final States: S

Transitions: $\Lambda \Longrightarrow S \qquad S \mid;\mid (in\delta; out\delta) \Longrightarrow S, \qquad \delta \in \Delta.$

To see the meaning of this specification we relate this specification with another description of the Simple Channel. We need the following basic concepts of the pomset framework ([Pr], [GP]):

A pomset $p = (V, <, \mu)$ is a **prefix** of $p' = (V', <', \mu')$, if p is a subpomset of p' and V is a prefix of V' under $<'$, i.e., $e' <' e \in V \Rightarrow e' \in V$.

We denote this by $p \sqsubseteq p'$.

Note that over strings $\sqsubseteq$ is the usual prefix ordering.

[If we regard a pomset as representing some (partially specified) complete computation, then a prefix represents some stage of the computation. A process should not be *prefix closed* (i.e., closed under prefixes) if the distinction between complete and incomplete computations is important.]

The **restriction** of a pomset p to the alphabet Σ, denoted p/Σ, is the subpomset of p consisting of the occurrences of members of Σ. In other words: p/Σ is the result of *hiding* the actions which are not in Σ.

Now consider the Simple Channel and, for each string s of actions, let $dat(s)$ be the string obtained by retaining in the actions only the data values,[3] e.g., $dat(in\delta_1\, in\delta_2 \ldots in\delta_n) = \delta_1\delta_2\ldots\delta_n$.

The Simple Channel process can be defined as the set of all pomsets which satisfy:

(i) p/In and p/Out are linear.

(ii) If $q \sqsubseteq p$ then $dat(q/Out) \sqsubseteq dat(q/In)$

(iii) $dat(p/Out) = dat(p/In)$

[3] In [GP] this has been generalized to a mapping which maps pomsets (not necessarily linear) into a cpo.

(i) says that each of the two channel ends performs sequentially. (ii) says that at every stage of the computation the output data string is a prefix of the input data string. This enforces the causal relation between input and output: the nth output event must be preceded by the nth input event (and their data-parts must be the same); otherwise the prefix of p consisting of the nth output and all $<$-smaller events does not contain the nth input, which contradicts (ii). The last condition, (iii), guarantees that in complete computations all messages arrive.

Now we have:

Theorem 3.1 *The set of pomsets defined recursively by the above given transition system is the core of the set of pomsets satisfying (i), (ii), (iii). This core is normal.*

Proof (Sketch) To show that the pomsets generated by the transition system satisfy the three properties, proceed by induction on the length of the generating transition sequence; the proof is easy. In the other direction, one has to show that a pomset satisfying the three properties augments some pomset producible via transitions. The idea is to consider only those arrows (order constraints) which are required in order to satisfy (i), (ii), (iii). This gives a pomset producible via transitions. The proof uses induction on the rank of events. The argument for normality was outlined at the end of the previous section. □

We shall now apply nonlinear transition systems to shared resource situations.

Dining Philosophers

A group AG of sequentially performing agents share resources belonging to some set RES. Agent i can perform actions from Σ_i. A mapping ρ defined over $\Sigma = \bigcup_{i \in Ag} \Sigma_i$ assigns each action a a set, $\rho(a)$, of resources used in doing a. Posession of $\rho(a)$ is necessary and sufficient for being able to perform a. No resource can be owned by two agents at the same time. If resource j is available agent i can acquire it by performing *i-acq-j*. He can release an owned resource via *i-rel-j*. (The acquiring and releasing actions are not included in Σ.)

Let $Ag(i)$ be the set of actions performable by agent i. $Ag(i)$ consists of all members of Σ_i and all *i-acq-j*, *i-rel-j*, $j \in RES$.

Let $Res(j)$ consist of all actions *i-acq-j*, *i-rel-j*, $i \in AG$

Consider the process defined by the following conditions:

(i) For all $i \in AG$, $p/Ag(i)$ is linear and satisfies:

For each occurrence, e, of $a \in \Sigma_i$: for every $j \in \rho(a)$ there is a preceding occurrence, e', of *i-acq-j*, such that no occurrence of *i-rel-j* is between e and e'.

(ii) For all $j \in RES$, $p/Res(j)$ is linear and satisfies:

Each (occurrence of) *i-rel-j* is immediately preceded by an *i-acq-j* and each *i-acq-j* which has a successor is immediately succeeded by an *i-rel-j*.

(i) means that no agent can perform an action without owning the necessary resources. (ii) guarantees that the computation will look as it should when regarded from the resource's point of view. It implies among the rest that no resource is owned by two agents at the same time.

Let DP be the process consisting of all pomsets satisfying (i) and (ii). Note that DP is augment closed (since each of the requirements is preserved under augmentation).

We can define DP as a composition of linear processes of the agents and linear processes of the resources, where each pomset entering the composition contributes its order constraints and the participating pomsets completely agree on the shared actions. (Pomset compositions were defined in [GP].) Here we shall offer a more constructive characterization of the process by a nonlinear transition system. With actions and sets of actions as just defined, the dependencies are:

$$Ag(i) \leftrightarrow_D Ag(i), \quad i \in AG \qquad\qquad Res(j) \leftrightarrow_D Res(j), \quad j \in RES$$

This is the most obvious dependency relation.[4] Note that the dependency relation here is a union of two equivalence relations, but it is *not* an equivalence.

States: States are vectors of the form $(J,\ K_i)_{i \in AG}$ (i.e., $(J, K_1 \ldots, K_i, \ldots)$ with i ranging over AG), such that the K_i's are disjoint subsets of RES and $J = RES - \bigcup_{i \in AG} K_i$. (It is convenient to accord J a separate coordinate even though it is determined by the rest). K_i is the resource set owned by i, it can be regarded as i's "local state". J is the set of available resources. Although such vectors amount to "global states", their meaning in the context of nonlinear transitions is somewhat different. They need not correspond to "real" time slices, as will become soon clear.

$(J, K_i)_{i \in AG}$ is a (possible) *deadlock state* if for each $i \in AG$ there exists $a_i \in \Sigma_i$ (the action that agent i wishes to perform) such that $\rho(a_i) \not\subseteq J \cup K_i$ for all $i \in AG$.

Since actions will have a limited effect on the state, we need not display the full state in writing a transition. We shall use $(J, K_i,\ -)$ to denote any state in which J and K_i are in the first and the ith coordinates. The "-" stands for the unspecified rest which is understood to be fixed throughout the transition.

Transitions:

$\Lambda \implies (RES,\ \emptyset,\ \emptyset, \ldots)$ (initially all resources are available.)

And for each $i \in AG$:

$(J, K_i, -)\ |;|\ i\text{-}acq\text{-}j \implies (J - \{j\}, K_i \cup \{j\}, -)$ where $j \in J$.

$(J, K_i, -)\ |;|\ a \implies (J, K_i, -)$, where $a \in \Sigma_i$ and $\rho(a) \subseteq K_i$.

$(J, K_i, -)\ |;|\ i\text{-}rel\text{-}j \implies (J \cup \{j\},\ K_i - \{j\}, -)$, where $j \in K_i$.

These transitions have obvious meanings: in the first an agent acquires an available resource, in the second an agents who owns the required resources performs an action and in the third a resource is released.

Here is an illustration of how the system generates pomsets:

Assume that there are two agents α and β and three resources $1, 2, 3$. Let a and b be actions such that $\rho(a) = \{1, 2\}$, $\rho(b) = \{2, 3\}$. consider the following transition sequence:

$(\{1,2,3\},\ \emptyset,\ \emptyset)$ α-*acq-1* $(\{2,3\},\ \{1\},\ \emptyset)$ α-*acq-2* $(\{3\},\ \{1,2\},\ \emptyset)$ a $(\{3\},\ \{1,2\}\ \emptyset)$ α-*rel-2* $(\{2,3\},\ \{1\},\ \emptyset)$ β-*acq-3* $(\{2\},\ \{1\},\ \{3\})$ β-*acq-2* $(\emptyset,\ \{1\},\ \{2,3\})$ b $(\emptyset,\ \{1\},\ \{2,3\})$

It produces the pomset: α-*acq-1* |;| α-*acq-2* |;| a |;| α-*rel-2* |;| β-*acq-3* |;| β-*acq-2* |;| b which is drawn below.

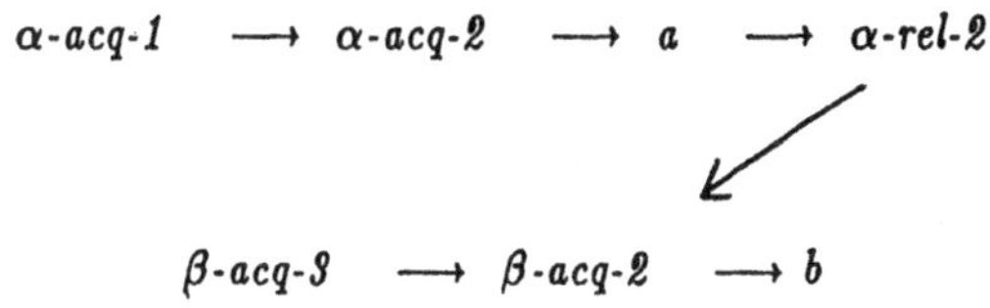

[4] We could have enlarged the relation, by making any two actions that use a common resource dependent, or we could have reduced it, by making only acquiring and releasing actions depend on each other. With states and transitions as defined below, the total effect would have come to the same.

Now each linearization of a generated pomset is a string of actions which determines in the obvious way a sequence of states. When the linearization is regarded as the true history of the computation, the sequence of states consists of "real" time slices.

Consider the following linearization of the pomset just given:

$$\beta\text{-}acq\text{-}3 \longrightarrow \alpha\text{-}acq\text{-}1 \longrightarrow \alpha\text{-}acq\text{-}2 \quad lar\ a \longrightarrow \alpha\text{-}rel\text{-}2 \longrightarrow \beta\text{-}acq\text{-}2 \longrightarrow b$$

For this history the sequence of states is:

$(\{1,2,3\},\emptyset,\emptyset)$ $(\{1,2\},\emptyset,\{3\})$ $(\{2\},\{1\},\{3\})$ $(\emptyset,\{1,2\},\{3\})$ $(\emptyset,\{1,2\},\{3\})$ $(\{2\},\{1\},\{3\})$ $(\emptyset,\{1\},\{2,3\})$ $(\emptyset,\{1\},\{2,3\})$

This sequence bears little resemblance to the sequence of states in the generating sequence. Half of the states of the generating sequence do not appear in the "real history" states and vice versa. Of course this cannot happen in linear systems. It shows that our states may, or may not, correspond to "real" time slices. They are only formally global. But in constructing the transition system we can play the "as if" game, using intuitions of linear constructions. The local concatenation will take care of the concurrencies. The following analog of Theorem 3.1 says among the rest that none of the right concurrencies are missed.

Theorem 3.2 *The set of pomsets generated by the last transition system is the core of DP. This core is normal.*

The proof follows the main outline of the proof of Theorem 3.1. One uses induction on the transition sequence to show that the generated pomsets satisfy the two conditions (this is straightforward). To show that these pomsets constitute the core of the DP process, take a pomset p satisfying the two conditions and reduce the ordering to the transitive closure of the union of all linear orders of $p/Ag(i)$ and $p/Res(j)$, $i \in AG$, $j \in RES$. One can show that the pomset thus obtained is generable via transitions (this is done by induction on the rank of events in the pomset). Moreover, one observes that in every transition-generated p the order is the transitive closure of the union of the linear orders of $p/Ag(i)$ and $p/Res(j)$ and these two restrictions determine p uniquely. This establishes normality.

We shall now use these results to establish properties of a deadlock-avoiding implementation by means of locks.

Dining Philosophers with Locking

Add to the action set Σ of DP actions of the form: *i-lock(A)*, *i-unlock(A)* where i ranges over agents and A over subsets of RES. An agent's activity is to be restricted as follows: In order to perform a he has to lock $\rho(a)$ by performing *i-lock(ρ(a))*. This can be done only if all members of $\rho(a)$ are unlocked. He then performs a and follows it by *i-unlock(A)*.

(We use this simple form for the sake of convenience. The differences between it and more detailed versions are unessential, as far as the results are considered.)

Let $Ag'(i)$ be the set consisting of the members of Σ_i and the actions *i-lock(A)*, *i-unlock(A)*, $A \subseteq RES$.

Let $Res'(j)$ consist of all *i-lock(A)*, *i-unlock(A)* $j \in A$, $i \in AG$

The DPL (Dining Philosophers with Locking) transition system is extremely simple. For dependencies we take:

$$Ag'(i) \leftrightarrow_D Ag'(i), \quad i \in AG \qquad\qquad Res'(j) \leftrightarrow_D Res'(j), \quad j \in RES$$

There is only one state S and, besides $\Lambda \Longrightarrow S$, the transitions are:

$S \,|;|\, (i\text{-}lock(\rho(a))\ ;\ a\ ;\ i\text{-}unlock(\rho(a))) \Longrightarrow S, \qquad i \in AG,\ a \in \Sigma_i.$

The simplicity is deceptive. Because of $|;|$ and the really complex, though easily defined, dependency relation, a lot of complicated concurrency goes on. In fact, as far as the actions of Σ are concerned, DPL computations are, we shall see, not poorer than DP computations.

First we note the following (proved by the same kind of argument used to establish previous analogous claims):

Theorem 3.3 *The pomsets generated by the DPL transition system constitute a normal core.*

Let DPL = the augment closure of the core generated by the DPL transition system.

To relate DPL with DP we interpret *i-lock(A)* as any sequence of successive acquiring actions, by which A is acquired by i, and we interpret *i-unlock(A)* as any sequence of successive releasing actions by which A is released.

Let DP$'$ be the process obtained from DPL via this interpretation. Formally, the definition is:

Let $i - acq(A)$ consist of all strings $i - acq - j_1; i - acq - j_2; \ldots; i - acq - j_n$, where $A = \{j_1, ..., j_n\}$. Let $i - rel(A)$ be similarly defined.

Then DP$'$ is the process consisting of all pomsets obtained from members of DPL by expanding each occurrence of *i-lock(A)* to any pomset of *i-acq(A)* and each occurrence of *i-unlock(A)* to any pomset of *i-rel(A)*. (Different occurrences of *i-lock(A)* can be replaced by different members of *i-acq(A)*; similarly for *i-unlock(A)*.

The "expanding" is done in the obvious way: events in the expansions inherit the order constraints governing their sources.

[The operation by which single actions are expanded into pomsets was defined by Gischer, [Gi], and appears in [Pr] under the name of *homomorphism*. The version used here differs slightly in that we allow more than one possible expansion for the same action.]

The relationship between the Dining Philosophers and its implementation via Locking is described in the following theorem.

We denote by P/Σ the process consisting of all p/Σ where $p \in P$. It is the result of hiding in the process all actions not in Σ. In our case Σ is the set of all "proper" actions of the agents, i.e., actions that are not locking, unlocking, acquiring or releasing of resources.

Theorem 3.4 *The following is true:*

(I) $DP' \subseteq DP$

(II) *There are no deadlock states in any sequence of states determined by a linearization of a member of DP'.*

(III) $DP'/\Sigma = DP/\Sigma$.

We can regard DP$'$ as an *implementation* of DP. (I) implies that the implemented computations are computations of the original process, thus the rules that characterize DP are not violated. (II) says that this implementation avoids deadlock.

(III) says that, as far as the actions of Σ are concerned, we have not lost any possibilities by locking. In particular, it implies that, over Σ, no concurrency is lost. In general, loss of concurrency (or loss of parallelism) is shown by additional constraints that are added to core members, i.e., core members of the implementation are proper augments of original core members.

The proof of (III) is via the core. One shows that both DP$'/\Sigma$ and DP$/\Sigma$ have as a core the set produced by the transition system consisting of a single state S and the transitions:

$S \; |;| \; a \implies S, \qquad a \in \Sigma$

Where the dependencies are:

$a \leftrightarrow_D b\,,\quad$ for all a, b such that $\rho(a) \cap \rho(b) \neq \emptyset$.

That no parallelism is lost is due here to the fact that the actions of Σ have no finer granularity than the locked chunks of resources. As a rule, there is some loss of parallelism when the actions have finer granularity; that is to say, when the agents have to perform transactions (strings of actions) such that different actions of a transaction may need different resources and the resources for the whole transaction have to be locked. The loss of parallelism is shown, in that case, by those core members of DP'/Σ which are proper augments of core members of DP/Σ.

A loss of parallelism of that kind is exemplified in our case if we consider the full action alphabet of DP (i.e., with all $i - acq - j$ and $i - rel - j$). As a rule there are core members of DP which are not in DP', only some of their augments are. (The inclusion in (I) is, in general, proper).

The analysis just given indicates how the proposed framework constitutes a setting within which questions such as deadlock, implementation and loss of parallelism can be discussed in precise terms. It is even possible to introduce some rough measures for loss of parallelism. But this lies outside the scope of this paper.

Other Topics and Further Research Directions

We have concentrated on cases where the specifications via nonlinear systems is straightforward and involves very simple transitions. Other cases are not as direct and require more effort. Thus, the well known "two way channel with disconnect" (problem 1 from the Cambridge 1983 Workshop [DHJW]) can be specified by a finite nonlinear transition system but the specification is not at all obvious. (This was presented in the REX lecture but is not included here for reasons of length).

We can make do with finite nonlinear transition system in cases where linear approaches would necessitate some infinite memory space (to be provided either by the states or by some equivalent device, like time stamped actions). The Simple Channel is such an example.

But finiteness should not, we think, be an overriding concern. The main goal is to produce formal specifications that enable us to see clearly various aspects of the process.

Various decidability questions for nonlinear transition systems are naturally suggested. For example, given two finite systems, do they produce the same sets of pomsets? On the whole one should expect negative answers. (The equality of the sets of all linearizations is undecidable, as is shown by the corresponding negative result for the less expressive model of traces.) For certain subcases the answer is positive, e.g., when the dependency relation is fixed and the pomsets that appear in the transitions are such that different strings give rise to different local concatenations; in that case the problem reduces to that of finite automata.

However we feel that the main thrust of our proposal is to provide a useful modeling tool. In particular, to extend in a natural way methods used in a linear context.

Linear transition systems have been used by Milner [Mi] to model hidden branching phenomena (known also as hidden nondeterminism). We can now extend the model by using nonlinear pomset-producing automata. In this way we can get a framework which does justice both to hidden branching and to true concurrency.

We can see already what the basic constructs of such a system might be:

Local concatenation $|;|$, a branching operation, say $+$, a composition operation for pomsets (which we have not treated in this paper), restriction to subalphabets: $/\Sigma$ (which is the same as hiding) and constructs for expressing dependencies and for constructing the finite pomsets p that appear in the left hand sides of the transitions: $S\ |;|\ p \Longrightarrow S'$. These finite pomsets replace the atomic actions of Milner's CCS.

Hidden branching will be expressed as the non-distributivity of |;| over +.

We can of course consider the employing of more than one dependency relation, getting thus several local concatenations. We can also consider non-symmetric dependencies. But one should be wary of overburdening the framework. Nonlinear transition systems seem to be expressive enough for dealing with many specification problems, while remaining within the bounds of manageability

REFERENCES

[AR] Aalbersberg, IJ. J. and G. Rozenberg "Theory of Traces" *Theoretical Computer Science* Vol. 60, 1-82, 1988.

[BA] Brock, J.D. and W.B. Ackerman "Scenarios: A Model of Non-Determinate Computation" *Formalization of Programming Concepts*, J. Diaz and I. Ramos, Eds, Lecture Notes in Computer Science 107, Springer-Verlag, 252-259, 1981.

[Fi] Fishbum, P. C. *Interval Orders and Interval Graphs*, John Wiley and Sons, 1985.

[GP] Gaifman, H. and V. Pratt "Partial Order Models of Concurrency and the Computation of Functions" *LICS (Symposium on Logic in Computer Science), June 1987*, IEEE Computer Society Press, 72-85, 1987.

[Gi] Gischer, J. *Partial Orders and the Axiomatic Theory of Shuffle*, Ph.D. Thesis, CS, Stanford University, 1984.

[Gr] Grabowski, J. "On Partial Languages" *Fundamenta Informaticae* IV.2, 427-498, 1981.

[Ho] Hoar, C. A. R. *Communicating Sequential Processes*, Prentice Hall, 1985.

[DHJW] Denvir, Harwood, Jackson and Wray, Editors *The Analysis of Concurrent Systems*, Proceedings of Workshop, Cambridge 1983, Lecture Notes in Computer Science, 207, Springer-Verlag, 1985.

[La] Lamport, L. "The Mutual Exclusion Problem, Parts I, II", *J. of the ACM*, Vol 33, No. 2 313-384, 1986.

[Ma] Mazurkiewicz, A. "Traces, histories, graphs: instances of a process monoid", *Lecture Notes in Computer Science 188*, 353-375, 1984.

[Mi] Milner, R. "Calculi for Synchrony and Asynchrony", *Theoretical Computer Science*, Vol. 25, 267-310, 1983.

[My] Myhill, J. "Finite Automata and the Representation of Trees", *WADD Technical Report 57-624* , Wright-Patterson Air Force Base, 1960.

[Pe] Petri, C. A. *Interpretations of Net Theory*, Gesellschaft fur Mathematik und Datenverarbeitung, Interner Bericht ISF-75-07, Second Edition, 1976.

[Pr] Pratt, V. "Modeling Concurrency with Partial Orders", *International Journal of Parallel Programming*, Vol. 15 No. 1 33-71, 1986.

[Re] Reisig, W. *Petri Nets, An Introduction*, EATC Monographs in Computer Science, vol 4. Springer Verlag, 1985.

[RT] Rozenberg, B. and P.S. Thiagarajan "Petri Nets: Basic Notions, Structure and Behavior", *Lecture Notes in Computer Science 224*, 585-668, 1986.

[St] Stark, E. W. "Concurrent Transition System Semantics of Process Networks" *POPL 14 (Fourteenth Annual ACM Symposium on Principles of Programming Languages) January 1987* ACM, 199-210, 1987.

An efficient verification method for parallel and distributed programs

(Preliminary version)

Shmuel Katz and Doron Peled

Department of Computer Science,
Technion, Haifa, Israel.

ABSTRACT. We present a formal proof method which is based on a partial order semantics for parallel or distributed programs. In this view, a program's semantics is given by a collection of partial orders of the events which can occur during execution. Rather than using the partial orders directly, the basis of the method assumes the sets of (linear) execution sequences with global states which are consistent with each partial order (each such set is called an *interleaving set*). The proof rules allow concluding the correctness of certain classes of properties for all execution sequences, even though the property is only demonstrated directly for a subset of the execution sequences. The subset used must include a representative sequence from each interleaving set, and the proof rules guarantee that this is the case when they may be applied. The method employs proof lattices, and is expressed using the temporal logic ISTL*. By choosing a subset with appropriate sequences, simpler intermediate assertions can be used than in previous formal approaches. Moreover, since less direct checking must be done, the method is often much more efficient.

Key words: Verification, Partial order semantics, Execution sequences, Temporal logic, Proof lattices.

CONTENTS

1. Introduction.

Verification of concurrent and distributed programs is traditionally treated using interleaving semantics. That is, first the program is modeled by a set of interleaving sequences of global states, and then properties of this set of sequences are proven using an appropriate formalism [MP1, MP2, OL]. Verifying using the set of all sequences related to a program can be tedious and unnatural with respect to the behavior of a program because all the possible interleavings of independent operations of a program are checked. This is usually expressed as a complex invariant needed to cover all possible global states. In fact, using only part of the interleaving sequences is often sufficient for verification. However, this cannot be exploited in verification methods which use the set of all sequences as a model.

Recently, there has been a trend towards using partial order semantics for distributed programs. New properties and phenomena are explained using the partial order model [L, R, M, KP]. However, verification using the partial order model is rare and is still done informally.

The purpose of this paper is twofold: First, to provide a rigorous method for proving new properties which stem from the partial order semantics and are expressible only in that model; second, to show how sets of interleaving execution sequences derived from the partial order semantics can be used to simplify the verification of interesting classes of properties which are expressible within interleaving semantics itself. Stated differently, it is valuable to use sets of sequences derived from partial order semantics even when the property itself is expressible within a simple interleaving semantics.

Using global states and execution sequences is convenient for verification, because the relative progress of different concurrent fragments of the program can easily be expressed, and induction on the sequences is convenient. On the other hand, in a pure interleaving semantics, one has to take care of various interleavings of independent events (events are executions of a program's operations), belonging to different processes. Grouping together sets of execution sequences will allow treating a subset of related events, while "freezing" processes doing an unrelated task concurrently. This technique, which will be formalized and illustrated, reduces the amount of work in the verification process by exploiting the locality of program fragments to prevent the combinatorial explosion of global states which must be handled.

The verification method introduced here is basically independent of any syntactic formalism. However, a temporal logic which combines partial orders with global states and execution sequences, such as ISTL* [KP], is useful to express these ideas in a rigorous manner. ISTL* is a temporal logic which combines the partial order model with "imaginary" global states generated by combining sets of execution events in a consistent way (these global states are obtained as a result of defining what is commonly called "slices" [L, R]). The global states are termed "imaginary" because it is not necessary that they really hold for a period of time in the computation. However, without an external observer, capable of observing the global state of the system, a proof that such a global state really did not occur cannot be given.

The rest of this paper is organized as follows: In Section 2, ISTL* is reviewed. In Section 3, the verification method is introduced. Section 4 shows how to prove eventuality properties and partial correctness. A detailed example using the proof method is given in Section 5. Section 6 concludes with a discussion and suggestions for further research.

2. Review of ISTL*.

The semantic model for the suggested verification method is based upon a set of branching structures, each representing the global states of a single partial order, and causal or temporal relations among these states.

Each substructure of ISTL [KP] and its extension ISTL* is a branching structure of global states obtained as *slices* (downward-closed sets of events) [L] of a single partial order execution. A path of a substructure is a sequence of global states. It can also be seen as a completion of the partial order on the set of events into a total order. However, not every sequence of global states is allowed. Only paths which include every event from the partial order execution are considered *acceptable*. A set of all acceptable paths consistent with a partial order is termed an *interleaving set*. A structure is then a set of such substructures.

ISTL* therefore distinguishes between nondeterminism caused by alternative choices in the code of a program, and that caused by concurrency. The former is a generator of different substructures, corresponding to different choices taken in the execution. The latter causes the substructures to be branched: when a global state has more than one successor, the set of operations causing the transitions from that global state can be executed concurrently.

ISTL* can assert about paths as well as global states. The syntactic modals of ISTL* are those of CTL* [EH]. It distinguishes between state formulas and path formulas. The state formulas are: Af (f holds for each acceptable path starting in a given global state) and Ef (there is an acceptable path starting in a given state which satisfies f). The path formulas are: Gf (f holds in each state on the path), Ff (f holds in some state on the path), Xf (f holds in the next state in the path) and fUg (there is a subsequent state in which g holds, and f holds in all the states of the path from the first one and up to, but not necessarily including, the first state in which g holds). A state formula can be interpreted over a path by evaluating the formula in the first state of the path, without using the remainder of the path.

Satisfaction for ISTL* formulas is defined on three levels. First, the fact that a substructure M and a global state s of M satisfy an ISTL* formula Φ is denoted by $s \models_M \Phi$. A substructure M satisfies the formula Φ (denoted $M \models \Phi$) if $s \models_M \Phi$ for each state s of M. Finally, a structure $\mathcal{A}$ satisfies a formula Φ if for every substructure M of $\mathcal{A}$, $M \models \Phi$, that is, if every state of every substructure of $\mathcal{A}$ satisfies Φ. For example, the formula $f \equiv P \rightarrow EGFQ$ asserts that in every partial order execution, from each state satisfying P there exists a path in which Q holds infinitely often.

3. A verification method.

In this section, principles for verification of distributed and concurrent programs using representative sequences are introduced. The technique generalizes the works of [EF] (layering of a program) and [AFR, Pn] (CSP [H] proof rules), where (although not stated explicitly), some of the interleavings of a program are not explicitly examined in the verification process. The method is general and can be applied to various models of concurrency, including CSP, shared variables and Petri nets [Pe].

3.1. Verification using representatives.

In the formalism presented below, an assertion about a program is expressed in terms of branching structures and verified for the interleaving sets generated from the set of all the different partial order executions derived from the program's semantics. This is in contrast with interleaving semantics, where the program is modeled by a set of sequences regardless of any underlying grouping according to partial order executions.

A program is constructed from a finite set of (atomic) operations T. Execution of a program's operation is called an *event*. For each operation $\tau \in T$ there exists an enabling condition $enabled(\tau)$ which must be satisfied in order that the operation may execute. The predicate transformer $wp(\tau, \Psi)$ ("weakest precondition") [D1] represents the transition of the program's variables and control caused by executing the operation τ and has the meaning: if the global state after executing τ satisfies Ψ whenever τ is executed, then the state before its execution satisfies $wp(\tau, \Psi)$.

The suggested method is based upon using only convenient representative paths instead of using the whole set of interleaving paths. We distinguish four steps:

(1) Select some subset of convenient paths.

(2) Show that each of the paths in the selected subset satisfy the property.

(3) Show that the subset of paths contains at least one representative from each interleaving set.

(4) In many cases, it is possible to infer from (1), (2) and (3) that the desired property holds for <u>all</u> the sequences generated by all of the possible partial orders (See Section 4.2).

The collection of paths needed in (1) may be specified by giving assertions about global states and the relative order in which the states appear. The "atomic" step of the proof technique is to show that for each partial order execution having a global state satisfying an assertion Φ, there exists a representative sequence, where this state is followed (immediately or eventually after a consecutive sequence of states satisfying Φ) by a global state satisfying Ψ. Note that checking all the possible transitions out of the global state satisfying Φ would be equivalent to an exhaustive check of all interleaving sequences. This is redundant, since some of the events are unordered according to the partial order relation. Paths which differ only in that these events appear in different orders, represent the same partial order execution. Moreover, from the definition of global states resulting from partial orders, interleaving unordered events in either order achieve eventually the same global state.

3.1.1. Definition. Let $I \subseteq T \times T$ be a symmetric and irreflexive relation (the *independency* relation [M]). Two operations $\tau_1, \tau_2 \in T$ such that $(\tau_1, \tau_2) \in I$ are said to be *independent* (denoted $\tau_1 || \tau_2$). Two events which appear adjacent in an interleaving sequence which is a linearization of some partial order, can be exchanged, resulting in a path which is a linearization of the same partial order iff they are executions of two independent operations.

This suggests decompositions of the program's operations depending on the current global state. Such a decomposition distinguishes a subset of the operations as "interesting". The transitions caused by the interesting operations are checked, while the others are proved to be either independent of them, or disabled. Therefore, although there might be other sequences which reach Φ but do not progress to Ψ (because some of the independent events were scheduled first), the appropriate representative sequences exist.

3.1.2. Definition. A *decomposition* of a program, $D = \langle Q, CON, \overline{Q} \rangle$ is a partition of the set of program's operations T, such that each operation from T belongs to exactly one of T's subsets in D, and each operation from Q is independent of each operation from $\overline{Q}$.

Proof rules which embody such decompositions are introduced in Section 3.2 to allow showing progress from one global state to another. They are combined using temporal logic assertions to show that the desired properties of (2) hold. The validity of the proof rules with respect to the set of interleaving sets associated with a program ensures that by using the proof rules, enough sequences are selected to contain representatives from each partial order (Thereby, achieving (3)).

When giving proof rules for a concurrent or distributed model, one has to deal with the semantic requirement of fairness, or at least the weaker assumption called justice. Let $J = \{J_1, J_2, \ldots, J_n\}$ be a set of sets of operations. Each of the justice sets J_i represents a set of operations which cannot be enabled continuously forever in a partial order execution without one of them being executed. Various definitions exist for justice sets [MP2, Fr]. In the sequel we assume at least the following:

3.1.3. Definition. *Operation justice* or *Maximality* [R]: the justice sets are singletons, containing the program's operations. (That is, no continuously enabled operation is ignored forever).

The language CSP [H] is used here to demonstrate the proof method. A mapping from CSP programs into operations appears in [MP2] and will be assumed in the forthcoming proof examples. It is important to notice that a communication operation is constructed from a matching pair of *send* $(A!x)$ and *receive* $(B?y)$ commands. For example, the operations τ_3 and τ_4 of the program in Figure 1. A communication command (send or receive) may participate in more than one communication operation. For example, the send command in process A of Figure 1 matches both receives of process B. There are many possible ways to define which operations in a CSP program are independent. One of these definitions is similar to the partial order defined in [L]. According to this definition, two operations in CSP are independent if they appear in different processes (notice again that a communication operation appears in two processes and therefore is not independent of other operations of both processes).

The CSP program in Figure 1 has the set of operations $T=\{\tau_1, \cdots, \tau_9\}$ where τ_8 and τ_9 are the exits from the two loops, respectively. (We will ignore these two operations for the moment. A precise treatment must take care of the folklore of the distributed termination assumption of CSP [H, AFR]). The pairs of independent operations in this example are those obtained from the Cartesian product $\{\tau_1, \tau_2, \tau_5\} \times \{\tau_6, \tau_7\}$.

3.2. Proof rules.

The next set of proof rules, given in Manna-Pnueli style [MP2], shorten proofs as well as pointing out explicitly when it is desirable to use the decomposition principles. We have to consider separately two cases. The first one handles the case where it is possible to show progress by executing a single operation. The second deals with the more complicated case of showing eventual progress using a justice assumption on the semantics of the program. Other proof rules allow combining simpler assertions. The proof rules may be justified using the semantic framework introduced in [KP].

3.2.1. Transition rule. To prove that a program eventually progresses from a global state satisfying Φ to a global state satisfying Ψ by executing a single operation, one should verify the following conditions:

```
          τ1       τ2                                  τ3               τ6
A ::*[a>0→a:=a-1                   B ::*[b≥0;A?tell(c)→b:=c×b
     □                      ||          □
          τ3/τ4       τ5                        τ4                τ7
     B!tell(a)→a:=0]                     b≤0;A?tell(c)→b:=b-1]
```

Figure 1.

Rule TRNS: Let $D=\langle Q, CON, \bar{Q}\rangle$.

1 $\delta \rightarrow \bigwedge_{\tau \in CON} \neg enabled(\tau)$ [When δ holds, no operation from CON is enabled.]

2 $\forall \tau \in \bar{Q}\ \ \delta \wedge enabled(\tau) \rightarrow wp(\tau, \delta)$ [δ is invariant under the operations of $\bar{Q}$.]

3 $\Phi \rightarrow (\delta \wedge \bigvee_{\tau \in Q} enabled(\tau))$ [Φ implies that δ holds and at least one operation from Q is enabled.]

4 $\forall \tau \in Q\ \ \Phi \wedge enabled(\tau) \rightarrow wp(\tau, \Psi)$ [Every operation from Q transforms Φ to Ψ.]

$\Phi \rightarrow EX\,\Psi$

To justify this rule, consider a situation where Φ holds. Unless an operation from Q is executed, any operation from CON is disabled (inductively, by 1, 2 and 3). By 3, at least one operation from Q is enabled when Φ holds. Assume no operation of Q is executed. Then only operations from $\bar{Q}$ can be executed. But, because of independence, executing operations from $\bar{Q}$ does not make the operations of Q disabled. Therefore, an operation of Q is kept enabled continuously, contradicting the maximality assumption. Using independence of Q and $\bar{Q}$ again, one can shuffle any adjacent appearance on a path of executions of operations from $\bar{Q}$ with execution of an operation from Q. Therefore, under these conditions, there exists a representative sequence in which an operation from Q appears immediately after the global state in which Φ holds. By 4, after the execution of such an operation, Ψ holds. Notice that the TRNS rule is valid only when communication justice (maximality) or a stronger requirement is assumed.

3.2.2. Eventual transition. To show progress, it is sometimes not enough to consider the immediate transition from a global state to an immediate successor. This is because an immediate successor in which some "real work" has been done might not exist and the program executes in some loop for a finite but unbounded time. Therefore, one proves instead that a global predicate Φ holds continuously until Ψ holds.

Rule JUST: Let $D=\langle Q, CON, \bar{Q}\rangle$ such that for some justice set J_i, $J_i \subset Q$.

1 $\delta \rightarrow \bigwedge_{\tau \in CON} \neg enabled(\tau)$ [When δ holds, no operation from CON is enabled.]

2 $\forall \tau \in \bar{Q}\ \ \delta \wedge enabled(\tau) \rightarrow wp(\tau, \delta)$ [δ is invariant under the operations of $\bar{Q}$.]

3 $\Phi \rightarrow (\delta \wedge \bigvee_{\tau \in J_i} enabled(\tau))$ [When Φ holds, δ holds and at least one operation of J_i is enabled.]

4 $\forall \tau \in Q\ \ \Phi \wedge enabled(\tau) \rightarrow wp(\tau, \Phi \vee \Psi)$ [Every $\tau \in Q$ transforms Φ to $\Phi \vee \Psi$.]

5 $\forall \tau \in J_i\ \ \Phi \wedge enabled(\tau) \rightarrow wp(\tau, \Psi)$ [Every operation of J_i transforms Φ to Ψ.]

$\Phi \rightarrow E[\Phi U \Psi]$

The reasoning behind this rule is similar to **TRNS** except that it uses the contradiction that if Ψ is never reached, there exists a justice set which is enabled continuously but never executed (by 3 and 4).

3.2.3. Well founded induction. The induction over well founded sets which is commonly used in liveness proofs is relativized here to the existence of representative sequences.

Rule WIND: Let W be a well founded set (a set having no infinite decreasing chain).

$$\Phi \rightarrow \exists \alpha P(\alpha) \wedge \alpha \in W$$

$$\forall \alpha P(\alpha) \rightarrow EF(\Psi \vee \exists \beta[\beta \in W \wedge \beta < \alpha \wedge P(\beta)])$$

$$\Phi \rightarrow EF\Psi$$

3.2.4. Confluence rule.

The existential confluence rule below is used to combine simple eventual assertions about representatives into more complicated ones. It is a counterpart to the linear temporal logic confluence [OL] which asserts about all the execution sequences associated with the program.

Rule CONF.

$$P \rightarrow EF(R_1 \vee \cdots \vee R_n)$$

for $1 \le i \le n$ $\ R_i \rightarrow EFQ$

$$P \rightarrow EFQ$$

4. Proving eventuality properties.

Following [OL, MP], this section suggests an efficient and natural verification method for using the proof rules of the logic to prove eventuality properties. Various applications are considered.

4.1. Proof lattices.

A proof lattice [OL, MP2] is basically a directed acyclic graph (DAG) whose nodes are labeled by state formulas. Basically, it is used in proving properties of the form $\Phi \rightarrow EF\Psi$. It represents the properties and the order which the representative paths leading from a global state satisfying a state formula Φ (a formula having no temporal modalities) to another global state satisfying state formula Ψ must satisfy. The proof lattices rigorously replace repetitive use of the confluence rule. To structure verification, proof lattices will have the feature of embedding more detailed proof lattices. This subroutine-like feature allows the verifier to stepwise refine his proofs.

4.1.1. Definition. A *proof lattice* is a quadruple $L=\langle root, last, V, E\rangle$, where (V, E) is a cycle-free finite graph, V is a set of nodes, E is a set of directed arrows, $root, last \in V$, and each node $v \in V$ is labeled with a state formula $\eta(v)$. In addition, there exists a path in the graph from *root* to every node in V and from any node in V to *last*.

Proof lattices were formerly used to prove properties of the form $\Phi \rightarrow AF\Psi$ ($\Phi \rightarrow \Diamond \Psi$ in linear temporal logic). In order to verify this, each of the program's interleaving paths starting from a global state satisfying Φ must have global states satisfying the state formulas according to the order they appear on at least one of the lattice's paths.

In our proof method, we are using the proof lattices to prove properties of the form $\Phi \rightarrow EF\Psi$. In view of this, the above requirement from the set of the program's interleaving paths is weakened to demand that from each partial order, there exists a representative path which satisfies the formulas along a path of the proof lattice. This is done inductively by showing that for each state formula η in the lattice, each partial order execution having a global state satisfying the formula has a successor global state satisfying one of η's descendants on the lattice. The proof rules of Section 3.2 can be used in order to establish this. For example, inferring $\Phi \rightarrow EX\Psi$ using TRNS means exactly that in every partial order, from each state satisfying Φ, there exists a path whose next state satisfies Ψ.

4.1.2. Definition. We say that a proof lattice L is a *verification* of an eventual property $\Phi \rightarrow EF\Psi$, if $\eta(root)=\Phi$, $\eta(last)=\Psi$, and for every transition between a node $v \in V$ and the set of its immediate successors, one of the following was used as a justification: (1) prove in classical (non temporal) logic the implication $\eta(v) \rightarrow \bigvee_{(v, v') \in E} \eta(v')$, (This represents a transition in which no step is taken in the program, and is the only justification possible when v has multiple immediate successors), (2) construct another proof lattice to show that $\eta(v) \rightarrow EF\eta(v')$ where (v, v') is in E, or (3) use one of the proof rules introduced in Section 3.2 (Notice that in order to prove the conditions of WIND, another proof lattice can be used).

4.1.3.Theorem. Each proof lattice satisfies that $\eta(root) \rightarrow EF\eta(last)$.

Proof. Using induction on the length of the longest path in the proof lattice (similar to the proof in [OL]).

4.2. Applicability of the method.

Assertions of type $\Phi \rightarrow EF\Psi$ or $\Phi \rightarrow [\Phi U \Psi]$ were shown to be interesting in [KP]. A few examples of phenomena described by such assertions are concurrency, layering of a program [EF], and some aspects of the snapshot algorithm of Chandy and Lamport [CL]. In many cases, it is easy to infer the more common $\Phi \rightarrow AF\Psi$ by first proving $\Phi \rightarrow EF\Psi$, and then showing that Ψ satisfies some easy to verify conditions. This is based on the semantic property called acceptability, mentioned in Section 2. One such condition is when Ψ is a stable property (i.e., $\Psi \rightarrow AG\Psi$) [KP]. This includes common properties such as total correctness or occurrence of deadlock. Another such interesting class is obtained by restricting the formula Ψ using the following definitions:

4.2.1. Definition. A set of operations P is a *sequential subset* of T (the set of all the operations of a program) if for any $\tau_1, \tau_2 \in P$ $\neg \tau_1 || \tau_2$.

4.2.2. Definition. A state (first order) formula Ψ is *invariant with respect* to L if $\forall \tau \in L$ $\Psi \wedge enabled(\tau) \rightarrow wp(\tau, \Psi)$.

4.2.3. Theorem. If P is a sequential subset of T and Ψ is invariant with respect to $T-P$, then for every first order formula Φ, $\Phi \rightarrow EF\Psi \models \Phi \rightarrow AF\Psi$.

Proof. Omitted.

One obvious use of the previous definitions is for truly disjoint state spaces. That is, suppose that the program is separated into processes with disjoint sets of variables and location counters. If Ψ is a local assertion, and $\Phi \rightarrow EF\Psi$ was proved, then $\Phi \rightarrow AF\Psi$ can be concluded. However, even when this is not the case, these ideas can be used. It is an interesting, and yet unsolved problem to characterize all classes of properties for which it is simple to move from the $EF\Psi$ assertion to the $AF\Psi$ assertion.

4.3. Adding the termination assumption.

In many cases, it is desired to prove a property which must hold in the executions in which the program terminates or deadlocks. Nonterminating, infinite executions are not considered. For example, partial correctness is such a property, asserting about the global states which occur after the program has terminated and ignoring nonterminating executions. This can be formulated as an implication with the condition $\Phi \wedge EF terminal$ (equally $\Phi \wedge AF terminal$ because of stability of *terminal*) at the left hand side, where *terminal* is a predicate which holds exactly when none of the program's operations is enabled.

A proof lattice used for verifying such a property may include cycles (because in the cases under consideration, the loops are assumed to be finite). Proving $\Phi \wedge EF terminal \rightarrow EF\Psi$ is similar to proving an eventuality of the kind $\Phi \rightarrow EF\Psi$ using proof rules and proof lattices. However, taking into account only the cases in which the program terminates, introduces an additional simplification into the program. The induction over well orders (WIND) is redundant (only the cases that the loops terminate are of interest). Thus, the inductions can be replaced by cycles.

It is also possible to treat properties of the type $\Phi \to EG\,\Psi$. This again uses a similar proof method using representatives. Here, again, loops are allowed. Special care must be taken for dealing with acceptability.

5. A detailed example.

The program in Figure 3 uses $N+1$ processes to sort a vector of N values. The process P_0 successively sends values to be sorted to the right (process P_1). Each process P_i $1 \le i \le N$ keeps the first value it receives from the left as its first current value (in $myval_i$). Successive values arriving from the left are compared with the current value. When a value greater than the current value arrives at a process, it is sent immediately to the right, while a value smaller than the process's current value replaces the current value, causing it to be sent to the right. This is an obvious pipeline algorithm.

```
P_0::init:a:=0
   main:*[a<N→inc:a:=a+1;decide:sendval:=V(a);transfer:P_1!value(sendval)]
   signal:P_1!finish(); end.

P_i::init:stopbit:=false; setval:hasval:=false;
   main:*[¬stopbit;P_{i-1}?finish()→setbit:stopbit:=true;signal:P_{i+1}!finish()
          □
          ¬stopbit∧¬hasval;P_{i-1}?value(myval)→sethas:hasval:=true
          □
          ¬stopbit∧hasval;P_{i-1}?value(newval)→
               decide:[newval≥myval→case1:sendval:=newval
                       □
                       newval≤myval→case2:sendval:=myval;update:myval:=newval];
               transfer:P_{i+1}!value(sendval)];
   end.

P_N::init:stopbit:=false; setval:hasval:=false;
    main:*[¬stopbit;P_{i-1}?finish()→setbit:stopbit:=true
           □
           ¬stopbit∧¬hasval;P_{i-1}?value(myval)→sethas:hasval:=true];
   end.
```

Figure 3. Program SORT.

Notice that a new value can start to migrate from the left while the migration caused by previous values is still taking place in higher indexed processes. This kind of behavior makes the verification of this algorithm using "linear" methods quite tricky, having to take care of various interleavings. The set notation "{" and "}" as well as the union operation in the proof refers to multisets.

In the Appendix, some of the proof lattices in the proof of total correctness for the program are depicted (note that the predicate which holds at termination is a stable property). The nodes of the proof lattices appear as (numbered) boxes with assertions inside. The comments on the arrows denote the kind of formal proof needed in the justification of that arrow in the lattice. In each arrow justified by using the TRNS rule, the arrow is annotated with the set Q chosen for the decomposition. The set CON of each decomposition used in this proof always contains all the other transitions of the processes including the operations referred to in Q. The state formula δ is in all of the cases, the predicate that states that the transitions in Q are enabled. (it can be easily checked that in this example, this condition disables any other operation from the sets CON described above. However, this is not true in general.)

In the first proof lattice in Figure 4 the following state formulas appear (the assertions for 5 and 6 are not shown in the figure):

1. The initial state.
2. The global state where P_0 has set the value of a to zero and all the other processes are in their initial state.
3. All the processes are exactly before entering the main loop for the first time.
4. The values of array V were sent and sorted into the processes. All the processes are at the outer level of their main loop.
5. Process P_0 has exited its main loop (because its only guard is *false*) and is waiting to send a *finish* message to P_1. All the other processes are in the outer level of their main loop.
6. Process P_0 has just sent a *finish* message to P_1 and terminated. P_1 is just before setting its *stopbit* to *true*. All the other processes are in the outer level of their main loop.
7. A global state similar to 6 except that P_1 has progressed and is waiting to send a *finish* message to P_2.
8. The processes $1..N-1$ are in the outer level of their main loop with their *stopbit* set to *true*. Process P_N is just before setting its *stopbit*.

9. The processes 1..N are in the outer level of their main loop with *stopbit* set to *true*.
10. All the processes have terminated.

Some of the justifications in the proof lattice will be explained below. Moving from 2 to 3 is proved by a simple induction on the number of processes. The inductive step is to show progress from a global state in which for each i $1 \le i \le n$, P_i is just before its local initialization, to the state in which P_i is before the start of its main loop. In each such step P_i is shown to move from $init_i$ to $setval_i$ and then to $main_i$ using trivial decompositions.

This simple handling of the variable initialization in all the processes, which is done prior to entering their main loop, demonstrates the simplicity and convenience of the proof method presented in this paper. If we would take into account all the interleaving sequences of the program, one would have to deal with all the possible interleavings of initialization statements in different processes. Furthermore, there exist some interleaving sequences in which some higher indexed processes are still initializing while lower indexed processes have already entered their main loop. Both of these lead to a very complex global invariant if all possible cases are to be covered.

The arrow from 3 to 4 is justified by induction on the length of the array V. The proof lattice in Figure 5 gives the induction step. The well ordering is the natural numbers between 0 and N and the order taken is opposite to the usual "less than". The formula $P(\alpha)$ appearing in WIND is the same as the formula in the *root* box (numbered 1) of Figure 5, except that x is replaced by α. The two conditions are justified by showing that: (1) the state formula in the box numbered 3 of Figure 4 implies $\exists \alpha P(alpha) \wedge \alpha \in W$ (for α=0), and (2) the *last* formula of Figure 5 (numbered 8) is the disjunction of formula 4 of Figure 4 and the *root* formula of Figure 5 with a "lower" value ($\beta = x+1$) of the parameter.

The arrow between state formulas 5 and 6 is justified using induction which is depicted in Figure 6. Justifications for other arrows are trivial.

6. Conclusions.

The proof method suggested in this paper provides a theoretical basis for many informal proofs which exist for properties of distributed or concurrent programs. Many errors in such proofs should be avoidable here, since the proof obligations are clear at each step and cannot be easily overlooked. We do *not* claim that the semantic model and temporal logic used here are the best for every purpose: (linear or branching) interleaved models and logics are often most natural for specification and are sufficient for some types of proofs, while a pure partial order model seems the most appropriate abstract framework for foundational issues of concurrency (such as computability). However, for the task of *proving properties* of complex concurrent programs, this approach gives what we view as an optimal mixture of invaluable information from the partial orders, along with the convenience of reasoning and induction on appropriately chosen sequences with global states.

In order to further understand the implications of this approach, we are currently investigating a number of complex examples from the areas of communication protocols and network algorithms using a nonblocking *send* operation. We also hope to further define when this view leads to thc greatest savings in effort, and to quantify this savings.

Acknowledgements. We appreciate the helpful conversations we have had on this subject with Nissim Francez, Amir Pnueli and Rob Gerth.

References:

[A] K. Abrahamson, Decidability and expressiveness of logics of programs, Ph.D. thesis, University of Washington at Seattle, 1980.

[AFR] K.R. Apt, N. Francez, W.P. de Roever, A proof system for Communicating Sequential Processes, ACM TOPLAS Vol 2(1980), 359-385.

[CL] K.M. Chandy, L. Lamport, Distributed snapshots: determining global states of distributed systems, ACM Transactions on Computer Systems, Vol. 3, No. 1, 63-75.

[DDM] P. Degano, R. De Nicola, U. Montanari, Partial ordering for CCS. In: Proceeding FCT 85, Lecture Notes in Computer Science, Springer-Verlag, 199, 520-533.

[D1] E.W. Dijkstra, Guarded commands, Nondeterminancy and Formal Derivation of Programs, Communication of the ACM, 18(1975), 453-457.

[D2] E.W. Dijkstra, The distributed snapshot algorithm of K.M. Chandy and L. Lamport, EWD864a.

[EF] Tz. Elrad, N. Francez, Decomposition of distributed programs into communication-closed layers, Science of Computer Programming 2(1982), 155-173

[E] E.A. Emerson, Alternative semantics for temporal logic, Theoretical Computer Science 26(1983), 121-130.

[EH] E.A. Emerson, J.Y. Halpern, "Sometimes" and "not never" revisited: on branching versus linear time temporal logic, Journal of the ACM 33(1986), 151-178. 30, 1985, 1-24.

[Fr] N. Francez, *Fairness*, texts and monographs in computer science (D. Gries, ed.), Springer-Verlag, New York, 1986.

[H] C.A.R. Hoare, Communicating sequential processes, Communications of the ACM, 21(1978), 666-677.

[KP] S. Katz, D. Peled, Interleaving Set Temporal Logic, 6th ACM Symposium on Principles of Distributed Computing, Vancouver, Canada, August 1987, 178-190.

[L] L. Lamport, Paradigms for distributed programs: computing global states, In: Distributed systems - Methods and tools for specification, An advanced course, Munich, 1985, Edited by M. Paul and H.J. Siegert, Lecture notes in Computer Science, Springer-Verlag, 190, 454-468.

[MP1] Z. Manna, A. Pnueli, Verification of concurrent programs: the temporal framework, In: The correctness problem in computer science, Edited by R.S. Boyer & J.S. Moore, 1981, 215-273.

[MP2] Z. Manna, A. Pnueli, How to cook a temporal proof system for your pet language, 10th Symposium on principles of programming languages, Austin, Texas, 1983, 141-154.

[M] A. Mazurkiewicz, Trace semantics, Proceedings of an advanced course, Bad Honnef, September 1986, Lecture Notes in Computer Science, 255.

[OL] S. Owicki, L. Lamport, Proving liveness properties of concurrent programs, ACM transactions on Programming languages and Systems, 4, 1982, 455-495.

[Pe] C. A. Petri, Kommunikation mit Automaten, Bonn: Institut fur Instrumentelle Matematik, Schriften des IIM Nr. 2(1962).

[Pn] A. Pnueli, Applications of temporal logic to the specification and verification of reactive systems, a survey of current trends.

[R] W. Reisig, Partial order semantics versus interleaving semantics for CSP like languages and its impact on fairness, 11th ICALP, Antwerp, Belgium, 1984, Lecture notes in Computer Science, Springer-Verlag, 172, 403-413.

ppendix. Proof lattices for program SORT.

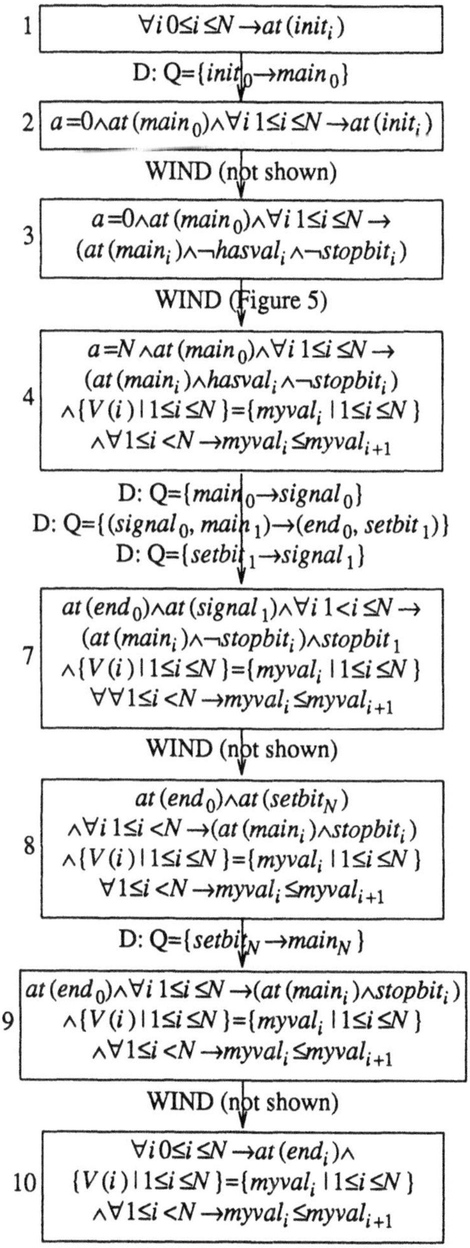
1
$\forall i\, 0 \le i \le N \rightarrow at(init_i)$
D: $Q=\{init_0 \rightarrow main_0\}$
2
$a=0 \wedge at(main_0) \wedge \forall i\, 1 \le i \le N \rightarrow at(init_i)$
WIND (not shown)
3
$a=0 \wedge at(main_0) \wedge \forall i\, 1 \le i \le N \rightarrow$
$(at(main_i) \wedge \neg hasval_i \wedge \neg stopbit_i)$
WIND (Figure 5)
4
$a=N \wedge at(main_0) \wedge \forall i\, 1 \le i \le N \rightarrow$
$(at(main_i) \wedge hasval_i \wedge \neg stopbit_i)$
$\wedge \{V(i) \mid 1 \le i \le N\} = \{myval_i \mid 1 \le i \le N\}$
$\wedge \forall 1 \le i < N \rightarrow myval_i \le myval_{i+1}$
D: $Q=\{main_0 \rightarrow signal_0\}$
D: $Q=\{(signal_0, main_1) \rightarrow (end_0, setbit_1)\}$
D: $Q=\{setbit_1 \rightarrow signal_1\}$
7
$at(end_0) \wedge at(signal_1) \wedge \forall i\, 1 < i \le N \rightarrow$
$(at(main_i) \wedge \neg stopbit_i) \wedge stopbit_1$
$\wedge \{V(i) \mid 1 \le i \le N\} = \{myval_i \mid 1 \le i \le N\}$
$\forall \forall 1 \le i < N \rightarrow myval_i \le myval_{i+1}$
WIND (not shown)
8
$at(end_0) \wedge at(setbit_N)$
$\wedge \forall i\, 1 \le i < N \rightarrow (at(main_i) \wedge stopbit_i)$
$\wedge \{V(i) \mid 1 \le i \le N\} = \{myval_i \mid 1 \le i \le N\}$
$\forall 1 \le i < N \rightarrow myval_i \le myval_{i+1}$
D: $Q=\{setbit_N \rightarrow main_N\}$
9
$at(end_0) \wedge \forall i\, 1 \le i \le N \rightarrow (at(main_i) \wedge stopbit_i)$
$\wedge \{V(i) \mid 1 \le i \le N\} = \{myval_i \mid 1 \le i \le N\}$
$\wedge \forall 1 \le i < N \rightarrow myval_i \le myval_{i+1}$
WIND (not shown)
10
$\forall i\, 0 \le i \le N \rightarrow at(end_i) \wedge$
$\{V(i) \mid 1 \le i \le N\} = \{myval_i \mid 1 \le i \le N\}$
$\wedge \forall 1 \le i < N \rightarrow myval_i \le myval_{i+1}$

Figure 4

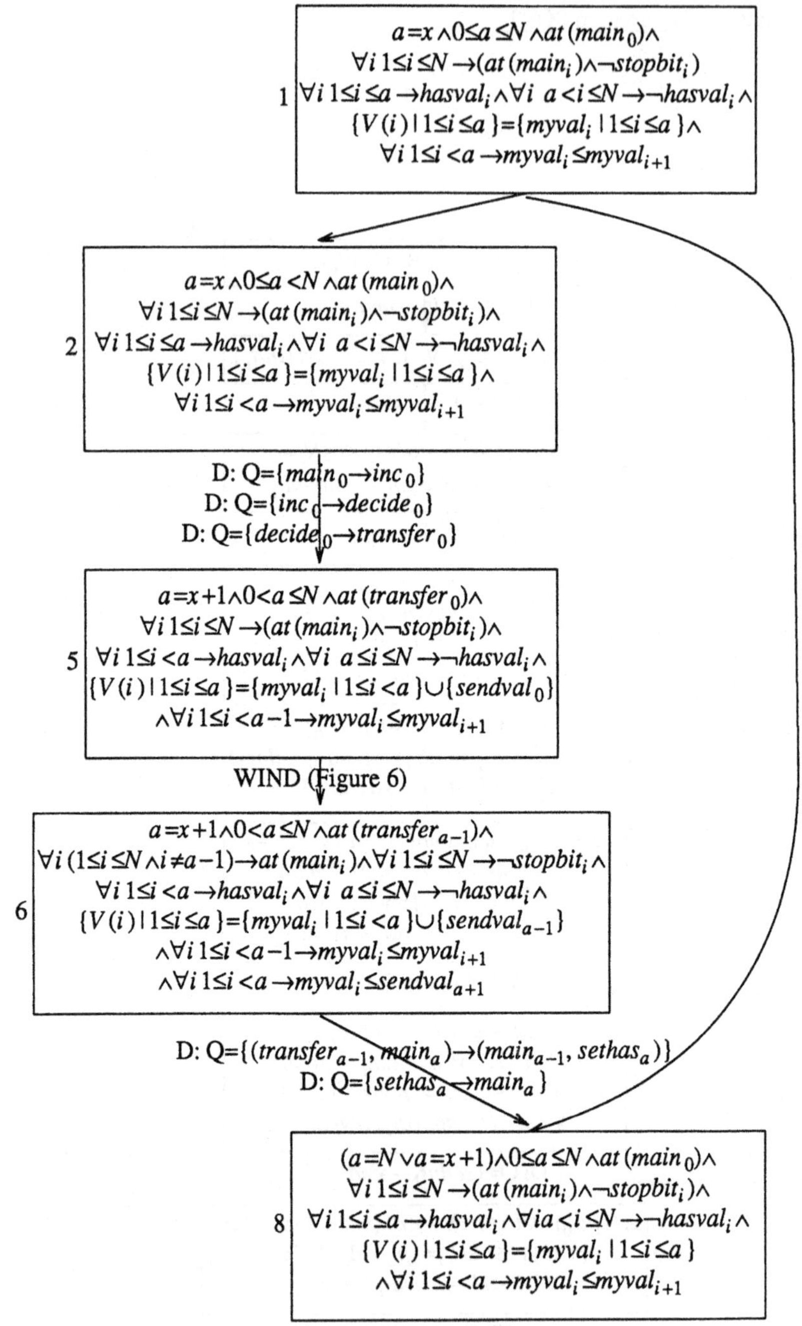
1
$a=x \wedge 0 \le a \le N \wedge at(main_0) \wedge$
$\forall i\ 1 \le i \le N \to (at(main_i) \wedge \neg stopbit_i)$
$\forall i\ 1 \le i \le a \to hasval_i \wedge \forall i\ \ a < i \le N \to \neg hasval_i \wedge$
$\{V(i) \mid 1 \le i \le a\} = \{myval_i \mid 1 \le i \le a\} \wedge$
$\forall i\ 1 \le i < a \to myval_i \le myval_{i+1}$
2
$a=x \wedge 0 \le a < N \wedge at(main_0) \wedge$
$\forall i\ 1 \le i \le N \to (at(main_i) \wedge \neg stopbit_i) \wedge$
$\forall i\ 1 \le i \le a \to hasval_i \wedge \forall i\ \ a < i \le N \to \neg hasval_i \wedge$
$\{V(i) \mid 1 \le i \le a\} = \{myval_i \mid 1 \le i \le a\} \wedge$
$\forall i\ 1 \le i < a \to myval_i \le myval_{i+1}$
D: Q=$\{main_0 \to inc_0\}$
D: Q=$\{inc_0 \to decide_0\}$
D: Q=$\{decide_0 \to transfer_0\}$
5
$a=x+1 \wedge 0 < a \le N \wedge at(transfer_0) \wedge$
$\forall i\ 1 \le i \le N \to (at(main_i) \wedge \neg stopbit_i) \wedge$
$\forall i\ 1 \le i < a \to hasval_i \wedge \forall i\ \ a \le i \le N \to \neg hasval_i \wedge$
$\{V(i) \mid 1 \le i \le a\} = \{myval_i \mid 1 \le i < a\} \cup \{sendval_0\}$
$\wedge \forall i\ 1 \le i < a-1 \to myval_i \le myval_{i+1}$
WIND (Figure 6)
6
$a=x+1 \wedge 0 < a \le N \wedge at(transfer_{a-1}) \wedge$
$\forall i\ (1 \le i \le N \wedge i \ne a-1) \to at(main_i) \wedge \forall i\ 1 \le i \le N \to \neg stopbit_i \wedge$
$\forall i\ 1 \le i < a \to hasval_i \wedge \forall i\ \ a \le i \le N \to \neg hasval_i \wedge$
$\{V(i) \mid 1 \le i \le a\} = \{myval_i \mid 1 \le i < a\} \cup \{sendval_{a-1}\}$
$\wedge \forall i\ 1 \le i < a-1 \to myval_i \le myval_{i+1}$
$\wedge \forall i\ 1 \le i < a \to myval_i \le sendval_{a+1}$
D: Q=$\{(transfer_{a-1}, main_a) \to (main_{a-1}, sethas_a)\}$
D: Q=$\{sethas_a \to main_a\}$
8
$(a=N \vee a=x+1) \wedge 0 \le a \le N \wedge at(main_0) \wedge$
$\forall i\ 1 \le i \le N \to (at(main_i) \wedge \neg stopbit_i) \wedge$
$\forall i\ 1 \le i \le a \to hasval_i \wedge \forall i a < i \le N \to \neg hasval_i \wedge$
$\{V(i) \mid 1 \le i \le a\} = \{myval_i \mid 1 \le i \le a\}$
$\wedge \forall i\ 1 \le i < a \to myval_i \le myval_{i+1}$

Figure 5

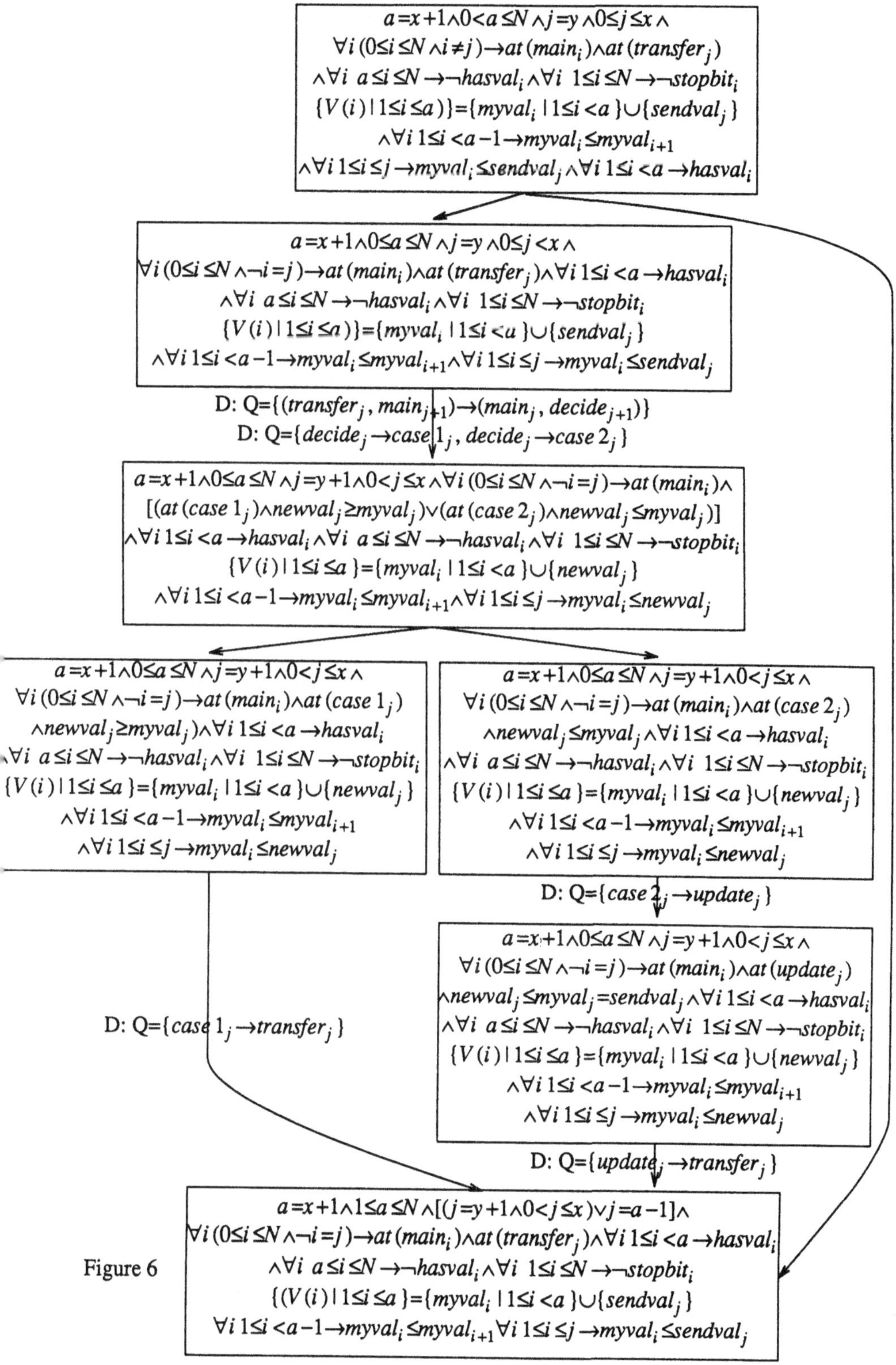
a=x+1∧0<a≤N∧j=y∧0≤j≤x∧
∀i (0≤i≤N∧i≠j)→at (main_i)∧at (transfer_j)
∧∀i a≤i≤N→¬hasval_i∧∀i 1≤i≤N→¬stopbit_i
{V(i) | 1≤i≤a)}={myval_i | 1≤i<a}∪{sendval_j}
∧∀i 1≤i<a−1→myval_i≤myval_{i+1}
∧∀i 1≤i≤j→myval_i≤sendval_j∧∀i 1≤i<a→hasval_i
a=x+1∧0≤a≤N∧j=y∧0≤j<x∧
∀i (0≤i≤N∧¬i=j)→at (main_i)∧at (transfer_j)∧∀i 1≤i<a→hasval_i
∧∀i a≤i≤N→¬hasval_i∧∀i 1≤i≤N→¬stopbit_i
{V(i) | 1≤i≤a)}={myval_i | 1≤i<a}∪{sendval_j}
∧∀i 1≤i<a−1→myval_i≤myval_{i+1}∧∀i 1≤i≤j→myval_i≤sendval_j
D: Q={(transfer_j, main_{j+1})→(main_j, decide_{j+1})}
D: Q={decide_j→case 1_j, decide_j→case 2_j}
a=x+1∧0≤a≤N∧j=y+1∧0<j≤x∧∀i (0≤i≤N∧¬i=j)→at (main_i)∧
[(at (case 1_j)∧newval_j≥myval_j)∨(at (case 2_j)∧newval_j≤myval_j)]
∧∀i 1≤i<a→hasval_i∧∀i a≤i≤N→¬hasval_i∧∀i 1≤i≤N→¬stopbit_i
{V(i) | 1≤i≤a}={myval_i | 1≤i<a}∪{newval_j}
∧∀i 1≤i<a−1→myval_i≤myval_{i+1}∧∀i 1≤i≤j→myval_i≤newval_j
a=x+1∧0≤a≤N∧j=y+1∧0<j≤x∧
∀i (0≤i≤N∧¬i=j)→at (main_i)∧at (case 1_j)
∧newval_j≥myval_j)∧∀i 1≤i<a→hasval_i
∧∀i a≤i≤N→¬hasval_i∧∀i 1≤i≤N→¬stopbit_i
{V(i) | 1≤i≤a}={myval_i | 1≤i<a}∪{newval_j}
∧∀i 1≤i<a−1→myval_i≤myval_{i+1}
∧∀i 1≤i≤j→myval_i≤newval_j
a=x+1∧0≤a≤N∧j=y+1∧0<j≤x∧
∀i (0≤i≤N∧¬i=j)→at (main_i)∧at (case 2_j)
∧newval_j≤myval_j∧∀i 1≤i<a→hasval_i
∧∀i a≤i≤N→¬hasval_i∧∀i 1≤i≤N→¬stopbit_i
{V(i) | 1≤i≤a}={myval_i | 1≤i<a}∪{newval_j}
∧∀i 1≤i<a−1→myval_i≤myval_{i+1}
∧∀i 1≤i≤j→myval_i≤newval_j
D: Q={case 2_j→update_j}
a=x+1∧0≤a≤N∧j=y+1∧0<j≤x∧
∀i (0≤i≤N∧¬i=j)→at (main_i)∧at (update_j)
∧newval_j≤myval_j=sendval_j∧∀i 1≤i<a→hasval_i
∧∀i a≤i≤N→¬hasval_i∧∀i 1≤i≤N→¬stopbit_i
{V(i) | 1≤i≤a}={myval_i | 1≤i<a}∪{newval_j}
∧∀i 1≤i<a−1→myval_i≤myval_{i+1}
∧∀i 1≤i≤j→myval_i≤newval_j
D: Q={case 1_j→transfer_j}
D: Q={update_j→transfer_j}
a=x+1∧1≤a≤N∧[(j=y+1∧0<j≤x)∨j=a−1]∧
∀i (0≤i≤N∧¬i=j)→at (main_i)∧at (transfer_j)∧∀i 1≤i<a→hasval_i
∧∀i a≤i≤N→¬hasval_i∧∀i 1≤i≤N→¬stopbit_i
{(V(i) | 1≤i≤a}={myval_i | 1≤i<a}∪{sendval_j}
∀i 1≤i<a−1→myval_i≤myval_{i+1}∀i 1≤i≤j→myval_i≤sendval_j

Figure 6

A Logic for Distributed Transition Systems

K. Lodaya, R. Ramanujam, P.S. Thiagarajan

The Institute of Mathematical Sciences
Madras 600 113, India

ABSTRACT. We present a logical characterization of a particular aspect of concurrency called the concurrent step notion. We do so by providing a sound and complete axiomatization of models called distributed transition systems. In a distributed transition system an old state is transformed into a new state through a set of actions occurring concurrently. Our logical language has the minimal features of linear time temporal logic and that of propositional dynamic logic. Our main result implies that satisfiability in our logical system is decidable.

Keywords: concurrent step, distributed transition systems, axiomatization, soundness, completeness.

CONTENTS

0. INTRODUCTION

The aim of this paper is to study the notion of concurrency from a logical standpoint. To do so, we define a simple transition system model called Distributed Transition Systems. Concurrency is captured in this model by permitting the system to go from an old state to a new state via a set of actions occurring concurrently; by this we mean a set of actions occurring independent of each other and hence with no order over their occurrences. The notion of concurrency is captured by demanding, in any such state transformation, the existence of a suitable set of intermediate states that form a "lattice" (with the old state as the "least" element and the new state as the "greatest" element).

Next we define a logical language which can be viewed - for all practical purposes - as a mild generalization of Propositional Dynamic Logic [FL]. Distributed transition systems can be viewed in a natural way as the underlying (Kripke) frames of the models for this language.

As the main contribution of this paper we provide a sound and complete axiomatization of the valid formulas of our language w.r.t. the chosen semantics. In this sense we expose the logical aspects of concurrency as captured in the distributed transition system model. An easy corollary of our main result is that satisfiability in our logical system is decidable in non-deterministic exponential time.

In the next section we introduce distributed transition systems. In section 2 we construct our logical language and define its semantics in terms of distributed transition systems. In section 3 we propose an axiomatization together with derived inference rules and theses. We also show that the proposed axiomatization is sound. The completeness of our axiomatization is established in section 4. Our proof of completeness at once implies the decidability of the logical system under study. In the concluding section, we review our results in the context of related literature. We also discuss briefly some strong negative results that have been obtained by R. Parikh [P] concerning the deterministic version of our logical system.

1. DISTRIBUTED TRANSITION SYSTEMS

We begin by recalling that a transition system is a triple $TS = (S,A,\rightarrow)$ where S is a set of states, A is a set of actions and $\rightarrow \subseteq S \times A \times S$ is the labelled transition relation. If $(s,a,s') \in \rightarrow$ then we say that the system can perform the action a at s and as a result achieve the state s'.

Our proposed generalization lies in defining the transition relation to be a subset of $S \times 2^A \times S$ where 2^A denotes the set of subsets of A. If (s,u,s') is a member of this generalized transition relation then this will be taken to mean that the members of u can occur independent of each other at s so as to result in the state s'. This is called a <u>concurrent</u> <u>step</u>. With this in mind we can now specify the class of objects investigated in this paper.

<u>Definition</u> <u>1.1</u> A distributed transition system (dts, for short) is a triple $TS = (S,A,\rightarrow)$ where

(i) S is a set of states

(ii) A is a finite set of actions

(iii) $\rightarrow \subseteq S \times 2^A \times S$ is the labelled (step) transition relation which is to satisfy the following requirements (throughout what follows we write $s \xrightarrow{u} s'$ instead of $(s,u,s') \in \rightarrow$).

(iii.a) $s \xrightarrow{\emptyset} s'$ iff $s = s'$.

(iii.b) if $s \xrightarrow{u} s'$ then there exists a function $f: 2^u \rightarrow S$ such that $f(\emptyset) = s$ and $f(u) = s'$ and for every $v_1 \subseteq v_2 \subseteq u$ it is the case that $f(v_1) \xrightarrow{v_2 - v_1} f(v_2)$. □

Two remarks concerning definition 1.1 are in order before proceeding to consider illustrative examples. Firstly we have required A to be a finite set because of the somewhat unusual mixture of temporal operators contained in our logical language. This will become clear once the material contained in the next section is encountered. Even otherwise, it seems reasonable to restrict our attention to distributed systems which exhibit only a "finite" amount of concurrency.

Secondly, the reader familiar with research on the "non-interleaved" operational semantics of CCS-like languages [DDM, O] will notice that the objects captured by definition 1.1 will arise naturally in such settings. However, there it would be more realistic to permit the transition system to go from an old state to a new state via a multi-set of actions occurring independent of each other. Here we have defined $\rightarrow$ to be a subset of $S \times 2^A \times S$ mainly for technical convenience.

Here is an example of a transition system in which three actions can occur independent of each other at $s_\emptyset$ to take the system to the state s_{abc} .

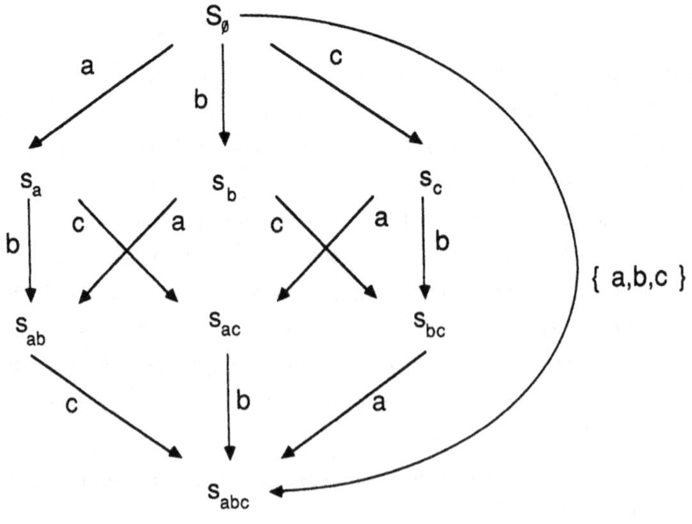

Figure 1.1

Here and throughout what follows we will often write the singleton {x} as simply x. In order to avoid cluttering up the diagram, we have not displayed all the members of the transition relation. Some of the members that have not been shown are:
$s_c \xrightarrow{\emptyset} s_c$, $s_a \xrightarrow{\{b,c\}} s_{abc}$ and $s_\emptyset \xrightarrow{\{a,c\}} s_{ac}$.

It is important to note that the condition stated in part (iii.b) of definition 1.1 is merely an implication. Here is an example illustrating this point.

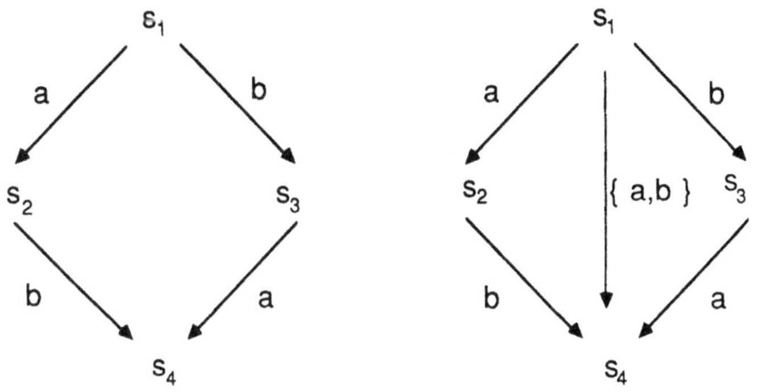

(i) (ii)

Figure 1.2

It is to be understood that the only members of the transition relation that have not been shown are of the form $s_i \xrightarrow{\emptyset} s_i$, for $1 \leq i \leq 4$. In particular, in Figure 1.2(i), (s_1 , {a,b}, s_4) is _not_ a member of the transition relation.

The ability to distinguish between these two transition systems could be used in a non-interleaving semantics of CCS/TCSP - like formalisms [DDM, O], where the terms a.b.nil + b.a.nil and a.nil $\|_\emptyset$ b.nil can be associated with figures 1.2(i) and 1.2(ii) respectively in the obvious manner.

Finally, we wish to point out that the choice function mentioned in part (iii.b) of definition 1.1 fixes _a priori_ one element of S for _each_ subset of u so as to yield a "u-lattice" within the state space of the transition system. This is crucial since our distributed transition system can be, in general, highly non-deterministic.

We conclude this section with a definition and an observation which will be used later.

Definition 1.2 Let (S,A,→) be a dts and s ∈ S. Then RC(s), the _reachability_

<u>set of s</u>, is the smallest subset of S containing s such that if $s' \in RC(s)$ and for some $u \subseteq A$, $s' \xrightarrow{u} s''$ then $s'' \in RC(s)$. □

<u>Proposition 1.1</u> Let $(S,A,\rightarrow)$ be a dts, $s \in S$ and $s' \in RC(s)$ such that $s \neq s'$. Then there exists a (finite) sequence of actions $a_1 a_2 \ldots a_n$ and a (finite) sequence of states $s_0 s_1 \ldots s_n$ such that $s = s_0$, $s_n = s'$ and for $1 \leq i \leq n$, $s_{i-1} \xrightarrow{a_i} s_i$.
<u>Proof</u>: Follows easily from the finiteness of A and the definitions. □

2. THE LANGUAGE

For the rest of the paper we fix a finite non-empty set of actions $A = \{ a_1 , a_2 , \ldots, a_n \}$. We also fix a finite non-empty set of propositions $P = \{ p_1 , p_2 , \ldots, p_m \}$. We let a, b and c range over A and u, v with or without subscripts range over 2^A. We let p, q and r range over P. The formulas of our language are then built up as follows.

<u>Definition 2.1</u>
(i) Every member of P is a formula.
(ii) If α and β are formulas then so are $\sim\alpha$, $\alpha \vee \beta$, $\langle u\rangle\alpha$ and $\Box\alpha$. □

We let $\alpha,\beta,\gamma,\delta$ with or without subscripts and/or superscripts range over F, the set of formulas. As before we will often write the singleton {a} as simply a. In particular, we will write $\langle a\rangle\alpha$ instead of $\langle\{a\}\rangle\alpha$ for $a \in A$ and $\alpha \in F$.

Before proceeding to consider the semantics of the formulas we wish to introduce some derived connectives and modalities. The connectives of PC (Propositional calculus) such as $\wedge$, $\supset$ and $\equiv$ are defined in terms of $\sim$ and $\vee$ in the usual way. In addition, we shall need:

(i) $\Diamond\alpha \overset{def}{\Longleftrightarrow} \sim\Box\sim\alpha$

(ii) $\bigcirc\alpha \overset{def}{\Longleftrightarrow} \langle a_1\rangle\, \alpha \vee \langle a_2\rangle\, \alpha \vee \ldots \vee \langle a_n\rangle\, \alpha$

(iii) $\odot\alpha \overset{def}{\Longleftrightarrow} \sim\bigcirc\sim\alpha$

(iv) $[u]\alpha \overset{def}{\Longleftrightarrow} \sim\langle u\rangle\sim\alpha$

The "weak" next state operator $\odot$ will play a crucial role in capturing the effect of the $\Box$ operator in terms of the indexed operator $\langle u\rangle$. It is for this reason that we require A to be a finite set. We are now ready to consider the semantics of our language.

A *frame* is a distributed transition system $Fr = (S,A,\rightarrow)$.

A *model* is an ordered pair $M = (Fr,V)$ where $Fr = (S,A,\rightarrow)$ is a frame and $V: S \rightarrow 2^P$ is the *valuation function*.

Let $M = ((S,A,\rightarrow),V)$ be a model, α a formula and $s \in S$. Then the notion of α being satisfied at the state s in the model M is denoted as $M,s \models \alpha$ and is defined inductively as follows:

Definition 2.2.

(i) $M,s \models p$ iff $p \in V(s)$

(ii) $M,s \models \sim\alpha$ iff $M,s \not\models \alpha$ ($M,s \not\models \alpha$ denotes that α is not satisfied at s in M)

(iii) $M,s \models \alpha \vee \beta$ iff $M,s \models \alpha$ or $M,s \models \beta$

(iv) $M,s \models \langle u\rangle\alpha$ iff there exists $s' \in S$ such that $s \xrightarrow{u} s'$ and $M,s' \models \alpha$

(v) $M,s \models \Box\alpha$ iff $M,s' \models \alpha$ for every $s' \in RC(s)$. □

We shall say that the formula α is *satisfiable* if there exists a model $M = ((S,A,\rightarrow),V)$ and a state $s \in S$ such that $M,s \models \alpha$. α is *M-valid* (denoted $M \models \alpha$) if $M,s \models \alpha$ for every $s \in S$. Finally, α is *valid* - and this will be denoted by $\models \alpha$ - if α is M-valid for every model M.

Hennessy and Milner [HM] have proposed the following logical language to reason about concurrency and nondeterminism:

HML (i) $\{ \top, \bot \} \subseteq$ HML

(ii) If $\alpha \in$ HML, so does $\sim\alpha$

(iii) If $\alpha \in$ HML and $a \in A$, then $\langle a\rangle\alpha \in$ HML

(iv) If $\alpha,\beta \in$ HML then $\alpha \vee \beta \in$ HML

Our language allows a set of propositions instead of just the truth-values. We also allow only finite conjunction but the □ operator can be used to reason about a potentially infinite number of states.

Moreover, we have the $\langle u\rangle$ modality, which explicitly represents concurrency.

Our indexed operator $\langle u\rangle$ can be viewed as a generalization of the $\langle a\rangle$ operator of Propositional Dynamic Logic [FL], where a is to be interpreted as an atomic program. Viewed in this light, a more natural language to consider (starting with A and P) would have been:

Programs (i) Every subset u of A is a program

(ii) If π_1 and π_2 are programs then so are $\pi_1 + \pi_2$, $\pi_1 ; \pi_2$ and π_1^*.

PDL^{set} (i) Every member of P is a formula of PDL^{set}

(ii) If α and β are formulas of PDL^{set}, then so are $\sim\alpha$, $\alpha \vee \beta$ and $\langle\pi\rangle\alpha$, where π is a program.

We could even allow A to be an infinite set here, provided condition (i) allows only <u>finite</u> subsets of A as programs. But there appears to be - from a logical standpoint - no loss of generality in demanding A to be a finite set.

However, we have chosen a syntax which includes only concurrent steps and the $\Box$ operator taken from temporal logic. We have done this mainly to reduce the number of cases to be dealt with in the completeness proof. We will have more to say about this in Section 5.

We are now ready to propose a sound and complete axiomatization of the valid formulas of our language.

3. AN AXIOMATIZATION

At present we have to use a countable set of axiom schemes to express the existence of a complete lattice of states whenever a concurrent step is performed. We shall use the notation F(u,k) to denote the set of functions $\{ f \mid f : 2^u \to \{ 1,2,\ldots,k\} \}$.

<u>Axiom schemes</u>

(A_0) All substitutional instances of the tautologies of propositional calculus

(A_1) $\Box(\alpha \supset \beta) \supset (\Box\alpha \supset \Box\beta)$

(A_2) $\Box\alpha \supset (\alpha \wedge \odot\Box\alpha)$

(A_3) $\Box(\alpha \supset \odot\alpha) \supset (\alpha \supset \Box\alpha)$

(A_4) $[u](\alpha \supset \beta) \supset ([u]\alpha \supset [u]\beta)$

(A_5) $[\emptyset]\alpha \equiv \alpha$

($A_{6,k}$) (for $k \geq 1$)

$$\langle u\rangle\alpha \wedge \bigwedge_{v\subseteq u} [v] \bigvee_{i=1}^{k} \beta_v^i \supset \bigvee_{f\in F(u,k)} \bigwedge_{v_1\subseteq u} \langle v_1\rangle (\gamma_{v_1} \wedge \bigwedge_{v_1\subseteq v_2\subseteq u} \langle v_2 - v_1\rangle\gamma_{v_2})$$

$$\text{where } \gamma_v = \begin{cases} \beta_v^{f(v)} \wedge \alpha, & \text{if } v = u \\ \beta_v^{f(v)}, & \text{if } v \subset u \end{cases}$$

<u>Inference rules</u>

(MP) $\dfrac{\alpha,\ \alpha \supset \beta}{\beta}$ (TG) $\dfrac{\alpha}{\Box\alpha}$ (u-Gen) $\dfrac{\alpha}{[u]\alpha}$

A formula which can be derived in a finite number of steps from the axioms using the inference rules will be called a thesis and thesishood of α will be denoted $\vdash \alpha$.

As usual, by a consistent formula, we shall mean a formula whose negation is not a thesis in our system. The finite set of formulas $\{ \alpha_1 , \ldots, \alpha_k \}$ is consistent iff $\alpha_1 \wedge \ldots \wedge \alpha_k$ is consistent. A set of formulas is consistent iff each of its finite subsets is.

Most of our axioms and inference rules are standard and have been assembled from [LPZ] and [K]. The characteristic axioms of our system are A_5 and the infinite set $A_{6,k}$, corresponding to the two clauses in our semantic definition of a concurrent step.

A_5 is easy to follow: each state can be reached from itself through the occurrence of the empty set of actions.

To understand $A_{6,k}$, it may be instructive to look at some of its implications. The first implication we can draw is

$$\vdash \langle u\rangle\alpha \supset \langle v\rangle\langle u-v\rangle\alpha, \quad \text{for } v \subseteq u$$

This says that a concurrent step can be broken up into a sequence of concurrent substeps.

We can generalize to $A_{6,1}$, which says

$$\vdash \langle u\rangle\alpha \wedge \bigwedge_{v\subseteq u} [v]\, \beta_v \supset \bigwedge_{v_1\subseteq u} \langle v_1\rangle \left(\gamma_{v_1} \wedge \bigwedge_{v_1\subseteq v_2\subseteq u} \langle v_2-v_1\rangle\gamma_{v_2}\right)$$

where the γ_v are defined as before.

This gives all the substeps of the concurrent step, forming the "lattice" structure.

However there is more to the semantics of the $\xrightarrow{u}$ relation: all the intermediate states are preassigned by the existence of a function. Hence if there are k possible v-successors (for instance due to nondeterminism), the function a priori chooses one, for each $v \subseteq u$. This is expressed by the set $A_{6,k}$, where k bounds the number of states from which a choice is to be made.

Theorem 3.1 (Soundness) If $\vdash \alpha$ then $\models \alpha$.

Proof: We shall only verify the soundness of $A_{6,k}$. It is routine to verify the soundness of the remaining axioms and to check that the inference rules preserve validity.

Suppose that $M = ((S,A,\rightarrow),V)$ is a model and $s \in S$ such that

$$M,s \models \langle u\rangle\alpha \wedge \bigwedge_{v\subseteq u} [v] \bigvee_{i=i}^{k} \beta_v^i .$$

Then there exists $s' \in S$ such that $s \xrightarrow{u} s'$ and $M,s' \models \alpha$.

From $s \xrightarrow{u} s'$ it follows that there exists $g\colon 2^u \rightarrow S$ such that $g(\emptyset) = s$

and $g(u) = s'$ and for every $v_1 \subseteq v_2 \subseteq u$, $g(v_1) \xrightarrow{v_2 - v_1} g(v_2)$. Consider now $v \subseteq u$. Since $M,s \models [v] \bigvee_{i=1}^{k} \beta_v^i$ and $s \xrightarrow{v} g(v)$, we must have $M,g(v) \models \bigvee_{i=1}^{k} \beta_v^i$. Hence for some $j \in \{ 1,2,\ldots,k \}$, it must be the case that $M,g(v) \models \beta_v^j$. This shows that for each $v \subseteq u$ there exists a $j_v \in \{ 1,2,\ldots,k \}$ dependent on g such that $M,g(v) \models \beta_v^{j_v}$. Let $f: 2^u \to \{ 1,2,\ldots,k \}$ be given by $f(v) = j_v$. Recalling that $\gamma_v = \beta_v^{f(v)} \wedge \alpha$ for $v = u$ and $\gamma_v = \beta_v^{f(v)}$ for $v \subset u$, it is easy to check that $M,g(v) \models \gamma_v$ for every $v \subseteq u$. The soundness of $A_{6,k}$ now follows easily from $s \xrightarrow{v_1} g(v_1)$ and $g(v_1) \xrightarrow{v_2 - v_1} g(v_2)$ for every $v_1 \subseteq v_2 \subseteq u$. □

We now wish to present some theses and derived inference rules which will be used in the completeness proof. The derivations are easy and hence we shall omit them.

Derived rules

(DR1) $\dfrac{\alpha \supset \beta,\ \alpha \supset \odot\alpha}{\alpha \supset \Box\beta}$ (DR2) $\dfrac{\alpha \supset \beta}{[u]\alpha \supset [u]\beta}$

(DR3) $\dfrac{\alpha \supset \beta}{\langle u\rangle\alpha \supset \langle u\rangle\beta}$ (DR4) $\dfrac{\alpha}{\odot\alpha}$

Theses

(T1) $[u]\alpha \wedge \langle u\rangle\beta \supset \langle u\rangle(\alpha \wedge \beta)$

(T2) $[u](\alpha \wedge \beta) \equiv [u]\alpha \wedge [u]\beta$

(T3) $\langle u\rangle(\alpha \wedge \beta) \supset \langle u\rangle\alpha \wedge \langle u\rangle\beta$

(T4) $\langle u\rangle\alpha \supset \langle v\rangle\langle u-v\rangle\alpha$ } for $v \subseteq u$

(T5) $[v][u-v]\ \alpha \supset [u]\alpha$ }

Proposition 3.2 If, for some u, $\langle u\rangle\alpha$ is consistent, then so is α.

Proof: Suppose α is not consistent. Then $\vdash \sim\alpha$.

By (u-Gen), $\vdash [u]\sim\alpha$, contradicting consistency of $\langle u\rangle\alpha$. □

4. COMPLETENESS

We will show that our proposed axiomatization is complete by proving that every consistent formula is satisfiable. To this end, we require the notion of the closure of a formula -often referred to as the Fischer-Ladner closure within the theory of PDL.

<u>Definition</u> <u>4.1</u>

(i) Let α_0 be a formula. Then $CL'(\alpha_0)$ is the least set of formulas containing α_0 which satisfies the following requirements.

(i.a) If $\sim\alpha \in CL'(\alpha_0)$ then $\alpha \in CL'(\alpha_0)$
(i.b) If $\alpha \vee \beta \in CL'(\alpha_0)$ then $\alpha,\beta \in CL'(\alpha_0)$
(i.c) If $<u>\alpha \in CL'(\alpha_0)$ then $\alpha \in CL'(\alpha_0)$
(i.d) If $\Box\alpha \in CL'(\alpha_0)$ then $\alpha, \bigcirc\Box\alpha \in CL'(\alpha_0)$

(ii) $CL(\alpha_0)$, the <u>closure</u> of α_0, is given by $CL(\alpha_0) \stackrel{def}{=} CL'(\alpha_0) \cup \{ \sim\alpha | \alpha \in CL'(\alpha_0) \}$.

(iii) An <u>atom</u> w.r.t. α_0 is a maximal consistent subset of $CL(\alpha_0)$.

(iv) $AT(\alpha_0)$ is the set of atoms w.r.t. α_0. □

It is easy to verify that there exists a constant $c > 0$ such that the size of $CL(\alpha_0)$ is at most cn, where n is the length of the formula α_0. Consequently $AT(\alpha_0)$ is of size at most 2^{cn}.

Through the rest of this section we fix a <u>consistent</u> formula α_0. We will use CL and AT to stand for $CL(\alpha_0)$ and $AT(\alpha_0)$ respectively.

If $\omega \in AT$ then we let $\hat{\omega}$ denote the conjunction of all the formulas in ω. If W is a nonempty subset of AT then $\check{W}$ will denote the disjunction $\hat{\omega}_1 \vee \hat{\omega}_2 \ldots \vee \hat{\omega}_k$ where $W = \{ \omega_1, \omega_2, \ldots, \omega_k \}$.

The next proposition states some properties of atoms; these can be proved using propositional reasoning.

<u>Proposition</u> <u>4.1</u> Let $\omega,\omega' \in AT$.

(i) If $\alpha \in \omega$ then $\vdash \hat{\omega} \supset \alpha$

(ii) If $\hat{\omega} \wedge \alpha$ is consistent and $\alpha \in CL$ then $\alpha \in \omega$

(iii) If $\hat{\omega} \wedge \hat{\omega}'$ is consistent then $w = \omega'$

(iv) $\vdash \omega_1 \vee \omega_2 \ldots \omega_k$ where $AT = \{ \omega_1, \omega_2, \ldots, \omega_k \}$

We now wish to construct a model for α_0 using its closure.

<u>Definition</u> <u>4.2</u>

(i) $TS_0 = (AT, A, \rightarrow_0)$

where $\rightarrow_0 \subseteq AT \times 2^A \times AT$ is given by:
$\omega \xrightarrow{u}_0 \omega'$ iff there exists $f: 2^u \rightarrow AT$ such that $f(\emptyset) = \omega$, $f(u) = \omega'$ and $\forall v_1 \subseteq v_2 \subseteq u$, $[v_2 - v_1]\alpha \in f(v_1)$ implies $\alpha \in f(v_2)$

It is easy to check that TS_0 is indeed a frame.

(ii) $M_0 = (TS_0, V_0)$
where $V_0 : AT \rightarrow 2^P$ is given by:
$V_0(\omega) = \omega \cap P$, for every $\omega \in AT$

The following intermediate results will be required in the proof of completeness.

<u>Lemma</u> <u>4.2</u> Let $\omega_1, \omega_2 \in AT$ and $v \subseteq A$. If $\hat{\omega}_1 \wedge \langle v\rangle\hat{\omega}_2$ is consistent and $[v]\alpha \in \omega_1$, then $\alpha \in \omega_2$.

<u>Proof</u>: Suppose not.
Then $\sim\alpha \in \omega_2$. Since $\hat{\omega}_1 \wedge \langle v\rangle\hat{\omega}_2$ is consistent we then have from T3 and part (i) of Proposition 4.1 and DR3 that $\hat{\omega}_1 \wedge \langle v\rangle\sim\alpha$ is consistent. But from $[v]\alpha \in \omega_1$ and once again from part (i) of Proposition 4.1 we now have the contradiction that $\langle v\rangle\sim\alpha \wedge [v]\alpha$ is consistent. □

<u>Lemma</u> <u>4.3</u> Let $\omega \in AT$ and $R = RC(\omega)$. (Here $RC(\omega)$, the reachability set of ω, is defined relative to TS_0.) Then $\vdash \check{R} \supset \odot\check{R}$.

<u>Proof</u>: Let $R = \{ x_1, x_2, \ldots, x_k \}$. Since $\omega \in R$, $k \geq 1$. Suppose $AT - R$ is empty. Then $AT = R$ so that $\vdash \odot\check{R}$ follows from part (iv) of Proposition 4.1 and DR4. Now $\vdash \check{R} \supset \odot\check{R}$ follows from the laws of propositional calculus. So assume that $AT - R = \{ y_1, y_2, \ldots, y_\ell \}$ with $\ell \geq 1$. Then once again from part (iv) of Proposition 4.1 it follows that $\vdash \sim(\hat{x}_1 \vee \hat{x}_2 \ldots \vee \hat{x}_k) \supset (\hat{y}_1 \vee \hat{y}_2 \ldots \vee \hat{y}_\ell)$. Suppose that $\check{R} \supset \odot\check{R}$ is not a thesis. Then there exists an $a \in A$ such that $(\hat{x}_1 \vee \hat{x}_2 \ldots \vee \hat{x}_k) \wedge \langle a\rangle (\hat{y}_1 \vee \ldots \vee \hat{y}_\ell)$ is consistent. This follows at once from the definitions and the thesis we have just established above. We now have that for some $i \in \{ 1, \ldots, k \}$ and some $j \in \{ 1, \ldots, \ell \}$, $\hat{x}_i \wedge \langle a\rangle\, \hat{y}_j$ is consistent. But this would imply by Lemma 4.2 and Definition 4.2 that $x_i \xrightarrow{a} y_j$. This leads to the contradiction that $y_j \in R$. □

<u>Theorem</u> <u>4.4</u> Let $\omega \in AT$ and $\alpha \in CL$.
Then $\alpha \in \omega$ iff $M_0, \omega \models \alpha$.

<u>Proof</u>: By induction on the structure of the formula α.

<u>Case</u> <u>1</u>: If $\alpha \in P$ or α is of the form $\sim\beta$ or $\beta \vee \gamma$, the proof is routine, so we omit it.

<u>Case</u> <u>2</u>: Suppose α is of the form $\Box\beta$. Let $R = RC(\omega)$.
$\Rightarrow$ First assume $\Box\beta \in \omega$, and let $\omega' \in R$.

Proposition 1.1 shows that there exist ω_0 , ..., ω_k , a_1 , ..., a_k , such that

$$\omega = \omega_0 \xrightarrow{a_1}_0 \omega_1 \xrightarrow{a_2}_0 \cdots \xrightarrow{a_{k-1}}_0 \omega_{k-1} \xrightarrow{a_k}_0 \omega_k = \omega' .$$

We show by induction on k that $\Box\beta \in \omega_k$.

<u>k = 0</u>. Then $\omega = \omega_0 = \omega_k = \omega'$ and by hypothesis $\Box\beta \in \omega$.

<u>k > 0</u>. By the induction hypothesis, $\Box\beta \in \omega_{k-1}$.

From the definition of $CL(\alpha_0)$ and A_2 , we have $\odot\Box\beta \in \omega_{k-1}$, therefore $[a_k]\Box\beta \in \omega_{k-1}$.

Since $\omega_{k-1} \xrightarrow{a_k}_0 \omega_k$, $\Box\beta \in \omega_k$.

Thus for all $\omega' \in R$, $\Box\beta \in \omega'$.

Using A_2 again, $\beta \in \omega'$, and therefore, by the induction hypothesis, $M_0,\omega' \models \beta$. Hence $M_0 , \omega \models \Box\beta$.

⇐ Next assume $\Box\beta \notin \omega$.

If there exists $\omega' \in R$ such that $\beta \notin \omega'$ then by the induction hypothesis $M_0,\omega' \not\models \beta$ and therefore $M_0,\omega \not\models \Box\beta$.

So assume that $\beta \in \omega'$ for every $\omega' \in R$.

By Proposition 4.1(i), $\vdash \hat{\omega}' \supset \beta$ for every $\omega' \in R$.

Combining using PC, $\vdash \check{R} \supset \beta$.

By Lemma 4.3, we know that $\vdash \check{R} \supset \odot \check{R}$.

Hence DR1 yields $\vdash \check{R} \supset \Box\beta$.

Since $\omega \in R$, we get $\vdash \hat{\omega} \supset \Box\beta$, and by Proposition 4.1 (ii) $\Box\beta \in \omega$, contradicting the hypothesis.

<u>Case</u> <u>3</u>: Finally suppose α is of the form $\langle u\rangle\beta$.

⇒ Assume $\langle u\rangle\beta \in \omega$.

By Proposition 4.1(i), $\vdash \hat{\omega} \supset \langle u\rangle\beta$.

By Proposition 4.1(iv), we know $\vdash \check{AT}$.

By repeated application of (u-Gen),

we get $\vdash \hat{\omega} \supset \langle u\rangle\beta \wedge \bigwedge_{v\subseteq u} [v]\, \check{AT}$.

Let AT = { ω_1 , ..., ω_j } . From $A_{6,j}$, we now infer that there exists $f: 2^u \to \{ 1, \ldots, j \}$ such that

$$\hat{\omega} \wedge \bigwedge_{v_1\subseteq u} \langle v_1\rangle(\gamma_{v_1} \wedge \bigwedge_{v_1\subseteq v_2\subseteq u} \langle v_2-v_1\rangle\gamma_{v_2}) \qquad -(1)$$

is consistent, where

$$\gamma_v = \begin{cases} \hat{\omega}_{f(v)}, & \text{if } v \subset u \\ \hat{\omega}_{f(v)} \wedge \beta, & \text{if } v = u \end{cases}$$

In what follows, we have often written x instead of $\hat{x}$ where x is an atom. This should cause no confusion.

Define $g : 2^u \to AT$ by $g(v) = \omega_{f(v)}$, for $v \subseteq u$.
From (1) and T3, we have $\hat{\omega} \wedge \langle\emptyset\rangle\, g(\emptyset)$ is consistent.
Hence by A_4, $\hat{\omega} \wedge g(\emptyset)$ is consistent, and by Proposition 4.1(iii), $\omega = g(\emptyset)$. -(2)
From (1) and T3, we can conclude for $v_1 \subseteq v_2 \subseteq u$,
$g(v_1) \wedge \langle v_2 - v_1\rangle\, g(v_2)$ is consistent.
By Lemma 4.2, we have for all $v_1 \subseteq v_2 \subseteq u$
$[v_2 - v_1]\alpha \in g(v_1)$ implies $\alpha \in g(v_2)$ -(3)
Putting (2) and (3) together, we have $\omega \xrightarrow{u}_0 g(u)$ -(4)
Using (1) and T3 again, we know that $\langle u\rangle(g(u) \wedge \beta)$ is consistent:
By Proposition 3.2, $g(u) \wedge \beta$ is consistent, which, with Proposition 4.1(ii), yields $\beta \in g(u)$.
By the induction hypothesis $M_0, g(u) \models \beta$ -(5)
(4) and (5) together imply $M_0, \omega \models \langle u\rangle\beta$.

$\Leftarrow$ Lastly assume $\langle u\rangle\beta \notin \omega$. Then $[u]\sim\beta \in \omega$.
Let $\omega \xrightarrow{u}_0 \omega'$.
By definition of $\to_0$, $\sim\beta \in \omega'$.
By the induction hypothesis $M_0, \omega' \models \sim\beta$.
Since this is true for arbitrary u-successors of ω, $M_0, \omega \not\models \langle u\rangle\beta$.□

<u>Corollary 4.5</u> (Completeness) $\vdash\alpha$ iff $\models\alpha$.
<u>Proof</u>: The 'if' part of the result is Theorem 3.1. The 'only if' part follows at once from Theorem 4.4. □

<u>Corollary 4.6</u> (Decidability). Satisfiability in our system is decidable in non-deterministic exponential time.
<u>Proof</u>: By Theorem 3.1, every satisfiable formula is consistent. By the definition of $CL(\alpha_0)$ and Theorem 4.4 it follows that every consistent formula α_0 has a model whose size is bounded by 2^{cn} where $c > 0$ is a constant and n is the length of the formula α_0 . □

5. DISCUSSION

In this paper, we have obtained a sound and complete axiomatization of distributed transition systems. The key aspect of a dts is that it captures the concurrency of action occurrences by postulating the existence of a suitable local "lattice" of states. Consequently, we can claim that through our axiomatization we have logically characterized this notion of concurrency.

Admittedly, our completeness result is slightly unsatisfactory in that it depends on an infinite set of axiom schemes. It is not clear whether this situation can be improved upon. All the evidence available to us at present suggests that a finite axiomatization may not be obtainable. Unfortunately, we do not have a proof of this conjecture at present. In this connection, it is worth pointing out some negative results that have been obtained by R. Parikh [P] concerning the class of deterministic distributed transition systems.

As might be expected, a dts TS = (S,A,→) is said to be <u>deterministic</u> if $s \xrightarrow{u} s'$ and $s \xrightarrow{u} s''$ together imply $s' = s''$, for every $s,s',s'' \in S$ and every $u \subseteq A$. Let DSAT denote the set of formulas of our language which are satisfiable over the class of deterministic models (i.e., by models whose underlying frames are deterministic distributed transition systems). Let DVAL be the set of formulas of our language that are valid over the class of deterministic models. Parikh has shown that DSAT is Σ_1^1-complete and hence satisfiability of a formula using deterministic models is highly undecidable. More, DVAL is Π_1^1-complete, and hence, unlike in the case of DPDL [BHP], it is impossible to obtain a sound and complete axiomatization of DVAL.

As we mentioned earlier, the work reported here could have been carried out as an extension of PDL. More specifically, by adding all the axioms $A_{6,k}$ $(k \geq 1)$, to the usual PDL axioms and inference rules [KP], we obtain a sound and complete axiomatization of the valid formulas of PDL^{set} defined in Section 2. The intended semantics of this language is the obvious one based on distributed transition systems. The details are straightforward and follow easily from [KP] and the contents of the previous section.

The language we have considered can be extended in many ways. Multi-sets can be admitted as steps. One can also consider introducing an UNTIL operator. Going over to a branching time logic framework is another possibility. These extensions will be considered in our future work.

ACKNOWLEDGEMENTS

We thank Rohit Parikh for fruitful discussions and suggestions. In particular, he suggested the transition relation specified in definition 4.2 and this has lead to considerable improvements in the axiomatization and in the completeness proof. We also thank Ms. Marloes van der Nat for the prompt and excellent typing of the manuscript.

REFERENCES

[BHP] Ben-Ari, M., Halpern, J.Y. and Pnueli, A. (1982): Deterministic Propositional Dynamic Logic: Finite Models, Complexity and Completeness. J. Comput. Syst. Sci., 25, pp. 402-417.

[DDM] Degano, P., De Nicola, R. and Montanari, U. (1987): A Distributed Operational Semantics for CCS based on Condition/Event Systems. Nota Interna I.E.I. - B4 - 21, Department of Computer Science, University of Pisa (To appear in Acta Informatica).

[FL] Fischer, M.J. and Ladner, R.E. (1979): Propositional Dynamic Logic of Regular Programs. J. Comput. Syst. Sci., 18, pp 194-211.

[HM] Hennessy, M. and Milner, R. (1980): On Observing Non-determinism and Concurrency, Springer Lecture Notes in Computer Science, 85, Springer-Verlag, pp 299-309.

[K] Kröger, F. (1987): Temporal Logic of Programs. EATCS Monograph on Theoretical Computer Science, 8, Springer-Verlag.

[KP] Kozen, D. and Parikh, R. (1982): An Elementary Proof of Completeness of PDL. Theor. Comput. Sci., 14, pp 113-118.

[LPZ] Lichtenstein, O., Pnueli, A. and Zuck, L. (1985): The Glory of the Past. In: Logic of Programs, Ed. R. Parikh, Springer Lecture Notes in Computer Science, 193, Springer-Verlag, pp 196-218.

[M] Milner, R., (1980): A Calculus of Communicating Systems. Springer Lecture Notes in Computer Science, 92, Springer-Verlag.

[O] Olderog, E.-R. (1987): Operational Petri Net Semantics for CCSP. In: Advances in Petri Nets, Ed. G. Rozenberg, Springer Lecture Notes in Computer Science, 266, Springer-Verlag, pp 381-400.

[P] Parikh, R. (1988): Decidability and Undecidability in Distributed Transition systems (Unpublished Manuscript).

Fully Abstract Models for a Process Language with Refinement

Mogens Nielsen* Uffe Engberg Kim S. Larsen

Computer Science Department
Aarhus University
Ny Munkegade
DK-8000 Aarhus C, Denmark

ABSTRACT. We study the use of sets of labelled partial orders (pomsets) as denotational models for process algebras. More specifically, we study their capability to capture degrees of nonsequentiality of processes. We present four full abstractness results. The operational equivalences are based on maximal action-sequences and step-sequences – defined for a very simple process language and its extensions with a refinement combinator (change of atomicity). The denotational models are all expressed as abstractions of a standard association of sets of labelled partial orders with processes.

Key words: concurrency, change of atomicity, noninterleaved models, labelled partial orders, semiwords, full abstraction.

CONTENTS

*Internet address: mn@daimi.DK

1 Introduction

In recent years one has studied a variety of behavioural equivalences for process algebras, - e.g. testing-, failure-, acceptance-, bisimulation equivalences for CCS, TCSP a.s.o.

Operationally these equivalences are basically defined in terms of different views on the branching structure of the labelled transition systems associated with expressions. Typically, they will distinguish expressions like

(1) $$a;(b+c) \text{ and } (a;b)+(a;c)$$

because of the obvious difference w.r.t. branching structure.

For a variety of process algebras, one has characterized these equivalences in terms of e.g. fully abstract models. And typically, these models may be viewed as abstractions of the computation trees (also called synchronization trees) associated with expressions.

For a detailed/short introduction to this line of research we refer to [6] and [8] respectively. In both of these, it is pointed out that the equivalences mentioned above do not distinguish between concurrent and purely nondeterministic processes. The corresponding models are all so-called interleaving models. E.g. they will all identify the following expressions:

(2) $$a \parallel b \text{ and } (a;b)+(b;a)$$

In [8] it is suggested to study process algebras similarly, but looking for distinctions w.r.t. the nonsequentiality of processes. In this paper we present some modest results following this suggestion.

It is easy to come up with equivalences distinguishing say (2) – see e.g. [4]. What we are particularly looking for are equivalences with a "natural" operational definition, and a fully abstract denotational model – a combination supporting the "naturalness" of both concepts.

We deliberately choose to study degrees of nonsequentiality as "orthogonal" to the existing study of degrees of branching. So, our equivalences will identify (1), but distinguish (2). We also deliberately choose to present our results for a very simple process language (see however conclusion). We present four full abstractness results. The operational equivalences are based on maximal action-sequences and step-sequences – defined for a very simple process language and its extensions with a refinement combinator (change of atomicity). Our main observation is that the corresponding denotational models may be viewed as abstractions of a standard association of labelled partial orders with expressions. So, sets of labelled partial orders in the study of nonsequentiality take the rôle of computation trees in the study of branching structure.

The outline of this paper will be as follows: Section 2 is about semiwords – a subset of labelled partial orders – which will be the basis for our denotational models. We define a number of operations on semiwords and prepare for denotational characterizations to come.

Each of the sections 3, 4 and 5 are presented along the same lines: We define a simple process language and an operational preorder. Using the appropriate abstraction of the standard association of labelled partial orders (here semiwords) with expressions, we find a fully abstract characterization of the operational preorder.

In sections 3 and 4 we consider our two different operational preorders for a simple process language, mainly clearing the way for the main results of the paper in sections 5 and 6 – characterizations of the same operational preorders for the language extended with a refinement operator.

2 Semiwords

As mentioned in the introduction, the concept of labelled partial orders will be central for the models we are going to present. The basic idea is that labelled partial orders will represent individual behaviours of processes. In particular we will look at semiwords (for clarity and technical tractability – see conclusion). Semiwords may be viewed as pomsets, [9], with no "autoparallelism" – that is pomsets for which any two identically labelled elements are ordered. We shall use the interpretation and graphical representation of pomsets from [12]. That is

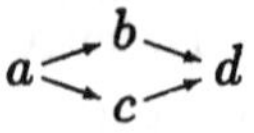

is used to represent a behaviour of a process with four action occurrences, where the d occurrence is causally dependent on the others, the b occurrence is causally dependent on a, but not on c, a.s.o.

Pomsets are usually defined as isomorphism classes of labelled partial orders ([3], [9]). Viewed as pomsets, semiwords have the nice property (see [12]) that they have canonical representations:

DEFINITION 2.1 *Semiword*

Given a finite multiset over Δ – that is a function $m : \Delta \rightarrow \mathbb{N}$ (multiplicity function – $\mathbb{N}$ stands for nonnegative integers). A semiword, s, over m is a tuple, $(A_s, \leq_s)$, where

$$A_s = \{a^i \mid a \in \Delta, 1 \leq i \leq m(a)\}$$
$$\subseteq \Delta \times \mathbb{N} \ (a^i \text{ shorthand notation for } (a, i))$$

$\leq_s$ is a partial order (causality ordering) over A_s satisfying for all $a^i, a^j \in A_s$

$$i \leq j \textit{ iff } a^i \leq_s a^j$$

□

SW denotes the set of semiwords over action alphabet Δ – a countably infinite alphabet (fixed through out the rest of this paper).

We overload notation and use ε and a to denote the empty semiword $(\emptyset, \emptyset)$ and the singleton semiword $(\{a^1\}, \{(a^1, a^1)\})$ respectively. Similarly if A is a finite subset of Δ then A will also denote the set semiword $(\{a^1 \mid a \in A\}, \{(a^1, a^1) \mid a \in A\})$. (Notice that by this notation we have $\emptyset = \varepsilon$ and $\{a\} = a$).

Intuitively a^i can be considered as the i'th occurrence of the action a in a semiword s, in which a occurs $m(a) =$ (notation)$|s|_a$ times. We shall use $x, y, \ldots$ to range over elements of $\Delta \times \mathbb{N}^+$.

x and y are said to be concurrent/causally independent,

$$x \ co_s \ y \textit{ iff } x \not\leq_s y \textit{ and } y \not\leq_s x$$

2.1 Operations on Semiwords

Semiwords have been equipped with a variety of operations ([3], [9]). In this paper we need only a few of these. The following two are both natural generalizations of concatenation of words: sequential and parallel composition.

DEFINITION 2.2 *Sequential Composition of Semiwords*

Given two semiwords, s and t. Their sequential composition, $s \cdot t$, is obtained (informally) by taking their disjoint union (componentwise), and making all elements of t causally dependent on all elements of s. □

Example:
$$a \mathrel{<}^{b}_{a} \cdot c \to d \;=\; a \mathrel{<}^{b}_{a} \mathrel{>} c \to d$$

DEFINITION 2.3 *Parallel Composition of Semiwords*

Given two semiwords, s and t, over disjoint multisets of actions. Their parallel composition, $s \times t$, is simply the union (componentwise) of s and t. □

Example:
$$a \mathrel{<}^{b}_{a} \times c \to d \;=\; \begin{matrix} a \mathrel{<}^{b}_{a} \\ c \to d \end{matrix}$$

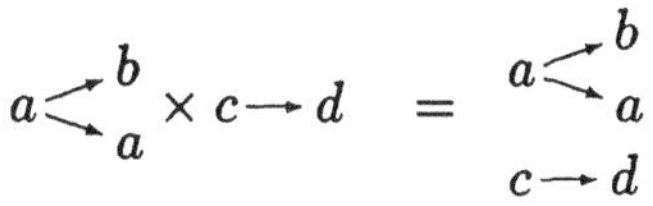

The next operator refines the different elements of a semiword into different semiwords (a formalization of the concept of "change of atomicity").

Example: Consider the semiword $a \mathrel{<}^{b}_{a}$. Suppose we would like to refine the first occurrence of a to $^{b}_{a} \mathrel{>} a$, the second to $c \to a$ and the b occurrence to $^{d}_{e} \mathrel{>} d$. Call this refinement π and the associated operator $<\pi>$ – then we would expect the refined semiword to be:

$$a \mathrel{<}^{b}_{a} <\pi> \;=\; \begin{matrix} b \mathrel{>} \\ a \mathrel{>} \end{matrix} a \mathrel{\to} e \begin{matrix} d \to d \\ c \to a \end{matrix}$$

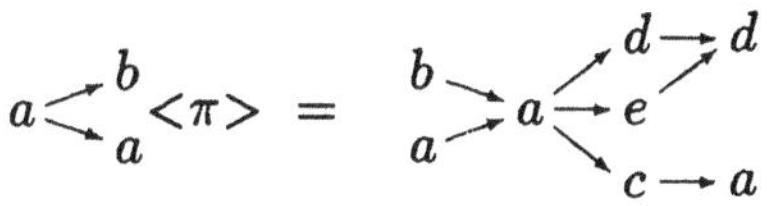

The operator is not as simple as the others, so we will be a bit more precise about its definition.

DEFINITION 2.4 *Particular Refinement*

A *particular refinement* is a mapping $\pi : \Delta \times \mathbb{N}^+ \rightarrow SW$ satisfying (for technical reasons) for all $x, y \in \Delta \times \mathbb{N}^+$,

$$L(x) \neq L(y) \Rightarrow L(\pi(x)) \cap L(\pi(y)) = \emptyset \tag{3}$$

where L is the set of actions from Δ occurring in the considered object, e.g. $L(a^i) = \{a\}$. □

With a particular refinement we associate an operator $<\pi> : SW \rightarrow SW$ as indicated above. The action occurrences of $s<\pi>$ will intuitively be the union of $A_{\pi(x)}$ for all $x \in A_s$. Viewed as a semiword the individual action occurrences will need to have appropriate occurrence numbers. Formally, the occurrence number associated with $b^j \in A_{\pi(a^i)}$ will be defined by:

$$f_\pi(a^i, b^j) := b^k,$$

where $k = (\Sigma_{l=1}^{i-1} |\pi(a^l)|_b) + j$. Notice that in this way an element of $A_{s<\pi>}$ has the unique representation of the form $f_\pi(a^i, b^j)$. In the example above $f_\pi(a^2, a^1) = a^3$.

DEFINITION 2.5 *Particular Refinement Operator*

The operator $<\pi> : SW \rightarrow SW$ associated with a particular refinement ρ is defined by $s<\pi> = (A, \leq)$, where

$$\begin{aligned} A &= \{f_\pi(x, x') \mid x \in A_s, x' \in A_{\pi(x)}\} \\ f_\pi(x, x') \leq f_\pi(y, y') \;\; &\textit{iff} \;\; x \leq_s y \textit{ and} \\ & \qquad x = y \Rightarrow x' \leq_{\pi(x)} y' \end{aligned}$$ □

Notice that (3) ensures $s<\pi>$ to be a semiword.

2.2 A Partial Order on Semiwords

We find it convenient to have the following relation between our representations of behaviours.

DEFINITION 2.6 *$\preceq$-ordering on Semiwords*

A semiword s is said to be smoother than [11]/ subsumed by [3]/less nonsequential than another semiword t,

$$s \preceq t \textit{ iff } (A_s = A_t \textit{ and } \leq_s \supseteq \leq_t)$$ □

Example: $a \rightarrow b \rightarrow c \;\preceq\; a \begin{smallmatrix} \nearrow b \\ \searrow c \end{smallmatrix} \;\preceq\; \begin{smallmatrix} a \rightarrow b \\ c \end{smallmatrix}$

The downwards closure of a semiword s, $\{s' \mid s' \preceq s\}$, is denoted $\delta(s)$. If P is a property of semiwords, $\delta_P(s)$ will be a shorthand for $\{s' \preceq s \mid P(s')\}$. Though we might have $s \notin \delta_P(s)$ for some property P, we call it the δ_P-closure. In the special case where $P(s)$ demands $\leq_s$ to be a total order we write $\delta_{lin}(s)$, because it is also known as the set of *linearizations* of s. The set of semiwords having this property is denoted W (words). Because of the one to one correspondence between Δ^* and W (see [11]) their elements will often be identified in the sequel. Notice that $<\pi>$ is $\preceq$-monotone and so are $\cdot$ and $\times$ in their left and right arguments.

2.3 Sets of Semiwords

Sets of semiwords and operators on them are used extensively in the models we shall present, so we briefly treat them here. The two operations on semiwords $\cdot$ and $\times$ generalize to sets in the natural way e.g. $S \cdot T = \{s \cdot t \mid s \in S, t \in T\}$. $\cup$ denotes the normal set union and $\mathcal{P}(\_)$ the powerset operator.

We shall need an operator which slightly differ from the natural extension of the particular refinement operator.

DEFINITION 2.7 *Refinements*

A $\mathcal{P}(SW)$-*refinement* is a mapping $\rho : \Delta \rightarrow \mathcal{P}(SW)$ satisfying for all $a, b \in \Delta$,

$$a \neq b \Rightarrow L(\rho(a)) \cap L(\rho(b)) = \emptyset$$

where L now is extended to sets by $L(A \cup B) = L(A) \cup L(B)$.

We say that a $\mathcal{P}(SW)$-refinement, ρ, is ε-*free* *iff* $\forall a \in \Delta.\, \varepsilon \notin \rho(a)$.

A particular refinement π is *consistent* with a $\mathcal{P}(SW)$-refinement ρ *iff* $\forall a^i \in \Delta \times I\!N^+.\, \pi(a^i) \in \rho(a)$

The mapping associated with ρ is now defined as $<\rho> : SW \rightarrow \mathcal{P}(SW)$ with $s<\rho> = \{s<\pi> \mid \pi \text{ is consistent with } \rho\}$ and generalized to sets by $S<\rho> = \bigcup_{s \in S} s<\rho>$.

The composition $\rho \circ \rho'$ of two refinements ρ and ρ' is defined by $(\rho \circ \rho')(a) = (\rho'(a))<\rho>$. □

Also for a semiword property P, δ_P generalize to sets: $\delta_P(S) = \ _{s \in S}\, \delta_P(s)$.

These operations enjoy a number of properties, many of them inherited from the corresponding properties of semiwords. Some of them are listed in:

PROPOSITION 2.8

- $\cdot$, $\times$ and $\cup$ are associative
- $\times$ and $\cup$ are commutative
- $a{<}\rho{>} = \rho(a)$ and ${<}\rho{>}$ distributes over $\cdot$, $\times$ and $\cup$

That ${<}\rho{>}$ distributes over $\cdot$ may seem surprising since ${<}\pi{>}$ does not. But if π is consistent with ρ one can also find a π' consistent with ρ such that $s{<}\pi{>}\cdot t{<}\pi'{>} = (s \cdot t){<}\pi{>}$ (let $\pi'(a^i) = \pi(a^{|s|_a + i})$).

The partial order $\subseteq$ on sets will be central to our models. $\cup$ and natural extensions to sets are $\subseteq$-monotone, so we get:

PROPOSITION 2.9 The operators $\cdot$, $\cup$, $\times$, ${<}\rho{>}$ and δ_P are $\subseteq$-monotone in all their arguments.

3 A Simple Process Language and some Semantic Considerations

As process expressions we shall use a very basic language, BL, over the abstract set of action symbols, Δ, containing combinators for sequencing, nondeterminism and parallelism (without communication).

BL consists of expressions of the form:

E	$::=$	a	individual action $a \in \Delta$
		$E_1;E_2$	sequential composition of E_1 and E_2
		$E_1 + E_2$	nondeterministic composition of E_1 and E_2
		$E_1 \parallel E_2$	parallel composition of E_1 and E_2.

In all models to come these binary operators are associative, a fact we shall make use of in examples together with the operator precedence:

$$+ \;<\; \parallel \;<\; ;$$

Remark
For mainly technical reasons we shall restrict ourselves to processes without what is called "autoparallelism" in [4] (see however the results in the conclusion). That is, we do not consider processes with the possibility of concurrent occurrences of the same action (symbol), as e.g. in the expression $a \parallel a$. Formally, we require for all subexpressions of the form $E_1 \| E_2$ that $L(E_1)$ and $L(E_2)$ are disjoint sets, where we overload notation by letting $L(E)$ denote the set of action symbols occurring in E. Notice, that formally all full abstraction results claimed in the following should be modified relative to this restriction. I.e. relations (precongruences) should only be considered in well defined "$\|$-contexts".

3.1 Operational Set-up

It is standard to define the operational behaviour of BL expressions in terms of a labelled transition system capturing its sequentialized/ interleaved behaviour. At the bottom of our operational preorders will be the notion of maximal/ terminating action-sequences associated with an expression in such a transition system. Importantly, this notion may also be seen as the bottom of most of the branching preorders studied in the literature (the most abstract among these, see e.g. [6]).

The action-sequence an expression can perform is built up from atomic action-relations $\xrightarrow{a}$ (one for each $a \in \Delta$) holding between configurations, with each BL-expression being a possible start configuration. Configurations are expressions from CL, which is like BL with Δ extended with $\dagger$ (a symbol distinct from those of Δ), but where subexpressions of the form $E_1 \parallel E_2$ do not have to be disjoint w.r.t. $\dagger$, i.e. $L(E_1) \cap L(E_2) \subseteq \{\dagger\}$. Intuitively $\dagger$ represents the extinct action. Notice that BL is contained in CL.

Two configurations E_1 and E_2 in the atomic action relation $\xrightarrow{a}$ is written $E_1 \xrightarrow{a} E_2$ to indicate that E_1 evolves to E_2 performing a. The relations $\xrightarrow{a} \subseteq CL \times CL$ are defined to be the least ones which can be inferred from the following labelled transition system:

$$a \xrightarrow{a} \dagger$$

$$\frac{E_1 \xrightarrow{a} E_1'}{E_1;E_2 \xrightarrow{a} E_1';E_2} \qquad \frac{E_1 \sim \dagger, E_2 \xrightarrow{a} E_2'}{E_1;E_2 \xrightarrow{a} E_2'}$$

$$\frac{E_1 \xrightarrow{a} E_1'}{\begin{array}{c} E_1 + E_2 \xrightarrow{a} E_1' \\ E_2 + E_1 \xrightarrow{a} E_1' \end{array}} \qquad \frac{E_1 \xrightarrow{a} E_1'}{\begin{array}{c} E_1 \parallel E_2 \xrightarrow{a} E_1' \parallel E_2 \\ E_2 \parallel E_1 \xrightarrow{a} E_2 \parallel E_1' \end{array}}$$

where $\sim$ is the least symmetric congruence satisfying

$$E = \dagger;E, \qquad E = \dagger + E, \qquad E = \dagger \parallel E$$

Example: $a;b + a;a \parallel b \xrightarrow{a} \dagger;a \parallel b \xrightarrow{b} \dagger;a \parallel \dagger \xrightarrow{a} \dagger \parallel \dagger \sim \dagger$.

The terminating action-sequences of $E \in BL$ may now be defined as follows:

$$E \xrightarrow{w} \text{ for } w \in \Delta^+, w = a_1a_2\ldots a_n$$

$$\Updownarrow$$

$$\exists E_1, \ldots, E_n \in CL.\, E \xrightarrow{a_1} E_1 \xrightarrow{a_2} \ldots \xrightarrow{a_n} E_n \sim \dagger$$

And our basic operational preorder is:

Definition 3.1 $\lesssim_{\mathsf{w}} \subseteq BL \times BL$

$$E_1 \lesssim_{\mathsf{w}} E_2$$

iff

$$\forall w \in \Delta^+.\, (E_1 \xrightarrow{w}) \Rightarrow (E_2 \xrightarrow{w})$$

□

Notice that as expected the equivalence of $\lesssim_{\mathsf{w}}$, $\approx_{\mathsf{w}}$, identifies $a;(b+c)$ and $a;b+a;c$.

3.2 Denotational Set-up

It is well-known that our operational preorder $\lesssim_{\mathsf{w}}$ may be characterized by a model based on sets of sequences of actions from Δ, (subsets of Δ^+) and using the shuffle operator when dealing with $\parallel$.

In order to clear the way for the more interesting models in the following sections we devise a corresponding model in the semiword framework.

Let us start out by presenting the natural association of sets of semiwords with BL-expressions through a mapping $\mathcal{S}$ which will be the basis of our denotational definitions in the following. $\mathcal{S} : BL \to \mathcal{P}(SW)$ is given compositionally by:

$$\begin{aligned}
\mathcal{S}(a) &= \{a\} \\
\mathcal{S}(E_1;E_2) &= \mathcal{S}(E_1) \cdot \mathcal{S}(E_2) \\
\mathcal{S}(E_1 + E_2) &= \mathcal{S}(E_1) \cup \mathcal{S}(E_2) \\
\mathcal{S}(E_1 \parallel E_2) &= \mathcal{S}(E_1) \times \mathcal{S}(E_2)
\end{aligned}$$

Example: $$\mathcal{S}((a+b);(a \parallel c)) = \left\{ a \substack{\nearrow a \\ \searrow c}, b \substack{\nearrow a \\ \searrow c} \right\}$$

Intuitively a maximal sequence of a +-free expression must respect the causal ordering imposed by the expression, and so intuitively also must be a linearization of the associated semiword. We therefore arrive at the denotation:

DEFINITION 3.2 $[\![\_]\!]_w : BL \rightarrow \mathcal{P}(W)$ $(\subseteq \mathcal{P}(SW))$ with $[\![E]\!]_w = \delta_{lin}(\mathcal{S}(E))$. □

So, our model is sets of P_{lin}-semiwords ($\mathcal{P}(W)$) partially ordered by inclusion.

$[\![\_]\!]_w$ together with the partial order $\subseteq$ induces a denotational preorder $\trianglelefteq_w$ by:

$$E_1 \trianglelefteq_w E_2 \textit{ iff } [\![E_1]\!]_w \subseteq [\![E_2]\!]_w$$

Having models using sets of sequences from Δ^+ in mind it is not hard to come up with:

THEOREM 3.3 $[\![\_]\!]_w$ can be defined compositionally by:

$$\begin{aligned}
[\![a]\!]_w &= \{a\} \\
[\![E_1;E_2]\!]_w &= [\![E_1]\!]_w \cdot [\![E_2]\!]_w \\
[\![E_1 + E_2]\!]_w &= [\![E_1]\!]_w \cup [\![E_2]\!]_w \\
[\![E_1 \parallel E_2]\!]_w &= \delta_{lin}([\![E_1]\!]_w \times [\![E_2]\!]_w)
\end{aligned}$$

Proof By structural induction.

a: Evident by inspecting the definitions.

$E_1;E_2$, $E_1 + E_2$: Follows from the compositional nature of $\mathcal{S}$ and the fact that δ_{lin} distributes over semiword sequential composition and $\cup$.

$E_1 \parallel E_2$: Similar, but instead of the distributivity of δ_{lin} using: $\delta_{lin}(s \times t) = \delta_{lin}(\delta_{lin}(s) \times \delta_{lin}(t))$ which generalizes to sets. □

3.3 Full Abstractness

The property of $\trianglelefteq_w$ being a preorder is inherited in all contexts:

PROPOSITION 3.4 $\trianglelefteq_w$ is a precongruence.

Proof From theorem 3.3 we know a compositional definition of $[\![\_]\!]_w$ using $\subseteq$-monotone operators (proposition 2.9), and hence $\trianglelefteq_w$ is a precongruence. □

THEOREM 3.5 $[\![\_]\!]_w$ is fully abstract w.r.t. $\lesssim_w$, because

a) $\lesssim_w$ is a precongruence w.r.t. BL

b) $E_1 \lesssim_w E_2$ *iff* $E_1 \trianglelefteq_w E_2$

Proof a) follows from proposition 3.4 and b). We get b) from:

$$\begin{aligned} E_1 \trianglelefteq_w E_2 &\Leftrightarrow [\![E_1]\!]_w \subseteq [\![E_2]\!]_w && \text{,by definition} \\ &\Leftrightarrow \{w \mid E_1 \xrightarrow{w}\} \subseteq \{w \mid E_2 \xrightarrow{w}\} && \text{,by the lemma 3.6 below} \\ &\Leftrightarrow (E_1 \xrightarrow{w}) \Rightarrow (E_2 \xrightarrow{w}) \\ &\Leftrightarrow E_1 \lesssim_w E_2 && \text{,by definition} \end{aligned}$$

□

This is, of course, not a major result on its own, but in the more interesting full abstractness results to come we shall follow the same pattern in proofs as here.

LEMMA 3.6 For $E \in BL$ we have: $[\![E]\!]_w = \{w \mid E \xrightarrow{w}\}$.

Proof The proof follows easily by induction in the structure of E using the compositional definition of $[\![\_]\!]_w$ and in the case of $E = E_1 \parallel E_2$:

$$(4) \qquad \begin{array}{c} \exists w_1, w_2.\, w \in \delta_{lin}(w_1 \times w_2), E_1 \xrightarrow{w_1}, E_2 \xrightarrow{w_2} \\ \textit{iff} \\ E_1 \parallel E_2 \xrightarrow{w} \end{array}$$

where $E \xrightarrow{\varepsilon}$ here should be read as $E \sim \dagger$. The if part of (4) is proven by induction in the length of w, $|w|$, and the only if part in $|w_1| \cdot |w_2|$. □

4 Step Semantics

4.1 Operational Set-up

In the theory of Petri Nets, [10], one often expresses the nonsequential behaviour of processes in terms of sequences of steps – a step being a set of concurrent actions. For BL an operational step semantics may be formalized by changing the labelled transition system from section 3 into a system where transitions are labelled by sets of actions.

The rules are changed in the obvious way, e.g.

$$a \xrightarrow{\{a\}} \dagger$$

and the following rule is added

$$\frac{E_1 \xrightarrow{U} E_1', E_2 \xrightarrow{V} E_2'}{E_1 \parallel E_2 \xrightarrow{U \cup V} E_1' \parallel E_2'}$$

Example: $a;b \parallel c;d \xrightarrow{\{a,c\}} \dagger;b \parallel \dagger;d \xrightarrow{\{d\}} \dagger;b \parallel \dagger \xrightarrow{\{b\}} \dagger \parallel \dagger \sim \dagger$

With the obvious extension of the notion of maximal sequences, we obtain the following generalized operational step-preorder $\lessapprox_s$:

DEFINITION 4.1 $\lessapprox_s \subseteq BL \times BL$

$$E_1 \lessapprox_s E_2$$

iff

$$\forall w \in (\mathcal{P}(\Delta))^+ . \, (E_1 \xrightarrow{w}) \Rightarrow (E_2 \xrightarrow{w})$$

□

4.2 Denotational Set-up

It is fairly easy to see that $\lessapprox_s$ is included in $\lessapprox_w$ (otherwise it will be proved formally in the following). So, looking for a model for $\lessapprox_s$, we follow the pattern from the previous section and look for a denotation for E of the form $\delta_P(\mathcal{S}(E))$ for some suitable semiword property P (weaker than lin). It seems natural here to look for a property reflecting the nature of step-sequences in terms of semiwords, i.e. semiwords of the form $A_1 \cdot A_2 \cdot \ldots \cdot A_n$. Semiwords of this form are not necessarily linearized, but "layered" in the sense that it may be viewed as "a linear order on top of a set of completely unordered semiwords (the individual A_i's)". One way to formalize this property is the following:

DEFINITION 4.2 *P_{and}-Property for Semiwords*

A semiword s is said to have the P_{and}-property, $P_{and}(s)$, *iff* for all x, x', y, y' in A_s we have:

	$x <_s x'$		$x <_s y'$
if	co_s	then	*and*
	$y <_s y'$		$y <_s x'$

□

Example: 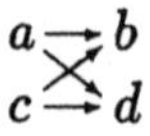 has the P_{and}-property, 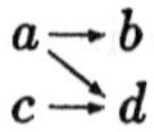 has not.

The denotation $[\![\_]\!]_s$ in the model can now be formalized.

DEFINITION 4.3 $[\![\_]\!]_s : BL \to \mathcal{P}(SW)$ is defined by $[\![E]\!]_s = \delta_{and}(\mathcal{S}(E))$ □

So, our model is here sets of P_{and}-semiwords partial ordered by inclusion.

The denotational preorder induced by $[\![\_]\!]_s$ and $\subseteq$ is denoted $\trianglelefteq_s$.

THEOREM 4.4 $[\![\_]\!]_s$ admits a simple compositional definition:

$$
\begin{aligned}
[\![a]\!]_s &= \{a\} \\
[\![E_1;E_2]\!]_s &= [\![E_1]\!]_s \cdot [\![E_2]\!]_s \\
[\![E_1 + E_2]\!]_s &= [\![E_1]\!]_s \cup [\![E_2]\!]_s \\
[\![E_1 \parallel E_2]\!]_s &= \delta_{and}([\![E_1]\!]_s \times [\![E_2]\!]_s)
\end{aligned}
$$

Proof Similar to that of theorem 3.3. □

4.3 Full Abstractness

PROPOSITION 4.5 $\trianglelefteq_s$ is a precongruence.

Proof As proposition 3.4. □

THEOREM 4.6 $[\![\_]\!]_s$ is fully abstract w.r.t. $\underset{\approx}{\sqsubset}_s$, because

a) $\underset{\approx}{\sqsubset}_s$ is a precongruence w.r.t. BL

b) $E_1 \underset{\approx}{\sqsubset}_s E_2$ *iff* $E_1 \trianglelefteq_s E_2$

Proof a) is a consequence of proposition 4.5 and b). b) is seen by first noticing

(5) $(s \neq \varepsilon \textit{ and } P_{and}(s))$ *iff* $\exists n \geq 1, A_1, \ldots, A_n \in (\mathcal{P}(\Delta) \setminus \emptyset).\ A_1 \cdot \ldots \cdot A_n = s$

and deducing

$$\begin{aligned}
& [\![E_1]\!]_s \subseteq [\![E_2]\!]_s \\
\Leftrightarrow\ & \delta_{and}(\mathcal{S}(E_1)) \subseteq \delta_{and}(\mathcal{S}(E_2)) && \text{,by definition} \\
\Leftrightarrow\ & P_{and}(t), t \preceq s_1 \in \mathcal{S}(E_1) \\
& \quad \Rightarrow t \preceq s_2 \in \mathcal{S}(E_2) \\
\Leftrightarrow\ & A_1 \cdot \ldots \cdot A_n \preceq s_1 \in \mathcal{S}(E_1) \\
& \quad \Rightarrow A_1 \cdot \ldots \cdot A_n \preceq s_2 \in \mathcal{S}(E_2) && \text{,by (5)} \\
\Leftrightarrow\ & E_1 \xrightarrow{A_1} \ldots \xrightarrow{A_n} E_1' \sim \dagger \\
& \quad \Rightarrow E_2 \xrightarrow{A_1} \ldots \xrightarrow{A_n} E_2' \sim \dagger && \text{,by lemma 4.7 below} \\
\Leftrightarrow\ & E_1 \sqsubseteq_s E_2 && \text{,by definition}
\end{aligned}$$

□

That $[\![\_]\!]_w$ is as abstract as $[\![\_]\!]_s$ can be seen from the definitions of $[\![\_]\!]_w$ and $[\![\_]\!]_s$, and the fact $P_{lin} \Rightarrow P_{and}$, – and it follows from the expressions in (2) that it is strictly more abstract (identified by $[\![\_]\!]_w$, but not by $[\![\_]\!]_s$).

For simplicity of the proof of the following lemma we shall temporarily adopt the notation $E \xrightarrow{\emptyset} E'$ to mean $E = E'$. For the same reason the lemma is formulated slightly stronger than needed in the proof of the theorem.

LEMMA 4.7 Suppose $A_1, \ldots, A_n$, $n \geq 1$ are subsets of Δ and $E \in BL$. Then $E \xrightarrow{A_1} \ldots \xrightarrow{A_n} E' \sim \dagger$ *iff* $\exists s \in \mathcal{S}(E).\, A_1 \cdot \ldots \cdot A_n \preceq s$.

Proof

If: By induction in the structure of E.

$E = a$: $\mathcal{S}(a) = \{a\}$ and we must have exactly one $A_i = \{a\}$, the rest of them equal to $\emptyset$, and hence the result follows from $a \xrightarrow{\{a\}} \dagger$.

$E = E_1;E_2$: $\mathcal{S}(E) = \mathcal{S}(E_1) \cdot \mathcal{S}(E_2)$ and $s = s_1 \cdot s_2$ for $s_i \in \mathcal{S}(E_i)$. Clearly $n \geq 2$ and it can be shown that $A_1 \cdot \ldots \cdot A_n \preceq s_1 \cdot s_2$ implies $A_1 \cdot \ldots \cdot A_j \preceq s_1$, $A_{j+1} \cdot \ldots \cdot A_n \preceq s_2$ for some $1 \leq j < n$. By hypothesis of induction then $E_1 \xrightarrow{A_1} \ldots \xrightarrow{A_j} E_1' \sim \dagger$ and $E_2 \xrightarrow{A_{j+1}} E_2'' \xrightarrow{A_{j+2}} \ldots \xrightarrow{A_n} E_2' \sim \dagger$. The rules for ; then give $E_1;E_2 \xrightarrow{A_1} \ldots \xrightarrow{A_j} E_1';E_2 \xrightarrow{A_{j+1}} E_2'' \xrightarrow{A_{j+2}} \ldots \xrightarrow{A_n} E_2' \sim \dagger$ as desired.

$E = E_1 + E_2$: $s \in \mathcal{S}(E_1) \cup \mathcal{S}(E_2)$ implies $s \in \mathcal{S}(E_1)$ or $s \in \mathcal{S}(E_2)$. Suppose w.l.o.g. $s \in \mathcal{S}(E_1)$. By hypothesis of induction $E_1 \xrightarrow{A_1} E_1'' \xrightarrow{A_2} \ldots \xrightarrow{A_n} E_1' \sim \dagger$. The + rules then yields $E_1 + E_2 \xrightarrow{A_1} E_1'' \xrightarrow{A_2} \ldots \xrightarrow{A_n} E_1' \sim \dagger$.

$E = E_1 \parallel E_2$: $s \in \mathcal{S}(E_1) \times \mathcal{S}(E_2)$ implies $s = s_1 \times s_2$ for some $s_i \in \mathcal{S}(E_i)$.

Since A_{s_1} and A_{s_2} are disjoint we can filter out from each A_i those elements belonging to A_{s_1}, B_i, and those belonging to A_{s_2}, C_i obtaining $B_1 \cdot \ldots \cdot B_n \preceq s_1$ and $C_1 \cdot \ldots \cdot C_n \preceq s_2$.

By hypothesis of induction then $E_1 \xrightarrow{B_1} \ldots \xrightarrow{B_n} E_1' \sim \dagger$ and $E_2 \xrightarrow{C_1} \ldots \xrightarrow{C_n} E_2' \sim \dagger$. It is then proven by induction in n that $E_1 \parallel E_2 \xrightarrow{A_1} \ldots \xrightarrow{A_n} E_1' \parallel E_2'$ and we have $E_1' \parallel E_2' \sim \dagger \parallel E_2' \sim E_2' \sim \dagger$.

Only if: Also by induction in the structure of E, but using $\preceq$-monotonicity of $\cdot$ in the case of ;, and in the case of $\parallel$ the $\preceq$-monotonicity of $\times$ together with the general fact

$$(s \times t) \cdot (s' \times t') \preceq (s \cdot s') \times (t \cdot t')$$

(to prove $A_1 \cdot \ldots \cdot A_n \preceq (B_1 \cdot \ldots \cdot B_n) \times (C_1 \cdot \ldots \cdot C_n)$). □

5 Change of Atomicity

5.1 Operational Set-up

It is well-known ([1], [4], [5]) that a distinction between concurrency and interleaving may be captured by adding a combinator to the process language, changing the atomicity of actions. We return to the labelled transition system from section 3 and investigate the consequences of adding a combinator allowing an expansion of an individual action into a process.

Formally, let a *BL-refinement* be a mapping $\rho : \Delta \to BL$ satisfying

$$a \neq b \Rightarrow L(\rho(a)) \cap L(\rho(b)) = \emptyset$$

For each BL-refinement ρ we introduce an combinator, $[\rho]$, into our language, with the operational meaning that $E[\rho]$ behaves operationally just like E with all a-occurrences substituted by $\rho(a)$. We denote this extended language by RBL. The substitution is "performed" by a compositionally defined mapping $\sigma : RBL \to BL$, using $\{\rho\}$ which (also compositionally) performs a single substitution in a refinement free expression. Because of their syntactic nature we write them postfix. The definitions of σ and $\{\rho\}$ are in full:

$$\begin{array}{rlrl} a\sigma &= a & a\{\rho\} &= \rho(a) \\ (E_1;E_2)\sigma &= E_1\sigma;E_2\sigma & (E_1;E_2)\{\rho\} &= E_1\{\rho\};E_2\{\rho\} \\ (E_1+E_2)\sigma &= E_1\sigma + E_2\sigma & (E_1+E_2)\{\rho\} &= E_1\{\rho\} + E_2\{\rho\} \\ (E_1 \parallel E_2)\sigma &= E_1\sigma \parallel E_2\sigma & (E_1 \parallel E_2)\{\rho\} &= E_1\{\rho\} \parallel E_2\{\rho\} \\ E[\rho]\sigma &= (E\sigma)\{\rho\} & & \end{array}$$

The composition $\rho \circ \rho'$ of two BL-refinements ρ and ρ' is defined using $\{\rho\}$ by: $(\rho \circ \rho')(a) = \rho'(a)\{\rho\}$.

Example: Let $\rho(a) = a;a$, $\rho(b) = b$, and $E_1 = a \parallel b$, $E_2 = a;b + b;a$. Then

$$E_1[\rho]\sigma = a;a \parallel b \text{ and } E_2[\rho]\sigma = a;a;b + b;a;a$$

With σ in hand we can define for $E \in RBL$, $w \in \Delta^+$

$$E \xrightarrow{w} \text{ if } E\sigma \xrightarrow{w}$$

One might claim that the meaning of a expression from RBL is not given strictly operationally in this way using σ. But intuitively it is clear that a possible transition system defined fully for RBL should behave exactly as if this substitution were done in advance. Mainly for reasons of clearity and space, we have taken this short cut. The doubting reader is referred to [7] where a similar language is considered.

Now the operational preorder $\lesssim_{\mathsf{w}}$ is not a precongruence for RBL! Let ρ, E_1 and E_2 be as in the example above. Then clearly $E_1 \lesssim_{\mathsf{w}} E_2$, but $E_1[\rho] \xrightarrow{aba}$ and $E_2[\rho] \not\xrightarrow{aba}$.

Our question is here: What is the precongruence associated with $\lesssim_{\mathsf{w}}$ for RBL, $\lesssim_{\mathsf{w}}^c$ (the largest precongruence contained in $\lesssim_{\mathsf{w}}$)? We will pursue this question in the following section through different considerations, gradually arriving at a model fully abstract with respect to $\lesssim_{\mathsf{w}}^c$.

5.2 Denotational Set-up

Similarly as the operational behaviour of a expression was extended to RBL, $[\![\_]\!]_{\mathsf{w}}$ is extended to RBL by letting

$$[\![E]\!]_{\mathsf{w}} = [\![E\sigma]\!]_{\mathsf{w}} \text{ for } E \in RBL$$

The induced denotational preorder $\trianglelefteq_{\mathsf{w}}$ then also extends to RBL and it follows from definitions and section 3 that $\lesssim_{\mathsf{w}} = \trianglelefteq_{\mathsf{w}}$ on RBL.

In the case of $\lesssim_{\mathsf{w}}^c$ it is much harder (than in the previous sections) to see intuitively that $\lesssim_{\mathsf{w}}^c$ should have a semiword based model at all – and if so what it should look like. But following the pattern from the previous sections we shall be looking for a model in which the denotation of E is expressible as $\delta_P(\mathcal{S}(E))$ for a suitable semiword property P, – but which?

Playing with examples, one soon realizes that a refinement context is quite a powerful tool in distinguishing expressions, because much of the information represented in $\mathcal{S}(E)$ may be reflected by suitable refinement contexts $\_[\rho]$, in the sense of "overlapping" occurrences of ρ-images of concurrent elements in $s \in \mathcal{S}(E)$ (as indicated above in the example of $\underset{\sim}{\sqsubset}{}_{w}$ not being a precongruence for RBL). One might be led to the conjecture that $\delta(\mathcal{S}(E))$ ordered under inclusion could be a model for $\underset{\sim}{\sqsubset}{}^{c}_{w}$. However, this is *not* the case, as can be seen by looking at:

$$E_1 = a;d \parallel b \parallel c + c;b \parallel a \parallel d \quad \text{and} \quad E_2 = a;b \parallel c;d$$

Then $E_1 \underset{\sim}{\sqsubset}{}^{c}_{w} E_1 + E_2$ and $E_1 + E_2 \underset{\sim}{\sqsubset}{}^{c}_{w} E_1$, but:

$$s = \begin{array}{c} a \rightarrow b \\ c \rightarrow d \end{array} \in \delta(\mathcal{S}(E_1 + E_2)), \qquad \begin{array}{c} a \rightarrow b \\ c \rightarrow d \end{array} \notin \delta(\mathcal{S}(E_1))$$

We don't intend to prove operational that $E_1 \underset{\sim}{\sqsubset}{}^{c}_{w} E_1+E_2$ and $E_1+E_2 \underset{\sim}{\sqsubset}{}^{c}_{w} E_1$ (it will follow easily from the denotational characterization to be developed), but invite the reader to find convincing arguments for this fact.

So, presumable s should not belong to the denotation of E in a model for $\underset{\sim}{\sqsubset}{}^{c}_{w}$. Intuitively, an argument could be that no single linearization of a refinement version $s{<}\rho{>}$ can reflect the full structure of s, in the sense that if the images of a and d overlap in such a linearization (reflecting a and d being concurrent) then the image of c must precede that of b, and vice versa. Following this intuition one may look for a property expressing when the full structure of a semiword may be reflected in a single linearization of a refined version of it (in the "overlapping" sense).

Based on our example, we suggest the following formalization of this property – expressed as a slight modification of the P_{and}-property.

DEFINITION 5.1 *P_{or}-Property for Semiwords*

A semiword s is said to have the P_{or}-property, $P_{or}(s)$, *iff* for all x, x', y, y' in A_s we have:

$$\text{if} \quad \begin{array}{l} x <_s x' \\ co_s \\ y <_s y' \end{array} \quad \text{then} \quad \begin{array}{l} x <_s y' \\ or \\ y <_s x' \end{array}$$

□

Example: $\begin{array}{c} a \rightarrow b \\ \searrow \\ c \rightarrow d \end{array}$ has the P_{or}-property, $\begin{array}{c} a \rightarrow b \\ c \rightarrow d \end{array}$ has not.

P_{or} has an alternative characterization (used extensively in the following), the proof of which is trivial:

PROPOSITION 5.2 A semiword s has the P_{or}-property *iff* for all x, x', y, y' in A_s:

$$\text{if} \quad \begin{matrix} x <_s x' \\ co_s \\ y <_s y' \end{matrix} \quad \text{then} \quad \begin{matrix} \forall z.\,(y <_s z) \Rightarrow (x <_s z) \\ or \\ \forall z.\,(x <_s z) \Rightarrow (y <_s z) \end{matrix}$$

After these manoeuvres we now give the denotation of a expression $E \in RBL$, $[\![E]\!]_r$, in the model we informally arrived at, that is, sets of P_{or}-semiwords partial ordered under inclusion.

DEFINITION 5.3 $[\![\_]\!]_r : RBL \rightarrow \mathcal{P}(SW)$ is defined by $[\![E]\!]_r = \delta_{or}(\mathcal{S}(E\sigma))$. □

As usual the induced denotational preorder is denoted $\trianglelefteq_r$.

For each BL-refinement ρ we associate the corresponding $\mathcal{P}(SW)$-refinement $\mathcal{S}(\rho)$, by letting $(\mathcal{S}(\rho))(a) = \mathcal{S}(\rho(a))$. Notice that $\mathcal{S}(\rho)$ is ε-free.

THEOREM 5.4 $[\![\_]\!]_r$ has the following compositional definition:

$$\begin{array}{ll} [\![a]\!]_r & = \{a\} \\ [\![E_1;E_2]\!]_r & = [\![E_1]\!]_r \cdot [\![E_2]\!]_r \\ [\![E_1 + E_2]\!]_r & = [\![E_1]\!]_r \cup [\![E_2]\!]_r \\ [\![E_1 \parallel E_2]\!]_r & = \delta_{or}([\![E_1]\!]_r \times [\![E_2]\!]_r) \\ [\![E[\rho]]\!]_r & = \delta_{or}([\![E]\!]_r{<}\mathcal{S}(\rho){>}) \end{array}$$

Proof Similar to that of theorem 3.3, but also using the compositional nature of σ. The case $E[\rho]$ is more difficult, so we use some lemma's proved in the sequel.

$$\begin{array}{lll} [\![E[\rho]]\!]_r & = \delta_{or}(\mathcal{S}(E[\rho]\sigma)) & \text{,by definition} \\ & = \delta_{or}((\mathcal{S}(E\sigma)){<}\mathcal{S}(\rho){>}) & \text{,by lemma 5.6} \\ & = \delta_{or}((\delta_{or}(\mathcal{S}(E\sigma))){<}\mathcal{S}(\rho){>}) & \text{,by lemma 5.5} \\ & = \delta_{or}([\![E]\!]_r{<}\mathcal{S}(\rho){>}) & \text{,by definition} \end{array}$$

□

LEMMA 5.5 Let S be a set of semiwords and ρ an ε-free $\mathcal{P}(SW)$-refinement. Then

$$\delta_{or}((\delta_{or}(S)){<}\rho{>}) = \delta_{or}(S{<}\rho{>})$$

Proof We prove this for a single semiword s and a particular refinement π from which the equation follows in general.

$\delta_{or}((\delta_{or}(s)){<}\pi{>}) \subseteq \delta_{or}(s{<}\pi{>})$ follows directly from ${<}\pi{>}$ being $\preceq$-monotone.

Now for $\delta_{or}((\delta_{or}(s))<\pi>) \supseteq \delta_{or}(s<\pi>)$, let $t \in \delta_{or}(s<\pi>)$ be given, i.e. $P_{or}(t)$ and $t \preceq s<\pi>$. We will find an $s' \in \delta_{or}(s)$ such that $t \preceq s'<\pi>$.

Define $s' := (A_s, \leq_{s'})$, where $\leq_{s'}$ is the reflexive closure of $<_{s'} \subseteq {A_s}^2$ defined by:

$$x <_{s'} y \quad (6) \quad \textit{iff} \quad \forall f_\pi(x, x'), f_\pi(y, y') \in A_t.\ f_\pi(x, x') <_t f_\pi(y, y')$$

That is, we order elements x, y in s' if and only if all elements from $\pi(y)$ are causally dependent on all elements $\pi(x)$ in t.

To see that s' in fact is a semiword notice that $\leq_{s'}$ by definition is reflexive, clearly also transitive and also antisymmetric from (6) and the antisymmetry of $\leq_t$. The property that equally labelled elements of s' are properly ordered follows from the same property of s, the way $<\pi>$ is defined and (6).

It is immediate from $t \preceq s<\pi>$ that $s' \preceq s$, so all we need to prove is that s' has the P_{or}-property.

Assume that s' does not have the P_{or}-property. That is $A_{s'}$ contain elements x_1, x_2, y_1, y_2 such that:

$$(7) \quad x_1 <_{s'} y_1 \ \ co_{s'} \ \ x_2 <_{s'} y_2 \qquad\qquad (8) \quad x_1 \not<_{s'} y_2 \ \ \textit{and} \ \ x_2 \not<_{s'} y_1$$

From the definition of s', the ε-freeness of ρ and (8) it then follows that there exists x_1', x_2', y_1', y_2' such that

$$(9) \quad f_\pi(x_1, x_1') \not<_t f_\pi(y_2, y_2') \ \ \textit{and} \ \ f_\pi(x_2, x_2') \not<_t f_\pi(y_1, y_1')$$

From (7) it follows that

$$(10) \quad f_\pi(x_1, x_1') <_t f_\pi(y_1, y_1') \qquad f_\pi(x_2, x_2') <_t f_\pi(y_2, y_2')$$

But from (9) and (10) it follows that:

$$f_\pi(x_1, x_1') \ co_t \ f_\pi(x_2, x_2')$$

and we have a contradiction to the fact that t has the P_{or}-property. □

LEMMA 5.6 $\mathcal{S}(E[\rho]\sigma) = (\mathcal{S}(E\sigma))\langle\mathcal{S}(\rho)\rangle$.

Proof By induction in the structure of E using:

- the compositional definitions of σ, $\{\}$ and $\mathcal{S}$
- the distributive nature of $\langle\rho\rangle$ (over $\cdot$, $\times$, $\cup$)

and in the case of $E = E'[\rho]$ that $\_\{\rho \circ \rho'\} = (\_\{\rho'\})\{\rho\}$ and $\_\langle\mathcal{S}(\rho \circ \rho')\rangle = \_\langle\mathcal{S}(\rho) \circ \mathcal{S}(\rho')\rangle = (\_\langle\mathcal{S}(\rho')\rangle)\langle\mathcal{S}(\rho)\rangle$. □

5.3 Full Abstractness

The connection between $[\![\_]\!]_r$ and $[\![\_]\!]_w$ is indicated by:

PROPOSITION 5.7 $[\![E]\!]_w = \delta_{lin}([\![E]\!]_r)$ for $E \in RBL$.

Proof
$$\begin{aligned}[\![E]\!]_w &= \delta_{lin}(\mathcal{S}(E\sigma)) && \text{,by definition} \\ &= \delta_{lin}(\delta_{or}(\mathcal{S}(E\sigma))) && \text{,since } \delta_{lin} \circ \delta_{or} = \delta_{lin} \\ &= \delta_{lin}([\![E]\!]_r) && \text{,by definition}\end{aligned}$$
□

Furthermore:

PROPOSITION 5.8 $\trianglelefteq_r$ is a precongruence.

Proof Similar to proposition 3.4, but with the additional case of $\langle\rho\rangle$, which also is $\subseteq$-monotone (proposition 2.9). □

And in fact:

THEOREM 5.9 The denotation $[\![\_]\!]_r$ is fully abstract w.r.t. $\sqsubseteq^c_w$.

Proof We show that $\trianglelefteq_r$ is the largest precongruence contained in $\sqsubseteq_w$ or equivalently the largest precongruence contained in $\trianglelefteq_w$.

By proposition 5.8 $\trianglelefteq_r$ is a precongruence and the containment is seen as follows:
$$\begin{aligned}E_1 \trianglelefteq_r E_2 &\Rightarrow [\![E_1]\!]_r \subseteq [\![E_2]\!]_r && \text{,by definition} \\ &\Rightarrow \delta_{lin}([\![E_1]\!]_r) \subseteq \delta_{lin}([\![E_2]\!]_r) && \text{,}\delta_{lin} \text{ is } \subseteq\text{-monotone} \\ &\Rightarrow [\![E_1]\!]_w \subseteq [\![E_2]\!]_w && \text{,by proposition 5.7} \\ &\Rightarrow E_1 \trianglelefteq_w E_2 && \text{,by definition}\end{aligned}$$

To show that $\trianglelefteq_r$ is the largest precongruence contained in $\trianglelefteq_w$ is harder, so we have deferred the crux of the matter to lemma 5.10 below, from which we see $E_1 \not\trianglelefteq_r E_2$ implies that there exists a BL-refinement ρ such that $E_1[\rho] \not\trianglelefteq_w E_2[\rho]$, and the result follows. □

It follows from $P_{and} \Rightarrow P_{or}$ and definitions that $[\![\_]\!]_s$ is as abstract as $[\![\_]\!]_r$ on BL. The following two expressions show that it is strictly more abstract:

$$E_1 = a;b \parallel c$$
$$E_2 = (a \parallel c);b + a;(b \parallel c)$$

In the following we will need a special type of refinements – *fission* refinements – which splits an atomic action into two. In this way the original action is no longer atomic. Our notation is inspired by Hennessy [5].

Since Δ is countably infinite, there exists BL-refinements ρ such that for all a in Δ we have $\rho(a) = a_S;a_F$ with $a_S \neq a_F$ (S = start, F = finish). We call such a BL-refinement ρ a fission refinement. The $\mathcal{P}(SW)$-refinement $\mathcal{S}(\rho)$ with $(\mathcal{S}(\rho))(a) = \{a_S \cdot a_F\}$ has only one consistent particular refinement, so for convenience we will not make any notational difference in the sequel. The operator $<\mathcal{S}(\rho)>$ corresponding to the RBL-combinator $[\rho]$ will for the same reason be abbreviated $<\rho>$. Notice that $\{f_\rho(a^i, x') \mid x' \in A_{\rho(a^i)}\} = \{f_\rho(a^i, a_S{}^1), f_\rho(a^i, a_F{}^1)\} =$ (notation) $\{a^i{}_S, a^i{}_F\}$. Given a semiword s and a fission refinement ρ, we say that a semiword t is *s-reflecting* if and only if any pair of concurrent elements from s have overlapping start/ finish occurrences in t, formally: *iff* $t \preceq s<\rho>$ and for all x, y in A_s:

$$\text{if } \begin{matrix} x \\ co_s \\ y \end{matrix} \text{ then } \begin{matrix} x_S <_t y_F \\ \textit{and} \\ y_S <_t x_F \end{matrix}$$

LEMMA 5.10 Suppose ρ is a fission refinement. Then

$$[\![E_1[\rho]]\!]_w \subseteq [\![E_2[\rho]]\!]_w \Rightarrow [\![E_1]\!]_r \subseteq [\![E_2]\!]_r$$

Proof Given $s \in [\![E_1]\!]_r$. Since $P_{or}(s)$ we can by lemma 5.11 choose a w in $\delta_{lin}(s<\rho>)$ such that w is s-reflecting.

Now $w \in \delta_{lin}(s<\rho>)$ and $s \in [\![E_1]\!]_r$ implies w in $\delta_{lin}([\![E_1]\!]_r<\rho>)$ which, because $\delta_{lin} \circ \delta_{or} = \delta_{lin}$, equals $\delta_{lin}(\delta_{or}([\![E_1]\!]_r<\rho>))$. By theorem 5.4 and proposition 5.7 then also $w \in [\![E_1[\rho]]\!]_w$ and so $w \in [\![E_2[\rho]]\!]_w$ from the antecedent of the implication. Reversing the arguments we find a $t \in [\![E_2]\!]_r$ such that w is a linearization of $t<\rho>$.

Then, of course, $A_s = A_t$, so if we can prove $\leq_t \subseteq \leq_s$ we have $s \preceq t$ and therefore $s \in [\![E_2]\!]_r$ because $P_{or}(s)$ and $[\![E_2]\!]_r$ is δ_{or}-closed.

So assume $x \leq_t y$. If $x = y$ then clearly $x \leq_s y$. If $x <_t y$ then $x_F <_{t<\rho>} y_S$, and hence $x_F <_w y_S$. Since w is also a linearization of $s<\rho>$ we cannot have $y <_s x$, and since w is s-reflecting we cannot have $x\ co_s\ y$ either, leaving $x <_s y$ as the only possibility. □

For a semiword s, let in the sequel $M_s \subseteq A_s$ denote the set of minimal elements of s (w.r.t. $\leq_s$).

We state and prove the lemma referred to in the proof of lemma 5.10 in a slightly stronger form than needed.

LEMMA 5.11 Let $s \neq \varepsilon$ be a semiword with the P_{or}-property, ρ a fission refinement, and assume that the minimal elements M_s of s listed in some arbitrary order are: $x_1, \ldots, x_n$. Then there exists an s-reflecting linearization w of $s<\rho>$ of the form:

$$w = x_{1S} \cdot \ldots \cdot x_{nS} \cdot v$$

Proof By induction in the size of A_s.
The basis, A_s a singleton, is clear.
So assume $|A_s| > 1$. From proposition 5.12 we can find an element $x_i \in M_s$ such that x_i is dominated in $\leq_s$ by all successors of M_s. Consider now the semiword, s', obtained by deleting x_i from s.

Notice that $M_s \setminus \{x_i\}$ is a subset of the minimal elements of s', hence we may list $M_{s'}$ as follows:

$$x_1, \ldots, x_{i-1}, x_{i+1}, \ldots, x_n, y_1, \ldots, y_m$$

Using the inductive hypothesis we can find an s'-reflecting linearization w' of $s'<\rho>$ of the form

$$w' = x_{1S} \cdot \ldots \cdot x_{i-1S} \cdot x_{i+1S} \cdot \ldots \cdot x_{nS} \cdot y_{1S} \cdot \ldots \cdot y_{mS} \cdot v'$$

Since x_i is minimal in s there are no other elements before x_{iS} and x_{iF} in $s<\rho>$, and so $x_{iS} \cdot x_{iF} \cdot w'$ is a possible linearization of $s<\rho>$. By the way x_i was chosen the elements concurrent to x_i are exactly $M_s \setminus \{x_i\}$. Then x_{iS} and x_{iF} are concurrent to $x_{1S}, \ldots, x_{i-1S}, x_{i+1S}, \ldots, x_{nS}$ in $s<\rho>$, from which it follows that

$$w = x_{1S} \cdot \ldots \cdot x_{iS} \cdot \ldots \cdot x_{nS} \cdot x_{iF} \cdot y_{1S} \cdot \ldots \cdot y_{mS} \cdot v'$$

also is a linearization of $s<\rho>$, which quite easily is seen to be s-reflecting as desired. □

PROPOSITION 5.12 Let s be a nonempty semiword with the P_{or}-property and M a subset of the minimal elements M_s of s. Then there is an element z of M dominated by all the successors of M.

Proof By induction in the size of M. The basis where $M = \{z\}$ is evident, and for the inductive step choose an $x \in M$. By hypothesis of induction we can find a $y \in M \setminus \{x\}$, which is dominated by the successors of $M \setminus \{x\}$. If y is dominated by the successors of x too, we can choose $z = y$. Otherwise, since s has the P_{or}-property, and minimal elements are mutual concurrent, the successors of y must dominate x. But the successors of y are also the successors of $M \setminus \{x\}$ and we can choose $z = x$. □

6 Summary

Let us sum up the three full abstractness results we have proved so far. If we let $\approx$ denote the equivalence associated with an operational preorder $\lesssim$, and if we extend $\lesssim_{\mathsf{s}}$ and $[\![\_]\!]_{\mathsf{s}}$ to RBL in the same simple way as $\lesssim_{\mathsf{w}}$ were extended in subsections 5.1 and 5.2, we get the following immediate corollary:

COROLLARY 6.1 For all $E_1, E_2 \in RBL$:

$$\begin{array}{lll} E_1 \approx_{\mathsf{w}} E_2 & \textit{iff} & [\![E_1]\!]_{\mathsf{w}} = [\![E_2]\!]_{\mathsf{w}} \\ E_1 \approx_{\mathsf{s}} E_2 & \textit{iff} & [\![E_1]\!]_{\mathsf{s}} = [\![E_2]\!]_{\mathsf{s}} \\ E_1 \approx_{\mathsf{w}}^{c} E_2 & \textit{iff} & [\![E_1]\!]_{\mathsf{r}} = [\![E_2]\!]_{\mathsf{r}} \end{array}$$

Furthermore, from the full abstractness results, the fact that $P_{lin} \Rightarrow P_{and} \Rightarrow P_{or}$, and the examples above we get:

COROLLARY 6.2 For all $E_1, E_2 \in RBL$:

$$(E_1 \lesssim_{\mathsf{w}}^{c} E_2) \Rightarrow (E_1 \lesssim_{\mathsf{s}} E_2) \Rightarrow (E_1 \lesssim_{\mathsf{w}} E_2)$$

and none of the implications hold in the other direction.

At this stage, it seems very natural to ask what would have happened, if we had chosen to look for a denotational characterization of the RBL congruence associated with the operational step-sequences rather than action-sequences, i.e. a characterization of $\lesssim_{\mathsf{s}}^{c}$ on RBL. Operationally it seems hard to say anything directly. However, from the above corollaries we get immediately that $\lesssim_{\mathsf{w}}^{c}$ must be the largest precongruence contained in $\lesssim_{\mathsf{s}}$. Hence the model for $\lesssim_{\mathsf{w}}^{c}$ is a model for $\lesssim_{\mathsf{s}}^{c}$ too, and we obtain the fourth full abstractness result.

COROLLARY 6.3 For all $E_1, E_2 \in RBL$:

$$\begin{array}{lll} E_1 \lesssim_{\mathsf{s}}^{c} E_2 & \textit{iff} & E_1 \lesssim_{\mathsf{w}}^{c} E_2 \\ E_1 \approx_{\mathsf{s}}^{c} E_2 & \textit{iff} & [\![E_1]\!]_{\mathsf{r}} = [\![E_2]\!]_{\mathsf{r}} \end{array}$$

7 Conclusion

We have deliberately chosen to present our full abstractness results for a very simple process language. A natural question to raise is the robustness of our results w.r.t. various extensions of this language. Let us look at a few of the most conspicuous omissions in RBL compared to most other process languages.

Inaction (Nil, $SKIP$) is easily included. In fact, all results go through for RBL extended with inaction, at the cost of slightly more complicated definitions and proofs.

Adding recursion is also straightforward – all our denotational models form c.p.o.'s as they are defined. However, these models obviously only reflect *finite* operational behaviours. Infinite operational behaviours may be distinguished by considering approximating sequences instead of maximal sequences. The modified operational equivalences may be characterized by semiword based models, but obviously more complicated models than just sets ordered by inclusion. For finite expressions (without recursion combinators) these models will agree with the models presented in this paper.

The fact that we have avoided the issue of autoparallelism may seem a severe restriction in our set-up. However, all definitions generalize smoothly to RBL with autoparallelism, where the denotational models obviously consist of sets of general pomsets, not just semiwords. And we do have proofs of all theorems from this paper generalized in this way. But notationally, all proofs get more complicated, and some have changed fundamentally. As one interesting example of this, it follows from our proofs that for RBL without autoparallelism the congruence of $\sqsubseteq_w$ w.r.t. our general refinement combinator is the same as the congruence w.r.t. fission refinements. This is *not* the case for RBL with autoparallelism, as may be seen from the following example:

$$E_1 = a;b;b \parallel b \qquad E_2 = E_1 + a;b \parallel b;b$$

We claim that E_1 are E_2 congruent w.r.t. fission refinement, but not w.r.t. general refinement (consider e.g. a refinement, ρ, with $\rho(b) = b_S;b_F + b'_S;b'_F$).

All these extensions will be dealt with in a forthcomming paper by the authors.

As a contrast to these extensions, adding communication seems to be considerably more difficult, also because it (in most cases) introduces aspects like deadlock, and hence forces also the models to reflect branching structure. We have deliberately carried out this work on nonsequentiality "orthogonally" to existing work on branching, but we find it an intriguing question, whether such an extension could be modeled by smooth combinations of pomset-models and existing tree-models

– capturing aspects of nonsequentiality as well as branching.

Another natural line of future research would be to look for equational characterizations and adequateness/expressiveness results w.r.t. modal logics for our equivalences. Here we have some preliminary results [2].

References

[1] G. Boudol, I. Castellani: Concurrency and Atomicity, *INRIA Rapports de Recherche No 748*, 1987.

[2] U. Engberg: Ph.D. *Thesis, Aarhus University, Denmark*, in preparation.

[3] J. Gischer: Partial Orders and the Axiomatic Theory of Shuffle, Ph.D. *Thesis, Stanford University*, 1984

[4] R. van Glabbeek, F. Vaandrager: Petri Net Models for Algebraic Theories of Concurrency, *Springer LNCS 259, 224-242*, 1987.

[5] M. Hennessy: Axiomatising Finite Concurrent Processes, *University of Sussex, Report No. 4/84*, 1987

[6] M. Hennessy: *An Algebraic Theory of Processes*, MIT Press, 1988.

[7] K. S. Larsen: A Fully Abstract Model for a Process Algebra with Refinement, *Thesis, Aarhus University, Denmark*, 1988.

[8] A. Pnueli: Linear and Branching Structures in the Semantics and Logics of Reactive Systems, *Springer LNCS 194, 15-32*, 1987.

[9] V.R. Pratt: Modelling Concurrency with Partial Orders, *Int. J. of Parallel Programming 15, 33-71*, 1986.

[10] G. Rozenberg, P.S. Thiagarajan: Petri Nets: Basic Notions, Structure, Behaviour, *Springer LNCS, 224, 585-668*, 1985.

[11] P.H. Starke: Processes in Petri Nets, *EIK 17, 8/9, 389 - 416*, 1981

[12] P.H. Starke: Traces and Semiwords, *Springer LNCS, 208, 332-349*, 1985.

1. INTRODUCTION

In a previous paper [Ol 87] we defined an operational Petri net semantics $\mathfrak{N}[\![\cdot]\!]$ for a language of process terms with operators from Milner's CCS and Hoare's CSP. "Operational" refers to Ploktin's structured approach to operational semantics [Pl 81]. Our definition uses and extends ideas of Degano, DeNicola and Montanari [DDM 87a, DDM 87b]. Since there are so many possibilities of defining such a semantics, we posed the following question:

What is a good Petri net semantics ?

In [Ol 87] we suggested four criteria for a good net semantics some of which were a bit ad hoc. We now suggest that a good net semantics should ...

(1) ... express the right transitions,
(2) ... represent the intended concurrency.

To define the adjectives "right" and "intended", we refer to the standard ...

(1) ... interleaving semantics $\mathfrak{A}[\![\cdot]\!]$ of process terms,
(2) ... compositional net operators $op_{\mathfrak{N}}$

associated with the operator symbols op for process terms and formulate two principles:

(1) *Retrievability.* The standard interleaving semantics for process terms should be retrievable from the net semantics in the sense that for every process term P the interleaving case graph of $\mathfrak{N}[\![P]\!]$ is strongly bisimilar to $\mathfrak{A}[\![P]\!]$.

Here strong bisimilarity refers to Park's original definition for automata [Pa 81]. Recall that under strong bisimilarity the state representation of the automata may differ, e.g. cycles may be expanded and common substructures may be shared. However, the transition behaviour of strongly bisimilar automata must coincide. Hence the retrievability principle requires that the net $\mathfrak{N}[\![P]\!]$ must neither contain fewer transitions than the automaton $\mathfrak{A}[\![P]\!]$ nor new "auxiliary transitions" not present in $\mathfrak{A}[\![P]\!]$, even no "hidden" τ-transitions. This is a very strong requirement which several of the proposed net semantics fail to satisfy (e.g. GM 84, Ta 87). In fact, statement and proof of the relationship between net semantics and interleaving semantics appears only in the most recent publications on this topic. Retrievability in this sense is shown in [DDM 87a, DDM 87b, Go 88a, Go 88b, Ol 89].

In this paper we shall not be concerned with retrievability, but with the formalisation of "intended concurrency". Since retrievability deals only with individual transitions, it does not reject semantics that exhibit "too little" concurrency. As an illustration of this point we might consider the original operational net semantics [DDM 87a], called here $\mathfrak{N}^*[\![\cdot]\!]$. As discussed in [Ol 87], this semantics fails to represent the intended concurrency when parallel composition interacts with choice or recursion. Using the symbols $\|$ for parallel

STRONG BISIMILARITY ON NETS: A NEW CONCEPT FOR COMPARING NET SEMANTICS

Ernst-Rüdiger Olderog

Institut für Informatik und Praktische Mathematik
Christian-Albrechts-Universität Kiel
2300 Kiel 1, Fed. Rep. Germany

ABSTRACT. We extend Park's notion of strong bisimilarity from automata to safe Petri nets. The underlying strong bisimulation is a relation on places which when lifted to the reachable markings preserves their token game and distribution over the places. As a consequence, strongly bisimilar nets have exactly the same concurrent computations as formalised by their causal nets.

We apply this concept of strong bisimilarity to the analysis of a previously defined operational Petri net semantics for process terms with operators from CCS, CSP and COSY. We show that the resulting Petri nets are strongly bisimilar to those obtained by the standard compositional net semantics. Hence the operational net semantics represents all the concurrency that is intended by the compositional net semantics. On the other hand, the operational net semantics yields more often finite nets than the compositional one.

Key words: Strong bisimilarity, labelled place / transitions nets, safeness, causal nets, process terms, CCS, CSP, COSY, operational and compositional net semantics.

CONTENTS

composition, + for choice and μ for recursion, this failure can be formalised by saying that the semantics $\mathfrak{N}^*[\![\cdot]\!]$ neither satisfies the *compositionality law* for choice, viz.

$$\mathfrak{N}^*[\![P_1 + P_2]\!] = \mathfrak{N}^*[\![P_1]\!] +_{\mathfrak{N}} \mathfrak{N}^*[\![P_2]\!]$$

with $+_{\mathfrak{N}}$ denoting the standard compositional net operator for choice [GM 84, Wi 84, Wi 87, GV 87, Go 88a] nor the *μ-expansion law* for recursion, viz.

$$\mathfrak{N}^*[\![\mu X.P]\!] = \mathfrak{N}^*[\![P\{\mu X.P/X\}]\!]$$

with $P\{\mu X.P/X\}$ denoting the result of substituting $\mu X.P$ for all free occurrences of the identifier X in P.

Thus to check whether a proposed net semantics represents the intended concurrency, we will require certain algebraic laws that relate the proposed semantics to the standard compositional net operators. However, to allow a greater flexibility for the proposed semantics, we shall not require equality in these laws as shown above. For example, as long as the concurrency is preserved we will accept that the nets differ by the expansion of cycles or the sharing of common substructures. This brings us to extend Park's notion of strong bisimilarity from automata to (safe) Petri nets. The underlying strong bisimulation is a relation on places which when lifted to the reachable markings preserves their token game and distribution over the places. As a consequence, strongly bisimilar nets have exactly the same concurrent computations as formalised by their causal nets. On the other hand, strong bisimilarity allows for expansion and sharing as in the case of automata. Thus a proposed net semantics may yield finite nets where the standard compositional semantics yields infinite ones.

Using the symbol $\approx$ for strong bisimilarity, we can now formulate our second principle for a good net semantics.

(2) *Compositionality.* Modulo strong bisimilarty the net semantics $\mathfrak{N}[\![\cdot]\!]$ should be compositional with respect to the standard compositional net operators $op_{\mathfrak{N}}$, i.e. for all operator symbols op and all closed process terms $P_1,\dots,P_n$ and $\mu X.P$ the laws

$$\mathfrak{N}[\![\ op(P_1,\dots,P_n)\ ]\!] \approx op_{\mathfrak{N}}(\mathfrak{N}[\![P_1]\!],\dots,\mathfrak{N}[\![P_n]\!])$$

and

$$\mathfrak{N}[\![\ \mu X.P\ ]\!] \approx \mathfrak{N}[\![\ P\{\mu X.P/X\}\ ]\!]$$

should hold.

The above definition has the advantage that we stay within the framework of nets. By contrast, Degano, DeNicola and Montanari have suggested two other formalisations of "intended concurrency" which both leave this framework. One refers to the so-called *step semantics* of process terms [DDM 87b] and a second one to *event structure semantics* [Wi 82, DDM 88].

2. PETRI NETS

By a Petri net we mean here a *labelled place/transition net* with arc weight 1 and place capacity ω [Re 85]. In fact, we will mainly work in the subclass of safe Petri nets. Moreover, we will slightly deviate slightly from the standard definition and use the following one which is inspired by [Go 88a, Go 88b].

We start from an infinite set Comm of *communications* and an element $\tau \notin$ Comm to build the set Act = Comm $\cup \{ \tau \}$ of *actions* . The element τ is called *internal* action and the communications are also called *external* actions. We let a, b, c range over Comm and u, v, w over Act. By a *communication alphabet* or simply *alphabet* we mean a finite subset of Comm. We let A, B range over alphabets.

Definition. A *Petri net* or simply *net* is a structure $\mathfrak{N} = (A, Pl, \longrightarrow, M_0)$ where

(1) A is a communication alphabet;

(2) Pl is a possibly infinite set of *places*;

(3) $\longrightarrow \subseteq \mathfrak{P}_{nf}(Pl) \times (A \cup \{ \tau \}) \times \mathfrak{P}_{nf}(Pl)$ is the *transition relation*;

(4) $M_0 \in \mathfrak{P}_{nf}(Pl)$ is the *initial marking.* □

Here $\mathfrak{P}_{nf}(Pl)$ denotes the set of all non-empty, finite subsets of Pl. An element (I, u, O) $\in \longrightarrow$ is called a *transition (labelled with the action u)* and will usually be written as

$$I \xrightarrow{u} O .$$

For a transition $t = I \xrightarrow{u} O$ its *preset* or *input* is given by pre(t) = I, its *postset* or *output* by post(t) = O and its action by act(t) = u.

The graphical representation of a net $\mathfrak{N} = (A, Pl, \longrightarrow, M_0)$ is as follows. We draw a rectangular box subdivided into an upper part diaplaying the alphabet A and a lower part displaying the remaining components Pl, $\longrightarrow$ and M_0 in the usual way. Thus places $p \in Pl$ are represented as *circles* with the name "p" outside and transitions

$$t = \{ p_1, ..., p_m \} \xrightarrow{u} \{ q_1, ..., q_n \}$$

as *boxes* carrying the label "u" inside and connected via directed arcs to the places in pre(t) and post(t). Since pre(t) and post(t) need not be disjoint, some of the outgoing arcs of u actually point back to places in pre(t) and thus introduce *cycles*. The initial marking is represented by putting a token into the circle of each $p \in M$.

Example. The graphical representation of nets can clearly visualise the basic concepts about processes. For instance, concurrency of two communications a and b is represented as follows:

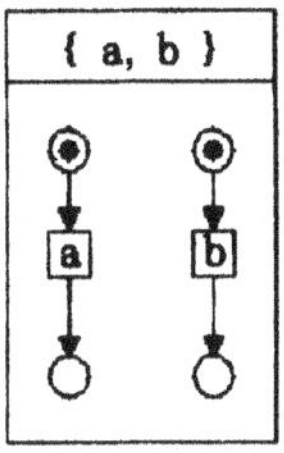

[]

The dynamic behaviour of a Petri net is defined by its *token game*; it describes which transitions are concurrently enabled at a given marking and what the result of their concurrent execution is. Though the initial marking of a net is defined to be a set of places, the token game can result in more general markings, viz. multisets.

Consider a net $\mathfrak{N}$ = (A, Pl, —>, M_0). A *marking* or *case* or *global state* of $\mathfrak{N}$ is a *multiset (over Pl)*, i.e. a mapping M: Pl —> $\mathbb{N}_0$. Graphically, such a marking M is represented by putting M(p) tokens into the circle drawn for each p $\in$ Pl. For simplicity any set N $\subseteq$ Pl, e.g. the initial marking M_0, will be identified with the multiset given by the characteristic function of N: N(p)=1 for p $\in$ N and N(p)=0 otherwise. For multisets M and N let

$$M \subseteq N,\ M \sqcup N \text{ and } M - N$$

denote *multiset inclusion, union* and *difference*. If M and N are sets then M $\subseteq$ N an M - N are just set inclusion and difference whereas M $\sqcup$ N in general differs from set-theoretic union. We write p $\in$ M if M(p) $\geq$ 1.

A *global transition* of $\mathfrak{N}$ is any non-empty, finite set $\mathfrak{T}$ of transitions of $\mathfrak{N}$. Define by using multiset union

$$\text{pre}(\mathfrak{T}) = \bigsqcup_{t \in \mathfrak{T}} \text{pre}(t)$$

and analogously for post($\mathfrak{T}$) and act($\mathfrak{T}$).

Definition. Let $\mathfrak{N}$ be a net, $\mathfrak{T}$ be a global transition of $\mathfrak{N}$ and M be a marking of $\mathfrak{N}$. Then

(1) the transitions in $\mathfrak{T}$ are *concurrently enabled at M* or simply $\mathfrak{T}$ is *enabled at M* if pre($\mathfrak{T}$) $\subseteq$ M,

(2) if enabled at M, the *concurrent execution* of the transitions in $\mathfrak{T}$ transforms M into a new marking M' of $\mathfrak{N}$; this is also called a *step from M to M' in (the token game of)* $\mathfrak{N}$. In symbols:

$$M \xrightarrow{\mathfrak{T}} M' \text{ in } \mathfrak{N}$$

if pre($\mathfrak{T}$) $\subseteq$ M and M' = (M - pre($\mathfrak{T}$)) $\sqcup$ post($\mathfrak{T}$). For $\mathfrak{T}$ = { t } we write $M \xrightarrow{t} M'$ instead. □

States of automata have both a static and dynamic facet: statically they are part of the structure of the automaton and dynamically each state which is currently active solely determines the future behaviour of the automaton. In nets the static and dynamic facet of states are separated into places and markings. Therefore we will distinguish two notions of reachability for a net $\mathfrak{N} = (\ A,\ Pl,\ \longrightarrow,\ M_0\ )$.

A *(dynamically) reachable marking* of $\mathfrak{N}$ is a marking M for which there exist intermediate markings $M_1, ..., M_n$ and global transitions $\mathfrak{T}_1, ..., \mathfrak{T}_n$ with

$$(*) \qquad M_0 \xrightarrow{\mathfrak{T}_1} M_1 \xrightarrow{\mathfrak{T}_2} \cdots \xrightarrow{\mathfrak{T}_n} M_n = M$$

Let mark($\mathfrak{N}$) denote the set of *reachable* markings of $\mathfrak{N}$. Note that the set mark($\mathfrak{N}$) does not change if in (*) we consider only singleton transitions $\mathfrak{T}_i = \{\ t_i\ \}$.

The set place($\mathfrak{N}$) of *statically reachable places* of $\mathfrak{N}$ is the smallest subset of Pl satisfying

(1) $M \ \subseteq$ place($\mathfrak{N}$) ,

(2) If $I \subseteq$ place($\mathfrak{N}$) and $I \xrightarrow{u} O$ for some $u \in A \cup \{\ \tau\ \}$ and $O \subseteq Pl$ then also $O \subseteq$ place($\mathfrak{N}$).

The term "statical" emphasizes that, by (2), the set place($\mathfrak{N}$) is closed under the execution of any transition $t = I \xrightarrow{u} O$ independently of whether t is ever enabled at some dynamically reachable marking of $\mathfrak{N}$. Consequently,

$$\text{place}(\mathfrak{N}) \subseteq \{\ p \mid \exists\ M \in \text{mark}(\mathfrak{N}):\ p \in M\ \}$$

and in general this inclusion is proper.

In the following we shall mainly work with safe nets where multiple tokens per place do not occur. Formally, a net $\mathfrak{N}$ is *safe* if

$$\forall\ M \in \text{mark}(\mathfrak{N})\ \forall\ p \in Pl:\ M(p) \le 1.$$

Thus in a safe net all reachable markings are sets.

Moreover, we mostly wish to ignore the identity of places and forget about places that are not statically reachable. We do this by introducing suitable notions of isomorphism and abstract net.

Definition. Two nets $\mathfrak{N}_i = (\ A_i,\ Pl_i,\ \longrightarrow_i,\ M_{0i}\ )$, i=1,2, are *weakly isomorphic*, abbreviated

$$\mathfrak{N}_1 =_{isom} \mathfrak{N}_2,$$

if $A_1 = A_2$ and there exists a bijection

$$\beta : \text{place}(\mathfrak{N}\ ) \longrightarrow \text{place}(\mathfrak{N}\ )$$

such that

$$\beta(M_{01}) = M_{02}$$

and for all $I, O \subseteq$ place($\mathfrak{N}_1$) and all $u \in A \cup \{\ \tau\ \}$

$$I \xrightarrow{u}_1 O \;\text{ iff }\; \beta(I) \xrightarrow{u}_2 \beta(O)$$

where $\beta(M_{01})$, $\beta(I)$, $\beta(O)$ are understood elementwise. The bijection β is called an *weak isomorphism between* $\mathfrak{N}_1$ *and* $\mathfrak{N}_2$. □

For an illustration of this concept look at the following example.

Example. Since place($\mathfrak{N}_1$) = { p_1, p_3 }, we have

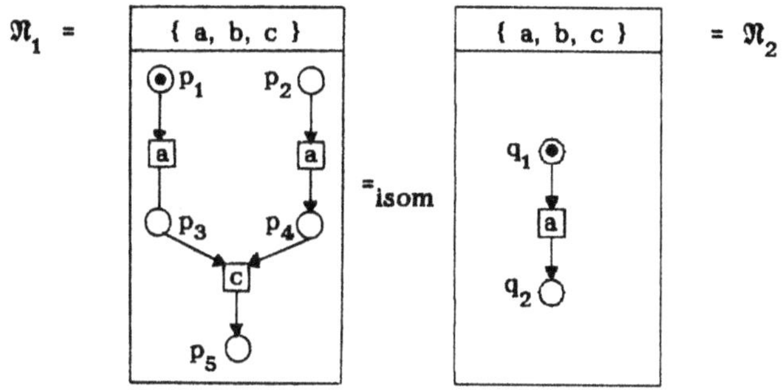

where the isomorphism maps p_1 onto q_1, and p_3 onto q_2. □

Clearly, $=_{isom}$ is an equivalence relation. An ***abstract net*** is defined as the isomorphism class

$$[\mathfrak{N}]_{=_{isom}} = \{ \mathfrak{N}' \mid \mathfrak{N} =_{isom} \mathfrak{N}' \}$$

of a net $\mathfrak{N}$. It will be written shorter as $[\mathfrak{N}]$. For abstract nets, we use the same graphical representation as for nets; we only have to make sure that all places are statically reachable and eliminate their names. Most concepts for nets can be lifted in a straightforward way to abstract nets. For example, we shall call an abstract net $[\mathfrak{N}]$ safe, if $\mathfrak{N}$ is safe. Let Net denote the set of nets and ANet the set of abstract nets.

3. STRONG BISIMILARITY ON SAFE NETS

Except for the identity of (statically reachable) places, isomorphisms preserve all information about the net structure. Often we wish to ignore a part of this information and concentrate on the rest. For example, we wish to express that nets have the same structure except that cycles may be (partially) unfolded or common substructures may be shared. For this purpose we will introduce a new notion of equivalence on nets inspired by the strong bisimmilarity on automata [Pa 81].

Recall that strong bisimilarity between two automata is shown by establishing a certain bisimulation relation $\mathfrak{B}$ between the *states* of these automata. When lifting such a definition to nets, the question arises what should replace the role of states ? Recently several versions of (strong and weak) bisimilarity on nets have been proposed and all definitions take *markings* as the right analogue for states [Po 85, GV 87]. This works well as far as the dynamic behaviour is concerned. However, one nice aspect of bisimulation on automata gets lost in this way, viz. that the bisimulation relation $\mathfrak{B}$ can be displayed on the static structure of the automata.

We wish to preserve this static property of bisimulation in our definition for nets and therefore start from a relation $\mathfrak{B}$ on *places* which will then be lifted to markings and transitions. For simplicity we state the definition only for safe nets. Consider safe nets $\mathfrak{N}_i = (A_i, Pl_i, \longrightarrow_i, M_{0i})$, i=1,2, and a relation $\mathfrak{B} \subseteq Pl_1 \times Pl_2$. Then *lifting* $\mathfrak{B}$ to markings and transitions is done by the following very strong relation $\hat{\mathfrak{B}}$.

(1) For sets $M_i \subseteq Pl_i$, i=1,2, we write $M_1 \hat{\mathfrak{B}} M_2$ if $\mathfrak{B} \cap (M_1 \times M_2)$ is a bijection.

(2) For transitions $t_i \in \longrightarrow_i$, i=1,2, we write $t_1 \hat{\mathfrak{B}} t_2$ if $pre(t_1) \hat{\mathfrak{B}} pre(t_2)$, $act(t_1) = act(t_2)$, $post(t_1) \hat{\mathfrak{B}} post(t_2)$.

Thus $\hat{\mathfrak{B}}$ preserves the distribution of markings over places. Now we can introduce the new notion of strong bisimilarity for safe nets.

Definition. Two safe nets $\mathfrak{N}_i = (A_i, Pl_i, \longrightarrow_i, M_{0i})$, i=1,2, are *strongly bisimilar*, abbreviated

$$\mathfrak{N}_1 \approx \mathfrak{N}_2 ,$$

if $A_1 = A_2$ and there exists a relation $\mathfrak{B} \subseteq Pl_1 \times Pl_2$ satisfying the following conditions:

(1) $M_{01} \hat{\mathfrak{B}} M_{02}$

(2) For all $M_1, N_1 \in mark(\mathfrak{N}_1)$, $M_2 \in mark(\mathfrak{N}_2)$ and all $t_1 \in \longrightarrow_1$ whenever

$$M_1 \hat{\mathfrak{B}} M_2 \text{ and } M_1 \xrightarrow{t_1}_1 N_1$$

then there exists some $t_2 \in \longrightarrow_2$ and some $N_2 \in mark(\mathfrak{N}_2)$ with

$$t_1 \hat{\mathfrak{B}} t_2 \text{ and } N_1 \hat{\mathfrak{B}} N_2 \text{ and } M_2 \xrightarrow{t_2}_2 N_2 .$$

(3) Conversely, for all $M_1 \in mark(\mathfrak{N}_1)$, $M_2, N_2 \in mark(\mathfrak{N}_2)$ and all $t_2 \in \longrightarrow_2$ whenever

$$M_1 \hat{\mathfrak{B}} M_2 \text{ and } M_2 \xrightarrow{t_2}_2 N_2$$

then there exist some $t_1 \in \longrightarrow_1$ and some $N_1 \in mark(\mathfrak{N}_1)$ with

$$t_1 \hat{\mathfrak{B}} t_2 \text{ and } N_1 \hat{\mathfrak{B}} N_2 \text{ and } M_1 \xrightarrow{t_1}_1 N_1 .$$

The relation $\mathfrak{B}$ is called a *strong bisimulation* between $\mathfrak{N}_1$ and $\mathfrak{N}_2$. □

Note that $\approx$ is an equivalence relation and

$$\mathfrak{N}_1 =_{\text{isom}} \mathfrak{N}_2 \text{ implies } \mathfrak{N}_1 \approx \mathfrak{N}_2$$

for all nets $\mathfrak{N}_1$ and $\mathfrak{N}_2$. Thus we can lift the definition of strong bisimilarity to abstract automata $[\mathfrak{N}_1]$ and $[\mathfrak{N}_2]$ by putting

$$[\mathfrak{N}_1] \approx [\mathfrak{N}_2] \quad \text{if} \quad \mathfrak{N}_1 \approx \mathfrak{N}_2 \ .$$

A specific way of defining a strong bisimulation $\hat{\mathfrak{B}}$ between two nets $\mathfrak{N}_1$ and $\mathfrak{N}_2$ is by giving *colours* to the places of $\mathfrak{N}_1$ and $\mathfrak{N}_2$. More precisely. we take a set C (of colours) and mappings f_i: Pl_i —> C, i=1,2, to define for all $p_i \in Pl_i$, i=1,2,

$$p_1 \ \mathfrak{B} \ p_2 \quad \text{if} \quad f_1(p_1) = f_2(p_2).$$

Example. The colours are given by natural numbers that appear inside the circles representing the places of the following abstract nets.

$\mathfrak{N}_1$ =

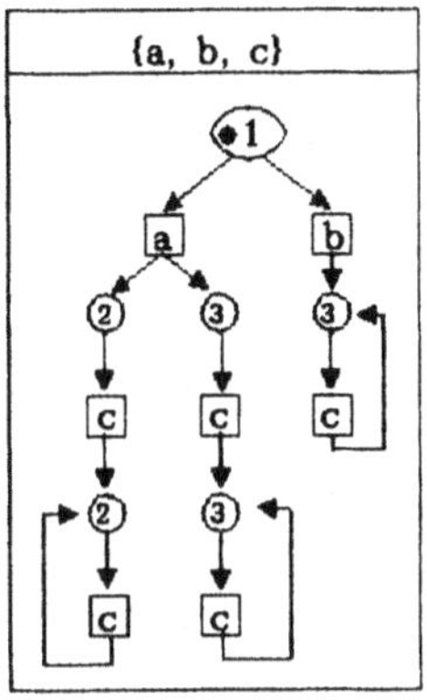

≈

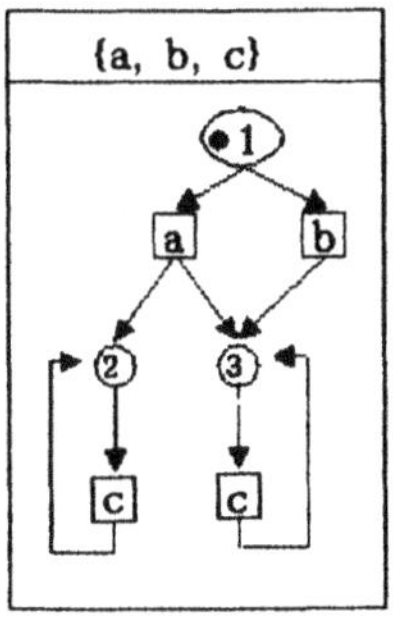

= $\mathfrak{N}_2$

Note that we cannot further identify the places 2 and 3 because because both appear in one reachable marking of $\mathfrak{N}_1$ resp. $\mathfrak{N}_2$ and the lifted relation $\hat{\mathfrak{B}}$ is required to be a bijection on markings. Thus strong bisimilarity preserves the concurrency of the two cycles in $\mathfrak{N}_2$. □

We wish to show that strong bisimilarity on nets always preserves concurrency. But how to formalise this property ? We will employ an idea of Petri that the concurrent computations of a net can be described with the help of *causal nets* [Pe 77, Re 85]. Informally, a causal net is an acyclic net where all choices have been resolved. It can be seen as a net-theoretic way of defining a partial order among the occurrences of transitions in a net representing their causal dependency. The formal definition requires some more notation.

Consider a net $\mathfrak{N}$ = (A, Pl, —>, M_0). We define *pre* – and *postsets of places* p ∈ Pl by

$$\text{pre}(p) = \{ t \in \longrightarrow \mid p \in \text{post}(t) \}$$

and

$$\text{post}(p) = \{ t \in \longrightarrow \mid p \in \text{pre}(t) \}.$$

We also need the *flow relation* $F_{\mathfrak{N}} \subseteq Pl \times Pl$ of $\mathfrak{N}$ given by

$$p\ F_{\mathfrak{N}}\ q \text{ if } \exists\ t \in \longrightarrow\ :\ p \in pre(t) \text{ and } q \in post(t).$$

$F_{\mathfrak{N}}$ is *well-founded* if there are no infinite backward chains ... $p_3\ F_{\mathfrak{N}}\ p_2\ F_{\mathfrak{N}}\ p_1$.

Definition. A *causal net* is a net $\mathfrak{N} = (\ A,\ Pl,\ \longrightarrow,\ M_0\ )$ satisfying the following conditions:

(1) all places are unbranched, i.e.

$$\forall\ p \in Pl : |\ pre(p)\ | \leq 1 \text{ and } |\ post(p)\ | \leq 1\ ,$$

(2) the flow relation F is well-founded,

(3) the initial marking consists of all places without ingoing arc, i.e.

$$M_0 = \{\ p \in Pl \mid pre(p) = \emptyset\ \}.$$

□

Condition (1) implies that there are no choices left in $\mathfrak{N}$. Condition (2) implies that $F_{\mathfrak{N}}^+$, the transitive closure of $F_{\mathfrak{N}}$, is irreflexive. Thus a causal net $\mathfrak{N}$ is acyclic so that each transition can occur only once. $\mathfrak{N}$ induces a partial order $\leq$ on transitions where $t_1 \leq t_2$ means that t_2 can occur only after t_1 has occured. In other words : t_2 *causally depends* on t_1. If neither $t_1 \leq t_2$ nor $t_2 \leq t_1$ then t_1 and t_2 are causally independent and can occur conccurrently. Conditions (2) and (3) together ensure that there are no superflous places and transitions in causal nets (see Lemma 2).

Following Petri's intuition, causal nets should describe the concurrent computations of a net. Thus we have to explain how causal nets relate to ordinary (safe) nets. To this end, we use the following notion of embedding.

Definition. Let $\mathfrak{N}_1 = (\ A_1,\ Pl_1,\ \longrightarrow_1,\ M_{01}\ )$ be a causal net and $\mathfrak{N}_2 = (\ A_2,\ Pl_2,\ \longrightarrow_2,\ M_{02}\ )$ be a safe net. $\mathfrak{N}_1$ is a *causal net of* $\mathfrak{N}_2$ if $A_1 = A_2$ and there exists a mapping

$$f : Pl_1 \longrightarrow Pl_2$$

such that

(1) $f\ (M_{01}) = M_{02}$

(2) $\forall\ M \in mark\ (\mathfrak{N}_1)\ :\ f \restriction M$ is injective,

(3) $\forall\ t \in \longrightarrow_1\ :\ f(t) \in \longrightarrow_2$

where f applied to sets of places is understood elementwise and where $f\ (t) = (\ f\ (pre\ (t)),\ act(t),\ f\ (post\ (t))\ )$. The mapping f is called an *embedding of* $\mathfrak{N}_1$ *into* $\mathfrak{N}_2$. □

In net theory an embedding is called a *process* [Pe 77, Re 85]. We prefer to leave the notion of process more general because the net-theoretic notion of process does not capture all our intentions, for example not the choices. But we like it as an explication of the concept of concurrent computation or history [By 86, DM 87].

Example. The following (abstract) net $\mathfrak{N}$ is a causal net of $\mathfrak{N}_2$ in the previous example.

$\mathfrak{N}$ =

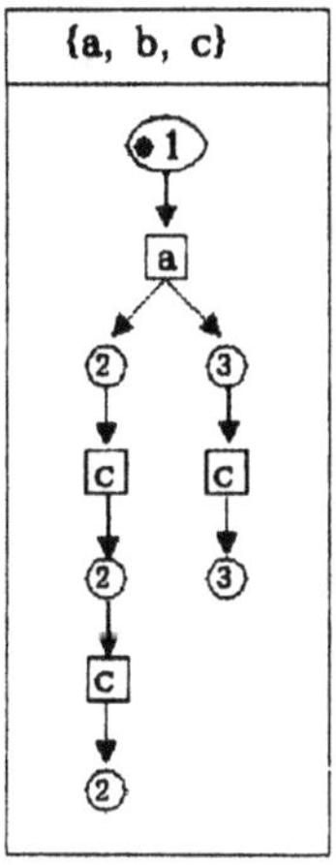

The embedding of $\mathfrak{N}$ into $\mathfrak{N}_2$ maps each place of $\mathfrak{N}$ onto that place of $\mathfrak{N}_2$ which is indicated by the corresponding number in $\mathfrak{N}$. □

Using causal nets we can now state formally that strong bisimilarity preserves concurrency.

Causality Theorem. Consider two strongly bisimilar safe nets $\mathfrak{N}_1$ and $\mathfrak{N}_2$. Then $\mathfrak{N}$ is a causal net of $\mathfrak{N}_1$ if $\mathfrak{N}$ is a causal net of $\mathfrak{N}_2$.

The proof relies on two lemmas investigating the properties of causal nets.

Lemma 1. Let $\mathfrak{N}$ = (A, Pl, —>, M_0) be a causal net. Then every transition sequence

(1) $$M_0 \xrightarrow{t_1} M_1 \xrightarrow{t_2} \cdots \xrightarrow{t_k} M_k$$

of $\mathfrak{N}$ satisfies

(2) $$M_j \cap \text{post}(t_k) = \emptyset$$

for all $j = 0, \ldots, k - 1$. □

Corollary. Every causal net is safe.

Lemma 2. Let $\mathfrak{N}$ = (A, Pl , —>, M_0) be a causal net. Then there exists one possibly infinite transition sequence

(1) $$M_0 \xrightarrow{t_1} M_1 \xrightarrow{t_2} \cdots \xrightarrow{t_k} M_k \xrightarrow{t_{k+1}} \cdots$$

of $\mathfrak{N}$ with

(2) $$Pl = \bigcup_{k=0} M_k \quad \text{and} \longrightarrow = \{ t_k \mid k \geq 0 \}.$$

Thus $\mathfrak{N}$ contains no superflous places and transitions because every place of $\mathfrak{N}$ is visited and every transition of $\mathfrak{N}$ is executed in the sequence (1). □

Proof of the Causality Theorem. Consider safe nets $\mathfrak{N}_i = (A, Pl_i, \longrightarrow_i, M_{0i})$, i = 1,2, and suppose that $\mathfrak{N} = (A, Pl_1, \longrightarrow, M_0)$ is a causal net of $\mathfrak{N}_1$ via the embedding $f_1 : Pl \longrightarrow Pl_1$ from $\mathfrak{N}$ into $\mathfrak{N}_1$ and let $\mathfrak{N}_1 \approx \mathfrak{N}_2$ via the strong bisimulation $\mathfrak{B}$ between $\mathfrak{N}_1$ and $\mathfrak{N}_2$. We have to construct an embedding $f_2 : Pl \longrightarrow Pl_2$ from $\mathfrak{N}$ into $\mathfrak{N}_2$. The idea is to obtain f_2 by composing f_1 and $\mathfrak{B}$.

More precisely, we consider a transition sequence

(1) $$M_0 \xrightarrow{t_1} M_1 \xrightarrow{t_2} \dots \xrightarrow{t_k} M_k \xrightarrow{t_{k+1}} \dots$$

of $\mathfrak{N}$ with

(2) $$Pl = \bigcup_{k \geq 0} M_k \quad \text{and} \quad \longrightarrow \; = \{ t_k \mid k \geq 0 \}$$

as in Lemma 2. Then, using f_1, there exists a transition sequence

(3) $$M_{01} \xrightarrow{t_{11}} M_{11} \xrightarrow{t_{21}} \dots \xrightarrow{t_{k1}} M_{k1} \xrightarrow{t_{k+1,1}} \dots$$

of $\mathfrak{N}_1$ with

(4) $$f_1(M_k) = M_{k1} \quad \text{and} \quad f_1(t_k) = t_{k1}$$

for every $k \geq 0$, and, using $\mathfrak{B}$, there exists a transition sequence

(5) $$M_{02} \xrightarrow{t_{12}} M_{12} \xrightarrow{t_{22}} \dots \xrightarrow{t_{k2}} M_{k2} \xrightarrow{t_{k+1,2}} \dots$$

of $\mathfrak{N}_2$ with

(6) $$M_{k1} \; \hat{\mathfrak{B}} \; M_{k2} \quad \text{and} \quad t_{k1} \; \hat{\mathfrak{B}} \; t_{k2}$$

for every $k \geq 0$. Define now

(7) $$f_2(p) = (\mathfrak{B} \cap (M_{k1} \times M_{k2}))\,(f_1(p))$$

where k is the smallest index with $p \in M_k$. Recall that by (6), $\mathfrak{B} \cap (M_{k1} \times M_{k2})$ is a bijection which is applied to $f_1(p)$.

First note that by (2) and Lemma 1, equation (7) yields a well-defined mapping $f_2 : Pl \longrightarrow Pl_2$. It remains to show that f_2 is indeed an embedding. This is done by checking the conditions (8) - (10) below.

(8) $f_2(M_0) = M_{02}$: By (4) and (6).

(9) $\forall\, M \in mark(\mathfrak{N}) : f_2 \restriction M$ is injective :

Clearly, f_2 is injective on all markings M_k, $k \geq 0$, that occur in (1), but in general there are more markings in $mark(\mathfrak{N})$. So consider some $M \in mark(\mathfrak{N})$. Then M can be generated from M_0 by executing some of the transitions t_1, t_2, ... of $\mathfrak{N}$ in some possibly different order than shown in (1). It follows that there exists a corresponding marking $M_2 \in mark(\mathfrak{N}_2)$ with $f_2(M) = M_2$ and $|M| = |M_2|$. Since all markings are finite, the restriction $f_2 \upharpoonright M$ is injective.

(10) $\forall\, t \in \longrightarrow\, : f_2\,(t) \longrightarrow_2\, :$

Every transition t of $\mathfrak{N}$ occurs in (1), i.e. $t = t_k$ for some $k \geq 0$. By construction, $f_2(t_k) = t_{k2}$ is a transition of $\mathfrak{N}_2$.

Thus $\mathfrak{N}$ is a causal net of $\mathfrak{N}_2$. Since $\approx$ is symmetric, this proves the theorem. □

4. PROCESS TERMS

Process terms are recursive terms over a certain signature of operator symbols taken from Lauer's COSY [LTS 79, Be 87], Milner's CCS [Mi 80] and Hoare's CSP as in [Ho 85]. More specifically, we take the parallel composition || from COSY, prefix a., choice + and action morphism [φ] from CCS, and deadlock *stop* : A , divergence *div* : A and the idea of using communication alphabets to state certain context-sensitive restrictions on process terms from CSP.

Recall that Comm denotes the infinite set of communications and Act = Comm ∪ { τ } the set of actions. As before letters a,b range over Comm and letters A,B over communication alphabets, i.e. finite subsets of Comm. The set of *(process) identifiers* is denoted by Idf; it is partitioned into sets Idf:A ⊆ Idf of *Identifiers with alphabet* A, one for each communication alphabet A. We let X,Y,Z range over Idf. By an *action morphism* we mean a mapping φ: Act ⟶ Act with $\varphi(\tau) = \tau$ and $\varphi(a) \neq a$ for only finitely many $a \in$ Comm. Communications a with $\varphi(a) = \tau$ are said to be hidden via φ and communications a with $\varphi(a) = b$ for some $b \neq a$ are said to be *renamed* into b via φ.

Definition. The set Rec of *(recursive) terms*, with typical elements P,Q,R, consists of all terms generated by the following context-free production rules:

P ::=	*stop* : A	(deadlock)
	| *div* : A	(divergence)
	| a. P	(prefix)
	| P + Q	(choice)
	| P || Q	(paralellism)
	| P [φ]	(morphism)
	| X	(identifier)
	| μX. P	(recursion)

□

An occurence of an identifier X in a term P is said to be *bound* if it occurs in P within a subterm of the form μX.Q. Otherwise the occurence is said to be *free*. A term P ∈ Rec without free occurences of identifiers is called *closed*. P{Q/X} denotes the result of *substituting* Q for every free occurence of X in P.

A term P is called *action-guarded* if in every recursive subterm $\mu X.Q$ of P every free occurence of X in Q occurs within a subterm of the form a.R of Q. For example,

$$\mu X.\ a.\ X,\ \mu X.\mu Y.\ a\ .Y\ ,\ (\ \mu X.\ a.X\ )\backslash a$$

are all action-guarded, but $a.\mu X.\ X$ is not.

To every term P we assign a communication alphabet $\alpha(P)$ defined inductively as follows :

$$\begin{aligned}
\alpha(\mathit{stop}:A) &= \alpha(\mathit{div}:A) = A,\\
\alpha(a.P) &= \{a\} \cup \alpha(P),\\
\alpha(P+Q) &= \alpha(P \,\|\, Q) = \alpha(P) \cup \alpha(Q),\\
\alpha(P[\varphi]) &= \varphi(\alpha(P)) - \{\tau\},\\
\alpha(X) &= A \quad \text{if } X \in Idf(A),\\
\alpha(\mu X.P) &= \alpha(X) \cup \alpha(P).
\end{aligned}$$

Definition. A *process term* is a term $P \in Rec$ which satisfies the following context-sensitive restrictions:

(1) P is action-guarded,
(2) every subterm a.Q of P satisfies $a \in \alpha(Q)$,
(3) every subterm Q+R of P satisfies $\alpha(Q) = \alpha(R)$,
(4) every subterm $\mu X.Q$ of P satisfies $\alpha(X) = \alpha(P)$.

Let Proc denote the set of all process terms and CProc the set of all closed process terms. □

5. OPERATIONAL NET SEMANTICS

A semantics is a mapping which assigns to every element of a syntactic domain a meaning or interpretation, i.e. an element of a semantic domain. Here we wish to define a Petri net semantics which assigns to every process term P an abstract net $\mathfrak{N}[\![P]\!]$. We pursue an approach which has been highly succesful in providing lucid interleaving semantics to CCS [Mi 80], CSP [BHR 84, OH 86] and various other languages: structured *operational* semantics as advocated by Plotkin [Pl 81, Pl 82]. Operational means that the states and transitions of an abstract machine are described. Plotkin's idea is that states are denoted by terms and that transitions are defined by structural induction using a deductive system. Until recently it was a challenge how to apply it to the distributed states and transitions of Petri nets.

Degano, De Nicola and Montanari were the first to attack this problem and to propose an operational Petri net semantics of CCS [DDM 87a]. Their main idea is to decompose each process term P syntactically into a set

$$\{ C_1,\dots, C_m \}$$

of *sequential components* which can be thought of as working concurrently. Sequential components denote the places of Petri nets. Consequently, net transitions are now of the form

$$\{C_1,\dots, C_m\} \xrightarrow{u} \{D_1,\dots, D_n\}$$

where $C_1,\dots, C_n, D_1,\dots, D_n$ are sequential components and u is an action, or represented graphically

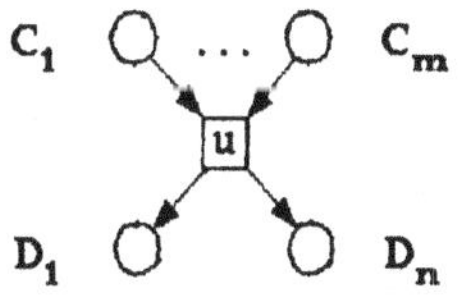

Except for a new treatment of choice and recursion, we follow [DDM 87a]. In particular, we make use of their idea of decomposition, only that we apply it here to the parallel operator of COSY rather than CCS. For example, if P and Q do not contain any further symbol ||, the sequential components of P || Q are the subterm P and Q equipped with some information about their synchronisation set. We will write

$$P\,||_A \text{ and } {}_A||\,Q$$

where $A=\alpha(P)\cap\alpha(Q)$. By postfixing P and prefixing Q with $||_A$ and ${}_A||$ we generate distinct names for places which can be active concurrently. New is that we treat recursion by an a priori expansion. Our treatment of choice, however, cannot be so simple.

Let us now explain the details of our approach. The set Sequ of *sequential components*, with typical elements C, D consists of all terms generated by the following production rules:

$$C ::= \textit{stop} : A \mid \textit{div}: A \mid a.P \mid C\,||_A \mid {}_A||\,D \mid C+D \mid C[\varphi]$$

where P ranges over CProc. Note that every process term a.P is also a sequential component regardless whether P contains any parallel composition. Thus sequentiality refers only to the set of initial actions; it states that this set does not contain any two actions that might occur concurrently.

We apply the operator symbols $||_A$, ${}_A||$, +, $[\varphi]$ also to *sets* of sequential components. Let $\mathbb{P}, \mathbb{Q}, \mathbb{R}$ range over $P_{nf}(\text{Sequ})$, the set of all non-empty, finite subsets of Sequ. Then

$$\mathbb{P}\,||_A,\ {}_A||\,\mathbb{Q}\ ,\ \mathbb{P}+\mathbb{Q}\ ,\ \mathbb{P}[\varphi]$$

are understood elementwise. For example, $\mathbb{P}\,||_A = \{ C\,||_A \mid C \in \mathbb{P} \}$. This notation is used in the following definition.

Definition. Decomposition and expansion of process terms into sequential components is archieved by a mapping

$$\text{dex: CProc} \longrightarrow \mathfrak{P}_{nf}\,(\text{Sequ})$$

defined as follows:

(1) $\text{dex}(\mathit{stop}{:}A) = \{\, \mathit{stop} : A \,\}$,
(2) $\text{dex}(\mathit{div}{:}A) = \{\, \mathit{div} : A \,\}$,
(3) $\text{dex}(a.P) = \{\, a.P \,\}$,
(4) $\text{dex}(P \| Q) = \text{dex}(P)\ \|_{A} \cup {}_{A}\|\ \text{dex}(Q)$ where $A = \alpha(P) \cap \alpha(Q)$,
(5) $\text{dex}(P + Q) = \text{dex}(P) + \text{dex}(Q)$,
(6) $\text{dex}(P[\varphi]) = \text{dex}(P)[\varphi]$,
(7) $\text{dex}(\mu X.P) = \text{dex}(P\{\mu X.P/X\})$

A set $\mathbb{P}$ of sequential components is called *complete* if there exists a closed process term Q with $\mathbb{P} = \text{dex}(Q)$. □

Next we define a transition relation

$$\longrightarrow\ \subseteq \mathfrak{P}_{nf}(\text{Sequ}) \times \text{Act} \times \mathfrak{P}_{nf}(\text{Sequ})$$

by induction on the syntactic structure of sequential components, using a deductive system. Thus transitions are now of the form

$$\mathbb{P} \xrightarrow{u} \mathbb{Q}$$

with $\mathbb{P}, \mathbb{Q} \in \mathfrak{P}_{nf}(\text{Sequ})$ and $u \in \text{Act}$. The deductive system consists of *transition rules* of the form

$$(\mathfrak{R}) \qquad \frac{T_1, \ldots, T_m}{T_{m+1}, \ldots, T_{m+n}} \qquad \text{where } \ldots$$

with $T_1, \ldots, T_{m+n}$ denoting transitions ($m \geq 0$, $n \geq 1$). $\mathfrak{R}$ states that if $T_1, \ldots, T_m$ are transitionssatisfying the condition "..." then also $T_{m+1}, \ldots, T_{m+n}$ are transitions. If $m = 0$ and $n = 1$, $\mathfrak{R}$ is called an *axiom* and written as "T_1 where ... "

Definition. The *Petri net transition relation* $\longrightarrow$ consists of all transitions that are deducible by the following transition axioms and rules:

(Prefix)

$$\{a.P\} \xrightarrow{a} \text{dex}(P)$$

(Divergence)

$$\{\mathit{div} : A\} \xrightarrow{\tau} \{\mathit{div} : A\}$$

(Parallel Composition)

Asynchrony:

$$\frac{\mathbb{P} \xrightarrow{u} \mathbb{P}'}{\mathbb{P}\,||_A \xrightarrow{u} \mathbb{P}'\,||_A\,,\ {}_A||\,\mathbb{P} \xrightarrow{u} {}_A||\,\mathbb{P}'} \qquad \text{where } u \notin A$$

Synchrony:

$$\frac{\mathbb{P} \xrightarrow{a} \mathbb{P}'\ ,\ \mathbb{Q} \xrightarrow{a} \mathbb{Q}'}{\mathbb{P}\,||_A \cup {}_A||\,\mathbb{Q} \xrightarrow{a} \mathbb{P}'\,||_A \cup {}_A||\,\mathbb{Q}'} \qquad \text{where } a \in A$$

(Choice)

$$\frac{\mathbb{P}_1 \cup \mathbb{P}_2 \xrightarrow{u} \mathbb{P}'}{\mathbb{P}_1 \cup (\mathbb{P}_2 + Q) \xrightarrow{u} \mathbb{P}'\,,\ \mathbb{P}_1 \cup (Q + \mathbb{P}_2) \xrightarrow{u} \mathbb{P}'} \qquad \text{where } \mathbb{P}_1 \cap \mathbb{P}_2 = \emptyset \text{ and } Q \text{ is complete}$$

(Morphism)

$$\frac{\mathbb{P} \xrightarrow{u} \mathbb{Q}}{\mathbb{P}[\varphi] \xrightarrow{\varphi(u)} \mathbb{Q}[\varphi]}$$

□

The essential new idea is embodied in the transition rule for choice. Firstly, only a part of the sequential components, viz. $\mathbb{P}_2$, need to have an alternative Q. Secondly Q need to be complete. This condition ensures that no sequential component in Q has been active previously. There is no analogue to these conditions in the case of operational interleaving semantics for choice.

For a given process term P the transition relation of its net $\mathfrak{N}[\![P]\!]$ is obtained by restricting the general relation $\longrightarrow$ to the alphabet of P and (via weak isomorphism) to the places that are statically reachable from the decomposition of P into its sequential components. Formally, this is expressed in the following definition.

Definition. The operational Petri net semantics for process terms is a mapping $\mathfrak{N}[\![\cdot]\!]$: CProc $\longrightarrow$ ANet which assigns to every $P \in$ CProc the abtract net

$$\mathfrak{N}[\![P]\!] = [(\alpha(P),\ Sequ,\ \longrightarrow \upharpoonright \alpha(P),\ dex(P))].$$

Here $\longrightarrow$ is the above transition relation and $\longrightarrow \upharpoonright \alpha(P) = \{\mathbb{P} \longrightarrow \mathbb{Q} \mid u \in \alpha(P) \cup \{\tau\}\}$ its restriction to the communications in $\alpha(P)$. □

To construct the abstract net $\mathfrak{N}[\![P]\!]$ we proceed as follows : first decompose P to yield dex(P) as initial marking, then starting from dex(P) explore all transitions that are successively applicable, and finally forget the particular names, here the sequential components, of places.

Example. In the following examples, however, these names are kept as an explanation of how the net was obtained.

(1) $a.\mathit{stop}:\{a\} \parallel b.\mathit{stop}:\{b\}$

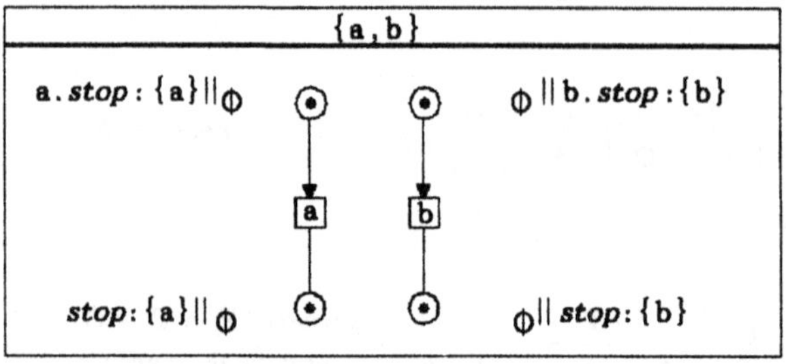

(2) $a.b.\mathit{stop}:\{a,b\} + b.a.\mathit{stop}:\{a,b\}$

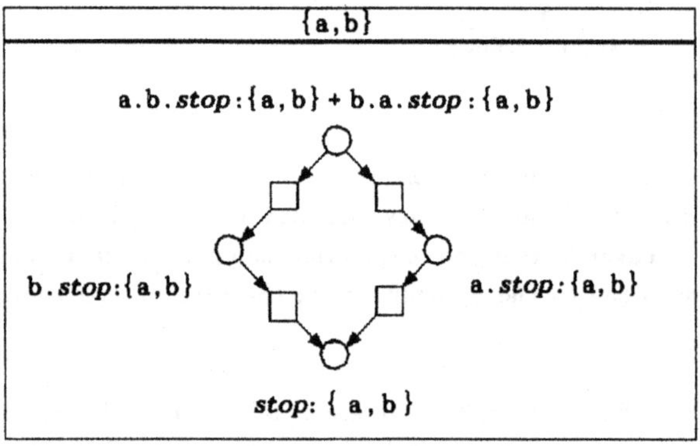

(3) $(a.\mathit{stop}:\{a,c\} \parallel b.\mathit{stop}:\{b,c\}) + c.\mathit{stop}:\{a,b,c\}$

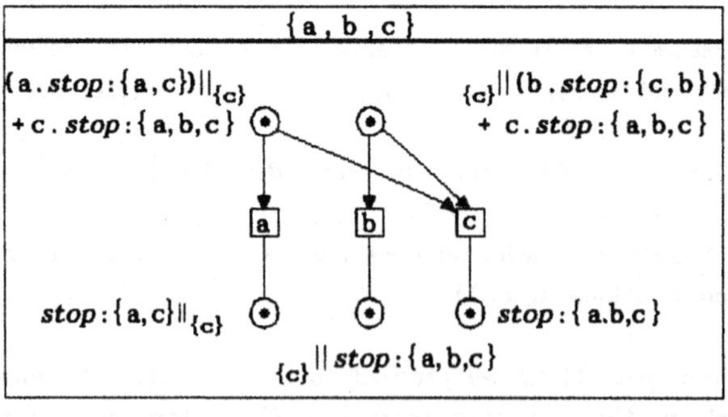

Here the preset of the transition labelled with c is $Q + c.\mathit{stop}:\{c\}$ where

$$Q = \{a.\mathit{stop}:\{a\} \parallel_{\Phi} ,\ _{\Phi}\parallel b.\mathit{stop}:\{b\}\}$$

is a complete set of sequential components. Note that by adding a choice of c the concurrency of a and b is preserved.

(4) a.b.c.*stop* : { a, b, c } || d.b.e.*stop* : { d, b, e }

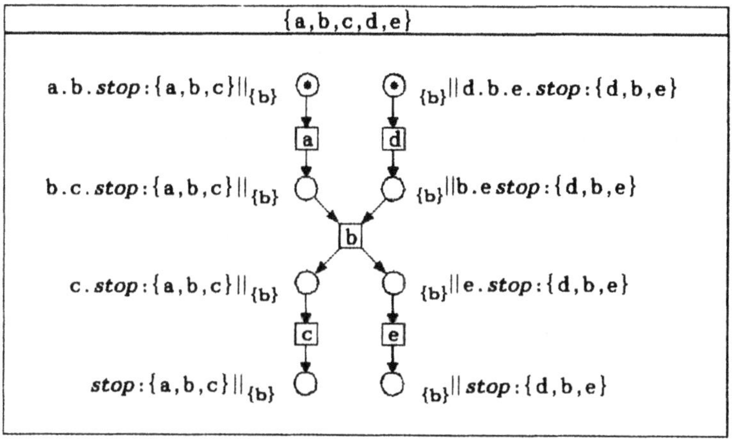

(5) $\mu X.a.b.X$ with $\alpha(X) = \{a,b\}$

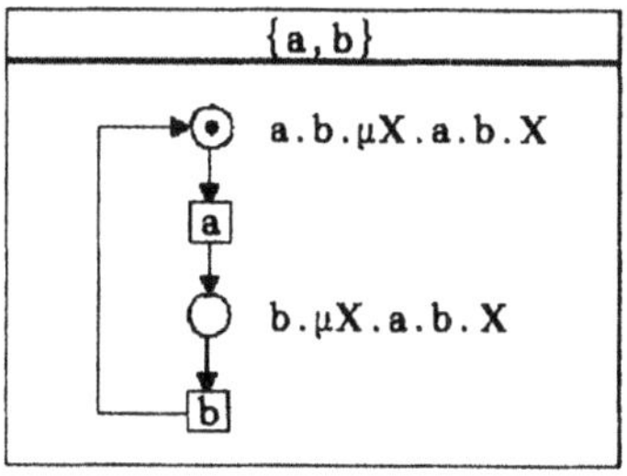

□

We conclude this section by stating the following property of the above nets semantics which is proved in [Ol 89].

Safeness Theorem. For every closed process term P the abstract net $\mathfrak{N}[\![P]\!]$ is safe. □

6. COMPOSITIONAL NET SEMANTICS

To show that our operational Petri net semantics satisfies the Compositionality Principle, we will first introduce the standard compositional net operators $op_{\mathfrak{N}}$.

Definition. Given an n-ary operator symbol op of CProc the corresponding net operator $op_{\mathfrak{N}}$ is a mapping

$$op_{\mathfrak{N}} : \underbrace{ANet \times \ldots \times ANet}_{n \text{ times}} \longrightarrow ANet$$

on abstract nets which is defined with the help of certain representatives in the isomorphism classes of abstract nets:

(1) *Deadlock.* For an arbitrary place p let

$$stop\colon A_{\mathfrak{N}} = [(A, \{p\}, \Phi, \{p\})].$$

(2) *Divergance.* For an arbitrary place p let

$$div\colon A_{\mathfrak{N}} = [\,(A, \{p\}, \{(\{p\}, \tau, \{p\})\}, \{p\}].$$

(3) *Prefix.* For $\mathfrak{N}_0 = (A_0, Pl_0, \longrightarrow_0, M_0)$ and $p \notin Pl_0$ let

$$a._{\mathfrak{N}} [\mathfrak{N}_0] = [(A_0 \cup \{a\}, Pl_0 \cup \{p\}, \longrightarrow, M_0)]$$

where $\longrightarrow\; = \;\longrightarrow_0 \cup \{(\{p\}, a, M_0)\}$.

(4) *Parallelism.* For $\mathfrak{N}_i = (A_i, Pl_i, \longrightarrow_i, M_{0i})$, $i = 1,2$, with $Pl_1 \cap Pl_2 = \Phi$ let

$$[\mathfrak{N}_1] \parallel_{\mathfrak{N}} [\mathfrak{N}_2] = [(A_1 \cup A_2, Pl_1 \cup Pl_2, \longrightarrow, M_{01} \cup M_{02})]$$

where
$$\begin{aligned}\longrightarrow\; = \;& \{\,(I,u,O) \in \longrightarrow_1 \cup \longrightarrow_2 \;|\; u \notin A_1 \cap A_2 \,\} \\ \cup\; & \{\,(I_1 \cup I_2, a, O_1 \cup O_2) \;|\; a \in A_1 \cap A_2 \text{ and } \\ & \quad (I_1, a, O_1) \in \longrightarrow_1 \text{ and } (I_2, a, O_2) \in \longrightarrow_2 \,\}\end{aligned}$$

(5) *Choice:* For $\mathfrak{N}_i = (A_i, Pl_i, \longrightarrow_i, M_{0i})$, $i = 1,2$, with $Pl_1 \cap Pl_2 = \Phi$ let

$$[\mathfrak{N}_1] +_{\mathfrak{N}} [\mathfrak{N}_2] = [(A_1 \cup A_2, Pl_1 \cup Pl_2 \cup (M_{01} \times M_{02}), \longrightarrow, M_{01} \times M_{02})$$

where
$$\begin{aligned}\longrightarrow\; = \;& \{\,((I_1 \times M_{02}) \cup I_2, u, O) \;|\; I_1 \subseteq M_{01} \text{ and } I_1 \cap I_2 = \Phi \\ & \qquad \text{and } (I_1 \cup I_2, u, O) \in \longrightarrow_1 \,\} \\ \cup\; & \{\,(I_1 \cup (M_{01} \times I_2)), u, O) \;|\; I_2 \subseteq M_{02} \text{ and } I_1 \cap I_2 = \Phi \\ & \qquad \text{and } (I_1 \cup I_2, u, O) \in \longrightarrow_2 \,\}\end{aligned}$$

(6) *Morphism.* For $\mathfrak{N}_0 = A_0, Pl_0, \longrightarrow_0, M_0)$ let

$$[\mathfrak{N}_0][\varphi]_{\mathfrak{N}} = [(\varphi A_0) - \{\tau\}, Pl_0, \longrightarrow, M_0)]$$

where $\longrightarrow\; = \{\,(I, \varphi(u), O) \;|\; (I, u, O) \in \longrightarrow_0 \,\}$

□

The operators are well-defined because for every abstract net we can find a representative satisfying the disjointness requirement and because the resulting abstract net is independent of the particular choice of this representive. Except for choice, the effect of these operators should be easy to understand. For example, prefix $a._{\mathfrak{N}}$ creates a new place as initial marking and links it via an a-transition to all places of the old initial marking. Parallel composition $\|_{\mathfrak{N}}$ puts the nets side by side and for transitions with the same action label takes the union of their individual pre- and postsets. In this way synchronisation is enforced.

The definition of $+_{\mathfrak{N}}$ is new and inspired by the transition rule for choice in Section 5: it combines the standard choice operator of [GM 84, Wi 84] with the idea of *root unwinding* due to [GV 87]. Root unwinding ensures that there are no cycles left at initially marked places. Only for such nets the operator of [GM 84, Wi 84] is applicable; it then uses a cartesian product construction to introduce choices between all pairs of initial transitions of the two nets involved. For example, we obtain:

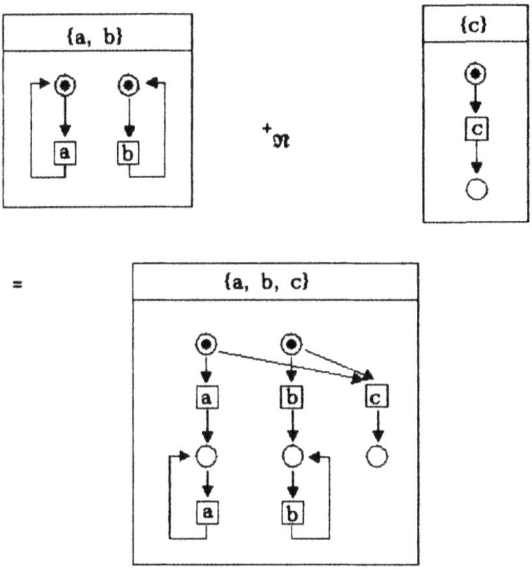

Actually, the definition of $+_{\mathfrak{N}}$ creates statically unreachable places which can be ignored modulo weak isomorphism. Hence they are not shown in the resulting net above.

The net operators respect strong bisimilarity on safe nets [Ol 89].

Congruence Theorem. (1) The net operators $a._{\mathfrak{N}}$, $\|_{\mathfrak{N}}$, $+_{\mathfrak{N}}$ and $[\varphi]_{\mathfrak{N}}$ preserve safeness.
(2) On safe abstract nets strong bisimilarity $\approx$ is a *congruence* with respect to the above net operators, i.e. whenever $[\mathfrak{N}_1] \approx [\mathfrak{N}_1'], \ldots, [\mathfrak{N}_n] \approx [\mathfrak{N}_1']$ for safe abstract nets then also

$$op_{\mathfrak{N}}([\mathfrak{N}_1], \ldots, [\mathfrak{N}_n]) \approx op_{\mathfrak{N}}([\mathfrak{N}_1'], \ldots, [\mathfrak{N}_n']).$$

for these operators. □

7. COMPARISON

We now compare the operational and compositional net semantics and show that the second principle for a good net semantics stated in Section 1 is obeyed.

Compositionality Theorem. For all n-ary operator symbols op of CProc and all process terms $P_1, \ldots, P_n, \mu X.P \in$ CProc

(1) $$\mathfrak{N}[\![op(P_1, \ldots, P_n)]\!] \approx op_{\mathfrak{N}}(\mathfrak{N}[\![P_1]\!], \ldots, \mathfrak{N}[\![P_n]\!]) ,$$

(2) $$\mathfrak{N}[\![\mu X.P]\!] \approx \mathfrak{N}[\![P\{\mu X.P/X\}]\!].$$

In fact, equality holds in (2) and in (1) except for op = a. and op = +.

Proof. The μ-expansion law (2) follows from the definition of the mapping dex(·). The compositionality laws (1) with equality obvious hold for

$$op \in \{stop{:}A,\ div{:}A,\ [\varphi] \mid A \text{ communication alphabet, } \varphi \text{ action morphism}\}.$$

Thus we are left with the following cases:

$$op \in \{\ a.,\ \|,\ + \mid a \text{ communication}\}$$

We shall deal here with the most difficult case, viz. op = +. Thus we wish to show

$$\mathfrak{N}[\![P_1 + P_2]\!] = \mathfrak{N}[\![P_1]\!] +_{\mathfrak{N}} \mathfrak{N}[\![P_2]\!]$$

for all $P_1, P_2 \in$ CProc. Let $A = \alpha(P_1) = \alpha(P_2)$ and consider

$$\mathfrak{N}_i = (A,\ Sequ,\ \longrightarrow\restriction A,\ dex(P_i)$$

for i = 1,2 and

$$\mathfrak{N} = (A,\ Sequ,\ \longrightarrow\restriction A,\ dex(P_1 + P_2)).$$

Since $place(\mathfrak{N}_1) \cap place(\mathfrak{N}_2) \neq \emptyset$ is possible, e.g. for P_1 = a.c.*stop*: {a,b,c} and P_2 = b.c.*stop*: {a,b,c}, we have in general

$$\mathfrak{N}[\![P_1 + P_2]\!] \neq \mathfrak{N}[\![P_1]\!] +_{\mathfrak{N}} \mathfrak{N}[\![P_2]\!] ,$$

but we will show that this difference is only modulo ≈. To this end, we create for every sequential component C two new copies denoted by C+ and +C. These are used to build two disjoint copies of $\mathfrak{N}_1$ and $\mathfrak{N}_2$ as required for applying $+_{\mathfrak{N}}$, viz.

$$\mathfrak{N}_{11} = (A,\ Sequ+,\ \longrightarrow_{11},\ dex(P_1)+)$$

where

$$\longrightarrow_{11} = \{(\mathbb{P}+,\ u,\ Q+) \mid \mathbb{P} \xrightarrow{u} Q \text{ and } u \in A \cup \{\tau\}\}$$

and

$$\mathfrak{N}_{21} = (A,\ +Sequ,\ \longrightarrow_{21},\ +dex(P_2))$$

where

$$\longrightarrow_{21} = \{(+\mathbb{P}, u, +Q) \mid \mathbb{P} \xrightarrow{u} Q \text{ and } u \in A \cup \{\tau\}\}.$$

Obviously

$$[\mathfrak{N}_1] = [\mathfrak{N}_{11}] \text{ and } [\mathfrak{N}_2] = [\mathfrak{N}_{21}].$$

Second, we introduce a version $\mathfrak{N}_0$ of the net $\mathfrak{N}$ with completely new transitions in it.

$$\mathfrak{N}_0 = (A, \text{Sequ} \cup \text{Sequ+} \cup \text{+Sequ}, \longrightarrow_0, \text{dex}(P+Q))$$

where

$$\longrightarrow_0 = \{(Q_1+ \cup (Q_2+ \text{dex}(P_2)), u, \mathbb{R}+) \mid Q_1 \cup Q_2 \xrightarrow{u} \mathbb{R}$$
$$\text{with } Q_1 \cap Q_2 = \emptyset \text{ and } u \in A \cup \{\tau\} \}$$
$$\cup \{((\text{dex}(P_1) + Q_1) \cup +Q_2, u, +\mathbb{R}) \mid Q_1 \cup Q_2 \xrightarrow{u} \mathbb{R}$$
$$\text{with } Q_1 \cap Q_2 = \emptyset \text{ and } u \in A \cup \{\tau\} \}.$$

In $\longrightarrow_0$ the transitions for choice keep track whether the left-hand or right-hand side of + was chosen. By the definition of $+_{\mathfrak{N}}$ and weak isomorphism, we realise:

$$[\mathfrak{N}_0] = [\mathfrak{N}_{11}] +_{\mathfrak{N}} [\mathfrak{N}_{21}].$$

It remains to show

$$\mathfrak{N} \approx \mathfrak{N}_0.$$

Consider the relation $\mathfrak{B} \subseteq \text{Sequ} \times (\text{Sequ} \cup \text{Sequ+} \cup \text{+Sequ})$ defined as follows:

$$\mathfrak{B} = id_{\text{Sequ}} \cup \{(C,C+) , (C,+C) \mid C \in \text{Sequ} \}.$$

$\mathfrak{B}$ is a strong bisimulation between $\mathfrak{N}$ and $\mathfrak{N}_0$. This is easily established by observing that every reachable marking of $\mathfrak{N}_0$ is either of the form

$$\{C_1+, \ldots, C_m+\} \cup (\{C_{m+1}, \ldots, C_{m+n}\} + \text{dex}(P_2))$$

or

$$\{+C_1, \ldots, +C_m\} \cup (\text{dex}(P_1) + \{C_{m+1}, \ldots, C_{m+n}\}).$$

The corresponding markings of $\mathfrak{N}$ are obtained by dropping the mary +'s. By the transition relation of $\mathfrak{N}$ and $\mathfrak{N}_0$, every transition of $\mathfrak{N}$ can be matched by a corresponding transition of $\mathfrak{N}_0$ and vice versa as required for the transfer property of $\mathfrak{B}$. Summarising, we obtain

$$\mathfrak{N}[\![P_1+P_2]\!] = [\mathfrak{N}] \approx [\mathfrak{N}_0] = [\mathfrak{N}_{11}] +_{\mathfrak{N}} [\mathfrak{N}_{21}] = \mathfrak{N}[\![P_1]\!] +_{\mathfrak{N}} \mathfrak{N}[\![P_2]\!].$$

This finishes the proof of the Compositionality Theorem. □

It may seem as a shortcoming of our operational Petri net semantics that we can show compositionality only modulo strong bisimilarity. But in fact, it is an advantage because by this deviation from the standard net operators our operational semantics yields finite nets for all regular process terms (cf. [Ol 89]). By contrast, equality

$$\mathfrak{N}[\![\mu X.a.X]\!] = \mathfrak{N}[\![a.\mu X.a.X]\!] = a._{\mathfrak{N}}\ \mathfrak{N}[\![\mu X.a.X]\!]$$

would force $\mathfrak{N}[\![\mu X.a.X]\!]$ to be infinite because the net operator $a._{\mathfrak{N}}$ always creates a completely new initial place. Thus strong bisimilarity allows a greater flexibility for the net semantics. On the other hand, it is strong enough to preserve concurrency. We have shown this in the Causality Theorem.

8. REFERENCES

[Be 87] E. Best, COSY: its relation to nets and CSP, in: W. Brauer, W. Reisig, G. Rozenberg (Eds.), Petri Nets: Applications and Relationships to Other Models of Concurrency, Lecture Notes in Comput. Sci. 255 (Springer-Verlag, 1987) 416-440.

[BHR 84] S.D. Brookes, C.A.R. Hoare, A.W. Roscoe, A theory of communicating sequential processes, J. ACM 31 (1984) 560-599.

[By 86] M. Broy, Process semantics of communicating concurrent processes, Bericht MIP-8602, Fak. Math. u. Inform., Univ. Passau,1986.

[DDM 87a] P. Degano, R. DeNicola, U. Montanari, CCS is an (augmented) contact-free C/E system, in: M. Venturini Zilli (Ed.), Math. Models for the Semantics of Parallelism, Lecture Notes in Comput. Sci. 280 (Springer-Verlag, 1987) 144-165.

[DDM 87b] P. Degano, R. DeNicola, U. Montanari, A distributed operational semantics for CCS based on condition/event systems, Nota Interna B4-21, Dept. Comput. Sci., Univ. of Pisa, 1987 (to appear in Acta Inform.).

[DDM 88] P. Degano, R. DeNicola, U. Montanari, On the consistency of "truly concurrent" operational and denotational semantics, in: Proc. Logics in Computer Science '88, Edinburgh, 1988.

[DM 87] P. Degano, U. Montanari, Concurrent histories: a basis for observing distributed systems, J. Comput. Syt. Sci. 34 (1987) 442-461.

[GV 87] R.J. van Glabbeek, F.W. Vaandrager, Petri net models for algebraic theories of concurrency, in: J.W. de Bakker; A.J. Nijman, P.C. Treleaven (Eds.), Proc. PARLE Conf., Eindhoven, Vol. II, Lecture Notes in Comput. Sci. 259 (Springer-Verlag, 1987) 224-242.

[GM 84] U. Goltz, A. Mycroft, On the relationship of CCS and Petri nets, in: J. Paredaens (Ed.), Proc. 11th Coll. Automata, Languages and Programming, Lecture Notes in Comput. Sci. 172 (Springer-Verlag, 1984) 196-208.

[Go 88a] U. Goltz, Über die Darstellung von CCS-Programmen durch Petrinetze, Doctoral Diss., RWTH Aachen, 1988.

[Go 88b] U. Goltz, On representing CCS programs by finite Petri nets, Arbeitspapiere der GMD 290, Gesellschaft Math. Datenverarb., St. Augustin, 1988.

[Ho 85] C.A.R. Hoare, Communicating Sequential Processes (Prentice-Hall, London, 1985).

[LTS 79] P.E. Lauer, P.R. Torrigiani, M.W. Shields, COSY - A system specification language based on paths and processes, Acta Inform. 12 (1979) 109-158.

[Mi 80] R. Milner, A Calculus of Communicating Systems, Lecture Notes in Comput. Sci. 92 (Springer-Verlag, 1980).

[Ol 87] E.-R. Olderog, Operational Petri net semantics for CCSP, in: G. Rozenberg (Ed.), Advances in Petri Nets 1987, Lecture Notes in Comput. Sci. 266 (Springer-Verlag, 1987) 196-223.

[Ol 89] E.-R. Olderog, Nets, terms and formulas: three views of concurrent processes and their relationship (to apear 1989).

[OH 86] E.-R. Olderog, C.A.R. Hoare, Specification-oriented semantics for communicating processes, Acta Inform. 23 (1986) 9-66.

[Pa 81] D. Park, Concurrency and automata on infinite sequences, in: P. Deussen (Ed.), Proc. 5th GI Conf. on Theoret. Comput. Sci., Lecture Notes in Comput. Sci. 104 (Springer-Verlag, 1981).

[Pe 77] C.A. Petri, Non-sequential processes, Internal Report GMD-ISF-77-5 Gesellschaft Math. Datenverarb., St. Augustin, 1977.

[Pl 81] G.D. Plotkin, Structured approach to operational semantics, Tech. Report DAIMI FN-19, Comput. Sci. Dept., Aarhus Univ., 1981.

[Pl 82] G.D. Plotkin, An operational semantics for CSP, in: D. Bjorner (Ed.), Formal Description of Programming Concepts II (North-Holland, Amsterdam, 1982) 199-225.

[Po 85] L. Pomello, Some equivalence notions for concurrent systems - an overview, in: G. Rozenberg (Ed.), Advances in Petri Nets 1985, Lecture Notes in Comput. Sci. 222 (Springer-Verlag, 185) 381-400.

[Re 85] W. Reisig, Petri Nets, An Introduction, EATCS Monographs on Theoret. Comput. Sci. (Springer-Verlag, 1985).

[Ta 87] D. Taubner, Theoretical CSP and formal languages, Bericht TUM-I8706, Inst. f. Inform., TU München, 1987.

[Wi 82] G. Winskel, Event structure semantics of CCS and related languages, in: E.M. Schmidt (Ed.), Proc. 9th Coll. Automata, Languages and Programming, Lecture Notes in Comput. Sci. 140 (Springer-Verlag, 1982).

[Wi 84] G. Winskel, A new definition of morphism on Petri nets, in: M. Fontet, K. Mehlhorn (Eds.), Proc. 1st Symp. Theoret. Aspects of Comput. Sci., Lecture Notes in Comput. Sci. 166 (Springer-Verlag, 1984) 140-150.

[Wi 87] G. Winskel, Event structures, in: W. Brauer, W. Reisig, G. Rozenberg (Eds.), Petri Nets: Application and Relationship to Other Models of Concurrency, Lecture Notes in Comput. Sci. 255 (Springer-Verlag, 1987) 325-392.

Nets of Processes and Data Flow

A. Rabinovich
B. A. Trakhtenbrot

School of Mathematical Sciences
Raymond and Beverly Sackler Faculty of Exact Sciences
Tel-Aviv University
Tel-Aviv, Israel 69978
e.mail: rabino@taurus.bitnet, trakhte@Math.Tau.Ac.IL

Abstract. Nets of Processes provide a unifying approach to semantics of concurrently executing agents. In this framework modularity and Kahn's principle are investigated for Data Flow Networks.

Keywords: Data Flow Computation, Synchronization, Processes, Denotational Semantics, Nondeterminism, Compositionality.

Contents

1. Introduction

A Data Flow Network N [Kahn] exhibits a clear operational semantics which relies on the asynchronous and concurrent firings of its components - the (elementary) computational agents A_i of the net. These agents are **buffered automata** with n input channels, m output channels and they are assumed to compute continuous stream functionals F_{A_i}. Kahn's principle refers to the global behaviour of the net N and claims that under appropriate conditions upon the A_i and upon the topology of N the net N as a whole also computes a functional F_N. Moreover, F_N is the least fixed point solution of a system of equations S which is assembled (in a clear pictorial way) from the component functionals F_{A_i}.

Figure 1 illustrates the situation for a net over agents L, M, N, P. Here S consists of the equations 1)-6) Note, that we use the "circles - boxes" drawing as in Petri Nets, with boxes representing the junctions of the channels.

Brock and Ackerman [BA] observed that in some Data Flow models which are a bit more general than Kahn's original one, modularity and therefore also the fixed point theorem fail. This result is known as the Brock-Ackerman Anomaly.

Recently there has been a proliferation of models for describing concurrent processes; they contrast Interleaving Concurrency with Partial-Order (causal) Concurrency on the one hand and Linear Time with Branching Time on the other hand. Note also that in the theory of processes a general construct "Nets of Processes" did emerge ([Pratt], [TRH]), which makes sense for all these models. In view of this one would like to know how the Kahn and Brock-Ackerman phenomena may be embodied into different models of nets of processes and to what extent do depend the proofs on the choice of the model.

Since Data Flow Nets refer to "computational stations" or "computing automata" there is no wonder that the interleaving and branching model of input-output processes was the first to be considered. In fact the first proofs ([Fa], see also

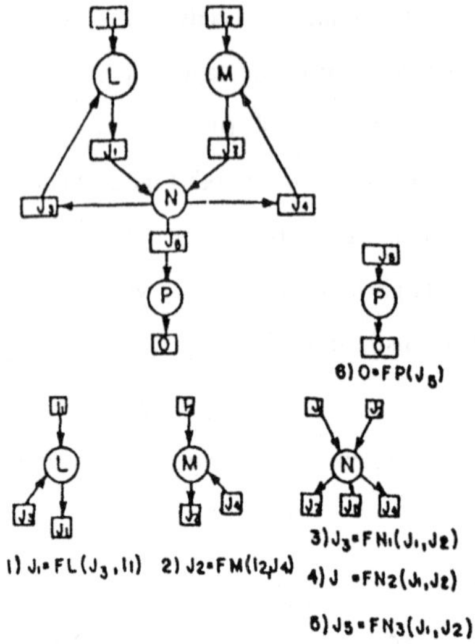

Fig. 1

recently [LS]) in a slightly disguised form deal with what one may call Nets of automata [TRH]. But automata (actually - transition diagrams) represent only one of the known models of process; other three models may be considered as well if one resigns from one or both features: interleaving and branching.

Hence the problem arises: under what conditions does Kahn's principle hold for nets over processes in these three models. In [GP] and [Rab] this problem was investigated for the case of Pomset processes, where each process P is a set of *pomsets* (partial order multisets); here P is intended to capture the causal scenarios, rather then branching time aspects. Indeed, the results look very much like for Kahn's original Data Flow Networks though the techniques are more elaborated. But what about the remaining two extremal cases:

a) The most liberal (linear time). A process is a prefix closed set P of strings.

b) The strongest (integrating both branching and causal aspects). A process is a Behaviour Structure [TRH].

One of our results is that Kahn's principle holds indeed for the Linear Model. The proof is only an adaptation (even a simplified version) of the proof proposed in [Rab] for the Pomset Model. One of the reason we reconsider it here in detail is that we need its analysis to justify the following conclusion:

Kahn's Principle is a linear interleaving phenomenon; its proof for more discriminating models does not require essentially additional techniques.

This is one of the main tasks of this paper. Other two tasks we are concerned with

(1) Recall that Brock and Ackerman argued [BA] the failure of Kahn's Princi-

ple in virtue of the failure of modularity. But is it the case that in order to prove modularity one must rely essentially on the proof of the Kahn Principle for the nets under consideration? We achieved a better understanding of the relation between modularity and the Kahn Principle.

(2) Most of the papers on the subject deal mainly with sufficient conditions which support the Kahn Principle. We show that our conditions are in a natural sense also necessary.

In this paper we deal almost exclusively with the functional (determinate) behaviour of Nets of Processes but we have the strong feeling that our notions and approach may be easily generalized to the nondeterminate case as well. Since we did not have enough time to elaborate the details we confine for the time being with some hints in the text and hope to return to the subject in forthcoming work.

In this sequel the exposition is organized as follows: Section 2 gives the conceptual background for input-output processes and nets of such processes. The main goal is to emphasize the circumstances which do not depend on the choice between alternatives: linear vs branching or interleaving vs partial order. In this way we aim at an unifying treatment of the subject, parametrized by the model of processes to be chosen. At the other hand in the next sections we deal with notions which heavily rely on the chosen model of processes. Therefore we start with the simplest model of linear processes and prepare the background for the main issues we are concerned with. Namely,

Section 4. Modularity Issues for Linear Processes.

Section 5. The Kahn Principle for Linear Processes.

Sections 4 and 5 contain the main technical results of the paper, so let us comment on them in more detail. There is a collision between two basic equivalences for I-O processes one has to consider. The first one $=_{ext}$ *(external equivalence)* amounts to hiding internal communications; actually it is a congruence wrt the net construct. The second one $=_{rel}$ (relational equivalence), which in particular may happen to be functional equivalence $=_{fun}$, is the most relevant from the view of data flow philosophy; the reason is that it deals with the observable input-output behaviour of the processes under considerations. It turns out that $=_{rel}$ is not a congruence wrt to the net construct, i.e. modularity fails for $=_{rel}$. That is an unfortunate circumstance if we regard the class of all nets as a programming language, whose programs compute (or specify) input-output behaviours. The remedy could be to confine with a more restricted but still reasonable class C of nets of processes for which modularity holds. In particular, assume that in C the equivalence $=_{rel}$ coincides with $=_{ext}$; then modularity wrt $=_{rel}$ would be guaranteed due to the status of $=_{ext}$. In Section 4 we show that for "reasonable" classes, there is no other alternative to get modularity. We define also the smoothness property and argue that classes of smooth processes are just the reasonable classes to be considered. Note that for these classes there is a direct proof of modularity without any fixed point arguments.

As a matter of fact for Kahn's fixed point theorem in its classical format to make sense, an additional restriction on the topology of the nets is usually assumed (no confluent output channels), which is not relevant for our analysis of modularity. This observation brings us in Section 5 to the challenge of revising (in fact - generalizing) the Kahn Principle in order to reveal its full connection to communication and process theoretical phenomena. We hope that this approach will be helpful in our forthcoming work on nondeterministic Data Flow.

2. Nets of Processes

2.1. Input-Output Processes

We have in mind four models of processes:

Non branching models: Linear processes and Pomset processes. Here a process is a *prefix closed* set of runs, which are respectively - strings and pomsets.

Branching models: Automata and Behaviour Structure [TRH]. Here a process is an appropriately labeled diagram.

Let us first recall some circumstances which are common to all these models.

1) *Action alphabet.* Each process P is equipped with a set alph(P) - the alphabet of the actions which are available in this process. Note that the runs (or labels) of P use actions only from alph(P), but not necessarily all of them.

2) *Equivalences.* There is a basic equivalence $\equiv$ between processes which may hold only for processes with the same action-alphabet. In the non branching cases equivalence amounts to the coincidence of the sets of runs for the processes under consideration. In the branching cases the labeled diagrams are required to be bissimilar: for automata the well known Milner-Park bissimulation is understood [Mil], whereas for Behaviour Structure there is a more elaborated notion of BS-bissimulation [TRH] [RT].

3) *Synchronization.* This operation is defined for sequences (finite or infinite) of processes; the alphabet of the result is union of the alphabets of the operands. It is *fully compositional* in the following sense:

   a) $Synch(P_1,P_2,...)$ does not depend on the order of the operands.

b) Whatever the disjoint partition of the set $\{P_i\}$ into sequences $seq_1, seq_2, \cdots$ might be, there holds:

$$Synch(P_1,P_2,...) \equiv Synch(Synch(seq_1), Synch(seq_2),...)$$

4) *Congruence* Theorem. Synchronization respects the equivalence $\equiv$:
If $P_i \equiv P_i'$ then $Synch(P_1,P_2,...) \equiv Synch(P_1',P_2',...)$

For Linear processes the definition of synchronization is very simple:

$$s \in Synch(P_1,P_2,...) \text{ iff for all } i \;\; s \,|alph(P_i) \in P_i$$

where $s\,|A$ is the notation for the string one gets from the string s omitting all the actions that are not in A.

For other models of processes the definitions are more elaborated; especially for Behaviour Structures it needs a very detailed and careful formulation [RT].

Input-Output Processes (shortly I-O processes). When dealing with Data Flow one has to be more specific about the action alphabet of the processes. Here are the relevant stipulations:

Communications. The action alphabet is structured as a Cartesian product $CH \times DATA$. An action <ch, d> is said to be a communication through channel ch which passes the data value d. Also a partition of CH into $CHinp$ (input channels), $CHout$ (output channels) and $CHint$ (internal channels) must be explicitly displayed.

We call this partition the *type* of the process. Correspondingly we use the terminology: *external type* (for the ports CHinp $\cup$ CHout), internal type, etc.. It may happen that $DATA$ is unary (consists of one element); usually in this case the data value is omitted, and communications are identified with the channels.

The status of input, output and internal channels will be formalized below in terms of *buffering;* informally it means that each input channel is always ready to absorb information from the environment, that input actions (respectively output actions) on different channels do not depend on each other and that input actions are independent of other actions.

2.2. Nets

Following the terminology of Petri Nets we use the term *Net* for a bipartite (oriented) graph with nodes of two kinds, pictured as circles and boxes and called respectively places and ports. The difference between the two kinds is relevant for the notion of subnet. A subgraph N' of N is considered to be a subnet if the set of its nodes consists of *some* places and of *all* ports which are adjacent to these places. In particular an *atomic subnet* contains a single place and all its neighboring ports. This is to be contrasted with an *atomic bunch* which contains a single port and all its neighboring places.

The following conditions are assumed:

No small loops (as in figures 2 a-b-c) are allowed.

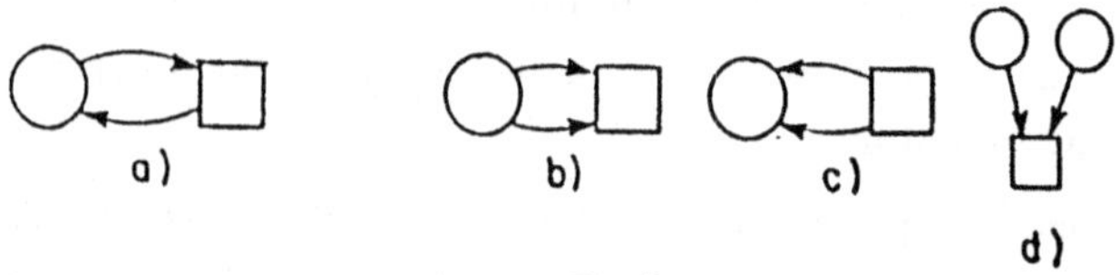

Fig. 2

The set of ports (boxes) of a net N is partitioned as follows:

(i) *Input ports.* Only exiting arrows - allowed.

(ii) *Output ports.* A single entering arrow allowed; no exiting arrows.

(iii) *Internal ports.* All the other.

A net of processes is an appropriately labeled net, that is a pair $<N,\psi>$ where N is a net and ψ is a labeling function which satisfies the following conditions:

a) ψ assigns to each port a channel name; different ports get different channel names

b) ψ assigns to each place p a process $P=\psi(p)$ in such a way that

  (i) The input and output channels of P coincide with the port names in the atomic subnet p. Moreover, input (output) channels of P corresponds to ports from which (to which) an arrow is directed to (from) p.

  (ii) For each $p \neq p'$ among the channels of $\psi(p')$ there is none which is internal to $\psi(p)$.

Finally, as semantics (behaviour) of $<N,\psi>$ one declares the following I-O process (notation - $S(N,\psi)$):

(1) As a process $S(N,\psi)$ is the synchronization of all the $\psi(p)$, $p \in N$.

(ii) Its input and output channels are respectively the labels of the input ports and the labels of the output ports of N.

Inheritance. We say that a property H of processes is inherited by nets if for each N, ψ the condition:

For all p in N $\psi(p)$ has property H

implies:

$$S(N,\ \psi) \text{ has the property H}$$

A relation R between processes is inherited by nets iff for each N, ψ_1, ψ_2 the condition:

$$\text{For all } p \text{ in } N \quad \psi_1(p) R \psi_2(p)$$

implies:

$$S(N,\ \psi_1) R S(N,\ \psi_2)$$

In particular if R is an equivalence relation - inheritance by nets means that R is a congruence wrt the net construct.

Most of the technical results in this sequel amount to the clarification if a given property (relation) is inherited or is not inherited by nets.

2.3. Net-Contexts

The definition is the same as for nets of processes except that the labeling function ψ is partial, namely some places (the "holes" of the context) are unlabeled. For a context $N[\ ]$ with one hole, $N[P]$ is the net of processes which arises when the hole is labeled by P. Clearly, this makes sense when the external type of P fits the type of the hole. Here (see Fig. 3) is an example, we shall refer to later: This is a very simple context with one hole. Note that there is an unique output port T and no input ports. Compare also the type $<I_1,...,I_n;\ O_1,...,O_m>$ of the hole with the type $<O_1,...,O_m;\ I_1,...,I_n,\ T>$ of the component R. Of course, we can parametrize also wrt the place p' and consider the context with two holes; we shall refer later to this specific context as to $Cont[p'][p]$.

After this survey we have to consider phenomena for which the peculiarities of the process model under consideration become relevant. We start in the next section with details concerning the "lowest" model of linear processes. The way how these things may (or should) be adapted for "higher" models will be discussed later in Section 6.

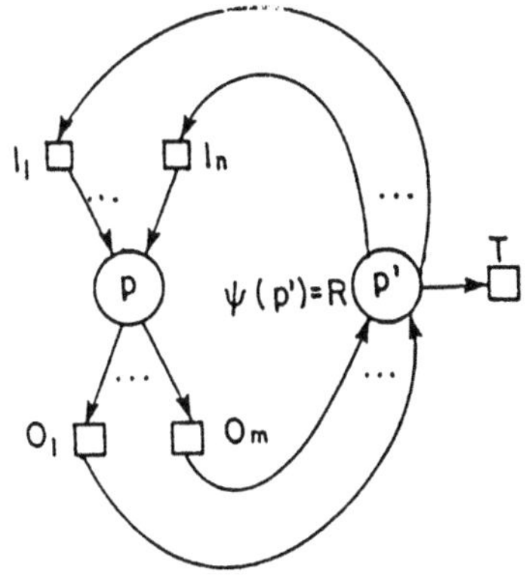

Fig. 3

3. I-O Linear Processes

Without lost of generality we assume below that $DATA$ is fixed, so we have only to specify the types of the processes under consideration. If $CHinp=\{I_1,...,I_n\}$ and $CHout=\{O_1,...,O_m\}$ we refer to the process as to a $(I_1,...,I_n;\ O_1,...,O_m)$-process. In the case when there are no internal channels at all that will be explicitly mentioned. A linear I-O process is a prefix closed set of finite communication strings and this strings inherit the type of the process. In other words, everywhere below when a string is considered it is assumed that it is equipped with a type of channels; again often we refer only to the external channels of the type.

3.1. External and Relational Equivalences and Approximations

First agree about the following notations and terminology.

(i) For a string s and a subset CH' of the set of channels let $s\,|CH'$ be the string which results when all the communications through channels not in CH' are deleted from s. In particular $s\,|ext=_{def} s\,|(CHinp \bigcup CHout)$.
Define external equivalence of strings:

$$s_1=_{ext}s_2 \text{ iff } s_1\,|ext=s_2\,|ext.$$

Accordingly we write $x\in_{ext}P$ if x is externally equivalent to a string in P.
For I-O processes P_1, P_2 the relation $P_1=_{ext}P_2$ (external equivalence of processes) holds iff they have the same external type and

$$\{s\,|ext:\ s\in P_1\}=\{s\,|ext:\ s\in P_2\} \qquad (*)$$

$P_1\leq_{ext}P_2$ (P_1 externally approximate P_2) holds iff $(*)$ is replaced by:

$$\{s\,|ext:\ s\in P_1\}\subset\{s\,|ext:\ s\in P_2\} \qquad (**)$$

From the definitions obviously follows

Claim 1. The relations $\leq_{ext}$ and $=_{ext}$ are inherited by nets.

(ii) For a string s and a sequence $\vec{CH}=(ch_1,..., ch_k)$ of channels stream$(s, \vec{CH})$ is the sequence $<s\,|ch_1,...,s\,|ch_k>$.

Now, we define the relational behaviour rel(P) of a I-O process P, relational equivalence $=_{rel}$, and relational approximation $\leq_{rel}$ for processes:

$$\text{rel}(s)=<\text{stream}(s, \vec{I}), \text{stream}(s, \vec{O})>$$

$$\text{rel}(P)=\{\text{rel}(s) : s\in P\}$$

$$P_1=_{rel}P_2 \text{ iff rel}(P_1)=\text{rel}(P_2)$$

$$P_1\leq_{rel}P_2 \text{ iff rel}(P_1)\subset \text{rel}(P_2)$$

Obviously $=_{ext}$ implies $=_{rel}$ and $\leq_{ext}$ implies $\leq_{rel}$.

It is very important to contrast Claim 1 with

Claim 2. The equivalence $=_{rel}$ (and hence also $\leq_{rel}$) is not inherited by nets.

This fact, which is known as the Brock-Ackerman Anomaly, is the source of most of the problems we are faced with in the paper. We postpone the proof (via counterexample) to the Section 4, after the definition of some appropriate processes.

3.2. Buffered Processes

Definition : A process $P(I_1,...,I_n, O_1,...,O_m)$ without internal channels is buffered iff whenever $s \in P$, P contains also the strings one may construct via the following "buffering" operations.

a) *Input extension.* Extend s appending to the right arbitrary many input communications.

b) *Input (output) permutation.* In the string $a_1 \cdots a_k a_{k+1} \cdots$ permute the adjacent a_k, a_{k+1} if they are both input (output) communications which refer to different channels.

c) *Input anticipation.* Permute the adjacent a_k, a_{k+1} whenever a_{k+1} is an input communication and a_k is an output communication.

A process with internal channels is buffered iff it is externally equivalent to a process without internal channels.

Examples of buffered processes.

1) *Buffers.* buf(I;O) is a process with no internal channels, with a single input channel I and a single output channel O; it is required that for each $s \in$ buf(I;O) there holds: the stream of data through O is a prefix of the stream of data through I.

2) *Buffering Closures.* A standard way to produce buffered processes is to start with an arbitrary given I-O process P and then to construct its closure Buf(P) under the buffering operations: input extension, input (output) permutation and input anticipation. It is now an easy exercise to check that Buf(P) is externally equivalent to the net N_P (see Fig. 4) where P' is the result of relabeling P ("priming" its channels) and where the other component are appropriate buffers.

This remark is useful in justifying that some manipulations with nets over buffered processes are $=_{ext}$ transformations, i.e. they produce a net which is external equivalent to the original one. Fig. 5 presents the following illustrations:

a) A chain of buffers is $=_{ext}$ to buffer.

b) Appending an input buffer to a "fork" of buffers is a $=_{ext}$ transformation.

c) A buffered process P is externally equivalent to the net N_P (see Fig. 4).

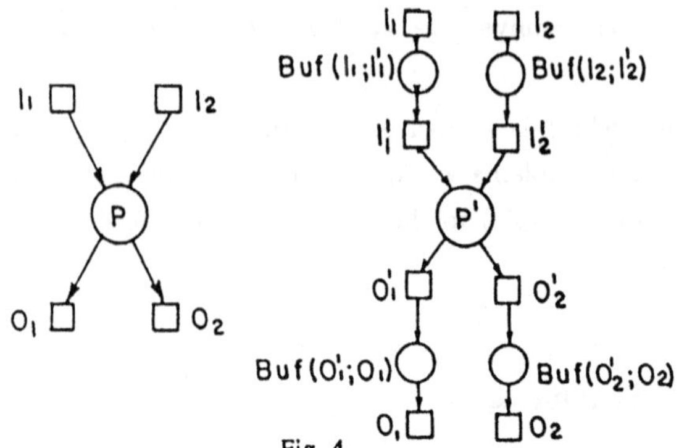

Fig. 4

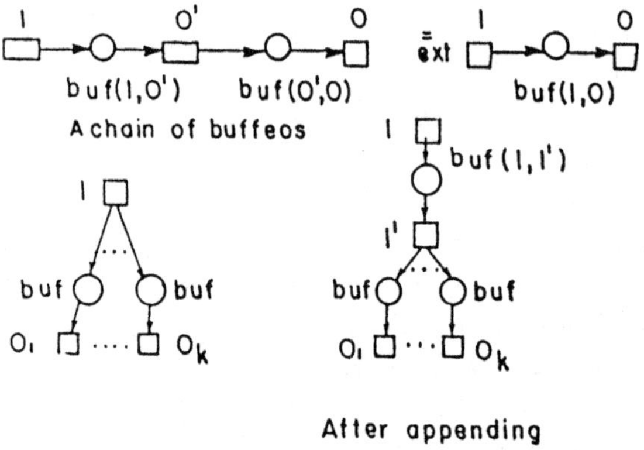

Fig. 5

3) *Rudimentary Processes.* Given an external channel type, say $(I_1,\ldots,I_n;\ O_1,\ldots,O_m)$, let s be a string of communications with (some of) these channels (note: no internal channels are involved). Construct first the process P_s which consists of all prefixes of s, and then the buffering closure Buf(P_s). An I-O process will be called ***rudimentary*** if it can be produced in this way.

4) *The process Ex_4.* Later we shall make use of the following example: Consider the pair of strings {IOO, O}. Closing them under prefixing and after then under buffering operations we get the buffered process Ex_4. Note that the only deviation from rudimentary processes is only in that we started with a pair of strings instead of a single string.

Returning to the general notion of buffered processes let us emphasize the following

Claim 3. Bufferness of processes is inherited by nets.

Proof: Given a net N of buffered processes. Apply equivalence transformation c) to each process of the net, and then apply equivalence transformation b) to the input ports of the resulting net. The net N' obtained after these transformations is externally equivalent to the net N, and it is buffered. Figure 6 illustrate the transformations .

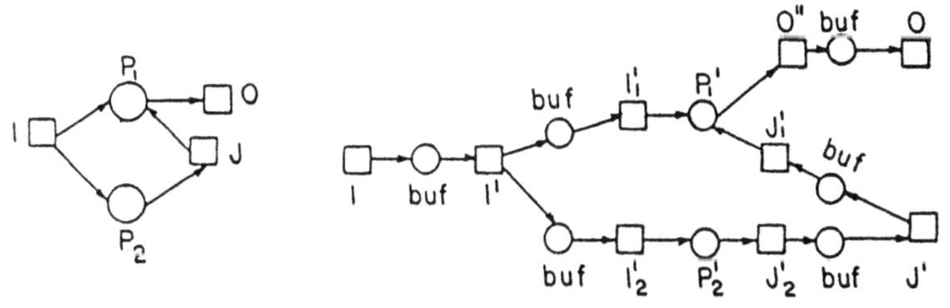

Fig. 6

From now on under process we have in mind a buffered (linear) I-O process.

3.3. Relational Behaviour vs Functional Behaviour

We are going to consider the case when the relational behaviour rel(P) of an I-O process is in fact functional. To this end we introduce and discuss some notations and terminology.

Consider $\overline{D}$ - the set of all finite and infinite strings over $DATA$, including the empty string. The relation $x \leq y$ "x is a prefix of y" is a partial order and obviously $<\overline{D}, \leq>$ is a complete partial order (CPO); we call it data-stream domain. Cartesian Powers of data-stream domains $<\overline{D}^n, \leq_n>$ are also CPO's. We can deal with monotonic and continuous functions from $<\overline{D}^n, \leq_n>$ into $<\overline{D}^m, \leq_m>$.

Clearly, each such function may be considered as m-tuple $f_1, \ldots, f_m$ of the respective monotonic and continuous functions from $<\overline{D}^n, \leq_n>$ into $<\overline{D}, \leq>$.

Yet in our process framework it is more convenient to deal with streams of communications than with streams of data. Therefore we adapt the notions above to streams of communications, called in the sequel simply "streams" (assuming that $DATA$ are fixed). For each channel ch let $[ch]$ be the set of all streams over ch. Similary, for a family CH of channels let $[CH]$ be the set of all tuples of streams, so that in a tuple each channel is presented by one stream. Partial order, continuity, etc. as defined for data-domains are obviously carried away upon domains of communication-streams.

A process P is said to be unambiguous if it satisfies the following *unambiguity* property:

Definition 2 (Unambiguity). Assume that $\xi_1 \in P$, $\xi_2 \in P$ and that for each input channel I the string $\xi_1\lceil I$ is consistent (in the sense of order on streams) with the string $\xi_2\lceil I$; then for each output channel O it is also the case that $\xi_1\lceil O$ is consistent with $\xi_2\lceil O$ and therefore sup($\xi_1\lceil O$, $\xi_2\lceil O$) exists.

It is evident from the definition that if P is unambiguous so is every process Q which is external equivalent to P.

If a process $P(I_1,...,I_n;\ O_1,...,O_m)$ is unambiguous and buffered the relational behaviour rel(P) induces actually a functional behaviour fun(P) as follows:

For a given n-tuple of streams $\vec{\sigma}=\sigma_1, \ldots, \sigma_n$, define fun(P)($\vec{\sigma}$) as the supremum over all m-tuples $\vec{\tau}=\tau_1, \ldots, \tau_m$ such that rel(P)($\vec{\sigma}$, $\vec{\tau}$) holds.

It is easy to check that the definition is correct and that fun(P) is indeed continuous; fun(P) is said to be specified by P.

Unambiguity seems to be the minimal condition to be imposed on a process P one would agree to consider as specifying a function.

Referring to the examples above it is easily seen that buffers, rudimentary processes and Ex_4 are actually unambiguous and buffered; they specify continuous stream functional. In particular the functional f=fun(Ex_4) acts as follows

$$f(\epsilon)=O$$

$$f(t)=OO \text{ for each non empty stream}$$

Clearly a buffer computes the identity function.

Let us call a functional *rudimentary* if it is the behaviour of a rudimentary process. Rudimentary functions have a lot of nice properties: they are effectively (i.e. algorithmically) computable, sequential and finite (in the sense of [KP],[Tra]). Moreover, every continuous stream function is the supremum of countable set of rudimentary functions. In Kahn's original model rudimentary functions are computed by very simple automata. That is best illustrated by the following example. Consider the rudimentary process generated by the sequence

$\langle I_1, 0\rangle\langle O, 1\rangle\langle O, 2\rangle\langle I_2, 2\rangle\langle O,3\rangle$.

Then the Kahn automaton acts as follows:

(1) Wait I_1;

(2) if I_1 different from 0 then Stop;

(3) output on O the daton 1;

(4) output on O the daton 2;

(5) Wait I_2;

(6) if I_2 different from 2 then Stop;

(7) output on O the daton 3;

(8) Stop.

Claim 4: Unambiguity is inherited by nets.

Proof: Easy follows from the following

Lemma. Consider a net $<N, \psi>$ over unambiguous processes. Assume that c is an output or internal port of the net and that s, $t \in S(N, \psi)$ are strings with consistent inputs (i.e. stream(s, $\vec{I}$) is consistent with stream(t, $\vec{I}$)). Then $s|c$ is consistent with $t|c$.

Proof. By induction on the length of s (whereas t is considered fixed).

Basis: $s=\epsilon$. Nothing to prove.

Otherwise s may be represented as $s=_{def} s_1<ch,d>$ where obviously the conditions of the lemma hold also for the pair s_1, t. We prove that $s|c$ is consistent with $t|c$, by cases.

Case 1: $ch \neq c$

Since s_1 is a prefix of s and the strings s, t are input consistent it follows that s_1 and t are input consistent as well; hence by the inductive hypothesis $s_1|c$ is consistent with $t|c$. At the other hand since $ch \neq c$ it follows that $s_1|c=s|c$; therefore $s|c$ is consistent with $t|c$.

Case 2: $ch=c$ and therefore ch is an output or internal port of the net.

In this case there exists a place p for which c is an output port. We introduce the notations (see Fig. 7)

(1) $input(p)$ - the set of input ports of p

(2) $P=\psi(p)$ - the process label of p.

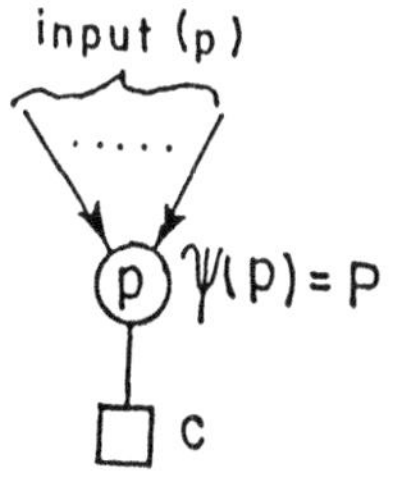

Fig. 7

Now consider the strings s', t'

(3) $s' =_{def} s|alph(P)$, $t' =_{def} t|alph(P)$

By these definitions the following equalities hold:

(4) $s|input(p)=s'|input(p)$, $t|input(p)=t'|input(p)$, $t'|c=t|c$, $s|c=s'|c$

Moreover, by the definition of synchronization

(5) $s' \in P$, $t' \in P$

Since there is no small loops in the net it follows that $c \notin input(p)$ and therefore

(6) $\quad s_1|I \Rightarrow s|I$ for each $I \in input(p)$

By the inductive hypothesis about the pair s_1, t consistency holds for the pairs $s_1|I$, $t|I$ where $I \in input(p)$; hence by (6)

(7) $\quad s|I$ is consistent with $t|I$ for each $I \in input(p)$

and by (4)

(8) $\quad s'|I$ is consistent with $t'|I$ for each $I \in input(p)$

P is an unambiguous process with input channels $input(p)$, an output channel c, and $t' \in P$, $s' \in P$. Therefore $t'|c$ is consistent with $s'|c$. Finally by (4) it follows that $s|c$ is consistent with $t|c$.

And this completes the proof of the lemma .

4. Modularity Issues for Buffered Linear Processes

4.1. The Brock-Ackerman Anomaly

Let us proceed with the proof of Claim 2. Consider the process Ex_4 (see Section 3) and the rudimentary process R_1 with one unary input channel I and one unary output channel O generated by the string OIO. Observe that $Ex_4 =_{rel} R_1$ and hence both processes specify the same function. Consider the following nets $<N, \psi_1>$ and $<N, \psi_2>$. N has three places and three ports; O_1 is an output port and the other ports are internal. Further (see also Fig. 8):

$$\psi_1(p_1) = Ex_3 =_{rel} R_1 = \psi_2(p_1)$$
$$\psi_1(p_2) = Buf(O,I) = \psi_2(p_2)$$
$$\psi_1(p_3) = Buf(O,O_1) = \psi_2(p_3)$$

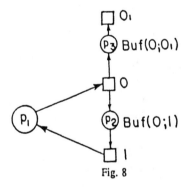

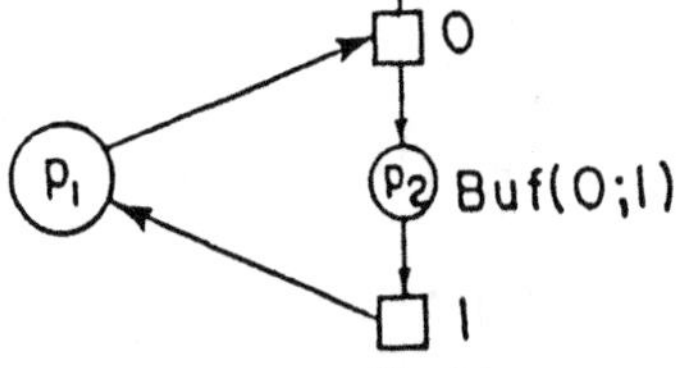

Fig. 8

It may be convenient to refer to these nets of processes in connection with the net-context $N[\ ]$ whose "hole" is the place p_1 and the buffers are assigned to the other places. Namely, $<N, \psi_1>$ and $<N, \psi_2>$ are nothing but $N[Ex_4]$ and $N[R_1]$. Since all the component processes are unambiguous so are the nets $<N,\psi_1>$ and $<N,\psi_1>$; therefore their behaviour is functional. But it is easy to check that $<N,\psi_1> \neq_{rel} <N,\psi_1>$ which implies that $<N,\psi_1> \neq_{fun} <N,\psi_1>$.

4.2. Smooth Processes

In view of the Brock-Ackerman Anomaly let us consider the class of *smooth* I-O processes for which the "anomaly" disappears.

A process P is said to be strong unambiguous if it satisfies the following *strong unambiguity* property.

Definition: (Strong Unambiguity). Assume that $\xi_1 \in P$, $\xi_2 \in P$ and that for each input channel I the string $\xi_1 |I$ is equal to the string $\xi_2 |I$; then for each output channel O there exists $\bar{\xi}$ such that

$$\bar{\xi}\,|ext \text{ extends } \xi_1\,|ext$$
$$\bar{\xi}|O = \sup(\xi_1|O, \xi_2|O)$$
$$\text{and } \bar{\xi}\,|I = \xi_1\,|I \text{ for each input channel I}$$

Finally

Definition (Smoothness). A process P is smooth iff it is both buffered and strong unambiguous.

Note that the Rudimentary processes are smooth.

Claim 5. Smoothness is inherited by nets.

Proof: The proof is similar to the proof of unambiguity and we omit it here.

Claim 6.

(i) (Universality) For each continuous stream functional f there is a smooth process P_f which specifies f.

(ii) P_f is unique up to $=_{ext}$.

(iii) Whatever unambiguous process Q specifies f there holds: $Q \leq_{ext} P_f$.

Proof: Let $CHinp = \{I_1,...,I_n\}$, $Chout = \{O_1,...,O_m\}$. Given a continuous stream function f from $[Chinp]$ to $[Chout]$, we will construct a smooth process P_f of type $(I_1,...,I_n,\ O_1,...,O_m)$ with no internal channels which computes f. We say that a string s is *consistent* with the function f if for each prefix s' of s there holds

$$\text{stream}(s', \vec{O}) \leq \text{f}(\text{stream}(s', \vec{I})) \quad (*)$$

We remark first that each process Q which specifies f consists only of strings consistent with f. Indeed, assume that $fun(Q)$=f and $s \in Q$; then according to the definition of fun (see 3.3) stream$(s, \vec{O}) \leq$f(stream$(s, \vec{I})$). Moreover, since Q is prefix closed each prefix s' of s is also in Q; hence, $(*)$ holds.

Finally, we define P_f as the set of all strings over channels $I_1,...,I_n$, $O_1,...,O_m$ consistent with f.

$$P_f =_{def} \{s\text{: } s \text{ is consistent with f}\}.$$

It is straightforward to check that P_f is smooth and that fun(P_f)=f. Moreover by the previous remark if Q specifies f then $Q \leq_{ext} P_f$.

Now, let us show that if Q is smooth and fun(Q)=f then $P_f \leq_{ext} Q$.

Lemma: Assume that $s \in P_f$ and fun(Q)=f. Then there is $t \in Q$ such that $t =_{ext} s$, that is $s \in Q\,|ext$.

Proof: By reduction to absurd.

Without lost of generality we assume that Q does not contain internal channels.

Let s be a shortest string in P_f which is not in $Q\,|ext$.

s cannot be ϵ. Therefore $s = s_1.\langle ch,\, d\rangle$. Since the lemma holds for s_1 there exists t_1 such that

$$(1) \quad t_1 \in Q \text{ and } s_1 =_{ext} t_1$$

Case 1: ch is an input port.

Use the fact that Q is buffered. Q is closed under input extension and $t_1 \in Q$; therefore $t_1.\langle ch,\, d\rangle \in Q$. But, $t_1.\langle ch,\, d\rangle =_{ext} s$; contradiction.

Case 2: ch is an output channel O_i.

Note the following facts:

(2) Since $s \in P_f$ there holds $stream(s,\, O_i) \leq f_i(stream(s,\, \vec{I}))$, where f_i is the i-th component of the stream functional f.

(3) $ch \notin \vec{I}$; therefore $s_1 |\vec{I} = s |\vec{I}$

Q specifies f; therefore

(4) there exists a string $t' \in Q$ such that $s\,|O_i \leq t'\,|O_i$ and $sream(s,\, \vec{I}) = stream(t',\, \vec{I})$

Now, remember that Q is smooth, so we may apply the strong unambiguity condition for the pair t_1 and t'. This and fact (4) guarantee that there exists $t'' \in Q$ such that t'' extends t_1 only through O_i and may be some internal communications and also that $s\,|O_i \leq t''\,|O_i$. Finally, since Q is both prefix closed and unambiguous, there exists a prefix t of t' such that $t =_{ext} s$.

Let us comment Claim 6. Assume that for smooth processes P_1, P_2 there holds $P_1 =_{rel} P_2$. This means that for an appropriate continuous function f there holds f=fun(P_1)=fun(P_2) and therefore due to (ii) in Claim 6 there holds $P_1 =_{ext} P_2$. Would we have the more general case $P_1 \leq_{rel} P_2$, one could conclude $P_1 \leq_{ext} P_2$, relying on the existence of continuous stream functions f_1 and f_2 such that

$$\text{fun}(P_1) = f_1 \leq f_2 = \text{fun}(P_2)$$

where $\leq$ denotes the partial order in the domain of continuous stream functions.

As a trivial consequence of these remarks we have the following fact, which should be compared with the Claim 2. It shows that the Brock-Ackerman Anomaly disappears if only smooth processes are considered.

Claim 7. Nets over smooth processes inherit $\leq_{rel}$ and $=_{rel}$.

But may be smoothness is too much to require in order to assure the inheritance of $\leq_{rel}$! We want to show that in some sense that is indeed the price one has to pay in order to avoid B-A-Anomaly. To this end we proceed first to some useful technicalities.

4.3. s - Testers

For a string s over channels $I_1,...,I_n$, $O_1,...,O_m$ we will construct a rudimentary context $Test_s[\ ]$ with the hole of type $\tau=(I_1,...,I_n;\ O_1,...,O_m)$ such that,

for each process P of external type τ there holds $Test_s[P]=\epsilon$ iff $s\notin_{ext}P$ (*)

Note that in P there may be internal channels.

The Construction of $Test_s[\ ]$.

Enrich the type τ with a fresh output channel T and consider the rudimentary process R^s of type $(O_1,...,O_m;\ I_1,...,I_n,\ T)$ generated by the string $s.<T,\ 0>$. Now define $Test_s[\ ]$ as $Cont[R^s]_1[\ ]_2$, where $Cont[\ ]_1[\ ]_2$ is the context from Section 2.3 (see Fig. 3).

Note that the only external channel of $Test_s[\ ]$ is T, and it is clear that for arbitrary process P of external type τ

$$Test_s[P]=_{ext}\epsilon \text{ or } Test_s[P]=_{ext}<T,\ 0> \quad (**)$$

Now, let us check that for $Test_s[\ ]$ as defined above the condition (*) indeed holds.

First, we introduce the following notations: Let θ be a renaming of the channels

For channels : $\theta(ch)$ - the result of renaming channel ch.

For Processes : $P\{\theta\}$ - the result of renaming process P.

To calculate $Test_s[P]$ recall first that

$R^s=_{ext}Synch(R,\ P_1,\ ...,\ P_n,\ P_{n+1},\ Q_1,..,\ Q_m)$ where $R=_{ext}prefix(s.<T,\ 0>)\{\theta\}$ and P_i, Q_j are the buffers attached to the channels of R as explained in 3.2 (see also Fig. 4), namely

For $i\leq n$ $\quad P_i=buf(\theta(I_i),\ I_i)$

$\qquad P_{n+1}=buf(\theta(T),\ T)$

For $j\leq m$ $\quad Q_j=buf(O_j,\ \theta(O_j))$

Now, $Test_s[P]=_{ext}Synch(R^s,\ P)$ (see Fig. 3). Hence, due to the full compositionality of synchronization and to $=_{ext}$ equivalent transformations: $Test_s[P]=_{ext}Synch(Synch(P,\ P_1,...P_n,\ Q_1,\ ...,\ Q_m),\ R,\ P_{n+1})$

Relying again on $=_{ext}$ equivalent transformation with buffers (see 3.2) one can observe that $Synch(P,\ P_1,...P_n,\ Q_1,\ ...,\ Q_m)=_{ext}P\{\theta\}$; therefore

$Test_s[P] =_{ext} Synch(\Pi,\ buf(\theta(T),\ T))$ where

$$\Pi =_{def} Synch(P\{\theta\},\ prefix(s.<T,0>)\{\theta\})$$

Π does not contain communications on T and has the only channel $\theta(T)$ in common with $buf(\theta(T),\ T)$. Therefore $Test_s[P]$ contains a communication on the channel T iff Π contains a communication on the channel $\theta(T)$. At the other hand $alph(P)\{\theta\} = \theta(I_1,...,I_n,\ O_1,...,O_m) \subset alph(prefix(s.<T,\ 0>)\{\theta\}$; Neither P, nor s contain a communication on the channel $\theta(T)$, therefore Π contains a communication on the channel $\theta(T)$ iff $s.<T,\ 0>\{\theta\}|\theta(alph(P)) \in_{ext} P\{\theta\}$. And this may happen only if $s \in_{ext} P$.

4.4. Observable Equivalence and Approximation

Given a class C of Processes. $N[p]$ is said to be a C-context if each place $p' \neq p$ is labeled by a process from C.

We define now a relation $\leq_{C-obs}$ which is parametrized wrt a set of Processes C. As a derivable relation (in fact an equivalence) we shall have C-observational equivalence $=_{C-obs}$, where $P_1 =_{C-obs} P_2$ iff $P_1 \leq_{C-obs} P_2$ and $P_2 \leq_{C-obs} P_1$.

$P_1 \leq_{C-obs} P_2$ (in words: P_1 C-observationally approximate P_2) iff for each C-context $N[\ ]$ there holds

$$N[P_1] \leq_{rel} N[P_2]$$

Note that the definition assumes that P_1 and P_2 have the same type. If C is the class of all processes we write $\leq_{obs}$; In the case that C is the class of rudimentary processes we write $\leq_{rud-obs}$.

The main technical fact, concerning the relation between processes P_1, P_2 in a R-class C is the following:

Claim 8: $P_1 \leq_{rud-obs} P_2 \leftrightarrow P_1 \leq_{ext} P_2 \leftrightarrow P_1 \leq_{obs} P_2$

Proof: It is clear that $P_1 \leq_{ext} P_2 \rightarrow P_1 \leq_{obs} P_2 \rightarrow P_1 \leq_{rud-obs} P_2$ therefore to prove the claim it is enough to show that $P_1 \leq_{rud-obs} P_2 \rightarrow P_1 \leq_{ext} P_2$. Now, assume that $P_1 \leq_{rud-obs} P_2$, and $s \notin P_2|ext$. Then $Test_s[P_1] \leq_{rel} Test_s[P_2] =_{rel} \epsilon$. Therefore $s \notin P_2|ext$ implies $s \notin P_1|ext$, i.e. $P_1 \leq_{ext} P_2$.

Note, unambiguity is not required for Claim 8.

4.5. Smoothness vs Strong Modularity

Call a class C of processes modular (strong modular) iff nets over C inherit $=_{rel}$ $(\leq_{rel})$.

As shown in 4.2 the class of all smooth processes (notations - SMOOTH) is strongly modular. Clearly, so is each subclass C⊂SMOOTH which satisfies the closeness conditions:

C is closed under the net-construct $(*)$

A class C is said to be an R-class if in addition to $(*)$ it satisfies also:

Rudim (the class of all rudimentary processes) $\subset$C $(**)$

This condition may be justifyed by the expectation that every class of nets of processes one would like to consider as a reasonable "programming language" should contain at least the rudimentary processes. Clearly each subclass C$\subset$SMOOTH which obeys $(*)$ is strongly modular even if $(**)$ is not assumed to hold. The following claim shows that smoothness almost coincides with strong modularity.

Claim 9. Assume that C is an R-class consisting of unambiguous processes. Then C is strongly modular iff each process P$\in$C is externally equivalent to a smooth process.

Proof. Let f be the function specified by P and let P_f be the smooth process which specifies f. Take an arbitrary $s \in P_f$.

Notations: T^s - the s Tester. P_s the rudimentary process generated by s

Clearly, $P_s \leq_{rel} P$ and hence by the assumption of strong modularity there holds

$$T^s[P_s] \leq_{rel} T^s[P].$$

Hence, $T^s[P] \neq_{ext} \epsilon$ and therefore $s \in_{ext} P$.

Comment 1. We consider the Claims 7 and 9 above as justifying the view on smoothness as on a relevant feature of linear processes which specify functionals and support modularity. In particular, from claim 7 we see that for nets over smooth agents modularity is established without any fixed point arguments. Moreover, modularity holds for arbitrary nets and among them for such nets for which the Kahn principle in each original format does not make sense. This is in particular the case when in a given net several outputs channels may confluent (as the channels x,y in Fig. 2d). In such a case the system of equations one would try to assign to the net may be inconsistent (i.e. may have no solution at all). That is why in Section 5 we revise the Kahn Principle, and we investigate it for nets without any specific restrictions (like prohibition of output confluences).

Comment 2. Claim 9 refers to R-Classes which consist only of unambiguous processes. Now consider the more general case, when nonambiguity is not assumed; this is a step to the consideration of processes specifying nondeterminate, i.e. non functional behaviours. It is an easy exercise to prove for this case:

Claim 9$'$. For each processes P_1, P_2 in a modular R-class C there holds

$$P_1 \equiv_{rel} P_2 \text{ iff } P_1 \equiv_{ext} P_2$$

Another variant of claims of this sort is

Claim 9$''$ (Saturation). The class SMOOTH is modular but enriching it with any buffered nonambiguous process which is not externally equivalent to a smooth process destroys modularity.

5. The Kahn Principle

5.1. Functional Nets

Kahn's Principle compares Nets over Processes with objects called Functional Nets we are going now to define.

First, let us recall some notations (see Section 3.3). Given a port *ch* we write $[ch]$ for the set of all streams of communications through *ch*. Accordingly, for a set $CH=\{ch_1, ch_2, \ldots ch_k\}$ of ports we use $[CH]$ for the set of tuples $[ch_1] \times [ch_2] \cdots \times [ch_k]$ and similary for infinite CH. The functions we shall deal with are mappings from some $[CH_1]$ into some $[CH_2]$. A functional net is a pair $[N, \phi]$, where N is a net and ϕ a labeling function which assigns names to the ports of N (different ports get different names) and functions to the places $p \in N$ under the following condition: Assume that in the atomic subnet with the place p there are labeled input ports $\pi_1, \pi_2, \ldots \pi_n$ and labeled output ports $q_1, q_2, \ldots q_m$; then then $f_p = \phi(p)$ is a mapping from $[\pi_1, \pi_2, \ldots \pi_n]$ into $[q_1, q_2, \ldots q_m]$.

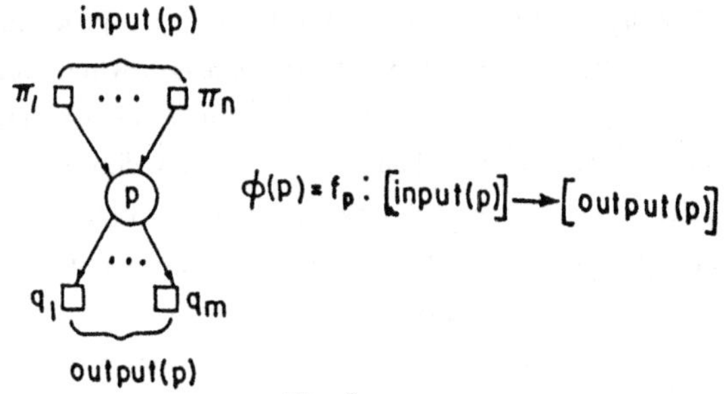

Fig. 9

We consider also the components f_{pq_i} $[\pi_1, \pi_2, \ldots \pi_n] \rightarrow [q_i]$ i=1...m of the mapping f_p. Let $e \in [CH]$ and $CH' \subset CH$; we use $e(CH')$ for the projection of e on $[CH']$.

5.1.1. Semantics of Functional Nets

Given a functional net $[N, \phi]$ first assign to each port *ch* of N a variable x_{ch} of type $[ch]$. Then using the signature $\{f_{pq}\}$ for all $p \in N$ and q an output port of p, consider the system of formal equations:

$$L^{=} \quad = \quad \{x_q = f_{pq}(x_{\pi_1}, \ldots x_{\pi_n})\} \qquad (*)$$

or the system of formal "upper" inequalities

$$L^{\geq} \quad = \quad \{x_q \geq f_{pq}(x_{\pi_1},...x_{\pi_n}\} \qquad (**)$$

or finally the system of formal "lower" inequalities

$$L^{\leq} \quad = \quad \{x_q \leq f_{pq}(x_{\pi_1},...x_{\pi_n}\} \qquad (***)$$

The idea is to assign to $[N, \phi]$ as its meaning a function $[CH] \rightarrow [CH]$ which is the least solution of an appropriate system of equations. We shall resume the technical details a bit later and for the time being let us give a comparative commentary to the three competing approaches $L^{=}$, $L^{\leq}$, $L^{\geq}$.

1. In $L^{=}$ semantics the format of the equations is just as in (*). Hence it may happen to be inconsistent, i.e. there may be no solution at all. This is because in the system $L^{=}$ there may be inconsistent equalities.

$$x_q = f_{pq}(x_{\pi_1},...x_{\pi_k})$$

$$x_q = f_{p'q}(x_{\pi'_1},...x_{\pi'_l})$$

That is why the "classical" Kahn Principle deals with nets where there is no confluence of output channels. In this way consistency is guaranteed and a solution via least fixed point techniques becomes possible.

2. In $L^{\geq}$ semantics there is a unique equation with lefthand side x_q:

$$x_q = lub\,\{f_{pq},\ f_{p'q} \cdots\}$$

where p, p',... are all the places in the net which have q as ab output port. Sometimes the least solution may exist for this system of equations, even if for $L^{=}$ it does not exist. Clearly, if the solution for $L^{=}$ exists then it is also a solution for $L^{\geq}$. The $L^{\geq}$ semantics is interested especially because it may produce

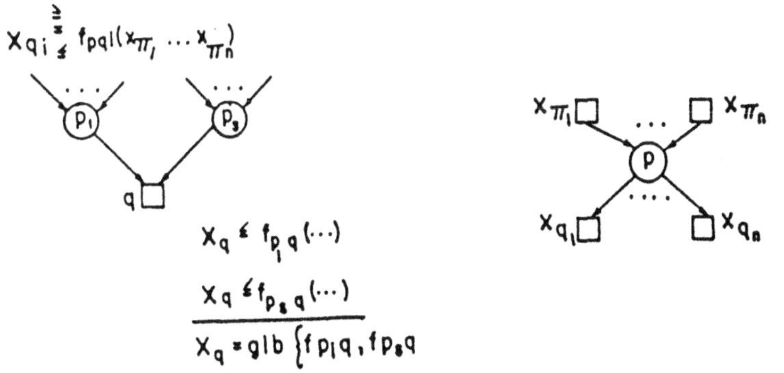

Fig. 10

as solutions **parallel** functions [Tra] even for the case when the f_{pq} are sequential.

3. Finally, in $L^{\leq}$ semantics it is required to use greatest low bounds (glb) instead of least upper bounds (lub) as in $L^{\geq}$. The crucial fact is that $L^{\leq}$ is

always consistent and hence the solution is defined for arbitrary nets (no restrictions like those we needed above). If $L^{=}$ semantics is defined it coincides with $L^{\leq}$, but if $L^{\geq}$ is defined it yields in general a different solution.

The Kahn semantics of a net $[N, \phi]$ will be defined below as $L^{\leq}$ semantics.

5.1.2. The Definition of $L^{\leq}$ Semantics

In the next paragraph 1.1.3 we associate with the net $[N, \phi]$ a function of type $[CH] \rightarrow [CH]$ for which we use the notation $F(N, \phi)$ and when it is clear from the context simply F. This function will be easily seen to have the following properties:

(a) F is monotonic and continuous.

(b) F preserves input in the following sense: if $f = F(e)$ then for each input channel ch

$$f(ch) = e(ch)$$

Assume that some $e \in [CH]$ is input-like, i.e. for each $ch \notin CHinp$ there holds $e(ch) = \epsilon$; then from (a) and (b) it follows that

(c) For each input-like e there holds

$$e \leq F(e) \leq F^2(e) \leq \cdots \leq F^k(e) \cdots \quad (*)$$

The least upper bound of (*) exists, and we use for it the notation $F^{\omega}(e)$. Finally the Kahn semantics Kahn(N, ϕ) of the net $[N, \phi]$ is described as follows: Given a stream $i \in [CHinp]$ extend it first to the input-like stream $\bar{i} \in [CH]$, take $F^{\omega}(\bar{i})$ and then restrict $F^{\omega}(\bar{i})$ to the output ports of N.

5.1.3. The Definition of $F(N, \phi)$

Let $[N, \phi]$ be a functional net with the set of ports CH. For a place p we denote by $input(p)$ the set of input ports of p and by $output(p)$ the set of its output ports. The function $F(N, \phi)$ from $[CH]$ to $[CH]$ is defined as follows:

(1) For $e \in [CH]$ and $q \in CHinp$

$$F(N, \phi)(e)(q) = e(q)$$

(2) For $q \notin Chinp$ let $p_1, p_2, \ldots p_k \cdots$ be the places for which $q \in output(p_i)$ and let $f_{p_1 q}, \ldots f_{p_k q}, \ldots$ be the functions specified by ϕ for these places.

$F(N, \phi)(e)(q)$ is the gratest lower bound of the set $\{f_{p_1 q}(e(input(p_1))), \ldots f_{p_k q}(e(input(p_k))), \ldots\}$

Figure 9 illustrate the situation.

5.2. The Kahn Semantics for Smooth Linear Processes

Let C be a class of unambiguous processes. We say that the Kahn Principle holds for C iff for all nets $<N, \psi>$ over C

$$\text{fun}(S(N, \psi)) = \text{Kahn}(N, \phi)$$

where $\phi(p) = \text{fun}(\psi(p))$ for all $p \in N$.

As a direct consequence from the definition of Kahn(N, ϕ) it follows

Claim 10. If for a class C there holds The Kahn Principle then C is strongly modular.

Below, adapting the proof from [Rab] we establish

Claim 11. The Kahn principle holds for the class of all smooth processes.

Comment. In virtue of Claim 10 and having in mind the characterization of strong modular R-Classes from Section 4.5 we see that Claim 11 establishs the Kahn Principle in the most general setting. Before we proceed to the proof of Claim 11 let us mention some notations.

Notations. Concerning a net $<N, \psi>$ over unambiguous processes.

(1) For a place p and $ch \in output(p)$ we use $fun(p,ch)$ for the function specified by $\psi(p)$ on ch. This is only a notational version of what we would write as $f_{p,ch}$ in the case of functional net. Clearly $fun(p,ch)$ is identical to the function $f_{p,ch}$ in the correspondent functional net $[N, \phi]$ and it maps $[input(p)]$ into $[ch]$.

(2) e with indexes will stay for finite streams in $[CH]$; s with indexes will stay for strings in the process $S(N, \psi)$.

(3) For a given s we take stream(s, $CHinp$) and extend it to an input-like stream; we use the notation $in(s)$ for the result.

Proof of Claim 11.

From the Lemma 1. (below) it follows that $S(N, \psi)$ contains only strings consistent with F^{ω}. Therefore

Fact 1. fun($S(N, \psi)$)$\leq$Kahn(N, ϕ) where $\phi(p)$=fun($\psi(p)$) for all $p \in N$.

Lemma. Strings of length k of the process $S(N, \psi)$ are F^k consistent.

Proof. By induction on k.

Formally the lemma says the following: Let $s \in S(N, \psi)$ be of length k. Then $stream(s,CH) \leq F^k(in(s))$.

Basis. Trivial.

Inductive step.

Let s be if length k+1; then $s = s_1.<ch, d>$, for s_1 of length k. We have to prove that

$$stream(s, CH) \leq F^{k+1}(in(s))$$

Now, recall that $S(N, \psi)$ is prefix closed hence

(1) $s_1 \in S(N, \psi)$, and stream(s_1,CH)$\leq F^k(in(s_1))$ by the inductive hypothesis.

Having in mind from now on the *ch* mentioned above we note that

(2) stream(s, CH)(c)=stream(s_1, CH)(c) for all $c \neq ch$

Note also that $F^k(in(t))$ increases with k and t; Thus by (1) and (2) it is enough to prove that

$$s\,|ch \leq F^{k+1}(\text{stream}(s, CH))(ch) \qquad (*)$$

If ch is an input channel then equality holds in (*) since F^{k+1} preserves inputs.

Assume ch is an output or internal channel and let p be a place for which ch is an output channel. Then

(3) $s_1\,|input(p) = s\,|input(p)$

Let $t =_{def} s\,|alph(\psi(p))$ then

(4) $t \in \psi(p)$, $t\,|ch = s\,|ch$ and $t\,|input(p) = s\,|input(p)$

Assume that the input ports of the place p absorb the stream generated by the string s; then at the output port ch there will be produced a stream which we designate as $R(s, p)$. Formally, it looks rather ugly

$$R(s, p) = fun(p, ch)(\text{stream}(s, input(p)))$$

Using the notation above we write down chains (5) and (6) of equalities and inequalities which completes the proof.

For each place p which has the output port ch there holds

(5) $s\,|ch = t\,|ch \leq R(t, p) = R(s_1, p)$

The first two steps hold by (4),the third by (3) and (4).

(6) $s\,|ch \leq F(\text{stream}(s_1, CH))(ch) \leq F^{k+1}(in(s_1))(ch) \leq F^{k+1}(in(s))(ch)$

The first step holds by the definition of F and (5), the second by (1) and the last holds by the monotonicity of F^{k+1} .

Note that this lemma holds for arbitrary nets over unambiguous processes (smoothness is not required at this stage).

From the next lemma it follows

Fact 2. $Kahn(N, \phi) \leq \text{fun}S(N, \psi)$.

Together with Fact 1 above - this completes the proof of Claim 11.

Lemma. Let e be a finite stream in $[CH]$ and let g be a finite input-like stream in $[CH]$. Assume that $e \leq F^k(g)$. Then there exists $s \in S(N, \psi)$ such that $e \leq \text{stream}(s, CH)$ and $g = in(s)$.

Proof: By the induction on k, whereas g is fixed.

Remark. Without loss of generality we assume that the component processes of the net use only communications through the ports of the net,

Basis. k=0.

e and g are input-like; $S(N, \psi)$ is buffered; hence there exists s satisfying the lemma.

Inductive step.

Let $e \leq F^{k+1}(g)$; then by the continuity of F there exists e_1 such that

(1) $e_1 \leq F^k(g)$

(2) $e \leq F(e_1)$

The inductive hypothesis for streams e_1 and g says that there exists s_1 such that

(3) $s_1 \in S(N, \psi)$ and

(4) $e_1 \leq \text{stream}(s_1, CH)$ and $g = in(s_1)$

Since e and $\text{stream}(s_1, CH)$ are consistent streams (both are majorized by $F^{\omega}(g)$) it follows that for each channel c either (a) $e(c) \leq \text{stream}(s, CH)(c)$ or (b) $\text{stream}(s, CH)(c) < e(c)$. e and s are finite; therefore (b) may hold only for finitely many channels. Let $c_1, \ldots, c_k$ be the channels of the net for which (b) holds. We designate by suf_i the suffix of $e(c_i)$ wrt the stream $(s, CH)(c_i)$. To finish the proof it is enough to show that

$$s =_{def} s_1 suf_1 suf_2 \ldots suf_k \in S(N, \psi) \quad (*)$$

For a process P not containing any of the channels $c_1, \ldots, c_k$ both strings s and s_1 have the same projection on alph(P). Therefore $s\,|\text{alph}(P) \in P$.

Assume that a place p contains c_i. The string $s_1\,|alph(\psi(p))$ is consistent with $fun(p, c_i)$ due to (3). Hence, due to (2), (4) and the definition of F the string $s\,|alph(\psi(p))$ is consistent with $fun(p, c_i)$. And since $\psi(p)$ is smooth it follows $s\,|alph(\psi(p)) \in \psi(p)$.

Finally, the definition of synchronization and the fact that $s\,|alph(\psi(p)) \in \psi(p)$ for each place p in the net imply that $s \in S(N, \psi)$. And this completes the proof of the lemma .

6. Concluding Remarks and Further Research

6.1. Comparing Higher Level Processes with Linear Processes

Let us give a rough idea about how things would go on with modularity issues and Kahn's Principle for higher level models: Automata, Pomset Processes, Behaviour Structures.

Ultimately, the task is to choose in the model under consideration a "reasonable" class C of processes (a "specification language") for specifying functions. Clearly, since the model is more discriminating than the Linear Model, it grants more opportunities to specify subtle features of computations. In this sense the level of the model is relevant; it is up to the designer how to choose the class C, in order to benefit in the best way of these opportunities. But what is the expected impact of the choice on the ideas and technicalities needed to deal with Kahn's Principle and modularity issues? What we are going to argue is only the following:

As far as these issues are concerned all one needs is essentially covered by the linear model.

More specifically we expect that the information about a process $P \in C$, which is relevant for the issues above is already contained in the process $Lin(P)$ - the linear projection of P. Hence, it may be possible to proceed according to the following scenario: Consider

$$Lin(C) =_{def} \{Q : \text{there exists } P \in C \text{ such that } Q = Lin(P)\}$$

We expect that if C is "reasonable" chosen then $Lin(C)$ will be an R-class of linear processes (see 4.5). Assuming that this is the case we would automatically lift the theorems about linear processes (Section 4 and Section 5) to the class C. Therefore, in order to justify the scenario above, we have only to become convinced that for a "reasonable" class C in the higher level model the following holds:

(1) $Lin(C)$ is closed under the net construct.

(2) $Lin(C)$ consists of only unambiguous processes.

(3) $Lin(C) \supset Rudim$

(4) $Lin(C)$ consists of only buffered processes.

Clearly C should be closed under the net construct, which ultimately amounts to synchronization of component processes. But for all known models, synchronization is inherited through linear projection (i.e the synchronization of linearizations is equivalent to the linearization of synchronization). Therefore - property 1 must hold.

Property 2 is hopefully also quite evident. Hence, we have to concentrate on the circumstances connected with rudimentary functions and buffers. It is reasonable to expect that C as a specification language, is enough powerful in order to specify at least all rudimentary functions. Note that Kahn's original model covers even all sequential functions and that is more then the family of rudimentary functions. Note also that beyond the sequential functions, there still are other continuous functions, the parallel functions [Tra]. As we have seen the linear rudimentary processes are extremely simple and natural specifications of rudimentary functions are possible at other levels as well; among them there are such that linearize to rudimentary processes in the sense of 3.3. There is no reason to exclude them from C. Hence - property 3.

Finally, from the very beginning - starting with Kahn's model - the prominent role of buffers and of buffered "computation stations". was clear and generally accepted Again, all known buffer-processes (in different models) linearize to the buffers from 3.3. That is why the property 4 is expected as well and this completes the justification of the scenario.

Now, for the class C under consideration let us look to its "closure" C' as below:

$P' \in C'$ iff there exists P in C such that $Lin(P') = Lin(P)$.

The same reasons which allow to lift the theory from $Lin(C)$ to C, allow to perform the lifting from $Lin(C')$ (which coincides with $Lin(C)$) to C'. In the case when C' is a proper extension of C we would get a more liberal class for which the Modularity theorems and Kahn's Principle hold. But the designer may feel uneasy with these extension for his specific reasons. That is the point where the peculiarities of the higher level come into play.

6.2. Non Deterministic Behaviour

Though we dealt with functional behaviour of input-output processes we have the strong feeling that the theory may be naturally extended to the more general nondeterministic case. Let us note two points where our approach, even at this stage allows to go beyond the functional case.

(a) First - we have in mind the s-Tester techniques, which (see Claim 9') is appropriate for nondeterminate relational behaviour.

(b) Further - basing Kahn's Principle on $L^{\leq}$ semantics , we removed the topological restriction (no confluent output channels) which seems natural in the "classical" format of the Kahn Principle, but is completely alien to the idea of nondeterminate behaviour.

Next, we are intended to provide a "smoothness" version for buffered relations removing the last essential obstacle to the full theory for nondeterminate behaviour.

6.3. Parallelism

Unlike $L^{\geq}$ semantics, $L^{\leq}$ semantics preserves sequentiality, i.e. if the component agents of a functional net specify sequential functions, so do the nets over them. This fact brings us to the (sounding a bit paradoxical) observation:

The concurrent work of agents is not a source of parallelism.

Hence also the task of investigating degrees of parallelism [Tra] for stream functions, i.e. the possibility to specify parallel functions through nets over "sequential" components and some specific parallel primitives.

7. References

[BA] Brock, J.D and Ackerman, W.B, Scenarios: A Model of Non-Deterministic Computations, In Formalization of Programming Concepts, LNCS 107, 1981, 252-259.

[Fa] Faustini, A.A., An Operational Semantics for Pure Dataflow., LNCS 140, 1982 , 212-224.

[GP] Gaifman, H., Pratt, V.R., Partial Order Models of Concurrency and the Computation of Functions, LICS 1987.

[K74] Kahn, G., The Semantics for a Simple Language for Parallel Programming, IFIP 74.

[KP] Kahn, G., Plotkin, G., Structure de donnes concretes. IRIA-LABORIA Report 336 1978

[LS] Lynch, N., Stark, E., A Proof of the Kahn Principle for Input/Output Automata Report Mit/LCS/TM-349 1988

[Mil] Milner, R., Calculi for Synchrony and Asynchrony, Theoretical Computer Science 25, 1983.

[Pr] Pratt, V., Modeling Concurrency with Partial Order, International Journal of Parallel Programming, Vol. 15, 1986

[Rab] Rabinovich, A., Pomset Semantics is Consistent with Data Flow Semantics, Bulletin of EATCS vol. 32, 1987.

[RT] Rabinovich, A., Trakhtenbrot, B. A., Behaviour Structures and Nets, to appear in Fundamenta Informatica 1988

[Tra] Trakhtenbrot, B. A., Recursive Program Schemes and Computable Functionals, LNCS, vol. 45, 1976.

[TRH] Trakhtenbrot, B. A., Rabinovich, A., Hirshfeld, J., Nets of Processes, Technical Report 97/88 Institute of Computer Science, Tel Aviv University.

Towards a Temporal Logic for Causality and Choice in Distributed Systems

Wolfgang Reisig

Technical University of Munich
Institut für Informatik
Postfach 20 24 20
8000 München 2
West Germany

and

Gesellschaft für Mathematik
und Datenverarbeitung – F1
Postfach 12 40
5205 Sankt Augustin 1
West Germany

ABSTRACT: Which kind of properties of nonsequential systems should be considered essential for specification and abstraction purposes, is still an open problem. In this paper we discuss some particular properties such as absence of delay and various notions of concurrency. They turn out to be adequately representable in partial order semantics. The most fundamental version of Petri Nets appears to be convenient for such investigations. A (generalized) temporal logic is introduced, covering the intricate relationship among causality (sequentiality), choice and concurrency appearing in distributed systems.

Key words: Concurrent System Properties, Temporal Logic, Petri Nets

CONTENTS

Introduction

Temporal Logic provides a recognized technique to specify systems, particularly nonsequential systems and to formulate and prove properties of such systems. It refers to conventional operational semantics, conceiving single runs of systems as sequences of states and transitions. Such sequences are gained by interleaving (arbitrarily ordering) transitions which occur independently in the reality to be modeled.

In recent years (and in Petri Nets more than a decade ago) it was understood that arbitrary interleavings conceal essential properties of runs of nonsequential systems: It is not clear whether two given sequences are different interleavings of the same run. Arbitrary interleavings furthermore introduce global states which do not correspond to the realm of nonsequential systems. So, the concept of *partial order semantics* found its way from Petri Nets to a couple of other system models. Properties such as absence of system–prone delay, the existence of alternatives in distributed situations, or particular questions of fairness can adequately be treated in this framework.

The first part of this paper concentrates on intuitive notions and concepts. We start with properties considered essential for nonsequential systems, and discuss their representability in conventional temporal logic. It turns out that new concepts are mandatory. Those new concepts concern the underlying semantic model. So, operational semantics is re–considered and the adequacy of partial order semantics is shown. As partial order semantics does not fit with conventional temporal logic, its roots in Modal Logic are discussed and a revised version of Temporal Logic is glanced.

The second part turns at formal aspects. The most elaborated system model for partial order semantics is introduced, viz *elementary net systems*, the basic system model of Petri Nets. Then a logical language, $\mathcal{F}(B)$ is introduced, fitting to the partially ordered concept of runs of elementary net systems.

The third part, finally, shows what is gained with partial order semantics and its logic. It is shown that a couple of essential system properties can be formulated in this language, including absence of delay and some notions in the area of concurrency.

I SYSTEM SPECIFICATION AND SYSTEM PROPERTIES

Intiuitive notions and concepts are discussed in this part. The first chapter reviews the kind fo properties representable by formulas of conventional temporal logic. It will be shown that the conventional eventuality operator is useful for representing properties fo previously constructed systems. But it can not be used to specify properties of systems to be built. A new operator, somewhere in between *eventually* and *next state* is needed. This is achieved on the base of *partial order semantics*, which is informally introduced and motivated for reactive systems in the second chapter. In the third chapter we reconsider the roots of temporal logic, viz. modal logic, in order to derive an interpretation of the temporal logic operators which fits with partial order semantics.

1 Temporal Logic and the Specification of Systems

Conventional Temporal Logic works with three modal operators, $\square$, $\diamond$ and $\circ$, denoting "It will always be the case that ...", "It will eventually be the case that ...", and "At next time it will be the case that ...", respectively. A binary operator, mostly " ... until ..." is in general also included. All these operators can be used to formulate system properties and to reason about them.

One usually distinguishes *safety properties*, separating acceptable states from unwandet states, and *liveness properties*, stating that some wanted state eventually will be reached [Lamport 83]. These two kinds of properties can be characterized with formulae formed $\square\ \varphi$ and $\diamond\ \varphi$ (with φ any formula).

In applications to computer science, temporal logic formulas are usually interpreted over well founded domains; mostly over domains isomorphic to the natural numbers. For such interpretations, a formula $\diamond\ \varphi$ can be conceived as representing the infinite alternative $\varphi \vee \circ\varphi \vee \circ^2\varphi \vee \ldots \vee \circ^i\varphi \vee \ldots$ (with $\circ^{i+1}\varphi := \circ\circ^i\varphi$ and $\circ^\circ\varphi := \varphi$). If $\diamond\varphi$ is valid for a concrete run of a system, there exists an integer, n, such that $\circ^n\varphi$ is valid. If $\diamond\varphi$ is valid for infinitely many runs, there might however not exist an integer, n, such that $\circ^n\varphi$ was valid for all of them. This situation may arise when reasoning about systems: A formula is valid for a system iff it is valid for each of its runs. Abstracting from concrete numbers n in formulas $\circ^n\varphi$, the eventually–operator $\diamond$ apperars quite convenient. The formulation of systems properties using $\diamond$ is detailed enough for many purposes. This particularly holds in case existing systems are analyzed: If necessary, more detailed descriptions may be gained by $\circ^n\varphi$–formulas.

The pragmatics of formulating properties of given systems differs substantially from specifying properties of systems to be built. A specification of such a system includes an agreement between a customer who wants to make use of a system that meets his requirements, and an engineer who is to install the system. The specification should include everything essential for the customer and should avoid unnecessary restrictions for the implementer. Upon agreement of the specification, the implementer is free to deliver any system as long as it meets the specification.

This implies that a specification including the eventuality operator is not acceptable for a customer: Each such specification can be implemented with delays inacceptable for the customer. To give a drastic example, the delay may cover the whole intended lifetime of the system.

Concrete implementations of specifications formulated in terms of the $\Diamond$–operator in fact always obey further hidden, i.e. not formulated assumptions about acceptable delays. Thus the $\Diamond$–operator has to be revised.

We discussed above already that the usual next state operator, $\circ$, can also not serve as a means for proper specifications. It would lead to overspecifications, just like $\Diamond$ leads to under–specifications. Additionally it was often mentioned in the literature (cf. [Lamport 83]) that the validity of formulas formed $\circ\varphi$ is in general not preserved under refinement. To overcome this problem, one could think obout level–dependent specifications with proper refinement procedures for formulas.

A further property of the $\circ$–operator appears even more inadequate: The validity of a $\circ\varphi$–formula is not preserved when a system is considered in its environment: Though the original system is not at all touched, due to interleaving its events with its environment's events, $\circ\varphi$–formulae may swap from true to false.

Thus we need a delay–independent operator excluding arbitrary delays, without enforcing events to occur in the next step. The operator just may express that an event is prepared to occur, that no other circumstances will prevent its occurrence, and that the event eventually will occur, independently from other event occurrences.

An example might clarify those aspects: Assume a producer/consumer system, linked by a buffer with n buffer cells. With the operators $\Box$ and $\Diamond$ one is able to formulate its behaviour: An item may eventually be placed into the buffer in case the buffer is not entirely filled, and vice versa, an item may eventually be removed from a non–empty buffer. Delays may arise due to internal moves of the buffer, or due to the overall system schedule. The Petri net of Fig. 1 shows an example of such a buffer with $n = 2$ cells. The internal buffer event, e, may delay an item be inserted or removed.

We now turn to a delay independent buffer: In case the buffer is not entirely filled, an item may be inserted *immediately* and not just eventually. Likewise, in case the buffer is not entirely empty, an item may be removed immediately. The buffer of Σ_2 in Fig. 2 meets this more strict requirement, in constrast to Σ_1 in Fig. 1.

The difference between both versions of the buffer may be essential for the user of the system: If (by further means) it is guaranteed that the buffer never is entirely filled or entirely empty, the system Σ_2 guarantees absence of delay, in contrast to Σ_1. This difference can not adequately be formulated in terms of

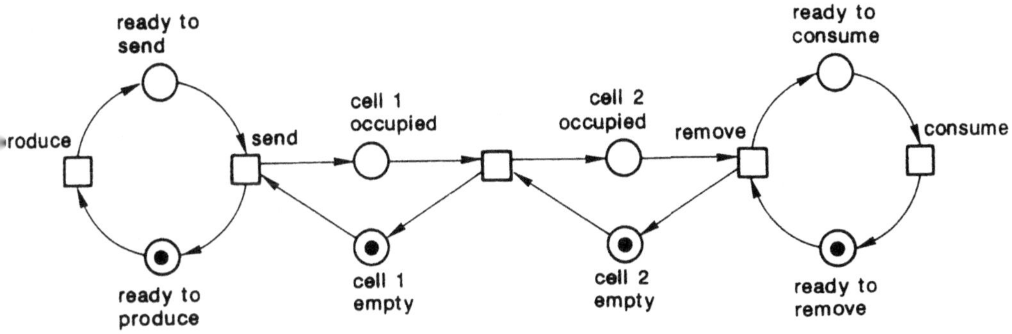

Figure 1: En–system Σ_1: A sequential buffer with two cells

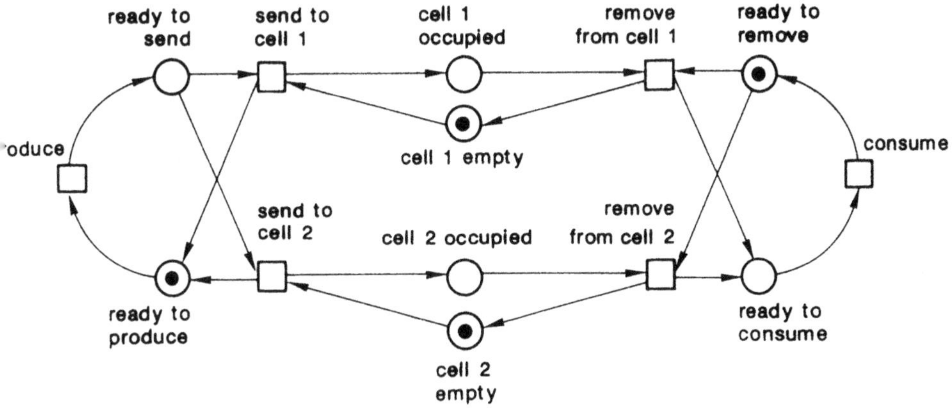

Figure 2: En–system Σ_2: A parallel buffer with two cells

conventional versions of temporal logic. The usual *at–next*–operator, $\circ$, can not serve for representing absence of delay because a couple of pairwise independent events may (but need not) occur without delay.

It turned out that a proper operator for absence of delay (or *local progress*) can not be based on the conventional notions of operational semantics. Thus we have to reconsider the notion of operational semantics. Based on a revised conception of system behaviour we then will suggest a logic with a proper operator for local progress.

2 Reactive Systems and Their Operational Semantics

Till the mid 70ies it was generally understood that the operational semantics of a system can be formulated in terms of its *execution sequences*. An execution sequence is a sequence of system states or system events or, alternatingly, of both. Intuitively, an execution sequence combines single system steps, thus describing a run of the system. Starting with a given initial state, one is essentially interested in terminating execution sequences and their final state, i.e. states with no action to follow. Nonterminating execution sequences in this setting are usually identified as representing divergence, hence failure prone system runs.

This approach has two implications. Firstly, in a run of a system it is assumed that global states can be identified and that the events of a run occur totally ordered. Secondly, no knowledge about alterntive continuations is explicitely provided during runs. Different ways to reach the same state are considered equivalent.

Execution sequences constitute an adequate model of system behaviour as long as systems are intended to compute functions or relations. Quite a lot of systems are however not intended to compute functions or relations. Among them are e.g. control systems for telephone, for factories, or for offices, or operating systems. [Pnueli 86] denotes such systems *reactive*.

Initial states do in general not exist for such systems, and terminal states might denote desaster rather than result. Operational semantics has to take into consideration the relative independence of system components and their cooperation. Consequently, global states can not naturally be identified in general, and the system–dependent order of events is not total but only partial. Additionally, the alternative continuations during a run are relevant for its comprehension, and thus are part of the system's semantics.

These requirements for an operational semantics of reactive systems contradict the above discussed consequences of approaches based on execution sequences. So, such sequences must be replaces by some other concept.

These aspects have been identified in the 70ies, and different approaches have been suggested to cover them. C.A. Petri in his work on Nonsequential Processes [Petri 77] suggested partial (instead of total) orders of event occurrences in each single run, thus avoiding the assumption of objective global states. This concept became part of the semantics of Petri Nets, and is meanwhile applied to other formalisms also, including data flow models, CCS and CSP. An example for a partially ordered run of the system Σ_2 is shown in Fig. 3. The circles and boxes in Fig. 3 represent occurrences of the corresponding elements in Σ_1 (indicated by inscriptions). The second aspect, i.e. knowledge about alternatives during a run, is taken into account with the concept of execution trees, failure semantics, and various notions of equivalence based on them. The recent workshop on combining compositionality and concurrency surveyed the stat–of–the–art in this field [Olderog et al 88].

Execution sequences can be re–gained from both partially ordered runs and execution trees: The interleavings (total extensions) of a partially ordered run, and the paths of an execution tree represent execution sequences; and all execution sequences can be gained this way. Partially ordered runs provide additional information about system specified (in–) dependence of events, and execution trees provide additional information about alternative continuations. Both kind of additional information is mandatory for a proper conception of reactive systems.

So far we identified two essential and new aspects of an operational semantics for

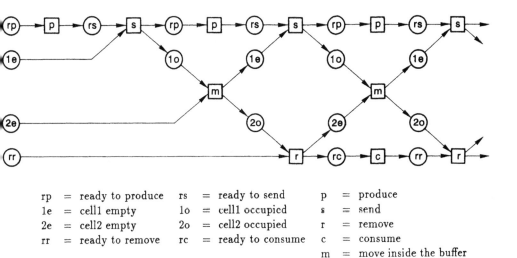

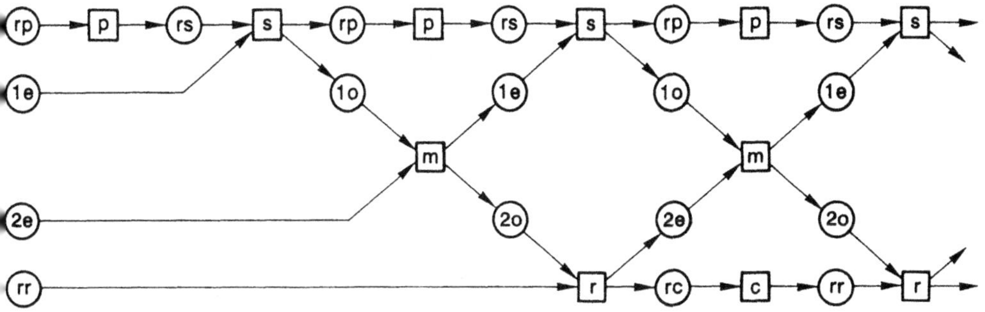

rp	=	ready to produce	rs	=	ready to send	p	=	produce
1e	=	cell1 empty	1o	=	cell1 occupied	s	=	send
2e	=	cell2 empty	2o	=	cell2 occupied	r	=	remove
rr	=	ready to remove	rc	=	ready to consume	c	=	consume
						m	=	move inside the buffer

Figure 3: A single run of the sequential buffer system

reactive systems: In each run of a system, independence among events and alternative continuations should be represented. Both these aspects should of course be represented *together*, i.e. partially ordered runs and synchronization trees should be combined. This was achieved with the notion of *event structures* introduced in [Nielsen, Plotkin, Winskel 80]. Fig. 4 shows an event structure, corresponding to the system of Σ_2.

To sum up, different concepts of operational semantics are gained by different answers to the following two questions: Firstly, what is a single run? Is it a sequence of events occurring totally ordered along a time scale? Or is it a set of events, partially ordered by system–specified dependencies (offen called "causal order")? The second question concerns the grouping of the runs of a system to its overall behaviour: Is the behaviour just the set of runs? Or is it a branched structure, indicating alternatives? The Matrix of Fig. 5 surveys these questions and the four variants for answering them.

3 Operational Semantics and Modal Logic

In the late 1970ies, Temporal Logic has been suggested as a means to formulate system properties and to reason about them, particularly for non–sequential systems and programs [Pnueli 81]. Two versions of Temporal Logic were identified and denoted *linear time* and *branching time*, respectively. Both versions consider system runs as being execution sequences, thus referring to the left column of Fig. 5. The linear time version considers detached runs, hence the upper entry of this column, whereas the branching time version assumes trees and thus corresponds to the column's lower entry.

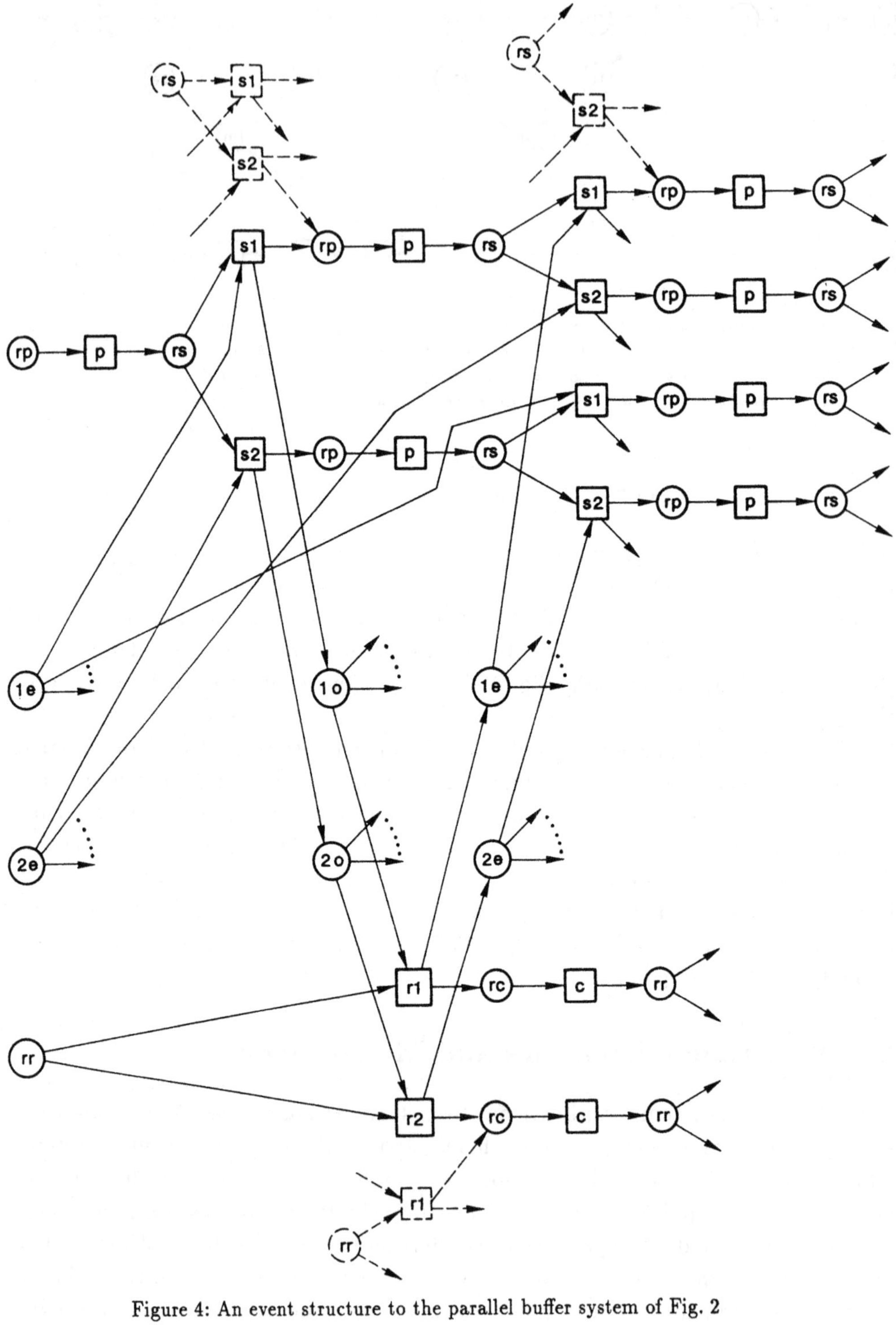

Figure 4: An event structure to the parallel buffer system of Fig. 2

		What is a Single run?	
		a sequence of events ordered in time	a partial order of events ordered by causality
how are runs grouped together, representing a system's behaviour?	a set of detached runs	*a set of sequences*	*a set of partial orders*
	a branched structure indicating alternatives	*a tree*	*an event structure with conflicts*

Figure 5: Taxonomy of operational semantics for concurrent systems

The meaning and the expressive power of both versions has extensively been discussed in the literature. *Computation tree logic* CTL* of [Emerson, Halpern 83] then introduced a systematic classification of the area. This approach fits perfectly with our above remark, stating that execution trees provide additional information to single runs: CTL* covers conventional linear time logic, but is more expressive.

In this paper we shall discuss logical systems for the right column of the matrix in Fig. 5. Such logical systems should be capable for expressing particular properties of partially ordered runs and event structures. Generally, there exists a couple of Temporal Logic concepts for partially ordered sets and detached, partially ordered runs of nonsequential systems, including [Lodaya, Thiagarajan 87], [Pinter, Wolper 84] and [Katz, Peled 87]. The case of detached, partially ordered runs of *elementary net systems* has in detail been considered in [Reisig 87a] and [Reisig 88].

	interleaved execution sequences	partially ordered, causality based runs
detached runs	linear time temporal logic	[Pinter, Wolper 84] [Katz, Peled 87] [Lodaya, Thiagarajan 87] [Reisig 88]
branching structure of runs with alternatives	CTL* etc.	?

Figure 6: Taxonomy of several versions of Temporal Logics

A Temporal Logic for the case of combining synchronization trees with partially ordered sets has — as far as we know — not yet been considered in the literature. (This is in Fig. 6 indicated by a question mark). Temporal Logic at first glance appears not too useful for this goal. As Fig. 4 shows, we need two kind of branchings: Branched palces (circles) denote alternatives, whereas branched transitions (boxes) denote concurrency. Temporal Logic in its branching time version concentrates on the first aspect, i.e. branching denoting alternatives. In [Reisig 88] we discussed however already the aspect of branchings denoting concurrency.

We shall discuss how a logic for the general case can be gained, by turning back to the roots of Temporal Logic.

Temporal Logic centers around particular interpretations of two operators, $\Box$ and $\Diamond$, occurring in logical expressions. These operators in their original *modal* interpretation denote "it is necessary that ..." and "it is possible that ...". Their precise meaning depends on *models*, over which they are interpreted. Models are usually constructed as *Kripke Structures*, consisting of a set W of objects (called *worlds*), a relation $R \subseteq W \times W$ denoting *reachability* and a mapping to return a truth value for each pair (w, p) of a world w and a modal logic formula p.

Different properties of the reachability relation R lead to different logical systems. Of interest for us is the S4 model where R is assumed to be reflexive and transitive (and some further axioms be valid). For details, see [Hughes, Creswell 68].

The Temporal Logic approach additionally assumes R be an order. In its applications to computer science, R is also discrete. The modal operators $\Box$ and $\Diamond$ then are interpreted "always in the future ..." and "sometime in the future ...". respectively. A binary operator is in general necessary, mostly called *until*. Additionally a *next time* operator, $\circ$, can be introduced, in case R is discrete. The above mentioned two versions of Temporal Logic both fit into this framework: Linear Time Temporal Logic assumes R to consist of total orders, thus apt for interleaved detached runs. Branching Time Temporal Logic assumes R a tree–like structure which fits with interleaved branched runs.

For the purposes discussed above, i.e. logical systems for the right column of Fig. 5, we retain the S4–model and assume R be an order. But R is not necessarily a collection of total orders or a tree. Instead, more general partial orders will occur. Additionally, and in principle even more important, the order has different interpretations: Different direct successers do no longer necessarily represent alternatives. They might instead also represent concurrency. This affects of course the formal concepts of the logic. Before turning to such details, we discuss a proper kind of models, called *elementary net systems.*

II REPRESENTATION AND ANALYSIS OF CONCURRENT SYSTEMS

On the background of the intuitive discussion of the first part, we develop here a system model fitting with partial order semantics, and a corresponding logical language. The system model to be defined in Chapter 4 are *Elementary Net Systems*, which are the base for more or less all approaches to partial order semantics. Their local state elements are *conditions*, constituting the base for the modal logic language to follow in Chapter 5.

4 Elementary Net Systems

We recall the basics of *Elementary Net Systems*, the fundamental Petri Net based system model, and develop the corresponding causality based operational semantics. The state elements of an elementary net system are *conditions*, apt to dynamic change of their current truth value. The transition elements are *events*, which upon occurring swap the truthvalues of their pre– and post–conditions.

Definition An elementary net system (en–system) $\Sigma = (B,\ E,\ F,\ c_0)$ consists of

- two disjoint sets B and E with elements called *conditions* and *events*, respectively,
- a relation $F \subseteq (S \times T) \cup (T \times S)$, called the *flow relation* of Σ,
- a set of conditions $c_0 \subseteq B$, called the *initial case* of Σ.

The above Figures 1 and 2 showed elementary net systems in the usual graphical form: Conditions and events are represented as circles and boxes, respectively. The elements of the flow relation F are represented by arcs between the respective circles and boxes. Dots inside circles denote the elements of the initial case.

As a technicality, the "dot notation" for neighbourhood is useful here:

Notation Let A be a set, and let $\rho \subseteq A \times A$ be a relation.

(i) For $a \in A$, let ${}^\bullet a = \{b \in A \mid (b,a) \in \rho\}$ and let $a^\bullet = \{b \in A \mid (a,b) \in \rho\}$.

(ii) For $B \subseteq A$, let ${}^\bullet B = \bigcup\{{}^\bullet b \mid b \in B\}$ and let $B^\bullet = \bigcup\{b^\bullet \mid b \in B\}$.

Whenever a relation is uniquely given from the context, this notation may be useful. It will particularly be applied to the flow relation of en–systems.

Our next topic is the dynamics of elementary net systems. In an en–system $\Sigma = (B,\ E,\ F,\ c_0)$, the truth values of conditions may change due to event occurrences. Global observations of such systems are called *cases*, formally described as subsets $c \subseteq B$ of conditions. One of them is the initial case, c_0. An event $e \in E$ may *occur* in a case c, iff all its pre–conditions ${}^\bullet e$ and none of its post–conditions $e^\bullet$ belong to c. Its occurrence swaps the truthvalues of the conditions in ${}^\bullet e$ and in $e^\bullet$.

Definition Let $\Sigma = (B,\ E,\ F,\ c_0)$ be an en–system.

(i) A *case* of Σ is a subset $c \subseteq B$ of conditions.

(ii) An event $e \in E$ is *enabled in a case* c if ${}^\bullet e \subseteq c$ and $e^\bullet \cap c = \emptyset$.

(iii) $c[e\rangle c'$ is a *step* in Σ iff e is an event, enabled in the case c, and $c' = (c \setminus {}^\bullet e) \cup e^\bullet$.

As an example in both Fig. 1 and Fig. 2, "produce" is the only enabled event in the indicated case.

Notice that in a step $c[e\rangle c'$, the conditions outside the scope ${}^\bullet e \cup e^\bullet$ of e are not relevant. Some of them belong to both c and c', the rest to neither of the two cases. The occurrence of an event is entirely fixed by swapping the truthvalues in its scope. Fig. 7 outlines this situation.

Figure 7: Outline of an event occurrence

Steps may form occurrence sequences $c_0[e_1\rangle c_1[e_2\rangle \ldots$ in the obvious way. Causality based semantics will be founded on the above discussed restriction of the events effect to their scope. Formally, a causality based run of a system Σ will be defined as a mapping from an acyclic net with unbranched places (an *occurrence net*) to Σ.

Definition An *occurrence net* $N = (S,\ T,\ F)$ consists of

- two disjoint sets S and T with elements called *places* and *transitions*, respectively,
- a relation $F \subseteq (S \times T) \cup (T \times S)$ such that
  (i) $< := F^+$ is irreflexive, and
  (ii) for all $s \in S$, $|{}^\bullet s| \leq 1$ and $|s^\bullet| \leq 1$.

The dot–notation in this definition refers of course to the involved relation F of N. Demanding F^+, the transitive closure of F under composition, be additionally irreflexive, $<$ in fact is a (partial, strict) order.

Fig. 3 shows an occurrence net (with inscribed places and transitions). Places and transitions of occurrence nets will represent instances of condition holdings and event occurrences, respectively. The order $<$ denotes system–defined, "causal" dependency, and consequently unorder represents concurrency.

Definition Let $N = (S, T, F)$ be an occurrence net.

(i) Two elements $x, y \in S \cup T$ are *concurrent* (written x $\underline{co}$ y) iff neither $x < y$ nor $y < x$.

(ii) A *slice of N* is a maximal subset $A \subseteq S$ of places such that x $\underline{co}$ y for all elements $x, y \in A$.

(iii) A slice A' is a *successor* of a slice A iff for some $t \in T$, $^\bullet t \subseteq A$ and $A' = (A \setminus {}^\bullet t) \cup t^\bullet$.

(iv) The order $<$ on N canonically defines an order on slices: $A \leq A'$ iff to each $s \in A$ there exists some $s' \in A'$ with $s \leq s'$ (where $\leq = < \cup\, id$).

We come now to a central notion, viz. causality based runs of en–systems. Such a run is formally defined as a mapping from an occurrence net to an en–system:

Definition Let $\Sigma = (B, E, F, c_0)$ be an en–system and let $N = (S, T, F')$ be an occurrence net. A mapping $r : S \cup T \longrightarrow B \cup E$ is a *run* of Σ (written $r : N \longrightarrow \Sigma$) iff

(i) for some slice A of N, $r(A) = c_0$,
(ii) for all $x, y \in S$: if $r(x) = r(y)$ then $x \leq y$ or $y \leq x$,
(iii) for each $t \in T$, $^\bullet r(t) = r(^\bullet t)$ and $r(t)^\bullet = r(t^\bullet)$.

Fig. 3 in fact shows a run of the system in Fig. 1. The mapping r is indicated by inscriptions of the elements of Fig. 3. Its places without predecessors form a slice which is mapped to the initial case of the system in Σ_1 (there indicated by dots).

Succession of slices corresponds in a run directly to the occurrence of events:

Proposition Let $r : N \longrightarrow \Sigma$ be a run. Let A' be a successor of a slice A in N. Then for the transition $t \in T$ with $^\bullet t \subseteq A$ and $t^\bullet \subseteq A'$, $r(A)[r(t)\rangle r(A')$ is a step in Σ.

The proof of this proposition follows directly from the involved definitions.

The above defined runs of en–systems fill the upper entry of the right column in Fig. 5. For its lower entry, we have to introduce a further branching structure on runs (besides the branching of transitions, which represents concurrency): Branching of places is an obvious means to represent alternatives in such runs. This has been the central idea of event structures [Nielsen, Plotkin, Winskel 80], which are a proper candidate for serving as domains of mappings to elementary net systems.

Fig. 4 shows an event structure and a mapping (represented by inscriptions) to the producer/consumer system of Fig. 2. The runs (in the above sense) of the system are in Fig. 4 contained as maximal subsets with unbranched places. As an example, Fig. 8 shows such a run describing alternative using of the buffer cells.

The paper [Strack 88] in an algebraic framework shows how event structures be mapped to en–systems. We refrain from formal details here, because we will not

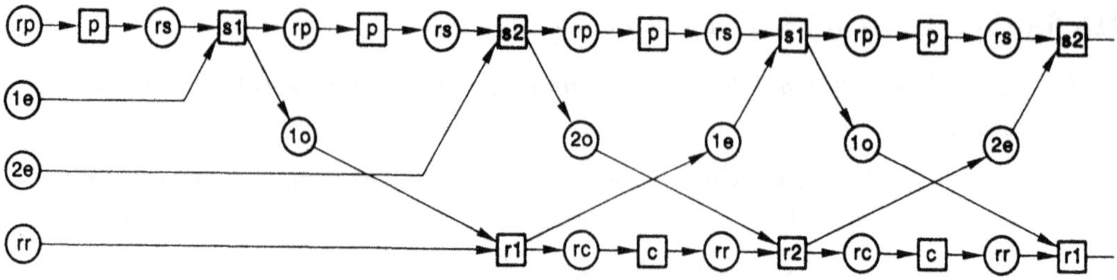

Figure 8: A single run of the parallel buffer system Σ_2

need them later on. Here it is sufficient to know that the net structure of Fig. 4 and the indicated mapping are examples for the branched structure of the lower entry in the right column of Fig. 5.

In the following we will stick to *simple* and *pure* elementary net systems: Simplicity means that different events can not have equal pre– and equal post– conditions. (If both sets were equal, there was no need for different events). Consequently, in a simple en–system an event is determined by its effect on the involved conditions. Pureness means that no condition is a precondition as well as a post–condition of one event, i.e. loops formed □ ○ are excluded. This means that causes and effects of events are uniquely determined by the changes of conditions. This leads to the following convention.

Convention In the rest of this paper, for all en–systems $\Sigma = (B,\ E,\ F,\ c_0)$ we assume:

(i) for all $e_0, e_1 \in E$: ${}^\bullet e_0 = {}^\bullet e_1$ and $e_0{}^\bullet = e_1{}^\bullet$ implies $e_0 = e_1$
(ii) for all $e \in E$: ${}^\bullet e \cap e^\bullet = \emptyset$.

5 The Logical Language $\mathcal{F}(B)$

In Chapter 4 we discussed the need of logical systems for the right column of Fig. 5. Chapter 4 provided corresponding models, consisting in sets of inscribed occurrence nets, and branched structures such as in Fig. 4, respectively.

One expects here two versions of logics for detached and for branched runs, respectively, in analogy to the above discussed Linear Time/Branching Time antonomy. For the case of detached runs, a logic has been introduced and used in [Reisig 87a] and [Reisig 88]. So we concentrate here on the case of branched runs (corresponding to Branching Time Temporal Logic). We develop the logic along the widely used logic CTL* of [Emerson, Halpern 83]. In this logic, the three temporal operators □, ◇, ○ are further refined by two quantifiers, "A" and "E", denoting "for each of the paths" and "for at least one of the paths" starting at the node under consideration. For reasons to become obvious later, we additionally use corresponding "past" operators, in the style of [Pinter, Wolper 84]. This leads to the following logical language:

Definition Let B be a finite set. The set $\mathcal{F}(B)$ of *(propositional) formulas over* B is the smallest set of formulas such that

(i) $B \subseteq \mathcal{F}(b)$

(ii) if $f \in \mathcal{F}(B)$ then $\neg f, \forall\Box f,\ \forall\Diamond f,\ \forall\circ f, \forall\overleftarrow{\Box} f,\ \forall\overleftarrow{\Diamond} f,\ \forall\overleftarrow{\circ} f \in \mathcal{F}(B)$

(iii) if $f, g \in \mathcal{F}(B)$ then $f \wedge g, f\ \forall\underline{until}\ g, f\ \forall\underline{since}\ g \in \mathcal{F}(B)$

Disjunction, implication, and the existential quantifier for the modal operators are introduced as shorthands:

Shorthands: Let $f, g \in \mathcal{F}(B)$. Then we write

$f \vee g$ for $\neg(\neg f \wedge \neg g)$, $f \rightarrow g$ for $\neg f \vee g$, $\exists\Box f$ for $\neg\forall\Diamond\neg f$, $\exists\Diamond f$ for $\neg\forall\Box\neg f$, $\exists\circ f$ for $\neg\forall\circ\neg f$, $\overleftarrow{\exists\Box} f$ for $\neg\forall\Diamond\neg f$, $\overleftarrow{\exists\Diamond} f$ for $\neg\forall\Box\neg f$, and $\overleftarrow{\exists\circ} f$ for $\neg\forall\circ\neg f$.

These formulas will be interpreted over elementary net systems. The set B of conditions of an en–system Σ is used to construct the corresponding set $\mathcal{F}(B)$ of formulas. A formula will be called *valid in a case* c of Σ iff all or some of its runs with a slice mapped onto c, fulfill certain requirements (defined below). A formula will be called *valid for* Σ iff it is valid in all cases of Σ.

The formal definition of validity will be based on the following notions:

Definition Let Σ be an en–system, let c be a case and let $r : N \rightarrow \Sigma$ be a run of Σ.

(i) A slice A of N is a *c–slice* iff $r(A) = c$

(ii) r is a *c–run* iff N has a c–slice.

Validity of formulas is defined for cases of en–systems, as follows:

Definition Let $\Sigma = (B,\ E,\ F,\ c_0)$ be an en–system, let c be a case of Σ and let $f \in \mathcal{F}(B)$. We define the validity of f in c, written $\Vdash_c f$, inductively as follows:

a) for the propositional operators:

for $b \in B$, $\Vdash_c b$ iff $b \in c$.

$\Vdash_c \neg f$ iff not $\Vdash_c f$.

$\Vdash_c f \wedge g$ iff $\Vdash_c f$ and $\Vdash_c g$.

b) for the forward oriented, $\forall$–quantified modal operators:

$\Vdash_c \forall\Box f$ iff for each run r of Σ with a c–slice A, $\Vdash_{r(A')}$ holds for all slices $A' \geq A$ of r;

$\Vdash_c \forall\Diamond f$ iff for each run r of Σ with a c–slice A,
$\Vdash_{r(A')} F$ holds for some slice $A' \geq A$ of r;

$\Vdash_c \forall\circ f$ iff for each run r of Σ with a c–slice A,
$\Vdash_{r(A')} f$ holds for some successor A' of A in r;

$\Vdash_c f \ \underline{\forall until}\ g$ iff for each run r of Σ with a c–slice A, there exists a slice $A' \geq A$ in r with $\Vdash_{r(A')} g$ and $\Vdash_{r(A'')} f$ holds for all $A \leq A'' \leq A'$.

c) for the backward oriented $\forall$–quantified modal operators:

$\Vdash_c \forall\overleftarrow{\Box} f$ iff for each run r of Σ with a c–slice A,
$\Vdash_{r(A')} f$ holds for all slices $A' \leq A$ in r;

$\Vdash_c \forall\overleftarrow{\Diamond} f$ iff for each run r of Σ with a c–slice A,
$\Vdash_{r(A')} f$ holds for some slice $A' \geq A$ in r;

$\Vdash_c \forall\overleftarrow{\circ} f$ iff for each run r of Σ with a c–slice A,
$\Vdash_{r(A')} f$ holds for some predecessor A' of A in r;

$\Vdash_c f \ \underline{\forall since}\ g$ iff for each run r of Σ with a c–slice A, there exists a slice $A' \leq A$ in r with $\Vdash_{r(A')} g$ and $\Vdash_{r(A'')}$ holds for all slices $A' \leq A'' \leq A$.

As an example, with the shorthands of Fig. 3 we get for the case $c = \{rs,\ 1e,\ 2e,\ rr$ of Σ_2 : $\Vdash_c \forall\circ rp$ and $\Vdash_c \forall\Box\forall\Diamond(1o \vee 2o)$.

The semantics of the above defined shorthand formulas $\exists\varphi$ is gained from the semantics of the corresponding $\forall\varphi$ formula upon replacing the phrase "... for each run r of Σ..." by " ... for some run r of Σ..." in the above definitions.

As an example, with the case $c = \{rs,\ 1e,\ 2e,\ rr\}$ of Σ_2 we get $\Vdash_c \exists\circ(1o)$, but not $\Vdash_c \forall\circ(1o)$.

Definition Let $\Sigma = (B,\ E,\ F,\ c_0)$ be an en–system and let $f \in \mathcal{F}(B)$.

Then f *is valid in* Σ (written $\Vdash_\Sigma f$) iff f is valid in each case of Σ.

As an example, with the case c of Σ_2 considered above, we get $\Vdash_\Sigma \forall\Box\exists\Diamond(1o)$. This formula says there is always a chance to use buffer cell 1. Likewise, $\Vdash_\Sigma \exists\Box 1e$ says that this cell may remain empty forever.

In Chapter 3 we mentioned that the logic $\mathcal{F}(B)$ is an S4–logic in the sense of [Hughes, Cresswell 68]. We can now more precisely describe what kind of Kripke structure we use: Its worlds are the slices of the runs of the considered en–system, its reachability relation is the (forward and backward) transitive closure of the next step relation, separate for each run. The labellings of the worlds (i.e. slices) is given by their mapping to en–systems.

III REPRESENTATION OF SYSTEM PROPERTIES

Here we discuss on a formal basis the properties of concurrent systems which are interesting enough to justify partial order semantics and a corresponding logic. First the parallel buffer introduced in the first chapter will be picked up and its property of minimal delay will be formulated in the logical language $\mathcal{F}(B)$. In Chapter 7 we turn to concurrency issues and show how several notions of this area can be formulated in the language $\mathcal{F}(B)$. Chapter 8 is devoted to a particular, strong form of concurrency. It introduces some kind of objectivity in definitely reaching distributed global states; a property essential for fairness notions.

6 Representable Properties: Examples

A typical property representable in the logig $\mathcal{F}(B)$ has already been mentioned in Chapter 1: In the producer/consumer system Σ_2 one always can continue with minimal delay: In case the buffer is not entirely occupied or not entirely empty, an item can be inserted or removed, respectively, without delay.

First we give formulas describing the buffer be not entirely occupied (NOC) and not entirely empty (NEM):

$$\begin{aligned} NOC &= em \vee em2 \\ NEM &= oc1 \vee oc2. \end{aligned}$$

The immediate chance to insert or to remove an item then is given by the formulas

$$\begin{aligned} IN &= rs \wedge NOC \longrightarrow \exists \bigcirc rp \quad , \quad and \\ OUT &= rr \wedge NEM \longrightarrow \exists \bigcirc rc \quad , \end{aligned}$$

respectively.

The requirement of minimal delay is represented by the conjunction

$$In \wedge OUT.$$

This formula is valid for Σ_2, but not for Σ_1.

IN is not valid in case the run shown in Fig. 9 was the only run of Σ_2. Hence, in the logic $\mathcal{L}(B)$ of [Reisig 88], IN is not true for Σ_2.

It is also not true in interleaving semantics, because direct succession then may be destroyed by interleaving events occurring elsewhere. This shows that IN (and likewise OUT) represents a typical effect of combining alternatives with concurrency.

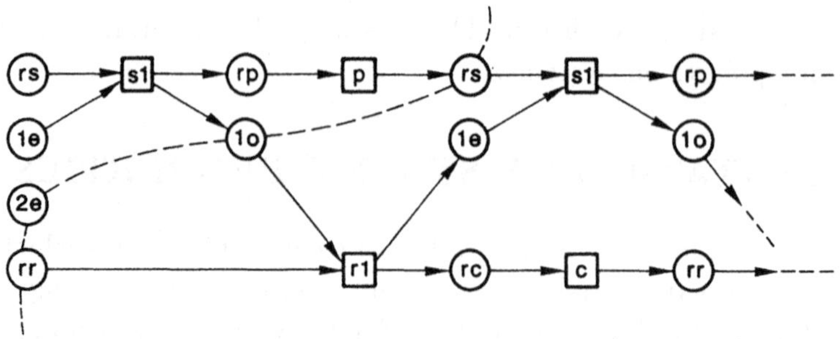

Figure 9: A run of Σ_2 with delay for the sender

7 Concurrency Formulas

Concurrency is usually defined as a binary relation over the elements of occurrence nets: Two such elements are concurrent iff they are unordered. This implies immediately a notion of concurrency for single event occurrences and condition holdings in elementary net systems. For the elements (i.e. conditions and events) of en–systems, the above notion can be extended in different ways.

Here we shall define two conditions b_0, b_1 of an en–system Σ to be *concurrent in a run* if each holding of b_0 is accompanied by a concurrent holding of b_1, and vice versa. This is equivalent to the property that whenever one of the conditions holds, at least one observer of the run sees the other one holding too. More formally this means that in the run $r : K \to \Sigma$ with an S–element $s_0 \in K$ being mapped to $r(s) = b_0$, there exists an S–element $s_1 \in K$ with $r(s_1) = b_1$ such that $s_0 \underline{co} s_1$ (and vice versa).

Definition Let $\Sigma = (B,\ E,\ F,\ c_0)$ be an en–system with $b_0, b_1 \in B$. Furthermore, let $r : N \to \Sigma$ be a run with $N = (S,\ T,\ F')$. b_0 and b_1 are *concurrent in* r iff for each $s_0 \in S$ with $r(s_0) = b_0$ there exists some $s_1 \in S$ with $r(s_1) = b_1$ and $s_0\ \underline{co}\ s_1$.

As an example, Fig. 10 shows an en–system, Σ_3, and Fig. 11 shows one of its runs r with b_0 and b_4 concurrent in r.

We generalize this notion to *concurrency in* Σ, considering all runs:

Definition Let $\Sigma = (B,\ E,\ F,\ c_0)$ be an en–system with $b_0, b_1 \in B$. b_0 and b_1 are *concurrent in* Σ iff they are concurrent in each run of Σ.

To give examples, in the systems Σ_1 and Σ_2 (Figs. 1 and 2), the conditions "ready to produce" and "ready to send" are not concurrent. But each of them is concurrent with each of the remaining conditions. In the system Σ_3 (Fig. 10), b_1 and b_4 are not concurrent. This is easily checked by help of the run in Fig. 12.

We are now after a characterization of the concurrency relation in terms of the language $\mathcal{F}(B)$. One can not argue about properties of single elements of occurrence nets, viz. their being mapped onto distinguished conditions, or about their unorder. Therefore we formulate concurrency in terms of what is going to

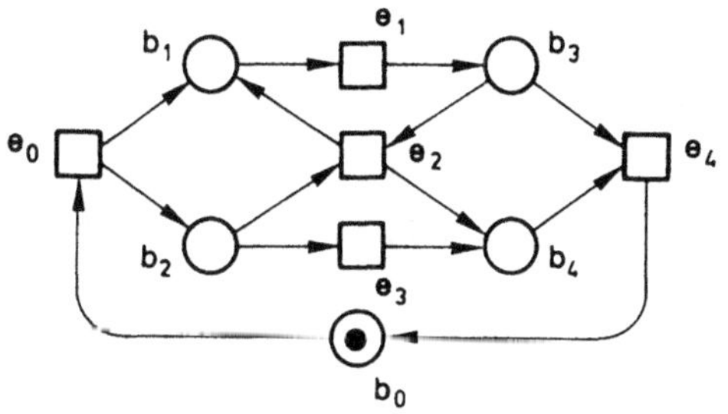

Figure 10: En–system Σ_3

happen in case one of the two considered conditions holds: In this case, we can seize this condition until the other one becomes valid, or we trace backwards and observe that the other one has been valid.

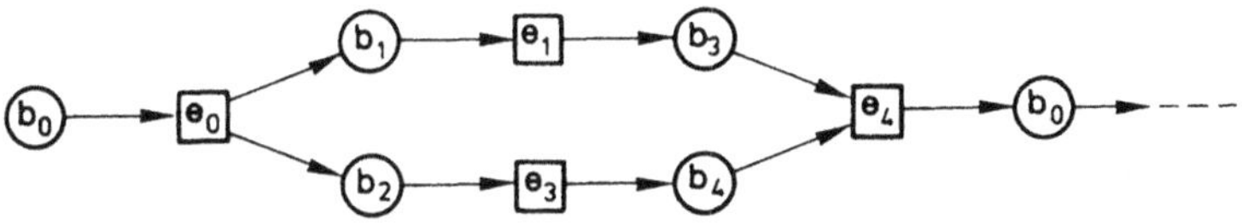

Figure 11: A run of Σ_3 with b_1 and b_4 concurrent

This leads to the following formula:

Definition For two conditions b_0 and b_1 of an elementary net system,

$$\begin{aligned} CO_{b_0 b_1} = \; & b_0 \;\rightarrow\; (b_0 \; \underline{\forall until} \; b_1 \;\vee\; b_0 \; \underline{\forall since} \; b_1) \;\; \wedge \\ & b_1 \;\rightarrow\; (b_1 \; \underline{\forall until} \; b_0 \;\vee\; b_1 \; \underline{\forall since} \; b_0) \end{aligned}$$

is the *concurrency formula of* b_0 *and* b_1.

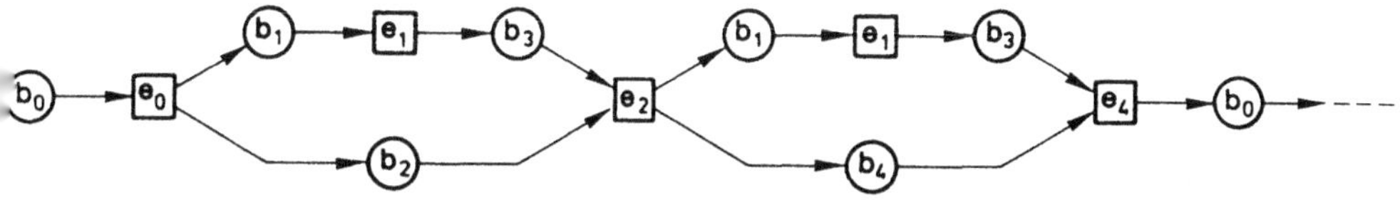

Figure 12: A run of Σ_3 with b_1 and b_4 lined

The following technical lemma prepares the central theorem of this section:

Lemma Let b_0, b_1 be conditions of an en–system Σ, and let c be a reachable case of Σ. b_0 and b_1 are concurrent in each run with a c–slice A iff $\Vdash_c CO_{b_0,b_1}$.

Proof We first show "$\Rightarrow$": Let $r : N \rightarrow \Sigma$ be a run with a c–slice. Let A be a slice of N with an element s_0 and $r(s_0) = b_0$. By definition of concurrency, there exists an element s_1 of N with $r(s_1) = b_1$ and s_0 $\underline{co}$ s_1. As A is a slice, for some $s \in A$ it holds $s \leq s_1$ or $s_1 \leq s$ (cf. Fig. 13). If $s \leq s_1$, there exists a slice $A' \geq A$ with $\{s_0, s_1\} \subseteq A'$. Furthermore, $s_0 \in A''$ for all A'' with $A \leq A'' \leq A'$. So, $\Vdash_{r(A')} b_1$ and $\Vdash_{r(A'')} b_0$ for all A'' with $A \leq A'' \leq A'$. This implies $\Vdash_{r(A)} b_0\ \underline{\forall until}\ b_1$. If $s_1 \leq s$, one likewise shows $\Vdash_{r(A)} b_0\ \underline{\forall since}\ b_1$. This completes "⇒".

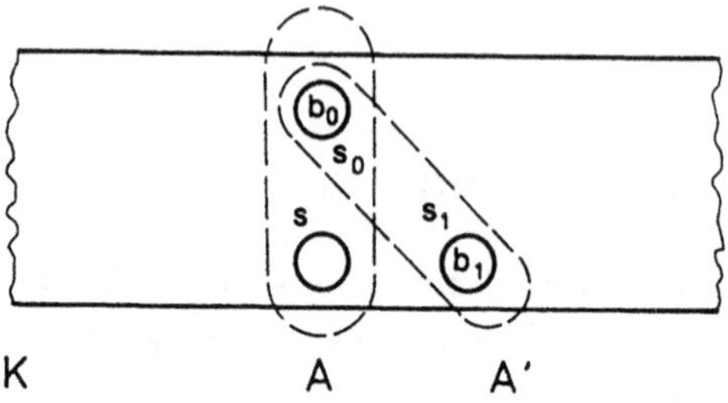

Figure 13: Illustrating the proof of the concurrency lemma

To show "⇐", we first assume $\Vdash_c b_0 \rightarrow (b_0\ \underline{\forall until}\ b_1)$. By definition of validity this is trivial in case not $b \in c$. Otherwise, this means that for each run r of Σ with a c–slice A, A has an element $s_0 \in A$ with $r(s_0) = b_0$. Furthermore, there exists a slice $A' \geq A$ in r with an element $s_1 \in A'$ and $r(s_1) = b_1$ (c.f. Fig. 13), and for all $A \leq A'' \leq A'$, $\Vdash_{A''} b_0$. Each such A'' contains s_0 (as loops ○ □ are excluded in en–systems.) So, $s_0, s_1 \in A'$ which means s_0 $\underline{co}$ s_1, implying b_0 and b_1 be concurrent.

The second part of CO_{b_0,b_1} is likewise shown.

■

Now we can show that CO–formulas in fact describe concurrency:

Theorem Let $\Sigma = (B,\ E,\ F,\ c_0)$ be an en–system with $b_0, b_1 \in B$. b_0 and b_1 are concurrent in Σ iff $\Vdash_\Sigma \forall \Box CO_{b_0 b_1}$.

Proof According to the above definition, b_0 and b_1 are concurrent in Σ iff they are concurrent in each run fo Σ. With the above lemma, this means that in each run of Σ, CO_{b_0,b_1} is valid in each slice. As each case of Σ is the image of at least one slice, we get $\Vdash_c \forall \Box CO_{b_0,b_1}$ for each case c. This is equivalent to $\Vdash_\Sigma \forall \Box CO_{b_0 b_1}$.

■

A further interesting formula,

$$\exists \Box CO_{b_0 b_1}$$

says that there exists always a chance for finding a run in which b_0 and b_1 are concurrent. As an example, we discussed above that $\forall \Box CO_{b_1 b_4}$ is not valid for the system Σ_3 (Fig. 10). But one easily shows

$$\Vdash_{\Sigma_3} \exists \Box CO_{b_1 b_4}$$

by help of the run in Fig. 11

The knowledge about conditions being concurrent is important for fairness concepts. As an example consider an event e with $^{\bullet}e = \{b_0, b_1\}$. b_0 and b_1 may infinitely often occur concurrently in a run r, but e may occur finitely often only. It is debatable whether or not r is unfair to e, because nothing guarantees b_0 and b_1 to occur definitely together. As examples, consider the conditions *ready to send* and *ready to remove* in Fig. 1 or in Fig. 2, and a corresponding event e with both these conditions in $^{\bullet}e$.

The situation changes when concurrent conditions are objectively reached. This is the topic of the following chapter.

8 Strong Concurrency Formulas

The above discussed concurrency relation covers an interesting sub–relation, called "strong concurrency". An intuitively nice relationship between both notions can be established along a new characterization of concurrency: Two S–elements of an occurrence net are concurrent (in the above defined sense) iff at least one observer of the corresponding run observes both of them at the same time — more formally: iff at least one interleaving sequence has a slice comprising both elements. Now, *strongly* concurrent elements are observed by *each* observer at the same time, i.e. *each* execution sequence of the run has a slice comprising both elements.

To discuss examples, all pairs of concurrent S–elements in the occurrence nets of Fig. 3 and Fig. 8, respectively, are strongly concurrent iff they have equal pre– or post–transitions. A less trivial example gives Fig. 14: here, s_0 and s_1 are strongly concurrent. Details of this notion and its consequences have been studied in [Reisig 87].

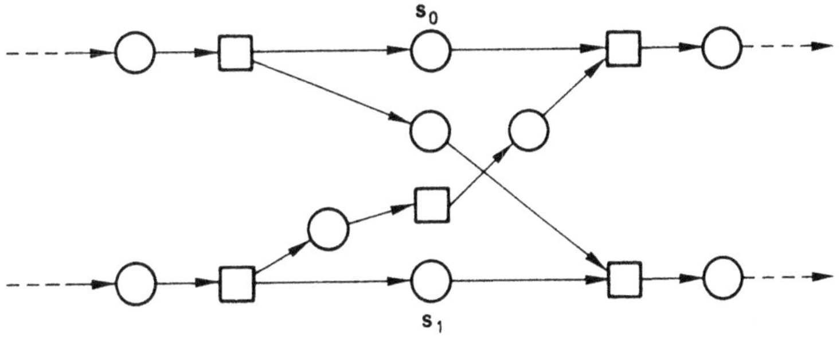

Figure 14: Occurrence Net with strongly concurrent S–elements s_0, s_1

First we formally relate partially ordered runs and occurrence sequences:

Definition Let $r : N \to \Sigma$ be a run. A sequence $A_0 t_1 A_1 \ldots t_n A_n$ of slices A_i and transitions t_i of N is an *interleaving sequence of* r, iff $\{t_1, \ldots, t_n\}$ is the set of all transitions of N and if for all $i = 1, \ldots, n$, $r(A_{i-1})[t_i\rangle r(A_i)$ is a step in Σ.

Now we define strong concurrency for occurrence nets:

Definition Let $r : N \to \Sigma$ be a run of an en–system Σ. Two S–elements s_0, s_1 of N are *strongly concurrent* in r iff each interleaving sequence $S_0\, t_1\, S_1 \ldots t_n\, S_n$ of r has a slice S_i with $\{s_0, s_1\} \subseteq S_i$.

We transfer this notion to en–systems as follows:

Definition Let Σ be an en–system and let b_0, b_1 be conditions of Σ. b_0 and b_1 are *strongly concurrent in* Σ iff they are concurrent in Σ and for each run $r : N \to \Sigma$ it holds: in case two concurrent S–elements s_0, s_1 of N exist with $r(s_0) = b_0$ and $r(s_1) = b_1$ then s_0 and s_1 are strongly concurrent in r.

An example for strongly concurrent conditons of an en–system shows Fig. 15.

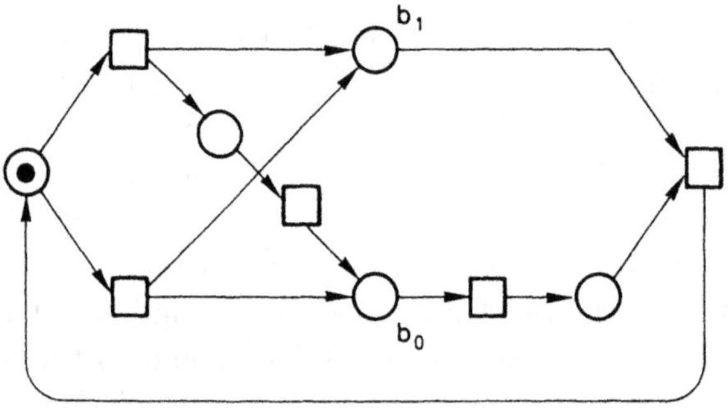

Figure 15: En–system Σ_4 with strongly concurrent conditions b_0 and b_1

We now derive a logical characterization of strong concurrency. Intuitively, the formula expressing strong concurrency will demand that concurrent conditions b_0 and b_1 are strongly concurrent and that furthermore holds: In case b_0 is valid and b_1 is to become valid in a next step, then b_0 is forced to "wait for b_1"

Definition For two conditions b_0 and b_1 of an elementary net system,

$$\begin{aligned} SCO_{b_0b_1} \;=\; CO_{b_0b_1} \;\wedge\; & (b_0 \wedge \neg b_1 \wedge \exists\circ b_1) \;\to\; \forall\circ b_0 \\ \wedge\; & (b_1 \wedge \neg b_0 b_0 \wedge \exists\circ b_0) \;\to\; \forall\circ b_1 \end{aligned}$$

is the *strong concurrency formula of* b_0 *and* b_1.

Strong concurrency formulas in fact describe strong concurrency:

Theorem Let $\Sigma = (B,\ E,\ F,\ c_0)$ be an en–system with $b_0, b_1 \in B$. b_0 and b_1 are strongly concurrent in Σ iff $\models_\Sigma \forall\Box SCO_{b_0b_1}$.

This Theorem has been shown in [Reisig 87a], pp. 19–20.

A further interesting formula,

$$\exists\Box SCO_{b_0b_1}$$

says that there exists always a chance for finding a run in which b_0 and b_1 are strongly concurrent.

A weaker property may also be of interest, stating that whenever two conditions occur concurrently, then this occurrence is even strongly concurrent:

$$CO_{b_0b_1} \longrightarrow SCO_{b_1b_1} .$$

As an example, this formula is not valid for the system Σ_3 (Fig. 10) with respect to b_1 and b_4. One finds however always a continuation to fulfill this formula, so it holds

$$\Vdash_{\Sigma_3} \exists\Box(CO_{b_0b_1} \longrightarrow SCO_{b_0b_1})$$

In fact, the run of Σ_3 shown in Fig. 12 indicates how to continue in any case, in order to meet this property.

Conclusion

We hope to have shown that partial order semantics leads to a couple of notions which are essential for concurrent systems, and that such notions can be covered by a revised version of temporal logic.

An adequate treatment of concurrency in terms of temporal logic has been the aim of several previous approaches: Some of them consider non-sequential systems consisting of sets of communicating agents, where each agent gets its "private" logic. [Emerson, Clarke 82] and [Manna, Wolper 84] synthesize the overall system behaviour as interleavings of the agent's sequences. this way they end up with conventional branching time and linear time temporal logic, respectively. [Enjalberg, Michel] take vector languages built from the agent's sequences and augment additional requirements. In [Lodaya, Thiagarajan 87] each agent is able to reason about the local states of other agents as long as they are forward or backward reachable from its own local state.

Some approaches directly consider partial orders as models of logics. [Pinter, Wolper 84] generate general partial orders via relations over (local) states and reason about such states with temporal logic. *Interleaving set temporal logic* of [Katz, Peled 87] considers the set of interleavings, gained by extending the partial orders of runs to total orders. Then properties are studies which can be derived from one interleaving but are valid for all interleavings of one interleaving set.

In this paper we concentrated on properties which can not be derived from each detached sequence of an interleaving set. Particularly the fairness issues glanced in Chapter 9 demand knowledge about the partially ordered sets. We hope the logic $\mathcal{F}(B)$ supports the representation of this kind of property.

The system model as well as the logic considered in this paper are both very basic. They are indended as a framework to deal with the fundamental phenomena of concurrent systems.

Much remains to be done to make $\mathcal{F}(B)$ a full-fledged logic. We did not give an axiomatization of the logic. Decidability and complexity issues have also not been discussed. We just concentrated on its expressiveness.

Practical applications of temporal logic and of Petri Nets require first order concepts in general. A first order version of the logic $\mathcal{F}(B)$, fitting with individual tokens in Petri nets, remains to be developed.

References

[**Clarke et al 83**] E. Clarke, M. Browne, E. Emerson, A. Sistla: *Using Temporal Logic for Automatic Verification of Finite State Systems.* in: Logics and Models of Concurrent Systems. K. Apt (ed.), Springer–Verlag, pp. 3–26 (1985)

[**Emerson, Clarke 82**] E. Allen Emerson, Edmund M. Clarke: *Using Branching Time Temporal Logic to Synthesize Synchronization Skeletons.* Science of Computer Programming 2, pp. 246–266 (1982

[**Emerson, Halpern 83**] E. Allen Emerson, Joseph Y. Halpern: *"Sometimes" and "Not Never" Revisited: On Branching versus Linear time.* Principles of programming languages 83, pp. 127–140, ACM (1983)

[**Enjalbert, Michel**] P. Enhalbert, M. Michel: *Many Sorted Temporal Logic for Multi–Process Systems.*

[**Hughes, Cresswell 68**] G.E. Hughes, M. J. Cresswell: *An Introduction to Modal Logic.* Methuen, London & New York (1968)

[**Katz, Peled 87**] Shmuel Katz, Doron Peled: *Interleaving Set Temporal Logic.* Proceedings of the ACM Symposium on Principles of Distributed Computation, Vancouver, B.C., (1987)

[**Lamport 80**] Leslie Lamport: *"Sometime" is sometimes " Not Never". On the Temporal Logic of Programs.* 7th Annual ACM Symp. on Principles of Programming Languages, pp. 174–185 (1980)

[**Lamport 83**] Leslie Lamport: *What Good is Temporal Logic?* Information Processing 83, R.E.A. Mason (ed.), North Holland, IFIP, pp. 657–667 (1983)

[**Lodaya, Thiagarajan 87**] K. Lodaya, P.S. Thiagarajan: *A Modal Logic for a Subclass of Event Structures.* 14th ICALP, Lecture Notes in Computer Science 267, Springer–Verlag pp. 290–303 (1987)

[Manna, Wolper 84] Zohar Manna, Pierre Wolper: *Synthesis of Communicating Processes from Temporal Logic Specifications.* ACM Transactions on Programming Languages and Systems, Vol. 6, No 1, pp. 68–93 (1984)

[Nielsen, Plotkin, Winskel 80] Mogns Nielsen, Gordon Plotkin, Glynn Winskel: *Petri Nets, Event Structures and Domains, Part I.* Theoretical Computer Science Vol. 13, No. 1, pp. 85–108 (1980)

[Olderog et al 88] Ernst Rüdiger Olderog, Ursula Goltz, Rob. v. Glabbeek: *Combining Compositionality and Concurrency.* Summary of a GMD–Workshop, Königswinter, March 1988. Gesellschaft für Mathematik und Datenverarbeitung, St. Augustin, Arbeitspapiere der GMD 320 (1988)

[Petri 77] Carl Adam Petri: *Non–sequential Processes.* Gesellschaft für Mathematik und Datenverarbeitung, Interner Bericht ISF–77–5 (1977)

[Pinter, Wolper 84] Shlomil S. Pinter, Pierre Wolper: *A Temporal Logic for Reasoning about Partially Ordered Computations.* Proceedings of the third ACM Symposium on Principles of Distributed Computing, Vancouver, Canada, pp. 28–37 (1984)

[Pnueli 81] Amir Pnueli: *The Temporal Logic of Concurrent Programs.* Theoretical Computer Science 13, pp. 45–60 (1981)

[Pnueli 86] Amir Pnueli: *Specification and Development of Reactive Systems.* Information Processing 86, H. J. Kugler (ed.), North–Holland, pp. 845–858 (1986)

[Reisig 84] Wolfgang Reisig: *Partial Order Semantics versus Interleaving Semantics for CSP–like Languages and its Impact on Fairness.* Lecture Notes in Computer Science Vol. 172, J. Paredaens (ed.), Springer–Verlag, pp. 403–413 (1984)

[Reisig 87a] Wolfgang Reisig: *Towards a Temporal Logic for True Concurrency Part I: Linear Time Propositional Logic.* Gesellschaft für Mathematik und Datenverarbeitung, St. Augustin, Arbeitspapiere der GMD 277 (1987)

[Reisig 87b] Wolfgang Reisig: *A Strong Part of Concurrency.* Advances in Petri Nets 1987, Lecture Notes in Computer Science 266; G. Rozenberg (ed.), Springer–Verlag, pp. 238–272 (1987)

[Reisig 88] Wolfgang Reisig: *Temporal Logic and Causality in Concurrent systems.* Proceedings of CONCURRENCY 88, Hamburg. Lecture Notes in Computer Science, Springer–Verlag (1988)

[Strack 88] Veronika Strack: *Occurrence Structures: A Model of Concurrency and Choice in Systems.* Gesellschaft für Mathematik und Datenverarbeitung, St. Augustin, Arbeitspapiere der GMD 328 (1988)

Correctness and full abstraction
of
metric semantics for concurrency

J.J.M.M. Rutten

Centre for Mathematics and Computer Science
P.O. Box 4079, 1009 AB Amsterdam, The Netherlands

ABSTRACT: Four different semantic models are given for a simple uniform programming language, containing constructs for parallel composition, global nondeterminism and communication: linear semantics, failure semantics, readiness semantics, and branching semantics. The mathematical framework used consists of complete metric spaces. All models and operators are given as fixed points of suitably defined contractions. This allows for a uniform presentation and an easy comparison of these models. It is shown that the latter three semantics all are correct and that the failure semantics is fully abstract with respect to the linear semantics. Although these results are not new, we believe the uniformity of the way they are presented here to be of some interest.

KEY WORDS AND PHRASES: concurrency, complete metric spaces, contractions, operational semantics, denotational semantics, compositionality, correctness, full abstraction.

CONTENTS

1. Introduction

The semantics of a uniform programming language $\mathcal{L}$ is studied, containing the following constructs: atomic actions, which are left uninterpreted and which can be either internal or communications; sequential composition, global nondeterminism and parallel composition; and recursion, modeled via the simultaneous declaration of statement variables. In the context of complete metric spaces, which is the mathematical framework we adopt, this language (and others similar to it) is treated in [BKMOZ86] and [BMOZ88]. There, an operational semantics $\mathcal{O}$ and a denotational semantics $\mathcal{D}$ for $\mathcal{L}$ are presented together with a proof of the correctness of $\mathcal{D}$ with respect to $\mathcal{O}$. In [KR88], this proof is simplified: For the denotational semantics an alternative formulation is given, based on the same transition relation which was used for the definition of $\mathcal{O}$. Then the correctness is proved by showing that both this alternative denotational semantics and $\mathcal{O}$ are a fixed point of the same contraction, which by Banach's theorem has a unique fixed point.

In this paper, we shall introduce, again in a metric setting, two other semantics for $\mathcal{L}$, which essentially are the well known readiness semantics ([OH86]) and failure semantics ([BHR84]). For both models, two alternative definitions will be given: an operational one, which is based on a transition relation for $\mathcal{L}$, and a *compositional* one, using explicit semantic operators. These differently defined models are shown to be equivalent along the lines of [KR88]. Then the readiness and failure semantics are related to $\mathcal{O}$ and $\mathcal{D}$: they are less distinctive than $\mathcal{D}$ is but are (still) correct with respect to $\mathcal{O}$. The importance of the failure model lies in the fact that it is *fully abstract* with respect to $\mathcal{O}$, that is, it makes *just enough* distinctions in order to be correct (and thus compositional) with respect to $\mathcal{O}$. This fact is proved along the lines of the proof of a similar statement in [BKO87].

2. A SIMPLE LANGUAGE

For the definition of $\mathcal{L}$ we introduce a (possibly infinite) set of *elementary actions* $(a,b\in)A$. (Throughout this paper, the notation $(x,y\in)X$ is used for the introduction of a set X ranged over by typical elements x and y.) We assume that A is partioned into $A=I\cup C$, where $(c\in)C$ is the set of *communication* actions and I (disjoint from C) is the set of *internal* actions. Similarly to CCS ([Mil80]) and CSP ([Ho85]), we assume given a bijection $\bar{\ }:C\to C$, which satisfies $\bar{\ }\circ\bar{\ }=id_C$. It yields, for every $c\in C$, a matching communication $\bar{c}$. In I, we have a special element τ denoting successful communication. Further, let $(x\in)Stmv$ be the set of statement variables.

DEFINITION 2.1 (Syntax for $\mathcal{L}$): The set of statements $(s,t\in)\mathcal{L}$ is defined by

$$s::=\ a\,|\,s_1;s_2\,|\,s_1+s_2\,|\,s_1\|s_2\,|\,x.$$

A statement is of one of five forms: an elementary action $a\in A$, which is either internal $(a\in I)$ or a communication action $(a\in C)$; the sequential composition of statements s_1 and s_2; the nondeterministic choice s_1+s_2, also called global nondeterminism; the parallel composition $s_1\|s_2$, which will be modeled by the arbitrary interleaving (or shuffle) of the elementary actions of s_1 and s_2; and finally a statement variable x, which will be bound to a statement with the use of so-called:

DEFINITION 2.2 (Declarations): The set of *declarations* $(\delta\in)\Delta$ is given by

$$\delta::\ =\ <x_1\Leftarrow g_1,\ldots,x_n\Leftarrow g_n>,$$

with $n\geq 0$, $x_i\in Stmv$, and $g_i\in\mathcal{L}^g$, the set of *guarded statements* which is defined below. We require all variables x_i to be different. We shall sometimes write $x\Leftarrow s\in\delta$ if there exists an $i\in\{1,\ldots,n\}$ with $x_i=x$ and $s_i=s$.

DEFINITION 2.3 (Guarded statements): The set $(g\in)\mathcal{L}^g$ of guarded statements is given by

$$g::\ =a\,|\,g;\ s\,|\,g_1+g_2\,|\,g_1\|g_2,$$

where $s\in\mathcal{L}$.

It will be useful to have the languages $\mathcal{L}$ and $\mathcal{L}^g$ contain a special element E, called the *empty statement.* We shall still write $\mathcal{L}$ and $\mathcal{L}^g$ for $\mathcal{L}\cup\{E\}$ and $\mathcal{L}^g\cup\{E\}$. Note that syntactic constructs like $s;E$ or $E\|s$ are *not* in $\mathcal{L}$ or $\mathcal{L}^g$.

A statement g is guarded if all occurrences of statement variables x in g are preceded by some guarded statement g', which by definition has to start with an elementary action. This requirement corresponds to the usual Greibach condition in formal language theory.

In $\mathcal{L}$, recursion is modeled via the simultaneous declaration of statement variables rather than using the μ-formalism, which allows nested constructs like: $\mu x[a;\mu y[x;b+c;y]]$. This limitation is not essential for what follows and entails a considerably more concise semantic treatment of the language $\mathcal{L}$.

In the next section, we shall define a number of operational semantic models for $\mathcal{L}$ which all are based on the same *transition relation* for $\mathcal{L}$, which we introduce next.

DEFINITION 2.4 (Transition relation for $\mathcal{L}$)
For every declaration $\delta \in \Delta$ we define a transition relation:

$$-\delta\rightarrow \ \subseteq \mathcal{L} \times A \times \mathcal{L}$$

For $(s, a, s') \in -\delta\rightarrow$ we shall write

$$s \xrightarrow[\delta]{a} s'.$$

Now let $-\delta\rightarrow$ be given as the smallest relation satisfying

(1) $a \xrightarrow[\delta]{a} E$

(2) if $s \xrightarrow[\delta]{a} s' \mid E$,

then: $s;\bar{s} \xrightarrow[\delta]{a} s';\bar{s} \mid \bar{s}$

$s+\bar{s} \xrightarrow[\delta]{a} s' \mid E$

$\bar{s}+s \xrightarrow[\delta]{a} s' \mid E$

$s \| \bar{s} \xrightarrow[\delta]{a} s' \| \bar{s} \mid \bar{s}$

$\bar{s} \| s \xrightarrow[\delta]{a} \bar{s} \| s' \mid \bar{s}$

$x \xrightarrow[\delta]{a} s' \mid E$, if $x \Leftarrow s \in \delta$

(3) if $s \xrightarrow[\delta]{c} s' \mid E$ and $t \xrightarrow[\delta]{\bar{c}} t'$,

then $s \| t \xrightarrow[\delta]{\tau} s' \| t' \mid t'$.

(Here one should read "if $s \rightarrow s_1 | s_2$ then $t \rightarrow t_1 | t_2$" as: "if $s \rightarrow s_1$ then $t \rightarrow t_1$" and "if $s \rightarrow s_2$ then $t \rightarrow t_2$".) We shall drop the δ labels on the arrows whenever they do not play a role or it is clear from the context which declaration is meant.

This transition relation gives a first operational interpretation of $\mathcal{L}$. Intuitively, $s \xrightarrow[\delta]{a} s'$ tells us that s can do the elementary action a as a first step, resulting in the statement s'. In general, we are interested in (possibly infinite) sequences of transitions. We give a few examples:

$$x \xrightarrow[\delta]{a} x \xrightarrow[\delta]{a} \cdots, \quad \text{with } x \Leftarrow a;x \in \delta$$

$$c \| \bar{c} \xrightarrow[\delta]{c} \bar{c} \xrightarrow[\delta]{\bar{c}} E$$

$$c \| \bar{c} \xrightarrow[\delta]{\tau} E.$$

We introduce an abbreviation which will be of use in many definitions.

DEFINITION 2.5 (Initial steps): For $s \in \mathcal{L}$ and $\delta \in \Delta$ we define:

$$Init(s)(\delta) = \{a: \exists s' \in \mathcal{L}\, [s \xrightarrow[\delta]{a} s']\}.$$

3. FOUR OPERATIONAL MODELS

In this section, we introduce four different semantic models for $\mathcal{L}$. They are called *operational* because their definitions are based on the transition relation given in definition 2.4. The models vary from a semantics $\mathcal{O}$ which yields sets of streams (or *traces*) as meanings, containing no branching structure at all, via the familiar *ready* and *failure* semantics, to a semantics $\mathcal{O}_B$, which yields tree-like, completely branching structures. (In subsection 3.5, we have collected some examples illustrating the different semantic models.)

3.1 Linear Semantics

We start with the definition of a semantic function $\mathcal{O}$ which is called *linear,* because it yields sets of non-branching streams as the meaning of a statement:

DEFINITION 3.1. ($\mathcal{O}$)
Let $(p,q \in) P = \mathcal{P}(I_{\partial}^{\infty})$, the set of subsets of I_{∂}^{∞}; here, the set $(w \in) I_{\partial}^{\infty}$ is defined as

$$I_{\partial}^{\infty} = I^{\infty} \cup I^{*} \cdot \partial$$

(with $I^{\infty} = I^{\omega} \cup I^{*}$), containing all finite and infinite words (or streams) over the alphabet I as well as the set of finite words over I ending in ∂, which is a special symbol not in A that denotes *deadlock.* We define a semantic function

$$\mathcal{O}: \mathcal{L} \to \Delta \to P$$

as follows. Let $s \in \mathcal{L}$ and $\delta \in \Delta$. We put

$$w \in \mathcal{O}[\![s]\!](\delta)$$

if and only if one of the following conditions is satisfied:

(1) there exist $a_1, \ldots, a_n$ in I and $s_1, \ldots, s_n$ in $\mathcal{L}$ such that

$$w = a_1 \cdots a_n \wedge s \xrightarrow[\delta]{a_1} s_1 \quad \cdots \quad \xrightarrow[\delta]{a_n} s_n = E$$

(2) there exist $a_1, \ldots, a_n$ in I and $s_1, \ldots, s_n$ in $\mathcal{L}$, with $s_n \neq E$, such that

$$w = a_1 \cdots a_n \cdot \partial \wedge s \xrightarrow[\delta]{a_1} s_1 \quad \cdots \xrightarrow[\delta]{a_n} s_n \wedge Init(s_n)(\delta) \subset C$$

(3) there exist an infinite sequence $a_1, a_2, \ldots$ in I and an infinite sequence $s_1, s_2, \ldots$ in $\mathcal{L}$ such that

$$w = a_1 a_2 \cdots \wedge s \xrightarrow[\delta]{a_1} s_1 \xrightarrow[\delta]{a_2} \cdots .$$

A word $w \in \mathcal{O}[\![s]\!](\delta)$ can be an element of I^*, indicating a finite, normally terminating computation starting in s; secondly, if $w \in I^* \cdot \{\partial\}$ it indicates that the computation first preforms the actions in w and next reaches a point (indicated by the statement s_n) from which only single-sided communication actions are possible: this is a situation of deadlock and thus w is followed by ∂; finally, w can be in I^ω, reflecting an infinite computation of s.

We can make P into a complete metric space by defining a suitable distance function on it. This will enable us to give a fixed point characterization of $\mathcal{O}$, which will be of use when relating $\mathcal{O}$ to other semantic models.

DEFINITION 3.2 (Semantic domain P_L)
We supply the set I_∂^∞ with the usual metric d_L, which is given by:

$$d_L(w_1, w_2) = \begin{cases} 0 & \text{if } w_1 = w_2 \\ 2^{-n} & \text{otherwise}, \end{cases}$$

where $n = \max\{k : w_1[k] = w_2[k]\}$ (with $w[k]$ denoting the prefix of w of length k). Next we put

$$(p, q \in)\ P_L = \mathcal{P}_{ncl}(I_\partial^\infty),$$

the set of all non-empty and closed subsets of I_∂^∞, which we supply with the Hausdorff metric $d_{P_L} = (d_L)_H$, induced by d_L (see definition A.6(d)). Since (I_∂^∞, d_L) is a complete metric space, so is (P_L, d_{P_L}). Sometimes we will use A_L to denote the set I_∂^∞.

(In this semantic domain we use the power set of *closed* subsets. For some technical reason, we shall sometimes use *compact* subsets (which are also closed).)

DEFINITION 3.3 (Alternative definition of $\mathcal{O}$)
Let Φ_L: $(\mathcal{L} \to \Delta \to P_L) \to (\mathcal{L} \to \Delta \to P_L)$ be defined as follows. Let $F \in \mathcal{L} \to \Delta \to P_L$, $s \in \mathcal{L}$, and $\delta \in \Delta$. We set: $\Phi_L(F)(E)(\delta) = \{\epsilon\}$; if $s \neq E$ we put

$$\Phi_L(F)(s)(\delta) = \begin{cases} \{\partial\} & \text{if } Init(s)(\delta) \subseteq C \\ \bigcup \{a \cdot F(s')(\delta) : s \xrightarrow{a}_\delta s' \wedge a \in I\} & \text{otherwise.} \end{cases}$$

We define:

$$\mathcal{O}_L = \text{Fixed Point}(\Phi_L).$$

It is straightforward to prove that $\Phi_L(F)(s)(\delta)$ is a closed set and that Φ_L is contracting.
Next, we show that $\mathcal{O}_L$ equals $\mathcal{O}$:

THEOREM 3.4 $\mathcal{O}_L = \mathcal{O}$

PROOF: Since Φ_L is a contraction and since contractions have unique fixed points, the result is immediate from the observation that also $\mathcal{O}$ is a fixed point of Φ_L, which is proved by the following argument. Let $s \in \mathcal{L}$ and $\delta \in \Delta$. From the fact that there are only a finite number of transitions possible from an arbitrary statement it follows that $\mathcal{O}[\![s]\!](\delta)$ is compact and hence closed: It is straightforward to show that in $\mathcal{O}[\![s]\!](\delta)$ every sequence has a converging subsequence. Thus $\mathcal{O}$ is an element of the domain of Φ_L, that is: $\mathcal{O} \in \mathcal{L} \to \Delta \to P_L$. Now let $w \in I_\partial^\infty$. For $w = \epsilon$ and $w = \partial$ we have: $w \in \mathcal{O}[\![s]\!](\delta) \Leftrightarrow w \in \Phi_L(\mathcal{O})(s)(\delta)$. Otherwise:

$$
\begin{aligned}
w \in \mathcal{O}[\![s]\!](\delta) \Leftrightarrow\ & [\text{definition } \mathcal{O}] \\
& \exists a \in I \exists s' \in \mathcal{L} \exists w' \in I_\partial^\infty \\
& [s - \mathcal{g} \to s' \wedge w' = a \cdot w' \wedge w' \in \mathcal{O}[\![s']\!](\delta)] \\
\Leftrightarrow\ & [\text{definition } \Phi_L] \\
& w \in \Phi_L(\mathcal{O})(s)(\delta).
\end{aligned}
$$

Thus $\mathcal{O} = \Phi_L(\mathcal{O})$.

The definition of $\mathcal{O}_L$ as a fixed point of Φ_L required the addition of some (metric) structure to the set $\mathcal{P}(I_\partial^\infty)$. For this we are rewarded with a concise definition on the one hand and an easy tool for comparing $\mathcal{O}_L$ to other models, Banach's theorem, that is, on the other.

3.2. Branching semantics

We follow [BKMOZ86] in introducing a *branching* time semantics for $\mathcal{L}$. First we have to define a suitable semantic universe. It is obtained as a solution of the following *domain equation*:

$$P \cong \{p_0\} \cup \mathcal{P}_{co}(A \times P). \qquad (*)$$

Such a solution we call a *domain*, and its elements are called *processes*. We can read the equation as follows: a process $p \in P$ is either p_0, the so-called *nil* process indicating termination, or it is a (compact) set X of pairs $<a,q>$, where a is the first action taken and q is the *resumption*, describing the rest of p's actions. If X is the empty set, it indicates deadlock (as does ∂ in the operational semantics). For reasons of cardinality, (*) has no solution when we take *all* subsets, rather than all *compact* subsets of $A \times P$. Moreover, we should be more precise about the metrics involved. We should have written (*) like this:

DEFINITION 3.5 (Semantic universe P_B)
Let (P_B, d_B) be a complete metric space satisfying the following reflexive domain equation:

$$P \cong \{p_0\} \overline{\cup} \mathcal{P}_{co}(A \times id_{1/2}(P)),$$

where, for any positive real number c, id_c maps a metric space (M,d) onto (M,d') with $d'(x,y) = c \cdot d(x,y)$, and $\overline{\cup}$ denotes the *disjoint* union. (For a formal definition of the metric on P we refer the reader to the appendix (definition A.6).) Typical elements of P_B are p and q.

We shall not go into the details of solving this equation. In [BZ82] it was first described how to solve this type of equations in a metric setting. In [AR88] this approach is reformulated and extended in a category-theoretic setting.

Examples of processes are

$$p_1 = \{<a, \{<b_1,p_0>, <b_2,p_0>\}>\}$$

$$p_2 = \{<a, \{<b_1,p_0>\}>, <a, \{<b_2,p_0>\}>\}.$$

Using this process domain P_B, we introduce a second semantic model for L.

DEFINITION 3.6 ($\mathcal{O}_B$)

Let Φ_B: $(\mathcal{L}\to\Delta\to P_B)\to(\mathcal{L}\to\Delta\to P_B)$ be defined as follows. Let $F\in\mathcal{L}\to\Delta\to P_B$, $s\in\mathcal{L}$, and $\delta\in\Delta$. If $s=E$ we put $\Phi_B(F)(s)(\delta)=p_0$. Otherwise:

$$\Phi_B(F)(s)(\delta) = \{<a, F(s')(\delta)>: s \xrightarrow{a}_{\delta} s'\}.$$

Now we put:

$$\mathcal{O}_B = \text{Fixed Point } (\Phi_B).$$

In defining $\mathcal{O}_B$, we follow [KR88], where (a variant of) $\mathcal{O}_B$ was used as an intermediate model between an operational and a denotational semantics.

Note that $\mathcal{O}_B$ does not signal deadlock explicitly, whereas $\mathcal{O}_L$ does by using ∂. However, the information about possible deadlocks is present in $\mathcal{O}_B[\![s]\!](\delta)$, because it gives the complete branching structure of all possible transition sequences starting in s. In subsection 3.5, it shown how to abstract from this branching structure and to translate it into an explicit representation of deadlock by the application of some abstraction operator.

Further, we observe that $\mathcal{O}_B$ is much more distinctive than $\mathcal{O}_L$ is, precisely because of the preservation of branching information. This is easily illustrated: We have, for $a, b_1, b_2\in I$:

$$\mathcal{O}_L[\![a;(b_1+b_2)]\!] = \mathcal{O}_L[\![(a;b_1)+(a;b_2)]\!] = \{ab_1, ab_2\},$$

as opposed to

$$\mathcal{O}_B[\![a;(b_1+b_2)]\!] = p_1 \neq p_2 = \mathcal{O}_B[\![(a;b_1)+(a;b_2)]\!],$$

with p_1 and p_2 as defined above.

We finish this subsection with a reference to [BK87], where a comparison is made between P_B and models based on process graphs.

3.3. Readiness semantics

Next, we introduce a semantics $\mathcal{O}_R$ which is based on the notion of *ready sets*, introduced in [OH86]. It is intermediate between $\mathcal{O}_L$ and $\mathcal{O}_B$ in the sense that it makes more distinctions than $\mathcal{O}_L$ and less distinctions than $\mathcal{O}_B$ makes. Moreover, unlike $\mathcal{O}_L$ it does not yield only streams but contains already some branching information (but less than is present in $\mathcal{O}_B$): Instead of using a single symbol to denote all possible deadlock situations, in $\mathcal{O}_R$ this information is refined by yielding in case of deadlock the set of all single-sided communication actions that could have been taken next (if only a matching communication partner for one of these were to be offered in parallel).

The formal definition of $\mathcal{O}_R$ can be given similarly to definition 3.1, using sequences of transitions. We leave such a formulation to the enthusiastic reader and continue with a fixed point definition in the style of definitions 3.3 and 3.6. First, we introduce a complete metric space of ready sets:

DEFINITION 3.7 (Ready domain P_R): Let $(\pi\in)A_R$ be given by

$$\begin{aligned} A_R &= A^{\infty} \cup A^{*}\cdot\mathcal{P}(C) \\ &= A^{*} \cup A^{\omega} \cup A^{*}\cdot\mathcal{P}(C). \end{aligned}$$

Elements of A^{∞} are indicated by w. Elements of $A^{*}\cdot\mathcal{P}(C)$ will be denoted by (w,X) (rather than $w\cdot X$) and are called *ready pairs.* The set A_R is supplied with the usual metric d_R (see definition 3.2), in the definition of which $\mathcal{P}(C)$, the set of all subsets of C, is regarded as an alphabet. Next we define

$$(p,q\in)\ \ P_R = \mathcal{P}_{nco}(A_R),$$

the set of non-empty compact subsets of A_R, which we supply with $d_{P_R}=(d_R)_H$, the Hausdorff metric induced by d_R. We have that (P_R,d_{P_R}) is a complete metric space. The elements of P_R are called *ready sets.*

DEFINITION 3.8 ($\mathcal{O}_R$)
We define a mapping $\Phi_R:(\mathcal{L}\to\Delta\to P_R)\to(\mathcal{L}\to\Delta\to P_R)$. Let $F\in\mathcal{L}\to\Delta\to P_R$, $s\in\mathcal{L}$, and $\delta\in\Delta$. We put $\Phi_R(F)(E)(\delta)=\{\epsilon\}$. Otherwise:

$$\Phi_R(F)(s)(\delta) = \bigcup\{a\cdot F(s')(\delta):\ s-\mathfrak{g}\to s'\} \cup \{(\epsilon,\ Init(s)(\delta)):\ Init(s)(\delta)\subseteq C\}.$$

(Here $a\cdot V$ is defined by $a\cdot V = \{a\cdot w:\ w\in V\} \cup \{(a\cdot w,X):(w,X)\in V\}$.) Now we set

$$\mathcal{O}_R = \text{Fixed Point }(\Phi_R).$$

We observe that $\mathcal{O}_R[\![s]\!](\delta)$ contains streams which are words over A rather than over I only. In other words, single-sided communication actions are visible. Further, as is indicated above, deadlock information in $\mathcal{O}_R[\![s]\!](\delta)$ is represented by ready pairs (w,X), which are interpreted as follows: After performing the actions in w, the computation has reached a point from which it can only perform communication actions; these are listed in X.

3.4. Failure semantics

The fourth model we introduce for $\mathcal{L}$ is a semantics $\mathcal{O}_F$ which is based on *failure sets,* as introduced in [BHR84]. It is, like $\mathcal{O}_B$, more distinctive than $\mathcal{O}_L$ but less than $\mathcal{O}_R$ is. Instead of ready pairs the function $\mathcal{O}_F$ yields *failure pairs* (w,X), which are again elements of $A^* \cdot \mathcal{P}(C)$, but now have a different interpretation: The set X is called a *refusal set* and contains those communication actions (but not necessarily all) that are to be refused, even if a matching communication would be offered in parallel. The complete metric space of *failure sets* is given in:

DEFINITION 3.9 (Failure domain P_F)
Let $(\pi \in) A_F = A_R$, which was given in definition 3.7. As a metric on A_F we take $d_F = d_R$. We set:

$$(p,q\in)\ P_F = \{V\colon V \subseteq A_F \wedge V \text{ is closed in } (A_F,d_F) \wedge\ V \text{ is downward closed }\},$$

where

$$V \text{ is downward closed} \Leftrightarrow$$

$$\forall w \in A^*\ \forall X,\ X' \in \mathcal{P}(C)\ [(w,X) \in V \wedge X' \subseteq X \Rightarrow (w,X') \in V].$$

The pair (P_F, d_{P_F}) (with $d_{P_F} = (d_F)_H$) is a complete metric space. Elements of P_F are called *failure sets.*

DEFINITION 3.10 ($\mathcal{O}_F$)
Let $\Phi_F\colon (\mathcal{L} \to \Delta \to P_F) \to (\mathcal{L} \to \Delta \to P_F)$ be given as follows. Let $G \in \mathcal{L} \to \Delta \to P_F$, $s \in \mathcal{L}$, and $\delta \in \Delta$. We put $\Phi_F(G)(E)(\delta) = \{\epsilon\}$. If $s \neq E$, then:

$$\Phi_F(G)(s)(\delta) = \bigcup \{a \cdot F(s')(\delta)\colon s \xrightarrow{a}_{\delta} s'\}$$

$$\cup\ \{(\epsilon, X)\colon X \subseteq C - Init(s)(\delta) \wedge Init(s)(\delta) \subseteq C\}.$$

(Here $-$ indicates the set-theoretic difference.) We define:

$$\mathcal{O}_F = \text{Fixed Point}(\Phi_F).$$

The fact that $\mathcal{O}_F$ is *less* distinctive than $\mathcal{O}_R$ is caused by the taking of the downward closure of $C - Init(s)(\delta)$ in the definition of $\mathcal{O}_F$ above. In a moment (in subsection 3.5) we shall see some examples illustrating the difference between $\mathcal{O}_F$ and $\mathcal{O}_R$.

A model isomorphic to $\mathcal{O}_F$ could be obtained in term of ready sets only by taking the *upward* closure, which could be defined similarly to the downward closure, of the ready sets in $\mathcal{O}_R[\![s]\!](\delta)$. Nevertheless, the separate notion of refusal sets has been introduced, because taking the downward closure of a refusal set can be nicely explained in intuitive terms: If, at a certain moment in a computation, a set of communications may be refused, then every subset of that set may be refused as well.

3.5. Some examples

Consider the following statements in $\mathcal{L}$ (with $a,b \in I$, $c_1,c_1 \in C$):

$$s_1 = a;b;(c_1+c_2)$$

$$s_2 = (a;b;c_1) + (a;b;(c_1+c_2)) + (a;b;c_2)$$

$$s_3 = (a;b;c_1) + (a;b;c_2)$$

$$s_4 = a;((b;c_1) + (b;c_2)).$$

We list the meaning of these statements according to the different semantic functions. (We omit the δ arguments because these do not matter here, a convention we shall use whenever we see the opportunity for doing so without causing confusion.)

(1)

$$\mathcal{O}_L[\![s_1]\!] = \{ab\partial\}$$

$$\mathcal{O}_F[\![s_1]\!] = \{abc_1, abc_2\} \cup \{(ab, X): X \subseteq C - \{c_1 c_2\}\}$$

$$\mathcal{O}_R[\![s_1]\!] = \{abc_1, abc_2, (ab, \{c_1, c_2\})\}$$

$$\mathcal{O}_B[\![s_1]\!] = \{<a, \{<b, \{<c_1, p_0>, <c_2, p_0>\}>\}>\}$$

(2)

$$\mathcal{O}_L[\![s_2]\!] = \mathcal{O}_L[\![s_1]\!]$$

$$\mathcal{O}_F[\![s_2]\!] = \{abc_1, abc_2\} \cup \{ab, X): X \subseteq C - \{c_1\}\} \cup \{(ab, X): X \subseteq C - \{c_2\}\}$$

$$\mathcal{O}_R[\![2]\!] = \{abc_1, abc_2, (ab, \{c_1\}), (ab, \{c_2\}), (ab, \{c_1, c_2\})\}$$

$$\mathcal{O}_B[\![s_2]\!] = \{<a, \{<b, \{<c_1, p_0>\}>\}>,$$
$$<a, \{<b, \{<c_1, p_0>, <c_2, p_0>\}>\}>,$$
$$<a, \{<b, \{<c_2, p_0>\}>\}>\}$$

(3)

$$\mathcal{O}_L[\![s_3]\!] = \mathcal{O}_L[\![s_2]\!] = \mathcal{O}_L[\![s_1]\!]$$

$$\mathcal{O}_F[\![s_3]\!] = \mathcal{O}_F[\![s_2]\!]$$

$$\mathcal{O}_R[\![s_3]\!] = \{abc_1, abc_2, (ab, \{c_1\}), (ab, \{c_2\})\}$$

$$\mathcal{O}_B[\![s_3]\!] = \{<a, \{<b, \{<c_1, p_0>\}>\}>, <a, \{<b, \{<c_2, p_0>\}>\}>\}$$

(4)

$$\mathcal{O}_L[\![s_4]\!] = \mathcal{O}_L[\![s_3]\!] = \mathcal{O}_L[\![s_2]\!] = \mathcal{O}_L[\![s_1]\!]$$

$$\mathcal{O}_F[\![s_4]\!] = \mathcal{O}_F[\![s_3]\!] = \mathcal{O}_F[\![s_2]\!]$$

$$\mathcal{O}_R[\![s_4]\!] = \mathcal{O}_R[\![s_3]\!]$$

$$\mathcal{O}_B[\![s_4]\!] = \{<a, \{<b, \{<c_1, p_0>\}>, <b, \{<c_2, p_0>\}>\}>\}$$

We see that from $\mathcal{O}_L$ to $\mathcal{O}_B$ the semantics get more distinctive.

3.6. *Relating the different operational models*

We can compare our four operational semantics via some abstraction operators which connect their respective domains:

DEFINITION 3.11 (Abstraction operators): We define three mappings

$$P_B \xrightarrow{\alpha_R} P_R \xrightarrow{\alpha_F} P_F \xrightarrow{\alpha_L} P_L$$

as follows:

(1) α_R: $P_B \rightarrow P_R$: We put $\alpha_R(p_0) = \{\epsilon\}$, and $\alpha_R(\emptyset) = \{(\epsilon, \emptyset)\}$. Otherwise:

$$\alpha_R(p) = \bigcup\{a\cdot(\alpha_R(p')): <a,p'>\in p\} \cup \{(\epsilon,\{c: \exists p'\in P_B\ [<c,p'>\in p]\}): p\subseteq C\times P_B\}$$

(2) α_F: $P_R \rightarrow P_F$:

$$\alpha_F(p) = \{w: w\in p\} \cup \{(w,Y): \exists X\in\mathcal{P}(C)\ [Y\subseteq C-X \wedge (w,X)\in p]\}$$

(3) α_L: $P_F \rightarrow P_L$:

$$\alpha_L(p) = \{w: w\in p\cap I^{\infty}\} \cup \{w\cdot\partial: w\in I^* \wedge \exists X\in\mathcal{P}(C)\ [(w,X)\in p]\}.$$

The definition of the first operator, α_R, is self-referential since $\alpha_R(p')$ occurs in the definition of $\alpha_R(p)$. It can, however, be correctly defined as the fixed point of the following contraction:

$$\theta: (P_B \rightarrow^1 P_R) \rightarrow (P_B \rightarrow^1 P_R)$$

(where $P_B \rightarrow^1 P_R$ is the set of non-expansive (see definition A.3(c)) functions from P_B to P_R), which is given by:

$$\theta(f)(p) = \bigcup\{a\cdot(f(p')): <a,p'>\in p\} \cup \{(\epsilon, \{c: \exists p'\in P_B[<c,p'>\in p]\}): p\subseteq C\times P_B\},$$

for $f\in P_B \rightarrow^1 P_R$ and $p\in P_B$. We observe (without proof) that $\theta(f)(p)$ is a compact set and that θ is indeed contracting. Now we can take $\alpha_R = \text{Fixed Point}(\theta)$.

The mapping α_R yields, for a given process $p\in P_B$, all its paths (or streams), and translates the deadlock information which p contains into ready pairs: if $p\subseteq C\times P_B$, that is, if p contains only pairs with a communication action as the first component, then we have a deadlock situation since, according to our operational intuition, no single-sided communications are allowed. Therefore, α_R delivers in that case the ready pair $(\epsilon, \{c\colon \exists p' \in P_B\ [<c,p'> \in p]\})$.

The operator α_F translates ready pairs (w,X) into the downward closure of a corresponding failure pair $(w, C-X)$:

$$\alpha_F(\{(w, X)\}) = \{(w, Y)\colon Y \subseteq C - X\}.$$

Finally, the mapping α_L distracts from a failure set $p \in P_F$ those streams that contain only internal actions, and maps failure pairs (w,X) (with $w \in I^*$) onto words $w \cdot \partial$: The deadlock information represented by the set X is replaced by the symbol ∂.

With these mappings we can easily formulate the precise relationship between our operational models:

THEOREM 3.12

The following rectangle commutes, which is indicated by the symbol $*$:

$$\begin{array}{ccc}
 & \Phi_B & \\
\mathcal{L}\to\Delta\to P_B & \to & \mathcal{L}\to\Delta\to P_B \\
\alpha_R\downarrow & *_1 & \downarrow\alpha_R \\
 & \Phi_R & \\
\mathcal{L}\to\Delta\to P_R & \to & \mathcal{L}\to\Delta\to P_R \\
\alpha_F\downarrow & *_2 & \downarrow\alpha_F \\
 & \Phi_F & \\
\mathcal{L}\to\Delta\to P_F & \to & \mathcal{L}\to\Delta\to P_F \\
\alpha_L\downarrow & *_3 & \downarrow\alpha_L \\
 & \Phi_L & \\
\mathcal{L}\to\Delta\to P_L & \to & \mathcal{L}\to\Delta\to P_L
\end{array}$$

(where the operators α are extended to sets of functions in the obvious way; for instance,

$$\alpha_R\colon (\mathcal{L}\to\Delta\to P_B)\to(\mathcal{L}\to\Delta\to P_R)$$

is defined by

$$\alpha_R(F) = \lambda s \in \mathcal{L}\, \lambda\delta \in \Delta \cdot\ \alpha_R(F(s)(\delta))).$$

PROOF: We only show $*_1$, the other cases being similar. We prove, for all $F \in \mathcal{L}\to\Delta\to P_B$, $s \in \mathcal{L}$, and $\delta \in \Delta$:

$$\alpha_R(\Phi_B(F)(s)(\delta)) = \Phi_R(\alpha_R(F))(s)(\delta).$$

For $s \neq E$ we have:

$$\Phi_R(\alpha_R(F))(s)(\delta) = \bigcup \{a \cdot (\alpha_R(F)(s)(\delta))\colon s \xrightarrow[\delta]{a} s'\} \cup \{(\epsilon,\ Init(s))\colon Init(s) \subseteq C\}$$

$$= \alpha_R(\{<a,\ F(s')(\delta)>\colon s \xrightarrow[\delta]{a} s'\})$$

$$= \alpha_R(\Phi_B(F)(s)(\delta)).$$

4. Three compositional models

We proceed with the introduction of three semantic models in a compositional way:

Definition 4.1 (Compositionality)
Let $\mathcal{M}:\mathcal{L}\to S$ be an arbitrary model for $\mathcal{L}$, with S an arbitrary set. We call $\mathcal{M}$ *compositional* (with respect to $\mathcal{L}$) if there exist operators $;^{\mathcal{M}}$, $+^{\mathcal{M}}$, and $\|^{\mathcal{M}}: S\times S\to S$ such that

$$\forall s,t\in\mathcal{L}\,[\mathcal{M}(s\ op\ t) = \mathcal{M}(s)\ op^{\mathcal{M}}\ \mathcal{M}(t)],$$

for $op=;,\ +,\ \|$.

In section 6, a relation between compositionality and the notion of a congruence relation is given (theorem 6.3). The models to be defined in this section, which will be called C_B, C_R and C_F, turn out to be equal to $\mathcal{O}_B, \mathcal{O}_R$, and $\mathcal{O}_F$, respectively, as will be proved in the next section. Therefore, their definitions can be seen as alternative characterizations of the operational models. We do *not* give a compositional version of $\mathcal{O}_L$ since this is impossible (see the remark following theorem 6.4).

Definition 4.2 (C_B, C_R, C_F)
Let λ be a label ranging over the set $\{B, R, F\}$. We define three compositional models for $\mathcal{L}$ as follows. Let $\delta\in\Delta$. Then:

(1) $\mathcal{C}_B[\![E]\!](\delta) = p_0$

$\mathcal{C}_R[\![E]\!](\delta) = \mathcal{C}_F[\![E]\!](\delta) = \{\epsilon\}$

(2) $\mathcal{C}_B[\![a]\!](\delta) = \{<a,p_0>\}$

$$\mathcal{C}_R[\![a]\!](\delta) = \begin{cases}\{a\} & \text{if } a\in I\\ \{a,(\epsilon,\{a\})\} & \text{if } a\in C\end{cases}$$

$$\mathcal{C}_F[\![a]\!](\delta) = \begin{cases}\{a\} & \text{if } a\in I\\ \{a\}\cup\{(\epsilon,X): X\subseteq C-\{a\}\} & \text{if } a\in C\end{cases}$$

(3) $\mathcal{C}_\lambda[\![s\ op\ t]\!](\delta) = \mathcal{C}_\lambda[\![s]\!](\delta)\ op^\lambda\,\mathcal{C}_\lambda[\![t]\!](\delta)$

with op ranging over the set $\{;,\ +,\ \|\}$ and the operator op^λ as given in definition 4.4 below.

(4) $\mathcal{C}_\lambda[\![x]\!](\delta) = \mathcal{C}_\lambda[\![g]\!](\delta)$, for $x\Leftarrow g\in\delta$.

The above definitions need some justification, since $\mathcal{C}_\lambda$ cannot be defined by a simple induction on the syntactic complexity of statements, as is apparent from clause (4) above. We give a formally correct definition of $\mathcal{C}_B$; the definitions of $\mathcal{C}_R$ and $\mathcal{C}_F$ can be treated similarly. (The occupied or impatient reader may wish to skip this part and continue with definition 4.4; it is not crucial for the understanding of the rest of the paper.)

We give $\mathcal{C}_B$ as the unique fixed point of a contraction

$$\Psi_B;\ (\mathcal{L}\to\Delta\to P_B)\to(\mathcal{L}\to\Delta\to P_B),$$

which is defined as follows. Let $F\in\mathcal{L}\to\Delta\to P_B$. We define $\Psi_B(F)$ in two stages: first for all $g\in\mathcal{L}^g$ and next for arbitrary s in $\mathcal{L}\,(\supseteq\mathcal{L}^g)$. We follow the inductive structure of $\mathcal{L}^g$; let $\delta\in\Delta$, then:

$$\Psi_B(F)(E)(\delta) = p_0$$

$$\Psi_B(F)(a)(\delta) = \{<a,\, p_0>\}$$

$$\Psi_B(F)(g;s)(\delta) = \Psi_B(F)(g)(\delta);^B\ F(s)(\delta)$$

$$\Psi_B(F)(g_1+g_2)(\delta) = \Psi_B(F)(g_1)(\delta)+^B\ \Psi_B(F)(g_2)(\delta)$$

$$\Psi_B(F)(g_1\|g_2)(\delta) = \Psi_B(F)(g_1)(\delta)\|^B\ \Psi_B(F)(g_2)(\delta).$$

Next, we extend this definition to $\mathcal{L}$, following the inductive structure of $\mathcal{L}$. We formulate the only new case: We have to add a clause for statement variables. Suppose $x\Leftarrow g\in\delta$. Then:

$$\Psi_B(F)(x)(\delta) = \Psi_B(F)(g)(\delta).$$

This is well defined, since $g\in\mathcal{L}^g$ and $\Psi_B(F)$ is already defined on $\mathcal{L}^g$. Now we can take $\mathcal{C}_B$ as the fixed point of Ψ_B as soon as we shall have verified that Ψ_B is a contraction:

THEOREM 4.3: *Ψ_B is a contraction on $\mathcal{L}\to\Delta\to P_B$*

PROOF: We prove that Ψ_B is contracting by showing, for all $F_1, F_2\in\mathcal{L}\to\Delta\to P_B,\ s\in\Delta$, that:

$$d_{P_B}(\Psi_B(F_1)(s)(\delta),\ \Psi_B(F_2)(s)(\delta)) \leqslant \frac{1}{2}\cdot d_{\mathcal{L}\to\Delta\to P_B}(F_1, F_2). \qquad (*)$$

Let F_1 and F_2 be in $\mathcal{L}\to\Delta\to P_B$. The proof falls apart into two parts: first $g\in\mathcal{L}^g$ is treated, next $s\in\mathcal{L}$. For $\mathcal{L}^g$ we only consider the most interesting case: suppose $g\in\mathcal{L}^g-\{E\}$, $s\in\mathcal{L}$ and $\delta\in\Delta$, such that (*) holds for g. The following argument shows that we also have (*) for $g\,;s$:

$$d_{P_B}(\Psi_B(F_1)(g\,;s)(\delta),\ \Psi_B(F_2)(g\,;s)(\delta))$$

$$= d_{P_B}(\Psi_B(F_1)(g)(\delta);^B F_1(s)(\delta),\ \Psi_B(F_2)(g)(\delta);^B F_2(s)(\delta))$$

$\leqslant$ [by lemma 4.5 (2), below]

$$\max\{d_{P_B}(\Psi_B(F_1)(g)(\delta),\ \Psi_B(F_2)(g)(\delta)),\ \frac{1}{2}\cdot d_{P_B}(F_1(s)(\delta),\ F_2(s)(\delta))\}$$

$\leqslant$ [induction hypothesis for g]

$$\frac{1}{2} \cdot d_{\mathfrak{L} \to \Delta \to P_B}(F_1, F_2).$$

The other operators, + and $\|$ can be treated similarly. Once the proof has been given for $\mathfrak{L}^g$, it can be easily extended to $\mathfrak{L}$ by adding the following proof for $x \in Stmv$. Suppose $x \Leftarrow g \in \delta$, with $g \in \mathfrak{L}^g$. Then:

$$d_{P_B}(\Psi_B(F_1)(x)(\delta), \Psi_B(F_2)(x)(\delta)) = d_{P_B}(\Psi_B(F_1)(g)(\delta), \Psi_B(F_2)(g)(\delta))$$

$\leqslant$ [induction, since $g \in \mathfrak{L}^g$]

$$\frac{1}{2} \cdot d_{\mathfrak{L} \to \Delta \to P_B}(F_1, F_2),$$

which concludes the proof. □

Next, we introduce the semantic operators.

DEFINITION 4.4 (Semantic operators)
Let λ range over $\{B,R,F\}$ and op over $\{;, +, \|\}$. We define semantic operators $op^\lambda: P_\lambda \times P_\lambda \to P_\lambda$.
(1) $op^B: P_B \times P_B \to P_B$

$$p_0 ;^B q = q$$

$$p ;^B q = \{<a, p' ;^B q>: <a, p'> \in p\}, \text{ for } p \neq p_0$$

$$p_0 +^B q = q +^B p_0 = q$$

$$p +^B q = p \cup q \text{ (set theoretic union) for } p, q \in p_B - \{p_0\}$$

$$p \|^B q = p \mathbin{⌊\!⌊}^B q \cup q \mathbin{⌊\!⌊}^B p \cup p |^B q,$$

where $p_0 \mathbin{⌊\!⌊}^B q = q$

$$p \mathbin{⌊\!⌊}^B q = \{<a, p' \|^B q>: <a, p'> \in p\}, \text{ for } p \neq p_0$$

$$p |^B q = \{<\tau, p' \|^B q'>: <c, p'> \in p \wedge <\bar{c}, q'> \in q\}$$

($⌊\!⌊$ is called the *left-merge* operator and | is called the *communication merge*);
(2) $op^R: P_R \times P_R \to P_R$

$$p ;^R q = \{a \cdot (p_a ;^R q): p_a \neq \emptyset\} \cup \{(\epsilon, X): (\epsilon, X) \in p\}$$

$$\cup \text{ (if } \epsilon \in p \text{ then } q \text{ else } \emptyset \text{ fi)}$$

where $p_a = \{\pi: \pi \in A_R \wedge a \cdot \pi \in p\}$, for $a \in A$,

with $a \cdot w$, for $w \in A^\infty$, as usual and $a \cdot (w, X) = (a \cdot w, X)$;

$$p+^R q = \{a{\cdot}p_a\colon p_a \neq \emptyset\} \cup \{a{\cdot}q_a\colon q_a \neq \emptyset\} \cup \{(\epsilon, X\cup Y)\colon (\epsilon,X)\in p \wedge (\epsilon,Y)\in q\};$$

(note that this definition is equivalent to

$$p+^R q = ((p\cup q)\cap(A^\infty \cup\{(w,X)\colon w\neq\epsilon\})) \cup \{(\epsilon, X\cup Y)\colon (\epsilon,X)\in p \;\wedge\; (\epsilon,Y)\in q\});$$

$$p\|^R q = p\,\|\!\!\lfloor^R q \cup q\,\|\!\!\lfloor^R p \cup p|^R q \cup p\#^R q,$$

where $p\,\|\!\!\lfloor^R q = \bigcup\{a{\cdot}(p_a\|^R q)\colon p_a\neq\emptyset\} \cup$ (if $\epsilon\in p$ then q else $\emptyset$ fi)

$$p|^R q = \bigcup\{\tau{\cdot}(p_c\|^R q_{\bar c})\colon p_c\neq\emptyset\neq q_{\bar c}\}$$

$$p\#^R q = \{(\epsilon, X\cup Y)\colon (\epsilon,X)\in p \wedge (\epsilon,Y)\in q \wedge X\cap\bar{Y}=\emptyset\}$$

(here $\bar{Y}=\{\bar{c}\colon c\in Y\}$);

(3) $op^F\colon P_F\times P_F\to P_F$

$$p;^F q = p;^R q$$

$$p+^F q = \{a{\cdot}p_a\colon p_a\neq\emptyset\} \cup \{a{\cdot}q_a\colon a_a\neq\emptyset\} \cup \{(\epsilon,X)\colon (\epsilon,X)\in p\cap q\}$$

$$p\|^F q = p\,\|\!\!\lfloor^F q \cup q\,\|\!\!\lfloor^F p \cup p|^F q \cup p\#^F q$$

where $p\,\|\!\!\lfloor^F q = p\,\|\!\!\lfloor^R q$

$$p|^F q = p|^R q$$

$$p\#^F q = \{(\epsilon,X)\colon \exists(\epsilon,Z_1)\in p\exists(\epsilon,Z_2)\in q$$
$$[(C-Z_1)\cap\overline{(C-Z_2)} = \emptyset \wedge X\subseteq Z_1\cap Z_2]\}.$$

By now, it will not come as a complete surprise that those operators above that are introduced by a self-referential definition (like $;^B$ and $\|^B$) can be formally defined as the fixed point of a suitably defined contraction (cf. the remark following definition 3.11).

The intuitive interpretation of the operators op^B is straightforward. Let us explain briefly the operators op^R and op^F.

The definition of $;^R$ implies that for all w, $w'\in A^*$, $X\in\mathcal{P}(C)$, and $q\in P_R$:

$$\{(w,X)\};^R q = \{(w,X)\} \text{ and } \{w\};^R\{(w',X)\} = \{(w{\cdot}w', X)\},$$

just as one would expect. The process $p+^R q$ can deadlock in its first step only if both p and q can deadlock immediately, that is, if both contain a ready pair of the form (ϵ,X). In all subsequent steps, $p+^R q$ behaves like $p\cup q$. In the definition of $p\|^R q$, the interleaving of actions of p and q is represented by $p\,\|\!\!\lfloor^R q$ and $q\,\|\!\!\lfloor^R p$. The communication between p and q are presented in $p|^R q$. Finally, $p\#^R q$ describes the immediate deadlock behavior of $p\|^R q$: if $(\epsilon,X)\in p$ and $(\epsilon,Y)\in q$ we include the ready pair $(\epsilon,X\cup Y)$ in $p\|^R q$ only if $X\cap\bar{Y}=\emptyset$. If $X\cap\bar{Y}\neq\emptyset$, then a communication between p and q is possible and hence the process $p\|^R q$ cannot deadlock immediately.

The definition of $p+^F q$ is like $p+^R q$ but for the difference that a failure pair (ϵ, X) is included only when $(\epsilon, X)\in p$ and $(\epsilon, X)\in q$: The communications that the process $p+^F q$ can refuse are those that can be refused by both p and q. Note that the downward closedness of $p+^F q$ follows from the downward closedness of p and q. The definition of $p\#^F q$ is very similar to $p\#^R q$. We observe that $p\#^F q$ is downward closed by definition. The following alternative definition of $p\#^F q$, which is simpler, would *not* do:

$$p(\#^F)'q = \{(\epsilon, X\cap Y)\colon (\epsilon, X)\in p \wedge (\epsilon, Y)\in q \wedge X\cap \bar{Y}=\varnothing\},$$

since it is not downward closed.

The next lemma, which can be easily verified, states some useful (with respect to, e.g., theorem 4.3) properties of the semantic operators:

LEMMA 4.5

(1) *For* $\lambda\in\{B, R, F\}$ *and* $op\in\{;, +, \|\}$: op^λ *is non-expansive (see definition A.3(c)).*

(2) *For* $p, p'\in P_B-\{p_0\}$ *and* $q, q'\in P_B$:

$$d_{P_B}(p;^B q, p';^B q') \leqslant \max\{d_{P_B}(p,p'), \tfrac{1}{2}\cdot d_{P_B}(q,q')\}.$$

For $\lambda\in\{R, F\}, p,p'\in P_\lambda$ *with* $\epsilon\notin p$ *and* $\epsilon\notin p'$, *and* $q, q'\in P_\lambda$:

$$d_{P_\lambda}(p;^\lambda q, p';^\lambda q') \leqslant \max\{d_{P_\lambda}(p,p'), \tfrac{1}{2}\cdot d_{P_\lambda}(q,q')\}.$$

We conclude this section by stating some properties of $\mathcal{C}_R$ and $\mathcal{C}_F$, which can be easily verified with induction on the complexity of statements. They are of use when comparing $\mathcal{C}_R$ and $\mathcal{C}_F$ with $\mathcal{O}_R$ and $\mathcal{O}_F$ (section 5).

LEMMA 4.6

$$(1)\ \ \forall X\in\mathcal{P}(C)\ \forall s\in\mathcal{L}\ \forall\delta\in\Delta\ [(\epsilon, X)\in\mathcal{C}_R[\![s]\!](\delta) \Leftrightarrow X=Init(s)(\delta)]$$

$$(2)\ \ \forall X\in\mathcal{P}(C)\ \forall s\in\mathcal{L}\ \forall\delta\in\Delta\ [(\epsilon, X)\in\mathcal{C}_F[\![s]\!](\delta) \Leftrightarrow X\subseteq C-Init(s)(\delta) \wedge Init(s)(\delta)\subseteq C]$$

$$(3)\ \ \forall X, Y\in\mathcal{P}(C)\ \forall s\in\mathcal{L}\ \forall\delta\in\Delta\ [(\epsilon, X)\in\mathcal{C}_F[\![s]\!](\delta) \wedge (\epsilon, Y)\in\mathcal{C}_F[\![s]\!](\delta)$$
$$\Rightarrow (\epsilon, X\cup Y)\in\mathcal{C}_F[\![s]\!](\delta)]$$

($Init(s)(\delta)$ was introduced in definition 2.5.)

Note that property (3) does not hold for arbitrary pairs (w, X) and (w, Y) with $w\in A^*$ and $w\neq\epsilon$.

5. Semantic equivalence

In this section, we compare the operational models $\mathcal{O}_\lambda$ and the compositional models $\mathcal{C}_\lambda$. We shall prove that $\mathcal{O}_\lambda = \mathcal{C}_\lambda$, for $\lambda \in \{B, R, F\}$. It is a corollary of the following

Theorem 5.1 *For* $\lambda \in \{B, R, F\}$: $\Phi_\lambda(\mathcal{C}_\lambda) = \mathcal{C}_\lambda$

Proof. Recall that Φ_λ is the defining contraction for $\mathcal{O}_\lambda$ as given in definitions 3.6, 3.8 and 3.10 for $\lambda = B, R$, and F, respectively. The theorem is proved by induction on the complexity of statements, first in $\mathcal{L}^g$ and then in $\mathcal{L}$. In part (1) and (2) below, the δ arguments have been omitted.

Part (1): It is obvious that $\Phi_\lambda(\mathcal{C}_\lambda)(E) = \mathcal{C}_\lambda(E)$. For $a \in A$ we have:

$$\Phi_B(\mathcal{C}_B)(a) = \{<a, p_0>\} = \mathcal{C}_B[\![a]\!]$$

$$\Phi_R(\mathcal{C}_R)(a) = \{a\} = \mathcal{C}_R[\![a]\!], \text{ if } a \in I$$

$$\Phi_R(\mathcal{C}_R)(a) = \{a, (\epsilon, \{a\})\} = \mathcal{C}_R[\![a]\!], \text{ if } a \in C.$$

Similarly for $\lambda = F$.

Part (2): Suppose we have $\Phi_\lambda(\mathcal{C}_\lambda)(s) = \mathcal{C}_\lambda[\![s]\!]$ and $\Phi_\lambda(\mathcal{C}_\lambda)(t) = \mathcal{C}_\lambda[\![t]\!]$, for $\lambda \in \{B, R, F\}$. We shall treat some typical cases:

$$\begin{aligned}
\Phi_B(\mathcal{C}_B)(s;t) &= \{<a, \mathcal{C}_B[\![s';t]\!]>: s - a \rightarrow s'\} \\
&= \{<a, \mathcal{C}_B[\![s']\!] ;^B \mathcal{C}_B[\![t]\!]>: s - a \rightarrow s'\} \\
&= \{<a, \mathcal{C}_B[\![s']\!]>: s - a \rightarrow s'\} ;^B \mathcal{C}_B[\![t]\!] \\
&= \Phi_B(\mathcal{C}_B)(s) ;^B \mathcal{C}_B[\![t]\!] \\
&= [\text{ induction }] \\
&\quad \mathcal{C}_B[\![s]\!] ;^B \mathcal{C}_B[\![t]\!] \\
&= \mathcal{C}_B[\![s;t]\!]
\end{aligned}$$

$$\begin{aligned}
\Phi_R(\mathcal{C}_R)(s+t) &= \bigcup \{a \cdot \mathcal{C}_R[\![s']\!]: s+t-a \rightarrow s'\} \cup \{(\epsilon, \mathit{Init}(s+t)): \mathit{Init}(s+t) \subseteq C\} \\
&= [\text{ by properties of } \rightarrow] \\
&\quad \bigcup \{a \cdot \mathcal{C}_R[\![s']\!]: s - a \rightarrow s'\} \cup \bigcup \{a \cdot \mathcal{C}_R[\![t']\!]: t - a \rightarrow t'\} \cup \\
&\quad \{(\epsilon, \mathit{Init}(s) \cup \mathit{Init}(t)): \mathit{Init}(s) \subseteq C \wedge \mathit{Init}(t) \subseteq C\} \\
&= [\text{ definition } +^R] \\
&\quad \bigcup \{a \cdot \mathcal{C}_R[\![s']\!]: s - a \rightarrow s'\} \cup \{(\epsilon, \mathit{Init}(s)): \mathit{Init}(s) \subseteq C\}
\end{aligned}$$

$$+^R$$

$$\bigcup \{a \cdot \mathcal{C}_R[\![t']\!];\ t - a \rightarrow t'\} \cup \{(\epsilon, Init(t)) \colon Init(t) \subseteq C\}$$

$$= [\text{ definition } \Phi_R \text{ }]$$

$$\Phi_R(\mathcal{C}_R)(s) \ +^R \Phi_R(\mathcal{C}_R)(t)$$

$$= [\text{ induction }]$$

$$\mathcal{C}_R[\![s]\!] \ +^R \mathcal{C}_R[\![t]\!]$$

$$= \mathcal{C}_R[\![s + t]\!]$$

$$\Phi_F(\mathcal{C}_F)(s \| t) = \bigcup \{a \cdot (\mathcal{C}_F[\![s' \| t]\!]) \colon s - a \rightarrow s'\} \cup$$

$$\bigcup \{a \cdot (\mathcal{C}_F[\![s \| t']\!]) \colon t - a \rightarrow t'\} \cup$$

$$\bigcup \{\tau \cdot (\mathcal{C}_F[\![s' \| t']\!]) \colon s - c \rightarrow s' \wedge t - \bar{c} \rightarrow t'\} \cup$$

$$\{(\epsilon, X) \colon X \subseteq (C - Init(s \| t)) \wedge Init(s \| t) \subseteq C\}$$

$$= \bigcup \{a \cdot (\mathcal{C}_F[\![s']\!] \|^F \mathcal{C}_F[\![t]\!]) \colon s - a \rightarrow s'\} \cup$$

$$\bigcup \{a \cdot (\mathcal{C}_F[\![s]\!] \|^F \mathcal{C}_F[\![t']\!]) \colon t - a \rightarrow t'\} \cup$$

$$\bigcup \{\tau \cdot (\mathcal{C}_F[\![s']\!] \|^F \mathcal{C}_F[\![t']\!]) \colon s - c \rightarrow s' \wedge t - \bar{c} \rightarrow t'\} \cup$$

$$\{(\epsilon, X) \colon X \subseteq (\mathcal{C} - Init(s \| t)) \wedge Init(s \| t) \subseteq C\}$$

$$= [\text{ definition } \Phi_F;\ Init(s \| t) \subseteq C \Rightarrow Init(s \| t) = Init(s) \cup Init(t) \text{ }]$$

$$\Phi_F(\mathcal{C}_F)(s) \mathbin{\|\!\!\_}^F \mathcal{C}_F[\![t]\!] \cup$$

$$\Phi_F(\mathcal{C}_F)(t) \mathbin{\|\!\!\_}^F \mathcal{C}_F[\![s]\!] \cup$$

$$\Phi_F(\mathcal{C}_F)(s) |^F \Phi_F(\mathcal{C}_F)(t) \cup$$

$$\{(\epsilon, X) \colon X \subseteq (C - Init(s)) \cap (C - Init(t)) \wedge Init(s) \subseteq C \wedge \ Init(t) \subseteq C\}$$

$$= [\text{ induction }]$$

$$(\mathcal{C}_F[\![s]\!] \mathbin{\|\!\!\_}^F \mathcal{C}_F[\![t]\!]) \cup (\mathcal{C}_F[\![t]\!] \mathbin{\|\!\!\_}^F \mathcal{C}_F[\![s]\!]) \cup (\mathcal{C}_F[\![s]\!] |^F \mathcal{C}_F[\![t]\!]) \cup$$

$$\{(\epsilon, X) \colon X \subseteq (C - Init(s)) \cap (C - Init(t)) \wedge Init(s) \subseteq C \wedge Init(t) \subseteq C\}$$

$$= [\text{ lemma 4.6 (2) }]$$

$$(\mathcal{C}_F[\![s]\!] \mathbin{\|\!\!\_}^F \mathcal{C}_F[\![t]\!]) \cup \mathcal{C}_F[\![t]\!] \mathbin{\|\!\!\_}^F \mathcal{C}_F[\![s]\!]) \cup (\mathcal{C}_F[\![s]\!] |^F \mathcal{C}_F[\![t]\!]) \cup$$

$$\{(\epsilon, X) \colon \exists (\epsilon, Z_1) \in \mathcal{C}_F[\![s]\!] \ \exists (\epsilon, Z_2) \in \mathcal{C}_F[\![t]\!]$$

$$[(C - Z_1) \cap \overline{(C - Z_2)} = \varnothing \wedge X \subseteq Z_1 \cap Z_2]\}$$

$$= [\text{ definition } \#^F\ ]$$

$$(\mathcal{C}_F[\![s]\!] \lfloor\!\lfloor^F \mathcal{C}_F[\![t]\!]) \cup (\mathcal{C}_F[\![t]\!] \lfloor\!\lfloor^F \mathcal{C}_F[\![s]\!]) \cup (\mathcal{C}_F[\![s]\!] |^F \mathcal{C}_F[\![t]\!]) \cup$$

$$(\mathcal{C}_F[\![s]\!] \#^F \mathcal{C}_F[\![t]\!])$$

$$= \mathcal{C}_F[\![s]\!] \|^F \mathcal{C}_F[\![t]\!]$$

$$= \mathcal{C}_F[\![s \| t]\!]$$

Part (3): Part (1) and (2) suffice to show: $\Phi_\lambda(\mathcal{C}_\lambda)(g) = \mathcal{C}_\lambda[\![g]\!]$ for all $g \in \mathcal{L}^g$. To deal with the entire language $\mathcal{L}$, we have to treat one other case: Let $\delta \in \Delta$, $x \in Stmw$; suppose $x \Leftarrow g \in \delta$. Then

$$\Phi_\lambda(\mathcal{C}_\lambda)(x)(\delta) = [\text{ definition } -\delta\rightarrow\ ]$$

$$\Phi_\lambda(\mathcal{C}_\lambda)(g)(\delta)$$

$$= [\text{ induction }]$$

$$\mathcal{C}_\lambda[\![g]\!](\delta)$$

$$= \mathcal{C}_\lambda[\![x]\!](\delta).$$

□

Since the functions Φ_λ are contractions, the following corollary is immediate:

COROLLARY 5.2: For $\lambda \in \{B, R, F\}$: $\mathcal{O}_\lambda = \mathcal{C}_\lambda$.

6. Correctness and full abstraction

In this section we show that $\mathcal{O}_F$, $\mathcal{O}_R$ and $\mathcal{O}_B$ are *correct* with respect to $\equiv_L$, the equivalence relation on $\mathcal{L}$ induced by $\mathcal{O}_L$, and that $\mathcal{O}_F$ is moreover *fully abstract* with respect to $\equiv_L$. We start by giving another characterization of the notion of compositionality (see definition 4.1). To this end, we first introduce two definitions.

DEFINITION 6.1

Let $\mathfrak{M}: \mathcal{L} \rightarrow S$ be a model for $\mathcal{L}$, with S an arbitrary set. Then $\mathfrak{M}$ induces an equivalence relation $\equiv_{\mathfrak{M}} \subseteq \mathcal{L} \times \mathcal{L}$ on $\mathcal{L}$ as follows. For all $s, t \in \mathcal{L}$:

$$s \equiv_{\mathfrak{M}} t \Leftrightarrow \mathfrak{M}[\![s]\!] = \mathfrak{M}[\![t]\!].$$

DEFINITION 6.2 (Congruence relation)

Let $\equiv \subseteq \mathcal{L} \times \mathcal{L}$ be an equivalence relation on $\mathcal{L}$. We say that $\equiv$ *respects* the operator *op* (where *op* ranges again over $\{;, +, \|\}$ if

$$\forall s, s', t, t' \in \mathcal{L}\, [(s \equiv s' \wedge t \equiv t') \Rightarrow (s\ op\ t) \equiv (s'\ op\ t')].$$

(We also say that $\equiv$ is *substitutive* with respect to *op*.) If $\equiv$ respects all of ;, +, and $\|$, it is called a *congruence relation* on $\mathcal{L}$. (Another term for this: $\equiv$ is substitutive for $\mathcal{L}$.)

The following theorem is immediate:

THEOREM 6.3: *$\mathfrak{M}$ is compositional for $\mathcal{L} \Leftrightarrow \equiv_{\mathfrak{M}}$ is a congruence on $\mathcal{L}$.*

From $\mathcal{O}_\lambda = \mathcal{C}_\lambda$, for $\lambda \in \{B, R, F\}$, it follows that $\mathcal{O}_B$, $\mathcal{O}_R$ and $\mathcal{O}_F$ are compositional. In other words:

THEOREM 6.4: *Let $\equiv_\lambda$ denote $\equiv_{\mathcal{O}_\lambda}$, for $\lambda \in \{B, R, F\}$. We have:*

$\equiv_\lambda$ is a congruence relation on $\mathcal{L}$.

This does not hold for $\equiv_L$ $(= \equiv_{\mathcal{O}_L})$: Consider the statements $s_1 = c$, $s_2 = \bar{c}$ and $t = c$; then

$$s_1 \equiv_L s_2, \text{ but not: } s_1 \| t \equiv_L s_2 \| t,$$

which is straightforward from the definition of $\mathcal{O}_L$. Intuitively, this can be explained by the observation that $\mathcal{O}_L$ makes too many identifications (like $\mathcal{O}_L[\![c]\!] = \mathcal{O}_L[\![\bar{c}]\!] = \{\partial\}$) in order to yield a congruence relation. In contrast, $\mathcal{O}_B$, $\mathcal{O}_R$ and $\mathcal{O}_F$ all make more distinctions, and, according to theorem 6.4, enough to obtain a congruence relation.

The question of *full abstraction*, for which we shall give a formal definition in a moment, is essentially the problem of finding, for a given equivalence relation $\equiv$ on $\mathcal{L}$, a model $\mathfrak{M}$ of $\mathcal{L}$ that makes precisely enough distinctions in order to yield a congruence relation $\equiv_{\mathfrak{M}}$ which is contained in $\equiv$. In other words, $\equiv_{\mathfrak{M}}$ should be the *largest* congruence relation that is contained in $\equiv$. Such a model will be called fully abstract with respect to $\equiv$.

With the above in mind, we next give for an arbitrary equivalence relation on $\mathcal{L}$ a characterization of the greatest congruence it contains. For this purpose, we use the notion of *contexts*:

DEFINITION 6.5 (Contexts)
The set of *contexts* $(C \in) Cont$ is given by

$$C ::= (\cdot) \mid a \mid C_1 ; C_2 \mid C_1 + C_2 \mid C_1 \| C_2 \mid x.$$

Here $(\cdot)$ denotes a so-called *hole*. Typical elements of *Cont* will also be indicated by $C(\cdot)$. Contexts can be interpreted as functions from $\mathcal{L}$ to $\mathcal{L}$: Given a context $C(\cdot)$ and a statement $s \in \mathcal{L}$, a new statement $C(s)$ is obtained by syntactically substituting s in all the holes occurring in $\mathcal{C}(\cdot)$.

DEFINITION 6.6
Let $\equiv \subseteq \mathcal{L} \times \mathcal{L}$ be an equivalence relation. We define a relation $\equiv^c$ on $\mathcal{L}$ by putting for $s, t \in \mathcal{L}$:

$$s \equiv^c t \Leftrightarrow \forall C(\cdot) \in Cont\ [C(s) \equiv C(t)].$$

The following theorem is straightforward:

THEOREM 6.7:
(1) $\equiv^c$ *is a congruence relation on* $\mathfrak{L}$
(2) $\equiv^c \subseteq \equiv$
(3) *For every congruence relation* $\equiv'$ *on* $\mathfrak{L}$: $\equiv' \subseteq \equiv \Rightarrow \equiv' \subseteq \equiv^c$

PROOF: We only prove (3). Let $\equiv' \subseteq \equiv$ be a congruence relation on $\mathfrak{L}$. One shows, by induction on the complexity of statements that for all s and t in $\mathfrak{L}$ with $s \equiv' t$:

$$\forall C(\cdot) \in Cont\ [C(s) \equiv' C(t)];$$

since $\equiv' \subseteq \equiv$ this implies:

$$\forall C(\cdot) \in Cont\ [C(s) \equiv C(t)],$$

thus $s \equiv^c t$.

We see that $\equiv^c$ is the largest congruence contained in $\equiv$.
Now we come to the formal definition of full abstraction:

DEFINITION 6.8 (Correctness and full abstraction)
Let $\mathfrak{M}: \mathfrak{L} \to S$ be a model for $\mathfrak{L}$, with S an arbitrary set. Then:
(1) $\mathfrak{M}$ is called *correct* (or *fully adequate*) *with respect to* $\equiv$ if

$$\equiv_{\mathfrak{M}} \subseteq \equiv^c$$

(2) $\mathfrak{M}$ is called *complete with respect to* $\equiv$ if

$$\equiv^c \subseteq \equiv_{\mathfrak{M}}$$

(3) $\mathfrak{M}$ is called *fully abstract* with respect to $\equiv$ if it is both correct and complete:

$$\equiv_{\mathfrak{M}} = \equiv^c$$

We have that $\mathcal{O}_B$, $\mathcal{O}_R$ and $\mathcal{O}_F$ all are correct with respect to $\equiv_L$. It is an immediate consequence of theorem 6.4 and the following theorem:

THEOREM 6.9: $\equiv_B \subsetneqq \equiv_R \subsetneqq \equiv_F \subsetneqq \equiv_L$

PROOF. We have the following implications, of which the premisses were stated in theorem 3.12:

$$\begin{aligned} \mathcal{O}_R &= \alpha_R \circ \mathcal{O}_B &\Rightarrow \equiv_B \subseteq \equiv_R \\ \mathcal{O}_F &= \alpha_F \circ \mathcal{O}_R &\Rightarrow \equiv_R \subseteq \equiv_F \\ \mathcal{O}_L &= \alpha_L \circ \mathcal{O}_F &\Rightarrow \equiv_F \subseteq \equiv_L. \end{aligned}$$

The $\neq$ signs are valid by the examples given in subsection 3.5.

COROLLARY 6.10
The models $\mathcal{O}_B$, $\mathcal{O}_R$ and $\mathcal{O}_F$ are correct with respect to $\equiv_L$:

$$\equiv_B \subsetneqq \equiv_R \subsetneqq \equiv_F \subsetneqq \equiv_{\mathcal{L}}^c \; (\subsetneqq \equiv_L).$$

It turns out that $\equiv_F = \equiv_{\mathcal{L}}^c$; in other words: $\mathcal{O}_F$ is fully abstract with respect to $\equiv_L$. We shall show this along the lines of the proof of a similar statement that was given in [BKO87]. The following definition facilitates the formulation of the proof.

DEFINITION 6.11 ($\tilde{w}$, $\hat{w}$): We define two mappings:

$$\sim: A^* \to I^* \quad \text{and} \quad \hat{}: A^* \to \mathcal{L}.$$

Let $w \in A^*$, say $w = a_1 \cdots a_n$. We set:

$$\begin{aligned} \sim(w) &= \tilde{w} \;\; \text{(notation)} \\ &= a_1'; \cdots ;a_n', \\ \hat{}(w) &= \hat{w} \;\; \text{(notation)} \\ &= \bar{a}_{i_1}; \cdots ;\bar{a}_{i_k}, \end{aligned}$$

where $\{a_{i_1}, \ldots, a_{i_k}\} = C \cap \{a_1, \ldots, a_n\}$ (with $i_1 < \cdots < i_k$) and for all $1 \leqslant j \leqslant n$:

$$\begin{aligned} a_j \in I &\Rightarrow a_j' = a_j \\ a_j \in C &\Rightarrow a_j' = \tau. \end{aligned}$$

(If $C \cap \{a_1, \ldots, a_n\} = \varnothing$ we define $\hat{w} = E$.)

We give a few examples:

if $w = c$, then: $\tilde{w} = \tau$, $\hat{w} = \bar{c}$;

if $w = abc_1\, abc_2$, then: $\tilde{w} = ab\tau\, ab\tau$, $\hat{w} = \bar{c}_1; \bar{c}_2$.

The definition is motivated by the following:

LEMMA 6.12: *Let $w = a_1 \cdots a_n$ and $s = a_1; \cdots ;a_n$. Then*

$$\mathcal{O}_L[\![s \| \hat{w}]\!] = \tilde{w}.$$

THEOREM 6.13: *$\mathcal{O}_F$ is fully abstract with respect to $\equiv_L$, that is: $\equiv_F = \equiv_{\mathcal{L}}^c$.*

Proof. We already know that $\equiv_F \subseteq \equiv_{\mathcal{L}}^c$. We prove that $\equiv_{\mathcal{L}}^c \subseteq \equiv_F$ by showing, for all $s, t \in \mathcal{L}$:

$$\forall C(\cdot) \in Cont \; [\mathcal{O}_L[\![C(s)]\!] = \mathcal{O}_L[\![C(t)]\!]] \qquad (*)$$

$$\Rightarrow \mathcal{O}_F[\![s]\!] = \mathcal{O}_F[\![t]\!].$$

Suppose that (*) holds for $s, t \in \mathcal{L}$. We prove:

(1) $\forall w \in A^\infty \; [w \in \mathcal{O}_F[\![s]\!] \Rightarrow w \in \mathcal{O}_F[\![t]\!]]$

(2) $\forall w \in A^* \forall X \in \mathcal{P}(C) \; [(w,X) \in \mathcal{O}_F[\![s]\!] \Rightarrow (w,X) \in \mathcal{O}_F[\![t]\!]]$.

From these properties and the symmetry of their proofs with respect to s and t, the theorem follows.

We prove (1): Suppose $w \in \mathcal{O}_F[\![s]\!]$, with $w \in A^\omega$, say $w = a_1 a_2 \cdots$. (The case that $w \in A^*$ is similar.) We show for all $N \in \mathbb{N}$:

$$d(w, \mathcal{O}_F[\![t]\!]) \leqslant 2^{-N}$$

(where $d(w, \mathcal{O}_F[\![t]\!]) = \inf_{w' \in \mathcal{O}_F[\![t]\!]} \{d_{A^\infty}(w, w')\}$). Because $\mathcal{O}_F[\![t]\!]$ is closed it then follows that $w \in \mathcal{O}_F[\![t]\!]$.

Let $N \in \mathbb{N}$ and let $w_1 = a_1 \cdots a_N$. We show:

$$\exists w_2 \in A_L \; [\tilde{w}_1 \cdot w_2 \in \mathcal{O}_L[\![s \| \hat{w}_1]\!]]:$$

there exist statements $s_1, \ldots, s_N$ such that

$$s \; -a_1\!\rightarrow s_1 \; -a_2\!\rightarrow \; \cdots \; -a_N\!\rightarrow s_n; \text{ thus:}$$

$$s \| \hat{w}_1 \; -a_1'\!\rightarrow \; \cdots \; -a_N'\!\rightarrow s_N,$$

where $a_1' \cdots a_N' = \tilde{w}_1$. By choosing w_2 in $\mathcal{O}_L[\![s_N]\!]$ we have: $\tilde{w}_1 \cdot w_2 \in \mathcal{O}_L[\![s \| \hat{w}_1]\!]$.

Because of (*) we also have $\tilde{w}_1 \cdot w_2 \in \mathcal{O}_L[\![t \| \hat{w}_1]\!]$. This implies the existence of statements $t_1, \ldots, t_N$ such that

$$t \; -a_1\!\rightarrow t_1 \; -a_2\!\rightarrow \; \cdots \; -a_N\!\rightarrow t_N$$

and such that $w_1 \cdot w_2 \in \mathcal{O}_L[\![t]\!]$. Hence: $d(w, \mathcal{O}_F[\![t]\!]) \leqslant 2^{-N}$.

Next, we prove (2): Let $w \in A^*$ and $X \in \mathcal{P}(C)$, and suppose $(w,X) \in \mathcal{O}_F[\![s]\!]$. We show that $(w,X) \in \mathcal{O}_F[\![t]\!]$. A first observation is that $\mathcal{O}_F[\![t]\!]$ must at least contain some failure pair (w, Y), since

$(w, X) \in \mathcal{O}_F[\![s]\!] \Rightarrow$

$(\tilde{w}, X) \in \mathcal{O}_F[\![s \| \hat{w}]\!] \Rightarrow$

$\tilde{w} \cdot \partial \in \mathcal{O}_L[\![s \| \hat{w}]\!] \Rightarrow$ (because (*))

$\tilde{w} \cdot \partial \in \mathcal{O}_L[\![t \| \hat{w}]\!] \Rightarrow$ (because $\mathcal{O}_L = \alpha_L \circ \mathcal{O}_F$)

$$\exists Y \in \mathcal{P}(C)\ [(\tilde{w}, Y) \in \mathcal{O}_F[\![t \| \hat{w}]\!]] \Rightarrow$$

$$\exists Y \in \mathcal{P}(C)\ [(w, Y) \in \mathcal{O}_F[\![t]\!]].$$

The latter implies (because $\mathcal{O}_F = \alpha_F \circ \mathcal{O}_R$)

$$\exists Y \in \mathcal{P}(C)\ [(w, Y) \in \mathcal{O}_R[\![t]\!]].$$

Now we distinguish between two cases. First, suppose

$$\forall Y \in \mathcal{P}(C)\ [(w, Y) \in \mathcal{O}_R[\![t]\!] \Rightarrow X \cap Y = \varnothing].$$

Consider a ready pair $(w, Y) \in \mathcal{O}_R[\![t]\!]$. Since $X \cap Y = \varnothing$ we have: $X \subseteq C - Y$. Because $(w, Y) \in \mathcal{O}_R[\![t]\!]$ this implies $(w, C - Y) \in \mathcal{O}_F[\![t]\!]$. Thus: $(w, X) \in \mathcal{O}_F[\![t]\!]$. So in this case we are done. We finish the proof by considering the second case; suppose:

$$\exists Y \in \mathcal{P}(C)\ [(w, Y) \in \mathcal{O}_R[\![t]\!] \wedge X \cap Y \neq \varnothing].$$

This property ensures that the following set is non-empty:

$$V = \{c: c \in C \wedge \exists y \in \mathcal{P}(C)\ [(w, Y) \in \mathcal{O}_R[\![t]\!] \wedge c \in X \cap Y]\}.$$

It is finite (since $V \subseteq \cup \{Y: (w, Y) \in \mathcal{O}_R[\![t]\!]\}$, which is finite); say $V = \{c_1, \ldots, c_k\}$. Now define the following statement:

$$u = \bar{c}_1 + \cdots + \bar{c}_k.$$

We have the following implications, of which the ones marked (A) and (B) are proved below:

$$(w, X) \in \mathcal{O}_F[\![s]\!] \Rightarrow$$

$$(\tilde{w}, X) \in \mathcal{O}_F[\![s \| \hat{w}]\!] \Rightarrow (A)$$

$$\tilde{w} \cdot \partial \in \mathcal{O}_L[\![s \| (\hat{w}; u)]\!] \Rightarrow \text{(because (*))}$$

$$\tilde{w} \cdot \partial \in \mathcal{O}_L[\![t \| (\hat{w}; u)]\!] \Rightarrow (B)$$

$$(\tilde{w}, X) \in \mathcal{O}_F[\![t \| \hat{w}]\!] \Rightarrow$$

$$(w, X) \in \mathcal{O}_F[\![t]\!].$$

So we are done if we can convince the reader of the validity of the implications marked by (A) and (B). We try to do so, first for (A).

Suppose $(\tilde{w}, X) \in \mathcal{O}_F[\![s \| \hat{w}]\!]$ and let $w = a_1 \cdots a_n$ and $\tilde{w} = a_1' \cdots a_n'$. Then there exist statements $s_1, \ldots, s_n$ such that

$$s \| \hat{w} \ -a_1'\rightarrow \ \cdots \ -a_n'\rightarrow s_n$$

and

$$Init(s_n) \subseteq C \wedge X \subseteq C - Init(s_n).$$

Because $V \subseteq X$ we have $Init(s_n) \cap V = \emptyset$. Thus $Init(s_n \| u) \subseteq C$, which implies

$$\tilde{w} \cdot \partial \in \mathcal{O}_L[\![s \| (\hat{w}; u)]\!].$$

Finally, we prove (B). Suppose $\tilde{w} \cdot \partial \in \mathcal{O}_L[\![t \| (\hat{w}; u)]\!]$ and, again, let $w = a_1 \cdots a_n$ and $\tilde{w} = a_1' \cdots a_n'$. Then there exist statements $t_1, \ldots, t_n$ such that

$$t \| (\hat{w}; u) \; -a_1' \rightarrow \; \cdots \; -a_n' \rightarrow \; t_n \| u$$

and $Init(t_n \| u) \subseteq C$. The latter implies $Init(t_n) \subseteq C$ and $Init(t_n) \cap V = \emptyset$ (since $\overline{V} = Init(u)$). Because

$$t \| \hat{w} \; -a_1' \rightarrow \; \cdots \; -a_n' \rightarrow \; t_n$$

we have $(\tilde{w}, Init(t_n)) \in \mathcal{O}_R[\![t \| \hat{w}]\!]$, and thus $(\tilde{w}, C - Init(t_n)) \in \mathcal{O}_F[\![t \| \hat{w}]\!]$. Because $Init(t_n) \cap V = \emptyset$ we have, by the definition of V, that $Init(t_n) \cap X = \emptyset$, which yields the desired result: $(\tilde{w}, X) \in \mathcal{O}_F[\![t \| \hat{w}]\!]$. □

7. Related work

Operational and denotational semantics of simple programming languages like $\mathcal{L}$ are, in a metric setting, extensively studied in [BMOZ88] and [BKMOZ86]. The problem of solving reflexive domain equations, like the one used for P_B (definition 3.5), over a category of complete metric spaces was first tackled in [BZ82] and is further explored for a wider class of equations in [AR88]. The technique of defining semantic models and operators as fixed points of contractions and the full exploration of this method with respect to the comparison of different models was introduced in [KR88]. Many application can be found in [BM88]. For readiness semantics we refer to [OH86]. Failure semantics was introduced in [BHR84]. In [De85], operational and denotational semantics of CCS and CSP like languages are studied, in which the notion of testing equivalences plays a key role. In the context of ACP (Algebra of Communicating Processes), a complete axiomatization for finite processes with communication (and without silent move) is given in [BKO87], for readiness and failure semantics; moreover, the fact that failure semantics induces the largest trace respecting congruence is proved there. For a treatment of full abstraction in the setting of partial orderings see [HP79]. In [Mu85], the question of semantic equivalence and full abstraction is tackled with the help of so-called inclusive predicates, again in an order-theoretic framework. In [St86], the general question concerning the existence of fully abstract models is treated in an algebraic context. In [AP86], an example is given of a language for which no fully abstract model exists.

8. REFERENCES

[AP86] K. APT, G. PLOTKIN, *Countable nondeterminism and random assignment,* Journal of the Association for Computing Machinery, Vol. 33, No. 4, 1986, pp. 724-767.

[AR88] P. AMERICA, J.J.M.M. RUTTEN, *Solving reflexive domain equations in a category of complete metric spaces,* in: Proceedings of the Third Workshop on Mathematical Foundations of Programming Language Semantics (M. Main, A. Melton, M. Mislove, D. Schmidt, Eds.), Lecture Notes in Computer Science 298, Springer-Verlag, 1988, pp. 254-288. (To appear in the Journal of Computer and System Sciences.)

[BHR84] S. BROOKES, C. HOARE, W. ROSCOE, *A theory of communicating sequential processes,* J. Assoc. Comput. Mach. 31, No. 3, 1984, pp. 560-599.

[BK87] J.A. BERGSTRA, J.W. KLOP, *A convergence theorem in process algebra,* Report CS-R8733, Centre for Mathematics and Computer Science, Amsterdam, 1987.

[BKO87] J.A. BERGSTRA, J.W. KLOP, E.-R. OLDEROG, *Readies and failures in the algebra of communicating processes (revised version),* Report CS-R8748, Centre for Mathematics and Computer Science, Amsterdam, 1987. (To appear in: SIAM Journal of Computing, 1988.)

[BM88] J.W. DE BAKKER, J.-J. CH. MEYER, *Metric semantics for concurrency,* Report CS-R8803, Centre for Mathematics and Computer Science, Amsterdam, 1988.

[BKMOZ86] J.W. DE BAKKER, J.N. KOK, J.-J. CH. MEYER, E.-R. OLDEROG, J.I. ZUCKER, *Contrasting themes in the semantics of imperative concurrency,* in: Current Trends in Concurrency (J.W. de Bakker, W.P. de Roever, G. Rozenberg, Eds.), Lecture Notes in Computer Science 224, Springer-Verlag, 1986, pp. 51-121.

[BMOZ88] J.W. DE BAKKER, J.-J. CH. MEYER, E.-R. OLDEROG, J.I. ZUCKER, *Transition systems, metric spaces and ready sets in the semantics of uniform concurrency,* Journal of Computer and System Sciences Vol 36 (number 2), 1988, pp. 158-224.

[BZ82] J.W. DE BAKKER, J.I. ZUCKER, *Processes and the denotational semantics of concurrency,* Information and Control 54 (1982), pp. 70-120.

[De85] R. DE NICOLA, *Testing equivalences and fully abstract models for communicating processes,* Ph.D. Thesis, report CST-36-85, Department of Computer Science, University of Edinburgh, 1985.

[Du66] J. DUGUNDJI, *Topology,* Allen and Bacon, Rockleigh, N.J., 1966.

[En77] E. ENGELKING, *General topology,* Polish Scientific Publishers, 1977.

[HP79] M. HENNESSY, G.D. PLOTKIN, *Full abstraction for a simple parallel programming language,* in: Proceedings 8th MFCS (J. Bečvář ed.), Lecture Notes in Computer Science 74, Springer-Verlag, 1979, pp. 108-120.

[Ho85] C.A.R. HOARE, *Communicating sequential processes,* Prentice Hall International, 1985.

[KR88] J.N. KOK, J.J.M.M. RUTTEN, *Contractions in comparing concurrency semantics,* in: Proceedings 15th ICALP, Tampere, 1988, Lecture Notes in Computer Science 317, Springer-Verlag, 1988, pp. 317-332.

[Mic51] E. MICHAEL, *Topologies on spaces of subsets,* in: Trans. AMS 71 (1951), pp. 152-182.

[Mil80] R. MILNER, *A Calculus of communicating systems,* Lecture Notes in Computer Science 92, Springer-Verlag, 1980.

[Mu85] K. MULMULEY, *Full abstraction and semantic equivalence,* Ph.D. Thesis, report CMU-CS-85-148, Computer Science Department, Carnegie-Mellon, 1985.

[OH86] E.-R. OLDEROG, C.A.R. HOARE, *Specification-oriented semantics for communicating processes,* Acta Informaticae 23, 1986, pp. 9-66.

[Pl76] G.D. PLOTKIN, *A powerdomain construction,* SIAM J. Comp. 5 (1976), pp. 452-487.

[Pl81] G.D. PLOTKIN, *A structural approach to operational semantics,* Report DAIMI FN-19, Comp. Sci. Dept., Aarhus Univ. 1981.

[Pl83] G.D. PLOTKIN, *An operational semantics for CSP,* in: Formal Description of Programming Concepts II (D. Bjørner ed.) North-Holland, Amsterdam (1983), pp. 199-223.

[St86] A. STOUGHTON, *Fully abstract models of programming languages,* Ph.D. Thesis, report CST-40-86, Department of Computer Science, University of Edinburgh, 1986.

9. APPENDIX: MATHEMATICAL DEFINITIONS

DEFINITION A.1 (Metric space)

A *metric space* is a pair (M,d) with M a non-empty set and d a mapping $d:M\times M\rightarrow[0,1]$ (a *metric* or *distance*) that satisfies the following properties:

(a) $\forall x,y\in M\,[d(x,y)=0 \Leftrightarrow x=y]$

(b) $\forall x,y\in M\,[d(x,y)=d(y,x)]$

(c) $\forall x,y,z\in M\,[d(x,y)\leqslant d(x,z)+d(z,y)]$.

We call (M,d) an *ultra-metric space* if the following stronger version of property (c) is satisfied:

(c′) $\forall x,y,z\in M\,[d(x,y)\leqslant\max\{d(x,z),d(z,y)\}]$.

Please note that we consider only metric spaces with bounded diameter: the distance between two points never exceeds 1.

EXAMPLES A.1.1

(a) Let A be an arbitrary set. The *discrete* metric d_A on A is defined as follows. Let $x,y\in A$, then

$$d_A(x,y)=\begin{cases}0 & \text{if } x=y\\ 1 & \text{if } x\neq y.\end{cases}$$

(b) Let A be an alphabet, and let $A^{\infty}=A^{*}\cup A^{\omega}$ denote the set of all finite and infinite words over A. Let, for $x \in A^{\infty}$, $x(n)$ denote the prefix of x of length n, in case $length(x) \geqslant n$, and x otherwise. We put

$$d(x,y) = 2^{-sup\{n \mid x(n)=y(n)\}},$$

with the convention that $2^{-\infty}=0$. Then (A^{∞},d) is a metric space.

DEFINITION A.2

Let (M,d) be a metric space, let $(x_i)_i$ be a sequence in M.

(a) We say that $(x_i)_i$ is a *Cauchy sequence* whenever we have:
$\forall \epsilon>0\ \exists N \in \mathbb{N}\ \forall n,m>N\ [d(x_n,x_m)<\epsilon]$.

(b) Let $x \in M$. We say that $(x_i)_i$ *converges to* x and call x the *limit* of $(x_i)_i$ whenever we have:
$\forall \epsilon>0\ \exists N \in \mathbb{N}\ \forall n>N\ [d(x,x_n)<\epsilon]$.
Such a sequence we call *convergent*. Notation: $\lim_{i\to\infty} x_i = x$.

(c) The metric space (M,d) is called *complete* whenever each Cauchy sequence converges to an element of M.

DEFINITION A.3

Let $(M_1,d_1),(M_2,d_2)$ be metric spaces.

(a) We say that (M_1,d_1) and (M_2,d_2) are *isometric* if there exists a bijection $f:M_1 \to M_2$ such that:
$\forall x,y \in M_1\ [d_2(f(x),f(y)) = d_1(x,y)]$. We then write $M_1 \cong M_2$. When f is not a bijection (but only an injection), we call it an *isometric embedding*.

(b) Let $f:M_1 \to M_2$ be a function. We call f *continuous* whenever for each sequence $(x_i)_i$ with limit x in M_1 we have that $\lim_{i\to\infty} f(x_i) = f(x)$.

(c) Let $A \geqslant 0$. With $M_1 \to^A M_2$ we denote the set of functions f from M_1 to M_2 that satisfy the following property:
$\forall x,y \in M_1\ [d_2(f(x),f(y)) \leqslant A \cdot d_1(x,y)]$.
Functions f in $M_1 \to^1 M_2$ we call *non-expansive*, functions f in $M_1 \to^{\epsilon} M_2$ with $0 \leqslant \epsilon < 1$ we call *contracting*.

PROPOSITION A.4

(a) *Let* $(M_1,d_1),(M_2,d_2)$ *be metric spaces. For every* $A \geqslant 0$ *and* $f \in M_1 \to^A M_2$ *we have:* f *is continuous.*

(b) *(Banach's fixed-point theorem)*
Let (M,d) *be a complete metric space and* $f:M \to M$ *a contracting function. Then there exists an* $x \in M$ *such that the following holds:*
(1) $f(x)=x$ *(x is a fixed point of f),*
(2) $\forall y \in M\ [f(y)=y \Rightarrow y=x]$ *(x is unique),*
(3) $\forall x_0 \in M\ [\lim_{n\to\infty} f^{(n)}(x_0)=x]$, *where* $f^{(n+1)}(x_0)=f(f^{(n)}(x_0))$ and $f^{(0)}(x_0)=x_0$.

DEFINITION A.5 (Compact subsets)

A subset X of a complete metric space (M,d) is called *compact* whenever each sequence in X has a subsequence that converges to an element of X.

DEFINITION A.6

Let $(M,d),(M_1,d_1),\ldots,(M_n,d_n)$ be metric spaces.

(a) With $M_1 \rightarrow M_2$ we denote the set of all continuous functions from M_1 to M_2. We define a metric d_F on $M_1 \rightarrow M_2$ as follows. For every $f_1,f_2 \in M_1 \rightarrow M_2$

$$d_F(f_1,f_2)=\sup_{x\in M_1}\{d_2(f_1(x),f_2(x))\}.$$

For $A \geqslant 0$ the set $M_1 \rightarrow^A M_2$ is a subset of $M_1 \rightarrow M_2$, and a metric on $M_1 \rightarrow^A M_2$ can be obtained by taking the restriction of the corresponding d_F.

(b) With $M_1 \overline{\cup} \cdots \overline{\cup} M_n$ we denote the *disjoint union* of $M_1,\ldots,M_n$, which can be defined as $\{1\}\times M_1 \cup \cdots \cup \{n\}\times M_n$. We define a metric d_U on $M_1 \overline{\cup} \cdots \overline{\cup} M_n$ as follows. For every $x,y \in M_1 \overline{\cup} \cdots \overline{\cup} M_n$

$$d_U(x,y) = \begin{cases} d_j(x,y) & \text{if } x,y \in \{j\}\times M_j,\ 1 \leqslant j \leqslant n \\ 1 & \text{otherwise.} \end{cases}$$

(c) We define a metric d_P on $M_1 \times \cdots \times M_n$ by the following clause.
For every $(x_1,\ldots,x_n), (y_1,\ldots,y_n) \in M_1 \times \cdots \times M_n$

$$d_P((x_1,\ldots,x_n),(y_1,\ldots,y_n))=\max_i\{d_i(x_i,y_i)\}.$$

(d) Let $\mathcal{P}_{nc}(M)=^{def}\{X \mid X \subseteq M \wedge X \text{ is compact and non-empty}\}$. We define a metric d_H on $\mathcal{P}_{nc}(M)$, called the *Hausdorff distance,* as follows. For every $X,Y \in \mathcal{P}_{nc}(M)$

$$d_H(X,Y)=\max\{\sup_{x\in X}\{d(x,Y)\},\sup_{y\in Y}\{d(y,X)\}\},$$

where $d(x,Z)=^{def}\inf_{z\in Z}\{d(x,z)\}$ for every $Z \subseteq M,\ x \in M$.
In $\mathcal{P}_{co}(M)=^{def}\{X \mid X \subseteq M \wedge X \text{ is compact}\}$ we also have the empty set as an element. We define d_H on $\mathcal{P}_{co}(M)$ as above but extended with the following case. If $X \neq \varnothing$, then

$$d_H(\varnothing,X)=d_H(X,\varnothing)=1.$$

(e) Let $c \in [0,\infty)$. We define: $id_c(M,d)=(M,c\cdot d)$.

PROPOSITION A.7

Let (M,d), $(M_1,d_1),\ldots,(M_n,d_n)$, d_F, d_U, d_P and d_H be as in definition A.6 and suppose that (M,d), $(M_1,d_1),\ldots,(M_n,d_n)$ are complete. We have that

(a) $(M_1 \rightarrow M_2,d_F)$, $(M_1 \rightarrow^A M_2,d_F)$,

(b) $(M_1 \overline{\cup} \cdots \overline{\cup} M_n,d_U)$,

(c) $(M_1 \times \cdots \times M_n,d_P)$,

(d) $(\mathcal{P}_{nc}(M),d_H)$, and $(\mathcal{P}_{co}(M),d_H)$

are complete metric spaces. If (M,d) and (M_i,d_i) are all ultra-metric spaces these composed spaces *are again ultra-metric. (Strictly spoken, for the completeness of $M_1 \rightarrow M_2$ and $M_1 \rightarrow^A M_2$ we do not need the completeness of M_1. The same holds for the ultra-metric property.)*

The proofs of proposition A.7 (a), (b) and (c) are straightforward. Part (d) is more involved. It can be proved with the help of the following characterization of the completeness of the Hausdorff metric.

PROPOSITION A.8
Let $(\mathcal{P}_{co}(M), d_H)$ be as in definition A.6. Let $(X_i)_i$ be a Cauchy sequence in $\mathcal{P}_{co}(M)$. We have:

$$\lim_{i \to \infty} X_i = \{\lim_{i \to \infty} x_i \mid x_i \in X_i, (x_i)_i \text{ a Cauchy sequence in } M\}.$$

The proof of proposition A.8 can be found in [Mic57] as a generalization of a similar result (for *closed* subsets) in [Du66] and [En77].

Temporal Logics for CCS

Colin Stirling
Department of Computer Science
University of Edinburgh
The King's Buildings
Edinburgh EH9 3JZ

ABSTRACT. Transition systems are focal structures in the study of concurrent systems. On the one hand they are used for defining operational semantics of such systems. And on the other hand they are fundamental structures for interpreting modal and temporal logics. Here we consider different transition systems associated with Milner's Calculus of Communicating Systems (CCS), these differ according to how silent actions are treated. Then a general framework for modal and temporal logics is outlined. Within this framework modal and temporal mu-calculi are highlighted, logics that are appropriate for describing CCS processes. Finally, the equivalences induced by these logics on processes is examined, in general terms.

Key-words: transition systems; modal logic; temporal logic; CCS.

CONTENTS

1. Transition Systems and Operational Semantics

Transition systems

Operational semantics of programs and systems are commonly defined in terms of labelled transition systems.

Definition 1.1 A labelled transition system is a triple $T = (S, L, R)$ where

i. S is a non-empty set (of states)
ii. L is a non-empty set (of action labels)
iii. For each $a \in L$, R_a is a binary relation on S

An example is the operational semantics of while programs. S is then a set of pairs (p, s) where p is a program and s a store. L consists of basic actions, such as assignment and boolean evaluation, dependent on the grain of atomicity. For each $a \in L$ the relation R_a is given as a set of rules. For basic a including booleans assume that R_a includes pairs of the form $\langle (a, s), (\Lambda, s') \rangle$ where s' is the appropriate update of s, and where Λ is the empty program (with the property $\Lambda; p = p = p; \Lambda$). Other elements of R_a are determined by closure conditions such as:

if $(\neg b, s) R_{\neg b} (\Lambda, s')$ then (if b then p else $q, s) R_{\neg b} (q, s')$
if $(p, s) R_a (p', s')$ then $(p; q, s) R_a (p'; q, s')$
if $(b, s) R_b (\Lambda, s')$ then (while b do $p, s) R_b (p$; while b do $p, s')$

The while language may also contain a choice operator, $\cup$, and the parallel operator $\|$. In which case each R_a is subject to further closure conditions including:

if $(p, s) R_a (p', s')$ then $(p \cup q, s) R_a (p', s')$
if $(p, s) R_a (p', s')$ then $(p \| q, s) R_a (p' \| q, s')$

A second type of example is the operational semantics of process languages such as Milner's CCS [1]. In fact, there is more than one transition system associated with CCS processes – this turns out to be very important when examining temporal logics for CCS. Here three systems are outlined; CCS, CCS$'$, and CCS$''$. In all three cases the sets S (S' and S'' respectively) are the same consisting of process expressions such as 0, nil, and closed under various operations including action prefixing, $a.$; nondeterminism, $+$; parallel, $|$; recursion, fix$Z.$ where Z is a variable; and restriction, $\backslash a$. The transition relations R_a(R'_a and R''_a respectively) define when a process p may perform the observable action a and thereby evolve into a process p'. The label sets L(L' and L'') depend on a little structure. Let $\triangle$ be a set of atomic action labels, and $\overline{\triangle}$ be a set of co-action labels disjoint from $\triangle$ and in bijection with it. The bijection is $^-$, so $\overline{a} \in \overline{\triangle}$ represents the co-action of $a \in \triangle$. Using $^-$ also for the inverse means that $a = \overline{\overline{a}}$, and therefore that a is also the co-action of $\overline{a}$. In CCS co-actions may synchronise, and the resultant action is represented by τ, the silent action. The three labels sets are defined as:

$$
\begin{aligned}
L &= \triangle \cup \overline{\triangle} \cup \{\tau\} \\
L' &= \triangle \cup \overline{\triangle} \\
L'' &= L' \cup \{\varepsilon\}
\end{aligned}
$$

Finally the transition relations R_a, R'_a and R''_a are defined. First, for $a \in L$ the relation R_a is given in terms of a set of rules which include the following:

$a.p \; R_a \; p$
if $p \; R_a \; p'$ then $p + q \; R_a \; p'$ and $p|q \; R_a \; p'|q$
if $p \; R_a \; p'$ and $q \; R_{\overline{a}} \; q'$ then $p|q \; R_\tau \; p'|q'$
if $p[Z := \text{fix}Z.p] \; R_a \; p'$ then $\text{fix}Z.p \; R_a \; p'$
if $p \; R_c \; p'$ and $c \notin \{a, \overline{a}\}$ then $p\backslash a \; R_c \; p'\backslash a$

There is no rule for the process 0 which represents inaction. Synchronisation of co-actions is given in the third example rule. The expression $p[Z := \text{fix}Z.p]$ in the subsequent rule means p with all free occurrences of Z substituted with fix$Z.p$. So the transition system CCS treats the silent action τ as observable. In contrast, CCS′ dispenses with an observable τ. The relations R'_a are defined in terms of R_a and R_τ:

$$R'_a = R^*_\tau \circ R_a \circ R^*_\tau$$

where $\circ$ is relational composition and R^*_τ is the reflexive and transitive closure of R_τ. So R'_a reflects the possible absorption of finite sequences of silent actions before and after a. However, CCS′ doesn't allow for a behavioural difference between the two processes $a.p + \tau.0$ and $a.p + 0$. Intuitively, the first may evolve to 0 autonomously by performing the silent event τ. CCS″ caters for this difference by including the relation R''_ϵ:

$$R''_\epsilon = R^*_\tau$$

So $a.p + \tau.0 \; R''_\epsilon 0$, unlike $a.p + 0$. For other labels $a \in L''$ the relation R''_a is just R'_a.

Extended transition systems

When developing temporal logics for concurrent while languages and CCS our concern is more with the overall behaviour of a program or a process rather than with the individual allowable transitions. Central to this overall behaviour is the notion of a computation, or a run of a system, understood as a (maximal) path through a transition system. A path σ through a transition system $T = (S, L, R)$ is a finite or infinite sequence of the form:

$$s_o \; R_{a_0} \; s_1 \; R_{a_1} \ldots s_i \; R_{a_i} \; s_{i+1} \ldots$$

where for each defined j, the pair $(s_j, s_{j+1}) \in R_{a_j}$. A path is maximal if either it contains no final state, or its final state has no transitions emanating from it. For instance, the following is a computation, a maximal path, in CCS′ when $p = \text{fix}Z.a.Z$:

$$p \; R'_a \; p \; R'_a \; p \ldots p \; R'_a \; p \ldots$$

For simplicity, it is usual to guarantee that a maximal path has infinite length by assuming that the union of transition relations in a transition system is total: for each $s \in S$ there is an $a \in L$ and a state s' such that $sR_a s'$. This practice is followed here – it can be guaranteed for arbitrary transition systems by grafting loops with imaginary labels onto states with no transitions emanating from them. It is already guaranteed in the case of CCS″ because of the relation R''_ϵ. Assume that an imaginary label λ is added to CCS and CCS′: the transition relation R_λ (and, similarly, R'_λ) is defined as follows

$$R_\lambda = \{(p, p) \mid \text{if } \forall a \in L. \, \forall q. \text{ not } (p \; R_a \; q)\}$$

Not all maximal paths through a transition system may count as a run, or a computation. For the notion of computation may be defined relative to fairness or liveness assumptions. For instance, in CCS″ the path where $p = a.0$

$$p \; R''_\epsilon \; p \; R''_\epsilon \; p \ldots p \; R''_\epsilon \; p \ldots$$

may be discounted as a computation because p doesn't make progress. Consequently, the notion of a transition system is extended to include the set of admissible paths through it. There are various definitions of such augmented systems, a small sample is [2,3,4]. For generality, we offer the following extension. Where σ is the path

$$s_o\ R_{a_0}\ s_1 \ldots s_i\ R_{a_i}\ s_{i+1} \ldots$$

then the ith suffix of σ, denoted by σ^i is the path

$$s_i\ R_{a_i}\ s_{i+1} \ldots$$

The principal condition imposed, in the following definition, is that if σ is an admissible path then so is any suffix of it.

Definition 1.2 An extended transition system is a quadruple $T = (S, L, R, \Sigma)$ where

i. (S, L, R) is a transition system
ii. R is total
iii. Σ is a non-empty suffix closed set of maximal paths through (S, L, R): if $\sigma \in \Sigma$ then for all $i > 0$. $\sigma^i \in \Sigma$

Let CCS, CCS′ (with additional label λ) and CCS″ also denote extended transition systems with path sets Σ, Σ' and Σ'' respectively. The sets Σ and Σ' consist of all maximal paths through CCS and CCS′ as transition systems. Σ'', in contrast, consists of all maximal paths σ through CCS″ which satisfy the following liveness assumption: if some suffix of σ has the form

$$p_o\ R''_\epsilon\ p_1 \ldots p_i\ R''_\epsilon\ p_{i+1} \ldots$$

then $\sigma \in \Sigma''$ just in case

$$\exists j \geq 0.\ \forall a \in \Delta \cup \overline{\Delta}.\ \forall q.\ \text{not}\ (p_j\ R''_a\ q)$$

This means that processes fix$Z.a.Z + \tau.Z$ and fix$Z.a.Z$ exhibit the same behaviour, they are in fact (weak) bisimulation equivalent. (For a more discriminating account which distinguishes these processes, by employing a pre-order rather than an equivalence, see [5].)

2. Modal and Temporal Logics

Modal logics

Modal logics are interpreted on labelled transition systems (definition 1.1). Propositional modal logic involves modalities expressing transitional change: for each label a the operator $[a]$ means 'after every a transition' while its dual $\neg[a]\neg$, abbreviated to $\langle a \rangle$ means 'after some a transition'. Where Q ranges over atomic sentences and a over labels then the syntax of modal logic is:

$$A ::= Q \mid \neg A \mid A \wedge A \mid [a]A$$

Really, the syntax specifies a family of languages parameterised by the atomic sentences and labels.

A modal logic with labels drawn from L is interpreted on labelled transition systems T whose label set is L. As with propositional logic atomic sentences also need to be interpreted. So a modal model is a pair $\mathcal{M} = (T, V)$ where V is a valuation which assigns to each atomic sentence Q a subset of the states of T, $V(Q)$ – the set of states where Q is deemed to hold. The set of states which hold of an arbitrary modal formula A in $\mathcal{M}$ is inductively defined as the set $\| A \|^T_V$. For ease of notation the index T is dropped:

$$\begin{array}{lcl} \| Q \|_V & = & V(Q) \\ \| \neg A \|_V & = & S_T - \| A \|_V \\ \| A \wedge B \|_V & = & \| A \|_V \cap \| B \|_V \\ \| [a]A \|_V & = & \overline{[a]} \| A \|_V \end{array}$$

Here S_T is the state set of T, and $\overline{[a]}$ is the state transformer which for $S' \subseteq S_T$ is defined as:

$$\overline{[a]}S' = \{s \mid \forall s'. \text{ if } sR_a s' \text{ then } s' \in S'\}$$

Modal logics naturally describe the transitional behaviour of CCS programs. Relevant is Hennessy-Milner logic [6], modal logic with the sole atomic sentence tt (the constant true), because of its characterization of bisimulation equivalence. However, it is less successful for describing properties of runs of CCS processes. For this we turn to temporal logics.

Temporal logics

Temporal logics emerge from modal logics when modal formulas are interpreted as holding on paths, and not just states. Modal logics themselves can be interpreted on paths by unravelling transition systems. If T is the transition system (S, L, R) where R is total then let T^+ be the system (S^+, L, R^+) where

$$S^+ = \{\sigma \mid \sigma \text{ is a maximal path through } T\}$$

The label set of T^+ is that of T. To define the transition relations R_a^+, a little notation is introduced. If σ is the maximal path

$$s_o\ R_{a_o}\ s_1 \ldots s_i\ R_{a_i} s_{i+1} \ldots$$

then $\sigma(i)$ denotes the ith state, s_i, of σ and $L_i(\sigma)$ denotes the ith label a_i. For $a \in L$

$$R_a^+ = \{(\sigma, \delta^1) \mid L_o(\delta) = a \text{ and } \sigma(o) = \delta(o)\}$$

When $\mathcal{M}$ is the modal model (T, V) then let $\mathcal{M}^+$ be the pair (T^+, V^+) with

$$V^+(Q) = \{\sigma \mid \sigma(o) \in V(Q)\}$$

The result is (by induction on A) that:

$$s \in \| A \|_V^T \text{ iff } \{\sigma \mid \sigma(o) = s\} \subseteq \| A \|_{V^+}^{T^+}$$

When the transition system T is CCS (or CCS′) of the previous section, with the imaginary label λ, then the set of states S^+ of T^+ is just the set of paths Σ (Σ') of CCS (CCS′) as an extended transition system. Unravelled models are richer in structure than their modal counterparts. Further operators expressing path features which are not naturally modally interpretable can be introduced. For instance, dropping the index T^+,

$$\begin{array}{ll} \| X_a A \|_{V^+} & = \{\sigma \mid L_o(\sigma) = a \text{ and } \sigma^1 \in \| A \|_{V^+}\} \\ \| A \mathcal{U} B \|_{V^+} & = \{\sigma \mid \exists i \geq 0.\ \sigma^i \in \| B \|_{V^+} \text{ and } \forall k : 0 \leq k < i.\ \sigma^k \in \| A \|_{V^+}\} \\ \| E_a A \|_{V^+} & = \{\sigma \mid L_o(\sigma) = a\} \\ \| \forall F A \|_{V^+} & = \{\sigma \mid \forall \delta. \text{ if } \delta(o) = \sigma(o) \text{ then } \exists i \geq 0.\ \delta^i \in \| A \|_{V^+}\} \\ \| G3n\ A \|_{V^+} & = \{\sigma \mid \forall n \geq 0.\ \sigma^{3n} \in \| A \|_{V^+}\} \end{array}$$

The first example, X_a, expresses a relativised 'next'. The second, $\mathcal{U}$, is the until operator of linear time. The operator E_a expresses 'somewhen a', while $\forall F$ is a strong eventually operator. Finally, $G3n$ expresses 'at every third moment'. All of these operators can be used to assert properties of CCS processes: for instance consider the single run of fix$Z.a.b.c.Z$: this path satisfies the formula $G3n < a > tt$, a notion that is not naturally expressible in modal logic. These operators are examples of temporal operators.

Generally, temporal logics are interpreted on extended transition systems. A propositional temporal logic has the following syntax where Q ranges over atomic sentences and O^n over n-ary operators, $n \geq 1$.

$$A \ ::= \ Q \mid \neg A \mid A \wedge A \mid O^n(A_1, \ldots, A_n)$$

A temporal logic with labels drawn from L is interpreted on extended transition systems, definition 1.2, with label sets L. A temporal model is a pair $\mathcal{M} = (T, V)$ where T is an extended transition system with state set S_T and path set Σ_T, and where V, as in a modal model, assigns to each atomic sentence Q a subset of S_T. Unlike the modal case, however, the set of paths which hold of a temporal formula A is inductively defined as the set $\| A \|_V^T$, where again the index T is dropped:

$$\begin{aligned}
\| Q \|_V &= \{\sigma \in \Sigma_T \mid \sigma(o) \in V(Q)\} \\
\| \neg A \|_V &= \Sigma_T - \| A \|_V \\
\| A \wedge B \|_V &= \| A \|_V \cap \| B \|_V \\
\| O^n(A_1, \ldots, A_n) \| &= \overline{O}^n(\| A_1 \|_V, \ldots, \| A_n \|_V)
\end{aligned}$$

Here $\overline{O}^n$ is a path transformer, operating on n subsets of Σ_T to yield a single subset.

To facilitate comparison between modal and temporal logics, the set of states in S_T which hold of a temporal formula is definable as a derived notion. For $s \in S_T$ appearing in some path in Σ_T let the set $\Sigma(s)$ be the set of paths $\{\sigma \mid \sigma(o) = s\}$. Now the set of states true of a formula A is defined as:

$$\{s \mid \Sigma(s) \subseteq \| A \|_V\}$$

Arbitrary temporal logics are interpretable on the various CCS extended transition systems of the previous section. For instance, using the derived notion of a temporal formula holding of a state, the temporal formula $\forall F\langle b\rangle tt$ is true of the process fix$Z.\tau.Z + a.b.Z$ in every CCS″ model. However, the choice of possible temporal logics for these systems is endless. Some appropriately restricted class needs to be isolated.

Linear and branching time temporal logics

Consider the interpretation of the modal operator $[a]$ in unravelled modal models:

$$\sigma \in \| [a]A \|_{V^+} \text{ iff } \forall \delta. \text{ if } \delta(o) = \sigma(o) \text{ and } L_o(\delta) = a \text{ then } \delta^1 \in \| A \|_{V^+}$$

Two general notions are involved here: on the one hand the idea of a path σ branching into those paths whose initial state is $\sigma(o)$, and on the other hand the notion of an immediate suffix of a path. Let us filter these aspects of the meaning of $[a]$ into separate temporal operators following [7,8].

$$\begin{aligned}
\sigma \in \| \forall A \|_V &\quad \text{iff} \quad \{\delta \mid \delta(o) = \sigma(o)\} \subseteq \| A \|_V \\
\sigma \in \| X_a A \|_V &\quad \text{iff} \quad L_o(\sigma) = a \text{ and } \sigma^1 \in \| A \|_V
\end{aligned}$$

Then $[a]$ is just $\forall \neg X_a \neg$ (and $\langle a\rangle$ is $\exists X_a$ where $\exists$ is the dual of $\forall$).

The contrast between the pair X_a and $\forall$ is the basis for an important division of temporal logics used for describing system properties into linear and branching time [9]. In this context, as described for CCS processes, the set of paths $\Sigma(s)$ represents the runs of s. Linear time temporal logics reason about s in terms of the common properties of paths in $\Sigma(s)$. However, paths in $\Sigma(s)$ can be organised into computation trees with choice points at a state s' representing the different ways that computations may proceed from s'. Branching time logics reason about s in terms of the properties of these trees. Logically the difference between a linear and a branching time operator resides with the possibility of path switching: the semantic clause for a branching time operator may involve constrained path switching expressed by $\forall$.

Unlike $[a]$, X_a is a linear time operator as its semantic clause does not involve path switching. A formal definition of a linear time operator appeals to the infinitary linear time language:

$$A ::= Q \mid \neg A \mid \bigwedge_{j \in J} A_j \mid X_a A$$

where J is a possibly infinite indexing set. The semantic clause for conjunction is:

$$\| \bigwedge_{j \in J} A_j \|_V = \bigcap_{j \in J} \| A_j \|_V$$

A temporal operator is *linear* if it is definable (in the usual logical sense) in this language. For instance, the unrelativized next operator X is definable as $\neg \bigwedge_{a \in L} \neg X_a$ where L is all labels. The operators G3n and $\mathcal{U}$ described above are linear. A temporal logic is *linear* if all its operators are. Standard linear time logics are described in [10,11].

Associated with any linear time operator O is the pair of *pure* branching time operators $\forall O$ and $\exists O$. For instance the two eventually operators $\forall F$ and $\exists F$, the former defined earlier and the latter as:

$$\| \exists F A \|_V = \{\sigma \mid \exists \delta . \delta(o) = \sigma(o) \text{ and } \exists i \geq 0.\ \delta^i \in \| A \|_V\}$$

Given a linear time logic with operators $0_1, \ldots, 0_n$ then its *pure* branching time version contains the operators $\forall 0_1, \ldots, \forall 0_n$ and $\exists 0_1, \ldots, \exists 0_n$. Pure branching time formulas cannot distinguish between paths with the same initial state: $\sigma \in \| A \|_V$ just in case $\Sigma(\sigma(o)) \subseteq \| A \|_V$. Standard branching time logics are discussed in [8,9].

A more general temporal logic encompassing a linear time logic and its pure branching version is its *full* branching time version. This temporal logic contains the linear operators together with the branching operator $\forall$. Generally, full branching time logics are very expressive, allowing arbitrary embedding of linear time and branching operators; see [9] for example.

Starting with a linear time logic there is a systematic method of generating pure and full branching time logics. The merits of using these logics for specification and verification have been widely discussed by a number of researchers. Before describing general versions of these logics, it should be pointed out that there are temporal logics that are neither linear nor branching. An example is the logic whose sole operator is E_a, described earlier.

Modal and temporal mu-calculi

Let $\mathcal{M} = (T, V)$ be the following modal model: $S_T = \{s_0, s_1, s_2\}; L = \{a\}$;
$R_a = \{(s_0, s_1), (s_0, s_2), (s_1, s_1), (s_2, s_2)\}$; and $V(Q) = \{s_1, s_2\}$. Consider the equation:

$$Z = Q \wedge \langle a \rangle Z$$

This can be thought of as a recursive equation to be solved in modal models. For instance, in the case of $\mathcal{M}$, a solution is a subset S' of $\{s_0, s_1, s_2\}$ with the property:

$$S' = \| Q \|_V \cap \overline{\langle a \rangle}\ S'$$

where $\overline{\langle a \rangle}$ is the expected dual transformer of $\overline{[a]}$. There are four solutions in $\mathcal{M}$ which can be ordered by the subset relation:

$$\begin{array}{ccc} \emptyset & \subseteq & \{s_1\} \\ |\cap & & |\cap \\ \{s_2\} & \subseteq & \{s_1, s_2\} \end{array}$$

Here $\{s_1, s_2\}$ is the maximal solution (with respect to $\subseteq$) while $\emptyset$ is the minimal solution. As T consists only of a finite set of states, these two solutions can be derived iteratively. Let $S_0 = \emptyset$ and $S_{i+1} = \| Q \|_V \cap \overline{\langle a \rangle} S_i$. Then the minimal solution is just $\bigcup_{i \geq 0} S_i$. Similarly, letting $S_0 = S_T$ and S_{i+1} be $\| Q \|_V \cap \overline{\langle a \rangle} S_i$ then the maximal solution is $\bigcap_{i \geq 0} S_i$.

Allowing such equations blurs the distinction between modal and pure branching time temporal logics for systems like CCS and CCS'. For the maximal solution of the equation above on the model $\mathcal{M}$ is expressed by a temporal formula in the associated temporal model $\mathcal{M}' = (T', V)$ where T' is the transition system T together with all maximal paths through T. This temporal formula is $\exists \neg F \neg Q$, expressing invariance of Q throughout some path. But this relationship between modal equations and temporal logics doesn't hold for the system CCS$''$ because its set of paths Σ'' does not consist of all paths through its underlying transition system.

Alternatively we can consider temporal equations. For instance, the linear time equation

$$Z = Q \wedge XXXZ$$

where X is the unrelativized next operator. Such an equation is to be solved on temporal models $\mathcal{M} = (T, V)$. Now a solution is a set of paths $\Sigma' \subseteq \Sigma_T$ with the property

$$\Sigma' = \| Q \|_V \cap \overline{X}\,\overline{X}\,\overline{X}\Sigma'$$

Its maximal solution is expressed by the temporal formula G3nQ. Similarly, there are equations of branching time such as $Z = \forall X_a \exists X_b Z$. The virtue of temporal equations is the possibility of very rich temporal logics built from a small number of primitive operators.

Not every modal and temporal equation has a solution. For instance, in the modal model $\mathcal{M}$ detailed above the following equation has no solution:

$$Z = Q \wedge \langle a \rangle \neg Z$$

The problem is that $Q \wedge \langle a \rangle \neg Z$ is not monotonic in Z in $\mathcal{M}$. For instance, $\{s_1\} \subseteq \{s_1, s_2\}$ but $\overline{\langle a \rangle}(S_T - \{s_1\}) \not\subseteq \overline{\langle a \rangle}(S_T - \{s_1, s_2\})$. These equations are ruled out by insisting that in any equation $Z = \psi$ all occurrences of Z in ψ are within the scope of an even number of equations. Any modal or temporal equation obeying this condition has a solution.

More generally, fixpoint quantifiers μZ and νZ can be introduced: $\mu Z.A$ represents the least solution to the equation $Z = A$ while $\nu Z.A$ stands for its maximal solution. This notation also allows these fixpoint quantifiers to be iterated, as in $\mu Z.\nu Y.A$. Their explicit introduction results in expressively rich modal and temporal logics. The syntax of these mu-calculi is given by closed formulas drawn from:

$$A ::= Q \mid \neg Z \mid \neg A \mid A \wedge A \mid OA \mid \nu Z.A$$

where Z ranges over propositional variables and in the case of $\mu Z.A$ all occurrences of Z in A are within the scope of an even number of negations. The formula $\mu Z.A$ is then definable as $\neg \nu Z.\neg A[Z := \neg Z]$. The type of mu-calculus depends on the operators that 0 ranges over. The modal mu-calculus results when 0 is $[a]$; the linear time mu-calculus when 0 ranges over the pair $\{X, X_a\}$; the pure branching time mu-calculus when it ranges over $\{\forall X, \forall X_a, \exists X_a\}$; and finally the full branching time mu-calculus is given when 0 ranges over $\{X, X_a, \forall\}$.

Models are pairs $\mathcal{M} = (T, V)$ where T is a transition system in the modal case, and an extended transition system in the temporal cases. When $\mathcal{M}$ is modal V assigns to each atomic sentence and to each variable a subset of S_T. However, when $\mathcal{M}$ is temporal V assigns to each variable a subset of Σ_T (and to each atomic sentence a subset of S_T). The usual updating notation is assumed: $V[W/Z]$ is the valuation V' which is like V except on the variable Z when $V'(Z) = W$, for $W \subseteq S_T$ or $W \subseteq \Sigma_T$. The set of paths in the temporal cases and the set of states in the modal case which hold of A in $\mathcal{M}$ is inductively defined as $\| A \|_V^T$, where T again is dropped. Let W range over state sets or path sets depending on whether the clause is read modally or temporally. The only clauses not covered by previous definitions are:

$$\| Z \|_V = V(Z)$$
$$\| \nu Z.A \|_V = \bigcup\{W \mid W \subseteq \| A \|_{V[W/Z]}\}$$

The derived clause for $\mu Z.A$ is

$$\| \mu Z.A \|_V = \bigcap\{W \mid \| A \|_{[W/Z]} \subseteq W\}$$

The linear time mu-calculus is a linear time logic according to the definition earlier. For every formula of it is equivalent to a formula of that infinitary linear time logic. For ordinals α and limit ordinals β let $(\nu Z.A)^{\circ} = tt$; $(\nu Z.A)^{\alpha+1} = A[Z := (\nu Z.A)^{\alpha}]$; and $(\nu Z.A)^{\beta} = \bigwedge_{\alpha<\beta}(\nu Z.A)^{\alpha}$. Then $\nu Z.A$ is equivalent to $\bigwedge_{\alpha \in I}(\nu Z.A)^{\alpha}$ where I is the class of ordinals.

The modal mu-calculus, introduced in [12,13], is a natural branching time temporal logic for CCS and CCS$'$, as discussed in [14]. Similarly, the temporal mu-calculi, introduced in [15,16], are natural temporal logics for all three CCS type extended transition systems.

3. Zig-Zags, Bisimulations and Histories

Various expressibility issues stem from modal and temporal logics. At the micro-level there is interest in the particular way that individual formulas express properties and delimit models. Pertinent here is the extent to which the metalanguage, the language the semantics is couched in, as a first or second-order language is itself reflected in the modal or temporal object languages. Instead the concern here is with the macro-level, the totality of modal or temporal formulas of a logic. We examine when two states of a model satisfy the same formulas and apply the results to equivalences on CCS type processes. A variety of behavioural equivalences between processes have been proposed. We are especially interested in the coincidence of a behavioural equivalence and an equivalence induced by a logic - when two states satisfy the same formulas. The classic result in this area is the Hennessy-Milner modal logic characterization of bisimulation equivalence [6]. The framework developed in section 2 allows us to offer similar general results for linear and branching time temporal logics which support the arguments in [2] that the distinction between linear and branching time is important to the difference between failures or testing and bisimulation equivalence. Further support can be found in the different testing framework [17]: the role of the test operators $\forall, \exists$ is analogous to their meaning in full branching time logics.

Zig-zag relations

Given a modal model $\mathcal{M} = (T, V)$ when do two states in S_T satisfy the same formulas? Equally, the question could be asked of two states from different models. The answer appeals to bisimulations with additional structure, or as they are called in modal logic zig-zag relations, [18].

Definition 3.1 A zig-zag on $\mathcal{M}$ is a relation $E \subseteq S_T \times S_T$ such that if sEs' then for all labels a and atomic Q

i. $s \in V(Q)$ iff $s' \in V(Q)$

ii. $\forall s_1.$ if sR_as_1 then $\exists s'_1.\ s'R_as'_1$ and $s_1Es'_1$

iii. $\forall s'_1.$ if $s'R_as'_1$ then $\exists s_1.\ sR_as_1$ and $s_1Es'_1$

The definition of a bisimulation relation omits clause i. Alternatively, it is a zig-zag for Hennessy-Milner logic, modal logic whose sole atomic sentence is tt, true, and for the modal mu-calculus with the single atomic sentence tt. When there is a zig-zag relation between two states s and s' we write $s \leftrightarrows s'$. The following result is a slight variant of one half of the Hennessy-Milner characterization of bisimulation equivalence. We use the notation $\| s \|_{\mathcal{M}}$ to denote the set $\{A \mid s \in \| A \|^{T}_{V}\}$. $\| s \|_{\mathcal{M}}$ is the set of modal formulas which hold of s.

Theorem 3.2 If $s \leftrightarrows s'$ then $\| s \|_{\mathcal{M}} = \| s' \|_{\mathcal{M}}$

Proof By structural induction on modal formulas. In the case of the modal mu-calculus by translation into infinitary modal logic and then by structural induction. □

The converse holds if infinitary conjunction is allowed in the modal logics. Alternatively, for modal logic and the modal mu-calculus, it holds if the transition system is finite branching in the sense that for each label a and state s the set $\{s' \mid sR_a s'\}$ is finite. Let $\mathcal{M}$ be finite branching if its transition system is. Then a slight variant of the other half of the Hennessy-Milner characterization is:

Theorem 3.3 If $\mathcal{M}$ is finite branching and $\| s \|_{\mathcal{M}} = \| s' \|_{\mathcal{M}}$ then $s \leftrightarrows s'$

Proof By showing that the particular relation $E \subseteq S_T \times S_T$ given by sEs' iff $\| s \|_{\mathcal{M}} = \| s' \|_{\mathcal{M}}$ is a zig-zag relation. □

A consequence of these theorems is that the modal mu-calculus with the single atomic sentence tt is an appropriate logic for CCS processes. The power of logical discrimination is intimately tied to bisimulation equivalence. Moreover, in the case of the transition systems CCS and CCS′ this modal mu-calculus can be understood as a branching time temporal logic.

History relations

We now consider when two states satisfy the same linear time logical formulas. Suppose $\mathcal{M} = (T, V)$ is a linear time temporal model. Recall that $\Sigma(s)$, for $s \in S_T$, is that subset of Σ_T where every path has initial state s. Moreover, recall that for $\sigma \in \Sigma_T, L_i(\sigma)$ denotes the i+1th label of σ. First the notion of history equivalence between paths is defined.

Definition 3.4 The paths $\sigma, \delta \in \Sigma_T$ are history equivalent, written as $\sigma \equiv \delta$, iff for all $i \geq 0$ and atomic Q
i. $L_i(\sigma) = L_i(\delta)$
ii. $\sigma^i(o) \in V(Q)$ iff $\delta^i(o) \in V(Q)$

If the only atomic sentence is tt then two paths are equivalent if they involve the same sequence of labels. Given a linear time logic, let $\| \sigma \|_{\mathcal{M}}$ be the set of formulas true of the path σ, the set $\{A \mid \sigma \in \| A \|^{T}_{V}\}$. The following result holds for any linear time logic.

Lemma 3.5 If $\sigma \equiv \delta$ then $\| \sigma \|_{\mathcal{M}} = \| \delta \|_{\mathcal{M}}$

Proof By structural induction on linear time formulas belonging to the infinitary linear time logic of the previous section. □

The converse of this lemma is guaranteed when the linear time logic includes the operators X_a, for each label a in T. However, our interest is when two states satisfy the same linear time formulas. For a given linear time logic, let $\| s \|_{\mathcal{M}}$ be the set $\{A \mid \Sigma(s) \subseteq \| A \|^{T}_{V}\}$. The linear time version of zig-zag equivalence is now as follows.

Definition 3.6 The states s and s' are history equivalent, written as $s \equiv s'$, iff
i. $\forall \sigma \in \Sigma(s).\ \exists \delta \in \Sigma(s').\ \sigma \equiv \delta$
ii. $\forall \delta \in \Sigma(s').\ \exists \sigma \in \Sigma(s).\ \delta \equiv \sigma$

The following result is almost a corollary of lemma 3.5.

Theorem 3.7 If $s \equiv s'$ then $\| s \|_{\mathcal{M}} = \| s' \|_{\mathcal{M}}$

Proof Straightforward. □

The converse of this theorem is guaranteed if infinitary conjunction is allowed in the linear time logic (or, for finitary logics, if one of the sets $\Sigma(s), \Sigma(s')$ is finite) and it contains the operator X_a for each a.

Consider now history equivalence of processes (drawn from the extended transition systems CCS, CCS′ and CCS″) with respect to the linear time mu-calculus. If the only atomic formula is tt then this logic cannot discriminate processes which are string (or traces) equivalent. Yet Hennessy-Milner logic is a sublogic of its pure (and hence full) branching time version, since $[a]$ is $\forall\neg X_a\neg$. So there is an enormous chasm in process distinguishability between the linear time mu-calculus with sole atomic sentence tt and its branching time versions. One way of closing this gap is to allow further atomic sentences. A general suggestion is to define for each $n \geq 0$ the atomic sentences to be the set of Hennessy-Milner logic formulas whose modal depth is at most n. The result is a family of increasingly discriminating linear time logics. History equivalence for $n = 0$ is string equivalence, and for $n = 1$ it is ready trace equivalence, [19].

Extended zig-zag relations

The notion of zig-zag needs to be extended when we examine states satisfying the same sets of branching time formulas. First, we extend zig-zags to be relations on paths. Assume $\mathcal{M} = (T, V)$ is a temporal model.

Definition 3.8 A path zig-zag on $\mathcal{M}$ is a relation $E \subseteq \Sigma_T \times \Sigma_T$ such that if $\sigma E \delta$ then for all $i \geq 0$
i. $\sigma \equiv \delta$
ii. $\forall \sigma_1 \in \Sigma(\sigma^i(o)).\exists \delta_1 \in \Sigma(\delta^i(o)).\sigma_1 E \delta_1$
iii. $\forall \delta_1 \in \Sigma(\delta^i(o)).\exists \sigma_1 \in \Sigma(\sigma^i(o)).\sigma_1 E \delta_1$

When there is a path zig-zag between σ and δ this is written as $\sigma \rightleftarrows \delta$. For branching time logics with tt as sole atomic formula then we call a path zig-zag a path bisimulation. The next result is the correlate of lemma 3.5, but now for any branching time logic.

Lemma 3.9 If $\sigma \rightleftarrows \delta$ then $\| \sigma \|_{\mathcal{M}} = \| \delta \|_{\mathcal{M}}$

Proof Similar to lemma 3.5 except for the additional induction case of a formula of the form $\forall A$. □

Path zig-zags are now extended to states, the result is a slight variant of extended bisimulations [4].

Definition 3.10 An extended zig-zag relation on $\mathcal{M}$ is a relation $E \subseteq S_T \times S_T$ such that if sEs' then
i. $\exists \sigma \in \Sigma(s).\exists \delta \in \Sigma(s').\ \sigma \rightleftarrows \delta$

We write $s \underline{\leftrightarrow}^{+} s'$ if s and s' are related by an extended zig-zag. In the case that the extended zig-zag depends on a path bisimulation we say that there is an extended bisimulation between the states. The branching time correlate of theorem 3.7 is:

Theorem 3.11 If $s \underline{\leftrightarrow}^{+} s'$ then $\| s \|_{\mathcal{M}} = \| s' \|_{\mathcal{M}}$

Proof A straightforward corollary of lemma 3.9 □

Extended zig-zag equivalence is associated with branching time temporal logics of processes. And in the case of the branching time mu-calculus with tt as the sole atomic formula then the associated equivalence is extended bisimulation equivalence. Generally, extended bisimulation equivalence is finer than bisimulation equivalence. However, this is not true for CCS, CCS′ and CCS″, as introduced in section 1. (In the particular case of a temporal model $\mathcal{M} = (T, V)$ if Σ_T consists of all paths through the underlying transition system as for CCS and CCS′ models then $\underline{\leftrightarrow}$ and $\underline{\leftrightarrow}^{+}$ coincide – a slight variant of this result is proved in [20]. The proof for CCS″ depends on the pervasiveness of the relation R''_{ϵ}.) Therefore, none of the branching time logics discriminates processes which are bisimulation equivalent when their only atomic formula is tt. The need in the case of CCS″ for liveness assumptions is purely pragmatic, to be able to describe progress of a process. In which circumstances might we want to distinguish processes that are bisimilar? One case is if we also include fairness assumptions about parallel processes. For instance, that every run of the process $p = \text{fix}Z.a.Z \mid \text{fix}Z.b.Z$ involves a and b happening infinitely often. In this case p is bisimulation equivalent to the process $q = \text{fix}Z.a.Z + b.Z$, but they are not extended bisimulation equivalent.

Acknowledgment
Many thanks to Dorothy McKie for typing.

References

1. R. Milner, A Calculus of Communicating Systems, Lecture Notes in Computer Science 92 (Springer, Berlin, 1980).

2. A. Pnueli, Specification and development of reactive systems, Information Processing 86 (Elsevier Science Publishers, North-Holland, 1986) 845-858.

3. J. Sifakis, A unified approach for studying the properties of transition systems, Theoretical Computer Science 18 (1982) 227-258.

4. M. Hennessy, Axiomatizing finite delay operators, Acta. Inform. 21 (1984), 61-88.

5. D. Walker, Bisimulations and divergence, 3rd Symposium on Logic in Computer Science (Computer Science Press, Washington, 1988) 186-192.

6. M. Hennessy and R. Milner, Algebraic laws for nondeterminism and concurrency, J. Assoc. Comput. Mach. 32 (1985) 137-161.

7. M. Ben-Ari, Z. Manna and A. Pnueli, The temporal logic of branching time, 8th Ann. ACM Symposium on Principles of Programming Languages (1981) 164-176.

8. E. Emerson and E. Clarke, Using branching time logic to synthesize synchronization skeletons, Sci. Comput. Programming 2 (1982) 241-266.

9. E. Emerson and J. Halpern, 'Sometimes' and 'not never' revisited: on branching versus linear time temporal logic, J. Assoc. Comput. Mach. 33 (1986) 151-178.

10. D. Gabbay, A. Pnueli, A. Shelah and J. Stavi, The temporal analysis of fairness, 7th Ann. ACM Symposium on Principles of Programming Languages (1980) 163-173.

11. P. Wolper, Temporal logic can be more expressive, Inform. and Control 56 (1983) 72-93.

12. V. Pratt, A decidable mu-calculus, 22nd ACM Foundations of Computer Science (1981) 421-427.

13. D. Kozen, Results on the propositional mu-calculus, Theoret. Comput. Sci. 27 (1983) 333-354.

14. K. Larsen, Proof systems for Hennessy-Milner logic with recursion, in Proceedings CAAP (1988).

15. E. Emerson and E. Clarke, Characterizing correctness properties of parallel programs as fixpoints, Lecture Notes in Computer Science 85 (Springer, Berlin, 1981).

16. H. Barringer, R. Kuiper and A. Pnueli, Now you may compose temporal logic specifications, 16th ACM Symposium of the Theory of Computing (1984).

17. S. Abramsky, Observational equivalence as a testing equivalence. Theoret. Comput. Sci. 53 (1987) 225-241.

18. J. Van Bentham, Correspondence theory, in Vol II of Handbook of Philosophical Logic, (Reidel D., 1984) 167-247.

19. J. Baeten, J. Bergstra and J. Klop, Ready trace semantics for concrete process algebra with priority operator, Report CS-R8517, Centrum voor Wiskunde en Informatica (1985).

20. M. Hennessy and C. Stirling, The power of the future perfect in program logics, Inform. and Control 67 (1985) 23-52.

Behavioural Presentations

M. W. Shields

Electronic Engineering Laboratories,
The University of Kent at Canterbury
United Kingdom

ABSTRACT. In this paper, we present a general behavioural model for parallel systems and a class of automata which accept them. We discuss the use of such automata in giving uniform, non-interleaving semantics for parallel specification languages.

KEYWORDS. Parallelism, concurrency, behavioural presentations, event structures, transition systems, asynchronous automata.

CONTENTS

1. Introduction

The purpose of this paper is to describe a number of low-level *non-interleaving* models of discrete systems and to sketch the relationships between these models and other existing models.

We begin by presenting a model of behaviour, that of the so-called behavioural presentations. These are mild generalisations of the event structures of [1] but are much more expressive. In particular, they are capable of describing a mixture of non-determinism, simultaneity and concurrency and can represent continuous as well as discrete systems. We shall only be concerned with the discrete subclass here, however.

We next describe a class of generalised automata, which we call *hybrid transition systems* and explain how these act as 'acceptors' for discrete behavioural presentations. The mechanics of this depend crucially on the relationship between behavioural presentations and *trace languages* [2].

Finally, we explain how hybrid transition systems may be used to provide a non-interleaving semantics for a variety of higher-level models.

Proofs have been omitted, for reasons of space. Many of them are to be found in [3]. A detailed presentation of the material presented here will appear in [4].

2. Behavioural Presentations

We postulate that the possible behaviour of any system may be characterised by a set of assertions concerning what has occurred during its evolution. An assertion will be valid relative to some point in the space-time of the system. We assume, therefore, that to each system there corresponds a set P of *points*. Points may be thought of as *time slices*. Furthermore, we assume that each point is associated with a set of *occurrences*, which have taken place prior to that point. We will not distinguish between two points having the same set of occurrences, and may therefore identify points with their associated sets. Thus, we have a set O of occurrences and $P \subseteq 2^O$. (If X is a set, 2^X denotes its powerset). We shall find it convenient to suppose that

$$\bigcup_{p \in P} p = O$$

We may wish to consider occurrences as occurrences of something. We assume that there is a set E of *events* and a function $\lambda: O \rightarrow E$. $\lambda(o) = e$ is to be interpreted as 'o is an occurrence of e. These four entities make up our basic behavioural model, that of the *behavioural presentation.*

2.1. Definition (Behavioural Presentations)

A behavioural presentation is a quadruple $B = (O, P, E, \lambda)$ where

2.1.1 O is a set of occurrences;

2.1.2 $P \subseteq 2^O$ is a non-empty set of points satisfying $\bigcup_{p \in P} p = O$;

2.1.3 E is a set of events;

2.1.4 $\lambda: O \rightarrow E$ is a labelling function.

2.2. Example (Waveforms)

Example 2.1 dealt with a notionally discrete system. Behavioural presentations may also be used to describe continuous or analogue systems. Consider an electronic black box with two output lines. The function of the box is to generate a signal f at one of its output lines and a signal g at its other output line. We consider the behaviour of the system between times t_1 and t_2.

We shall let the occurrences of this system be the attaining of a given voltage at a given time by a given signal, so that

$$O = [t_1, t_2) \times \{f, g\}$$

Points correspond to instants in the time interval, so that

$$P = \{p_t \mid t \in [t_1, t_2]\}$$

and the set of all things that have happened prior to a point t is therefore

$$p_t = [t_1, t) \times \{f, g\}$$

Finally, $\lambda(t, f) = f(t)$ and $\lambda(t, g) = g(t)$.

2.3. Example (Special Relativity)

This example is based on the famous thought-experiment of Einstein in [5]. Two trains are travelling at a constant speed in opposite directions along a pair of straight parallel tracks. Observers O_1 and O_2 are sitting at the middle of the two trains. At a given instant, the two observers are on a line at right angles to the side of the train with a third observer, O_3, sitting on the embankment, and at that instant two forks of lightning strike the ends of the first train in such a way that O_3 sees them strike simultaneously. Observer O_2, travelling towards the light coming from the first strike, sees that before he sees the light coming from the second. Observer O_1 travelling towards the light coming from the second strike, sees that before he sees the light coming from the first.

Let o_1 denote the occurrence of the first bolt striking and let o_2 denote the occurrence of the second, so that $O = \{o_1, o_2\}$.

From the point of view of observer O_3, there are two distinct time points; $p_0 = \emptyset$ when nothing has happened yet and $p_{both} = \{o_1, o_2\}$, when both have. O_3 never sees one without the other. O_2 sees the first bolt strike before the second, so that from his point of view, there are three points; p_0 and p_{both} and a third point $p_{first} = \{o_1\}$, when o_1 has occurred but not o_2. Likewise, O_1 has three points; p_0, p_{both} and $p_{second} = \{o_2\}$.

Thus, $P = \{p_0, p_{both}, p_{first}, p_{second}\}$. We may take $E = \{flash\}$ and $\lambda(o_1) = \lambda(o_2) = flash$.

2.4. Example (Coin Tossing)

The next example is a description of a system consisting of a coin being tossed and coming down either head or tail. Let $E = \{H, T\}$.

Recall that if X is a set, then X^* denotes the set of all finite sequences of elements of X. Let Ω denote the null sequence. Let $X^+ = X^* - \{\Omega\}$. xy denotes the string concatenation of $x, y \in X^*$. Define $x \leq y \Leftrightarrow \exists u \in X^* : xu = y$.

We suppose that two occurrences of the same action are the same if and only if they have been preceded by the same sequences of events. The third 'tail' in the sequence *HTHHTT* is not the same occurrence as the third 'tail' in the sequence *HHTHHTT*; they take place in different 'possible worlds'. We may refer to events by giving the sequence of which they are the last occurrence. Thus, $O = \{o_x \mid x \in E^+\}$ and $P = \{p_x \mid x \in E^*\}$, with $p_x = \{o_y \mid y \leq x\}$. If $x = ua$, with $a \in E$, then set $\lambda(o_x) = a$.

Now, let us return to the general case. We introduce two fundamental relations.

2.5. Definition

Suppose $o_1, o_2 \in O$. We define.

2.5.1. $o_1 \# o_2 \Leftrightarrow \forall p \in P : o_2 \in p \Rightarrow o_1 \notin p$:

2.5.2. $o_1 \rightarrow o_2 \Leftrightarrow \forall p \in P : o_2 \in p \Rightarrow o_1 \in p$.

These two definitions introduce concepts of *mutual exclusion* and *time ordering*. If $o_1 \# o_2$, then an occurrence o_2 excludes the future occurrence o_1 - and vice versa. It is this relation that allows us to introduce notions of *non-determinism* into the theory. If $o_1 \rightarrow o_2$, on the other hand, then if o_2 has occurred, then so must o_1. We may read $o_1 \rightarrow o_2$ as meaning, 'occurrence o_1 either preceded or was at the same time as occurrence o_2'.

The following remark gives the basic properties of these two relations. First, recall that a *pre-order* is a reflexive, transitive relation. An *independence relation* is an irreflexive, symmetric relation.

2.6. Remark

2.6.1. # is an independence relation on O satisfying the following property $o_1 \# o_2 \;\&\; o_1 \rightarrow o'_1 \;\&\; o_2 \rightarrow o'_2 \Rightarrow o'_1 \# e'_2$;

2.6.2. $\rightarrow$ is a pre-order on O.

□

Let us see how these relations manifest themselves in our examples.

• In example 2.2, we may check that $O = p_{t_2}$, from which it follows that $o, o' \in p_{t_2}$, for all $o, o' \in O$. Thus, $\# = \varnothing$ in this example. On the other hand, if $x, y \in \{f, g\}$ and $t, t' \in [t_1, t_2)$, then $(t, x) \rightarrow (t', y) \Longleftrightarrow t \leq t'$. This is consistent with our view of the system as having no non-determinacy and in which the occurrences are ordered according to the (global) time at which they occurred.

• In example 2.3, we may check that $O = p_{both}$, so that $\# = \varnothing$ in this example. However, neither $o_1 \rightarrow o_2$ nor $o_2 \rightarrow o_1$. We shall return to this phenomenon later.

• In example 2.4, we may check that $o_x, o_y \in p_z \Longleftrightarrow x, y \leq z$ and that this is the case only if $x \leq y$ or $y \leq x$. Thus, we have $o_x \# o_y \Longleftrightarrow x \not\leq y \;\&\; y \not\leq x$. Here at last we have an example of non-determinism. For example $o_{HTHHTT} \# o_{HHTHHTT}$. We may check that $o_x \rightarrow o_y \Longleftrightarrow x \leq y$.

When we come to consider the relationships between arbitrary pairs of occurrences then devotees of the law of the excluded middle will have no difficulty in demonstrating that exactly one of the following holds

(TR1) $o_1 \# o_2$

(TR2) $o_1 \rightarrow o_2 \;\&\; o_2 \rightarrow o_1$

(TR3) $o_1 \rightarrow o_2 \;\&\; \neg\, o_2 \rightarrow o_1$

(TR4) $\neg\, o_1 \rightarrow o_2 \;\&\; o_2 \rightarrow o_1$

(TR5) $\neg\, o_1 \# o_2 \;\&\; \neg\, o_1 \rightarrow o_2 \;\&\; \neg\, o_2 \rightarrow o_1$

We have already discussed (TR1). Let us examine the others. First, (TR2). Define

$$o_1 \approx o_2 \Longleftrightarrow o_1 \rightarrow o_2 \;\&\; o_2 \rightarrow o_1.$$

$\approx$ is the equivalence relation generated by the pre-order $\rightarrow$, so the following result (the proof of which is elementary) is standard.

2.7. Remark

2.7.1. $\approx$ is an equivalence relation.

2.7.2 Let $o, o_1, o_2 \in O$ and suppose that $o_1 \approx o_2$ then

(a) $o_1 \rightarrow o \Longleftrightarrow o_2 \rightarrow o$.

(b) $o \rightarrow o_1 \Longleftrightarrow o \rightarrow o_2$.

(c) $o \approx o_1 \Longleftrightarrow o \approx o_2$.

□

We shall write $[o]_{\approx}$ for the $\approx$ class of o and write $O/\approx$ for the set of all such classes: $O/\approx = \{[o]_{\approx} \mid o \in O\}$.

We see that two occurrences in the relation $\approx$ stand in exactly the same relationship to other occurrences. Our interpretation is that o_1 and o_2 are *simultaneous*.

If we now go through our examples, we see that in example 2.3, $(t, x) \rightarrow (t', y) \Longleftrightarrow t \leq t'$ and so $(t, x) \approx (t', y) \Longleftrightarrow t = t'$. Thus, $(t, f) \approx (t, g)$. Thus, there *is* non-trivial simultaneity in this example.

It is worth pointing out that example 2.4 is based on a thought-experiment whose point was to demonstrate the non-objectivity of simultaneity in relativistic mechanics. C.A. Petri in [6] refers to this principle when adopting a different form of contemporaneity for his Net Theory, namely *concurrency*. In Net theory, the only type of simultaneity is coincidence.

However, simultaneity is sometimes a convenient fiction; for example, Classical mechanics, in which the contemporaneous relation is simultaneity, is a workable approximation to relativistic mechanics in most cases. However, the contemporaneous relation in example 2.4 is not simultaneity. The two occurrences o_1 and o_2 are clearly contemporaneous but not simultaneous. Two such events will be said to be *concurrent* and we define

$$o_1 \; co \; o_2 \Longleftrightarrow \neg\, o_1 \# o_2 \;\&\; \neg\, o_1 \rightarrow o_2 \;\&\; \neg\, o_2 \rightarrow o_1$$

This deals with case (TR5). The remaining cases, (TR3) and (TR4) are merely mirror images of each other. Define

$$o_1 < o_2 \Longleftrightarrow o_1 \rightarrow o_2 \;\&\; \neg\, o_2 \rightarrow o_1$$

then $o_1 < o_2$ may be read 'o_1 strictly preceded o_2'. It is easy enough to show that $<$ is a strict pre-order - that is to say, a transitive, irreflexive relation - and co is an independence relation. Having dressed up the case analysis of (TR1 - 5) in (hopefully) more intuitive terms, we may now state:

2.8. Proposition

Two occurrences are either strictly ordered in time, simultaneous, concurrent or mutually exclusive, but only one of these relations holds.

□

The systems described in examples 2.2 - 2.4 are of different types. In example 2.5, there can be only one occurrence at a time. In examples 2.2 and 2.3 this is not the case, but in the former case contemporaneous occurrences are simultaneous whereas in the latter they are concurrent. In examples 2.2 and 2.3, the behaviours of the systems are predictable, whereas in example 2.4 they are not.

Behavioural presentations may be classified according to the nature of their co, $\approx$ and # relations.

2.9. Definition (Types of Behavioural Presentation)

Let B be a behavioural presentation, then

(1) B is *sequential* $\Longleftrightarrow co = \emptyset$ and $\approx \; = id_O$. Here, id_O denotes the identity relation on O.

(2) B is (non-sequentially) *synchronous* $\Longleftrightarrow co = \emptyset$ and $\approx \; \neq id_O$.

(3) B is (non-sequentially) *asynchronous* $\Longleftrightarrow co \neq \emptyset$ and $\approx \; = id_O$.

(4) B is (non-sequentially) *hybrid* $\iff$ $co \neq \emptyset$ and $\approx \neq id_O$.

By synchronous (respectively asynchronous, hybrid), we usually mean non-sequentially synchronous or sequential (respectively non-sequentially asynchronous or sequential, non-sequentially hybrid or sequential).

2.10. Definition

Let B be a behavioural presentation, then B is *determinate* $\iff$ $\# = \emptyset$, otherwise, B is *non-determinate*.

Our examples classify as follows. Example 2.2 is of a determinate, non-sequentially synchronous system. Example 2.3 is of a determinate, non-sequentially asynchronous system. Example 2.4 is of a non-determinate, sequential system. These give us three out of a possible eight kinds, which are listed in the following result.

2.11. Remark (Classification of Behavioural Presentations)

Let B be a behavioural presentation, then precisely one of the following holds.

(1) B is sequential and determinate.

(2) B is sequential and non-determinate.

(3) B is non-sequentially synchronous and determinate.

(4) B is non-sequentially synchronous and non-determinate.

(5) B is non-sequentially asynchronous and determinate.

(6) B is non-sequentially asynchronous and non-determinate.

(7) B is non-sequentially hybrid and determinate.

(8) B is non-sequentially hybrid and non-determinate.

□

There is one further distinction, that between example 2.2 and the other examples, namely that example 2.2 deals with a non-discrete system whereas the other examples deal with discrete systems (at least, on the level of abstraction on which they are described). We shall be exclusively concerned with discrete systems from now on. We begin our examination of them in the next section.

3. Discrete Behavioural Presentations

We now consider the subclass that interests us, the *discrete* behavioural presentations.

3.1. Definition (Left-Closure Relation)

Let $X, Y \subseteq O$, then X is *left closed* in Y and we write $X \leq Y \iff$

3.12.1 $X \subseteq Y$

3.12.2 $\forall o_1 \in X\ \forall o_2 \in Y: o_2 \to o_1 \Rightarrow o_2 \in X$.

It is easy to verify that $\leq$ is a partial order on 2^O and that for $p_1, p_2 \in P$, $p_1 \subseteq p_2 \iff p_1 \leq p_2$.

3.2. Definition (Left-Closed Behavioural Presentations)

A behavioural presentation will be said to be *left closed* $\Longleftrightarrow$

$$\forall p \in P\ \forall X \subseteq O : X \leq p \Rightarrow X \in P \qquad [3.1]$$

3.3. Definition (Discrete Behavioural Presentations)

A behavioural presentation B will be said to be *discrete* $\Longleftrightarrow$

3.3.1. B is left closed;

3.3.2. B is *finitary*, that is $\forall p \in P : |p| < \infty$.

Discrete behavioural presentations have nice order theoretic properties. The following results are slight generalisations of theorems presented in [7]. First, let us denote greatest lower bound of a set X by $glb(X)$ and its least upper bound by $lub(X)$.

3.4. Proposition (Consistent Completeness)

Let B be a left-closed behavioural presentation, then $(P, \subseteq)$ is *consistently complete*, that is

$$\forall \mathbf{U} \subseteq P : \mathbf{U} \neq \varnothing \Rightarrow glb(\mathbf{U}) \text{ exists.} \qquad [3.2]$$

Furthermore if $\mathbf{U} \neq \varnothing$, then

3.4.1 $glb(\mathbf{U}) = \bigcap_{p \in \mathbf{U}} p$;

3.4.2 $lub(\mathbf{U}) = \bigcup_{p \in \mathbf{U}} p$, if the former exists.

□

3.5. Definition (Primes and Prime Algebraic Posets)

Let $(D, \leq)$ be a poset. An element $x \in D$ is a *complete prime* of D
$\Longleftrightarrow \forall X \subseteq D : x \leq lub(X) \Rightarrow \exists y \in D : x \leq y$.

$(D, \leq)$ is *prime algebraic* $\Longleftrightarrow \forall x \in D : lub(\{y \in Pr(D) \mid y \leq x\})$ exists and equals x.

3.6. Proposition (Prime Algebraicity)

Suppose B is left closed, then $(P, \subseteq)$ is prime algebraic. The complete primes of $(P, \subseteq)$ are the elements $\downarrow o$, $o \in O$, where

$$\downarrow o = \{o' \in O \mid o' \rightarrow o\} \qquad [3.3]$$

□

3.7. Proposition

Suppose $(D, \leq)$ is prime algebraic and consistently complete, then there exists a left-closed behavioural presentation B_D such that $(P_D, \subseteq)$ is isomorphic to $(D, \leq)$. Specifically, $O_D = Primes(D)$ and $P_D = \{p_d \mid d \in D\}$, where $p_d = \{u \in D \mid u \leq p \ \&\ u \text{ is prime}\}$.

□

4. Trace Languages

We seek automata theoretic objects which correspond to discrete behavioural presentations in the same sort of way that transition systems [8] correspond to sequential behavioural presentations. Transition systems themselves are not adequate for this purpose because they cannot distinguish between an asynchronous system and an interleaved version of it. There are cases in which the distinction may be important. We have more to say about this point in the conclusions section.

The simplest way to establish a connection is to recall that transition systems may be regarded as acceptors for *string languages* - their sets of *execution sequences*. *Trace languages*, introduced in [2], allow us to relate certain asynchronous behavioural presentations to some language theoretic object which may be accepted by a generalisation of transition systems. Recall that an *independence relation* is an irreflexive, symmetric relation.

4.1. Definition (Traces and Trace Languages [2])

Let A be a set and let ι be an independence relation on A. We define a relation $\equiv_\iota^{(1)}$ on A^* by:

$$x \equiv_\iota^{(1)} y \iff \exists\, u, v \in A^*\ \exists\, a, b \in A : x = u.a.b.v\ \&\ y = u.b.a.v\ \&\ a\ \iota\ b \qquad [4.1]$$

Let $\equiv_\iota$ be the reflexive, transitive closure of $\equiv_\iota^{(1)}$. By definition, $\equiv_\iota$ is an equivalence relation on A^*. We denote the equivalence class of $x \in A$ by $\langle x \rangle_\iota$.

Let $A_\iota^* = \{\langle x \rangle_\iota \mid x \in A^*\}$. A_ι^* is the set of *traces* of A with independence relation ι. Any subset L of A_ι^* is called a *trace language*.

Let us first make some observations concerning the basic properties of traces.

4.2. Proposition

Suppose ι is an independence relation on a set S, then

4.2.1. A_ι^* is a monoid with respect to a composition defined by

$$\forall x, y \in A^* : \langle x \rangle_\iota . \langle y \rangle_\iota = \langle xy \rangle_\iota \qquad [4.2]$$

The identity of the monoid is $\langle \Omega \rangle_\iota$.

4.2.2. A_ι^* is a partial order with respect to the relation $\leq$ defined by

$$\forall x, y \in A^* : \langle x \rangle_\iota \leq \langle y \rangle_\iota \iff \exists\, z \in A^* : \langle xz \rangle_\iota = \langle y \rangle_\iota \qquad [4.3]$$

□

In view of proposition 3.7, the following property of trace languages is not without interest.

4.3. Theorem

Suppose that $L \subseteq A_\iota^*$ is *left-closed*, that is

$$\forall \langle x \rangle_\iota \in L\ \forall \langle y \rangle_\iota \in A_\iota^* : \langle y \rangle_\iota \leq \langle x \rangle_\iota \Rightarrow \langle y \rangle_\iota \in L \qquad [4.4]$$

then $(L, \leq)$ is prime algebraic and consistently complete. The complete primes of L are the elements $\langle x \rangle_\iota \in L$ such that

$$\forall u, v \in A^*\ \forall a, b \in A : \langle ua \rangle_\iota = \langle x \rangle_\iota = \langle vb \rangle_\iota \Rightarrow a = b \qquad [4.5]$$

□

Proposition 3.7 shows that we may construct a behavioural presentation from a given left-closed trace language, $L \subseteq A_\iota{}^*$, as follows. Define $B_L = (O_L, P_L, E_L, \lambda_L)$, where $O_L = Primes(L)$, $P_L = \{p_x \mid x \in L\}$, $p_x = \{u \in O_L \mid u \leq x\}$, $E_L = A$ and $\lambda_L(<u.a>_\iota) = a$.

Note, incidentally, that the behavioural presentation of example 2.4 is precisely $B_{\{H,T\}^*}$.

What kind of behavioural presentation is B_L? It may be shows that B_L is discrete and asynchronous, but there is more to it than that. The relation ι constrains the ways in which occurrences may be concurrent.

We now describe the class of behavioural presentations to which B_L belongs. First, we need a little notation.

Let $o_1, o_2 \in O$, then we shall say that they are *unseparated*, and write $unsep(o_1, o_2)$, if $\neg\, o_1 \# o_2$ and $\neg \exists o'' \in O: (o < o'' < o' \text{ or } o' < o'' < o)$.

Suppose $p_1, p_2 \in P$, then p_1 and p_2 are *isomorphic*, and we write $p_1 \equiv p_2$, if there exists a bijection $\phi: p_1 \rightarrow p_2$ such that

$$\forall o_1, o_2 \in p_1: o_1 \rightarrow o_2 \Leftrightarrow \phi(o_1) \rightarrow \phi(o_2) \qquad [4.6]$$

$$\forall o \in p_1: \lambda(o) = \lambda(\phi(o)) \qquad [4.7]$$

4.4. Definition

Let B be a behavioural presentation and ι an independence relation on E, then B will be said to be ι-*linguistic* $\Leftrightarrow$

4.4.1 B is discrete and asynchronous;

4.4.2 If $\forall o_1, o_2 \in O: o_1 \; co \; o_2 \Rightarrow \lambda(o_1) \;\iota\; \lambda(o_2)$;

4.4.3 $\forall o_1, o_2 \in O: unsep(o_1, o_2) \Rightarrow (\lambda(o_1) \;\iota\; \lambda(o_2) \Rightarrow o_1 \; co \; o_2)$;

4.4.4 $\forall p_1, p_2 \in P: p_1 \equiv p_2 \Rightarrow p_1 = p_2$.

4.5. Proposition

Suppose $L \subseteq A_\iota{}^*$ is left-closed, then B_L is ι-linguistic.

□

4.6. Theorem

Suppose B is ι-linguistic. For each $p \in P$, let $\rho(p)$ denote the set of all strings $\lambda(o_1)\ldots\lambda(o_n)$, where $p = \{o_1, \ldots, o_n\}$ and $o_1 < \ldots < o_n$ is a total order extending $\rightarrow$ on p. Then $L = \rho(P) \subseteq E_\iota{}^*$ and is left closed.

Furthermore, $\rho: (P, \subseteq) \rightarrow (L, \leq)$ is an isomorphism of posets and if $L \subseteq A_\iota{}^*$ is left-closed, then $\rho(B_L) = L$ is ι-linguistic.

□

What if $\rho(B_1) = \rho(B_2)$?

4.7. Definition (Isomorphisms)

Let B_1, B_2 be behavioural presentations, then they are *isomorphic*, and we write $B_1 \equiv B_2$ if there exists bijective mappings $\omega: O_1 \rightarrow O_2$ and $\pi: P_1 \rightarrow P_2$ such that

$$\forall p \in P_1: \pi(p) = \{\omega(o) \mid o \in p\} \quad [4.8]$$

4.8. Proposition

Suppose B_1, B_2 are ι-linguistic, then $\rho(B_1) = \rho(B_2) \Longleftrightarrow B_1 \equiv B_2$.

□

5. Asynchronous and Hybrid Transition Systems

What sort of automata could accept discrete behavioural presentations? Let us ask a less general question: what sort of automata could accept ι-linguistic behavioural presentations? We have several routes towards an answer to this question. First, given B, we may construct $\rho(P) \subseteq E_\iota{}^*$ and from $\rho(P)$ we may construct a transition system through the usual quotient construction. That is, we define, for $\forall x, y \in \rho(P)$,

$$\forall x, y \in \rho(P): x \equiv y \Longleftrightarrow \forall u \in E_\iota{}^*: x.u \in \rho(P) \Longleftrightarrow y.u \in \rho(P) \quad [4.9]$$

and note that $\equiv$ is a right congruence and that we may therefore define a transition system $(Q, E, \rightarrow)$, where Q is the set of $\equiv$ classes of $\rho(P)$ and $[x] \rightarrow^e [y] \Longleftrightarrow x.e \equiv y$.

Alternatively, we could take advantage of the fact that B comes with its own transition structure.

5.1. Definition (Steps or Derivations)

Let B be a behavioural presentation. A derivation or step in B is a triple (p, X, p') where $p, p' \in P$ and $X \in O/\approx$ such that

5.1.1 $p \subseteq p'$;

5.1.2 $p' - p = X$.

We shall write $p \vdash^X p'$ to indicate that (p, X, p') is a step and we shall refer to it as a step from p to p' via the occurrences in X. By abuse of terminology we shall refer to the expression $p \vdash^X p'$ as a step. If $X = \{o\}$, for $o \in O$, then we write $p \vdash^o p'$.

5.2. Lemma (Existence of Steps)

Let B be a discrete behavioural presentation, then

$$\forall p, p' \in P: p \subset p' \Rightarrow \exists p'' \in P \ \ \exists X \in O/\approx: p \vdash^X p'' \subseteq p' \quad [5.1]$$

□

If B is ι-linguistic, then we may define a transition system $(P, E, \rightarrow)$, where $p_1 \rightarrow^e p_2 \Longleftrightarrow \exists o \in O: \lambda(o) = e \ \& \ p_1 \vdash^o p_2$.

In either case, we obtain the following type of structure.

5.3. Definition (ι Asynchronous Transition Systems [3,9])

An ι asynchronous transition system is quadruple $C = (Q, A, \rightarrow, \iota)$ where

5.3.1 $T(C) = (Q, A, \rightarrow)$ is a transition system and it is *unambiguous*, that is;

$$\forall q, q_1, q_2 \in Q\ \forall a \in A: q \rightarrow^a q_1\ \&\ q \rightarrow^a q_2 \Rightarrow q_1 = q_2 \quad [5.2]$$

5.3.2 ι is an independence relation;

5.3.3 $\forall q, q_1, q_2 \in Q\ \forall a, b \in A: a\ \iota\ b\ \&\ q \rightarrow^a q_1\ \&\ q_1 \rightarrow^b q_2 \Rightarrow$
$\exists q'_1 \in Q: q \rightarrow^b q'_1\ \&\ q'_1 \rightarrow^a q_2$.

Recall that if $q \in Q$, then an *execution sequence* of $T(C)$ from q is a string $x \in A^*$ such that $q \rightarrow^x q'$, some $q' \in Q$, where $q \rightarrow^\Omega q$ (Ω is the null string) and for $y \in A^*$ and $a \in A$

$$q \rightarrow^{ya} q' \Leftrightarrow \exists q' \in Q: q \rightarrow^y q''\ \&\ q'' \rightarrow^a q' \quad [5.3]$$

Write $L(T(C), q)$ for the set of all execution sequences. Let

$$L(C, q) = \{<x>_\iota \mid x \in L(T(C), q)\} \quad [5.4]$$

It may be shown that $L(C, q)$ is left-closed. By proposition 4.5, it gives rise to an ι-linguistic behavioural presentation $B_{L(C,q)}$.

5.4. Definition (Acceptors for ι-Linguistic Behavioural Presentations)

Let B be a behavioural presentation and suppose C is an ι-asynchronous transition system with $q \in Q$, then (C, q) *accepts* $B \Leftrightarrow B \equiv B_{L(C,q)}$.

Note that by 4.6 and 4.7,

$$B \equiv B_{L(C,q)} \Leftrightarrow \rho(P) = L \quad [5.5]$$

If B is ι-linguistic and $C_B = (P, E, \rightarrow, \iota)$, where $p_1 \rightarrow^e p_2 \Leftrightarrow$
$\exists o \in O: \lambda(o) = e\ \&\ p_1 \vdash^o p_2$, then it may be shown that $\rho(P) = L(C_B, \varnothing)$. Hence $(C_B, \varnothing)$ accepts B. Thus:

5.5. Theorem

Every ι-linguistic behavioural presentation is accepted by some pair (C, q), where C is an ι-asynchronous transition system and $q \in Q$. Conversely, every pair (C, q), where C is an ι-asynchronous transition system and $q \in Q$, accepts some ι-linguistic behavioural presentation.

□

Turning to the general case, we are faced with the problem of representing the simultaneous executions of elements. Following [10], we shall use elements of a free algebra generated by E, except that in our case it suffices to use the free commutative semigroup generated by E.

5.6. Definition

Let E be a non-empty set and consider the set $S(E)$ of all expressions $x = e_1^{m_1} \ldots e_n^{m_n}$, where $e_1, \ldots, e_n$ are distinct elements of E and the m_i are positive integers. Define $\exp_e(x)$, the exponent of $e \in E$ in x, to be m_i if $e = e_i$ and 0 otherwise. If $x, y \in E$, define

$$x = y \Leftrightarrow \forall e \in E: \exp_e(x) = \exp_e(y) \quad [5.6]$$

If $x, y \in S(E)$, then define their product $x.y$ to be the expression $e_1^{m_1} \ldots e_n^{m_n}$, where $\{e_1, \ldots, e_n\} = \{e \in E: \exp_e(x) + \exp_e(y) > 0\}$ and $m_i = \exp_e(x) + \exp_e(y)$, each i. It is easy to see that $S(E)$ is a commutative semigroup. We call it the *free commutative semigroup generated by* E.

This construction allows us to 'factor' discrete behavioural presentations into two parts. Let B be a discrete behavioural presentation. Define $B/\approx$ to be the tuple $(O/\approx, P/\approx, S(E), \mu)$, where

- $O/\approx$ is the set of $\approx$ classes of O;
- $P/\approx = \{p/\approx \mid p \in P\}$, where for any $X \subseteq O$, $X/\approx = \{U \in O/\approx \mid U \subseteq X\}$;
- $\mu: O/\approx \to S(E)$ is defined $\forall e \in E: \exp_e(\mu(U)) = |\{o \in U \mid \lambda(o) = e\}|$.

We shall call $B/\approx$ the *$\approx$-quotient* of B.

$B/\approx$ gives us two things. The first is a behavioural presentation, $B' = (O/\approx, P/\approx, O/\approx, \lambda)$, where λ is the identity function on $O/\approx$, and the second is the function $\mu: O/\approx \to S(E)$. B' may actually be shown to be *co-linguistic*, so by theorem 5.5, it is accepted by some *co*-asynchronous transition system C from some state q. C will be of the form $(Q, O, \to, co)$. Now the tuple $(Q, O, \to, co, E, \mu)$ not only allows us to recapture B' (up to isomorphism) but also $B/\approx$. From $B/\approx$ we may recapture B (up to isomorphism) via the following construction.

Let B be a behavioural presentation of the form $(O, P, S(E), \mu)$. For $o \in O$ and $X \subseteq O$, we define

- $\varepsilon(o, \mu) = \{(o, e, i) \mid 1 \le i \le \exp_e(\mu(o))\}$;
- $\varepsilon(X, \mu) = \bigcup_{o \in X} \varepsilon(o, \mu)$;

and we define $\varepsilon(B, \mu)$ to be the quadruple $(\hat{O}, \hat{P}, \hat{E}, \hat{\lambda})$, where $\hat{O} = \varepsilon(O, \mu)$, $\hat{P} = \{\varepsilon(p, \mu) \mid p \in P\}$, $\hat{E} = E$ and $\hat{\lambda}(o, e, i) = e$.

It begins to appear that tuples $(Q, O, \to, co, E, \mu)$, together with initial states, determine behavioural presentations. Let us first describe the tuples.

5.7. Definition (Hybrid Transition Systems)

A hybrid transition system is sextuple $H = (Q, A, \to, \iota, E, \mu)$ where

(1) $C(H) = (Q, A, \to, \iota)$ is an ι-asynchronous transition system;

(2) $\mu: A \to S(E)$.

5.8. Definition (Acceptors for Discrete Behavioural Presentations)

Given $q \in Q$, we may construct $B_{L(C(H), q)}$ which will be of the form (O, P, A, λ) and hence a behavioural presentation $(O, P, S(E), \mu')$, where $\mu' = \mu \circ \lambda$. We shall say that (H, q) *accepts* a behavioural presentation $B \Leftrightarrow B \equiv \varepsilon((O, P, S(E), \mu'), \mu')$.

Given a discrete behavioural presentation, may we find an hybrid transition system that accepts it? Indeed we may.

5.9. Proposition

Let B be a discrete behavioural presentation and let $H_B = (P/\approx, O/\approx, \vdash, co, E, \mu)$, where $\vdash$ is the relation of definition 5.1, co is the co relation of $B/\approx$ and $\mu: O/\approx \to S(E)$ is defined $\forall e \in E: \exp_e(\mu(U)) = |\{o \in U \mid \lambda(o) = e\}|$. Then H_B is an hybrid transition system and $(H_B, \emptyset)$ accepts B.

□

5.10. Theorem

Every discrete behavioural presentation is accepted by some pair (H, q), where H is an hybrid transition system and $q \in Q$. Conversely, every pair (H, q), where H is an hybrid transition system and $q \in Q$, accepts some discrete behavioural presentation.

□

6. Connections with Other Models

In this section, we indicate briefly relationships between the material presented here and other approaches to the modelling of parallelism. Shortage of space requires us to be a trifle terse. The readers are referred to the appropriate literature.

6.1. Event Structures

There is a close connection between behavioural presentations and the various event structure models [7, 1, 11], which we shall now sketch. If B is an asynchronous, left-closed behavioural presentation, then $\Sigma(B) = (O, \rightarrow, \#)$ is an event structure. Conversely, if $S = (O, \leq, \#)$ is an event structure, then $\Lambda(S) = (O, P, O, id_O)$ is an asynchronous, left-closed behavioural presentation, where P is the set of *processes* of S namely sets X for which (a) $\forall o, o' \in O: \neg\, o \# o'$ and (b) $\forall o \in X\ \forall o' \in O: o' \leq o \Rightarrow o' \in X$

We always have $\Sigma(\Lambda(S) = S$, but in general, $B \subseteq \Lambda(\Sigma(B))$. Define $\overline{B} = \Lambda(\Sigma(B))$ and say that B is *closed* if $B = \overline{B}$. It may be shown that B is closed $\Leftrightarrow$ B is left-closed and coherent. It follows that event structures of [7] correspond to the class of asynchronous, left-closed and coherent behavioural presentations.

6.2. Petri Nets

Suppose $\mathbf{N} = (S, T, F)$. We are considering $\mathbf{N}$ operating under the so-called 'safe firing rule', Markings of $\mathbf{N}$ may be identified with subsets of S. Writing $x^\bullet = \{y \in S \cup T \mid x\ F\ y\}$ and ${}^\bullet x = \{y \in S \cup T \mid y\ F\ x\}$, then the rule is

$* \; c, c' \subseteq S\ \forall t \in T: c \rightarrow^t c' \Leftrightarrow c - c' = {}^\bullet t \ \&\ c' - c = t^\bullet$ [6.1]

We also have an independence relation co defined on T by

$\forall t, t' \in T: t\ co\ t' \Leftrightarrow ({}^\bullet t \cup t^\bullet) \cap ({}^\bullet t' \cup t'^\bullet) = \varnothing$ [6.2]

6.1. Remark

$C_{\mathbf{N}} = (2^O, T, \rightarrow, co)$ is a co–asynchronous transition system.

□

Every net $\mathbf{N}$, together with an initial marking, M, operating under the firing rule [6.2], determines a set of so-called process nets. Each of these is a cycle-free and forward- and backward-conflict free net exhibiting a possible period of asynchronous activity. (See, e.g. [12] for more detail). If one threw away the places of these process nets, then the result would be a set of partial orders labelled by elements of T. It may be shown that every element of this set is isomorphic to a unique element of $B_{L(C_{\mathbf{N}}, M)}$. That is to say, as far as time ordering of transition firings is concerned, the semantics of $\mathbf{N}$ given by $C_{\mathbf{N}}$ coincides with the semantics in terms of process nets.

6.3. CCS and Related Models

Many very important models of parallelism do not set out explicitly to model concurrency. This seems to be the case for theories such as CCS [13], and its variants, and 'Theoretical CSP', as described in [14]. An event structure semantics for CCS is described in [1]; we would like to know whether it is possible to construct a semantics based on hybrid transition systems directly.

In one sense, it is trivial to give a semantics for such languages in terms of hybrid transition systems, since we may use their operations semantics to associate each of their objects with a standard transition system; if $T = (Q, A, \rightarrow)$, then we may regard it as an hybrid transition system $H_T = (Q, A, \rightarrow, \varnothing, A, id_A)$, which will accept the same sequential behavioural presentations as T.

However, the intention of these theories is to describe concurrent systems and, at least from an informal view, they do this in an elegant manner. What is absent is a formalised notion of concurrency.

In a sense, it is easy to add in a concurrent semantics; if $H = (Q, A, \rightarrow, \iota, E, \lambda)$ is a hybrid transition system such that $(Q, A, \rightarrow, \varnothing, E, \lambda)$ - which we might call the 'sequentialisation of H' - corresponds to a transition system of a given system description, then H describes the same system, but with concurrency introduced into it.

However, things are not as simple as that. Consider, for example, the following two CCS expressions:

$$X \Leftarrow a.b.NIL + b.a.NIL \qquad [6.3]$$

$$Y \Leftarrow a.NIL \mid b.NIL \qquad [6.4]$$

Informally, [6.3] asks for the two actions a and b to be performed in either order, while [6.4] asks for them to be performed in parallel. From a formal point of view, the two are equal (strongly congruent). Indeed, an implementation of Y on a sequential processor would quite likely be the same as an implementation of X. However, it is not as clear that an implementation of Y would serve also as an implementation of X; the designer might *require* that a and b be mutually exclusive and has chosen the form [6.3] rather than [6.4] to make that clear.

It would seem prudent, therefore, only to enrich transition systems of CCS or CSP systems with concurrency when doing so is consistent with the degree of parallelism suggested by the syntax of the description.

The main problem seems to be the construction of the underlying asynchronous transition system. In general a CCS system would not correspond to something ι-linguistic. $a.NIL \mid a.NIL$ has two actions with the same name concurrent with each other; we would need to regard this as system $e_1.NIL \mid e_2.NIL$ - so that $e_1 \iota e_2$ - in which each e_i is labelled by a. Broadly speaking, CCS lies at a higher level of abstraction than the 1-safe nets we mentioned in section 6.2.

What seems to be required is a subclass of CCS (or whatever) such that

- Each action comes from a specific process and is not in conflict with itself, so that concurrency may be unambiguously defined by being simultaneously enabled and belonging to distinct processes;
- Every description may be regarded as a labelled form of a description in the subclass.

Asynchronous transition systems may be defined for the subclass; each description then becomes a labelled ,asynchronous transition system that is, an hybrid transition system.

A possible candidate for such a subclass, constructed using a labelling operation which eliminates ambiguities, is given in [15]. The details of the construction of the class of asynchronous transition systems corresponding to such a subclass is sketched in [16].

7. Conclusions

Why bother with non-interleaving models at all; won't interleaving models do just as well? There are two questions involved here: Are interleaving models an adequate abstraction from non-interleaving models? That is to say, in analysing (say) an asynchronous transition system to discover its properties, is it sufficient to consider the transition system which is its interleaving? Do interleaving models adequately represent the real world?

The first is a purely technical question; basically, it asks whether an asynchronous transition system and its interleaving have the same properties - where one supposes that one has a 'sensible' definition of 'properties'. It is clear that any property which may be defined in terms of potential finite reachability - properties such as absence of deadlock - remain unchanged. We should expect things to go wrong where it is essential not to confuse concurrency with non-deterministic choice - in situations described by the Net Theoretic notion of *confusion* [12].

Let us give an example of such a situation.[1] Consider the transition system of figure 1, in which $a \iota c$. We suppose that we are trying to establish a fixed priority of b over c - whenever both are enabled then b should be taken. We shall say that an execution sequence x *respects the priority* if whenever $x = u.d.v$, where $d \in \{b, c\}$, and both $u.b$ and $u.c$ are execution sequences, then $d = b$.

The question is, which terminating execution sequences - that is execution sequences leading to a state with no output arcs - respect the priority?

Considering figure 1 merely as a transition system, we see that *ab* and *ca* both respect the priority, but that *ac* doesn't. As an asynchronous transition system, however, we have $ac \equiv_\iota ca$. Does $<ac>_\iota$ respect the priority or not?

This problem is typical of situations in which it is not possible to say whether a non-deterministic choice has arisen during a behaviour. In the example, it seems to have done during *ac* but not during *ca*. Such problems crop up in studies of fairness, where of two $\equiv$ -equivalent sequences, one may enable some action and infinity of times and the other may never enable it at all. In such a case, some definitions of fairness break down - depending as they do on the idea of something being enabled an infinite number of times.

Whether or not these matters are crucial, it seems arguable that the assumption that an interleaved and non-interleaved representation of the same system have the same properties is dubious.

---

[1] Janicki, in [17], discusses this example, presented in the form of a set of path expressions. He forcefully rejects the idea that such systems are ill-defined, but does so on the basis that the priority relation changes the independence relation; that is, the fixed priority may be imposed in an unambiguous way providing the independence relation is suitably modified. This is surely true, and it is a quite valid *construction* - although one of several possible constructions. However, our example is not concerned with a construction but the properties of a *given system*.

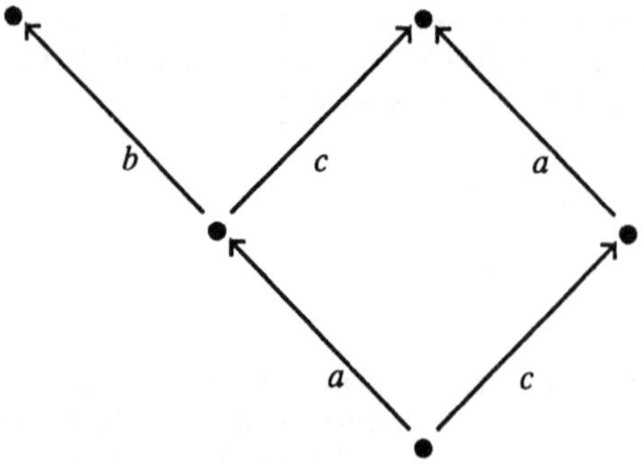

Figure 1

This wouldn't matter at all if interleaving models were adequate for a representation of the real world - or at least those parts of it that concern theoretical computer science.

Possibly, the easiest place to find examples of where the interleaving approach may oversimplify is in the area of digital systems. (Some models of parallelism have been proposed as means of specifying hardware).

As a contribution towards the search, I offer the following. A J-K Flip-flop is a binary storage device with three input lines (J, K and Clock) and two output lines (Q and $\overline{\text{Q}}$). On receiving a clock pulse, the logic levels on (Q and $\overline{\text{Q}}$) are set according to their current level and the levels on J and K. Events in such a system are arrivals and propagation of rises and falls in logic level. Writing 01 for a rise from logic level 0 to logic level 1, and writing 10 for the fall from logic level 1 to logic level 0, we might describe the flip-flop as follows.

$$JK(j,k,q) \Leftarrow \alpha_K(x).JK(g(x,j),k,q) + \alpha_K(x).JK(j,g(x,k),q)$$

$$alpha_{CLK}(x).(IF\ x = 01\ THEN\ JK(j,k,q)\ ELSEJK(j,x,f(j,k,q))$$

where $g(01,0) = 1$ and $g(10,1) = 0$ and $f(j,k,q)$ is given by

$$f(j,k,q) = \begin{cases} q & \text{if } j = k = 0 \\ 1 & \text{if } j = 1 \ \& \ k = 0 \\ 0 & \text{if } j = 0 \ \& \ k = 1 \\ 1 - q & \text{if } j = k = 1 \end{cases}$$

This description embodies an assumption that seems quite important to the interleaving approach, namely that the system is capable of discriminating between arrivals of events, that it can 'see them' happening in some order.

Unfortunately, this is not the case. It takes time for the flip-flop to reset itself and if there is a change to the logic levels on the J or K lines *while it is clocking*, the result is not as described by the CCS expression above.

Hardware can behave in an unpredictable way if it receives inputs which are too close together in time for it to be able to distinguish an order in their arrivals. 'Too close together' is a relation on occurrences which, ignoring equality, is precisely an independence relation. The description above fails to take into account what amounts to the *possible concurrent occurrences of the three input events*.

The situation we have met with our flip-flop, the 'concurrent' arrival of two signals, is called a *race condition*. Race conditions are not so unusual in digital systems that they may be ignored.

One might like to argue that - well, one could always fix the interleaving description somehow. Perhaps. But it is worth pointing out that race conditions tend to give rise to the phenomenon that Net Theorists call confusion - and it was the presence of confusion that caused the anomalies of the example concerning figure 6.

References

1. G. Winskel, "Event Structure Semantics for CCS and Related Languages.," Tech. Rep. DAIMIPB-159, Computer Science Department, University of Aarhus, April, 1983.
2. A. Mazurkiewicz, "Concurrent Program Schema and their Interpretations," in *Procedings Aarhus Workshop on Verification of Parallel Programs*, 1977.
3. M. W. Shields, "Concurrent Machines," *Computer Journal*, vol. 28, pp. 449-465, 1985.
4. M. W. Shields, *Elements of a Theory of Parallelism*, MIT Press, In Preparation.
5. A. Einstein, *Relativity: The Special and General Theory*, Methuen.
6. C. A. Petri, "Non-Sequential Processes," Interner Bericht ISF-77-05, Gesellschaft fur Mathematik und Datenverarbeitung, 1977.
7. M. Neilsen, G. Plotkin, and G. Winskel, "Petri Nets, Event Structures and Domains," in *Proceedings, Symposium on the Semantics of Concurrent Computation*, Lecture Notes in Computer Science, vol. 70, pp. 266-283, Springer Verlag, 1979.
8. R. M. Keller, "Formal Verification of Parallel Programs," *CACM*, vol. 19(7), 1975.
9. M. A. Bednarcztk, *Categories of Asynchronous Systems*, Ph.D. Thesis, University of Sussex, October 1987.
10. A. R. J. G. Milner, "Calculi for Synchrony and Asynchrony," Tech. Rep. CSR-104-82, Computer Science Department, University of Edinburgh, 1982.
11. G. Winskel, *Events in Computation,*, Ph.D. Thesis, Computer Science Department, University of Sussex, October 1980.
12. H. J. Genrich, K. Lautenbach, and P. S. Thiagarajan, "Elements of General Net Theory," in *Proceedings, Advanced Course on General Net Theory of Processes and Systems*, Lecture Notes in Computer Science, vol. 84, pp. 21-164, Springer Verlag, 1979.
13. A. R. J. G. Milner, *A Calculus of Communicating Systems*, Lecture Notes in Computer Science, 92, Springer Verlag, 1980.
14. C. A. R. Hoare, *Communicating Sequential Processes*, Prentice-Hall International Series in Computer Science, 1985.
15. G. Costa and C. Stirling, "Fair Calculus of Communicating Systems," Tech. Rep. CSR-137-83, Computer Science Department, University of Edinburgh, 1983.
16. M. W. Shields, "Algebraic Models of Parallelism and Net Theory," in *Concurrency and Nets*, ed. K. Voss, H. J. Genrich and G. Rozenburg, pp. 423-434, Springer Verlag, 1987.
17. R. Janicki, "A Formal Semantics for Concurrent Systems with a Priority Relation," Tech. Rep. R 84-16, Institut for Elektroniske Systemer, University of Aalborg, 1984.

Computation Tree Logic and Regular ω-Languages

Wolfgang Thomas

Lehrstuhl für Informatik II, RWTH Aachen
D-5100 Aachen

ABSTRACT. The expressive power of branching time logics is studied in the framework of the theory of ω-automata and ω-languages. The systems CTL* (computation tree logic) and ECTL* (extended computation tree logic) are characterized in terms of star-free, resp. regular ω-languages. A further characterization of CTL* by a "non-counting property" for sets of trees shows that it is decidable whether an ECTL*-formula can be written as a CTL*-formula.

Key words: Branching time logic, computation tree logic, Büchi automata, Rabin tree automata, noncounting property, group-free monoids.

CONTENTS

1. Introduction

In the specification and verification of concurrent programs two main categories of temporal logic systems have been used: logics of linear time and logics of branching time. The purpose of the present paper is to study a possible integration of the two approaches, making use of results from the theory of automata over infinite words. We discuss a treatment of two standard systems of branching time logic (the computation tree logic CTL* of [EH86], and the extended computation tree logic ECTL* of [VW84], [CGK87]) in the framework of Büchi automata and regular ω-languages. As it turns out, it is possible in this way

- to "embed" branching time logics in the theory of Büchi automata and regular ω-languages,
- to simplify certain aspects in the syntax of branching time logic (e.g. to eliminate "path formulas" and keep only "state formulas"),
- to apply results from the structure theory of regular ω-languages for characterizations of (the expressive power of) branching time logics.

We give an intuitive outline of the main ideas; formal definitions are provided in the following sections. In the analysis of concurrent systems, linear time temporal logic serves as a specification formalism which allows to express conditions on the ongoing behaviour of a system. A standard approach is to use temporal logic formulas for describing desired (or assumed) properties of "execution sequences", i.e. sequences $\sigma = s_0 s_1 \ldots$ of states which the program should (or can) realize. If n state properties are relevant for the specification under consideration, formulas are used which are built up from n atomic formulas $p_1,\ldots,p_n$, each representing one state property. In this case, states need to be distinguished only by the possible truth valuations for $p_1,\ldots,p_n$ which are given by 0-1-vectors of length n. Accordingly, the satisfaction of a (linear time) temporal logic formula in an execution sequence $\sigma = s_0 s_1 \ldots$ is determined by the associated ω-sequence $\alpha = \alpha(0)\alpha(1)\ldots$ consisting of vectors from $\{0,1\}^n$ (where the i-th component of $\alpha(j)$ is 1 iff s_j satisfies p_i.) This motivates the choice of sequences $\alpha \in (\{0,1\}^n)^\omega$ as possible models: The meaning of a formula with the atomic formulas $p_1,\ldots,p_n$ is given by the set of sequences $\alpha \in (\{0,1\}^n)^\omega$ which satisfy it, i.e. by an ω-language over the finite alphabet $\{0,1\}^n$. As a result, it is possible to treat temporal logics of linear time directly in the framework of ω-language theory.

In the context of branching time logic, one does not consider the individual execution sequences as the models of specifications, but the totality of execution sequences, collected in a computation tree. (Usually one assumes that there is a designated initial state which serves as the root of the computation tree.) A branching time logic formula expresses properties of computation trees; as in the linear time case we can assume that each node (representing a state) carries a value from $\{0,1\}^n$ when n atomic formulas $p_1,\ldots,p_n$ are involved. The main ingredients of systems of branching time logic are quantifiers over paths through computation trees (i.e., over execution sequences). This constitutes an essential difference to systems of linear time logic: In branching time logic one can express the existence of execution sequences with certain properties, and path quantifiers can be nested, whereas linear time logic specifications are understood as conditions on arbitrary single execution sequences and hence only involve one implicit universal quantification over paths.

Concerning linear time logic, we are interested here in the systems propositional temporal logic PTL (cf. [Pn81], [Pn86]) and the extended temporal logic ETL of [Wo83], [WVS83]. PTL-formulas are built up from the atomic formulas p_i by means of boolean connectives and the temporal operators X ("next"), ◊ ("eventually"), □ ("henceforth"), and U ("until"). For example, the PTL-formula

(*) $$\Box(p_1 \rightarrow X((\neg p_2)\ U\ p_1)$$

expresses the following condition on state sequences $\sigma = s_0 s_1 \ldots$:

> "in any state s_i of σ, if p_1 holds in s_i, then from the next state s_{i+1} of σ onwards p_2 does not hold until eventually a state s_j $(i+1 \leq j)$ of σ is reached where p_1 holds."

The formula defines the ω-language L over $\{0,1\}^2$ such that $\alpha \in L$ iff

> after any letter in α with first component 1 there follow only letters with second component 0 until eventually a letter with first component 1 occurs.

In ETL, one allows arbitrary finite automata over infinite words as temporal operators. The model we use is the (nondeterministic) Büchi automaton of [Bü62] which accepts an ω-word by a run that passes infinitely often through a final state. The following illustration, which yields an ETL-formulation of the above PTL-formula (*), will clarify the idea: The Büchi automaton (given in state graph representation)

$\mathcal{B}_0$:

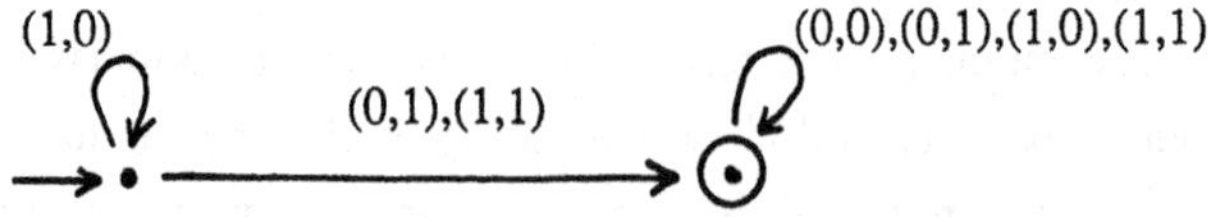

accepts those infinite words over $\{0,1\}^2$ where the first components are 1 until eventually some letter with second component 1 is reached. Since a PTL-formula $\varphi_1 U \varphi_2$ is satisfied iff precisely this condition holds for the sequence of truth value pairs for (φ_1,φ_2), $\mathcal{B}_0$ describes the semantics of the "until"-operator. Similarly, the meaning of the formula $\Box(\varphi_1 \rightarrow X\ \varphi_2)$ in terms of φ_1, φ_2 is expressed by the Büchi automaton

$\mathcal{A}_0$:

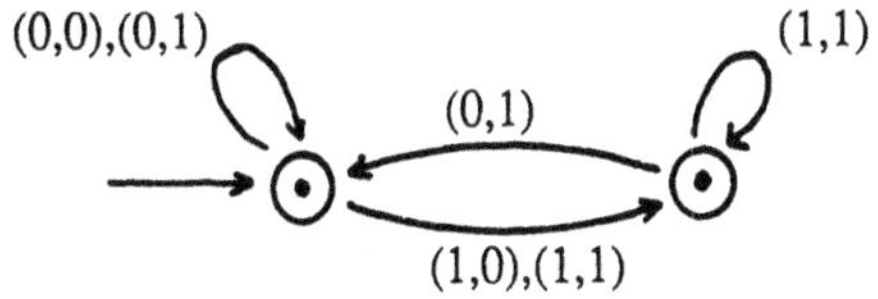

because $\mathcal{A}_0$ accepts those infinite words where after any letter with first component 1 there follows immediately a letter with second component 1. In this way a Büchi automaton $\mathcal{A}$ over $\{0,1\}^n$ can be used as an n-ary connective, written $\mathcal{A}(\varphi_1,...,\varphi_n)$ if applied to given formulas $\varphi_1,...,\varphi_n$. Thus, by substitution of $\mathcal{B}_0$ in $\mathcal{A}_0$ one obtains the following formulation of the above PTL-formula (*) as an ETL-formula:

$$\mathcal{A}_0(p_1,\mathcal{B}_0(\neg p_2,p_1)).$$

Since all four temporal operators of PTL are easily described by appropriate Büchi automata, ETL is an extension of PTL. (For the reader acquainted with the approach of [Wo83] and [WVS83] we note a difference in terminology: In those papers the alphabet for the automata does not consist of truth value vectors but of indices for the relevant subformulas, in the cases discussed above of the indices 1, 2. The definition of the present paper is somewhat more general than [Wo83], [WVS83] and fits better to the subsequent discussion.)

PTL and ETL correspond to well-known classes of ω-languages: From [GPSS80] and [Th79] it follows that PTL allows to define exactly the star-free ω-languages, and [Wo83], [WVS83] show that in the extended temporal logic ETL one can define precisely the regular ω-languages (recognized by Büchi automata). Thus known results on the relation between star-free and regular ω-languages can be transferred to the logics PTL and ETL. For instance, the examples of ω-languages which are regular but not star-free show that ETL is strictly more expressive than PTL. Moreover, since there is an effective criterion for the decision when a Büchi automaton defines a star-free ω-language (by [Per84]), one can decide effectively whether an ETL-formula can be written as a PTL-formula or not.

Both results can be shown by a characterization of star-free ω-languages in terms of the noncounting property (within the class of regular ω-languages). This property was introduced by [MNP71] in the context of languages of finite words. For a regular language the noncounting property is equivalent to the algebraic condition that the finite syntactic monoid of the language is group-free. Intuitively, a language is noncounting if it cannot "count modulo a number m > 1". A language W of finite words is said to count modulo m if there are words u, v, w such that for arbitrary large k we have $uv^{k\cdot m}w \in W$ but $uv^{k\cdot m+1}w \notin W$. In section 4 this condition will be transferred to ω-languages, yielding a characterization of the star-free ω-languages. An example of an ω-language which counts modulo 2 is the set of ω-words over $\{0,1\}$ where between any two letters 1 there is an even number of letters 0. So this ω-language violates the noncounting property and hence is not star-free.

The aim of this paper is to apply these results to branching time logic. For formulas of branching time logic we use a semantics based on similar conventions as above: The possible models for branching time logic formulas with atomic formulas $p_1,...,p_n$ will be infinite trees whose nodes are valued with vectors from $\{0,1\}^n$. Hence the meaning of a branching time logic formula is given by a tree language, consisting of infinite $\{0,1\}^n$-valued trees. The starting point is the computation tree logic CTL* introduced by [EH86]. It allows to use quantifiers over paths of infinite trees and conditions on paths which are formalizable in the linear time logic PTL. Systems of extended computation tree logic ECTL* have been introduced in [VW84] and [CGK87]. The underlying idea is similar as in the step from PTL to ETL: Instead of writing out linear time conditions on paths with some selected temporal operators, one describes these conditions directly by automata, gaining in this way both flexibility and expressive power. We follow here the approach of [CGK87]; however, where [CGK87] use the model of (deterministic) Muller automaton over infinite words we refer to the equivalent model of (nondeterministic) Büchi automaton.

It is easy to verify that CTL* is characterized by those ECTL* formulas where all occurring Büchi automata recognize star-free ω-languages. In the present work also the decidability result on star-freeness of regular ω-languages (or PTL-expressibility of ETL-formulas) is transferred to the case of branching time logic: Given an ECTL*-formula, one can decide whether it can be written as a CTL*-formula. The proof is based on a generalization of the notion of noncounting property from ω-languages to tree languages; but also additional technical work is needed to reduce arbitrary ECTL*-formulas to a form such that the results known from the linear time case are applicable. In the present preliminary version of the paper some proofs concerning this reduction are only outlined.

The present work originates in [Th87], where an embedding of logics over trees into the framework of regular ω-languages is developed for fragments of monadic second-order logic ("chain logic" and "path logic"), and where the corresponding results for branching time logic are announced. A second background is [VW84] and [CGK87] where a similar approach for branching time logic is developed, by integrating automata over ω-words into the syntax of computation tree logic. However, [VW84] and [CGK87] investigate (the complexity of) satisfiability tests and model checking procedures for the logic and do not consider decision problems on expressiveness.

The remainder of the paper is organized as follows: Section 2 collects prerequisites and terminology. In section 3 we introduce CTL* and ECTL*. Sections 4 and 5 discuss the noncounting property for sets of (ω-)words and sets of trees, and give the main result.

2. Notation and Basic Definitions

Let Σ be a finite alphabet. For an ω-sequence $\alpha = \alpha(0)\alpha(1)\ldots$ from Σ^ω denote by α^i the i-th suffix $\alpha(i)\alpha(i+1)\ldots$. If $\Sigma = \{0,1\}^n$, then $(\alpha(i))_j$ is the j-th component of $\alpha(i)$.

A tree domain is a subset D of ω^* (the set of finite sequences of natural numbers) which is closed under prefixes and such that, for any $x \in \omega^*$, $xi \in D$ and $j < i$ imply $xj \in D$. A Σ-valued tree is a map $t:\mathrm{dom}(t) \rightarrow \Sigma$ where $\mathrm{dom}(t) \subseteq \omega^*$ is a tree domain. If $\mathrm{dom}(t) \subseteq \{0,\ldots,k-1\}^*$ we say that t is a k-ary tree; in case $\mathrm{dom}(t) = \{0,\ldots,k-1\}^*$ we speak of a full k-ary tree. To avoid technical details which arise by the treatment of terminating branches, we shall restrict to trees t which are infinite and where any node has at least one successor in dom(t). By T_Σ we denote the set of Σ-valued trees of this kind. In section 4, however, we shall introduce also "special trees" having exactly one frontier node, i.e. a node without successors in the tree domain. For $x \in \mathrm{dom}(t)$, the subtree t_x at node x is given by $\mathrm{dom}(t_x) = \{y \mid xy \in \mathrm{dom}(t)\}$ and $t_x(y) = t(xy)$ for $y \in \mathrm{dom}(t_x)$. A path in the tree t is a sequence $\pi = \pi(0)\pi(1)\ldots$ of elements of dom(t) where for each n, $\pi(n+1) = \pi(n)j$ for some j; here $\pi(0)$ is not necessarily the root. Note that $t_{\pi(n)}$ is the subtree of t whose root is the n-th node of π. By a chain we mean a subset of a path, i.e. a set which is linearly ordered in the partial tree ordering (the prefix relation $<$ on ω^*).

We recall some facts on regular ω-languages. An ω-language $L \subseteq \Sigma^\omega$ is regular if it is recognized by a Büchi automaton in the sense of [Bü62]: A Büchi automaton over Σ is a nondeterministic finite automaton $\mathcal{A} = (Q,q_0,\Delta,F)$ with finite state set Q, initial state q_0, transition relation $\Delta \subseteq Q\times\Sigma\times Q$ and final state set F. The ω-language $L(\mathcal{A})$ recognized by $\mathcal{A}$ contains those ω-words $\alpha \in \Sigma^\omega$ on which there is a run of $\mathcal{A}$ that assumes infinitely often a final state. A basic representation result states that an ω-language over Σ is regular iff it is a finite union of sets $U\cdot V^\omega$ where $U,V \subseteq \Sigma^*$ are regular sets of finite words and $V\cdot V \subseteq V$. The star-free ω-languages are obtained in an analogous way, by taking U, V to be star-free sets of finite words. (A set of finite words is called star-free if it is constructible from finite word-sets by applications of boolean operations and of concatenation.) It is known that an ω-language is regular, resp. star-free, iff it is definable in monadic second-order logic, resp. first-order logic, over the ordering $(\omega,<)$. For a more detailed discussion of Büchi automata and regular ω-languages see e.g. the survey papers [HR86], [Th88].

Let us now introduce formally the propositional temporal logic of linear time, denoted PTL. PTL-formulas are constructed from propositional variables p_i (as atomic formulas) by application of the boolean connectives (here $\neg$, $\vee$), the unary connective X ("nexttime") and the binary connective U ("until"). For simplicity we do not include the (definable) operators "eventually" and "henceforth". A PTL-formula φ in which at most the atomic formulas $p_1,\ldots,p_n$ occur is also written $\varphi(p_1,\ldots,p_n)$; the notation $\varphi(p_1/\psi_1,\ldots,p_n/\psi_n)$ will indicate the result of substituting formula ψ_i for p_i in φ. PTL-formulas $\varphi(p_1,\ldots,p_n)$ are interpreted in ω-sequences over the alphabet $\Sigma = \{0,1\}^n$. The satisfaction relation $\alpha \models \varphi$ is given by the clauses

$\alpha \models p_i$	iff	$(\alpha(0))_i = 1$;
$\alpha \models \neg\varphi$	iff	not $\alpha \models \varphi$; similarly for $\vee$;
$\alpha \models X\varphi$	iff	$\alpha^1 \models \varphi$;
$\alpha \models \varphi_1 U \varphi_2$	iff	there is $j \geq 0$ such that $\alpha^j \models \varphi_2$ and for all i with $0 \leq i < j$ $\alpha^i \models \varphi_1$.

Set <u>true</u> $= p_1 \vee \neg p_1$ and <u>false</u> $= \neg$ <u>true</u>. The operators $\Diamond$ ("eventually") and $\Box$ ("henceforth") are introduced in terms of U: $\Diamond\varphi$ abbreviates <u>true</u> U φ, and $\Box\varphi$ abbreviates $\neg\Diamond\neg\varphi$.

3. Systems of Computation Tree Logic

3.1 Computation Tree Logic CTL*. In this section we list only the basic definitions concerning CTL* which are needed in the sequel; a more exhaustive introduction is given in [EH86], [Em88]. Let $P_n = \{p_1,\ldots,p_n\}$ be a set of propositional variables. The CTL*-formulas over P_n are defined inductively in two categories, as "state formulas" (sf) and "path formulas" (pf). Their formation is described by the following BNF-rules:

sf ::= p_i | $\neg$ sf | sf $\vee$ sf | E pf

pf ::= sf | $\neg$ pf | pf $\vee$ pf | X pf | pf U pf.

The constants <u>true</u>, <u>false</u> and the operators $\Diamond$ and $\Box$ are introduced as for PTL. We define the semantics of CTL*-formulas over $\{0,1\}^n$-valued trees. Intuitively, nodes of trees are viewed as states, and the components of the values from $\{0,1\}^n$ indicate which of the atomic formulas $p_1,\ldots,p_n$ are true in the states. The operator E means "there is a path", and X, U stand for "next" and "until" as in PTL. Formally, state formulas (denoted φ below) will be true of (the root of) trees, and path formulas (denoted ψ) will be satisfied in trees with a distinguished path. The satisfaction relation $t \models \varphi$, resp. $(t,\pi) \models \psi$, is defined by the following clauses:

$t \models p_i$	iff	$(t(\varepsilon))_i = 1$;
$t \models \neg\varphi$	iff	not $t \models \varphi$; similarly for $\vee$;
$t \models E\psi$	iff	there is a path π through t, starting at the root of t, such that $(t,\pi) \models \psi$;
$(t,\pi) \models \varphi$	iff	$t \models \varphi$;
$(t,\pi) \models \neg\psi$	iff	not $(t,\pi) \models \psi$; similarly for $\vee$;

$(t,\pi) \models X\psi$ iff $(t_{\pi(1)},\pi^1) \models \psi$;

$(t,\pi) \models \psi_1 U \psi_2$ iff there is $j \geq 0$ such that $(t_{\pi(j)},\pi^j) \models \psi_2$ and for all i $(0 \leq i < j)$ $(t_{\pi(i)},\pi^i) \models \psi_1$.

A set T of $\{0,1\}^n$-valued trees is said to be CTL*-definable if for some state formula φ of CTL* (over P_n) we have $t \in T$ iff $t \models \varphi$.

For inductive proofs it is convenient to classify the CTL*-formulas by the nesting of the E-operators. Here we refer only to state formulas; by their E-depth we mean the maximal nesting of E's in them. Define, for $d \geq 0$, the set E_d of state formulas of E-depth $\leq d$ (over P_n) as follows:

> E_0 contains all boolean combinations of atomic formulas.
>
> E_{d+1} contains the formulas of E_d and all boolean combinations of formulas $E\ \varphi(q_1/\varphi_1,\ldots,q_m/\varphi_m)$, where $\varphi(q_1,\ldots,q_m)$ is a PTL-formula and $\varphi_1,\ldots,\varphi_m$ belong to E_d.

We say that the state formula φ is of E-depth $\leq d$ if $\varphi \in E_d$. The classification by E-depth condenses the formation of a path formula from state formulas (by applications of $\neg$, $\vee$, X, U) into a single step (yielding a PTL-formula). It is easy to see that the set of CTL*-formulas is the union over all sets E_d.

3.2 Extended Computation Tree Logic ECTL*. Assume a set $P_n = \{p_1,\ldots,p_n\}$ of propositional variables is given. The ECTL*-formulas over P_n are built up inductively from the p_i by the boolean connectives $\neg$, $\vee$, and the following inductive clause:

> if $\varphi_1,\ldots,\varphi_m$ are ECTL*-formulas and $\mathcal{A}$ is a Büchi automaton over the alphabet $\{0,1\}^m$, then $E(\mathcal{A},\varphi_1,\ldots,\varphi_m)$ is an ECTL*-formula.

The definition of E-depth is transferred from CTL* to ECTL* in the canonical way. Note that the generality of the clause involving the automata $\mathcal{A}$ results in a simplification compared with the syntax of CTL*: there is no more a distinction between state and path formulas (indeed, path formulas are eliminated), and the temporal operators are replaced by the unifying (and more general) framework of automata.

The semantics for ECTL*-formulas is based on the idea that the formula $E(\mathcal{A},\varphi_1,\ldots\varphi_m)$ is true of the tree t iff there is a path through t such that $\mathcal{A}$ accepts the sequence of m-tuples of truth values which record satisfaction of the formulas $\varphi_1,\ldots,\varphi_m$ along that path. Formally, we associate with any path π through a tree t and an m-tuple $(\varphi_1,\ldots,\varphi_m)$ of ECTL*-formulas a sequence $\alpha = \alpha(t,\pi,\varphi_1,\ldots,\varphi_m)$ over $\{0,1\}^m$ by setting

$$(\alpha(i))_j = 1 \text{ iff } t_{\pi(i)} \models \varphi_j.$$

(Later on we also refer to tree languages T_i instead of defining formulas φ_i and write $\alpha(t,\pi,T_1,\ldots,T_m)$; then $(\alpha(i))_j = 1$ iff $t_{\pi(i)} \in T_j$.) Now the satisfaction relation "$t \models \varphi$"

between $\{0,1\}^n$-valued trees and ECTL*-formulas φ over P_n is defined by induction:

$t \models p_i$	iff	$(t(\varepsilon))_i = 1$;
$t \models \neg\varphi$	iff	not $t \models \varphi$; similarly for $\vee$;
$t \models E(\mathcal{A}, \varphi_1, ..., \varphi_m)$	iff	there is a path π through t, starting at the root of t, s.t. $\mathcal{A}$ accepts the ω-word $\alpha(t, \pi, \varphi_1, ..., \varphi_m)$.

For an ECTL*-formula φ over the set P_n of atomic formulas let $T(\varphi)$ be the set of $\{0,1\}^n$-valued trees which satisfy φ. A set T is called ECTL*-definable if $T = T(\varphi)$ for some ECTL*-formula φ.

3.3 Example. Consider the CTL*-formula

$$E\,\underline{[](p_1 \rightarrow X\Diamond}\,E\,\underline{[]\Diamond\, p_2})$$

which says intuitively

> "there is a path π such that after any state on π satisfying p_1 there starts eventually some path on which p_2 is satisfied infinitely often".

To write this as an ECTL*-formula, we use two Büchi automata $\mathcal{A}$ and $\mathcal{B}$ corresponding to the two occurrences of the path quantifier E. The first automaton $\mathcal{A}$ checks existence of a path which satisfies the first underlined part of the formula (in terms of the two subformulas $\varphi_1 = p_1$, $\varphi_2 = E[]\Diamond p_2$. The second automaton $\mathcal{B}$ checks existence of a path which satisfies $[]\Diamond p_2$, i.e. the second underlined part of the formula (in terms of the subformula p_2). We obtain the ECTL*-formula $E(\mathcal{A}, p_1, E(\mathcal{B}, p_2))$, where $\mathcal{A}$ (over $\{0,1\}^2$) and $\mathcal{B}$ (over $\{0,1\}$) are given by the following state graphs:

$\mathcal{A}$:

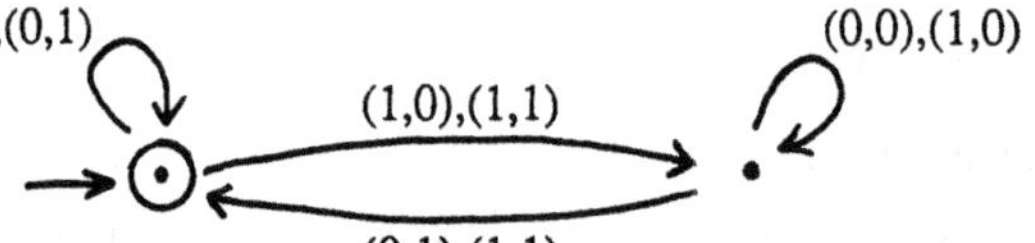

($\mathcal{A}$ accepts those ω-words over $\{0,1\}^2$ in which after any entry with first component 1 there follows eventually an entry with second component 1.)

$\mathcal{B}$:

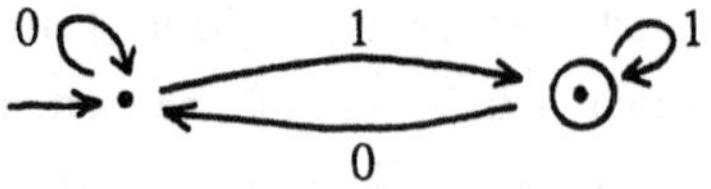

($\mathcal{B}$ accepts those ω-words over $\{0,1\}$ in which 1 occurs infinitely often.) ❑

Let us verify that CTL* may be regarded as a fragment of ECTL*.

3.4 Proposition.

Any CTL*-formula is equivalent to an ECTL*-formula.

Proof. Use induction over the E-depth of state formulas of CTL*. A CTL*-formula of E-depth 0 is already an ECTL*-formula. In the induction step, assuming that the claim is shown for CTL*-formulas of E-depth $\leq$ d, it suffices to consider a state formula $E\varphi$ where φ is of form $\varphi(q_1/\varphi_1,...,q_m/\varphi_m)$ for some PTL-formula $\varphi(q_1,...,q_m)$ and CTL*-formulas $\varphi_1,...,\varphi_m$ of E-depth $\leq$ d. By induction hypothesis, there are ECTL*-formulas $\psi_1,...,\psi_m$, equivalent to $\varphi_1,...,\varphi_m$. Moreover, since PTL-formulas define regular ω-languages, there is a Büchi automaton $\mathcal{A}$ which recognizes the same ω-language over $\{0,1\}^m$ as $\varphi(q_1,...,q_m)$ defines. So $E(\mathcal{A},\psi_1,...,\psi_m)$ is an ECTL*-formula as desired. ❑

Note that by the equivalence between PTL and star-free ω-languages the Büchi automaton $\mathcal{A}$ of the preceding proof recognizes an ω-language which is star-free. Conversely, assume that an ECTL*-formula contains only Büchi automata of this kind. The ω-language recognized by such a Büchi automaton $\mathcal{A}$, say over the alphabet $\{0,1\}^\omega$, is definable by a PTL-formula $\varphi(q_1,...,q_m)$. Hence $E(\mathcal{A},\varphi_1,...,\varphi_m)$ is expressible in CTL* by $E\varphi(q_1/\varphi_1,...,q_m/\varphi_m)$. Altogether we obtain:

3.5 Proposition.

A CTL*-formula can be written as an ECTL*-formula which contains only Büchi automata recognizing star-free ω-languages, and conversely an ECTL*-formula in which all occurring Büchi automata recognize star-free ω-languages is equivalent to a CTL*-formula. ❑

3.6 Computation Tree Logic, Rabin tree automata and Monadic Second-Order Logic.

It is instructive to compare ECTL* and CTL* with the model of Rabin tree automaton and monadic second-order logic over infinite trees [Ra69]. Since Rabin tree automata work over full binary trees, this comparison requires a coding from arbitrary countably branching trees into binary trees. For this, we represent the node $x = (n_1,...,n_m) \in \omega^*$ of an arbitrary tree by the node $\underline{x} = 1^{n_1}0...1^{n_m}0$ of the binary tree. Given t:dom(t) $\rightarrow \Sigma$, let $\underline{t}:\{0,1\}^* \rightarrow \Sigma\cup\{\$\}$ be the full binary tree defined by $\underline{t}(\underline{x}) = t(x)$ for all $x \in$ dom(t) and $\underline{t}(y) = \$$ for all y which are not of the form $\underline{x}$ with $x \in$ dom(t). For $T \subseteq T_\Sigma$ set $\underline{T} = \{\underline{t} \mid t \in T\}$.

A Rabin tree automaton over Σ is of the form $\mathcal{A} = (Q,q_o,\Delta,\mathcal{F})$ with finite state set Q, initial state q_o, transition relation $\Delta \subseteq Q\times\Sigma\times Q^2$, and a system $\mathcal{F}$ of final state sets. $\mathcal{A}$ accepts a tree t if there is a run r of $\mathcal{A}$ on t(i.e. a tree r with $r(\varepsilon) = q_o$, $(r(x),t(x),r(x0),r(x1)) \in \Delta$ for $x \in \{0,1\}^*$) such that the states on each path of r form a set in $\mathcal{F}$. Note that Rabin tree automata distinguish the successors of a node x (as being left successor x0 or right successor x1).

As shown in [Ra 69], Rabin tree automata over binary trees are equivalent in expressive power to the system S2S of monadic second-order logic. S2S has variables x,y,... ranging over nodes of binary trees, and variables X,Y,... ranging over sets of nodes. It is built up from atomic formulas $x \in X$ ("node x is in set X"), $x\ S_i\ y$ ("node x has y as i-th successor", for i = 0,1), and $x \in P_a$ ("node x carries value a", for $a \in \Sigma$) by means of the boolean connectives and the quantifiers $\exists$, $\forall$. Relations like the partial tree ordering < or the set predicates of being a path or being a chain are definable in this language.

We compare ECTL* with Rabin tree automata and S2S via the coding $t \to \underline{t}$ mentioned above. Since Büchi recognizable sets of ω-sequences can be defined in monadic second-order logic over the ordering (ω,<), an easy induction over ECTL*-formulas shows:

3.7 Proposition.

If $T \subseteq T_\Sigma$ is ECTL*-definable, then $\underline{T}$ is definable in S2S (and hence Rabin recognizable). ❑

Moreover, the set quantifiers in the S2S-formula may be restricted to range over chains (= subsets of paths) only. For translations of CTL*-formulas it even suffices to use set quantifiers ranging over maximal chains (= paths).

The resulting fragments of S2S (called chain logic and path logic) have been studied in more detail in [Th87]. As it turns out, chain logic (resp. path logic) is still strictly more expressive than ECTL* (resp. CTL*). There are two defects by which ECTL* differs from chain logic (and by which CTL* differs from path logic): First, in ECTL* and CTL* one does not refer to an ordering of the successors of a node. So ECTL* and CTL* should better be compared with a logic where in the signature the primitives S_i are replaced by < for the partial tree ordering. But even if we consider chain logic in the signature <, we obtain a system which has more expressive power than ECTL*. For example, the statement

"there are at least n paths X through node x such that φ(X)"

can be expressed in chain logic by saying

"there are at least n nodes $y_1,...,y_n > x$ which are pairwise incomparable w.r.t. <, and paths $Y_1,...,Y_n$ through $y_1,...,y_n$, respectively, such that $\varphi(Y_i)$ holds".

It can be shown that conditions of this form are in general not expressible in CTL* or ECTL* for $n \geq 2$ (cf. [HT87] for an example). As a result, one may say that CTL* and

ECTL* do not allow to count beyond cardinality 1 on sets of pairwise < -incomparable elements.

It is interesting to note that this defect vanishes when one restricts the interpretation of (E)CTL*-formulas to binary tree models only: As shown in the main result of [HT87], ECTL* and chain logic in the signature with < are expressively equivalent over binary trees, as are CTL* and path logic in the signature < over binary trees.

4. Monoids Associated with Sets of Strings and Sets of Trees

One of the first results in the algebraic theory of regular languages was Schützenberger's characterization of the star-free languages in terms of group-free monoids ([Sch65]). An equivalent characterization, presented in [MNP71], refers to the "noncounting property" of regular languages. We briefly recall the relevant definitions.

A language $W \subseteq \Sigma^*$ is called noncounting if there is $k \geq 1$ such that for all $n \geq k$ and for arbitrary $x,y,u \in \Sigma^*$ we have

$$xu^n y \in W \text{ iff } xu^{n+1} y \in W.$$

This means that for any given $x,y,u \in \Sigma^*$ either almost all words $xu^n y$ or only finitely many words $xu^n y$ belong to W. If a language does not share the noncounting property we sometimes say it is counting. For arbitrary languages the noncounting property was studied in [BCG71]. In the context of regular languages it is especially useful to formulate it in terms of the syntactic monoid. The syntactic monoid M(W) of a language W is the structure $\Sigma^*/\sim_W$ where $\sim_W$ denotes the syntactic congruence of W on Σ^*, defined by

$$u \sim_W v \text{ iff for all } x,y \in \Sigma^* \ (xuy \in W \leftrightarrow xvy \in W),$$

and the product operation is concatenation (extended to $\sim_W$-classes). A language W is regular iff M(W) is finite.

4.1 Theorem. ([Sch65], [MNP71])

For regular $W \subseteq \Sigma^*$, the following conditions are equivalent:

(a) W is star-free (i.e., constructible from finite sets of words by boolean operations and concatenation),

(b) W is noncounting,

(c) M(W) is group-free (i.e., contains no subsets which form a nontrivial group under the product of M(W)). ❑

Since M(W) is effectively constructible from a representation of W (say by a finite automaton), and the property "group-free" can be checked effectively for finite monoids, conditions (a) and (b) are decidable for regular languages.

An analogous result holds for regular ω-languages, based on the following definitions of noncounting property and syntactic monoid: A set $L \subseteq \Sigma^\omega$ is said to be noncounting with index k if for all $n \geq k$ and any $x,y,z,u \in \Sigma^*$, $xu^nyz^\omega \in L$ iff $xu^{n+1}yz^\omega \in L$, and $x(yu^nz)^\omega \in L$ iff $x(yu^{n+1}z)^\omega \in L$. L is called noncounting if there exists $k \geq 1$ such that L is noncounting with index k. So one refers only to ultimately periodic ω-words and considers repetitions of segments in the initial part as well as in the period of such ω-words. Also the definition of the syntactic monoid M(L) for $L \subseteq \Sigma^\omega$, defined by [Arn85], is based on an analogous step from finite words to ultimately periodic ω-words: M(L) is the structure $\Sigma^*/{\sim_L}$, given by the following congruence $\sim_L$ over Σ^*:

$$u \sim_L v \text{ iff for all } x,y,z \in \Sigma^*: (xuyz^\omega \in L \leftrightarrow xvyz^\omega \in L) \text{ and } (x(yuz)^\omega \in L \leftrightarrow x(yvz)^\omega \in L).$$

Again, if L is regular, then M(L) is finite and effectively constructible. (It can be shown that the converse fails in general; an example is given by the set of ω-words over {0,1} which are ultimately periodic.)

4.2 Theorem. ([Arn85],[Pe84])

For a regular ω-language $L \subseteq \Sigma^\omega$, the following conditions are equivalent:

(a) L is star-free (i.e., a finite union of sets $U \cdot V^\omega$ with star-free sets $U,V \subseteq \Sigma^*$ and $V \cdot V \subseteq V$),

(b) L is noncounting,

(c) M(L) is group-free. ❑

We now introduce corresponding definitions for sets of trees. The idea is to use "special trees" which have a designated node where concatenation takes place. If Σ is an alphabet, c a new symbol not in Σ, we call a $(\Sigma \cup \{c\})$-valued tree special over Σ if it has exactly one occurrence of a c-valued node which moreover belongs to the frontier of the tree (i.e., has no successors in the tree). If this c-valued node is the root, the special tree is just the symbol c. Let S_Σ be the set of special trees over Σ. For $s,t \in S_\Sigma$, the product $s \cdot t$ (or simply st) is the special tree which results from s by substituting its c by the tree t. Clearly S_Σ is a monoid under this product (with neutral element c). Referring to this product for special trees, one defines canonically for $s \in S_\Sigma$ the powers s^n and the ω-power s^ω. For $s \neq c$ the concatenation symbol c vanishes in s^ω and we have $s^\omega \in T_\Sigma$.

We associate with any set T of Σ-valued trees a monoid M(T) based on this concatenation. Given $T \subseteq T_\Sigma$, define for $s,t \in S_\Sigma$

$$s \sim_T t \text{ iff } \forall s_1,s_2,s_3 \in S_\Sigma: (s_1 s s_2 (s_3)^\omega \in T \leftrightarrow s_1 t s_2 (s_3)^\omega \in T) \text{ and } (s_1(s_2 s s_3)^\omega \in T \leftrightarrow s_1(s_2 t s_3)^\omega \in T).$$

The relation $\sim_T$ is a congruence over S_Σ. Let M(T) be the monoid $S_\Sigma/\sim_T$ where the product is the above tree concatenation (extended to $\sim_T$-classes).

4.3 Lemma.

If T is ECTL*-definable, then M(T) is finite and effectively constructible (from an ECTL*-formula defining T).

Proof. We show the claim in two steps, using Rabin tree automata over binary trees and the coding $t \rightarrow \underline{t}$ form arbitrary to binary trees as introduced in section 3.6 above. We shall prove:

(a) For any Rabin recognizable set T (of binary trees), the monoid M(T) is finite and effectively constructible (from a Rabin tree automaton recognizing T).

(b) For an arbitrary set T of (countably branching) trees one obtains from an effective presentation of $M(\underline{T})$ as a finite monoid an effective presentation of M(T) as a finite monoid.

This shows the claim of the lemma, because for any ECTL*-definable set T we obtain that $\underline{T}$ is Rabin recognizable (cf. 3.6), find an effective presentation of $M(\underline{T})$ by (a), and get an effective presentation of M(T) by (b).

Proof of (a). Assume $T \subseteq T_\Sigma$ is a Rabin recognizable set of binary trees. Let $\mathcal{A} = (Q,q_0,\Delta,\mathcal{F})$ be a Rabin tree automaton over Σ recognizing T. We define a relation $\sim_{\mathcal{A}}$ over S_Σ which has the following properties:

(1) $\sim_{\mathcal{A}}$ is a finite congruence, and the finite monoid $S_\Sigma/\sim_{\mathcal{A}}$ is effectively presentable.

(2) $\sim_{\mathcal{A}}$ is a refinement of $\sim_T$, and it can be checked effectively whether two $\sim_{\mathcal{A}}$-classes are contained in one $\sim_T$-class.

Clearly, this will establish (a).

We shall say that a run of $\mathcal{A}$ on a special tree s is essentially successful if the acceptance condition for Rabin tree automata is satisfied on all infinite paths of the run (which do not pass the node x where s(x) = c). Given $q,q' \in Q$, a state set $R \subseteq Q$, and a binary special tree s, we write

$q \rightarrow_s q'(R)$ iff there is an essentially successful run $r:\text{dom}(s) \rightarrow Q$ of $\mathcal{A}$ on s such that $r(\varepsilon) = q$, $r(x) = q'$ for the unique x with $s(x) = c$, and the set of states on the path from the root ε to this node x is R.

Now define for binary special Σ-valued trees s,t:

$s \sim_{\mathcal{A}} t$ iff for all $q,q' \in Q$ and all $R \subseteq Q$: $(q \rightarrow_s q'(R) \text{ iff } q \rightarrow_t q'(R))$.

Proof of (1). It is immediate from the definition that $\sim_{\mathcal{A}}$ is a congruence. The $\sim_{\mathcal{A}}$-class of the special tree s, henceforth denoted [s], is determined by the set D_s of triples $(q,q',R) \in Q \times Q \times 2^Q$ such that $q \rightarrow_s q'(R)$. If we define, for such a triple $d = (q,q',R)$,

$$T_d = \{s \in S_\Sigma \mid q \rightarrow_s q'(R)\},$$

then [s] is the intersection of those T_d where $d \in D_s$ and those complement sets $\sim T_d$ where $d \in Q \times Q \times 2^Q - D_s$. Since Q is finite, we obtain that $\sim_{\mathcal{A}}$ has only finitely many congruence classes. Moreover, given two $\sim_{\mathcal{A}}$-classes [s],[t], we can compute $D_{s \cdot t}$ from D_s and D_t and hence obtain the mentioned intersection representation for $[s \cdot t]$ from the corresponding representations of [s] and [t]. Hence $S_\Sigma / \sim_{\mathcal{A}}$ is effectively presentable.

For later use (in the proof of (b)), let us also note that each of the sets T_d, and hence each $\sim_{\mathcal{A}}$-class and each $\sim_T$-class, is Rabin recognizable. (In this case we use Rabin automata with an acceptance condition which covers also finite paths as they appear in special trees: at frontier nodes a certain designated final state should be reached.)

Proof of (2). We first show that the $\sim_{\mathcal{A}}$-classes [s] are compatible with T (the tree language recognized by $\mathcal{A}$) in the following sense:

(+) if $s_1 s s_2 (s_3)^\omega \in T$ then $[s_1][s][s_2][s_3]^\omega \subseteq T$; similarly for the products $s_1(s_2 s s_3)^\omega$.

For the proof consider $t_1 \in [s_1]$, $t \in [s]$, $t_2 \in [s_2]$, $t_3 \in [s_3]$. Existence of a successful run of $\mathcal{A}$ on the tree $t_1 t t_2 (t_3)^\omega$ is obtained from the existence of a successful run on $s_1 s s_2 (s_3)^\omega$: By $s \sim_{\mathcal{A}} t$ and $s_i \sim_{\mathcal{A}} t_i$ (i = 1,2,3) one obtains runs on t and the t_i which are successful on the paths which avoid the special c-labelled nodes and which at these nodes can be concatenated to yield a run on $t_1 t t_2 (t_3)^\omega$. This run is successful; note that on the path through the sequence of nodes where concatenation was applied infinitely often the set of states assumed infinitely often is (by $s_3 \sim_{\mathcal{A}} t_3$) the same as on the corresponding path through $s_1 s s_2 (s_3)^\omega$. The argument for the case of trees $s_1(s_2 s s_3)^\omega$ is analogous.

Now we show that $\sim_T$ is refined by $\sim_{\mathcal{A}}$: Assume $s \sim_{\mathcal{A}} t$. To verify $s \sim_T t$ suppose $s_1 s s_2 (s_3)^\omega \in T$. By (+) above we have $[s_1][s][s_2][s_3]^\omega \subseteq T$. Since [s] = [t] we obtain $s_1 t s_2 (s_3)^\omega \in T$. The converse and the case of trees $s_1(s_2 s s_3)^\omega$ are handled similarly.

Finally, we verify that it can be tested effectively whether two $\sim_{\mathcal{A}}$-classes are contained in one $\sim_T$-class. Consider the $\sim_{\mathcal{A}}$-classes [s],[t] for special trees s,t. To check $s \sim_T t$, it suffices by (+) to verify whether

(*) for all $\sim_{\mathcal{A}}$-classes $[s_1],[s_2],[s_3]$: $[s_1][s][s_2][s_3]^\omega \subseteq T$ iff $[s_1][t][s_2][s_3]^\omega \subseteq T$,
and $[s_1]([s_2][s][s_3])^\omega \subseteq T$ iff $[s_1]([s_2][t][s_3])^\omega \subseteq T$.

Any of these product languages is recognized by a Rabin automaton which can be constructed effectively, and (by [Ra69]) set inclusion is decidable for Rabin recognizable sets of trees. Since there are only finitely many $\sim_{\mathcal{A}}$-classes, we obtain a procedure which decides (*) and hence whether $s \sim_{T} t$ holds.

Proof of (b). By definition of $\sim_T$ we have $s \sim_T t$ iff $\underline{s} \sim_{\underline{T}} \underline{t}$. Hence a copy of M(T) is given by those $\sim_{\underline{T}}$-classes of $M(\underline{T})$ which contain some tree $\underline{s}$. Since each $\sim_{\underline{T}}$-class is Rabin recognizable (see proof of (a)) and also the set of trees of form $\underline{s}$ is Rabin recognizable, it can be tested effectively by [Ra69] whether the two have a nonempty intersection. Thus one obtains an effective representation of M(T) within $M(\underline{T})$. ❑

5. Noncounting Sets of Trees

Let us call a set $T \subseteq T_\Sigma$ noncounting with index k if for all $n \geq k$ and all $s_1,s_2,s_3,s \in S_\Sigma$, $s_1 s^n s_2(s_3)^\omega \in T$ iff $s_1 s^{n+1} s_2(s_3)^\omega \in T$, and $s_1(s_2 s^n s_3)^\omega \in T$ iff $s_1(s_2 s^{n+1} s_3)^\omega \in T$. The set T is called noncounting if T is noncounting with some index k.

5.1 Lemma.

An ECTL*-definable set T of trees is noncounting iff M(T) is group-free.

Proof. The argument follows the pattern of the corresponding proof for sets of finite words [MNP71]. If M(T) contains a proper group, pick $\sim_T$-classes $\langle s\rangle$, $\langle t\rangle$ as elements of M(T) such that $\langle s\rangle$ is the neutral element and $\langle t\rangle$ a nonneutral element of that group. The element $\langle t\rangle$ generates a finite cyclic group with neutral element $\langle s\rangle$, say of order m. Since s, t are not in relation $\sim_T$, there are special trees s_1,s_2,s_3 such that

not ($s_1 s s_2(s_3)^\omega \in T$ iff $s_1 t s_2(s_3)^\omega \in T$), or not ($s_1(s_2 s s_3)^\omega \in T$ iff $s_1(s_2 t s_3)^\omega \in T$).

Since $\langle s\rangle = \langle t\rangle^m$, we may replace s by $t^{i\cdot m}$ and t by $t^{i\cdot m+1}$ for any $i \geq 1$. Hence T does not share the noncounting property.

Conversely, assume that T is counting. Then there is a special tree t such that for arbitrary large n we find s_1,s_2,s_3 with

not ($s_1 t^n s_2(s_3)^\omega \in T$ iff $s_1 t^{n+1} s_2(s_3)^\omega \in T$),
or not ($s_1(s_2 t^n s_3)^\omega \in T$ iff $s_1(s_2 t^{n+1} s_3)^\omega \in T$).

Hence the sequence of $\sim_T$-classes $\langle t\rangle, \langle t\rangle^2, \langle t\rangle^3, \ldots$ cannot be ultimately stationary but will be periodic (with period > 2) from some exponent k onwards. This period defines a nontrivial cyclic group in M(T). ❑

In 3.5 above we noted that CTL*-formulas can be viewed as those ECTL*-formulas where all occurring Büchi automata recognize star-free (i.e., noncounting regular) ω-languages.

This leaves open the question how to decide whether a given ECTL*-formula can be reduced to an equivalent ECTL*-formula which has this form. The theorem which follows yields such a decision procedure. It connects CTL*-definability directly with the noncounting property for tree languages (and not only with the noncounting property for the ω-languages appearing in the linear time parts of ECTL*-definitions).

5.2 Theorem.

An ECTL*-definable set of trees is CTL*-definable iff it is noncounting.

Together with Lemmas 4.3 and 5.1 this yields

5.3 Corollary.

For an ECTL*-formula one can decide effectively whether it is equivalent to a CTL*-formula. ❑

The two directions of Theorem 5.2 are shown in the subsequent Lemmas 5.4 and 5.7.

5.4 Lemma.

Any CTL*-definable set of trees is noncounting.

Proof. We apply 3.5 and show the claim for those ECTL*-formulas where all occurring Büchi automata recognize star-free (and hence noncounting) ω-languages. Proceed by induction over CTL*-formulas, as in the proof that star-free languages are noncounting (cf. [MNP71]). For atomic ECTL*-formulas the statement of the lemma is trivial. In the induction step, consider given ECTL*-formulas $\varphi_1,\dots,\varphi_m$ containing only Büchi automata which recognize star-free ω-languages, and assume by induction hypothesis that the sets $T_1,\dots,T_m$ of Σ-valued trees defined by $\varphi_1,\dots,\varphi_m$ are noncounting, say with index $k_1,\dots,k_m$ respectively. We have to show that the formulas $\varphi_1 \vee \varphi_2$, $\neg\, \varphi_1$, and $E(\mathcal{A},\varphi_1,\dots,\varphi_m)$, where $\mathcal{A}$ is a Büchi automaton recognizing a star-free ω-language, define noncounting sets of trees. From the assumptions it follows immediately that the set $T_1 \cup T_2$ is noncounting with index $\max(k_1,k_2)$ and that the complement $T_\Sigma - T_1$ is noncounting with index k_1.

In the quantifier step, suppose that the star-free ω-language recognized by $\mathcal{A}$ is noncounting with index k. We show that the set T defined by $E(\mathcal{A},\varphi_1,\dots,\varphi_m)$ is noncounting with index $k+\max(k_1,\dots,k_m)+1$. Assume that for some n which is equal or greater than this number a tree of form $t = s_1 s^n s_2 (s_3)^\omega$ belongs to T. Since t satisfies $E(\mathcal{A},\varphi_1,\dots,\varphi_m)$, we may choose a path π through t such that the induced ω-word $\alpha(t,\pi,\varphi_1,\dots,\varphi_m)$ of truth value vectors is accepted by $\mathcal{A}$. Compare this path π with the unique path σ in t given by the sequence of nodes where the special trees s_1, s, s_2, and s_3 are concatenated. We distinguish two cases, depending on whether the common initial segment of π and σ extends beyond the special node of s_1s^k within t or whether π and σ branch inside this part. In the first case, the noncounting property of the ω-language recognized by $\mathcal{A}$ (with index k) can be applied. It yields an ω-word α' again accepted by $\mathcal{A}$, coding the path π' through the tree $t' = s_1s^{n+1}s_2(s_3)^\omega$ which starts like π through s_1, continues through k+1 copies of s (instead of k copies as π does), and then proceeds in t' like π in t. Since $\mathcal{A}$ accepts α', the tree t' also satisfies $E(\mathcal{A},\varphi_1,\dots,\varphi_m)$. In the second case the paths π and σ branch within the part s_1s^k of t. Let $\pi(j)$ be the last node common to π and σ, and consider the truth value vector $\alpha(j)$ where $\alpha = \alpha(t,\pi,\varphi_1,\dots,\varphi_m)$. This vector records satisfaction of $\varphi_1,\dots,\varphi_m$ in the tree $t_{\pi(j)}$, which is of form $s_os^rs_2(s_3)^\omega$ for some special tree $s_o \neq c$ and $r \geq \max(k_1,\dots,k_m)$. Since the sets T_i are noncounting with index k_i, replacement of $t_{\pi(j)}$ by $s_os^{r+1}s_2(s_3)^\omega$ does not change the truth values for $\varphi_1,\dots,\varphi_m$. So again $t' = s_1s^{n+1}s_2(s_3)^\omega$ satisfies $E(\mathcal{A},\varphi_1,\dots,\varphi_m)$. The converse step from n+1 to n is shown analogously. Also for the trees of the form $s_1(s_2s^ns_3)^\omega$ the above argument is applied; in this case the replacement of s^n by s^{n+1}, resp. the reverse, is carried out simultaneously in all copies of the period, using the corresponding clause of the non-counting property for the ω-language recognized by $\mathcal{A}$ and for the sets T_i. ❑

For the converse of 5.4 we need two preparations, summarized in Lemmas 5.5 and 5.6 below and given here in an outline only. First we introduce certain equivalence relations on ω-words and on trees, defined in terms of the size of Büchi automata and the nesting of path quantifiers in ECTL*-formulas. Via these relations, ECTL*-definable sets of trees are represented in a "distributive normal form" which is motivated by the distributive normal form of first-order logic. Secondly, we study the operation of "noncounting extension for index k and automaton size n", which yields for a Büchi recognizable ω-language (resp. a Rabin recognizable tree language) a larger set of ω-words (resp. trees) which is noncounting with index k and small in the sense that it is included in any superset which is recognized a Büchi (resp. Rabin) automaton with $\leq$ n states and non-counting with index k.

Let us introduce the mentioned normal form for ECTL*-formulas. Given an alphabet $\Sigma = \{0,1\}^m$ define for two ω-words $\alpha, \beta \in \Sigma^\omega$

$\alpha \sim_n \beta$ iff for all Büchi automata $\mathcal{A}$ over Σ with $\leq$ n states, $\mathcal{A}$ accepts α iff $\mathcal{A}$ accepts β.

The relation $\sim_n$ is of finite index, and clearly any ω-language recognized by a Büchi automaton with at most n states is a union of $\sim_n$-classes.

The next step is to add the E-depth as a second criterion for the classification of ECTL*-formulas. Call two Σ-valued trees t, t' (n,d)-equivalent (and write $t \sim_{(n,d)} t'$) if for all ECTL*-formulas φ of E-depth d, in which only the atomic formulas $p_1,...,p_n$ and Büchi automata with $\leq$ n states occur, we have t $\models \varphi$ iff t' $\models \varphi$. By induction over d one can show that the relation $\sim_{(n,d)}$ is of finite index, and any ECTL*-definable set of trees is a union of $\sim_{(n,d)}$-classes for suitable n and d. These classes are ECTL*-definable; and defining formulas can be introduced by induction on the E-depth (for fixed n) as follows:

(1) Any $\sim_{(n,0)}$-class is defined by a boolean combination of $p_1,...,p_n$.

(2) Any $\sim_{(n,d+1)}$-class is defined by a formula of the form

$$E(\mathcal{A}_1,\varphi_1,...,\varphi_m) \wedge ... \wedge E(\mathcal{A}_r,\varphi_1,...,\varphi_m) \wedge \neg E(\mathcal{A}_{r+1},\varphi_1,...,\varphi_m) \wedge \neg E(\mathcal{A}_q,\varphi_1,...,\varphi_m)$$

where $\varphi_1,...,\varphi_m$ is the sequence of ECTL*-definitions of all $\sim_{(n,d)}$-classes and the $\mathcal{A}_i$ range over the Büchi automata with $\leq$ n states (over the alphabet $\{0,1\}^m$).

(The proof of this definability claim for the $\sim_{(n,d)}$-classes is a copy of the argument which yields Hintikka's normal form for first-order logic [Hi65].) Clause (2) above states that a $\sim_{(n,d+1)}$-class C is determined by the collection of path languages $L(\mathcal{A}_1),...,L(\mathcal{A}_r)$: A tree t belongs to C iff each path through t is in some $L(\mathcal{A}_i)$ and each set $L(\mathcal{A}_i)$ contains a path through t. Summarizing we obtain the distributive normal form for ECTL*-formulas:

5.5 Lemma.

Any ECTL*-formula of E-depth d+1 (and containing only Büchi automata with $\leq$ n states) is equivalent to a disjunction of formulas

$$E(\mathcal{A}_1,\varphi_1,...,\varphi_m) \wedge ... \wedge E(\mathcal{A}_r,\varphi_1,...,\varphi_m) \wedge \neg E(\mathcal{A},\varphi_1,...,\varphi_m)$$

where the φ_i define the $\sim_{(n,d)}$-classes, the $\mathcal{A}_i$ are Büchi automata over $\{0,1\}^m$ with $\leq$n states, and $\mathcal{A}$ is a Büchi automaton recognizing the complement of the union of the sets $L(\mathcal{A}_i)$. ❑

Sometimes it will be convenient to to refer to the ω-languages instead of the defining Büchi automata and to tree languages instead of defining formulas (or Rabin tree automata). For sets $T_1,...,T_m$ of Σ-valued trees and ω-languages $L_1,...,L_r \subseteq \{0,1\}^m$ we shall denote by

$$<L_1\cdot(T_1,...,T_m),...,L_r\cdot(T_1,...,T_m)>$$

the set of Σ-valued trees t such that an ω-word $\alpha \in \{0,1\}^m$ is induced by a path π through t (i.e., $\alpha = \alpha(t,\pi,T_1,...,T_m)$) iff $\alpha \in L_i$ for some i = 1,...,r.

We now turn to the second preparation, an automaton construction concerning the noncounting property. The trees we consider in this context are full binary ones, i.e. trees to which Rabin tree automata can be applied. Fix an alphabet Σ and numbers n,k.

We associate with any Büchi recognizable ω-language $L \subseteq \Sigma^{\omega}$ a larger ω-language, the (n,k)-extension of L, denoted (n,k)-ext(L), which will be noncounting with index k and satisfy the following smallness property: For any ω-language $L' \supseteq L$ which is recognized by a Büchi automaton with $\leq n$ states and is noncounting with index k, we have (n,k)-ext(L) $\subseteq L'$. Similarly, for a Rabin recognizable set T of trees the (n,k)-extension (n,k)-ext(T) will be defined. (The (n,k)-extensions themselves will not be recognized by automata with $\leq n$ states.)

Consider the following equivalence relation $\equiv_n$ on Σ^*:

$u \equiv_n v$ iff for all nondeterministic finite automata $\mathcal{A}$ with $\leq n$ states and for all states q,q' of $\mathcal{A}$ there is a finite run from q to q' via u iff there is such a run via v, and the first run can be chosen to contain a final state iff the second run can.

Clearly $\equiv_n$ is a congruence of finite index. Using $\equiv_n$, we construct from any Büchi automaton $\mathcal{A}$ the (n,k)-extension of its ω-language $L(\mathcal{A})$: Let $\mathcal{A} = (Q,q_0,\Delta,F)$ be a Büchi automaton over Σ, with finite state set Q, initial state q_0, transition relation $\Delta \subseteq Q\times\Sigma\times Q$, and final state set F. Consider any loop λ in $\mathcal{A}$, consisting of states $q_1,\ldots,q_r,q_1$ such that

- for some word w, q_{i+1} is reached from q_i (for $i = 1,\ldots,r-1$) and q_1 from q_r via w,
- no state repetition occurs in $q_1,\ldots,q_r$,
- at least two states q_i,q_j are inequivalent (in the sense that there is an ω-word α which admits a successful run of $\mathcal{A}$ from one state but not from the other).

Since the length of w may be bounded (by the number of states) and since inequivalence of states can be checked effectively, there is an algorithm to find these loops. $\mathcal{A}$ violates the noncounting property iff at least one loop with these properties is found. For any such loop λ and any $\equiv_n$-class C (which is a regular language!) we introduce new states and transitions to prohibit any modulo counting beyond the threshold k by means of λ via a word from C. For fixed C and $\lambda = q_1,\ldots,q_r,q_1$ adjoin the states $q_i(1),\ldots,q_i(k)$ where $i = 1,\ldots,r$, and insert transitions such that from q_i to $q_i(1)$, from $q_i(j)$ to $q_i(j+1)$, and from $q_i(k)$ to $q_i(k)$ one can pass exactly via the words from C. Finally add, for $j < k$, such transitions between $q_i(j)$ and the state q_k such that $j+1 \equiv m \pmod r$, declare $q_i(j)$ as final iff q_m with $j \equiv m \pmod r$ is final, and declare $q_i(m)$ as final state iff one state of $q_1,\ldots,q_r$ is final.

Define (n,k)-ext($L(\mathcal{A})$) to be the ω-language which is recognized by the Büchi automaton $\mathcal{B}$ which results by these supplements to the loops of $\mathcal{A}$. Obviously $L(\mathcal{B})$ is noncounting with index k, and we have $L(\mathcal{A}) \subseteq L(\mathcal{B})$.

Let us verify that (n,k)-ext($L(\mathcal{A})$) is contained in any ω-language $L' \supseteq L(\mathcal{A})$ which is recognized by a Büchi automaton $\mathcal{A}'$ with $\leq n$ states and is noncounting with index k:

Suppose L' = L($\mathcal{A}$') has these properties and assume $\beta \in L(\mathcal{B})$. To show that $\beta \in L(\mathcal{A}')$, we shall find a sequence α such that two conditions are satisfied:

(i) $\mathcal{A}$ accepts α iff $\mathcal{B}$ accepts β,

(ii) $\mathcal{A}$ accepts α iff $\mathcal{A}$' accepts β,

Consider a successful run of $\mathcal{B}$ on β. Any run segment leading $\mathcal{B}$ into a state $q_i(j)$ can be realized already in $\mathcal{A}$, excepting the case that a state $q_i(k)$ is reached. Consider those segments of β for which the run passes through states $q_i(j)$ and reaches $q_i(k)$. Replace these β-segments (from the respective classes C) by fixed representatives $w \in C$, and obtain an ω-word β' which admits a successful run of $\mathcal{B}$ iff β does. By insertion of additional copies of the chosen words w in β' ensure that in each case w is repeated an appropriate number of times modulo the respective loop length r. In this way an ω-word α is obtained which is accepted by $\mathcal{A}$. Condition (i) is satisfied because L($\mathcal{B}$) is noncounting with index k. Finally, we have (ii) by definition of $\equiv_n$ (and since the C are $\equiv_n$-classes), and by the assumption that L($\mathcal{A}$') is noncounting with index k.

For Rabin tree automata $\mathcal{A}$ the construction of $\mathcal{B}$ is similar, based on a modification of $\equiv_n$ which refers to finite path segments through trees instead of finite words. By a finite path segment (of a binary Σ-valued tree) we mean a word from $(\Sigma\cdot\{0,1\})^*\cdot\Sigma$, coding a sequence of values and directions from $\{0,1\}$. Define, for finite path segments u,v

$u =_n v$ iff for all Rabin tree automata $\mathcal{A}$ with $\leq n$ states, any states q,q' from $\mathcal{A}$ and any set R of transitions of $\mathcal{A}$, there is a sequence of $\mathcal{A}$-transitions via u from q to q' which forms the set R on u iff there is such a sequence of transitions via v.

The extension of a given Rabin tree automaton $\mathcal{A}$ is now defined in the same way as for Büchi automata, using $=_n$ in place of $\equiv_n$, and considering finite path segments of trees in place of finite segments of ω-words. The extension of $\mathcal{A}$ has additional chains of transitions, obtained by copying finite loops consisting of $\mathcal{A}$-transitions. This defines the (n,k)-extension (n,k)-ext(T) for a Rabin recognizable tree language T. The set (n,k)-ext(T) is noncounting of index k, and again is contained in any superset of T which is noncounting of index k and is recognized by a Rabin tree automaton with $\leq$ n states. Moreover, from the latter property of the (n,k)-extensions we obtain a compatibility with the operations occurring in the normal form of Lemma 5.5. (In the present paper we omit the proof.)

5.6 Lemma.

(a) Suppose T, T_1, T_2 are recognized by Rabin automata with $\leq$ n states. Then for any $k \geq 1$

$$(n,k)\text{-ext}(T_1) \cup (n,k)\text{-ext}(T_2) = (n,k)\text{-ext}(T_1 \cup T_2).$$

(b) Let $T, T_1, \ldots, T_m$ be tree languages and $L_1, \ldots, L_r \subseteq \Sigma^\omega$ be ω-languages recognized by Rabin tree automata, resp. Büchi automata with $\leq n$ states, and assume $T = \langle L_1 \cdot (T_1, \ldots, T_m), \ldots, L_r \cdot (T_1, \ldots, T_m) \rangle$. Then for any $k \geq 1$,

$$(n,k)\text{-ext}(T) = \langle (n,k)\text{-ext}(L_1) \cdot ((n,k)\text{-ext}(T_1), \ldots, (n,k)\text{-ext}(T_m)), \ldots, (n,k)\text{-ext}(L_r) \cdot ((n,k)\text{-ext}(T_1), \ldots, (n,k)\text{-ext}(T_m)) \rangle. \quad \square$$

For sets T of arbitrary (not necessarily binary) trees, define the (n,k)-extension using the coding $t \rightarrow \underline{t}$ into binary trees (cf. 3.6): Let

$$(n,k)\text{-ext}(T) := \{ t \in T_\Sigma \mid \underline{t} \in (n,k)\text{-ext}(\underline{T}) \}.$$

5.7 Lemma.

An ECTL*-definable set of trees which is noncounting is CTL*-definable.

Proof. Let T_o be an ECTL*-definable set of trees which is noncounting with index k. If d_o is the E-depth of a defining ECTL*-formula, we shall apply a reduction procedure d_o times to obtain an equivalent ECTL*-formula in which all occurring Büchi automata recognize noncounting ω-languages: In each of the d_o steps, a set T defined by an ECTL*-formula of E-depth d+1 is given. For sufficiently large n, the set (n,k)-ext(T) will be represented as a boolean combination of sets $L \cdot (T_1, \ldots, T_m)$ where L is regular and noncounting with index k, and where the T_i are (n,k)-extensions of sets defined by ECTL*-formulas of E-depth d. Starting with T_o, which is equal to (n,k)-ext(T_o) by assumption (for n sufficiently large), one obtains after d_o steps sets of trees defined by quantifier-free ECTL*-formulas (which are CTL*-formulas). Since all ω-languages constructed are noncounting and recognized by Büchi automata, it follows (by 3.5 and 4.2) that T_o is CTL*-definable.

It remains to describe one step of the above procedure (from E-depth d+1 to E-depth d). By 5.5 we may assume that any set T defined by an ECTL*-formula of E-depth d+1 is a union of sets $S_1, \ldots, S_q$, each of the form

$$S_j = \langle L_1 \cdot (T_1, \ldots, T_m), \ldots, L_r \cdot (T_1, \ldots, T_m) \rangle$$

where the L_i are regular ω-languages and the T_i are defined by ECTL*-formulas of E-depth d. For sufficiently large n (namely, equal or greater than the size of Büchi and Rabin automata recognizing $L_1, \ldots, L_r, T, T_1, \ldots, T_m$) and for arbitrary $k \geq 1$ we have by 5.6(a)

$$(n,k)\text{-ext}(T) = (n,k)\text{-ext}(S_1) \cup \ldots \cup (n,k)\text{-ext}(S_q).$$

Each union member (n,k)-ext(S_j), for S_j as mentioned above, is by 5.6(b) equal to

$$\langle L'_1 \cdot (T'_1, \ldots, T'_m), \ldots, L'_r \cdot (T'_1, \ldots, T'_m) \rangle$$

with noncounting ω-languages L_i' and tree languages T_i' which are (n,k)-extensions of sets defined by ECTL*-formulas of E-depth d. This yields the desired reduction from E-depth d+1 to d. ❑

6. Conclusion

In this paper we discussed a tight connection between ω-language theory and modal logics (of programs) interpreted over infinite trees. The essence of this connection may be found in the fact that modal logics are variants of path logic (second-order logic with set quantification restricted to paths through trees), and that path properties are naturally represented by ω-languages.

Several interesting problems which are motivated by this work remain to be investigated. We mention the following three: First, can the characterization of modal logics via properties of monoids be extended to other systems (than CTL*) and other conditions on monoids (than group-free)? Secondly, is there a natural automaton model, say a variant or a restriction of Rabin tree automaton, which characterizes logics with path quantifiers, like CTL* or ECTL*? And finally: Is it decidable whether a given Rabin recognizable set of trees (specified by a Rabin automaton) is definable in CTL* (or ECTL*)?

7. References

[Arn85] A. Arnold, A syntactic congruence for rational ω-languages, Theor. Comput. Sci. 39 (1985), 333-335.

[Bü62] J.R. Büchi, On a decision method in restricted second order arithmetic, in: Logic, Methodology, and Philosophy of Science (E. Nagel et al., Eds.), Stanford Univ. Press 1962, pp. 1-11.

[CGK87] E.M. Clarke, O. Grümberg, R.P. Kurshan, A synthesis of two approaches for verifying finite state concurrent systems, manuscript, Carnegie Mellon Univ., Pittsburgh 1987.

[BCG71] J.A. Brzozowski, K. Culik II, A. Gabrielian, Classification of noncounting events, J. Comput. System Sci. 5 (1971), 41-53.

[EH86] E.A. Emerson, J.Y. Halpern, "Sometimes" and "Not Never" revisited: On branching time versus linear time, J. Assoc. Comput. Mach. 33 (1986), 151-178.

[Em88] E.A. Emerson, Temporal and modal logic, in: Handbook of Theoretical Computer Science (J. v. Leeuwen, Ed.), North-Holland, Amsterdam (to appear).

[GPSS80] D. Gabbay, A. Pnueli, S. Shelah, J. Stavi, On the temporal analysis of fairness, in: 7th ACM Symp. on Principles of Programming Languages, Las Vegas, Nevada, 1980, 163-173.

[Hi65] J. Hintikka, Distributive normal forms in first-order logic, in: "Formal Systems and Recursive Functions" (J.N. Crossley, M.A.E. Dummett, Eds.), pp. 47-90, North-Holland, Amsterdam 1965.

[HT87] T. Hafer, W. Thomas, Computation tree logic CTL* and path quantifiers in the monadic theory of the binary tree, in: Proc. 14th ICALP, Karlsruhe (T. Ottmann, Ed.), LNCS 267 (1987), 269-279.

[HR86] H.J. Hoogeboom, G. Rozenberg, Infinitary languages: Basic theory and applications to concurrent systems, in: Current Trends in Concurrency (J.W. de Bakker et alt., Eds.), LNCS 224 (1986), 266-342.

[MNP71] R. McNaughton, S. Papert, Counter-Free Automata, MIT Press, Cambridge, Mass. 1971

[Per84] D. Perrin, Recent results on automata and infinite words, in: Math. Found. of Comput. Sci. (M.P. Chytil, V. Koubek, Eds.), LNCS 176 (1984), 134-148.

[Pn81] A. Pnueli, The temporal logic of concurrent programs, Theor. Comput. Sci. 13 (1981), 45-60.

[Pn86] A. Pnueli, Applications of temporal logic to the specification and verification of reactive systems: a survey of current trends, in: Current Trends in Concurrency (J.W. de Bakker et alt., Eds.), LNCS 224 (1986), 510-584.

[Ra69] M.O. Rabin, Decidability of second-order theories and automata on infinite trees, Trans. Amer. Math. Soc. 141 (1969), 1-35.

[Sch65] M.P. Schützenberger, On finite monoids having only trivial subgroups, Inform. Contr. 8 (1965),190-194.

[Th79] W. Thomas, Star-free regular sets of ω-sequences, Inform. Contr. 42 (1979), 148-156.

[Th87] W. Thomas, On chain logic, path logic, and first-order logic over infinite trees, Proc. 2nd Symp. on Logic in Computer Sci., Ithaca, N.Y., 1987, 245-256.

[Th88] W. Thomas, Automata on infinite objects (preliminary version), Aachener Informatik-Berichte 88/17, RWTH Aachen (to appear in: Handbook of Theoretical Computer Science, J.v. Leeuwen, Ed., North-Holland, Amsterdam).

[VW84] M.Y. Vardi, P. Wolper, Yet another process logic, in: Logics of Programs (E. Clarke, D. Kozen, Eds.), LNCS 164 (1984), 501-512.

[Wo83] P. Wolper, Temporal logic can be more expressive, Inform. Contr. 56 (1983), 72-99.

[WVS83] P. Wolper, M.Y. Vardi, A.P. Sistla, Reasoning about infinite computation paths, Proc. 24th Symp. on Found. of Comput. Sci., Tucson, Arizona, 1983, 185-194.

_ecture Notes in Computer Science

'ol. 270: E. Börger (Ed.), Computation Theory and Logic. IX, 442 ages. 1987.

'ol. 271: D. Snyers, A. Thayse, From Logic Design to Logic Programming. IV, 125 pages. 1987.

'ol. 272: P. Treleaven, M. Vanneschi (Eds.), Future Parallel Computers. Proceedings, 1986. V, 492 pages. 1987.

'ol. 273: J.S. Royer, A Connotational Theory of Program Structure. ', 186 pages. 1987.

'ol. 274: G. Kahn (Ed.), Functional Programming Languages and Computer Architecture. Proceedings. VI, 470 pages. 1987.

'ol. 275: A.N. Habermann, U. Montanari (Eds.), System Development and Ada. Proceedings, 1986. V, 305 pages. 1987.

'ol. 276: J. Bézivin, J.-M. Hullot, P. Cointe, H. Lieberman (Eds.), ECOOP '87. European Conference on Object-Oriented Programming. Proceedings. VI, 273 pages. 1987.

'ol. 277: B. Benninghofen, S. Kemmerich, M.M. Richter, Systems of Reductions. X, 265 pages. 1987.

'ol. 278: L. Budach, R.G. Bukharajev, O.B. Lupanov (Eds.), Fundamentals of Computation Theory. Proceedings, 1987. XIV, 505 pages. 987.

'ol. 279: J.H. Fasel, R.M. Keller (Eds.), Graph Reduction. Proceedings, 1986. XVI, 450 pages. 1987.

'ol. 280: M. Venturini Zilli (Ed.), Mathematical Models for the Semantics of Parallelism. Proceedings, 1986. V, 231 pages. 1987.

'ol. 281: A. Kelemenová, J. Kelemen (Eds.), Trends, Techniques, and Problems in Theoretical Computer Science. Proceedings, 1986. VI, 13 pages. 1987.

'ol. 282: P. Gorny, M.J. Tauber (Eds.), Visualization in Programming. Proceedings, 1986. VII, 210 pages. 1987.

'ol. 283: D.H. Pitt, A. Poigné, D.E. Rydeheard (Eds.), Category Theory and Computer Science. Proceedings, 1987. V, 300 pages. 987.

'ol. 284: A. Kündig, R.E. Bührer, J. Dähler (Eds.), Embedded Systems. Proceedings, 1986. V, 207 pages. 1987.

'ol. 285: C. Delgado Kloos, Semantics of Digital Circuits. IX, 124 ages. 1987.

'ol. 286: B. Bouchon, R.R. Yager (Eds.), Uncertainty in Knowledge-Based Systems. Proceedings, 1986. VII, 405 pages. 1987.

'ol. 287: K.V. Nori (Ed.), Foundations of Software Technology and Theoretical Computer Science. Proceedings, 1987. IX, 540 pages. 987.

'ol. 288: A. Blikle, MetaSoft Primer. XIII, 140 pages. 1987.

'ol. 289: H.K. Nichols, D. Simpson (Eds.), ESEC '87. 1st European Software Engineering Conference. Proceedings, 1987. XII, 404 pages. 1987.

'ol. 290: T.X. Bui, Co-oP A Group Decision Support System for Cooperative Multiple Criteria Group Decision Making. XIII, 250 pages. 1987.

'ol. 291: H. Ehrig, M. Nagl, G. Rozenberg, A. Rosenfeld (Eds.), Graph-Grammars and Their Application to Computer Science. VIII, 09 pages. 1987.

'ol. 292: The Munich Project CIP. Volume II: The Program Transformation System CIP-S. By the CIP System Group. VIII, 522 pages. 987.

'ol. 293: C. Pomerance (Ed.), Advances in Cryptology – CRYPTO 87. Proceedings. X, 463 pages. 1988.

'ol. 294: R. Cori, M. Wirsing (Eds.), STACS 88. Proceedings, 1988. (, 404 pages. 1988.

'ol. 295: R. Dierstein, D. Müller-Wichards, H.-M. Wacker (Eds.), Parallel Computing in Science and Engineering. Proceedings, 1987. ', 185 pages. 1988.

Vol. 296: R. Janßen (Ed.), Trends in Computer Algebra. Proceedings, 1987. V, 197 pages. 1988.

Vol. 297: E.N. Houstis, T.S. Papatheodorou, C.D. Polychronopoulos (Eds.), Supercomputing. Proceedings, 1987. X, 1093 pages. 1988.

Vol. 298: M. Main, A. Melton, M. Mislove, D. Schmidt (Eds.), Mathematical Foundations of Programming Language Semantics. Proceedings, 1987. VIII, 637 pages. 1988.

Vol. 299: M. Dauchet, M. Nivat (Eds.), CAAP '88. Proceedings, 1988. VI, 304 pages. 1988.

Vol. 300: H. Ganzinger (Ed.), ESOP '88. Proceedings, 1988. VI, 381 pages. 1988.

Vol. 301: J. Kittler (Ed.), Pattern Recognition. Proceedings, 1988. VII, 668 pages. 1988.

Vol. 302: D.M. Yellin, Attribute Grammar Inversion and Source-to-source Translation. VIII, 176 pages. 1988.

Vol. 303: J.W. Schmidt, S. Ceri, M. Missikoff (Eds.), Advances in Database Technology – EDBT '88. X, 620 pages. 1988.

Vol. 304: W.L. Price, D. Chaum (Eds.), Advances in Cryptology – EUROCRYPT '87. Proceedings, 1987. VII, 314 pages. 1988.

Vol. 305: J. Biskup, J. Demetrovics, J. Paredaens, B. Thalheim (Eds.), MFDBS 87. Proceedings, 1987. V, 247 pages. 1988.

Vol. 306: M. Boscarol, L. Carlucci Aiello, G. Levi (Eds.), Foundations of Logic and Functional Programming. Proceedings, 1986. V, 218 pages. 1988.

Vol. 307: Th. Beth, M. Clausen (Eds.), Applicable Algebra, Error-Correcting Codes, Combinatorics and Computer Algebra. Proceedings, 1986. VI, 215 pages. 1988.

Vol. 308: S. Kaplan, J.-P. Jouannaud (Eds.), Conditional Term Rewriting Systems. Proceedings, 1987. VI, 278 pages. 1988.

Vol. 309: J. Nehmer (Ed.), Experiences with Distributed Systems. Proceedings, 1987. VI, 292 pages. 1988.

Vol. 310: E. Lusk, R. Overbeek (Eds.), 9th International Conference on Automated Deduction. Proceedings, 1988. X, 775 pages. 1988.

Vol. 311: G. Cohen, P. Godlewski (Eds.), Coding Theory and Applications 1986. Proceedings, 1986. XIV, 196 pages. 1988.

Vol. 312: J. van Leeuwen (Ed.), Distributed Algorithms 1987. Proceedings, 1987. VII, 430 pages. 1988.

Vol. 313: B. Bouchon, L. Saitta, R.R. Yager (Eds.), Uncertainty and Intelligent Systems. IPMU '88. Proceedings, 1988. VIII, 408 pages. 1988.

Vol. 314: H. Göttler, H.J. Schneider (Eds.), Graph-Theoretic Concepts in Computer Science. Proceedings, 1987. VI, 254 pages. 1988.

Vol. 315: K. Furukawa, H. Tanaka, T. Fujisaki (Eds.), Logic Programming '87. Proceedings, 1987. VI, 327 pages. 1988.

Vol. 316: C. Choffrut (Ed.), Automata Networks. Proceedings, 1986. VII, 125 pages. 1988.

Vol. 317: T. Lepistö, A. Salomaa (Eds.), Automata, Languages and Programming. Proceedings, 1988. XI, 741 pages. 1988.

Vol. 318: R. Karlsson, A. Lingas (Eds.), SWAT 88. Proceedings, 1988. VI, 262 pages. 1988.

Vol. 319: J.H. Reif (Ed.), VLSI Algorithms and Architectures – AWOC 88. Proceedings, 1988. X, 476 pages. 1988.

Vol. 320: A. Blaser (Ed.), Natural Language at the Computer. Proceedings, 1988. III, 176 pages. 1988.

Vol. 321: J. Zwiers, Compositionality, Concurrency and Partial Correctness. VI, 272 pages. 1989.

Vol. 322: S. Gjessing, K. Nygaard (Eds.), ECOOP '88. European Conference on Object-Oriented Programming. Proceedings, 1988. VI, 410 pages. 1988.

Vol. 323: P. Deransart, M. Jourdan, B. Lorho, Attribute Grammars. IX, 232 pages. 1988.

Vol. 324: M.P. Chytil, L. Janiga, V. Koubek (Eds.), Mathematical Foundations of Computer Science 1988. Proceedings. IX, 562 pages. 1988.

Vol. 325: G. Brassard, Modern Cryptology. VI, 107 pages. 1988.

Vol. 326: M. Gyssens, J. Paredaens, D. Van Gucht (Eds.), ICDT '88. 2nd International Conference on Database Theory. Proceedings, 1988. VI, 409 pages. 1988.

Vol. 327: G.A. Ford (Ed.), Software Engineering Education. Proceedings, 1988. V, 207 pages. 1988.

Vol. 328: R. Bloomfield, L. Marshall, R. Jones (Eds.), VDM '88. VDM – The Way Ahead. Proceedings, 1988. IX, 499 pages. 1988.

Vol. 329: E. Börger, H. Kleine Büning, M.M. Richter (Eds.), CSL '87. 1st Workshop on Computer Science Logic. Proceedings, 1987. VI, 346 pages. 1988.

Vol. 330: C.G. Günther (Ed.), Advances in Cryptology – EUROCRYPT '88. Proceedings, 1988. XI, 473 pages. 1988.

Vol. 331: M. Joseph (Ed.), Formal Techniques in Real-Time and Fault-Tolerant Systems. Proceedings, 1988. VI, 229 pages. 1988.

Vol. 332: D. Sannella, A. Tarlecki (Eds.), Recent Trends in Data Type Specification. V, 259 pages. 1988.

Vol. 333: H. Noltemeier (Ed.), Computational Geometry and its Applications. Proceedings, 1988. VI, 252 pages. 1988.

Vol. 334: K.R. Dittrich (Ed.), Advances in Object-Oriented Database Systems. Proceedings, 1988. VII, 373 pages. 1988.

Vol. 335: F.A. Vogt (Ed.), CONCURRENCY 88. Proceedings, 1988. VI, 401 pages. 1988.

Vol. 336: B.R. Donald, Error Detection and Recovery in Robotics. XXIV, 314 pages. 1989.

Vol. 337: O. Günther, Efficient Structures for Geometric Data Management. XI, 135 pages. 1988.

Vol. 338: K.V. Nori, S. Kumar (Eds.), Foundations of Software Technology and Theoretical Computer Science. Proceedings, 1988. IX, 520 pages. 1988.

Vol. 339: M. Rafanelli, J.C. Klensin, P. Svensson (Eds.), Statistical and Scientific Database Management. Proceedings, 1988. IX, 454 pages. 1989.

Vol. 340: G. Rozenberg (Ed.), Advances in Petri Nets 1988. VI, 439 pages. 1988.

Vol. 341: S. Bittanti (Ed.), Software Reliability Modelling and Identification. VII, 209 pages. 1988.

Vol. 342: G. Wolf, T. Legendi, U. Schendel (Eds.), Parcella '88. Proceedings, 1988. 380 pages. 1989.

Vol. 343: J. Grabowski, P. Lescanne, W. Wechler (Eds.), Algebraic and Logic Programming. Proceedings, 1988. 278 pages. 1988.

Vol. 344: J. van Leeuwen, Graph-Theoretic Concepts in Computer Science. Proceedings, 1988. VII, 459 pages. 1989.

Vol. 345: R.T. Nossum (Ed.), Advanced Topics in Artificial Intelligence. VII, 233 pages. 1988 (Subseries LNAI).

Vol. 346: M. Reinfrank, J. de Kleer, M.L. Ginsberg, E. Sandewall (Eds.), Non-Monotonic Reasoning. Proceedings, 1988. XIV, 237 pages. 1989 (Subseries LNAI).

Vol. 347: K. Morik (Ed.), Knowledge Representation and Organization in Machine Learning. XV, 319 pages. 1989 (Subseries LNAI).

Vol. 348: P. Deransart, B. Lorho, J. Maluszyński (Eds.), Programming Languages Implementation and Logic Programming. Proceedings, 1988. VI, 299 pages. 1989.

Vol. 349: B. Monien, R. Cori (Eds.), STACS 89. Proceedings, 1989. VIII, 544 pages. 1989.

Vol. 350: A. Törn, A. Žilinskas, Global Optimization. X, 255 pages. 1989.

Vol. 351: J. Díaz, F. Orejas (Eds.), TAPSOFT '89. Volume 1. Proceedings, 1989. X, 383 pages. 1989.

Vol. 352: J. Díaz, F. Orejas (Eds.), TAPSOFT '89. Volume 2. Proceedings, 1989. X, 389 pages. 1989.

Vol. 354: J.W. de Bakker, W.-P. de Roever, G. Rozenberg (Eds Linear Time, Branching Time and Partial Order in Logics and Mod for Concurrency. VIII, 713 pages. 1989.